HALSBURY'S
Laws of England

FIFTH EDITION
2017

Volume 95

This is volume 95 of the Fifth Edition of Halsbury's Laws of England, containing the titles SOCIAL SERVICES and SPECIFIC PERFORMANCE.

The titles SOCIAL SERVICES and SPECIFIC PERFORMANCE replace the titles SOCIAL SERVICES AND COMMUNITY CARE and SPECIFIC PERFORMANCE contained in volume 95 (2013). Upon receipt of volume 95 (2017), volume 95 (2013) may be archived.

For a full list of volumes comprised in a current set of Halsbury's Laws of England please see overleaf.

Fifth Edition volumes:

1 (2008), 2 (2017), 3 (2011), 4 (2011), 5 (2013), 6 (2011), 7 (2015), 8 (2015), 9 (2017), 10 (2017), 11 (2015), 12 (2015), 12A (2015), 13 (2009), 14 (2016), 15 (2016), 15A (2016), 16 (2011), 17 (2011), 18 (2009), 19 (2011), 20 (2014), 21 (2016), 22 (2012), 23 (2016), 24 (2010), 25 (2016), 26 (2016), 27 (2015), 28 (2015), 29 (2014), 30 (2012), 31 (2012), 32 (2012), 33 (2013), 34 (2011), 35 (2015), 36 (2015), 37 (2013), 38 (2013), 38A (2013), 39 (2014), 40 (2014), 41 (2014), 41A (2014), 42 (2011), 43 (2011), 44 (2011), 45 (2010), 46 (2010), 47 (2014), 47A (2014), 48 (2015), 49 (2015), 50 (2016), 50A (2016), 51 (2013), 52 (2014), 53 (2014), 54 (2017), 54A (2017), 55 (2012), 56 (2017), 57 (2012), 58 (2014), 58A (2014), 59 (2014), 59A (2014), 60 (2011), 61 (2010), 62 (2016), 63 (2016), 64 (2016), 65 (2015), 66 (2015), 67 (2016), 68 (2016), 69 (2009), 70 (2012), 71 (2013), 72 (2015), 73 (2015), 74 (2011), 75 (2013), 76 (2013), 77 (2016), 78 (2010), 79 (2014), 80 (2013), 81 (2010), 82 (2010), 83 (2010), 84 (2013), 84A (2013), 85 (2012), 86 (2013), 87 (2012), 88 (2012), 88A (2013), 89 (2011), 90 (2011), 91 (2012), 92 (2015), 93 (2008), 94 (2008), 95 (2017), 96 (2012), 97 (2015), 97A (2014), 98 (2013), 99 (2012), 100 (2009), 101 (2009), 102 (2016), 103 (2016), 104 (2014)

Consolidated Index and Tables:

2016 Consolidated Index (A–E), 2016 Consolidated Index (F–O), 2016 Consolidated Index (P–Z), 2017 Consolidated Table of Statutes, 2017 Consolidated Table of Statutory Instruments, etc, 2017 Consolidated Table of Cases (A–G), 2017 Consolidated Table of Cases (H–Q), 2017 Consolidated Table of Cases (R–Z, ECJ Cases)

Updating and ancillary materials:

2017 annual Cumulative Supplement; monthly Noter-up; annual Abridgments 1974–2016

May 2017

DLA Piper UK LLP Leeds

Property of DLA Piper UK LLP
Information Centre
1 St Paul's Place
DLA Piper UK LLP Leeds
Sheffield
S1 2JX

DLA Piper UK LLP Leeds

HALSBURY'S
Laws of England

Volume 95

2017

Members of the LexisNexis Group worldwide

United Kingdom	RELX (UK) Ltd, trading as LexisNexis, 1–3 Strand, London WC2N 5JR and 9–10 St Andrew Square, Edinburgh EH2 2AF
Australia	Reed International Books Australia Pty Ltd trading as LexisNexis, Chatswood, New South Wales
Austria	LexisNexis Verlag ARD Orac GmbH & Co KG, Vienna
Benelux	LexisNexis Benelux, Amsterdam
Canada	LexisNexis Canada, Markham, Ontario
China	LexisNexis China, Beijing and Shanghai
France	LexisNexis SA, Paris
Germany	LexisNexis GmbH, Dusseldorf
Hong Kong	LexisNexis Hong Kong, Hong Kong
India	LexisNexis India, New Delhi
Italy	Giuffrè Editore, Milan
Japan	LexisNexis Japan, Tokyo
Malaysia	Malayan Law Journal Sdn Bhd, Kuala Lumpur
New Zealand	LexisNexis New Zealand Ltd, Wellington
Singapore	LexisNexis Singapore, Singapore
South Africa	LexisNexis, Durban
USA	LexisNexis, Dayton, Ohio

FIRST EDITION	*Published in 31 volumes between 1907 and 1917*
SECOND EDITION	*Published in 37 volumes between 1931 and 1942*
THIRD EDITION	*Published in 43 volumes between 1952 and 1964*
FOURTH EDITION	*Published in 56 volumes between 1973 and 1987, with reissues between 1988 and 2008*
FIFTH EDITION	*Published between 2008 and 2014, with reissues from 2014*

© 2017 RELX (UK) Ltd

A CIP Catalogue record for this book is available from the British Library.

ISBN 978-1-4743-0599-0

9 781474 305990

ISBN for the set: 9781405734394
ISBN for this volume: 9781474305990
Typeset by LexisNexis
Printed and bound by CPI Group (UK) Ltd, Croydon, CR0 4YY

Visit LexisNexis at www.lexisnexis.co.uk

HALSBURY ADVISORY BOARD

SOCIAL SERVICES

Consultant Editor

IAN CLARK, MA,

Former Consultant Solicitor with Kent County Council

SPECIFIC PERFORMANCE

Consultant Editor

ANDREW TETTENBORN, LLB (Cantab),

Professor of Commercial Law,
Institute of International Shipping and Trade Law, Swansea University;
Barrister (non-practising)

The law stated in this volume is in general that in force on 1 April 2017, although subsequent changes have been included wherever possible.

Any future updating material will be found in the Noter-up and annual Cumulative Supplement to Halsbury's Laws of England.

TABLE OF CONTENTS

HOW TO USE HALSBURY'S LAWS
OF ENGLAND

Volumes

Each text volume of Halsbury's Laws of England contains the law on the titles contained in it as at a date stated at the front of the volume (the operative date).

Information contained in Halsbury's Laws of England may be accessed in several ways.

First, by using the tables of contents.

Each volume contains both a general Table of Contents, and a specific Table of Contents for each title contained in it. From these tables you will be directed to the relevant part of the work.

Readers should note that the current arrangement of titles can be found in the Noter-up.

Secondly, by using tables of statutes, statutory instruments, cases or other materials.

If you know the name of the Act, statutory instrument or case with which your research is concerned, you should consult the Consolidated Tables of statutes, cases and so on (published as separate volumes) which will direct you to the relevant volume and paragraph.

(Each individual text volume also includes tables of those materials used as authority in that volume.)

Thirdly, by using the indexes.

If you are uncertain of the general subject area of your research, you should go to the Consolidated Index (published as separate volumes) for reference to the relevant volume(s) and paragraph(s).

(Each individual text volume also includes an index to the material contained therein.)

Updating publications

The text volumes of Halsbury's Laws should be used in conjunction with the annual Cumulative Supplement and the monthly Noter-up.

The annual Cumulative Supplement

The Supplement gives details of all changes between the operative date of the text volume and the operative date of the Supplement. It is arranged in the same volume, title and paragraph order as the text volumes. Developments affecting particular points of law are noted to the relevant paragraph(s) of the text volumes.

For narrative treatment of material noted in the Cumulative Supplement, go to the annual Abridgment volume for the relevant year.

Destination Tables

In certain titles in the annual *Cumulative Supplement*, reference is made to Destination Tables showing the destination of consolidated legislation. Those Destination Tables are to be found either at the end of the titles within the annual *Cumulative Supplement*, or in a separate *Destination Tables* booklet provided from time to time with the *Cumulative Supplement*.

The Noter-up

The Noter-up is issued monthly and notes changes since the publication of the annual Cumulative Supplement. Also arranged in the same volume, title and paragraph order as the text volumes, the Noter-up follows the style of the Cumulative Supplement.

For narrative treatment of material noted in the Noter-up, go to the annual Abridgment volume for the relevant year.

REFERENCES AND ABBREVIATIONS

ACT	Australian Capital Territory
A-G	Attorney General
Admin	Administrative Court
Admlty	Admiralty Court
Adv-Gen	Advocate General
affd	affirmed
affg	affirming
Alta	Alberta
App	Appendix
art	article
Aust	Australia
B	Baron
BC	British Columbia
C	Command Paper (of a series published before 1900)
c	chapter number of an Act
CA	Court of Appeal
CAC	Central Arbitration Committee
CA in Ch	Court of Appeal in Chancery
CB	Chief Baron
CCA	Court of Criminal Appeal
CCR	County Court Rules 1981 (as subsequently amended)
CCR	Court for Crown Cases Reserved
CJEU	Court of Justice of the European Union
C-MAC	Courts-Martial Appeal Court
CO	Crown Office
COD	Crown Office Digest
CPR	Civil Procedure Rules
Can	Canada
Cd	Command Paper (of the series published 1900–18)
Cf	compare
Ch	Chancery Division
ch	chapter
cl	clause
Cm	Command Paper (of the series published 1986 to date)
Cmd	Command Paper (of the series published 1919–56)
Cmnd	Command Paper (of the series published 1956–86)
Comm	Commercial Court

Comr	Commissioner
Court Forms (2nd Edn)	Atkin's Encyclopaedia of Court Forms in Civil Proceedings, 2nd Edn. See note 2 post.
CrimPR	Criminal Procedure Rules
DC	Divisional Court
DPP	Director of Public Prosecutions
EAT	Employment Appeal Tribunal
EC	European Community
ECJ	Court of Justice of the European Community (before the Treaty of Lisbon (OJ C306, 17.12.2007, p 1) came into force on 1 December 2009); European Court of Justice (after the Treaty of Lisbon (OJ C306, 17.12.2007, p 1) came into force on 1 December 2009)
EComHR	European Commission of Human Rights
ECSC	European Coal and Steel Community
ECtHR Rules of Court	Rules of Court of the European Court of Human Rights
EEC	European Economic Community
EFTA	European Free Trade Association
EGC	European General Court
EWCA Civ	Official neutral citation for judgments of the Court of Appeal (Civil Division)
EWCA Crim	Official neutral citation for judgments of the Court of Appeal (Criminal Division)
EWHC	Official neutral citation for judgments of the High Court
Edn	Edition
Euratom	European Atomic Energy Community
EU	European Union
Ex Ch	Court of Exchequer Chamber
ex p	ex parte
Fam	Family Division
Fed	Federal
Forms & Precedents (5th Edn)	Encyclopaedia of Forms and Precedents other than Court Forms, 5th Edn. See note 2 post
GLC	Greater London Council
HC	High Court
HC	House of Commons
HK	Hong Kong
HL	House of Lords
IAT	Immigration Appeal Tribunal
ILM	International Legal Materials
INLR	Immigration and Nationality Law Reports

IRC	Inland Revenue Commissioners
Ind	India
Int Rels	International Relations
Ir	Ireland
J	Justice
JA	Judge of Appeal
Kan	Kansas
LA	Lord Advocate
LC	Lord Chancellor
LCC	London County Council
LCJ	Lord Chief Justice
LJ	Lord Justice of Appeal
LoN	League of Nations
MR	Master of the Rolls
Man	Manitoba
n.	note
NB	New Brunswick
NI	Northern Ireland
NS	Nova Scotia
NSW	New South Wales
NY	New York
NZ	New Zealand
OHIM	Office for Harmonisation in the Internal Market
OJ	The Official Journal of the European Union published by the Publications Office of the European Union
Ont	Ontario
P.	President
PC	Judicial Committee of the Privy Council
PEI	Prince Edward Island
Pat	Patents Court
q.	question
QB	Queen's Bench Division
QBD	Queen's Bench Division of the High Court
Qld	Queensland
Que	Quebec
r	rule
RDC	Rural District Council
RPC	Restrictive Practices Court
RSC	Rules of the Supreme Court 1965 (as subsequently amended)
reg	regulation
Res	Resolution
revsd	reversed

Rly	Railway
s	section
SA	South Africa
S Aust	South Australia
SC	Supreme Court
SI	Statutory Instruments published by authority
SR & O	Statutory Rules and Orders published by authority
SR & O Rev 1904	Revised Edition comprising all Public and General Statutory Rules and Orders in force on 31 December 1903
SR & O Rev 1948	Revised Edition comprising all Public and General Statutory Rules and Orders and Statutory Instruments in force on 31 December 1948
SRNI	Statutory Rules of Northern Ireland
STI	Simon's Tax Intelligence (1973–1995); Simon's Weekly Tax Intelligence (1996-current)
Sask	Saskatchewan
Sch	Schedule
Sess	Session
Sing	Singapore
TCC	Technology and Construction Court
TS	Treaty Series
Tanz	Tanzania
Tas	Tasmania
UDC	Urban District Council
UKHL	Official neutral citation for judgments of the House of Lords
UKPC	Official neutral citation for judgments of the Privy Council
UN	United Nations
V-C	Vice-Chancellor
Vict	Victoria
W Aust	Western Australia
Zimb	Zimbabwe

NOTE 1. A general list of the abbreviations of law reports and other sources used in this work can be found at the beginning of the Consolidated Table of Cases.

NOTE 2. Where references are made to other publications, the volume number precedes and the page number follows the name of the publication; eg the reference '12 Forms & Precedents (5th Edn) 44' refers to volume 12 of the Encyclopaedia of Forms and Precedents, page 44.

NOTE 3. An English statute is cited by short title or, where there is no short title, by regnal year and chapter number together with the name by which it is commonly known or a description of its subject matter and date. In the case of a foreign statute, the mode of citation generally follows the style of citation in use in the country concerned with the addition, where necessary, of the name of the country in parentheses.

NOTE 4. A statutory instrument is cited by short title, if any, followed by the year and number, or, if unnumbered, the date.

TABLE OF STATUTES

TABLE
OF STATUTORY INSTRUMENTS

TABLE OF PROCEDURE

Civil Procedure

Practice Directions relating to Civil Procedure

TABLE OF CASES

H

PARA

M

Decisions of the European Court of Justice are listed below numerically. These decisions are also included in the preceding alphabetical list.

SOCIAL SERVICES

1. THE PROVISION OF CARE AND SUPPORT

(1) LOCAL AUTHORITY DUTY TO PROVIDE CARE AND SUPPORT

1. Local authorities in England. The provision of care and support for adults and adult carers in England[1] is governed by the Care Act 2014[2]. The provision of care and support for children and young carers in England is governed by the provisions of the Children Act 1989 relating to the provision of support for children and families and the care, supervision and protection of children[3]. In either case, the statutory duty to provide care and support falls on local authorities, that is to say:

(1)   in relation to duties under the Care Act 2014, county councils[4], district councils for areas for which there are no county councils[5], London borough councils[6] and the Common Council of the City of London[7]; and

(2)   in relation to duties under the Children Act 1989, county councils, metropolitan districts, London Borough councils and the Common Council of the City of London[8].

A local authority in England may meet care and support needs under the Care Act 2014[9] by itself providing a service[10], by arranging for a person other than it to provide a service[11], or by making direct payments[12], and may also authorise a person to exercise on its behalf a function[13] relating to the provision of care and support for adults and adult carers[14]. The means by which care and support needs may be met under the Children Act 1989 are set out in that legislation[15].

1   In any Act, unless the contrary intention appears, 'England' means, subject to any alteration of the boundaries of local government areas, the areas consisting of the counties established by the Local Government Act 1972 s 1 (see LOCAL GOVERNMENT vol 69 (2009) PARAS 5, 22), and Greater London and the Isles of Scilly: see the Interpretation Act 1978 s 5, Sch 1. As to local government areas and authorities in England and Wales see LOCAL GOVERNMENT vol 69 (2009) PARA 22 et seq. As to boundary changes see LOCAL GOVERNMENT vol 69 (2009) PARA 54 et seq. 'Adult' means a person aged 18 or over: Care Act 2014 s 2(8). As to the meaning of 'carer' see PARA 33 note 2. As to the social services functions of local authorities in England generally see PARAS 315–323.

2   Ie the Care Act 2014 Pt 1 (ss 1–80). As to the provision of care and support for adults in England see PARAS 8–14; as to the provision of care and support for carers in England see PARAS 33–53.

3   Ie the Children Act 1989 Pt 3 (ss 16B–30A), Pt IV (ss 31–42) and Pt V (ss 43–52): see PARA 21; and CHILDREN AND YOUNG PERSONS.

4   Care Act 2014 s 1(4)(a).

5   Care Act 2014 s 1(4)(b).

6   Care Act 2014 s 1(4)(c). As to the London boroughs and their councils see LONDON GOVERNMENT vol 71 (2013) PARAS 15, 20, 34–38.

7   Care Act 2014 s 1(4)(d). As to the Common Council of the City of London see LONDON GOVERNMENT vol 71 (2013) PARA 16.

8   See the Children Act 1989 105(1); and CHILDREN AND YOUNG PERSONS vol 9 (2017) PARA 154.

9   Ie needs under the Care Act 2014 ss 18–20 (see PARAS 12–13 (adults), and PARAS 36, 37 (carers)), or s 62(1) (child's carers: see PARA 44): s 8(2); Care and Support (Children's Carer's) Regulations 2015, SI 2015/305, reg 4 (made under the Care Act 2014 s 62(2)) (see PARA 44 note 6) (and see also the general power to make regulations and orders under s 125). Note that the ways by which a local authority may meet care needs under these provisions are described as 'examples': s 8(2). For examples of what may be provided to meet needs see PARA 3.

10   Care Act 2014 s 8(2)(b).

11   Care Act 2014 s 8(2)(a).

12   Care Act 2014 s 8(2)(a). As to the making of direct payments see PARAS 106–110.

13   Ie a function under the Care Act 2014 Pt 1, apart from s 3 (see PARA 322), ss 6, 7 (see PARA 320), s 14 (see PARA 111), ss 42–47 (see PARAS 234–235) or s 79 (see note 14): s 79(2)(a)–(e). The

Secretary of State may by order amend s 79(2) so as to add to or remove from the list a provision of Pt 1 (s 79(9)(a), (10)): at the date at which this volume states the law no such order had been made.

'Function' includes a power to do anything that is calculated to facilitate, or is conducive or incidental to, the exercise of a function: s 79(11). An authorisation under s 79 may authorise the exercise of the function to which it relates either wholly or to the extent specified in the authorisation (s 79(4)(a)), either generally or in cases, circumstances or areas so specified (s 79(4)(b)), and either unconditionally or subject to conditions so specified (s 79(4)(c)). The power to delegate also applies to functions under the Mental Health Act 1983 s 117 (after-care services: see MENTAL HEALTH AND CAPACITY vol 75 (2013) PARA 945): Care Act 2014 s 79(1)(b).

14 Care Act 2014 s 79(1)(a). The Secretary of State may by order amend s 79(1) so as to add to or remove from the list a provision relating to care and support for adults or support for carers (s 79(9)(b)) or impose conditions or other restrictions on the exercise of the power under s 79(1), whether by amending s 79 or otherwise (s 79(9)(c)). At the date at which this volume states the law no such order had been made.

An authorisation under s 79 may authorise an employee of the authorised person to exercise the function to which the authorisation relates; and for that purpose, where the authorised person is a body corporate, 'employee' includes a director or officer of the body: s 79(3). An authorisation is for the period specified in the authorisation (s 79(5)(a)), may be revoked by the local authority (s 79(5)(b)), and does not prevent the local authority from exercising the function to which the authorisation relates (s 79(5)(c)). Anything done or omitted to be done by or in relation to a person so authorised under in, or in connection with, the exercise or purported exercise of the function to which the authorisation relates is to be treated for all purposes as done or omitted to be done by or in relation to the local authority (s 79(6)), although this does not apply either for the purposes of the terms of any contract between the authorised person and the local authority which relate to the function (s 79(7)(a)) or for the purposes of any criminal proceedings brought in respect of anything done or omitted to be done by the authorised person (s 79(7)(b)).

The Deregulation and Contracting Out Act 1994 (which permits disclosure of information between local authorities and contractors where that is necessary for the exercise of the functions concerned, even if that would otherwise be unlawful) applies to an authorisation under the Care Act 2014 s 79 as it applies to an authorisation by virtue of an order under the Deregulation and Contracting Out Act 1994 s 70(2) (see LOCAL GOVERNMENT vol 69 (2009) PARA 407): Care Act 2014 s 79(8).

15 See note 3.

2. Local authorities in Wales.

2. Local authorities in Wales. The provision of care and support[1] for adults (that is, persons aged 18 or over[2]), children (persons aged under 18[3]) and carers in Wales[4] is governed by the Social Services and Well-being (Wales) Act 2014[5]. The statutory duty to provide care and support falls on local authorities, that is to say, the councils of counties or county boroughs in Wales[6]. A local authority in Wales may meet care needs[7] by itself providing something[8], by arranging for a person other than it to provide something[9], or by providing something, or by arranging for something to be provided, to a person other than the person with needs for care and support (or, in the case of a carer, support)[10].

1   In the Social Services and Well-being (Wales) Act 2014 any reference to 'care' and 'support' is to be construed as a reference to care, support, and both care and support: s 4.
2   Social Services and Well-being (Wales) Act 2014 s 3(1), (2).
3   Social Services and Well-being (Wales) Act 2014 s 3(3).
4   'Wales' means the combined areas of the counties created by the Local Government Act 1972 s 20 (as originally enacted) (see LOCAL GOVERNMENT vol 69 (2009) PARAS 5, 37), but subject to any alteration made under s 73 (consequential alteration of boundary following alteration of watercourse: see LOCAL GOVERNMENT vol 69 (2009) PARA 90): see the Interpretation Act 1978 Sch 1 (definition substituted by the Local Government (Wales) Act 1994 s 1(3), Sch 2 para 9). As to local government areas and authorities in England and Wales see LOCAL GOVERNMENT vol 69 (2009) PARA 22 et seq. As to boundary changes see LOCAL GOVERNMENT vol 69 (2009) PARA 54 et seq. As to the meaning of 'carer' see PARA 54 note 2.
5   Ie the Social Services and Well-being (Wales) Act 2014 Pts 1–4 (ss 1–58). As to the provision of care and support for adults in Wales see PARAS 15–20; as to the provision of care and support for children in Wales see PARAS 26–32; as to the provision of care and support for carers in Wales see PARAS 54–63.
6   Social Services and Well-being (Wales) Act 2014 s 197(1). This definition also applies for the purposes of the Health and Social Care (Community Health and Standards) Act 2003 Pt 2

    (ss 45–149) (see s 148 (amended in relation to local authorities in Wales by SI 2016/413)) and for the purposes of the Regulation and Inspection of Social Care (Wales) Act 2016 (see s 189).

7   Ie needs under the Social Services and Well-being (Wales) Act 2014 ss 35–45 (see PARAS 19–20 (adults), PARAS 30–32 (children) and PARAS 58–63 (carers)). Note that the ways by which a local authority may meet care needs under these provisions are described as 'examples': s 34(1). For examples of what may be provided to meet needs see PARA 3.

8   Social Services and Well-being (Wales) Act 2014 s 34(1)(b).

9   Social Services and Well-being (Wales) Act 2014 s 34(1)(a).

10 Social Services and Well-being (Wales) Act 2014 s 34(1)(c).

3. What may be provided to meet needs. The following are examples of what may be provided[1] in England to meet the care and support needs of adults and adult carers[2]:

    (1)   accommodation in a care home[3] or in premises of some other type[4];

    (2)   care and support at home or in the community[5];

    (3)   counselling and other types of social work[6];

    (4)   goods and facilities[7];

    (5)   information, advice and advocacy[8].

The following are examples of what may be provided or arranged[9] in Wales to meet the care and support needs of adults, children and carers[10]:

    (a)   accommodation in a care home[11], children's home[12] or premises of some other type[13];

    (b)   care and support[14] at home or in the community[15];

    (c)   services[16], goods and facilities[17];

    (d)   information and advice[18];

    (e)   counselling and advocacy[19];

    (f)   social work[20];

    (g)   payments (including direct payments)[21];

    (h)   aids and adaptations[22];

    (i)   occupational therapy[23].

1   Ie under the Care Act 2014 ss 18–20 (see PARAS 12–13 (adults), and PARAS 36, 37 (carers)) and under s 48(2) (business failure: see PARA 184) as it applies to meeting needs under s 18: ss 8(1), 52(2). As to what may not be provided see PARA 5.

2   For the duty of local authorities in England to provide care and support for adults and adult carers see PARA 1 (noting that the care and support needs of children in England are dealt with under the Children Act 1989 Pt 3 (ss 16B–30A): see PARA 21; and CHILDREN AND YOUNG PERSONS. As to the meaning of 'carer' see PARA 33 note 2.

3   An establishment is a 'care home' if it provides accommodation, together with nursing or personal care, for:

    (1)   persons who are or have been ill (Care Standards Act 2000 s 3(1), (2)(a); Care Act 2014 s 8(3));

    (2)   persons who have or have had a mental disorder (Care Standards Act 2000 s 3(2)(b));

    (3)   persons who are disabled or infirm (s 3(2)(c)); or

    (4)   persons who are or have been dependent on alcohol or drugs (s 3(2)(d)).

    However an establishment in Wales is not a care home if it is:

    (a)   a hospital (s 3(3)(a) (s 3(3) amended, s 3(4) added, by the Health and Social Care Act 2008 Sch 5 para 4));

    (b)   an independent clinic (Care Standards Act 2000 s 3(3)(b)); or

    (c)   a children's home (s 3(3)(c)),

    or if it is of a description excepted by the Care Homes (Wales) Regulations 2002, SI 2002/324, and an establishment in England is not a care home if it is:

    (i)   a hospital (within the meaning of the National Health Service Act 2006: see HEALTH SERVICES vol 54 (2017) PARA 26) (Care Standards Act 2000 s 3(4)(a) (as so added)); or

    (ii)   a children's home (s 3(4)(b) (as so added)),

    or if it is of a description excepted by regulations (none of which had been made at the date on which this volume states the law) (s 3(4) (as so added)).

As from a day to be appointed, the Care Standards Act 2000 s 3(3) is repealed in relation to Wales by the Regulation and Inspection of Social Care (Wales) Act 2016 Sch 3 para 2. At the date at which this volume states the law no such day had been appointed.

In connection with the provision of accommodation in a care home see PARA 4 (provision of preferred accommodation).

4 Care Act 2014 s 8(1)(a). The National Assistance Act 1948 ss 21–24, 26, 32, which applies in relation to local authorities in England only (see the Social Services and Well-being (Wales) Act 2014 (Consequential Amendments) Regulations 2016, SI 2016/413, regs 6, 8) imposes duties on local authorities to provide accommodation for persons in need (and associated provisions) which have been superseded by the overall effect of the Care Act 2014 s 8(1), although the National Assistance Act 1948 ss 21–24, 26, 32 remain in force for England.

5 Care Act 2014 s 8(1)(b).

6 Care Act 2014 s 8(1)(c).

7 Care Act 2014 s 8(1)(d).

8 Care Act 2014 s 8(1)(e). In connection with the provision of information and advice by local authorities in England see also s 4; and PARA 326.

9 Ie under the Social Services and Well-being (Wales) Act 2014 ss 35–45 (see PARAS 19–20 (adults), PARAS 30–32 (children) and PARAS 58–63 (carers)). As to what may not be provided or arranged see PARA 5.

10 For the duty of local authorities in Wales to provide care and support for adults, children and carers see PARA 2. As to the meanings of 'care' and 'support' see PARA 2 note 1. As to the meaning of 'carer' see PARA 54 note 2.

11 As to the meaning of 'care home' in the context of the provision of care and support in Wales see, until a day to be appointed, the Care Standards Act 2000 s 3; and note 3 (definition applied by the Social Services and Well-being (Wales) Act 2014 s 197(1) (prospectively amended by the Regulation and Inspection of Social Care (Wales) Act 2016 Sch 3 para 36)); as from the appointed day 'care home' means premises at which a care home service within the meaning of the Regulation and Inspection of Social Care (Wales) Act 2016 Pt 1 (ss 1–64) (see Sch 1 para 1; and PARA 205) is provided wholly or mainly to adults (Social Services and Well-being (Wales) Act 2014 s 197(1) (as so prospectively amended)). At the date at which this volume states the law no day had been appointed for this purpose. In connection with the provision of accommodation in a care home see PARA 4 (provision of preferred accommodation).

12 In the Social Services and Well-being (Wales) Act 2014 (except s 86) 'children's home' means, until a day to be appointed, a children's home within the meaning of the Care Standards Act 2000 (see s 1; and CHILDREN AND YOUNG PERSONS vol 10 (2017) PARA 1003) in respect of which a person is registered under Pt 2 (ss 11–42: see CHILDREN AND YOUNG PERSONS vol 10 (2017) PARA 1017 et seq); as from the appointed day 'children's home' means premises at which a care home service within the meaning of the Regulation and Inspection of Social Care (Wales) Act 2016 Pt 1 is provided wholly or mainly to children: Social Services and Well-being (Wales) Act 2014 s 197(1) (prospectively amended by the Regulation and Inspection of Social Care (Wales) Act 2016 Sch 3 para 36). At the date at which this volume states the law no day had been appointed for this purpose.

13 Social Services and Well-being (Wales) Act 2014 s 34(2)(a).

14 As to the meaning of 'care and support' see PARA 2 note 1.

15 Social Services and Well-being (Wales) Act 2014 s 34(2)(b). Where a local authority is meeting a person's needs under ss 35–45 by providing or arranging care and support at the person's home, the authority must satisfy itself that any visits to the person's home for that purpose are of sufficient length to provide the person with the care and support required to meet the needs in question: s 34(3).

16 'Services' includes facilities: Social Services and Well-being (Wales) Act 2014 s 197(1).

17 Social Services and Well-being (Wales) Act 2014 s 34(2)(c).

18 Social Services and Well-being (Wales) Act 2014 s 34(2)(d). In connection with the provision of information and advice by local authorities in England see also s 17; and PARA 392.

19 Social Services and Well-being (Wales) Act 2014 s 34(2)(e).

20 Social Services and Well-being (Wales) Act 2014 s 34(2)(f).

21 Social Services and Well-being (Wales) Act 2014 s 34(2)(g). As to the making of direct payments see PARAS 125–130.

22 Social Services and Well-being (Wales) Act 2014 s 34(2)(h).

23 Social Services and Well-being (Wales) Act 2014 s 34(2)(i).

4. Provision of preferred accommodation. Where:

(1) a local authority in England[1] is going to meet adult's or carer's needs[2] (but not a child's carer's needs[3]) by providing or arranging for the provision of care home accommodation[4], shared lives scheme accommodation[5] or supported living accommodation[6] in England[7] and the adult for whom the accommodation is to be provided expresses a preference for particular accommodation[8] of a specified type[9]; or

(2) a local authority in Wales[10] which are going to meet adult's or children's needs[11] by providing or arranging for the provision of care home accommodation in the United Kingdom which is not short term[12] and the person for whom the accommodation is to be provided expresses a preference for a particular care home[13],

the authority must provide or arrange for the provision of the preferred accommodation if:

(a) the care and support plan for the person[14] specifies that his needs are going to be met by the provision of specified[15] accommodation[16];

(b) (in relation to local authorities in England only) the preferred accommodation is of the same type as that specified in the adult's care and support plan[17];

(c) the preferred accommodation is suitable to the person's needs[18] and is available[19]; and

(d) where the preferred accommodation is not provided by the local authority, the provider of the accommodation agrees to provide the accommodation to the adult on the local authority's terms[20].

If the cost to the authority of providing or arranging for the provision of the preferred accommodation is excessive[21] the additional cost condition[22] must also be met[23]. The application of this power is also restricted in the case of detained persons and persons in other residential accommodation[24].

A local authority must explain a refusal to provide preferred accommodation[25].

In relation to local authorities in England, similar provisions apply in connection with the provision of after-care under mental health legislation[26].

1 For the duty of local authorities in England to provide care and support for adults and adult carers see PARA 1 (noting that the care and support needs of children in England are dealt with under the Children Act 1989 Pt 3 (ss 16B–30A): see PARA 21; and CHILDREN AND YOUNG PERSONS).

2 Ie under the Care Act 2014 ss 18–20: see PARAS 12, 13 (adults) and PARAS 36, 37 (carers). As to the meanings of 'adult' and 'carer' see PARAS 1 note 1, 33 note 2.

3 The Care Act 2014 s 30 and the Care and Support and After-care (Choice of Accommodation) Regulations 2014, SI 2014/2670, do not apply to the exercise of the power to meet a child's carer's needs for support under the Care Act 2014 s 62(1) (see PARA 44): Care and Support (Children's Carer's) Regulations 2015, SI 2015/305, reg 2(2)(a).

4 Care and Support and After-care (Choice of Accommodation) Regulations 2014, SI 2014/2670, reg 2(2)(a) (made under the Care Act 2014 s 30). 'Care home accommodation' means accommodation in a care home within the meaning given by the Care Standards Act 2000 s 3 (see PARA 3 note 3): Care and Support and After-care (Choice of Accommodation) Regulations 2014, SI 2014/2670, reg 6.

5 Care and Support and After-care (Choice of Accommodation) Regulations 2014, SI 2014/2670, reg 2(2)(b). 'Shared lives scheme accommodation' means accommodation which is provided for an adult by a shared lives carer, and for this purpose 'shared lives carer' means an individual who, under the terms of a shared lives agreement, provides, or intends to provide, personal care for adults together with, where necessary, accommodation in the individual's home; 'shared lives agreement' means an agreement entered into between a person carrying on a shared lives scheme and an individual for the provision, by that individual, of personal care to an adult together with, where necessary, accommodation in the individual's home; and 'shared lives scheme' means a scheme carried on (whether or not for profit) by a local authority or other person for the purposes of recruiting and training shared lives carers, making arrangements for the placing of adults with shared lives carers, and supporting and monitoring placements: reg 7.

'Personal care' means (by virtue of reg 1(3)):

(1)   physical assistance given to a person in connection with eating or drinking (including the administration of parenteral nutrition), toileting (including in relation to the process of menstruation), washing or bathing, dressing, oral care, and the care of skin, hair and nails (with the exception of nail care provided by a chiropodist or podiatrist); or

(2)   the prompting, together with supervision, of a person in relation to the performance of any of the activities listed under head (1) above, where that person is unable to make a decision for themselves in relation to performing the activity without such prompting or supervision.

6 Care and Support and After-care (Choice of Accommodation) Regulations 2014, SI 2014/2670, reg 2(2)(c). 'Supported living accommodation' means accommodation in premises which are specifically designed or adapted for occupation by adults with needs for care and support to enable them to live as independently as possible (not including adapted premises where the adult had occupied those premises as their home before the adaptations were made), and accommodation which is provided in premises which are intended for occupation by adults with needs for care and support (whether or not the premises are specifically designed or adapted for that purpose), and in circumstances in which personal care is available if required (for which purposes personal care may be provided by a person other than the person who provides the accommodation): reg 8.

7 Care and Support and After-care (Choice of Accommodation) Regulations 2014, SI 2014/2670, reg 2(1)(a).

8 Ie identifiable by reference to its address or provider.

9 Care and Support and After-care (Choice of Accommodation) Regulations 2014, SI 2014/2670, reg 2(1)(b).

10 For the duty of local authorities in Wales to provide care and support for adults, children and carers see PARA 2.

11 Ie under the Social Services and Well-being (Wales) Act 2014 ss 35–38: see PARAS 19, 20 (adults) and PARAS 30, 31 (children). As to the meanings of 'adult' and 'child' see PARA 2.

12 Care and Support (Choice of Accommodation) (Wales) Regulations 2015, SI 2015/1840, reg 2(a) (amended by SI 2017/214). The Care and Support (Choice of Accommodation) (Wales) Regulations 2015, SI 2015/1840, are made under the Social Services and Well-being (Wales) Act 2014 s 57. 'Care home accommodation' means accommodation in a care home within the meaning given by the Care Standards Act 2000 s 3 where the accommodation is in Wales or England, or accommodation in a care home in Scotland or Northern Ireland within the meaning given by the appropriate Scotland or Northern Ireland legislation: Care and Support (Choice of Accommodation) (Wales) Regulations 2015, SI 2015/1840, reg 1(3). 'Short term' means a period not exceeding 8 weeks: reg 1(3).

In any Act, 'United Kingdom' means Great Britain and Northern Ireland (see the Interpretation Act 1978 s 5, Sch 1); and 'Great Britain' means England, Scotland and Wales (see the Union with Scotland Act 1706, preamble art I; Interpretation Act 1978 s 22(1), Sch 2 para 5(a)). Neither the Channel Islands nor the Isle of Man are within the United Kingdom. See further CONSTITUTIONAL AND ADMINISTRATIVE LAW vol 10 (2014) PARA 3.

13 Care and Support (Choice of Accommodation) (Wales) Regulations 2015, SI 2015/1840, reg 2(b).

14 As to care and support plans for adults and carers in England see PARAS 78–80; as to care and support plans for adults and children in Wales see PARAS 81–83.

15 Ie care home accommodation or (in relation to local authorities in England only) shared lives scheme accommodation or supported living accommodation: Care and Support and After-care (Choice of Accommodation) Regulations 2014, SI 2014/2670, reg 3(1)(a); Care and Support (Choice of Accommodation) (Wales) Regulations 2015, SI 2015/1840, reg 3(1)(a).

16 Care and Support and After-care (Choice of Accommodation) Regulations 2014, SI 2014/2670, regs 2(1)(c), 3(1)(a); Care and Support (Choice of Accommodation) (Wales) Regulations 2015, SI 2015/1840, regs 2(c), 3(1)(a).

17 Care and Support and After-care (Choice of Accommodation) Regulations 2014, SI 2014/2670, reg 3(1)(b).

18 Care and Support and After-care (Choice of Accommodation) Regulations 2014, SI 2014/2670, reg 3(1)(c); Care and Support (Choice of Accommodation) (Wales) Regulations 2015, SI 2015/1840, reg 3(1)(b).

19 Care and Support and After-care (Choice of Accommodation) Regulations 2014, SI 2014/2670, reg 3(1)(d); Care and Support (Choice of Accommodation) (Wales) Regulations 2015, SI 2015/1840, reg 3(1)(c).

20 Care and Support and After-care (Choice of Accommodation) Regulations 2014, SI 2014/2670, reg 3(1)(e); Care and Support (Choice of Accommodation) (Wales) Regulations 2015, SI 2015/1840, reg 3(1)(d).

21 Ie is greater:

(1)   in relation to local authorities in England, than the amount specified in the adult's personal budget that relates to the provision of accommodation of that type (Care and Support and After-care (Choice of Accommodation) Regulations 2014, SI 2014/2670, reg 3(2)); or

(2)   in relation to local authorities in Wales, than the cost that the local authority would usually expect to incur in providing or arranging the provision of care home accommodation to meet the needs of the person concerned (Care and Support (Choice of Accommodation) (Wales) Regulations 2015, SI 2015/1840, reg 3(2)).

As to personal budgets in England see PARAS 121–122.

22 The additional cost condition is set out in the Care and Support and After-care (Choice of Accommodation) Regulations 2014, SI 2014/2670, reg 5 and the Care and Support (Choice of Accommodation) (Wales) Regulations 2015, SI 2015/1840, reg 4.

23 Care and Support and After-care (Choice of Accommodation) Regulations 2014, SI 2014/2670, reg 3(2); Care and Support (Choice of Accommodation) (Wales) Regulations 2015, SI 2015/1840, reg 3(2).

24 See the Care Act 2014 s 76(4) and the Social Services and Well-being (Wales) Act 2014 s 187(3) (the power under the Care Act 2014 s 30 and the Care and Support and After-care (Choice of Accommodation) Regulations 2014, SI 2014/2670, and the power under the Social Services and Well-being (Wales) Act 2014 s 57 and the Care and Support (Choice of Accommodation) (Wales) Regulations 2015, SI 2015/1840, may not be exercised in the case of an adult (or a person in Wales) who is detained in prison (or, in Wales, in youth detention accommodation) or residing in approved premises except for the purpose of making provision with respect to accommodation for the adult or person on his or her release from prison (or youth detention accommodation) (including temporary release) or on ceasing to reside in approved premises); and (particularly in connection with the interpretation of these provisions) PARA 87.

25 See the Care and Support and After-care (Choice of Accommodation) Regulations 2014, SI 2014/2670, reg 9 (England) (a local authority must give the adult its written reasons for a refusal to provide or arrange for the provision of preferred accommodation) and the Care and Support (Choice of Accommodation) (Wales) Regulations 2015, SI 2015/1840, reg 5 (where a local authority refuses to provide or arrange for the provision of preferred accommodation it must provide a statement in writing setting out which of the conditions in reg 3(1) (see the text and notes 13–19) or regulation 4(1) (see note 22) is not met and specifying the reasons).

26 See the Mental health Act 1983 s 117(2); the Care and Support and After-care (Choice of Accommodation) Regulations 2014, SI 2014/2670, reg 4; and MENTAL HEALTH AND CAPACITY vol 75 (2013) PARA 945).

5.   What may not be provided to meet needs. A local authority in England[1] or Wales[2] may not meet the needs for care and support of, or provide or arrange for the provision of services, facilities or resources aimed at preventing or delaying the development of needs for care and support[3] by, an adult[4] who is subject to immigration control and excluded from entitlement to benefits[5] whose needs for care and support have arisen[6] solely because he is destitute[7] or because of the physical effects, or anticipated physical effects, of being destitute[8].

A local authority may not meet needs[9] or perform its preventive duty[10] by providing or arranging for:

(1)   the provision of a service or facility that is required to be provided under the principal health service legislation[11] unless doing so would be merely incidental or ancillary to doing something else to meet such needs or perform such duty[12] and (in England only) the service or facility in question would be of a nature that the local authority could be expected to provide[13]; or

(2)   nursing care[14] by a registered nurse[15],

although an authority may[16] arrange for the provision of accommodation together with the provision of nursing care by a registered nurse if either it has obtained consent for it to arrange for the provision of the nursing care from the applicable[17] health body[18] or the case is urgent and the arrangements for accommodation are only temporary[19].

A local authority may not meet needs[20] or perform its preventive duty[21] by doing anything which it or another local authority[22] is required to do under applicable housing legislation[23].

1 For the duty of local authorities in England to provide care and support for adults and adult carers see PARA 1 (noting that the care and support needs of children in England are dealt with under the Children Act 1989 Pt 3 (ss 16B–30A): see PARA 21; and CHILDREN AND YOUNG PERSONS).

2 For the duty of local authorities in Wales to provide care and support for adults, children and carers see PARA 2.

3 Ie, perform the duty under the Care Act 2014 s 2(1), s 48(2) (business failure: see PARA 184) as it applies to meeting needs under s 18, or the Social Services and Well-being (Wales) Act 2014 s 15 (see PARA 376): Care Act 2014 ss 21(5), 52(7); Social Services and Well-being (Wales) Act 2014 s 46(1).

4 As to the meaning of 'adult' see PARA 1 note 1 (England) and PARA 2 (Wales). The reference to meeting an adult's needs for care and support includes a reference to providing care and support to the adult in order to meet a carer's needs for support: Care Act 2014 s 21(4); Social Services and Well-being (Wales) Act 2014 s 46(4). As to the meanings of 'care' and 'support' (in Wales only) see PARA 2 note 1.

5 Ie an adult to whom the Immigration and Asylum Act 1999 s 115 (see IMMIGRATION AND ASYLUM vol 57 (2012) PARA 335) applies.

6 Or, in the case of the exercise of the duty under the Care Act 2014 s 2(1), for whom needs for care and support may in the future arise: s 21(5). As to the meaning of 'care and support' (in the context of Wales only) see PARA 2 note 1.

7 Care Act 2014 ss 2(7), 21(1)(a), (5); Social Services and Well-being (Wales) Act 2014 ss 15(9), 46(1)(a). In connection with the meaning of 'destitute' see the Immigration and Asylum Act 1999 s 95(2)–(7) (and IMMIGRATION AND ASYLUM vol 57 (2012) PARAS 344–346) (definition applied with modifications by the Care Act 2014 s 21(2), (3) and the Social Services and Well-being (Wales) Act 2014 s 46(2), (3)).

8 Care Act 2014 s 21(1)(b); Social Services and Well-being (Wales) Act 2014 s 46(1)(b).

9 Ie, England, needs under the Care Act 2014 ss 18–20 (adults and carers: see PARAS 12–13 (adults), and PARAS 36, 37 (carers)) and s 62(1) (child's carers: see PARA 44) or, in Wales, needs for care and support (including a carer's needs for care and support) under ss 35–45 (see PARAS 19–20 (adults), PARAS 30–32 (children) and PARAS 58–63 (carers)).

10 Ie perform the duty under the Care Act 2014 s 2(1) (ss 22(10), 23(3)) or secure services or facilities for a person under the Social Services and Well-being (Wales) Act 2014 s 15 (s 47(2)).

11 Ie, in England, the National Health Service Act 2006 (Care Act 2014 s 22(1)) or, in Wales, the National Health Service (Wales) Act 2006 or corresponding England, Scotland or Northern Ireland legislation ('health enactments') (Social Services and Well-being (Wales) Act 2014 s 47(10)). Regulations may specify (by virtue of the Care Act 2014 s 22(2) and the Social Services and Well-being (Wales) Act 2014 s 47(3)):

(1) types of services or facilities which, despite these restrictions, may be provided or the provision of which may be arranged by a local authority, or circumstances in which such services or facilities may be so provided or the provision of which may be so arranged;

(2) types of services or facilities which may not be provided or the provision of which may not be arranged by a local authority, or circumstances in which such services or facilities may not be so provided or the provision of which may not be so arranged;

(3) services or facilities, or a method for determining services or facilities, the provision of which is, or is not, to be treated as meeting the conditions in the Care Act 2014 s 22(1) or the Social Services and Well-being (Wales) Act 2014 s 47(1).

At the date at which this volume states the law no such regulations had been made. See however the Care and Support (Provision of Health Services) Regulations 2014, SI 2014/2821, regs 3, 4 and the Care and Support (Provision of Health Services) (Wales) Regulations 2015, SI 2015/1919, reg 4 (joint working with relevant bodies and arrangements for the resolution of disputes) (made under the Care Act 2014 s 22(6) and the Social Services and Well-being (Wales) Act 2014 s 47(8)). Nothing in the Care Act 2014 s 22 or the Social Services and Well-being (Wales) Act 2014 s 47 affects what a local authority may do under the National Health Service Act 2006 or the National Health Service Act (Wales) 2006, including entering into arrangements under regulations under the National Health Service Act 2006 s 75 or the National Health Service Act (Wales) 2006 s 33 (arrangements with NHS bodies: see HEALTH SERVICES vol 54 (2017) PARA 282): Care Act 2014 s 22(7); Social Services and Well-being (Wales) Act 2014 s 47(9).

The Care Act 2014 s 22 is modified in the context of its application to adults placed in accommodation in Wales, Scotland or Northern Ireland by English local authorities): see Sch 1 para 1(2), (5); and PARA 85.

12 Care Act 2014 s 22(1)(a); Social Services and Well-being (Wales) Act 2014 s 47(1); Care and Support (Children's Carer's) Regulations 2015, SI 2015/305, regs 7, 8 (see PARA 44 note 6).

13 Care Act 2014 s 22(1)(b).

14 For the purposes of Wales only, 'nursing care' means a service which involves either the provision of care or the planning, supervision or delegation of the provision of care, but does not include a service which, by its nature and in the circumstances in which it is to be provided, does not need to be provided by a registered nurse: Social Services and Well-being (Wales) Act 2014 s 47(10).

15 Care Act 2014 s 22(3); Social Services and Well-being (Wales) Act 2014 s 47(4), (5). In the context of the provision of care under the Care Act 2014 s 22 a reference to the provision of nursing care by a registered nurse is a reference to the provision by a registered nurse of a service involving the provision of care or the planning, supervision or delegation of the provision of care other than a service which, having regard to its nature and the circumstances in which it is provided, does not need to be provided by a registered nurse: s 22(8). As to registered nurses see MEDICAL PROFESSIONS vol 74 (2011) PARA 713.

16 Ie despite the prohibitions in the Care Act 2014 s 22(3) and the Social Services and Well-being (Wales) Act 2014 s 47(4).

17 In the context of care being provided under the Care Act 2014 s 22(4) or care being provided under the Services and Well-being (Wales) Act 2014 s 47(6) where the authority proposes to accommodate the person in England, this is a reference to the clinical commissioning group (see HEALTH SERVICES vol 54 (2017) PARA 35 et seq) which has responsibility for arranging for the provision of nursing care by a registered nurse in respect of the person, pursuant to the provisions of the National Health Service Act 2006 s 3(1), (1A), (1E) and regulations made under s 3(1B) or (1D) (see HEALTH SERVICES vol 54 (2017) PARA 36) (Care and Support (Provision of Health Services) Regulations 2014, SI 2014/2821, reg 2; Care and Support (Provision of Health Services) (Wales) Regulations 2015, SI 2015/1919, reg 3(1)(c), (2)) or (where the National Health Service Commissioning Board (see HEALTH SERVICES vol 54 (2017) PARA 32) has responsibility for arranging for the provision of the nursing care, the Board (Care Act 2014 s 22(9))); in the context of care being provided under the Services and Well-being (Wales) Act 2014 s 46(6) where the authority proposes to accommodate the person in Wales, it is a reference to the Local Health Board for the area in which accommodation is provided (Care and Support (Provision of Health Services) (Wales) Regulations 2015, SI 2015/1919, reg 3(1)(a)); and in the context of care being provided under the Services and Well-being (Wales) Act 2014 s 46(6) where the authority proposes to accommodate the person in Scotland or Northern Ireland it is a reference to corresponding Scotland or Northern Ireland bodies (Care and Support (Provision of Health Services) (Wales) Regulations 2015, SI 2015/1919, reg 3(1)(b)). As to Local Health Boards see HEALTH SERVICES vol 54 (2017) PARA 97.

18 Care Act 2014 s 22(4)(a); Social Services and Well-being (Wales) Act 2014 s 47(6)(a).

19 Care Act 2014 s 22(4)(b); Social Services and Well-being (Wales) Act 2014 s 47(6)(b). As soon as is feasible after the temporary arrangements are made, the local authority must seek to obtain the consent mentioned in, as the case may be, the Care Act 2014 s 22(4)(a) or the Social Services and Well-being (Wales) Act 2014 s 46(6)(a): Care Act 2014 s 22(5); Social Services and Well-being (Wales) Act 2014 s 47(7).

20 See note 9.

21 See note 10.

22 In the context of care provided under the Care Act 2014 'another local authority' includes a district council for an area in England for which there is also a county council: s 23(2).

23 Care Act 2014 s 23(1); Social Services and Well-being (Wales) Act 2014 s 48 (amended by the Housing (Wales) Act 2014 Sch 3 para 22). The 'applicable housing legislation' is the Housing Act 1996, the Housing (Wales) Act 2014 (see HOUSING) and any other enactment specified in regulations: Care Act 2014 s 23(1); Social Services and Well-being (Wales) Act 2014 s 48 (as so amended).

6. Meeting needs by the making of payments. Local authorities in England may make provision towards the cost of meeting adult care needs[1] by making direct payments[2] or by entering into deferred payment agreements[3]. Direct payments may be made where that authority is satisfied that making such payments is an appropriate way to meet the needs in question and that the recipient is capable of managing the payments[4]. Deferred payment agreements involve the authority financing the adult's care and being reimbursed at a later date, usually from the realisation of such equity as the adult has in his home[5].

Local authorities in Wales may not provide payments to meet an adult's[6] or child's[7] needs for care and support, or a carer's needs for support[8], unless:

(1)   the payments are direct payments[9];

(2)   the authority considers that the person's needs are urgent and that it would not be reasonably practicable to meet those needs in any other way[10];

(3)   the payments are provided under or by virtue of a contract[11]; or

(4)   the payments are provided in circumstances specified in regulations[12].

1   For the duty of local authorities in England to provide care and support for adults and adult carers see PARA 1 (noting that the care and support needs of children in England are dealt with under the Children Act 1989 Pt 3 (ss 16B–30A): see PARA 21; and CHILDREN AND YOUNG PERSONS).

2   See PARAS 106–110.

3   See PARAS 113–116.

4   See PARA 106.

5   See PARA 113.

6   Ie an adult's needs for care and support under the Social Services and Well-being (Wales) Act 2014 ss 35–36: see PARAS 19–20.

7   Ie a child's needs for care and support under the Social Services and Well-being (Wales) Act 2014 ss 37–39: see PARAS 30–32.

8   Ie a carer's needs for support under the Social Services and Well-being (Wales) Act 2014 ss 40–45: see PARAS 58–63.

9   Social Services and Well-being (Wales) Act 2014 s 49(1)(a). As to the making of direct payments see ss 50–53; and PARAS 125–130.

10 Social Services and Well-being (Wales) Act 2014 s 49(1)(b).

11 Social Services and Well-being (Wales) Act 2014 s 49(1)(c).

12 Social Services and Well-being (Wales) Act 2014 s 49(1)(d).

7. Local authority provision of care within scope of Human Rights Act. Where a registered care provider in England and Wales[1] provides care and support to an adult[2] or support to a carer[3], in the course of providing personal care[4] in a place where the adult receiving the personal care is living when the personal care is provided[5] or residential accommodation together with nursing[6] or personal care[7], the provider is to be taken for human rights purposes[8] to be exercising a function of a public nature in providing the care or support[9] if:

(1)   the care or support is arranged by a local authority in England[10] or Wales[11] or corresponding Scotland or Northern Ireland authorities or paid for (directly or indirectly, and in whole or in part) by such an authority[12]; and

(2)   the authority arranges or pays for the care or support under a applicable statutory provision imposing a duty or conferring a power to meet needs[13].

1   Ie, in England, a person registered under the Health and Social Care Act 2008 Pt 1 Ch 2 (ss 8–44: see PARAS 152–165) or, in Wales, a person registered under the Care Standards Act 2000 Pt 2 (ss 11–42) (see CHILDREN AND YOUNG PERSONS vol 10 (2017) PARA 1017 et seq): Care Act 2014 ss 48(1), 73(1)(a), (b). As to the meanings of 'England' and 'Wales' see PARAS 1, 2.

2   As to the meaning of 'adult' see PARAS 1 note 1, 2. As to the provision of support for adults see PARAS 8–14. As to the meanings of 'care' and 'support' (in Wales only) see PARA 2 note 1.

3   As to the provision of support for carers see PARAS 33–53. As to the meaning of 'carer' see PARA 33 note 2 (England) and PARA 54 note 2 (Wales).

4   As to the meaning of 'personal care' see the Health and Social Care Act 2010 (Regulated Activities) Regulations 2014, SI 2014/2936, reg 2(1); and PARA 152 (definition applied by the Care Act 2014 s 73(4)).

5   Care Act 2014 s 73(1)(a)(i), (b)(i).

6   As to the meaning of 'nursing care' see the Health and Social Care Act 2010 (Regulated Activities) Regulations 2014, SI 2014/2936, reg 2(1); and PARA 153 note 1 (definition applied by the Care Act 2014 s 73(4)).

7   Care Act 2014 s 73(1)(a)(ii), (b)(ii).

8   Ie for the purposes of the Human Rights Act 1998 of s 6(3)(b) (acts of public authorities: see RIGHTS AND FREEDOMS vol 88A (2013) PARA 24).

9 Care Act 2014 s 73(2). For these purposes 'the care or support' means the care and support, support, advice, guidance, assistance or services provided as mentioned in s 73, and 'the provider' means the person who provides the care or support: s 73(1).
10 'Local authority in England' means a local authority for the purposes of the Care Act 2014 Pt 1 (ss 1–80): see s 73(4); and for the duty of local authorities in England to provide care and support for adults and adult carers see PARA 1 (noting that the care and support needs of children in England are dealt with under the Children Act 1989 Pt 3 (ss 16B–30A): see PARA 21; and CHILDREN AND YOUNG PERSONS).
11 'Local authority in Wales' means a local authority for the purposes of the Social Services and Well-being (Wales) Act 2014: see the Care Act 2014 s 73(4); and for the duty of local authorities in Wales to provide care and support for adults, children and carers see PARA 2.
12 Care Act 2014 s 73(3)(a).
13 Care Act 2014 s 73(3)(b). The applicable statutory provisions are (by virtue of s 73(3)):
     (1)   in the case of a local authority in England, ss 2, 18, 19, 20, 38, 48; and
     (2)   in the case of a local authority in Wales, s 50, and the Social Services and Well-being (Wales) Act 2014 Pt 4 (ss 32–58) and s 189.

(2) PROVISION OF CARE AND SUPPORT FOR ADULTS

(i) England

8. Duty to carry out assessment of an adult's care needs. Where it appears to a local authority in England[1] that an adult[2] may have needs for care and support, the authority must assess whether the adult does have needs for care and support[3] and if he does, what those needs are[4]. Such an assessment is referred to as a 'needs assessment'[5], and the duty to carry one out applies regardless of the authority's view of the level of the adult's needs for care and support[6] or the level of the adult's financial resources[7]. An adult may refuse a needs assessment, in which event the local authority concerned is not required to carry one out[8], although the authority may not rely on this[9] if the adult lacks capacity[10] to refuse the assessment and the authority is satisfied that carrying out the assessment would be in the adult's best interests[11] or the adult is experiencing, or is at risk of, abuse[12] or neglect[13]. An authority is also required to carry out an assessment (subject to a further refusal) where an adult has refused an assessment and the authority thinks that the adult's needs or circumstances have changed[14], and, to the extent that the authority considers appropriate, where circumstances have changed in a way that affects a care and support plan[15].

1 As to the meaning of 'local authority' see PARA 1. As to the social services functions of local authorities in England generally, and the overarching principles in accordance with which functions relating to the provision of care and support must be exercised, see PARAS 315–323.
2 As to the meaning of 'adult' see PARA 1 note 1.
3 Care Act 2014 s 9(1)(a).
4 Care Act 2014 s 9(1)(b).
5 Care Act 2014 s 9(2).
6 Care Act 2014 s 9(3)(a). A reference to a needs assessment includes a reference to a needs assessment which forms part of a combined assessment under s 12(5) (see PARA 66): s 12(8). A reference to an assessment includes a reference to part of an assessment: s 12(9). As to the carrying out of needs assessments for adults see the Care and Support (Assessment) Regulations 2014, SI 2014/2827; and PARAS 64–65. As to what must be included in a needs assessment see PARA 9. The local authority must give a written record of a needs assessment to the adult to whom the assessment relates (s 12(3)(a)), any carer that the adult has, if the adult asks the authority to do so (s 12(3)(b)), and any other person to whom the adult asks the authority to give a copy (s 12(3)(c)). As to the meaning of 'carer' see PARA 33 note 2.
7 Care Act 2014 s 9(3)(b).
8 Care Act 2014 ss 9(7), 11(1). In these circumstances s 9(1) (see the text and notes 1–4) will not apply: s 11(1). Where, having refused a needs assessment, an adult requests the assessment, s 9(1) applies in the adult's case (and s 11(1) does not): s 11(3).

9   And so must carry out a needs assessment: Care Act 2014 s 11(2).
10 A reference in the Care Act 2014 Pt 1 (ss 1–80) to having or lacking capacity, or to a person's best interests, is to be interpreted in accordance with the Mental Capacity Act 2005 (see ss 2–4; and MENTAL HEALTH AND CAPACITY vol 75 (2013) PARAS 603–605) (Care Act 2014 s 80(2)); and a reference in the Social Services and Well-being (Wales) Act 2014 to a person having, or lacking, capacity in relation to a matter is to be interpreted as a reference to a person having, or lacking, capacity within the meaning of the Mental Capacity Act 2005 in relation to that matter (Social Services and Well-being (Wales) Act 2014 s 197(5)).
11 Care Act 2014 s 11(2)(a).
12 'Abuse' includes financial abuse; and for that purpose 'financial abuse' includes:
     (1)   having money or other property stolen (Care Act 2014 s 42(3)(a));
     (2)   being defrauded (s 42(3)(b));
     (3)   being put under pressure in relation to money or other property (s 42(3)(c)); and
     (4)   having money or other property misused (s 42(3)(d)).
13 Care Act 2014 s 11(2)(b).
14 Care Act 2014 s 11(4). In these circumstances s 9(1) applies in the adult's case (but subject to further refusal as mentioned in s 11(1)): s 11(4).
15 See the Care Act 2014 s 27(4)(a); and PARA 80.

9.   What must be included in a needs assessment. A needs assessment for an adult in England[1] must include an assessment of the impact of the adult's[2] needs for care and support on his well-being[3], the outcomes that the adult wishes to achieve in day-to-day life[4] and whether, and if so to what extent, the provision of care and support could contribute to the achievement of those outcomes[5]. In carrying out a needs assessment a local authority[6] must involve the adult[7], any carer[8] that the adult has[9] and any person whom the adult asks the authority to involve or, where the adult lacks capacity[10] to ask the authority to do that, any person who appears to the authority to be interested in the adult's welfare[11].

Where it appears to a local authority carrying out a needs assessment that the individual to whom the assessment relates may be eligible for NHS continuing healthcare[12], the local authority must refer the individual to the relevant body[13].

1   See PARA 8; and as to the carrying out of assessments see PARAS 64–65.
2   As to the meaning of 'adult' see PARA 1 note 1.
3   Care Act 2014 s 9(4)(a). The reference in the text to the adult's 'well-being' is a reference to the matters specified in s 1(2) (see PARA 317).
4   Care Act 2014 s 9(4)(b). When carrying out a needs assessment a local authority must also consider whether, and if so to what extent, matters other than the provision of care and support could contribute to the achievement of the outcomes that the adult wishes to achieve in day-to-day life: s 9(6)(a).
5   Care Act 2014 s 9(4)(c). When carrying out a needs assessment a local authority must also consider whether the adult would benefit from the provision of anything under s 2 or s 4 (preventative and educational measures: see PARAS 318, 326) or of anything which might be available in the community: s 9(6)(b).
6   As to the meaning of 'local authority' see PARA 1. As to the social services functions of local authorities in England generally, and the overarching principles in accordance with which functions relating to the provision of care and support must be exercised, see PARAS 315–323.
7   Care Act 2014 s 9(5)(a). A local authority which is required to involve an individual in its exercise of a function under s 9(5)(a), (b) may be required to arrange for an independent advocate to be available to represent and support the individual: see s 67 (in particular s 67(3)(a)); the Care and Support (Independent Advocacy Support) (No 2) Regulations 2014, SI 2014/2889; and PARAS 100–103.
8   As to the meaning of 'carer' see PARA 33 note 2.
9   Care Act 2014 s 9(5)(b). See note 7.
10 As to having or lacking capacity see PARA 8 note 10.
11 Care Act 2014 s 9(5)(c).
12 'NHS continuing health care' is to be construed in accordance with standing rules under the National Health Service Act 2006 s 6E (see HEALTH SERVICES vol 54 (2017) PARA 22): Care Act 2014 s 12(10).
13 Care and Support (Assessment) Regulations 2014, SI 2014/2827, reg 7(1) (made under the Care Act 2014 ss 12(1), (2), 65(1)). The 'relevant body' means the National Health Service Commissioning Board (see HEALTH SERVICES vol 54 (2017) PARA 32) or a clinical

commissioning group (see HEALTH SERVICES vol 54 (2017) PARA 35 et seq) as the case may be, which appears to the local authority to have responsibility for the individual by reason of the National Health Service Commissioning Board and Clinical Commissioning Groups (Responsibilities and Standing Rules) Regulations 2012, SI 2012/2996, reg 20(2): Care and Support (Assessment) Regulations 2014, SI 2014/2827, reg 7(4). In performing its duties under reg 7, a local authority must have regard to the National Framework for NHS Continuing Healthcare and NHS-funded Nursing Care issued by the Secretary of State and dated 28 November 2012: Care and Support (Assessment) Regulations 2014, SI 2014/2827, reg 7(3).

10. Determination of eligibility and the eligibility criteria. Where a local authority in England[1] is satisfied on the basis of a needs assessment[2] that an adult[3] has needs for care and support it must determine whether any of the needs meet the eligibility criteria[4]. An adult's needs meet the eligibility criteria if:

(1)   his needs arise from or are related to a physical or mental impairment or illness[5];

(2)   as a result of his needs he is unable to achieve two or more of the following outcomes[6]:

   (a)   managing and maintaining nutrition[7];
   (b)   maintaining personal hygiene[8];
   (c)   managing toilet needs[9];
   (d)   being appropriately clothed[10];
   (e)   being able to make use of the adult's home safely[11];
   (f)   maintaining a habitable home environment[12];
   (g)   developing and maintaining family or other personal relationships[13];
   (h)   accessing and engaging in work, training, education or volunteering[14];
   (i)   making use of necessary facilities or services in the local community including public transport, and recreational facilities or services[15]; and
   (j)   carrying out any caring responsibilities the adult has for a child[16]; and

(3)   as a consequence there is, or is likely to be, a significant impact on the adult's well-being[17].

1   As to the meaning of 'local authority' see PARA 1. As to the social services functions of local authorities in England generally, and the overarching principles in accordance with which functions relating to the provision of care and support must be exercised, see PARAS 315–323.
2   As to the duty to assess an adult's needs, and the meaning of 'needs assessment', see PARA 8; as to what must be included in a needs assessment see PARA 9.
3   As to the meaning of 'adult' see PARA 1 note 1.
4   Care Act 2014 s 13(1). An authority must also make a determination under s 13(1), to the extent that it considers appropriate, where it is satisfied that circumstances have changed in a way that affects a care and support plan: see s 27(4)(a); and PARA 80. As to care and support plans see PARAS 78–80. As to the duty to consider what can be done to meet eligible and ineligible needs see PARA 11. Regulations may make provision about the making of such determination: s 13(6). At the date at which this volume states the law no such regulations had been made. Having made a determination under s 13(1), the local authority must give the adult concerned a written record of the determination and the reasons for it: s 13(2).
5   Care and Support (Eligibility Criteria) Regulations 2015, SI 2015/313, reg 2(1)(a) (made under the Care Act 2014 s 13(7), (8)). Where the level of an adult's needs fluctuates, in determining whether his needs meet the eligibility criteria the local authority must take into account his circumstances over such period as it considers necessary to establish accurately his level of need: Care and Support (Eligibility Criteria) Regulations 2015, SI 2015/313, art 2(4).
6   For these purposes an adult is to be regarded as being unable to achieve an outcome if he:
   (1)   is unable to achieve it without assistance (Care and Support (Eligibility Criteria) Regulations 2015, SI 2015/313, reg 2(3)(a));
   (2)   is able to achieve it without assistance but doing so causes him significant pain, distress or anxiety (reg 2(3)(b));

(3) is able to achieve it without assistance but doing so endangers or is likely to endanger the health or safety of him, or of others (reg 2(3)(c)); or

(4) is able to achieve it without assistance but takes significantly longer than would normally be expected (reg 2(3)(d)).

7 Care and Support (Eligibility Criteria) Regulations 2015, SI 2015/313, art 2(1)(b), (2)(a).
8 Care and Support (Eligibility Criteria) Regulations 2015, SI 2015/313, art 2(2)(b).
9 Care and Support (Eligibility Criteria) Regulations 2015, SI 2015/313, art 2(2)(c).
10 Care and Support (Eligibility Criteria) Regulations 2015, SI 2015/313, art 2(2)(d).
11 Care and Support (Eligibility Criteria) Regulations 2015, SI 2015/313, art 2(2)(e).
12 Care and Support (Eligibility Criteria) Regulations 2015, SI 2015/313, art 2(2)(f).
13 Care and Support (Eligibility Criteria) Regulations 2015, SI 2015/313, art 2(2)(g).
14 Care and Support (Eligibility Criteria) Regulations 2015, SI 2015/313, art 2(2)(h).
15 Care and Support (Eligibility Criteria) Regulations 2015, SI 2015/313, art 2(2)(i).
16 Care and Support (Eligibility Criteria) Regulations 2015, SI 2015/313, art 2(2)(j).
17 Care and Support (Eligibility Criteria) Regulations 2015, SI 2015/313, art 2(1)(c). As to the meaning of 'well-being' see PARA 317.

11.   Duty to consider what can be done to meet needs. Where at least some of an adult's needs for care and support[1] meet the eligibility criteria[2], a local authority in England[3] must:

(1) consider what could be done to meet those needs that do[4];

(2) ascertain whether the adult wants to have those needs met[5] by the local authority[6]; and

(3) establish whether the adult is ordinarily resident[7] in the local authority's area[8].

Where none of the needs of the adult concerned meet the eligibility criteria, the local authority must give him or her written advice and information about:

(a) what can be done to meet or reduce the needs[9]; and

(b) what can be done to prevent or delay the development of needs for care and support, or the development of needs for support, in the future[10].

1 As to the duty to assess an adult's needs, and the meaning of 'needs assessment', see PARA 8; as to what must be included in a needs assessment see PARA 9. As to the meaning of 'adult' see PARA 1 note 1.
2 As to the eligibility criteria see PARA 10.
3 As to the meaning of 'local authority' see PARA 1. As to the social services functions of local authorities in England generally, and the overarching principles in accordance with which functions relating to the provision of care and support must be exercised, see PARAS 315–323.
4 Care Act 2014 s 13(3)(a).
5 Ie in accordance with the Care Act 2014 Pt 1 (ss 1–80).
6 Care Act 2014 s 13(3)(b).
7 In connection with a person's residence see PARAS 84–87.
8 Care Act 2014 s 13(3)(c).
9 Care Act 2014 s 13(5)(a).
10 Care Act 2014 s 13(5)(b).

12.   Circumstances where local authority must meet adult's needs for care and support. Where a local authority in England[1] has made a determination as to whether an adult's needs[2] meet the eligibility criteria[3] the authority must meet such of the adult's needs which meet the criteria if the adult is ordinarily resident in the authority's area or is present in its area but of no settled residence[4] and his accrued costs exceed the cap on care costs[5]. Where the eligibility requirement is met and the residence requirement satisfied[6] but the person's accrued costs do not exceed the cap on care costs[7], the authority must also meet his needs if either there is no charge[8] for meeting the needs[9] or in so far as there is, either:

(1) the authority is satisfied on the basis of the financial assessment it carried out[10] that the adult's financial resources are at or below the financial limit[11];

(2)   the authority is satisfied on the basis of the financial assessment it carried out that the adult's financial resources are above the financial limit[12] but the adult nonetheless asks the authority to meet the adult's needs[13]; or

(3)   the adult lacks capacity to arrange for the provision of care and support[14] but there is no person authorised to do so[15] or otherwise in a position to do so on the adult's behalf[16].

These duties do not apply to such of the adult's needs as are being met by a carer[17].

1   As to the meaning of 'local authority' see PARA 1. As to the social services functions of local authorities in England generally, and the overarching principles in accordance with which functions relating to the provision of care and support must be exercised, see PARAS 315–323. See also PARA 327 (local authority duty to protect property of adults being cared for away from home).

2   As to the duty to assess an adult's needs, and the meaning of 'needs assessment', see PARA 8; as to what must be included in a needs assessment see PARA 9; as to the duty to consider what can be done to meet needs see PARA 11. As to the meaning of 'adult' see PARA 1 note 1.

3   As to such determinations see the Care Act 2014 s 13(1); and PARA 10.

4   Care Act 2014 s 18(5)(a). In connection with a person's residence see PARAS 84–87.

5   Care Act 2014 s 18(5)(b). As to the meaning of 'accrued costs' see s 15(5); and PARA 112. As to the cap on care costs see s 15(4); and PARA 112. As to the next steps after making a decision as to the provision of care see PARA 14.

6   Care Act 2014 s 18(1)(a).

7   Care Act 2014 s 18(1)(b).

8   Ie under the Care Act 2014 s 14: see PARA 111. The reference in this provision and in s 19 (see PARA 13) to there being no charge under s 14 for meeting an adult's needs for care and support is a reference to there being no such charge because the authority is prohibited by regulations under s 14 from making such a charge (ss 18(6)(a), 19(5)) or the authority is entitled to make such a charge but decides not to do so (s 18(6)(b)).

9   Care Act 2014 s 18(1)(c).

10 As to financial assessments see PARAS 119–120.

11 Care Act 2014 s 18(2). The 'financial limit' is £23,250: see PARA 105.

12 Care Act 2014 s 18(3)(a).

13 Care Act 2014 s 18(3)(b).

14 As to a person having or lacking capacity see PARA 8 note 10.

15 Ie under the Mental Capacity Act 2005. A reference in the Care Act 2014 Pt 1 or the Social Services and Well-being (Wales) Act 2014 to being authorised under the Mental Capacity Act 2005 is a reference to being authorised (whether in general or specific terms) as a donee of a lasting power of attorney granted under that Act (see AGENCY vol 1 (2008) PARA 217 et seq) (Care Act 2014 s 80(3)(a); Social Services and Well-being (Wales) Act 2014 s 197(6)(a)) or a deputy appointed by the Court of Protection under the Mental Capacity Act 2005 s 16(2)(b) (see MENTAL HEALTH AND CAPACITY vol 75 (2013) PARA 734) (Care Act 2014 s 80(3)(b); Social Services and Well-being (Wales) Act 2014 s 197(6)(b)).

16 Care Act 2014 s 18(4)(b).

17 Care Act 2014 s 13(7). As to the meaning of 'carer' see PARA 33 note 2.

13.   Circumstances where local authority may meet adult's needs for care and support. Where a local authority in England[1] has carried out a needs assessment[2] and (if required to do so) a financial assessment[3] it may meet an adult's[4] needs for care and support if the adult is ordinarily resident in the authority's area or is present in its area but of no settled residence[5] and the authority is satisfied that it is not required[6] to meet the adult's needs[7]. Where an authority has made a determination[8] as to whether an adult's needs meet the eligibility criteria[9] it may meet such of the needs which meet the criteria if:

(1)   the adult is ordinarily resident in the area of another local authority[10];

(2)   there is no charge[11] for meeting the needs or, in so far as there is such a charge:

    (a)   the authority is satisfied on the basis of the financial assessment it carried out that the adult's financial resources are at or below the financial limit[12];

    (b)   the authority is satisfied on the basis of the financial assessment it carried out that the adult's financial resources are above the financial limit[13] but the adult nonetheless asks the authority to meet the adult's needs[14]; or

    (c)   the adult lacks capacity to arrange for the provision of care and support[15] but there is no person authorised to do so[16] or otherwise in a position to do so on the adult's behalf[17]; and

(3)   the authority has notified the other local authority of its intention to meet the needs[18].

A local authority may meet an adult's needs for care and support which appear to it to be urgent (regardless of whether the adult is ordinarily resident in its area) without having yet carried out a needs assessment or a financial assessment[19] or made[20] an eligibility determination[21].

1   As to the meaning of 'local authority' see PARA 1. As to the social services functions of local authorities in England generally, and the overarching principles in accordance with which functions relating to the provision of care and support must be exercised, see PARAS 315–323. See also PARA 327 (local authority duty to protect property of adults being cared for away from home).

2   As to the duty to assess an adult's needs, and the meaning of 'needs assessment', see PARA 8; as to what must be included in a needs assessment see PARA 9; as to the duty to consider what can be done to meet needs see PARA 11.

3   As to financial assessments see PARAS 119–120.

4   As to the meaning of 'adult' see PARA 1 note 1.

5   Care Act 2014 s 19(1)(a). In connection with a person's residence see PARAS 84–87.

6   Ie under the Care Act 2014 s 18 (see PARA 12).

7   Care Act 2014 s 19(1)(b). As to the next steps after making a decision as to the provision of care see PARA 14.

8   Ie under the Care Act 2014 s 13(1) (see PARA 12).

9   As to the eligibility criteria for adults in England see PARA 10.

10 Care Act 2014 s 19(2)(a).

11 Ie under the Care Act 2014 s 14: see PARA 111; and PARA 12 note 8.

12 Care Act 2014 ss 18(2), 19(2)(b). Ie £23,250: see PARA 105.

13 Care Act 2014 s 18(3)(a).

14 Care Act 2014 s 18(3)(b).

15 Care Act 2014 s 18(4)(a). As to 'having' and 'lacking' capacity see PARA 8 note 10.

16 Ie under the Mental Capacity Act 2005: see PARA 12 note 15.

17 Care Act 2014 s 18(4)(b).

18 Care Act 2014 s 19(2)(c).

19 Care Act 2014 s 19(3)(a).

20 See note 8.

21 Care Act 2014 s 19(3)(b). A local authority may meet an adult's needs under s 19(3) where, for example, the adult is terminally ill (within the meaning given in the Welfare Reform Act 2012 s 82(4): see WELFARE BENEFITS AND STATE PENSIONS vol 104 (2014) PARA 135): Care Act 2014 s 19(4).

14. Next steps after making decision as to provision of care. Where a local authority in England[1] is required to meet an adult's needs[2] or decides to do so[3] it must prepare a care and support plan for the adult concerned[4], tell the adult which (if any) of the needs that it is going to meet may be met by direct payments[5] and help the adult with deciding how to have the needs met[6]. Where an authority has carried out a needs assessment[7] but is not required, and does not decide, to meet needs[8], it must give the adult concerned its written reasons for not meeting the needs[9] and[10] advice and information about what can be done to meet or reduce the needs[11] and to prevent or delay the development by the adult concerned of needs for care and support or of needs for support in the future[12].

Where an authority is not going to meet an adult's needs for care and support it must nonetheless prepare an independent personal budget for the adult[13] if the needs meet the eligibility criteria[14], at least some of the needs are not being met by a carer[15] and the adult is ordinarily resident in the authority's area or is present in its area but of no settled residence[16].

1   As to the meaning of 'local authority' see PARA 1. As to the social services functions of local authorities in England generally, and the overarching principles in accordance with which functions relating to the provision of care and support must be exercised, see PARAS 315–323.
2   Ie under the Care Act 2014 s 18 (see PARAS 12, 13). As to the meaning of 'adult' see PARA 1 note 1.
3   Ie under the Care Act 2014 s 19(1) or (2) (see PARA 13).
4   Care Act 2014 s 24(1)(a). As to care and support plans see PARAS 78–80.
5   Care Act 2014 s 24(1)(b). As to direct payments see PARA 106–110.
6   Care Act 2014 s 24(1)(c).
7   As to the meaning of 'needs assessment' see PARA 8.
8   See notes 2, 3.
9   Care Act 2014 s 24(2)(a).
10 Ie unless the authority has already done so under the Care Act 2014 s 13(5) (see PARA 11).
11 Care Act 2014 s 24(2)(b)(i).
12 Care Act 2014 s 24(2)(b)(ii).
13 As to independent personal budgets see PARA 122.
14 Care Act 2014 s 24(3)(a). As to the eligibility criteria for adults in England see PARA 10.
15 Care Act 2014 s 24(3)(b). As to the meaning of 'carer' see PARA 33 note 2.
16 Care Act 2014 s 24(3)(c). In connection with a person's residence see PARAS 84–87.

(ii) Wales

15.   Assessment of an adult's care needs. Where it appears to a local authority in Wales[1] that an adult[2] may have needs for care and support[3] the authority must assess whether the adult does have needs for care and support[4] and if he does, what those needs are[5]. This duty applies regardless of the authority's view of the level of the adult's needs for care and support[6] or the level of the adult's financial resources[7]: it does not, however, apply where an adult (or, where applicable, an authorised person[8]) refuses a needs assessment[9] (unless the adult in question lacks capacity[10] or is at risk[11]), although the duty will be re-engaged, subject to any further refusal, if the adult (or, where applicable, an authorised person) subsequently asks for an assessment[12] or the authority considers that the adult's needs or circumstances have changed[13].

1   As to the meaning of 'local authority' see PARA 2. As to the social services functions of local authorities in Wales generally, and the overarching principles in accordance with which functions relating to the provision of care and support must be exercised, see PARAS 373–383.
2   As to the meaning of 'adult' see PARA 2. This duty applies in relation to an adult who is ordinarily resident in the authority's area (Social Services and Well-being (Wales) Act 2014 s 19(2)(a)) and any other adult who is within the authority's area (s 19(2)(b)). In connection with a person's residence see PARAS 84–87.
3   As to the meanings of 'care' and 'support' see PARA 2 note 1.
4   Social Services and Well-being (Wales) Act 2014 s 19(1)(a). The nature of the needs assessment required by these provisions is one that the local authority considers proportionate in the circumstances, subject to any requirement in the Care and Support (Assessment) (Wales) Regulations 2015, SI 2015/1305 (see PARAS 66–77): Social Services and Well-being (Wales) Act 2014 s 19(6). As to what must be included in a needs assessment see PARA 16.
5   Social Services and Well-being (Wales) Act 2014 s 19(1)(b).
6   Social Services and Well-being (Wales) Act 2014 s 19(3)(a).
7   Social Services and Well-being (Wales) Act 2014 s 19(3)(b).
8   In this context 'authorised person' means a person authorised under the Mental Capacity Act 2005 (whether in general or specific terms) to decide whether to refuse, or ask for, a needs assessment

on the adult's behalf: Social Services and Well-being (Wales) Act 2014 s 20(4). As to a person being 'authorised' under the Mental Capacity Act 2005 see PARA 12 note 15.

9 Social Services and Well-being (Wales) Act 2014 s 20(1).

10 As to a person having or lacking capacity see PARA 8 note 10.

11 Ie a refusal under the Social Services and Well-being (Wales) Act 2014 s 20(1) does not discharge a local authority from its duty under s 19 (see the text and notes 1–7) in the following cases (s 20(2)):

(1) where the local authority is satisfied, in the case of a refusal given by the adult, that the adult lacks capacity to decide whether to refuse to have the assessment but there is an authorised person to make the decision on the adult's behalf;

(2) where the local authority is satisfied, in the case of a refusal given by the adult, that the adult lacks capacity to decide whether to refuse to have the assessment, there is no authorised person to make the decision on the adult's behalf, and having the assessment would be in the adult's best interests; or

(3) where the local authority suspects that the adult is experiencing or at risk of abuse or neglect.

For the purposes the Social Services and Well-being (Wales) Act 2014 'abuse' means (by virtue of s 197(1)) physical, sexual, psychological, emotional or financial abuse (and includes abuse taking place in any setting, whether in a private dwelling, an institution or any other place); and 'financial abuse' includes:

(a) having money or other property stolen;

(b) being defrauded;

(c) being put under pressure in relation to money or other property;

(d) having money or other property misused.

For the purposes of the Social Services and Well-being (Wales) Act 2014 'neglect' means a failure to meet a person's basic physical, emotional, social or psychological needs, which is likely to result in an impairment of the person's well-being (for example, an impairment of the person's health or, in the case of a child, an impairment of the child's development): s 197(1). As to the meaning of 'well-being' see PARA 375.

12 Social Services and Well-being (Wales) Act 2014 s 20(3)(a).

13 Social Services and Well-being (Wales) Act 2014 s 20(3)(b).

16. What must be included in a needs assessment. In carrying out a needs assessment for an adult in Wales[1] the local authority[2] must:

(1) seek to identify the outcomes that the adult[3] wishes to achieve in day to day life[4];

(2) assess whether, and if so, to what extent, the provision of care and support[5], preventative services[6], or information, advice or assistance[7], could contribute to the achievement of those outcomes or otherwise meet needs identified by the assessment[8]; and

(3) assess whether, and if so, to what extent, other matters could contribute to the achievement of those outcomes or otherwise meet those needs[9].

In carrying out a needs assessment the authority must involve the adult[10] and where feasible, any carer that the adult has[11].

1 See PARA 15; and as to the carrying out of assessments see PARAS 66–77.

2 As to the meaning of 'local authority' see PARA 2. As to the social services functions of local authorities in Wales generally, and the overarching principles in accordance with which functions relating to the provision of care and support must be exercised, see PARAS 373–383.

3 As to the meaning of 'adult' see PARA 2.

4 Social Services and Well-being (Wales) Act 2014 s 19(4)(a).

5 Social Services and Well-being (Wales) Act 2014 s 19(4)(b)(i). As to the meanings of 'care' and 'support' see PARA 2 note 1.

6 Social Services and Well-being (Wales) Act 2014 s 19(4)(b)(ii). 'Preventative services' means services that may be provided by virtue of s 15 (see PARA 376): s 31.

7 Social Services and Well-being (Wales) Act 2014 s 19(4)(b)(iii). 'Information, advice or assistance' means information, advice or assistance that may be provided by virtue of s 17 (see PARA 392): s 31.

8 Social Services and Well-being (Wales) Act 2014 s 19(4)(b).

9 Social Services and Well-being (Wales) Act 2014 s 19(4)(c).

10 Social Services and Well-being (Wales) Act 2014 s 19(5)(a).

11 Social Services and Well-being (Wales) Act 2014 s 19(5)(b). As to the meaning of 'carer' see
   PARA 54 note 2.

17. Determination of eligibility and the eligibility criteria. Where a local
authority in Wales[1] is satisfied on the basis of a needs assessment[2] that an adult[3]
has one or more needs for care and support[4] it must determine whether any of the
needs meet the eligibility criteria[5]. Any one of those needs meets the eligibility
criteria if:

(1)   it arises from the adult's physical or mental ill-health, age, disability,
       dependence on alcohol or drugs, or other similar circumstances[6];

(2)   it relates to one or more of:
       (a)   ability to carry out self-care or domestic routines[7];
       (b)   ability to communicate[8];
       (c)   protection from abuse or neglect[9];
       (d)   involvement in work, education, learning or in leisure activities[10];
       (e)   maintenance or development of family or other significant
              personal relationships[11];
       (f)   development and maintenance of social relationships and
              involvement in the community[12]; or
       (g)   fulfilment of caring responsibilities for a child[13];

(3)   it is such that the adult is not able to meet that need either alone[14], with
       the care and support of others who are willing to provide that care and
       support[15] or with the assistance of services in the community to which
       the adult has access[16]; and

(4)   the adult is unlikely to achieve one or more of his personal outcomes[17]
       unless the local authority provides or arranges care and support to meet
       the need[18] or the authority enables the need to be met by making direct
       payments[19].

1 As to the meaning of 'local authority' see PARA 2. As to the social services functions of local
   authorities in Wales generally, and the overarching principles in accordance with which functions
   relating to the provision of care and support must be exercised, see PARAS 373–383.
2 As to the duty to assess an adult's needs see PARA 15; as to what must be included in a needs
   assessment see PARA 16.
3 As to the meaning of 'adult' see PARA 2.
4 As to the meanings of 'care' and 'support' see PARA 2 note 1.
5 Social Services and Well-being (Wales) Act 2014 s 32(1)(a).
6 Care and Support (Eligibility) (Wales) Regulations 2015, SI 2015/1578, regs 2(1), 3(a) (made
   pursuant to the Social Services and Well-being (Wales) Act 2014 ss 32(3)–(5), 33).
7 Care and Support (Eligibility) (Wales) Regulations 2015, SI 2015/1578, reg 3(b)(i). 'Self-care'
   means (by virtue of reg 2(3)) tasks that a person carries out as part of daily life including:
       (1)   eating and drinking;
       (2)   maintaining personal hygiene;
       (3)   getting up and getting dressed;
       (4)   moving around the home;
       (5)   preparing meals; and
       (6)   keeping the home clean, safe and hygienic.
8 Care and Support (Eligibility) (Wales) Regulations 2015, SI 2015/1578, reg 3(b)(ii).
9 Care and Support (Eligibility) (Wales) Regulations 2015, SI 2015/1578, reg 3(b)(iii). As to the
   meanings of 'abuse' and 'neglect' see PARA 15 note 11.
10 Care and Support (Eligibility) (Wales) Regulations 2015, SI 2015/1578, reg 3(b)(iv).
11 Care and Support (Eligibility) (Wales) Regulations 2015, SI 2015/1578, reg 3(b)(v).
12 Care and Support (Eligibility) (Wales) Regulations 2015, SI 2015/1578, reg 3(b)(vi).
13 Care and Support (Eligibility) (Wales) Regulations 2015, SI 2015/1578, reg 3(b)(vii).
14 Care and Support (Eligibility) (Wales) Regulations 2015, SI 2015/1578, reg 3(c)(i). For the
   purposes of reg 3(c), reg 4(1)(c) (see PARA 28) and reg 5(c) (see PARA 56) a person who is able to
   meet the need, alone or with the assistance of others is to be regarded as unable to meet the need
   if doing so:
       (1)   causes significant pain, anxiety or distress to that person (reg 6(a));

(2)   endangers or is likely to endanger the health or safety of that person or another person (reg 6(b)); or

(3)   takes that person significantly longer than would normally be expected (reg 6(c)).

15 Care and Support (Eligibility) (Wales) Regulations 2015, SI 2015/1578, reg 3(c)(ii). See note 14.

16 Care and Support (Eligibility) (Wales) Regulations 2015, SI 2015/1578, reg 3(c)(iii). See note 14.

17 'Personal outcomes' means the outcomes which have been identified in relation to a person by an assessment under the Social Services and Well-being (Wales) Act 2014 s 19, s 21 or s 24, as the case may be: Care and Support (Eligibility) (Wales) Regulations 2015, SI 2015/1578, reg 2(3).

18 Care and Support (Eligibility) (Wales) Regulations 2015, SI 2015/1578, reg 3(d)(i).

19 Care and Support (Eligibility) (Wales) Regulations 2015, SI 2015/1578, reg 3(d)(ii).

18. Duty to consider what can be done to meet needs.

If a local authority in Wales[1] determines that any adult needs must be met, or are to be met[2], it must:

(1)   consider what could be done to meet those needs[3]; and

(2)   consider whether it would impose a charge for doing those things, and if so, determine the amount of that charge[4].

Where an authority is satisfied on the basis of a needs assessment[5] that an adult[6] has needs for care and support[7] it must determine whether the needs call for the exercise of any social care function it has[8], in so far as the function is relevant to that person[9], and consider whether the person would benefit from the provision of preventative or advisory services[10] or anything else that may be available in the community[11].

If an adult's needs do not meet the eligibility criteria[12] the authority must determine whether it is nevertheless necessary to meet the needs in order to protect him from abuse or neglect or a risk of abuse or neglect[13].

1   As to the meaning of 'local authority' see PARA 2. As to the social services functions of local authorities in Wales generally, and the overarching principles in accordance with which functions relating to the provision of care and support must be exercised, see PARAS 373–383.

2   Ie, in the context of adult needs, under the Social Services and Well-being (Wales) Act 2014 ss 35, 36 (see PARAS 19, 20).

3   Social Services and Well-being (Wales) Act 2014 s 32(2)(a).

4   Social Services and Well-being (Wales) Act 2014 s 32(2)(b). See Pt 5 (ss 59–73); and PARAS 131–142.

5   As to the duty to assess an adult's needs see PARA 15; as to what must be included in a needs assessment see PARA 16.

6   As to the meaning of 'adult' see PARA 2.

7   As to the meanings of 'care' and 'support' see PARA 2 note 1.

8   Ie under the Social Services and Well-being (Wales) Act 2014.

9   Social Services and Well-being (Wales) Act 2014 s 32(1)(c).

10 Ie anything that may be provided by virtue of the Social Services and Well-being (Wales) Act 2014 s 15 (preventative services: see PARA 376) or 17 (information, advice and assistance: see PARA 392).

11 Social Services and Well-being (Wales) Act 2014 s 32(1)(d).

12 As to the eligibility criteria see PARA 10.

13 Social Services and Well-being (Wales) Act 2014 s 32(1)(b)(i). As to the meanings of 'abuse' and 'neglect' see PARA 15 note 11.

19. Circumstances where local authority must meet adult's needs for care and support.

A local authority in Wales[1] must meet an adult's needs[2] for care and support[3] if it is satisfied that:

(1)   the adult is ordinarily resident in the authority's area or of no settled residence but within the authority's area[4];

(2)   either the needs meet the eligibility criteria[5] or the authority considers it necessary to meet the needs in order to protect the adult from abuse[6] or neglect[7] or a risk of abuse or neglect[8]; and

(3)   either there is no charge for the care and support needed to meet those needs[9] or there is a charge for that care and support but:

(a)   the authority is satisfied on the basis of a financial assessment[10] that the adult's financial resources are at or below the financial limit[11];

(b)   the authority is satisfied on the basis of a financial assessment that the adult's financial resources are above the financial limit but the adult nonetheless asks the authority to meet his or her needs[12]; or

(c)   the authority is satisfied that the adult lacks capacity to arrange for the provision of care and support[13] and there is no person authorised to make such arrangements[14] or otherwise in a position to do so on the adult's behalf[15].

These duties do not apply to the extent that the authority is satisfied that an adult's needs are being met by a carer[16].

1   As to the meaning of 'local authority' see PARA 2. As to the social services functions of local authorities in Wales generally, and the overarching principles in accordance with which functions relating to the provision of care and support must be exercised, see PARAS 373–383.

2   As to the duty to assess an adult's needs see PARA 15; as to what must be included in a needs assessment see PARA 16; as to the duty to consider what can be done to meet needs see PARA 18.

3   As to the meanings of 'care' and 'support' see PARA 2 note 1. Where a local authority in Wales is required to meet needs under these provisions it must prepare a care and support plan: see the Social Services and Well-being (Wales) Act 2014 s 54; and PARA 81. Where advocacy services are being provided for a person under s 35 and regulations under s 181 (provision of advocacy services: see PARA 104) would (apart from this provision) impose a requirement upon a local authority to make advocacy services available to that person in respect of the same matters, that requirement does not apply: s 182(2).

4   Social Services and Well-being (Wales) Act 2014 s 35(1), (2). In connection with a person's residence see PARAS 84–87.

5   Social Services and Well-being (Wales) Act 2014 s 35(3)(a). As to the eligibility criteria for adults in Wales see PARA 17.

6   As to the meaning of 'abuse' see PARA 15 note 11.

7   As to the meaning of 'neglect' see PARA 15 note 11.

8   Social Services and Well-being (Wales) Act 2014 s 35(3)(b).

9   Social Services and Well-being (Wales) Act 2014 s 35(4)(a).

10   As to the meaning of 'financial assessment' see (by virtue of the Social Services and Well-being (Wales) Act 2014 s 35(5)) s 63; and PARA 132.

11   Social Services and Well-being (Wales) Act 2014 s 35(4)(b)(i). As to the meaning of 'financial limit' see (by virtue of s 35(5)) s 66(5); and PARA 132.

12   Social Services and Well-being (Wales) Act 2014 s 35(4)(b)(ii).

13   As to 'having' and 'lacking' capacity see PARA 8 note 10.

14   Ie under the Mental Capacity Act 2005: see PARA 12 note 15.

15   Social Services and Well-being (Wales) Act 2014 s 35(4)(b)(iii).

16   Social Services and Well-being (Wales) Act 2014 s 35(6). As to the meaning of 'carer' see PARA 54 note 2.

20.   Circumstances where local authority may meet adult's needs for care and support. A local authority in Wales[1] may meet an adult's[2] needs for care and support[3] if the adult is within the local authority's area[4] or ordinarily resident in the authority's area, but outside its area[5]. An authority has the power to meet needs under these provisions whether or not it has completed a needs assessment[6] or[7] a financial assessment[8].

1   As to the meaning of 'local authority' see PARA 2. As to the social services functions of local authorities in Wales generally, and the overarching principles in accordance with which functions relating to the provision of care and support must be exercised, see PARAS 373–383.

2   As to the meaning of 'adult' see PARA 2. As to the duty to assess an adult's needs see PARA 15; as to what must be included in a needs assessment see PARA 16; as to the duty to consider what can be done to meet needs see PARA 18.

3   As to the meanings of 'care' and 'support' see PARA 2 note 1. Where advocacy services are being provided for a person under the Social Services and Well-being (Wales) Act 2014 s 36 and regulations under s 181 (provision of advocacy services: see PARA 104) would (apart from this

provision) impose a requirement upon a local authority to make advocacy services available to that person in respect of the same matters, that requirement does not apply: s 182(2).

4 Social Services and Well-being (Wales) Act 2014 s 36(1)(a). If a local authority meets the needs of an adult who is ordinarily resident in the area of another local authority under s 36(1), it must notify the local authority in whose area the adult is ordinarily resident that it is doing so: s 36(2). In connection with a person's residence see PARAS 84–87.

5 Social Services and Well-being (Wales) Act 2014 s 36(1)(b).

6 Ie in accordance with the Social Services and Well-being (Wales) Act 2014 Pt 3 (ss 19–31): in connection with assessments of adults' needs in Wales see PARAS 66–77.

7 Ie in accordance with the Social Services and Well-being (Wales) Act 2014 Pt 5 (ss 59–73): in connection with assessments of adults' finances in Wales see PARAS 131–142.

8 Social Services and Well-being (Wales) Act 2014 s 36(3).

(3) PROVISION OF CARE AND SUPPORT FOR CHILDREN

(i) England

A. CARE FOR CHILDREN GENERALLY

21. Provision of care by local authorities under the Children Act 1989. It is the general duty of local authorities in England[1] to safeguard and promote the welfare of children within their area who are in need and so far as is consistent with that duty, to promote the upbringing of such children by their families, by providing a range and level of services appropriate to those children's needs[2]. Care may be provided by means of direct payments[3], by means of day care[4] or by the provision of accommodation[5]. Local authorities are required to comply with a number of statutory duties relating to the accommodation and maintenance of children in their care[6], to make provision for visiting and contact[7], to provide advice and assistance for formerly looked-after children[8], and to provide personal advisors and pathway plans for children who are becoming adults[9]. Provision is also made for the issue and operation of care and supervision orders[10] and child assessment orders[11].

1 Ie under the Children Act 1989 Pt 3 (ss 16B–30A), which by virtue of the Social Services and Well-being (Wales) Act 2014 (Consequential Amendments) Regulations 2016, SI 2016/413, reg 57(1) applies only in relation to local authorities in England. As to the meaning of 'local authority' in the Children Act 1989 see s 105(1); and CHILDREN AND YOUNG PERSONS vol 9 (2017) PARA 154. Note also the provisions of Pt 3 dealing with young carers' (see ss 17ZA–17ZC; and PARAS 47–49) and parent carers' (see ss 17ZD–17ZF; and PARAS 39–40) needs, and the provisions relating to the transition from child to adult care (see s 17ZH; and PARAS 25, 46, 53).

2 See the Children Act 1989 s 17(1); and CHILDREN AND YOUNG PERSONS vol 10 (2017) PARAS 789, 796. Section 17(2)–(3), Sch 2 Pt 1 makes provision for the identification of children in need, the assessment of needs and the taking of steps to meet needs: see CHILDREN AND YOUNG PERSONS vol 10 (2017) PARA 789 et seq.

3 See the Children Act 1989 s 17A; and CHILDREN AND YOUNG PERSONS vol 10 (2017) PARA 804.

4 See the Children Act 1989 s 18; and CHILDREN AND YOUNG PERSONS vol 10 (2017) PARA 799.

5 See the Children Act 1989 ss 20, 21; and CHILDREN AND YOUNG PERSONS vol 10 (2017) PARAS 822–825.

6 See the Children Act 1989 ss 22, 22A–22G, 23; and CHILDREN AND YOUNG PERSONS vol 10 (2017) PARAS 829 et seq, 886.

7 See the Children Act 1989 ss 23ZA, 23ZB; and CHILDREN AND YOUNG PERSONS vol 10 (2017) PARAS 834, 835.

8 See the Children Act 1989 ss 23A–23CA; and CHILDREN AND YOUNG PERSONS vol 10 (2017) PARAS 849–853.

9 See the Children Act 1989 ss 23D, 23E, 24, 24A–24D; and CHILDREN AND YOUNG PERSONS vol 10 (2017) PARAS 850–862, 1101.

10 Ie under the Children Act 1989 Pt 4 (ss 31–42); and CHILDREN AND YOUNG PERSONS vol 9 (2017) PARA 349 et seq. Part 4 applies to England and Wales.

11 Ie under the Children Act 1989 Pt 5 (ss 43–52); and CHILDREN AND YOUNG PERSONS vol 9 (2017) PARA 249 et seq. Part 5 applies to England and Wales.

B.   CHILDREN TRANSITIONING TO ADULT SUPPORT

22.   Assessment of care needs of child attaining age of 18. Where:

(1)   it appears to a local authority in England[1] that a child is likely to have needs for care and support after becoming 18[2];

(2)   the authority is satisfied that it would be of significant benefit to the child to assess his needs[3]; and

(3)   either the child has capacity[4] or is competent to consent to an assessment being carried out and the child does so consent[5], or the child lacks capacity or is not competent so to consent but the authority is satisfied that carrying out an assessment would be in the child's best interests[6],

the authority must assess:

(a)   whether the child has needs for care and support and, if so, what those needs are[7]; and

(b)   whether the child is likely to have needs for care and support after becoming 18 and, if so, what those needs are likely to be[8].

Such an assessment is referred to as a 'child's needs assessment'[9]. Where a child refuses a child's needs assessment and the consent condition[10] is accordingly not met, the authority must nonetheless carry out the assessment if the child is experiencing, or is at risk of, abuse or neglect[11].

A child's needs assessment may, subject to consent, be combined with another assessment being carried out by the authority[12], and a local authority carrying out a child's needs assessment and another assessment may carry out that other assessment jointly or on behalf of the other body carrying it out[13].

1   As to the meaning of 'local authority' see PARA 1. As to the social services functions of local authorities in England generally, and the overarching principles in accordance with which functions relating to the provision of care and support must be exercised, see PARAS 315–323.

2   Care Act 2014 s 58(1).

3   Care Act 2014 s 58(1).

4   As to a person having or lacking capacity see PARA 8 note 10.

5   Care Act 2014 s 58(3)(a). The provisions of s 58(3) are referred to as 'the consent condition': s 58(3).

6   Care Act 2014 s 58(3)(b).

7   Care Act 2014 s 58(1)(a).

8   Care Act 2014 s 58(1)(b).

9   Care Act 2014 s 58(2). As to the carrying out of needs assessments see the Care and Support (Assessment) Regulations 2014, SI 2014/2827; and PARAS 64–65. As to what must be included in a child's needs assessment see PARA 23; as to consideration of a child's needs assessment see PARA 24. As to the duty to continue to provide care during the transition to adult support see PARA 25.

   Where a local authority, having received a request to carry out a child's needs assessment from the child concerned or a parent or carer of the child, decides not to comply with the request, it must give the person who made the request written reasons for its decision (Care Act 2014 s 58(5)(a)) and advice and information about what can be done to prevent or delay the development by the child of needs for care and support in the future (s 58(5)(b)).

   In the context of ss 58, 59 'parent', in relation to a child, includes a parent of the child who does not have parental responsibility for the child (s 58(6)(a)) and a person who is not a parent of the child but who has parental responsibility for the child (s 58(6)(b)). As to the meaning of 'parental responsibility' see the Children Act 1989 s 3; and CHILDREN AND YOUNG PERSONS vol 9 (2017) PARA 150. 'Carer', in relation to a child, means a person, other than a parent, who is providing care for the child, whether or not under or by virtue of a contract or as voluntary work: Care Act 2014 ss 58(7), 59(8). The reference to providing care includes a reference to providing practical or emotional support: s 58(8).

10 See the text and notes 4–6.

11 Care Act 2014 s 58(4). As to the meaning of 'abuse' see PARA 8 note 12.

12 A local authority may combine a child's needs assessment with an assessment it is carrying out (whether or not under the Care Act 2014 Pt 1) in relation to another person only if the consent condition is met in relation to the child to whom the child's needs assessment relates and:

    (1)   where the combination would include an assessment relating to another child, the consent condition is met in relation to that other child (s 65(2)(a));

    (2)   where the combination would include an assessment relating to an adult, the adult agrees (s 65(2)(b)).

    For the purposes of s 65 the consent condition is met in relation to a child if:

    (a)   the child has capacity or is competent to agree to the assessments being combined and does so agree (s 65(4)(a)); or

    (b)   the child lacks capacity or is not competent so to agree but the local authority is satisfied that combining the assessments would be in the child's best interests (s 65(4)(b)).

    In s 65 a reference to an assessment includes a reference to part of an assessment: s 65(6).

13 Where a local authority is carrying out a child's needs assessment and there is some other assessment being or about to be carried out in relation to the person to whom the assessment relates or in relation to a relevant person, the local authority may carry out that other assessment:

    (1)   on behalf of or jointly with the body responsible for carrying it out (Care Act 2014 s 65(5)(a)); or

    (2)   if that body has arranged to carry out the other assessment jointly with another person, jointly with that body and the other person (s 65(5)(b)).

    A person is a 'relevant person', in relation to a child's needs, child's carer's or young carer's assessment, if it would be reasonable to combine an assessment relating to that person with the child's needs, child's carer's or young carer's assessment (as mentioned in s 65(2) (see note 12) and (as the case may be) s 65(3) (see PARA 42)): s 65(7).

23. What must be included in a child's needs assessment of a person attaining age of 18.

A child's needs assessment[1] must include an assessment of:

    (1)   the impact on matters pertaining to the child's well-being[2] of what the child's needs for care and support are likely to be after the child becomes 18[3];

    (2)   the outcomes that the child wishes to achieve in day-to-day life[4]; and

    (3)   whether, and if so to what extent, the provision of care and support could contribute to the achievement of those outcomes[5].

In carrying out a child's needs assessment the local authority[6] must involve the child[7], his parents[8] and any carer[9] that he has[10], and any person whom the child or a parent or carer of the child requests the authority to involve[11], and must also consider whether, and if so to what extent, matters other than the provision of care and support could contribute to the achievement of the outcomes that the child wishes to achieve in day-to-day life[12].

Where it appears to a local authority carrying out a child's needs assessment that the child may, after becoming 18, be eligible for NHS continuing healthcare[13], the authority must refer the individual to the relevant body[14].

1 As to the duty to carry out a child's needs assessment see PARA 22; as to consideration of a child's needs assessment see PARA 24. As to the duty to continue to provide care during the transition to adult support see PARA 25.

2 Ie the matters specified in the Care Act 2014 s 1(2) (see PARA 12).

3 Care Act 2014 s 59(1)(a).

4 Care Act 2014 s 59(1)(b).

5 Care Act 2014 s 59(1)(c).

6 As to the meaning of 'local authority' see PARA 1. As to the social services functions of local authorities in England generally, and the overarching principles in accordance with which functions relating to the provision of care and support must be exercised, see PARAS 315–323.

7 Care Act 2014 s 59(2)(a). A local authority which is required to involve an individual in its exercise of a function under s 59(2)(a), (b) may be required to arrange for an independent advocate to be available to represent and support the individual: see s 67 (in particular s 67(3)(g)); the Care and Support (Independent Advocacy Support) (No 2) Regulations 2014, SI 2014/2889; and PARAS 100–103.

8   As to the meaning of 'parents' in this context see PARA 23 note 9.
9   As to the meaning of 'carer' in this context see PARA 23 note 9.
10 Care Act 2014 s 59(2)(b). See note 7.
11 Care Act 2014 s 59(2)(c).
12 Care Act 2014 s 59(3).
13 As to the meaning of 'NHS continuing healthcare' see PARA 9 note 12.
14 Care and Support (Assessment) Regulations 2014, SI 2014/2827, reg 7(2). As to the meaning of 'relevant body' see PARA 9 note 13 (noting also reg 7(4)).

24. Consideration of a child's needs assessment. Having carried out a child's needs assessment[1] a local authority[2] must give the child (or, where he lacks capacity[3], his parents[4]):

(1)   an indication as to whether any of the needs for care and support which it thinks the child is likely to have after becoming 18 are likely to meet the eligibility criteria[5] (and, if so, which ones are likely to do so)[6]; and

(2)   advice and information about what can be done to meet or reduce the needs for support which it thinks the child is likely to have after becoming 18[7] and what can be done to prevent or delay the development by the child of needs for care and support in the future[8].

1   As to the duty to carry out a child's needs assessment see PARAS 23–24. As to the duty to continue to provide care during the transition to adult support see PARA 25.
2   As to the meaning of 'local authority' see PARA 1. As to the social services functions of local authorities in England generally, and the overarching principles in accordance with which functions relating to the provision of care and support must be exercised, see PARAS 315–323.
3   Ie, in a case where the child is not competent or lacks capacity to understand the things which the local authority is required to give under the Care Act 2014 s 59(4) (see the text and notes 4–8): s 59(5). As to a person having or lacking capacity see PARA 8 note 10.
4   As to the meaning of 'parents' in this context see PARA 23 note 8.
5   As to the eligibility criteria for adults see PARA 10.
6   Care Act 2014 s 59(4)(a).
7   Care Act 2014 s 59(4)(b)(i).
8   Care Act 2014 s 59(4)(b)(ii).

25. Duty to continue to provide care during transition to adult support. Where a person to whom a child's needs assessment[1] relates becomes 18, the local authority[2] must decide whether to treat the assessment as a needs assessment[3]; and if the authority decides to do so, the care and support provisions[4] apply to the child's needs assessment as if it were a needs assessment that had been carried out after the person had become 18[5]. Where a local authority[6] providing services for a child in need[7], or a local authority[8] in England making arrangements for a disabled child[9], are required to carry out a child's needs assessment[10] in relation to the child[11] and carry out the assessment before the child reaches the age of 18 and decide to treat it as a needs assessment[12], the authority must continue to provide such services[13] or make such arrangements[14] after the child reaches the age of 18 until they reach a conclusion in his case[15]. If the local authority carry out the assessment before the child reaches the age of 18 but decide not to treat it as a needs assessment[16]:

(1)   they must carry out a needs assessment after the child reaches the age of 18[17]; and

(2)   they must continue to provide services or make arrangements[18] after he reaches that age until they reach a conclusion in his case[19],

and if the authority do not carry out the assessment before the child reaches the age of 18, they must continue to provide services or make arrangements after he reaches that age until:

(a)   they decide that the duty to carry out a needs assessment[20] does not apply[21]; or

(b)   having decided that the duty applies and having discharged it, they reach a conclusion in his case[22].

Where a local authority providing services for a child in need[23] or making arrangements for a disabled child[24] receive a request for a child's needs assessment to be carried out in relation to the child[25] but have yet to be required[26] to carry out the assessment[27], then if the authority do not decide, before the child reaches the age of 18, whether or not to comply with the request, they must continue to provide services or make arrangements after he reaches that age until:

(i)   they decide that the duty to carry out a needs assessment[28] does not apply[29]; or

(ii)   having decided that the duty applies and having discharged it, they reach a conclusion in his case[30].

1   As to the duty to carry out a child's needs assessment see the Care Act 2014 s 58(1), (2);and PARAS 23–24.

2   As to the meaning of 'local authority' in the context of the Care Act 2014 see PARA 1. As to the social services functions of local authorities in England generally, and the overarching principles in accordance with which functions relating to the provision of care and support must be exercised, see PARAS 315–323.

3   Care Act 2014 s 59(6). As to needs assessments see PARAS 64–65 (and see also, as to persons leaving hospital, PARAS 69–72). In considering what to decide under s 59(6), the authority must have regard to when the child's needs assessment was carried out (s 59(7)(a)) and whether it appears to the authority that the circumstances of the person to whom the child's needs assessment relates have changed in a way that might affect the assessment (s 59(7)(b)).

4   Ie the Care Act 2014 Pt 1 (ss 1–80).

5   Care Act 2014 s 59(6).

6   As to the meaning of 'local authority' in the context of the Children Act 1989 see s 105(1); and CHILDREN AND YOUNG PERSONS vol 9 (2017) PARA 154.

7   Ie in the exercise of functions conferred by the Children Act 1989 s 17: see PARA 21; and CHILDREN AND YOUNG PERSONS).

8   The local authorities for the purposes of the Chronically Sick and Disabled Persons Act 1970 are (by virtue of the National Assistance Act 1948 s 33(1) (amended by the Local Government Act 1972 Sch 23 para 2; and by SI 2015/914 (which is partly made under the Care Act 2014 s 123 (power to make consequential provision)); the Local Authority Social Services Act 1970 s 1; and the Chronically Sick and Disabled Persons Act 1970 s 2(1)) the councils of non-metropolitan counties and metropolitan districts in England, the councils of London boroughs and the Common Council of the City of London. As to local government areas and authorities in England see LOCAL GOVERNMENT vol 69 (2009) PARA 22 et seq. As to the London boroughs and their councils see LONDON GOVERNMENT vol 71 (2013) PARAS 15, 20, 34–38. As to the Common Council of the City of London see LONDON GOVERNMENT vol 71 (2013) PARA 16.

9   Ie under the Chronically Sick and Disabled Persons Act 1970 s 2 (see PARA 330).

10   Ie an assessment under the Care Act 2014 s 58(1): see PARAS 22, 23.

11   Ie in the Chronically Sick and Disabled Persons Act 1970 s 2A(1), (8) (s 2A added by the Care Act 2014 s 66(3)); Children Act 1989 s 17ZH(1)(a), (8) (s 17ZH added by the Care Act 2014 s 66(1)).

12   Ie in accordance with the Care Act 2014 s 59(6) (see the text and notes 1–4), with Pt 1 applying to the assessment as a result: Chronically Sick and Disabled Persons Act 1970 s 2A(2) (as added: see note 11); Children Act 1989 s 17ZH(2) (as so added).

13   Ie must continue to comply with the Children Act 1989 s 17.

14   Ie must continue to comply with the Chronically Sick and Disabled Persons Act 1970 s 2.

15   Chronically Sick and Disabled Persons Act 1970 s 2A(2) (as added: see note 11); Children Act 1989 s 17ZH(2) (as so added). A local authority reach a conclusion in a person's case when:

(1)   they conclude that he does not have needs for care and support or (as the case may be) for support (Chronically Sick and Disabled Persons Act 1970 s 2A(7)(a) (as so added); Children Act 1989 s 17ZH(7)(a) (as so added)); or

(2)   having concluded that he has such needs and that they are going to meet some or all of them, they begin to do so (Chronically Sick and Disabled Persons Act 1970 s 2A(7)(b) (as so added); Children Act 1989 s 17ZH(7)(b) (as so added)); or

(3)   having concluded that he has such needs, they conclude that they are not going to meet any of those needs (whether because those needs do not meet the eligibility criteria or for some other reason) (Chronically Sick and Disabled Persons Act 1970 s 2A(7)(c) (as so added); Children Act 1989 s 17ZH(7)(c) (as so added)).

As to the eligibility criteria see PARAS 10 (adults) and PARAS 35 (carers).

16 See note 12.
17 Chronically Sick and Disabled Persons Act 1970 s 2A(3)(a) (as added: see note 11); Children Act 1989 s 17ZH(3)(a) (as so added).
18 See notes 13, 14.
19 Chronically Sick and Disabled Persons Act 1970 s 2A(3)(a) (as added: see note 11); Children Act 1989 s 17ZH(3)(b) (as so added).
20 Ie under the Care Act 2014 s 9: see PARA 8.
21 Chronically Sick and Disabled Persons Act 1970 s 2A(4)(a) (as added: see note 11); Children Act 1989 s 17ZH(4)(a) (as so added).
22 Chronically Sick and Disabled Persons Act 1970 s 2A(4)(b) (as added: see note 11); Children Act 1989 s 17ZH(4)(b) (as so added).
23 See note 7.
24 See note 9.
25 Chronically Sick and Disabled Persons Act 1970 s 2A(5)(a) (as added: see note 11); Children Act 1989 s 17ZH(5)(a) (as so added).
26 Ie under the Care Act 2014 s 58(1).
27 Chronically Sick and Disabled Persons Act 1970 s 2A(5)(b) (as added: see note 11); Children Act 1989 s 17ZH(5)(b) (as so added).
28 See note 20.
29 Chronically Sick and Disabled Persons Act 1970 s 2A(6)(a) (as added: see note 11); Children Act 1989 s 17ZH(6)(a) (as so added).
30 Chronically Sick and Disabled Persons Act 1970 s 2A(6)(b) (as added: see note 11); Children Act 1989 s 17ZH(6)(b) (as so added).

(ii) Wales

26. Assessment of child's care needs. Where it appears to a local authority in Wales[1] that a child[2] (other than a child looked after by a local authority[3] or a Health and Social Care Trust[4]) may need care and support[5] in addition to, or instead of, the care and support provided by the child's family[6], the authority must assess whether the child does need care and support of that kind[7] and if he does, what those needs are[8]. This duty applies regardless of the authority's view of the level of the child's needs for care and support[9] or the level of the financial resources of the child or any person with parental responsibility for the child[10]: it does not, however, apply where the assessment is refused by or on behalf of the child[11] (subject to safeguarding provisions[12]), although the duty will be re-engaged, subject to any further refusal, if an assessment is subsequently requested by or on behalf of the child[13] or the authority considers that the child's needs or circumstances, or the needs or circumstances of a person with parental responsibility for the child, have changed[14].

1 As to the meaning of 'local authority' see PARA 2. As to the social services functions of local authorities in Wales generally, and the overarching principles in accordance with which functions relating to the provision of care and support must be exercised, see PARAS 373–383.
2 As to the meaning of 'child' see PARA 2. This duty applies in relation to a child who is ordinarily resident in the authority's area (Social Services and Well-being (Wales) Act 2014 s 21(2)(a)) and any other child who is within the authority's area (s 21(2)(b)): however, ss 21, 37, 38 do not apply in relation to a child who having been convicted of an offence is detained in youth detention accommodation or in prison or is residing in approved premises, and immediately before being convicted, was provided with accommodation by a local authority in England under the Children Act 1989 s 20 (see CHILDREN AND YOUNG PERSONS vol 10 (2017) PARAS 822–825) (Social Services and Well-being (Wales) Act 2014 s 186(6), (7)). In connection with the residence of detained persons and persons in approved and other residential premises generally (in particular with reference to interpretation) see PARA 87; in connection with the ordinary residence of children see PARA 86.
3 The Social Services and Well-being (Wales) Act 2014 ss 21, 37, 38 (assessments of needs and meeting needs: see the text and notes 4–14; and PARAS 27–31) do not apply to a child looked after by a local authority in Wales, England or Scotland: ss 21(8)(a)–(c), 37(6)(a)–(c), 38(4)(a)–(c). As to children looked after by local authorities in Wales see Pt 6 (ss 74–125); and CHILDREN AND

YOUNG PERSONS vol 10 (2017) PARA 826 et seq. As to children looked after by local authorities in England see the Children Act 1989 ss 20–30; and CHILDREN AND YOUNG PERSONS vol 10 (2017) PARA 822 et seq.

4   The Social Services and Well-being (Wales) Act 2014 ss 21, 37, 38 do not apply to a child looked after by a Health and Social Care Trust: ss 21(8)(d), 37(6)(d), 38(4)(d).

5   As to the meanings of 'care' and 'support' see PARA 2 note 1.

6   For these purposes a disabled child is presumed to need care and support in addition to, or instead of, the care and support provided by his family: Social Services and Well-being (Wales) Act 2014 s 21(7). A person is 'disabled' if he has a disability for the purposes of the Equality Act 2010 (see DISCRIMINATION vol 33 (2013) PARA 50), although this is subject to any provision made under the Social Services and Well-being (Wales) Act 2014 s 3(6), under which regulations may provide that a person falling within a specified category is or is not to be treated as disabled for these purposes. At the date at which this volume states the law no such regulations had been made.

7   Social Services and Well-being (Wales) Act 2014 s 21(1)(a). The nature of the needs assessment required by these provisions is one that the local authority considers proportionate in the circumstances, subject to any requirement in the Care and Support (Assessment) (Wales) Regulations 2015, SI 2015/1305 (see PARAS 66–77): Social Services and Well-being (Wales) Act 2014 s 21(6). As to what must be included in a needs assessment see PARA 27.

8   Social Services and Well-being (Wales) Act 2014 s 21(1)(b).

9   Social Services and Well-being (Wales) Act 2014 s 21(3)(a).

10 Social Services and Well-being (Wales) Act 2014 s 21(3)(b). As to the meaning of 'parental responsibility' see the Children Act 1989 s 3; and CHILDREN AND YOUNG PERSONS vol 9 (2017) PARA 150 (definition applied by the Social Services and Well-being (Wales) Act 2014 s 197(1)).

11 Ie where:

    (1)   a child aged 16 or 17 (or, where applicable, an authorised person) refuses a needs assessment under the Social Services and Well-being (Wales) Act 2014 s 21 (s 22(1));

    (2)   a person with parental responsibility for a child aged 16 or 17 refuses a needs assessment for that child under s 21 in circumstances in which the local authority is satisfied that the child lacks capacity to decide whether to refuse to have the assessment (s 22(2)(a)) and there is no authorised person to make the decision on the child's behalf (s 22(2)(b));

    (3)   a child aged under 16 refuses a needs assessment under s 21 (s 23(1)(a)) and the authority is satisfied that the child has sufficient understanding to make an informed decision about the refusal of the assessment (s 23(1)(b)); or

    (4)   a person with parental responsibility for a child aged under 16 refuses a needs assessment for that child under s 21 (s 23(2)).

In this context 'authorised person' means a person authorised under the Mental Capacity Act 2005 (whether in general or specific terms) to decide whether to refuse, or ask for, a needs assessment on the child's behalf: Social Services and Well-being (Wales) Act 2014 s 22(5). As to a person being 'authorised' under the Mental Capacity Act 2005 see PARA 12 note 15. As to a person having or lacking capacity see PARA 8 note 10.

12 A refusal by or on behalf a child aged 16 or 17 under the Social Services and Well-being (Wales) Act 2014 s 22(1) or (2) does not discharge a local authority from its duty under s 21 (see the text and notes 1–10) if (s 22(3)):

    (1)   the authority is satisfied, in the case of a refusal given by a child, that the child lacks capacity to decide whether to refuse to have the assessment;

    (2)   the authority is satisfied, in the case of a refusal given by a person with parental responsibility for the child, that the person lacks capacity to decide whether to refuse the assessment;

    (3)   the authority is satisfied, in the case of a refusal given by a person with parental responsibility for the child, that not having the assessment would not be in the child's best interests; or

    (4)   the authority suspects that the child is experiencing or at risk of abuse, neglect or other kinds of harm.

A refusal by or on behalf a child aged under 16 under s 23(1) or (2) does not discharge an authority from its duty under s 21 if (s 23(3)):

    (a)   the authority is satisfied, in the case of a refusal given by a person with parental responsibility for the child, that the person lacks capacity to decide whether to refuse the assessment;

    (b)   the authority is satisfied, in the case of a refusal given by a person with parental responsibility for the child, that the child has sufficient understanding to make an informed decision about the refusal of the assessment and does not agree with the refusal given by the person with parental responsibility for the child;

(c)   the authority is satisfied, in the case of a refusal given by a person with parental responsibility for the child, that not having the assessment would be inconsistent with the child's well-being; or

(d)   the authority suspects that the child is experiencing or at risk of abuse, neglect or other kinds of harm.

As to the meaning of 'well-being' see PARA 375. As to the meanings of 'abuse' and 'neglect' see PARA 15 note 11.

13 Ie:

(1)   in the case of a child aged 16 or 17, if:

(a)   the child (or, where applicable, an authorised person) subsequently asks for an assessment (Social Services and Well-being (Wales) Act 2014 s 22(4)(a)); or

(b)   a person with parental responsibility for the child subsequently asks for an assessment in circumstances where the authority is satisfied that the child lacks capacity to decide whether to refuse to have the assessment and there is no authorised person to make the decision on the child's behalf (s 22(4)(b)), or

(2)   in the case of a child aged under 16, if:

(a)   the child subsequently asks for an assessment and the authority is satisfied that the child has sufficient understanding to make an informed decision about having an assessment (s 23(4)(a)); or

(b)   a person with parental responsibility for the child subsequently asks for an assessment (s 23(4)(b)).

14 Social Services and Well-being (Wales) Act 2014 ss 22(4)(c), 23(4)(c).

27. What must be included in a needs assessment. In carrying out a needs assessment for a child[1] in Wales[2] the local authority[3] must:

(1)   assess the developmental needs of the child[4];

(2)   seek to identify the outcomes that the child wishes to achieve, to the extent it considers appropriate having regard to the child's age and understanding[5], the persons with parental responsibility[6] for the child wish to achieve in relation to the child, to the extent it considers appropriate having regard to the need to promote the child's well-being[7], and persons specified in regulations (if any) wish to achieve in relation to the child[8];

(3)   assess whether, and if so, to what extent, the provision of care and support[9], preventative services[10], or information, advice or assistance[11], could contribute to the achievement of those outcomes or otherwise meet needs identified by the assessment[12];

(4)   assess whether, and if so, to what extent, other matters could contribute to the achievement of those outcomes or otherwise meet those needs[13]; and

(5)   take account of any other circumstances affecting the child's well-being[14].

In carrying out a needs assessment the authority must involve the child[15] and any person with parental responsibility for the child[16].

1   As to the meaning of 'child' see PARA 2 (and as to the exclusion from these provisions of children in care see PARA 26 notes 3, 4).

2   See PARA 26; and as to the carrying out of assessments see PARAS 66–77.

3   As to the meaning of 'local authority' see PARA 2. As to the social services functions of local authorities in Wales generally, and the overarching principles in accordance with which functions relating to the provision of care and support must be exercised, see PARAS 373–383.

4   Social Services and Well-being (Wales) Act 2014 s 21(4)(a).

5   Social Services and Well-being (Wales) Act 2014 s 21(4)(b)(i).

6   As to the meaning of 'parental responsibility' see PARA 26 note 10.

7   Social Services and Well-being (Wales) Act 2014 s 21(4)(b)(ii). As to the meaning of 'well-being' see PARA 375.

8   Social Services and Well-being (Wales) Act 2014 s 21(4)(b)(iii). At the date at which this volume states the law no regulations had been made for this purpose.

9 Social Services and Well-being (Wales) Act 2014 s 21(4)(c)(i). As to the meanings of 'care' and 'support' see PARA 2 note 1.
10 Social Services and Well-being (Wales) Act 2014 s 21(4)(c)(ii). As to the meaning of 'preventative services' see PARA 16 note 6.
11 Social Services and Well-being (Wales) Act 2014 s 21(4)(c)(iii). As to the meaning of 'information, advice or assistance' see PARA 16 note 7.
12 Social Services and Well-being (Wales) Act 2014 s 21(4)(c).
13 Social Services and Well-being (Wales) Act 2014 s 21(4)(d).
14 Social Services and Well-being (Wales) Act 2014 s 21(4)(e).
15 Social Services and Well-being (Wales) Act 2014 s 21(5)(a).
16 Social Services and Well-being (Wales) Act 2014 s 21(5)(b).

28. Determination of eligibility and the eligibility criteria. Where a local authority in Wales[1] is satisfied on the basis of a needs assessment[2] that a child[3] has one or more needs for care and support[4] it must determine whether any of the needs meet the eligibility criteria[5]. Any one of those needs meets the eligibility criteria if:

(1) either the need arises from the child's physical or mental ill-health, age, disability, dependence on alcohol or drugs, or other similar circumstances[6] or the need is one that if unmet is likely to have an adverse effect on the child's development[7];

(2) the need relates to one or more of:
  (a) ability to carry out self-care or domestic routines[8];
  (b) ability to communicate[9];
  (c) protection from abuse or neglect[10];
  (d) involvement in work, education, learning or in leisure activities[11];
  (e) maintenance or development of family or other significant personal relationships[12];
  (f) development and maintenance of social relationships and involvement in the community[13]; or
  (g) achieving developmental goals[14];

(3) the need is one that neither the child, the child's parents nor other persons in a parental role[15] are able to meet, either alone or together[16], with the care and support of others who are willing to provide that care and support[17], or with the assistance of services in the community to which the child, the parents or other persons in a parental role have access[18]; and

(4) the child is unlikely to achieve one or more of his personal outcomes unless the local authority provides or arranges care and support to meet the need[19] or enables the need to be met by making direct payments[20].

1 As to the meaning of 'local authority' see PARA 2. As to the social services functions of local authorities in Wales generally, and the overarching principles in accordance with which functions relating to the provision of care and support must be exercised, see PARAS 373–383.
2 As to the duty to assess a child's needs see PARA 26; as to what must be included in a needs assessment see PARA 27.
3 As to the meaning of 'child' see PARA 2 (and as to the exclusion from these provisions of children in care see PARA 26 notes 3, 4).
4 As to the meanings of 'care' and 'support' see PARA 2 note 1.
5 Social Services and Well-being (Wales) Act 2014 s 32(1)(a).
6 Care and Support (Eligibility) (Wales) Regulations 2015, SI 2015/1578, regs 2(2), 4(1)(a)(i).
7 Care and Support (Eligibility) (Wales) Regulations 2015, SI 2015/1578, reg 4(1)(a)(ii). References to a child's development include the physical, intellectual, emotional, social and behavioural development of that child: reg 4(2)(i).
8 Care and Support (Eligibility) (Wales) Regulations 2015, SI 2015/1578, reg 4(1)(b)(i).
9 Care and Support (Eligibility) (Wales) Regulations 2015, SI 2015/1578, reg 4(1)(b)(ii).
10 Care and Support (Eligibility) (Wales) Regulations 2015, SI 2015/1578, reg 4(1)(b)(iii). As to the meanings of 'abuse' and 'neglect' see PARA 15 note 11.

11 Care and Support (Eligibility) (Wales) Regulations 2015, SI 2015/1578, reg 4(1)(b)(iv).
12 Care and Support (Eligibility) (Wales) Regulations 2015, SI 2015/1578, reg 4(1)(b)(v).
13 Care and Support (Eligibility) (Wales) Regulations 2015, SI 2015/1578, reg 4(1)(b)(vi).
14 Care and Support (Eligibility) (Wales) Regulations 2015, SI 2015/1578, reg 4(1)(b)(vii).
15 'Other persons in a parental role' includes persons with parental responsibility or relatives who
    play a role in looking after the child: Care and Support (Eligibility) (Wales) Regulations 2015, SI
    2015/1578, reg 4(2)(ii). As to the meaning of 'parental responsibility' see PARA 26 note 10.
    'Relative', in relation to a child, means a step-parent, grandparent, brother, sister, uncle or aunt
    (including any person who is in that relationship by virtue of a marriage or civil partnership or an
    enduring family relationship): Social Services and Well-being (Wales) Act 2014 s 197(1); Care and
    Support (Eligibility) (Wales) Regulations 2015, SI 2015/1578, reg 4(2)(iii).
16 Care and Support (Eligibility) (Wales) Regulations 2015, SI 2015/1578, reg 4(1)(c)(i). As to when
    a person who is able to meet the need, alone or with the assistance of others is to be regarded as
    unable to meet the need see reg 6; and PARA 17 note 14.
17 Care and Support (Eligibility) (Wales) Regulations 2015, SI 2015/1578, reg 4(1)(c)(ii).
18 Care and Support (Eligibility) (Wales) Regulations 2015, SI 2015/1578, reg 4(1)(c)(iii).
19 Care and Support (Eligibility) (Wales) Regulations 2015, SI 2015/1578, reg 4(1)(d)(i). As to the
    meaning of 'personal outcomes' see PARA 17 note 17.
20 Care and Support (Eligibility) (Wales) Regulations 2015, SI 2015/1578, reg 4(1)(d)(ii).

29. Duty to consider what can be done to meet needs. If a local authority in
Wales[1] determines that any child needs must be met, or are to be met[2], it must:

(1)   consider what could be done to meet those needs[3]; and
(2)   consider whether it would impose a charge for doing those things, and
        if so, determine the amount of that charge[4].

Where an authority is satisfied on the basis of a needs assessment[5] that a child[6]
has needs for care and support[7] it must determine whether the needs call for the
exercise of any social care function it has[8], in so far as the function is relevant to
that person[9], and consider whether the person would benefit from the provision of
preventative or advisory services[10] or anything else that may be available in the
community[11].

If a child's needs do not meet the eligibility criteria[12] the authority must
determine whether it is nevertheless necessary to meet the needs in order to protect
him from abuse or neglect or a risk of abuse or neglect, or other harm or a risk
of such harm[13].

1   As to the meaning of 'local authority' see PARA 2. As to the social services functions of local
    authorities in Wales generally, and the overarching principles in accordance with which functions
    relating to the provision of care and support must be exercised, see PARAS 373–383.
2   Ie, in the context of a child's needs, under the Social Services and Well-being (Wales) Act 2014
    ss 37–39 (see PARAS 30–32).
3   Social Services and Well-being (Wales) Act 2014 s 32(2)(a).
4   Social Services and Well-being (Wales) Act 2014 s 32(2)(b). See Pt 5 (ss 59–73); and
    PARAS 131–142.
5   As to the duty to assess a child's needs see PARA 26; as to what must be included in a needs
    assessment see PARA 27.
6   As to the meaning of 'child' see PARA 2 (and as to the exclusion from these provisions of children
    in care see PARA 26 notes 3, 4).
7   As to the meanings of 'care' and 'support' see PARA 2 note 1.
8   Ie under the Social Services and Well-being (Wales) Act 2014 or the Children Act 1989 Pt 4
    (ss 31–42) (care and supervision: see CHILDREN AND YOUNG PERSONS vol 9 (2017) PARA 349
    et seq) or Pt 5 (ss 43–52) (protection of children: see CHILDREN AND YOUNG PERSONS vol 9
    (2017) PARA 249 et seq).
9   Social Services and Well-being (Wales) Act 2014 s 32(1)(c).
10 Ie anything that may be provided by virtue of the Social Services and Well-being (Wales) Act 2014
    s 15 (preventative services: see PARA 376) or 17 (information, advice and assistance: see
    PARA 392).
11 Social Services and Well-being (Wales) Act 2014 s 32(1)(d).
12 As to the eligibility criteria see PARA 28.
13 Social Services and Well-being (Wales) Act 2014 s 32(1)(b)(ii). As to the meanings of 'abuse' and
    'neglect' see PARA 15 note 11.

30. Circumstances where local authority must meet child's needs for care and support. A local authority in Wales[1] must meet a child's needs[2] for care and support[3] if it is satisfied that:

(1)   the child is within the authority's area[4]; and

(2)   either the needs meet the eligibility criteria[5] or the authority considers it necessary to meet the needs in order to protect the child from abuse[6] or neglect[7] or other harm or a risk of such harm[8].

Further conditions may be specified by regulations[9].

These duties do not apply to the extent that the authority is satisfied that a child's needs are being met by the child's family or a carer[10].

1   As to the meaning of 'local authority' see PARA 2. As to the social services functions of local authorities in Wales generally, and the overarching principles in accordance with which functions relating to the provision of care and support must be exercised, see PARAS 373–383.
2   As to the meaning of 'child' see PARA 2; as to the application of these provisions in relation to children in detention or care see PARA 26 notes 2–4. As to the duty to assess a child's needs see PARA 26; as to what must be included in a needs assessment see PARA 27; as to the duty to consider what can be done to meet needs see PARA 29.
3   As to the meanings of 'care' and 'support' see PARA 2 note 1. Where a local authority in Wales is required to meet needs under these provisions it must prepare a care and support plan: see the Social Services and Well-being (Wales) Act 2014 s 54; and PARA 81. Where advocacy services are being provided for a person under s 37 and regulations under s 181 (provision of advocacy services: see PARA 104) would (apart from this provision) impose a requirement upon a local authority to make advocacy services available to that person in respect of the same matters, that requirement does not apply: s 182(2).
4   Social Services and Well-being (Wales) Act 2014 s 37(1), (2). In connection with a person's residence see PARAS 84–87. If local authority has been notified about a child under s 120(2)(a) or the Children Act 1989 s 85(1) (assessment of children accommodated by health or education authorities: see CHILDREN AND YOUNG PERSONS vol 10 (2017) PARA 1268), it must treat the child as being within its area for these purposes: Social Services and Well-being (Wales) Act 2014 s 37(4) (amended by SI 2016/413).
5   Social Services and Well-being (Wales) Act 2014 s 37(3)(a). As to the eligibility criteria for children in Wales see PARA 28.
6   As to the meaning of 'abuse' see PARA 15 note 11.
7   As to the meaning of 'neglect' see PARA 15 note 11.
8   Social Services and Well-being (Wales) Act 2014 s 37(3)(b).
9   Social Services and Well-being (Wales) Act 2014 s 37(1). At the date at which this volume states the law no such regulations had been made.
10 Social Services and Well-being (Wales) Act 2014 s 37(5). See however s 39 (maintenance of family contact); and PARA 32. As to the meaning of 'carer' see PARA 54 note 2.

31. Circumstances where local authority may meet child's needs for care and support. A local authority in Wales[1] may meet a child's[2] needs for care and support[3] if the child is within the local authority's area[4] or ordinarily resident in the authority's area, but outside its area[5]. An authority has the power to meet needs under these provisions whether or not it has completed a needs assessment[6] or[7] a financial assessment[8].

1   As to the meaning of 'local authority' see PARA 2. As to the social services functions of local authorities in Wales generally, and the overarching principles in accordance with which functions relating to the provision of care and support must be exercised, see PARAS 373–383.
2   As to the meaning of 'child' see PARA 2; as to the application of these provisions in relation to children in detention or care see PARA 26 notes 2–4. As to the duty to assess a child's needs see PARA 26; as to what must be included in a needs assessment see PARA 27; as to the duty to consider what can be done to meet needs see PARA 29.
3   As to the meanings of 'care' and 'support' see PARA 2 note 1. Where advocacy services are being provided for a person under the Social Services and Well-being (Wales) Act 2014 s 38 and regulations under s 181 (provision of advocacy services: see PARA 104) would (apart from this provision) impose a requirement upon a local authority to make advocacy services available to that person in respect of the same matters, that requirement does not apply: s 182(2).
4   Social Services and Well-being (Wales) Act 2014 s 38(1)(a). If a local authority meets the needs of a child who is ordinarily resident in the area of another local authority under s 38(1), it must notify

the local authority in whose area the child is ordinarily resident that it is doing so: s 38(2). In connection with a person's residence see PARAS 84–87.
5 Social Services and Well-being (Wales) Act 2014 s 38(1)(b).
6 Ie in accordance with the Social Services and Well-being (Wales) Act 2014 Pt 3 (ss 19–31): in connection with assessments of children's needs in Wales see PARAS 66–77.
7 Ie in accordance with the Social Services and Well-being (Wales) Act 2014 Pt 5 (ss 59–73): in connection with assessments of finances in Wales see PARAS 131–142.
8 Social Services and Well-being (Wales) Act 2014 s 38(3).

32. Maintenance of family contact. Where a child[1] within the area of a local authority[2] is living apart from his family[3] and is not looked after by the authority[4], and the authority considers that he has needs for care and support[5] in addition to the care and support provided by his family[6], the authority must, if it considers it necessary in order to promote the well-being[7] of the child, take such steps as are reasonably practicable to enable the child to live with his family[8] or promote contact between the child and his family[9].

1 As to the meaning of 'child' see PARA 2 (and as to the exclusion from these provisions of children in care see PARA 26 notes 3, 4). As to the duty to assess a child's needs see PARA 26; as to what must be included in a needs assessment see PARA 27; as to the duty to consider what can be done to meet needs see PARA 29.
2 Social Services and Well-being (Wales) Act 2014 s 39(1)(a). As to the meaning of 'local authority' see PARA 2. As to the social services functions of local authorities in Wales generally, and the overarching principles in accordance with which functions relating to the provision of care and support must be exercised, see PARAS 373–383.
3 Social Services and Well-being (Wales) Act 2014 s 39(1)(c).
4 Social Services and Well-being (Wales) Act 2014 s 39(1)(d). As to children looked after by local authorities in Wales see Pt 6 (ss 74–125); and CHILDREN AND YOUNG PERSONS vol 10 (2017) PARA 826 et seq.
5 As to the meanings of 'care' and 'support' see PARA 2 note 1.
6 Social Services and Well-being (Wales) Act 2014 s 39(1)(b).
7 As to the meaning of 'well-being' see PARA 375.
8 Social Services and Well-being (Wales) Act 2014 s 39(2)(a).
9 Social Services and Well-being (Wales) Act 2014 s 39(2)(b).

(4) PROVISION OF SUPPORT FOR CARERS

(i) England

A.   ADULT CARERS

(A)   Adult Carers Generally

33. Assessment of a carer's care needs. Where it appears to a local authority in England[1] that a carer[2] may have needs for care and support (whether currently or in the future) the authority must assess whether the adult does have needs for care and support (or is likely to do so in the future)[3] and if he does, what those needs are (or are likely to be in the future)[4]. Such an assessment is referred to as a 'carer's assessment'[5], and the duty to carry one out applies regardless of the authority's view of the level of the carer's needs for care and support[6] or the level of the carer's financial resources or those of the adult needing care[7]. A carer may refuse a carer's assessment, in which event the local authority concerned is not required to carry one out[8], although an authority is required to carry out an assessment (subject to a further refusal) where a carer has refused an assessment and the authority thinks that his needs or circumstances, or those of the adult needing care, have changed[9]. An authority must also carry out a carer's assessment, to the extent that the authority considers appropriate, where circumstances have changed in a way that affects a support plan in respect of a carer[10].

1   As to the meaning of 'local authority' see PARA 1. As to the social services functions of local authorities in England generally, and the overarching principles in accordance with which functions relating to the provision of care and support must be exercised, see PARAS 315–323.
2   'Carer' means an adult who provides or intends to provide care for another adult (an 'adult needing care'): Care Act 2014 s 10(3). An adult is not, however, to be regarded as a carer if he provides or intends to provide care under or by virtue of a contract (s 10(9)(a)) or as voluntary work (s 10(9)(b)), although in a case where the local authority considers that the relationship between the adult needing care and the adult providing or intending to provide care is such that it would be appropriate for the latter to be regarded as a carer, that adult is to be regarded as such (and s 10(9) is therefore to be ignored in that case) (s 10(10)). The references in s 10 to 'providing care' include a reference to providing practical or emotional support: s 10(11). As to the meaning of 'adult' see PARA 1 note 1.
3   Care Act 2014 s 10(1)(a).
4   Care Act 2014 s 10(1)(b). As to the carrying out of assessments see the Care and Support (Assessment) Regulations 2014, SI 2014/2827; and PARAS 64–65. As to what must be included in a needs assessment see PARA 34.
5   Care Act 2014 s 10(2). A child's carer's assessment (see PARAS 42–43) concerning a child who attains the age of 18 may be treated as a carer's assessment: see s 61(6), (7); and PARA 46.
6   Care Act 2014 s 10(4)(a). A reference to a carer's assessment includes a reference to a carer's assessment which forms part of a combined assessment under s 12(5) (see PARA 66): s 12(8). A reference to an assessment includes a reference to part of an assessment: s 12(9). As to the carrying out of carer's assessments see the Care and Support (Assessment) Regulations 2014, SI 2014/2827; and PARAS 64–65. The local authority must give a written record of a carer's assessment to the carer to whom the assessment relates (s 12(4)(a)), the adult needing care, if the adult asks the authority to do so (s 12(4)(b)), and any other person to whom the carer asks the authority to give a copy (s 12(4)(c)).
7   Care Act 2014 s 10(4)(b).
8   Care Act 2014 ss 10(12), 11(5). In these circumstances s 10(1) (see the text and notes 1–4) will not apply: s 11(5). Where, having refused a carer's assessment, an adult requests the assessment, s 10(1) applies in the carer's case (and s 11(5) does not): s 11(6).
9   Care Act 2014 s 11(7). In these circumstances s 10(1) applies in the carer's case (but subject to further refusal as mentioned in s 11(5)): s 11(7).
10 See the Care Act 2014 s 27(4)(a); the Care and Support (Children's Carer's) Regulations 2015, SI 2015/305, reg 11(g) (see PARA 44 note 6); and PARA 80. Where the authority is satisfied that circumstances have changed in a way that affects a support plan in respect of a child's carer, the authority must, to the extent that it thinks appropriate, carry out a child's carer's assessment: see the Care Act 2014 s 27(4A)(a); the Care and Support (Children's Carer's) Regulations 2015, SI 2015/305, reg 11(h); and PARA 80.

34. What must be included in a carer's assessment. A carer's assessment in England[1] must include an assessment of:

(1)   whether the carer[2] is able, and is likely to continue to be able, to provide care for the adult[3] needing care[4];

(2)   whether the carer is willing, and is likely to continue to be willing, to do so[5];

(3)   the impact of the carer's needs for support on his well-being[6];

(4)   the outcomes that the carer wishes to achieve in day-to-day life[7]; and

(5)   whether, and if so to what extent, the provision of support could contribute to the achievement of those outcomes[8].

In carrying out a carer's assessment a local authority[9] must have regard to whether the carer works or wishes to do so[10] and whether the carer is participating in or wishes to participate in education, training or recreation[11]. The assessment must also involve the carer[12] and any person whom the carer asks the authority to involve[13].

1   See PARA 33; and as to the carrying out of assessments see PARAS 64–65.
2   As to the meaning of 'carer' see PARA 33 note 2.

3 As to the meaning of 'adult' see PARA 1 note 1.
4 Care Act 2015 s 10(5)(a).
5 Care Act 2015 s 10(5)(b).
6 Care Act 2014 s 10(5)(c). The reference in the text to the carer's 'well-being' is a reference to the matters specified in s 1(2) (see PARA 317).
7 Care Act 2014 s 10(5)(d). When carrying out a carer's assessment a local authority must also consider whether, and if so to what extent, matters other than the provision of support could contribute to the achievement of the outcomes that the carer wishes to achieve in day-to-day life: s 10(8)(a).
8 Care Act 2014 s 10(5)(e). When carrying out a carer's assessment a local authority must also consider whether the carer would benefit from the provision of anything under s 2 or s 4 (preventative and educational measures: see PARAS 318, 326) or of anything which might be available in the community: s 10(8)(b).
9 As to the meaning of 'local authority' see PARA 1. As to the social services functions of local authorities in England generally, and the overarching principles in accordance with which functions relating to the provision of care and support must be exercised, see PARAS 315–323.
10 Care Act 2015 s 10(6)(a).
11 Care Act 2015 s 10(6)(b).
12 Care Act 2014 s 10(7)(a). A local authority which is required to involve an individual in its exercise of a function under s 10(7)(a) may be required to arrange for an independent advocate to be available to represent and support the individual: see s 67 (in particular s 67(3)(b)); the Care and Support (Independent Advocacy Support) (No 2) Regulations 2014, SI 2014/2889; and PARAS 100–103.
13 Care Act 2014 s 10(7)(b).

35. Determination of eligibility and the eligibility criteria. Where a local authority in England[1] is satisfied on the basis of a carer's assessment[2] that a carer[3] has needs for care and support it must determine whether any of the needs meet the eligibility criteria[4]. A carer's needs meet the eligibility criteria if:

(1) the needs arise as a consequence of providing necessary care for an adult[5];

(2) the effect of the carer's needs is that his physical or mental health is, or is at risk of, deteriorating[6] or he is unable to achieve any of the following outcomes[7]:

  (a) carrying out any caring responsibilities the carer has for a child[8];
  (b) providing care to other persons for whom the carer provides care[9];
  (c) maintaining a habitable home environment in the carer's home (whether or not this is also the home of the adult needing care)[10];
  (d) managing and maintaining nutrition[11];
  (e) developing and maintaining family or other personal relationships[12];
  (f) engaging in work, training, education or volunteering[13];
  (g) making use of necessary facilities or services in the local community, including recreational facilities or services[14]; or
  (h) engaging in recreational activities[15] and

(3) as a consequence of that fact there is, or is likely to be, a significant impact on the carer's well-being[16].

Where at least some of a carer's needs for support meet the eligibility criteria the local authority must consider what could be done to meet those needs that do[17] and establish whether the adult needing care is ordinarily resident in the local authority's area[18].

1 As to the meaning of 'local authority' see PARA 1. As to the social services functions of local authorities in England generally, and the overarching principles in accordance with which functions relating to the provision of care and support must be exercised, see PARAS 315–323.
2 As to the duty to assess an carer's needs, and the meaning of 'carer's assessment', see PARA 33; as to what must be included in a carers assessment see PARA 34.

3 As to the meaning of 'carer' see PARA 33 note 2.
4 Care Act 2014 s 13(1). Regulations may make provision about the making of such determination: s 13(6). At the date at which this volume states the law no such regulations had been made. Having made a determination under s 13(1), the local authority must give the person concerned a written record of the determination and the reasons for it: s 13(2). An authority must also make a determination under s 13(1), to the extent that it considers appropriate, where it is satisfied that circumstances have changed in a way that affects a support plan in respect of a carer: see s 27(4)(a); the Care and Support (Children's Carer's) Regulations 2015, SI 2015/305, reg 11(g) (see PARA 44 note 6); and PARA 80.
5 Care and Support (Eligibility Criteria) Regulations 2015, SI 2015/313, reg 3(1)(a) (made under the Care Act 2014 s 13(7), (8)). As to the meaning of 'adult' see PARA 1 note 1. Where the level of a carer's needs fluctuates, in determining whether his needs meet the eligibility criteria the local authority must take into account his circumstances over such period as it considers necessary to establish accurately his level of need: Care and Support (Eligibility Criteria) Regulations 2015, SI 2015/313, art 3(4).
6 Care and Support (Eligibility Criteria) Regulations 2015, SI 2015/313, art 3(1)(b), (2)(a).
7 For these purposes a carer is to be regarded as being unable to achieve an outcome if he:
　　(1)　　is unable to achieve it without assistance (Care and Support (Eligibility Criteria) Regulations 2015, SI 2015/313, reg 3(3)(a));
　　(2)　　is able to achieve it without assistance but doing so causes him significant pain, distress or anxiety (reg 3(3)(b)); or
　　(3)　　is able to achieve it without assistance but doing so endangers or is likely to endanger the health or safety of him, or of others (reg 3(3)(c)).
8 Care and Support (Eligibility Criteria) Regulations 2015, SI 2015/313, art 3(2)(b)(i).
9 Care and Support (Eligibility Criteria) Regulations 2015, SI 2015/313, art 3(2)(b)(ii).
10 Care and Support (Eligibility Criteria) Regulations 2015, SI 2015/313, art 3(2)(b)(iii).
11 Care and Support (Eligibility Criteria) Regulations 2015, SI 2015/313, art 3(2)(b)(iv).
12 Care and Support (Eligibility Criteria) Regulations 2015, SI 2015/313, art 3(2)(b)(v).
13 Care and Support (Eligibility Criteria) Regulations 2015, SI 2015/313, art 3(2)(b)(vi).
14 Care and Support (Eligibility Criteria) Regulations 2015, SI 2015/313, art 3(2)(b)(vii).
15 Care and Support (Eligibility Criteria) Regulations 2015, SI 2015/313, art 3(2)(b)(viii).
16 Care and Support (Eligibility Criteria) Regulations 2015, SI 2015/313, art 3(1)(c). As to the meaning of 'well-being' see PARA 317.
17 Care Act 2014 s 13(4)(a).
18 Care Act 2014 s 13(4)(b). In connection with a person's residence see PARAS 84–87.

36. Circumstances where local authority must meet carer's needs for support.
Where a local authority in England[1] has made a determination as to whether a carer's needs[2] meet the eligibility criteria[3] the authority must meet such of the carer's needs which meet the criteria if:

(1)　　the adult[4] needing care is ordinarily resident in the authority's area or is present in its area but of no settled residence[5];

(2)　　in so far as meeting the carer's needs involves the provision of support to the carer, there is no charge[6] for meeting the needs or, in so far as there is, either the authority is satisfied on the basis of the financial assessment it carried out[7] that the carer's financial resources are at or below the financial limit[8] or the authority is satisfied on the basis of the financial assessment it carried out that the carer's financial resources are above the financial limit[9] but the carer nonetheless asks the authority to meet the needs in question[10]; and

(3)　　in so far as meeting the carer's needs involves the provision of care and support to the adult needing care, either there is no charge[11] for meeting the needs and the adult needing care agrees to the needs being met in that way[12] or, in so far as there is such a charge, either the authority is satisfied on the basis of the financial assessment it carried out that the financial resources of the adult needing care are at or below the financial limit[13] and the adult needing care agrees to the authority meeting the needs in question by providing care and support to him or her[14], or the authority is satisfied on the basis of the financial assessment it carried out that the financial resources of the adult needing care are above the financial limit[15] but the adult needing care nonetheless asks the authority to meet the needs in question by providing care and support to him or her[16].

1 As to the meaning of 'local authority' see PARA 1. As to the social services functions of local authorities in England generally, and the overarching principles in accordance with which functions relating to the provision of care and support must be exercised, see PARAS 315–323.

2 As to the duty to assess a carer's needs see PARA 8; as to what must be included in a carer's assessment see PARA 34. As to the meaning of 'carer' see PARA 33 note 2.

3 As to the making of such determinations see the Care Act 2014 s 13(1); and PARA 35. As to the next steps after making a decision as to the provision of care see PARA 38. Where a local authority is required by s 20 to meet some or all of a carer's needs for support but it does not prove feasible for it to do so by providing care and support to the adult needing care, it must, so far as it is feasible to do so, identify some other way in which to do so: s 20(8).

4 As to the meaning of 'adult' see PARA 1 note 1.

5 Care Act 2014 s 20(1)(a). In connection with a person's residence see PARAS 84–87.

6 Ie under the Care Act 2014 s 14: see PARA 111. The reference in this provision to there being no charge under s 14 for meeting a carer's needs for support is a reference to there being no such charge because the authority is prohibited by regulations under s 14 from making such a charge (s 20(9)(a)) or the authority is entitled to make such a charge but decides not to do so (s 20(9)(b)).

7 As to financial assessments see PARAS 119–120.

8 Care Act 2014 s 20(1)(b), (2). The 'financial limit' is £23,250: see PARA 105.

9 Care Act 2014 s 20(3)(a).

10 Care Act 2014 s 20(3)(b).

11 Ie under the Care Act 2014 s 14. The reference in this provision to there being no charge under s 14 for meeting an adult's needs for care and support is to be construed in accordance with s 18(6) (see PARA 12): s 20(10).

12 Care Act 2014 s 20(1)(c)(i).

13 Care Act 2014 s 20(1)(c)(ii), (4)(a).

14 Care Act 2014 s 20(4)(b).

15 Care Act 2014 s 20(5)(a).

16 Care Act 2014 s 20(5)(b).

37. Circumstances where local authority may meet carer's needs for care and support. A local authority in England[1] may meet a carer's needs for support[2] if it is satisfied that it is not required to meet his needs[3]; but, in so far as meeting the carer's needs involves the provision of care and support to the adult[4] needing care, it may do so only if the adult needing care agrees to the needs being met in that way[5]. An authority may meet some or all of a carer's needs for support in a way which involves the provision of care and support to the adult needing care, even if the authority would not be required[6] to meet the adult's needs for care and support[7].

1 As to the meaning of 'local authority' see PARA 1. As to the social services functions of local authorities in England generally, and the overarching principles in accordance with which functions relating to the provision of care and support must be exercised, see PARAS 315–323.

2 As to the duty to assess a carer's needs see PARA 8; as to what must be included in a carer's assessment see PARA 34. As to the meaning of 'carer' see PARA 33 note 2. As to the next steps after making a decision as to the provision of care see PARA 38.

3 Ie under the Care Act 2014 s 20: see PARA 36.

4 As to the meaning of 'adult' see PARA 1 note 1.

5 Care Act 2014 s 20(6).

6 Ie under the Care Act 2014 s 18: see PARA 12.

7 Care Act 2014 s 20(7).

38. Next steps after making decision as to provision of care. Where a local authority in England[1] is required to meet a carer's needs[2] or decides to do so[3] it must prepare a support plan for the carer concerned[4], tell the person which (if any) of the needs that it is going to meet may be met by direct payments[5] and help the person with deciding how to have the needs met[6]. Where an authority has carried out a carer's assessment[7] but is not required, and does not decide, to meet needs[8], it must give the person concerned its written reasons for not meeting the needs[9] and[10] advice and information about what can be done to meet or reduce the needs[11] and to prevent or delay the development by the person concerned of needs for care and support or of needs for support in the future[12].

1 As to the meaning of 'local authority' see PARA 1. As to the social services functions of local authorities in England generally, and the overarching principles in accordance with which functions relating to the provision of care and support must be exercised, see PARAS 315–323.
2 Ie under the Care Act 2014 s 20(1) (see PARA 36). As to the meaning of 'carer' see PARA 33 note 2.
3 Ie under the Care Act 2014 s 20(6) (see PARA 37).
4 Care Act 2014 s 24(1)(a). As to support plans see PARAS 78–80.
5 Care Act 2014 s 24(1)(b). As to direct payments see PARAS 106–110.
6 Care Act 2014 s 24(1)(c).
7 As to the meaning of 'carer's assessment' see PARA 33. As to what must be included in a carer's assessment see PARA 34.
8 See notes 2, 3.
9 Care Act 2014 s 24(2)(a).
10 Ie unless the authority has already done so under the Care Act 2014 s 13(5) (see PARA 11).
11 Care Act 2014 s 24(2)(b)(i).
12 Care Act 2014 s 24(2)(b)(ii).

(B) Adult Carers of Children for whom they have Parental Responsibility

39. Assessment of care needs of parent carer. A local authority in England[1] must assess whether a parent carer — ie a person aged 18 or over who provides or intends to provide care for a disabled child[2] for whom the person has parental responsibility[3] — within their area has needs for support[4] and, if so, what those needs are, if:

(1)   it appears to the authority that the parent carer may have needs for support[5] or the authority receive a request from the parent carer to assess his needs for support[6]; and

(2)   the authority are satisfied that the disabled child cared for and the disabled child's family are persons for whom they may[7] provide or arrange for the provision of services[8].

Such an assessment is referred to as a 'parent carer's needs assessment'[9]. The obligation to carry out an assessment does not apply[10] in relation to a parent carer if the authority have previously carried out a care-related assessment[11] of the parent carer in relation to the same disabled child cared for[12], although an assessment must be carried out[13] if it appears to the authority that the needs or circumstances of the parent carer or the disabled child cared for have changed since the last care-related assessment[14].

Where a local authority are required to carry out a parent carer's needs assessment and are required or have decided to carry out some other assessment of the parent carer or of the disabled child cared for, the authority may combine the assessments[15].

1 As to the meaning of 'local authority' see PARA 25 note 6.
2 As to the meanings of 'disabled' and 'child' in the context of the Children Act 1989 see ss 17(11), 105(1); and CHILDREN AND YOUNG PERSONS vol 9 (2017) PARA 3, CHILDREN AND YOUNG PERSONS vol 10 (2017) PARA 789. The references in the Children Act 1989 s 17ZD to providing care include a reference to providing practical or emotional support: s 17ZE(1), (2) (ss 17ZD, 17ZE added by the Children and Families Act 2014 s 97(1)).
3 Children Act 1989 s 17ZD(2) (as added: see note 2). As to the meaning of 'parental responsibility' see the Children Act 1989 s 3; and CHILDREN AND YOUNG PERSONS vol 9 (2017) PARA 150.
4 A local authority in England must take reasonable steps to identify the extent to which there are parent carers within their area who have needs for support: Children Act 1989 s 17ZD(14) (as added: see note 2).
5 Children Act 1989 s 17ZD(1), (3)(a) (as added: see note 2).

6   Children Act 1989 s 17ZD(3)(b) (as added: see note 2).

7   Ie under the Children Act 1989 s 17: see PARA 21; and CHILDREN AND YOUNG PERSONS vol 10 (2017) PARA 789 et seq).

8   Children Act 1989 s 17ZD(4) (as added: see note 2).

9   Children Act 1989 s 17ZD(5) (as added: see note 2). As to the carrying out of assessments see PARAS 64–65. As to what must be included in a parent-carer's assessment see PARA 40; as to the consideration of a parent-carer's assessment see PARA 41. A local authority that have carried out a parent carer's needs assessment must give a written record of the assessment to the parent carer (s 17ZD(13)(a) (as so added)) and any person to whom the parent carer requests the authority to give a copy (s 17ZD(13)(b) (as so added)).

10   Ie the Children Act 1989 s 17ZD(1) (see the text and notes 1–8) does not apply.

11   'Care-related assessment' means a parent carer's needs assessment (Children Act 1989 s 17ZD(8)(a) (as added: see note 2)), or an assessment under any of the Carers (Recognition and Services) Act 1995 s 1 (Children Act 1989 s 17ZD(8)(b)(i) (as so added)), the Carers and Disabled Children Act 2000 s 6 (repealed) (Children Act 1989 s 17ZD(8)(b)(ii) (as so added)), the Community Care (Delayed Discharges) Act 2003 s 4(3) (see PARA 69) (Children Act 1989 s 17ZD(8)(b)(iii) (as so added)) and the Care Act 2014 Pt 1 (ss 1–80) (see PARAS 33–38) (Children Act 1989 s 17ZD(8)(b)(iv)) (as so added; further added by SI 2015/914 (made under the Children Act 1989 s 17ZE(5) (as so added))).

12   Children Act 1989 s 17ZD(6) (as added: see note 2).

13   And the Children Act 1989 s 17ZD(1) applies.

14   Children Act 1989 s 17ZD(7) (as added: see note 2).

15   Children Act 1989 s 17ZE(3) (as added: see note 2).

40. What must be included in a parent-carer's assessment. A parent carer's needs assessment[1] must include an assessment of whether it is appropriate for the parent carer to provide, or continue to provide, care for the disabled child[2], in the light of the parent carer's needs for support, other needs and wishes[3]. In carrying out a parent carer's needs assessment local authority[4] must have regard to the well-being of the parent carer[5] and the need to safeguard and promote the welfare of the disabled child cared for and any other child for whom the parent carer has parental responsibility[6], and must involve the parent carer[7], any child for whom the parent carer has parental responsibility[8] and any person who the parent carer requests the authority to involve[9].

1   As to the circumstances in which a parent carer's needs assessment must be carried out see PARA 39; as to the consideration of a parent-carer's assessment see PARA 41.

2   As to the meanings of 'disabled' and 'child' see PARA 39 note 2. As to 'providing care' see PARA 39 note 2.

3   Children Act 1989 s 17ZD(9) (ss 17ZD, 17ZE added by the Children and Families Act 2014 s 97(1)). The Secretary of State may by regulations make further provision about carrying out a parent carer's needs assessment; the regulations may, in particular:

     (1)   specify matters to which a local authority is to have regard in carrying out an assessment (Children Act 1989 s 17ZE(4)(a) (as so added));

     (2)   specify matters which a local authority is to determine in carrying out an assessment (s 17ZE(4)(b) (as so added));

     (3)   make provision about the manner in which an assessment is to be carried out (s 17ZE(4)(c) (as so added));

     (4)   make provision about the form an assessment is to take (s 17ZE(4)(d) (as so added)).

     At the date at which this volume states the law no such regulations had been made. As to the Secretary of State see PARA 333.

4   As to the meaning of 'local authority' see PARA 25 note 6.

5   Children Act 1989 s 17ZD(10)(a) (as added: see note 3). As to the meaning of 'well-being' see the Care Act 2014 s 1(2); and PARA 317 (definition applied by the Children Act 1989 s 17D(11) (as so added)).

6   Children Act 1989 s 17ZD(10)(b) (as added: see note 3). As to the meaning of 'parental responsibility' see PARA 39 note 3.

7   Children Act 1989 s 17ZD(12)(a) (as added: see note 3).

8   Children Act 1989 s 17ZD(12)(b) (as added: see note 3).

9   Children Act 1989 s 17ZD(12)(c) (as added: see note 3).

41. Consideration of a parent-carer's assessment. A local authority[1] that carry out a parent carer's needs assessment[2] must consider the assessment and decide:

(1)   whether the parent carer[3] has needs for support in relation to the care which he or she provides or intends to provide[4];

(2)   whether the disabled child[5] cared for has needs for support[6];

(3)   if either head (1) or head (2) above applies, whether those needs could be satisfied (wholly or partly) by services which the authority may provide[7] pursuant to its general powers relating to the provision of services for children in need[8]; and

(4)   if they could be so satisfied, whether or not to provide any such services in relation to the parent carer or the disabled child cared for[9].

1   As to the meaning of 'local authority' see PARA 25 note 6.
2   As to the circumstances in which a parent carer's needs assessment must be carried out see PARA 39; as to what must be included in a parent-carer's assessment see PARA 40.
3   As to the meaning of 'parent carer' see PARA 39.
4   Children Act 1989 s 17ZF(a) (s 17ZF added by the Children and Families Act 2014 s 97(1)). As to 'providing care' see PARA 39 note 2.
5   As to the meanings of 'disabled' and 'child' see PARA 39 note 2.
6   Children Act 1989 s 17ZF(b) (as added: see note 4).
7   Ie under the Children Act 1989 s 17: see PARA 21; and CHILDREN AND YOUNG PERSONS vol 10 (2017) PARA 789 et seq).
8   Children Act 1989 s 17ZF(c) (as added: see note 4).
9   Children Act 1989 s 17ZF(d) (as added: see note 4).

(C)   Adult Carers of Children Attaining the Age of 18

42. Assessment of care needs of adult carer of child becoming 18. Where it appears to a local authority in England[1] that an adult carer[2] of a child[3] is likely to have needs for support after the child becomes 18 the authority must, if it is satisfied that it would be of significant benefit to the carer to do so, assess whether the carer has needs for support and, if so, what those needs are[4] and whether the carer is likely to have needs for support after the child becomes 18 and, if so, what those needs are likely to be[5]. Such an assessment is referred to as a 'child's carer's assessment'[6]. A carer may refuse an assessment, in which event the local authority is not required to carry one out[7], although a carer who has refused an assessment may subsequently request one and the authority's duty to consider carrying one out will be revived[8]. The authority's duty to consider carrying out an assessment is also revived[9], subject to further refusal, where a child's carer has refused an assessment and the local authority concerned thinks that his needs or circumstances have changed[10].

A child's carer's assessment may, subject to consent, be combined with another assessment being carried out by the authority[11], and a local authority carrying out a child's carer's assessment and another assessment may carry out that other assessment jointly or on behalf of the other body carrying it out[12].

1   As to the meaning of 'local authority' see PARA 1. As to the social services functions of local authorities in England generally, and the overarching principles in accordance with which functions relating to the provision of care and support must be exercised, see PARAS 315–323.
2   In this context 'carer', in relation to a child, means an adult (including one who is a parent of the child) who provides or intends to provide care for the child (Care Act 2014 ss 60(7), 61(8), 62(4)), although an adult is not a carer for these purposes if he provides or intends to provide care under or by virtue of a contract (s 60(8)(a)) or as voluntary work (s 60(8)(b)). However in a case where the local authority considers that the relationship between the child and the adult providing or intending to provide care is such that it would be appropriate for the adult to be regarded as a carer, the adult is to be regarded as such (and s 60(8) is therefore to be ignored in that case): s 60(9). The references to 'providing care' include a reference to providing practical or emotional support: s 60(10). As to the meaning of 'carer' generally see PARA 33 note 2. As to the meaning of 'adult' see PARA 1 note 1.
3   As to the meaning of 'child' see PARA 1.
4   Care Act 2014 s 60(1)(a).

5   Care Act 2014 s 60(1)(b).
6   Care Act 2014 s 60(2). As to the carrying out of assessments see the Care and Support
     (Assessment) Regulations 2014, SI 2014/2827; and PARAS 64–65. As to the duty to continue to
     provide care during the transition to adult support see PARA 46.
7   Care Act 2014 s 60(3). In these circumstances s 60(1) does not apply.
8   Care Act 2014 s 60(4). In these circumstances the Care Act 2014 s 60(1) (see the text and notes
     1–5) applies in the carer's case (and s 60(3) (see the text and note 7) does not): s 60(4). Where a
     local authority, having received a request to carry out an assessment from the carer concerned,
     decides not to comply with the request, it must give the carer written reasons for its decision
     (s 60(6)(a)) and information and advice about what can be done to prevent or delay the
     development by the carer of needs for support in the future (s 60(6)(b)).
9   Ie the Care Act 2014 s 60(1) applies in the carer's case.
10 Care Act 2014 s 60(5).
11 A local authority may combine a child's carer's assessment with an assessment it is carrying out
     (whether or not under the Care Act 2014 Pt 1) in relation to another person only if the adult to
     whom the child's carer's assessment relates agrees and:
         (1)   where the combination would include an assessment relating to another adult, that other
                adult agrees (s 65(3)(a)); and
         (2)   where the combination would include an assessment relating to a child, the consent
                condition is met in relation to that child (s 65(3)(b)).
         As to when the consent condition is met, and as to partial assessment, see s 65(4), (6); and
     PARA 22 note 12.
12 Where a local authority is carrying out a child's carer's assessment and there is some other
     assessment being or about to be carried out in relation to the person to whom the assessment
     relates or in relation to a relevant person (as to which see PARA 22 note 13), the local authority
     may carry out that other assessment:
         (1)   on behalf of or jointly with the body responsible for carrying it out (Care Act 2014
                s 65(5)(a)); or
         (2)   if that body has arranged to carry out the other assessment jointly with another person,
                jointly with that body and the other person (s 65(5)(b)).

43.   What must be included in a carer's assessment. A child's carer's assessment[1]
must include an assessment of:
   (1)   whether the carer is able to provide care for the child and is likely to
          continue to be able to do so after the child becomes 18[2];
   (2)   whether the carer is willing to do so and is likely to continue to be
          willing to do so after the child becomes 18[3];
   (3)   the impact on matters pertaining to the child's well-being[4] of what the
          carer's needs for support are likely to be after the child becomes 18[5];
   (4)   the outcomes that the carer wishes to achieve in day-to-day life[6]; and
   (5)   whether, and if so to what extent, the provision of support could
          contribute to the achievement of those outcomes[7].

In carrying out a child's carer's assessment the local authority[8] must have
regard to whether the carer works or wishes to do so[9] and whether the carer is
participating in or wishes to participate in education, training or recreation[10], and
must involve the carer[11] and any person whom the carer asks the local authority
to involve[12]. When carrying out a child's carer's assessment a local authority must
also consider whether, and if so to what extent, matters other than the provision
of support could contribute to the achievement of the outcomes that the carer
wishes to achieve in day-to-day life[13].

1   As to the requirement for an assessment see PARA 42; as to the meaning of 'carer' see PARA 42 note
     2; as to the meaning of 'child' see PARA 1.
2   Care Act 2014 s 61(1)(a).
3   Care Act 2014 s 61(1)(b).
4   Ie the matters specified in the Care Act 2014 s 1(2) (see PARA 12).
5   Care Act 2014 s 61(1)(c).
6   Care Act 2014 s 61(1)(d).
7   Care Act 2014 s 61(1)(e).

8   As to the meaning of 'local authority' see PARA 1. As to the social services functions of local authorities in England generally, and the overarching principles in accordance with which functions relating to the provision of care and support must be exercised, see PARAS 315–323.

9   Care Act 2014 s 61(2)(a).

10 Care Act 2014 s 61(2)(b).

11 Care Act 2014 s 61(3)(a). A local authority which is required to involve an individual in its exercise of a function under s 61(3)(a) may be required to arrange for an independent advocate to be available to represent and support the individual: see s 67 (in particular s 67(3)(h)); the Care and Support (Independent Advocacy Support) (No 2) Regulations 2014, SI 2014/2889; and PARAS 100–103.

12 Care Act 2014 s 61(3)(b).

13 Care Act 2014 s 61(4).

44. Local authority duties and powers with regard to meeting child's carer's needs for support.

Having carried out a child's carer's assessment[1] a local authority[2] must give the child's carer an indication as to whether any of the needs for support which it thinks the carer is likely to have after the child becomes 18 are likely to meet the eligibility criteria (and, if so, which ones are likely to do so)[3] and advice and information about:

(1)   what can be done to meet or reduce the needs which it thinks the carer is likely to have after the child becomes 18[4];

(2)   what can be done to prevent or delay the development by the carer of needs for support in the future[5].

Where a local authority, having carried out a child's carer's assessment, is satisfied that the carer has needs for support, it may meet such of those needs as it considers appropriate[6].

1   As to the requirement for an assessment see PARA 42; as to what must be included in an assessment see PARA 43; as to the meaning of 'carer' see PARA 42 note 2; as to the meaning of 'child' see PARA 1.

2   As to the meaning of 'local authority' see PARA 1. As to the social services functions of local authorities in England generally, and the overarching principles in accordance with which functions relating to the provision of care and support must be exercised, see PARAS 315–323.

3   Care Act 2014 s 61(5)(a). As to the eligibility criteria for carers see PARA 35.

4   Care Act 2014 s 61(5)(b)(i).

5   Care Act 2014 s 61(5)(b)(ii).

6   Care Act 2014 s 62(1). A local authority may not meet a child's carer's needs for support under s 62(1) by providing care and support to the child: Care and Support (Children's Carer's) Regulations 2015, SI 2015/305, reg 3. In deciding whether or how to exercise the power under s 62(1) a local authority must have regard to any services being provided to the carer under the Children Act 1989 s 17 (see PARA 21; and CHILDREN AND YOUNG PERSONS vol 10 (2017) PARA 789 et seq) or, where applicable, the Social Services and Well-being (Wales) Act 2014 ss 37–39 (see PARAS 30–32): Care Act 2014 s 62(3) (amended in relation to local authorities in Wales by SI 2016/413).

    The Care Act 2014 Pt 1 (ss 1–80) applies to the exercise of the power to meet a child carer's needs for support under s 62(1) in so far as they apply to the exercise of the power to meet a carer's needs for support under s 20(6) (see PARA 44) and do not already apply to the exercise of the power under s 62(1): see the Care and Support (Children's Carer's) Regulations 2015, SI 2015/305, reg 2(1)(a). This application is subject to specified modifications, noted to the affected provisions.

45. Next steps after making decision as to provision of care.

Where a local authority in England[1] decides to meet a child's carer's needs[2] it must prepare a support plan for the carer concerned[3], tell the person which (if any) of the needs that it is going to meet may be met by direct payments[4] and help the person with deciding how to have the needs met[5]. Where an authority has carried out a carer's assessment[6] but does not decide to meet needs[7], it must give the person concerned its written reasons for not meeting the needs[8] and[9] advice and information about what can be done to meet or reduce the needs[10] and to prevent or delay the development by the person concerned of needs for care and support or of needs for support in the future[11].

1 As to the meaning of 'local authority' see PARA 1. As to the social services functions of local authorities in England generally, and the overarching principles in accordance with which functions relating to the provision of care and support must be exercised, see PARAS 315–323.
2 Ie under the Care Act 2014 s 20(1) (see PARA 36). As to the meaning of 'carer' see PARA 33 note 2.
3 Care Act 2014 s 24(1)(a); Care and Support (Children's Carer's) Regulations 2015, SI 2015/305, reg 9 (see PARA 44 note 6). As to support plans see PARAS 78–80.
4 Care Act 2014 s 24(1)(b). As to direct payments see PARAS 106–110.
5 Care Act 2014 s 24(1)(c).
6 As to the meaning of 'carer's assessment' see PARA 33. As to what must be included in a carer's assessment see PARA 34.
7 See note 2.
8 Care Act 2014 s 24(2)(a).
9 Ie unless the authority has already done so under the Care Act 2014 s 13(5) (see PARA 11).
10 Care Act 2014 s 24(2)(b)(i).
11 Care Act 2014 s 24(2)(b)(ii).

46. Duty to continue to provide care during transition to adult support. Where, in the case of a carer to whom a child's carer's assessment[1] relates, the child becomes 18, the local authority[2] must decide whether to treat the assessment as a carer's assessment[3]; and if the authority decides to do so, the care and support provisions[4] apply to the child's carer's assessment as if it were a carer's assessment that had been carried out after the child had become 18[5]. Where a local authority[6] providing services for a child in need[7] are required to carry out a young carer's assessment in relation to the child[8] and the authority carry out the assessment before the child reaches the age of 18 and decide to treat it as a carer's assessment[9], the authority must continue to provide such services[10] after the child reaches the age of 18 until they reach a conclusion in his case[11]. If the local authority carry out the assessment before the child reaches the age of 18 but decide not to treat it as a carer's assessment[12]:

(1) they must carry out a carer's assessment after the child reaches the age of 18[13]; and

(2) they must continue to provide services[14] after he reaches that age until they reach a conclusion in his case[15],

and if the authority do not carry out the assessment before the child reaches the age of 18, they must continue to provide services after he reaches that age until:

(a) they decide that the duty to carry out a carer's assessment[16] does not apply[17]; or

(b) having decided that the duty applies and having discharged it, they reach a conclusion in his case[18].

Where a local authority providing services for a child in need[19] receive a request for a child's carer's assessment to be carried out in relation to the carer of the child[20] but have yet to be required[21] to carry out the assessment[22], then if the authority do not decide, before the child reaches the age of 18, whether or not to comply with the request, they must continue to provide services after he reaches that age until:

(i) they decide that the duty to carry out a carer's assessment[23] does not apply[24]; or

(ii) having decided that the duty applies and having discharged it, they reach a conclusion in his case[25].

1 As to the duty to carry out a child's carer's assessment see the Care Act 2014 s 60(1), (2);and PARAS 42–43.

2 As to the meaning of 'local authority' in the context of the Care Act 2014 see PARA 1. As to the social services functions of local authorities in England generally, and the overarching principles in accordance with which functions relating to the provision of care and support must be exercised, see PARAS 315–323.

3 Care Act 2014 s 61(6). As to carer's assessments see PARAS 33–38. In considering what to decide under s 61(6), the authority must have regard to when the child's carer's assessment was carried out (s 61(7)(a)) and whether it appears to the authority that the circumstances of the carer to whom the child's carer's assessment relates have changed in a way that might affect the assessment (s 61(7)(b)).

4 Ie the Care Act 2014 Pt 1 (ss 1–80).

5 Care Act 2014 s 61(6).

6 As to the meaning of 'local authority' in the context of the Children Act 1989 see PARA 25 note 2.

7 Ie in the exercise of functions conferred by the Children Act 1989 s 17: see PARA 21; and CHILDREN AND YOUNG PERSONS vol 10 (2017) PARA 789 et seq).

8 Children Act 1989 s 17ZH(1)(b) (s 17ZH added by the Care Act 2014 s 66(1)).

9 Ie in accordance with the Care Act 2014 s 61(6) (see the text and notes 1–5), with Pt 1 applying to the assessment as a result: Children Act 1989 s 17ZH(2) (as added: see note 8).

10 Ie he must continue to comply with the Children Act 1989 s 17.

11 Children Act 1989 s 17ZH(2) (as added: see note 8). As to when a local authority reaches a conclusion in a person's case see PARA 25 note 11.

12 See note 9.

13 Children Act 1989 s 17ZH(3)(a) (as added: see note 8).

14 See note 10.

15 Children Act 1989 s 17ZH(3)(b) (as added: see note 8).

16 Ie under the Care Act 2014 s 10: see PARA 33.

17 Children Act 1989 s 17ZH(4)(a) (as added: see note 8).

18 Children Act 1989 s 17ZH(4)(b) (as added: see note 8).

19 See note 7.

20 Children Act 1989 s 17ZH(5)(a) (as added: see note 8).

21 Ie under the Care Act 2014 s 60(1).

22 Children Act 1989 s 17ZH(5)(b) (as added: see note 8).

23 See note 16.

24 Children Act 1989 s 17ZH(6)(a) (as added: see note 8).

25 Children Act 1989 s 17ZH(6)(b) (as added: see note 8).

B.   YOUNG CARERS

(A)   Young Carers Generally

47.   Assessment of care needs of young carer. A local authority in England[1] must assess whether a young carer — ie a person aged under 18 who provides or intends to provide care for another person[2] — within their area has needs for support[3] and, if so, what those needs are, if it appears to the authority that the young carer may have needs for support[4] or the authority receive a request from the young carer or a parent of the young carer[5] to assess his needs for support[6]. Such an assessment is referred to as a 'young carer's needs assessment'[7]. The obligation to carry out an assessment does not apply[8] in relation to a young carer if the authority have previously carried out a care-related assessment[9] of the young carer in relation to the same person cared for[10], although an assessment must be carried out[11] if it appears to the authority that the needs or circumstances of the young carer or the person cared for have changed since the last care-related assessment[12].

Where a local authority are required to carry out a young carer's needs assessment and are required or have decided to carry out some other assessment of the young carer or of the person cared for, the authority may combine the assessments[13].

1 As to the meaning of 'local authority' see PARA 25 note 6.

2 Children Act 1989 s 17ZA(3) (ss 17ZA, 17ZB added by the Children and Families Act 2014 s 97(1)): a person is not a 'young carer' if he provides or intends to provide care under or by virtue

of a contract or as voluntary work (Children Act 1989 s 17ZB(1), (3) (as so added)): however, in a case where the local authority consider that the relationship between the person cared for and the person under 18 providing or intending to provide care is such that it would be appropriate for the person under 18 to be regarded as a young carer, that person is to be regarded as such (and s 17ZB(3) is therefore to be ignored in that case): s 17ZB(4) (as so added). The references in ss 17ZA, 17ZB to providing care include a reference to providing practical or emotional support: s 17ZB(5) (as so added).

3   A local authority in England must take reasonable steps to identify the extent to which there are young carers within their area who have needs for support: Children Act 1989 s 17ZA(12) (as added: see note 2).

4   Children Act 1989 s 17ZA(1)(a) (as added: see note 2).

5   'Parent', in relation to a young carer, includes a parent of the young carer who does not have parental responsibility for the young carer (Children Act 1989 s 17ZB(2)(a) (as added: see note 2)) and a person who is not a parent of the young carer but who has parental responsibility for the young carer (s 17ZB(2)(b) (as so added). As to the meaning of 'parental responsibility' see PARA 39 note 3.

6   Children Act 1989 s 17ZA(1)(b) (as added: see note 2).

7   Children Act 1989 s 17ZA(2) (as added: see note 2). As to what must be included in a young carer's needs assessment see PARA 48; as to the consideration of a young carer's needs assessment see PARA 49. A local authority that have carried out a young carer's needs assessment must give a written record of the assessment to the young carer (Care Act 2014 s 17ZD(10)(a) (as so added)), the young carer's parents carer (s 17ZD(10)(b) (as so added)) and any person to whom the young carer requests the authority to give a copy (s 17ZD(10)(c) (as so added)). Where the person cared for is under 18, the written record must state whether the local authority consider him or her to be a child in need: (s 17ZD(11) (as so added).

8   Ie the Children Act 1989 s 17ZA(1) (see the text and notes 1–6) does not apply.

9   'Care-related assessment' means a young carer's needs assessment (Children Act 1989 s 17ZA(6)(a) (as added: see note 2)) or an assessment under any of the Carers (Recognition and Services) Act 1995 s 1 (Children Act 1989 s 17ZA(6)(b)(i) (as added: see note 2)), the Carers and Disabled Children Act 2000 s 6 (repealed) (Children Act 1989 s 17ZA(6)(b)(ii) (as so added)), the Community Care (Delayed Discharges) Act 2003 s 4(3) (see PARA 69) (Children Act 1989 s 17ZA(6)(b)(ii) (as so added)) and the Care Act 2014 Pt 1 (ss 1–80) (see PARAS 33–38) (Children Act 1989 s 17ZA(6)(b)(iv) (as so added; further added by SI 2015/914 (made under the Children Act 1989 s 17ZB(9) (as so added))).

10 Children Act 1989 s 17ZA(4) (as added: see note 2).

11 And the Children Act 1989 s 17ZA(1) applies.

12 Children Act 1989 s 17ZA(5) (as added: see note 2).

13 Children Act 1989 s 17ZB(6) (as added: see note 2). A young carer's needs assessment may be combined with an assessment of the person cared for only if the young carer and the person cared for agree: s 17ZB(7) (as so added).

48. What must be included in a young carer's needs assessment.

A young carer's needs assessment[1] must include an assessment of whether it is appropriate for the young carer to provide, or continue to provide[2], care for the person in question, in the light of the young carer's needs for support, other needs and wishes[3]. In carrying out a young carer's needs assessment, the local authority[4] must have regard to the extent to which the young carer is participating in or wishes to participate in education, training or recreation[5] and the extent to which the young carer works or wishes to work[6], and must involve the young carer[7], the young carer's parents[8] and any person who the young carer requests the authority to involve[9].

1   As to the circumstances in which a young carer's needs assessment must be carried out see PARA 47; as to the consideration of a young carer's needs assessment see PARA 49.

2   As to 'providing care' see PARA 47 note 2.

3   Children Act 1989 s 17ZA(7) (ss 17ZA, 17ZB added by the Children and Families Act 2014 s 97(1)). Regulations make provision about carrying out a young carer's needs assessment: see the Young Carers (Needs Assessments) Regulations 2015, SI 2015/527 (made under the Children Act 1989 s 17ZB(8) (as so added)).

4   As to the meaning of 'local authority' see PARA 25 note 6.

5   Children Act 1989 s 17ZA(8)(a) (as added: see note 3).

6   Children Act 1989 s 17ZA(8)(b) (as added: see note 3).

7   Children Act 1989 s 17ZA(9)(a) (as added: see note 3).

8 Children Act 1989 s 17ZA(9)(b) (as added: see note 3). As to the parents of a young carer see PARA 47 note 5.
9 Children Act 1989 s 17ZA(9)(c) (as added: see note 3).

49. Consideration of a young carer's needs assessment. A local authority[1] that carry out a young carer's needs assessment[2] must consider the assessment and decide:

(1) whether the young carer[3] has needs for support in relation to the care which he or she provides or intends to provide[4];

(2) if so, whether those needs could be satisfied (wholly or partly) by services which the authority may provide[5] pursuant to its general powers relating to the provision of services for children in need[6]; and

(3) if they could be so satisfied, whether or not to provide any such services in relation to the young carer[7].

1 As to the meaning of 'local authority' see PARA 25 note 6.
2 As to the circumstances in which a young carer's needs assessment must be carried out see PARA 47; as to what must be included in a young carer's needs assessment see PARA 48.
3 As to the meaning of 'young carer' see PARA 47.
4 Children Act 1989 s 17ZC(a) (s 17ZC added by the Children and Families Act 2014 s 97(1)). As to 'providing care' see PARA 39 note 2.
5 Ie under the Children Act 1989 s 17: see PARA 21; and CHILDREN AND YOUNG PERSONS vol 10 (2017) PARA 789 et seq).
6 Children Act 1989 s 17ZC(b) (as added: see note 4).
7 Children Act 1989 s 17ZC(c) (as added: see note 4).

(B) Young Carers Attaining the Age of 18

50. Assessment of care needs of young carer attaining age of 18. Where:

(1) it appears to a local authority in England[1] that a young carer[2] is likely to have needs for support after becoming 18[3];

(2) the authority is satisfied that it would be of significant benefit to the young carer to assess his needs[4]; and

(3) either the young carer has capacity[5] or is competent to consent to an assessment being carried out and the young carer does so consent[6], or the young carer lacks capacity or is not competent so to consent but the authority is satisfied that carrying out an assessment would be in the young carer's best interests[7],

the authority must assess:

(a) whether the young carer has needs for support and, if so, what those needs are[8]; and

(b) whether the young carer is likely to have needs for support after becoming 18 and, if so, what those needs are likely to be[9].

Such an assessment is referred to as a 'young carer's assessment'[10]. Where a young carer refuses a young carer's assessment and the consent condition[11] is accordingly not met, the authority must nonetheless carry out the assessment if the young carer is experiencing, or is at risk of, abuse or neglect[12].

A young carer's assessment may, subject to consent, be combined with another assessment being carried out by the authority[13], and a local authority carrying out a young carer's assessment and another assessment may carry out that other assessment jointly or on behalf of the other body carrying it out[14].

1 As to the meaning of 'local authority' see PARA 1. As to the social services functions of local authorities in England generally, and the overarching principles in accordance with which functions relating to the provision of care and support must be exercised, see PARAS 315–323.
2 'Young carer' means a person under 18 who provides or intends to provide care for an adult (Care Act 2014 s 63(6)), although a person is not a young carer for these purposes if he provides or intends to provide care under or by virtue of a contract (s 63(7)(a)) or as voluntary work

(s 63(7)(b)). However in a case where the local authority considers that the relationship between the adult and the person under 18 providing or intending to provide care is such that it would be appropriate for the person under 18 to be regarded as a young carer, that person is to be regarded as such (and s 63(7) is therefore to be ignored in that case): s 63(8). The references to providing care include a reference to providing practical or emotional support: s 63(9).

3   Care Act 2014 s 63(1).
4   Care Act 2014 s 63(1).
5   As to a person having or lacking capacity see PARA 8 note 10.
6   Care Act 2014 s 63(3)(a). The provisions of s 63(3) are referred to as 'the consent condition': s 63(3).
7   Care Act 2014 s 63(3)(b).
8   Care Act 2014 s 63(1)(a).
9   Care Act 2014 s 63(1)(b).
10 Care Act 2014 s 63(2). As to the carrying out of assessments see the Care and Support (Assessment) Regulations 2014, SI 2014/2827; and PARAS 64–65. As to what must be included in a young carer's assessment see PARA 51; as to consideration of a young carer's assessment see PARA 52. As to the duty to continue to provide care during the transition to adult support see PARA 53.

   Where a local authority, having received a request to carry out a young carer's assessment from the young carer concerned or a parent of the young carer, decides not to comply with the request, it must give the person who made the request written reasons for its decision (Care Act 2014 s 63(5)(a)) and advice and information about what can be done to prevent or delay the development by the young carer of needs for support in the future (s 63(5)(b)).
11 See the text and notes 5–7.
12 Care Act 2014 s 63(4). As to the meaning of 'abuse' see PARA 8 note 12.
13 A local authority may combine a young carer's assessment with an assessment it is carrying out (whether or not under the Care Act 2014 Pt 1) in relation to another person only if the consent condition is met in relation to the child to whom the young carer's assessment relates and:
    (1)   where the combination would include an assessment relating to another child, the consent condition is met in relation to that other child (s 65(2)(a));
    (2)   where the combination would include an assessment relating to an adult, the adult agrees (s 65(2)(b)).
    As to when the consent condition is met, and as to partial assessment, see s 65(4), (6); and PARA 22 note 12.
14 Where a local authority is carrying out a young carer's assessment and there is some other assessment being or about to be carried out in relation to the person to whom the assessment relates or in relation to a relevant person (as to which see PARA 22 note 13), the local authority may carry out that other assessment:
    (1)   on behalf of or jointly with the body responsible for carrying it out (Care Act 2014 s 65(5)(a)); or
    (2)   if that body has arranged to carry out the other assessment jointly with another person, jointly with that body and the other person (s 65(5)(b)).

51. What must be included in an assessment of a young carer attaining age of 18. A young carer's assessment[1] must include an assessment of:

(1)   whether the young carer is able to provide care[2] for the person in question and is likely to continue to be able to do so after becoming 18[3];

(2)   whether the young carer is willing to do so and is likely to continue to be willing to do so after becoming 18[4];

(3)   the impact on matters pertaining to the young carer's well-being[5] of what his needs for support are likely to be after the carer becomes 18[6];

(4)   the outcomes that the young carer wishes to achieve in day-to-day life[7]; and

(5)   whether, and if so to what extent, the provision of support could contribute to the achievement of those outcomes[8].

In carrying out a young carer's assessment the authority must have regard to:

(a)   the extent to which the young carer works or wishes to work (or is likely to wish to do so after becoming 18)[9]; and

(b)   the extent to which the young carer is participating in or wishes to participate in education, training or recreation (or is likely to wish to do so after becoming 18)[10].

In carrying out a young carer's assessment the local authority[11] must involve the young carer[12], his parents[13], and any person whom the young carer or a parent of the young carer requests the authority to involve[14], and must also consider whether, and if so to what extent, matters other than the provision of support could contribute to the achievement of the outcomes that the young carer wishes to achieve in day-to-day life[15].

1   As to the duty to carry out a young carer's assessment see PARA 50; as to consideration of a young carer's assessment see PARA 52. As to the duty to continue to provide care during the transition to adult support see PARA 53.
2   As to the meaning of 'young carer', and as to 'providing care', see PARA 50 note 2.
3   Care Act 2014 s 64(1)(a).
4   Care Act 2014 s 64(1)(b).
5   Ie the matters specified in the Care Act 2014 s 1(2) (see PARA 12).
6   Care Act 2014 s 64(1)(c).
7   Care Act 2014 s 64(1)(d).
8   Care Act 2014 s 64(1)(e).
9   Care Act 2014 s 64(2)(a).
10 Care Act 2014 s 64(2)(b).
11 As to the meaning of 'local authority' see PARA 1. As to the social services functions of local authorities in England generally, and the overarching principles in accordance with which functions relating to the provision of care and support must be exercised, see PARAS 315–323.
12 Care Act 2014 s 64(3)(a). A local authority which is required to involve an individual in its exercise of a function under s 64(3)(a), (b) may be required to arrange for an independent advocate to be available to represent and support the individual: see s 67 (in particular s 67(3)(i)); the Care and Support (Independent Advocacy Support) (No 2) Regulations 2014, SI 2014/2889; and PARAS 100–103.
13 Care Act 2014 s 64(3)(b). See note 12.
14 Care Act 2014 s 64(3)(c).
15 Care Act 2014 s 64(4).

52. Consideration of a young carer's assessment. Having carried out a young carer's assessment[1] a local authority[2] must give the young carer (or, where the young carer lacks capacity[3], his parents):

(1)   an indication as to whether any of the needs for support which it thinks the young carer is likely to have after becoming 18 are likely to meet the eligibility criteria[4] (and, if so, which ones are likely to do so)[5]; and

(2)   advice and information about what can be done to meet or reduce the needs for support which it thinks the young carer is likely to have after becoming 18[6] and what can be done to prevent or delay the development by the young carer of needs for support in the future[7].

1   As to the duty to carry out a young carer's assessment see PARAS 50–51. As to the duty to continue to provide care during the transition to adult support see PARA 25.
2   As to the meaning of 'local authority' see PARA 1. As to the social services functions of local authorities in England generally, and the overarching principles in accordance with which functions relating to the provision of care and support must be exercised, see PARAS 315–323.
3   Ie, in a case where the young carer is not competent or lacks capacity to understand the things which the local authority is required to give under the Care Act 2014 s 64(5) (see the text and notes 4–7): s 64(6). As to a person having or lacking capacity see PARA 8 note 10. As to the meaning of 'young carer' see PARA 50 note 2.
4   As to the eligibility criteria for young carers see PARA 35.
5   Care Act 2014 s 64(5)(a).
6   Care Act 2014 s 64(5)(b)(i).
7   Care Act 2014 s 64(5)(b)(ii).

53. Duty to continue to provide care during transition to adult support. Where a person to whom a young carer's assessment[1] relates becomes 18, the local authority[2] must decide whether to treat the assessment as a carer's assessment[3]; and if the authority decides to do so, the care and support provisions[4] apply to the young carer's assessment as if it were a carer's assessment that had been carried out after the person had become 18[5]. Where a local authority[6] providing services for a child in need[7] are required to carry out a young carer's assessment in relation to a carer of the child[8] and the authority carry out the assessment before the child reaches the age of 18 and decide to treat it as a carer's assessment[9], the authority must continue to provide such services[10] after the child reaches the age of 18 until they reach a conclusion in his case[11]. If the local authority carry out the assessment before the child reaches the age of 18 but decide not to treat it as a carer's assessment[12]:

(1)   they must carry out a carer's assessment after the child reaches the age of 18[13]; and

(2)   they must continue to provide services[14] after he reaches that age until they reach a conclusion in his case[15],

and if the authority do not carry out the assessment before the child reaches the age of 18, they must continue to provide services after he reaches that age until:

(a)   they decide that the duty to carry out a carer's assessment[16] does not apply[17]; or

(b)   having decided that the duty applies and having discharged it, they reach a conclusion in his case[18].

Where a local authority providing services for a child in need[19] receive a request for a young carer's assessment to be carried out in relation to the child[20] but have yet to be required[21] to carry out the assessment[22], then if the authority do not decide, before the child reaches the age of 18, whether or not to comply with the request, they must continue to provide services after he reaches that age until:

(i)   they decide that the duty to carry out a carer's assessment[23] does not apply[24]; or

(ii)   having decided that the duty applies and having discharged it, they reach a conclusion in his case[25].

1   As to the duty to carry out a young carer's assessment see the Care Act 2014 s 63(1), (2);and PARAS 50–51.
2   As to the meaning of 'local authority' in the context of the Care Act 2014 see PARA 1. As to the social services functions of local authorities in England generally, and the overarching principles in accordance with which functions relating to the provision of care and support must be exercised, see PARAS 315–323.
3   Care Act 2014 s 64(7). As to carer's assessments see PARAS 33–38. In considering what to decide under s 64(7), the authority must have regard to when the young carer's assessment was carried out (s 64(8)(a)) and whether it appears to the authority that the circumstances of the person to whom the young carer's assessment relates have changed in a way that might affect the assessment (s 64(8)(b)).
4   Ie the Care Act 2014 Pt 1 (ss 1–80).
5   Care Act 2014 s 64(7).
6   As to the meaning of 'local authority' in the context of the Children Act 1989 see PARA 25 note 2.
7   Ie in the exercise of functions conferred by the Children Act 1989 s 17: see PARA 21; and CHILDREN AND YOUNG PERSONS vol 10 (2017) PARA 789 et seq).
8   Children Act 1989 s 17ZH(1)(a) (s 17ZH added by the Care Act 2014 s 66(1)).
9   Ie in accordance with the Care Act 2014 s 64(7) (see the text and notes 1–5), with Pt 1 applying to the assessment as a result: Children Act 1989 s 17ZH(2) (as added: see note 8).
10 Ie must continue to comply with the Children Act 1989 s 17.
11 Children Act 1989 s 17ZH(2) (as added: see note 8). As to when a local authority reaches a conclusion in a person's case see PARA 25 note 11.
12 See note 9.
13 Children Act 1989 s 17ZH(3)(a) (as added: see note 8).
14 See note 10.

15 Children Act 1989 s 17ZH(3)(b) (as added: see note 8).
16 Ie under the Care Act 2014 s 10: see PARA 33.
17 Children Act 1989 s 17ZH(4)(a) (as added: see note 8).
18 Children Act 1989 s 17ZH(4)(b) (as added: see note 8).
19 See note 7.
20 Children Act 1989 s 17ZH(5)(a) (as added: see note 8).
21 Ie under the Care Act 2014 s 63(1).
22 Children Act 1989 s 17ZH(5)(b) (as added: see note 8).
23 See note 16.
24 Children Act 1989 s 17ZH(6)(a) (as added: see note 8).
25 Children Act 1989 s 17ZH(6)(b) (as added: see note 8).

(ii) Wales

54. Assessment of a carer's care needs. Where it appears to a local authority in Wales[1] that a carer[2] may have needs for support the authority must assess whether the carer does have needs for care and support (or is likely to do so in the future)[3] and if he does, what those needs are (or are likely to be in the future)[4]. This duty applies in relation to a carer who is providing or intends to provide care for an adult[5] or disabled child[6] who is ordinarily resident in the authority's area[7] or any other adult or disabled child who is within the authority's area[8], and applies regardless of the authority's view of the level of the carer's needs for support[9] or the level of the financial resources of the carer or the person for whom he provides or intends to provide care[10]: it does not, however, apply where a carer (or, where applicable an authorised person[11]) refuses an assessment[12] (although the right of refusal is qualified if the carer lacks capacity[13]), although the duty will be re-engaged, subject to any further refusal, if the carer subsequently asks for an assessment[14] or the authority considers that the carer's needs or circumstances (or, in the case of a carer aged under 18, the needs or circumstances of a person with parental responsibility for the carer) have changed[15].

1 As to the meaning of 'local authority' see PARA 2. As to the social services functions of local authorities in Wales generally, and the overarching principles in accordance with which functions relating to the provision of care and support must be exercised, see PARAS 373–383.
2 'Carer' means a person who provides or intends to provide care for an adult or disabled child: Social Services and Well-being (Wales) Act 2014 s 3(4). A person is not a carer for these purposes if he provides or intends to provide care under or by virtue of a contract (s 3(7)(a)) or as voluntary work (s 3(7)(b)), although a local authority may treat a person as a carer for the purposes of any of its functions under the Social Services and Well-being (Wales) Act 2014 if the authority considers that the relationship between the person providing or intending to provide care and the person for whom that care is, or is to be, provided is such that it would be appropriate for the former to be treated as a carer for the purposes of that function or those functions (s 3(8)). A person is not a carer for these purposes if he is detained in prison or youth detention accommodation, or having been convicted of an offence, is residing in approved premises: ss 185(7), 186(8), 187(1). As to the meanings of 'prison', 'youth detention accommodation' and 'approved premises': see PARA 87 notes 2–4.
    A person is 'disabled' if he has a disability for the purposes of the Equality Act 2010 (see DISCRIMINATION vol 33 (2013) PARA 50), although this is subject to any provision made under the Social Services and Well-being (Wales) Act 2014 s 3(6), under which regulations may provide that a person falling within a specified category is or is not to be treated as disabled for these purposes. At the date at which this volume states the law no such regulations had been made.
3 Social Services and Well-being (Wales) Act 2014 s 24(1)(a). As to the meanings of 'care' and 'support' see PARA 2 note 1. The nature of the assessment required by these provisions is one that the local authority considers proportionate in the circumstances, subject to any requirement in the Care and Support (Assessment) (Wales) Regulations 2015, SI 2015/1305 (see PARAS 66–77): Social Services and Well-being (Wales) Act 2014 s 24(7). As to the carrying out of assessments see PARAS 66–77. As to what must be included in a carer's assessment PARA 55.
4 Social Services and Well-being (Wales) Act 2014 s 24(1)(b).
5 As to the meaning of 'adult' see PARA 2.
6 As to the meaning of 'child' see PARA 2. As to the meaning of 'disabled' see PARA 26 note 6.

7   Social Services and Well-being (Wales) Act 2014 s 24(2)(a). In connection with a person's residence see PARAS 84–87.
8   Social Services and Well-being (Wales) Act 2014 s 24(2)(b).
9   Social Services and Well-being (Wales) Act 2014 s 24(3)(a).
10 Social Services and Well-being (Wales) Act 2014 s 24(3)(b).
11 In this context 'authorised person' means a person authorised under the Mental Capacity Act 2005 (whether in general or specific terms) to decide whether to refuse, or ask for, a needs assessment on the carer's behalf: Social Services and Well-being (Wales) Act 2014 ss 25(4), 26(5). As to a person being 'authorised' under the Mental Capacity Act 2005 see PARA 12 note 15.
12 The duty under the Social Services and Well-being (Wales) Act 2014 s 24 (see the text and notes 1–10) to assess the carer's needs does not apply if:
    (1)   a carer who is an adult or is aged 16 or 17 (or, where applicable, an authorised person) refuses a needs assessment under s 24 (ss 25(1), 26(1));
    (2)   if a person with parental responsibility for a carer aged 16 or 17 refuses a needs assessment for the carer under s 24 in circumstances in which the local authority is satisfied that the carer lacks capacity to decide whether to refuse to have the assessment (s 26(2)(a)) and there is no authorised person to make the decision on the carer's behalf (s 26(2)(b));
    (3)   if a carer aged under 16 refuses such an assessment (s 27(1)(a)) and the local authority is satisfied that the carer has sufficient understanding to make an informed decision about the refusal of the assessment (s 27(1)(b)); or
    (4)   if a person with parental responsibility for a carer aged under 16 refuses a needs assessment for the carer under s 24 (s 27(2)).
    As to the meaning of 'parental responsibility' see PARA 26 note 10.
13 A refusal of a needs assessment for an adult carer under the Social Services and Well-being (Wales) Act 2014 s 25(1) (see note 12) does not discharge a local authority from its duty under s 24 in the following cases (s 25(2)):
    (1)   where the local authority is satisfied, in the case of a refusal given by the carer, that the carer lacks capacity to decide whether to refuse to have the assessment but there is an authorised person to make the decision on the carer's behalf; or
    (2)   where the local authority is satisfied, in the case of a refusal given by the carer, that the carer lacks capacity to decide whether to refuse to have the assessment, there is no authorised person to make the decision on the carer's behalf, and having the assessment would be in the carer's best interests.
    A refusal of a needs assessment for a carer aged 16 or 17 under s 26(1) or (2) (see note 12) does not discharge a local authority from its duty under s 24 in the following cases (s 26(3)):
    (a)   where the local authority is satisfied, in the case of a refusal given by the carer, that the carer lacks capacity to decide whether to refuse to have the assessment;
    (b)   where the local authority is satisfied, in the case of a refusal given by a person with parental responsibility for the carer, that the person lacks capacity to decide whether to refuse the assessment; or
    (c)   where the local authority is satisfied, in the case of a refusal given by a person with parental responsibility for the carer, that not having the assessment would not be in the carer's best interests.
    A refusal of a needs assessment for a carer aged under 16 or 17 under s 27(1) or (2) (see note 12) does not discharge a local authority from its duty under s 24 in the following cases (s 27(3)):
    (i)   where the local authority is satisfied, in the case of a refusal given by a person with parental responsibility for the carer, that the person lacks capacity to decide whether to refuse the assessment;
    (ii) where the local authority is satisfied, in the case of a refusal given by a person with parental responsibility for the carer, that the carer has sufficient understanding to make an informed decision about the refusal of the assessment and does not agree with the refusal given by the person with parental responsibility for the carer; or
    (iii) where the local authority is satisfied, in the case of a refusal given by a person with parental responsibility for the carer, that not having the assessment would be inconsistent with the carer's well-being.
    As to the meaning of 'well-being' see PARA 375.
14 Ie:
    (1)   where a local authority has been discharged from its duty under the Social Services and Well-being (Wales) Act 2014 s 24 by a refusal under s 25 (adult carers) or s 26 (carers aged 16 or 17), the carer (or where applicable, an authorised person) subsequently asks for an assessment (ss 25(3)(a), 26(4)(a)) or (in the case of a refusal under s 26 only), a

person with parental responsibility for the carer subsequently asks for an assessment in the circumstances described in s 26(2) (see note 12) (s 26(4)(b)); or

(2)   where a local authority has been discharged from its duty under s 24 by a refusal under s 27 (carers aged under 16), the carer subsequently asks for an assessment and the local authority is satisfied that the carer has sufficient understanding to make an informed decision about having an assessment (s 27(4)(a)) or a person with parental responsibility for the carer subsequently asks for an assessment (s 27(4)(b)).

15 Social Services and Well-being (Wales) Act 2014 ss 25(3)(b), 26(4)(c), 27(4)(c).

55. What must be included in a carer's assessment.

In carrying out a carer's assessment in Wales[1] the local authority[2] must:

(1)   assess the extent to which the carer[3] is able, and will continue to be able, to provide care for the person for whom the carer provides or intends to provide care[4];

(2)   assess the extent to which the carer is willing, and will continue to be willing, to do so[5];

(3)   in the case of a carer who is an adult[6], seek to identify the outcomes that the carer wishes to achieve[7];

(4)   in the case of a carer who is a child[8], seek to identify the outcomes that:

    (a)   the carer wishes to achieve, to the extent it considers appropriate having regard to the carer's age and understanding[9];

    (b)   the persons with parental responsibility[10] for the carer wish to achieve in relation to the carer, to the extent it considers appropriate having regard to the need to promote the carer's well-being[11]; and

    (c)   persons specified in regulations (if any) wish to achieve in relation to the carer[12];

(5)   assess whether, and if so, to what extent, the provision of support[13], preventative services[14] or information, advice or assistance[15], could contribute to the achievement of those outcomes or otherwise meet needs identified by the assessment[16]; and

(6)   assess whether, and if so, to what extent, other matters could contribute to the achievement of those outcomes or otherwise meet those needs[17].

In carrying out a carer's assessment a local authority must have regard to whether the carer works or wishes to do so[18], whether the carer is participating in or wishes to participate in education, training or any leisure activity[19], and, in the case of a carer who is a child, the developmental needs of the child[20] and whether it is appropriate for the child to provide the care (or any care) in light of those needs[21], and must involve the carer[22] and where feasible, the person for whom the carer provides or intends to provide care[23].

1   See PARA 54; and as to the carrying out of assessments generally see PARAS 66–77.
2   As to the meaning of 'local authority' see PARA 2. As to the social services functions of local authorities in Wales generally, and the overarching principles in accordance with which functions relating to the provision of care and support must be exercised, see PARAS 373–383.
3   As to the meaning of 'carer' see PARA 54 note 2.
4   Social Services and Well-being (Wales) Act 2014 s 24(4)(a). As to the meanings of 'care' and 'support' see PARA 2 note 1.
5   Social Services and Well-being (Wales) Act 2014 s 24(4)(b).
6   As to the meaning of 'adult' see PARA 2.
7   Social Services and Well-being (Wales) Act 2014 s 24(4)(c).
8   As to the meaning of 'child' see PARA 2.
9   Social Services and Well-being (Wales) Act 2014 s 24(4)(d)(i).
10   As to the meaning of 'parental responsibility' see PARA 26 note 10.
11   Social Services and Well-being (Wales) Act 2014 s 24(4)(d)(ii). As to the meaning of 'well-being' see PARA 375.

12 Social Services and Well-being (Wales) Act 2014 s 24(4)(d)(iii). At the date at which this volume states the law no regulations had been made for this purpose.
13 Social Services and Well-being (Wales) Act 2014 s 24(4)(e)(i).
14 Social Services and Well-being (Wales) Act 2014 s 24(4)(e)(ii). As to the meaning of 'preventative services' see PARA 16 note 6.
15 Social Services and Well-being (Wales) Act 2014 s 24(4)(e)(iii). As to the meaning of 'information, advice or assistance' see PARA 16 note 7.
16 Social Services and Well-being (Wales) Act 2014 s 24(4)(e).
17 Social Services and Well-being (Wales) Act 2014 s 24(4)(f).
18 Social Services and Well-being (Wales) Act 2014 s 24(5)(a).
19 Social Services and Well-being (Wales) Act 2014 s 24(5)(b).
20 Social Services and Well-being (Wales) Act 2014 s 24(5)(c)(i).
21 Social Services and Well-being (Wales) Act 2014 s 24(5)(c)(ii).
22 Social Services and Well-being (Wales) Act 2014 s 24(6)(a).
23 Social Services and Well-being (Wales) Act 2014 s 24(6)(b).

56. Determination of eligibility and the eligibility criteria. Where a local authority in Wales[1] is satisfied on the basis of a needs assessment[2] that a carer[3] has one or more needs for support it must determine whether any of the needs meet the eligibility criteria[4]. Any one of those needs meets the eligibility criteria if:

(1)   the need arises as a result of providing care for either an adult[5] with eligible needs[6] or a disabled child[7];

(2)   the need relates to one or more of the following:

(a)   ability to carry out self-care or domestic routines[8];

(b)   ability to communicate[9];

(c)   protection from abuse or neglect[10];

(d)   involvement in work, education, learning or in leisure activities[11];

(e)   maintenance or development of family or other significant personal relationships[12];

(f)   development and maintenance of social relationships and involvement in the community[13]; or

(g)   in the case of an adult carer, fulfilment of caring responsibilities for a child[14];

(h)   in the case of a child carer, achieving developmental goals[15];

(3)   the carer cannot meet the need whether alone[16], with the support of others who are willing to provide that support[17] or with the assistance of services in the community to which the carer has access[18]; and

(4)   the carer is unlikely to achieve one or more of their personal outcomes unless the local authority provides or arranges support to the carer to meet the carer's need[19], the local authority provides or arranges care and support to the person for whom the carer provides care, in order to meet the carer's need[20], or the local authority enables the need to be met by making direct payments[21].

1   As to the meaning of 'local authority' see PARA 2. As to the social services functions of local authorities in Wales generally, and the overarching principles in accordance with which functions relating to the provision of care and support must be exercised, see PARAS 373–383.
2   As to the duty to assess a carer's needs see PARA 54; as to what must be included in a needs assessment see PARA 55.
3   As to the meaning of 'carer' see PARA 54 note 2.
4   Social Services and Well-being (Wales) Act 2014 s 32(1)(a). As to the meanings of 'care' and 'support' see PARA 2 note 1.
5   Ie an adult who has needs which fall within the Care and Support (Eligibility) (Wales) Regulations 2015, SI 2015/1578, reg 3(a), (b) (see PARA 17).
6   Care and Support (Eligibility) (Wales) Regulations 2015, SI 2015/1578, regs 2(3), 5(a)(i).
7   Care and Support (Eligibility) (Wales) Regulations 2015, SI 2015/1578, reg 5(a)(ii). As to the meaning of 'disabled' see PARA 26 note 6; as to the meaning of 'child' see PARA 2.

8 Care and Support (Eligibility) (Wales) Regulations 2015, SI 2015/1578, reg 5(b)(i). As to the meaning of 'self-care' see PARA 17 note 7.
9 Care and Support (Eligibility) (Wales) Regulations 2015, SI 2015/1578, reg 5(b)(ii).
10 Care and Support (Eligibility) (Wales) Regulations 2015, SI 2015/1578, reg 5(b)(iii). As to the meanings of 'abuse' and 'neglect' see PARA 15 note 11.
11 Care and Support (Eligibility) (Wales) Regulations 2015, SI 2015/1578, reg 5(b)(iv).
12 Care and Support (Eligibility) (Wales) Regulations 2015, SI 2015/1578, reg 5(b)(v).
13 Care and Support (Eligibility) (Wales) Regulations 2015, SI 2015/1578, reg 5(b)(vi).
14 Care and Support (Eligibility) (Wales) Regulations 2015, SI 2015/1578, reg 5(b)(vii).
15 Care and Support (Eligibility) (Wales) Regulations 2015, SI 2015/1578, reg 5(b)(viii).
16 Care and Support (Eligibility) (Wales) Regulations 2015, SI 2015/1578, reg 5(c)(i). As to when a person who is able to meet the need, alone or with the assistance of others is to be regarded as unable to meet the need see reg 6; and PARA 17 note 14.
17 Care and Support (Eligibility) (Wales) Regulations 2015, SI 2015/1578, reg 5(c)(ii).
18 Care and Support (Eligibility) (Wales) Regulations 2015, SI 2015/1578, reg 5(c)(iii).
19 Care and Support (Eligibility) (Wales) Regulations 2015, SI 2015/1578, reg 5(d)(i).
20 Care and Support (Eligibility) (Wales) Regulations 2015, SI 2015/1578, reg 5(d)(ii).
21 Care and Support (Eligibility) (Wales) Regulations 2015, SI 2015/1578, reg 5(d)(iii).

57. Duty to consider what can be done to meet needs. If a local authority in Wales[1] determines that any carer[2] needs must be met, or are to be met[3], it must:

    (1)   consider what could be done to meet those needs[4]; and

    (2)   consider whether it would impose a charge for doing those things, and if so, determine the amount of that charge[5].

Where an authority is satisfied on the basis of a needs assessment[6] that a carer[7] has needs for support it must determine whether the needs call for the exercise of any social care function it has[8], in so far as the function is relevant to that person[9], and consider whether the person would benefit from the provision of preventative or advisory services[10] or anything else that may be available in the community[11].

If a carer's needs do not meet the eligibility criteria[12] the authority must determine whether it is nevertheless necessary to meet the needs in order to protect him from abuse or neglect or a risk of abuse or neglect (if the person is an adult)[13] or other harm or a risk of such harm (if the other person is a child)[14].

1 As to the meaning of 'local authority' see PARA 2. As to the social services functions of local authorities in Wales generally, and the overarching principles in accordance with which functions relating to the provision of care and support must be exercised, see PARAS 373–383.
2 As to the meaning of 'carer' see PARA 54 note 2.
3 Ie, in the context of carer needs, under the Social Services and Well-being (Wales) Act 2014 ss 40–45 (see PARAS 58–63).
4 Social Services and Well-being (Wales) Act 2014 s 32(2)(a).
5 Social Services and Well-being (Wales) Act 2014 s 32(2)(b). See Pt 5 (ss 59–73); and PARAS 131–142.
6 As to the duty to assess a carer's needs see PARA 54; as to what must be included in a needs assessment see PARA 55.
7 As to the meaning of 'adult' see PARA 2.
8 Ie under the Social Services and Well-being (Wales) Act 2014 or the Children Act 1989 Pt 4 (ss 31–42) (care and supervision: see CHILDREN AND YOUNG PERSONS vol 9 (2017) PARA 349 et seq) or Pt 5 (ss 43–52) (protection of children: see CHILDREN AND YOUNG PERSONS vol 9 (2017) PARA 249 et seq). As to the meanings of 'care' and 'support' see PARA 2 note 1.
9 Social Services and Well-being (Wales) Act 2014 s 32(1)(c).
10 Ie anything that may be provided by virtue of the Social Services and Well-being (Wales) Act 2014 s 15 (preventative services: see PARA 376) or 17 (information, advice and assistance: see PARA 392).
11 Social Services and Well-being (Wales) Act 2014 s 32(1)(d).
12 As to the eligibility criteria see PARA 56.
13 Social Services and Well-being (Wales) Act 2014 s 32(1)(b)(i). As to the meanings of 'abuse' and 'neglect' see PARA 15 note 11.
14 Social Services and Well-being (Wales) Act 2014 s 32(1)(b)(ii).

58. Circumstances where local authority must meet carer's needs for support. A local authority in Wales[1] must meet the needs for support of a carer[2] who is an adult[3] or a child[4] if it is satisfied[5]:

(1) that the person cared for by the carer is an adult who is ordinarily resident in the local authority's area[6] or of no settled residence and within the authority's area[7], or a disabled child[8] who is within the authority's area[9]; and

(2) that the carer's needs meet the eligibility criteria[10]; and

(3) the applicable financial conditions, if any, are met[11].

Meeting some or all of a carer's needs for support may involve the provision of care and support[12] to the person cared for by the carer, even where there would be no duty[13] to meet the person's needs for that care and support[14]. Where a local authority is required[15] to meet some or all of a carer's needs for support, but it does not prove feasible for it to do so by providing care and support to the person cared for by the carer, it must, so far as it is feasible to do so, identify some other way in which to do so[16].

1 As to the meaning of 'local authority' see PARA 2. As to the social services functions of local authorities in Wales generally, and the overarching principles in accordance with which functions relating to the provision of care and support must be exercised, see PARAS 373–383.

2 As to the meaning of 'carer' see PARA 54 note 2. As to the meanings of 'care' and 'support' see PARA 2 note 1.

3 As to the meaning of 'adult' see PARA 2.

4 As to the meaning of 'child' see PARA 2.

5 Additional conditions to those listed in the text may be specified in regulations (Social Services and Well-being (Wales) Act 2014 ss 40(1), 42(1)): at the date at which this volume states the law no such regulations had been made.

6 Social Services and Well-being (Wales) Act 2014 ss 40(2)(a)(i), 42(2)(a)(i). In connection with a person's residence see PARAS 84–87.

7 Social Services and Well-being (Wales) Act 2014 ss 40(2)(a)(ii), 42(2)(a)(ii).

8 As to the meaning of 'disabled' see PARA 26 note 6.

9 Social Services and Well-being (Wales) Act 2014 ss 40(2)(b), 42(2)(b).

10 Social Services and Well-being (Wales) Act 2014 ss 40(3), 42(3). As to the eligibility criteria see PARA 56.

11 As to the applicable financial conditions see PARA 59 (financial condition where carer's needs involve provision of support to carer), PARA 60 (financial condition where carer's needs involve provision of care and support to cared-for adult), PARA 61 (financial condition where carer's needs involve provision of care and support to cared-for disabled child aged 16 or 17) and PARA 62 (financial condition where carer's needs involve provision of care and support to cared-for disabled child aged under 16).

12 As to the meaning of 'care' and 'support' see PARA 2 note 1.

13 Ie under the Social Services and Well-being (Wales) Act 2014 s 35 (see PARA 19) or s 37 (see PARA 30).

14 Social Services and Well-being (Wales) Act 2014 s 44(1), (2).

15 Ie by the Social Services and Well-being (Wales) Act 2014 s 40 or 42 (see the text and notes 1–11).

16 Social Services and Well-being (Wales) Act 2014 s 44(3).

59. Financial condition where carer's needs involve provision of support to carer. In so far as meeting an adult carer's[1] needs involves the provision of support to the carer, a local authority in Wales[2] must meet the adult carer's needs for support if[3] either there is not a charge[4] for meeting those needs[5] or in so far as there is a charge either:

(1) the authority is satisfied on the basis of a financial assessment[6] that the carer's financial resources are at or below the financial limit[7]; or

(2) the authority is satisfied on the basis of a financial assessment that the carer's financial resources are above the financial limit[8] and the carer nonetheless asks the authority to meet the needs in question[9].

There are no applicable financial conditions where a child carer's needs involve the provision of support to the carer.

1   As to the meaning of 'adult' see PARA 2; as to the meaning of 'carer' see PARA 54 note 2. As to the meanings of 'care' and 'support' see PARA 2 note 1.
2   As to the meaning of 'local authority' see PARA 2. As to the social services functions of local authorities in Wales generally, and the overarching principles in accordance with which functions relating to the provision of care and support must be exercised, see PARAS 373–383.
3   Ie where the conditions as to the residence of the cared-for person and the eligibility of the carer's needs (see PARA 58) are met.
4   Ie under the Social Services and Well-being (Wales) Act 2014 s 59 (see PARA 131).
5   Social Services and Well-being (Wales) Act 2014 s 40(4)(a)(i).
6   As to financial assessments see PARA 141.
7   Social Services and Well-being (Wales) Act 2014 ss 40(4)(a)(ii), 41(1).
8   Social Services and Well-being (Wales) Act 2014 s 41(2)(a).
9   Social Services and Well-being (Wales) Act 2014 s 41(2)(b).

60. Financial condition where carer's needs involve provision of care and support to cared-for adult. In so far as meeting an adult or child carer's[1] needs involves the provision of care and support[2] to an adult cared for by the carer, a local authority in Wales[3] must meet the carer's needs for support if[4]:

(1)   there is not a charge[5] for meeting those needs and either:

   (a)   the authority is satisfied that the person cared for by the carer has capacity[6] to decide whether to have the needs in question met by the provision of care and support to that person[7] and the person agrees to have those needs met in that way[8];

   (b)   an authorised person[9] agrees, on behalf of the person cared for by the carer, to have the needs in question met by the provision of care and support to that person[10]; or

   (c)   the authority is satisfied that the adult cared for by the carer lacks capacity to decide whether to have the needs in question met by the provision of care and support to that adult[11], there is no authorised person to make the decision on the adult's behalf[12] and the authority is satisfied that it is in the adult's best interests to have those needs met in that way[13]; or

(2)   in so far as there is a charge either:

   (a)   the authority is satisfied on the basis of a financial assessment that the financial resources of the adult cared for by the carer are at or below the financial limit[14] and head (a), head (b) or head (c) above applies[15]; or

   (b)   the authority is satisfied on the basis of a financial assessment that the financial resources of the adult cared for by the carer are above the financial limit[16] and head (a), head (b) or head (c) above applies[17].

1   As to the meanings of 'adult' and 'child' see PARA 2; as to the meaning of 'carer' see PARA 54 note 2.
2   As to the meaning of 'care' and 'support' see PARA 2 note 1.
3   As to the meaning of 'local authority' see PARA 2. As to the social services functions of local authorities in Wales generally, and the overarching principles in accordance with which functions relating to the provision of care and support must be exercised, see PARAS 373–383.
4   Ie where the conditions as to the residence of the cared-for person and the eligibility of the carer's needs (see PARA 58) are met.
5   Ie under the Social Services and Well-being (Wales) Act 2014 s 59 (see PARA 131).
6   As to a person having or lacking capacity see PARA 8 note 10.
7   Social Services and Well-being (Wales) Act 2014 ss 40(4)(b)(i), 41(7)(a), 42(4)(a)(i), 43(5)(a) (s 42(4)(a)(i), (ii) amended by the Regulation and Inspection of Social Care (Wales) Act 2016 Sch 3 para 62).

8   Social Services and Well-being (Wales) Act 2014 ss 41(7)(b), 43(5)(b).
9   'Authorised person' means a person authorised under the Mental Capacity Act 2005 (whether in
    general or specific terms) (see PARA 12 note 15) to decide on behalf of the person cared for by the
    carer whether to have the needs in question met by the provision of care and support to that
    person: Social Services and Well-being (Wales) Act 2014 ss 41(15), 43(13).
10 Social Services and Well-being (Wales) Act 2014 ss 41(8), 43(6).
11 Social Services and Well-being (Wales) Act 2014 ss 41(9)(a), 43(7)(a).
12 Social Services and Well-being (Wales) Act 2014 ss 41(9)(b), 43(7)(b).
13 Social Services and Well-being (Wales) Act 2014 ss 41(9)(c), 43(7)(c).
14 Social Services and Well-being (Wales) Act 2014 ss 40(4)(b)(ii), 41(3)(a), 42(4)(a)(ii), 43(1)(a)
    (s 42(4)(a)(ii) as amended: see note 7). As to the meanings of 'financial assessment' and 'financial
    resources' see Pt 5 (ss 59–73) (in particular ss 63(4)); and PARAS 141 (definitions applied by
    ss 41(16), 43(14)).
15 Social Services and Well-being (Wales) Act 2014 ss 41(3)(b), 43(1)(b).
16 Social Services and Well-being (Wales) Act 2014 ss 41(4)(a), 43(2)(a).
17 Social Services and Well-being (Wales) Act 2014 ss 41(4)(b), 43(2)(b).

61. Financial condition where carer's needs involve provision of care and support to cared-for disabled child aged 16 or 17. In so far as meeting an adult or child carer's[1] needs involves the provision of care and support[2] to a disabled child[3] aged 16 or 17 who is cared for by the carer, a local authority in Wales[4] must meet the carer's needs for support if[5]:

(1)   there is not a charge[6] for meeting those needs and either:

    (a)   the authority is satisfied that the person cared for by the carer has capacity[7] to decide whether to have the needs in question met by the provision of care and support to that person[8] and the person agrees to have those needs met in that way[9];

    (b)   an authorised person[10] agrees, on behalf of the person cared for by the carer, to have the needs in question met by the provision of care and support to that person[11]; or

    (c)   the authority is satisfied that the disabled child cared for by the carer lacks capacity to decide whether to have the needs in question met by the provision of care and support to that child[12], there is no authorised person to make the decision on the child's behalf[13], and no objection has been made by a person with parental responsibility[14] for the child to having those needs met in that way[15]; or

(2)   in so far as there is a charge, either:

    (a)   in respect of an adult upon whom the authority thinks it would impose a charge for the provision of care and support to the disabled child cared for by the carer, the authority is satisfied on the basis of a financial assessment[16] that it would not be reasonably practicable for the adult to pay any amount for the care and support[17] and head (a), head (b) or head (c) above applies[18]; or

    (b)   in respect of an adult upon whom the authority thinks it would impose a charge for the provision of care and support to the disabled child cared for by the carer, the authority is satisfied on the basis of a financial assessment that it would be reasonably practicable for the adult to pay the standard charge[19] for the care and support[20] or to pay any other amount for the care and support[21], the adult does not object to the provision of the care and support[22], and head (a), head (b) or head (c) above applies[23].

1   As to the meanings of 'adult' and 'child' see PARA 2; as to the meaning of 'carer' see PARA 54 note
    2.

2   As to the meaning of 'care' and 'support' see PARA 2 note 1.

3   As to the meaning of 'disabled' see PARA 26 note 6.

4   As to the meaning of 'local authority' see PARA 2. As to the social services functions of local authorities in Wales generally, and the overarching principles in accordance with which functions relating to the provision of care and support must be exercised, see PARAS 373–383.

5   Ie where the conditions as to the residence of the cared-for person and the eligibility of the carer's needs (see PARA 58) are met.

6   Ie under the Social Services and Well-being (Wales) Act 2014 s 59 (see PARA 131).

7   As to a person having or lacking capacity see PARA 8 note 10.

8   Social Services and Well-being (Wales) Act 2014 ss 40(4)(c)(i), 41(7)(a), 42(4)(b)(i), 43(5)(a) (s 42(4)(b)(i), (ii) amended by the Regulation and Inspection of Social Care (Wales) Act 2016 Sch 3 para 62).

9   Social Services and Well-being (Wales) Act 2014 s 41(7)(b).

10 As to the meaning of 'authorised person' see PARA 60 note 9).

11 Social Services and Well-being (Wales) Act 2014 ss 41(8), 43(6).

12 Social Services and Well-being (Wales) Act 2014 ss 41(10)(a), 43(8)(a).

13 Social Services and Well-being (Wales) Act 2014 ss 41(10)(b), 43(8)(b).

14 As to the meaning of 'parental responsibility' see PARA 26 note 10.

15 Social Services and Well-being (Wales) Act 2014 ss 41(10)(c), 43(8)(c). The local authority may disregard an objection for the purposes of s 41(10)(c) or s 43(8)(c) if it is satisfied that it would not be in the disabled child's best interests: ss 41(11), 43(9).

16 As to the meaning of 'financial assessment' see PARA 60 note 14.

17 Social Services and Well-being (Wales) Act 2014 ss 40(4)(c)(ii), 41(5)(a), 42(4)(b)(ii) (s 42(4)(b)(ii) as amended: see note 8), 43(3)(a).

18 Social Services and Well-being (Wales) Act 2014 ss 41(5)(b)(i), 43(3)(b)(i).

19 As to the meaning of 'standard charge' see the Social Services and Well-being (Wales) Act 2014 s 63(3); and PARA 132 (definition applied by ss 41(15), 43(13)).

20 Social Services and Well-being (Wales) Act 2014 ss 41(6)(a)(i), 43(4)(a)(i).

21 Social Services and Well-being (Wales) Act 2014 ss 41(6)(a)(ii), 43(4)(a)(ii).

22 Social Services and Well-being (Wales) Act 2014 ss 41(6)(b), 43(4)(b).

23 Social Services and Well-being (Wales) Act 2014 ss 41(6)(c)(i), 43(4)(c)(i).

62. Financial condition where carer's needs involve provision of care and support to cared-for disabled child aged under 16. In so far as meeting an adult or child carer's[1] needs involves the provision of care and support[2] to a disabled child[3] aged under 16 who is cared for by the carer, a local authority in Wales[4] must meet the carer's needs for support if[5]:

(1)   there is not a charge[6] for meeting those needs and either:

    (a)   the authority is satisfied that the disabled child cared for by the carer has sufficient understanding to make an informed decision about having the needs in question met by the provision of care and support to that child[7] and the child agrees to have those needs met in that way[8]; or

    (b)   the authority is satisfied that the disabled child cared for by the carer does not have sufficient understanding to make an informed decision about having the needs in question met by the provision of care and support to that child[9] and no objection has been made by a person with parental responsibility for the child to having those needs met in that way[10]; or

(2)   in so far as there is a charge:

    (a)   in respect of an adult upon whom the authority thinks it would impose a charge for the provision of care and support to the disabled child cared for by the carer, the authority is satisfied on the basis of a financial assessment[11] that it would not be reasonably practicable for the adult to pay any amount for the care and support[12] and head (a) or head (b) above applies[13]; or

(b)   in respect of an adult upon whom the authority thinks it would impose a charge for the provision of care and support to the disabled child cared for by the carer, the authority is satisfied on the basis of a financial assessment that it would be reasonably practicable for the adult to pay the standard charge[14] for the care and support[15] or to pay any other amount for the care and support[16], the adult does not object to the provision of the care and support[17], and head (a) or head (b) above applies[18].

1   As to the meanings of 'adult' and 'child' see PARA 2; as to the meaning of 'carer' see PARA 54 note 2.
2   As to the meaning of 'care' and 'support' see PARA 2 note 1.
3   As to the meaning of 'disabled' see PARA 26 note 6.
4   As to the meaning of 'local authority' see PARA 2. As to the social services functions of local authorities in Wales generally, and the overarching principles in accordance with which functions relating to the provision of care and support must be exercised, see PARAS 373–383.
5   Ie where the conditions as to the residence of the cared-for person and the eligibility of the carer's needs (see PARA 58) are met.
6   Ie under the Social Services and Well-being (Wales) Act 2014 s 59 (see PARA 131).
7   Social Services and Well-being (Wales) Act 2014 ss 40(4)(d)(i), 41(12)(a), 42(4)(c)(i), 43(10)(a) (s 42(4)(c)(i), (ii) amended by the Regulation and Inspection of Social Care (Wales) Act 2016 Sch 3 para 62).
8   Social Services and Well-being (Wales) Act 2014 ss 41(12)(b), 43(10)(b).
9   Social Services and Well-being (Wales) Act 2014 ss 41(13)(a), 43(11)(a).
10 Social Services and Well-being (Wales) Act 2014 ss 41(13)(b), 43(11)(b). The local authority may disregard an objection for the purposes of s 41(13)(b) or s 43(11)(b) if it is satisfied that it would not be consistent with the disabled child's well-being: ss 41(14), 43(12). As to the meaning of 'parental responsibility' see PARA 26 note 10. As to the meaning of 'well-being' see PARA 375.
11 As to the meaning of 'financial assessment' see PARA 60 note 14.
12 Social Services and Well-being (Wales) Act 2014 ss 40(4)(d)(ii), 41(5)(a), 42(4)(c)(ii), 43(3)(a) (s 42(4)(c)(ii) as amended: see note 7).
13 Social Services and Well-being (Wales) Act 2014 ss 41(5)(b)(ii), 43(3)(b)(ii).
14 As to the meaning of 'standard charge' see PARA 61 note 19.
15 Social Services and Well-being (Wales) Act 2014 ss 41(6)(a)(i), 43(4)(a)(i).
16 Social Services and Well-being (Wales) Act 2014 ss 41(6)(a)(ii), 43(4)(a)(ii).
17 Social Services and Well-being (Wales) Act 2014 ss 41(6)(b), 43(4)(b).
18 Social Services and Well-being (Wales) Act 2014 ss 41(6)(c)(ii), 43(4)(c)(ii).

63.   Circumstances where local authority may meet carer's needs for care and support. A local authority in Wales[1] may meet a carer's[2] needs for support if the person cared for by the carer is within the local authority's area[3] or ordinarily resident in the authority's area, but outside its area[4]. A local authority has the power to meet needs under these provisions whether or not it has completed a needs assessment[5] or a financial assessment[6].

1   As to the meaning of 'local authority' see PARA 2. As to the social services functions of local authorities in Wales generally, and the overarching principles in accordance with which functions relating to the provision of care and support must be exercised, see PARAS 373–383.
2   As to the meaning of 'carer' see PARA 54 note 2.
3   Social Services and Well-being (Wales) Act 2014 s 45(1)(a).
4   Social Services and Well-being (Wales) Act 2014 s 45(1)(b). In connection with a person's residence see PARAS 84–87.
5   Ie in accordance with the Social Services and Well-being (Wales) Act 2014 Pt 3 (ss 19–31) (see PARAS 66–77).
6   Social Services and Well-being (Wales) Act 2014 s 45(2). Financial assessments are completed under Pt 5 (ss 59–73) (see PARAS 131–142).

(5) ASSESSMENTS

(i) England

A. NEEDS AND CARER'S ASSESSMENTS

64. Assessments must be appropriate and proportionate. A local authority in England[1] must carry out a needs or carer's assessment[2] in a manner which is appropriate and proportionate to the needs and circumstances of the individual to whom it relates[3] and ensures that the individual is able to participate in the process as effectively as possible[4]. In seeking to ensure that an assessment is carried out in an appropriate and proportionate manner, an authority must have regard to the wishes and preferences of the individual to whom it relates[5], the outcome the individual seeks from the assessment[6], and the severity and overall extent of the individual's needs[7].

An authority carrying out an assessment must consider the impact of the needs of the individual to whom the assessment relates on any person who is involved in caring for the individual[8] and any person the local authority considers to be relevant[9]. If it appears to an authority carrying out an assessment that a child[10] is involved in providing care to any individual, the authority must consider the impact of the needs of the individual concerned on the child's well-being[11], welfare, education and development[12], and identify whether any of the tasks which the child is performing for the individual are inappropriate for the child to perform having regard to all the circumstances[13].

1   As to the meaning of 'local authority' see PARA 1. As to the social services functions of local authorities in England generally, and the overarching principles in accordance with which functions relating to the provision of care and support must be exercised, see PARAS 315–323.
2   Ie a needs assessment (see PARA 8), a child's needs assessment (see PARA 22), a carer's assessment (see PARA 33), a child's carer's assessment (see PARA 42) or a young carer's assessment (see PARA 50) (an 'assessment'): Care and Support (Assessment) Regulations 2014, SI 2014/2827, reg 1(2) (made under the Care Act 2014 ss 12(1), (2), 65(1)). Note that these provisions apply only to assessments under the Care Act 2014, and do not apply to a young carer's needs assessment under the Children Act 1989 s 17ZA (see PARAS 47–49).
3   Care and Support (Assessment) Regulations 2014, SI 2014/2827, reg 3(1)(a).
4   Care and Support (Assessment) Regulations 2014, SI 2014/2827, reg 3(1)(b).
5   Care and Support (Assessment) Regulations 2014, SI 2014/2827, reg 3(2)(a).
6   Care and Support (Assessment) Regulations 2014, SI 2014/2827, reg 3(2)(b).
7   Care and Support (Assessment) Regulations 2014, SI 2014/2827, reg 3(2)(c). In a case where the level of the individual's needs fluctuates, the authority must take into account the individual's circumstances over such period as it considers necessary to establish accurately the individual's level of needs: reg 3(3).
8   Care and Support (Assessment) Regulations 2014, SI 2014/2827, reg 4(1)(a).
9   Care and Support (Assessment) Regulations 2014, SI 2014/2827, reg 4(1)(b).
10   As to the meaning of 'child' see PARA 1.
11   As to the meaning of 'well-being' see PARA 317.
12   Care and Support (Assessment) Regulations 2014, SI 2014/2827, reg 4(3)(a).
13   Care and Support (Assessment) Regulations 2014, SI 2014/2827, reg 4(3)(b).

65. Supported self-assessments. A local authority[1] proposing to carry out a needs or carer's assessment[2] must ascertain whether the individual to whom the assessment is to relate wishes the assessment to be a supported self-assessment[3], that is, an assessment carried out jointly by the authority and the individual to whom it relates[4]. A supported self-assessment must be carried out if the individual concerned is an adult[5] and wishes the assessment to be a supported self-assessment[6] and has the capacity[7] to take part in a supported self-assessment[8], and may be carried out if the individual concerned is a child[9] and wishes the assessment to be a supported self-assessment[10], has the capacity, and is competent, to take part in a supported self-assessment[11], and the authority believes it appropriate for a self-supported assessment to be carried out having regard to all the circumstances[12].

1   As to the meaning of 'local authority' see PARA 1. As to the social services functions of local authorities in England generally, and the overarching principles in accordance with which functions relating to the provision of care and support must be exercised, see PARAS 315–323.
2   As to the carrying out of assessments see PARA 64.
3   Care and Support (Assessment) Regulations 2014, SI 2014/2827, reg 2(2).
4   Care and Support (Assessment) Regulations 2014, SI 2014/2827, reg 2(1). To facilitate the carrying out of a supported self-assessment an authority must provide an individual taking part in a supported self-assessment with relevant information: see reg 2(5)–(7); and PARA 67.
5   As to the meaning of 'adult' see PARA 1 note 1.
6   Care and Support (Assessment) Regulations 2014, SI 2014/2827, reg 2(3)(a).
7   As to a person having or lacking capacity see PARA 8 note 10.
8   Care and Support (Assessment) Regulations 2014, SI 2014/2827, reg 2(3)(b).
9   As to the meaning of 'child' see PARA 1.
10 Care and Support (Assessment) Regulations 2014, SI 2014/2827, reg 2(4)(a).
11 Care and Support (Assessment) Regulations 2014, SI 2014/2827, reg 2(4)(b).
12 Care and Support (Assessment) Regulations 2014, SI 2014/2827, reg 2(4)(c).

66. Combined assessments. A local authority[1] may combine a needs or carer's assessment[2] with an assessment it is carrying out[3] in relation to another person only if the adult[4] to whom the assessment relates agrees and:

   (1)   where the combination would include an assessment relating to another adult, that other adult agrees[5];

   (2)   where the combination would include an assessment relating to a child[6] (including a young carer[7]), the consent condition is met in relation to the child[8].

Where a local authority is carrying out a needs or carer's assessment, and there is some other assessment being or about to be carried out in relation to the adult to whom the assessment relates or in relation to a relevant person[9], the authority may carry out that other assessment on behalf of or jointly with the body responsible for carrying it out[10] or if that body has arranged to carry out the other assessment jointly with another person, jointly with that body and the other person[11].

Provision is made in connection with arrangements for independent advocacy where assessments are combined[12].

1   As to the meaning of 'local authority' see PARA 1. As to the social services functions of local authorities in England generally, and the overarching principles in accordance with which functions relating to the provision of care and support must be exercised, see PARAS 315–323.
2   As to the carrying out of assessments see PARA 64.
3   Ie whether or not under the Care Act 2014 Pt 1 (ss 1–80).
4   As to the meaning of 'adult' see PARA 1 note 1.
5   Care Act 2014 s 12(5)(a).
6   As to the meaning of 'child' see PARA 1.
7   As to the meaning of 'young carer' see PARA 50 note 2.
8   Care Act 2014 s 12(5)(b). The consent condition is met in relation to a child if:
        (1)   the child has capacity or is competent to agree to the assessments being combined and does so agree (s 12(6)(a)); or
        (2)   the child lacks capacity or is not competent so to agree but the local authority is satisfied that combining the assessments would be in the child's best interests (s 12(6)(b)).
        As to a person having or lacking capacity see PARA 8 note 10.
9   A person is a 'relevant person', in relation to a needs or carer's assessment, if it would be reasonable to combine an assessment relating to that person with the needs or carer's assessment (as mentioned in the Care Act 2014 s 12(5): see the text and notes 1–8): s 12(11).
10 Care Act 2014 s 12(7)(a).
11 Care Act 2014 s 12(7)(b).

12 Where a local authority combines an assessment of an individual under the Care Act 2014 Pt 1 with an assessment under Pt 1 that relates to another individual (Care and Support (Independent Advocacy Support) (No 2) Regulations 2014, SI 2014/2889, reg 7(1)(a)) (made under the Care Act 2014 s 67(7)(e))) and that authority is required to make arrangements for independent advocacy under s 67(2) (see PARAS 100–103) in respect of each of those individuals (Care and Support (Independent Advocacy Support) (No 2) Regulations 2014, SI 2014/2889, reg 7(1)(b)), then each of those individuals may be represented and supported by the same independent advocate in circumstances where the authority is satisfied that there would be no conflict of interest on a material issue between the individuals (reg 7(2)(a)) or between the independent advocate and either of the individuals (reg 7(2)(b)). As to the meaning of 'independent advocate' see PARA 100. As to the meaning of 'the individual' see PARA 100 note 6. The authority must ensure that each of those individuals is represented and supported by different independent advocates if so requested by either of those individuals (Care and Support (Independent Advocacy Support) (No 2) Regulations 2014, SI 2014/2889, reg 7(3)(a)) or any independent advocate who has already begun to represent and support one of those individuals under arrangements made under the Care Act 2014 s 67(2) (Care and Support (Independent Advocacy Support) (No 2) Regulations 2014, SI 2014/2889, reg 7(3)(b)).

67. Information and consultation. A local authority[1] must give information about the assessment process[2] to the individual whose needs are being assessed[3] or, in the case of a child's needs assessment[4] or a young carer's assessment[5], if the child[6] or young carer[7] is not competent or lacks capacity[8] to understand the assessment process, to all parents of that child or young carer[9]. Where an authority considers that any person would benefit from the provision of information and advice relating to care and support for individuals or support for carers[10], it must advise that person how to obtain such information and advice[11].

To facilitate the carrying out of a supported self-assessment[12] or an assessment which relates to an individual who is deafblind[13] an authority must provide an individual taking part in a supported self-assessment, or any person carrying out an assessment which relates to an individual who is deafblind, with any relevant information it may have about that individual[14] and (in the case of a supported self-assessment, providing the consent condition[15] is met), about the person[16] needing care[17].

1 As to the meaning of 'local authority' see PARA 1. As to the social services functions of local authorities in England generally, and the overarching principles in accordance with which functions relating to the provision of care and support must be exercised, see PARAS 315–323.
2 As to the carrying out of assessments see PARA 64. The information must be provided prior to the assessment wherever practicable, and in a format which is accessible to the individual to whom it is given: Care and Support (Assessment) Regulations 2014, SI 2014/2827, reg 3(5).
3 Care and Support (Assessment) Regulations 2014, SI 2014/2827, reg 3(4)(a).
4 See PARA 22.
5 See PARA 47.
6 As to the meaning of 'child' see PARA 1.
7 As to the meaning of 'young carer' see PARA 50 note 2.
8 As to a person having or lacking capacity see PARA 8 note 10.
9 Care and Support (Assessment) Regulations 2014, SI 2014/2827, reg 3(4)(b).
10 As to the meaning of 'carer' see PARA 33 note 2.
11 Care and Support (Assessment) Regulations 2014, SI 2014/2827, reg 4(2).
12 As to supported self-assessments see PARA 65.
13 An individual is 'deafblind' if he has combined sight and hearing impairment which causes difficulties with communication, access to information and mobility: Care and Support (Assessment) Regulations 2014, SI 2014/2827, reg 6(3).
14 Care and Support (Assessment) Regulations 2014, SI 2014/2827, regs 2(5)(a), 6(2)(a). In the case of information provided pursuant to a supported self-assessment the information must be provided in a format which is accessible to the individual to whom it is given: reg 2(7).
15 The consent condition is met if:
   (1)   the adult or child needing care has capacity or is competent to agree to the information in reg 2(5)(b) being provided and does so agree (reg 2(6)(a)); or
   (2)   the adult or child needing care does not have capacity or is not competent so to agree but the local authority is satisfied that providing the information in reg 2(5)(b) would be in the best interests of the adult or child needing care (reg 2(6)(b)).

16 Ie the adult needing care (in the case of a carer's assessment (Care and Support (Assessment) Regulations 2014, SI 2014/2827, regs 2(5)(b)(i), 6(2)(b)(i)) or a young carer's assessment (if, where the assessment is a supported self-assessment, the local authority believes it is appropriate for the young carer to have that information having regard to all the circumstances) (regs 2(5)(b)(iii), 6(2)(b)(iii)), or the child needing care (in the case of a child's carer's assessment (regs 2(5)(b)(ii), 6(2)(b)(ii)).
17 Care and Support (Assessment) Regulations 2014, SI 2014/2827, regs 2(5)(b), 6(2)(b).

68. Training and competence. A local authority[1] must ensure that any person (other than in the case of a supported self-assessment[2], the individual to whom it relates) carrying out a needs or carer's assessment[3] has the skills, knowledge and competence to carry out the assessment in question[4] and is appropriately trained[5]. An authority carrying out an assessment must consult a person who has expertise in relation to the condition or other circumstances of the individual whose needs are being assessed in any case where it considers that the needs of the individual concerned require it to do so[6]. An assessment which relates to an individual who is deafblind[7] must be carried out by a person who has specific training and expertise relating to individuals who are deafblind[8].

1   As to the meaning of 'local authority' see PARA 1. As to the social services functions of local authorities in England generally, and the overarching principles in accordance with which functions relating to the provision of care and support must be exercised, see PARAS 315–323.
2   As to supported self-assessments see PARA 65.
3   As to the carrying out of assessments see PARA 64.
4   Care and Support (Assessment) Regulations 2014, SI 2014/2827, reg 5(1)(a).
5   Care and Support (Assessment) Regulations 2014, SI 2014/2827, reg 5(1)(b).
6   Care and Support (Assessment) Regulations 2014, SI 2014/2827, reg 5(2). Such consultation may take place before, or during, the carrying out of the assessment: reg 5(3).
7   As to when an individual is deafblind see PARA 67 note 13.
8   Care and Support (Assessment) Regulations 2014, SI 2014/2827, reg 6(1).

B.   PERSONS LEAVING HOSPITAL

69. Discharge of hospital patients with care and support needs. English NHS bodies[1] discharging patients into local authority areas in England are required by the Care Act 2014 to coordinate and consult with that local authority in assessing the patient's ongoing care needs[2]. The duty arises where:

(1)   an English NHS body is responsible for a patient[3] ordinarily resident in England[4] who is being accommodated either in an English NHS hospital[5] or at an independent hospital anywhere in the United Kingdom[6] as a result of arrangements made by the English NHS body[7], and is receiving (or has received or can reasonably be expected to receive) acute care[8] (a 'hospital patient'[9]); and

(2)   the NHS body considers that it is not likely to be safe to discharge the patient unless arrangements for meeting his needs for care and support are in place[10].

The NHS body must give notice (an 'assessment notice'[11]) to the applicable English local authority[12], which is then required to carry out a needs assessment and (where applicable) a carer's assessment[13]. Failure to carry out an assessment attracts ongoing financial sanctions[14].

Patients may also be discharged into local authority areas in England by NHS bodies in Wales, in which circumstances a similar process governed by different statutory provisions applies[15].

1   For the purposes of the Care Act 2014 s 74, Sch 3 'NHS body' means an NHS trust established under the National Health Service Act 2006 s 25 (see HEALTH SERVICES vol 54 (2017) PARA 235), an NHS foundation trust (see HEALTH SERVICES vol 54 (2017) PARA 244), the

National Health Service Commissioning Board (see HEALTH SERVICES vol 54 (2017) PARA 32) or a clinical commissioning group (see HEALTH SERVICES vol 54 (2017) PARA 35 et seq): Care Act 2014 Sch 3 para 7(4).

2   See the Care Act 2014 s 74, Sch 3; the text and notes 3–15; and PARAS 70–72. Section 74 and Sch 3 do not apply to the exercise of the power to meet a child's carer's needs for support under s 62(1) (see PARA 44): Care and Support (Children's Carer's) Regulations 2015, SI 2015/305, reg 2(2)(c).
    An NHS body may make arrangements with any person connected with the management of an independent hospital (see note 6) for that person (or an employee of that person) to do, on behalf of the NHS body and in accordance with the arrangements, anything which is required or authorised to be done by the NHS body by or under Sch 3 in relation to hospital patients accommodated in that hospital: Care Act 2014 Sch 3 para 5(1). Anything done or omitted to be done by or in relation to the authorised person (or an employee of that person) under such arrangements is to be treated as done or omitted to be done by or in relation to the NHS body: Sch 3 para 5(2). Nothing in Sch 3 para 5 prevents anything being done by or in relation to the NHS body: Sch 3 para 5(3).

3   A reference to the NHS body responsible for a hospital patient is if the hospital is an NHS hospital, a reference to the NHS body managing it, or if the hospital is an independent hospital, a reference to the NHS body that arranged for the patient to be accommodated in it: Care Act 2014 Sch 3 para 7(5).

4   As to the meaning of 'England' see PARA 1 note 1. In connection with a person's residence see PARAS 84–87.

5   For the purposes of the Care Act 2014 Sch 3 'NHS hospital' means a health service hospital (as defined by the National Health Service Act 2006: see s 275(1); and HEALTH SERVICES vol 54 (2017) PARA 26) in England: Care Act 2014 Sch 3 para 7(2).

6   For the purposes of the Care Act 2014 Sch 3 'independent hospital' means a hospital (as defined by the National Health Service Act 2006: see s 275(1); and HEALTH SERVICES vol 54 (2017) PARA 26) in the United Kingdom which is not an NHS hospital or a health service hospital as defined by the National Health Service (Wales) Act 2006 s 206 (see HEALTH SERVICES vol 54 (2017) PARA 26) or corresponding Scotland or Northern Ireland provisions: Care Act 2014 Sch 3 para 7(3). As to the meaning of 'United Kingdom' see PARA 4 note 12.

7   Care Act 2014 Sch 3 para 7(1)(a).

8   Care Act 2014 Sch 3 para 7(1)(b). 'Acute care' means intensive medical treatment provided by or under the supervision of a consultant, that lasts for a limited period after which the person receiving the treatment no longer benefits from it: Sch 3 para 7(6). Care is not 'acute care' if the patient has given an undertaking (or one has been given on the patient's behalf) to pay for it; nor is any of the following 'acute care': care of an expectant or nursing mother; mental health care; palliative care; a structured programme of care provided for a limited period to help a person maintain or regain the ability to live at home; or care provided for recuperation or rehabilitation: Sch 3 para 7(7). 'Mental health care' means psychiatric services, or other services provided for the purpose of preventing, diagnosing or treating illness, the arrangements for which are the primary responsibility of a consultant psychiatrist: Sch 3 para 7(8).

9   Care Act 2014 Sch 3 para 7(1).

10 Care Act 2014 Sch 3 para 1(1).

11 Care Act 2014 Sch 3 para 1(2).

12 Ie the authority in whose area the patient is ordinarily resident (Care Act 2014 Sch 3 para 1(1)(a)) or if it appears to the body that the patient is of no settled residence, the local authority in whose area the hospital is situated (Sch 3 para 1(1)(b)). As to the meaning of 'local authority' see PARA 1. The local authority to which an assessment notice is given is referred to in Sch 3 as 'the relevant authority': Sch 3 para 1(2). As to the social services functions of local authorities in England generally, and the overarching principles in accordance with which functions relating to the provision of care and support must be exercised, see PARAS 315–323.

13 See PARA 71. A local authority to which an assessment notice has been given must accept that notice and carry out the duties of a relevant authority arising from it even though it may wish to dispute that it was the correct authority to which to give the notice: Care and Support (Discharge of Hospital Patients) Regulations 2014, SI 2014/2823, reg 12(1) (made under the Care Act 2014 Sch 3 paras 6, 8). If for one of the reasons set out below it is agreed or determined that the patient to whom the notice relates is ordinarily resident in the area of another local authority then that local authority is to become the relevant authority in the patient's case: the reasons are:
    (1)   the other local authority agrees that it is the correct authority (Care and Support (Discharge of Hospital Patients) Regulations 2014, SI 2014/2823, reg 12(2), (3)(a)); or
    (2)   a determination is made under the Care Act 2014 s 40 (see PARA 96) to the effect that the patient is ordinarily resident in the area of the other local authority (Care and Support (Discharge of Hospital Patients) Regulations 2014, SI 2014/2823, reg 12(3)(b)).

14 See PARA 72.
15 See the Community Care (Delayed Discharges) Act 2003 Pt 1 (ss 1–14). That Act has been brought
    into force only in relation to England, and imposes duties similar to those under the Care Act 2014
    Sch 3 on Welsh NHS bodies (ie NHS Trusts (or, as from a day to be appointed, NHS Trusts in
    Wales) and local health boards in Wales) in respect of persons accommodated at health service
    hospitals in Wales (ie within the meaning given by the National Health Service (Wales) Act 2006
    (see note 6)) or independent hospitals in England or Wales in pursuance of arrangements made by
    Welsh NHS bodies: see the Community Care (Delayed Discharges) Act 2003 s 1(1)–(3) (amended
    by the Health and Social Care Act 2012 Sch 5 para 109; prospectively amended by Sch 14
    para 84); and the definitions 'health service hospital' and 'independent hospital' in the Community
    Care (Delayed Discharges) Act 2003 s 12 (amended by the National Health Service (Consequential
    Provisions) Act 2006 Sch 1 para 231; by SI 2012/813; and by SI 2015/914). As to Local Health
    Boards see HEALTH SERVICES vol 54 (2017) PARA 97.

70. Assessment notices and discharge notices. An English NHS body[1]
discharging a hospital patient[2] with care and support needs[3] must give the relevant
local authority[4] an assessment notice relating to the patient[5] and the authority
must carry out a needs assessment and (where applicable) a carer's assessment[6].
An assessment notice must describe itself as such, and may not be given more than
seven days before the day on which the patient is expected to be admitted to
hospital[7]. Before giving the assessment notice, the NHS body responsible for the
patient must consult him and, where it is feasible to do so, any carer that he has[8],
and having given the notice, must consult the authority before deciding what it
will do for the patient in order for discharge to be safe[9] and give the authority
notice (a 'discharge notice'[10]) of the day on which it proposes to discharge the
patient[11]. The discharge notice must specify whether the responsible NHS body
will be providing or arranging for the provision of services[12] to the patient after
discharge[13] and if it will, what those services are[14]. A discharge notice may be
withdrawn where the patient's safety requires[15].

1   As to the meanings of 'NHS body' and 'England' see PARA 69 note 1; as to the application of the
    Care Act 2014 s 74 and Sch 3 see PARA 69.
2   As to the meaning of 'hospital patient' generally see PARA 69. As to when an English NHS body
    is 'responsible' for a hospital patient see PARA 69 note 3. A reference in the Care Act 2014 Sch 3
    para 1 to a 'hospital patient' includes a reference to a person who it is reasonable to expect is about
    to become one: Sch 3 para 1(6).
3   Ie where the conditions set out in see PARA 69 are met.
4   As to the local authority for these purposes see PARA 69 note 12.
5   See the Care Act 2014 Sch 3 para 1(1), (2); and PARA 69. As to the form and content of an
    assessment notice see the Care and Support (Discharge of Hospital Patients) Regulations 2014, SI
    2014/2823, regs 2, 3. An assessment notice remains in force until the patient is discharged
    (whether by the NHS body responsible for him or by himself) or dies or the NHS body responsible
    for the patient withdraws the notice by giving a notice (a 'withdrawal notice') to the relevant
    authority: Sch 3 para 1(5). As to the form of a withdrawal notice and when a withdrawal notice
    must be given see the Care and Support (Discharge of Hospital Patients) Regulations 2014, SI
    2014/2823, regs 2, 4.
6   See PARA 71.
7   Care Act 2014 Sch 3 para 1(3). An assessment notice which is given after 2pm on any day is to be
    treated as having been given on the following day: Care and Support (Discharge of Hospital
    Patients) Regulations 2014, SI 2014/2823, reg 11.
8   Care Act 2014 Sch 3 para 1(4).
9   Care Act 2014 Sch 3 para 2(1)(a).
10 Care Act 2014 Sch 3 para 2(2). As to the form and content of a discharge notice see the Care and
    Support (Discharge of Hospital Patients) Regulations 2014, SI 2014/2823, regs 2, 6. A discharge
    notice remains in force until the end of the relevant day, or the NHS body responsible for the
    patient withdraws the notice by giving a withdrawal notice to the relevant authority: Care Act
    2014 Sch 3 para 2(4). As to the form of a withdrawal notice see the Care and Support (Discharge
    of Hospital Patients) Regulations 2014, SI 2014/2823, reg 2. The 'relevant day' is the later of the
    day specified in the discharge notice and the last day of the period beginning with the day after that
    on which the assessment notice is given or treated as given in accordance with the Care and
    Support (Discharge of Hospital Patients) Regulations 2014, SI 2014/2823, reg 11 and ending two

days after that date: Care Act 2014 Sch 3 paras 2(5), (6), 4(5); Care and Support (Discharge of Hospital Patients) Regulations 2014, SI 2014/2823, reg 8.

11 Care Act 2014 Sch 3 para 2(1)(b). A discharge notice may not be given less than one day in advance of the proposed discharge date: Care and Support (Discharge of Hospital Patients) Regulations 2014, SI 2014/2823, reg 5. A discharge notice which is given after 2pm on any day is to be treated as having been given on the following day: reg 11.

12 Ie services under the National Health Service Act 2006.

13 Care Act 2014 Sch 3 para 2(3)(a).

14 Care Act 2014 Sch 3 para 2(3)(b).

15 A notice withdrawing a discharge notice must be given where the NHS body responsible for the patient considers that it is no longer likely to be safe to discharge the patient on the proposed discharge date (Care and Support (Discharge of Hospital Patients) Regulations 2014, SI 2014/2823, reg 7(1)), unless the only reason that the NHS body considers that it is no longer likely to be safe to discharge the patient on the proposed discharge date is that the relevant authority has not discharged its duty to carry out a needs assessment or (where applicable) a carer's assessment in relation to the patient (reg 7(2)(a)) or not put in place arrangements for meeting some or all of those needs that it proposes to meet under the Care Act 2014 ss 18–20 (see PARAS 12–13 (adults), and PARAS 36, 37 (carers)) in the case of the patient or (where applicable) the patient's carer (Care and Support (Discharge of Hospital Patients) Regulations 2014, SI 2014/2823, reg 7(2)(b)).

71. Needs assessments and carer's assessments. The relevant local authority[1], having received an assessment notice[2] and having in light of it carried out a needs assessment and (where applicable) a carer's assessment[3], must inform the NHS body responsible for the patient[4]:

(1)   whether the patient has needs for care and support[5];

(2)   (where applicable) whether a carer has needs for support[6];

(3)   whether any of the needs referred to in heads (1) and (2) above meet the eligibility criteria[7]; and

(4)   how the authority plans to meet such of those needs as meet the eligibility criteria[8].

Where, having carried out a needs assessment or carer's assessment in a case where the person's circumstances have changed[9], the relevant authority considers that the patient's needs for care and support or (as the case may be) the carer's needs for support have changed, it must inform the NHS body responsible for the patient of the change[10].

1 As to the relevant local authority see PARA 69 note 12; as to the application of the Care Act 2014 s 74 and Sch 3 see PARA 69.

2 As to the duty to issue assessment notices in respect of patients being discharged from hospital see PARAS 70–71.

3 As to the meaning of 'needs assessment' see PARA 8; as to the meaning of 'carer's assessment' see PARA 33. As to the carrying out of needs and carer's assessments generally see PARAS 64–65. Failure to carry out an assessment attracts ongoing financial sanctions: see PARA 72.

4 As to the meaning of 'NHS body' see PARA 69 note 2. As to the meaning of 'hospital patient' generally see PARA 69. As to when an English NHS body is 'responsible' for a hospital patient see PARA 69 note 3.

5 Care Act 2014 Sch 3 para 3(1)(a).

6 Care Act 2014 Sch 3 para 3(1)(b).

7 Care Act 2014 Sch 3 para 3(1)(c). As to the eligibility criteria see PARA 10 (adults) and PARA 35 (carers).

8 Care Act 2014 Sch 3 para 3(1)(d).

9 Ie a case within the Care Act 2014 s 27(4) (see PARA 80).

10 Care Act 2014 Sch 3 para 3(2).

72. Delayed discharge payments. If the relevant local authority[1]:

(1)   having received an assessment notice and a discharge notice[2], has not carried out a needs or (where applicable) carer's assessment[3] and the patient[4] has not been discharged by the end of the relevant day[5]; or

(2)   has not put in place arrangements for meeting some or all of those of the needs[6] that it proposes to meet in the case of the patient or (where applicable) a carer, and the patient has for that reason alone not been discharged by the end of the relevant day[7],

the NHS body responsible for the patient[8] may require the relevant authority to pay the specified amount[9] for each day of the specified period[10]. Such payment must be made to the NHS body responsible for the patient[11].

1   As to the relevant local authority see PARA 69 note 12; as to the application of the Care Act 2014 s 74 and Sch 3 see PARA 69.
2   As to the duty to issue assessment notices in respect of patients being discharged from hospital see PARAS 70–71. If, in a case within the Care Act 2014 Sch 3 para 4(1), (2) (see the text and notes 3–10), the assessment notice ceases to be in force, any liability arising thereunder before it ceased to be in force is unaffected: Care Act 2014 Sch 3 para 4(3).
3   See PARA 71. As to the meaning of 'needs assessment' see PARA 8; as to the meaning of 'carer's assessment' see PARA 33. As to the carrying out of needs and carer's assessments generally see PARAS 64–65.
4   As to the meaning of 'hospital patient' generally see PARA 69. As to when an English NHS body is 'responsible' for a hospital patient see PARA 69 note 3.
5   Care Act 2014 Sch 3 para 4(1). As to the 'relevant day' see PARA 70 note 10.
6   Ie under the Care Act 2014 ss 18–20 (see PARAS 12–13 (adults), and PARAS 36, 37 (carers)).
7   Care Act 2014 Sch 3 para 4(2).
8   As to the meaning of 'NHS body' see PARA 69 note 1. As to the meaning of 'hospital patient' generally see PARA 69. As to when an English NHS body is 'responsible' for a hospital patient see PARA 69 note 3.
9   Ie £155 where the authority is a London Borough Council or the Common Council of the City of London or £130 in any other case: Care and Support (Discharge of Hospital Patients) Regulations 2014, SI 2014/2823, reg 10 (made under the Care Act 2014 Sch 3 para 4(6), (7)). As to the London boroughs and their councils see LONDON GOVERNMENT vol 71 (2013) PARAS 15, 20, 34–38. As to the Common Council of the City of London see LONDON GOVERNMENT vol 71 (2013) PARA 16.
10 Care Act 2014 Sch 3 para 4(1). The specified period is determined in accordance with the Care and Support (Discharge of Hospital Patients) Regulations 2014, SI 2014/2823, reg 9. Where reg 12(2) applies (see PARA 69 note 13), the local authority to which the notice was given may recover from the local authority which is the correct authority in relation to that case any expenditure it has incurred in relation to making a payment under the Care Act 2014 Sch 3 para 4 in that case: Care and Support (Discharge of Hospital Patients) Regulations 2014, SI 2014/2823, reg 12(3).
11 Care Act 2014 Sch 3 para 4(4)(a). Regulations may specify alternative persons to whom payments must be made (Sch 3 para 4(4)(b)): at the date at which this volume states the law no such regulations had been made.

(ii) Wales

73. Considerations to which local authority must have regard. In carrying out an assessment of the needs of an adult[1] or child[2] for care and support, or of the needs of a carer[3] for support (an 'assessment'[4]), a local authority in Wales[5] must:
(1)   assess and have regard to the person's circumstances[6];
(2)   have regard to the personal outcomes[7];
(3)   assess and have regard to any barriers to achieving those outcomes[8];
(4)   assess and have regard to any risks to the person or to other persons if those outcomes are not achieved[9]; and
(5)   assess and have regard to the person's strengths and capabilities[10].

1   Ie an assessment under the Social Services and Well-being (Wales) Act 2014 s 19 (see PARA 15). As to the meaning of 'adult' see PARA 2.
2   Ie an assessment under the Social Services and Well-being (Wales) Act 2014 s 21 (see PARA 26). As to the meaning of 'child' see PARA 2.
3   Ie an assessment under the Social Services and Well-being (Wales) Act 2014 s 24 (see PARA 54). As to the meaning of 'carer' see PARA 54 note 2.

4   Care and Support (Assessment) (Wales) Regulations 2015, SI 2015/1305, reg 1(3) (made under the
    Social Services and Well-being (Wales) Act 2014 s 30).
5   As to the meaning of 'local authority' see PARA 2. As to the social services functions of local
    authorities in Wales generally, and the overarching principles in accordance with which functions
    relating to the provision of care and support must be exercised, see PARAS 373–383.
6   Care and Support (Assessment) (Wales) Regulations 2015, SI 2015/1305, reg 4(a).
7   Care and Support (Assessment) (Wales) Regulations 2015, SI 2015/1305, reg 4(b). 'Personal
    outcomes' means the outcomes which have been identified in relation to a person in accordance
    with the Social Services and Well-being (Wales) Act 2014 s 19(4)(a) (adults: see PARA 16),
    s 21(4)(b) (children: see PARA 26) or s 24(4)(c) or (d) (carers: see PARA 55), as the case may be:
    Care and Support (Assessment) (Wales) Regulations 2015, SI 2015/1305, reg 1(3).
8   Care and Support (Assessment) (Wales) Regulations 2015, SI 2015/1305, reg 4(c).
9   Care and Support (Assessment) (Wales) Regulations 2015, SI 2015/1305, reg 4(d).
10 Care and Support (Assessment) (Wales) Regulations 2015, SI 2015/1305, reg 4(e).

74. Combined assessments. Where a person who appears to need care and
support[1] has a carer[2], a local authority[3] may combine his needs[4] assessment[5] and
the carer's needs[6] assessment[7], although:

(1)   an authority may not combine a needs assessment for an adult[8] with a
        needs assessment for another person unless the adult (or, where
        applicable, an authorised person[9]) gives valid consent[10] or the
        requirement for valid consent may be dispensed with[11];

(2)   an authority may not combine a needs assessment for a child aged 16 or
        17[12] with a needs assessment for another person unless the child (or,
        where applicable, an authorised person) gives valid consent[13], a person
        with parental responsibility for the child gives valid consent in
        circumstances in which the local authority is satisfied that the child lacks
        capacity to decide whether to consent to the combining of the needs
        assessments[14] and there is no authorised person to make the decision on
        the child's behalf[15], or the requirement for valid consent may be
        dispensed with[16]; and

(3)   an authority may not combine a needs assessment for a child aged under
        16[17] with a needs assessment for another person unless the child or a
        person with parental responsibility for the child gives valid consent[18] or
        the requirement for valid consent may be dispensed with[19].

Where a person who appears to need support as a carer also appears to have
needs for care and support in his own right, a local authority may combine his
carer's needs assessment[20] with his needs[21] assessment[22]. An authority may carry
out a needs assessment for a person at the same time as it or another body carries
out another assessment under any enactment in relation to that person[23].

1   As to the meanings of 'care' and 'support' see PARA 2 note 1.
2   As to the meaning of 'carer' see PARA 54 note 2.
3   As to the meaning of 'local authority' see PARA 2. As to the social services functions of local
    authorities in Wales generally, and the overarching principles in accordance with which functions
    relating to the provision of care and support must be exercised, see PARAS 373–383.
4   Ie his assessment under the Social Services and Well-being (Wales) Act 2014 s 19 (adults: see
    PARA 15) or s 21 (children: see PARA 26).
5   Social Services and Well-being (Wales) Act 2014 s 28(1)(a).
6   Ie the assessment under the Social Services and Well-being (Wales) Act 2014 s 24 (see PARA 54).
7   Social Services and Well-being (Wales) Act 2014 s 28(1)(b).
8   Ie whether under the Social Services and Well-being (Wales) Act 2014 s 19 or s 24: s 28(2)(a). As
    to the meaning of 'adult' see PARA 2.
9   In this context 'authorised person' means a person authorised under the Mental Capacity Act 2005
    (whether in general or specific terms) to decide whether to consent to the combination of the needs
    assessments on the adult or child's behalf: Social Services and Well-being (Wales) Act 2014 s 28(9).
    As to a person being 'authorised' under the Mental Capacity Act 2005 see PARA 12 note 15.
10 Social Services and Well-being (Wales) Act 2014 s 28(2)(a). Consent given under s 28(2), (3) or (4)
    is valid except (s 28(5)):

(1)   where the authority is satisfied, in the case of consent given by an adult or a child aged 16 or 17, that the adult or child lacks capacity to consent to the combination of the needs assessments;

(2)   where the authority is satisfied, in the case of consent given by a child aged under 16, that the child does not have sufficient understanding to make an informed decision about the combination of the needs assessments; or

(3)   where the authority is satisfied, in the case of consent given by a person with parental responsibility for a child aged under 16 in relation to the child's needs assessment, that the child has sufficient understanding to make an informed decision about the combination of the needs assessments and does not agree with the consent given by the person with parental responsibility.

As to the meaning of 'child' see PARA 2. As to a person having or lacking capacity see PARA 8 note 10. As to the meaning of 'parental responsibility' see PARA 26 note 10.

11 Social Services and Well-being (Wales) Act 2014 s 28(2)(b). An authority may dispense with the requirement for valid consent if (s 28(6)):

(1)   the authority is satisfied, with regard to the needs assessment of an adult, that there is no person who may give valid consent and combining the needs assessments would be in the adult's best interests;

(2)   the authority is satisfied, with regard to the needs assessment of a child aged 16 or 17, that the child lacks capacity to give valid consent, there is no authorised person who may give valid consent on the child's behalf, and combining the needs assessments would be in the child's best interests; or

(3)   that the authority is satisfied, with regard to the needs assessment of a child aged under 16, that the child does not have sufficient understanding to make an informed decision about the combination of the needs assessments and combining the needs assessments would be consistent with the child's well-being.

As to the meaning of 'well-being' see PARA 375.

12 Ie whether under the Social Services and Well-being (Wales) Act 2014 s 21 or s 24.

13 Social Services and Well-being (Wales) Act 2014 s 28(3)(a).

14 Social Services and Well-being (Wales) Act 2014 s 28(3)(b)(i).

15 Social Services and Well-being (Wales) Act 2014 s 28(3)(b)(ii).

16 Social Services and Well-being (Wales) Act 2014 s 28(3)(c).

17 See note 12.

18 Social Services and Well-being (Wales) Act 2014 s 28(4)(a).

19 Social Services and Well-being (Wales) Act 2014 s 28(4)(b).

20 See note 6.

21 See note 4.

22 Social Services and Well-being (Wales) Act 2014 s 29(1).

23 Social Services and Well-being (Wales) Act 2014 s 29(2). For this purpose the authority may carry out the other assessment on behalf of or jointly with the other body (s 29(3)(a)) or if the other body has already arranged for the other assessment to be carried out jointly with another person, the local authority may carry out the other assessment jointly with the other body and that other person (s 29(3)(b)).

75. Individuals carrying out assessments.

The local authority[1] responsible for carrying out a needs or carer's assessment[2] must ensure that there is a named individual whose function is to co-ordinate the carrying out of the assessment[3]. An authority must ensure that any person carrying out an assessment has the skills, knowledge and competence to carry out the assessment in question[4] and has received training in the carrying out of assessments[5]. When carrying out an assessment, an authority must consider whether the nature of the person's needs calls for the involvement of a person who has specialist skills, knowledge or expertise[6], and if the authority decides that such involvement is called for, it must either consult with a person who it considers will be able to provide those skills or that knowledge or expertise or arrange for the assessment to be carried out by a person with the required specialist skills, knowledge or expertise[7].

1   As to the meaning of 'local authority' see PARA 2. As to the social services functions of local authorities in Wales generally, and the overarching principles in accordance with which functions relating to the provision of care and support must be exercised, see PARAS 373–383.

2   As to the meaning of 'assessment' see PARA 73.

3   Care and Support (Assessment) (Wales) Regulations 2015, SI 2015/1305, reg 2.
4   Care and Support (Assessment) (Wales) Regulations 2015, SI 2015/1305, reg 3(1)(a).
5   Care and Support (Assessment) (Wales) Regulations 2015, SI 2015/1305, reg 3(1)(b).
6   Care and Support (Assessment) (Wales) Regulations 2015, SI 2015/1305, reg 3(2).
7   Care and Support (Assessment) (Wales) Regulations 2015, SI 2015/1305, reg 3(3).

76.   Reviews of assessments. A local authority[1] must review an assessment[2] if it appears to it that there has been a significant change in the person's circumstances or in their personal outcomes[3]. Also, where the assessment is of an adult's[4] needs (including the needs of an adult carer[5]) the adult and any person authorised to act on his behalf[6] may request a review of an assessment[7]; and where the assessment is of a child's needs (including the needs of a child carer) the child, any person with parental responsibility[8] for the child, and any person authorised to act on behalf of the child, may request a review of an assessment[9]. The authority must comply with the request if it is satisfied that there has been a significant change in the person's circumstances or in their personal outcomes[10], but may refuse to comply with the request if it is satisfied that there has not been any significant change in the person's circumstances or in their personal outcomes since the assessment was completed[11].

1   As to the meaning of 'local authority' see PARA 2. As to the social services functions of local authorities in Wales generally, and the overarching principles in accordance with which functions relating to the provision of care and support must be exercised, see PARAS 373–383.
2   As to the meaning of 'assessment' see PARA 73.
3   Care and Support (Assessment) (Wales) Regulations 2015, SI 2015/1305, reg 7(1). As to the meaning of 'personal outcomes' see PARA 73 note 7.
4   As to the meaning of 'adult' see PARA 2.
5   As to the meaning of 'carer' see PARA 54 note 2.
6   In the Care and Support (Assessment) (Wales) Regulations 2015, SI 2015/1305, regs 6, 7, a person is authorised to act on behalf of an adult or a child if the adult or the child has requested the person to act on their behalf (reg 6(3)(a)) or the adult or child lacks capacity and the person is authorised under the Mental Capacity Act 2005 (whether in general or in specific terms) to make decisions about the assessment of the person's needs (Care and Support (Assessment) (Wales) Regulations 2015, SI 2015/1305, reg 6(3)(b)). As to the meaning of 'child' see PARA 2. As to a person being 'authorised' under the Mental Capacity Act 2005 see PARA 12 note 15.
7   Care and Support (Assessment) (Wales) Regulations 2015, SI 2015/1305, reg 7(2)(a).
8   As to the meaning of 'parental responsibility' see PARA 26 note 10.
9   Care and Support (Assessment) (Wales) Regulations 2015, SI 2015/1305, reg 7(2)(b).
10   Care and Support (Assessment) (Wales) Regulations 2015, SI 2015/1305, reg 7(3).
11   Care and Support (Assessment) (Wales) Regulations 2015, SI 2015/1305, reg 7(4).

77.   Records of assessments. When an assessment[1] has been completed, the local authority[2] must make a written record of the results of the assessment and the matters to which the authority has had regard[3] in carrying out the assessment[4]. If, in the course of carrying out the assessment, the local authority considers that the provision of preventative services, the provision of information, advice or assistance or other matters could contribute to the achievement of the personal outcomes or otherwise meet needs identified in the assessment, the written record must include details of that provision or those matters[5] and include details of how that provision or those matters could contribute to the achievement of the personal outcomes or otherwise meet needs identified in the assessment[6].

Where the assessment is of an adult's[7] needs (including the needs of an adult carer[8]), the authority must offer to give a copy of the record to the adult[9], any person authorised to act on behalf of the adult[10], and where the adult lacks capacity[11] to be able to request a person to act on their behalf and there is no person authorised to act on their behalf, any person who the authority considers to be acting in the best interests of the adult[12]. Where the assessment is of a child's[13] needs (including the needs of a child carer), the authority must offer to give a copy of the record to the child[14], any person with parental responsibility[15] for the child, unless doing so would be inconsistent with the child's well-being[16], any person authorised to act on behalf of the child[17] and, where the child lacks capacity or is not competent to request a person to act on their behalf and there is no person authorised to act on their behalf, any person who the authority considers to be acting in the best interests of the child[18].

1   As to the meaning of 'assessment' see PARA 73.
2   As to the meaning of 'local authority' see PARA 2. As to the social services functions of local authorities in Wales generally, and the overarching principles in accordance with which functions relating to the provision of care and support must be exercised, see PARAS 373–383.
3   As to the matters to which the authority must have regard see PARA 73.
4   Care and Support (Assessment) (Wales) Regulations 2015, SI 2015/1305, reg 5(1).
5   Care and Support (Assessment) (Wales) Regulations 2015, SI 2015/1305, reg 5(2)(a).
6   Care and Support (Assessment) (Wales) Regulations 2015, SI 2015/1305, reg 5(2)(b).
7   As to the meaning of 'adult' see PARA 2.
8   As to the meaning of 'carer' see PARA 54 note 2.
9   Care and Support (Assessment) (Wales) Regulations 2015, SI 2015/1305, reg 6(1)(i).
10 Care and Support (Assessment) (Wales) Regulations 2015, SI 2015/1305, reg 6(1)(ii). As to when a person is authorised to act on behalf of an adult or a child see PARA 76 note 6.
11 As to a person having or lacking capacity see PARA 8 note 10.
12 Care and Support (Assessment) (Wales) Regulations 2015, SI 2015/1305, reg 6(1)(iii).
13 As to the meaning of 'child' see PARA 2.
14 Care and Support (Assessment) (Wales) Regulations 2015, SI 2015/1305, reg 6(2)(i).
15 As to the meaning of 'parental responsibility' see PARA 54.
16 Care and Support (Assessment) (Wales) Regulations 2015, SI 2015/1305, reg 6(2)(ii). As to the meaning of 'well-being' see PARA 375.
17 Care and Support (Assessment) (Wales) Regulations 2015, SI 2015/1305, reg 6(2)(iii).
18 Care and Support (Assessment) (Wales) Regulations 2015, SI 2015/1305, reg 6(2)(iv).

(6) CARE AND SUPPORT PLANS

(i) England

78. Matters to be specified in care and support plans and support plans. After making a decision as to the provision of care for an adult[1] or a carer or child's carer[2] a local authority in England[3] is required to prepare a care and support plan (in the case of care for an adult) or a support plan (in the case of care for a carer)[4]. This is a document prepared by the authority[5] which:

(1)   specifies the needs identified by the needs assessment[6] or carer's assessment or child's carer's assessment[7];

(2)   except in the case of a child's carer, specifies whether, and if so to what extent, the needs meet the eligibility criteria[8];

(3)   specifies the needs that the local authority is going to meet and how it is going to meet them[9];

(4)   specifies to which of the matters relating to impacts and outcomes[10] could be relevant[11];

(5)   includes the personal budget[12] for the adult concerned[13]; and

(6)   includes advice and information about what can be done to meet or reduce the needs in question[14] and what can be done to prevent or delay the development of needs for care and support or of needs for support in the future[15].

Where some or all of the needs are to be met by making direct payments[16], the plan must also specify the needs which are to be so met[17] and the amount and frequency of the direct payments[18].

1 As to decisions relating to the provision of care for an adult see PARAS 8–14. As to the meaning of 'adult' see PARA 1 note 1.
2 As to decisions relating to the provision of care for a carer see PARAS 33–38. As to the meaning of 'carer' see PARA 33 note 2.
3 As to the meaning of 'local authority' see PARA 1. As to the social services functions of local authorities in England generally, and the overarching principles in accordance with which functions relating to the provision of care and support must be exercised, see PARAS 315–323.
4 See the Care and Support (Children's Carer's) Regulations 2015, SI 2015/305, reg 10(a) (see PARA 44 note 6); and PARAS 14, 38. As to the preparation of plans see PARA 79; as to the review and revision of plans see PARA 80. The authority must give a copy of a care and support plan to:
    (1)   the adult for whom it has been prepared (Care Act 2014 s 25(9)(a));
    (2)   any carer that the adult has, if the adult asks the authority to do so (s 25(9)(b)); and
    (3)   any other person to whom the adult asks the authority to give a copy (s 25(9)(c)),
  and must give a copy of a support plan to:
    (a)   the carer or child's carer for whom it has been prepared (s 25(10)(a); Care and Support (Children's Carer's) Regulations 2015, SI 2015/305, reg 10(l));
    (b)   in the case of a carer, the adult needing care, if the carer asks the authority to do so (Care Act 2014 s 25(10)(b); Care and Support (Children's Carer's) Regulations 2015, SI 2015/305, reg 10(m));
    (c)   in the case of a child's carer, the child the child's carer cares for, if the child's carer asks the authority to do so (Care Act 2014 s 25(10)(ba); Care and Support (Children's Carer's) Regulations 2015, SI 2015/305, reg 10(n)); and
    (d)   any other person to whom the carer or child's carer asks the authority to give a copy (Care Act 2014 s 25(10)(c); Care and Support (Children's Carer's) Regulations 2015, SI 2015/305, reg 10(o)).
  Regulations may specify cases or circumstances in which such of the Care Act 2014 s 25(1)(a)–(f) and s 25(2)(a), (b) as are specified do not apply: s 25(13). The regulations may in particular specify that the provisions in question do not apply as regards specified needs or matters: s 25(14). At the date at which this volume states the law no such regulations had been made.
5 The authority may authorise a person (including the person for whom the plan is to be prepared) to prepare the plan jointly with the authority: Care Act 2014 s 25(7). The authority may do things to facilitate the preparation of the plan in a case within s 25(7); it may, for example, provide a person so authorised with:
    (1)   in the case of a care and support plan, information about the adult for whom the plan is being prepared (s 25(8)(a));
    (2)   in the case of a support plan, information about the carer or child's carer and the adult needing care or child the child's carer cares for (s 25(8)(b); Care and Support (Children's Carer's) Regulations 2015, SI 2015/305, reg 10(k)); and
    (3)   in either case, whatever resources, or access to whatever facilities, the authority thinks are required to prepare the plan (Care Act 2014 s 25(8)(c)).
6 As to the meaning of 'needs assessment' see PARA 8.
7 Care Act 2014 s 25(1)(a); Care and Support (Children's Carer's) Regulations 2015, SI 2015/305, reg 10(b). As to the meaning of 'carer's assessment' see PARA 33; as to the meaning of 'child's carer's assessment' see PARA 42.
8 Care Act 2014 s 25(1)(b); Care and Support (Children's Carer's) Regulations 2015, SI 2015/305, reg 10(c). As to the eligibility criteria see PARA 10 (adults) and PARA 35 (carers).
9 Care Act 2014 s 25(1)(c).
10 Ie the matters referred to in the Care Act 2014 s 9(4) (adult's needs and outcomes: see PARA 8), s 10(5), (6) (carer's needs and outcomes: see PARA 33) or s 61(1), (2) (child's carer: see PARA 43).
11 Care Act 2014 s 25(1)(d); Care and Support (Children's Carer's) Regulations 2015, SI 2015/305, reg 10(d).
12 As to personal budgets see the Care Act 2014 s 26; and PARA 121.
13 Care Act 2014 s 25(1)(e).
14 Care Act 2014 s 25(1)(f)(i).
15 Care Act 2014 s 25(1)(f)(ii).
16 As to direct payments see PARAS 106–110.
17 Care Act 2014 s 25(2)(a).
18 Care Act 2014 s 25(2)(b).

79. Preparation of plans and proportionality. In preparing a care and support plan in respect of an adult's care needs[1] the local authority[2] must involve:

(1) the adult[3] for whom it is being prepared[4];

(2) any carer[5] that the adult has[6]; and

(3) any person whom the adult asks the authority to involve or, where the adult lacks capacity[7] to ask the authority to do that, any person who appears to the authority to be interested in the adult's welfare[8].

In preparing a support plan in respect of a carer's care needs[9] the authority must involve:

(a) the carer or child's carer for whom it is being prepared[10];

(b) in the case of a carer, the adult needing care, if the carer asks the authority to do so[11];

(c) in the case of a child's carer, the child the child's carer cares for, if the child's carer asks the authority to do so[12]; and

(d) any other person whom the carer or child's carer asks the authority to involve[13].

In seeking to ensure that a plan is proportionate to the needs to be met, the authority must have regard in particular to the matters relating to impacts and outcomes[14].

A care and support plan or a support plan may, subject to consent, be combined with a plan relating to another person[15].

1 As to the duty to prepare, and the matters to be specified in, care and support plans for adults see PARA 78.

2 As to the meaning of 'local authority' see PARA 1. As to the social services functions of local authorities in England generally, and the overarching principles in accordance with which functions relating to the provision of care and support must be exercised, see PARAS 315–323.

3 As to the meaning of 'adult' see PARA 1 note 1.

4 Care Act 2014 s 25(3)(a). In performing the duty under s 25(3)(a) the local authority must take all reasonable steps to reach agreement with the adult for whom the plan is being prepared about how the authority should meet the needs in question: s 25(5). A local authority which is required to involve an individual in its exercise of a function under s 25(3)(a), (b) or s 25(4)(a), (b) may be required to arrange for an independent advocate to be available to represent and support the individual: see s 67 (in particular s 67(3)(c), (d)); the Care and Support (Independent Advocacy Support) (No 2) Regulations 2014, SI 2014/2889; and PARAS 100–103.

5 As to the meaning of 'carer' see PARA 33 note 2.

6 Care Act 2014 s 25(3)(b). See note 4.

7 As to a person having or lacking capacity see PARA 8 note 10.

8 Care Act 2014 s 25(3)(b).

9 As to the duty to prepare, and the matters to be specified in, support plans for carers see PARA 78.

10 Care Act 2014 s 25(4)(a); Care and Support (Children's Carer's) Regulations 2015, SI 2015/305, reg 10(e) (see PARA 44 note 6). In performing the duty under the Care Act 2014 s 25(4)(a), the local authority must take all reasonable steps to reach agreement with the carer or child's carer for whom the plan is being prepared about how the authority should meet the needs in question: s 25(5); Care and Support (Children's Carer's) Regulations 2015, SI 2015/305, reg 10(i). See note 4.

11 Care Act 2014 s 25(4)(b); Care and Support (Children's Carer's) Regulations 2015, SI 2015/305, reg 10(f). See note 4.

12 Care Act 2014 s 25(4)(ba); Care and Support (Children's Carer's) Regulations 2015, SI 2015/305, reg 10(g).

13 Care Act 2014 s 25(4)(c); Care and Support (Children's Carer's) Regulations 2015, SI 2015/305, reg 10(h).

14 Ie, in the case of a care and support plan, to the matters referred to in the Care Act 2014 s 9(4) (adult's needs and outcomes: see PARA 8) (s 25(6)(a)) or, in the case of a support plan, to the matters referred to in s 10(5), (6) (carer's needs and outcomes: see PARA 33) or s 61(1) or (2) (child's carer: see PARA 43) (s 25(6)(b); Care and Support (Children's Carer's) Regulations 2015, SI 2015/305, reg 10(j)).

15 A local authority may combine a care and support plan or a support plan with a plan (whether or not prepared by it and whether or not under the Care Act 2014 Pt 1 (ss 1–80)) relating to another person only if the adult for whom the care and support plan or the support plan is being prepared agrees and:

(1)   where the combination would include a plan prepared for another adult, that other adult agrees (s 25(11)(a));

(2)   where the combination would include a plan prepared for a child (including a young carer), the consent condition is met in relation to the child (s 25(11)(b)).

The consent condition is met in relation to a child if:

(a)   the child has capacity or is competent to agree to the plans being combined and does so agree (s 25(12)(a)), or

(b)   the child lacks capacity or is not competent so to agree but the local authority is satisfied that the combining the plans would be in the child's best interests (s 25(12)(b)).

80. Review of plans. A local authority[1] must keep under review generally care and support plans, and support plans[2], that it has prepared[3], and on a reasonable request by or on behalf of the adult to whom a care and support plan relates or the carer or child's carer to whom a support plan relates, review the plan[4]. An authority may also revise a plan[5]. Where an authority is satisfied that circumstances have changed in a way that affects a care and support plan or a support plan in respect of a carer, the authority must to the extent it thinks appropriate, carry out a needs[6] or carer's[7] assessment, carry out a financial assessment[8] and make[9] an eligibility determination[10] and revise the care and support plan or support plan accordingly[11].

1   As to the meaning of 'local authority' see PARA 1. As to the social services functions of local authorities in England generally, and the overarching principles in accordance with which functions relating to the provision of care and support must be exercised, see PARAS 315–323.
2   As to the duty to prepare, and the matters to be specified in, care and support plans for adults and support plans for carers see PARA 78.
3   Care Act 2014 s 27(1)(a).
4   Care Act 2014 s 27(1)(d).
5   Care Act 2014 s 27(2), (3); Care and Support (Children's Carer's) Regulations 2015, SI 2015/305, reg 11(a) (see PARA 44 note 6). In deciding whether or how to revise a care and support plan an authority must have regard in particular to the matters referred to in the Care Act 2014 s 9(4) (see PARA 8) (and specified in the plan under s 25(1)(d) (see PARA 78))) (s 27(2)(a)) and must involve the adult to whom the plan relates (s 27(2)(b)(i)), any carer that the adult has (s 27(2)(b)(ii)), and any person whom the adult asks the authority to involve or, where the adult lacks capacity to ask the authority to do that, any person who appears to the authority to be interested in the adult's welfare (s 27(2)(b)(iii)). As to a person having or lacking capacity see PARA 8 note 10. In deciding whether or how to revise a support plan an authority must have regard in particular to the matters referred to in s 10(5), (6) (see PARA 33) or, in the case of a child's carer, s 61(1), (2) (see PARA 43) (and specified in the plan under s 25(1)(d)) (s 27(3)(a); Care and Support (Children's Carer's) Regulations 2015, SI 2015/305, reg 11(b)), and must involve the carer or child's carer to whom the plan relates (Care Act 2014 s 27(3)(b)(i); Care and Support (Children's Carer's) Regulations 2015, SI 2015/305, reg 11(c)), in the case of a carer, the adult needing care, if the carer asks the authority to do so (Care Act 2014 s 27(3)(b)(ii); Care and Support (Children's Carer's) Regulations 2015, SI 2015/305, reg 11(d)), in the case of a child's carer, the child the child's carer cares for, if the child's carer asks the authority to do so (Care Act 2014 s 27(3)(b)(iia); Care and Support (Children's Carer's) Regulations 2015, SI 2015/305, reg 11(e)), and any other person whom the carer asks the authority to involve (Care Act 2014 s 27(3)(b)(iii)). A local authority which is required to involve an individual in its exercise of a function under s 27(2)(b)(i), (ii) or s 27(3)(b)(i), (ii) may be required to arrange for an independent advocate to be available to represent and support the individual: see s 67 (in particular s 67(3)(e), (f)); the Care and Support (Independent Advocacy Support) (No 2) Regulations 2014, SI 2014/2889; and PARAS 100–103.
6   See PARA 8.
7   See PARA 33. Where the authority is satisfied that circumstances have changed in a way that affects a support plan in respect of a child's carer, the authority must, to the extent that it thinks appropriate, carry out a child's carer's assessment: Care Act 2014 s 27(4A)(a); the Care and Support (Children's Carer's) Regulations 2015, SI 2015/305, reg 11(h).
8   As to financial assessments see PARAS 119–120.
9   Ie under the Care Act 2014 s 13(1): see PARAS 10 (adults), 35 (carers).

10 Care Act 2014 s 27(4)(a); Care and Support (Children's Carer's) Regulations 2015, SI 2015/305, reg 11(g).

11 Care Act 2014 s 27(4)(b), (4A)(b); Care and Support (Children's Carer's) Regulations 2015, SI 2015/305, reg 11(h). Where, in a case within the Care Act 2014 s 27(4), the authority is proposing to change how it meets the needs in question, it must, in performing the duty under s 27(2)(b)(i) or s 27(3)(b)(i) (see note 5) take all reasonable steps to reach agreement with the adult concerned about how it should meet those needs: s 27(5).

(ii) Wales

81. Duty to prepare and maintain care and support plans and support plans. Where a local authority in Wales[1] is required[2] to meet the needs of an adult or a child it must prepare and maintain a care and support plan in relation to that adult or child[3], and where an authority is required[4] to meet the needs of a carer it must prepare and maintain a support plan in relation to that carer[5]. Regulations must make provision about how plans are to be prepared[6] and what a plan is to contain[7], and must include provision about recording in a care and support plan the conclusions of enquiries made[8] about adults at risk[9]. At the date at which this volume states the law no such regulations had been made.

1 As to the meaning of 'local authority' see PARA 2. As to the social services functions of local authorities in Wales generally, and the overarching principles in accordance with which functions relating to the provision of care and support must be exercised, see PARAS 373–383.

2 Ie under the Social Services and Well-being (Wales) Act 2014 ss 35–37: see PARAS 19, 20 (adults), and PARA 30 (children).

3 Social Services and Well-being (Wales) Act 2014 s 54(1). As to the meanings of 'adult' and 'child' see PARA 2.

4 Ie under the Social Services and Well-being (Wales) Act 2014 ss 40–42: see PARAS 58–63.

5 Social Services and Well-being (Wales) Act 2014 s 54(2). As to the meaning of 'carer' see PARA 54 note 2. As to the preparation of plans see PARA 82; as to the review and revision of plans see PARA 83.

6 Social Services and Well-being (Wales) Act 2014 s 54(5)(a). Regulations under s 54(5) may, for example:
    (1) require plans to be in a specified form (s 55(a));
    (2) require plans to contain specified things(s 55(b));
    (3) make provision about further persons whom a local authority must involve in the preparation, review or revision of plans(s 55(c));
    (4) require plans to be prepared, reviewed or revised by specified persons (s 55(d));
    (5) confer functions on persons specified in the regulations in connection with the preparation, review or revision of plans (s 55(e));
    (6) specify persons to whom written copies of a plan must be provided (including, in specified cases, the provision of copies without the consent of the person to whom the plan relates) (s 55(f)); and
    (7) specify further circumstances in which plans must be reviewed (s 55(g)).

7 Social Services and Well-being (Wales) Act 2014 s 54(5)(b).

8 Ie under the Social Services and Well-being (Wales) Act 2014 s 126 (see PARA 379).

9 Social Services and Well-being (Wales) Act 2014 s 126(3).

82. Preparation of plans. When preparing, reviewing or revising a care and support plan or a support plan[1] a local authority[2] must involve:
    (1)   in the case of a care and support plan relating to an adult[3], the adult and, where feasible, any carer[4] that the adult has[5];
    (2)   in the case of a care and support plan relating to a child[6], the child and any person with parental responsibility[7] for the child[8];
    (3)   in the case of a support plan relating to a carer, the carer and, where feasible, the person for whom the carer provides or intends to provide care[9].

The local authority may prepare, review or revise a plan at the same time as it or another body is preparing, reviewing or revising another document in the case of the person concerned[10], and include the other document in the plan[11].

1 Ie under the Social Services and Well-being (Wales) Act 2014 s 54: see PARA 81 (preparation) and PARA 83 (revision).
2 As to the meaning of 'local authority' see PARA 2. As to the social services functions of local authorities in Wales generally, and the overarching principles in accordance with which functions relating to the provision of care and support must be exercised, see PARAS 373–383.
3 As to the meaning of 'adult' see PARA 2.
4 As to the meaning of 'carer' see PARA 54 note 2.
5 Social Services and Well-being (Wales) Act 2014 s 54(7)(a).
6 As to the meaning of 'child' see PARA 2.
7 As to the meaning of 'parental responsibility' see PARA 26 note 10.
8 Social Services and Well-being (Wales) Act 2014 s 54(7)(b).
9 Social Services and Well-being (Wales) Act 2014 s 54(7)(c).
10 Social Services and Well-being (Wales) Act 2014 s 54(8)(a).
11 Social Services and Well-being (Wales) Act 2014 s 54(8)(b).

83. Review and revision of plans. A local authority[1] must keep under review the care and support plans and support plans[2] that it maintains[3], and where an authority is satisfied that the circumstances of the person to whom a plan relates have changed in a way that affects the plan, the authority must carry out such assessments as it considers appropriate[4] and revise the plan[5]. Regulations must make provision about the review and revision of plans[6]: at the date at which this volume states the law no such regulations had been made.

1 As to the meaning of 'local authority' see PARA 2. As to the social services functions of local authorities in Wales generally, and the overarching principles in accordance with which functions relating to the provision of care and support must be exercised, see PARAS 373–383.
2 Ie the plans the authority maintains under the Social Services and Well-being (Wales) Act 2014 s 54 (see PARAS 81, 82).
3 Social Services and Well-being (Wales) Act 2014 s 54(3).
4 Social Services and Well-being (Wales) Act 2014 s 54(4)(a). As to the carrying out of assessments see PARAS 66–77.
5 Social Services and Well-being (Wales) Act 2014 s 54(4)(b).
6 Social Services and Well-being (Wales) Act 2014 s 54(5)(c). Regulations under s 54(5)(c) must specify, in particular the persons who may request a review of a plan (on their own behalf or on behalf of another person) (s 54(6)(a)) and the circumstances in which a local authority may refuse to comply with a request for a review of a plan (s 54(6)(b)(i)) and may not refuse to do so (s 54(6)(b)(ii)). As to the making of regulations under s 54(5) generally see s 55; and PARA 81 note 6.

(7) ESTABLISHING RESIDENCE AND CONTINUITY OF CARE

(i) A Person's 'Ordinary Residence'

84. Adults in residential accommodation. Where an adult[1] in England[2] or Wales[3] has needs for care and support[4] which can be met only if he is living in care home accommodation[5] or (in England) shared lives scheme accommodation[6] or supported living accommodation[7], and he is living in such accommodation in England[8] or, as the case may be, Wales, he is to be treated[9] as ordinarily resident:

(1)   in the area in which he was ordinarily resident immediately before he began to live in accommodation of the specified type[10]; or

(2)   if he was of no settled residence immediately before he began to live in accommodation of the specified type, in the area in which he was present at that time[11].

Where an adult is being provided by a local authority with NHS accommodation or accommodation under a health enactment[12] he is to be treated[13] as ordinarily resident:

(a)   in the area in which he was ordinarily resident immediately before the accommodation was provided[14]; or

(b)   if he was of no settled residence immediately before the accommodation was provided, in the area in which he was present at that time[15].

An adult who is being provided with accommodation pursuant to the provision of after-care under mental health legislation[16] is to be treated[17] as ordinarily resident in the area of the local authority in England[18] or Wales[19], as applicable, on which the duty to provide him with services[20] is imposed[21].

Provision is made for the resolution of disputes about a person's residence[22].

1   As to the meaning of 'adult' see PARA 1 note 1 (England) and PARA 2 (Wales).
2   As to the meaning of 'England' see PARA 1 note 1.
3   As to the meaning of 'Wales' see PARA 2 note 4.
4   As to the meanings of 'care' and 'support' (in Wales only) see PARA 2 note 1.
5   Care and Support (Ordinary Residence) (Specified Accommodation) Regulations 2014, SI 2014/2828, reg 2(1)(a) (reg 2(1) amended, reg 2(2) added, by SI 2015/644) (made under the Care Act 2014 s 39(1), (3)); Care and Support (Ordinary Residence) (Specified Accommodation) (Wales) Regulations 2015, SI 2015/1499, reg 2 (made under the Social Services and Well-being (Wales) Act 2014 s 194(1), (3)). 'Care home accommodation' means accommodation in a care home within the meaning given by the Care Standards Act 2000 s 3 (see PARA 3 note 3): Care and Support (Ordinary Residence) (Specified Accommodation) Regulations 2014, SI 2014/2828, reg 3; Care and Support (Ordinary Residence) (Specified Accommodation) (Wales) Regulations 2015, SI 2015/1499, reg 3.
6   Care and Support (Ordinary Residence) (Specified Accommodation) Regulations 2014, SI 2014/2828, reg 2(1)(b) (as amended: see note 5). 'Shared lives scheme accommodation' means accommodation which is provided for an adult by a shared lives carer, and for this purpose 'shared lives carer' means an individual who, under the terms of a shared lives agreement, provides, or intends to provide, personal care for adults together with, where necessary, accommodation in the individual's home; 'shared lives agreement' means an agreement entered into between a person carrying on a shared lives scheme and an individual for the provision, by that individual, of personal care to an adult together with, where necessary, accommodation in the individual's home; and 'shared lives scheme' means a scheme carried on (whether or not for profit) by a local authority or other person for the purposes of recruiting and training shared lives carers, making arrangements for the placing of adults with shared lives carers, and supporting and monitoring placements: reg 4.
       'Personal care' means (by virtue of reg 1(2)):
       (1)   physical assistance given to a person in connection with eating or drinking (including the administration of parenteral nutrition), toileting (including in relation to the process of menstruation), washing or bathing, dressing, oral care, and the care of skin, hair and nails (with the exception of nail care provided by a chiropodist or podiatrist); or
       (2)   the prompting, together with supervision, of a person in relation to the performance of any of the activities listed under head (1) above, where that person is unable to make a decision for themselves in relation to performing the activity without such prompting or supervision.
       As to the meaning of 'local authority' see PARA 1. As to the social services functions of local authorities in England generally, and the overarching principles in accordance with which functions relating to the provision of care and support must be exercised, see PARAS 315–323.
7   Care and Support (Ordinary Residence) (Specified Accommodation) Regulations 2014, SI 2014/2828, reg 2(1)(c) (as amended: see note 5). 'Supported living accommodation' means accommodation in premises which are specifically designed or adapted for occupation by adults with needs for care and support to enable them to live as independently as possible (not including adapted premises where the adult had occupied those premises as their home before the adaptations were made), and accommodation which is provided in premises which are intended for occupation by adults with needs for care and support (whether or not the premises are

specifically designed or adapted for that purpose), and in circumstances in which personal care is available if required (for which purposes personal care may be provided by a person other than the person who provides the accommodation): reg 5.

8 Care Act 2014 s 39(1); Social Services and Well-being (Wales) Act 2014 s 194(1); Care and Support (Ordinary Residence) (Specified Accommodation) Regulations 2014, SI 2014/2828, reg 2(2) (as added: see note 5).

9 Ie for the purposes of the Care Act 2014 Pt 1 (ss 1–80), apart from s 28 (independent personal budget: see PARA 122) (s 39(7)) or, as the case may be, the Social Services and Well-being (Wales) Act 2014 (s 194(1)).

10 Care Act 2014 s 39(1)(a); Social Services and Well-being (Wales) Act 2014 s 194(1)(a). Where, before beginning to live in his or her current accommodation, the adult was living in care home accommodation or (in England) shared lives scheme accommodation or supported living accommodation (whether or not of the same type of accommodation as the current accommodation), the reference in the Care Act 2014 s 39(1)(a) and the Social Services and Well-being (Wales) Act 2014 s 194(1)(a) to when the adult began to live in accommodation of the specified type is a reference to the beginning of the period during which he has been living in accommodation of one or more of the specified types for consecutive periods: Care Act 2014 s 39(2); Social Services and Well-being (Wales) Act 2014 s 194(2).

11 Care Act 2014 s 39(1)(b); Social Services and Well-being (Wales) Act 2014 s 194(1)(b).

12 Ie accommodation under the National Health Service Act 2006, the National Health Service (Wales) Act 2006, or corresponding Scotland or Northern Ireland legislation: Care Act 2014 s 39(6), Sch 1 para 12(10) (referring to 'NHS accommodation'); Social Services and Well-being (Wales) Act 2014 s 194(5) (referring to 'accommodation under a health enactment').

13 Ie for the purposes of the Care Act 2014 Pt 1 or, as the case may be, the Social Services and Well-being (Wales) Act 2014.

14 Care Act 2014 s 39(5)(a); Social Services and Well-being (Wales) Act 2014 s 194(4)(a).

15 Care Act 2014 s 39(5)(b); Social Services and Well-being (Wales) Act 2014 s 194(4)(b).

16 Ie under the Mental Health Act 1983 s 117 (after-care services: see MENTAL HEALTH AND CAPACITY vol 75 (2013) PARA 945).

17 See note 14.

18 Ie a local authority for the purposes of the Care Act 2014 Pt 1 (see PARA 1).

19 Ie a local authority for the purposes of the Social Services and Well-being (Wales) Act 2014 (see PARA 2).

20 See note 14.

21 Care Act 2014 s 39(4); Social Services and Well-being (Wales) Act 2014 s 194(4A) (added by SI 2016/413).

22 See PARAS 96–99.

85. Adults placed in accommodation in Wales, Scotland or Northern Ireland.

Where a local authority in England[1] is meeting an adult's[2] needs for care and support by arranging for the provision of accommodation[3] in Wales[4], Scotland[5] or Northern Ireland[6], or a local authority in Wales[7] is meeting an adult's needs for care and support[8] by arranging for the provision of accommodation in England[9], Scotland or Northern Ireland, the adult is to be treated[10] as ordinarily resident (or, as the case may require, remaining[11]) in the local authority's area[12]. Similar provision is made in respect of placements from Scotland to England, Wales or Northern Ireland[13] and placements from Northern Ireland to England, Wales or Scotland[14].

In a case where[15] an adult is treated as ordinarily resident in an area in England, Wales or Northern Ireland (as the case may be), he does not cease to be so treated merely because he is provided with NHS accommodation[16]; and in a case where an adult is not treated as ordinarily resident anywhere in England or Wales (as the case may be), he continues not to be so treated even if he is provided with NHS accommodation[17].

1 Ie a local authority for the purposes of the Care Act 2014 Pt 1 (see PARA 1): s 39(8), Sch 1 para 12(1), (6); Social Services and Well-being (Wales) Act 2014 s 194(8) (added by the Care Act 2014 Sch 1 para 13). As to the meaning of 'England' see PARA 1 note 1. Disputes about who is the responsible authority in cross-border cases are resolved by the appropriate national authority: see Sch 1 para 5; and the Care and Support (Cross-border Placements and Business Failure: Temporary Duty) (Dispute Resolution) Regulations 2014, SI 2014/2843.

2   As to the meaning of 'adult' see PARA 1 note 1.
3   Regulations may provide for the Care Act 2014 Sch 1 to apply, with such modifications as may be
    specified, to a case where an adult has needs for care and support which can be met only if he is
    living in accommodation of a type specified in the regulations, the adult is living in accommodation
    in England, Wales, Scotland or Northern Ireland (see notes 3, 4, 5, 8) that is of a type so specified,
    and his needs for care and support are being met by an authority in another of the territories
    providing or arranging for the provision of services other than the accommodation: Sch 1
    para 10(1). At the date at which this volume states the law no such regulations had been made.
4   'Accommodation in Wales' means accommodation in Wales of a type specified in the Care and
    Support (Ordinary Residence) (Specified Accommodation) (Wales) Regulations 2015, SI
    2015/1499 (see PARA 84) but not of a type specified in regulations under the Care Act 2014 Sch 1
    para 12: Sch 1 para 12(3). At the date at which this volume states the law no such regulations had
    been made.
5   'Accommodation in Scotland' means residential accommodation in Scotland of a type which may
    be provided under or by virtue of the Social Work (Scotland) Act 1968 s 12 or s 13A, or the Mental
    Health (Care and Treatment) (Scotland) Act 2003 s 25, but not of a type specified in regulations
    under the Care Act 2014 Sch 1 para 12: Sch 1 para 12(4).
6   'Accommodation in Northern Ireland' means residential or other accommodation in Northern
    Ireland of a type which may be provided under the Health and Personal Social Services (Northern
    Ireland) Order 1972, SI 1962/1265 (NI 14), art 15: Care Act 2014 Sch 1 para 12(5).
7   Ie a local authority for the purposes of the Social Services and Well-being (Wales) Act 2014 (see
    PARA 2): Care Act 2014 Sch 1 para 12(7).
8   Ie its duty under the Social Services and Well-being (Wales) Act 2014 s 35 (see PARA 19) or its
    power under s 36 (see PARA 20).
9   'Accommodation in England' means accommodation in England of a type specified in the Care and
    Support (Ordinary Residence) (Specified Accommodation) Regulations 2014, SI 2014/2828 (see
    PARA 84) but not of a type specified in regulations under the Care Act 2014 Sch 1 para 12: Sch 1
    para 12(2).
10 Ie for the purposes of the Care Act 2014 Pt 1 (ss 1–80) (local authorities in England) or, as the case
    may be, the Social Services and Well-being (Wales) Act 2014 (local authorities in Wales).
11 Where a local authority in Wales is arranging for the provision of accommodation in England,
    Scotland or Northern Ireland in the exercise of its power under the Social Services and Well-being
    (Wales) Act 2014 s 36 the adult concerned is to be treated for the purposes of that Act: (1) in a case
    where he was within the local authority's area immediately before being provided by the local
    authority with accommodation in England, Scotland or Northern Ireland, as remaining within that
    area (Care Act 2014 Sch 1 para 2(2)(a)(i), (4)(a)(i), (7)(a)(i)); or (2) in a case where the adult was
    outside but ordinarily resident in the local authority's area immediately before being provided by
    the local authority with accommodation in England, Scotland or Northern Ireland, as remaining
    outside but ordinarily resident in that area (Sch 1 para 2(2)(a)(ii), (4)(a)(ii), (7)(a)(ii)). In a case
    where, as a result of Sch 1 para 2(2), (4) or (7), an adult is treated as remaining within, or as
    remaining outside but ordinarily resident in, an area in Wales, he does not cease to be so treated
    merely because he is provided with NHS accommodation: Sch 1 para 8(4). As to the meaning of
    'NHS accommodation' see PARA 84 note 13.
12 Care Act 2014 Sch 1 paras 1(1)(a), (3)(a), (4)(a), 2(1)(a), (3)(a), (6)(a). An adult whose needs are
    being met by a local authority in England is accordingly not to be treated for the purposes of the
    Social Services and Well-being (Wales) Act 2014 as ordinarily resident anywhere in Wales (Care
    Act 2014 Sch 1 para 1(1)(b)), and no duty under the Social Work (Scotland) Act 1968 Pt 2 or the
    Mental Health (Care and Treatment) (Scotland) Act 2003 ss 25–27, or under the Health and
    Personal Social Services (Northern Ireland) Order 1972, SI 1962/1265 (NI 14), or the Health and
    Social Care (Reform) Act (Northern Ireland) 2009, to provide or secure the provision of
    accommodation or other facilities applies in his case (Care Act 2014 Sch 1 para 1(3)(b), (4)(b)). An
    adult whose needs are being met by a local authority in Wales is accordingly not to be treated for
    the purposes of the Care Act 2014 as ordinarily resident anywhere in England (unless, in the case
    of an adult in respect of whom a local authority in Wales is arranging for the provision of
    accommodation in England in the exercise of its power under the Social Services and Well-being
    (Wales) Act 2014 s 36, the adult was so ordinarily resident immediately before being provided by
    the local authority with accommodation in England) (Sch 1 para 2(1)(b), (2)(b)), and no duty
    under the Social Work (Scotland) Act 1968 Pt 2 or the Mental Health (Care and Treatment)
    (Scotland) Act 2003 ss 25–27, or under the Health and Personal Social Services (Northern Ireland)
    Order 1972, SI 1962/1265 (NI 14), or the Health and Social Care (Reform) Act (Northern Ireland)
    2009, to provide or secure the provision of accommodation or other facilities applies in his case
    (Care Act 2014 Sch 1 para 2(3)(b), (4)(b), (6)(b), (7)(b)). Schedule 1 para 2(4)(b), (7)(b) do not
    prevent a duty mentioned in Sch 1 para 2(4) or Sch 1 para 7(4) (see note 10) from applying in the

case of an adult who was ordinarily resident in Scotland or Northern Ireland immediately before being provided by the local authority with accommodation in Scotland or Northern Ireland: Sch 1 para 2(5), (8). In a case where, as a result of Sch 1, no duty under the Social Work (Scotland) Act 1968 Pt 2, the Mental Health (Care and Treatment) (Scotland) Act 2003 ss 25–27, the Health and Personal Social Services (Northern Ireland) Order 1972, SI 1962/1265 (NI 14), or the Health and Social Care (Reform) Act (Northern Ireland) 2009, applies, the duty does not apply merely because the adult in question is provided with NHS accommodation: Care Act 2014 Sch 1 para 8(3). See also the Care and Support (Cross-border Placements) (Business Failure Duties of Scottish Local Authorities) Regulations 2014, SI 2014/2839 (amended by SI 2016/1641; SI 2015/644; SI 2016/481). In connection with disputes about residence see PARAS 96–99.

13 See the Care Act 2014 Sch 1 para 3.
14 See the Care Act 2014 Sch 1 para 4.
15 Ie as a result of the Care Act 2014 Sch 1.
16 Care Act 2014 Sch 1 para 8(1).
17 Care Act 2014 Sch 1 para 8(2).

86. Ordinary residence of children. In the context of the duties of local authorities in Wales to provide care and support for children[1], in determining the ordinary residence of a child his residence in any of the following places must be disregarded[2]:

(1)   a school or other institution[3];
(2)   a place in which he is placed in accordance with the requirements of a supervision order[4];
(3)   a place in which he is placed in accordance with the requirements of a youth rehabilitation order[5]; or
(4)   accommodation by or on behalf of a local authority in England or Wales[6].

Local authorities in England have a general statutory duty to safeguard and promote the welfare of children within their area who are in need[7], and for that purpose the ordinary residence of a child is similarly defined[8].

1 Ie for the purposes of the Social Services and Well-being (Wales) Act 2014: see, in particular, PARAS 26–32. As to the meaning of 'child' see s 3(3); and PARA 2.
2 Regulations may prescribe additional places for the purposes of the Social Services and Well-being (Wales) Act 2014: s 194(6)(e). At the date at which this volume states the law no such regulations had been made. In connection with disputes about residence see PARAS 96–99.
3 Social Services and Well-being (Wales) Act 2014 s 194(6)(a).
4 Social Services and Well-being (Wales) Act 2014 s 194(6)(b). A supervision order is an order under the Children Act 1989 s 31(1)(b): see s 31(11); and CHILDREN AND YOUNG PERSONS vol 9 (2017) PARA 351.
5 Social Services and Well-being (Wales) Act 2014 s 194(6)(c). A youth rehabilitation order is an order under the Criminal Justice and Immigration Act 2008 Pt 1 (ss 1–8); see s 1; and SENTENCING vol 92 (2015) PARA 73 et seq.
6 Social Services and Well-being (Wales) Act 2014 s 194(6)(d). As to local authorities in England and Wales see PARAS 1, 2.
7 See the Children Act 1989 Pt 3 (ss 16B–30A), Pt 4 (ss 31–42) and Pt 5 (ss 43–52); and PARA 21. As to the meaning of 'child' for the purposes of the Children Act 1989 see s 105(1); and CHILDREN AND YOUNG PERSONS vol 9 (2017) PARA 3.
8 See the Children Act 1989 s 105(6); and CHILDREN AND YOUNG PERSONS vol 9 (2017) PARA 351. See also s 30(2), (2A), (2B); and CHILDREN AND YOUNG PERSONS vol 10 (2017) PARA 822.

87. Detained persons and persons in approved and other residential premises. In their application to an adult[1] who is :

(1)   detained in prison in England or Wales[2];
(2)   detained in youth detention accommodation in Wales[3];
(3)   residing in approved premises in England or Wales[4]; or
(4)   residing in any other premises in England or Wales because a requirement to do so has been imposed on him as a condition of the grant of bail in criminal proceedings[5],

the statutory provisions relating to the provision of care and support in England[6] and Wales[7] have effect as if references to being ordinarily resident in an area were, as the case may be, references to being detained in prison in that area, to being detained in youth detention accommodation in that area, to being resident in approved premises in that area or to being resident in premises in that area because of such a requirement[8].

In the context of the provision of care and support for children in Wales[9], where a child (a 'relevant child') is detained[10] or is in residential accommodation[11] and immediately before being convicted of an offence:

(a)   has needs for care and support[12] that are being met[13] by a local authority[14];

(b)   is looked after by a local authority by virtue of being provided with accommodation by the authority[15]; or

(c)   is ordinarily resident in the area of a local authority, but does not come within head (1) or (2) above[16],

The child is to be treated[17] as being within that local authority's area while he or she is a relevant child (and is not to be treated as being ordinarily resident or within any other local authority's area)[18].

1   As to the meaning of 'adult' see PARA 1 note 1 (England) and PARA 2 (Wales).

2   As to the meaning of 'prison' see the Prison Act 1952 s 53(1); and PRISONS AND PRISONERS vol 85 (2012) PARA 403 (definition applied by the Care Act 2014 s 76(11); and the Social Services and Well-being (Wales) Act 2014 s 188(1)). In the context of a person detained in England a reference to a prison includes a reference to a young offender institution (see PRISONS AND PRISONERS vol 85 (2012) PARAS 487–490), a secure training centre (see PRISONS AND PRISONERS vol 85 (2012) PARAS 491–514) or a secure children's home (see CHILDREN AND YOUNG PERSONS vol 10 (2017) PARA 1044): s 76(11)(a). For these purposes a person who is temporarily absent from prison is to be treated as detained in prison for the period of absence: Care Act 2014 s 76(14)(a); Social Services and Well-being (Wales) Act 2014 s 188(2)(a)). As to the meanings of 'England' and 'Wales' see PARAS 1, 2.

3   'Youth detention accommodation' means (by virtue of the Social Services and Well-being (Wales) Act 2014 s 188(1) (amended by the Criminal Justice and Courts Act 2015 Sch 9 para 32(4); prospectively amended by the Regulation and Inspection of Social Care (Wales) Act 2016 Sch 3 para 32)):

    (1)   a secure children's home;

    (2)   a secure training centre;

    (3)   a secure college (see PRISONS AND PRISONERS);

    (4)   a young offender institution;

    (5)   accommodation provided, equipped and maintained by the Welsh Ministers under the Children Act 1989 s 82(5) (see CHILDREN AND YOUNG PERSONS vol 9 (2017) PARA 173) for the purpose of restricting the liberty of children;

    (6)   accommodation, or accommodation of a description, for the time being specified by order under the Powers of Criminal Courts (Sentencing) Act 2000 s 107(1)(e) (youth detention accommodation for purposes of detention and training orders: see CHILDREN AND YOUNG PERSONS vol 10 (2017) PARA 1389); and

    (7)   as from a day to be appointed, a secure accommodation service (within the meaning of the Regulation and Inspection of Social Care (Wales) Act 2016 Pt 1 (ss 1–64) (see s 2(1)(b), Sch 1 para 2; and PARA 206)).

     At the date at which this volume states the law no day had been appointed for the purpose of head (7) above.

     For these purposes a person who is temporarily absent from youth detention accommodation is to be treated as detained in youth detention accommodation for the period of absence: Social Services and Well-being (Wales) Act 2014 s 188(2)(a).

4   As to the meaning of 'approved premises' see the Offender Management Act 2007 s 13; and SENTENCING vol 92 (2015) PARA 745 (definition applied by the Care Act 2014 s 76(12) and the Social Services and Well-being (Wales) Act 2014 s 188(1)). A person who is temporarily absent from approved premises is to be treated as residing in approved premises for the period of absence: Care Act 2014 s 76(14)(b); Social Services and Well-being (Wales) Act 2014 s 188(2)(b).

5   As to the meaning of 'bail in criminal proceedings' see the Bail Act 1976 s 1; and CRIMINAL PROCEDURE vol 27 (2015) PARA 67 (definition applied by the Care Act 2014 s 76(13) and the

Social Services and Well-being (Wales) Act 2014 s 188(1)). A person who is temporarily absent from other premises in which he is required to reside as a condition of the grant of bail in criminal proceedings is to be treated as residing in the premises for the period of absence: Care Act 2014 s 76(14)(c); Social Services and Well-being (Wales) Act 2014 s 188(2)(c).

6   Ie the Care Act 2014 Pt 1 (ss 1–80).
7   Ie the Social Services and Well-being (Wales) Act 2014.
8   Care Act 2014 s 76(1)–(3); Social Services and Well-being (Wales) Act 2014 s 185(1)–(3). In connection with disputes about residence see PARAS 96–99.
9   Ie under the Social Services and Well-being (Wales) Act 2014. As to the meaning of 'child' see PARA 2. The provision of care and support for children in England is governed by provisions of the Children Act 1989 described in PARA 21: see also, in connection with the ordinary residence of children in both England and Wales, PARA 86.
10   Ie detained in youth detention accommodation or prison: Social Services and Well-being (Wales) Act 2014 s 186(1)(a).
11   Ie is residing in approved premises (Social Services and Well-being (Wales) Act 2014 s 186(1)(b)) or is residing in any other premises because a requirement to do so has been imposed on the child as a condition of the grant of bail in criminal proceedings (s 186(1)(c)).
12   As to the meanings of 'care' and 'support' see PARA 2 note 1.
13   Ie under the Social Services and Well-being (Wales) Act 2014 Pt 4 (ss 32–58).
14   Social Services and Well-being (Wales) Act 2014 s 186(2)(a). As to the meaning of 'local authority' see PARA 2. As to the social services functions of local authorities in Wales generally, and the overarching principles in accordance with which functions relating to the provision of care and support must be exercised, see PARAS 373–383.
15   Social Services and Well-being (Wales) Act 2014 s 186(2)(b).
16   Social Services and Well-being (Wales) Act 2014 s 186(2)(c).
17   Ie for the purposes of the Social Services and Well-being (Wales) Act 2014.
18   Social Services and Well-being (Wales) Act 2014 s 186(2).

(ii) Continuity of Care when a Person Moves

A.   ENGLAND

88. Continuing care for adults moving between local authorities. Provision is made for the continuity of care of adults[1] who move between local authorities in England[2], ie where:

(1)   an adult's needs for care and support are being met[3] by a local authority ('the first authority')[4] (or are not being so met but such authority is nonetheless keeping a care account[5] in the adult's case[6]), the adult notifies another local authority ('the second authority') (or that authority is notified on the adult's behalf) that he intends to move to the area of the second authority[7], and the second authority is satisfied that his intention is genuine[8]; or

(2)   an adult's needs for care and support are being met[9] by a local authority ('the first authority') arranging for the provision of accommodation in the area of another local authority ('the second authority')[10], the adult notifies the second authority (or that authority is notified on the adult's behalf) that he intends to move out of that accommodation but to remain, and be provided with care and support at home or in the community, in its area[11], and the second authority is satisfied that the adult's intention is genuine[12].

The continuity provisions involve the exchange of information between the relevant local authorities[13] and the receiving authority carrying out a needs or carer's assessment[14], and they also apply in the case of an adult detained in prison or residing in approved premises[15].

Provision is also made for the continuity of care where the person moves before the necessary consultation and assessments are completed[16].

1   As to the meaning of 'adult' see PARA 1 note 1.

2   As to the meaning of 'local authority' in England see PARA 1. As to the social services functions
    of local authorities in England generally, and the overarching principles in accordance with which
    functions relating to the provision of care and support must be exercised, see PARAS 315–323. In
    connection with disputes between local authorities about continuity of care see PARAS 96–99.
3   Ie under the Care Act 2014 s 18 or s 19: see PARAS 12, 13.
4   Care Act 2014 s 37(1)(a).
5   As to care accounts see PARA 123.
6   Care Act 2014 s 37(2)(a).
7   Care Act 2014 s 37(1)(b), (2)(b). A reference to moving to an area is a reference to moving to that
    area with a view to becoming ordinarily resident there: s 37(15)(b).
8   Care Act 2014 s 37(1)(c), (2)(c).
9   See note 3.
10 Care Act 2014 s 37(3)(a).
11 Care Act 2014 s 37(3)(b). A reference to remaining in an area is a reference to remaining ordinarily
    resident there: s 37(15)(c).
12 Care Act 2014 s 37(3)(c).
13 See PARA 89.
14 See PARA 90.
15 The Care Act 2014 ss 37, 38, in their application to an adult who is detained in prison or residing
    in approved premises, also apply where it is decided that the adult is to be detained in prison, or
    is to reside in approved premises, in the area of another local authority; and accordingly references
    to the adult's intention to move are to be read as references to that decision, and references to
    carers are to be ignored: s 76(6). In connection with detained persons (particularly in connection
    with the interpretation of these provisions) see PARA 87.
16 See PARA 91.

89. Notification and exchange of information. Where a qualifying adult intends
to move from the area of a local authority in England which is meeting his needs
for care and support into the area of another local authority in England[1] the
second authority[2] must provide[3] the adult and, if he has or is proposing to have
a carer[4], the carer with such information as it considers appropriate[5] and notify
the first authority that it is satisfied[6] that the adult qualifies for continuing care[7].
Having received such notification the first authority must provide the second
authority with:

(1)   a copy of any care and support plan[8] prepared for the adult[9];
(2)   a copy of any independent personal budget[10] prepared for the adult[11];
(3)   in a case where care is not being provided[12], a copy of the most recent
        needs assessment in the adult's case[13];
(4)   if the first authority has been keeping a care account[14] in the adult's case,
        a copy of that account[15];
(5)   if the adult has a carer and that carer is to continue as his carer after the
        move, a copy of any support plan prepared for the carer[16]; and
(6)   such other information relating to the adult and, if he has a carer
        (whether or not one with needs for support), such other information
        relating to the carer as the second authority may request[17].

Pending the adult's move[18], the first authority must keep in contact with the
second authority in order to ascertain the progress that the second authority is
making in preparing to meet any needs for care and support[19] in the adult's case[20]
and where the adult is proposing to have a carer immediately after the move, any
needs for support[21] in the carer's case[22], and the first authority must keep the adult
(and, where applicable, the carer) informed about such contact with the second
authority and must involve the adult (and, where applicable, the carer) in the
contact[23].

1   Ie where any of the circumstances set out in PARA 88 are satisfied. As to the meaning of 'adult' see
    PARA 1 note 1. As to the meaning of 'local authority' see PARA 1. As to the social services functions
    of local authorities in England generally, and the overarching principles in accordance with which
    functions relating to the provision of care and support must be exercised, see PARAS 315–323.

2 As to the meanings of 'the first authority' and 'the second authority' see PARA 88.
3 Ie in so far as it would not do so under the Care Act 2014 s 4: see PARA 326.
4 As to the meaning of 'carer' see PARA 33 note 2.
5 Care Act 2014 s 37(4)(a).
6 Ie as mentioned in the Care Act 2014 s 37(1)(c), (2)(c) or (3)(c) (see PARA 88). Regulations may specify steps which a local authority must take for the purpose of being satisfied as mentioned in s 37(1)(c), (2)(c) or (3)(c) (s 37(14)): at the date at which this volume states the law no such regulations had been made.
7 Care Act 2014 s 37(4)(b).
8 As to care and support plans for adults in England see PARAS 78–80.
9 Care Act 2014 s 37(5)(a).
10 As to independent personal budgets see PARA 122.
11 Care Act 2014 s 37(5)(b).
12 Ie in a case within the Care Act 2014 s 37(2) (see PARA 88).
13 Care Act 2014 s 37(5)(c). As to the requirement to carry out needs assessments see PARAS 8, 9.
14 As to care accounts see PARA 123.
15 Care Act 2014 s 37(5)(d).
16 Care Act 2014 s 37(5)(e). As to support plans for carers in England see PARAS 78–80.
17 Care Act 2014 s 37(5)(f).
18 As to references to moving to an area see PARA 88 note 7.
19 Ie under the Care Act 2014 s 18 or s 19: see PARAS 12, 13.
20 Care Act 2014 s 37(9)(a).
21 Ie under the Care Act 2014 s 20: see PARAS 36, 37.
22 Care Act 2014 s 37(9)(b).
23 Care Act 2014 s 37(10).

90. Duty of receiving authority to carry out needs or carer's assessment. Where a qualifying adult is moving from the area of a local authority in England which is meeting his needs for care and support into the area of another local authority in England[1] and the authorities have exchanged the required information[2] the second authority[3] must assess whether the adult has needs for care and support and, if he does, what those needs are[4] and, where the adult has or is proposing to have a carer and it is appropriate to do so, assess whether the carer has or is likely to have needs for support and, if the carer does or is likely to, what those needs are or are likely to be[5].

1 Ie where any of the circumstances set out in PARA 88 are satisfied. As to the meaning of 'adult' see PARA 1 note 1. As to the meaning of 'local authority' see PARA 1. As to the social services functions of local authorities in England generally, and the overarching principles in accordance with which functions relating to the provision of care and support must be exercised, see PARAS 315–323.
2 See PARA 89.
3 As to the meanings of 'the first authority' and 'the second authority' see PARA 88.
4 Care Act 2014 s 37(6)(a). In carrying out an assessment under s 37(6)(a) or (b), the second authority must have regard to the care and support plan provided under s 37(5)(a) (see PARA 89) or (as the case may be) the support plan provided under s 37(5)(e) (see PARA 89): s 37(7). Part 1 (ss 1–80) applies to an assessment under s 37(6)(a) as it applies to a needs assessment (s 37(8)(a)): as to needs assessments see PARAS 8, 9. Where the needs identified by an assessment under s 37(6)(a) carried out by the second authority are different from those specified in the care and support plan provided under s 37(5)(a) (see PARA 89), or where the cost to the second authority of meeting the adult's eligible needs is different from the cost to the first authority of doing so, the second authority must provide a written explanation of the difference to the adult, any carer that the adult has, if the adult asks the authority to do so, and any other person to whom the adult asks the authority to provide the explanation: s 37(11), (12). As to the meaning of 'carer' see PARA 33 note 2. An adult's needs are 'eligible needs' if they meet the eligibility criteria (see PARA 10) and are not being met by a carer: s 37(15)(a).
5 Care Act 2014 s 37(6)(b). See note 4. Part 1 applies to an assessment under s 37(6)(b) as it applies to a carer's assessment (s 37(8)(b)): as to carer's assessments see PARAS 33, 34. Where the needs identified by an assessment under s 37(6)(b) carried out by the second authority are different from those in the support plan provided under s 37(5)(e) (see PARA 89), the second authority must provide a written explanation of the difference to the carer, the adult needing care, if the carer asks the authority to do so, and any other person to whom the carer asks the authority to provide an explanation: s 37(13).

91. Continuity of care where person moves before consultation and assessments are completed. Where a qualifying adult is moving from the area of a local authority in England which is meeting his needs for care and support into the area of another local authority in England[1] and on the day of the intended move[2] the second authority[3] has yet to carry out the necessary needs or carer's assessment[4], or has done so but has yet to take the other necessary steps[5] in the adult's case, it must:

(1)   meet the adult's needs for care and support[6], and the needs for support of any carer who is continuing as the adult's carer[7], which the first authority has been meeting[8]; and

(2)   where the first authority has been keeping a care account[9] in the adult's case, itself keep that account on the same basis as the first authority has been keeping it[10].

The second authority is subject to this duty until it has carried out[11] the assessment or assessments[12] and taken the other steps required[13] in the adult's case[14], and the first authority is not required to meet the adult's needs for care and support or, if the adult has a carer, such needs for support as the carer has, for so long as the second authority is subject to the duty[15].

1   Ie where any of the circumstances set out in PARA 88 are satisfied. As to the meaning of 'adult' see PARA 1 note 1. As to the meaning of 'local authority' see PARA 1. As to the social services functions of local authorities in England generally, and the overarching principles in accordance with which functions relating to the provision of care and support must be exercised, see PARAS 315–323.
2   Ie as mentioned in the Care Act 2014 s 37(1)(b), (2)(b) or (3)(b) (see PARA 88).
3   As to the meanings of 'the first authority' and 'the second authority' see PARA 88.
4   Ie under the Care Act 2014 s 37(6) (see PARA 90).
5   Ie the steps required under the Care Act 2014 Pt 1 (ss 1–80) by virtue of s 37(8) (see PARA 90).
6   In deciding how to meet the adult's needs for care and support the second authority must involve the adult (Care Act 2014 s 38(3)(a)), any carer who is continuing as the adult's carer (s 38(3)(b)), and any person whom the adult asks the authority to involve or, where the adult lacks capacity to ask the authority to do that, any person who appears to the authority to be interested in the adult's welfare (s 38(3)(c)). In performing the duty under s 37(3)(a), the second authority must take all reasonable steps to reach agreement with the adult about how it should meet the needs in question: s 38(5). As to the meaning of 'carer' see PARA 33 note 2.

     The second authority must have regard to the following matters in deciding how to perform its duty under s 38(1) in respect of an adult ('the relevant adult'):
(1)   the contents of any care and support plan supplied to the authority under s 37(5)(a) (documents to be supplied by first authority where second authority is satisfied as to genuineness of intention to move: see PARA 89) in relation to the relevant adult (Care and Support (Continuity of Care) Regulations 2014, SI 2014/2825, reg 2(1)(a) (made under the Care Act 2014 s 38(8)));
(2)   the contents of any support plan supplied to the authority under s 37(5)(e) (see PARA 89) in relation to any relevant carer of the relevant adult (Care and Support (Continuity of Care) Regulations 2014, SI 2014/2825, reg 2(1)(b));
(3)   the outcomes that the relevant adult wishes to achieve in day-to-day life (reg 2(1)(c));
(4)   the outcomes that any relevant carer of that adult wishes to achieve in day-to-day life (reg 2(1)(d));
(5)   the views and preferences of the relevant adult as to how the authority should meet his needs for care and support (reg 2(1)(e));
(6)   the views and preferences of any relevant carer of that adult as to how the authority should meet that carer's needs for support (reg 2(1)(f));
(7)   any relevant difference between the relevant adult's circumstances before and after the day of his intended move, including in relation to access to a carer, suitability of living accommodation, location of living accommodation in terms of its proximity and accessibility to necessary facilities or services in the local community including medical services, public transport, educational facilities and recreational facilities or services, and the availability of support from family members, friends, neighbours and the wider community (reg 2(1)(g)). For the purposes of reg 2(1)(g), a difference is 'relevant' if it is likely to have a significant effect on the well-being of the relevant adult during the period when that adult's needs for care and support are being met under the Care Act 2014 s 38(1).

7   In deciding how to meet the needs for support of any carer who is continuing as the adult's carer, the second authority must involve the carer (Care Act 2014 s 38(4)(a)), the adult needing care, if the carer asks the authority to do so (s 38(4)(b)), and any other person whom the carer asks the authority to involve (s 38(4)(c)). In performing the duty under s 38(4)(a), the second authority must take all reasonable steps to reach agreement with the carer about how it should meet the needs in question: s 38(5).
8   Care Act 2014 s 38(1)(a).
9   As to care accounts see PARA 123.
10 Care Act 2014 s 38(1)(b).
11 See note 4.
12 Care Act 2014 s 38(2)(a).
13 See note 5.
14 Care Act 2014 s 38(2)(b). Where, having complied with the duty under s 38(1), the second authority is not required to meet the adult's needs for care and support under s 18 (see PARAS 12, 13) because the adult is still ordinarily resident in the area of the first authority, the second authority may recover from the first authority the costs it incurs in complying with the duty under s 38(1): s 38(7).
15 Care Act 2014 s 38(6).

B.   WALES

92. Continuing care for adults and children moving between local authorities. Provision is made for the continuity of care of adults[1] and children[2] who move between local authorities in Wales[3], ie where an authority ('the sending authority') is notified by or on behalf of a person in respect of whom it has a duty[4] to meet needs for care and support that the person is going to move to the area of another local authority[5] ('the receiving authority') and it is satisfied that the move is likely to happen[6]. The continuity provisions involve the exchange of information between the relevant local authorities[7] and the receiving authority carrying out a needs or carer's assessment[8].

1   As to the meaning of 'adult' see PARA 2.
2   As to the meaning of 'child' see PARA 2.
3   For the duty of local authorities in Wales to provide care and support for adults, children and carers see PARA 2. As to the meanings of 'care' and 'support' see PARA 2 note 1. As to the meaning of 'carer' see PARA 54 note 2. In connection with disputes between local authorities about continuity of care see PARAS 96–99.
4   Ie under the Social Services and Well-being (Wales) Act 2014 s 35 (adults) or s 37 (children): see PARAS 19, 30.
5   A reference in the Social Services and Well-being (Wales) Act 2014 s 56 to moving to an area is a reference to moving to that area with a view to becoming ordinarily resident there: s 56(7).
6   Social Services and Well-being (Wales) Act 2014 s 56(1). Regulations may specify steps which a local authority must take to satisfy itself in respect of the matters mentioned in s 56(1), (2) (s 56(6)(a)) and cases in which the duties under s 56(1), (2) do not apply (s 56(6)(c)). At the date at which this volume states the law no such regulations had been made.
7   See PARA 93.
8   See PARA 94.

93. Notification and exchange of information. Where a qualifying adult or child is going to move from the area of a local authority in Wales which is meeting his needs for care and support into the area of another local authority in Wales[1] the sending authority[2] must notify the receiving authority that it is satisfied that the move is likely to happen[3] and provide the receiving authority with a copy of the care and support plan prepared for the person[4] and such other information relating to the person and, if the person has a carer[5], such other information relating to the carer as the receiving authority may request[6].

1   Ie where any of the circumstances set out in PARA 92 are satisfied. As to the meanings of 'adult', 'child' and 'local authority' see PARA 2. As to the social services functions of local authorities in Wales generally, and the overarching principles in accordance with which functions relating to the provision of care and support must be exercised, see PARAS 373–383.

2 As to the meanings of 'the sending authority' and 'the receiving authority' see PARA 92.
3 Social Services and Well-being (Wales) Act 2014 s 56(1)(a). See PARA 92 note 6.
4 Social Services and Well-being (Wales) Act 2014 s 56(1)(b)(i). As to care and support plans see PARAS 81–83.
5 As to the meaning of 'carer' see PARA 54 note 2.
6 Social Services and Well-being (Wales) Act 2014 s 56(1)(b)(ii).

94. Duty of receiving authority to carry out needs or carer's assessment. Where a qualifying adult or child intends to move from the area of a local authority in Wales which is meeting his needs for care and support into the area of another local authority in Wales[1], the sending authority has sent the required information[2], and the receiving authority[3] is notified by or on behalf of a person in respect of whom the sending authority has a duty[4] to meet needs for care and support[5] that the person is going to move to the receiving authority's area, and the receiving authority is satisfied that the move is likely to happen, it must:

(1)   notify the sending authority that it is so satisfied[6];

(2)   provide the person and, if the person has a carer, the carer with such information as it considers appropriate[7];

(3)   if the person is a child, provide the persons with parental responsibility[8] for the child with such information as it considers appropriate[9]; and

(4)   assess the person[10] having regard in particular to any change in the person's needs for care and support arising from the move[11].

1 Ie where any of the circumstances set out in PARA 92 are satisfied. As to the meanings of 'adult', 'child' and 'local authority' see PARA 2. As to the social services functions of local authorities in Wales generally, and the overarching principles in accordance with which functions relating to the provision of care and support must be exercised, see PARAS 373–383.
2 See PARA 93.
3 As to the meanings of 'the sending authority' and 'the receiving authority' see PARA 92.
4 Ie under the Social Services and Well-being (Wales) Act 2014 s 35 (adults) or s 37 (children): see PARAS 19, 30.
5 As to the meanings of 'care' and 'support' see PARA 2 note 1.
6 Social Services and Well-being (Wales) Act 2014 s 56(2)(a). See PARA 92 note 6.
7 Social Services and Well-being (Wales) Act 2014 s 56(2)(b).
8 As to the meaning of 'parental responsibility' see PARA 26 note 10.
9 Social Services and Well-being (Wales) Act 2014 s 56(2)(c).
10 Ie under the Social Services and Well-being (Wales) Act 2014 s 19 (if the person is an adult: see PARAS 15, 16) or s 21 (if the person is a child: see PARAS 26, 27).
11 Social Services and Well-being (Wales) Act 2014 s 56(2)(d). In carrying out the assessment required by s 56(2)(d), the receiving authority must have regard to the care and support plan provided under s 56(1)(b) (see PARA 93): s 56(4).

95. Continuity of care where person moves before consultation and assessments are completed. Where a qualifying adult or child moves from the area of a local authority in Wales which is meeting his needs for care and support into the area of another local authority in Wales[1], and on the day the person moves to its area the receiving authority[2] has yet to carry out the needs or carer's assessment[3], or has done so but has yet to carry out the other statutory steps[4], it must meet the person's needs for care and support[5] in accordance with the care and support plan[6] prepared by the sending authority, in so far as that is reasonably practicable[7]. The receiving authority is subject to this duty until it has carried out the assessment required[8] and taken the other statutory steps[9].

1 Ie where any of the circumstances set out in PARA 92 are satisfied. As to the meanings of 'adult', 'child' and 'local authority' see PARA 2. As to the social services functions of local authorities in Wales generally, and the overarching principles in accordance with which functions relating to the provision of care and support must be exercised, see PARAS 373–383.
2 As to the meanings of 'the sending authority' and 'the receiving authority' see PARA 92.
3 Ie the assessment required by the Social Services and Well-being (Wales) Act 2014 s 56(2)(d) (see PARA 94).

4　Ie the steps required by the Social Services and Well-being (Wales) Act 2014 Pt 4 (ss 32–58) or Pt 5 (ss 59–73).

5　As to the meanings of 'care' and 'support' see PARA 2 note 1.

6　As to care and support plans see PARAS 81–83.

7　Social Services and Well-being (Wales) Act 2014 s 56(3). Regulations may specify matters to which a receiving authority must have regard in deciding how to comply with the duty under s 56(3) (s 56(6)(b)) and cases in which the duties under s 56(3) do not apply (s 56(6)(c)). At the date at which this volume states the law no such regulations had been made.

8　Social Services and Well-being (Wales) Act 2014 s 56(5)(a).

9　Social Services and Well-being (Wales) Act 2014 s 56(5)(b).

(iii) Disputes about Residence and Continuity

96. The resolution procedure. Provision is made for the resolution of disputes between local authorities[1] about where an adult[2] is ordinarily resident[3] and about the application of the statutory provisions about continuity and portability of care where a person moves[4]. Disputes are determined, wherever possible, by dialogue between the authorities concerned[5]: only if the authorities cannot resolve the dispute between themselves within four months of the date on which it arose, the lead authority must refer[6] it for determination to the Secretary of State or, as the case may be, the Welsh Ministers[7].

These provisions also apply[8] to the resolution of disputes about the application of the provisions about the duties of local authorities[9] to carry on regulated activities in the event of provider failure[10].

1　As to the meaning of 'local authority' see PARA 1 (England) and PARA 2 (Wales).

2　As to the meaning of 'adult' see PARA 1 note 1 (England) and PARA 2 (Wales).

3　Ie for the purposes of the Care Act 2014 Pt 1 (ss 1–80) or the Social Services and Well-being (Wales) Act 2014: Care and Support (Disputes Between Local Authorities) Regulations 2014, SI 2014/2829, reg 1(2) (made under the Care Act 2014 s 40(4)); Care and Support (Disputes about Ordinary Residence, etc) (Wales) Regulations 2015, SI 2015/1494, reg 1(3) (made under the Social Services and Well-being (Wales) Act 2014 s 195(2)).

4　Ie the application of the Care Act 2014 s 37 (see PARAS 88–91) and the Social Services and Well-being (Wales) Act 2014 s 56 (see PARAS 92–95): Care and Support (Disputes Between Local Authorities) Regulations 2014, SI 2014/2829, reg 1(2); Care and Support (Disputes about Ordinary Residence, etc) (Wales) Regulations 2015, SI 2015/1494, reg 1(3). In relation to a local authority in Wales, where the dispute is one to which the Children Act 1989 s 30(2C) (questions of whether child ordinarily resident in England or Wales: see CHILDREN AND YOUNG PERSONS vol 10 (2017) PARA 822) applies, then these provisions (ie the Social Services and Well-being (Wales) Act 2014 s 195(1)) does not apply: s 195(1A) (added by SI 2016/413).

5　As to the actions which the disputing authorities must take pursuant to the resolution of a dispute see PARA 98. A reference to 'the authorities' is a reference to the local authorities who are parties to a dispute and includes (where different) a reference to the lead authority in relation to that dispute: Care and Support (Disputes Between Local Authorities) Regulations 2014, SI 2014/2829, reg 1(4); Care and Support (Disputes about Ordinary Residence, etc) (Wales) Regulations 2015, SI 2015/1494, reg 1(5). 'The lead authority' means, in relation to a dispute, the local authority which is meeting the needs of the person to whom the dispute relates at the date on which the dispute arises, or if no local authority is meeting those needs at that date, is required to do so by the Care and Support (Disputes Between Local Authorities) Regulations 2014, SI 2014/2829, reg 2(3) or, as the case may be, the Care and Support (Disputes about Ordinary Residence, etc) (Wales) Regulations 2015, SI 2015/1494, reg 2(3) (see PARA 97): Care and Support (Disputes Between Local Authorities) Regulations 2014, SI 2014/2829, reg 1(2); Care and Support (Disputes about Ordinary Residence, etc) (Wales) Regulations 2015, SI 2015/1494, reg 1(3). As to the meaning of 'local authority' see PARA 1 (England) and PARA 2 (Wales).

6　'Referred' means referred for determination by the appropriate person, and 'refer' and 'referral' are construed accordingly: Care and Support (Disputes Between Local Authorities) Regulations 2014, SI 2014/2829, reg 1(2); Care and Support (Disputes about Ordinary Residence, etc) (Wales) Regulations 2015, SI 2015/1494, reg 1(3). As to the documents, information and legal arguments that must be included with a referral see the Care and Support (Disputes Between Local Authorities) Regulations 2014, SI 2014/2829, regs 4–6; and the Care and Support (Disputes about Ordinary Residence, etc) (Wales) Regulations 2015, SI 2015/1494, regs 4–6.

7 Care Act 2014 s 40(1)(a); Social Services and Well-being (Wales) Act 2014 s 195(1)(a); Care and Support (Disputes Between Local Authorities) Regulations 2014, SI 2014/2829, reg 3(8); Care and Support (Disputes about Ordinary Residence, etc) (Wales) Regulations 2015, SI 2015/1494, reg 3(7). Where the Secretary of State or the Welsh Ministers appoint a person for this purpose, disputes are to be determined by that person: Care Act 2014 s 40(1)(b); Social Services and Well-being (Wales) Act 2014 s 195(1)(b).

8 Ie by virtue of the Care Act 2014 s 48(8) and the Social Services and Well-being (Wales) Act 2014 s 189(8).

9 Ie under the Care Act 2014 s 48 (see PARA 180) and the Social Services and Well-being (Wales) Act 2014 s 189 (see PARA 230).

10 Care and Support (Disputes Between Local Authorities) Regulations 2014, SI 2014/2829, reg 1(2); Care and Support (Disputes about Ordinary Residence, etc) (Wales) Regulations 2015, SI 2015/1494, reg 1(3).

97. Responsibility for meeting needs whilst dispute is unresolved. The authorities[1] must not allow the existence of a dispute[2] to prevent, delay, interrupt or otherwise adversely affect the meeting of the needs of the person[3] to whom the dispute relates[4], and accordingly the local authority which is meeting the person's needs on the date on which the dispute arises[5] must continue to meet those needs until the dispute is resolved[6]. If no local authority is meeting the needs on the date on which the dispute arises the local authority in whose area the person is living[7], or if the person is not living in the area of any local authority, the local authority in whose area he is present[8], must, until the dispute is resolved, perform the statutory duties[9] in respect of the person as if the person was ordinarily resident in its area[10]. Moreover, where the dispute is about continuity of care[11], the authorities must perform their statutory duties[12] notwithstanding the existence of the dispute[13].

1 As to the meaning of 'the authorities' see PARA 96 note 5.

2 As to the disputes to which these provisions apply see PARA 96.

3 The Care and Support (Disputes Between Local Authorities) Regulations 2014, SI 2014/2829, do not apply to the care of children (see PARA 21) and refer to an 'adult or carer' and an 'adult needing care' in the context of the person to whom a dispute relates. The Care and Support (Disputes about Ordinary Residence, etc) (Wales) Regulations 2015, SI 2015/1494, apply to adults, children and carers so refer to the 'person or carer' or the 'person to whom the dispute relates'. As to the meaning of 'adult' see PARA 1 note 1 (England) and PARA 2 (Wales); as to the meaning of 'carer' see PARA 33 note 2 (England) and PARA 54 (Wales).

4 Care and Support (Disputes Between Local Authorities) Regulations 2014, SI 2014/2829, reg 2(1); Care and Support (Disputes about Ordinary Residence, etc) (Wales) Regulations 2015, SI 2015/1494, reg 2(1).

5 References in the Care and Support (Disputes Between Local Authorities) Regulations 2014, SI 2014/2829, and the Care and Support (Disputes about Ordinary Residence, etc) (Wales) Regulations 2015, SI 2015/1494, to the date on which a dispute arises are references to the first date on which a written communication is sent by one of the local authorities ('the first authority') to another of the local authorities ('the second authority') which (as the case may be):

(1) asserts that, in the first authority's view, the person to whom the dispute relates is not ordinarily resident in its area for the purposes of the Care Act 2014 Pt 1 (ss 1–80) or the Social Services and Well-being (Wales) Act 2014 (as the case may be), or that that person is ordinarily resident in the second authority's area for those purposes (Care and Support (Disputes Between Local Authorities) Regulations 2014, SI 2014/2829, reg 1(3)(a); Care and Support (Disputes about Ordinary Residence, etc) (Wales) Regulations 2015, SI 2015/1494, reg 1(4)(a));

(2) raises an issue about the application of the Care Act 2014 s 37 (see PARAS 88–91) or the Social Services and Well-being (Wales) Act 2014 s 56 (see PARAS 92–95) (Care and Support (Disputes Between Local Authorities) Regulations 2014, SI 2014/2829, reg 1(3)(b); Care and Support (Disputes about Ordinary Residence, etc) (Wales) Regulations 2015, SI 2015/1494, reg 1(4)(b)); or

(3) raises an issue about the application of the Care Act 2014 s 48 (see PARA 180) or the Social Services and Well-being (Wales) Act 2014 s 189 (see PARA 230) (Care and Support (Disputes Between Local Authorities) Regulations 2014, SI 2014/2829, reg 1(3)(c); Care and Support (Disputes about Ordinary Residence, etc) (Wales) Regulations 2015, SI 2015/1494, reg 1(4)(c)).

6 Care and Support (Disputes Between Local Authorities) Regulations 2014, SI 2014/2829, reg 2(2); Care and Support (Disputes about Ordinary Residence, etc) (Wales) Regulations 2015, SI 2015/1494, reg 2(2).

7 Care and Support (Disputes Between Local Authorities) Regulations 2014, SI 2014/2829, reg 2(3)(a); Care and Support (Disputes about Ordinary Residence, etc) (Wales) Regulations 2015, SI 2015/1494, reg 2(3)(a).

8 Care and Support (Disputes Between Local Authorities) Regulations 2014, SI 2014/2829, reg 2(3)(b); Care and Support (Disputes about Ordinary Residence, etc) (Wales) Regulations 2015, SI 2015/1494, reg 2(3)(b).

9 Ie the duties under the Care Act 2014 Pt 1 or the Social Services and Well-being (Wales) Act 2014.

10 Care and Support (Disputes Between Local Authorities) Regulations 2014, SI 2014/2829, reg 2(3); Care and Support (Disputes about Ordinary Residence, etc) (Wales) Regulations 2015, SI 2015/1494, reg 2(3). If the duty under the Care and Support (Disputes Between Local Authorities) Regulations 2014, SI 2014/2829, reg 2(3) or the Care and Support (Disputes about Ordinary Residence, etc) (Wales) Regulations 2015, SI 2015/1494, reg 2(3) falls to be discharged by a local authority ('A') which is not one of the authorities already party to the dispute, those authorities must, without delay, bring to A's attention A's duty thereunder and A's status as the lead authority for these purposes: Care and Support (Disputes Between Local Authorities) Regulations 2014, SI 2014/2829, reg 2(4); Care and Support (Disputes about Ordinary Residence, etc) (Wales) Regulations 2015, SI 2015/1494, reg 2(4). A is not under the duties set out in the Care and Support (Disputes Between Local Authorities) Regulations 2014, SI 2014/2829 or the Care and Support (Disputes about Ordinary Residence, etc) (Wales) Regulations 2015, SI 2015/1494, until the date on which it is aware of, or could reasonably be expected to have been aware of, its status as the lead authority: Care and Support (Disputes Between Local Authorities) Regulations 2014, SI 2014/2829, reg 2(5); Care and Support (Disputes about Ordinary Residence, etc) (Wales) Regulations 2015, SI 2015/1494, reg 2(5). As to the meaning of 'the lead authority' see PARA 96 note 5.

11 Ie where the dispute is about the application of the Care Act 2014 s 37 or the Social Services and Well-being (Wales) Act 2014 s 56.

12 Ie duties under the Care Act 2014 s 37 or s 38 or the Social Services and Well-being (Wales) Act 2014 s 56.

13 Care and Support (Disputes Between Local Authorities) Regulations 2014, SI 2014/2829, reg 2(6); Care and Support (Disputes about Ordinary Residence, etc) (Wales) Regulations 2015, SI 2015/1494, reg 2(6).

98. Resolution of dispute by dialogue between authorities. As soon as reasonably practicable after the date on which the dispute arises[1] and prior to the referral of the dispute[2] the lead authority[3] must seek to identify all the other authorities[4] concerned in the dispute and co-ordinate discussions between those authorities in an attempt to resolve the dispute[5]. The lead authority must also, prior to the referral of the dispute:

(1)   co-ordinate the discharge, by the authorities, of their statutory[6] duties[7];

(2)   take steps to obtain from the other authorities information which may be relevant to the determination of the dispute[8];

(3)   disclose that information to the other authorities[9]; and

(4)   disclose to the other authorities any information the lead authority itself holds that may help to resolve the dispute[10].

The authorities must take all reasonable steps to resolve the dispute between themselves[11] and co-operate with each other in the discharge of their statutory duties[12]. Each of the authorities must:

(a)   engage in a constructive dialogue with the other authorities, with a view to bringing about the speedy resolution of the dispute[13];

(b)   comply, without delay, with any reasonable request for relevant information made by the lead authority[14]; and

(c)   keep the other authorities informed of any developments which appear to it to be relevant to the determination of the dispute[15].

Parties to the dispute must be kept informed of progress[16].

1   As to the disputes to which these provisions apply see PARA 96. As to the date on which the dispute arises see PARA 97 note 5.

2   As to the meaning of 'referred' see PARA 96 note 6. Disputes may be referred only of they have not been resolved by agreement four months after the date on which they arose: see the Care and Support (Disputes Between Local Authorities) Regulations 2014, SI 2014/2829, reg 3(7); the Care and Support (Disputes about Ordinary Residence, etc) (Wales) Regulations 2015, SI 2015/1494, reg 3(8); and PARA 96.

3   As to the meaning of 'the lead authority' see PARA 96 note 5.

4   As to the meaning of 'the authorities' see PARA 96 note 5.

5   Care and Support (Disputes Between Local Authorities) Regulations 2014, SI 2014/2829, reg 3(1), (2)(a); Care and Support (Disputes about Ordinary Residence, etc) (Wales) Regulations 2015, SI 2015/1494, reg 3(1), (2)(a). Each of the authorities must nominate an individual who will act as the point of contact within that authority in relation to the dispute, and provide the other authorities with the contact details of that individual: Care and Support (Disputes Between Local Authorities) Regulations 2014, SI 2014/2829, reg 3(2)(b); Care and Support (Disputes about Ordinary Residence, etc) (Wales) Regulations 2015, SI 2015/1494, reg 3(2)(b).

6   Ie duties under the Care and Support (Disputes Between Local Authorities) Regulations 2014, SI 2014/2829 or the Care and Support (Disputes about Ordinary Residence, etc) (Wales) Regulations 2015, SI 2015/1494, as the case may be.

7   Care and Support (Disputes Between Local Authorities) Regulations 2014, SI 2014/2829, reg 3(3)(a); Care and Support (Disputes about Ordinary Residence, etc) (Wales) Regulations 2015, SI 2015/1494, reg 3(3)(a).

8   Care and Support (Disputes Between Local Authorities) Regulations 2014, SI 2014/2829, reg 3(3)(b); Care and Support (Disputes about Ordinary Residence, etc) (Wales) Regulations 2015, SI 2015/1494, reg 3(3)(b).

9   Care and Support (Disputes Between Local Authorities) Regulations 2014, SI 2014/2829, reg 3(3)(c); Care and Support (Disputes about Ordinary Residence, etc) (Wales) Regulations 2015, SI 2015/1494, reg 3(3)(c).

10 Care and Support (Disputes Between Local Authorities) Regulations 2014, SI 2014/2829, reg 3(3)(d); Care and Support (Disputes about Ordinary Residence, etc) (Wales) Regulations 2015, SI 2015/1494, reg 3(3)(d).

11 Care and Support (Disputes Between Local Authorities) Regulations 2014, SI 2014/2829, reg 3(4)(a); Care and Support (Disputes about Ordinary Residence, etc) (Wales) Regulations 2015, SI 2015/1494, reg 3(4)(a).

12 Care and Support (Disputes Between Local Authorities) Regulations 2014, SI 2014/2829, reg 3(4)(b); Care and Support (Disputes about Ordinary Residence, etc) (Wales) Regulations 2015, SI 2015/1494, reg 3(4)(b).

13 Care and Support (Disputes Between Local Authorities) Regulations 2014, SI 2014/2829, reg 3(5)(a); Care and Support (Disputes about Ordinary Residence, etc) (Wales) Regulations 2015, SI 2015/1494, reg 3(5)(a).

14 Care and Support (Disputes Between Local Authorities) Regulations 2014, SI 2014/2829, reg 3(5)(b); Care and Support (Disputes about Ordinary Residence, etc) (Wales) Regulations 2015, SI 2015/1494, reg 3(5)(b).

15 Care and Support (Disputes Between Local Authorities) Regulations 2014, SI 2014/2829, reg 3(5)(c); Care and Support (Disputes about Ordinary Residence, etc) (Wales) Regulations 2015, SI 2015/1494, reg 3(5)(c).

16 In England, the lead authority must provide to the adult or carer to whom the dispute relates, or to that person's representatives, such information as appears to it to be appropriate about progress in resolving the dispute: Care and Support (Disputes Between Local Authorities) Regulations 2014, SI 2014/2829, reg 3(6). In Wales, the lead authority must provide to the person to whom the dispute relates, the carer of that person (if the dispute is about which authority is to meet the needs of a carer), and a representative of the person or carer, such information as appears to it to be appropriate about progress in resolving the dispute: Care and Support (Disputes about Ordinary Residence, etc) (Wales) Regulations 2015, SI 2015/1494, reg 3(6), (7). As to the 'person' to whom the dispute relates see PARA 97 note 3.

99. Review of determinations. Where the Secretary of State or an appointed person has made a determination[1] with respect to a dispute between local authorities in England, the Secretary of State or the appointed person may review that determination, provided that the review begins within three months of the date of the determination[2]. Where the Welsh Ministers or an appointed person has made a determination[3] with respect to a dispute between local authorities in Wales an authority may make a request to the Welsh Ministers, within three months of the date of the determination, to review the determination[4]. A review may also be carried out by the Welsh Ministers without a request having been made[5].

In either case, the Secretary of State (or the appointed person) or the Welsh Ministers may confirm the determination or substitute a different determination[6].

1   Ie under the Care Act 2014 s 40(1) (see PARA 96).
2   Care Act 2014 s 40(2).
3   Ie under the Social Services and Well-being (Wales) Act 2014 s 195(1) (see PARA 96).
4   Care and Support (Disputes about Ordinary Residence, etc) (Wales) Regulations 2015, SI 2015/1494, reg 7(1), (2).
5   Care and Support (Disputes about Ordinary Residence, etc) (Wales) Regulations 2015, SI 2015/1494, reg 7(3).
6   Care Act 2014 s 40(3); Care and Support (Disputes about Ordinary Residence, etc) (Wales) Regulations 2015, SI 2015/1494, reg 7(4). Where a review of a determination has been carried out in accordance with the Care Act 2014 s 40(2) or the Care and Support (Disputes about Ordinary Residence, etc) (Wales) Regulations 2015, SI 2015/1494, reg 7, and a different determination substituted, in consequence of the first determination a local authority ('A') has paid an amount to another local authority ('B'), and the effect of the second determination is that some or all of the amount paid by A to B was not required to have been paid, B must repay to A the sum that was not required to have been paid: Care and Support (Disputes Between Local Authorities) Regulations 2014, SI 2014/2829, reg 7; Care and Support (Disputes about Ordinary Residence, etc) (Wales) Regulations 2015, SI 2015/1494, reg 8.

(8) INDEPENDENT ADVOCACY

(i) England

100. Role of independent advocate. Where a local authority in England[1] is required[2] to involve an individual in its exercise of a function[3], and the authority considers that, were a person who is independent of the authority (an 'independent advocate') not to be available, the individual would be disadvantaged in his dealing with the authority[4], the authority must arrange for an independent advocate to be available to represent and support the individual for the purpose of facilitating the individual's involvement[5].

Where a local authority has arranged for an independent advocate it must, in exercising any assessment or planning function:

(1)   take into account any representations the independent advocate makes on behalf of the individual[6] in question in relation to its exercise of that function or the impact of such exercise on the individual[7]; and

(2)   take reasonable steps to assist the independent advocate to represent and support the individual[8].

There are certain circumstances in which the duty to make independent advocacy available does not apply[9], and provision is made in connection with the requirements a person must comply with in order to be an independent advocate[10], the manner in which independent advocates are to carry out their functions[11], and the provision of independent advocacy in cases involving combined assessments[12].

1   As to the meaning of 'local authority' see PARA 1. As to the social services functions of local authorities in England generally, and the overarching principles in accordance with which functions relating to the provision of care and support must be exercised, see PARAS 315–323.
2   Ie by the Care Act 2014 s 9(5)(a), (b) (carrying out needs assessment: see PARA 9), s 10(7)(a) (carrying out carer's assessment: see PARA 34), s 25(3)(a), (b) (preparing care and support plan: see

PARA 79), s 25(4)(a), (b) (preparing support plan: see PARA 79), s 27(2)(b)(i), (ii) (revising care and support plan: see PARA 80), s 27(3)(b)(i), (ii) (revising support plan: see PARA 80), s 59(2)(a), (b) (carrying out child's needs assessment: see PARA 23), s 61(3)(a) (carrying out child's carer's assessment: see PARA 43) or s 64(3)(a), (b) (carrying out young carer's assessment: see PARA 51) (a 'relevant provision'): s 67(3)(a)–(i).

3 Care Act 2014 s 67(1).

4 Ie, absent the assistance of an independent advocate, the individual would experience substantial difficulty in doing one or more of understanding relevant information (Care Act 2014 s 67(4)(a)), retaining that information (s 67(4)(b)), using or weighing that information as part of the process of being involved (s 67(4)(c)) and communicating his views, wishes or feelings (whether by talking, using sign language or any other means) (s 67(4)(d)). In deciding whether an individual would experience substantial difficulty of the kind mentioned in s 67(4), a local authority must have regard to:

   (1)   any health condition the individual has (Care and Support (Independent Advocacy Support) (No 2) Regulations 2014, SI 2014/2889, reg 3(a)) (made under the Care Act 2014 s 67(7)(b), (c));
   (2)   any learning difficulty the individual has (Care and Support (Independent Advocacy Support) (No 2) Regulations 2014, SI 2014/2889, reg 3(b));
   (3)   any disability the individual has (reg 3(c));
   (4)   the degree of complexity of the individual's circumstances, whether in relation to the individual's needs for care and support or otherwise (reg 3(d));
   (5)   where the assessment or planning function is the carrying out of an assessment, whether the individual has previously refused an assessment (reg 3(e)); and
   (6)   whether the individual is experiencing, or at risk of, abuse or neglect (reg 3(f)).

   'Assessment or planning function' means a function, in the exercise of which a local authority is required by a relevant provision (see note 2) to involve an individual: reg 1(2). As to assessments see PARAS 64–72. As to the meaning of 'abuse' see PARA 8 note 12.

   The Care and Support (Independent Advocacy Support) (No 2) Regulations 2014, SI 2014/2889, apply to the exercise of the power to meet a child's carer's needs for support under the Care Act 2014 s 62(1) (see PARA 44) in so far as they apply to the exercise of the power to meet a carer's needs for support under s 20(6) (see PARA 37): Care and Support (Children's Carer's) Regulations 2015, SI 2015/305, reg 2(3)(a).

5 Care Act 2014 s 67(2). Section 67 does not restrict the provision that may be made under any other provision of the Care Act 2014: s 67(8). A local authority may make reasonable requests for information in connection with the performance of an independent advocate's functions and the independent advocate must comply with such requests: Care and Support (Independent Advocacy Support) (No 2) Regulations 2014, SI 2014/2889, reg 6(3).

6 'The individual' refers to the individual in relation to whom the duty under the Care Act 2014 s 67(2) would apply but for the exception in s 67(5) (see PARA 101): Care and Support (Independent Advocacy Support) (No 2) Regulations 2014, SI 2014/2889, reg 4(4).

7 Care and Support (Independent Advocacy Support) (No 2) Regulations 2014, SI 2014/2889, reg 6(1)(a).

8 Care and Support (Independent Advocacy Support) (No 2) Regulations 2014, SI 2014/2889, reg 6(1)(b).

9 See PARA 101.

10 See PARA 102.

11 See PARA 103.

12 See PARA 66.

101. Circumstances in which duty to make arrangements for independent advocacy does not apply.

The duty imposed on a local authority[1] to arrange for an independent advocate[2] to be made available to a person who would otherwise be disadvantaged in his dealings with the authority[3] does not apply if the authority is satisfied that there is a person who would be an appropriate person[4] to represent and support the individual for the purpose of facilitating the individual's involvement[5] and who is not engaged in providing care or treatment for the individual in a professional capacity or for remuneration[6]. This exception, however, does not apply if:

   (1)   the exercise of the assessment or planning function[7] in relation to the individual[8] is likely to result in an NHS body[9] making arrangements for the provision to that individual of accommodation in a hospital[10] for a

period of 28 days or more[11] or a care home[12] for a period of 8 weeks or more[13], and the local authority is satisfied that it would be in the best interests of the individual to make arrangements for independent advocacy[14] in relation to that individual[15]; or

(2)   there is disagreement on a material issue between the authority and the appropriate person[16] in the case of the individual[17] and the authority and that person agree that making arrangements for independent advocacy in relation to the individual would be in the best interests of that individual[18].

1   As to the meaning of 'local authority' see PARA 1. As to the social services functions of local authorities in England generally, and the overarching principles in accordance with which functions relating to the provision of care and support must be exercised, see PARAS 315–323.
2   As to the meaning of 'independent advocate' and the scope of the provision of independent advocacy see PARA 100.
3   Ie the duty under the Care Act 2014 s 67(2): see PARA 100.
4   For these purposes a person is not to be regarded as an 'appropriate person' unless:
    (1)   where the individual has capacity or is competent to consent to being represented and supported by that person, the individual does so consent (Care Act 2014 s 67(6)(a)); or
    (2)   where the individual lacks capacity or is not competent so to consent, the local authority is satisfied that being represented and supported by that person would be in the individual's best interests (s 67(6)(b)).
    As to having or lacking capacity see PARA 8 note 10.
5   Care Act 2014 s 67(5)(a).
6   Care Act 2014 s 67(5)(b).
7   As to the meaning of 'assessment or planning function' see PARA 100 note 4.
8   As to the meaning of 'the individual' see PARA 100 note 6.
9   'NHS body' means the National Health Service Commissioning Board (see HEALTH SERVICES vol 54 (2017) PARA 32), a clinical commissioning group (see HEALTH SERVICES vol 54 (2017) PARA 35 et seq) or a NHS trust or foundation trust (see HEALTH SERVICES vol 54 (2017) PARAS 235, 244): Care and Support (Independent Advocacy Support) (No 2) Regulations 2014, SI 2014/2889, reg 4(4).
10 'Hospital' means (by virtue of the Care and Support (Independent Advocacy Support) (No 2) Regulations 2014, SI 2014/2889, reg 4(4)):
    (1)   any institution for the reception and treatment of persons suffering from illness;
    (2)   any maternity home; or
    (3)   any institution for the reception and treatment of persons during convalescence or persons requiring medical rehabilitation;
11 Care and Support (Independent Advocacy Support) (No 2) Regulations 2014, SI 2014/2889, reg 4(1), (2)(a)(i).
12 'Care home' means a care home (within the meaning given in the Care Standards Act 2000 s 3: see PARA 3 note 3) in respect of a which a person is registered under the Health and Social Care Act 2008 for the regulated activity of the provision of residential accommodation together with nursing or personal care: Care and Support (Independent Advocacy Support) (No 2) Regulations 2014, SI 2014/2889, reg 4(4).
13 Care and Support (Independent Advocacy Support) (No 2) Regulations 2014, SI 2014/2889, reg 4(2)(a)(ii).
14 Ie arrangements under the Care Act 2014 s 67(2).
15 Care and Support (Independent Advocacy Support) (No 2) Regulations 2014, SI 2014/2889, reg 4(2)(b).
16 Ie the person referred to in the Care Act 2014 s 67(5).
17 Care and Support (Independent Advocacy Support) (No 2) Regulations 2014, SI 2014/2889, reg 4(3)(a).
18 Care and Support (Independent Advocacy Support) (No 2) Regulations 2014, SI 2014/2889, reg 4(3)(b).

102.   Requirements a person must comply with in order to be an independent advocate. A local authority[1] must not make arrangements for a person to be an independent advocate[2] unless the authority is satisfied that the person:
    (1)   has appropriate experience[3];
    (2)   has undertaken appropriate training[4];

(3)   is competent to represent and support the individual[5] for the purpose of facilitating that individual's involvement in any assessment and planning function[6];

(4)   has integrity and is of good character[7]; and

(5)   has arrangements in place to receive appropriate supervision[8].

A local authority must not make arrangements for a person to be an independent advocate where that person is engaged in providing care or treatment in a professional capacity, or for remuneration:

(a)   for the individual to whom representation and support are to be made available[9]; or

(b)   for that individual's carer[10], where the individual is an adult[11] with care and support needs[12], or the adult in respect of whom that individual is providing care, where the individual is a carer[13].

The requirements that must be met for a person to be 'independent' for these purposes are that:

(i)   the local authority[14] is satisfied that the person demonstrates the ability to act independently of the local authority[15]; and

(ii)   the person is not employed by, or otherwise working for, the local authority[16].

1   As to the meaning of 'local authority' see PARA 1. As to the social services functions of local authorities in England generally, and the overarching principles in accordance with which functions relating to the provision of care and support must be exercised, see PARAS 315–323.

2   Ie under the Care Act 2014 s 67(2): see PARA 100 (meaning of 'independent advocate' and scope of the provision of independent advocacy).

3   Care and Support (Independent Advocacy Support) (No 2) Regulations 2014, SI 2014/2889, reg 2(1)(a) (made under the Care Act 2014 s 67(7)(a)).

4   Care and Support (Independent Advocacy Support) (No 2) Regulations 2014, SI 2014/2889, reg 2(1)(b).

5   As to the meaning of 'the individual' see PARA 100 note 6.

6   Care and Support (Independent Advocacy Support) (No 2) Regulations 2014, SI 2014/2889, reg 2(1)(c). As to the meaning of 'assessment or planning function' see PARA 100 note 4.

7   Care and Support (Independent Advocacy Support) (No 2) Regulations 2014, SI 2014/2889, reg 2(1)(d). Before deciding whether a person has integrity and is of good character as mentioned in reg 2(1)(d), the authority must obtain, in respect of that person, an enhanced criminal record certificate issued under the Police Act 1997 s 113B (see SENTENCING vol 92 (2015) PARAS 640–642) which includes:

    (1)   where the individual to whom representation and support are being made available is under 18 years of age, suitability information relating to children (within the meaning of s 113BA: see SENTENCING vol 92 (2015) PARA 638) (Care and Support (Independent Advocacy Support) (No 2) Regulations 2014, SI 2014/2889, reg 2(4)(a)); and

    (2)   where the individual to whom representation and support are being made available is 18 years of age or older, suitability information relating to vulnerable adults (within the meaning of the Police Act 1997 s 113BB: see SENTENCING vol 92 (2015) PARA 638) (Care and Support (Independent Advocacy Support) (No 2) Regulations 2014, SI 2014/2889, reg 2(4)(b)).

8   Care and Support (Independent Advocacy Support) (No 2) Regulations 2014, SI 2014/2889, reg 2(1)(e).

9   Care and Support (Independent Advocacy Support) (No 2) Regulations 2014, SI 2014/2889, reg 2(2)(a).

10   As to the meaning of 'carer' see PARA 33 note 2.

11   As to the meaning of 'adult' see PARA 1 note 1.

12   Care and Support (Independent Advocacy Support) (No 2) Regulations 2014, SI 2014/2889, reg 2(2)(b)(i).

13   Care and Support (Independent Advocacy Support) (No 2) Regulations 2014, SI 2014/2889, reg 2(2)(b)(ii).

14   Where a local authority has made arrangements with any other person for that person to carry out the assessment or planning function on the local authority's behalf, the references in the Care and Support (Independent Advocacy Support) (No 2) Regulations 2014, SI 2014/2889, reg 2(3)(a), (b) to a local authority include a reference to that other person: reg 2(5).

15 Care and Support (Independent Advocacy Support) (No 2) Regulations 2014, SI 2014/2889, reg 2(3)(a).
16 Care and Support (Independent Advocacy Support) (No 2) Regulations 2014, SI 2014/2889, reg 2(3)(b).

103. Manner in which independent advocates are to carry out their functions. In performing his functions an independent advocate[1] must determine in all the circumstances how best to represent and support the individual[2] in question but at all times must act with a view to promoting the individual's well-being[3]. In particular, an independent advocate must, to the extent that it is practicable and appropriate to do so:

(1)   meet the individual in private[4]; and
(2)   provided that the individual's capacity allows[5], with a view to promoting the individual's well-being, consult with persons who are, or have been, engaged in providing care or treatment for the individual in a professional capacity or for remuneration[6] and other persons who may be in a position to comment on the individual's wishes, beliefs or values, for example family members, carers or friends of the individual[7].

In particular, an independent advocate must:

(a)   assist the individual in understanding the function in the exercise of which the individual is involved[8], communicating the individual's views, wishes or feelings[9], understanding how the individual's care and support, or support, needs could be met by the local authority or otherwise[10], making decisions in respect of care and support arrangements[11] and challenging the local authority's decisions if the individual so wishes[12];
(b)   so far as is practicable, ensure that the individual understands the local authority's duties relating to the provision of care and support for adults and adult carers[13] and the individual's corresponding rights and obligations[14] and any other rights and obligations of the individual which may be relevant to those obligations[15];
(c)   make such representations as are necessary for the purpose of securing the individual's rights in relation to the exercise of the function[16]; and
(d)   where the independent advocate has concerns about the manner in which the assessment or planning function[17] has been exercised or the outcomes arising from it, prepare a report for the local authority outlining those concerns[18].

In particular, an independent advocate may examine and take copies of any relevant records[19] relating to the individual in circumstances where:

(i)   the individual has capacity, or is competent, to consent to the records being made available to the independent advocate and does so consent[20]; or
(ii)   the individual does not have capacity, or is not competent, to consent to the records being made available to the independent advocate but the independent advocate considers it is in the best interests of the individual[21].

Where the individual does not have capacity, or is not competent, to communicate his or her views, wishes or feelings, the independent advocate must do so to the extent the independent advocate can ascertain them[22]; and where the individual does not have capacity, or is not competent, to challenge a decision made in the exercise of the assessment or planning function, the independent advocate must challenge the decision if the independent advocate considers the decision to be inconsistent with the authority's general duty[23] to promote the individual's well-being[24].

1   As to the meaning of 'independent advocate', the circumstances in which an independent advocate will be required and the scope of the provision of independent advocacy see PARA 100; as to the requirements a person must comply with in order to be an independent advocate see PARA 102.
2   As to the meaning of 'the individual' see PARA 100 note 6.
3   Care and Support (Independent Advocacy Support) (No 2) Regulations 2014, SI 2014/2889, reg 5(1), (2) (made under the Care Act 2014 s 67(7)(d), (f)). As to the meaning of 'well-being' see PARA 317.
4   Care and Support (Independent Advocacy Support) (No 2) Regulations 2014, SI 2014/2889, reg 5(3)(a).
5   Ie provided that:
    (1)   the individual has capacity, or is competent, to consent to the independent advocate consulting with a person mentioned in the Care and Support (Independent Advocacy Support) (No 2) Regulations 2014, SI 2014/2889, reg 5(3)(b) (see the text and notes 6–7), and does so consent (reg 5(4)(a)); or
    (2)   the individual does not have capacity, or is not competent, so to consent but the independent advocate is satisfied that consulting with a person mentioned in reg 5(3)(b) would be in the individual's best interests (reg 5(4)(b)).
    As to having or lacking capacity see PARA 8 note 10.
6   Care and Support (Independent Advocacy Support) (No 2) Regulations 2014, SI 2014/2889, reg 5(3)(b)(i).
7   Care and Support (Independent Advocacy Support) (No 2) Regulations 2014, SI 2014/2889, reg 5(3)(b)(ii).
8   Care and Support (Independent Advocacy Support) (No 2) Regulations 2014, SI 2014/2889, reg 5(5)(a)(i).
9   Care and Support (Independent Advocacy Support) (No 2) Regulations 2014, SI 2014/2889, reg 5(5)(a)(ii).
10 Care and Support (Independent Advocacy Support) (No 2) Regulations 2014, SI 2014/2889, reg 5(5)(a)(iii). As to the meaning of 'local authority' see PARA 1. As to the social services functions of local authorities in England generally, and the overarching principles in accordance with which functions relating to the provision of care and support must be exercised, see PARAS 315–323.
11 Care and Support (Independent Advocacy Support) (No 2) Regulations 2014, SI 2014/2889, reg 5(5)(a)(iv).
12 Care and Support (Independent Advocacy Support) (No 2) Regulations 2014, SI 2014/2889, reg 5(5)(a)(v).
13 Ie the authority's duties under the Care Act 2014 Pt 1 (ss 1–80).
14 Ie the individual's corresponding rights and obligations under the Care Act 2014 Pt 1 (ss 1–80).
15 Care and Support (Independent Advocacy Support) (No 2) Regulations 2014, SI 2014/2889, reg 5(5)(b).
16 Care and Support (Independent Advocacy Support) (No 2) Regulations 2014, SI 2014/2889, reg 5(5)(c).
17 As to the meaning of 'assessment or planning function' see PARA 100 note 4.
18 Care and Support (Independent Advocacy Support) (No 2) Regulations 2014, SI 2014/2889, reg 5(5)(d). A local authority must provide an independent advocate with a written response to any report prepared for the authority by the advocate under reg 5(5)(d): reg 6(2).
19 'Relevant record' means:
    (1)   a health record (within the meaning given in the Data Protection Act 1998 s 68 (as read with s 69) (see CONFIDENCE AND INFORMATIONAL PRIVACY vol 19 (2011) PARAS 30, 97) (Care Act 2014 s 67(9)(a));
    (2)   a record of, or held by, a local authority and compiled in connection with a function under the Care Act 2014 Pt 1 or a social services function (within the meaning given in the Local Authority Social Services Act 1970 s 1A: see PARA 315) (Care Act 2014 s 67(9)(b));
    (3)   a record held by a person registered under the Care Standards Act 2000 Pt 2 (ss 11–42: see CHILDREN AND YOUNG PERSONS vol 10 (2017) PARA 1017 et seq) or the Health and Social Care Act 2008 Pt 1 Ch 2 (ss 8–44: see PARAS 152–165) (Care Act 2014 s 67(9)(c)); or
    (4)   a record of such other description as may be specified in regulations (Care Act 2014 s 67(9)(d)).

At the date at which this volume states the law no additional description of record had been prescribed.

20 Care and Support (Independent Advocacy Support) (No 2) Regulations 2014, SI 2014/2889, reg 5(6)(a).
21 Care and Support (Independent Advocacy Support) (No 2) Regulations 2014, SI 2014/2889, reg 5(6)(b).
22 Care and Support (Independent Advocacy Support) (No 2) Regulations 2014, SI 2014/2889, reg 5(7).
23 Ie the authority's duty under the Care Act 2014 s 1 (see PARA 317).
24 Care and Support (Independent Advocacy Support) (No 2) Regulations 2014, SI 2014/2889, reg 5(8).

(ii) Wales

104. Provision of advocacy services. Regulations may require a local authority in Wales[1] to arrange for advocacy services[2] to be made available to people with needs for care and support[3] (whether or not those needs are being met by a local authority)[4]. Such regulations may not, however, require advocacy services to be made available to a person:

(1)   for the purpose of making a complaint in respect of which a local authority is required[5] to make arrangements for the provision of assistance to the person[6];

(2)   for the purpose of making representations in respect of which a local authority is required[7] to make arrangements for the provision of assistance to the person[8];

(3)   for purposes in respect of which the Welsh Ministers[9] are required[10] to make arrangements to enable an independent mental health advocate to be available[11];

(4)   for purposes in respect of which a local authority is required[12] to make arrangements for the provision of independent advocacy services[13];

(5)   for purposes in respect of which the Welsh Ministers are required[14] to make arrangements to enable an independent mental capacity advocate to be available[15];

(6)   for the purpose of making a complaint in respect of which the Welsh Ministers are required[16] to arrange for the provision of independent advocacy services[17].

1   As to the meaning of 'local authority' see PARA 2. As to the social services functions of local authorities in Wales generally, and the overarching principles in accordance with which functions relating to the provision of care and support must be exercised, see PARAS 373–383.
2   'Advocacy services' are services which provide assistance (by way of representation or otherwise) to persons for purposes relating to their care and support: Social Services and Well-being (Wales) Act 2014 s 181(2).
3   As to the meanings of 'care' and 'support' see PARA 2 note 1.
4   Social Services and Well-being (Wales) Act 2014 s 181(1). The regulations may specify:
    (1)   the persons, or description of persons, to whom advocacy services are to be made available (s 181(3)(a));
    (2)   the circumstances in which advocacy services are to be made available (s 181(3)(b)); and
    (3)   the persons, or description of persons, by whom advocacy services may, or may not, be provided (s 181(3)(c)),
    and must require a local authority to give publicity to its arrangements for making advocacy services available (s 181(4)).
5   Ie by virtue of regulations under the Social Services and Well-being (Wales) Act 2014 s 173 (assistance for complainants: see PARA 391).
6   Social Services and Well-being (Wales) Act 2014 s 182(1)(a).
7   Ie by virtue of regulations under the Social Services and Well-being (Wales) Act 2014 s 178 (assistance for persons making representations).
8   Social Services and Well-being (Wales) Act 2014 s 182(1)(b).

9 As to the Welsh Ministers see PARA 395.
10 Ie under the Mental Health Act 1983 s 130E: see MENTAL HEALTH AND CAPACITY vol 75 (2013) PARA 807.
11 Social Services and Well-being (Wales) Act 2014 s 182(1)(c).
12 Ie under the Education Act 1996 s 332BB (see EDUCATION vol 36 (2015) PARA 1031) or the Equality Act 2010 Sch 17 para 6D (see DISCRIMINATION vol 33 (2013) PARA 343).
13 Social Services and Well-being (Wales) Act 2014 s 182(1)(d).
14 Ie under the Mental Capacity Act 2005 s 35 (see MENTAL HEALTH AND CAPACITY vol 75 (2013) PARA 635).
15 Social Services and Well-being (Wales) Act 2014 s 182(1)(e).
16 Ie under the National Health Service (Wales) Act 2006 s 187 (HEALTH SERVICES vol 54A (2017) PARA 660).
17 Social Services and Well-being (Wales) Act 2014 s 182(1)(f).

2. FINANCING THE PROVISION OF CARE

(1) CARE PROVIDED BY LOCAL AUTHORITIES

(i) England

A. LIMIT ON LOCAL AUTHORITY LIABILITY FOR COSTS

105. Local authority not liable for costs in respect of adult or carer whose financial resources exceed £23,250. If the financial resources[1] of an adult[2] who is a permanent resident[3] in a care home exceed £23,250, a local authority in England[4] is not permitted to pay towards the cost of the provision of accommodation in a care home for that adult[5]. If the financial resources[6] of an adult who has needs for care and support other than as a permanent resident exceed £23,250, the local authority may (but need not) pay towards the cost of that care and support[7]. If the financial resources[8] of a carer[9] whose needs involve the provision of support exceed £23,250, the local authority may (but need not) pay towards the cost of the provision of that support for the carer[10]. The amount of £23,250 is referred to[11] as the 'financial limit'[12], and is susceptible to periodic review by the Secretary of State[13].

1 Ie in terms of capital: Care and Support (Charging and Assessment of Resources) Regulations 2014, SI 2014/2672, reg 12(1)–(3) (made under the Care Act 2014 s 17(7)–(10)).
2 As to the meaning of 'adult' see PARA 1 note 1. As to the means of assessment of a person's financial resources see PARAS 119–120.
3 'Permanent resident' means a resident who is not a temporary resident or a short-term resident; 'resident' means a person who is provided with accommodation in a care home under the Care Act 2014; 'temporary resident' means a resident whose stay is unlikely to exceed 52 weeks or in exceptional circumstances, unlikely to substantially exceed that period; 'short-term resident' means a person who is provided with accommodation in a care home under the Care Act 2014 for a period not exceeding 8 weeks; and 'care home' means a care home (within the meaning given the Care Standards Act 2000 s 3: see PARA 3 note 3) in respect of which a person is registered under the Health and Social Care Act 2008 for the regulated activity of the provision of residential accommodation together with nursing or personal care: Care and Support (Charging and Assessment of Resources) Regulations 2014, SI 2014/2672, reg 2(1).
4 As to the meaning of 'local authority' see PARA 1.
5 Care and Support (Charging and Assessment of Resources) Regulations 2014, SI 2014/2672, reg 12(1). In connection with local authority payments for care see PARAS 106–110 (direct payments) and PARAS 113–116 (deferred payments and loans).
6 See note 1.
7 Care and Support (Charging and Assessment of Resources) Regulations 2014, SI 2014/2672, reg 12(2).
8 See note 1.
9 As to the meaning of 'carer' see PARA 33 note 2.
10 Care and Support (Charging and Assessment of Resources) Regulations 2014, SI 2014/2672, reg 12(3).
11 Ie for the purposes of the Care Act 2014 Pt 1 (ss 1–80).
12 Care Act 2014 s 17(10).
13 As from a day to be appointed the Secretary of State must review the level at which the financial limit is for the time being set under the Care and Support (Charging and Assessment of Resources) Regulations 2014, SI 2014/2672: Care Act 2014 s 71(1)(c) (not yet in force). In carrying out a review under s 71 the Secretary of State must have regard to:
    (1)   the financial burden on the state of each of those matters being at the level in question (s 71(2)(a) (not yet in force));
    (2)   the financial burden on local authorities of each of those matters being at the level in question (s 71(2)(b) (not yet in force));
    (3)   the financial burden on adults who have needs for care and support of each of those matters being at the level in question (s 71(2)(c) (not yet in force));

(4)   the length of time for which people can reasonably be expected to live in good health (s 71(2)(d) (not yet in force));

(5)   changes in the ways or circumstances in which adults' needs for care and support are being or are likely to be met (s 71(2)(e) (not yet in force));

(6)   changes in the prevalence of conditions for which the provision of care and support is or is likely to be required (s 71(2)(f) (not yet in force)); and

(7)   such other factors as the Secretary of State considers relevant (s 71(2)(g) (not yet in force)).

At the date at which this volume states the law no such day had been appointed. The Secretary of State must prepare and publish a report on the outcome of the review: s 71(3) (not yet in force). The first report must be published before the end of the period of five years beginning with the day on which s 15 (the cap on care costs: see PARA 112) comes into force (s 71(4) (not yet in force)), and each subsequent report must be published before the end of the period of five years beginning with the day on which the previous report was published (s 71(5) (not yet in force)). The Secretary of State may arrange for some other person to carry out the whole or part of a review under s 71 on the Secretary of State's behalf: s 71(6) (not yet in force). The Secretary of State must lay before Parliament a report prepared under s 71: s 71(7) (not yet in force). As to the Secretary of State see PARA 333.

B.   DIRECT PAYMENTS

106.   Duty to make direct payments on request. Local authorities in England[1] are required to make direct payments[2] towards the cost of meeting an adult's care needs[3], provided that the authority is satisfied that making such payments[4] is an appropriate way to meet those needs[5] and that the recipient[6] is capable[7] of managing such payments[8], and provided also that the adult in question is not subject to certain drug or alcohol treatment requirements[9]. Additional conditions are imposed in respect of adults who lack capacity[10]. All the conditions (ie Conditions 1 to 4 in the case of a person having capacity and Conditions 1 to 5 in the case of a person lacking capacity) must be met in order for the duty to make payments to arise[11], and if one or more of the applicable conditions is no longer met the authority must terminate the making of direct payments[12]. Where the adult has capacity, payments are made to him or to a nominated person; where the adult lacks capacity payments are made to the authorised person[13]. The duty to make payments is triggered on request[14], and the payments themselves are made subject to conditions[15].

A local authority may not make a direct payment for the provision of accommodation in a care home[16] for an adult for a period of more than four consecutive weeks in any 12 month period[17].

1   As to the meaning of 'local authority' see PARA 1. Provision for the care and support of children in England is made by the Children Act 1989 (see PARA 21) and not by the Care Act 2014 Pt 1 (ss 1–80), and accordingly the Care Act 2014 makes no corresponding provision for children.

2   Ie payments under the Care Act 2014 s 31 or s 32: ss 31(3), 32(3).

3   Ie the needs to which an adult's personal budget relates: Care Act 2014 ss 31(1)(a), 32(1)(a). As to the meaning of 'adult' see PARA 1 note 1. As to the meaning of 'personal budget' see PARA 121.

4   See the text and note 12.

5   Care Act 2014 ss 31(7), 32(9). This condition is 'Condition 4' in relation to a person having capacity and 'Condition 5' in relation to a person lacking capacity: ss 31(7), 32(9). As to having or lacking capacity see PARA 8 note 10. These conditions being no longer met is grounds for a review of direct payments: see Care and Support (Direct Payments) Regulations 2014, SI 2014/2871, reg 7(1)(c)(ii), (d)(iii); and PARA 110.

A local authority must take the following steps before it can be satisfied that condition 5 in relation to a person lacking capacity (ie in the Care Act 2014 s 32) is met:

(1)   so far as is reasonably practicable and appropriate, consult and take into account the views of anyone named by the adult as someone to be consulted on the matter of whether direct payments should be made to the authorised person, anyone engaged in caring for the adult or interested in the adult's welfare and any person who is authorised under the Mental Capacity Act 2005 (see MENTAL HEALTH AND CAPACITY) to make

decisions about the adult's needs for care and support (Care and Support (Direct Payments) Regulations 2014, SI 2014/2871, reg 5(1), (2)(a) (made under the Care Act 2014 s 33(1), (2)(d))); and

(2)   so far as is reasonably ascertainable, consider the adult's past and present wishes and feelings (and, in particular, any relevant written statement made by the adult when the adult had capacity to request the local authority to meet his or her needs by making direct payments), the beliefs and values that would be likely to influence the adult's decision if the adult had such capacity, and other relevant factors that the adult would be likely to consider if he or she were able to do so (Care and Support (Direct Payments) Regulations 2014, SI 2014/2871, reg 5(2)(b)); and

(3)   obtain an enhanced criminal record certificate issued under the Police Act 1997 s 113B (see SENTENCING vol 92 (2015) PARAS 640–642) in respect of the authorised person (see note 12) if he or she is an individual who is neither family member (ie a person mentioned in the Care and Support (Direct Payments) Regulations 2014, SI 2014/2871, reg 3(3): see PARA 109 note 2) nor a friend of the adult who is involved in the provision of care for the adult, and (in a case where the authorised person is a body corporate or an unincorporated body of persons) in respect of the individual who will, on behalf of that body, have overall responsibility for the day to day management of the adult's direct payments (reg 5(2)(c)).

6   See the text and note 12.
7   Ie either by himself (Care Act 2014 ss 31(6)(a), 32(8)(a)) or with whatever help the authority thinks the adult, the nominated person or the authorised person, as the case may be (see note 12) will be able to access (ss 31(6)(b), 32(8)(b)).
8   Care Act 2014 ss 31(6), 32(8). This condition is 'Condition 3' in relation to a person having capacity and 'Condition 4' in relation to a person lacking capacity: ss 31(6), 32(8). These conditions being no longer met is grounds for a review of direct payments: see Care and Support (Direct Payments) Regulations 2014, SI 2014/2871, reg 7(1)(c)(ii), (d)(iii); and PARA 110.
9   See the Care Act 2014 ss 31(5), 32(6); the Care and Support (Direct Payments) Regulations 2014, SI 2014/2871, reg 2, Sch 1; and PARA 107.
10 See the Care Act 2014 s 32(5), (7); and PARA 108.
11 Care Act 2014 ss 31(2), 32(2).
12 Care Act 2014 s 33(4). For the purpose of ascertaining whether s 33(4) applies, an adult who lacks capacity to request the making of direct payments may nonetheless be regarded by a local authority as having capacity to do so where:

(1)   the authority is satisfied that the adult's lack of capacity to make the request is temporary (Care and Support (Direct Payments) Regulations 2014, SI 2014/2871, reg 8(1), (2)(a) (made under the Care Act 2014 s 33(2)(e))); and

(2)   another person who appears to the authority to be capable of managing a direct payment is prepared to accept and manage such payments on behalf of the adult during the period of the adult's incapacity (Care and Support (Direct Payments) Regulations 2014, SI 2014/2871, reg 8(2)(b)).

13 Care Act 2014 ss 31(2), (6), (7), 32(2), (8), (9). Where an adult has capacity to make a request for payments (s 31(4)(a)) and there is a nominated person, that person agreeing to receive the payments (s 31(4)(b)) is 'Condition 1' in relation to such payments. A person is 'authorised' for the purposes of s 32 if:

(1)   he is authorised under the Mental Capacity Act 2005 to make decisions about the adult's needs for care and support (Care Act 2014 s 32(4)(a));

(2)   where he is not so authorised, a person who is so authorised agrees with the local authority that the person is a suitable person to whom to make direct payments (s 32(4)(b)); or

(3)   where he is not so authorised and there is no person who is so authorised, the local authority considers that the person is a suitable person to whom to make direct payments (s 32(4)(c)).

14 Where:

(1)   a personal budget for an adult specifies an amount which a local authority in England must pay towards the cost of meeting the needs to which the personal budget relates (Care Act 2014 ss 31(1)(a), 32(1)(a)); and

(2)   either the adult (having capacity) requests the authority to meet some or all of those needs by making payments to him or a person nominated by him (s 31(1)(b)), or (the adult lacking capacity to make such request (s 32(1)(b))) an authorised person requests the authority to meet some or all of those needs by making payments to the authorised person (s 32(2)(c)),

the authority must, where the applicable Conditions are satisfied (see the text and note 11) and subject to the Care and Support (Direct Payments) Regulations 2014, SI 2014/2871 (see PARAS 106–110), make the payments to which the request relates (Care Act 2014 ss 31(2), 32(2)).

For the purpose of ascertaining whether s 32(1)(b) ceases to apply, an adult who no longer lacks capacity to request the making of direct payments may nonetheless be regarded by a local authority as lacking capacity to do so where:

(a)   the authority is satisfied that the adult's capacity to request the authority to meet the needs to which the adult's personal budget relates by making a direct payment is temporary (Care and Support (Direct Payments) Regulations 2014, SI 2014/2871, reg 9(1), (2)(a) (made under the Care Act 2014 s 33(2)(f))); and

(b)   the direct payments made during the period that the adult has the capacity to make such a request are made subject to an additional condition that the authorised person shall allow the adult to manage the direct payments themselves for any period in respect of which the authority is satisfied that the adult has the capacity to request the making of direct payments (Care and Support (Direct Payments) Regulations 2014, SI 2014/2871, reg 9(2)(b)).

15 See PARA 109.

16 As to the meaning of 'care home' in this context see the Care Standards Act 2000 s 3; and PARA 3 note 3 (definition applied by the Care and Support (Direct Payments) Regulations 2014, SI 2014/2871, reg 6(1)). In calculating this period of 4 weeks a period of accommodation in a care home of less than 4 weeks must be added to any succeeding period in such accommodation where the two periods are separated by a period of less than 4 weeks but not otherwise: reg 6(2). This restriction does not apply to the following local authorities: Bristol City Council; Cornwall Council; Gateshead Council; Hertfordshire County Council; Hull City Council; Lincolnshire County Council; the London Boroughs of Enfield and Redbridge; Milton Keynes Council; Norfolk County Council; North Lincolnshire Council; Nottinghamshire County Council; Stockport Council; Surrey County Council: Sch 2 (amended by SI 2015/644; SI 2016/167).

17 Care and Support (Direct Payments) Regulations 2014, SI 2014/2871, reg 6(1).

107. No duty to make payments in respect of persons subject to drug or alcohol treatment orders or detained persons. A local authority in England must not meet needs by making a direct payment[1] if the adult whose needs are to be met is:

(1)   subject to a drug rehabilitation requirement[2] specified in a community order[3] or a suspended sentence order[4];

(2)   subject to an alcohol treatment requirement[5] specified in a community order or a suspended sentence order;

(3)   released from prison on licence[6] subject to a non-standard licence condition requiring the offender to undertake offending behaviour work to address drug or alcohol related behaviour or subject to a drug testing requirement[7] or a drug appointment requirement[8];

(4)   required to comply with a drug testing or a drug appointment requirement[9];

(5)   required to submit to treatment for their drug or alcohol dependency by virtue of a community rehabilitation order[10] or a community punishment and rehabilitation order[11];

(6)   subject to a drug treatment and testing order[12]; or

(7)   subject to corresponding Scottish provision,

The duty to make direct payments does not arise[13] in the case of an adult who, having been convicted of an offence, is detained in prison[14] or residing in approved premises[15].

1   Ie by virtue of the Care and Support (Direct Payments) Regulations 2014, SI 2014/2871, reg 2, Sch 1 (made under the Care Act 2014 s 33(2)(a)). As to the meaning of 'local authority' see PARA 1. As to the duty of local authorities in England to make direct payments, and the conditions relating to that duty, see PARA 106. Sections 31(5), 32(6) provide that Condition 2 for the making of direct payments is that:

(1)   the local authority is not prohibited by such regulations from meeting the adult's needs by making direct payments to the adult or nominated person or authorized person (as the case may be: see PARA 106 note 12); and

    (2)   if regulations under s 33 give the local authority discretion to decide not to meet the adult's needs by making direct payments to such person, it does not exercise that discretion.

    No such discretion is conferred by the regulations. As to the meaning of 'adult' see PARA 1 note 1.

2 Ie as defined by the Criminal Justice Act 2003 s 209: see SENTENCING vol 92 (2015) PARA 124.
3 Ie as defined by the Criminal Justice Act 2003 s 177: see SENTENCING vol 92 (2015) PARA 48.
4 Ie as defined by the Criminal Justice Act 2003 s 189: see SENTENCING vol 92 (2015) PARA 100.
5 Ie as defined by the Criminal Justice Act 2003 s 212: see SENTENCING vol 92 (2015) PARA 122.
6 Ie under the Criminal Justice Act 2003 Pt 12 Ch 6 (ss 237–268) (sentencing: release, licenses and recall: see SENTENCING) or the Crime (Sentences) Act 1997 Pt 2 Ch 2 (ss 28–34) (effect of custodial sentences: life sentences: see SENTENCING).
7 Ie under the Criminal Justice and Courts Services Act 2000 s 64 (release on licence etc: drug testing: see SENTENCING vol 92 (2015) PARA 743).
8 Ie under the Criminal Justice and Courts Services Act 2000 s 64A (release on licence etc: drug appointment: see SENTENCING).
9 Ie specified in a notice given under the Criminal Justice Act 2003 s 256AA (supervision after end of sentence of prisoners serving less than 2 years: see SENTENCING vol 92 (2015) PARA 741).
10 Ie within the meaning of the Powers of Criminal Courts (Sentencing) Act 2000 s 41 (repealed).
11 Ie within the meaning of the Powers of Criminal Courts (Sentencing) Act 2000 s 51 (repealed).
12 Ie imposed under the Powers of Criminal Courts (Sentencing) Act 2000 s 52 (repealed).
13 Ie the Care Act 2014 ss 31–33 (see PARA 106) do not apply.
14 Care Act 2014 s 76(5)(a). As to the meanings of 'prison', 'detained in prison' and 'approved premises', and as to detained persons and persons in approved and other residential premises generally in this context, see PARA 87.
15 Care Act 2014 s 76(5)(b). See note 14.

108. Additional protections for adults lacking capacity. There are two additional conditions which must be satisfied in order to trigger the duty of a local authority in England to make direct payments in respect of the needs of an adult who lacks capacity[1]:

    (1)   that where the authorised person[2] is not authorised[3] to make decisions about the adult's needs for care and support[4] but there is at least one person who is so authorised, a person who is so authorised supports the authorised person's request for payments[5]; and

    (2)   that the local authority is satisfied that the authorised person will act in the adult's best interests in arranging for the provision of the care and support for which the direct payments would be used[6].

1 As to the duty of local authorities in England to make direct payments, and the generally applicable conditions relating to that duty, see PARA 106. As to having or lacking capacity see PARA 8 note 10. As to the meaning of 'local authority' see PARA 1. As to the meaning of 'adult' see PARA 1 note 1.
2 Ie the person to whom any payments will be made: see PARA 106 note 12.
3 Ie under the Mental Capacity Act 2005 (see MENTAL HEALTH AND CAPACITY).
4 Ie is not authorised as mentioned in the Care Act 2014 s 32(4)(a) (see PARA 106 note 12).
5 Care Act 2014 s 32(5). As to the making of requests for payment in this context see s 32(1); and PARA 106 note 13. This condition is 'Condition 1' in relation to a person lacking capacity: s 32(5).
6 Care Act 2014 s 32(7). This condition is 'Condition 3' in relation to a person lacking capacity: s 32(7). Condition 3 in relation to a person lacking capacity being no longer met is grounds for a review of direct payments: see Care and Support (Direct Payments) Regulations 2014, SI 2014/2871, reg 7(1)(d)(iii); and PARA 110.

109. Conditions to which direct payments must or may be subject. A direct payment[1] is made on condition that it be used only to pay for arrangements under which the needs specified in the care and support plan or (as the case may be) the support plan[2] are met[3].

Direct payments must be made subject to the condition that they must not be used to pay specified family members[4] to meet the needs of the adult in respect of whose needs the payment is made, unless, and in specific circumstances, the local authority considers it is necessary to do so[5]. A direct payment in respect of a person lacking capacity[6] must be made subject to the condition that the authorised person[7] must notify the local authority if he reasonably believes that the adult no longer lacks the capacity to request the making of direct payments[8] and, in certain circumstances[9], must obtain a criminal record certificate[10] in respect of any person from whom a service in respect of which a direct payment is made is secured[11]. A local authority may also make a direct payment subject to other conditions[12] which may, in particular, require that the needs may not be met by a particular person[13] or that the adult or[14] authorised person must provide information to the authority[15].

In a case where any condition relating to the making of a direct payment[16] is breached, the local authority may terminate the making of direct payments[17] and may require repayment[18] of the whole or part of a direct payment[19].

1   As to the duty of local authorities in England to make direct payments, and the generally applicable conditions relating to that duty, see PARA 106. As to the meaning of 'local authority' see PARA 1.
2   Ie under the Care Act 2014 s 25(2)(a) (see PARA 78).
3   Care Act 2014 s 33(3). Where a direct payment is made for an adult for whom payments are made under the National Health Service Act 2006 12A (direct payments for health care: see HEALTH SERVICES vol 54A (2017) PARA 688), the local authority must take reasonable steps to co-ordinate the systems, processes and requirements which it applies or imposes in relation to the direct payment with those which apply in relation to the payments made under the 2006 Act with a view to minimising the administrative or other burdens which they place on the adult for whom, or the nominated or authorised person to whom, the local authority makes the direct payment: Care and Support (Direct Payments) Regulations 2014, SI 2014/2871, reg 10. See also reg 11 (direct payments made in respect of after-care under the Mental Health Act 1983 s 117 (see MENTAL HEALTH AND CAPACITY vol 75 (2013) PARA 945)); and the Care Act 2014 Sch 4 para 1 (modifying ss 31–33 in this context).
4   Ie:
   (1)   the spouse or civil partner of the adult (Care and Support (Direct Payments) Regulations 2014, SI 2014/2871, reg 3(1), (3)(a) (made under the Care Act 2014 s 33(2)(b)));
   (2)   a person who lives with the adult as if their spouse or civil partner (Care and Support (Direct Payments) Regulations 2014, SI 2014/2871, reg 3(3)(b));
   (3)   a person living in the same household as the adult who is the adult's parent or parent-in-law, son or daughter, son-in-law or daughter-in-law, stepson or stepdaughter, brother or sister, aunt or uncle, or grandparent (reg 3(3)(c));
   (4)   the spouse or civil partner of any person specified in head (3) above who lives in the same household as the adult (reg 3(3)(d)); and
   (5)   a person who lives with any person specified in head (3) above as if that person's spouse or civil partner (reg 3(3)(e)).
   As to the meaning of 'adult' see PARA 1 note 1.
5   If the local authority considers it is necessary to do so, direct payments may be used to pay a person mentioned in note 4 to meet the care needs of the adult (Care and Support (Direct Payments) Regulations 2014, SI 2014/2871, reg 3(2)(a)) or to provide administrative and management support or services for the purpose of enabling a person to whom the direct payments are made to comply with legal obligations arising from the making of and use of the direct payment or monitor the receipt and expenditure of the direct payment (reg 3(2)(b)).
6   Ie a direct payment under the Care Act 2014 s 32 (see PARA 106). As to having or lacking capacity see PARA 8 note 10.
7   As to the meaning of 'authorised person' see PARA 106 note 12.
8   Care and Support (Direct Payments) Regulations 2014, SI 2014/2871, reg 3(4)(a).
9   Ie if the authorised person is a body corporate, an unincorporated body of persons, an individual who is not a person mentioned in the Care and Support (Direct Payments) Regulations 2014, SI 2014/2871, reg 3(3) (see note 4) or an individual who is not a friend of the adult who is involved in the provision of care for the adult: reg 3(5).
10 Ie an enhanced criminal record certificate issued under the Police Act 1997 s 113B (see SENTENCING vol 92 (2015) PARAS 640–642) or verification that a satisfactory certificate of that type under that Act has been obtained: Care and Support (Direct Payments) Regulations 2014, SI 2014/2871, reg 3(4)(b).
11 Care and Support (Direct Payments) Regulations 2014, SI 2014/2871, reg 3(4).
12 Care and Support (Direct Payments) Regulations 2014, SI 2014/2871, reg 4(1).

13 Care and Support (Direct Payments) Regulations 2014, SI 2014/2871, reg 4(2)(a). Conditions may not, however, require the needs of the adult to be met by any particular person: reg 4(3)(a).
14 Ie in the case of direct payments made under the Care Act 2014 s 32.
15 Care and Support (Direct Payments) Regulations 2014, SI 2014/2871, reg 4(2)(b). Conditions may not, however, require information to be provided to the authority:
    (1)   more frequently and in more detail than is reasonably required by the authority for the purpose of enabling it to ascertain that making direct payments is an appropriate way to meet the needs in question or the conditions upon which it is made are complied with (reg 4(3)(b)(i)); or
    (2)   in a format which is not reasonably practicable for the adult or authorised person to provide (reg 4(3)(b)(ii)).
16 Ie a condition mentioned in the Care Act 2014 s 33(3) or specified in the Care and Support (Direct Payments) Regulations 2014, SI 2014/2871, reg 3 or reg 4 (see the text and notes 1–15).
17 Care Act 2014 s 33(5)(a). A local authority must review the making of direct payments in respect of an adult if it considers that there has been the breach of a condition and it may exercise its discretion under s 33(5) to terminate the payments or require repayment: see the Care and Support (Direct Payments) Regulations 2014, SI 2014/2871, reg 7(1)(b); and PARA 110.
18 Ie with the Care Act 2014 s 69 (see PARA 118) accordingly applying to sums which the local authority requires to be repaid.
19 Care Act 2014 s 33(5)(b). See note 17.

110. Review of direct payments. A local authority in England must conduct a review for the purpose of ascertaining whether the making of direct payments[1] is an appropriate way to meet the adult's[2] needs:

    (1)   at least once within the first six months of the direct payment being made and at intervals not exceeding 12 months thereafter[3];

    (2)   if it considers that there has been a breach of a condition and that it may exercise its discretion[4] to terminate payments or require repayment in respect of that breach[5];

    (3)   in the case of a direct payment made to meet the needs of an adult not lacking capacity[6], whenever the local authority considers that that adult no longer has the capacity to request it to meet any of those needs by the making of direct payments to him[7] or Condition 3 (adult or nominated person is capable[8]) or Condition 4 (making direct payments to adult or nominated person is appropriate[9]) is no longer met[10]; and

    (4)   in the case of a direct payment made to meet the needs of an adult lacking capacity[11], whenever the local authority considers that the adult no longer lacks the capacity to request the local authority to meet any of those needs by the making of direct payments to the adult[12], is notified by any person of concerns that the direct payment may not have been used to meet the needs for which the payment was made[13], or considers, or is notified by any person of concerns, that Condition 3, 4 or 5[14] is no longer met[15].

When complying with its duty to conduct a review the local authority must involve the adult[16] and other specified persons involved in his care[17] and must take all reasonable steps to reach agreement[18] as to the outcome of the review[19].

1 As to the duty of local authorities in England to make direct payments, and the generally applicable conditions relating to that duty, see PARA 106. As to the meaning of 'local authority' see PARA 1.
2 As to the meaning of 'adult' see PARA 1 note 1.
3 Care and Support (Direct Payments) Regulations 2014, SI 2014/2871, reg 7(1)(a) (made under the Care Act 2014 s 33(2)(g)).
4 Ie its discretion under the Care Act 2014 s 33(5) (see PARA 109).
5 Care and Support (Direct Payments) Regulations 2014, SI 2014/2871, reg 7(1)(b).
6 Ie a payment under the Care Act 2014 s 31 (see PARA 106). As to having or lacking capacity see PARA 8 note 10.
7 Care and Support (Direct Payments) Regulations 2014, SI 2014/2871, reg 7(1)(c)(i).

8   As to Condition 3 in relation to a person having capacity see the Care Act 2014 s 31(6); and
    PARA 106.
9   As to Condition 4 in relation to an adult having capacity see the Care Act 2014 s 31(7); and
    PARA 106.
10 Care and Support (Direct Payments) Regulations 2014, SI 2014/2871, reg 7(1)(c)(ii).
11 Ie a payment under the Care Act 2014 s 32 (see PARA 106).
12 Care and Support (Direct Payments) Regulations 2014, SI 2014/2871, reg 7(1)(d)(i).
13 Care and Support (Direct Payments) Regulations 2014, SI 2014/2871, reg 7(1)(d)(ii).
14 As to Conditions 3–5 in relation to an adult lacking capacity see the Care Act 2014 s 32(7)–(9);
    and PARAS 106, 108.
15 Care and Support (Direct Payments) Regulations 2014, SI 2014/2871, reg 7(1)(d)(iii).
16 Care and Support (Direct Payments) Regulations 2014, SI 2014/2871, reg 7(2)(a).
17 Ie any carer that the adult has (Care and Support (Direct Payments) Regulations 2014, SI
    2014/2871, reg 7(2)(b)), the authorised person to whom the direct payment is being made (in the
    case of direct payments made under the Care Act 2014 s 32) (Care and Support (Direct Payments)
    Regulations 2014, SI 2014/2871, reg 7(2)(c)), any person who is providing administrative or
    management support or services in accordance with reg 3(2)(b) (see PARA 109) (reg 7(2)(d)) and
    either any person whom the adult asks the authority to involve (reg 7(2)(e)(i)) or, if the adult lacks
    the capacity to do that, the person who is authorised under the Mental Capacity Act 2005 (see
    MENTAL HEALTH AND CAPACITY) to make decisions about the adult's needs for care and
    support (if different to the person in the Care and Support (Direct Payments) Regulations 2014, SI
    2014/2871, reg 7(2)(c)) or if there is no such person, any person who appears to the authority to
    be interested in the adult's welfare (reg 7(2)(e)(ii)). As to the meaning of 'carer' see PARA 33 note
    2.
18 Ie with the adult concerned (Care and Support (Direct Payments) Regulations 2014, SI 2014/2871,
    reg 7(3)(a)) or, if the adult lacks capacity to reach such agreement, the person who is authorised
    under the Mental Capacity Act 2005 to make decisions about the adult's needs for care and
    support (Care and Support (Direct Payments) Regulations 2014, SI 2014/2871, reg 7(3)(b)(i)) or
    where there is no such person, any person who appears to the authority to be interested in the
    adult's welfare (reg 7(3)(b)(ii)).
19 Care and Support (Direct Payments) Regulations 2014, SI 2014/2871, reg 7(3)(b).

C.   CHARGES FOR SERVICES AND THE 'CAP ON CARE COSTS'

111.   Power of local authority to make a charge for meeting needs. A local
authority in England may[1] make a charge for meeting an adult's needs for care and
support[2] and a carer's needs for support[3]. Certain services, consisting of the
provision of community equipment or intermediate care and reablement support
services, may not be the subject of a charge[4], and a charge may not be imposed
where care and support is provided[5] in respect of an adult suffering from variant
Creutzfeldt-Jakob disease[6]. Additionally, a local authority may not make a charge
if the income of the adult concerned would, after deduction of the charge, fall
below a specified amount[7]. Charges may only be levied after a financial assessment
of the adult or carer has been carried out[8]. As from a day to be appointed[9], where
the authority has a duty to meet an adult's needs[10], it may not make such a charge
if the total of the costs accrued in meeting the adult's eligible needs exceeds the
'cap on care costs'[11].

1   Ie by virtue of the Care Act 2014 s 14(1)(a). A charge under s 14(1)(a) may cover only the cost that
    the local authority incurs in meeting the needs to which the charge applies: s 14(4). As to the
    meaning of 'local authority' see PARA 1.
2   Ie needs under the Care Act 2014 ss 18, 19 (see PARAS 12, 13). As to the meaning of 'adult' see
    PARA 1 note 1. Where it is meeting needs in circumstances where the adult's financial resources are
    above £23,250 (the 'financial limit': see PARA 105) (ie because Condition 2 in s 18(2) (see
    PARA 12) is satisfied, the authority may also make a charge (in addition to the charge it makes
    under s 14(1)(a)) for putting in place the arrangements for meeting those needs (s 14(1)(b)): such
    a charge may only cover the cost that the authority incurs in putting in place the arrangements for
    meeting those needs (Care and Support (Charging and Assessment of Resources) Regulations
    2014, SI 2014/2672, reg 5 (made under the Care Act 2014 s 14(5), (6)).
        The National Assistance Act 1948 Pt III (ss 21–36) imposes duties on local authorities to
    provide accommodation for persons in need which, while remaining in force for England, have
    been superseded by the overall effect of the Care Act 2014 s 8(1) (how to meet needs: see PARA 3

note 4): the National Assistance Act 1948 ss 22, 26, 32, and the Health and Social Care Act 2001 ss 54, 55 make provision corresponding to that made by the Care Act 2014 s 14, and have therefore been similarly superseded.

Provision for the care and support of children in England is made by the Children Act 1989 (see PARA 21) and not by the Care Act 2014 Pt 1 (ss 1–80), and accordingly the Care Act 2014 makes no corresponding provision for children.

3   Ie needs under the Care Act 2014 s 20 (see PARAS 36, 37). As to the meaning of 'carer' see PARA 33 note 2. The power to make a charge under s 14(1) for meeting a carer's needs for support under s 20 by providing care and support to the adult needing care may not be exercised so as to charge the carer: s 14(3). Where it is meeting needs in circumstances where the financial resources of the carer or the adult needing care are above £23,250 (ie because Condition 2 or 4 in s 20(3) or (5) (see PARA 36) is satisfied, the authority may also make a charge (in addition to the charge it makes under s 14(1)(a)) for putting in place the arrangements for meeting those needs (s 14(1)(b)): such a charge may only cover the cost that the authority incurs in putting in place the arrangements for meeting those needs (Care and Support (Charging and Assessment of Resources) Regulations 2014, SI 2014/2672, reg 5).

4   See the Care and Support (Charging and Assessment of Resources) Regulations 2014, SI 2014/2672, reg 3. A local authority may, if it thinks fit, financially assess and charge a short-term resident (see PARA 105 note 3) as if they are receiving care and support, or support under the Care Act 2014 s 18, s 19 or s 20 other than the provision of accommodation in a care home: Care and Support (Charging and Assessment of Resources) Regulations 2014, SI 2014/2672, reg 8.

5   Ie under the Care Act 2014 s 18, s 19 or s 20.

6   Care and Support (Charging and Assessment of Resources) Regulations 2014, SI 2014/2672, reg 4.

7   See the Care Act 2014 s 14(7), (8); and as to the specified amounts see the Care and Support (Charging and Assessment of Resources) Regulations 2014, SI 2014/2672, regs 6, 7 (amended by SI 2015/644).

8   See PARA 119.

9   At the date at which this volume states the law the Care Act 2014 s 15 (the cap on care costs: see PARA 112) had yet to be brought into force.

10 Ie where the authority is meeting an adult's needs under the Care Act 2014 s 18.

11 See the Care Act 2014 s 15(1)–(6), (8); and PARA 112. As from a day to be appointed, where the cost to a local authority of meeting an adult's needs under s 18 includes daily living costs, and the accrued costs exceed the cap on care costs (with the result that s 14(1) applies), the local authority may nonetheless make a charge to cover the amount attributable to those daily living costs (see PARA 112 note 4): s 15(7) (not yet in force).

112.   The 'cap on care costs'. As from a day to be appointed[1], where a local authority in England has a duty to meet an adult's needs for care and support[2] it may not make a charge for meeting those needs[3] if the total of the costs accrued[4] in meeting[5] the adult's eligible needs[6] exceeds the cap on care costs[7]. The 'cap on care costs' is the amount specified as such in regulations, which may in particular[8] specify different amounts for persons of different age groups[9] and specify zero as the amount for persons of a specified description[10]. Regulations may also vary the cap on care costs in accordance with changes in the level of average earnings in England[11]. At the date at which this volume states the law no such regulations had been made.

1   At the date at which this volume states the law the Care Act 2014 ss 15, 16, 71(1)(a), (b) (the cap on care costs: see the text and notes 2–11) had yet to be brought into force. As to the meaning of 'local authority' see PARA 1.

2   Ie where the authority is meeting an adult's needs under the Care Act 2014 s 18: see PARA 111. As to the meaning of 'adult' see PARA 1 note 1.

3   Ie may not make a charge under the Care Act 2014 s 14: see PARA 111.

4   The reference to 'costs accrued' in meeting 'eligible needs' (see note 6) is a reference:

(1)   in so far as the authority met those needs, to the cost to the authority of having done so (as reckoned from the costs specified in the personal budget for meeting those needs (see the Care Act 2014 s 26; and PARA 121)) (s 15(2)(a) (not yet in force));

(2)   in so far as another local authority met the needs, to the cost to that other local authority of having done so (as reckoned from the costs so specified for meeting those needs) (s 15(2)(b)) (not yet in force);

(3)   in so far as a person other than a local authority met the needs, to what the cost of doing so would have been to the local authority which would otherwise have done so (as reckoned from the costs specified in the independent personal budget for meeting those needs (see s 28; and PARA 122) (s 15(2)(c)) (not yet in force).

The total of the costs accrued in meeting an adult's eligible needs after the bringing into force of s 15 is referred to in Pt 1 (ss 1–80) as the adult's 'accrued costs': s 15(5) (not yet in force). Where the costs accrued include daily living costs, the amount attributable to the daily living costs is to be disregarded in working out for these purposes the total of the costs accrued in meeting an adult's eligible needs after the coming into force of s 15: s 15(6) (not yet in force). For the purposes of Pt 1, the amount attributable to an adult's daily living costs is the amount specified in, or determined in accordance with, regulations: s 15(8) (not yet in force). At the date at which this volume states the law no such regulations had been made. The Secretary of State must review the level at which the amount attributable to an adult's daily living costs is for the time being set under regulations under s 15(8): s 71(1)(b) (not yet in force). As to such reviews see further s 71(2)–(7); and PARA 105 note 13. As to the Secretary of State see PARA 333.

5   Ie after the coming into force of the Care Act 2014 s 15.
6   An adult's needs are 'eligible needs' if, at the time they were met they met the eligibility criteria (Care Act 2014 s 15(3)(a) (not yet in force)), they were not being met by a carer (s 15(3)(b) (not yet in force)), and the adult was ordinarily resident or present in the area of a local authority (s 15(3)(c) (not yet in force)). As to the eligibility criteria see PARA 10.
7   Care Act 2014 ss 14(2), 15(1) (s 15(1) not yet in force). A financial assessment must be carried out: see PARA 120.
8   Ie in reliance on the Care Act 2014 s 125(7).
9   Care Act 2014 s 15(4)(a) (not yet in force). The Secretary of State must review the level at which the cap on care costs is for the time being set under regulations under s 15(4): s 71(1)(a) (not yet in force). As to such reviews see further s 71(2)–(7); and PARA 105 note 13.
10   Care Act 2014 s 15(4)(b) (not yet in force).
11   See the Care Act 2014 s 16 (not yet in force).

D.   DEFERRED PAYMENTS AND LOANS

113.   Deferred payment agreements. A 'deferred payment agreement' is an agreement under which a local authority in England[1] agrees not to require until the specified time either or both of:

(1)   the payment of the specified part of the amounts due[2] from an adult[3] to the authority[4]; and

(2)   the repayment of the specified part of a loan[5] made under the agreement by the authority to an adult for the purpose of assisting him to obtain the provision of care and support for him[6].

Local authorities are required to enter into a deferred payment agreement where the value of the adult's interest in his home does not exceed £23,250[7]. Authorities may also enter into such agreements at their own discretion[8]. The authority must obtain adequate security for repayment of the deferred amounts[9] and the consent of other interested persons[10]. The 'specified time' for repayment[11] is the sooner of:

(a)   the date of sale or disposal of the land or other asset in respect of which the authority has a charge[12]; or

(b)   90 days after the date of the death of the adult with whom the agreement is made or such longer time as the authority may permit[13],

although the adult may terminate the agreement at any time prior to the specified time by giving the authority reasonable notice in writing and paying the outstanding amount[14]. Provision is made as to the terms and conditions which must be included in agreements[15].

1   As to the meaning of 'local authority' see PARA 1.
2   Ie under such provision of the Care Act 2014 Pt 1 or of regulations thereunder as is specified in regulations. 'Specified', in relation to a time or a part of an amount or loan, means specified in or determined in accordance with regulations; and the specified part of an amount or loan may be 100%: s 34(7).
3   As to the meaning of 'adult' see PARA 1 note 1. Provision for the care and support of children in England is made by the Children Act 1989 (see PARA 21) and not by the Care Act 2014 Pt 1 (ss 1–80), and accordingly the Care Act 2014 makes no corresponding provision for children.
4   Care Act 2014 s 34(2)(a).

5   The Care Act 2014 s 34 (see the text and note 6; and PARAS 114–116) applies subject to specified
     modifications, in relation to an agreement under which a local authority agrees to make a loan to
     an adult for the purpose of assisting the adult to obtain the provision of care and support for the
     adult as it applies in relation to a deferred payment agreement: s 34(8).
6   Care Act 2014 s 34(2)(b). The care and support mentioned in s 34(2)(b) (or, in the case of a loan,
     s 34(8) (see note 5)) includes care and support the provision of which the authority does not
     consider to be necessary to meet the adult's needs (ss 34(3)(a), (8)(a)) and is in addition to care and
     support which is being provided, arranged for, or paid for (in whole or in part) by the authority
     (s 34(3)(b)).
7   See PARA 114.
8   See PARA 115.
9   Ie the deferred amount and any interest and administration costs which have been treated in the
     same way as the deferred amount: see the Care and Support (Deferred Payment) Regulations 2014,
     SI 2014/2671, reg 4(1)(a); and PARA 116. The 'deferred amount' is determined in accordance with
     the Care and Support (Deferred Payment) Regulations 2014, SI 2014/2671, regs 5, 6 (reg 6
     prospectively amended by SI 2015/644). The authority's interest and administration costs may be
     charged in accordance with the Care and Support (Deferred Payment) Regulations 2014, SI
     2014/2671, regs 9, 10 (made under the Care Act 2014 s 35(1), (2), (4)).
         Regulations may, in such cases or circumstances and subject to such conditions as may be
     specified, require or permit a local authority in England to enter into alternative financial
     arrangements of a specified description with an adult: s 36(1). 'Alternative financial arrangements'
     means arrangements which in the Secretary of State's opinion equate in substance to a deferred
     payment agreement or an agreement of the kind mentioned in s 34(8) (see note 5) (s 36(2)(a)), but
     achieve a similar effect to an agreement of the kind in question without including provision for the
     payment of interest (s 36(2)(b)). The regulations may make provision in connection with
     alternative financial arrangements to which they apply, including, in particular, provision of the
     kind that may (or must) be made in regulations under s 34 or s 35 (apart from provision for the
     payment of interest): s 36(3). At the date at which this volume states the law no such regulations
     had been made.
10   See the Care and Support (Deferred Payment) Regulations 2014, SI 2014/2671, reg 4(1)(b); and
     PARA 116.
11   Ie for repayment of the deferred amount and any interest and administration costs which have been
     treated in the same way as the deferred amount: Care and Support (Deferred Payment) Regulations
     2014, SI 2014/2671, reg 7.
12   Care and Support (Deferred Payment) Regulations 2014, SI 2014/2671, reg 7(a).
13   Care and Support (Deferred Payment) Regulations 2014, SI 2014/2671, reg 7(b).
14   Ie paying to the authority the deferred amount and any interest and administration costs which
     have been treated in the same way as the deferred amount: Care and Support (Deferred Payment)
     Regulations 2014, SI 2014/2671, reg 8 (made under the Care Act 2014 s 35(5), (6)).
15   See the Care and Support (Deferred Payment) Regulations 2014, SI 2014/2671, reg 11 (made
     under the Care Act 2014 s 35(7)–(10)).

114. Local authority required to enter into deferred payment agreement where adult's assets do not exceed £23,250. A local authority in England is required to enter into a deferred payment agreement[1] with an adult[2] if:

(1)   either the adult's needs for care and support are being met or are going
       to be met[3] and the care and support plan[4] for the adult specifies that the
       local authority is going to meet the adult's needs by the provision of
       accommodation in a care home[5], or are not being or going to be met by
       the authority and the authority considers that if it had been asked to
       meet the adult's needs it would have done so[6] and it would have met the
       adult's needs by the provision to the adult of accommodation in a care
       home[7]; and

(2)   the authority is satisfied that the adult has a legal or beneficial interest
       in a property which is his main or only home[8] which does not exceed
       £23,250[9].

Additionally, the authority must obtain security for the payment (ie the 'security condition'[10] must be met)[11] and the adult must agree to all the terms and conditions included[12] in the agreement[13].

1 As to the making of deferred payment agreements and loans by local authorities in England see PARA 113. As to the meaning of 'local authority' see PARA 1.
2 As to the meaning of 'adult' see PARA 1 note 1.
3 Ie under the Care Act 2014 s 18 (see PARA 12) or s 19(1) or (2) (see PARA 13).
4 As to care and support plans in England see PARAS 78–80.
5 Care and Support (Deferred Payment) Regulations 2014, SI 2014/2671, reg 2(1)(a), (2)(a)(i) (made under the Care Act 2014 s 34(1)). 'Care home' means a care home, within the meaning given in the Care Standards Act 2000 s 3 (see PARA 3 note 3) in respect of which a person is registered under the Health and Social Care Act 2008 for the regulated activity of the provision of accommodation together with nursing or personal care: Care and Support (Deferred Payment) Regulations 2014, SI 2014/2671, reg 1(2). An authority is only required to enter into a deferred payment agreement with an adult for amounts due from the adult to the authority under the Care Act 2014 s 14 (see PARA 111), or for costs of care and support the provision of which the local authority considers to be necessary to meet the adult's needs: Care and Support (Deferred Payment) Regulations 2014, SI 2014/2671, reg 2(3).
6 See note 3.
7 Care and Support (Deferred Payment) Regulations 2014, SI 2014/2671, reg 2(2)(a)(ii).
8 Care and Support (Deferred Payment) Regulations 2014, SI 2014/2671, reg 2(2)(b).
9 Ie:
   (1) where a financial assessment within the meaning of the Care Act 2014 s 17(5) (see PARA 119) has been carried out in respect of the adult, that the value of that interest has not been disregarded for the purposes of calculating the amount of the adult's capital (Care and Support (Deferred Payment) Regulations 2014, SI 2014/2671, reg 2(2)(b)(i)(aa)) and the adult's capital less the value of that interest does not exceed £23,250 (reg 2(2)(b)(i)(bb)); or
   (2) where such a financial assessment has not been carried out in respect of the adult head (1) above would be satisfied if such an assessment were carried out (reg 2(2)(b)(ii)).
10 Ie the condition in the Care and Support (Deferred Payment) Regulations 2014, SI 2014/2671, reg 4 (see PARA 116).
11 Care and Support (Deferred Payment) Regulations 2014, SI 2014/2671, reg 2(1)(b) (made under the Care Act 2014 ss 34(4), (8)(b)).
12 Ie included in accordance with in the Care and Support (Deferred Payment) Regulations 2014, SI 2014/2671, reg 11 (see PARA 113).
13 Care and Support (Deferred Payment) Regulations 2014, SI 2014/2671, reg 2(1)(c).

115. Power of local authority to enter into deferred payment agreement at its discretion. A local authority in England is permitted to enter into a deferred payment agreement[1] with an adult[2] if either the adult's needs for care and support are being met or are going to be met[3] and the care and support plan[4] for him specifies that the local authority is going to meet his needs by the provision to him of accommodation in a care home[5] or supported living accommodation[6], or those needs are not being or going to be met by the authority and the authority considers that if it had been asked to meet those needs it would have done so[7] and it would have met the needs by the provision to the adult of accommodation in a care home or supported living accommodation[8].

Additionally, the authority must obtain security for the payment (ie the 'security condition'[9] must be met)[10] and the adult must agree to all the terms and conditions included[11] in the agreement[12].

1 As to the making of deferred payment agreements and loans by local authorities in England see PARA 113. As to the meaning of 'local authority' see PARA 1.
2 As to the meaning of 'adult' see PARA 1 note 1.
3 Ie under the Care Act 2014 s 18 (see PARA 12) or s 19(1) or (2) (see PARA 13).
4 As to care and support plans see PARAS 78–80.
5 As to the meaning of 'care home' see PARA 114 note 5.
6 Care and Support (Deferred Payment) Regulations 2014, SI 2014/2671, reg 3(1)(a)(i). For these purposes 'supported living accommodation' means accommodation which is not a care home and is:

(1)   in premises which are specifically designed or adapted for occupation by adults with needs for care and support to enable them to live as independently as possible (reg 3(2)(a)); or

(2)   provided in premises which are intended for occupation by adults with needs for care and support (whether or not the premises are specifically designed or adapted for that purpose) (reg 3(2)(b)(i)) and in circumstances in which personal care is available if required (reg 3(2)(b)(ii)).

For the purposes of reg 3(2)(b)(ii), personal care may be provided by a person other than the person who provides the accommodation: reg 3(3). The accommodation referred to in reg 3(2) does not include premises in respect of which the adult is for the time being entitled to dispose of the fee simple, whether or not with the consent of other joint owners (reg 3(4)(a)) or which the adult occupies other than under a licence or tenancy agreement (reg 3(4)(b)). In reg 3(4) 'tenancy' means a tenancy which is not a long tenancy: reg 3(5). A 'long tenancy' is a tenancy granted for a term of years certain exceeding 21 years, whether or not the tenancy is, or may become, terminable before the end of that term by notice given by or to the tenant or by re-entry, forfeiture or otherwise and includes a lease for a term fixed by law under a grant with a covenant or obligation for perpetual renewal unless it is a lease by sub-demise from one which is not a long tenancy: reg 1(2).

7   See note 3.
8   Care and Support (Deferred Payment) Regulations 2014, SI 2014/2671, reg 3(1)(a)(ii).
9   Ie the condition in the Care and Support (Deferred Payment) Regulations 2014, SI 2014/2671, reg 4 (see PARA 116).
10 Care and Support (Deferred Payment) Regulations 2014, SI 2014/2671, reg 3(1)(b).
11 Ie included in accordance with in the Care and Support (Deferred Payment) Regulations 2014, SI 2014/2671, reg 11 (see PARA 113).
12 Care and Support (Deferred Payment) Regulations 2014, SI 2014/2671, reg 3(1)(c).

116. Local authority must obtain security for, and consent to, deferred agreement or loan. Before entering into a deferred payment agreement[1] a local authority in England must obtain adequate security for the payment of the adult's[2] deferred amount[3] and any interest or administration costs[4] which are treated in the same way as the adult's deferred amount[5]. For these purposes[6] 'adequate security' is a charge by way of legal mortgage for an amount which is at least equal to the deferred amount and any interest or administration costs which are to be treated in the same way as the adult's deferred amount and which is capable of being registered as a first legal charge in favour of the local authority in the land register[7]: for the purposes of an agreement made at the authority's discretion[8], 'adequate security' may alternatively be any other security which the authority considers is sufficient to secure payment of the deferred amount and any interest and administration costs which are to be treated in the same way as the adult's deferred amount[9]. If the authority considers it is necessary to do so, it must also obtain the genuine and informed consent to the agreement or loan of all interested persons[10].

1   As to the making of deferred payment agreements and loans by local authorities in England see PARAS 113–115. The security condition (ie the Care and Support (Deferred Payment) Regulations 2014, SI 2014/2671, reg 4: see the text and notes 2–10) has to be complied with in order for a local authority to enter into a deferred payment agreement: see the Care and Support (Deferred Payment) Regulations 2014, SI 2014/2671, regs 2(1)(b), 3(1)(b); and PARAS 114, 115. As to the meaning of 'local authority' see PARA 1.
2   As to the meaning of 'adult' see PARA 1 note 1.
3   As to the deferred amount see PARA 113 note 9.
4   As to the authority's power to charge interest and administration costs see PARA 113 note 9.
5   Care and Support (Deferred Payment) Regulations 2014, SI 2014/2671, reg 4(1)(a) (made under the Care Act 2014 ss 34(5), (6), 35(3)).
6   Ie for the purposes of an agreement made under the Care and Support (Deferred Payment) Regulations 2014, SI 2014/2671, reg 2 (see PARA 114) or reg 3 (see PARA 115).
7   Care and Support (Deferred Payment) Regulations 2014, SI 2014/2671, reg 4(2), (3)(a).
8   Ie an agreement made under the Care and Support (Deferred Payment) Regulations 2014, SI 2014/2671, reg 3.
9   Care and Support (Deferred Payment) Regulations 2014, SI 2014/2671, reg 4(3)(b).

10 Care and Support (Deferred Payment) Regulations 2014, SI 2014/2671, reg 4(1)(b). The consent so required is consent which in the authority's opinion is genuine and informed consent given in writing to the matters specified below by any person:

    (1)   who the authority considers has an interest in the land or other asset in respect of which a charge will be obtained (reg 4(4)(a)); and

    (2)   whose interest the authority considers may prevent it from exercising a power of sale of the land or asset or recovering the deferred amount (reg 4(4)(b)).

  The matters specified are:

    (a)   the creation of a charge (reg 4(5)(a)); and

    (b)   the charge taking priority to and ranking before any interest the person has in the land or other asset which will be the subject of the charge (reg 4(5)(b)).

E.   ANTI-AVOIDANCE AND RECOVERY

117. Transfer of assets to avoid charges. Where an adult's[1] needs have been or are being met by a local authority in England[2] and:

    (1)   the adult has transferred an asset to another person (a 'transferee')[3];

    (2)   the transfer was undertaken with the intention of avoiding charges for having the adult's needs met[4]; and

    (3)   either the consideration for the transfer was less than the value of the asset[5] or there was no consideration for the transfer[6],

the transferee is liable to pay to the local authority an amount equal to the difference between the amount the authority would have charged the adult were it not for the transfer of the asset[7] and the amount it did in fact charge the adult[8]. The transferee is not liable to pay to the authority an amount which exceeds the benefit accruing to the transferee from the transfer[9].

1 As to the meaning of 'adult' see PARA 1 note 1.

2 Ie under the Care Act 2014 ss 18–20: see PARAS 12, 13 (adults) and PARAS 36, 37 (carers). As to the meaning of 'local authority' see PARA 1.

3 Care Act 2014 s 70(1)(a). 'Asset' means anything which may be taken into account for the purposes of a financial assessment: s 70(5). As to financial assessments see PARAS 119–120.

4 Care Act 2014 s 70(1)(b). For the power of local authority to make a charge for meeting needs see PARA 111.

5 The value of an asset (other than cash) is the amount which would have been realised if it had been sold on the open market by a willing seller at the time of the transfer, with a deduction for the amount of any incumbrance on the asset (Care Act 2014 s 70(6)(a)) and a reasonable amount in respect of the expenses of the sale (s 70(6)(b)).

6 Care Act 2014 s 70(1)(c).

7 Care Act 2014 s 70(2)(a).

8 Care Act 2014 s 70(2)(b). Where an asset has been transferred to more than one transferee, the liability of each transferee under these provisions is in proportion to the benefit accruing to that transferee from the transfer: s 70(4). Regulations may specify cases or circumstances in which liability under s 70(2) does not arise: s 70(7). At the date at which this volume states the law no such regulations had been made.

9 Care Act 2014 s 70(3).

118. Recovery of charges and interest. Any sum due to a local authority in England[1] for the provision of care and support[2] is recoverable by the authority as a debt due to it[3]. A sum is so recoverable:

    (1)   in a case in which the sum becomes due to the local authority on or after 1 April 2015[4], within six years of the date the sum becomes due[5]; and

    (2)   in any other case, within three years of the date on which it becomes due[6].

Where a person misrepresents or fails to disclose (whether fraudulently or otherwise) to a local authority any material fact in connection with the provision of care and support[7], the following sums are due to the authority from the person:

    (a)   any expenditure incurred by the authority as a result of the misrepresentation or failure[8]; and

(b)   any sum recoverable[9] which the authority has not recovered as a result of the misrepresentation or failure[10].

The costs incurred by a local authority in recovering or seeking to recover a sum due to it[11] are recoverable by the authority as a debt due to it[12].

1   As to the meaning of 'local authority' see PARA 1.
2   Ie any sum due under the Care Act 2014 Pt 1 (ss 1–80).
3   Care Act 2014 s 69(1). This provision does not apply in a case where a deferred payment agreement could, in accordance with the Care and Support (Deferred Payment) Regulations 2014, SI 2014/2671 (see PARAS 113–116), be entered into, unless the local authority has sought to enter into such an agreement with the adult from whom the sum is due (Care Act 2014 s 69(2)(a)) and the adult has refused (s 69(2)(b)). As to the meaning of 'adult' see PARA 1 note 1. Regulations may:
     (1)   make provision for determining the date on which a sum becomes due to a local authority for the purposes of s 69 (s 69(6)(a));
     (2)   specify cases or circumstances in which a sum due to a local authority under Pt 1 is not recoverable by it under s 69 (s 69(6)(b));
     (3)   specify cases or circumstances in which a local authority may charge interest on a sum due to it under Pt 1 (s 69(6)(c));
     (4)   where interest is chargeable, provide that it must be charged at a rate specified in or determined in accordance with the regulations or may not be charged at a rate that exceeds the rate specified in or determined in accordance with the regulations (s 69(6)(d)).
     At the date at which this volume states the law no such regulations had been made.
     The National Assistance Act 1948 Pt III (ss 21–36) imposes duties on local authorities to provide accommodation for persons in need which, while remaining in force for England, have been superseded by the overall effect of the Care Act 2014 s 8(1) (how to meet needs: see PARA 3 note 4): the National Assistance Act 1948 ss 45, 56 make provision corresponding to that made by the Care Act 2014 s 69, and have therefore been similarly superseded.
4   Ie the date on which the Care Act 2014 s 69 was brought into force by the Care Act 2014 (Commencement No 4) Order 2015, SI 2015/993, art 2(q).
5   Care Act 2014 s 69(3)(a).
6   Care Act 2014 s 69(3)(b).
7   Ie in connection with the Care Act 2014 Pt 1.
8   Care Act 2014 s 69(4)(a).
9   Ie under the Care Act 2014 s 69.
10 Care Act 2014 s 69(4)(b).
11 See note 2.
12 Care Act 2014 s 69(5).

F.   FINANCIAL ASSESSMENT AND ADMINISTRATION

119. Financial assessments relating to charges for meeting needs. Where a local authority in England, having made an eligibility determination[1], thinks that, if it were to meet an adult's[2] needs for care and support, or a carer's[3] needs for support, it would charge[4] the adult, the carer, or the adult needing care, for meeting at least some of the needs, it must assess the level of the financial resources of the adult, the carer, or the adult needing care[5] and the amount (if any) which the adult, the carer, or the adult needing care would be likely to be able to pay towards the cost of meeting the needs for care and support[6]. An authority is also required to carry out an assessment where, to the extent that the authority considers appropriate, circumstances have changed in a way that affects a care and support plan[7]. Such an assessment is referred to[8] as a 'financial assessment'[9].

An authority is to be treated as having carried out a financial assessment in an adult's case and being satisfied on that basis that the adult's financial resources exceed the financial limit[10] where:
    (1)   the adult has refused a financial assessment[11], or the authority has been unable to carry out a full financial assessment because of the adult's refusal to co-operate with the assessment and the local authority nevertheless decides to meet some or all of the adult's needs for care and support, or for support[12]; or

(2) with the consent of the adult, the authority has not carried out[13] a financial assessment[14] but the authority is satisfied from the evidence available to it that the adult's financial resources do exceed the financial limit[15].

A local authority is also to be treated as having carried out a financial assessment in an adult's case and being satisfied on that basis that the adult's financial resources do not exceed the financial limit where with the consent of the adult, the authority has not carried out[16] a financial assessment[17] and the authority is satisfied from the evidence available to it that the adult's financial resources do not exceed the financial limit[18].

1   Ie a determination under the Care Act 2014 s 13(1): see PARA 10 (adults) and PARA 35 (carers). As to the meaning of 'local authority' see PARA 1.
2   As to the meaning of 'adult' see PARA 1 note 1.
3   As to the meaning of 'carer' see PARA 33 note 2.
4   Ie under the Care Act 2014 s 14(1): see PARA 111.
5   Care Act 2014 s 17(1)(a), (3)(a), (4)(a). Provision for calculating a person's income is made by the Care and Support (Charging and Assessment of Resources) Regulations 2014, SI 2014/2672, regs 11, 13–17, Sch 1 (Sch 1 amended by SI 2015/644; SI 2017/555) (made under the Care Act 2014 s 17(11), (12)); provision for calculating capital is made by the Care and Support (Charging and Assessment of Resources) Regulations 2014, SI 2014/2672, regs 18–25, Sch 2.
6   Care Act 2014 s 17(1)(b), (3)(b), (4)(b).
7   See the Care Act 2014 s 27(4)(a), (4A)(a); and PARA 80. As to the duty to prepare, and the matters to be specified in, care and support plans for adults and support plans for carers see PARA 78.
8   Ie in the Care Act 2014 Pt 1 (ss 1–80).
9   Care Act 2014 s 17(5). A local authority, having carried out a financial assessment, must give a written record of the assessment to the adult to whom it relates: s 17(6).
10 Ie £23,250: see PARA 105.
11 Care and Support (Charging and Assessment of Resources) Regulations 2014, SI 2014/2672, regs 9, 10(1)(a) (made under the Care Act 2014 s 17(13)).
12 Care and Support (Charging and Assessment of Resources) Regulations 2014, SI 2014/2672, reg 10(1)(b).
13 Ie in accordance with the Care and Support (Charging and Assessment of Resources) Regulations 2014, SI 2014/2672.
14 Care and Support (Charging and Assessment of Resources) Regulations 2014, SI 2014/2672, reg 10(3)(a).
15 Care and Support (Charging and Assessment of Resources) Regulations 2014, SI 2014/2672, reg 10(3)(b).
16 See note 13.
17 Care and Support (Charging and Assessment of Resources) Regulations 2014, SI 2014/2672, reg 10(2)(a).
18 Care and Support (Charging and Assessment of Resources) Regulations 2014, SI 2014/2672, reg 10(2)(b).

120. Financial assessments relating to the cap on care costs. Where a local authority in England thinks that, in meeting an adult's[1] needs for care and support, it would make a charge[2] for daily living costs that exceed the cap on care costs, it must assess the level of the adult's financial resources[3] and the amount (if any) which the adult would be likely to be able to pay towards the amount attributable to the adult's daily living costs[4]. Such an assessment is referred to[5] as a 'financial assessment'[6].

1   As to the meaning of 'adult' see PARA 1 note 1.
2   Ie under the Care Act 2014 s 15(7): see PARA 112.
3   Care Act 2014 s 17(2)(a).
4   Care Act 2014 s 17(2)(b). As to the meaning of 'local authority' see PARA 1.
5   Ie in the Care Act 2014 Pt 1 (ss 1–80).
6   Care Act 2014 s 17(5).

121. Personal budget. In England, a 'personal budget' for an adult[1] is a statement which specifies:

(1)   the cost to the local authority[2] of meeting those of the adult's needs which it is required or decides[3] to meet[4];

(2)   the amount which, on the basis of the financial assessment[5], the adult must pay towards that cost[6]; and

(3)   if on that basis the local authority must itself pay towards that cost, the amount which it must pay[7].

In the case of an adult with needs for care and support which the local authority is required to meet[8], the personal budget must also specify:

(a)   the cost to the local authority of meeting those adult's needs[9]; and

(b)   where that cost includes daily living costs the amount attributable to those daily living costs[10] and the balance of the cost referred to above[11].

A personal budget for an adult may also specify other amounts of public money that are available in the adult's case including, for example, amounts available for spending on matters relating to housing, health care or welfare[12].

The costs to a local authority of meeting needs where it meets those needs by the provision of intermediate care and reablement services[13] must be excluded from a personal budget if:

(i)   it is not permitted[14] to make a charge for meeting needs by the provision of such services[15]; or

(ii)   it is permitted to make a charge but nevertheless it does not make a charge to any adult to whom it provides such services[16].

1   As to the meaning of 'adult' see PARA 1 note 1. Provision for the care and support of children in England is made by the Children Act 1989 (see PARA 21) and not by the Care Act 2014 Pt 1 (ss 1–80), and accordingly the Care Act 2014 makes no corresponding provision for children.
2   As to the meaning of 'local authority' see PARA 1.
3   Ie as mentioned in the Care Act 2014 s 24(1) (see PARA 14).
4   Care Act 2014 s 26(1)(a).
5   As to financial assessments see PARAS 119–120.
6   Care Act 2014 s 26(1)(b).
7   Care Act 2014 s 26(1)(c).
8   Ie under the Care Act 2014 s 18 (see PARA 12).
9   Care Act 2014 s 26(2)(a).
10 Care Act 2014 s 26(2)(b)(i).
11 Care Act 2014 s 26(2)(b)(ii).
12 Care Act 2014 s 26(3).
13 'Intermediate care and reablement support services' means (by virtue of the Care and Support (Personal Budget: Exclusion of Costs) Regulations 2014, SI 2014/2840, reg 1(2) (made under the Care Act 2014 s 26(4)); and the Care and Support (Children's Carer's) Regulations 2015, SI 2015/305, reg 14) care and support or support provided to an adult by a local authority under the Care Act 2014 s 18, s 19 (see PARA 13), s 20 (see PARA 36) or s 62(1) (see PARA 44) which:
    (1)   consists of a programme of care and support or support;
    (2)   is for a specified period of time; and
    (3)   has as its purpose the provision of assistance to an adult to enable the adult to maintain or regain the ability needed to live independently in their own home.
    The Care and Support (Personal Budget: Exclusion of Costs) Regulations 2014, SI 2014/2840, apply to the exercise of the power to meet a child's carer's needs for support under the Care Act 2014 s 62(1) (see PARA 44) in so far as they apply to the exercise of the power to meet a carer's needs for support under s 20(6) (see PARA 37): Care and Support (Children's Carer's) Regulations 2015, SI 2015/305, reg 2(3)(c).
14 Ie by the Care and Support (Charging and Assessment of Resources) Regulations 2014, SI 2014/2672 (made under the Care Act 2014 s 14) (see PARAS 105, 111, 119).
15 Care and Support (Personal Budget: Exclusion of Costs) Regulations 2014, SI 2014/2840, reg 2(1), (2)(a).
16 Care and Support (Personal Budget: Exclusion of Costs) Regulations 2014, SI 2014/2840, reg 2(2)(b).

122. Independent personal budget. In England, an 'independent personal budget'[1] is a statement which specifies what the cost would be to the local authority concerned[2] of meeting the adult's eligible needs[3] for care and support[4]. Where this amount includes daily living costs, the independent personal budget for the adult must specify the amount attributable to those daily living costs[5] and the balance of the amount referred to above[6]. Independent personal budgets must be kept under review and, where necessary, revised[7].

1 As to personal budgets see PARA 121.
2 See the Care Act 2014 s 24(3); and PARA 14. As to the meaning of 'local authority' see PARA 1.
3 As to the meaning of 'adult' see PARA 1 note 1. An adult's needs are 'eligible needs' if, at the time they were met:
    (1)   they met the eligibility criteria (Care Act 2014 s 28(3)(a));
    (2)   they were not being met by a carer (s 28(3)(b)); and
    (3)   the adult was ordinarily resident or present in the area of the local authority (s 28(3)(c)).
    As to the eligibility criteria for adults see PARA 10. As to the meaning of 'carer' see PARA 33 note 2. In connection with a person's residence see PARAS 84–87. Provision for the care and support of children in England is made by the Children Act 1989 (see PARA 21) and not by the Care Act 2014 Pt 1 (ss 1–80), and accordingly the Care Act 2014 makes no corresponding provision for children.
4 Care Act 2014 s 28(1).
5 Care Act 2014 s 28(2)(a).
6 Care Act 2014 s 28(2)(b).
7 A local authority must keep under review generally independent personal budgets that it has prepared (Care Act 2014 s 28(4)(a)) and on a reasonable request by or on behalf of the adult to whom an independent personal budget relates, review the independent personal budget (s 28(4)(b)). A local authority may revise an independent personal budget; and in deciding whether or how to do so, it must, in so far as it is feasible to do so, involve the adult to whom the budget relates (s 28(5)(a)), any carer that the adult has (s 28(5)(b)), and any other person whom the adult asks the authority to involve or, where the adult lacks capacity to ask the authority to do that, any person who appears to the authority to be interested in the adult's welfare (s 28(5)(c)). As to the meaning of 'carer' see PARA 33 note 2. Where a local authority is satisfied that the circumstances of the adult to whom an independent personal budget applies have changed in a way that affects the budget, the authority must to the extent it thinks appropriate, carry out a needs assessment and make a determination under s 13(1) (see PARA 12) (s 28(6)(a)) and revise the independent personal budget accordingly (s 28(6)(b)). Having reviewed an independent personal budget, a local authority must:
    (1)   if it revises the budget, notify the adult to whom the budget relates of the revisions and provide an explanation of the effect of each revision (s 28(8)(a)); or
    (2)   if it does not revise the budget, notify the adult accordingly (s 28(8)(b)).

123. Care account. Where an adult[1] in England has needs for care and support which meet the eligibility criteria[2], the local authority[3] in whose area the adult is ordinarily resident[4] or, if the adult is of no settled residence, in whose area the adult is present, must keep an up-to-date record of the adult's accrued costs (a 'care account')[5] and once those costs exceed the cap on care costs[6], must inform the adult[7]. Where a local authority which has been keeping a care account is no longer required to do so, it must nonetheless retain the account that it has kept so far until the end of the period of 99 years beginning with the day on which it last updated the account[8] or where the adult dies, the local authority becomes aware of the death[9].

1 As to the meaning of 'adult' see PARA 1 note 1. Provision for the care and support of children in England is made by the Children Act 1989 (see PARA 21) and not by the Care Act 2014 Pt 1 (ss 1–80), and accordingly the Care Act 2014 makes no corresponding provision for children.
2 As to the eligibility criteria for adults see PARA 10.
3 As to the meaning of 'local authority' see PARA 1.
4 In connection with a person's residence see PARAS 84–87.
5 Care Act 2014 s 29(1)(a). A care account must specify such amount as is attributable to the adult's daily living costs: s 29(3). A local authority which is keeping a care account must, at such times as regulations may specify, provide the adult concerned with a statement which sets out the adult's accrued costs (s 29(4)(a)) and includes such other matters as regulations may specify (s 29(4)(b)). Regulations may specify circumstances in which the duty under s 29(4) does not apply: s 29(5). At the date at which this volume states the law no such regulations had been made.

Where, in a case within s 28(6) (needs assessment for purposes of independent personal budget: see PARA 122) an adult refuses a needs assessment and the local authority thinks that his refusal is unreasonable, it need no longer keep an up-to-date care account in the adult's case: s 28(7).

6   As to the cap on care costs see PARA 112.
7   Care Act 2014 s 29(1)(b).
8   Care Act 2014 s 29(2)(a).
9   Care Act 2014 s 29(2)(b).

124.   Financial adjustments between local authorities. Where:

(1)   a local authority in England[1] has been meeting an adult's[2] needs for care and support[3] but it transpires[4] that the adult was, for some or all of the time that the authority has been meeting the adult's needs, ordinarily resident[5] in the area of another local authority[6]; or

(2)   a local authority has been meeting a carer's[7] needs for support[8] but it transpires[9] that the adult needing care was, for some or all of the time that the authority has been meeting the carer's needs, ordinarily resident in the area of another local authority[10],

the local authority concerned may recover from the other local authority the amount of any payments it made towards meeting the needs in question at a time when the other local authority was instead liable[11] to meet them[12].

1   As to the meaning of 'local authority' see PARA 1.
2   As to the meaning of 'adult' see PARA 1 note 1. Provision for the care and support of children in England is made by the Children Act 1989 (see PARA 21) and not by the Care Act 2014 Pt 1 (ss 1–80), and accordingly the Care Act 2014 makes no corresponding provision for children.
3   Care Act 2014 s 41(1)(a).
4   Ie whether following the determination of a dispute under the Care Act 2014 s 40 (see PARA 96) or otherwise.
5   As to residence see PARAS 84–87.
6   Care Act 2014 s 41(1)(b).
7   As to the meaning of 'carer' see PARA 33 note 2.
8   Care Act 2014 s 41(2)(a).
9   See note 4.
10 Care Act 2014 s 41(2)(b).
11 Ie under the Care Act 2014 s 18 (see PARA 12) or 20(1) (see PARA 36) (as the case may be).
12 Care Act 2014 s 41(3). Section 41(3) does not apply to payments which are the subject of a deferred payment agreement (see PARAS 113–116) entered into by the local authority in question, unless it agrees with the other local authority to assign its rights and obligations under the deferred payment agreement to that other authority: s 41(4). Any period during which a local authority was meeting the needs in question under s 19 (see PARA 13) or s 20(6) (see PARA 37) is to be disregarded for these purposes: s 41(5). See also, in connection with financial adjustments relating to adults placed in accommodation in Wales, Scotland or Northern Ireland by English local authorities, Sch 1 paras 6, 9; and PARA 85.

(ii) Wales

A.   DIRECT PAYMENTS

125.   Duty to make direct payments to meet an adult's needs. Where a local authority in Wales[1] is under a duty to meet an adult's[2] needs for care and support[3], or has decided to meet that adult's needs for care and support[4], it must make direct payments towards the cost of meeting those needs[5], provided that it is satisfied that making such payments[6] is an appropriate way to meet the recipient (A)'s needs[7], the payments are consented to[8], and A is capable of managing the payments[9]. Additional conditions are imposed in relation to adults lacking capacity[10], and there are also generally applicable conditions relating to the making of payments[11]. Where the potential recipient of the payments is subject to certain drug or alcohol treatment requirements, the duty to make direct payments is discretionary, and any payments must be made subject to conditions[12].

Payments may be made net or gross and may be subject to conditions requiring contribution and reimbursement[13]. Payments are made to A[14] or, where A does not have, or the local authority believes that he does not have, capacity to consent to the making of the payments, to a 'suitable person'[15]. A local authority may terminate its arrangements for making direct payments, and may require repayment of all or part of the direct payments which it has made, if it is satisfied either that the payments have not been used to meet the need to which they relate[16] or that an applicable condition[17] has not been complied with[18].

1   As to the meaning of 'local authority' see PARA 2.
2   As to the meaning of 'adult' see PARA 2.
3   Ie under the Social Services and Well-being (Wales) Act 2014 s 35: see PARA 19. As to the meanings of 'care' and 'support' see PARA 2 note 1.
4   Ie under the Social Services and Well-being (Wales) Act 2014 s 36: see PARA 20.
5   Care and Support (Direct Payments) (Wales) Regulations 2015, SI 2015/1815, reg 2(a)(i), (ii) (made under the Social Services and Well-being (Wales) Act 2014 ss 50(1), (7), 187(2)). Where a local authority makes direct payments to a person, the making of the payments displaces the authority's duty or power to provide, directly or indirectly, to meet the needs, or that aspect of the needs, in relation to which the payments are made and for the duration of the period for which payments are made: Care and Support (Direct Payments) (Wales) Regulations 2015, SI 2015/1815, reg 3 (made under the Social Services and Well-being (Wales) Act 2014 s 53(1)(i)). Payments are subject to review: see PARA 130. See also s 53(11), Sch A1 (amended and added by SI 2016/413); the Care and Support (Direct Payments) (Wales) Regulations 2015, SI 2015/1815, reg 15 (direct payments made in respect of after-care under the Mental Health Act 1983 s 117 (see MENTAL HEALTH AND CAPACITY vol 75 (2013) PARA 945)); and the Care Act 2014 Sch 4 para 2 (modifying the Services and Well-being (Wales) Act 2014 ss 50, 51, 53 in this context).
6   As to the persons to whom the payments must be made see the text and notes 14–15. 'P' ('P') is used to refer to a person who is, or who it is proposed, will be a recipient of direct payments and who is a 'suitable person' for the purposes of the Social Services and Well-being (Wales) Act 2014 s 50(4) (see note 15) or a person with parental responsibility for A to whom direct payments may be made for the benefit of A (see note 7) under s 51 (see PARA 126): Care and Support (Direct Payments) (Wales) Regulations 2015, SI 2015/1815, reg 1(4). As to the meaning of 'parental responsibility' see PARA 26 note 10.
7   Social Services and Well-being (Wales) Act 2014 s 50(2), (3)(c)(i), (4)(d)(i); Care and Support (Direct Payments) (Wales) Regulations 2015, SI 2015/1815, reg 2(b). 'A' ('A') is used to refer to a person whose care and support needs or support needs are being or will be met by making direct payments: reg 1(4). Before considering whether direct payments are an appropriate way of meeting the needs of A where A is an adult without capacity, a local authority must:
    (1)   consult anyone named by A as someone to be consulted on the issue, anyone engaged in caring for A or with a significant interest in his welfare, P, and a person authorised under the Mental Capacity Act 2005 (whether in general or specific terms: see MENTAL HEALTH AND CAPACITY) to make decisions about A's needs for care and support (Care and Support (Direct Payments) (Wales) Regulations 2015, SI 2015/1815, reg 5(a) (made under the Social Services and Well-being (Wales) Act 2014 s 53(1)(d), (f));
    (2)   where A is an adult who previously had capacity, consider, so far as reasonably practicable his past and present views, wishes and feelings and, in particular, any relevant written statement made by him while still with capacity, the beliefs and values which would be likely to influence his decision, and any other relevant factors that he would in the local authority's view be likely to consider, if able to do so (Care and Support (Direct Payments) (Wales) Regulations 2015, SI 2015/1815, reg 5(b)); and
    (3)   obtain an enhanced criminal record certificate issued under the Police Act 1997 s 113B (see SENTENCING vol 92 (2015) PARAS 640–642) in respect of P where P is an individual but is neither a relative of the adult nor a friend of his who is involved in his care (Care and Support (Direct Payments) (Wales) Regulations 2015, SI 2015/1815, reg 5(c)).
    'Relative' means (by virtue of reg 1(4)):
    (a)   a spouse or civil partner;
    (b)   a person who lives with a person as if a spouse or civil partner;
    (c)   parent, parent-in-law or step-parent;
    (d)   son or daughter;
    (e)   son-in-law or daughter-in-law;
    (f)   stepson or stepdaughter;
    (g)   brother or sister;

    (h)   aunt or uncle;

    (i)   grandparent; or

    (j)   the spouse or civil partner of any person specified in heads (c) to (i).

8 Ie where A has, or the local authority believes that he has, capacity to consent to the making of the payments (Social Services and Well-being (Wales) Act 2014 s 50(3)(b)) and he has consented to the making of the payments (s 50(3)(d)), or, where A does not have, or the local authority believes that he does not have, capacity to consent to the making of the payments (s 50(4)(a)), the necessary consent has been obtained to make the payments to him (s 50(4)(e)). As to a person having or lacking capacity see PARA 8 note 10. For the purposes of s 50(4)(e), the 'necessary consent' means:

    (1)   the consent of P (s 50(6)(a)); and

    (2)   where P is a suitable person by virtue of s 50(5)(b) (see note 15), the consent of a person authorised under the Mental Capacity Act 2005 (whether in general or specific terms) to make decisions about A's needs for care and support (Social Services and Well-being (Wales) Act 2014 s 50(6)(a)).

    A local authority that has decided to make direct payments must provide information to A so that he can decide whether to consent to the payments: see the Care and Support (Direct Payments) (Wales) Regulations 2015, SI 2015/1815, reg 4 (made under the Social Services and Well-being (Wales) Act 2014 s 53(5), (6)).

9 In the case of an adult having capacity, the authority must be satisfied that A is capable of managing the payments (either by himself or herself or with the support that is available to him) (Social Services and Well-being (Wales) Act 2014 s 50(3)(c)(ii)); where A does not have, or the local authority believes that he does not have, capacity to consent to the making of the payments, the authority must be satisfied that P is capable of managing the payments (either by himself or herself or with the support that is available to him) (s 50(4)(d)(ii)) and will act in A's best interests in managing the payments (s 50(4)(d)(iii)).

10 Where a local authority makes direct payments under the Services and Well-being (Wales) Act 2014 s 50 to P because A lacks capacity, it must impose conditions that:

    (1)   P acts in the best interests of A when securing the provision of care and support (Care and Support (Direct Payments) (Wales) Regulations 2015, SI 2015/1815, reg 7(1), (2)(a) (made under the Social Services and Well-being (Wales) Act 2014 s 53(1)(e)); and

    (2)   notifies the local authority if P believes that A no longer lacks capacity (Care and Support (Direct Payments) (Wales) Regulations 2015, SI 2015/1815, reg 7(2)(b)).

    Where P is not a relative of A (reg 7(4)(a)) or a friend of A who is involved in the provision of his care (reg 7(4)(b)) the authority must also impose a condition that P obtains:

    (a)   an enhanced criminal record certificate issued under the Police Act 1997 s 113B including suitability information relating to vulnerable adults (within the meaning of s 113BB: see SENTENCING vol 92 (2015) PARA 638) or children (within the meaning of s 113BA: see SENTENCING vol 92 (2015) PARA 638) (Care and Support (Direct Payments) (Wales) Regulations 2015, SI 2015/1815, reg 7(3)(a)); or

    (b)   verification that a satisfactory certificate of that sort has been obtained (reg 7(3)(b)),

in respect of any person from whom a service is secured being a service for which the direct payments are made. See also, in connection with an adult who loses capacity, reg 13; and note 18.

11 See the Care and Support (Direct Payments) (Wales) Regulations 2015, SI 2015/1815, regs 6, 8; and PARA 129.

12 See the Care and Support (Direct Payments) (Wales) Regulations 2015, SI 2015/1815, reg 14; and PARA 128.

13 When a local authority decides to make direct payments, whether under the Care and Support (Direct Payments) (Wales) Regulations 2015, SI 2015/1815, reg 2 (see the text and notes 1–12; and PARAS 126–127) or reg 14, it must decide whether to make them as net payments or gross payments: reg 9(1) (made under the Social Services and Well-being (Wales) Act 2014 s 53(1)(b)):

    (1)   'gross payments' means direct payments which are made at a rate that the authority estimates to be equivalent to the reasonable cost of securing the provision of the care and support (or, in the case of carers, the support) in respect of which the payments are made, but which may be made subject to the condition that a specified person pays to the authority, by way of reimbursement, a specified amount or amounts; and

    (2)   'net payments' means direct payments which are made on the basis that a specified person will pay a specified amount or amounts by way of contribution towards the cost of securing the provision of the care and support (or, in the case of carers, the support) in respect of which the payments are made, and which are accordingly made at a rate below the rate the local authority estimates to be equivalent to the reasonable cost of securing the provision of that care and support (or, in the case of carers, that support) so as to reflect the contribution to be made by that person (s 53(2)).

    In connection with contribution and reimbursement see further PARAS 136–137. In deciding whether to make net payments or gross payments a local authority must take into account the

effect on A having regard to his financial circumstances: Care and Support (Direct Payments) (Wales) Regulations 2015, SI 2015/1815, reg 9(2).
14 Social Services and Well-being (Wales) Act 2014 s 50(3)(a).
15 Social Services and Well-being (Wales) Act 2014 s 50(4)(a)–(c). A person (P) is a 'suitable person':
    (1)   if he is authorised under the Mental Capacity Act 2005 (whether in general or specific terms) to make decisions about A's needs for care and support (Social Services and Well-being (Wales) Act 2014 s 50(5)(a));
    (2)   where P is not so authorised, if a person who is so authorised agrees with the local authority that P is suitable to receive payments towards the cost of meeting A's needs for care and support (s 50(5)(b)); or
    (3)   where P is not so authorised and there is no person who is so authorised, if the local authority considers that P is suitable to receive payments of that kind (s 50(5)(c)).
16 Care and Support (Direct Payments) (Wales) Regulations 2015, SI 2015/1815, reg 10(a) (made under the Social Services and Well-being (Wales) Act 2014 s 53(1)(m), (n)).
17 Ie, in the case of direct payments generally, the conditions about using payments to pay relatives and relating to the meeting of needs by particular persons (see the Care and Support (Direct Payments) (Wales) Regulations 2015, SI 2015/1815, regs 6, 8; and PARA 129) and the conditions relating to making payments persons subject to drug or alcohol treatment orders (see reg 14; and PARA 128); and in the case of payments in respect of adults lacking capacity, the condition requiring vetting (see reg 7; and note 10): reg 10(b).
18 Care and Support (Direct Payments) (Wales) Regulations 2015, SI 2015/1815, reg 10(b). A local authority need not terminate the making of direct payments under the Social Services and Well-being (Wales) Act 2014 s 50 in relation to A where A is an adult in relation to whom the condition in s 50(3)(b) (see the text and note 8) was met because A had capacity to consent to the making of payments at the time the arrangement started, but who subsequently loses capacity, and either:
    (1)   the authority is satisfied that A's loss of capacity to consent to the making of payments is temporary and either the period or periods of loss of capacity are not likely to affect A's ability to manage the payments (Care and Support (Direct Payments) (Wales) Regulations 2015, SI 2015/1815, reg 13(1), (2), (3)(a)(i) (made under the Social Services and Well-being (Wales) Act 2014 s 53(1)(k)) or another person who appears to the authority to be capable of managing the payments is prepared to accept and manage the payments on behalf of A during the periods of A's incapacity (Care and Support (Direct Payments) (Wales) Regulations 2015, SI 2015/1815, reg 13(3)(a)(ii)); or
    (2)   the conditions in the Social Services and Well-being (Wales) Act 2014 s 50(4) (see the text and notes 7–9) are met (Care and Support (Direct Payments) (Wales) Regulations 2015, SI 2015/1815, reg 13(3)(b)).

126. Duty to make direct payments to meet a child's needs.

Where a local authority in Wales[1] is under a duty to meet a child's[2] needs for care and support[3], or has decided to meet that child's needs for care and support[4], it must make direct payments towards the cost of meeting the child's needs[5], provided that it is satisfied that making such payments[6] is an appropriate way to meet those needs[7], the payments are consented to[8], P is capable of managing the payments[9], and the well-being[10] of the child will be safeguarded and promoted by the making of the payments[11]. There are also generally applicable conditions relating to the making of payments[12]. Where the potential recipient of the payments is subject to certain drug or alcohol treatment requirements, the duty to make direct payments is discretionary, and any payments must be made subject to conditions[13].

Payments may be made net or gross, but may not be subject to conditions requiring contribution and reimbursement[14]. Payments are made to the child who has needs for care and support[15] or to a person with parental responsibility for such a child[16]. Particular provision is made where A or P is in receipt of specified child benefits[17]. A local authority may terminate its arrangements for making direct payments, and may require repayment of all or part of the direct payments which it has made, if it is satisfied either that the payments have not been used to meet the need to which they relate or that an applicable condition has not been complied with[18].

1   As to the meaning of 'local authority' see PARA 2.

2   As to the meaning of 'child' see PARA 2.
3   Ie under the Social Services and Well-being (Wales) Act 2014 s 37 (see PARA 30) or s 39 (see PARA 32). As to the meanings of 'care' and 'support' see PARA 2 note 1.
4   Ie under the Social Services and Well-being (Wales) Act 2014 s 38: see PARA 31.
5   Care and Support (Direct Payments) (Wales) Regulations 2015, SI 2015/1815, reg 2(a)(i), (ii) (made under the Social Services and Well-being (Wales) Act 2014 ss 51(1), (7), 187(2)). As to the effect of making direct payments see PARA 125 note 5. Payments are subject to review: see PARA 130. See also s 53(11), Sch A1 (added by SI 2016/413); the Care and Support (Direct Payments) (Wales) Regulations 2015, SI 2015/1815, reg 15 (direct payments made in respect of after-care under the Mental Health Act 1983 s 117 (see MENTAL HEALTH AND CAPACITY vol 75 (2013) PARA 945)).
6   As to the persons to whom the payments must be made see the text and notes 15–16.
7   Social Services and Well-being (Wales) Act 2014 s 51(2), (5)(a); Care and Support (Direct Payments) (Wales) Regulations 2015, SI 2015/1815, reg 2(b).
8   Ie:
    (1)   where P (as to which see PARA 125 note 6) is an adult or a child aged 16 or 17, he has, or the authority believes that he has, capacity to consent to the making of the payments (Care Act 2014 s 51(4)(a)); or
    (2)   where P is a child aged under 16, the authority is satisfied that he has sufficient understanding to make an informed decision about receiving direct payments (s 51(4)(b)).
    and that P has consented to the making of the payments (s 51(6)). As to the meaning of 'adult' see PARA 2. A local authority that has decided to make direct payments must provide information to A so that he can decide whether to consent to the payments: see the Care and Support (Direct Payments) (Wales) Regulations 2015, SI 2015/1815, reg 4; and PARA 125 note 8. As to 'A' see PARA 125 note 7.
9   Ie, the local authority must be satisfied that P is capable of managing the payments (either by himself or herself or with the support that is available to him): Social Services and Well-being (Wales) Act 2014 s 50(5)(c).
10 As to the meaning of 'well-being' see PARA 375.
11 Social Services and Well-being (Wales) Act 2014 s 50(5)(b).
12 See the Care and Support (Direct Payments) (Wales) Regulations 2015, SI 2015/1815, regs 6, 8; and PARA 129.
13 See the Care and Support (Direct Payments) (Wales) Regulations 2015, SI 2015/1815, reg 14; and PARA 128.
14 See PARA 125 note 15.
15 Social Services and Well-being (Wales) Act 2014 s 51(3)(b).
16 Social Services and Well-being (Wales) Act 2014 s 51(3)(a). As to the meaning of 'parental responsibility' see PARA 26 note 10.
17 Where A is a child and a local authority makes direct payments under the Social Services and Well-being (Wales) Act 2014 s 51 towards the cost of meeting his care and support needs, and either A or P is in receipt of specified benefits, the authority must make the payments at the rate which it estimates to be the reasonable cost of provision to meet the care and support needs in respect of which the payments are made and must not make the payments subject to any condition requiring either the child A or, the recipient of the payment P, to pay any amount to the authority by way of reimbursement: see the Care and Support (Direct Payments) (Wales) Regulations 2015, SI 2015/1815, reg 12 (made under the Social Services and Well-being (Wales) Act 2014 s 53(7), (8)).
18 See the Care and Support (Direct Payments) (Wales) Regulations 2015, SI 2015/1815, reg 10; and PARA 125 notes 16–18.

127.   Duty to make direct payments to meet a carer's needs. Where a local authority in Wales[1] is under a duty to meet a carer's[2] needs for support[3], or has decided to meet that carer's needs for support[4], it must make direct payments towards the cost of meeting those needs[5], provided that it is satisfied that making such payments[6] is an appropriate way to meet those needs[7], the payments are consented to[8], and the recipient is capable of managing the payments[9]. There are also generally applicable conditions relating to the making of payments[10]. Where the potential recipient of the payments is subject to certain drug or alcohol treatment requirements, the duty to make direct payments is discretionary, and any payments must be made subject to conditions[11].

Payments may be made net or gross and may be subject to conditions requiring contribution and reimbursement[12]. Payments are made to the carer who has needs for support[13]. A local authority may terminate its arrangements for making direct payments, and may require repayment of all or part of the direct payments which it has made, if it is satisfied either that the payments have not been used to meet the need to which they relate or that an applicable condition has not been complied with[14].

1   As to the meaning of 'local authority' see PARA 2.
2   As to the meaning of 'carer' see PARA 54 note 2.
3   Ie under the Social Services and Well-being (Wales) Act 2014 s 40 or s 42 (see PARA 58–62).
4   Ie under the Social Services and Well-being (Wales) Act 2014 s 45: see PARA 63.
5   Care and Support (Direct Payments) (Wales) Regulations 2015, SI 2015/1815, regs 1(5), 2(a)(i), (ii) (made under the Social Services and Well-being (Wales) Act 2014 s 52(1), (7)). As to the effect of making direct payments see PARA 125 note 5. Payments are subject to review: see PARA 130.
6   As to the persons to whom the payments must be made see the text and note 13.
7   Social Services and Well-being (Wales) Act 2014 s 52(2), (5)(a); Care and Support (Direct Payments) (Wales) Regulations 2015, SI 2015/1815, reg 2(b).
8   Ie:
    (1)   where the carer is an adult or a child aged 16 or 17 he has, or the authority believes that he has, capacity to consent to the making of the payments (Social Services and Well-being (Wales) Act 2014 s 52(4)(a)); or
    (2)   where the carer is a child aged under 16, the authority is satisfied that he has sufficient understanding to make an informed decision about receiving direct payments (s 52(4)(b)),
    and that the carer has consented to the making of the payments (s 52(6)). As to the meanings of 'adult' and 'child' see PARA 2. A local authority that has decided to make direct payments must provide information to the potential recipient so that he can decide whether to consent to the payments: see the Care and Support (Direct Payments) (Wales) Regulations 2015, SI 2015/1815, reg 4; and PARA 125 note 8.
9   Ie, the local authority must be satisfied that the recipient (see note 11) is capable of managing the payments (either by himself or herself or with the support that is available to him): Social Services and Well-being (Wales) Act 2014 s 52(5)(b).
10 See the Care and Support (Direct Payments) (Wales) Regulations 2015, SI 2015/1815, regs 6, 8; and PARA 129.
11 See the Care and Support (Direct Payments) (Wales) Regulations 2015, SI 2015/1815, reg 14; and PARA 128.
12 See PARA 125 note 15.
13 Social Services and Well-being (Wales) Act 2014 s 52(3).
14 See the Care and Support (Direct Payments) (Wales) Regulations 2015, SI 2015/1815, reg 10; and PARA 125 notes 16–18.

128.   No duty to make payments in respect of persons subject to drug or alcohol treatment orders. A local authority in Wales is not required to make a direct payment[1] to persons who are:
    (1)   subject to a drug rehabilitation requirement[2] imposed by a community order[3] or by a suspended sentence order[4];
    (2)   subject to an alcohol treatment requirement[5] imposed by a community order or a suspended sentence order;
    (3)   released on licence[6] subject to a non-standard licence condition requiring the offender to undertake offending behaviour work to address drug or alcohol related behaviour;
    (4)   required to submit to treatment for their drug or alcohol dependency by virtue of a community rehabilitation order[7] or a community punishment and rehabilitation order[8];
    (5)   subject to a drug treatment and testing order[9]; or
    (6)   subject to corresponding Scottish provision,
although an authority may make a direct payment to such a person if it attaches conditions in the following terms:

(a)   that A agrees and remains in agreement that the payments are made to a person ('B') to manage on A's behalf[10]; and

(b)   that B agrees and remains in agreement to receive the payments and to manage the payments to meet A's needs for care and support[11].

and the authority is satisfied that B is an appropriate person to receive and manage payments on A's behalf[12].

1 Ie by virtue of the Care and Support (Direct Payments) (Wales) Regulations 2015, SI 2015/1815, regs 2, 14(1), Schedule (made under the Social Services and Well-being (Wales) Act 2014 s 53(1)(j)). As to the duty of local authorities in Wales to make direct payments, and the conditions relating to that duty, see PARAS 125–127. As to the meaning of 'local authority' see PARA 2.
2 Ie as defined by the Criminal Justice Act 2003 s 209: see SENTENCING vol 92 (2015) PARA 124.
3 Ie as defined by the Criminal Justice Act 2003 s 177: see SENTENCING vol 92 (2015) PARA 48.
4 Ie as defined by the Criminal Justice Act 2003 s 189: see SENTENCING vol 92 (2015) PARA 100.
5 Ie as defined by the Criminal Justice Act 2003 s 212: see SENTENCING vol 92 (2015) PARA 122.
6 Ie under the Criminal Justice Act 1991 Pt 2 (ss 32–51); the Criminal Justice Act 2003 Pt 12 Ch 6 (ss 237–268) (sentencing: release, licenses and recall: see SENTENCING) or the Crime (Sentences) Act 1997 Pt 2 Ch 2 (ss 28–34) (effect of custodial sentences: life sentences: see SENTENCING).
7 Ie within the meaning of the Powers of Criminal Courts (Sentencing) Act 2000 s 41 (repealed).
8 Ie within the meaning of the Powers of Criminal Courts (Sentencing) Act 2000 s 51 (repealed).
9 Ie imposed under the Powers of Criminal Courts (Sentencing) Act 2000 s 52 (repealed).
10 Care and Support (Direct Payments) (Wales) Regulations 2015, SI 2015/1815, reg 14(2), (3)(a). As to 'A' see PARA 125 note 7.
11 Care and Support (Direct Payments) (Wales) Regulations 2015, SI 2015/1815, reg 14(3)(b).
12 Care and Support (Direct Payments) (Wales) Regulations 2015, SI 2015/1815, reg 14(2), (4).

129. Generally applicable conditions relating to the making of direct payments. A person to whom a local authority in Wales makes a direct payment[1] may[2] use the payment to purchase care and support[3] (or, in the case of a carer[4], support) from any person (including, among others, the authority which made the payment)[5]. An authority may authorise the use of direct payments to pay a relative of A[6] who is living in the same household if it considers that it is necessary to promote the well-being[7] of A[8]. Payments may be authorised to pay the relative either for the provision of care and support to A[9] or for help to A in managing the payments[10]. Where a local authority does not consider that it is necessary to promote A's well-being, it must impose a condition that direct payments are not to be used to pay a relative of A who is living in the same household[11].

An authority may make a direct payment subject to further conditions which may, for example, include a requirement that:

(1)   the needs in respect of which payment is being made may not be met by a particular person[12];

(2)   the recipient of the payments must provide information reasonably required by the authority for the purposes of ensuring that direct payments are an appropriate way of meeting A's needs[13].

Failure to comply with these conditions may result in the termination, and repayment, of payments[14].

1 As to the duty of local authorities in Wales to make direct payments, and the specific conditions relating to that duty, see PARAS 125–127. As to the meaning of 'local authority' see PARA 2.
2 Ie subject to the Care and Support (Direct Payments) (Wales) Regulations 2015, SI 2015/1815; the Care and Support (Charging) (Wales) Regulations 2015, SI 2015/1815; and the Care and Support (Financial Assessment) (Wales) Regulations 2015, SI 2015/1844.
3 As to the meanings of 'care' and 'support' see PARA 2 note 1.
4 As to the meaning of 'carer' see PARA 54 note 2.
5 Social Services and Well-being (Wales) Act 2014 s 53(9).
6 As to 'A', and as to the meaning of 'relative', see PARA 125 note 7.
7 As to the meaning of 'well-being' see PARA 375.

8 Care and Support (Direct Payments) (Wales) Regulations 2015, SI 2015/1815, reg 6(1). In considering whether it is necessary to promote the well-being of A in accordance with reg 6(1) a local authority must take into account the views of A and the other persons mentioned in reg 11(3) (reviews: see PARA 130): reg 6(3).
9 Care and Support (Direct Payments) (Wales) Regulations 2015, SI 2015/1815, reg 6(2)(a).
10 Care and Support (Direct Payments) (Wales) Regulations 2015, SI 2015/1815, reg 6(2)(b).
11 Care and Support (Direct Payments) (Wales) Regulations 2015, SI 2015/1815, reg 6(4).
12 Care and Support (Direct Payments) (Wales) Regulations 2015, SI 2015/1815, reg 8(1), (2)(a). A condition so imposed must not require that A's needs may only be met by a particular person: reg 8(3).
13 Care and Support (Direct Payments) (Wales) Regulations 2015, SI 2015/1815, reg 8(2)(b).
14 See the Care and Support (Direct Payments) (Wales) Regulations 2015, SI 2015/1815, reg 10; and PARA 125 notes 16–18.

130. Review of direct payments. A local authority in Wales must review the arrangements for the making of direct payments[1] and the use which is being made of them:

(1)   at intervals which the authority determines appropriate at the point of starting to make direct payments to A, having regard to the circumstances in A's case[2];

(2)   when A or P call for a review[3];

(3)   when the authority calls for a review either because it is concerned that the use being made of the direct payments is not meeting the needs of A[4], it is concerned that a condition attached to the making of the payments is not being complied with[5], or there is a significant change in A or P's circumstances[6]; and

(4)   in any event, at intervals not greater than six months after the first payment is made[7] and 12 months following the first review[8].

When carrying out a review the authority must involve A[9], P (where payments are made to P)[10] and other specified persons involved in A's care[11].

1 As to the duty of local authorities in Wales to make direct payments, and the generally applicable conditions relating to that duty, see PARAS 125–129. As to the meaning of 'local authority' see PARA 2.
2 Care and Support (Direct Payments) (Wales) Regulations 2015, SI 2015/1815, reg 11(1)(a) (made under the Social Services and Well-being (Wales) Act 2014 s 53(1)(l)). As to 'A' see PARA 125 note 7.
3 Care and Support (Direct Payments) (Wales) Regulations 2015, SI 2015/1815, reg 11(1)(b). As to 'P' see PARA 125 note 6. Where A, P or the local authority call for a review under reg 11(1)(b) or (c), the period before the next review is due will be extended accordingly: reg 11(2).
4 Care and Support (Direct Payments) (Wales) Regulations 2015, SI 2015/1815, reg 11(1)(c)(i). See note 3.
5 Care and Support (Direct Payments) (Wales) Regulations 2015, SI 2015/1815, reg 11(1)(c)(ii). See note 3.
6 Care and Support (Direct Payments) (Wales) Regulations 2015, SI 2015/1815, reg 11(1)(c)(iii). See note 3.
7 Care and Support (Direct Payments) (Wales) Regulations 2015, SI 2015/1815, reg 11(1)(d)(i).
8 Care and Support (Direct Payments) (Wales) Regulations 2015, SI 2015/1815, reg 11(1)(d)(ii).
9 Care and Support (Direct Payments) (Wales) Regulations 2015, SI 2015/1815, reg 11(3)(a).
10 Care and Support (Direct Payments) (Wales) Regulations 2015, SI 2015/1815, reg 11(3)(b).
11 Ie:
(1)   any carer of A (Care and Support (Direct Payments) (Wales) Regulations 2015, SI 2015/1815, reg 11(3)(c));
(2)   any person whom A asks the authority to involve (reg 11(3)(d)(i));
(3)   if A is an adult who lacks the capacity to decide who to involve, any person authorised under the Mental Capacity Act 2005 (see MENTAL HEALTH AND CAPACITY) to make decisions about A's needs for care and support (Care and Support (Direct Payments) (Wales) Regulations 2015, SI 2015/1815, reg 11(3)(d)(ii));
(4)   if A is a child aged 16 or 17 who does not have capacity to decide who to involve, any person authorised to make decisions about A's needs for care and support under the

Mental Capacity Act 2005 (Care and Support (Direct Payments) (Wales) Regulations 2015, SI 2015/1815, reg 11(3)(d)(iii)(aa)) or a person with parental responsibility for A (reg 11(3)(d)(iii)(bb));

(5)   if A is a child below the age of 16, A's parent or other person in a parental role (reg 11(3)(d)(iv)); and

(6)   any other person who the local authority considers to have sufficient involvement in the care or support arrangements for A (reg 11(3)(e)).

The requirement to involve a parent or other person in a parental role in a review under reg 11(3)(d)(iv) does not apply where, in the view of the local authority, involving that person would not be consistent with the child's well-being: reg 11(4). As to the meaning of 'carer' see PARA 54 note 2. As to the meanings of 'adult' and 'child' see PARA 2. As to the meanings of 'care' and 'support' see PARA 2 note 1. As to the meaning of 'parental responsibility' see PARA 26 note 10. In reg 11, 'person in a parental role' includes a parent, a person with parental responsibility or other person who is looking after the child: reg 11(5).

B.   CHARGING, REIMBURSEMENT AND CONTRIBUTION

(A)   Charges and Deferred Payment Agreements

131. Power of local authority to impose a charge for meeting needs. A local authority in Wales[1] may require a person to pay a charge to the authority for providing or arranging the provision of care and support[2] to meet[3] an adult's[4] needs or support to meet[5] a carer's[6] needs[7]. An authority may not impose a charge for care and support provided or arranged[8] to meet the needs of a child[9]. A charge so imposed is referred to as the 'standard charge'[10]. The standard charge may cover only the cost that the authority incurs in meeting the needs to which the charge applies[11], although an additional charge may be imposed where the authority chooses to provide care and support, rather than where it is under a duty to do so[12]. Certain services, consisting of specified transportation, reablement and advocacy services, may not be the subject of a charge[13], and a charge may also not be imposed in respect of a person suffering from variant Creutzfeldt-Jakob disease[14] or a person receiving after-care following detention for mental health treatment[15].

A charge for providing or arranging the provision of care and support to meet an adult's needs, or for putting in place the arrangements for that care and support, may be imposed on that adult[16]. A charge for providing or arranging the provision of support to meet a carer's needs, or for putting in place the arrangements for that support, may be imposed either on that carer[17] or on an adult with parental responsibility for that carer[18]. Any charge so imposed is susceptible to review[19].

1   As to the meaning of 'local authority' see PARA 2.
2   As to the meaning of 'care' and 'support' see PARA 2 note 1.
3   Ie under the Social Services and Well-being (Wales) Act 2014 ss 35–36: see PARAS 19–20.
4   As to the meaning of 'adult' see PARA 2.
5   As to the meaning of 'carer' see PARA 54 note 2.
6   Ie under the Social Services and Well-being (Wales) Act 2014 ss 40–45: see PARAS 58–62.
7   Social Services and Well-being (Wales) Act 2014 s 59(1). See also s 53(10) (a local authority may impose a reasonable charge for the provision of care and support (or, in the case of a carer, support) to meet needs in respect of which a direct payment has been made). A local authority's power to impose a charge under s 59 is subject to Care and Support (Charging) (Wales) Regulations 2015, SI 2015/1843 (see the text and notes 8–19; and PARAS 132, 136, 137) and its duties under the Social Services and Well-being (Wales) Act 2014 ss 63, 66, 67 (if applicable) (see PARAS 132, 136): s 59(4).
8   Ie under the Social Services and Well-being (Wales) Act 2014 ss 37–39: see PARAS 30–32.
9   Care and Support (Charging) (Wales) Regulations 2015, SI 2015/1843, reg 3(a) (made under the Social Services and Well-being (Wales) Act 2014 ss 61(1), 62). Statutory provision is nonetheless made to enable an authority to impose a charge in respect of a child's needs should this exemption be removed: see s 59(1), (3), 60(3).

10 In the Social Services and Well-being (Wales) Act 2014 Pt 4 (ss 32–58) 'standard charge' means the amount that a local authority would charge under s 59 if no determination were made under s 66 (see PARAS 136–137) as to a person's ability to pay that amount: s 63(3). As to determining the standard charge see PARA 132.

11 Social Services and Well-being (Wales) Act 2014 s 59(2).

12 Where an authority is meeting needs because the Social Services and Well-being (Wales) Act 2014 s 35(4)(b)(ii) (see PARA 19), s 36 (see PARA 20), s 41(2), (4) or (6)(a)(i) (see PARAS 59–61), s 43(2) or (4)(a)(i) (see PARAS 60–61) or s 45 (see PARA 63) applies, it may require a person to pay a charge to the authority (in addition to any charge imposed under s 59(1)) for putting in place the arrangements for meeting those needs: s 59(3).

13 See the Care and Support (Charging) (Wales) Regulations 2015, SI 2015/1843, reg 4. 'Reablement' means care and support provided or arranged by a local authority under the Social Services and Well-being (Wales) Act 2014 Pt 2 (ss 5–18) or Pt 4 (ss 59–73), or secured or arranged by the person, where he is or will be receiving direct payments made in accordance with s 50 or s 52, and which consists of a programme of care and support, is for a specified period of time ('the specified period'), and has as its purpose the provision of assistance to the person to enable him to maintain or regain the ability to live independently in his only or main home: Care and Support (Charging) (Wales) Regulations 2015, SI 2015/1843, reg 1(4).

14 A local authority may not impose a charge for care and support provided or arranged for a person who is suffering from any form of Creutzfeldt-Jakob disease where that disease has been clinically diagnosed by a registered medical practitioner: Care and Support (Charging) (Wales) Regulations 2015, SI 2015/1843, reg 3(b). As to the meaning of 'registered medical practitioner' see MEDICAL PROFESSIONS vol 74 (2011) PARA 176.

15 A local authority may not impose a charge for care and support provided or arranged for a person who has been offered or is receiving a service provided as part of a package of after care services in accordance with the Mental Health Act 1983 s 117 (see MENTAL HEALTH AND CAPACITY vol 75 (2013) PARA 945): Care and Support (Charging) (Wales) Regulations 2015, SI 2015/1843, reg 3(c).

16 Social Services and Well-being (Wales) Act 2014 s 60(1), (2); Care and Support (Charging) (Wales) Regulations 2015, SI 2015/1843, reg 2.

17 Ie where the support is provided to a carer who is an adult: Social Services and Well-being (Wales) Act 2014 s 60(4)(a). Where a carer's needs for support are met by the provision of care and support to a person for whom the carer provides or intends to provide care, s 60(4) does not apply; a charge for providing or arranging the provision of that support, or for putting in place the arrangements for that support, may instead be imposed:

    (1)   where the carer's needs for support are met by the provision of care and support to an adult, on that adult (s 60(5)(a));

    (2)   where the carer's needs for support are met by the provision of care and support to a child, on an adult with parental responsibility for that child (s 60(5)(b)).

18 Ie where the support is provided to a carer who is a child: Social Services and Well-being (Wales) Act 2014 s 60(4)(b). As to the meaning of 'parental responsibility' see the Children Act 1989 s 3; and CHILDREN AND YOUNG PERSONS vol 9 (2017) PARA 150. See note 15.

19 Social Services and Well-being (Wales) Act 2014 s 73(1)(a). The following persons may request a review of any of the decisions relating to charging set out in s 73(1) or a determination of a reimbursement or contribution made in accordance with the Care and Support (Charging) (Wales) Regulations 2015, SI 2015/1843 and the Care and Support (Financial Assessment) (Wales) Regulations 2015, SI 2015/1844 (see PARAS 136–141):

    (1)   persons upon whom a charge may be imposed in accordance with the Social Services and Well-being (Wales) Act 2014 s 60 (see the text and notes 1–18) (Care and Support (Review of Charging Decisions and Determinations) (Wales) Regulations 2015, SI 2015/1842, reg 3(a));

    (2)   a person who is required to pay a reimbursement or contribution in respect of a direct payment determined as stated above (reg 3(b));

    (3)   a liable transferee (ie a transferee within the meaning of the Social Services and Well-being (Wales) Act 2014 72 (see PARAS 138) against whom liability arises under s 72 (Care and Support (Review of Charging Decisions and Determinations) (Wales) Regulations 2015, SI 2015/1842, reg 3(c)); or

    (4)   subject to reg 6 (representatives), any representative appointed to make the request on behalf of persons falling within heads 1 to 3 above (reg 3(d)).

Provision for the circumstances under which a review may be requested, and the procedure for reviews, is made by regs 4–17 (made under the Social Services and Well-being (Wales) Act 2014 s 73(2)).

132. Determining a person's ability to pay the standard charge, and the 'capital limit'. Where a local authority in Wales has carried out a financial assessment[1]:

(1)   it must determine, in light of the assessment, whether it would be reasonably practicable for the assessed person[2] to pay the standard charge[3] for the care and support or (in the case of carers) the support in respect of which a charge would be imposed on that person[4] and if so, what that amount should be[5]; and

(2)   if the authority determines that it would not be reasonably practicable for the assessed person to pay the standard charge, the authority must determine the amount (if any) that it would be reasonably practicable for that person to pay for that care and support or that support[6].

Where the person has capital above £24,000 (in the context of non-residential care) or £30,000 (in the context of residential care)[7] the authority must determine that it is reasonably practicable for him to pay the standard charge, subject to the maximum weekly charge[8] in relation to non-residential care and support[9]. There are also levels below which a person's net weekly income may not be reduced by the imposition of a charge[10]. Any determination so made is susceptible to review[11].

1   Where a local authority in Wales thinks it would impose a charge under the Social Services and Well-being (Wales) Act 2014 s 59 (see PARA 131) were it to meet an adult's needs for care and support or (if he is a carer) his needs for support (s 63(1), (4)), the authority must assess the level of the person's financial resources in order to determine whether it would be reasonably practicable for the person to pay the standard charge (subject to s 65: see PARA 141): s 63(2); Care and Support (Financial Assessment) (Wales) Regulations 2015, SI 2015/1844, reg 6(1)(a). As to the meaning of 'local authority' see PARA 2. As to the meaning of 'carer' see PARA 54 note 2. As to the carrying out of financial assessments, and the circumstances in which a financial assessment will not be required, see PARA 141.
2   Ie the person whose financial resources have been assessed under the Social Services and Well-being (Wales) Act 2014 s 63: s 66(2).
3   As to the power of the local authority to impose the standard charge see the Social Services and Well-being (Wales) Act 2014 s 59; and PARA 131.
4   Social Services and Well-being (Wales) Act 2014 s 66(1)(a).
5   Where a local authority thinks it would impose a charge under the Social Services and Well-being (Wales) Act 2014 s 59 and has carried out a financial assessment of a person in accordance with the requirements of the Care and Support (Financial Assessment) (Wales) Regulations 2015, SI 2015/1844, it must make a determination about what amount, if any, it is reasonably practicable for the person to pay in accordance with the requirements of the Care and Support (Charging) (Wales) Regulations 2015, SI 2015/1843: reg 5. A local authority need not make a determination under those Regulations where the only services provided are either those to which a flat-rate charge applies or to which no charge applies: reg 6. Procedure for determining a charge is set out in regs 8, 9 (amended by SI 2017/214); provision for the notification and revision of determinations is made by the Care and Support (Charging) (Wales) Regulations 2015, SI 2015/1843, regs 14, 15 (made under the Social Services and Well-being (Wales) Act 2014 s 67) (reg 15 amended by SI 2017/214). As to the meaning of 'flat-rate charge' see PARA 376 note 24.
6   Social Services and Well-being (Wales) Act 2014 s 66(1)(b).
7   Ie the 'relevant capital limit', which is the financial limit for the purposes of the Social Services and Well-being (Wales) Act 2014 s 66(5): Care and Support (Charging) (Wales) Regulations 2015, SI 2015/1843, reg 11(2) (amended by SI 2017/214). See also the Care and Support (Charging) (Wales) Regulations 2015, SI 2015/1843, reg 1(4) (amended by SI 2017/214) ('relevant capital limit' means the maximum amount of capital, assessed in accordance with the Care and Support (Financial Assessment) (Wales) Regulations 2015, SI 2015/1844, which a chargeable person may have depending on whether their need is for care and support which is residential or non-residential, above which that person will be required, in accordance with the Care and Support (Charging) (Wales) Regulations 2015, SI 2015/1843, reg 11 (see the text and notes 9–10) to meet the standard charge in full).
8   See the Care and Support (Charging) (Wales) Regulations 2015, SI 2015/1843, reg 7(1) (amended by SI 2017/214) (made under the Social Services and Well-being (Wales) Act 2014 s 61(2), (3)), which provides that except where the care and support which is provided, or is to be provided consists of provision of care and accommodation in a care home, a local authority may not determine that it is reasonably practicable for A to pay a total charge greater than £70 per week

for the care and support. A local authority must, however, in calculating the total charge for the care and support which the person receives for the purpose of applying the maximum weekly charge in the Care and Support (Charging) (Wales) Regulations 2015, SI 2015/1843, reg 7(1), exclude any charges in relation to care and support for which it imposes a flat-rate charge so that any flat-rate charges are separate to the charges for care and support to which the maximum weekly charge applies: reg 7(2). As to the meaning of 'care home' see PARA 3 note 11.

9   Care and Support (Charging) (Wales) Regulations 2015, SI 2015/1843, reg 11(1) (amended by SI 2017/214). 'Non-residential care and support' means any care and support provided to meet a person's need for care and support other than provision of accommodation in a care home: Care and Support (Charging) (Wales) Regulations 2015, SI 2015/1843, reg 1(4). As to the maximum weekly charge see PARA 131. Where the person has capital at or below the relevant capital limit then a local authority must determine that it is not reasonably practicable for him to pay the standard charge or any lesser amount from capital: reg 11(3) (amended by SI 2017/214).

10 See the Care and Support (Charging) (Wales) Regulations 2015, SI 2015/1843, regs 12, 13 (reg 13 amended by SI 2017/214). 'Net weekly income' means the weekly income which A has, or would have left, after the deduction from A's assessed income of the standard charge (or any other charge) imposed under the Social Services and Well-being (Wales) Act 2014 Pt 5 (ss 59–73) and the Care and Support (Charging) (Wales) Regulations 2015, SI 2015/1843: reg 1(4). 'Assessed income' means that part of A's income calculated in accordance with the Care and Support (Financial Assessment) (Wales) Regulations 2015, SI 2015/1855, which a local authority may take into account in making a determination under the Care and Support (Charging) (Wales) Regulations 2015, SI 2015/1843: reg 1(4).

11 Social Services and Well-being (Wales) Act 2014 s 73(1)(b). In connection with who may request reviews, the circumstances under which a review may be requested, and the procedure for reviews, see the Care and Support (Review of Charging Decisions and Determinations) (Wales) Regulations 2015, SI 2015/1842; and PARA 131 note 19.

133. Deferred payment agreements. A 'deferred payment agreement' is an agreement under which:

(1)   a local authority in Wales[1] agrees not to require payment of the whole or a portion of a person's statutory charge[2] until the specified time[3]; and

(2)   the person agrees to give the authority a charge over his interest in his home[4] to secure payment of his required amount[5].

Local authorities are required to enter into a deferred payment agreement where the value of the adult's interest in his home does not exceed £24,000[6]. The authority must obtain adequate security for repayment of the required amounts[7] and the consent of other interested persons[8]. The 'specified time' for repayment[9] is the sooner of:

(a)   the date of sale or disposal of the adult's property[10]; or

(b)   90 days after the date of the death of the adult with whom the agreement is made or such longer time as the authority may permit[11],

although the adult may terminate the agreement at any time prior to the specified time by giving the authority reasonable notice in writing and paying the required amount[12]. Provision is made as to the terms and conditions which must be included in agreements[13].

1   As to the meaning of 'local authority' see PARA 2.
2   Ie the 'required amount', that is to say, so much of the charge that the adult is required (or is going to be required) to pay under the Social Services and Well-being (Wales) Act 2014 s 59 (see PARAS 131–136) and any amount the adult is required to pay in accordance with the Care and Support (Choice of Accommodation) (Wales) Regulations 2015, SI 2015/1840 (see PARA 4) as is specified or determined in accordance with the Care and Support (Deferred Payment) (Wales) Regulations 2015, SI 2015/1841, reg 5 (see note 7): Social Services and Well-being (Wales) Act 2014 s 68(3); Care and Support (Deferred Payment) (Wales) Regulations 2015, SI 2015/1841, reg 2. As to the meaning of 'adult' see PARA 2.
3   Social Services and Well-being (Wales) Act 2014 s 68(2)(a).
4   A reference to a person's home is a reference to the property which he occupies as his only or main residence; and a reference to a person's interest in a property is a reference to his legal or beneficial interest in that property: Social Services and Well-being (Wales) Act 2014 s 68(10).
5   Social Services and Well-being (Wales) Act 2014 s 68(2)(b).

6   See PARA 134.
7   Ie the required amount and any interest and administration costs which are to be treated in the
    same way as the deferred amount: see the Care and Support (Deferred Payment) (Wales)
    Regulations 2015, SI 2015/1841, reg 4(1)(a); and PARA 135. The 'required amount' is determined
    in accordance with regs 5, 6. The authority's interest and administration costs may be charged in
    accordance with regs 9, 10 (made under the Social Services and Well-being (Wales) Act 2014
    s 68(4)–(7)).
8   See the Care and Support (Deferred Payment) (Wales) Regulations 2015, SI 2015/1841,
    reg 4(1)(b); and PARA 135.
9   Ie for repayment of the required amount and any interest and administration costs which have
    been treated in the same way as the required amount: Care and Support (Deferred Payment)
    (Wales) Regulations 2015, SI 2015/1841, reg 7.
10 Care and Support (Deferred Payment) (Wales) Regulations 2015, SI 2015/1841, reg 7(a).
11 Care and Support (Deferred Payment) (Wales) Regulations 2015, SI 2015/1841, reg 7(b).
12 Ie paying to the authority the required amount together with any amount of interest and any
    amount which is required to be paid towards administrative costs which the adult has agreed is to
    be treated in the same way as the required amount: Care and Support (Deferred Payment) (Wales)
    Regulations 2015, SI 2015/1841, reg 8 (made under the Social Services and Well-being (Wales) Act
    2014 s 68(8)).
13 See the Care and Support (Deferred Payment) (Wales) Regulations 2015, SI 2015/1841, reg 8
    (made under the Social Services and Well-being (Wales) Act 2014 s 68(9)).

134. Local authority required to enter into deferred payment agreement where adult's assets do not exceed £24,000. A local authority in Wales[1] is required to enter into a deferred payment agreement[2] with an adult[3] if:

(1)   the adult's needs for care and support[4] are being met or are going to be
       met[5] and the care and support plan[6] for the adult specifies that the
       authority is going to meet the adult's needs by the provision of
       accommodation in a care home[7];

(2)   the adult is required (or is going to be required) to pay a charge[8] for his
       care and support[9];

(3)   the authority has carried out[10] a financial assessment[11];

(4)   the authority is satisfied that the adult has an interest in a property
       which he occupies as his home[12], or which he used to occupy as his
       home, and that the value of that interest has not been disregarded for the
       purposes of calculating[13] the amount of the adult's capital[14] and the
       adult's capital, less the value of that interest, does not exceed £24,000[15];
       and

(5)   the adult's weekly assessed income is insufficient to meet the full amount
       due from the adult[16] for the provision of care and support in a care home
       and any amount the adult is required[17] (where applicable) to pay for his
       choice of accommodation[18].

Additionally, the authority must obtain security for the payment (ie the 'security condition'[19] must be met)[20] and the adult must agree to all the terms and conditions included[21] in the agreement[22].

1   As to the meaning of 'local authority' see PARA 2.
2   As to the making of deferred payment agreements by local authorities in Wales see PARA 133.
3   As to the meaning of 'adult' see PARA 2.
4   As to the meanings of 'care' and 'support' see PARA 2 note 1.
5   Ie under the Social Services and Well-being (Wales) Act 2014 s 35 (see PARA 19) or s 36(1) (see
    PARA 20).
6   'Care and support plan' means a plan prepared in accordance with the Social Services and
    Well-being (Wales) Act 2014 s 54 (see PARA 81), or a plan which a local authority prepares when
    it meets an adult's needs for care and support under s 36: Care and Support (Deferred Payment)
    (Wales) Regulations 2015, SI 2015/1841, reg 2.
7   Care and Support (Deferred Payment) (Wales) Regulations 2015, SI 2015/1841, reg 3(1)(a), (2)(a)
    (made under the Social Services and Well-being (Wales) Act 2014 s 68(1), (11)). As to the meaning
    of 'care home' see PARA 3 note 11.

8 Ie under the Social Services and Well-being (Wales) Act 2014 s 59(1): see PARAS 131–136.
9 Care and Support (Deferred Payment) (Wales) Regulations 2015, SI 2015/1841, reg 3(2)(b).
10 As to the duty to carry out a financial assessment in connection with charges see the Social Services
   and Well-being (Wales) Act 2014 s 63(1); and PARA 132; as to the carrying out of financial
   assessments generally see PARA 141.
11 Care and Support (Deferred Payment) (Wales) Regulations 2015, SI 2015/1841, reg 3(2)(c).
12 As to the meaning of 'home' see PARA 133 note 4.
13 Ie under the Care and Support (Financial Assessment) (Wales) Regulations 2015, SI 2015/1844,
   regs 18–24, Sch 2 (see PARA 141).
14 Care and Support (Deferred Payment) (Wales) Regulations 2015, SI 2015/1841, reg 3(2)(d)(i).
15 Care and Support (Deferred Payment) (Wales) Regulations 2015, SI 2015/1841, reg 3(2)(d)(ii).
   £24,000 is the 'capital limit', which is the financial limit for the purposes of the Social Services and
   Well-being (Wales) Act 2014 s 66(5): see the Care and Support (Charging) (Wales) Regulations
   2015, SI 2015/1843, reg 11(2); and PARA 132.
16 See note 8. As to the meaning of 'assessed income' see the Care and Support (Charging) (Wales)
   Regulations 2015, SI 2015/1843, reg 1(4); and PARA 132 note 10 (definition applied by the Care
   and Support (Deferred Payment) (Wales) Regulations 2015, SI 2015/1841, reg 2).
17 Ie under the Care and Support (Choice of Accommodation) (Wales) Regulations 2015, SI
   2015/1840 (see PARA 4).
18 Care and Support (Deferred Payment) (Wales) Regulations 2015, SI 2015/1841, reg 3(2)(e).
19 Ie the condition in the Care and Support (Deferred Payment) (Wales) Regulations 2015, SI
   2015/1841, reg 4 (see PARA 135).
20 Care and Support (Deferred Payment) (Wales) Regulations 2015, SI 2015/1841, reg 3(1)(b).
21 Ie included in accordance with in the Care and Support (Deferred Payment) (Wales) Regulations
   2015, SI 2015/1841, reg 11 (see PARA 133).
22 Care and Support (Deferred Payment) (Wales) Regulations 2015, SI 2015/1841, reg 3(1)(c).

**135. Local authority must obtain security for, and consent to, deferred payment
agreement.** Before entering into a deferred payment agreement[1] a local authority
in Wales must obtain adequate security for the payment of the adult's[2] required
amount[3] and any interest or administration costs[4] which are to be treated in the
same way as the adult's deferred amount[5]. For these purposes 'adequate security'
is a charge by way of legal mortgage for an amount which is at least equal to the
adult's required amount and any interest or administration costs which are to be
treated in the same way as the adult's required amount and which is capable of
being registered as a first legal charge in favour of the local authority in the land
register[6]. If the authority considers it is necessary to do so, it must also obtain the
genuine and informed consent to the agreement of all interested persons[7].

1 As to the making of deferred payment agreements by local authorities in Wales see
   PARAS 133–134. The security condition (ie the Care and Support (Deferred Payment) (Wales)
   Regulations 2015, SI 2015/1841, reg 4: see the text and notes 2–7) has to be complied with in
   order for a local authority to enter into a deferred payment agreement: see reg 3(1)(b); and
   PARA 134. As to the meaning of 'local authority' see PARA 2.
2 As to the meaning of 'adult' see PARA 2.
3 As to the required amount see PARA 133.
4 As to the authority's power to charge interest and administration costs see PARA 133.
5 Care and Support (Deferred Payment) (Wales) Regulations 2015, SI 2015/1841, reg 4(1)(a).
6 Care and Support (Deferred Payment) (Wales) Regulations 2015, SI 2015/1841, reg 2.
7 Care and Support (Deferred Payment) (Wales) Regulations 2015, SI 2015/1841, reg 4(1)(b). The
   consent so required is consent which in the authority's opinion is genuine and informed consent
   given in writing to the matters specified below by any person:
   (1)   who the authority considers has an interest in the land or other asset in respect of which
          a charge will be created (reg 4(2)(a)); and
   (2)   whose interest the authority considers may prevent it from exercising a power of sale of
          the property or recovering the required amount and any interest or administration costs
          which are to be treated in the same way as the required amount (reg 4(2)(b)).
   The matters specified are:
   (a)   the creation of a charge (reg 4(3)(a)); and
   (b)   the charge taking priority to and ranking before any interest the person has in the
          property over which the charge will be created (reg 4(3)(b)).

(B)   Reimbursement and Contribution

136.   Power of local authority to require reimbursement of, and contributions towards, direct payments. A local authority in Wales has a discretion to require a person to whom it makes direct payments[1] to make a contribution or reimbursement towards the cost of securing the provision of the care and support in respect of which the payments are made[2]. 'Contributions' are made when the direct payments are net payments; 'reimbursement' may be a condition of gross payments[3]. Payments made in connection with the provision of care and support for children, and payments for certain services, consisting of specified transportation, reablement and advocacy services, may not be subject to reimbursement or contribution[4]. Payments also may not be subject to reimbursement or contribution where they are made in respect of a person suffering from variant Creutzfeldt-Jakob disease[5] or a person receiving after-care following detention for mental health treatment[6].

1   As to the making of direct payments see PARAS 125–130.
2   Care and Support (Charging) (Wales) Regulations 2015, SI 2015/1843, reg 17(1) (made under the Social Services and Well-being (Wales) Act 2014 ss 50(1), 52(1), 53(1)(c), (3), (4)). As to the making of determinations about contributions and reimbursements see PARA 137. As to the meaning of 'local authority' see PARA 2.
3   See the Social Services and Well-being (Wales) Act 2014 s 53(2); and PARA 125 note 13. 'Contribution', in relation to a person whose needs are met by the local authority making direct payments has the meaning ascribed in the definition of 'net payments' in s 53(2); 'reimbursement', in relation to a person whose needs are met by the local authority making direct payments has the meaning ascribed in the definition of 'gross payments' in s 53(2): Care and Support (Charging) (Wales) Regulations 2015, SI 2015/1843, reg 1(4).
4   A local authority may not require a contribution or impose a condition for reimbursement in relation to a person whose needs for care and support a local authority is meeting in accordance with a duty or a power conferred by the Care and Support (Direct Payments) (Wales) Regulations 2015, SI 2015/1815, by virtue of the Social Services and Well-being (Wales) Act 2014 s 51 (see PARA 126): Care and Support (Charging) (Wales) Regulations 2015, SI 2015/1843, regs 17(2), (3), 18(2). In connection with transportation, reablement and advocacy services see reg 19. As to the meaning of 'reablement' see PARA 131 note 13.
5   A local authority may not require a contribution or impose a condition for reimbursement in relation to B where B is suffering from any form of Creutzfeldt-Jakob disease where that disease has been clinically diagnosed by a registered medical practitioner: Care and Support (Charging) (Wales) Regulations 2015, SI 2015/1843, reg 18(1)(a). As to the meaning of 'registered medical practitioner' see MEDICAL PROFESSIONS vol 74 (2011) PARA 176.
6   A local authority may not require a contribution or impose a condition for reimbursement in relation to B where B has been offered or is receiving a service provided as part of a package of after care services in accordance with the Mental Health Act 1983 s 117 (see MENTAL HEALTH AND CAPACITY vol 75 (2013) PARA 945): Care and Support (Charging) (Wales) Regulations 2015, SI 2015/1843, reg 18(1)(b).

137.   Determining a person's liability to make contribution or reimbursement. Where a local authority in Wales thinks it would require a contribution or a reimbursement in relation to direct payments which it is making or proposing to make[1], and has carried out a financial assessment[2] of the recipient ('B')[3], it must make a determination about what amount, if any, it is reasonably practicable for B to contribute towards the cost of securing the care and support in respect of which the payments are made, whether by way of contribution or reimbursement[4]. Where the person has capital above £24,000 (in the context of non-residential care) or £30,000 (in the context of residential care)[5] the authority must determine that it is reasonably practicable for him to make contribution or reimbursement equal to the reasonable cost of securing the care and support in respect of which payments are made, subject to the maximum weekly contribution or reimbursement[6] in relation to non-residential service[7]. There are also levels below which a person's net weekly income may not be reduced by the imposition of a charge[8].

A determination of liability to make a contribution or reimbursement under these provisions is susceptible to review[9].

1　See PARA 136.
2　Where a local authority thinks that if it were to make payments towards meeting the cost of his needs for care and support by making direct payments by virtue of the Social Services and Well-being (Wales) Act 2014 s 50 or s 52 (see PARAS 125, 127), it would require him to pay by way of reimbursement (in the case of a gross payment) or contribution (in the case of a net payment) towards the costs of securing the provision of that care and support, it must carry out an assessment of his financial resources in accordance with the Care and Support (Financial Assessment) (Wales) Regulations 2015, SI 2015/1844: reg 6(1)(b). As to the meaning of 'local authority' see PARA 2. As to the carrying out of financial assessments, and the circumstances in which a financial assessment will not be required, see PARA 141.
3　'B' ('B') is used to refer to a person in relation to whose needs a local authority is providing direct payments or may be required to make direct payments pursuant to regulations made under the Social Services and Well-being (Wales) Act 2014 s 50 or s 52 and who is liable to make a contribution or reimbursement: Care and Support (Charging) (Wales) Regulations 2015, SI 2015/1843, reg 1(4).
4　Care and Support (Charging) (Wales) Regulations 2015, SI 2015/1843, reg 20. A local authority need not make a determination under these provisions where the only care and support in respect of which direct payments are made is either that to which a flat-rate charge applies or to which no charge applies: reg 21. Procedure for determining the amount of a contribution or reimbursement is set out in regs 23, 24 (reg 23 amended by SI 2017/214); provision for the notification and revision of determinations is made by the Care and Support (Charging) (Wales) Regulations 2015, SI 2015/1843, regs 29, 30 (reg 30 amended by SI 2017/214). As to the meaning of 'flat-rate charge' see PARA 376 note 24.
5　Ie the 'relevant capital limit', which is the financial limit for the purposes of the Social Services and Well-being (Wales) Act 2014 s 66(5): Care and Support (Charging) (Wales) Regulations 2015, SI 2015/1843, reg 11(2) (amended by SI 2017/214) (see also the Care and Support (Charging) (Wales) Regulations 2015, SI 2015/1843, reg 1(4) (amended by SI 2017/214) ('financial limit' means the limit in relation to A's capital set by the relevant capital limit)).
6　See the Care and Support (Charging) (Wales) Regulations 2015, SI 2015/1843, reg 22(1) (amended by SI 2017/214), which provides that except where the care and support in respect of which direct payments are made consists of provision of care and accommodation in a care home, a local authority may not determine that it is reasonably practicable for B to make a contribution or reimbursement greater than £70 per week towards the costs of the care and support. When calculating the maximum reasonable amount that B may be required to pay, however, a local authority must disregard the cost of securing any care and support for which it imposes a flat-rate charge and may impose the charges in respect of such a service in addition to the maximum weekly contribution or reimbursement (Care and Support (Charging) (Wales) Regulations 2015, SI 2015/1843, reg 22(2)), and where B receives a direct payment to enable the purchase of equipment, which would otherwise be provided by a local authority, the local authority must disregard the cost of the equipment when calculating the maximum weekly contribution or reimbursement that B may be required to pay and may require B to pay an amount in addition to the maximum weekly contribution or reimbursement towards the cost of securing the equipment (reg 22(3)). As to the meaning of 'care home' see PARA 3 note 11.
7　Care and Support (Charging) (Wales) Regulations 2015, SI 2015/1843, reg 26(1) (amended by SI 2017/214). Where the person has capital at or below the relevant capital limit then a local authority must determine that it is not reasonably practicable for him to make any contribution or reimbursement from capital: Care and Support (Charging) (Wales) Regulations 2015, SI 2015/1843, reg 26(2) (amended by SI 2017/214).
8　See the Care and Support (Charging) (Wales) Regulations 2015, SI 2015/1843, regs 27, 28 (reg 28 amended by SI 2017/214). As to the meaning of 'net weekly income' see PARA 132 note 10.
9　See the Care and Support (Review of Charging Decisions and Determinations) (Wales) Regulations 2015, SI 2015/1842, reg 3; and PARA 131 note 19.

C.　ANTI-AVOIDANCE AND RECOVERY

138.　Transfer of assets to avoid charges. Where a person's ('P's') needs have been or are being met by a local authority in Wales[1] and:

(1)   a person ('the transferor'[2]) has transferred an asset to another person (a 'transferee')[3];

(2)   the transfer was undertaken with the intention of avoiding charges for having P's needs met[4]; and

(3)   either the consideration for the transfer was less than the value of the asset[5] or there was no consideration for the transfer[6],

the transferee is liable to pay to the local authority an amount equal to the difference between the amount the authority would have charged the transferor were it not for the transfer of the asset[7] and the amount it did in fact charge the transferor[8]. The transferee is not liable to pay to the authority an amount which exceeds the benefit accruing to the transferee from the transfer[9].

A decision under these provisions relating to the liability of a transferee to pay an amount is susceptible to review[10].

1   Ie under the Social Services and Well-being (Wales) Act 2014 ss 35–42 (see PARAS 19, 20, 30–32, 58–62) or s 45 (see PARA 63). As to the meaning of 'local authority' see PARA 2.
2   The transferor may be P but need not be so: Social Services and Well-being (Wales) Act 2014 s 72(1)(a).
3   Social Services and Well-being (Wales) Act 2014 s 72(1)(a). 'Asset' means anything which may be taken into account for the purposes of a financial assessment: s 72(5). As to financial assessments see PARA 141.
4   Social Services and Well-being (Wales) Act 2014 s 72(1)(b). For the power of local authority to make a charge for meeting needs see PARA 131.
5   The value of an asset (other than cash) is the amount which would have been realised if it had been sold on the open market by a willing seller at the time of the transfer, with a deduction for the amount of any encumbrance on the asset (Social Services and Well-being (Wales) Act 2014 s 72(6)(a)) and a reasonable amount in respect of the expenses of the sale (s 72(6)(b)).
6   Social Services and Well-being (Wales) Act 2014 s 72(1)(c).
7   Social Services and Well-being (Wales) Act 2014 s 72(2)(a).
8   Social Services and Well-being (Wales) Act 2014 s 72(2)(b). Where an asset has been transferred to more than one transferee, the liability of each transferee under these provisions is in proportion to the benefit accruing to that transferee from the transfer: s 72(4). Regulations may specify cases or circumstances in which liability under s 72(2) does not arise: s 72(7). At the date at which this volume states the law no such regulations had been made.
9   Social Services and Well-being (Wales) Act 2014 s 72(3).
10 Social Services and Well-being (Wales) Act 2014 s 73(1)(c). In connection with who may request reviews, the circumstances under which a review may be requested, and the procedure for reviews, see the Care and Support (Review of Charging Decisions and Determinations) (Wales) Regulations 2015, SI 2015/1842; and PARA 131 note 19.

139. Recovery of charges and interest. Any sum due to a local authority in Wales[1] for the provision of care and support[2] is recoverable by the authority as a debt due to it[3]. An amount so recoverable is recoverable summarily as a civil debt (but this does not affect any other method of recovery)[4], and is recoverable within six years of the date on which the amount becomes due[5].

Where a person[6] misrepresents or fails to disclose (whether fraudulently or otherwise) to a local authority any material fact in connection with the provision of care and support[7], the following amounts are due to the authority from the person:

(1)   any expenditure incurred by the authority as a result of the misrepresentation or failure[8]; and

(2)   any amount recoverable[9] which the authority has not recovered as a result of the misrepresentation or failure[10].

The reasonable costs incurred by a local authority in recovering or seeking to recover an amount due to it[11] are recoverable by the authority as a debt due to it[12].

1   As to the meaning of 'local authority' see PARA 2.
2   Ie any sum due under the Social Services and Well-being (Wales) Act 2014 Pt 5 (ss 59–73).

3 Social Services and Well-being (Wales) Act 2014 s 70(1). This provision does not apply in a case where a deferred payment agreement could, in accordance with the Care and Support (Deferred Payment) (Wales) Regulations 2015, SI 2015/1841 (see PARAS 133–135), be entered into, unless the local authority has sought to enter into such an agreement with the person from whom the sum is due (Social Services and Well-being (Wales) Act 2014 s 70(2)(a)) and that person has refused (s 70(2)(b)). As to the meaning of 'adult' see PARA 2. Regulations may:

    (1)   make provision for determining the date on which an amount becomes due to a local authority for the purposes of s 70 (s 70(8)(a));

    (2)   specify cases or circumstances in which a sum due to a local authority under Pt 5 is not recoverable by it under s 70 (s 70(8)(b));

    (3)   specify cases or circumstances in which a local authority may charge interest on an amount (including any costs recoverable by the authority under s 70(7)) due to it under Pt 5 (s 70(8)(c));

    (4)   where interest is chargeable, provide that it must be charged at a rate specified in or determined in accordance with the regulations or may not be charged at a rate that exceeds the rate specified in or determined in accordance with the regulations (s 70(8)(d)).

See the Care and Support (Review of Charging Decisions and Determinations) (Wales) Regulations 2015, SI 2015/1842; and PARA 131 note 19.

4 Social Services and Well-being (Wales) Act 2014 s 70(3).

5 Social Services and Well-being (Wales) Act 2014 s 70(4).

6 The persons are:

    (1)   an adult who appears to the local authority to have needs for care and support or (in the case of a carer) support under the Social Services and Well-being (Wales) Act 2014 Pt 3 (ss 19–31), and who has capacity to understand whether a fact may be material in connection with the provisions of Pt 5 (s 70(6)(a));

    (2)   an adult to whom something is provided in order to meet another person's needs for care and support or (in the case of a carer) support under Pt 3 and who has capacity to understand whether a fact may be material in connection with the provisions of Pt 5 (s 70(6)(b)); and

    (3)   an adult of a description specified in regulations in relation to care and support or (in the case of a carer) support which appears to the local authority to be needed by a child, or an adult who does not have capacity to understand whether a fact may be material in connection with the provisions of Pt 5 (s 70(6)(c)).

As to the meanings of 'adult' and 'child' see PARA 2; as to the meaning of 'carer' see PARA 54 note 2. As to a person having or lacking capacity see PARA 8 note 10. At the date at which this volume states the law no such regulations had been made.

7 Ie in connection with the Social Services and Well-being (Wales) Act 2014 Pt 5.

8 Social Services and Well-being (Wales) Act 2014 s 70(5)(a).

9 Ie under the Social Services and Well-being (Wales) Act 2014 s 70.

10 Social Services and Well-being (Wales) Act 2014 s 70(5)(b).

11 See note 2.

12 Social Services and Well-being (Wales) Act 2014 s 70(7). Section 70(3) (see the text and note 4) applies to the recovery of those costs as if they were amounts to which s 70(1) applies: s 70(7).

140. Creation of charge over interest in land. Where a person fails to pay to a local authority in Wales[1] an amount that is recoverable[2] by the authority[3] and has a legal or beneficial interest in land in Wales or England[4], the authority may create a charge in its favour over the person's interest in the land to secure payment of that amount[5]. Where the person has interests in more than one parcel of land, the local authority may create the charge over whichever one of those interests it chooses[6]. The charge may be in respect of any amount that is so recoverable by the authority[7], subject to the proviso that where the charge is created over the interest of an equitable joint tenant in land, the amount of the charge must not exceed the value of the interest that the person would have in the land if the joint tenancy were severed (but the creation of the charge does not sever the joint tenancy)[8].

On the death of an equitable joint tenant in land whose interest in the land is subject to a charge under these provisions, the following persons' interests in land become subject to a charge[9]:

    (1)   if there are surviving joint tenants, their interests in the land[10]; and

(2)   if the land vests in one person, or one person is entitled to have it vested in himself or herself, that person's interest in the land[11].

Where an amount is charged over a person's interest in land under these provisions, interest is chargeable upon that amount from the day on which the person[12] dies[13].

1   As to the meanings of 'local authority' and 'Wales' see PARA 2.
2   Ie under the Social Services and Well-being (Wales) Act 2014 Pt 5 (ss 59–73).
3   Social Services and Well-being (Wales) Act 2014 s 71(1)(a).
4   Social Services and Well-being (Wales) Act 2014 s 71(1)(b).
5   Social Services and Well-being (Wales) Act 2014 s 71(1). A charge under s 71 must be created by a declaration in writing made by the local authority: s 71(7). Such a charge, other than a charge over the interest of an equitable joint tenant in land:
    (1)   in the case of unregistered land, is a Class B land charge within the meaning of the Land Charges Act 1972 s 2 (see REAL PROPERTY AND REGISTRATION vol 87 (2012) PARA 717) (Social Services and Well-being (Wales) Act 2014 s 71(8)(a));
    (2)   in the case of registered land, is a registrable charge taking effect as a charge by way of legal mortgage (s 71(8)(b)).
6   Social Services and Well-being (Wales) Act 2014 s 71(2).
7   Social Services and Well-being (Wales) Act 2014 s 71(3).
8   Social Services and Well-being (Wales) Act 2014 s 71(4).
9   The amount of the charge so created must not exceed the amount of the charge to which the interest of the deceased joint tenant was subject: Social Services and Well-being (Wales) Act 2014 s 71(6).
10 Social Services and Well-being (Wales) Act 2014 s 71(4)(a).
11 Social Services and Well-being (Wales) Act 2014 s 71(4)(b).
12 Ie the person mentioned in the Social Services and Well-being (Wales) Act 2014 s 71(1).
13 Social Services and Well-being (Wales) Act 2014 s 71(9). The rate of interest so chargeable is a rate specified in or determined in accordance with regulations or if no regulations are made, a rate determined by the local authority: s 71(10). At the date at which this volume states the law no such regulations had been made.

D.   FINANCIAL ASSESSMENT AND ADMINISTRATION

141. Carrying out financial assessments. A local authority in Wales must carry out a financial assessment[1] where it thinks it would impose a charge for meeting a person's needs for care and support[2] and where it thinks that if it were to make direct payments for a person's care and support it would require that person to make payments by way of reimbursement or contribution towards the cost of securing the provision of that care and support[3]. The duty to carry out a financial assessment does not apply (ie the authority is under no duty to carry out an assessment of the person's financial resources) where the person:

(1)   has been assessed as needing or is receiving care and support, assistance or a service or any combination of the same for which the local authority applies a flat-rate charge[4];

(2)   declines to undergo a financial assessment[5];

(3)   fails to provide the local authority with the information or documents required by the authority[6] within a reasonable time or at all[7];

(4)   is suffering from any form of Creutzfeldt-Jakob disease, where that disease has been diagnosed by a registered medical practitioner[8];

(5)   has been offered or is receiving care and support, advice or a service, or has been offered or provided with direct payments to secure the provision of care and support as part of a package of after-care services[9] following mental health treatment[10];

(6)   has been offered or is receiving reablement[11] for the first six weeks of the specified period or, if the specified period is less than six weeks, for that period[12]; or

(7)   has been assessed as needing, or is receiving, only advocacy services[13].

1   For the financial assessment process see the Care and Support (Financial Assessment) (Wales) Regulations 2015, SI 2015/1844, regs 3–5, 8–11 (process generally), regs 12, 13–17, Sch 1 (Sch 1 amended by SI 2017/214) provision for calculating a person's income) and the Care and Support (Financial Assessment) (Wales) Regulations 2015, SI 2015/1844, regs 18–24, Sch 2 (provision for calculating capital) (made under the Social Services and Well-being (Wales) Act 2014 ss 64, 66(3), (4), (6)–(11)). As to the meaning of 'local authority' see PARA 2.
2   See the Social Services and Well-being (Wales) Act 2014 s 63(1), (4); the Care and Support (Financial Assessment) (Wales) Regulations 2015, SI 2015/1844, reg 6(1)(a); and PARA 132.
3   See the Care and Support (Financial Assessment) (Wales) Regulations 2015, SI 2015/1844, reg 6(1)(b); and PARA 137.
4   Care and Support (Financial Assessment) (Wales) Regulations 2015, SI 2015/1844, regs 6(2), 7(1)(a) (made under the Social Services and Well-being (Wales) Act 2014 s 65). 'Flat-rate charge' means a fixed rate charge which is imposed by a local authority regardless of the means of the person who is liable to be charged for care and support arranged or provided by a local authority under Pt 4 (ss 32–58) (meeting needs) or services provided under s 15 (preventative services: see PARA 376) or for assistance provided under s 17 (provision of information, advice and assistance: see PARA 392): Care and Support (Financial Assessment) (Wales) Regulations 2015, SI 1844, reg 2(1).
5   Care and Support (Financial Assessment) (Wales) Regulations 2015, SI 2015/1844, reg 7(1)(b). Where reg 7(1)(b) or (c) applies, a local authority must determine that it is reasonably practicable for a person to pay the standard charge (subject to the maximum weekly charge in relation to non-residential care and support) or (as the case may be) to contribute by way of contribution or reimbursement an amount equal to the reasonable cost of securing the care and support in respect of which the payments are made: Care and Support (Charging) (Wales) Regulations 2015, SI 2015/1843, regs 10, 25(1). In a contribution or reimbursement case, where direct payments are made or are to be made to meet B's needs for non-residential care and support, the requirement in reg 25(1) is subject to the maximum weekly contribution or reimbursement in relation to non-residential services imposed by reg 22 (see PARA 137): reg 25(2). As to the meaning of 'non-residential care and support' see PARA 132 note 9.
6   Ie in accordance with the Care and Support (Financial Assessment) (Wales) Regulations 2015, SI 2015/1844, reg 3(f) (see note 1).
7   Care and Support (Financial Assessment) (Wales) Regulations 2015, SI 2015/1844, reg 7(1)(c). Where reg 7(1)(c) applies, a local authority may, if it considers that it has sufficient information, make an assessment of A's financial resources on the basis of the partial information or partial document (or both) that is in its possession: reg 7(2).
8   Care and Support (Financial Assessment) (Wales) Regulations 2015, SI 2015/1844, reg 7(1)(d). As to the meaning of 'registered medical practitioner' see MEDICAL PROFESSIONS vol 74 (2011) PARA 176.
9   Ie in accordance with the Mental Health Act 1983 s 117 (after-care: see MENTAL HEALTH AND CAPACITY vol 75 (2013) PARA 945).
10 Care and Support (Financial Assessment) (Wales) Regulations 2015, SI 1844, reg 7(1)(e).
11 'Reablement' means care and support provided or arranged by a local authority under the Social Services and Well-being (Wales) Act 2014 Pt 2 (ss 5–18) or Pt 4, or secured or arranged by the person, where he is or will be receiving direct payments made in accordance with s 50 or s 52, and which consists of a programme of care and support, is for a specified period of time ('the specified period'), and has as its purpose the provision of assistance to the person to enable him to maintain or regain the ability to live independently in his only or main home: Care and Support (Financial Assessment) (Wales) Regulations 2015, SI 1844, reg 2(1).
12 Care and Support (Financial Assessment) (Wales) Regulations 2015, SI 1844, reg 7(1)(f).
13 Care and Support (Financial Assessment) (Wales) Regulations 2015, SI 1844, reg 7(1)(g).

142. Recovery of costs between local authorities. Where a local authority in Wales[1] ('authority A') provides or arranges care and support[2] to a person who is ordinarily resident in the area of another local authority in Wales ('authority B')[3], and the care and support was provided either to meet urgent needs in order to safeguard the person's well-being[4] or with the consent of authority B[5], authority A may recover from authority B any reasonable expenses incurred by it in providing or arranging the care and support[6].

Where a local authority in Wales complies with any request for co-operation or information[7] in relation to a person who is not ordinarily resident within its area, it may recover from the local authority in Wales, or local authority in England, in whose area the person is ordinarily resident any reasonable expenses incurred by it in respect of that person[8].

1   As to the meanings of 'local authority' and 'Wales' see PARA 2.
2   As to the meaning of 'care and support' see PARA 2 note 1.
3   Social Services and Well-being (Wales) Act 2014 s 193(1)(a).
4   Social Services and Well-being (Wales) Act 2014 s 193(1)(b)(i). As to the meaning of 'well-being' see PARA 375.
5   Social Services and Well-being (Wales) Act 2014 s 193(1)(b)(ii).
6   Social Services and Well-being (Wales) Act 2014 s 193(2).
7   Ie under the Social Services and Well-being (Wales) Act 2014 s 164(1) or (2) (see PARA 378), or under the Children Act 1989 s 27(2) (co-operation between authorities: see CHILDREN AND YOUNG PERSONS vol 10 (2017) PARA 808).
8   Social Services and Well-being (Wales) Act 2014 s 193(6) (amended in relation to local authorities in Wales by SI 2016/413). As to local authorities in England see PARA 1. This does not apply where the Social Services and Well-being (Wales) Act 2014 s 193(7) or (8) (see CHILDREN AND YOUNG PERSONS vol 10 (2017) PARAS 826, 828) applies: s 193(6). Where a local authority in Wales ('authority A') complies with any request for co-operation or information under s 164(1) or (2) from another local authority ('authority B') in relation to a person for whom authority B is the responsible local authority within the meaning of the Social Services and Well-being (Wales) Act 2014 s 104: see CHILDREN AND YOUNG PERSONS vol 10 (2017) PARA 868), authority A may recover from authority B any reasonable expenses incurred by it in exercising its functions under ss 105–115) (see CHILDREN AND YOUNG PERSONS vol 10 (2017) PARAS 869–880) in respect of that person: s 193(7). See also s 193(3)–(5), (8); CHILDREN AND YOUNG PERSONS vol 10 (2017) PARAS 808, 827, 828.

(2) FINANCIAL ASSISTANCE FOR LOCAL AUTHORITIES AND CARE ORGANISATIONS

(i) England

A.   FINANCIAL ASSISTANCE FOR QUALIFYING BODIES

143. Bodies which qualify for financial assistance. Provision is made for the giving of financial assistance[1] to 'qualifying bodies' which are engaged in the provision in England of health services[2] or social care services[3] or in the provision to other persons of services that are connected with the provision in England by those other persons of health services or of social care services[4]. For these purposes a body is a 'qualifying body' if:

(1)   a reasonable person might consider that its activities are being carried on for the benefit of the community in England[5];

(2)   the constitution[6] of the body states, or contains provisions which ensure, that not less than 50 per cent of its distributable profits[7] in each financial year[8] will be used or applied for the purpose of the activities of that body[9];

(3)   it is carrying on a business[10];

(4)   the constitution of the body contains a statement or condition that the body is carrying on its activities for the benefit of the community in England[11];

(5)   the constitution of the body, where appropriate, contains provisions relating to the distribution of assets which take effect when that body is dissolved or wound up[12]; and

(6)   the body must, if it is an unincorporated body, have a constitution[13].

Financial assistance may also be given to persons for the purposes of the establishment by them of qualifying bodies which satisfy any of the conditions set out above which are to be engaged in the provision in England of health services or of social care services[14] or the provision to other persons of services that will be connected with the provision in England by those other persons of health services or of social care services[15].

1 As to who may give such assistance see PARA 144. As to the forms of assistance and terms on which assistance is given see PARA 145.

2 For the purposes of the Health and Social Care Act 2008 ss 149–156 'health services' means services which must or may be provided for the purposes of the health service continued under the National Health Service Act 2006 s 1(1) (see HEALTH SERVICES vol 54 (2017) PARA 9) or services which are similar to such services: Health and Social Care Act 2008 s 156(2).

3 Health and Social Care Act 2008 s 149(1)(a). For the purposes of ss 149–156 'social care services' means services which an English local authority must or may provide or arrange to be provided under the Care Act 2014 Pt 1 (ss 1–80) (see PARA 1 et seq) or the Mental Health Act 1983 s 117 (see MENTAL HEALTH AND CAPACITY vol 75 (2013) PARA 945): Health and Social Care Act 2008 s 156(2) (amended by SI 2015/914).

4 Health and Social Care Act 2008 s 149(1)(b).

5 Health and Social Care Act 2008 ss 150(1)(a), 156(2). 'Community' includes a section of the community; and for these purposes any group of individuals may constitute a section of the community if they share a readily identifiable characteristic and other members of the community of which that group forms part do not share that characteristic: s 150(3); Health and Social Care (Financial Assistance) Regulations 2009, SI 2009/649, reg 4. For the purposes of the Health and Social Care Act 2008 s 150(1)(a), (2)(b), the following activities are treated as not being activities which a reasonable person might consider are activities carried on for the benefit of the community in England:

(1) the promotion of, or opposition to, changes in any law applicable in the United Kingdom or elsewhere, or the policy adopted by any governmental or public authority in relation to any matter (Health and Social Care (Financial Assistance) Regulations 2009, SI 2009/649, reg 3(1)(a) (made under the Health and Social Care Act 2008 s 150(1)));

(2) the promotion of, or opposition (including the promotion of changes) to, the policy which any governmental or public authority proposes to adopt in relation to any matter (Health and Social Care (Financial Assistance) Regulations 2009, SI 2009/649, reg 3(1)(b)); and

(3) activities which can reasonably be regarded as intended or likely to provide or affect support (whether financial or otherwise) for a political party or political campaigning organisation or influence voters in relation to any election or referendum (reg 3(1)(c)).

However activities of these descriptions are to be treated as being activities which a reasonable person might consider are activities carried on for the benefit of the community in England if they can reasonably be regarded as incidental to other activities, which a reasonable person might consider are being carried on for the benefit of the community (reg 3(2)(a)), and those other activities cannot reasonably be regarded as incidental to the activities prescribed in reg 3(1) (reg 3(2)(b)).

'Governmental authority' includes any national, regional or local government in the United Kingdom or elsewhere, including any organ or agency of any such government, the EU or any of its institutions or agencies, and any organisation which is able to make rules or adopt decisions which are legally binding on any such governmental authority; 'public authority' includes a court or tribunal and any person certain of whose functions are functions of a public nature; 'political party' includes any person standing, or proposing to stand, as a candidate at any election, and any person holding public office following election to that office; 'political campaigning organisation' means any person carrying on, or proposing to carry on activities to promote, or oppose, changes in any law applicable in the United Kingdom or elsewhere, or any policy of a governmental or public authority (unless such activities are incidental to other activities carried on by that person), or which could reasonably be regarded as intended to affect public support for a political party, or to influence voters in relation to any election or referendum (unless such activities are incidental to other activities carried on by that person); and 'referendum' includes any national or regional referendum or other poll held in pursuance of any provisions made by or under the law of any state on one or more questions or propositions specified in or in accordance with any such provision: reg 2 (amended by SI 2011/1043).

6　'Constitution' means (by virtue of the Health and Social Care (Financial Assistance) Regulations 2009, SI 2009/649, reg 2)):
　　(1)　in the case of a company, the company's memorandum and articles of association; and
　　(2)　in the case of any other body, a written instrument which sets out the purpose, objectives, proposed activities and provisions for the governance of the body, including any provisions relating to the membership of the body and the distribution of profits and assets.

7　'Distributable profits' means (by virtue of the Health and Social Care (Financial Assistance) Regulations 2009, SI 2009/649, reg 2)):
　　(1)　in relation to a company, the company's profits available for distribution, within the meaning of the Companies Act 2006 s 830 (see COMPANIES vol 15A (2016) PARA 1563);
　　(2)　in relation to any other body, its accumulated, realised profits, so far as not previously utilised by distribution, less its accumulated, realised losses, so far as not previously written off.
　　'Realised losses' and 'realised profits' means the losses or profits of the business carried on by the body as fall to be treated as realised in accordance with generally accepted accounting practice: Health and Social Care (Financial Assistance) Regulations 2009, SI 2009/649, reg 2.

8　'Financial year; means the 12 month period that a body uses for accounting purposes: Health and Social Care (Financial Assistance) Regulations 2009, SI 2009/649, reg 2.

9　Health and Social Care (Financial Assistance) Regulations 2009, SI 2009/649, reg 5(1) (made under the Health and Social Care Act 2008 s 150(2)). The following bodies are excluded for this purpose and for the purpose of heads (4) and (5) in the text: a company limited by guarantee and registered as a charity in England and Wales; a community interest company registered as a company limited by guarantee; and a charitable incorporated organisation (within the meaning of the Charities Act 1993 s 69A: see CHARITIES): Health and Social Care (Financial Assistance) Regulations 2009, SI 2009/649, regs 5(2), 6(2). 'Charity' has the meaning given in the Charities Act 2006 s 1 (see CHARITIES vol 8 (2015) PARA 1); 'community interest company' means a company as referred to in the Companies (Audit, Investigations and Community Enterprise) Act 2004 s 26 (see COMPANIES vol 14 (2016) PARA 75): Health and Social Care (Financial Assistance) Regulations 2009, SI 2009/649, reg 2.

10　Health and Social Care Act 2008 s 150(1)(c).

11　Health and Social Care (Financial Assistance) Regulations 2009, SI 2009/649, regs 6(1), 7. Certain bodies are excluded: see note 9.

12　Health and Social Care (Financial Assistance) Regulations 2009, SI 2009/649, reg 8(1). Certain bodies are excluded: see note 9. The provisions are ones which:
　　(1)　require that the residual assets of the body be distributed to those members of the body (if any) who are entitled to share in any distribution of assets on the dissolution or winding up of that body according to those members' rights and interests in that body (reg 8(2)(a));
　　(2)　in the case of a company not limited by guarantee and registered as a charity in England and Wales, provide that no member shall receive an amount which exceeds the paid up value of the shares which the member holds in the company (reg 8(2)(b)); and
　　(3)　designate another qualifying body (for the purposes of the Health and Social Care Act 2008 ss 149–156) to which any remaining residual assets of the body will be distributed after any distribution to members of the body (Health and Social Care (Financial Assistance) Regulations 2009, SI 2009/649, reg 8(2)(c)).
　　'Residual assets' means, in relation to the dissolution or winding up of a body, the assets of the body which remain after satisfaction of the body's liabilities: reg 2.

13　Health and Social Care (Financial Assistance) Regulations 2009, SI 2009/649, reg 9.

14　Health and Social Care Act 2008 s 149(2)(a).

15　Health and Social Care Act 2008 s 149(2)(b).

144. Who may give financial assistance. The power to give financial assistance to qualifying bodies[1] may be exercised by the Secretary of State[2], who may exercise the power himself[3] or direct a Special Health Authority[4] or, until a day to be appointed, a National Health Service trust[5], to exercise any functions of the Secretary of State[6] in relation to financial assistance[7]. The Secretary of State may also make arrangements for financial assistance to be given[8], or other functions relating to such assistance to be exercised[9], by a person other than such an NHS body or an English local authority[10] ('P')[11]. Such arrangements may provide for the functions concerned to be exercised by P either wholly or to such extent as may be specified in the arrangements[12] and either generally or in such cases or circumstances as may be so specified[13].

The Secretary of State may also form, or participate in forming, one or more companies[14] with a view to making such arrangements[15] with the companies for financial assistance[16] to be given, or other functions relating to such assistance to be exercised, by the company[17].

1 Ie arrangements under the Health and Social Care Act 2008 s 149(1): see PARA 143.
2 As to the Secretary of State see PARA 333.
3 Health and Social Care Act 2008 s 149(1).
4 Ie a Special Health Authority performing functions only or mainly in respect of England: Health and Social Care Act 2008 s 153(1). As to Special Health Authorities see HEALTH SERVICES vol 54 (2017) PARA 180 et seq.
5 Ie a National Health Service trust all or most of whose hospitals, establishments and facilities are situated in England: Health and Social Care Act 2008 s 153(1) (amended and prospectively amended by the Health and Social Care Act 2012 Sch 5 para 167). At the date at which this volume states the law no day had been appointed for the prospective element of this amendment. As to National Health Service trusts see HEALTH SERVICES vol 54 (2017) PARA 234 et seq.
6 Ie functions under the Health and Social Care Act 2008 s 149: see PARA 143.
7 Health and Social Care Act 2008 s 153(1). The Secretary of State may also give directions to any such body about the exercise by it of any function of the Secretary of State which it exercises by virtue of these provisions: s 153(2). As to directions generally see s 165; and PARA 337 note 13.
8 Health and Social Care Act 2008 s 154(1)(a).
9 Health and Social Care Act 2008 s 154(1)(b).
10 'English local authority' means a county council in England, a metropolitan district council, a non-metropolitan district council for an area for which there is no county council, a London borough council, the Common Council of the City of London or the Council of the Isles of Scilly: Health and Social Care Act 2008 s 156(2). As to local government areas and authorities in England see LOCAL GOVERNMENT vol 69 (2009) PARA 22 et seq. As to the London boroughs and their councils see LONDON GOVERNMENT vol 71 (2013) PARAS 15, 20, 34–38. As to the Common Council of the City of London see LONDON GOVERNMENT vol 71 (2013) PARA 16. For these purposes 'English local authority' includes a non-metropolitan district council for an area for which there is a county council: s 154(6).
11 Health and Social Care Act 2008 s 154(1), (2). Such arrangements may make provision as to the forms of financial assistance which may be given by P (subject to s 151(3): see PARA 145) (s 154(4)(a)) and as to the terms on which financial assistance may be given by P (s 154(4)(b)), and may provide for the Secretary of State to make payments to P (s 154(5)(a)) and make provision as to the circumstances in which any such payments are to be repaid to the Secretary of State (s 154(5)(b)).
12 Health and Social Care Act 2008 s 154(3)(a).
13 Health and Social Care Act 2008 s 154(3)(b).
14 For the purposes of the Health and Social Care Act 2008 ss 149–156, 'company' means a company as defined by the Companies Act 2006 s 1 (see COMPANIES vol 14 (2016) PARA 21): Health and Social Care Act 2008 s 156(2).
15 Ie arrangements under the Health and Social Care Act 2008 s 154(1) (see the text and notes 8–11).
16 See note 1.
17 Health and Social Care Act 2008 s 155.

145. Forms of assistance and terms on which assistance is given. Financial assistance[1] may be given in any form[2] and may, in particular, be given by way of grants[3], loans[4], guarantees[5] or, in the case of assistance given to a company which is a qualifying body[6], purchasing share capital of the company[7]. Assistance may be given on such terms as the Secretary of State[8] considers appropriate[9]. Terms may, in particular, include provisions as to:

(1)   circumstances in which the assistance is to be repaid, or otherwise made good, to the Secretary of State, and the manner in which that is to be done[10]; and

(2)   the keeping, and making available for inspection, of accounts and other records[11].

The person receiving assistance[12] must comply with the terms on which it is given, and compliance may be enforced by the Secretary of State[13].

1   Ie financial assistance under the Health and Social Care Act 2008 s 149: see PARA 143.
2   Health and Social Care Act 2008 s 151(1). This is subject to s 151(3) (see the text and notes 6–7): s 151(3).
3   Health and Social Care Act 2008 s 151(2)(a).
4   Health and Social Care Act 2008 s 151(2)(b).
5   Health and Social Care Act 2008 s 151(2)(c).
6   Ie financial assistance under the Health and Social Care Act 2008 s 149(1): see PARA 143. As to the meaning of 'company' see PARA 144 note 14.
7   Health and Social Care Act 2008 s 151(2). Financial assistance for establishing a qualifying body given under s 149(2) (see PARA 143) may not be given by way of purchasing share capital of the company: s 151(3).
8   As to the Secretary of State see PARA 333.
9   Health and Social Care Act 2008 s 152(1).
10 Health and Social Care Act 2008 s 152(2)(a).
11 Health and Social Care Act 2008 s 152(2)(b).
12 See note 1.
13 Health and Social Care Act 2008 s 152(3).

B.   GRANTS

146. Grants to local authorities for the provision of welfare services. The Secretary of State[1] may, with the consent of the Treasury[2], pay grants to local authorities in England[3] towards expenditure incurred by them in providing, or contributing to the provision of, such welfare services[4] as may be determined by the Secretary of State[5] or in connection with any such welfare services[6]. The amount of any such grants and the manner of their payment are to be such as may be determined by the Secretary of State[7], and grants may be paid on such terms and conditions as the Secretary of State may determine[8].

A local authority must supply the Secretary of State with such information as he may require for these purposes[9], and a local authority must have regard to any guidance for the time being issued by the Secretary of State with respect to the administration and application of grants which are paid to it[10]. A local authority must also comply with any directions for the time being given by the Secretary of State with respect to the administration and application of grants which are paid to it[11].

1   As to the Secretary of State see PARA 333.
2   As to the Treasury see CONSTITUTIONAL AND ADMINISTRATIVE LAW vol 20 (2014) PARA 262 et seq.
3   For these purposes, 'local authority' means, in relation to England, a county council, a district council, a London borough council, the Common Council of the City of London or the Council of the Isles of Scilly: Local Government Act 2000 s 93(12). As to local government areas and authorities in England see LOCAL GOVERNMENT vol 69 (2009) PARA 22 et seq. As to the London boroughs and their councils see LONDON GOVERNMENT vol 71 (2013) PARAS 15, 20, 34–38. As to the Common Council of the City of London see LONDON GOVERNMENT vol 71 (2013) PARA 16. As to the meaning of 'England' see PARA 1 note 1. Grants under the Local Government Act 2000 s 93 may be paid to all local authorities (s 93(4)(a)), to particular local authorities (s 93(4)(b)) or to particular descriptions of local authority (including descriptions framed by reference to authorities in particular areas) (s 93(4)(c)).
4   For the purposes of the Local Government Act 2000 s 93 'welfare services' includes services which provide support, assistance, advice or counselling to individuals with particular needs: Local Government Act 2000 s 93(12).
5   Local Government Act 2000 s 93(1)(a) (s 93(1)(a), (b) substituted, s 93(6A) added, by the Adoption and Children Act 2002 s 136(1), (2), (4)). Any determination, guidance or directions under the Local Government Act 2003 s 93 may make different provision in relation to different local authorities or descriptions of local authority (including descriptions framed by reference to authorities in particular areas): s 93(10). Before making any determination, issuing any guidance or giving any directions relating to all local authorities in England or any description of such

authorities, the Secretary of State must consult such local authorities or representatives of local authorities as appear to him to be appropriate (s 93(11)(a)), such recipients, or representatives of recipients, of welfare services as appear to him to be appropriate (s 93(11)(b)), and such providers, or representatives of providers, of welfare services as appear to him to be appropriate (s 93(11)(c)).

6   Local Government Act 2000 s 93(1)(b) (as substituted: see note 5).
7   Local Government Act 2000 s 93(3). Before making any determination under s 93(3) or (5) the Secretary of State must obtain the consent of the Treasury: s 93(6A) (as added: see note 5).
8   Local Government Act 2000 s 93(5). See note 7. Terms and conditions may include provision as to the circumstances in which the whole or any part of a grant under s 93 must be repaid to the Secretary of State: s 93(6). Nothing in s 93(6) affects the generality of s 93(5): s 93(5).
9   Local Government Act 2000 s 93(7).
10 Local Government Act 2000 s 93(8). See note 5.
11 Local Government Act 2000 s 93(9). See note 5.

147.   Grants to local authorities in respect of services to the mentally ill. The Secretary of State[1] may make grants out of money provided by Parliament[2] towards any expenses of local authorities[3] incurred in connection with the exercise of social services functions[4] in relation to persons suffering from mental illness[5].

1   As to the Secretary of State see PARA 333. By virtue of the Social Services and Well-being (Wales) Act 2014 (Consequential Amendments) Regulations 2016, SI 2016/413, reg 19, 20, the Local Authority Social Services Act 1970 s 7E applies only in relation to local authorities in England.
2   Grants are made with the approval of the Treasury. As to the Treasury see CONSTITUTIONAL AND ADMINISTRATIVE LAW vol 20 (2014) PARA 262 et seq.
3   The local authorities for the purposes of the Local Authority Social Services Act 1970 are the councils of non-metropolitan counties and metropolitan districts in England, the councils of London boroughs and the Common Council of the City of London: s 1. As to local government areas and authorities in England see LOCAL GOVERNMENT vol 69 (2009) PARA 22 et seq. As to the London boroughs and their councils see LONDON GOVERNMENT vol 71 (2013) PARAS 15, 20, 34–38. As to the Common Council of the City of London see LONDON GOVERNMENT vol 71 (2013) PARA 16.
4   As to the social services functions of a local authority for the purposes of the Local Authority Social Services Act 1970 see s 1A; and PARA 315.
5   Local Authority Social Services Act 1970 s 7E (added by the National Health Service and Community Care Act 1990 s 50). As to social services functions in relation to persons suffering from mental illness see MENTAL HEALTH AND CAPACITY vol 75 (2013) PARA 579 et seq.

148.   Grants for resettlement. The Secretary of State[1] may pay such grants, to such persons, as he considers appropriate in relation to expenditure in connection with the provision or maintenance of resettlement places[2]. Any such grant may be made on such terms and subject to such conditions as the Secretary of State considers appropriate[3], and must be paid out of money provided by Parliament[4].

There is older legislation which makes provision to assist displaced Poles and their dependents in regard to accommodation and other needs[5].

1   As to the Secretary of State see PARA 333.
2   Jobseekers Act 1995 s 30(1). 'Resettlement places' means places at which persons without a settled way of life are afforded temporary accommodation with a view to assisting them to lead a more settled life: s 30(2). As to provisions relating to jobseekers generally see WELFARE BENEFITS AND STATE PENSIONS vol 104 (2014) PARAS 262 et seq, 419 et seq.
3   Jobseekers Act 1995 s 30(3).
4   Jobseekers Act 1995 s 30(5). Any sums received by way of the repayment of any such grant must be paid into the Consolidated Fund: s 30(6). As to the Consolidated Fund see CONSTITUTIONAL AND ADMINISTRATIVE LAW vol 20 (2014) PARA 480; PARLIAMENT vol 78 (2010) PARA 1028 et seq.
5   See the Polish Resettlement Act 1947 which is still in force but unlikely to be used further.

149.   Grants to Motability. The Secretary of State[1] may make grants to Motability[2] for such purposes as he may determine[3]. Any grant made may be of such amount, and subject to such conditions, as the Secretary of State may with the consent of the Treasury[4] determine[5]; and is payable out of money provided by Parliament[6].

1 As to the Secretary of State see PARA 333.
2 Disability (Grants) Act 1993 s 1(1)(c). Motability is the company set up under that name as a charity and originally incorporated under the Companies Act 1985 and subsequently incorporated by Royal Charter: see the Universal Credit, Personal Independence Payment, Jobseeker's Allowance and Employment and Support Allowance (Claims and Payments) Regulations 2013, SI 2013/380, reg 62(5); and as to Motability see WELFARE BENEFITS AND STATE PENSIONS vol 104 (2014) PARA 143. These provisions also enable the Secretary of State to make grants to:
    (1)   the Independent Living Fund (2006) established by a deed dated 10 April 2006 and made between the Secretary of State for Work and Pensions of the one part and Margaret Rosemary Cooper, Michael Beresford Boyall and Marie Theresa Martin of the other part (Disability (Grants) Act 1993 s 1(1)(d) (s 1(1)(a), (b) prospectively repealed, s 1(1)(d) added, by the Welfare Reform Act 2007 s 61(1), Sch 8);
    (2)   until a day to be appointed, the Independent Living (Extension) Fund established by a deed dated 25 February 1993 and made between the Secretary of State for Social Security of the one part and Robin Glover Wendt and John Fletcher Shepherd of the other part (Disability (Grants) Act 1993 s 1(1)(a) (as so prospectively repealed)); and
    (3)   until a day to be appointed, the Independent Living (1993) Fund established by a deed of the same date made between the same parties (s 1(1)(b) (as so prospectively repealed)).
    At the date at which this volume states the law no day had been appointed for the coming into force of the amendments cited as prospective. However, the Independent Living Fund was closed on 30 June 2015.
3 Disability Grants Act 1993 s 1(1).
4 As to the Treasury see CONSTITUTIONAL AND ADMINISTRATIVE LAW vol 20 (2014) PARA 262 et seq.
5 Disability Grants Act 1993 s 1(2).
6 Disability Grants Act 1993 s 1(3).

(ii) Wales

150. Grants to local authorities for the provision of welfare services. The Welsh Ministers[1] may pay grants to local authorities in Wales[2] towards expenditure incurred by them in providing, or contributing to the provision of, such welfare services[3] as may be determined by the Welsh Ministers[4] or in connection with any such welfare services[5]. The amount of any such grants and the manner of their payment are to be such as may be determined by the Welsh Ministers[6], and grants may be paid on such terms and conditions as the Welsh Ministers may determine[7].

A local authority must supply the Welsh Ministers with such information as they may require for these purposes[8], and a local authority must have regard to any guidance for the time being issued by the Welsh Ministers with respect to the administration and application of grants which are paid to it[9]. A local authority must also comply with any directions for the time being given by the Welsh Ministers with respect to the administration and application of grants which are paid to it[10].

1 As to the Welsh Ministers see PARA 395.
2 For these purposes, 'local authority' means, in relation to Wales, a county council or a county borough council: Local Government Act 2000 s 93(12). As to local government areas and authorities in England and Wales see LOCAL GOVERNMENT vol 69 (2009) PARA 22 et seq. Grants under the Local Government Act 2000 s 93 may be paid to all local authorities (s 93(4)(a)), to particular local authorities (s 93(4)(b)) or to particular descriptions of local authority (including descriptions framed by reference to authorities in particular areas) (s 93(4)(c)).
3 As to the meaning of 'welfare services' see PARA 146 note 4.
4 Local Government Act 2000 s 93(2)(a) (s 93(2)(a), (b) substituted by the Adoption and Children Act 2002 s 136(3)). Any determination, guidance or directions under the Local Government Act 2000 s 93 may make different provision in relation to different local authorities or descriptions of

local authority (including descriptions framed by reference to authorities in particular areas): s 93(10). Before making any determination, issuing any guidance or giving any directions relating to all local authorities in England or any description of such authorities, the Welsh Ministers must consult such local authorities or representatives of local authorities as appear to them to be appropriate (s 93(11)(a)), such recipients, or representatives of recipients, of welfare services as appear to them to be appropriate (s 93(11)(b)), and such providers, or representatives of providers, of welfare services as appear to them to be appropriate (s 93(11)(c)).

5 Local Government Act 2000 s 93(2)(b) (as substituted: see note 4).
6 Local Government Act 2000 s 93(3).
7 Local Government Act 2000 s 93(5). Terms and conditions may include provision as to the circumstances in which the whole or any part of a grant under s 93 must be repaid to the Welsh Assembly Government: s 93(6). Nothing in s 93(6) affects the generality of s 93(5): s 93(5).
8 Local Government Act 2000 s 93(7).
9 Local Government Act 2000 s 93(8). See note 4.
10 Local Government Act 2000 s 93(9). See note 4.

151. Grants for resettlement. The Welsh Ministers[1] may pay such grants, to such persons, as they consider appropriate in relation to expenditure in connection with the provision or maintenance of resettlement places[2]. Any such grant may be made on such terms and subject to such conditions as the Ministers consider appropriate[3], and must be paid out of money provided by the Welsh Assenbly[4].

1 As to the Welsh Ministers: see PARA 395.
2 Jobseekers Act 1995 s 30(1). As to 'resettlement places' see PARA 148 note 2.
3 Jobseekers Act 1995 s 30(3).
4 Jobseekers Act 1995 s 30(5). See also s 30(6); and see PARA 148 note 4.

3. REGULATION OF PERSONS PROVIDING CARE

(1) ENGLAND

(i) The Regulated Activities

152. Personal care. The provision of personal care for persons who, by reason of old age, illness or disability are unable to provide it for themselves, and which is provided in a place where those persons are living at the time the care is provided, is a 'regulated activity' for the purpose of the statutory provisions[1] governing the registration of health or social care providers in England[2]. 'Personal care' means[3] physical assistance given to a person in connection with:

(1)   eating or drinking (including the maintenance of established parenteral nutrition);

(2)   toileting (including in relation to the process of menstruation);

(3)   washing or bathing;

(4)   dressing;

(5)   oral care; or

(6)   the care of skin, hair and nails (with the exception of nail care provided by a chiropodist or podiatrist[4]),

or the prompting, together with supervision, of a person, in relation to the performance of any of the activities listed above, where that person is unable to make a decision for themselves in relation to performing such an activity without such prompting and supervision.

The following types of provision are excepted:

(a)   the supply of carers[5] to a service provider[6] by an undertaking acting as an employment agency or employment business[7] for the purposes of that provider carrying on a regulated activity[8];

(b)   the introduction of carers to an individual (other than a service provider) by a person (including an employment agency or an employment business) having no ongoing role in the direction or control of the service provided to that individual[9];

(c)   the services of a carer employed by an individual or related third party[10], without the involvement of an undertaking acting as an employment agency or employment business, and working wholly under the direction and control of that individual or related third party in order to meet the individual's own care requirements[11]; and

(d)   the provision of personal care by a person managing a prison or other similar[12] custodial establishment[13].

Additionally, the provision of personal care is not a 'regulated activity' in the context of the accommodation or persons requiring nursing or personal care[14].

1   Ie for the purposes of the Health and Social Care Act 2008 Pt 1 (ss 1–97).

2   Health and Social Care Act 2008 (Regulated Activities) Regulations 2014, SI 2014/2936, reg 3(1), Sch 1 para 1(1) (made under the Health and Social Care Act 2008 s 8). 'Health care' includes all forms of health care provided for individuals, whether relating to physical or mental health, and also includes procedures that are similar to forms of medical or surgical care but are not provided in connection with a medical condition: ss 9(1), (2), 97(1). Any reference in Pt 1 (ss 1–97) to the provision of health care, or adult social services, by a person includes a reference to the provision of that care, or those services, by that person's agent or sub-contractor: s 97(6). 'Social care' includes all forms of personal care and other practical assistance provided for individuals who by

reason of age, illness, disability, pregnancy, childbirth, dependence on alcohol or drugs, or any other similar circumstances, are in need of such care or other assistance: s 9(3). 'Health or social care' means health care or social care: s 9(4).

An activity is a regulated activity for these purposes only if it is carried on in England: see the Health and Social Care Act 2008 (Regulated Activities) Regulations 2014, SI 2014/2936, reg 3(3); and PARA 158. Provision is made for the modification by regulations of any provision of the Health and Social Care Act 2008 Pt 1 Ch 2 (ss 8–44) in their application to a 'newly regulated activity' (as defined): see s 43. At the date at which this volume states the law no such regulations had been made. An activity which is ancillary to, or is carried on wholly or mainly in relation to, a regulated activity treated as part of that activity: Health and Social Care Act 2008 (Regulated Activities) Regulations 2014, SI 2014/2936, reg 3(2). Any reference in the Health and Social Care Act 2008 Pt 1 to a person who carries on a regulated activity includes a reference to a person who carries it on otherwise than for profit: s 97(5).

Regulations may require the person carrying on a regulated activity to make a return to the Care Quality Commission at such intervals as may be prescribed: s 40(1). Provision may be made by the regulations as to the contents of the return and the period in respect of which and date by which it is to be made: s 40(2). At the date this volume states the law no such regulations had been made. As to the Care Quality Commission see PARA 336 et seq.

3   Ie by virtue of the Health and Social Care Act 2008 (Regulated Activities) Regulations 2014, SI 2014/2936, reg 2(1).

4   Ie a person registered as such with the Health and Care Professions Council pursuant to the Health and Social Work Professions Order 2001, SI 2002/254, art 5 (see MEDICAL PROFESSIONS vol 74 (2011) PARA 928).

5   In this context 'carer' means an individual who provides personal care to a person referred to in the Health and Social Care Act 2008 (Regulated Activities) Regulations 2014, SI 2014/2936, Sch 1 para 1(1): Sch 1 para 1(4).

6   'Service provider' means, in respect of a regulated activity, a person registered with the Care Quality Commission under the Health and Social Care Act 2008 Pt 1 Ch 2 as a service provider in respect of that activity: Care Quality Commission (Registration) Regulations 2009, SI 2009/3112, reg 2; Health and Social Care Act 2008 (Regulated Activities) Regulations 2014, SI 2014/2936, reg 2(1).

7   As to the meanings of 'employment agency' and 'employment business' see the Employment Agencies Act 1973 s 13; and TRADE AND INDUSTRY vol 97 (2015) PARA 974 (definition applied by the Health and Social Care Act 2008 (Regulated Activities) Regulations 2014, SI 2014/2936, reg 2(1)).

8   Health and Social Care Act 2008 (Regulated Activities) Regulations 2014, SI 2014/2936, Sch 1 para 1(3)(a).

9   Health and Social Care Act 2008 (Regulated Activities) Regulations 2014, SI 2014/2936, Sch 1 para 1(3)(b).

10   'Related third party' means (by virtue of the Health and Social Care Act 2008 (Regulated Activities) Regulations 2014, SI 2014/2936, Sch 1 para 1(4)):

(1)   an individual with parental responsibility (within the meaning of the Children Act 1989 s 3: see CHILDREN AND YOUNG PERSONS vol 9 (2017) PARA 150) for a child to whom personal care services are to be provided;

(2)   an individual with power of attorney or other lawful authority to make arrangements on behalf of the person to whom personal care services are to be provided;

(3)   a group of individuals mentioned in either of heads (1) and (2) above making arrangements on behalf of one or more persons to whom personal care services are to be provided;

(4)   a trust established for the purpose of providing services to meet the health or social care needs of a named individual.

11   Health and Social Care Act 2008 (Regulated Activities) Regulations 2014, SI 2014/2936, Sch 1 para 1(3)(c).

12   Ie other than a hospital within the meaning of the Mental Health Act 1983 Pt II (ss 2–34): see MENTAL HEALTH AND CAPACITY vol 75 (2013) PARA 577.

13   Health and Social Care Act 2008 (Regulated Activities) Regulations 2014, SI 2014/2936, Sch 1 para 1(3)(d).

14   Ie the Health and Social Care Act 2008 (Regulated Activities) Regulations 2014, SI 2014/2936, Sch 1 para 1(1) does not apply where Sch 1 para 2 (see PARA 153) applies: Sch 1 para 1(2).

153. Provision of residential accommodation.

The provision of residential accommodation together with nursing[1] or personal care[2] is a 'regulated activity'[3] for the purpose of the statutory provisions[4] governing the registration of health or social care providers in England[5]. This does not apply to the provision of accommodation:

(1)   to an individual by a shared lives carer[6] under the terms of a shared lives agreement[7];

(2)   in a school[8];

(3)   in an institution within the further education sector or in a 16 to 19 Academy[9]; or

(4)   in an institution within the further education sector where the number of persons to whom nursing or personal care and accommodation are provided is not more than one-tenth of the number of students to whom both education and accommodation are provided[10].

The provision of residential accommodation for a person together with treatment[11] for drug or alcohol misuse, where acceptance by the person of such treatment is a condition of the provision of the accommodation, is also a 'regulated activity' for these purposes[12].

1   'Nursing care' means any services provided by a nurse and involving the provision of care or the planning, supervision or delegation of the provision of care, other than any services which, having regard to their nature and the circumstances in which they are provided, do not need to be provided by a nurse; and 'nurse' means a registered nurse: Health and Social Care Act 2008 (Regulated Activities) Regulations 2014, SI 2014/2936, reg 2(1). As to registered nurses see MEDICAL PROFESSIONS vol 74 (2011) PARA 713.

2   As to the meaning of 'personal care' see PARA 152.

3   As to the meaning of 'regulated activity' for these purposes see PARA 152 note 2.

4   Ie for the purposes of the Health and Social Care Act 2008 Pt 1 (ss 1–97).

5   Health and Social Care Act 2008 (Regulated Activities) Regulations 2014, SI 2014/2936, Sch 1 para 2(1). An activity is a regulated activity for these purposes only if it is carried on in England: see reg 3(3); and PARA 158. The Care Standards Act 2000 Pts I, II (ss 1–42), which makes provision for the registration and regulation of various types of non-local authority residential care providers, is dealt with in CHILDREN AND YOUNG PERSONS and HEALTH SERVICES.

6   'Shared lives carer' means an individual who, under the terms of a shared lives agreement, provides, or intends to provide, personal care for service users together with, where necessary, accommodation in the individual's home; 'shared lives agreement' means an agreement entered into between a person carrying on a shared lives scheme and an individual for the provision, by that individual, of personal care to a service user together with, where necessary, accommodation in the individual's home; 'shared lives scheme' means a scheme carried on (whether or not for profit) by a local authority or other person for the purposes of recruiting and training shared lives carers, making arrangements for the placing of service users with shared lives carers, and supporting and monitoring placements; and 'service user' means a person who receives services provided in the carrying on of a regulated activity: Health and Social Care Act 2008 (Regulated Activities) Regulations 2014, SI 2014/2936, reg 2(1).

7   Health and Social Care Act 2008 (Regulated Activities) Regulations 2014, SI 2014/2936, Sch 1 para 2(2)(a).

8   Health and Social Care Act 2008 (Regulated Activities) Regulations 2014, SI 2014/2936, Sch 1 para 2(2)(b). As to the meaning of 'school' see the Education Act 1996 s 4; and EDUCATION vol 35 (2015) PARA 91 (definition applied by the Health and Social Care Act 2008 (Regulated Activities) Regulations 2014, SI 2014/2936, reg 2(1)).

9   Health and Social Care Act 2008 (Regulated Activities) Regulations 2014, SI 2014/2936, Sch 1 para 2(2)(c). As to the meanings of 'institution within the further education sector' and '16 to 19 academy' see the Further and Higher Education Act 1992 s 91; the Academies Act 2010 s 1B; and EDUCATION vol 35 (2015) PARAS 346, 555 (definitions applied by the Health and Social Care Act 2008 (Regulated Activities) Regulations 2014, SI 2014/2936, reg 2(1)).

10   Health and Social Care Act 2008 (Regulated Activities) Regulations 2014, SI 2014/2936, Sch 1 para 2(2)(d).

11   'Treatment', except in the Health and Social Care Act 2008 (Regulated Activities) Regulations 2014, SI 2014/2936, Sch 1 para 5 (see MENTAL HEALTH AND CAPACITY vol 75 (2013) PARA 760), includes (by virtue of the Health and Social Care Act 2008 (Regulated Activities) Regulations 2014, SI 2014/2936, reg 2(1)):
     (1)   a diagnostic or screening procedure carried out for medical purposes;

(2)   the ongoing assessment of a service user's mental or physical state;
(3)   nursing, personal and palliative care; and
(4)   the giving of vaccinations and immunisations.

12 Health and Social Care Act 2008 (Regulated Activities) Regulations 2014, SI 2014/2936, Sch 1 para 3.

154. Medical activities and activities concerned with mentally disordered persons. 'Regulated activities'[1] for the purposes of the statutory provisions[2] governing the registration of health or social care providers in England include the provision of health care, such as:

(1)   the treatment of disease, disorder or injury[3];
(2)   surgical, diagnostic and screening procedures[4];
(3)   the provision of nursing care[5];
(4)   the management of the supply of blood and blood derived products[6];
(5)   maternity, midwifery and family planning services[7];
(6)   the provision of services in slimming clinics[8];
(7)   transport services, triage and the provision of remote medical services[9];
(8)   the assessment and treatment of mentally disordered persons[10].

1   As to the meaning of 'regulated activity' for these purposes see PARA 152 note 2.
2   Ie for the purposes of the Health and Social Care Act 2008 Pt 1 (ss 1–97).
3   See the Health and Social Care Act 2008 (Regulated Activities) Regulations 2014, SI 2014/2936, Sch 1 para 4; and MEDICAL PROFESSIONS.
4   See the Health and Social Care Act 2008 (Regulated Activities) Regulations 2014, SI 2014/2936, Sch 1 paras 6, 7; and MEDICAL PROFESSIONS.
5   See the Health and Social Care Act 2008 (Regulated Activities) Regulations 2014, SI 2014/2936, Sch 1 para 13; and MEDICAL PROFESSIONS.
6   See the Health and Social Care Act 2008 (Regulated Activities) Regulations 2014, SI 2014/2936, Sch 1 para 8; and MEDICAL PROFESSIONS.
7   See the Health and Social Care Act 2008 (Regulated Activities) Regulations 2014, SI 2014/2936, Sch 1 paras 10, 11, 14; and MEDICAL PROFESSIONS.
8   See the Health and Social Care Act 2008 (Regulated Activities) Regulations 2014, SI 2014/2936, Sch 1 para 12; and MEDICAL PROFESSIONS.
9   See the Health and Social Care Act 2008 (Regulated Activities) Regulations 2014, SI 2014/2936, Sch 1 para 9; and MEDICAL PROFESSIONS.
10 See the Health and Social Care Act 2008 (Regulated Activities) Regulations 2014, SI 2014/2936, Sch 1 para 5; and MENTAL HEALTH AND CAPACITY vol 75 (2013) PARA 760.

155. Certain family or personal relationships. Any activity which is carried on:
(1)   in the course of a family[1] or personal relationship[2]; and
(2)   for no commercial consideration[3],
is not a 'regulated activity'[4] for the purpose of the statutory provisions[5] governing the registration of health or social care providers in England[6].

1   A family relationship includes a relationship between two persons who live in the same household and treat each other as though they were members of the same family: Health and Social Care Act 2008 (Regulated Activities) Regulations 2014, SI 2014/2936, reg 3(4), Sch 2 para 1(2).
2   Health and Social Care Act 2008 (Regulated Activities) Regulations 2014, SI 2014/2936, Sch 2 para 1(1)(a). A personal relationship is a relationship between or among friends: Sch 2 para 1(3). A friend of a person ('A') includes a person who is a friend of a member of A's family: Sch 2 para 1(4).
3   Health and Social Care Act 2008 (Regulated Activities) Regulations 2014, SI 2014/2936, Sch 2 para 1(1)(b).
4   As to the meaning of 'regulated activity' for these purposes see PARA 152 note 2.
5   Ie for the purposes of the Health and Social Care Act 2008 Pt 1 (ss 1–97).
6   Health and Social Care Act 2008 (Regulated Activities) Regulations 2014, SI 2014/2936, Sch 2 para 1(1).

156. Carrying on of establishment or agency. Any activity which involves the carrying on of an establishment or agency[1] for which Her Majesty's Chief Inspector of Education, Children's Services and Skills[2] is the registration authority is not a 'regulated activity'[3] for the purpose of the statutory provisions[4] governing the registration of health or social care providers in England[5].

1 Ie within the meaning of the Care Standards Act 2000: see s 22; the regulations made thereunder; and CHILDREN AND YOUNG PERSONS vol 10 (2017) PARA 1017.
2 As to Her Majesty's Chief Inspector of Education, Children's Services and Skills see EDUCATION vol 36 (2015) PARA 1133 et seq.
3 As to the meaning of 'regulated activity' for these purposes see PARA 152 note 2.
4 Ie for the purposes of the Health and Social Care Act 2008 Pt 1 (ss 1–97).
5 Health and Social Care Act 2008 (Regulated Activities) Regulations 2014, SI 2014/2936, Sch 2 para 2.

157. Specified medical activities. 'Regulated activities'[1] for the purposes of the statutory provisions[2] governing the registration of health or social care providers in England do not include:

(1)   the provision of treatment in a surgery or consulting room by certain medical practitioners[3];
(2)   the provision of certain medical or dental services[4];
(3)   the provision of certain primary ophthalmic services[5];
(4)   the provision of certain pharmaceutical services[6]; and
(5)   the provision of first aid[7]; and
(6)   the provision of treatment by a school nurse[8].

1 As to the meaning of 'regulated activity' for these purposes see PARA 152 note 2.
2 Ie for the purposes of the Health and Social Care Act 2008 Pt 1 (ss 1–97).
3 See the Health and Social Care Act 2008 (Regulated Activities) Regulations 2014, SI 2014/2936, Sch 2 para 3, Sch 2 para 4 (exclusions); and MEDICAL PROFESSIONS.
4 See the Health and Social Care Act 2008 (Regulated Activities) Regulations 2014, SI 2014/2936, Sch 2 paras 5, 6, 10; and MEDICAL PROFESSIONS.
5 See the Health and Social Care Act 2008 (Regulated Activities) Regulations 2014, SI 2014/2936, Sch 2 para 7; and MEDICAL PROFESSIONS.
6 See the Health and Social Care Act 2008 (Regulated Activities) Regulations 2014, SI 2014/2936, Sch 2 para 8; and MEDICAL PROFESSIONS.
7 See the Health and Social Care Act 2008 (Regulated Activities) Regulations 2014, SI 2014/2936, Sch 2 para 9; and MEDICAL PROFESSIONS.
8 See the Health and Social Care Act 2008 (Regulated Activities) Regulations 2014, SI 2014/2936, Sch 2 para 11; and MEDICAL PROFESSIONS.

(ii) Registration of Service Providers and Managers

158. Provision of regulated activities by unregistered persons. An activity is only a regulated activity for these purposes[1] if it is carried on in England[2]. Any person who, with intent to deceive any person:

(1)   applies any name to any concern[3] carried on in England or to any premises in England[4]; or
(2)   in any way describes such a concern or such premises or holds such a concern or such premises out[5],

so as to indicate, or reasonably be understood to indicate, that the carrying on of the concern is a regulated activity or that the premises are used for the carrying on of a regulated activity, is guilty of an offence[6] unless:

(a)   a person is registered[7] as a service provider in respect of the regulated activity in question[8]; and
(b)   the registration has not been suspended[9].

1 Ie for the purposes of the Health and Social Care Act 2008 Pt 1 (ss 1–97). As to the regulated activities see PARAS 152–157 (noting in particular PARA 152 note 2).
2 Health and Social Care Act 2008 (Regulated Activities) Regulations 2014, SI 2014/2936, reg 3(3).
3 For these purposes 'concern' includes any organisation: Health and Social Care Act 2008 s 36(5).
4 Health and Social Care Act 2008 s 36(1)(a).

5 Health and Social Care Act 2008 s 36(1)(b).
6 A person guilty of an offence under the Health and Social Care Act 2008 s 36(1) or (3) is liable
   on summary conviction to a fine not exceeding level 5 on the standard scale: s 36(4). As to the
   powers of magistrates' courts to issue fines on summary conviction see SENTENCING vol 92 (2015)
   PARA 176. A conviction for a Part 1 offence (ie an offence under Pt 1 (s 197(1))), and where
   applicable the payment of a penalty notice, must be publicised by the Care Quality Commission:
   see the Care Quality Commission (Registration) Regulations 2009, SI 2009/3112, reg 7, Sch 2
   paras 2, 4, 6, 7, 8(3)–(5), 9, 11, 12 (made under the Health and Social Care Act 2008 s 89
   (amended by the Care Act 2014 s 82(4))). As to the Care Quality Commission see PARA 336 et seq.
      Proceedings in respect of a Part 1 offence may not, without the written consent of the Attorney
   General, be taken by any person other than the Commission or, in relation to any functions of
   the Commission which the Secretary of State is for the time being discharging by virtue of the
   Health and Social Care Act 2008 s 82, the Secretary of State: s 90(1). As to the Attorney General
   see CONSTITUTIONAL AND ADMINISTRATIVE LAW vol 20 (2014) PARA 273. Proceedings for a
   Part 1 offence may be brought within a period of 12 months from the date on which evidence
   sufficient in the opinion of the prosecutor to warrant the proceedings came to the
   prosecutor's knowledge; but no such proceedings are to be brought by virtue of s 90(2) more than
   three years after the commission of the offence: s 90(2).
      Where a Part 1 offence is committed by a body corporate, if the offence is proved to have been
   committed by, or with the consent or connivance of, or to be attributable to any neglect on the part
   of any director, manager or secretary of the body corporate; or any person who was purporting to
   act in any such capacity, that director, manager, secretary or person purporting to act as such (as
   well as the body corporate) is guilty of the offence and liable to be proceeded against and punished
   accordingly: s 91(1), (2). The reference above to a director, manager or secretary of a body
   corporate includes a reference to any other similar officer of the body; and where the body is an
   English NHS body or English local authority, to any officer or member of the NHS body or local
   authority: s 91(3). 'English local authority' means a county council in England, a metropolitan
   district council, a non-metropolitan district council for an area for which there is no county
   council, a London borough council, the Common Council of the City of London, or the Council
   of the Isles of Scilly: s 97(1). As to local government areas and authorities in England see LOCAL
   GOVERNMENT vol 69 (2009) PARA 22 et seq. As to the London boroughs and their councils see
   LONDON GOVERNMENT vol 71 (2013) PARAS 15, 20, 34–38. As to the Common Council of the
   City of London see LONDON GOVERNMENT vol 71 (2013) PARA 16. 'English NHS body' means
   the National Health Service Commissioning Board (see HEALTH SERVICES vol 54 (2017)
   PARA 32), a clinical commissioning group (see HEALTH SERVICES vol 54 (2017) PARA 35 et seq),
   an NHS foundation trust (see HEALTH SERVICES vol 54 (2017) PARA 244), a Special Health
   Authority (see HEALTH SERVICES vol 54A (2017) PARA 532 et seq) performing functions only or
   mainly in respect of England or, until a day to be appointed, a National Health Service trust (see
   HEALTH SERVICES vol 54 (2017) PARA 235) all or most of whose hospitals, establishments and
   facilities are situated in England: s 97(1) (definition amended by the Health and Social Care Act
   2012 Sch 5 para 166(1), (2); prospectively amended by Sch 14 Pt 2 paras 108, 109(a). At the date .
   at which this volume states the law no such day had been appointed.
      Proceedings for a Part 1 offence alleged to have been committed by an unincorporated
   association are to be brought in the name of the association (and not in that of any of the
   members): Health and Social Care Act 2008 s 92(1). Rules of court relating to the service of
   documents have effect as if the unincorporated association were a body corporate: s 92(2). In
   proceedings for a Part 1 offence brought against an unincorporated association, the Criminal
   Justice Act 1925 s 33 (see CRIMINAL PROCEDURE vol 27 (2015) PARAS 373–374) and the
   Magistrates' Courts Act 1980 Sch 3 (see CRIMINAL PROCEDURE vol 27 (2015) PARA 198) apply
   as they apply in relation to a body corporate: Health and Social Care Act 2008 s 92(3). A fine
   imposed on an unincorporated association on its conviction for a Part 1 offence is to be paid out
   of the funds of the association: s 92(4). If a Part 1 offence committed by an unincorporated
   association is proved to have been committed with the consent or connivance of an officer of the
   association or a member of its governing body; or to be attributable to any neglect on the part of
   such an officer or member, the officer or member (as well as the association) is guilty of the offence
   and liable to be proceeded against and punished accordingly: s 92(5). For the power of the Care
   Quality Commission to issue guidance in this regard see PARA 197.
      The Secretary of State must carry out a review of the Care Quality Commission (Registration)
   Regulations 2009, SI 2009/3112, and the Health and Social Care Act 2008 (Regulated Activities)
   Regulations 2014, SI 2014/2936: Care Quality Commission (Registration) Regulations 2009, SI
   2009/3112, reg 27(1)(a) (reg 27 added by SI 2012/921); Health and Social Care Act 2008
   (Regulated Activities) Regulations 2014, SI 2014/2936, reg 27(1)(a). The review of the 2009
   regulations must take place before 1 October 2017, and the review of the 2014 regulations must
   take place before 1 April 2020: Care Quality Commission (Registration) Regulations 2009, SI
   2009/3112, reg 27(1) (as so added); Health and Social Care Act 2008 (Regulated Activities)

Regulations 2014, SI 2014/2936, reg 27(1) (amended by SI 2015/64). The Secretary of State must set out conclusions of the review in a report and publish the report: Care Quality Commission (Registration) Regulations 2009, SI 2009/3112, reg 27(1)(b), (c) (as so added); Health and Social Care Act 2008 (Regulated Activities) Regulations 2014, SI 2014/2936, reg 27(1)(b), (c). The reports must, in particular, set out the objectives intended to be achieved by the regulatory system established by the relevant regulations, assess the extent to which those objectives are achieved, and assess whether those objectives remain appropriate and, if so, the extent to which they could be achieved with a system that imposes less regulation Care Quality Commission (Registration) Regulations 2009, SI 2009/3112, reg 27(2) (as so added); Health and Social Care Act 2008 (Regulated Activities) Regulations 2014, SI 2014/2936, reg 27(2).

7   Ie under the Health and Social Care Act 2008 Pt 1 Ch 2 (ss 8–44).
8   Health and Social Care Act 2008 s 36(2)(a).
9   Health and Social Care Act 2008 s 36(2)(b).

159. Requirement to register as a service provider or manager. Any person who carries on a regulated activity in England[1] without being registered[2] as a 'service provider'[3] in respect of the carrying on of that activity is guilty of an offence[4]. Where the service provider (S) is:

(1)   a body of persons corporate or unincorporated (other than an English NHS body or NHS Blood and Transplant[5]); or

(2)   an individual who is not a fit person[6] to manage the carrying on of the regulated activity, or is not, or does not intend to be, in full-time day to day charge of the carrying on of the regulated activity[7],

his registration as a service provider in respect of a regulated activity must be subject to a 'registered manager condition', ie a condition that the activity as carried on by S, or the activity as carried on by S at or from particular premises, must be managed by an individual who is registered[8] as a manager in respect of the activity, or the activity as carried on at or from those premises[9].

1   As to the meaning of 'regulated activity' for these purposes, and the restriction of these provisions to activities carried on in England, see PARA 152 note 2; as to the regulated activities see PARAS 152–157. Provision for determining who is carrying on a regulated activity for this purpose when it is carried on by more than one person is made by the Care Quality Commission (Registration) Regulations 2009, SI 2009/3112, reg 4 (made under the Health and Social Care Act 2008 s 10(2)).

2   Ie under the Health and Social Care Act 2008 Pt 1 Ch 2 (ss 8–44). Where there is more than one registered person in respect of a regulated activity, or in respect of that activity as carried on at or from particular premises, anything which is required under the Care Quality Commission (Registration) Regulations 2009, SI 2009/3112 to be done by the registered person, if done by one of the registered persons, is not be required to be done by any of the other registered persons: reg 23.

3   In the Health and Social Care Act 2008 ss 11–97 the registration of a person under Pt 1 Ch 2 in respect of the carrying on of a regulated activity by that person is referred to as registration 'as a service provider' in respect of that activity: s 10(3).

4   Health and Social Care Act 2008 s 10(1). A person guilty of an offence under s 10 is liable on summary conviction to a fine or to imprisonment for a term not exceeding 6 months, or to both; and conviction on indictment to a fine or to imprisonment for a term not exceeding 6 months, or to both: s 10(4) (amended by SI 2015/64). When the Criminal Justice Act 2003 s 154(1) (general limit on magistrates' court's power to impose imprisonment) is brought into force, the maximum sentence on summary conviction increases to 12 months: Health and Social Care Act 2008 s 10(5).

    As to the powers of magistrates' courts to issue fines on summary conviction see SENTENCING vol 92 (2015) PARA 176. As to proceedings for offences see PARA 158 note 6. The offence under s 10(1) is a 'fixed penalty offence', the monetary amount of which is £4,000: see the Health and Social Care Act 2008 (Regulated Activities) Regulations 2014, SI 2014/2936, reg 24 (which also set out the mechanism for the issue and payment of fixed penalties), Sch 5 (made under the Health and Social Care Act 2008 ss 35, 86, 87 (s 35 amended by SI 2015/64)). For the power of the Care Quality Commission to issue guidance in this regard see PARA 197.

5   Care Quality Commission (Registration) Regulations 2009, SI 2009/3112, regs 2, 5(1), (2) (reg 2 (definition 'health service body') amended by SI 2013/2325) (made under the Health and Social Care Act 2008 s 13(1)).

6   A service provider ('P') is not a fit person to manage the carrying on of a regulated activity unless P is of good character; is physically and mentally fit to manage the carrying on of the regulated

activity; has the necessary qualifications, skills and experience to do so; and is able to supply to the Commission, or arrange for the availability of, information relating to themselves specified in the Care Quality Commission (Registration) Regulations 2009, SI 2009/3112, Sch 1: reg 5(3).

7   Care Quality Commission (Registration) Regulations 2009, SI 2009/3112, reg 5(1)(b).
8   See note 2.
9   Health and Social Care Act 2008 s 13(3).

160. Applications for registration and grant and refusal of applications. A person seeking to be registered in England[1] as a service provider or[2] manager must make an application to the Care Quality Commission[3]. Where an application for registration has been made the Commission must grant it if it is satisfied that the statutory requirements for the protection of persons for whom the services are provided and for ensuring quality of service[4] are being and will continue to be complied with (so far as applicable) in relation to the carrying on of the regulated activity[5]. If the Commission is not so satisfied, it must refuse the application[6]. Where an application is granted, it may be granted either unconditionally or subject to such conditions[7] as the Commission thinks fit[8].

A decision of the Commission under these provisions is subject to appeal[9].

1   As to the requirement to register as a service provider or manager see PARA 159.
2   Ie where a person seeks to be registered as a manager in respect of a regulated activity in respect of which a registered manager condition has, or is to have, effect: Health and Social Care Act 2008 s 14(1). As to the meaning of 'regulated activity' for these purposes, and the restriction of these provisions to activities carried on in England, see PARA 152 note 2; as to the regulated activities see PARAS 152–157.
3   Health and Social Care Act 2008 ss 11(1), 14(1). As to the Care Quality Commission see PARA 336 et seq. The application must be made in such form, and contain or be accompanied by such information, as the Commission requires: ss 11(2), 14(2). In such cases as the Commission may determine, a person seeking to be registered as a service provider or manager in respect of two or more regulated activities (in the case of an application for registration as a manager, two or more regulated activities carried on by a person registered as a service provider) may make a single application in respect of them: ss 11(3), 14(3).

    If, in an application for registration, a person knowingly makes a statement which is false or misleading in a material respect, he is guilty of an offence: s 37(1)(a), (2). A person guilty of an offence under s 37 is liable on summary conviction to a fine not exceeding level 4 on the standard scale: s 37(3). As to proceedings for offences see PARA 158 note 6.

    The Commission may with the consent of the Secretary of State from time to time make and publish provision requiring a fee to be paid in respect of an application for registration as a service provider or manager under Pt 1 Ch 2 (ss 8–44) or the grant or subsistence of any such registration: s 85(1)(a)(i), (ii). The amount of a fee payable under s 85(1) is to be such as may be specified in, or calculated or determined under, the provision: s 85(2). Provision under s 85(1) may include provision for different fees to be paid in different cases (s 85(3)(a)), for different fees to be paid by persons of different descriptions (s 85(3)(b)), for the amount of a fee to be determined by the Commission in accordance with specified factors (s 85(3)(c)), and, for determining the time by which a fee is to be payable (s 85(3)(d)). Before making provision under s 85(1), the Commission must consult such persons as it thinks appropriate: s 85(4). At the date at which this volume states the law no fees had been prescribed for the purposes of s 85(1)(a)(i), (ii).

    If the Secretary of State considers it necessary or desirable to do so, he may by regulations make provision determining the amount of a fee payable to the Commission by virtue of s 85, and the time at which it is payable, instead of those matters being determined in accordance with provision so made: s 85(5). Before making any such regulations, the Secretary of State must consult the Commission and such other persons as he thinks appropriate: s 85(6). For the purpose of determining the fee payable by a person, the person must provide the Commission with such information, in such form, as the Commission may require: s 85(7). A fee so payable may, without prejudice to any other method of recovery, be recovered summarily as a civil debt: s 85(8). At the date at which this volume states the law no such regulations had been made.
4   Ie the requirements contained in the Care Quality Commission (Registration) Regulations 2009, SI 2009/3112 and the Health and Social Care Act 2008 (Regulated Activities) Regulations 2014, SI 2014/2936 (in so far as those regulations are made under the Health and Social Care Act 2008 s 20(1)–(5B), (8), (9) (amended by the Health and Social Care (Safety and Quality) Act 2015 s 1; and the Care Act 2014 ss 81, 95)), and the requirements of any other enactment which appears to the Commission to be relevant.

5   Health and Social Care Act 2008 ss 12(1), (2), 15(1), (2). On granting the application, the Commission must issue a certificate of registration to the applicant: ss 12(4), 15(4).

6   Health and Social Care Act 2008 ss 12(2), 15(2). The Commission must give the applicant notice in writing of a proposal to refuse the application: s 26(1), (3). A notice under s 26 must give the Commission's reasons for its proposal: s 26(6). A notice under s 26 must state that within 28 days of service of the notice any person on whom it was served may make written representations to the Commission concerning any matter which that person wishes to dispute: s 27(1). Where a notice has been served under s 26, the Commission must not determine any matter to which the notice relates until either any person on whom the notice was served has made written representations to it concerning the matter (s 27(2)(a)), any such person has notified the Commission in writing that the person does not intend to make such representations (s 27(2)(b)), or the period during which any such person could have made representations has elapsed (s 27(2)(c)). If the Commission decides to adopt a proposal of which it was required to give notice under s 26, it must give notice in writing of its decision to any person to whom it was required to give notice of the proposal: s 28(3). A notice under s 28(3) must:

(1)   explain the right of appeal conferred by s 32 (see note 9) (s 28(4)(a));

(2)   in the case of a decision to adopt a proposal under s 26(2) (see note 7), state the conditions subject to which the application is granted (s 28(4)(b));

(3)   in the case of a decision to adopt a proposal under s 26(4)(b) (see PARA 161), state the period (or extended period) of suspension (s 28(4)(c)); and

(4)   in the case of a decision to adopt a proposal under s 26(4)(c) or (d) (see PARA 161), state the condition as varied, the condition which is removed or (as the case may be) the additional condition imposed (s 28(4)(d)).

Where a person ('M') is registered as a manager in respect of a regulated activity, the Commission must give him a copy of any notice given under s 28(3) to the person ('S') registered as a service provider in respect of the regulated activity (s 28(5)(a)) and give S a copy of any such notice given to M (s 28(5)(b)). A decision of the Commission to adopt a proposal under s 26(2) or (4) takes effect at the end of the period of 28 days referred to in s 32(2) (see note 9) (s 28(6)(a)) or if an appeal is brought, on the determination or abandonment of the appeal (s 28(6)(b)). Section 28(6) is subject to s 28(7)–(9) (s 28(6) (s 28(6) amended, s 28(8), (9) added, by the Care Act 2014 s 87)), which provide:

(a)   that where the applicant notifies the Commission in writing before the end of the period mentioned in the Health and Social Care Act 2008 s 28(6)(a) that the applicant does not intend to appeal, the decision is to take effect when the Commission receives the applicant's notification (s 28(7));

(b)   that in a case where notice of the proposal has been given to an individual under s 26(4A) (see PARA 161), s 28(7) does not apply unless, by the time the Commission receives the applicant's notification, it has received notification from the individual that he does not intend to appeal (s 28(8) (as so added)); and

(c)   that if the Commission receives notification from the individual after it receives the applicant's notification and before the end of the period mentioned in s 28(6)(a), the decision is to take effect when the Commission receives the individual's notification (s 28(9) (as so added)).

Where the Commission gives notice under the Health and Social Care Act 2008 s 26, s 28(1) or (3), s 29 (see PARA 165), s 29A (see HEALTH SERVICES vol 54 (2017) PARA 243) or s 31 (see PARA 161) in respect of a regulated activity it must give a copy of the notice:

(i)   the National Health Service Commissioning Board (see HEALTH SERVICES vol 54 (2017) PARA 32) (in the circumstances prescribed in the Care Quality Commission (Registration) Regulations 2009, SI 2009/3112, reg 9(6A), (6B) (reg 9(1), (2), (4), (6) amended, reg 9(6A), (6B) added, by SI 2013/235)) (Health and Social Care Act 2008 s 39(1)(za), (2), (3) (s 39(1)(za) added, s 39(1)(a) amended, s 39(1)(c) substituted, by the Health and Social Care Act 2012 Sch 5 para 156));

(ii)   to a clinical commissioning group (see HEALTH SERVICES vol 54 (2017) PARA 35 et seq) or English local authority (in the circumstances prescribed in the Care Quality Commission (Registration) Regulations 2009, SI 2009/3112, reg 9(1)(a), (2)–(6) (as so amended)) (Health and Social Care Act 2008 s 39(1)(a) (as so amended));

(iii)   where the person registered as a service provider in respect of the activity is a person who holds a licence under the Health and Social Care Act 2012 Pt 3 Ch 3 (ss 81–110) (see HEALTH SERVICES vol 54A (2017) PARA 636 et seq), to Monitor (Health and Social Care Act 2008 s 39(1)(c) (as so substituted)); and

(iv)   to such other persons as the Commission considers appropriate (s 39(1)(d)).

As to Monitor see HEALTH SERVICES vol 54 (2017) PARA 195. The Commission must notify each of the persons mentioned above of either of the following events in relation to a registered person: the payment of a penalty in accordance with a penalty notice issued under s 86 (s 39(3)(a)) or the commencement of proceedings in respect of a Part 1 offence (s 39(3)(b)). These requirements (ie s 39(1)) do not apply to a notice of proposal given under s 26(2) or (3) or s 28(1) or (3) (Care Quality Commission (Registration) Regulations 2009, SI 2009/3112, reg 8(a)) to a notice of decision given under the Health and Social Care Act 2008 s 28(3) which relates to the variation or removal of any condition for the time being in force in relation to a registration or the imposition of an additional condition in relation to a registration and appears to the Commission not to have a material impact on the regulated activity being carried on (Care Quality Commission (Registration) Regulations 2009, SI 2009/3112, reg 8(b)), or to a notice of decision given under the Health and Social Care Act 2008 s 28(3) to refuse an application by the registered person under s 19(1) (Care Quality Commission (Registration) Regulations 2009, SI 2009/3112, reg 8(c)).

7   Where a person applies for registration as a service provider or manager in respect of a regulated activity and the Care Quality Commission proposes to grant the application subject to any condition which has not been agreed in writing between it and the applicant, other than a registered manager condition as required by the Health and Social Care Act 2008 s 13(1) (see PARA 159), it must give the applicant notice in writing of its proposal and of the conditions subject to which it proposes to grant the application: s 26(2). If the Commission decides to grant an application for registration as a service provider or manager in respect of a regulated activity unconditionally; or subject only to conditions each of which is either required by s 13(1) or agreed in writing between the Commission and the applicant, it must give the applicant notice in writing of the decision: s 28(1). Such a notice must state the conditions subject to which registration is granted: s 28(2). As to the right to make representations in response to notices under s 26, and as to the persons who must be notified where notice is given under s 26 or s 28, see ss 27, 39; and note 6. As to conditions of registration see further PARA 161.

8   Health and Social Care Act 2008 ss 12(3), 15(3). Section 12(3)–(5) have effect subject to s 13, which makes provision in connection with the registered manager condition: s 12(6). In deciding whether to impose a registered manager condition under s 12(3) or (5), in a case where s 13(1) (see PARA 159) does not require such a condition to be imposed, the Care Quality Commission must have regard to prescribed matters: s 13(2).

9   An appeal against any decision of the Commission under the Health and Social Care Act 2008 Pt 1 Ch 2 (ss 8–44), other than a decision to give a warning notice under s 29 or s 29A, lies to the First-tier Tribunal: s 32(1)(a) (s 32(1), (3)–(7) amended by SI 2009/56; Health and Social Care Act 2008 s 32(1)(a) amended by the Care Act 2014 s 82(4)(a))). As to the First-tier Tribunal see generally COURTS AND TRIBUNALS vol 24 (2010) PARA 874 et seq. No appeal against a decision or order may be brought by a person more than 28 days after service on the person of notice of the decision or order: Health and Social Care Act 2008 s 32(2). On an appeal against a decision of the Commission (other than a decision to which a notice under s 31 (see PARAS 161, 164) relates, the First-tier Tribunal may confirm the decision or direct that it is not to have effect: s 32(3) (as so amended). On an appeal against a decision or order, the First-tier Tribunal also has power to vary any discretionary condition for the time being in force in respect of the regulated activity to which the appeal relates (s 32(6)(a)), to direct that any such discretionary condition is to cease to have effect (s 32(6)(b)), to direct that any such discretionary condition as the First-tier Tribunal thinks fit has effect in respect of the regulated activity (s 32(6)(c)), or to vary the period of any suspension (s 32(6)(d)). For these purposes, 'discretionary condition', in relation to registration under Pt 1 Ch 2, means any condition other than a registered manager condition required by s 13(1) (see PARA 159): s 32(7).

161. Conditions of registration and variation and removal of conditions. A person who is registered in respect of a regulated activity in England (whether as a service provider or manager)[1] who fails, without reasonable excuse, to comply with any condition for the time being in force[2] in relation to the registration, is guilty of an offence[3]. Any person who, with intent to deceive any person, in any way describes or holds out any person registered as a service provider in respect of a regulated activity as able to provide a service or do any thing the provision or doing of which would contravene a condition for the time being in force[4] in relation to the regulated activity is guilty of an offence[5].

The Care Quality Commission[6] may also at any time vary or remove any condition for the time being in force in relation to a person's registration as a service provider or manager[7] or impose any additional condition[8]. There is an expedited procedure for the making of such variation where a person is at risk[9]. Except where it would be pre-empting a decision by the Commission to cancel a registration[10] or to vary[11] or remove[12] a condition, a person registered as a service provider or manager may apply to the Commission for the variation or removal of any condition (other than a registered manager condition)[13].

A decision of the Commission under these provisions is subject to appeal[14].

1   As to registration see the Health and Social Care Act 2008 Pt 1 Ch 2 (ss 8–44); and
    PARAS 159–160. As to the meaning of 'regulated activity' for these purposes, and the restriction
    of these provisions to activities carried on in England, see PARA 152 note 2; as to the regulated
    activities see PARAS 152–157.
2   Ie by virtue of the Health and Social Care Act 2008 Pt 1 Ch 2 (ss 8–44).
3   Health and Social Care Act 2008 s 33. A person who commits this offence is liable on summary
    conviction to a fine: s 33 (amended by SI 2015/64). As to proceedings for offences see PARA 158
    note 6. The offence under the Health and Social Care Act 2008 s 33 is a fixed penalty offence: see
    the Health and Social Care Act 2008 (Regulated Activities) Regulations 2014, SI 2014/2936,
    reg 24, Sch 5; and PARA 159 note 4.
4   Ie by virtue of the Health and Social Care Act 2008 Pt 1 Ch 2.
5   Health and Social Care Act 2008 s 36(3). As to offences under s 36 see PARA 158 note 6.
6   As to the Care Quality Commission see PARA 336 et seq. For the power of the Commission to issue
    guidance in this regard see PARA 197.
7   Health and Social Care Act 2008 ss 12(5)(a), 15(5)(a).
8   Health and Social Care Act 2008 ss 12(5)(b), 15(5)(b). Except where it makes an application under
    s 30 (see PARA 162) or gives notice under s 31 (see note 9), the Commission must give any person
    registered as a service provider or manager in respect of a regulated activity notice in writing of a
    proposal to vary or remove (otherwise than in accordance with an application under s 19(1)(a) (see
    the text and notes 10–13)) any condition for the time being in force in relation to the registration
    (s 26(4)(c)) or to impose in relation to the registration any additional condition (s 26(4)(d)). Where
    a proposal under s 26(4) names an individual and specifies action that the Commission would
    require the registered person to take in relation to that individual, the Commission must give that
    individual notice in writing of the proposal: s 26(4A) (added by the Care Act 2014 s 87(1)). A
    notice under the Health and Social Care Act 2008 s 26 must give the Commission's reasons for its
    proposal: s 26(6). As to the right to make representations in response to notices under s 26 and the
    information that must be provided, and as to the persons who must be notified where notice is
    given under s 26, see ss 27, 28, 39; and PARA 160 note 6. Section 39 does not apply to a notice
    of proposal given under s 26(4)(c) or (d) which relates to the variation or removal of any condition
    for the time being in force in relation to a registration or the imposition of an additional condition
    in relation to a registration and appears to the Commission not to have a material impact on the
    regulated activity being carried on (Care Quality Commission (Registration) Regulations 2009, SI
    2009/3112, reg 8(b)). Information about the variation or removal of a condition, or the imposition
    of an additional condition, under the Health and Social Care Act 2008 s 12(5) must be publicised
    by the Commission: see the Care Quality Commission (Registration) Regulations 2009, SI
    2009/3112, Sch 2 paras 3, 5, 8(1), (2). Certain information about decisions under the Health and
    Social Care Act 2008 s 12(5) must be publicised by the Care Quality Commission: see the Care
    Quality Commission (Registration) Regulations 2009, SI 2009/3112, Sch 2 para 10.
9   If the Commission has reasonable cause to believe that unless it acts expeditiously (ie under the
    Health and Social Care Act 2008 s 31) any person will or may be exposed to the risk of harm,
    the Commission may, by giving notice in writing under s 31 to a person registered as a service
    provider or manager in respect of a regulated activity, provide for any decision of the Commission
    under s 12(5) or s 15(5) to take effect from the time when the notice is given: s 31(1), (2)(a). A
    notice under s 31 must:
    (1)   state that it is given under s 31 (s 31(3)(a));
    (2)   state the Commission's reasons for believing that the circumstances fall within s 31(1)
           (s 31(3)(b));
    (3)   specify the condition as varied, removed or imposed or (in the case of a decision under
           s 31(2)(b) the period (or extended period) of suspension (s 31(3)(c));and
    (4)   explain the right of appeal conferred by s 32 (see the text and note 14) (s 31(3)(d)).
10 Ie except where:
    (1)   the Commission has given R notice under the Health and Social Care Act 2008
           s 26(4)(a) of a proposal to cancel the registration and the Commission has not decided
           not to take that step (Case A) (s 19(1), (2) (s 19(1) amended, s 19(3A)–(3F) added, by
           the Care Act 2014 s 86)); or
    (2)   the Commission has given R notice under the Health and Social Care Act 2008 s 28(3)
           of its decision to cancel the registration, and either the time within which an appeal may
           be brought has not expired or, if an appeal has been brought, it has not yet been
           determined (Case B) (s 19(3)).
11 A person may not apply under these provisions for the variation of a condition where either:
    (1)   the Commission has given him notice under the Health and Social Care Act 2008
           s 26(4)(c) of a proposal to make that variation (or a variation which would have

substantially the same effect as that variation) and the Commission has not decided not to take that step (s 19(3A), (3B) (as added: see note 10)); or

(2)   the Commission has given him notice under s 28(3) of its decision to make that variation (or a variation which would have substantially the same effect as that variation) and either the time within which an appeal may be brought has not expired or, if an appeal has been brought, it has not yet been determined (s 19(3C) (as so added)).

12   A person may not apply under these provisions for the removal of a condition where either:

(1)   the Commission has given him notice under the Health and Social Care Act 2008 s 26(4)(c) of a proposal to remove that condition and the Commission has not decided not to take that step (s 19(3D), (3E) (as added: see note 10)); or

(2)   the Commission has given him notice under s 28(3) of its decision to remove that condition, and either the time within which an appeal may be brought has not expired or, if an appeal has been brought, it has not yet been determined (s 19(3F) (as so added)).

13   Health and Social Care Act 2008 s 19(1)(a). As to the meaning of 'registered manager condition' see PARA 159. An application under s 19(1) must be made in such form, and contain or be accompanied by such information, as the Commission requires: s 19(4). If the Commission decides to grant an application under s 19(1)(a), it must serve notice in writing of its decision on the applicant (stating, where applicable, the condition as varied) and issue a new certificate of registration: s 19(5). The Commission must give the applicant notice in writing of a proposal to refuse an application: s 26(5). A notice must give the Commission's reasons for its proposal: s 26(6). If, in an application for the variation or removal of a condition, a person knowingly makes a statement which is false or misleading in a material respect, he is guilty of an offence: s 37(1)(b), (2). A person guilty of an offence under s 37 is liable on summary conviction to a fine not exceeding level 4 on the standard scale: s 37(3). As to proceedings for offences see PARA 158 note 6. The Commission may with the consent of the Secretary of State from time to time make and publish provision requiring a fee to be paid in respect of an application under s 19(1): s 85(1)(a)(iii). As to such fees see PARA 160 note 3.

14   See the Health and Social Care Act 2008 s 32(1)(a), (2), (3), (6), (7); and PARA 160 note 9. On an appeal against a decision to which a notice under s 31 (see the text and note 9) relates, the Tribunal may confirm the decision or direct that it is to cease to have effect: s 32(5).

162.   Cancellation of registrations in urgent cases where persons are at risk. If:

(1)   the Care Quality Commission[1] applies to a justice of the peace[2] for an order cancelling the registration of a person as a service provider or manager[3] in respect of a regulated activity in England[4]; and

(2)   it appears to the justice that, unless the order is made, there will be a serious risk to a person's life, health or well-being[5],

the justice may make the order, and the cancellation has effect from the time when the order is made[6]. Where such an order is made, the Commission must, as soon as practicable after the making of the order, serve on the person registered as a service provider or manager in respect of the regulated activity a copy of the order[7] and notice of the right of appeal[8].

A person ('M') whose registration as a manager in respect of a regulated activity has been cancelled is guilty of an offence[9] if he manages that activity at a time when:

(a)   a person ('S') remains registered as a service provider in respect of the activity[10];

(b)   S's registration remains subject to a registered manager condition[11]; and

(c)   no one has been registered as a manager in respect of the activity since the cancellation of M's registration[12].

1   As to the Care Quality Commission see PARA 336 et seq.
2   As to justices of the peace see MAGISTRATES vol 71 (2013) PARA 401 et seq. An application may, if the justice thinks fit, be made without notice having been given to the registered person: Health and Social Care Act 2008 s 30(2). As soon as practicable after the making of an application the Commission must give notice of the application to:

(1)   the National Health Service Commissioning Board (see HEALTH SERVICES vol 54 (2017) PARA 32) (in the circumstances prescribed in the Care Quality Commission (Registration) Regulations 2009, SI 2009/3112, reg 9(6A), (6B) (reg 9(1), (2), (4), (6) amended, reg 9(6A), (6B) added, by SI 2013/235)) (Health and Social Care Act 2008 s 30(3)(za) (s 30(3)(za) added, s 30(3)(a) amended, s 30(3)(c) substituted, by the Health and Social Care Act 2012 Sch 5 para 155));

(2)   to a clinical commissioning group (see HEALTH SERVICES vol 54 (2017) PARA 35 et seq) or English local authority (in the circumstances prescribed in the Care Quality Commission (Registration) Regulations 2009, SI 2009/3112, reg 9(1)(a), (2)–(6) (as so amended)) (Health and Social Care Act 2008 s 30(3)(a) (as so amended));

(3)   where the person registered as a service provider in respect of the activity is a person who holds a licence under the Health and Social Care Act 2012 Pt 3 Ch 3 (ss 81–110) (see HEALTH SERVICES vol 54A (2017) PARA 636 et seq), to Monitor (Health and Social Care Act 2008 s 30(3)(c) (as so substituted)); and

(4)   to such other persons as the Commission considers appropriate (s 30(3)(d)).

As to Monitor see HEALTH SERVICES vol 54 (2017) PARA 195.

3   Ie under the Health and Social Care Act 2008 Pt 1 Ch 2 (ss 8–44). As to registration as a service provider or manager see PARA 159 et seq.
4   Health and Social Care Act 2008 s 30(1)(a). As to the meaning of 'regulated activity' for these purposes, and the restriction of these provisions to activities carried on in England, see PARA 152 note 2; as to the regulated activities see PARAS 152–157.
5   Health and Social Care Act 2008 s 30(1)(b).
6   Health and Social Care Act 2008 s 30(1). An order must be in writing: s 30(4). As to cancellations in other circumstances see PARA 163. Information about the cancellation of a person's registration must be publicised by the Care Quality Commission: see the Care Quality Commission (Registration) Regulations 2009, SI 2009/3112, Sch 2 paras 1, 5, 8(1), (2).
7   Health and Social Care Act 2008 s 30(5)(a).
8   Health and Social Care Act 2008 s 30(5)(b). An appeal against an order made by a justice of the peace under s 30 lies to the First-tier Tribunal: s 32(1)(b) (s 32(1), (3)–(7) amended by SI 2009/56). On an appeal against an order made by a justice of the peace the First-tier Tribunal may confirm the order or direct that it is to cease to have effect: s 32(4) (as so amended). As to appeals under the Health and Social Care Act 2008 s 32 generally, and the powers of justices, see further PARA 160 note 9.
9   A person guilty of an offence under the Health and Social Care Act 2008 s 34 is liable on summary conviction to a fine: s 34(5) (amended by SI 2015/64). As to proceedings for offences see PARA 158 note 6. The offence under the Health and Social Care Act 2008 s 34 is a fixed penalty offence: see the Health and Social Care Act 2008 (Regulated Activities) Regulations 2014, SI 2014/2936, reg 24, Sch 5; and PARA 159 note 4.
10 Health and Social Care Act 2008 s 34(3)(a).
11 Health and Social Care Act 2008 s 34(3)(b).
12 Health and Social Care Act 2008 s 34(3)(c).

163. Cancellation of registrations on administrative grounds or on application of registered person. The Care Quality Commission[1] may at any time cancel the registration of a person as a service provider or manager[2] in respect of a regulated activity in England[3] on the ground that:

(1)   R has been convicted of, or admitted, a relevant offence[4];

(2)   any other person has been convicted of any relevant offence in relation to the regulated activity[5];

(3)   the regulated activity is being, or has at any time been, carried on otherwise than in accordance with the relevant requirements[6];

(4)   R has failed to comply with another[7] requirement[8];

(5)   the registered person has made a statement which is false or misleading in a material respect, or provided false information, in relation to any application for registration or for the variation or removal of a condition in relation to his registration[9];

(6)   the registered person has failed to pay any applicable[10] fees[11]; and

(7)   if the registered person is a service provider he is not, and has not been for a continuous period of 12 months ending with the date of the decision to cancel registration, carrying on that regulated activity[12].

The Commission must cancel the registration of a person as a manager in respect of a regulated activity if no-one is registered as a service provider in respect of the activity[13] or the registration of a person as a service provider in respect of the activity ceases to be subject to a registered manager condition[14]. Except where it would be pre-empting a decision by the Commission to cancel a registration[15], a person registered as a service provider or manager may apply to the Commission for the cancellation of the registration[16].

There are particular offences relating to a person continuing to manage a regulated activity after his registration as a manager has been cancelled[17].

A decision of the Commission under these provisions is subject to appeal[18].

1　As to the Care Quality Commission see PARA 336 et seq. For the power of the Commission to issue guidance in this regard see PARA 197.

2　Ie under the Health and Social Care Act 2008 Pt 1 Ch 2 (ss 8–44). As to registration as a service provider or manager see PARA 159 et seq. Except where it makes an application under s 30 (see PARA 162) or gives notice under s 31 (see PARA 161), the Commission must give any person registered as a service provider or manager in respect of a regulated activity notice in writing of a proposal to cancel the registration (otherwise than by virtue of s 17(2) (see the text and notes 13–14) or in accordance with an application under s 19(1)(b) (see PARA 161): s 26(4)(a). As to such notifications see further PARA 161 note 8. As to the right to make representations in response to notices under s 26 and the information that must be provided, and as to the persons who must be notified where notice is given under s 26, see ss 27, 28, 39; and PARA 160 note 6. Information about the cancellation of a person's registration must be publicised by the Care Quality Commission: see the Care Quality Commission (Registration) Regulations 2009, SI 2009/3112, Sch 2 paras 1, 5, 8(1), (2).

3　As to the meaning of 'regulated activity' for these purposes, and the restriction of these provisions to activities carried on in England, see PARA 152 note 2; as to the regulated activities see PARAS 152–157.

4　Health and Social Care Act 2008 s 17(1)(a). For these purposes the following are (by virtue of s 17(3)) relevant offences:
　　(1)　a Part 1 offence (PARA 158 note 6);
　　(2)　an offence under the Registered Homes Act 1984 (repealed) or regulations made under it;
　　(3)　an offence under the Care Standards Act 2000 Pt II (ss 11–42) (see CHILDREN AND YOUNG PERSONS vol 10 (2017) PARA 1017 et seq) or regulations made under it; and
　　(4)　any other offence which appears to the Commission to be relevant.

5　Health and Social Care Act 2008 s 17(1)(b).

6　Health and Social Care Act 2008 s 17(1)(c). For these purposes, 'relevant requirements' means any requirements or conditions imposed by or under Pt 1 Ch 2 (ss 17(4)(a), 18(5)) and the requirements of any other enactment which appears to the Commission to be relevant (s 17(4)(b)).

7　Ie a requirement imposed by or under the Health and Social Care Act 2008 Pt 1 Ch 6 (ss 60–97). For the purposes of ss 17, 18, a requirement imposed on a registered care provider or by virtue of any of the Care Act 2014 ss 54–56 (see PARAS 180–185) (or by virtue of s 57(1) or (2) (see PARA 355)) is to be treated as a requirement imposed by or under the Health and Social Care Act 2008 Pt 1 Ch 6: Care Act 2014 s 57(3).

8　Health and Social Care Act 2008 s 17(1)(d).

9　Health and Social Care Act 2008 s 17(1)(e); Care Quality Commission (Registration) Regulations 2009, SI 2009/3112, reg 6(1)(a). As to applications for registration see PARA 160; as to application for the variation or removal of a condition see PARA 161.

10　Ie payable pursuant to provision under s 85 (see PARA 160 note 3).

11　Care Quality Commission (Registration) Regulations 2009, SI 2009/3112, reg 6(1)(b).

12　Care Quality Commission (Registration) Regulations 2009, SI 2009/3112, reg 6(1)(c).

13　Health and Social Care Act 2008 s 17(2)(a).

14　Health and Social Care Act 2008 s 17(2)(b). As to the meaning of 'registered manager condition' see PARA 159.

15　Ie except where the circumstances described in the Health and Social Care Act 2008 s 19(2), (3) (see PARA 161 note 10) apply.

16　Health and Social Care Act 2008 s 19(1)(b). An application under s 19(1) must be made in such form, and contain or be accompanied by such information, as the Commission requires: s 19(4). The Commission must give the applicant notice in writing of a proposal to refuse an application: s 26(5). A notice must give the Commission's reasons for its proposal: s 26(6). If, in an application for cancellation of registration, a person knowingly makes a statement which is false or misleading in a material respect, he is guilty of an offence: s 37(1)(d), (2). A person guilty of an offence under s 37 is liable on summary conviction to a fine not exceeding level 4 on the standard scale: s 37(3). As to proceedings for offences see PARA 158 note 6.

17　See the Health and Social Care Act 2008 s 34; and PARA 162.

18　See the Health and Social Care Act 2008 s 32(1)(a), (2), (3), (6), (7); and PARA 160 note 9.

164. Suspension of registration. The Care Quality Commission[1] may at any time suspend a person's registration as a service provider or manager[2] for a specified period[3]. This power is exercisable only on the ground that the regulated activity[4] is being, or has at any time been, carried on otherwise than in accordance with the relevant requirements[5] or the person has failed to comply with another[6] requirement[7], and there is an expedited procedure for the exercise of this power where a person is at risk[8]. The suspension of a person's registration does not affect the continuation of the registration[9]: however, a person is guilty of an offence[10] if:

(1)   he is registered as a service provider in respect of a regulated activity and carries on that activity while his registration is suspended[11];

(2)   his registration as a manager in respect of a regulated activity is suspended and during the period of suspension he manages that activity at a time when no one else has been registered as a manager in respect of the activity since the suspension of his registration[12]; or

(3)   he is registered as a manager in respect of a regulated activity and manages that activity while the registration of the person registered as a service provider in respect of the activity is suspended, and he knows or could reasonably be expected to know of the suspension[13].

Except where it would be pre-empting a decision by the Commission to cancel a registration[14], a person registered as a service provider or manager may apply to the Commission for the cancellation of, or the variation of the period of, any suspension of the registration[15]. A period of suspension may be extended[16] on one or more occasions[17]. A decision of the Commission under these provisions is subject to appeal[18].

1   As to the Care Quality Commission see PARA 336 et seq. For the power of the Commission to issue guidance in this regard see PARA 197.

2   Ie under the Health and Social Care Act 2008 Pt 1 Ch 2 (ss 8–44). As to registration as a service provider or manager see PARA 159 et seq. As to registration as a service provider or manager see PARA 159 et seq. Except where it makes an application under s 30 (see PARA 162) or gives notice under s 31 (see PARA 161), the Commission must give any person registered as a service provider or manager in respect of a regulated activity notice in writing of a proposal to suspend the registration or extend a period of suspension: s 26(4)(b). As to such notifications see further PARA 161 note 8. As to the right to make representations in response to notices under s 26 and the information that must be provided, and as to the persons who must be notified where notice is given under s 26, see ss 27, 28, 39; and PARA 160 note 6. Section 39 does not apply to a notice of proposal given under s 26(5) (see note 15) to refuse an application by the registered person under s 19(1): Care Quality Commission (Registration) Regulations 2009, SI 2009/3112, reg 8(c). Information about the suspension of a person's registration must be publicised by the Commission: see Sch 2 paras 1, 5, 8(1), (2).

3   Health and Social Care Act 2008 s 18(1).

4   As to the meaning of 'regulated activity' for these purposes, and the restriction of these provisions to activities carried on in England, see PARA 152 note 2; as to the regulated activities see PARAS 152–157.

5   Health and Social Care Act 2008 s 18(2)(a). As to the meaning of 'relevant requirements' see PARA 163 note 6.

6   Ie a requirement imposed by or under the Health and Social Care Act 2008 Pt 1 Ch 6 (ss 60–97). See the Care Act 2014 s 57(3); and PARA 163 note 7.

7   Health and Social Care Act 2008 s 18(2)(b).

8   If the Commission has reasonable cause to believe that unless it acts expeditiously (ie under the Health and Social Care Act 2008 s 31) any person will or may be exposed to the risk of harm, the Commission may, by giving notice in writing under s 31 to a person registered as a service provider or manager in respect of a regulated activity, provide for any decision of the Commission under s 18 to take effect from the time when the notice is given: s 31(1), (2)(b). As to the content of such a notice see PARA 161 note 9.

9   Health and Social Care Act 2008 s 18(3). However reference should be had to s 34 (see the text and notes 10–13) and s 36 (see PARA 158) as to offences: s 18(3).

10   A person guilty of an offence under the Health and Social Care Act 2008 s 18 is liable on summary conviction to a fine: s 34(5) (amended by SI 2015/64). As to proceedings for offences see PARA 158

note 6. The offence under the Health and Social Care Act 2008 s 34 is a fixed penalty offence: see the Health and Social Care Act 2008 (Regulated Activities) Regulations 2014, SI 2014/2936, reg 24, Sch 5; and PARA 159 note 4.

11 Health and Social Care Act 2008 s 34(1).

12 Health and Social Care Act 2008 s 34(2).

13 Health and Social Care Act 2008 s 34(4).

14 Ie except where the circumstances described in the Health and Social Care Act 2008 s 19(2), (3) (see PARA 161 note 10) apply.

15 Health and Social Care Act 2008 s 19(1)(c). An application under s 19(1) must be made in such form, and contain or be accompanied by such information, as the Commission requires: s 19(4). If the Commission decides to grant an application under subsection (1)(c), it must serve notice in writing of its decision on the applicant (stating, where applicable, the period as varied): s 19(6). The Commission must give the applicant notice in writing of a proposal to refuse an application: s 26(5). A notice must give the Commission's reasons for its proposal: s 26(6). If, in an application for variation or cancellation of a suspension, a person knowingly makes a statement which is false or misleading in a material respect, he is guilty of an offence: s 37(1)(c), (2). A person guilty of an offence under s 37 is liable on summary conviction to a fine not exceeding level 4 on the standard scale: s 37(3). As to proceedings for offences see PARA 158 note 6.

16 Ie under the Health and Social Care Act 2008 s 18(1).

17 Health and Social Care Act 2008 s 18(4).

18 See the Health and Social Care Act 2008 s 32(1)(a), (2), (3), (6), (7); and PARA 160 note 9. On an appeal against a decision to which a notice under s 31 (see the text and note 8) relates, the Tribunal may confirm the decision or direct that it is to cease to have effect: s 32(5).

165. Warning notices. If it appears to the Care Quality Commission[1] that a person who is registered as a service provider or manager in respect of a regulated activity in England[2] has failed to comply with the registration requirements[3], the Commission may give the registered person a warning notice[4]. Where a warning notice has been given to any person[5] and where any failure to comply with a requirement is specified[6], the requirement has been complied with within the specified time[7] then:

(1) the failure to which the notice relates, so far as occurring before the relevant time[8], is not to constitute a ground for the cancellation or suspension of registration, the variation of the conditions of registration, the removal of a condition or the imposition of any additional condition[9]; and

(2) no proceedings may be brought against any person registered in respect of the regulated activity for a Part 1 offence[10] that arises out of the failure to which the notice relates, so far as occurring before the relevant time[11].

1 As to the Care Quality Commission see PARA 336 et seq. For the power of the Commission to issue guidance in this regard see PARA 197.

2 Ie under the Health and Social Care Act 2008 Pt 1 Ch 2 (ss 8–44). As to registration as a service provider or manager see PARA 159 et seq. As to registration as a service provider or manager see PARA 159 et seq. As to the meaning of 'regulated activity' for these purposes, and the restriction of these provisions to activities carried on in England, see PARA 152 note 2; as to the regulated activities see PARAS 152–157.

3 Ie the 'relevant requirements', which means:

(1) any requirements or conditions imposed by or under the Health and Social Care Act 2008 Pt 1 Ch 2 or Pt Ch 6 (ss 60–97) (s 29(7)(a)); and

(2) the requirements of any other enactment which appears to the Commission to be relevant (s 29(7)(b)).

4 Health and Social Care Act 2008 s 29(1). A warning notice under s 29 may not be given to an NHS trust established under the National Health Service Act 2006 s 25, or an NHS foundation trust (see HEALTH SERVICES vol 54 (2017) PARA 244): Health and Social Care Act 2008 s 29(1A) (s 29(1A) added, s 29(2), (3)(a) amended, by the Care Act 2014 s 82). A warning notice under the Health and Social Care Act 2008 s 29 is a notice in writing:

(1) specifying the conduct which appears to the Commission to constitute a failure to comply with the relevant requirements (s 29(2)(a) (as so amended));

(2) specifying the requirement concerned (s 29(2)(b)); and

(3)   where it appears to the Commission that the failure is continuing, requiring the registered person to comply with the requirement concerned within a specified time (s 29(2)(c)(i)) and stating that, if the registered person fails to do so within that time, the Commission may take action to secure compliance with the relevant requirements (s 29(2)(c)(ii)).

As to service of notices and electronic communications generally see the Health and Social Care Act 2008 ss 93, 94; and PARA 179 note 14. The notification requirements (ie s 39(1): see PARA 160 note 6) do not apply to a warning notice given under s 29 which appears to the Commission not to have a material impact on the regulated activity being carried on: Care Quality Commission (Registration) Regulations 2009, SI 2009/3112, reg 8(d). Certain information about warning notices under the Health and Social Care Act 2008 s 29 must be publicised by the Care Quality Commission: see the Care Quality Commission (Registration) Regulations 2009, SI 2009/3112, Sch 2 para 13.

5   Health and Social Care Act 2008 s 29(3)(a).
6   Ie under the Health and Social Care Act 2008 s 29(2)(c): see note 4.
7   Health and Social Care Act 2008 s 29(3)(b).
8   In the Health and Social Care Act 2008 s 29(4), (5) 'the relevant time' means:
    (1)   where a time is specified under s 29(2)(c)(i) (see note 4), the time so specified (s 29(6)(a)); and
    (2)   in any other case, the date on which the notice was given (s 29(6)(b)).
9   Health and Social Care Act 2008 s 29(4). As to conditions, cancellation and suspension see PARAS 161–164.
10 As to the meaning of 'Part 1 offence' see PARA 158 note 6.
11 Health and Social Care Act 2008 s 29(5).

(iii) Fitness to Carry on Regulated Activity

166. Registered individual must be fit to carry on regulated activity. Where a service provider[1] is an individual[2] he must not carry on a regulated activity in England[3] unless he is fit to do so[4]. A service provider who is an individual is not fit to carry on a regulated activity unless he carries on the activity otherwise than in partnership[5] with others and:
(1)   is of good character[6];
(2)   is able by reason of his health, after reasonable adjustments are made, of properly performing tasks which are intrinsic to the carrying on of the regulated activity[7];
(3)   is able to supply to the Care Quality Commission[8], or arrange for the availability of, specified information relating to his identity, employment history and criminal record and satisfactory information about any relevant physical or mental health conditions[9]; and
(4)   has the necessary qualifications, skills and experience to carry on the regulated activity[10].

1   As to the meaning of 'service provider' see PARA 152 note 6.
2   Health and Social Care Act 2008 (Regulated Activities) Regulations 2014, SI 2014/2936, reg 4(1).
3   As to the meaning of 'regulated activity' for these purposes, and the restriction of these provisions to activities carried on in England, see PARA 152 note 2; as to the regulated activities see PARAS 152–157.
4   Health and Social Care Act 2008 (Regulated Activities) Regulations 2014, SI 2014/2936, reg 4(2).
5   'Partnership' does not include a limited liability partnership: Health and Social Care Act 2008 (Regulated Activities) Regulations 2014, SI 2014/2936, reg 2(1).
6   Health and Social Care Act 2008 (Regulated Activities) Regulations 2014, SI 2014/2936, reg 4(3)(a)(i), (4)(a). In assessing an individual's character for the purposes of regs 4(4)(a), 5(3)(a), 6(3)(a), 7(2)(a), the matters considered must include whether the person has been convicted in the United Kingdom of any offence or been convicted elsewhere of any offence which, if committed in any part of the United Kingdom, would constitute an offence, and whether he has been erased, removed or struck-off a register of professionals maintained by a regulator of health care or social work professionals: regs 4(7), 5(4), 6(4), 7(3), Sch 4 paras 7, 8 (regs 4(5) amended, regs 4(7), 6(4), 7(3) added, by SI 2015/64).
7   Health and Social Care Act 2008 (Regulated Activities) Regulations 2014, SI 2014/2936, reg 4(4)(b)(i).

8   As to the Care Quality Commission see PARA 336 et seq.
9   Health and Social Care Act 2008 (Regulated Activities) Regulations 2014, SI 2014/2936, reg 4(4)(c). The information is specified in Sch 3.
10 Health and Social Care Act 2008 (Regulated Activities) Regulations 2014, SI 2014/2936, reg 4(3)(a)(ii), (5) (as amended: see note 6).

167. Registered partnership must be fit to carry on regulated activity. Where a service provider[1] is a partnership[2], the partnership must not carry on a regulated activity in England[3] unless he is fit to do so[4]. A service provider who is an individual is not fit to carry on a regulated activity unless each of the partners:

(1)   is of good character[5];
(2)   is able by reason of their health, after reasonable adjustments are made, of properly performing tasks which are intrinsic to their role in the carrying on of the regulated activity[6];
(3)   is able to supply to the Care Quality Commission[7], or arrange for the availability of, specified information relating to their identity, employment history and criminal record and satisfactory information about any relevant physical or mental health conditions[8]; and
(4)   through the combination of the qualifications, skills and experience of the partners, the partnership has the necessary qualifications, skills and experience to carry on the regulated activity[9].

1   As to the meaning of 'service provider' see PARA 152 note 6.
2   Health and Social Care Act 2008 (Regulated Activities) Regulations 2014, SI 2014/2936, reg 4(1). As to the meaning of 'partnership' see PARA 166 note 5.
3   As to the meaning of 'regulated activity' for these purposes, and the restriction of these provisions to activities carried on in England, see PARA 152 note 2; as to the regulated activities see PARAS 152–157.
4   Health and Social Care Act 2008 (Regulated Activities) Regulations 2014, SI 2014/2936, reg 4(2).
5   Health and Social Care Act 2008 (Regulated Activities) Regulations 2014, SI 2014/2936, reg 4(3)(b)(i), (4)(a). As to matters to be taken into account PARA 166 note 6.
6   Health and Social Care Act 2008 (Regulated Activities) Regulations 2014, SI 2014/2936, reg 4(4)(b)(ii).
7   As to the Care Quality Commission see PARA 336 et seq.
8   Health and Social Care Act 2008 (Regulated Activities) Regulations 2014, SI 2014/2936, reg 4(4)(c). The information is specified in Sch 3.
9   Health and Social Care Act 2008 (Regulated Activities) Regulations 2014, SI 2014/2936, reg 4(3)(b)(ii), (6) (reg 4(6) amended by SI 2015/64).

168. Directors and supervisors must be fit and proper persons. Where a service provider[1] is a body other than a partnership[2] it must not appoint or have in place an individual as a director[3] unless that individual:

(1)   is of good character[4];
(2)   has the qualifications, competence, skills and experience which are necessary for the relevant office or position or the work for which he is employed[5];
(3)   is able by reason of his health, after reasonable adjustments are made, of properly performing tasks which are intrinsic to the office or position for which he is appointed or to the work for which he is employed[6];
(4)   has not been responsible for, been privy to, contributed to or facilitated any serious misconduct or mismanagement (whether unlawful or not) in the course of carrying on a regulated activity in England[7] or providing a service elsewhere which, if provided in England, would be a regulated activity[8]; and
(5)   is not an unfit person[9] for reasons of finance or safeguarding[10].

Recruitment procedures must be established and operated effectively to ensure, where applicable, that persons employed meet these conditions[11]. The registered person in relation to such a body[12] must take all reasonable steps to ensure that the 'nominated individual'[13]:

(a)   is of good character[14];

(b)   has the necessary qualifications, competence, skills and experience to properly supervise the management of the carrying on of the regulated activity[15];

(c)   is able by reason of his health, after reasonable adjustments are made, of properly doing so[16]; and

(d)   is able to supply to the registered person, or arrange for the availability of, specified information relating to his identity, employment history and criminal record[17].

1 As to the meaning of 'service provider' see PARA 152 note 6.
2 Health and Social Care Act 2008 (Regulated Activities) Regulations 2014, SI 2014/2936, regs 5(1), 6(1) (reg 5(1) substituted, regs 5(2), 6(3)(b) amended, by SI 2015/64). As to the meaning of 'partnership' see PARA 166 note 5.
3 Ie a director of the service provider (Health and Social Care Act 2008 (Regulated Activities) Regulations 2014, SI 2014/2936, reg 5(2)(a) (as amended: see note 2)) or an individual performing the functions of, or functions equivalent or similar to the functions of, a director (reg 5(2)(b)). Information relating to each such individual's identity, employment history and criminal record (ie the information specified in Sch 3: reg 5(5)(a)), and such other information as is required to be kept by the service provider under any enactment which is relevant to that director (reg 5(5)(b)), must be available to be supplied to the Care Quality Commission (reg 5(5)). Where any such individual no longer meets the requirements in reg 5(3) (see the text and notes 4–10) the service provider must take such action as is necessary and proportionate to ensure that the office or position in question is held by an individual who meets such requirements (reg 5(6)(a)) and if the individual is a health care professional, social worker or other professional registered with a health care or social care regulator, inform the regulator in question (reg 5(6)(b)). 'Health care professional', except in Sch 1 para 4, means a person who is registered as a member of any profession to which the Health Act 1999 s 60(2) (regulation of health professions, social workers, other care workers, etc: see MEDICAL PROFESSIONS vol 74 (2011) PARA 3) applies; and 'social worker' means a person who is registered as such in Part 16 of the register maintained by the Health and Care Professions Council under the Health and Social Work Professions Order 2001, SI 2002/254, art 5 (see MEDICAL PROFESSIONS vol 74 (2011) PARA 928): Health and Social Care Act 2008 (Regulated Activities) Regulations 2014, SI 2014/2936, reg 2(1). As to the Care Quality Commission see PARA 336 et seq.
4 Health and Social Care Act 2008 (Regulated Activities) Regulations 2014, SI 2014/2936, reg 5(3)(a). As to matters to be taken into account PARA 166 note 6.
5 Health and Social Care Act 2008 (Regulated Activities) Regulations 2014, SI 2014/2936, reg 5(3)(b).
6 Health and Social Care Act 2008 (Regulated Activities) Regulations 2014, SI 2014/2936, reg 5(3)(c).
7 As to the meaning of 'regulated activity' for these purposes, and the restriction of these provisions to activities carried on in England, see PARA 152 note 2; as to the regulated activities see PARAS 152–157.
8 Health and Social Care Act 2008 (Regulated Activities) Regulations 2014, SI 2014/2936, reg 5(3)(d).
9 Ie none of the grounds of unfitness specified in the Health and Social Care Act 2008 (Regulated Activities) Regulations 2014, SI 2014/2936, Sch 4 paras 1–6 apply to the individual.
10 Health and Social Care Act 2008 (Regulated Activities) Regulations 2014, SI 2014/2936, reg 5(3)(e).
11 Health and Social Care Act 2008 (Regulated Activities) Regulations 2014, SI 2014/2936, reg 19(2)(b).
12 'Registered person' means, in respect of a regulated activity, a person who is the service provider or registered manager in respect of that activity; and 'registered manager' means, in respect of a regulated activity, a person registered with the Commission under the Health and Social Care Act 2008 Pt 1 Ch 2 (ss 8–44) as a manager in respect of that activity: Care Quality Commission (Registration) Regulations 2009, SI 2009/3112, reg 2; Health and Social Care Act 2008 (Regulated Activities) Regulations 2014, SI 2014/2936, reg 2(1). For the purposes of compliance with the

requirements set out in the Care Quality Commission (Registration) Regulations 2009, SI 2009/3112, the registered person must have regard to guidance issued by the Commission pursuant to the Health and Social Care Act 2008 s 23 (see PARA 196) in relation to the requirements set out in the Care Quality Commission (Registration) Regulations 2009, SI 2009/3112, Pt 4 (regs 11–20): reg 24. For the purposes of compliance with the requirements set out in the Health and Social Care Act 2008 (Regulated Activities) Regulations 2014, SI 2014/2936, the registered person must have regard to guidance issued by the Care Quality Commission under the Health and Social Care Act 2008 s 23 (see PARA 196) in relation to the requirements set out in the Health and Social Care Act 2008 (Regulated Activities) Regulations 2014, SI 2014/2936, Pt 3 (regs 4–20) (with the exception of reg 12 in so far as it applies to health care associated infections), and in relation to reg 12, in so far as it applies to health care associated infections, any code of practice issued by the Secretary of State under the Health and Social Care Act 2008 s 21 (see PARA 196) in relation to the prevention or control of health care associated infections: Health and Social Care Act 2008 (Regulated Activities) Regulations 2014, SI 2014/2936, reg 21. As to the meaning of 'health care associated infection' see PARA 173 note 14.

13 A service provider which is a body other than a partnership must give notice to the Care Quality Commission of the name, address and position in the body of an individual ('the nominated individual') who is employed as a director, manager or secretary of the body (Health and Social Care Act 2008 (Regulated Activities) Regulations 2014, SI 2014/2936, reg 6(2)(a)) and is responsible for supervising the management of the carrying on of the regulated activity by the body (reg 6(2)(b)).

14 Health and Social Care Act 2008 (Regulated Activities) Regulations 2014, SI 2014/2936, reg 6(3)(a). As to matters to be taken into account PARA 166 note 6.

15 Health and Social Care Act 2008 (Regulated Activities) Regulations 2014, SI 2014/2936, reg 6(3)(b) (as amended: see note 2).

16 Health and Social Care Act 2008 (Regulated Activities) Regulations 2014, SI 2014/2936, reg 6(3)(c).

17 Health and Social Care Act 2008 (Regulated Activities) Regulations 2014, SI 2014/2936, reg 6(3)(d). The information is specified in Sch 3.

169. Registered managers must be fit and proper persons. A person must not manage the carrying on of a regulated activity in England[1] as a registered manager[2] unless he is fit to do so[3]. A person is not fit to be a registered manager in respect of a regulated activity unless he is:

(1)   of good character[4];

(2)   has the necessary qualifications, competence, skills and experience to manage carrying on of the regulated activity[5];

(3)   is able by reason of his health, after reasonable adjustments are made, of doing so[6]; and

(4)   is able to supply to the Care Quality Commission[7], or arrange for the availability of, specified information relating to his identity, employment history and criminal record[8].

1   As to the meaning of 'regulated activity' for these purposes, and the restriction of these provisions to activities carried on in England, see PARA 152 note 2; as to the regulated activities see PARAS 152–157.

2   As to the meaning of 'registered manager' see PARA 168 note 12.

3   Health and Social Care Act 2008 (Regulated Activities) Regulations 2014, SI 2014/2936, reg 7(1).

4   Health and Social Care Act 2008 (Regulated Activities) Regulations 2014, SI 2014/2936, reg 7(2)(a). As to matters to be taken into account PARA 166 note 6.

5   Health and Social Care Act 2008 (Regulated Activities) Regulations 2014, SI 2014/2936, reg 7(2)(b) (amended by SI 2015/64).

6   Health and Social Care Act 2008 (Regulated Activities) Regulations 2014, SI 2014/2936, reg 7(2)(c).

7   As to the Care Quality Commission see PARA 336 et seq.

8   Health and Social Care Act 2008 (Regulated Activities) Regulations 2014, SI 2014/2936, reg 7(2)(d). The information is specified in Sch 3.

170. Employees must be fit and proper persons. Persons employed[1] for the purposes of carrying on a regulated activity in England must be of good character[2], have the qualifications, competence, skills and experience which are necessary for the work to be performed by them[3], and be able by reason of their health, after reasonable adjustments are made, of properly performing tasks which are intrinsic to the work for which they are employed[4]. Recruitment procedures must be established and operated effectively to ensure that persons employed meet these conditions[5]. Specified information relating to identity, employment history and criminal record[6], and such other information as is required under any enactment to be kept by the registered person in relation to such persons employed[7], must be available in relation to each such persons employed[8]. Persons employed must be registered[9] with the relevant professional body[10].

Sufficient numbers of suitably qualified, competent, skilled and experienced persons must be deployed in order to meet the statutory[11] requirements[12]. Persons employed by the service provider in the provision of a regulated activity must:

(1)   receive such appropriate support, training, professional development, supervision and appraisal as is necessary to enable them to carry out the duties they are employed to perform[13];

(2)   be enabled where appropriate to obtain further qualifications appropriate to the work they perform[14]; and

(3)   where such persons are health care professionals, social workers or other professionals registered with a health care or social care regulator, be enabled to provide evidence to the regulator in question demonstrating, where it is possible to do so, that they continue to meet the professional standards which are a condition of their ability to practise or a requirement of their role[15].

1   'Employment' means employment under a contract of service, an apprenticeship, a contract for services or otherwise than under a contract, and the grant of practising privileges by a service provider to a registered medical practitioner, giving permission to practice as a registered medical practitioner in a hospital managed by the service provider; and 'employed' and 'employer' are to be construed accordingly: Health and Social Care Act 2008 (Regulated Activities) Regulations 2014, SI 2014/2936, reg 2(1). In this definition of 'employment', the reference to otherwise than under a contract includes under a shared lives agreement, under an agreement between the service provider and a temporary work agency for the supply of an agency worker to the service provider, and under arrangements for persons to provide their services voluntarily: reg 2(2). As to the meaning of 'service provider' see PARA 152 note 6. 'Hospital', except in Sch 1 para 1(3)(d) (see PARA 152) and Sch 1 para 5 (see MENTAL HEALTH AND CAPACITY vol 75 (2013) PARA 760) has the same meaning as in the National Health Service Act 2006 s 275 (see HEALTH SERVICES vol 54 (2017) PARA 26): Health and Social Care Act 2008 (Regulated Activities) Regulations 2014, SI 2014/2936, reg 2(1). 'Agency worker' and 'temporary work agency' have the same meaning as in the Agency Workers Regulations 2010, SI 2010/93 (see regs 3, 4; and EMPLOYMENT vol 39 (2014) PARA 97) (Health and Social Care Act 2008 (Regulated Activities) Regulations 2014, SI 2014/2936, reg 2(3)). As to the meaning of 'shared lives agreement' see PARA 153 note 6. As to the meaning of 'registered medical practitioner' see MEDICAL PROFESSIONS vol 74 (2011) PARA 176.
    A registered person must comply with regs 9–20A (see the text and notes 2–15; and PARAS 171–178) in carrying on a regulated activity in England (reg 8(1) (regs 8(1)–(3) amended by SI 2015/64)), although the Health and Social Care Act 2008 (Regulated Activities) Regulations 2014, SI 2014/2936, reg 8(1) does not require a person to do something to the extent that what is required to be done to comply with regs 9–20A has already been done by another person who is a registered person in relation to the regulated activity concerned (reg 8(2) (as so added)). As to the meaning of 'regulated activity' for these purposes, and the restriction of these provisions to activities carried on in England, see PARA 152 note 2; as to the regulated activities see PARAS 152–157.
    Regulation 19(1), (3) does not apply in a case to which reg 5 (directors: see PARA 168) applies: reg 19(6).
2   Health and Social Care Act 2008 (Regulated Activities) Regulations 2014, SI 2014/2936, reg 19(1)(a). Where a person employed by the registered person no longer meets the criteria in reg 19(1), the registered person must take such action as is necessary and proportionate to ensure that such requirement is complied with (reg 19(5)(a)) and if the person is a health care professional, social worker or other professional registered with a health care or social care regulator, inform the

regulator in question (reg 19(5)(b)). As to the meanings of 'health care professional' and 'social worker' see PARA 168 note 3; as to the meanings of 'health care' and 'social care' see PARA 152 note 2.

3 Health and Social Care Act 2008 (Regulated Activities) Regulations 2014, SI 2014/2936, reg 19(1)(b). See note 2.

4 Health and Social Care Act 2008 (Regulated Activities) Regulations 2014, SI 2014/2936, reg 19(1)(c). See note 2.

5 Health and Social Care Act 2008 (Regulated Activities) Regulations 2014, SI 2014/2936, reg 19(2)(a).

6 Health and Social Care Act 2008 (Regulated Activities) Regulations 2014, SI 2014/2936, reg 19(3)(a). The information is specified in Sch 3.

7 Health and Social Care Act 2008 (Regulated Activities) Regulations 2014, SI 2014/2936, reg 19(3)(b).

8 Health and Social Care Act 2008 (Regulated Activities) Regulations 2014, SI 2014/2936, reg 19(3).

9 Ie where such registration is required by, or under, any enactment in relation to the work that the person is to perform (Health and Social Care Act 2008 (Regulated Activities) Regulations 2014, SI 2014/2936, reg 19(4)(a)) or the title that the person takes or uses (reg 19(4)(b)).

10 Health and Social Care Act 2008 (Regulated Activities) Regulations 2014, SI 2014/2936, reg 19(4).

11 Ie the requirements of the Health and Social Care Act 2008 (Regulated Activities) Regulations 2014, SI 2014/2936, Pt 3 (regs 4–20A).

12 Health and Social Care Act 2008 (Regulated Activities) Regulations 2014, SI 2014/2936, reg 18(1).

13 Health and Social Care Act 2008 (Regulated Activities) Regulations 2014, SI 2014/2936, reg 18(2)(a).

14 Health and Social Care Act 2008 (Regulated Activities) Regulations 2014, SI 2014/2936, reg 18(2)(b).

15 Health and Social Care Act 2008 (Regulated Activities) Regulations 2014, SI 2014/2936, reg 18(2)(c).

(iv) Standards of Service Provision

171. Provision of person-centred care. The care and treatment[1] of service users in England[2] must[3] be appropriate[4], meet the user's needs[5], and reflect the user's preferences[6]. Without limiting this requirement, the things which a registered person[7] must do to comply with these requirements include:

(1)   carrying out, collaboratively with the relevant person[8], an assessment of the needs and preferences for care and treatment of the service user[9];

(2)   designing care or treatment with a view to achieving service users' preferences and ensuring their needs are met[10];

(3)   enabling and supporting relevant persons to understand the care or treatment choices available to the service user and to discuss, with a competent health care professional[11] or other competent person, the balance of risks and benefits involved in any particular course of treatment[12];

(4)   enabling and supporting relevant persons to make, or participate in making, decisions relating to the service user's care or treatment to the maximum extent possible[13];

(5)   providing opportunities for relevant persons to manage the service user's care or treatment[14];

(6)   involving relevant persons in decisions relating to the way in which the regulated activity is carried on in so far as it relates to the service user's care or treatment[15];

(7)   providing relevant persons with the information they would reasonably need for the purposes of heads (3) to (6) above[16];

(8)   making reasonable adjustments[17] to enable the service user to receive their care or treatment[18]; and

(9)   where meeting a service user's nutritional and hydration needs, having regard to the service user's well-being[19].

1   As to the meaning of 'treatment' see PARA 153 note 11.
2   As to the meaning of 'service user' see PARA 153 note 6.
3   These provisions do not apply to the extent that the provision of care or treatment would result in a breach of the Health and Social Care Act 2008 (Regulated Activities) Regulations 2014, SI 2014/2936, reg 11 (see PARA 172): reg 9(2).
4   Health and Social Care Act 2008 (Regulated Activities) Regulations 2014, SI 2014/2936, reg 9(1)(a).
5   Health and Social Care Act 2008 (Regulated Activities) Regulations 2014, SI 2014/2936, reg 9(1)(b).
6   Health and Social Care Act 2008 (Regulated Activities) Regulations 2014, SI 2014/2936, reg 9(1)(c).
7   As to the meaning of 'registered person' see PARA 168 note 12. If the service user is 16 or over and lacks capacity in relation to a matter to which reg 9 applies, reg 9(1)–(3) are subject to any duty on the registered person under the Mental Capacity Act 2005 in relation to that matter: Health and Social Care Act 2008 (Regulated Activities) Regulations 2014, SI 2014/2936, reg 9(4), (5). However if the Mental Health Act 1983 Pt 4 (ss 56–64) (see MENTAL HEALTH AND CAPACITY vol 75 (2013) PARA 924 et seq) or Pt 4A (ss 64A–64K) (see MENTAL HEALTH AND CAPACITY vol 75 (2013) PARA 935 et seq) applies to a service user, care and treatment must be provided in accordance with the provisions of that Act: Health and Social Care Act 2008 (Regulated Activities) Regulations 2014, SI 2014/2936, reg 9(6). For the purposes of determining under regs 9–20A whether a service user who is 16 or over lacks capacity, the Mental Capacity Act 2005 ss 2, 3 (people who lack capacity: see MENTAL HEALTH AND CAPACITY vol 75 (2013) PARAS 603–605) apply as they apply for the purposes of that Act: Health and Social Care Act 2008 (Regulated Activities) Regulations 2014, SI 2014/2936, reg 8(3) (as so amended).
8   'Relevant person', except in the Health and Social Care Act 2008 (Regulated Activities) Regulations 2014, SI 2014/2936, reg 20, means the service user or, where the service user is under 16 and not competent to make a decision in relation to their care or treatment, a person lawfully acting on their behalf: reg 2(1).
9   Health and Social Care Act 2008 (Regulated Activities) Regulations 2014, SI 2014/2936, reg 9(3)(a).
10 Health and Social Care Act 2008 (Regulated Activities) Regulations 2014, SI 2014/2936, reg 9(3)(b).
11 As to the meaning of 'health care professional' see PARA 168 note 3.
12 Health and Social Care Act 2008 (Regulated Activities) Regulations 2014, SI 2014/2936, reg 9(3)(c).
13 Health and Social Care Act 2008 (Regulated Activities) Regulations 2014, SI 2014/2936, reg 9(3)(d).
14 Health and Social Care Act 2008 (Regulated Activities) Regulations 2014, SI 2014/2936, reg 9(3)(e).
15 Health and Social Care Act 2008 (Regulated Activities) Regulations 2014, SI 2014/2936, reg 9(3)(f).
16 Health and Social Care Act 2008 (Regulated Activities) Regulations 2014, SI 2014/2936, reg 9(3)(g).
17 'Reasonable adjustments' means such reasonable adjustments as would be required under the Equality Act 2010 (see DISCRIMINATION vol 33 (2013) PARA 84): Health and Social Care Act 2008 (Regulated Activities) Regulations 2014, SI 2014/2936, reg 2(1).
18 Health and Social Care Act 2008 (Regulated Activities) Regulations 2014, SI 2014/2936, reg 9(3)(h).
19 Health and Social Care Act 2008 (Regulated Activities) Regulations 2014, SI 2014/2936, reg 9(3)(i).

172. Dignity, respect and consent. Service users[1] must be treated with dignity and respect[2], and without limiting this requirement, the things which a registered person[3] is required to do to comply with this requirement include, in particular, ensuring the privacy of the service user[4], supporting the autonomy, independence and involvement in the community of the service user[5], and having due regard to any relevant protected characteristics[6] of the service user[7].

Care and treatment of service users must only be provided with the consent of the relevant person[8]. Provision is made in connection with the giving of consent where a service user lacks capacity[9]. Failure to comply with this requirement is an offence[10].

1 As to the meaning of 'service user' see PARA 153 note 6.
2 Health and Social Care Act 2008 (Regulated Activities) Regulations 2014, SI 2014/2936, reg 10(1).
3 As to the meaning of 'registered person' see PARA 168 note 12.
4 Health and Social Care Act 2008 (Regulated Activities) Regulations 2014, SI 2014/2936, reg 10(2)(ai).
5 Health and Social Care Act 2008 (Regulated Activities) Regulations 2014, SI 2014/2936, reg 10(2)(b).
6 Ie as defined by the Equality Act 2010 s 149(7) (see DISCRIMINATION vol 33 (2013) PARA 48).
7 Health and Social Care Act 2008 (Regulated Activities) Regulations 2014, SI 2014/2936, reg 10(2)(c).
8 Health and Social Care Act 2008 (Regulated Activities) Regulations 2014, SI 2014/2936, reg 11(1).
9 If the service user is 16 or over and is unable to give such consent because he lacks capacity to do so, the registered person must act in accordance with the Mental Capacity Act 2005 (see MENTAL HEALTH AND CAPACITY) in relation to that matter: Health and Social Care Act 2008 (Regulated Activities) Regulations 2014, SI 2014/2936, reg 11(2), (3). However if the Mental Health Act 1983 Pt 4 (ss 56–64) (see MENTAL HEALTH AND CAPACITY vol 75 (2013) PARA 924 et seq) or Pt 4A (ss 64A–64K) (see MENTAL HEALTH AND CAPACITY vol 75 (2013) PARA 935 et seq) applies to a service user, the registered person must act in accordance with the provisions of that Act: Health and Social Care Act 2008 (Regulated Activities) Regulations 2014, SI 2014/2936, reg 11(4). In connection with determining whether a service user who is 16 or over lacks capacity see reg 8(3); and PARA 171 note 7. Nothing in reg 11 affects the operation of the Mental Capacity Act 2005 s 5, as read with s 6 (acts in connection with care or treatment: see MENTAL HEALTH AND CAPACITY vol 75 (2013) PARA 611): Health and Social Care Act 2008 (Regulated Activities) Regulations 2014, SI 2014/2936, reg 11(5).
10 It is an offence for a registered person to fail to comply with any of the requirements in the Health and Social Care Act 2008 (Regulated Activities) Regulations 2014, SI 2014/2936, reg 11, reg 16(3) (see PARA 177), reg 17(3) (see PARA 177), reg 20(2)(a), (3) (see PARA 178), or reg 20A (see PARA 179), as read with reg 8 (see PARA 170 note 1) (reg 22(1) (regs 22(1), (4), 23(4), (5) amended, reg 22(5A) added, by SI 2015/64)), although it is a defence for a registered person to prove that they took all reasonable steps and exercised all due diligence to prevent the breach of any of those regulations that has occurred (Health and Social Care Act 2008 (Regulated Activities) Regulations 2014, SI 2014/2936, reg 22(4) (as so amended)). A person guilty of an offence under reg 22(1) for breach of reg 11 is liable on summary conviction to a fine (reg 22(4) (as so amended)); a person guilty of an offence under reg 22(1) for breach of reg 16(3), reg 17(3) or reg 20(2)(a), (3) is liable, on summary conviction, to a fine not exceeding level 4 on the standard scale (reg 22(5) (as so amended)); and a person guilty of an offence under reg 22(1) for breach of reg 20A is liable, on summary conviction, to a fine not exceeding level 2 on the standard scale (reg 22(5A) (as so added)). As to the powers of magistrates' courts to issue fines on summary conviction see SENTENCING vol 92 (2015) PARA 176. The offence under reg 22(1) is a fixed penalty offence: see reg 24, Sch 5; and PARA 159 note 4. In connection with offences under the Health and Social Care Act 2008 Pt 1 generally see PARA 158 note 6.

173. Care and welfare of service users. Care and treatment[1] must be provided in a safe way for service users[2], and (without limiting this requirement), the things which a registered person[3] must do to comply with that requirement include:

(1) assessing the risks to the health and safety of service users of receiving the care or treatment[4];

(2) doing all that is reasonably practicable to mitigate any such risks[5];

(3) ensuring that persons providing care or treatment to service users have the qualifications, competence, skills and experience to do so safely[6];

(4) ensuring that the premises[7] used by the service provider are safe to use for their intended purpose and are used in a safe way[8];

(5) ensuring that the equipment[9] used by the service provider for providing care or treatment to a service user is safe for such use and is used in a safe way[10];

(6)   where equipment or medicines are supplied by the service provider[11], ensuring that there are sufficient quantities of these to ensure the safety of service users and to meet their needs[12];

(7)   the proper and safe management of medicines[13];

(8)   assessing the risk of, and preventing, detecting and controlling the spread of, infections, including those that are health care associated[14];

(9)   where responsibility for the care and treatment of service users is shared with, or transferred to, other persons, working with such other persons, service users and other appropriate persons to ensure that timely care planning takes place to ensure the health, safety and welfare of the service users[15].

Failure to comply with these requirements, where such failure causes harm or loss, is an offence[16].

1   As to the meaning of 'treatment' see PARA 153 note 11.
2   Health and Social Care Act 2008 (Regulated Activities) Regulations 2014, SI 2014/2936, reg 12(1). As to the meaning of 'service user' see PARA 153 note 6.
3   As to the meaning of 'registered person' see PARA 168 note 12.
4   Health and Social Care Act 2008 (Regulated Activities) Regulations 2014, SI 2014/2936, reg 12(2)(a).
5   Health and Social Care Act 2008 (Regulated Activities) Regulations 2014, SI 2014/2936, reg 12(2)(b).
6   Health and Social Care Act 2008 (Regulated Activities) Regulations 2014, SI 2014/2936, reg 12(2)(c).
7   'Premises' means any building or other structure, including any machinery, engineering systems or other objects which are physically affixed and integral to such building or structure, and any surrounding grounds, or a vehicle, but in the Health and Social Care Act 2008 (Regulated Activities) Regulations 2014, SI 2014/2936, regs 12, 14, 15 does not include the service user's accommodation where such accommodation is not provided as part of the service user's care or treatment: reg 2(1).
8   Health and Social Care Act 2008 (Regulated Activities) Regulations 2014, SI 2014/2936, reg 12(2)(d).
9   'Equipment' includes a medical device (as defined in the Medical Devices Regulations 2002, SI 2002/618, reg 2(1) (see MEDICAL PRODUCTS AND DRUGS vol 75 (2013) PARA 472) and materials used in, or used by persons employed in, the carrying on of a regulated activity in England: Health and Social Care Act 2008 (Regulated Activities) Regulations 2014, SI 2014/2936, reg 2(1). As to the meaning of 'regulated activity' for these purposes, and the restriction of these provisions to activities carried on in England, see PARA 152 note 2; as to the regulated activities see PARAS 152–157.
10   Health and Social Care Act 2008 (Regulated Activities) Regulations 2014, SI 2014/2936, reg 12(2)(e).
11   As to the meaning of 'service provider' see PARA 152 note 6.
12   Health and Social Care Act 2008 (Regulated Activities) Regulations 2014, SI 2014/2936, reg 12(2)(f).
13   Health and Social Care Act 2008 (Regulated Activities) Regulations 2014, SI 2014/2936, reg 12(2)(g).
14   Health and Social Care Act 2008 (Regulated Activities) Regulations 2014, SI 2014/2936, reg 12(2)(h). In the Health and Social Care Act 2008 Pt 1 Ch 2 (ss 8–44) 'health care associated infection' means any infection to which an individual may be exposed or made susceptible (or more susceptible) in circumstances where health or social care is being, or has been, provided to that or any other individual (s 20(6)(a)) and the risk of exposure to the infection, or of susceptibility (or increased susceptibility) to it, is directly or indirectly attributable to the provision of that care (s 20(6)(b)), but does not include an infection to which the individual is deliberately exposed as part of any health care (s 20(7)). As to the meanings of 'health care' and 'social care' see PARA 152 note 2.
15   Health and Social Care Act 2008 (Regulated Activities) Regulations 2014, SI 2014/2936, reg 12(2)(i).
16   A registered person commits an offence if he fails to comply with a requirement of the Health and Social Care Act 2008 (Regulated Activities) Regulations 2014, SI 2014/2936, reg 12, reg 13(1)–(4) (see PARA 174) or reg 14 (see PARA 175), as read with reg 8 (see PARA 170 note 1), and such failure results in avoidable harm (whether of a physical or psychological nature) to a service user,

a service user being exposed to a significant risk of such harm occurring, or in a case of theft, misuse or misappropriation of money or property, any loss by a service user of the money or property concerned (reg 22(2)), although it is a defence for a registered person to prove that he took all reasonable steps and exercised all due diligence to prevent the breach of any of those regulations that has occurred (reg 22(4) (regs 22(4), 23(4) amended by SI 2015/64)). A person guilty of an offence under the Health and Social Care Act 2008 (Regulated Activities) Regulations 2014, SI 2014/2936, reg 22(2) is liable on summary conviction to a fine: reg 22(4) (as so amended). As to the powers of magistrates' courts to issue fines on summary conviction see SENTENCING vol 92 (2015) PARA 176. In connection with offences under the Health and Social Care Act 2008 Pt 1 generally see PARA 158 note 6.

174. Safeguarding service users from abuse and improper treatment. Service users[1] must be protected[2] from abuse and improper treatment[3], and systems and processes must be established and operated effectively to prevent abuse of service users[4] and to investigate, immediately upon becoming aware of, any allegation or evidence of such abuse[5]. Care or treatment for service users must not be provided in a way that:

(1)   includes discrimination against a service user on grounds of any protected characteristic[6] of the service user[7];

(2)   includes acts intended to control or restrain a service user[8] that are not necessary to prevent, or not a proportionate response to, a risk of harm posed to the service user or another individual if the service user was not subject to control or restraint[9];

(3)   is degrading for the service user[10]; or

(4)   significantly disregards the needs of the service user for care or treatment[11].

Failure to comply with these requirements, where such failure causes harm or loss, is an offence[12].

A service user must not be deprived of his liberty for the purpose of receiving care or treatment without lawful authority[13].

1   As to the meaning of 'service user' see PARA 153 note 6.
2   Ie in accordance with the Health and Social Care Act 2008 (Regulated Activities) Regulations 2014, SI 2014/2936, reg 13 (see the text and notes 3–13).
3   Health and Social Care Act 2008 (Regulated Activities) Regulations 2014, SI 2014/2936, reg 13(1). For these purposes 'abuse' means any behaviour towards a service user that is an offence under the Sexual Offences Act 2003 (see CRIMINAL LAW vol 25 (2016) PARA 196 et seq), ill-treatment (whether of a physical or psychological nature) of a service user, theft, misuse or misappropriation of money or property belonging to a service user, or neglect of a service user: Health and Social Care Act 2008 (Regulated Activities) Regulations 2014, SI 2014/2936, reg 13(6).
4   Health and Social Care Act 2008 (Regulated Activities) Regulations 2014, SI 2014/2936, reg 13(2).
5   Health and Social Care Act 2008 (Regulated Activities) Regulations 2014, SI 2014/2936, reg 13(3).
6   Ie as defined in the Equality Act 2010 s 4 (see DISCRIMINATION vol 33 (2013) PARA 48).
7   Health and Social Care Act 2008 (Regulated Activities) Regulations 2014, SI 2014/2936, reg 13(4)(a).
8   For these purposes a person controls or restrains a service user if he uses, or threatens to use, force to secure the doing of an act which the service user resists or restricts the service user's liberty of movement, whether or not the service user resists, including by use of physical, mechanical or chemical means: Health and Social Care Act 2008 (Regulated Activities) Regulations 2014, SI 2014/2936, reg 13(7).
9   Health and Social Care Act 2008 (Regulated Activities) Regulations 2014, SI 2014/2936, reg 13(4)(b).
10 Health and Social Care Act 2008 (Regulated Activities) Regulations 2014, SI 2014/2936, reg 13(4)(c).
11 Health and Social Care Act 2008 (Regulated Activities) Regulations 2014, SI 2014/2936, reg 13(4)(d). As to the meaning of 'treatment' see PARA 153 note 11.
12 See the Health and Social Care Act 2008 (Regulated Activities) Regulations 2014, SI 2014/2936, reg 22(2); and PARA 173 note 16.

13 Health and Social Care Act 2008 (Regulated Activities) Regulations 2014, SI 2014/2936, reg 13(5).

175. Nutritional and hydration needs. The nutritional and hydration needs[1] of service users must be met[2]. This requirement applies where:

(1)   care or treatment[3] involves the provision of accommodation by the service provider[4] or an overnight stay for the service user on premises[5] used by the service for the purposes of carrying on a regulated activity in England[6]; or

(2)   the meeting of the nutritional or hydration needs of service users is part of the arrangements made for the provision of care or treatment by the service provider[7].

However this requirement does not apply to the extent that the meeting of such nutritional or hydration needs would breach consent[8] requirements[9] not be in the service user's best interests[10].

Failure to comply with these requirements, where such failure causes harm or loss, is an offence[11].

1   For these purposes 'nutritional and hydration needs' means:
(1)   receipt by a service user of suitable and nutritious food and hydration which is adequate to sustain life and good health (Health and Social Care Act 2008 (Regulated Activities) Regulations 2014, SI 2014/2936, reg 14(4)(a));
(2)   receipt by a service user of parenteral nutrition and dietary supplements when prescribed by a health care professional (reg 14(4)(b));
(3)   the meeting of any reasonable requirements of a service user for food and hydration arising from the service user's preferences or their religious or cultural background (reg 14(4)(c)); and
(4)   if necessary, support for a service user to eat or drink (reg 14(4)(d)).
    As to the meaning of 'service user' see PARA 153 note 6. As to the meaning of 'health care professional' see PARA 168 note 3.
2   Health and Social Care Act 2008 (Regulated Activities) Regulations 2014, SI 2014/2936, reg 14(1).
3   As to the meaning of 'treatment' see PARA 153 note 11.
4   Health and Social Care Act 2008 (Regulated Activities) Regulations 2014, SI 2014/2936, reg 14(2)(a)(i). As to the meaning of 'service provider' see PARA 152 note 6.
5   As to the meaning of 'premises' see PARA 173 note 7.
6   Health and Social Care Act 2008 (Regulated Activities) Regulations 2014, SI 2014/2936, reg 14(2)(a)(ii). As to the meaning of 'regulated activity' for these purposes, and the restriction of these provisions to activities carried on in England, see PARA 152 note 2; as to the regulated activities see PARAS 152–157.
7   Health and Social Care Act 2008 (Regulated Activities) Regulations 2014, SI 2014/2936, reg 14(2)(b).
8   Ie would result in a breach of the Health and Social Care Act 2008 (Regulated Activities) Regulations 2014, SI 2014/2936, reg 11 (see PARA 171).
9   Health and Social Care Act 2008 (Regulated Activities) Regulations 2014, SI 2014/2936, reg 14(3)(a).
10   Health and Social Care Act 2008 (Regulated Activities) Regulations 2014, SI 2014/2936, reg 14(3)(b). The Mental Capacity Act 2005 s 4 (best interests: see MENTAL HEALTH AND CAPACITY vol 75 (2013) PARA 606) applies for the purposes of determining the best interests of a service user who is 16 or over under these provisions as it applies for the purposes of that Act: Health and Social Care Act 2008 (Regulated Activities) Regulations 2014, SI 2014/2936, reg 14(5).
11   See the Health and Social Care Act 2008 (Regulated Activities) Regulations 2014, SI 2014/2936, reg 22(2); and PARA 173 note 16.

176.   Cleanliness and infection control. All premises[1] and equipment[2] used by the service provider must be:

(1)   clean[3];

(2)   secure[4];

(3)   suitable for the purpose for which they are being used[5];

(4)   properly used[6];
(5)   properly maintained[7]; and
(6)   appropriately located for the purpose for which they are being used[8].

The registered person[9] must, in relation to such premises and equipment, maintain standards of hygiene appropriate for the purposes for which they are being used[10].

1   As to the meaning of 'premises' see PARA 173 note 7.
2   As to the meaning of 'equipment' see PARA 173 note 9. For the purposes of heads (2), (3), (5), (6) in the text 'equipment' does not include equipment at the service user's accommodation if such accommodation is not provided as part of the service user's care or treatment (Health and Social Care Act 2008 (Regulated Activities) Regulations 2014, SI 2014/2936, reg 15(3)(a)) and such equipment is not supplied by the service provider (reg 15(3)(b)). As to the meaning of 'service provider' see PARA 152 note 6.
3   Health and Social Care Act 2008 (Regulated Activities) Regulations 2014, SI 2014/2936, reg 15(1)(a).
4   Health and Social Care Act 2008 (Regulated Activities) Regulations 2014, SI 2014/2936, reg 15(1)(b).
5   Health and Social Care Act 2008 (Regulated Activities) Regulations 2014, SI 2014/2936, reg 15(1)(c).
6   Health and Social Care Act 2008 (Regulated Activities) Regulations 2014, SI 2014/2936, reg 15(1)(d).
7   Health and Social Care Act 2008 (Regulated Activities) Regulations 2014, SI 2014/2936, reg 15(1)(e).
8   Health and Social Care Act 2008 (Regulated Activities) Regulations 2014, SI 2014/2936, reg 15(1)(f).
9   As to the meaning of 'registered person' see PARA 168 note 12.
10 Health and Social Care Act 2008 (Regulated Activities) Regulations 2014, SI 2014/2936, reg 15(2).

177. Complaints and good governance. Any complaint received must be investigated and necessary and proportionate action must be taken in response to any failure identified by the complaint or investigation[1]. The registered person[2] must establish and operate effectively an accessible system for identifying, receiving, recording, handling and responding to complaints by service users[3] and other persons in relation to the carrying on of the regulated activity in England[4]. The registered person must provide to the Care Quality Commission[5] a summary of:

(1)   complaints made under such complaints system[6];
(2)   responses made by the registered person to such complaints and any further correspondence with the complainants in relation to such complaints[7]; and
(3)   any other relevant information in relation to such complaints as the Commission may request[8].

Failure to comply with these requirements[9] is an offence[10].

Systems or processes must be established and operated effectively to ensure compliance with the statutory[11] requirements[12]: without limiting this, such systems or processes must enable the registered person, in particular, to:

(a)   assess, monitor and improve the quality and safety of the services provided in the carrying on of the regulated activity (including the quality of the experience of service users in receiving those services)[13];
(b)   assess, monitor and mitigate the risks relating to the health, safety and welfare of service users and others who may be at risk which arise from the carrying on of the regulated activity[14];

(c) maintain securely an accurate, complete and contemporaneous record in respect of each service user, including a record of the care and treatment[15] provided to the service user and of decisions taken in relation to the care and treatment provided[16];

(d) maintain securely such other records as are necessary to be kept in relation to persons employed[17] in the carrying on of the regulated activity[18] and the management of the regulated activity[19];

(e) seek and act on feedback from relevant persons[20] and other persons on the services provided in the carrying on of the regulated activity, for the purposes of continually evaluating and improving such services[21]; and

(f) evaluate and improve their practice in respect of the processing of the information referred to in heads (a) to (e) above[22].

1   Health and Social Care Act 2008 (Regulated Activities) Regulations 2014, SI 2014/2936, reg 16(1).

2   As to the meaning of 'registered person' see PARA 168 note 12.

3   As to the meaning of 'service user' see PARA 153 note 6.

4   Health and Social Care Act 2008 (Regulated Activities) Regulations 2014, SI 2014/2936, reg 16(2). As to the meaning of 'regulated activity' for these purposes, and the restriction of these provisions to activities carried on in England, see PARA 152 note 2; as to the regulated activities see PARAS 152–157.

5   Ie when requested to do so and by no later than 28 days beginning on the day after receipt of the request: Health and Social Care Act 2008 (Regulated Activities) Regulations 2014, SI 2014/2936, reg 16(3). As to the Care Quality Commission see PARA 336 et seq.

6   Health and Social Care Act 2008 (Regulated Activities) Regulations 2014, SI 2014/2936, reg 16(3)(a).

7   Health and Social Care Act 2008 (Regulated Activities) Regulations 2014, SI 2014/2936, reg 16(3)(b).

8   Health and Social Care Act 2008 (Regulated Activities) Regulations 2014, SI 2014/2936, reg 16(3)(c).

9   Ie the requirements of the Health and Social Care Act 2008 (Regulated Activities) Regulations 2014, SI 2014/2936, reg 16(3).

10 See the Health and Social Care Act 2008 (Regulated Activities) Regulations 2014, SI 2014/2936, regs 22(1), 23; and PARA 172 note 10.

11 Ie the requirements of the Health and Social Care Act 2008 (Regulated Activities) Regulations 2014, SI 2014/2936, Pt 3 (regs 4–20A).

12 Health and Social Care Act 2008 (Regulated Activities) Regulations 2014, SI 2014/2936, reg 18(1).

13 Health and Social Care Act 2008 (Regulated Activities) Regulations 2014, SI 2014/2936, reg 17(2)(a). The registered person must send to the Commission, when requested to do so and by no later than 28 days beginning on the day after receipt of the request, a written report setting out how, and the extent to which, in the opinion of the registered person, the requirements of reg 17(2)(a), (b) are being complied with (reg 17(3)(a)) and any plans that the registered person has for improving the standard of the services provided to service users with a view to ensuring their health and welfare (reg 17(3)(b)). Failure to comply with reg 17(3) is an offence: see regs 22(1), 23.

14 Health and Social Care Act 2008 (Regulated Activities) Regulations 2014, SI 2014/2936, reg 17(2)(b).

15 As to the meaning of 'treatment' see PARA 153 note 11.

16 Health and Social Care Act 2008 (Regulated Activities) Regulations 2014, SI 2014/2936, reg 17(2)(c).

17 As to the meaning of 'employed' see PARA 170 note 1.

18 Health and Social Care Act 2008 (Regulated Activities) Regulations 2014, SI 2014/2936, reg 17(2)(d)(i).

19 Health and Social Care Act 2008 (Regulated Activities) Regulations 2014, SI 2014/2936, reg 17(2)(d)(ii).

20 As to the meaning of 'relevant person' see PARA 171 note 8.

21 Health and Social Care Act 2008 (Regulated Activities) Regulations 2014, SI 2014/2936, reg 17(2)(e).

22 Health and Social Care Act 2008 (Regulated Activities) Regulations 2014, SI 2014/2936, reg 17(2)(f).

178. Duty of candour. Registered persons[1] must act in an open and transparent way with relevant persons[2] in relation to care and treatment[3] provided to service users in carrying on a regulated activity in England[4]. As soon as reasonably practicable after becoming aware that a notifiable safety incident[5] has occurred a registered person must notify the relevant person that the incident has occurred[6] and provide reasonable support to the relevant person in relation to the incident, including when giving such notification[7]. However, if the relevant person cannot be contacted in person or declines to speak to the representative of the registered person these requirements[8] are not to apply[9] a written record is to be kept of attempts to contact or to speak to the relevant person[10]. Failure to comply with the notification requirements[11] is an offence[12].

1 As to the meaning of 'registered person' see PARA 168 note 12.
2 'Relevant person' means (by virtue of the Health and Social Care Act 2008 (Regulated Activities) Regulations 2014, SI 2014/2936, reg 20(7) (reg 20(1), (2), (3)(a)–(c), (e), (5)–(7) amended, reg 20(8), (9) added, by SI 2015/64)) the service user or, in the following circumstances, a person lawfully acting on their behalf:
    (1)   on the death of the service user;
    (2)   where the service user is under 16 and not competent to make a decision in relation to their care or treatment; or
    (3)   where the service user is 16 or over and lacks capacity in relation to the matter.
    As to the meaning of 'service user' see PARA 153 note 6. In connection with determining whether a service user who is 16 or over lacks capacity see the Health and Social Care Act 2008 (Regulated Activities) Regulations 2014, SI 2014/2936, reg 8(3); and PARA 171 note 7.
3 As to the meaning of 'treatment' see PARA 153 note 11.
4 Health and Social Care Act 2008 (Regulated Activities) Regulations 2014, SI 2014/2936, reg 20(1) (as amended: see note 2). As to the meaning of 'regulated activity' for these purposes, and the restriction of these provisions to activities carried on in England, see PARA 152 note 2; as to the regulated activities see PARAS 152–157.
5 In relation to a health service body, 'notifiable safety incident' means any unintended or unexpected incident that occurred in respect of a service user during the provision of a regulated activity that, in the reasonable opinion of a health care professional, could result in, or appears to have resulted in the death of the service user, where the death relates directly to the incident rather than to the natural course of the service user's illness or underlying condition (Health and Social Care Act 2008 (Regulated Activities) Regulations 2014, SI 2014/2936, reg 20(7), (8)(a) (as amended and added: see note 2)) or severe harm, moderate harm or prolonged psychological harm to the service user (reg 20(8)(b) (as so added)). In relation to any other registered person, 'notifiable safety incident' means any unintended or unexpected incident that occurred in respect of a service user during the provision of a regulated activity that, in the reasonable opinion of a health care professional:
    (1)   appears to have resulted in the death of the service user, where the death relates directly to the incident rather than to the natural course of the service user's illness or underlying condition (reg 20(9)(a)(i) (as so added)), an impairment of the sensory, motor or intellectual functions of the service user which has lasted, or is likely to last, for a continuous period of at least 28 days (reg 20(9)(a)(ii) (as so added)), changes to the structure of the service user's body (reg 20(9)(a)(iii) (as so added)), the service user experiencing prolonged pain or prolonged psychological harm (reg 20(9)(a)(iv) (as so added)), or the shortening of the life expectancy of the service user (reg 20(9)(a)(v) (as so added)); or
    (2)   requires treatment by a health care professional in order to prevent the death of the service user (reg 20(9)(b)(i) (as so added)) or any injury to the service user which, if left untreated, would lead to one or more of the outcomes mentioned head (1) above (reg 20(9)(b)(ii) (as so added)).
    'Health service body' means an NHS trust established under the National Health Service Act 2006 s 25, an NHS foundation trust (see HEALTH SERVICES vol 54 (2017) PARA 244), or a Special Health Authority (see HEALTH SERVICES vol 54A (2017) PARA 532 et seq) (reg 2(1)); 'moderate harm' means harm that requires a moderate increase in treatment and significant, but not permanent, harm (reg 20(7)); 'severe harm' means a permanent lessening of bodily, sensory, motor, physiologic or intellectual functions, including removal of the wrong limb or organ or brain damage, that is related directly to the incident and not related to the natural course of the service user's illness or underlying condition (reg 20(7)); 'prolonged pain' means pain which a service user

has experienced, or is likely to experience, for a continuous period of at least 28 days (reg 20(7)); 'prolonged psychological harm' means psychological harm which a service user has experienced, or is likely to experience, for a continuous period of at least 28 days (reg 20(7)); and 'moderate increase in treatment' means an unplanned return to surgery, an unplanned re-admission, a prolonged episode of care, extra time in hospital or as an outpatient, cancelling of treatment, or transfer to another treatment area (such as intensive care) (reg 20(7)). As to the meaning of 'health care professional' see PARA 168 note 3.

6   Health and Social Care Act 2008 (Regulated Activities) Regulations 2014, SI 2014/2936, reg 20(2)(a) (as amended: see note 2). The notification to be given under reg 20(2)(a) must:

    (1)   be given in person by one or more representatives of the registered person (reg 20(3)(a) (as so amended));

    (2)   provide an account, which to the best of the registered person's knowledge is true, of all the facts the registered person knows about the incident as at the date of the notification (reg 20(3)(b) (as so amended));

    (3)   advise the relevant person what further enquiries into the incident the registered person believes are appropriate (reg 20(3)(c) (as so amended));

    (4)   include an apology (reg 20(3)(d)); and

    (5)   be recorded in a written record which is kept securely by the registered person (reg 20(3)(e) (as so amended)).

'Apology' means an expression of sorrow or regret in respect of a notifiable safety incident: reg 20(7). The notification given under reg 20(2)(a) must be followed by a written notification given or sent to the relevant person containing:

    (a)   the information provided under reg 20(3)(b) (reg 20(4)(a));

    (b)   details of any enquiries to be undertaken in accordance with reg 20(3)(c) (reg 20(4)(b));

    (c)   the results of any further enquiries into the incident (reg 20(4)(c)); and

    (d)   an apology (reg 20(4)(d)).

The registered person must keep a copy of all correspondence with the relevant person under reg 20(4): reg 20(6) (as so amended).

7   Health and Social Care Act 2008 (Regulated Activities) Regulations 2014, SI 2014/2936, reg 20(2)(b).

8   Ie the Health and Social Care Act 2008 (Regulated Activities) Regulations 2014, SI 2014/2936, reg 20(2)–(4) (see the text and notes 5–7).

9   Health and Social Care Act 2008 (Regulated Activities) Regulations 2014, SI 2014/2936, reg 20(5)(a) (as amended: see note 2).

10 Health and Social Care Act 2008 (Regulated Activities) Regulations 2014, SI 2014/2936, reg 20(5)(b) (as amended: see note 2).

11 Ie the Health and Social Care Act 2008 (Regulated Activities) Regulations 2014, SI 2014/2936, reg 20(2)(a), (3) (see the text and notes 6–7).

12 See the Health and Social Care Act 2008 (Regulated Activities) Regulations 2014, SI 2014/2936, regs 22(1), 23; and PARA 172 note 10.

179. Periodic reviews and assessments of registered providers. The Care Quality Commission[1] must conduct reviews of the carrying on of regulated activities[2] by registered service providers[3] which are NHS Trusts, NHS foundation trusts, independent hospitals or other providers of primary medical services[4]. The Commission must also conduct reviews of the carrying on of personal care[5], the provision of residential accommodation[6] or nursing care[7] by any other service provider[8]. The Commission must assess the performance of the service providers following each such review[9] and publish a report of its assessment[10]. Service providers must display, at its premises and online, its performance assessments[11].

Where the Commission conducts a review under these provisions in respect of an English local authority[12] and considers that the authority is failing to discharge any of its adult social services functions[13] to an acceptable standard, the Commission must inform the Secretary of State of that fact and recommend any special measures which it considers the Secretary of State should take[14].

1   As to the Care Quality Commission see PARA 336 et seq.

2   As to the meaning of 'regulated activity' for these purposes see PARA 152 note 2. Regulated activities are not prescribed for these purposes if they are provided in a prison within the meaning of the Prison Act 1952 (see s 53(1); and PRISONS AND PRISONERS vol 85 (2012) PARA 403): Care Quality Commission (Reviews and Performance Assessments) Regulations 2014, SI 2014/1788, reg 2(2) (made under the Health and Social Care Act 2008 s 46(2) (s 46 substituted

by the Care Act 2014 s 91(1), (2))). The Commission must prepare a statement setting out the frequency with which reviews under the Health and Social Care Act 2008 s 46 are to be conducted and the period to which they are to relate (s 46(4)(a) (as so substituted)) and describing the method that it proposes to use in assessing and evaluating the performance of a registered service provider under s 46 (s 46(4)(b) (as so substituted)). The Commission may make different provision about frequency and period of reviews for different cases (s 46(5)(b) (as so substituted)) and describe different methods for different cases (s 46(5)(c) (as so substituted)). The Commission must publish the statement it prepares for the purpose of s 46(4): s 46(6)(a) (as so substituted). Before publishing under s 46(6) the Commission must consult the Secretary of State and such other persons, or other persons of such a description, as may be prescribed (s 46(7)(a) (as so substituted)) and may also consult any other persons it considers appropriate (s 46(7)(b) (as so substituted)). The Commission may from time to time revise the statement it prepares for the purpose of s 46(4) and, if it does so, it must publish the statement as revised: s 46(8)(b) (as so substituted)). Section 46(7) applies to revised indicators (see note 9) and a revised statement, so far as the Commission considers the revisions in question to be significant: s 46(9) (as so substituted). As to the Secretary of State see PARA 333. Provision is made for the periodic review of the Care Quality Commission (Reviews and Performance Assessments) Regulations 2014, SI 2014/1788: see reg 3.

3   In the Health and Social Care Act 2008 'registered service provider' means a person registered under Pt 1 Ch 2 (ss 8–44) as a service provider: s 46(10) (as substituted: see note 2). Provision is also made for the inspection of the carrying out of regulated activities: see PARA 341.

4   Care Quality Commission (Reviews and Performance Assessments) Regulations 2014, SI 2014/1788, reg 2(1), Schedule. As to NHS Trusts (ie trusts established under the National Health Service Act 2006 s 25) see HEALTH SERVICES vol 54 (2017) PARA 235; as to NHS foundation trusts and independent hospitals (ie hospitals which are not health service hospitals as defined in the National Health Service Act 2006 s 275) (see HEALTH SERVICES vol 54 (2017) PARA 244; HEALTH SERVICES vol 54A (2017) PARA 633). The 'other providers of primary medical services' referred to are providers whose sole or main purpose is the provision of primary medical services under arrangements made pursuant to the National Health Service Act 2006 s 83(2) (primary medical services: see HEALTH SERVICES vol 54 (2017) PARA 295), a contract entered into pursuant to s 84 (general medical services contracts: see HEALTH SERVICES vol 54 (2017) PARA 296) or arrangements made pursuant to s 92 (arrangements by the Board for the provision of primary medical services: see HEALTH SERVICES vol 54 (2017) PARA 307): Care Quality Commission (Reviews and Performance Assessments) Regulations 2014, SI 2014/1788, Schedule. Specified activities relating to human fertilization and embryology are excluded, but the Schedule continues to refer to the Health and Social Care Act 2008 (Regulated Activities) Regulations 2010, SI 2010/781 (which were replaced by the Health and Social Care Act 2008 (Regulated Activities) Regulations 2014, SI 2014/2936) in this matter.

5   Ie as referred to in the Health and Social Care Act 2008 (Regulated Activities) Regulations 2014, SI 2014/2936, Sch 1 para 1 (see PARA 152).

6   Ie as referred to in the Health and Social Care Act 2008 (Regulated Activities) Regulations 2014, SI 2014/2936, Sch 1 para 2 (see PARA 153).

7   Ie as referred to in the Health and Social Care Act 2008 (Regulated Activities) Regulations 2014, SI 2014/2936, Sch 1 para 13 (see MEDICAL PROFESSIONS).

8   Health and Social Care Act 2008 s 46(1)(a) (as substituted: see note 2); Care Quality Commission (Reviews and Performance Assessments) Regulations 2014, SI 2014/1788, Schedule.

9   Health and Social Care Act 2008 s 46(1)(b) (as substituted: see note 2). The assessment of the performance of a registered service provider is to be by reference to whatever indicators of quality the Commission devises: s 46(3) (as so substituted). The Commission may use different indicators for different cases: s 46(5)(a) (as so substituted). The Commission must publish any indicators it devises for the purpose of s 46(3): s 46(6)(a) (as so substituted). The Commission may from time to time revise any indicators it devises for the purpose of s 46(3) and, if it does so, it must publish the indicators and statement as revised: s 46(8)(a) (as so substituted). See s 46(7), (9); and note 2.

10   Health and Social Care Act 2008 s 46(1)(c) (as substituted: see note 2). Where a report is published by the Commission under any provision of Pt 1 (ss 1–97) (see PARA 152 et seq) or of the Mental Health Act 1983 (see MENTAL HEALTH AND CAPACITY) the Commission must make copies of the report available for inspection at its offices by any person at any reasonable time and any person who requests a copy of the report is entitled to have one on payment of such reasonable fee (if any) as the Commission considers appropriate: Health and Social Care Act 2008 s 84(1)–(3). The Commission may charge a person such reasonable fee as it considers appropriate where it provides the person, on request, with any other information relevant to the exercise of the Commission's functions under the Health and Social Care Act 2008 Pt 1: s 84(4). See the Care Quality Commission (Fees) (Reviews and Performance Assessments) Regulations 2016, SI 2016/249 (made under the Health and Social Care Act 2008 s 85(1)(b)).

11   See the Health and Social Care Act 2008 (Regulated Activities) Regulations 2014, SI 2014/2936, reg 20A (added by SI 2015/64). Failure to comply with these requirements is an offence: see the

Health and Social Care Act 2008 (Regulated Activities) Regulations 2014, SI 2014/2936, regs 22(1), 23; and PARA 172 note 10.

12 As to the meaning of 'English local authority' see PARA 158 note 6.

13 'Adult social services' means services which are provided or commissioned by an English local authority in the exercise of its adult social services functions, and services which are provided or commissioned by an English local authority under the Local Government Act 2000 s 2(1)(b) (see LOCAL GOVERNMENT vol 69 (2009) PARA 463) or the Localism Act 2011 s 1 (see LOCAL GOVERNMENT) and which are similar in nature to a service which could be provided by the authority in the exercise of any of its adult social services functions; and 'adult social services functions' means social services functions (within the meaning of the Local Authority Social Services Act 1970: see s 1A, Sch 1; and PARA 315) so far as relating to persons aged 18 or over, excluding any function to which Chapter 4 of Part 8 of the Education and Inspections Act 2006 Pt 8 Ch 4 (ss 135–142) (see EDUCATION vol 36 (2015) PARAS 1289–1292) applies: Health and Social Care Act 2008 s 97(1) (definition amended by SI 2012/961).

14 Health and Social Care Act 2008 s 50(1), (2) (s 50(1) amended by the Care Act 2014 s 91(9)(a)). If the Commission considers that the failure is not substantial, it may instead give the authority a notice specifying the respects in which the Commission considers that the authority is failing, the action which the Commission considers the authority should take to remedy the failure, and the time by which the Commission considers the action should be taken, and inform the Secretary of State that it has done so: Health and Social Care Act 2008 s 50(3), (4). If the Commission recommends that the Secretary of State should take special measures in relation to the authority it must, if the Secretary of State so requests, conduct a further review under s 48 (see PARA 340) in relation to the authority, and include in its report under s 48(4) a report on such matters as the Secretary of State may specify: s 50(5). Provision for the giving of notices is made by ss 93, 94 (s 93 amended by SI 2009/3023).

(v) Financial Sustainability and Business Failure

180. Assessment of financial sustainability of care providers. The Care Quality Commission[1] must assess the financial sustainability[2] of a registered provider[3] of:

(1)   personal care[4]; or
(2)   residential care[5],

where that provider's business is of sufficient size to qualify for such an assessment[6]. Following such assessment, the Commission may work with the provider to formulate strategies for mitigating or eliminating financial risk[7].

1 As to the Care Quality Commission see PARA 336 et seq. The Commission must, in exercising any of its functions under the Care Act 2014 ss 54–56 (see the text and notes 2–7; and PARAS 181–182), have regard to the need to minimise the burdens it imposes on others: s 57(4).

2 Ie the financial sustainability of the care provider's business of carrying on in England of the regulated activity in respect of which it is registered: Care Act 2014 s 55(1). As to the meaning of 'regulated activity' for these purposes, and the restriction of these provisions to activities carried on in England, see PARA 152 note 2; as to the regulated activities see PARAS 152–157. Regulations may make provision about the making of the assessment required by s 55(1): s 55(6). At the date at which this volume states the law no such regulations had been made. The Commission may consult such persons as it considers appropriate on the method for assessing the financial sustainability of a registered care provider's business; and, having done so, it must publish guidance on the method it expects to apply in making the assessment: s 55(7).

3 Ie a person who is registered under the Health and Social Care Act 2008 Pt 1 Ch 2 (ss 8–44) in respect of the carrying on of a regulated activity in England: Care Act 2014 s 48(1). As to the meaning of 'regulated activity' for these purposes, and the restriction of these provisions to activities carried on in England, see PARA 152 note 2; as to the regulated activities see PARAS 152–157.

4 Ie a registered care provider who is not a local authority and who is registered in respect of the carrying on of the regulated activity set out in the Health and Social Care Act 2008 (Regulated Activities) Regulations 2014, SI 2014/2936, Sch 1 para 1 (see PARA 152): Care and Support (Market Oversight Criteria) Regulations 2015, SI 2015/314, reg 2(1) (made under the Care Act 2014 s 53). As to the meaning of 'local authority' see PARA 1.

5 Ie a registered care provider who is not a local authority and who is registered in respect of the carrying on of the regulated activity set out in the Health and Social Care Act 2008 (Regulated

Activities) Regulations 2014, SI 2014/2936, Sch 1 para 2 (see PARA 153): Care and Support (Market Oversight Criteria) Regulations 2015, SI 2015/314, reg 3(1).

6 A registered provider of personal care (see note 4) may be assessed under these provisions if:
   (1) the number of hours of regulated care (ie care provided in connection with the carrying on of the regulated activity referred to in note 4) provided by the provider in a week is 30,000 or more (Care and Support (Market Oversight Criteria) Regulations 2015, SI 2015/314, reg 2(1)(a), (2));
   (2) the number of people to whom regulated care is provided by the registered care provider in a week is 2,000 or more (reg 2(1)(b)); or
   (3) the number of people to whom regulated care is provided by the registered care provider in a week is 800 or more and hours of regulated care provided by that provider in the same week divided by that number of people exceeds 30 (reg 2(1)(c)).
   For this purpose, where a registered care provider is an undertaking:
   (a) the hours of regulated care provided by the provider include hours of regulated care provided by any group undertaking of the provider (reg 2(3)(a)); and
   (b) the number of people to whom regulated care is provided by the provider includes people to whom regulated care is provided by any group undertaking of the provider (reg 2(3)(b)).
   As to the meanings of 'undertaking' and 'group undertaking' see the Companies Act 2006 s 1161(1), (5); and COMPANIES vol 14 (2016) PARAS 23–24 (definitions applied by the Care and Support (Market Oversight Information) Regulations 2014, SI 2014/2822, reg 1(2); and by the Care and Support (Market Oversight Criteria) Regulations 2015, SI 2015/314, reg 1(2)).
   A registered provider of residential care (see note 5) may be assessed under these provisions if the bed capacity of that provider is:
   (i) 1,000 or more but less than 2,000 and where the bed capacity of that provider is at least 1 in each of 16 or more local authority areas or the bed capacity of that provider in each of 3 or more local authority areas exceeds 10% of the total bed capacity in each of those local authority areas (reg 3(1)(a)); or
   (ii) 2,000 or more (reg 3(1)(b)).
   For this purpose 'bed capacity' means the number of beds made available by a registered care provider in connection with the carrying on of the regulated activity set out in the Health and Social Care Act 2008 (Regulated Activities) Regulations 2014, SI 2014/2936, Sch 1 para 2; and 'total bed capacity' means the number of beds made available by all registered care providers in connection with the carrying on of that activity: Care and Support (Market Oversight Criteria) Regulations 2015, SI 2015/314, reg 3(2). For these purposes, where the registered care provider is an undertaking, the bed capacity of the provider includes the bed capacity of any group undertaking of the provider: reg 3(3).
   The Care Quality Commission must determine, in the case of each registered care provider, whether the provider satisfies one or more of these criteria (Care Act 2014 s 54(1)), and if the Commission determines that the provider satisfies one or more of those criteria, the assessment provisions (ie s 55) apply to that provider unless, or except in so far as, the Care and Support (Market Oversight Criteria) Regulations 2015, SI 2015/314, provide that it does not apply (Care Act 2014 s 54(2)). Where the assessment provisions apply to a registered care provider (whether as a result of s 54(2) or as a result of the Care and Support (Market Oversight Criteria) Regulations 2015, SI 2015/314), the Commission must inform the provider accordingly: Care Act 2014 s 54(3).

7 See PARAS 181–182.

181. Strategies for mitigating or eliminating financial risk. Where the Care Quality Commission[1], in light of a financial sustainability assessment[2], considers that there is a significant risk to the financial sustainability of a registered care provider's[3] business, it may require the provider to develop a plan for how to mitigate or eliminate the risk[4] and arrange for, or require the provider to arrange for, a person with appropriate professional expertise to carry out an independent review of the business[5].

1 See PARA 180 note 1.
2 Ie an assessment under the Care Act 2014 s 55(1) (see PARA 180).
3 As to the meaning of 'registered care provider' see PARA 180 note 3.
4 Care Act 2014 s 55(2)(a). Where the Commission imposes a requirement on a care provider under s 55(2)(a), it may also require the provider to co-operate with it in developing the plan (s 55(3)(a)) and to obtain its approval of the finalised plan (s 55(3)(b)).

5   Care Act 2014 s 55(2)(b). Where the Commission arranges for a review under s 55(2)(b), it may
    recover from the provider such costs as the Commission incurs in connection with the
    arrangements (other than its administrative costs in making the arrangements): s 55(4).

182.   Provision of financial information. Where a registered care provider[1] who
may be subject to a financial sustainability assessment[2] is an undertaking[3], the
Care Quality Commission[4] may require the provider to obtain from a group
undertaking of the provider an 'information undertaking' to provide
the Commission with such information as the Commission requests[5]. An
information undertaking must be in a form which is legally enforceable by the
registered care provider[6].

1   As to the meaning of 'registered care provider' see PARA 180 note 3.
2   Ie a provider to whom the Care Act 2014 s 55 (see PARAS 180–181) applies.
3   Care and Support (Market Oversight Information) Regulations 2014, SI 2014/2822, reg 2(1)
    (made under the Care Act 2014 s 55(5)). As to the meanings of 'undertaking' and 'group
    undertaking' see PARA 180 note 6.
4   See PARA 180 note 1.
5   Care and Support (Market Oversight Information) Regulations 2014, SI 2014/2822, reg 2(2).
    'Information' means any information, documents, records or other material: reg 1(2).
6   Care and Support (Market Oversight Information) Regulations 2014, SI 2014/2822, reg 2(3).
    The Commission may specify the form of an information undertaking and may provide in
    particular that:
      (1)   information must be provided at such times and such places as may be specified by
            the Commission (reg 3(a));
      (2)   an explanation of any information must be provided at such times and such places as
            may be specified by the Commission (reg 3(b));
      (3)   information and explanations must be provided in such manner or format as may be
            specified by the Commission (reg 3(c));
      (4)   the group undertaking must co-operate with the Commission in connection with
            providing information and explanations (reg 3(d)); and
      (5)   information and explanations must be complete and accurate (reg 3(e)).
    The provider must obtain the information undertaking within such period as the Commission
    specifies (reg 4(1)) and must send to the Commission a copy of the undertaking within such period
    as the Commission specifies (reg 4(2)). The undertaking must remain in force for as long as the
    person required to provide information remains a group undertaking of the registered care
    provider and the Care Act 2014 s 55 continues to apply to the provider: Care and Support (Market
    Oversight Information) Regulations 2014, SI 2014/2822, reg 4(3). The provider must inform
    the Commission immediately in writing if it becomes aware that the information undertaking has
    ceased to be in force, the information undertaking has ceased to be legally enforceable, or any
    terms of the undertaking have been breached: reg 5(1). The provider must comply with any request
    made by the Commission to enforce the undertaking: reg 5(2).

183.   'Business failure'. A registered care provider[1] who is not an individual
suffers 'business failure'[2] if, in respect of that provider:
      (1)   the appointment of an administrator[3] takes effect[4];
      (2)   a receiver is appointed[5];
      (3)   an administrative receiver[6] is appointed[7];
      (4)   a resolution for a voluntary winding up is passed other than in a
            members' voluntary winding up[8];
      (5)   a winding up order is made[9];
      (6)   a joint bankruptcy petition[10] is made[11];
      (7)   the charity trustees of the provider become unable to pay their debts as
            they fall due[12];
      (8)   every member of the partnership (in a case where the provider is a
            partnership) is adjudged bankrupt[13]; or
      (9)   a voluntary arrangement[14] has been approved[15].
In relation to a provider who is an individual, 'business failure'[16] means that:
      (a)   the individual is made bankrupt[17]; or

(b)   a voluntary arrangement[18] is proposed by or entered into by the individual[19].

1   As to the meaning of 'registered care provider' see PARA 180 note 3.
2   Ie for the purposes of the Care Act 2014 ss 48, 50–52 (see PARA 184).
3   Ie within the meaning given by the Insolvency Act 1986 Sch B1 para 1(1) (see COMPANY AND PARTNERSHIP INSOLVENCY vol 16 (2011) PARA 159) or corresponding Northern Ireland legislation.
4   Care and Support (Business Failure) Regulations 2015, SI 2015/301, reg 2(1)(a), (2)(a) (made under the Care Act 2014 s 52(12)).
5   Care and Support (Business Failure) Regulations 2015, SI 2015/301, reg 2(2)(b).
6   Ie as defined in the Insolvency Act 1986 s 251 (see COMPANIES vol 15A (2016) PARA 1618) or corresponding Northern Ireland legislation.
7   Care and Support (Business Failure) Regulations 2015, SI 2015/301, reg 2(2)(c).
8   Care and Support (Business Failure) Regulations 2015, SI 2015/301, reg 2(2)(d). 'A members' voluntary winding up' means a winding up where a statutory declaration has been made under the Insolvency Act 1986 s 89 (see COMPANY AND PARTNERSHIP INSOLVENCY vol 17 (2011) PARA 900) or corresponding Northern Ireland legislation: Care and Support (Business Failure) Regulations 2015, SI 2015/301, reg 1(4).
9   Care and Support (Business Failure) Regulations 2015, SI 2015/301, reg 2(2)(e).
10 Ie an order by virtue of the Insolvent Partnerships Order 1994, SI 1994/2421, art 11 (joint bankruptcy petition by individual members of insolvent partnership: see COMPANY AND PARTNERSHIP INSOLVENCY vol 17 (2011) PARA 1323) or corresponding Northern Ireland legislation.
11 Care and Support (Business Failure) Regulations 2015, SI 2015/301, reg 2(2)(f), (g).
12 Care and Support (Business Failure) Regulations 2015, SI 2015/301, reg 2(2)(h). For these purposes of a person is a charity trustee of a provider if the provider is a charity that is unincorporated and the person is a trustee of that charity (reg 2(4)), and the charity trustees of a provider are to be treated as becoming unable to pay their debts as they fall due if:
    (1)   a creditor to whom the trustees are indebted in a sum exceeding the relevant amount then due has served on the trustees a written demand requiring the trustees to pay the sum so due and the trustees have for 3 weeks thereafter neglected to pay the sum or to secure or compound for it to the reasonable satisfaction of the creditor (reg 2(5)(a)); or
    (2)   in England and Wales, execution or other process issued on a judgment, decree or order of a court in favour of a creditor of the trustees is returned unsatisfied in whole or in part (reg 2(5)(b)).
    'The relevant amount' means the amount specified in the Insolvency Act 1986 s 123(1)(a) (definition of inability to pay debts) (see COMPANY AND PARTNERSHIP INSOLVENCY vol 17 (2011) PARA 1281) or corresponding Northern Ireland legislation: Care and Support (Business Failure) Regulations 2015, SI 2015/301, reg 1(4).
13 Care and Support (Business Failure) Regulations 2015, SI 2015/301, reg 2(2)(i).
14 Ie a voluntary arrangement proposed for the purposes of the Insolvency Act 1986 Pt 1 (ss 1–7B) (see COMPANY AND PARTNERSHIP INSOLVENCY) or corresponding Northern Ireland legislation.
15 Care and Support (Business Failure) Regulations 2015, SI 2015/301, reg 2(2)(j).
16 See note 2.
17 Care and Support (Business Failure) Regulations 2015, SI 2015/301, reg 2(3)(a) (amended by SI 2016/481).
18 Ie a voluntary arrangement proposed pursuant to the Insolvency Act 1986 Pt 8 (ss 252–263) (see COMPANY AND PARTNERSHIP INSOLVENCY) or corresponding Northern Ireland legislation.
19 Care and Support (Business Failure) Regulations 2015, SI 2015/301, reg 2(3)(b).

184.   Duty of local authority to meet needs in event of business failure. Where a registered care provider[1] becomes unable to carry on a regulated activity in England[2] because of business failure[3], a local authority[4] must for so long as it considers necessary (and in so far as it is not already required to do so) meet those of an adult's[5] needs for care and support and those of a carer's[6] needs for support which were, immediately before the registered care provider became unable to carry on the regulated activity, being met by the carrying on of that activity in the authority's area by the provider[7]. An authority is accordingly required to meet such needs regardless of:
    (1)   whether the relevant adult[8] is ordinarily resident in its area[9];

(2) whether the authority has carried out a needs assessment, a carer's assessment or a financial assessment[10]; or

(3) whether any of the needs meet the eligibility criteria[11].

In deciding how to meet an adult's or carer's needs for care and support under these provisions an authority must involve:

(a) the adult or carer[12];

(b) any carer that the adult has[13];

(c) any person whom the adult or carer asks the authority to involve or, in the case of an adult lacking capacity[14] to ask the authority to do that, any person who appears to the authority to be interested in the adult's welfare[15].

1 As to the meaning of 'registered care provider' see PARA 180 note 3.

2 Ie a regulated activity within the meaning of the Health and Social Care Act 2008 Pt 1 (ss 1–97): Care Act 2014 s 48(1). As to the meaning of 'regulated activity' for these purposes, and the restriction of these provisions to activities carried on in England, see PARA 152 note 2; as to the regulated activities see PARAS 152–157.

3 As to the meaning of 'business failure' see PARA 183. A provider is to be treated as unable to carry on a regulated activity or to carry on or manage an establishment or agency because of business failure if the provider's inability to do so follows business failure: Care and Support (Business Failure) Regulations 2015, SI 2015/301, reg 2(1)(b). An authority becomes subject to the duty under these provisions as soon as it becomes aware of the business failure: Care Act 2014 s 52(1). See also the Care and Support (Cross-border Placements) (Business Failure Duties of Scottish Local Authorities) Regulations 2014, SI 2014/2839 (made under the Care Act 2014 Sch 1 para 1(6), (7)); and PARA 85.

4 As to the meaning of 'local authority' see PARA 1.

5 As to the meaning of 'adult' see PARA 1 note 1.

6 As to the meaning of 'carer' see PARA 33 note 2.

7 Care Act 2014 s 48(1), (2). As to what may and may not be provided to meet needs see ss 8, 21–23; and PARAS 3, 5. Where a local authority considers it necessary to do so for the purpose of carrying out its duty under s 48(2), it may request the registered care provider, or such other person involved in the provider's business as it considers appropriate, to provide it with specified information: s 52(11). A local authority may make a charge for meeting needs under s 48(2) (except in so far as doing so involves the provision of information or advice); and a charge under this provision may cover only the cost that the local authority incurs in meeting the needs to which the charge applies: s 48(5). Section 48(5) does not apply if a 49 (cross-border cases: see note 9) applies (see s 49(3)): s 48(6).

8 'The relevant adult' means:

  (1) in a case involving an adult's needs for care and support, that adult (Care Act 2014 s 48(9)(a)); or

  (2) in a case involving a carer's needs for support, the adult needing care (s 48(9)(b)).

9 Care Act 2014 s 48(3)(a). In connection with a person's residence see PARA 84–87. If the relevant adult is not ordinarily resident in the area of the local authority which is required to meet needs under s 48(2), that authority:

  (1) must, in meeting needs under that provision which were being met under arrangements made by another local authority, co-operate with that authority (in so far as it is not already required to do so by s 6 (see PARA 320)) (s 48(7)(a));

  (2) must, in meeting needs under that provision which were being met under arrangements all or part of the cost of which was paid for by another local authority by means of direct payments, co-operate with that authority (in so far as it is not already required to do so by s 6) (s 48(7)(b)); and

  (3) may recover from the other local authority mentioned in head (1) or (2) above (as the case may be) the cost it incurs in meeting those of the adult's or carer's needs referred to in provision in question (s 48(7)(c)).

  Any dispute between local authorities about the application of s 48 is to be determined under s 40 (see PARAS 96–99) as if it were a dispute of the type mentioned in s 40(1): s 48(8). Provision is also made in connection with cross-border cases: see ss 49–51, 52(3), (8), (13), (14).

10 Care Act 2014 s 48(3)(b). As to needs and carer's assessments see PARAS 64–72; as to financial assessments see PARAS 119–120. Where a local authority is meeting needs under s 48(2), it is not required to carry out a needs assessment, a carer's assessment or a financial assessment: s 48(4).

11 Care Act 2014 s 48(3)(c). As to the eligibility criteria see PARA 10 (adults) and PARA 35 (carers). Where a local authority is meeting needs under s 48(2), it is not required to determine whether any of the needs meet the eligibility criteria: s 48(4).

12 Care Act 2014 s 52(4)(a), (5)(a). In carrying out the duty under s 52(4)(a) or (5)(a) an authority must take all reasonable steps to reach agreement with the adult or carer about how it should meet the needs in question: s 52(6).

13 Care Act 2014 s 52(4)(b).

14 As to having or lacking capacity see PARA 8 note 10.

15 Care Act 2014 s 52(4)(c), (5)(b).

185. Duty to inform local authorities. Where the Care Quality Commission[1] is satisfied that a registered care provider[2] is likely to become unable to carry on the regulated activity in respect of which it is registered[3] because of business failure[4], the Commission must inform the local authorities[5] which it thinks will be required to carry out the duty[6] to meet the needs which that provider is likely to become unable to meet if the provider becomes unable to carry on the regulated activity in question[7]. Where the Commission considers it necessary to do so for the purpose of assisting a local authority to carry out such duty, it may request the provider, or such other person involved in the provider's business as the Commission considers appropriate, to provide it with specified information[8].

1 See PARA 180 note 1.

2 Ie a registered care provider to whom the Care Act 2014 s 55 (financial sustainability assessments: see PARAS 180–181) applies: s 56(1). As to the meaning of 'registered care provider' see PARA 180 note 3.

3 As to the meaning of 'regulated activity' for these purposes, and the restriction of these provisions to activities carried on in England, see PARA 152 note 2; as to the regulated activities see PARAS 152–157.

4 Ie as mentioned in the Care Act 2014 s 48: see PARAS 183–184. The Commission may consult such persons as it considers appropriate on the methods to apply in assessing likelihood for these purposes and, having carried out that consultation, it must publish guidance on the methods it expects to apply in making the assessment: s 56(6). Regulations may make provision as to the circumstances in which the Commission is entitled to be satisfied for these purposes that a registered care provider is likely to become unable to carry on a regulated activity: s 56(5). At the date at which this volume states the law no such regulations had been made.

5 As to the meaning of 'local authority' see PARA 1.

6 Ie the duty under the Care Act 2014 s 48(2) (see PARAS 183–184). Where (as a result of s 56(3) or otherwise) the Commission has information about the provider's business that it considers may assist a local authority in carrying out the duty under s 48(2), the Commission must give the information to the local authority: s 56(4).

7 Care Act 2014 s 56(1), (2).

8 Care Act 2014 s 56(3).

(vi) **Administrative Matters**

186. Statement of purpose. The registered person[1] must give the Care Quality Commission[2] a statement of purpose containing specified information about the provider and senior staff[3]. The registered person must keep under review and, where appropriate, revise the statement of purpose[4]. The registered person must provide written details of any revision to the statement of purpose to the Commission within 28 days of any such revision[5].

A contravention of, or failure to comply with, these provisions is an offence[6].

1 As to the meaning of 'registered person' see PARA 168 note 12. A registered person must, in so far as they are applicable, comply with the requirements specified in the Care Quality Commission (Registration) Regulations 2009, SI 2009/3112, regs 12–20 (see the text and notes 2–6; and PARAS 187–192) in relation to any regulated activity in England in respect of which they are registered: reg 11. As to the meaning of 'regulated activity' for these purposes, and the restriction of these provisions to activities carried on in England, see PARA 152 note 2; as to the regulated activities see PARAS 152–157.

2 As to the Care Quality Commission see PARA 336 et seq.

3 Care Quality Commission (Registration) Regulations 2009, SI 2009/3112, reg 12(1). The information referred to in the text is that listed in Sch 3.

4 Care Quality Commission (Registration) Regulations 2009, SI 2009/3112, reg 12(2).

5 Care Quality Commission (Registration) Regulations 2009, SI 2009/3112, reg 12(3).
6 A contravention of, or failure to comply with, any of the provisions of the Care Quality Commission (Registration) Regulations 2009, SI 2009/3112, regs 12, 14–20, is an offence: reg 25(1). A person guilty of an offence under reg 25(1) is liable, on summary conviction, to a fine not exceeding level 4 on the standard scale: reg 25(2). As to the powers of magistrates' courts to issue fines on summary conviction see SENTENCING vol 92 (2015) PARA 176. The offence under reg 25 is a fixed penalty offence: see the Health and Social Care Act 2008 (Regulated Activities) Regulations 2014, SI 2014/2936, reg 24, Sch 5; and PARA 159 note 4.

187. Financial responsibility and contractual arrangements. The service provider[1] (except where it is an English local authority or a health service body[2]) must take all reasonable steps to carry on the regulated activity[3] in such a manner as to ensure the financial viability of the carrying on of that activity for the purposes of achieving the aims and objectives set out in the statement of purpose[4] and meeting the registration requirements prescribed[5].

Where a service user[6] will be responsible for paying the costs of that user's care or treatment (either in full or partially), the registered person[7] must provide a statement[8] to the service user, or to a person acting on the service user's behalf:

(1) specifying the terms and conditions in respect of the services to be provided to the service user, including as to the amount and method of payment of fees[9]; and

(2) including, where applicable, the form of contract for the provision of services by the service provider[10].

A contravention of, or failure to comply with, these requirements is an offence[11].

1 As to the meaning of 'service provider' see PARA 152 note 6.
2 'Local authority' has the same meaning as in the National Health Service Act 2006 s 2B (see HEALTH SERVICES vol 54 (2017) PARA 17): Care Quality Commission (Registration) Regulations 2009, SI 2009/3112, reg 2 (definition added by SI 2013/235). As to the meaning of 'health service body' see PARA 159.
3 As to the meaning of 'regulated activity' for these purposes, and the restriction of these provisions to activities carried on in England, see PARA 152 note 2; as to the regulated activities see PARAS 152–157.
4 Care Quality Commission (Registration) Regulations 2009, SI 2009/3112, reg 13(1)(a), (2). As to the statement of purpose see PARA 186. The reference in the text to the registration requirements prescribed is pursuant to the Care Quality Commission (Registration) Regulations 2009, SI 2009/3112 and the Health and Social Care Act 2008 (Regulated Activities) Regulations 2014, SI 2014/2936 (see PARA 160 note 4).
5 Care Quality Commission (Registration) Regulations 2009, SI 2009/3112, reg 13(1)(b).
6 'Service user' means a person who receives services provided in the carrying on of a regulated activity: Care Quality Commission (Registration) Regulations 2009, SI 2009/3112, reg 2.
7 As to the meanings of 'registered person' and 'registered manager' see PARA 168 note 12; as to the duty of registered persons to comply with these requirements see PARA 186 note 1.
8 The statement must be in writing (Care Quality Commission (Registration) Regulations 2009, SI 2009/3112, reg 19(2)(a)) and as far as reasonably practicable, provided prior to the commencement of the services to which the statement relates (reg 19(2)(b)).
9 Care Quality Commission (Registration) Regulations 2009, SI 2009/3112, reg 19(1)(a).
10 Care Quality Commission (Registration) Regulations 2009, SI 2009/3112, reg 19(1)(a).
11 See the Care Quality Commission (Registration) Regulations 2009, SI 2009/3112, reg 25; and PARA 186 note 6.

188. Notification of manager's absence. Where the service provider[1] (except where it is a health service body[2]) or the registered manager[3] proposes to be absent from carrying on or managing the regulated activity in England[4] for a continuous period of 28 days or more, the registered person[5] must give notice in writing to the Care Quality Commission[6] of the proposed absence[7]. Where the service provider[8] or registered manager has been absent for a continuous period of 28 days or more, and the Commission has not been given notice of the absence, the registered person must forthwith give notice in writing to the Commission[9]. The registered person must notify the Commission of the return to duty of the service provider or (as the case may be) the registered manager not later than seven working days after the date of that return[10]. A contravention of, or failure to comply with, these requirements is an offence[11].

1   Ie if the provider is the person in day to day charge of the carrying on of the regulated activity (see note 3): Care Quality Commission (Registration) Regulations 2009, SI 2009/3112, reg 14(1)(a), (4)(a). As to the meaning of 'service provider' see PARA 152 note 6.
2   Care Quality Commission (Registration) Regulations 2009, SI 2009/3112, reg 14(7). As to the meaning of 'health service body' see PARA 159. Where the service provider is a health service body and is subject to a registered manager condition pursuant to reg 5 (see PARA 159) or the Health and Social Care Act 2008 s 12(3) or (5) (see PARA 160), the Care Quality Commission (Registration) Regulations 2009, SI 2009/3112, reg 14 has effect in relation to any absence, proposed absence or return to duty of that registered manager: reg 14(8).
3   Care Quality Commission (Registration) Regulations 2009, SI 2009/3112, reg 14(1)(b). As to the meaning of 'registered manager' see PARA 168 note 12.
4   As to the meaning of 'regulated activity' for these purposes, and the restriction of these provisions to activities carried on in England, see PARA 152 note 2; as to the regulated activities see PARAS 152–157.
5   As to the meaning of 'registered person' see PARA 168 note 12; as to the duty of registered persons to comply with these requirements see PARA 186 note 1.
6   As to the Care Quality Commission see PARA 336 et seq. Notifications made pursuant to the Care Quality Commission (Registration) Regulations 2009, SI 2009/3112, reg 14 must be made using the forms provided by the Commission for this purpose: see reg 22A (added by SI 2012/921).
7   Care Quality Commission (Registration) Regulations 2009, SI 2009/3112, reg 14(1). Except in the case of an emergency, such notice must be given no later than 28 days before the proposed absence commences or within such shorter period as may be agreed with the Commission and must contain the following information in relation to the proposed absence:
    (1)   its length or expected length (reg 14(2)(a));
    (2)   the reason for it (reg 14(2)(b));
    (3)   the arrangements which have been made for the management of the carrying on of the regulated activity during the period of absence (reg 14(2)(c));
    (4)   the name, address and qualifications of the person who will be responsible for the management of the carrying on of the regulated activity during that absence (reg 14(2)(d));
    (5)   in the case of the absence of the registered manager, the arrangements that have been, or are proposed to be, made for appointing another person to manage the carrying on of the regulated activity during that absence, including the proposed date by which the appointment is to be made (reg 14(2)(e)).
    Where the absence arises as the result of an emergency, the registered person must give notice of the absence to the Commission within five working days of its occurrence specifying the matters set out in heads (1) to (5) above: reg 14(3). For these purposes, 'working day' means any day other than a Saturday, a Sunday, Christmas Day, Good Friday or a day which is a bank holiday in England and Wales within the meaning of the Banking and Financial Dealings Act 1971 (see FINANCIAL INSTRUMENTS AND TRANSACTIONS vol 49 (2015) PARA 221): Care Quality Commission (Registration) Regulations 2009, SI 2009/3112, reg 14(6). As to the meanings of 'England' and 'Wales' see PARAS 1 note 1, 2 note 4.
8   See note 1.
9   Care Quality Commission (Registration) Regulations 2009, SI 2009/3112, reg 14(4). The notice must specify the matters set out in note 7.
10 Care Quality Commission (Registration) Regulations 2009, SI 2009/3112, reg 14(5).
11 See the Care Quality Commission (Registration) Regulations 2009, SI 2009/3112, reg 25; and PARA 186 note 6.

189. Notification of organisational changes. The registered person[1] must give notice in writing to the Care Quality Commission[2], as soon as it is reasonably practicable to do so, if any of the following events takes place or is proposed to take place:
    (1)   a person other than the registered person carries on or manages the regulated activity in England[3];
    (2)   a registered person ceases to carry on or manage the regulated activity[4];

(3)   the name of a registered person (where that person is an individual) changes[5];

(4)   where the service provider[6] is a partnership, any change in the membership of the partnership[7];

(5)   where the service provider is a body other than a partnership, a change in the name or address of the body[8], a change of director, secretary or other similar officer of the body[9], or a change of nominated individual[10]; and

(6)   relevant insolvency arrangements[11].

A contravention of, or failure to comply with, these requirements is an offence[12].

1   As to the meaning of 'registered person' see PARA 168 note 12; as to the duty of registered persons to comply with these requirements see PARA 186 note 1.
2   As to the Care Quality Commission see PARA 336 et seq. Notifications made pursuant to the Care Quality Commission (Registration) Regulations 2009, SI 2009/3112, reg 15 must be made using the forms provided by the Commission for this purpose: see reg 22A (added by SI 2012/921)
3   Care Quality Commission (Registration) Regulations 2009, SI 2009/3112, reg 15(1)(a). As to the meaning of 'regulated activity' for these purposes, and the restriction of these provisions to activities carried on in England, see PARA 152 note 2; as to the regulated activities see PARAS 152–157.
4   Care Quality Commission (Registration) Regulations 2009, SI 2009/3112, reg 15(1)(b).
5   Care Quality Commission (Registration) Regulations 2009, SI 2009/3112, reg 15(1)(c).
6   As to the meaning of 'service provider' see PARA 152 note 6.
7   Care Quality Commission (Registration) Regulations 2009, SI 2009/3112, reg 15(1)(d).
8   Care Quality Commission (Registration) Regulations 2009, SI 2009/3112, reg 15(1)(e)(i).
9   Care Quality Commission (Registration) Regulations 2009, SI 2009/3112, reg 15(1)(e)(ii). Regulation 15(1)(e)(ii) does not apply where the service provider is a health service body: reg 15(2). As to the meaning of 'health service body' see PARA 159.
10   Care Quality Commission (Registration) Regulations 2009, SI 2009/3112, reg 15(1)(e)(iii). For these purposes, 'nominated individual' means the individual who is employed as a director, manager or secretary of the body and whose name has been notified to the Commission as being the person who is responsible for supervising the management of the carrying on of the regulated activity by that body: reg 15(3).
11   Ie:
      (1)   where the service provider is an individual, the appointment of a trustee in bankruptcy in relation to that individual (Care Quality Commission (Registration) Regulations 2009, SI 2009/3112, reg 15(1)(f)(i)); or
      (2)   where the service provider is a company or partnership, the appointment of a receiver, manager, liquidator or provisional liquidator in relation to that company or partnership (reg 15(1)(f)(ii)).
12   See the Care Quality Commission (Registration) Regulations 2009, SI 2009/3112, reg 25; and PARA 186 note 6.

190. Notification of death or unauthorised absence of service user. The registered person[1] must notify the Care Quality Commission[2] without delay of the death of a service user[3] whilst services were being provided in the carrying on of a regulated activity in England[4] or which has, or may have, resulted from the carrying on of a regulated activity in England[5]. Where the service provider[6] is a health service body[7], a local authority[8] exercising public health functions[9], or a provider of primary medical services[10], the registered person must notify the Commission[11] without delay of the death of a service user where the death:

(1)   either:

      (a)   occurred whilst services were being provided in the carrying on of a regulated activity in England[12];

      (b)   has, or may have, resulted from the provision of services by a health service body or local authority exercising public health functions in the course of carrying on a regulated activity[13]; or

(c) has, or may have, resulted from the provision of primary medical services in the course of carrying on a regulated activity and those services were provided within the period of two weeks prior to the death of the service user[14]; and

(2) cannot, in the reasonable opinion of the registered person, be attributed to the course which that service user's illness or medical condition would naturally have taken if that service user was receiving appropriate care and treatment[15].

The registered person must notify the Commission without delay of the death in any location or unauthorised absence from a relevant location[16] of a service user who is liable to be detained[17] by the registered person under the Mental Health Act 1983[18] or pursuant to an order or direction made under another enactment (which applies in relation to England), where that detention takes effect as if the order or direction were made pursuant to the provisions of the 1983 Act[19]. The registered person must notify the Commission without delay of the return to a relevant location after a period of unauthorised absence of a service user whose absence is required to be notified[20].

A contravention of, or failure to comply with, these requirements is an offence[21].

1 As to the meaning of 'registered person' see PARA 168 note 12; as to the duty of registered persons to comply with these requirements see PARA 186 note 1.
2 As to the Care Quality Commission see PARA 336 et seq. Notifications made pursuant to the Care Quality Commission (Registration) Regulations 2009, SI 2009/3112, reg 16 must be made using the forms provided by the Commission for this purpose: see reg 22A (added by SI 2012/921). Notification of the death of a service user must include a description of the circumstances of the death: Care Quality Commission (Registration) Regulations 2009, SI 2009/3112, reg 16(3). The requirement to notify does not apply where reg 17 (see the text and notes 16–20) applies: reg 16(5).
3 As to the meaning of 'service user' see PARA 187 note 6.
4 Care Quality Commission (Registration) Regulations 2009, SI 2009/3112, reg 16(1)(a). As to the meaning of 'regulated activity' for these purposes, and the restriction of these provisions to activities carried on in England, see PARA 152 note 2; as to the regulated activities see PARAS 152–157.
5 Care Quality Commission (Registration) Regulations 2009, SI 2009/3112, reg 16(1)(b) (substituted by SI 2012/921).
6 As to the meaning of 'service provider' see PARA 152 note 6.
7 As to the meaning of 'health service body' see PARA 159.
8 As to the meaning of 'local authority' see PARA 187 note 2.
9 Ie within the meaning of the National Health Service Act 2006: see s 1H(5); and HEALTH SERVICES vol 54 (2017) PARA 32.
10 For these purposes, 'provider of primary medical services' means a person who provides primary medical services pursuant to one of the following provisions of the National Health Service Act 2006: s 3A (power of clinical commissioning groups as to commissioning certain health services); s 83(2)(b) (primary medical services); s 84 (general medical services contracts); or s 92 (arrangements for the provision of primary medical services): see the Care Quality Commission (Registration) Regulations 2009, SI 2009/3112, reg 16(6) (added by SI 2012/921; amended by SI 2013/235); and HEALTH SERVICES vol 54 (2008) PARAS 37, 295, 296, 307. As to clinical commissioning groups see HEALTH SERVICES vol 54 (2017) PARA 35 et seq.
11 See note 2. The requirement to notify does not apply (ie the Care Quality Commission (Registration) Regulations 2009, SI 2009/3112, reg 16(2) does not apply) if, and to the extent that, the registered person has reported the death to the National Health Service Commissioning Board (see HEALTH SERVICES vol 54 (2017) PARA 32): reg 16(4) (amended by SI 2012/1641). For these purposes, where a person has reported a death to the NHS Commissioning Board Authority, established under the NHS Commissioning Board Authority (Establishment and Constitution) Order 2011, SI 2011/2237, art 2, before the establishment of the National Health Service Commissioning Board ('the Board'), that report is to be treated as having been made to the Board: Care Quality Commission (Registration) Regulations 2009, SI 2009/3112, reg 16(4A) (added by SI 2012/1641).
12 Care Quality Commission (Registration) Regulations 2009, SI 2009/3112, reg 16(2)(a)(i) (reg 16(2) substituted by SI 2012/921).

13 Care Quality Commission (Registration) Regulations 2009, SI 2009/3112, reg 16(2)(a)(ii) (as substituted (see note 12); amended by SI 2013/235).

14 Care Quality Commission (Registration) Regulations 2009, SI 2009/3112, reg 16(2)(a)(iii) (as substituted: see note 12).

15 Care Quality Commission (Registration) Regulations 2009, SI 2009/3112, reg 16(2)(b) (as substituted: see note 12).

16 For these purposes, 'relevant location' means a location used to provide secure psychiatric services under a contract with an English NHS body or the Secretary of State: Care Quality Commission (Registration) Regulations 2009, SI 2009/3112, reg 17(3)(ca) (added by SI 2012/921). As to the Secretary of State see PARA 333.

17 For these purposes, references to persons 'liable to be detained' include a community patient who has been recalled to hospital in accordance with the Mental Health Act 1983 s 17E (see MENTAL HEALTH AND CAPACITY vol 75 (2013) PARA 801), but do not include a patient who has been conditionally discharged and not recalled to hospital in accordance with s 42 (see MENTAL HEALTH AND CAPACITY vol 75 (2013) PARA 876), s 73 (see MENTAL HEALTH AND CAPACITY vol 75 (2013) PARA 969) or s 74 (see MENTAL HEALTH AND CAPACITY vol 75 (2013) PARA 970): Care Quality Commission (Registration) Regulations 2009, SI 2009/3112, reg 17(3)(a). 'Community patient' has the same meaning as in the Mental Health Act 1983 s 17A (see MENTAL HEALTH AND CAPACITY vol 75 (2013) PARA 797): Care Quality Commission (Registration) Regulations 2009, SI 2009/3112, reg 17(3)(b). 'Hospital' means a hospital within the meaning of the Mental Health Act 1983 Pt II (ss 2–34) (see MENTAL HEALTH AND CAPACITY vol 75 (2013) PARA 577): Care Quality Commission (Registration) Regulations 2009, SI 2009/3112, reg 17(3)(c).

18 Care Quality Commission (Registration) Regulations 2009, SI 2009/3112, reg 17(1)(a) (reg 17(1) amended by SI 2012/921). Notifications made pursuant to the Care Quality Commission (Registration) Regulations 2009, SI 2009/3112, reg 17 must be made using the forms provided by the Commission for this purpose: see reg 22A (as added: see note 2). Notification of the death of a service user must include a description of the circumstances of the death: Care Quality Commission (Registration) Regulations 2009, SI 2009/3112, reg 17(2).

19 Care Quality Commission (Registration) Regulations 2009, SI 2009/3112, reg 17(1)(b) (as amended: see note 18). See note 18. As to the meaning of 'England' see PARA 1 note 1.

20 Care Quality Commission (Registration) Regulations 2009, SI 2009/3112, reg 17(2A) (added by SI 2012/921).

21 See the Care Quality Commission (Registration) Regulations 2009, SI 2009/3112, reg 25; and PARA 186 note 6.

191. Notification of injury, abuse and criminal incidents. The registered person[1] must notify the Care Quality Commission[2] without delay of certain injury, abuse and criminal incidents[3] which occur whilst services are being provided in the carrying on of a regulated activity in England, or as a consequence of the carrying on of a regulated activity[4]. Where the service provider[5] is a health service body[6], this requirement does not apply if, and to the extent that, the registered person has reported the incident to the National Health Service Commissioning Board[7].

The registered person must also notify the Commission of the following events, which occur whilst services are being provided in the carrying on of a regulated activity, or as a consequence of the carrying on of a regulated activity:

(1)   any request to a supervisory body[8] made pursuant to the Mental Capacity Act 2005[9] by the registered person for a standard authorisation[10]; and

(2)   any application made to a court in relation to depriving a service user of that service user's liberty[11].

A contravention of, or failure to comply with, these requirements is an offence[12].

1 As to the meaning of 'registered person' see PARA 168 note 12; as to the duty of registered persons to comply with these requirements see PARA 186 note 1.

2 As to the Care Quality Commission see PARA 336 et seq.

3 Ie:

    (1)   any injury to a service user which, in the reasonable opinion of a health care professional, has resulted in an impairment of the sensory, motor or intellectual

functions of the service user which is not likely to be temporary (Care Quality Commission (Registration) Regulations 2009, SI 2009/3112, reg 18(2)(a)(i)), changes to the structure of a service user's body (reg 18(2)(a)(ii)), the service user experiencing prolonged pain or prolonged psychological harm (reg 18(2)(a)(iii)) or the shortening of the life expectancy of the service user (reg 18(2)(a)(iv));

(2) any injury to a service user which, in the reasonable opinion of a health care professional, requires treatment by that, or another, health care professional in order to prevent the death of the service user (reg 18(2)(b)(i)) or an injury to the service user which, if left untreated, would lead to one or more of the outcomes mentioned in head (1) above (reg 18(2)(b)(ii));

(3) any abuse or allegation of abuse in relation to a service user (reg 18(2)(e));

(4) (except where the service provider is an English NHS body), any incident which is reported to, or investigated by, the police (reg 18(2)(f), (3));

(5) any event which prevents, or appears to the service provider to be likely to threaten to prevent, the service provider's ability to continue to carry on the regulated activity safely, or in accordance with the registration requirements, including an insufficient number of suitably qualified, skilled and experienced persons being employed for the purposes of carrying on the regulated activity in England (reg 18(2)(g)(i)), an interruption in the supply to premises owned or used by the service provider for the purposes of carrying on the regulated activity of electricity, gas, water or sewerage where that interruption has lasted for longer than a continuous period of 24 hours (reg 18(2)(g)(ii)), physical damage to premises owned or used by the service provider for the purposes of carrying on the regulated activity which has, or is likely to have, a detrimental effect on the treatment or care provided to service users (reg 18(2)(g)(iii)), and the failure, or malfunctioning, of fire alarms or other safety devices in premises owned or used by the service provider for the purposes of carrying on the regulated activity where that failure or malfunctioning has lasted for longer than a continuous period of 24 hours (reg 18(2)(g)(iv));

(6) any placement of a service user under the age of 18 in a psychiatric unit whose services are intended for persons over that age where that placement has lasted for longer than a continuous period of 48 hours (reg 18(2)(h) (added by SI 2012/921)).

As to the meaning of 'service user' see PARA 187 note 6. 'Health care professional' means a person who is registered as a member of any profession to which the Health Act 1999 s 60(2) (see MEDICAL PROFESSIONS vol 74 (2011) PARA 3) applies: Care Quality Commission (Registration) Regulations 2009, SI 2009/3112, reg 18(5)(c). 'Abuse', in relation to a service user, means sexual abuse, physical or psychological ill-treatment, theft, misuse or misappropriation of money or property, or neglect and acts of omission which cause harm or place at risk of harm: reg 18(5)(b). As to the meaning of 'regulated activity' for these purposes, and the restriction of these provisions to activities carried on in England, see PARA 152 note 2; as to the regulated activities see PARAS 152–157. 'Registration requirements' means any requirements or conditions imposed on the registered person by or under the Health and Social Care Act 2008 Pt 1 Ch 2 (ss 8–44): Care Quality Commission (Registration) Regulations 2009, SI 2009/3112, reg 18(5)(d). As to the meaning of 'English NHS body' see PARA 158 note 6.

For the purposes of reg 18(2)(a) (see head (1) above) 'prolonged pain' and 'prolonged psychological harm' means pain or harm which a service user has experienced, or is likely to experience, for a continuous period of at least 28 days; and a sensory, motor or intellectual impairment is not temporary if such an impairment has lasted, or is likely to last, for a continuous period of at least 28 days: reg 18(5)(g).

4 Care Quality Commission (Registration) Regulations 2009, SI 2009/3112, reg 18(1). Notifications made pursuant to reg 18 must be made using the forms provided by the Commission for this purpose: see reg 22A (added by SI 2012/921).

5 As to the meaning of 'service provider' see PARA 152 note 6.

6 As to the meaning of 'health service body' see PARA 159.

7 Care Quality Commission (Registration) Regulations 2009, SI 2009/3112, reg 18(4) (amended by SI 2012/1641). For these purposes, where a person has reported an incident to the NHS Commissioning Board Authority, established under the NHS Commissioning Board Authority (Establishment and Constitution) Order 2011, SI 2011/2237, art 2, before the establishment of the National Health Service Commissioning Board ('the Board'), that report is to be treated as having been made to the Board: Care Quality Commission (Registration) Regulations 2009, SI 2009/3112, reg 18(4ZA) (added by SI 2012/1641). As to the National Health Service Commissioning Board see HEALTH SERVICES vol 54 (2017) PARA 32.

8 'Supervisory body' has the meaning given in the Mental Capacity Act 2005 Sch A1 para 180 (in relation to a hospital in England) (see MENTAL HEALTH AND CAPACITY vol 75 (2013)

PARA 664) or Sch A1 para 182 (in relation to a care home) (see MENTAL HEALTH AND CAPACITY vol 75 (2013) PARA 664): Care Quality Commission (Registration) Regulations 2009, SI 2009/3112, reg 18(5)(f). As to the meaning of 'England' see PARA 1 note 1.

9 Ie made pursuant to the Mental Capacity Act 2005 Sch A1 Pt 4: see MENTAL HEALTH AND CAPACITY vol 75 (2013) PARA 661 et seq.

10 Care Quality Commission (Registration) Regulations 2009, SI 2009/3112, reg 18(4A)(a) (reg 18(4A), (4B) added by SI 2012/921). 'Standard authorisation' has the meaning given under the Mental Capacity Act 2005 Sch A1 Pt 4 (see MENTAL HEALTH AND CAPACITY vol 75 (2013) PARA 663): Care Quality Commission (Registration) Regulations 2009, SI 2009/3112, reg 18(5)(e). Any notification required to be given in respect of an event in reg 18(4A) must be given once the outcome of the request or application is known or, if the request or application is withdrawn, at the point of withdrawal and must include a statement as to the date and nature of the request or application (reg 18(4B)(a) (as so added)), whether the request or application was preceded by the use of an urgent authorisation, within the meaning of the Mental Capacity Act 2005 Sch A1 para 9 (see MENTAL HEALTH AND CAPACITY vol 75 (2013) PARA 713) (Care Quality Commission (Registration) Regulations 2009, SI 2009/3112, reg 18(4B)(b) (as so added)), the outcome of the request or application or reason for its withdrawal (reg 18(4B)(c) (as so added)) and the date of the outcome or withdrawal (reg 18(4B)(d) (as so added)).

11 Care Quality Commission (Registration) Regulations 2009, SI 2009/3112, reg 18(4A)(b) (as added: see note 10). See note 10. The reference in the text is to depriving a service user of liberty pursuant to the Mental Capacity Act 2005 s 16(2)(a): see MENTAL HEALTH AND CAPACITY vol 75 (2013) PARA 724.

12 See the Care Quality Commission (Registration) Regulations 2009, SI 2009/3112, reg 25; and PARA 186 note 6.

192. Termination of pregnancies. The registered person[1] must ensure that, unless two certificates of opinion[2] have been received in respect of the service user[3], no termination of pregnancy is carried out[4] and no fee is demanded or accepted from a service user[5]. The registered person must ensure that no termination of pregnancy is undertaken after the twentieth week of gestation, unless the service user is treated by persons who are suitably qualified, skilled and experienced in the late termination of pregnancy[6] and appropriate procedures are in place to deal with any medical emergency which occurs during or as a result of the termination[7]. The registered person must ensure that no termination of a pregnancy is undertaken after the twenty-fourth week of gestation[8].

The registered person must ensure that a register of service users undergoing a termination of pregnancy is maintained, which is completed in respect of each service user at the time the termination is undertaken[9] and retained for a period of not less than three years beginning on the date of the last entry[10]. The registered person must also ensure that a record is maintained of the total numbers of terminations of pregnancies undertaken[11].

The registered person must ensure that notice in writing is sent to the Chief Medical Officer of the Department of Health of each termination of pregnancy[12].

If the registered person receives information concerning the death of a service user who has undergone termination of a pregnancy during the period of 12 months ending on the date on which the information is received[13], and has reason to believe that the service user's death may be associated with the termination, the registered person must give notice in writing to the Care Quality Commission[14] of that information, within the period of 14 days beginning on the day on which the information is received[15].

The registered person must prepare and implement appropriate procedures to ensure that foetal tissue is treated with respect[16].

A contravention of, or failure to comply with, these requirements is an offence[17].

1 The Care Quality Commission (Registration) Regulations 2009, SI 2009/3112, reg 20 applies to a registered person who carries on or manages a regulated activity in England consisting of the termination of pregnancies (reg 20(1)(a)) and is not an English NHS body (reg 20(1)(b)). The

registered person must ensure that a certificate of opinion in respect of a service user undergoing termination of a pregnancy is completed and included with the service user's medical record: reg 20(3). As to the meaning of 'registered person' see PARA 168 note 12; as to the duty of registered persons to comply with these requirements see PARA 186 note 1. As to the meaning of 'regulated activity' for these purposes, and the restriction of these provisions to activities carried on in England, see PARA 152 note 2; as to the regulated activities see PARAS 152–157. As to the meaning of 'English NHS body' see PARA 158 note 6.

2 For these purposes 'certificate of opinion' means a certificate required by regulations made under the Abortion Act 1967 s 2(1) (see MEDICAL PROFESSIONS vol 74 (2011) PARA 33): Care Quality Commission (Registration) Regulations 2009, SI 2009/3112, reg 20(12).

3 As to the meaning of 'service user' see PARA 187 note 6.

4 Care Quality Commission (Registration) Regulations 2009, SI 2009/3112, reg 20(2)(a).

5 Care Quality Commission (Registration) Regulations 2009, SI 2009/3112, reg 20(2)(b).

6 Care Quality Commission (Registration) Regulations 2009, SI 2009/3112, reg 20(4)(a).

7 Care Quality Commission (Registration) Regulations 2009, SI 2009/3112, reg 20(4)(b).

8 Care Quality Commission (Registration) Regulations 2009, SI 2009/3112, reg 20(5).

9 Care Quality Commission (Registration) Regulations 2009, SI 2009/3112, reg 20(6)(a).

10 Care Quality Commission (Registration) Regulations 2009, SI 2009/3112, reg 20(6)(b).

11 Care Quality Commission (Registration) Regulations 2009, SI 2009/3112, reg 20(7). The registered person must ensure that the record referred to in reg 20(7) (which may be in paper or electronic form) is accurate, kept securely and can be located promptly when required, retained for an appropriate period of time, and securely destroyed when it is appropriate to do so: reg 20(8).

12 Care Quality Commission (Registration) Regulations 2009, SI 2009/3112, reg 20(9).

13 Care Quality Commission (Registration) Regulations 2009, SI 2009/3112, reg 20(10)(a).

14 As to the Care Quality Commission see PARA 336 et seq.

15 Care Quality Commission (Registration) Regulations 2009, SI 2009/3112, reg 20(10)(b).

16 Care Quality Commission (Registration) Regulations 2009, SI 2009/3112, reg 20(11).

17 See the Care Quality Commission (Registration) Regulations 2009, SI 2009/3112, reg 25; and PARA 186 note 6.

193.   Death of service provider. Where the service provider[1] is a partnership and a partner dies, the surviving partner must without delay notify the Care Quality Commission[2] of the death in writing[3]. Where the service provider is an individual and that individual dies, that individual's personal representative must notify the Commission in writing without delay of the death[4] and within 28 days of the date of death of their intentions regarding the future carrying on of the regulated activity in England[5]. The personal representative of the deceased service provider may carry on the regulated activity without being registered in respect of it for a period not exceeding 28 days[6].

1 As to the meaning of 'service provider' see PARA 152 note 6.

2 As to the Care Quality Commission see PARA 336 et seq.

3 Care Quality Commission (Registration) Regulations 2009, SI 2009/3112, reg 21(1) (made under the Health and Social Care Act 2008 s 42). Notifications under these provisions must be made using the forms provided by the Commission for this purpose: Care Quality Commission (Registration) Regulations 2009, SI 2009/3112, reg 22A (added by SI 2012/921).

4 Care Quality Commission (Registration) Regulations 2009, SI 2009/3112, reg 21(2)(a).

5 Care Quality Commission (Registration) Regulations 2009, SI 2009/3112, reg 21(2)(b). As to the meaning of 'regulated activity' for these purposes, and the restriction of these provisions to activities carried on in England, see PARA 152 note 2; as to the regulated activities see PARAS 152–157.

6 Care Quality Commission (Registration) Regulations 2009, SI 2009/3112, reg 21(3)(a). The Commission may extend this period by such further period, not exceeding one year, as it determines, and must notify any such determination to the personal representative in writing: reg 21(4). The personal representative of the deceased service provider may carry on the regulated activity without being registered for such period as may be so determined: reg 21(3)(b). The personal representative of the deceased service provider must appoint a person to take full-time day to day charge of the carrying on of the regulated activity during any period in which, in accordance with reg 21(3), that person carries on the regulated activity without being registered in respect of it: reg 21(5).

194. Appointment of liquidators. Where a company or partnership is registered[1] as a service provider[2] in respect of a regulated activity in England[3] it must[4]:

(1) notify the Care Quality Commission[5] of that person's appointment and the reasons for the appointment[6];

(2) appoint a manager to manage the regulated activity in any cases where there is not a registered manager[7]; and

(3) before the end of the period of 28 days beginning with the date of the person's appointment, notify the Commission of the person's intentions regarding the future carrying on of the regulated activity[8].

1 Ie under the Health and Social Care Act 2008 Pt 1 Ch 2 (ss 8–44). Such a company or partnership is referred to in these provisions as 'the relevant company'.
2 As to the meaning of 'service provider' see PARA 152 note 6.
3 Health and Social Care Act 2008 s 41(3). As to the meaning of 'regulated activity' for these purposes, and the restriction of these provisions to activities carried on in England, see PARA 152 note 2; as to the regulated activities see PARAS 152–157.
4 These requirements must be carried out by any person appointed as a receiver or manager of the property of the relevant company, the liquidator or provisional liquidator of a relevant company or the trustee in bankruptcy of a relevant individual: Health and Social Care Act 2008 s 41(2); Care Quality Commission (Registration) Regulations 2009, SI 2009/3112, reg 22(2) (made under the Health and Social Care Act 2008 s 41(1)). 'Relevant individual' means an individual who is registered under Pt 1 Ch 2 as a service provider in respect of a regulated activity: s 41(3).
5 As to the Care Quality Commission see PARA 336 et seq. Notifications must be made using the forms provided by the Commission for this purpose: Care Quality Commission (Registration) Regulations 2009, SI 2009/3112, reg 22A (added by SI 2012/921).
6 Care Quality Commission (Registration) Regulations 2009, SI 2009/3112, reg 22(1)(a).
7 Care Quality Commission (Registration) Regulations 2009, SI 2009/3112, reg 22(1)(b). As to the meaning of 'registered manager' see PARA 168 note 12.
8 Care Quality Commission (Registration) Regulations 2009, SI 2009/3112, reg 22(1)(c).

(vii) Registers, Codes of Practice and Guidance

195. Keeping of registers. The Care Quality Commission[1] must establish and maintain a register containing such information as appears to the Commission to be necessary to keep the public informed about the identity of registered persons[2] and their carrying on of regulated activities in England[3]. The Commission must secure that copies of any register are available at its offices for inspection at all reasonable times by any person[4]. Any person who asks the Commission for a copy of, or an extract from, a register is entitled to have one[5].

1 As to the Care Quality Commission see PARA 336 et seq.
2 As to the meaning of 'registered person' see PARA 168 note 12.
3 Care Quality Commission (Registration) Regulations 2009, SI 2009/3112, reg 3 (made under the Health and Social Care Act 2008 s 16). As to the meaning of 'regulated activity' for these purposes, and the restriction of these provisions to activities carried on in England, see PARA 152 note 2; as to the regulated activities see PARAS 152–157.
4 Health and Social Care Act 2008 s 38(1). Regulations may provide that s 38(1), (2) do not apply in such circumstances as may be prescribed (s 38(3)(a)) or to such parts of a register as may be prescribed (s 38(3)(b)). At the date at which this volume states the law no such regulations had been made.
5 Health and Social Care Act 2008 s 38(2). See note 4. A fee determined by the Commission is payable for the copy or extract except in prescribed circumstances (s 38(4)(a)) or in any case where the Commission considers it appropriate to provide the copy or extract free of charge (s 38(4)(b)). At the date at which this volume states the law no fee had been prescribed.

196. Code of practice and guidance relating to compliance with statutory requirements. The Secretary of State[1] may issue a code of practice, and the Care Quality Commission[2] may issue guidance, about compliance with statutory requirements[3] relating to the registration of health and social care providers in

England[4]. The Secretary of State's Code of Practice may be concerned only with such of those requirements as relate to the prevention or control of health care associated infections[5]; the Commission's guidance may be concerned only with requirements other than those relating to the prevention or control of such infections[6]. The Commission's guidance may, if the Commission thinks fit, also relate to compliance with the requirements of any other enactments[7].

The Secretary of State must keep the code under review and may from time to time revise the whole or any part of the code; and he may issue a revised code[8]. The Commission may from time to time revise guidance issued by it under these provisions and issue the revised guidance[9].

Any such code or guidance are to be taken into account:

(1)   in the making of any relevant decision[10] by the Care Quality Commission[11];

(2)   in any proceedings[12] for the making of an order for cancellation of registration[13];

(3)   in any proceedings on an appeal against such a decision or order[14];

(4)   in any proceedings for an offence of failing to comply with conditions[15] or for a statutory[16] offence[17].

A code of practice or guidance is also admissible in evidence in other criminal or civil proceedings[18]. A failure to observe any provision of a code of practice or guidance does not of itself make a person liable to any criminal or civil proceedings[19].

1   As to the Secretary of State see PARA 333.
2   As to the Care Quality Commission see PARA 336 et seq.
3   Ie any requirements of the Care Quality Commission (Registration) Regulations 2009, SI 2009/3112 or the Health and Social Care Act 2008 (Regulated Activities) Regulations 2014, SI 2014/2936 (see PARA 159 note 4). Where the Secretary of State or the Commission proposes to issue a code of practice or guidance under these provisions, or proposes to issue a revised code or revised guidance which in his or its opinion would result in a substantial change in the code or the guidance, he or it must prepare a draft of the code or guidance and consult such persons as he or it considers appropriate about the draft: Health and Social Care Act 2008 ss 22(1), (2), 24(1), (2). Where, following such consultation, the Secretary of State or the Commission issues the code or revised code or the guidance or revised guidance (whether in the form of the draft or with such modifications as the Secretary of State or the Commission thinks fit), it comes into force at the time when it is issued by him or it: ss 22(3), 24(3).
4   Health and Social Care Act 2008 ss 21(1), 23(1). The code and guidance may:
       (1)   operate by reference to provisions of other documents specified in it (whether published by the Secretary of State or, as the case may be, the Commission, or otherwise) (ss 21(2)(a), 23(3)(a));
       (2)   provide for any reference in it to such a document to take effect as a reference to that document as revised from time to time (ss 21(2)(b), 23(3)(b)); and
       (3)   make different provision for different cases or circumstances (ss 21(2)(c), 23(3)(c)).
       Where:
       (a)   any document by reference to whose provisions the code or guidance operates as mentioned in s 21(2)(a), (b) or s 23(3)(a), (b) is a document published by the Secretary of State in connection with his functions relating to health or social care or, as the case may be, published by the Commission (ss 22(4)(a), 24(4)(a));
       (b)   the Secretary of State or the Commission proposes to revise the document (ss 22(4)(b), 24(4)(b)); and
       (c)   in the opinion of the Secretary of State or the Commission, the revision would result in a substantial change in the code or the guidance (ss 22(4)(c), 24(4)(c)),
       the Secretary of State or, as the case may be, the Commission must, before revising the document, consult such persons as he or it considers appropriate about the change (ss 22(4), 24(4)).
       Where:
       (i)   any document by reference to whose provisions the code or guidance operates as mentioned in s 21(2)(a), (b) or s 23(3)(a), (b) is not one to which s 22(4)(a) or s 24(4)(a) applies (ss 22(5)(a), 24(5)(a));
       (ii)   the document is revised (ss 22(5)(b), 24(5)(b)); and

(iii)　in the opinion of the Secretary of State or, as the case may be, the Commission, the revision results in a substantial change in the code or the guidance (ss 22(5)(c), 24(5)(c)), the Secretary of State or, as the case may be, the Commission, must consult such persons as he or it considers appropriate about whether the code or guidance should be revised in connection with the change (ss 22(5), 24(5)). As to the meanings of 'health care' and 'social care' see PARA 152 note 2.

5　As to the meaning of 'health care associated infection' see PARA 173 note 14.
6　Health and Social Care Act 2008 ss 21(1), 23(1).
7　Health and Social Care Act 2008 s 23(2).
8　Health and Social Care Act 2008 s 21(3). See notes 3, 4.
9　Health and Social Care Act 2008 s 23(4). See notes 3, 4.
10　Ie any decision by the Commission under the Health and Social Care Act 2008 Pt 1 Ch 2: s 25(1)(a).
11　Health and Social Care Act 2008 s 25(1)(a).
12　Ie under the Health and Social Care Act 2008 s 30 (see PARA 162).
13　Health and Social Care Act 2008 s 25(1)(b).
14　Health and Social Care Act 2008 s 25(1)(c). As to appeals see PARA 160 note 9.
15　Ie under the Health and Social Care Act 2008 s 33: see PARA 161.
16　Ie an offence under the Care Quality Commission (Registration) Regulations 2009, SI 2009/3112 or the Health and Social Care Act 2008 (Regulated Activities) Regulations 2014, SI 2014/2936 (see PARA 159 note 4).
17　Health and Social Care Act 2008 s 25(1)(d).
18　Health and Social Care Act 2008 s 25(2).
19　Health and Social Care Act 2008 s 25(3).

197. Guidance relating to functions of Care Quality Commission. The Care Quality Commission[1] must issue guidance about how it will exercise its functions in regard to:

(1)　the variation, removal or imposition of a condition in relation to registration as a service provider or manager[2];
(2)　cancellation or suspension of registration[3];
(3)　the giving of warning notices[4];
(4)　the giving of penalty notices[5]; and
(5)　the publication of information[6].

The guidance may also include guidance, in relation to any Part 1 offence[7], as to the circumstances in which the Commission is likely to take criminal proceedings for the offence[8]. The Commission may from time to time revise guidance published by it under these provisions and issue the revised guidance[9]. Before issuing any guidance or revised guidance, the Commission must consult such persons as may be prescribed[10] and such other persons as the Commission considers appropriate[11].

1　As to the Care Quality Commission see PARA 336 et seq.
2　Ie its functions under the Health and Social Care Act 2008 s 12(5) (service providers) and s 15(5) (managers) (see PARA 161): s 88(1)(a), (b).
3　Ie its functions under the Health and Social Care Act 2008 s 17 (cancellation: see PARA 163) and s 18 (registration: see PARA 164): s 88(1)(c).
4　Ie its functions under the Health and Social Care Act 2008 s 29 (see PARA 165) and s 29A (see HEALTH SERVICES vol 54A (2017) PARA 423): s 88(1)(d) (amended by the Care Act 2014 s 82(5)).
5　Ie its functions under the Health and Social Care Act 2008 s 86 (see PARA 159 note 4): s 88(1)(e).
6　Ie its functions under the Health and Social Care Act 2008 s 89 (see PARA 158 note 6): s 88(1)(f).
7　As to the meaning of 'Part 1 offence' see PARA 158 note 6.
8　Health and Social Care Act 2008 s 88(2).
9　Health and Social Care Act 2008 s 88(3).
10　Health and Social Care Act 2008 s 88(4)(a). At the date at which this volume states the law no persons had been prescribed for this purpose.
11　Health and Social Care Act 2008 s 88(4)(b).

(2) WALES

(i) Regulation of Social Workers

198. Meanings of 'social care worker' and 'social worker'. 'Social worker' means[1] a person who engages in relevant social work[2], that is, social work which is required in connection with any health, education or social services provided in Wales[3]. 'Social care worker' means[4] a social worker[5], a person who manages at a place at or from which a regulated service is provided[6], and a person who, either in the course of his employment with a service provider[7] or under a contract for services, provides care and support to any person in Wales in connection with a regulated service provided by the service provider that employs or contracts with him[8]. Additional persons and categories of persons are treated as 'social care workers' for specified purposes[9].

1   Ie for the purposes of the Regulation and Inspection of Social Care (Wales) Act 2016 Pts 3–8 (ss 67–175).
2   Regulation and Inspection of Social Care (Wales) Act 2016 s 79(1)(a), (5).
3   Regulation and Inspection of Social Care (Wales) Act 2016 s 79(4).
4   See note 1. The Welsh Ministers may by regulations except persons of a specified description from the definition of 'social care worker': Regulation and Inspection of Social Care (Wales) Act 2016 s 79(2)(a). At the date at which this volume states the law no such regulations had been made. As to the Welsh Ministers see PARA 395.
5   Regulation and Inspection of Social Care (Wales) Act 2016 s 79(1)(a).
6   Regulation and Inspection of Social Care (Wales) Act 2016 s 79(1)(b). Such a person is referred to in Pts 3–8 as a 'social care manager': s 79(1)(b) (amended by SI 2016/1030).
7   As to the meaning of 'service provider' see PARA 203 note 4.
8   Regulation and Inspection of Social Care (Wales) Act 2016 s 79(1)(c), (d). Provision is made in connection with codes of practice and continuing professional development for social care workers: see ss 112, 113 (s 113 amended by SI 2016/1030).
9   Persons of any of the following descriptions, and categories of person falling within any of these descriptions, are to be treated as social care workers for the purposes only of the functions of Social Care Wales under the Regulation and Inspection of Social Care (Wales) Act 2016 s 68(2), s 112, s 114 and s 116:
     (1)   a person designated under Pt 1 Ch 2 (ss 5–31) (registration etc of service providers: see PARA 203 et seq) as a responsible individual in respect of a place at, from or in relation to which a regulated service is provided (s 79(2)(b), (3)(a); Social Care Wales (Extension of Meaning of 'Social Care Worker') Regulations 2016, SI 2016/1251);
     (2)   a person engaged in work for the purposes of a local authority's social services functions (within the meaning of the Social Services and Well-being (Wales) Act 2014: see Sch 2; and PARA 373), or in the provision of services similar to services which may or must be provided by local authorities in Wales in the exercise of those functions (Regulation and Inspection of Social Care (Wales) Act 2016 s 79(3)(b));
     (3)   a person providing care and support which would, but for Sch 1 para 8(2)(a) (see PARA 210), constitute the provision of a domiciliary support service (s 79(3)(c));
     (4)   a person registered under the Children and Families (Wales) Measure 2010 Pt 2 (ss 19–56) (see CHILDREN AND YOUNG PERSONS vol 10 (2017) PARA 1242 et seq) as a child minder or a provider of day care for children (Regulation and Inspection of Social Care (Wales) Act 2016 s 79(3)(d));
     (5)   a person who manages, or is employed in, an undertaking carrying on an employment business (within the meaning of the Employment Agencies Act 1973 s 13: see TRADE AND INDUSTRY vol 97 (2015) PARA 974) which supplies persons to provide care and support to any person in Wales (Regulation and Inspection of Social Care (Wales) Act 2016 s 79(3)(e));
     (6)   a person who manages, or is employed in, an undertaking carrying on an employment agency (within the meaning of the Employment Agencies Act 1973 s 13: see TRADE AND INDUSTRY vol 97 (2015) PARA 974) which provides services for the purpose of supplying persons to provide care and support to any person in Wales (Regulation and Inspection of Social Care (Wales) Act 2016 s 79(3)(f));
     (7)   a person undertaking a course approved by Social Care Wales under s 114 (courses for persons who are or wish to become social care workers) (s 79(3)(g));

(8)   an inspector carrying out inspections of regulated services on behalf of the Welsh Ministers under Pt 1 Ch 3 (ss 32–37) (information and inspections see PARAS 224–227) (s 79(3)(h));

(9)   an inspector carrying out inspections under the Social Services and Well-being (Wales) Act 2014 s 161 (inspections in connection with local authority social services functions: see PARA 407) (Regulation and Inspection of Social Care (Wales) Act 2016 s 79(3)(i));

(10)   a person employed in connection with the discharge of the functions of the Welsh Ministers under the Children Act 1989 s 80 (inspection of children's homes etc: see CHILDREN AND YOUNG PERSONS vol 9 (2017) PARA 171) (Regulation and Inspection of Social Care (Wales) Act 2016 s 79(3)(j));

(11)   staff of the Welsh Government who inspect premises under the Children Act 1989 s 87 (welfare of children accommodated in independent schools and colleges: see CHILDREN AND YOUNG PERSONS vol 10 (2017) PARA 1276) or the Children and Families (Wales) Measure 2010 s 40 (inspection of child minding and day care in Wales: see CHILDREN AND YOUNG PERSONS vol 10 (2017) PARA 1257) (Regulation and Inspection of Social Care (Wales) Act 2016 s 79(3)(k)); and

(12)   a person who manages staff mentioned in head (10) or (11) above (s 79(3)(l)).

As to the meaning of 'regulated service' see PARA 203. As to the meaning of 'responsible individual' see PARA 212. As to the meanings of 'local authority' and 'Wales' see PARA 2. As to the meanings of 'care' and 'support' see PARA 2 note 1. As to Social Care Wales see PARAS 412–414.

199. Offence of claiming to be a social worker. It is an offence for a person in Wales[1] who is not registered in a relevant register[2] as a social worker[3] to, with intent to deceive another:

(1)   take or use the title of social worker[4];

(2)   take or use any title or description implying registration as a social worker[5]; or

(3)   pretend to be a social worker in any other way[6].

It is also an offence for a person in Wales who is not registered in a relevant register as a social care worker[7] of such other description as may be prescribed[8] to, with intent to deceive another:

(a)   take or use the title of that description of social care worker[9];

(b)   take or use any title or description implying registration as such a social care worker[10]; or

(c)   pretend to be such a social care worker in any other way[11].

A person guilty of such an offence is liable on summary conviction to a fine[12].

1   As to the meaning of 'Wales' see PARA 2 note 4.
2   For these purposes a register is a 'relevant register' if it is a register kept by Social Care Wales (see PARAS 412–414), the Health and Care Professions Council (see MEDICAL PROFESSIONS vol 74 (2011) PARA 928), the Scottish Social Services Council or the Northern Ireland Social Care Council: Regulation and Inspection of Social Care (Wales) Act 2016 s 111(4). The Welsh Ministers may amend s 111(4) by regulations (s 111(5): at the date at which this volume states the law no such regulations had been made. As to Social Care Wales see PARAS 412–414.
3   As to the meaning of 'social worker' see PARA 198.
4   Regulation and Inspection of Social Care (Wales) Act 2016 s 111(1)(a).
5   Regulation and Inspection of Social Care (Wales) Act 2016 s 111(1)(b).
6   Regulation and Inspection of Social Care (Wales) Act 2016 s 111(1)(c).
7   As to the meaning of 'social care worker' see PARA 198.
8   At the date at which this volume states the law nothing had been prescribed for this purpose.
9   Regulation and Inspection of Social Care (Wales) Act 2016 s 111(2)(a).
10 Regulation and Inspection of Social Care (Wales) Act 2016 s 111(2)(b).
11 Regulation and Inspection of Social Care (Wales) Act 2016 s 111(2)(c).
12 Regulation and Inspection of Social Care (Wales) Act 2016 s 111(3). As to the powers of magistrates' courts to issue fines on summary conviction see SENTENCING vol 92 (2015) PARA 176.

200. Fitness to practise. A person's fitness to practise may be regarded as impaired[1] by reason only of one or more of the following grounds:

(1)   deficient performance as a social care worker[2];

(2)   serious misconduct (whether as a social care worker or otherwise)[3];

(3)   the inclusion of the person in a barred list[4];

(4)   a determination by a relevant body[5] to the effect that the person's fitness to practise is impaired[6];

(5)   adverse physical or mental health[7];

(6)   a conviction or caution in the United Kingdom for a criminal offence, or a conviction or caution elsewhere for an offence which, if committed in England and Wales[8], would constitute a criminal offence[9].

A person's fitness to practise may be regarded as impaired by reason of matters arising or incidents occurring:

(a)   whether inside or outside of Wales[10];

(b)   whether or not the person was registered on the register at the time[11];

(c)   whether before or after the commencement of these provisions[12].

Allegations of impaired fitness to practice are considered and investigated through procedures governed by Social Care Wales[13].

1   Ie for the purposes of the Regulation and Inspection of Social Care (Wales) Act 2016 Pt 4 (ss 79–111) and Pt 6 (ss 117–164). The Welsh Ministers may by regulations amend s 117(1) for the purpose of adding, modifying or removing a ground of impairment: s 117(6). At the date at which this volume states the law no such regulations had been made. There is provision for the collection of information relating to a person's fitness to practice: see s 107.

2   Regulation and Inspection of Social Care (Wales) Act 2016 s 117(1)(a). As to the meaning of 'social care worker' see PARA 198. For this purpose 'deficient performance as a social care worker' may include:
    (1)   an instance of negligence (s 117(2)(a));
    (2)   a breach of an undertaking agreed with Social Care Wales under the Regulation and Inspection of Social Care (Wales) Act 2016 (s 117(2)(b)) and
    (3)   a breach of an undertaking agreed with a fitness to practice panel under the Regulation and Inspection of Social Care (Wales) Act 2016 (s 117(2)(b)).
    As to Social Care Wales see PARAS 412–414.

3   Regulation and Inspection of Social Care (Wales) Act 2016 s 117(1)(b).

4   Regulation and Inspection of Social Care (Wales) Act 2016 s 117(1)(c). In this context 'barred list' means a list maintained under the Safeguarding Vulnerable Groups Act 2006 s 2 (see PARAS 265, 266) or under corresponding Scotland or Northern Ireland legislation: Regulation and Inspection of Social Care (Wales) Act 2016 s 117(3).

5   For these purposes 'relevant body' means the Health and Care Professions Council (see MEDICAL PROFESSIONS vol 74 (2011) PARA 928), the Nursing and Midwifery Council (see MEDICAL PROFESSIONS vol 74 (2011) PARA 692 et seq), the Scottish Social Services Council, the Northern Ireland Social Care Council, a body outside of the United Kingdom which is responsible for the regulation of activities which would, in Wales, be regulated by Social Care Wales, or a prescribed body: Regulation and Inspection of Social Care (Wales) Act 2016 s 117(4). At the date at which this volume states the law no further bodies had been prescribed for this purpose.

6   Regulation and Inspection of Social Care (Wales) Act 2016 s 117(1)(d).

7   Regulation and Inspection of Social Care (Wales) Act 2016 s 117(1)(e).

8   As to the meanings of 'England' and 'Wales' see PARAS 1 note 1, 2 note 4.

9   Regulation and Inspection of Social Care (Wales) Act 2016 s 117(1)(f).

10 Regulation and Inspection of Social Care (Wales) Act 2016 s 117(5)(a).

11 Regulation and Inspection of Social Care (Wales) Act 2016 s 117(5)(b).

12 Regulation and Inspection of Social Care (Wales) Act 2016 s 117(5)(c).

13 See the Regulation and Inspection of Social Care (Wales) Act 2016 ss 118–133 (consideration, investigation and review), ss 134–142 (disposal), ss 143–149 (interim orders), ss 150–157 (review), s 158 (appeals) and ss 159–164 (s 164 amended by SI 2016/1030) (administration).

201. Registration of social workers and social care workers. Inclusion in the register of social workers and social care workers[1] is by application[2], and an application must be granted if the applicant meets the registration requirements[3], which are that:

(1)   the person is appropriately qualified[4];

(2)   the person's fitness to practise is not[5] impaired[6]; and

(3)   the person intends to practise the work of persons registered in the part of the register to which the application relates[7].

Social Care Wales may provide that registration is time-limited and renewable[8]; and registration will as a rule lapse if not renewed[9]. A person may also be removed from the register by agreement[10], or on death[11], or if his entry is based on false information[12]. Provision is also made for the restoration of registrations[13].

1   Ie the register maintained by Social Care Wales under the Regulation and Inspection of Social Care (Wales) Act 2016: see s 80; and the Social Care Wales (Specification of Social Care Workers) (Registration) Regulations 2016, SI 2016/1235. As to Social Care Wales see PARAS 412–414. As to the meanings of 'social worker' and 'social care worker' see PARA 198 (noting in particular note 9).

2   See the Regulation and Inspection of Social Care (Wales) Act 2016 s 82. Visiting social workers and social care managers are also entitled to be registered: see s 90 and s 90A (amended and added by SI 2016/1030).

3   See the Regulation and Inspection of Social Care (Wales) Act 2016 ss 83(1)(c), 89. Applications must also be in the prescribed form and be accompanied by the prescribed fee: see s 83(1)(a), (b), There is a right of appeal against refusal: see ss 101(1)(a), (2) 102–105 (s 105 amended by SI 2016/1030); and see also the Regulation and Inspection of Social Care (Wales) Act 2016 ss 174, 175; the Social Care Wales (Constitution of Panels: Prescribed Persons) Regulations 2016, SI 2016/1099; and the Social Care Wales (Proceedings before Panels) Regulations 2016, SI 2016/1100 (registration appeals panels).

4   Regulation and Inspection of Social Care (Wales) Act 2016 s 83(2)(a). For the purposes of s 83 a person is 'appropriately qualified' if:
    (1)   in the case of an application for registration as a social worker, the applicant has successfully completed a course approved by Social Care Wales under s 114 for persons wishing to become social workers, satisfies the requirements of s 85 (amended by SI 2016/1030) (qualifications gained outside of Wales), or satisfies any requirements as to training which Social Care Wales may by rules impose (Regulation and Inspection of Social Care (Wales) Act 2016 s 84(a));
    (2)   in the case of an application for registration as a social care manager, the applicant has successfully completed a course approved by Social Care Wales under s 114 for persons wishing to become social care managers, satisfies the requirements of s 85A (added by SI 2016/1030) (qualifications gained outside Wales—social care managers), or satisfies any requirements as to training which Social Care Wales may by rules impose in relation to social care managers (Regulation and Inspection of Social Care (Wales) Act 2016 s 84(aa) (added by SI 2016/1030)); or
    (3)   in the case of an applicant for registration as a social care worker of any other description, the applicant has successfully completed a course approved by Social Care Wales under the Regulation and Inspection of Social Care (Wales) Act 2016 s 114 for persons wishing to become a social care worker of that description, or satisfies any requirements as to training which Social Care Wales may by rules impose in relation to social care workers of that description (s 84(b)).
    In connection with courses and education see also s 115 and s 116 (ensuring adequacy pf provision). As to the meaning of 'social care manager' see PARA 198 note 6.

5   Ie on one or more of the grounds in the Regulation and Inspection of Social Care (Wales) Act 2016 s 117(1) (see PARA 200). Determinations as to fitness to practise are made in accordance with rules made by Social Care Wales: see s 88.

6   Regulation and Inspection of Social Care (Wales) Act 2016 s 83(2)(b). As to the consideration and disposal of fitness to practice cases see PARA 200.

7   Regulation and Inspection of Social Care (Wales) Act 2016 s 83(2)(c). For the purposes of s 83(2)(c), Social Care Wales may by rules specify activities that are to be regarded as practising the work of persons registered in a part of the register and the criteria to be applied by the registrar for determining whether a person intends to practice: s 83(3).

8   See the Regulation and Inspection of Social Care (Wales) Act 2016 s 86. There is a right of appeal against refusal of renewal: see s 101(1)(b).

9   See the Regulation and Inspection of Social Care (Wales) Act 2016 s 87.

10   See the Regulation and Inspection of Social Care (Wales) Act 2016 s 92.

11   See the Regulation and Inspection of Social Care (Wales) Act 2016 s 93.

12   See the Regulation and Inspection of Social Care (Wales) Act 2016 s 94. There is a right of appeal against removal: see s 101(1)(c).

13 See the Regulation and Inspection of Social Care (Wales) Act 2016 ss 95–100, 101(1)(d) (rights of appeal), 109.

202. Persons prohibited from working in social care. The Welsh Ministers[1] may by regulations designate:

(1)   practising as a social care worker[2] of a prescribed description[3];

(2)   carrying out a prescribed activity as a social care worker[4];

(3)   the use by an individual of a prescribed title relating to an activity within head (1) or (2) above[5],

as a 'regulated activity'[6], and authorise the making of prohibition orders in respect of the regulated activity[7]. A 'prohibition order' is an order made by a fitness to practise panel prohibiting a person from carrying out a regulated activity[8], and regulations must also prescribe the circumstances in which a fitness to practise panel may make such an order[9], authorise the making of interim orders[10], and make provision as to the operation and review of an order or interim order[11] and appeals[12]. It is an offence for a person to fail to comply with a prohibition order or interim order[13].

At the date at which this volume states the law no such regulations had been made and nothing had been prescribed for the other purposes referred to above.

1   As to the Welsh Ministers see PARA 395. Before making regulations under these provisions the Welsh Ministers must consult any persons they think appropriate: Regulation and Inspection of Social Care (Wales) Act 2016 s 165(5). However the requirement to consult does not apply to regulations which amend other regulations made under s 155 and do not, in the opinion of the Welsh Ministers, effect any substantial change in the provision made by the regulations to be amended: s 165(6).

2   As to the meanings of 'social worker' and 'social care worker' see PARA 198. In this context references to 'social care worker' do not include a reference to a social worker or a social care worker of a description specified for the time being by regulations under s 80(1)(b) (descriptions of social care worker in respect of whom Social Care Wales keeps an added part of the register): Regulation and Inspection of Social Care (Wales) Act 2016 s 165(3).

3   Regulation and Inspection of Social Care (Wales) Act 2016 s 165(1)(a), (2)(a).

4   Regulation and Inspection of Social Care (Wales) Act 2016 s 165(2)(b).

5   Regulation and Inspection of Social Care (Wales) Act 2016 s 165(2)(c).

6   Ie for the purposes of the Regulation and Inspection of Social Care (Wales) Act 2016 Pt 7 (ss 165–173).

7   Regulation and Inspection of Social Care (Wales) Act 2016 s 165(1)(b).

8   Regulation and Inspection of Social Care (Wales) Act 2016 s 165(4).

9   See the Regulation and Inspection of Social Care (Wales) Act 2016 s 166.

10   See the Regulation and Inspection of Social Care (Wales) Act 2016 s 167.

11   See the Regulation and Inspection of Social Care (Wales) Act 2016 ss 168, 169, 172, 173.

12   See the Regulation and Inspection of Social Care (Wales) Act 2016 s 170.

13   See the Regulation and Inspection of Social Care (Wales) Act 2016 s 171(1). A person who commits an offence under s 171(1) is liable on summary conviction to a fine: s 171(2). As to the powers of magistrates' courts to issue fines on summary conviction see SENTENCING vol 92 (2015) PARA 176. The Welsh Ministers may by regulations create summary offences relating to the employment or appointment of a person to do anything that the person is prohibited from doing by a prohibition order or an interim prohibition order: regulations creating an offence may not provide for the offence to be punishable otherwise than by a fine (whether an unlimited fine or a fine not exceeding a specified level on the standard scale): s 171(3), (4).

(ii) Regulation of Providers

A.   REQUIREMENT FOR REGISTRATION

203. Offence of providing regulated services without registration. As from a day to be appointed[1] it is an offence for a person to provide a regulated service without being registered[2] in respect of that service[3], for a service provider[4] to fail to comply with any condition relating to his registration which is[5] for the time being in force[6], or for a person, with intent to deceive another, pretend to be a service provider[7] or to pretend that a place is one at, from or in relation to which a regulated service is provided[8]. The 'regulated services' are[9]:

(1)　a care home service[10];
(2)　a secure accommodation service[11];
(3)　a residential family centre service[12];
(4)　an adoption service[13];
(5)　a fostering service[14];
(6)　an adult placement service[15];
(7)　an advocacy service[16]; and
(8)　a domiciliary support service[17].

1　At the date at which this volume states the law the Regulation and Inspection of Social Care (Wales) Act 2016 Pt 1 (ss 1–64) had yet to be brought into force.

2　Ie in accordance with the Regulation and Inspection of Social Care (Wales) Act 2016 Pt 1 Ch 2 (ss 5–31).

3　Regulation and Inspection of Social Care (Wales) Act 2016 s 5 (not yet in force: see note 1). A person guilty of an offence under s 5, s 43, s 44, s 47, s 49 or s 50 or under regulations made under s 45 or s 46 is liable on summary conviction, to a fine, or to imprisonment for a term not exceeding 6 months, or to both, or on conviction on indictment, to a fine, or to imprisonment for a term not exceeding 2 years, or to both: s 51(1) (not yet in force). As to the powers of magistrates' courts to issue fines on summary conviction see SENTENCING vol 92 (2015) PARA 176.

Where an offence under Pt 1 or under regulations made thereunder is committed by a body corporate a director, manager, secretary or other similar officer of the body corporate, a member (where a body corporate's affairs are managed by its members) or any person purporting to act in any of those capacities also commits the offence if the offence is proved to have been committed with the consent or connivance of, or to have been attributable to any neglect on the part of, that person: s 53(1)–(3) (not yet in force). Where a body corporate is a local authority, the reference in these provisions to a director, manager or secretary of the body is to be read as a reference to an officer or member of the authority: s 53(4) (not yet in force). Proceedings for an offence under Pt 1 and under regulations made thereunder alleged to have been committed by an unincorporated body may be brought in the name of the body instead of in the name of any of its members and, for the purposes of any such proceedings, any rules of court relating to the service of documents have effect as if that body were a body corporate: s 54(1), (2) (not yet in force). Any fine imposed on an unincorporated body on its conviction of an offence is to be paid out of the funds of that body: s 54(3) (not yet in force). If an unincorporated body is charged with an offence, the Criminal Justice Act 1925 s 33 and the Magistrates' Courts Act 1980 Sch 3 (see CRIMINAL PROCEDURE vol 27 (2015) PARAS 198, 373–374) have effect as if a body corporate had been charged: Regulation and Inspection of Social Care (Wales) Act 2016 s 53(4) (not yet in force). Proceedings in respect of an offence under Pt 1 or regulations made thereunder may not, without the written consent of the Counsel General to the Welsh Government, be brought by any person other than the Counsel General or the Welsh Ministers: s 55(1) (not yet in force). As to the Welsh Ministers see PARA 395. Summary proceedings in respect of an offence under Pt 1 or regulations made thereunder must be brought within the period of 12 months beginning on the date on which sufficient evidence to warrant the proceedings came to the prosecutor's knowledge: s 55(2) (not yet in force). However no such proceedings may be brought more than three years after the offence is committed: s 55(3) (not yet in force).

The Welsh Ministers must notify each local authority of proceedings brought against it in respect of offence under Pt 1 or regulations made thereunder: s 39(1)(e) (not yet in force). A notification under s 39 must contain such other information as may be prescribed: s 39(2) (not yet in force). At the date at which this volume states the law no further information had been prescribed. As to the meaning of 'local authority' see PARA 2: in s 39(1) the reference to 'local authority' includes a reference to a county council in England, a district council for an area in England for which there is no county council, a London borough council, the Common Council of the City of London, and the Council of the Isles of Scilly: s 39(3) (not yet in force). As to local government areas and authorities in England see LOCAL GOVERNMENT vol 69 (2009) PARA 22 et seq. As to the London boroughs and their councils see LONDON GOVERNMENT vol 71 (2013) PARAS 15, 20, 34–38. As to the Common Council of the City of London see LONDON GOVERNMENT vol 71 (2013) PARA 16. Further matters to be notified to local authorities under these provisions may be prescribed (s 39(1)(g) (not yet in force)): at the date at which this volume states the law no further matters had been prescribed.

4 'Service provider' means a person registered under the Regulation and Inspection of Social Care (Wales) Act 2016 s 7 (see PARA 216) to provide a regulated service: s 3(1)(c) (not yet in force: see note 1). As to the register of service providers see s 38; and PARA 398.
5 Ie by virtue of the Regulation and Inspection of Social Care (Wales) Act 2016 Pt 1.
6 Regulation and Inspection of Social Care (Wales) Act 2016 s 43(1) (not yet in force: see note 1). A service provider does not commit an offence under s 43(1) by failing to have a responsible individual designated in respect of a place at, from or in relation to which the provider provides a regulated service if:
    (1) the time limit prescribed under s 11(2) (see PARA 223) has not expired (prescribed time limit for applying to designate a new responsible individual) (s 43(2)(a) (not yet in force)); or
    (2) that time limit has expired but the service provider made the application for variation within the time limit and the Welsh Ministers have not made a decision on it (s 43(2)(b) (not yet in force)).
7 Regulation and Inspection of Social Care (Wales) Act 2016 s 44(1)(a) (not yet in force: see note 1). Any of the following may (among other things) be an act constituting an offence under s 44(1):
    (1) applying a name to a service or place to give the impression that it is specified in a service provider's registration when it is not (s 44(2)(a) (not yet in force));
    (2) describing a service or place in a manner intended to give that impression (s 44(2)(b) (not yet in force));
    (3) holding a service out to be a regulated service specified in a service provider's registration when it is not (s 44(2)(c) (not yet in force));
    (4) holding a place out to be a place specified in a service provider's registration when it is not (s 44(2)(d) (not yet in force));
    (5) acting in a manner that gives the impression of being a responsible individual when not designated as one (s 44(2)(e) (not yet in force)).
8 Regulation and Inspection of Social Care (Wales) Act 2016 s 44(1)(b) (not yet in force: see note 1). See note 7.
9 Other services comprising the provision of care and support in Wales may be prescribed as 'regulated services' for these purposes: Regulation and Inspection of Social Care (Wales) Act 2016 s 2(1)(i) (not yet in force: see note 1). The Welsh Ministers may also by regulations prescribe things which, despite Sch 1 (see PARAS 205–210), are not to be treated as regulated services for these purposes: s 2(3) (not yet in force). At the date at which this volume states the law no services or things had been prescribed for these purposes. Before making regulations under s 2 the Welsh Ministers must consult such persons as they think appropriate: s 2(4) (not yet in force).
10 Regulation and Inspection of Social Care (Wales) Act 2016 ss 2(1)(a), 79(5) (not yet in force: see note 1). See PARA 205.
11 Regulation and Inspection of Social Care (Wales) Act 2016 s 2(1)(b) (not yet in force: see note 1). See PARA 206.
12 Regulation and Inspection of Social Care (Wales) Act 2016 s 2(1)(c) (not yet in force: see note 1). See PARA 206.
13 Regulation and Inspection of Social Care (Wales) Act 2016 s 2(1)(d) (not yet in force: see note 1). See PARA 207.
14 Regulation and Inspection of Social Care (Wales) Act 2016 s 2(1)(e) (not yet in force: see note 1). See PARA 207.
15 Regulation and Inspection of Social Care (Wales) Act 2016 s 2(1)(f) (not yet in force: see note 1). See PARA 208.
16 Regulation and Inspection of Social Care (Wales) Act 2016 s 2(1)(g) (not yet in force: see note 1). See PARA 209.
17 Regulation and Inspection of Social Care (Wales) Act 2016 s 2(1)(h) (not yet in force: see note 1). See PARA 210.

204. 'Care' and 'support'. 'Care' means care relating to the day to day physical tasks and needs of the person cared for (for example, eating and washing) and the mental processes related to those tasks and needs (for example, the mental process of remembering to eat and wash)[1]. 'Support' means counselling, advice or other help, provided as part of a plan prepared for the person receiving support by a service provider[2] or other person providing care and support to the person or a local authority (even if the authority does not provide care and support to the person)[3]; references to 'care and support' are read as references to care, support, or both care and support[4].

As from a day to be appointed the Welsh Ministers may by regulations prescribe things which[5] are not to be treated as 'care' and 'support' for these purposes[6].

1   Regulation and Inspection of Social Care (Wales) Act 2016 s 3(1)(a) (at the date at which this volume states the law Pt 1 (ss 1–64) had yet to be brought into force).
2   As to the meaning of 'service provider' see PARA 203 note 4.
3   Regulation and Inspection of Social Care (Wales) Act 2016 s 3(1)(d) (not yet in force: see note 1).
4   Regulation and Inspection of Social Care (Wales) Act 2016 s 3(2) (not yet in force: see note 1).
5   Ie despite the Regulation and Inspection of Social Care (Wales) Act 2016 s 3(1)(a), (d).
6   Regulation and Inspection of Social Care (Wales) Act 2016 s 3(3) (not yet in force: see note 1). At the date at which this volume states the law no such regulations had been made.

205. 'Care home service'. A 'care home service' is the provision of accommodation, together with nursing or care[1] at a place in Wales[2], to persons because of their vulnerability or need[3]. However accommodation together with nursing or care provided at the following places does not constitute a 'care home service':

(1)   a hospital[4];
(2)   a school[5];
(3)   a residential family centre[6];
(4)   a place providing a secure accommodation service[7];
(5)   a place providing accommodation for an adult arranged as part of an adult placement service[8].

The provision of accommodation and care to a child by a parent[9], relative or foster parent[10] does not constitute a 'care home service'[11].

1   As to the meaning of 'care' see PARA 204.
2   As to the meaning of 'Wales' see PARA 2.
3   Regulation and Inspection of Social Care (Wales) Act 2016 s 2(2), Sch 1 para 1(1) (at the date at which this volume states the law Pt 1 (ss 1–64) had yet to be brought into force).
4   Regulation and Inspection of Social Care (Wales) Act 2016 Sch 1 para 1(2)(a) (not yet in force: see note 3). 'Hospital' means (by virtue of Sch 1 para 9 (not yet in force)):
    (1)   a health service hospital within the meaning given by the National Health Service (Wales) Act 2006 (see s 206(1); and HEALTH SERVICES vol 54 (2017) PARA 26);
    (2)   an independent hospital within the meaning given by the Care Standards Act 2000 (see s 2; and HEALTH SERVICES vol 54A (2017) PARA 633); and
    (3)   an independent clinic within the meaning given by the Care Standards Act 2000 (see s 2; and HEALTH SERVICES vol 54A (2017) PARA 633).
5   Regulation and Inspection of Social Care (Wales) Act 2016 Sch 1 para 1(2)(b) (not yet in force: see note 3). As to the meaning of 'school' see the Education Act 1996 s 4; and EDUCATION vol 35 (2015) PARA 91 (definition applied by the Regulation and Inspection of Social Care (Wales) Act 2016 Sch 1 para 1(5) (not yet in force)). Accommodation together with nursing or care provided at a school does constitute a care home service if, at the time accommodation is provided for children at the school:
    (1)   accommodation has been provided at the school or under arrangements made by the school's proprietor for at least one child for more than 295 days in any period of 12 months falling within the previous 24 months (Sch 1 para 1(3)(a) (not yet in force)); or
    (2)   such accommodation is intended to be provided for at least one child for more than 295 days in any period of 12 months falling within the following 24 months (Sch 1 para 1(3)(b) (not yet in force)).
6   Regulation and Inspection of Social Care (Wales) Act 2016 Sch 1 para 1(2)(c) (not yet in force: see note 3). As to residential family centre services see PARA 206.
7   Regulation and Inspection of Social Care (Wales) Act 2016 Sch 1 para 1(2)(d) (not yet in force: see note 3). As to secure accommodation services see PARA 206.
8   Regulation and Inspection of Social Care (Wales) Act 2016 Sch 1 para 1(2)(e) (not yet in force: see note 3). As to adult placement services see PARA 208.
9   For this purpose 'parent' means a person who has parental responsibility for a child (within the meaning given by the Children Act 1989 s 3: see CHILDREN AND YOUNG PERSONS vol 9 (2017) PARA 150): Regulation and Inspection of Social Care (Wales) Act 2016 Sch 1 para 1(6) (not yet in force: see note 3).

10 For these purposes a person is a foster parent in relation to a child if he is a local authority foster parent or fosters the child privately: Regulation and Inspection of Social Care (Wales) Act 2016 Sch 1 para 1(7) (not yet in force: see note 3). As to the meaning of 'local authority foster parent' see the Social Services and Well-being (Wales) Act 2014 s 197; and CHILDREN AND YOUNG PERSONS vol 10 (2017) PARA 873 (definition applied by the Regulation and Inspection of Social Care (Wales) Act 2016 Sch 1 para 9 (not yet in force)).
11 Regulation and Inspection of Social Care (Wales) Act 2016 Sch 1 para 1(4) (not yet in force: see note 3).

206. 'Secure accommodation service' and 'residential family centre service'. A 'secure accommodation service' is the provision of accommodation for the purpose of restricting the liberty of children at residential premises in Wales[1] where care and support[2] is provided to those children[3]. A 'residential family centre service' is the provision of accommodation for children and their parents[4] at a place in Wales where the parents' capacity to respond to the children's needs and to safeguard their well-being[5] is monitored[6] or assessed and the parents are given such care and support as is thought necessary[7].

1 As to the meaning of 'Wales' see PARA 2.
2 As to the meanings of 'care' and 'support' see PARA 204.
3 Regulation and Inspection of Social Care (Wales) Act 2016 Sch 1 para 2 (at the date at which this volume states the law Pt 1 (ss 1–64) had yet to be brought into force).
4 For this purpose 'parent', in relation to a child, means any person who is looking after the child: Regulation and Inspection of Social Care (Wales) Act 2016 Sch 1 para 3(2) (not yet in force: see note 3).
5 As to the meaning of 'well-being' see PARA 375.
6 Regulation and Inspection of Social Care (Wales) Act 2016 Sch 1 para 3(1)(a) (not yet in force: see note 3).
7 Regulation and Inspection of Social Care (Wales) Act 2016 Sch 1 para 3(1)(b) (not yet in force: see note 3).

207. 'Adoption' and 'fostering' service. An 'adoption service' is a service provided in Wales[1] by an adoption society[2] which is a voluntary organisation[3] or an adoption support agency[4]. A 'fostering service' means any service provided in Wales by a person other than a local authority[5] which consists of or includes the placement of children with local authority foster parents[6] or exercising functions in connection with such placement[7].

1 As to the meaning of 'Wales' see PARA 2.
2 Ie within the meaning of the Adoption and Children Act 2002: see s 2(5); and CHILDREN AND YOUNG PERSONS vol 9 (2017) PARA 475.
3 Regulation and Inspection of Social Care (Wales) Act 2016 Sch 1 para 4(a) (at the date at which this volume states the law Pt 1 (ss 1–64) had yet to be brought into force). The reference is to a voluntary organisation within the meaning of the Adoption and Children Act 2002: see s 2(5); and CHILDREN AND YOUNG PERSONS vol 9 (2017) PARA 475.
4 Regulation and Inspection of Social Care (Wales) Act 2016 Sch 1 para 4(b) (not yet in force: see note 3). The reference is to an adoption support agency within the meaning of the Adoption and Children Act 2002 s 8 (see CHILDREN AND YOUNG PERSONS vol 9 (2017) PARA 463).
5 As to the meaning of 'local authority' see PARA 2.
6 Regulation and Inspection of Social Care (Wales) Act 2016 Sch 1 para 5(a) (not yet in force: see note 3).
7 Regulation and Inspection of Social Care (Wales) Act 2016 Sch 1 para 5(b) (not yet in force: see note 3).

208. 'Adult placement service'. An 'adult placement service' means a service carried on (whether or not for profit) by a local authority[1] or other person for the purposes of placing adults with an individual in Wales[2] under a carer agreement[3] (and includes any arrangements for the recruitment, training and supervision of such individuals)[4].

1 As to the meaning of 'local authority' see PARA 2.

2   As to the meaning of 'Wales' see PARA 2.
3   'Carer agreement' means an agreement for the provision by an individual of accommodation at the
    individual's home together with care and support for up to three adults: Regulation and Inspection
    of Social Care (Wales) Act 2016 Sch 1 para 6(2) (at the date at which this volume states the law
    Pt 1 (ss 1–64) had yet to be brought into force). As to the meanings of 'care' and 'support' see
    PARA 204.
4   Regulation and Inspection of Social Care (Wales) Act 2016 Sch 1 para 6(1) (not yet in force: see
    note 3).

209. 'Advocacy service'. An 'advocacy service' is a service specified for these
purposes by regulations made by the Welsh Ministers[1]. A service may be specified
as an advocacy service only if, and to the extent that, the following requirements
are satisfied in relation to the service:
(1)   that the service is a service which is carried on (whether or not for profit)
       for the purpose of representing the views of individuals, or assisting
       individuals to represent those views, in respect of matters relating to
       those individuals' needs for care and support[2] (including matters
       relating to assessing whether those needs exist)[3];
(2)   that the service is not carried on by a person, in the course of a legal
       activity[4], who is an authorised person[5] or a European lawyer[6];
At the date at which this volume states the law no such regulations had been
made.

1   Regulation and Inspection of Social Care (Wales) Act 2016 Sch 1 para 7(1) (at the date at which
    this volume states the law Pt 1 (ss 1–64) had yet to be brought into force). As to the Welsh
    Ministers see PARA 395. Before making such regulations the Welsh Ministers must consult any
    persons they think appropriate: Sch 1 para 7(5) (not yet in force). However the requirement to
    consult does not apply to regulations which amend other regulations made under Sch 1 para 7(1)
    and do not, in the opinion of the Welsh Ministers, effect any substantial change in the provision
    made by the regulations to be amended: Sch 1 para 7(6) (not yet in force).
2   As to the meanings of 'care' and 'support' see PARA 204.
3   Regulation and Inspection of Social Care (Wales) Act 2016 Sch 1 para 7(2), (3)(a) (not yet in force:
    see note 1).
4   Ie within the meaning of the Legal Services Act 2007: see s 12(3); and LEGAL PROFESSIONS vol 65
    (2015) PARA 352.
5   Ie for the purposes of the Legal Services Act 2007: see s 1(4); and LEGAL PROFESSIONS vol 65
    (2015) PARA 202.
6   Regulation and Inspection of Social Care (Wales) Act 2016 Sch 1 para 7(4) (not yet in force: see
    note 1). The reference is to a person who is a European lawyer within the meaning of the
    European Communities (Services of Lawyers) Order, SI 1978/1910 (see LEGAL PROFESSIONS
    vol 65 (2015) PARAS 377–381).

210. 'Domiciliary support service'. A 'domiciliary support service' is the
provision of care and support[1] to a person who by reason of vulnerability or need
(other than vulnerability or need arising only because the person is of a young age)
is unable to provide it for him or herself and is provided at the place in Wales[2]
where the person lives (including making arrangements for or providing services
in connection with such provision)[3]. However the provision of care and support
does not constitute a 'domiciliary support service' if:
(1)   it is provided by an individual without the involvement of an
       undertaking acting as an employment agency or employment business[4]
       and who works wholly under the direction and control of the person
       receiving the care and support[5]; or
(2)   it is provided at a place where a care home service[6], secure
       accommodation service[7], residential family centre service[8] or
       accommodation arranged as part of an adult placement service[9] is
       provided[10], or at a hospital[11].

As from a day to be appointed a person who introduces individuals who provide a domiciliary support service to individuals who may wish to receive it but has no ongoing role in the direction or control of the care and support provided is not treated as providing a domiciliary support service (regardless of whether or not the introduction is for profit)[12].

1   As to the meanings of 'care' and 'support' see PARA 204.
2   As to the meaning of 'Wales' see PARA 2.
3   Regulation and Inspection of Social Care (Wales) Act 2016 Sch 1 para 8(1) (at the date at which this volume states the law Pt 1 (ss 1–64) had yet to be brought into force).
4   Ie within the meaning given to those expressions by the Employment Agencies Act 1973 s 13: see TRADE AND INDUSTRY vol 97 (2015) PARA 974.
5   Regulation and Inspection of Social Care (Wales) Act 2016 Sch 1 para 8(2)(a) (not yet in force: see note 3).
6   See PARA 205.
7   See PARA 206.
8   See PARA 206.
9   See PARA 208.
10 Regulation and Inspection of Social Care (Wales) Act 2016 Sch 1 para 8(2)(b)(i) (not yet in force: see note 3).
11 Regulation and Inspection of Social Care (Wales) Act 2016 Sch 1 para 8(2)(b)(ii) (not yet in force: see note 3). As to the meaning of 'hospital' see PARA 205 note 4.
12 Regulation and Inspection of Social Care (Wales) Act 2016 Sch 1 para 8(3) (not yet in force: see note 3).

211.   Fit and proper person test. As from a day to be appointed[1], in making a decision as to whether a service provider[2], a person applying to be a service provider[3], a responsible individual[4] or a person to be designated as a responsible individual[5] is a fit and proper person to be a service provider or, as the case may be, a responsible individual, the Welsh Ministers[6] must have regard to all matters they think appropriate[7]. In particular, the Welsh Ministers must have regard to evidence which shows that the person:

(1)   has committed any offence involving fraud or other dishonesty, violence, firearms or drugs[8];

(2)   has committed any offence[9] attracting notification requirements[10];

(3)   has committed an offence relating to[11] the regulation and inspection of social care in England and Wales[12];

(4)   committed any other offence which the Welsh Ministers think is relevant[13];

(5)   has practised unlawful discrimination or harassment on the grounds of any protected characteristic[14], or victimised another person[15], in or in connection with the carrying on of any business[16];

(6)   has been responsible for, contributed to or facilitated misconduct or mismanagement in the provision of a regulated service[17] or a service provided outside Wales which, if provided in Wales, would be a regulated service, or of a service which would been such a service had the current regulatory system[18] been operating at the time the service was being provided[19]; or

(7)   has previously failed to comply with an undertaking[20] relating to an application for registration, a condition of registration[21] or a requirement imposed by regulations[22] relating to regulated services and responsible individuals[23].

The Welsh Ministers must also have regard to evidence which shows that any other person associated or formerly associated with the person (whether on a personal, work or other basis) has done any of the things set out in heads (1) to (5) above, where it appears to the Welsh Ministers that the evidence is relevant to the question as to whether the person is a fit and proper person to be a service provider or, as the case may be, a responsible individual[24].

1   At the date at which this volume states the law the Regulation and Inspection of Social Care (Wales) Act 2016 Pt 1 (ss 1–64) had yet to be brought into force.
2   Regulation and Inspection of Social Care (Wales) Act 2016 s 9(1)(a) (not yet in force: see note 1). As to the meaning of 'service provider' see PARA 203 note 4.
3   Regulation and Inspection of Social Care (Wales) Act 2016 s 9(1)(b) (not yet in force: see note 1).
4   Regulation and Inspection of Social Care (Wales) Act 2016 s 9(1)(c) (not yet in force: see note 1). As to the meaning of 'responsible individual' see PARA 212.
5   Regulation and Inspection of Social Care (Wales) Act 2016 s 9(1)(d) (not yet in force: see note 1).
6   As to the Welsh Ministers see PARA 395. The Welsh Ministers may by regulations amend the Regulation and Inspection of Social Care (Wales) Act 2016 s 9 to vary the evidence to which they must have regard: s 9(9) (not yet in force: see note 1). At the date at which this volume states the law no such regulations had been made.
7   Regulation and Inspection of Social Care (Wales) Act 2016 s 9(2) (not yet in force: see note 1).
8   Regulation and Inspection of Social Care (Wales) Act 2016 s 9(3), (4)(a)(i) (not yet in force: see note 1).
9   Ie any offence listed in the Sexual Offences Act 2003 Sch 3: see SENTENCING vol 92 (2015) PARA 329.
10 Regulation and Inspection of Social Care (Wales) Act 2016 s 9(4)(a)(i) (not yet in force: see note 1).
11 Ie an offence under the Regulation and Inspection of Social Care (Wales) Act 2016, the Care Standards Act 2000 Pt 2 (ss 11–42) (see CHILDREN AND YOUNG PERSONS vol 10 (2017) PARA 1017 et seq) or regulations made under that legislation.
12 Regulation and Inspection of Social Care (Wales) Act 2016 s 9(4)(a)(ii), (iii) (not yet in force: see note 1).
13 Regulation and Inspection of Social Care (Wales) Act 2016 s 9(4)(a)(iv) (not yet in force: see note 1).
14 Ie any characteristic which is a protected characteristic under the Equality Act 2010 s 4 (see DISCRIMINATION vol 33 (2013) PARA 48).
15 Ie contrary to the Equality Act 2010.
16 Regulation and Inspection of Social Care (Wales) Act 2016 s 9(4)(b) (not yet in force: see note 1).
17 As to the meaning of 'regulated service' see PARA 203.
18 Ie the regulatory system established by the Regulation and Inspection of Social Care (Wales) Act 2016 Pt 1 (ss 1–64).
19 Regulation and Inspection of Social Care (Wales) Act 2016 s 9(6) (not yet in force: see note 1). When having regard to evidence within s 9(6), the Welsh Ministers must, among other things, take account of the seriousness and duration of the misconduct or mismanagement, harm caused to any person, or any evidence of an intent to cause harm, any financial gain made by the person, and any action taken by the person to remedy the misconduct or mismanagement: s 9(7) (not yet in force).
20 Ie an undertaking given under the Regulation and Inspection of Social Care (Wales) Act 2016 s 7(1)(a)(ii) (see PARA 216) or s 11(3)(a)(ii) (see PARA 223).
21 Ie a condition imposed under the Regulation and Inspection of Social Care (Wales) Act 2016 Pt 1.
22 Ie regulations under the Regulation and Inspection of Social Care (Wales) Act 2016 s 27(1) (see PARA 214) or s 28(1) (see PARA 214).
23 Regulation and Inspection of Social Care (Wales) Act 2016 s 9(8) (not yet in force: see note 1).
24 Regulation and Inspection of Social Care (Wales) Act 2016 s 9(5) (not yet in force: see note 1).

212. The 'responsible individual'. 'Responsible individual' means[1] an individual:

(1)   who is eligible[2] to be a responsible individual[3];
(2)   who the Welsh Ministers[4] are satisfied is a fit and proper person to be a responsible individual[5]; and
(3)   designated by a service provider[6] in respect of a place at, from or in relation to which the provider provides a regulated service[7] and specified as such in the service provider's registration[8].

As from a day to be appointed, to be eligible to be a responsible individual the individual must[9]:

(a)   where the service provider is an individual, be the service provider[10];
(b)   where the service provider is a partnership, be one of the partners[11];

(c)   where the service provider is a body corporate other than a local authority[12], be a director or similar officer of the body[13], a director or company secretary (in the case of a public limited company)[14], or be a member of the body (in the case of a body corporate whose affairs are managed by its members)[15];

(d)   where the service provider is an unincorporated body, be a member of the body[16]; or

(e)   where the service provider is a local authority, be an officer of the local authority designated by the authority's director of social services[17].

The Welsh Ministers may cancel a responsible individual's designation only on one or more of the following grounds:

(i)   they have reason to believe the individual no longer satisfies the eligibility[18] requirements[19];

(ii)   they have reason to believe the individual has been convicted of, or has been given a caution in respect of, a relevant offence[20] in connection with a regulated service provided by the service provider[21];

(iii)   they are no longer satisfied that the individual is a fit and proper person to be a responsible individual[22];

(iv)   they have reason to believe that the individual has not complied with an applicable[23] requirement[24].

If the Welsh Ministers propose to cancel a responsible individual's designation they must give the individual an improvement notice[25], and if they are not satisfied that action specified in such notice has been taken or information so specified has been provided within the time limit specified in the notice they may give a notice of cancellation[26]. The Welsh Ministers may give a notice of cancellation of a responsible individual's designation without taking these steps if they have reasonable cause to believe that unless the designation is cancelled a person will or may be exposed to a risk of harm[27]. A decision to cancel a responsible individual's designation is subject to appeal[28].

It is an offence for a person for a person, with intent to deceive another, to pretend to be a responsible individual[29].

1   Ie for the purposes of the Regulation and Inspection of Social Care (Wales) Act 2016 Pt 1 (ss 1–64). At the date at which this volume states the law Pt 1 had yet to be brought into force. The same responsible individual may be designated in relation to more than one place at, from or in relation to which a regulated service is provided: s 21(4) (not yet in force).

2   Ie under the Regulation and Inspection of Social Care (Wales) Act 2016 s 21(2) (see the text and notes 9–17).

3   Regulation and Inspection of Social Care (Wales) Act 2016 s 21(1)(a) (not yet in force: see note 1).

4   As to the Welsh Ministers see PARA 395.

5   Regulation and Inspection of Social Care (Wales) Act 2016 s 21(1)(b) (not yet in force: see note 1). As to the fit and proper person test see s 9; and PARA 211.

6   As to the meaning of 'service provider' see PARA 203 note 4.

7   As to the meaning of 'regulated service' see PARA 203.

8   Regulation and Inspection of Social Care (Wales) Act 2016 s 21(1)(c) (not yet in force: see note 1).

9   The Welsh Ministers may, by regulations specify circumstances in which the Welsh Ministers (instead of a service provider) may designate an individual to be a responsible individual despite the requirements of the Regulation and Inspection of Social Care (Wales) Act 2016 s 21(2) not being met in respect of the individual and make provision for Pt 1 to apply with prescribed modifications to such a responsible individual: s 21(5) (not yet in force: see note 1). At the date at which this volume states the law no such regulations had been made.

10   Regulation and Inspection of Social Care (Wales) Act 2016 s 21(2)(a) (not yet in force: see note 1).

11   Regulation and Inspection of Social Care (Wales) Act 2016 s 21(2)(b) (not yet in force: see note 1).

12   As to the meaning of 'local authority' see PARA 2.

13   Regulation and Inspection of Social Care (Wales) Act 2016 s 21(2)(c)(i) (not yet in force: see note 1).

14 Regulation and Inspection of Social Care (Wales) Act 2016 s 21(2)(c)(ii) (not yet in force: see note 1).
15 Regulation and Inspection of Social Care (Wales) Act 2016 s 21(2)(c)(iii) (not yet in force: see note 1).
16 Regulation and Inspection of Social Care (Wales) Act 2016 s 21(2)(d) (not yet in force: see note 1).
17 Regulation and Inspection of Social Care (Wales) Act 2016 s 21(2)(e) (not yet in force: see note 1). For the purposes of s 21(2)(e) a local authority's director of social services may designate an officer only if the director thinks that the officer has the necessary experience and expertise to be a responsible individual: s 21(3) (not yet in force). As to a local authority's director of social services see PARA 384.
18 Ie the requirements of the Regulation and Inspection of Social Care (Wales) Act 2016 s 21(2) (see the text and notes 9–17).
19 Regulation and Inspection of Social Care (Wales) Act 2016 s 22(1)(a) (not yet in force: see note 1).
20 For the purposes of the Regulation and Inspection of Social Care (Wales) Act 2016 s 22 and s 15(1)(d), (e) (see PARA 220), the following are relevant offences:
    (1)   an offence under the Regulation and Inspection of Social Care (Wales) Act 2016, the Care Standards Act 2000 Pt 2 (ss 11–42) (see CHILDREN AND YOUNG PERSONS vol 10 (2017) PARA 1017 et seq) or regulations made under that legislation (Regulation and Inspection of Social Care (Wales) Act 2016 ss 15(2)(a), (b), 22(2) (not yet in force: see note 1)); and
    (2)   any offence which, in the opinion of the Welsh Ministers, makes it appropriate for the registration to be cancelled (including an offence committed outside England and Wales which, if committed in England and Wales, would constitute a criminal offence) (s 15(2)(c) (not yet in force)).
21 Regulation and Inspection of Social Care (Wales) Act 2016 s 22(1)(b) (not yet in force: see note 1).
22 Regulation and Inspection of Social Care (Wales) Act 2016 s 22(1)(c) (not yet in force: see note 1).
23 Ie requirement imposed on the individual by regulations under the Regulation and Inspection of Social Care (Wales) Act 2016 s 28(1) (see PARA 214).
24 Regulation and Inspection of Social Care (Wales) Act 2016 s 22(1)(d) (not yet in force: see note 1).
25 Regulation and Inspection of Social Care (Wales) Act 2016 s 22(3) (not yet in force: see note 1). An improvement notice must specify:
    (1)   the reason why the Welsh Ministers propose to cancel the responsible individual's designation (s 22(4)(a) (not yet in force));
    (2)   either action that they think the individual must take or information they think the individual must provide, in order to satisfy them that the individual's designation should not be cancelled (s 22(4)(b) (not yet in force)); and
    (3)   a time limit within which the action must be taken or the information must be provided (s 22(4)(c) (not yet in force)).
26 Regulation and Inspection of Social Care (Wales) Act 2016 s 22(5) (not yet in force: see note 1). A notice of cancellation must be given to the responsible individual and the service provider who designated the individual: s 22(7) (not yet in force). An individual ceases to be designated as a responsible individual when the notice of cancellation is given to the service provider: s 22(8) (not yet in force). A notice of cancellation must give reasons for the decision, explain the right of appeal conferred by s 26 (see the text and note 28), explain the requirement on the service provider to apply for variation of registration (see s 11(1)(c); and PARA 223), and state the time limit prescribed under s 11(2) (prescribed time limit for applying to designate a new responsible individual: see PARA 223): s 22(9) (not yet in force).
The Welsh Ministers must notify each local authority of the cancellation of a designation of a responsible individual under s 22: s 39(1)(d) (not yet in force). As to such notifications (and in particular as to the meaning of 'local authority' in this context) see further s 39(2), (3); and PARA 203 note 3.
27 Regulation and Inspection of Social Care (Wales) Act 2016 s 22(6) (not yet in force: see note 1). In this context 'harm' means abuse or impairment of physical or mental health or physical, intellectual, emotional, social or behavioural development, and in a case where the harm relates to the impairment of a child's health or development, the child's health or development is to be compared with that which could reasonably be expected of a similar child: s 22(10) (not yet in force).
28 An appeal lies to the First-tier tribunal against a decision contained in a notice given under the Regulation and Inspection of Social Care (Wales) Act 2016 s 22(5) or (6) (see the text and notes 26–27): s 26(1) (not yet in force: see note 1). An appeal under s 26(1) must be made no later than 28 days after the date on which the decision notice is given (s 26(2) (not yet in force)), although the tribunal may allow an appeal to be made after the expiry of that 28 day period if it is satisfied

that there is a good reason for the failure to appeal before the expiry of that period (and for any delay in applying for permission to appeal out of time) (s 26(3) (not yet in force)). On an appeal under s 26(1) the tribunal may—

(1) confirm the decision (s 26(4)(a) (not yet in force));

(2) direct that the decision is not to take effect (or, if the decision has taken effect, direct that the decision is to cease to have effect) (s 26(4)(b) (not yet in force));

(3) substitute for the decision appealed against another decision that the Welsh Ministers could have made (s 26(4)(c) (not yet in force));

(4) make such other order (including an interim order) as the tribunal thinks appropriate (s 26(4)(d) (not yet in force)).

An interim order may, among other things, suspend the effect of a decision for such period as the tribunal may specify: s 26(5) (not yet in force). As to the establishment of the First-tier Tribunal see COURTS AND TRIBUNALS vol 24 (2010) PARA 874; as to membership, constitution etc see COURTS AND TRIBUNALS vol 24 (2010) PARAS 888–894, 903–917.

29 Regulation and Inspection of Social Care (Wales) Act 2016 s 44(1)(c) (not in force: see note 1). See further s 44(2); and PARA 203 note 7. As to offences see PARA 203 note 3.

213. Annual returns. As from a day to be appointed[1] a service provider[2] must submit an annual return to the Welsh Ministers[3] following the end of each financial year[4] during which the provider is registered[5]. An annual return must contain the following information:

(1) the regulated services[6] that the service provider is registered to provide[7];

(2) the places at, from or in relation to which the provider is registered to provide those services[8];

(3) the name of the responsible individual[9] registered in respect of each such place[10];

(4) the date on which the provider's registration took effect in respect of each such regulated service and place[11];

(5) details of any other conditions imposed on the service provider's registration[12];

(6) details of the number of persons to whom the provider provided care and support[13] during the year in the course of providing each such service[14];

(7) such information about training offered or undertaken in relation to each such service as may be prescribed[15];

(8) such information about workforce planning as may be prescribed[16]; and

(9) such other information as may be prescribed[17].

An annual return must also contain a statement setting out how the service provider has complied with any regulations about the provision of regulated services[18], specifying the standard of care and support that must be provided[19] by a service provider[20].

It is an offence:

(a) for a service provider to fail to submit an annual return to the Welsh Ministers within the prescribed time limit[21]; and

(b) for a person to make statement which he knows is false or materially misleading in an annual return submitted under these provisions[22].

1 At the date at which this volume states the law the Regulation and Inspection of Social Care (Wales) Act 2016 Pt 1 (ss 1–64) had yet to be brought into force.

2 As to the meaning of 'service provider' see PARA 203 note 4.

3 As to the Welsh Ministers see PARA 395.

4 'Financial year' means the period of one year beginning on 1 April and ending on 31 March: Regulation and Inspection of Social Care (Wales) Act 2016 s 189.

5 Regulation and Inspection of Social Care (Wales) Act 2016 s 10(1) (not yet in force: see note 1). An annual return must be in the prescribed form (s 10(2) (not yet in force)) and must be submitted to the Welsh Ministers within the prescribed time limit (s 10(3) (not yet in force)). At the date at

which this volume states the law nothing had been prescribed for this purpose. The Welsh Ministers must publish each annual return so submitted: s 10(5) (not yet in force).

6 As to the meaning of 'regulated service' see PARA 203.

7 Regulation and Inspection of Social Care (Wales) Act 2016 s 10(2)(a)(i) (not yet in force: see note 1).

8 Regulation and Inspection of Social Care (Wales) Act 2016 s 10(2)(a)(ii) (not yet in force: see note 1).

9 As to the responsible individual see PARA 212.

10 Regulation and Inspection of Social Care (Wales) Act 2016 s 10(2)(a)(iii) (not yet in force: see note 1).

11 Regulation and Inspection of Social Care (Wales) Act 2016 s 10(2)(a)(iv) (not yet in force: see note 1).

12 Regulation and Inspection of Social Care (Wales) Act 2016 s 10(2)(a)(v) (not yet in force: see note 1).

13 As to the meanings of 'care' and 'support' see PARA 204.

14 Regulation and Inspection of Social Care (Wales) Act 2016 s 10(2)(a)(vi) (not yet in force: see note 1).

15 Regulation and Inspection of Social Care (Wales) Act 2016 s 10(2)(a)(vii) (not yet in force: see note 1).

16 Regulation and Inspection of Social Care (Wales) Act 2016 s 10(2)(a)(viii) (not yet in force: see note 1).

17 Regulation and Inspection of Social Care (Wales) Act 2016 s 10(2)(a)(ix) (not yet in force: see note 1).

18 Ie any regulations under the Regulation and Inspection of Social Care (Wales) Act 2016 s 27(1) (see PARA 214).

19 See the Regulation and Inspection of Social Care (Wales) Act 2016 s 27(2); and PARA 214.

20 Regulation and Inspection of Social Care (Wales) Act 2016 s 10(2)(b) (not yet in force: see note 1).

21 Regulation and Inspection of Social Care (Wales) Act 2016 s 48 (not yet in force: see note 1). As to the prescribed time limit see s 10(1); and note 5. A person guilty of an offence under s 48 is liable on summary conviction to a fine: s 51(2) (not yet in force). As to the powers of magistrates' courts to issue fines on summary conviction see SENTENCING vol 92 (2015) PARA 176. As to proceedings, offences by bodies corporate etc see PARA 203 note 3. The Welsh Ministers may give a penalty notice to a person if they are satisfied that he has committed a prescribed offence (s 52(1) (not yet in force)); only offences under s 48, s 47 (see the text and note 22; and PARAS 216, 222, 224) or s 49 (see PARA 224), or under regulations made under s 45 or s 46 (see PARA 214), may be so prescribed (s 52(2) (not yet in force)). A penalty notice is a notice offering the person the opportunity of discharging any liability to conviction for the offence to which the notice relates by payment to the Welsh Ministers of a sum specified in the notice in accordance with the terms of the notice: s 52(3) (not yet in force). Where a person is given a penalty notice, proceedings for the offence to which the notice relates may not be brought before the end of such period as may be specified in the notice: s 52(4) (not yet in force). If a person who is given a penalty notice pays the sum specified in the notice in accordance with the terms of the notice, the person cannot be convicted of the offence to which the notice relates: s 52(5) (not yet in force). The Welsh Ministers may by regulations make provision:

(1) as to the form and content of penalty notices (s 52(6)(a) (not yet in force));

(2) as to the sum payable under a penalty notice and the time within which it is to be paid (including provision permitting a different sum to be payable in relation to different offences and according to the time by which it is paid) (s 52(6)(b) (not yet in force));

(3) determining the ways in which a sum may be paid (s 52(6)(c) (not yet in force));

(4) as to the records to be kept in relation to penalty notices (s 52(6)(d) (not yet in force));

(5) about the circumstances in which a penalty notice may be withdrawn, including provision about the repayment of any sum paid before a notice is withdrawn and the circumstances in which proceedings for an offence may not be brought despite the withdrawal of a notice (s 52(6)(e) (not yet in force)).

Regulations under s 52(6)(b) may not make provision for a sum to be payable under a penalty notice which exceeds two and a half times level 4 on the standard scale: s 52(7) (not yet in force).

As to the powers of magistrates' courts to issue fines on summary conviction see SENTENCING vol 92 (2015) PARA 176. At the date at which this volume states the law no such regulations had been made. The Welsh Ministers must notify each local authority of s penalty notice given under s 52: s 39(1)(f) (not yet in force). As to such notifications (and in particular as to the meaning of 'local authority' in this context) see further s 39(2), (3); and PARA 203 note 3.

22 Regulation and Inspection of Social Care (Wales) Act 2016 s 47(c) (not yet in force: see note 1).

B.   IMPOSITION OF STANDARDS

214. Imposition of requirements on service providers and responsible individuals. As from a day to be appointed[1] the Welsh Ministers[2] may by regulations[3] impose requirements on a service provider[4] in relation to a regulated service[5]. Requirements so imposed must include requirements as to the standard of care and support[6] to be provided by a service provider[7] and when making regulations imposing requirements of this kind the Ministers must have regard to the importance of the well-being[8] of any individuals to whom care and support will be provided[9] and the quality standards included in any code[10] relating to the achievement of well-being outcomes[11].

The Ministers may also by regulations impose requirements on a responsible individual[12] in relation to a place in respect of which the individual is designated[13]. Such regulations may include provision requiring a responsible individual to appoint an individual of a prescribed description to manage the place in respect of which the responsible individual is designated[14], and may make provision for a function conferred on a responsible individual by the regulations to be delegated to another person only in prescribed circumstances[15].

The Ministers may also by regulations provide that it is an offence for a service provider or responsible individual to fail to comply with a specified provision of such regulations[16].

At the date at which this volume states the law no such regulations had been made.

1 At the date at which this volume states the law the Regulation and Inspection of Social Care (Wales) Act 2016 Pt 1 (ss 1–64) had yet to be brought into force.
2 As to the Welsh Ministers see PARA 395.
3 Before making regulations under these provisions the Welsh Ministers must consult any persons they think appropriate and, in the case of regulations under the Regulation and Inspection of Social Care (Wales) Act 2016 s 27, publish a statement about the consultation: ss 27(4), 28(4) (not yet in force: see note 1). The Welsh Ministers must lay a copy of a statement published under s 27(4) before the National Assembly for Wales: s 27(5) (not yet in force). The requirement to consult and (where applicable) publish a statement does not apply to regulations which amend other regulations made under s 27 or s 28 and do not, in the opinion of the Welsh Ministers, effect any substantial change in the provision made by the regulations to be amended: ss 27(6), 28(5) (not yet in force).
    The Welsh Ministers must publish guidance about how service providers may comply with requirements imposed by regulations under s 27(1) (including how providers may meet any standards for the provision of a regulated service specified by such regulations) and how responsible individuals may comply with requirements imposed by regulations under s 28(1): s 29(1) (not yet in force). The Ministers may revise such guidance and must publish the revised guidance: s 29(2) (not yet in force). Service providers and responsible individuals must have regard to guidance published under s 29: s 29(3) (not yet in force).
4 As to the meaning of 'service provider' see PARA 203 note 4.
5 Regulation and Inspection of Social Care (Wales) Act 2016 s 27(1) (not yet in force: see note 1). As to the meaning of 'regulated service' see PARA 203.
6 As to the meanings of 'care' and 'support' see PARA 204.
7 Regulation and Inspection of Social Care (Wales) Act 2016 s 27(2) (not yet in force: see note 1).
8 As to the meaning of 'well-being' see PARA 375.
9 Regulation and Inspection of Social Care (Wales) Act 2016 s 27(3)(a) (not yet in force: see note 1).
10 Ie a code issued under the Social Services and Well-being (Wales) Act 2014 s 9 (see PARA 396).
11 Regulation and Inspection of Social Care (Wales) Act 2016 s 27(3)(b) (not yet in force: see note 1).
12 As to the responsible individual see PARA 212.
13 Regulation and Inspection of Social Care (Wales) Act 2016 s 28(1) (not yet in force: see note 1). See note 2.
14 Regulation and Inspection of Social Care (Wales) Act 2016 s 28(2) (not yet in force: see note 1).
15 Regulation and Inspection of Social Care (Wales) Act 2016 s 28(3) (not yet in force: see note 1). Such provision may not affect the liability or responsibility of the responsible individual for exercising the function: s 28(3) (not yet in force).

16 Regulation and Inspection of Social Care (Wales) Act 2016 ss 45, 46 (not yet in force: see note 1). As to offences see PARA 203 note 3. An offence under regulations made under s 45 or s 46 may be prescribed as an offence in relation to which a penalty notice may be issued: see s 52; and PARA 213 note 21.

215. Service providers who are liquidated or have died. As from a day to be appointed[1] the Welsh Ministers[2] may by regulations make provision requiring an insolvency practitioner[3] (an 'appointed person') to notify them of his appointment[4] and requiring the personal representatives of a service provider who is an individual who has died to notify them of the death[5].

1 At the date at which this volume states the law the Regulation and Inspection of Social Care (Wales) Act 2016 Pt 1 (ss 1–64) had yet to be brought into force.
2 As to the Welsh Ministers see PARA 395.
3 Ie a person appointed as:
   (1) a receiver or administrative receiver of the property of a service provider who is a body corporate or a partnership (Regulation and Inspection of Social Care (Wales) Act 2016 s 30(2)(a) (not yet in force: see note 1));
   (2) a liquidator, provisional liquidator or administrator of a service provider who is a body corporate or a partnership (s 30(2)(b) (not yet in force));
   (3) a trustee in bankruptcy of a service provider who is an individual or a partnership (s 30(2)(2) (not yet in force)).
   As to the meaning of 'service provider' see PARA 203 note 4.
4 Regulation and Inspection of Social Care (Wales) Act 2016 s 30(1)(a) (not yet in force: see note 1). Regulations under s 30 or s 31 may also make provision for Pt 1 (ss 1–64) to apply with prescribed modifications to service providers in relation to whom an insolvency practitioner has been appointed (s 30(1)(b) (not yet in force)), or where a service provider who is an individual has died (s 31(1)(a) (not yet in force)).
5 Regulation and Inspection of Social Care (Wales) Act 2016 s 31(1)(b) (not yet in force: see note 1). Regulations under s 31(1) may in particular provide for a prescribed person who is not a service provider to act in that capacity for a prescribed period and for that period to be extended in prescribed circumstances: s 31(2) (not yet in force).

C. APPLICATIONS FOR REGISTRATION

216. Making and granting of applications. As from a day to be appointed[1] a person who wants to provide a regulated service[2] must make an application for registration to the Welsh Ministers[3]:
   (1) specifying the regulated service that he wants to provide[4];
   (2) specifying the places at, from or in relation to which the service is to be provided[5];
   (3) designating an individual as the responsible individual[6] in respect of each place and stating each such individual's name and address[7]; and
   (4) including such other information as may be prescribed[8].
The Welsh Ministers must grant such an application, subject to conditions and notification[9], if satisfied that:
   (a) the application is in the prescribed form[10] and contains everything required under heads (1) to (4) above[11];
   (b) the applicant is a fit and proper person to be a service provider[12];
   (c) each individual to be designated as a responsible individual[13] is eligible[14] to be a responsible individual, is a fit and proper person to be a responsible individual and will comply with any regulatory[15] requirements[16];
   (d) the requirements of any regulations about the provision of regulated services[17] and any other enactment which appears to the Welsh Ministers to be relevant, will be complied with (so far as applicable) in relation to the provision of the regulated service[18].
In any other case the Welsh Ministers must refuse an application[19].

It is an offence for a person to make a statement which he knows is false or materially misleading in an application for registration as a service provider[20].

1   At the date at which this volume states the law the Regulation and Inspection of Social Care (Wales) Act 2016 Pt 1 (ss 1–64) had yet to be brought into force.
2   As to the meaning of 'regulated service' see PARA 203.
3   As to the Welsh Ministers see PARA 395. An application must be in the prescribed form: Regulation and Inspection of Social Care (Wales) Act 2016 s 6(2) (not yet in force: see note 1). At the date at which this volume states the law no form had been prescribed for this purpose. A person who wants to be registered as a service provider in respect of two or more regulated services may make a single application in respect of them (s 6(3) (not yet in force)), and where a person has made a single application in respect of two or more regulated services the Ministers may separately grant or refuse the application in respect of each service (s 7(4) (not yet in force)).
    The Welsh Ministers may by regulations make provision requiring a fee to be paid by a person making an application for registration as a service provider under s 6 (s 40(1)(a) (not yet in force)) or to allow the person to continue to be registered as a service provider for such period as may be prescribed in the regulations (s 40(1)(c) (not yet in force)). Such regulations may include provision:
    (1)   specifying the amount of any fee or permitting the Welsh Ministers to determine the amount of any fee (subject to any limits or other factors as may be specified in the regulations) (s 40(2)(a) (not yet in force));
    (2)   specifying circumstances in which a fee, which would otherwise be payable under the regulations, is not payable (s 40(2)(b) (not yet in force));
    (3)   specifying the time by which a fee is to be payable or specifying factors by which that time is to be determined by the Welsh Ministers (s 40(2)(c) (not yet in force));
    (4)   about the consequences of failing to pay a fee (which may include refusal to register, or cancellation of registration) (s 40(2)(d) (not yet in force)).
    Before making regulations under s 40(1) the Ministers must take reasonable steps to consult persons who the Ministers think may be required to pay a fee by virtue of the regulations and such other persons as they think appropriate: s 40(3) (not yet in force). A fee payable by virtue of regulations made under s 40(1) may, without prejudice to any other method of recovery, be recovered summarily as a civil debt: s 40(4) (not yet in force).
    At the date at which this volume states the law no fees had been prescribed for this purpose.
4   Regulation and Inspection of Social Care (Wales) Act 2016 s 6(1)(a) (not yet in force: see note 1).
5   Regulation and Inspection of Social Care (Wales) Act 2016 s 6(1)(b) (not yet in force: see note 1).
6   As to the responsible individual see PARA 212.
7   Regulation and Inspection of Social Care (Wales) Act 2016 s 6(1)(c) (not yet in force: see note 1).
8   Regulation and Inspection of Social Care (Wales) Act 2016 s 6(1)(d) (not yet in force: see note 1). At the date at which this volume states the law no further information had been prescribed for this purpose.
9   The grant of an application must be subject to a condition specifying the places at, from or in relation to which the service provider is to provide a regulated service, and the individual designated as the responsible individual for each place (Regulation and Inspection of Social Care (Wales) Act 2016 s 7(3)(a) (not yet in force: see note 1)), and may be subject to such further conditions as the Welsh Ministers think appropriate (s 7(3)(b) (not yet in force)). As to the meaning of 'service provider' see PARA 203 note 4. See also PARA 217 (notification requirements).
10 Ie meets the requirements prescribed under the Regulation and Inspection of Social Care (Wales) Act 2016 s 6(2) (see note 3).
11 Regulation and Inspection of Social Care (Wales) Act 2016 s 7(1)(a)(i), (iii) (not yet in force: see note 1). An additional undertaking is prescribed in connection with an application relating to a domiciliary support service (as to which see PARA 210): see ss 7(1)(a)(ii), 8 (not yet in force).
12 Regulation and Inspection of Social Care (Wales) Act 2016 s 7(1)(b) (not yet in force: see note 1). As to the 'fit and proper person' test see PARA 211.
13 As to the responsible individual see PARA 212.
14 Ie in accordance with the Regulation and Inspection of Social Care (Wales) Act 2016 s 21(2) (see PARA 212).
15 Ie an requirements of regulations under the Regulation and Inspection of Social Care (Wales) Act 2016 s 28 (so far as applicable) (see PARA 214).
16 Regulation and Inspection of Social Care (Wales) Act 2016 s 7(1)(c) (not yet in force: see note 1).
17 Ie any regulations under the Regulation and Inspection of Social Care (Wales) Act 2016 s 27 (including any requirements as to the standard of care and support that must be provided) (see PARA 214).
18 Regulation and Inspection of Social Care (Wales) Act 2016 s 7(1)(d) (not yet in force: see note 1).
19 Regulation and Inspection of Social Care (Wales) Act 2016 s 7(2) (not yet in force: see note 1).

20 Regulation and Inspection of Social Care (Wales) Act 2016 s 47(a) (not yet in force: see note 1). As to offences see PARA 203 note 3. An offence under s 47 may be prescribed as an offence in relation to which a penalty notice may be issued: see s 52; and PARA 213 note 21.

217. Notification requirements. As from a day to be appointed[1], where the Welsh Ministers[2] propose to grant an application for registration as a service provider[3] subject to a condition that has not been agreed in writing with the applicant[4], or to refuse such an application[5], they must give a notice of the proposal to the service provider specifying the action they propose to take[6], giving reasons for the proposal[7], and specifying a time limit of no less than 28 days from the date on which the notice is given within which the service provider may make representations to them[8].

Where the Welsh Ministers have given a notice of proposal[9], in making a decision on the proposal, the Ministers must have regard to any representations made to them (whether made by the service provider or any other person who the Welsh Ministers think has an interest)[10]. The Ministers must give a notice of decision to the service provider no later than 28 days after the expiry of the later of the specified[11] time limit[12]. A notice of decision must:

(1)   state whether the Ministers have decided to take the action specified in the notice of proposal[13];

(2)   give reasons for the decision[14]; and

(3)   if the Ministers have decided to take the action specified in the notice of proposal, explain the right of appeal[15].

Where the Welsh Ministers have decided to grant an application for registration as a service provider subject only to conditions that have been agreed in writing with the applicant[16], they must give a notice of decision to the service provider[17]. A decision on a proposal is subject to appeal[18].

The grant of an application for registration[19] takes effect only if the notification requirements[20] are met (so far as applicable)[21].

1   At the date at which this volume states the law the Regulation and Inspection of Social Care (Wales) Act 2016 Pt 1 (ss 1–64) had yet to be brought into force.

2   As to the Welsh Ministers see PARA 395.

3   As to the making and granting of applications see PARA 216. As to the meaning of 'service provider' see PARA 203 note 4. In the case of a refusal of an application for registration as a service provider references in the Regulation and Inspection of Social Care (Wales) Act 2016 ss 18, 19 (see the text and notes 4–21) to a 'service provider' are to be treated as references to the person who applied to be registered as a service provider: s 18(4) (not yet in force: see note 1).

       Note that these provisions (ie ss 18–20) apply also to the Welsh Ministers' power to grant or refuse an application for the variation of a service provider's registration on the application of that provider: see s 12; and PARA 223.

4   Regulation and Inspection of Social Care (Wales) Act 2016 s 18(1)(a) (not yet in force: see note 1).

5   Regulation and Inspection of Social Care (Wales) Act 2016 s 18(1)(b) (not yet in force: see note 1).

6   Regulation and Inspection of Social Care (Wales) Act 2016 s 18(2)(a) (not yet in force: see note 1). A notice of proposal under s 18(2) may specify action which, if taken by a provider within the time limit specified in the notice, would result in the Ministers not taking the action they propose in the notice: s 18(3) (not yet in force). Where the Welsh Ministers have given a notice of proposal and are satisfied that a service provider has taken such action as may be specified under s 18(3) within the time limit specified in the notice of proposal, they must not take the action proposed in the notice: s 19(3) (not yet in force).

7   Regulation and Inspection of Social Care (Wales) Act 2016 s 18(2)(b) (not yet in force: see note 1).

8   Regulation and Inspection of Social Care (Wales) Act 2016 s 18(2)(c) (not yet in force: see note 1).

9   Ie a notice of proposal under the Regulation and Inspection of Social Care (Wales) Act 2016 s 18: see the text and notes 1–8; and see also PARA 218 (notification of Welsh Ministers' intention to vary or cancel registration).

10   Regulation and Inspection of Social Care (Wales) Act 2016 s 19(1), (2) (not yet in force: see note 1).

11   Ie the time limit specified under the Regulation and Inspection of Social Care (Wales) Act 2016 s 18(2)(c) (see the text and note 8) or any time limit as may be specified under s 18(3) (see note 6).

12 Regulation and Inspection of Social Care (Wales) Act 2016 s 19(4) (not yet in force: see note 1). Notwithstanding s 19(4), a notice of decision given after the 28 day period mentioned therein is valid if the notice gives reasons for the delay in making the decision and is given no later than 56 days after the expiry of the later of the time limits mentioned in note 9: s 19(5) (not yet in force). The Welsh Ministers may by regulations amend the 28 day period mentioned in s 19(4) and the 56 day period mentioned in s 19(5) (s 19(8) (not yet in force)); at the date at which this volume states the law no such regulations had been made. A decision stated in a notice given under s 19(4) to take action specified in a notice of proposal takes effect:

    (1)   if no appeal is made against the decision, on the day after the last day of the 28 day period referred to in s 26(2) (s 19(7)(a) (not yet in force)); or

    (2)   if an appeal is made, on the day specified by the tribunal in determining the appeal or on the day the appeal is withdrawn (s 19(7)(b) (not yet in force)).

13 Regulation and Inspection of Social Care (Wales) Act 2016 s 19(6)(a) (not yet in force: see note 1).
14 Regulation and Inspection of Social Care (Wales) Act 2016 s 19(6)(b) (not yet in force: see note 1).
15 Regulation and Inspection of Social Care (Wales) Act 2016 s 19(6)(c) (not yet in force: see note 1) (not yet in force: see note 1).
16 Regulation and Inspection of Social Care (Wales) Act 2016 s 20(1)(a) (not yet in force: see note 1).
17 Regulation and Inspection of Social Care (Wales) Act 2016 s 20(2) (not yet in force: see note 1). A decision stated in a notice given under s 20(2) takes effect on the date on which the notice is given: s 20(3) (not yet in force).
18 An appeal lies to the First-tier tribunal against a decision contained in a notice given under the Regulation and Inspection of Social Care (Wales) Act 2016 s 19(4): s 26(1) (not yet in force: see note 1). As to appeals see further s 26(2)–(5); and PARA 212 note 28.
19 Ie an application under the Regulation and Inspection of Social Care (Wales) Act 2016 s 6 (see PARA 216).
20 Ie the requirements of the Regulation and Inspection of Social Care (Wales) Act 2016 ss 18–20 (see the text and notes 1–17).
21 Regulation and Inspection of Social Care (Wales) Act 2016 s 7(5) (not yet in force: see note 1).

D.   VARIATION AND CANCELLATION OF REGISTRATION

218. Welsh Ministers' power to vary or cancel. As from a day to be appointed[1] the Welsh Ministers[2] may vary any condition[3] of a person's registration[4] or impose a further condition on a service provider's[5] registration[6]. Where the Welsh Ministers propose to make such a variation[7] they must give a notice of the proposal to the service provider[8] specifying the action they propose to take[9], giving reasons for the proposal[10], and specifying a time limit of no less than 28 days from the date on which the notice is given within which the service provider may make representations to them[11]. No variation of a provider's registration may be made under these provisions unless the notification requirements[12] are met[13].

1 At the date at which this volume states the law the Regulation and Inspection of Social Care (Wales) Act 2016 Pt 1 (ss 1–64) had yet to be brought into force.
2 As to the Welsh Ministers see PARA 395.
3 Ie any condition imposed under the Regulation and Inspection of Social Care (Wales) Act 2016 s 7(3)(b) (see PARA 216), s 12(2) (see PARA 223) or s 13(1)(b) (see the text and note 6).
4 Regulation and Inspection of Social Care (Wales) Act 2016 s 13(1)(a) (not yet in force: see note 1).
5 As to the meaning of 'service provider' see PARA 203 note 4.
6 Regulation and Inspection of Social Care (Wales) Act 2016 s 13(1)(b) (not yet in force: see note 1).
7 Ie where the Welsh Ministers propose to vary the registration of a service provider other than in accordance with an application for variation made under the Regulation and Inspection of Social Care (Wales) Act 2016 s 11 (see PARA 223) or under s 13(3) or (4) (see PARA 218), s 23(1)(b) (see PARA 221) or s 25(2)(a) (see PARA 221): s 18(1)(c) (not yet in force: see note 1).
8 In connection with notices of proposal see the Regulation and Inspection of Social Care (Wales) Act 2016 ss 18(3), 19 (remedial action and decision following notice); and PARA 217.
9 Regulation and Inspection of Social Care (Wales) Act 2016 s 18(2)(a) (not yet in force: see note 1). A notice of proposal may specify action which, if taken by a provider within the time limit specified in the notice, would result in the Ministers not taking the action they propose in the notice: s 18(3) (not yet in force). Where the Welsh Ministers have given a notice of proposal and are satisfied that a service provider has taken such action as may be specified under s 18(3) within the time limit specified in the notice of proposal, they must not take the action proposed in the notice: s 19(3) (not yet in force).

10 Regulation and Inspection of Social Care (Wales) Act 2016 s 18(2)(b) (not yet in force: see note 1).
11 Regulation and Inspection of Social Care (Wales) Act 2016 s 18(2)(c) (not yet in force: see note 1).
12 Ie the requirements of the Regulation and Inspection of Social Care (Wales) Act 2016 ss 18, 19 (see
    PARA 217).
13 Regulation and Inspection of Social Care (Wales) Act 2016 s 13(2) (not yet in force: see note 1).
    This does not affect the Welsh Ministers' power to urgently vary a registration under s 25) (see
    PARA 221): s 13(2) (not yet in force).

219. Welsh Ministers' power to remove a regulated service from a person's registration. As from a day to be appointed[1] if a service provider[2] provides more than one regulated service[3] the Welsh Ministers[4] may vary the provider's registration by removing a regulated service if satisfied that the service provider no longer provides that service[5] or the service is not being provided in accordance with the regulatory[6] requirements[7]. If a service provider provides a regulated service at, from or in relation to more than one place, the Welsh Ministers may vary his registration by removing a place if satisfied that:

(1)   the service provider no longer provides a regulated service at, from or in relation to that place[8];

(2)   the service provided at, from or in relation to that place is not being provided in accordance with the regulatory requirements[9]; or

(3)   there is no responsible individual designated in respect of that place (and the applicable time limit[10] has expired)[11].

Where the Welsh Ministers propose to vary a provider's registration under these provisions[12] they must give an improvement notice to the service provider before varying the registration[13]. An improvement notice must specify:

(a)   the ground on which the Ministers propose to vary the registration and the manner of the variation[14];

(b)   action the Ministers think the provider must take, or information the provider must provide, in order to satisfy them that variation on the basis of that ground is not appropriate[15]; and

(c)   a time limit within which the action must be taken or the information must be provided and the service provider may make representations[16].

If the Welsh Ministers are satisfied that action specified in an improvement notice has been taken[17] or information so specified has been provided[18], within the time limit specified in the notice they must notify the service provider that they have decided not to vary the provider's registration on the ground specified in the improvement notice[19]. If the Ministers are not satisfied that information specified in an improvement notice has been provided within the time limit specified in the notice they must give the service provider a decision notice stating that the provider's registration is to be varied on the ground specified in the improvement notice[20]. If the Ministers are not satisfied that action specified in an improvement notice has been taken within the time limit specified in the notice they must either:

(i)   give the service provider a decision notice stating that the provider's registration is to be varied on the ground specified in the improvement notice[21]; or

(ii)   notify the provider that the action has not been taken, of a new date by which the action must be taken, that, following that date, an inspection[22] of the regulated service or place to which the improvement notice relates will be carried out, and that, following that inspection, if the action has not been taken they will proceed to vary the provider's registration on the ground specified in the improvement notice[23].

A decision to remove a regulated service under these provisions is subject to appeal[24].

No variation may be made under these provisions unless the notification requirements[25] are met[26].

1   At the date at which this volume states the law the Regulation and Inspection of Social Care (Wales) Act 2016 Pt 1 (ss 1–64) had yet to be brought into force.
2   As to the meaning of 'service provider' see PARA 203 note 4.
3   As to the meaning of 'regulated service' see PARA 203.
4   As to the Welsh Ministers see PARA 395.
5   Regulation and Inspection of Social Care (Wales) Act 2016 s 13(3)(a) (not yet in force: see note 1).
6   Ie the requirements mentioned in the Regulation and Inspection of Social Care (Wales) Act 2016 s 7(1)(d) (see PARA 216) so far as applicable to that service.
7   Regulation and Inspection of Social Care (Wales) Act 2016 s 13(3)(b) (not yet in force: see note 1).
8   Regulation and Inspection of Social Care (Wales) Act 2016 s 13(4)(a) (not yet in force: see note 1).
9   Regulation and Inspection of Social Care (Wales) Act 2016 s 13(4)(b) (not yet in force: see note 1). See note 6.
10 Ie the time limit prescribed under the Regulation and Inspection of Social Care (Wales) Act 2016 s 11(2) (see PARA 223).
11 Regulation and Inspection of Social Care (Wales) Act 2016 s 13(4)(c) (not yet in force: see note 1). See note 6.
12 Regulation and Inspection of Social Care (Wales) Act 2016 s 16(1)(b) (not yet in force: see note 1). The Welsh Ministers must notify each local authority of the variation of the registration of a service provider by removing from the registration a regulated service or a place at, from or in relation to which the provider is providing a regulated service: s 39(1)(b) (not yet in force). As to such notifications (and in particular as to the meaning of 'local authority' in this context) see further s 39(2), (3); and PARA 203 note 3.
13 Regulation and Inspection of Social Care (Wales) Act 2016 s 16(2) (not yet in force: see note 1).
14 Regulation and Inspection of Social Care (Wales) Act 2016 s 16(3)(a) (not yet in force: see note 1).
15 Regulation and Inspection of Social Care (Wales) Act 2016 s 16(3)(b) (not yet in force: see note 1).
16 Regulation and Inspection of Social Care (Wales) Act 2016 s 16(3)(c) (not yet in force: see note 1). The service provider may make representations to the Ministers before the expiry of the time limit specified in the improvement notice and the Ministers must have regard to those representations when deciding what to do under s 17 (see the text and notes 17–23): s 16(4) (not yet in force).
17 Regulation and Inspection of Social Care (Wales) Act 2016 s 17(1)(a) (not yet in force: see note 1).
18 Regulation and Inspection of Social Care (Wales) Act 2016 s 17(1)(b) (not yet in force: see note 1).
19 Regulation and Inspection of Social Care (Wales) Act 2016 s 17(1) (not yet in force: see note 1).
20 Regulation and Inspection of Social Care (Wales) Act 2016 s 17(2) (not yet in force: see note 1). A decision notice given under s 17(2), (3)(a) or (5) must state the reasons for the decision (including the grounds for variation) and explain the right of appeal conferred by s 26 (see PARA 212 note 28): s 17(6) (not yet in force). A decision stated in a notice given under s 17(2), (3)(a) or (5) takes effect:
    (1)   if no appeal is made against the decision, on the day after the last day of the 28 day period referred to in s 26(2) (s 17(7)(a) (not yet in force:)); or
    (2)   if an appeal is made, on the day specified by the tribunal in determining the appeal or on the day the appeal is withdrawn (s 17(7)(b) (not yet in force)).
21 Regulation and Inspection of Social Care (Wales) Act 2016 s 17(3)(a) (not yet in force: see note 1). See note 20.
22 Ie under the under Regulation and Inspection of Social Care (Wales) Act 2016 s 33 (see PARA 225).
23 Regulation and Inspection of Social Care (Wales) Act 2016 s 17(3)(b) (not yet in force: see note 1). If, after the inspection, the Ministers are satisfied that the action specified in the improvement notice has been taken they must notify the service provider that they have decided not to vary the provider's registration on the ground specified in the improvement notice: s 17(4) (not yet in force). If, after the inspection, the Ministers are still not satisfied that the action specified in the improvement notice has been taken they must give the service provider a decision notice stating that the provider's registration is to be varied on the ground specified in the improvement notice: s 17(5) (not yet in force). See note 20.
24 An appeal lies to the First-tier tribunal against a decision contained in a notice given under the Regulation and Inspection of Social Care (Wales) Act 2016 s 17(2), (3)(a) or (5): s 26(1) (not yet in force: see note 1). As to appeals see further s 26(2)–(5); and PARA 212 note 28.
25 Ie the requirements of the Regulation and Inspection of Social Care (Wales) Act 2016 ss 16, 17 (see the text and notes 11–23).

26 Regulation and Inspection of Social Care (Wales) Act 2016 s 13(5) (not yet in force: see note 1). This does not affect the Welsh Ministers' power to urgently vary a registration under s 23) (see PARA 221): s 13(5) (not yet in force).

220. Welsh Ministers' power to cancel a registration. As from a day to be appointed[1] the Welsh Ministers[2] may cancel the registration of a service provider[3] if:

(1)   the service provider no longer provides any regulated services[4];

(2)   the Welsh Ministers are no longer satisfied that the service provider is a fit and proper person to be a service provider[5];

(3)   there is no responsible individual[6] designated in respect of each place at, from or in relation to which the provider provides a regulated service (and the time limit for applying to vary the registration[7] has expired)[8];

(4)   the service provider or a responsible individual designated in respect of a place at, from or in relation to which the provider provides a regulated service has been convicted of, or has been given a caution in respect of, a relevant offence[9] in connection with a regulated service provided by the service provider[10];

(5)   any other person has been convicted of, or has been given a caution in respect of, a relevant offence in connection with a regulated service provided by the service provider[11]; or

(6)   a regulated service provided by the service provider is not being provided in accordance with the regulatory[12] requirements[13].

Where the Welsh Ministers propose to cancel the registration of a service provider under these provisions[14] they must give an improvement notice to the service provider before cancelling the registration[15]. An improvement notice must specify:

(a)   the ground on which the Ministers propose to cancel the registration[16];

(b)   action the Ministers think the provider must take, or information the provider must provide, in order to satisfy them that cancellation on the basis of that ground is not appropriate[17]; and

(c)   a time limit within which the action must be taken or the information must be provided and the service provider may make representations[18].

If the Ministers are satisfied that action specified in an improvement notice has been taken[19] or information so specified has been provided[20], within the time limit specified in the notice they must notify the service provider that they have decided not to cancel the provider's registration on the ground specified in the improvement notice[21]. If the Ministers are not satisfied that information specified in an improvement notice has been provided within the time limit specified in the notice they must give the service provider a decision notice stating that the provider's registration is to be cancelled on the ground specified in the improvement notice[22]. If the Ministers are not satisfied that action specified in an improvement notice has been taken within the time limit specified in the notice they must either:

(i)   give the service provider a decision notice stating that the provider's registration is to be cancelled on the ground specified in the improvement notice[23]; or

(ii)   notify the provider that the action has not been taken, of a new date by which the action must be taken, that, following that date, an inspection[24] of the regulated service or place to which the improvement notice relates will be carried out, and that, following that inspection, if the action has not been taken they will proceed to cancel the provider's registration on the ground specified in the improvement notice[25].

No cancellation may be made under these provisions unless the notification requirements[26] are met[27].

1 At the date at which this volume states the law the Regulation and Inspection of Social Care (Wales) Act 2016 Pt 1 (ss 1–64) had yet to be brought into force.

2 As to the Welsh Ministers see PARA 395.

3 As to the meaning of 'service provider' see PARA 203 note 4. The Welsh Ministers must notify each local authority of the cancellation of the registration of a service provider: Regulation and Inspection of Social Care (Wales) Act 2016 s 39(1)(a) (not yet in force: see note 1). As to such notifications (and in particular as to the meaning of 'local authority' in this context) see further s 39(2), (3); and PARA 203 note 3.

4 Regulation and Inspection of Social Care (Wales) Act 2016 s 15(1)(a) (not yet in force: see note 1). As to the meaning of 'regulated service' see PARA 203.

5 Regulation and Inspection of Social Care (Wales) Act 2016 s 15(1)(b) (not yet in force: see note 1). As to the fit and proper person test see s 9; and PARA 211.

6 As to the responsible individual see PARA 212.

7 Ie prescribed in regulations made under the Regulation and Inspection of Social Care (Wales) Act 2016 s 11(2) (see PARA 223).

8 Regulation and Inspection of Social Care (Wales) Act 2016 s 15(1)(c) (not yet in force: see note 1).

9 As to the meaning of 'relevant offence' see PARA 212 note 20.

10 Regulation and Inspection of Social Care (Wales) Act 2016 s 15(1)(d) (not yet in force: see note 1).

11 Regulation and Inspection of Social Care (Wales) Act 2016 s 15(1)(e) (not yet in force: see note 1).

12 Ie the requirements mentioned in the Regulation and Inspection of Social Care (Wales) Act 2016 s 7(1)(d) (see PARA 216) so far as applicable to that service.

13 Regulation and Inspection of Social Care (Wales) Act 2016 s 15(1)(f) (not yet in force: see note 1).

14 Regulation and Inspection of Social Care (Wales) Act 2016 s 16(1)(a) (not yet in force: see note 1).

15 Regulation and Inspection of Social Care (Wales) Act 2016 s 16(2) (not yet in force: see note 1).

16 Regulation and Inspection of Social Care (Wales) Act 2016 s 16(3)(a) (not yet in force: see note 1).

17 Regulation and Inspection of Social Care (Wales) Act 2016 s 16(3)(b) (not yet in force: see note 1).

18 Regulation and Inspection of Social Care (Wales) Act 2016 s 16(3)(c) (not yet in force: see note 1). The service provider may make representations to the Ministers before the expiry of the time limit specified in the improvement notice and the Ministers must have regard to those representations when deciding what to do under s 17 (see the text and notes 19–25): s 16(4) (not yet in force).

19 Regulation and Inspection of Social Care (Wales) Act 2016 s 17(1)(a) (not yet in force: see note 1).

20 Regulation and Inspection of Social Care (Wales) Act 2016 s 17(1)(b) (not yet in force: see note 1).

21 Regulation and Inspection of Social Care (Wales) Act 2016 s 17(1) (not yet in force: see note 1).

22 Regulation and Inspection of Social Care (Wales) Act 2016 s 17(2) (not yet in force: see note 1). A decision notice given under s 17(2), (3)(a) or (5) must state the reasons for the decision (including the grounds for cancellation) and explain the right of appeal conferred by s 26 (see PARA 212 note 28): s 17(6) (not yet in force). A decision stated in a notice given under s 17(2), (3)(a) or (5) takes effect:

(1) if no appeal is made against the decision, on the day after the last day of the 28 day period referred to in s 26(2) (s 17(7)(a) (not yet in force)); or

(2) if an appeal is made, on the day specified by the tribunal in determining the appeal or on the day the appeal is withdrawn (s 17(7)(b) (not yet in force)).

23 Regulation and Inspection of Social Care (Wales) Act 2016 s 17(3)(a) (not yet in force: see note 1). See note 22.

24 Ie under the Regulation and Inspection of Social Care (Wales) Act 2016 s 33 (see PARA 225).

25 Regulation and Inspection of Social Care (Wales) Act 2016 s 17(3)(b) (not yet in force: see note 1). If, after the inspection, the Ministers are satisfied that the action specified in the improvement notice has been taken they must notify the service provider that they have decided not to cancel the provider's registration on the ground specified in the improvement notice: s 17(4) (not yet in force). If, after the inspection, the Ministers are still not satisfied that the action specified in the improvement notice has been taken they must give the service provider a decision notice stating that the provider's registration is to be cancelled on the ground specified in the improvement notice: s 17(5) (not yet in force). See note 22.

26 Ie the requirements of the Regulation and Inspection of Social Care (Wales) Act 2016 ss 16, 17 (see the text and notes 14–25).

27 Regulation and Inspection of Social Care (Wales) Act 2016 s 15(3) (not yet in force: see note 1). This does not affect the Welsh Ministers' power to urgently cancel a registration under s 23) (see PARA 221): s 15(3) (not yet in force).

221. Urgent cases. As from a day to be appointed[1] the Welsh Ministers may apply[2] to a justice of the peace for an order authorising them to cancel the registration of a service provider[3], or to vary the registration of a service provider by removing from the registration a regulated service[4] or a place at, from or in relation to which the provider is providing a regulated service[5], on the ground that unless the registration is cancelled or varied there is a serious risk to a person's life or physical or mental health[6], or of a person suffering from abuse or neglect[7]. The justice may make the order only if he is satisfied as to the ground on which the Welsh Ministers made the application[8]. As soon as is practicable after such an order is made the Ministers must give a notice to the service provider to whom the order relates explaining the terms of the order[9] and that the service provider may appeal to the First-tier tribunal against the making of the order no later than 14 days after the day on which such notice is given[10]. On such an appeal the tribunal may confirm or revoke the order or make such other order (including an interim order[11]) as it thinks appropriate[12].

The Welsh Ministers may give a decision notice to a service provider varying or imposing a condition[13] if they think that unless they do so there is, or may be, a risk to a person's life or physical or mental health, or of a person suffering from abuse or neglect[14]. Such a notice must:

(1)   state that it is so given[15];
(2)   specify the condition to be varied or imposed[16];
(3)   give reasons for imposing or varying the condition[17];
(4)   explain the right to make representations[18]; and
(5)   explain the right[19] of appeal[20].

The Ministers may vary or remove a condition so varied or imposed[21] by giving a further decision notice to the service provider, but before doing so they must have regard to any representations made to them by the service provider about the original decision notice[22]. Such a notice must:

(a)   state that it is so given[23];
(b)   specify the condition to be varied or removed[24];
(c)   give reasons for the decision[25]; and
(d)   explain the right[26] of appeal[27].

There is a right of appeal against the variation, imposition or removal of a condition by the Welsh Ministers[28].

1   At the date at which this volume states the law the Regulation and Inspection of Social Care (Wales) Act 2016 Pt 1 (ss 1–64) had yet to be brought into force.
2   As to the Welsh Ministers see PARA 395. As soon as practicable after making such an application the Ministers must notify each local authority and Local Health Board in whose area the service provider provides a regulated service and any other person they think it appropriate to notify: Regulation and Inspection of Social Care (Wales) Act 2016 s 23(3) (not yet in force: see note 1). As to the meaning of 'local authority' see PARA 2. As to Local Health Boards see HEALTH SERVICES vol 54 (2017) PARA 97.
3   Regulation and Inspection of Social Care (Wales) Act 2016 s 23(1)(a) (not yet in force: see note 1). As to the meaning of 'service provider' see PARA 203 note 4. The Welsh Ministers must notify each local authority of the cancellation of the registration of a service provider, of the variation of the registration of a service provider by removing from the registration a regulated service or a place at, from or in relation to which the provider is providing a regulated service, and of the making of an order by a justice of the peace under s 23: s 39(1)(a)–(c) (not yet in force). As to such notifications (and in particular as to the meaning of 'local authority' in this context) see further s 39(2), (3); and PARA 203 note 3.
4   As to the meaning of 'regulated service' see PARA 203.
5   Regulation and Inspection of Social Care (Wales) Act 2016 s 23(1)(b) (not yet in force: see note 1).

6 Regulation and Inspection of Social Care (Wales) Act 2016 s 23(2)(a) (not yet in force: see note 1).
7 Regulation and Inspection of Social Care (Wales) Act 2016 s 23(2)(b) (not yet in force: see note 1).
8 Regulation and Inspection of Social Care (Wales) Act 2016 s 23(4) (not yet in force: see note 1). An order under s 23 may be made in the absence of the service provider to whom it relates if the justice is satisfied that the Welsh Ministers have taken all reasonable steps to notify the service provider of their intention to apply for an order under this section or it is not appropriate to take any such steps: s 23(5) (not yet in force). An order made under s 23 has effect as soon as it is made or at such other time as the justice of the peace thinks appropriate (s 23(6) (not yet in force)): in particular, the justice may specify that the order is not to take effect until such time following the giving of notice under s 24(1) (see the text and notes 9–10) as he thinks appropriate (s 23(7) (not yet in force)).
9 Regulation and Inspection of Social Care (Wales) Act 2016 s 24(1)(a) (not yet in force: see note 1).
10 Regulation and Inspection of Social Care (Wales) Act 2016 s 24(1)(b), (2) (not yet in force: see note 1). The tribunal may allow an appeal to be made after the expiry of that 14 day period if it is satisfied that there is a good reason for the failure to appeal before the expiry of that period (and for any delay in applying for permission to appeal out of time): s 24(3) (not yet in force). As to the establishment of the First-tier Tribunal see COURTS AND TRIBUNALS vol 24 (2010) PARA 874; as to membership, constitution etc see COURTS AND TRIBUNALS vol 24 (2010) PARAS 888–894, 903–917.
11 An interim order of the tribunal may, among other things, suspend the effect of an order made under the Regulation and Inspection of Social Care (Wales) Act 2016 s 23 for such period as the tribunal may specify: s 24(5) (not yet in force).
12 Regulation and Inspection of Social Care (Wales) Act 2016 s 24(4) (not yet in force: see note 1).
13 Ie varying a condition imposed, or imposing a condition that could have been imposed, under the Regulation and Inspection of Social Care (Wales) Act 2016 s 7(3)(b) (see PARA 216), s 12(2) (see PARA 223), s 13(1) (see PARA 218) or previously imposed under s 25.
14 Regulation and Inspection of Social Care (Wales) Act 2016 s 25(1), (2) (not yet in force: see note 1). Such a decision notice takes effect on the day it is given: s 25(3) (not yet in force).
15 Regulation and Inspection of Social Care (Wales) Act 2016 s 25(4)(a) (not yet in force: see note 1).
16 Regulation and Inspection of Social Care (Wales) Act 2016 s 25(4)(b) (not yet in force: see note 1).
17 Regulation and Inspection of Social Care (Wales) Act 2016 s 25(4)(c) (not yet in force: see note 1).
18 Regulation and Inspection of Social Care (Wales) Act 2016 s 25(4)(d) (not yet in force: see note 1). As to the right to make representations see s 25(5); and the text and notes 19–22.
19 Ie the right conferred by the Regulation and Inspection of Social Care (Wales) Act 2016 s 26 (see the text and note 28).
20 Regulation and Inspection of Social Care (Wales) Act 2016 s 25(4)(e) (not yet in force: see note 1).
21 Ie varied or imposed under the Regulation and Inspection of Social Care (Wales) Act 2016 s 25(2) (see the text and notes 13–14).
22 Regulation and Inspection of Social Care (Wales) Act 2016 s 25(5) (not yet in force: see note 1). Such a notice given takes effect on the day it is given: s 25(6) (not yet in force).
23 Regulation and Inspection of Social Care (Wales) Act 2016 s 25(7)(a) (not yet in force: see note 1).
24 Regulation and Inspection of Social Care (Wales) Act 2016 s 25(7)(b) (not yet in force: see note 1).
25 Regulation and Inspection of Social Care (Wales) Act 2016 s 25(7)(c) (not yet in force: see note 1).
26 See note 19.
27 Regulation and Inspection of Social Care (Wales) Act 2016 s 25(7)(d) (not yet in force: see note 1).
28 An appeal lies to the First-tier tribunal against a decision contained in a notice given under the Regulation and Inspection of Social Care (Wales) Act 2016 s 25(2) or (5): s 26(1) (not yet in force: see note 1). As to appeals see further s 26(2)–(5); and PARA 212 note 28.

222. Cancellation of registration on application of service provider. As from a day to be appointed[1] if a service provider[2] applies to the Welsh Ministers[3] for cancellation of the provider's registration, the Ministers must grant the application unless they have taken action[4] with a view to cancelling the registration[5]. The Ministers must give notice of the granting of an application for cancellation under these provisions to the service provider[6].

It is an offence for a person to make a statement which he knows is false or materially misleading in an application for cancellation of registration[7].

1 At the date at which this volume states the law the Regulation and Inspection of Social Care (Wales) Act 2016 Pt 1 (ss 1–64) had yet to be brought into force.
2 As to the meaning of 'service provider' see PARA 203 note 4.
3 As to the Welsh Ministers see PARA 395.

4   Ie under the Regulation and Inspection of Social Care (Wales) Act 2016 s 15 (see PARA 220) or
     s 23 (see PARA 221).
5   Regulation and Inspection of Social Care (Wales) Act 2016 s 14(1) (not yet in force: see note 1).
     Cancellation under s 14 takes effect on the day falling 3 months after the day on which the service
     provider receives the notice or such earlier day as the Welsh Ministers may specify in the notice:
     s 14(3) (not yet in force). The Welsh Ministers must notify each local authority of the cancellation
     of the registration of a service provider: s 39(1)(a) (not yet in force). As to such notifications (and
     in particular as to the meaning of 'local authority' in this context) see further s 39(2), (3); and
     PARA 203 note 3.
6   Regulation and Inspection of Social Care (Wales) Act 2016 s 14(2) (not yet in force: see note 1).
7   Regulation and Inspection of Social Care (Wales) Act 2016 s 47(b) (not yet in force: see note 1).
     As to offences see PARA 203 note 3. An offence under s 47 may be prescribed as an offence in
     relation to which a penalty notice may be issued: see s 52; and PARA 213 note 21.

223. Variation of registration on application of service provider. As from a day
to be appointed[1] a service provider[2] must apply to the Welsh Ministers[3] for a
variation of the provider's registration if he wants:

(1)   to provide a regulated service[4] which he is not already registered to
         provide[5], or wants to provide a regulated service or at, from or in
         relation to a place which is not already specified in his registration in
         relation to that service[6];

(2)   to cease to provide a regulated service[7] or cease to provide a regulated
         service at, from or in relation to a place[8];

(3)   a condition[9] to be varied or removed[10]; or

(4)   to designate a different responsible individual[11] in respect of a place or
         is required to designate a responsible individual because there is no such
         individual designated in respect of a place at, from or in relation to
         which the provider provides a regulated service[12].

The Welsh Ministers may grant or refuse such an application[13]. The notification
requirements applicable to the Welsh Ministers' powers to grants applications for
registration, variations etc, apply to an application under these provisions[14]. It is
an offence for a person to make a statement which he knows is false or materially
misleading in an application for the variation of a registration[15].

Where the Welsh Ministers have decided to vary the registration of a service
provider in accordance with an application made under these provisions[16], they
must give a notice of decision to the service provider[17].

1   At the date at which this volume states the law the Regulation and Inspection of Social Care
     (Wales) Act 2016 Pt 1 (ss 1–64) had yet to be brought into force.
2   As to the meaning of 'service provider' see PARA 203 note 4.
3   As to the Welsh Ministers see PARA 395. An application under these provisions must be in the
     prescribed form (Regulation and Inspection of Social Care (Wales) Act 2016 s 11(3)(b) (not yet in
     force: see note 1)) and contain details of the variation sought by the provider and such other
     information as may be prescribed (s 11(3)(a)(i), (iii) (not yet in force)). An additional undertaking
     is prescribed in connection with an application relating to a domiciliary support service (as to
     which see PARA 210): see ss 11(3)(a)(ii), 8 (not yet in force).
4   As to the meaning of 'regulated service' see PARA 203.
5   Regulation and Inspection of Social Care (Wales) Act 2016 s 11(1)(a)(i) (not yet in force: see note
     1).
6   Regulation and Inspection of Social Care (Wales) Act 2016 s 11(1)(a)(ii) (not yet in force: see note
     1).
7   Regulation and Inspection of Social Care (Wales) Act 2016 s 11(1)(a)(iii) (not yet in force: see note
     1). The Welsh Ministers must notify each local authority of the variation of the registration of a
     service provider by removing from the registration a regulated service or a place at, from or in
     relation to which the provider is providing a regulated service: s 39(1)(b) (not yet in force). As to
     such notifications (and in particular as to the meaning of 'local authority' in this context) see
     further s 39(2), (3); and PARA 203 note 3.
8   Regulation and Inspection of Social Care (Wales) Act 2016 s 11(1)(a)(iv) (not yet in force: see note
     1). See note 7.

9   Ie a condition imposed under the Regulation and Inspection of Social Care (Wales) Act 2016
    s 7(3)(b) (see PARA 216), s 12(2) (see PARA 223) or s 13(1) (see PARA 218).
10 Regulation and Inspection of Social Care (Wales) Act 2016 s 11(1)(b) (not yet in force: see note 1).
11 As to the responsible individual see PARA 212.
12 Regulation and Inspection of Social Care (Wales) Act 2016 s 11(1)(c) (not yet in force: see note 1).
    The Welsh Ministers must by regulations prescribe a time limit within which an application for
    variation of a provider's registration must be made in circumstances where there is no responsible
    individual designated in respect of a place at, from or in relation to which the provider provides
    a regulated service: s 11(2) (not yet in force). At the date at which this volume states the law no
    such regulations had been made.
13 Regulation and Inspection of Social Care (Wales) Act 2016 s 12(1) (not yet in force: see note 1).
    In the case of an application under s 11(1)(b) (see the text and notes 9–10), the Welsh Ministers
    may (instead of granting or refusing the application) vary a condition on different terms to those
    specified in the application or impose another condition on the provider's registration (whether in
    place of or in addition to the condition which the provider applied to have varied or removed):
    s 12(2) (not yet in force). The Welsh Ministers may by regulations make provision requiring a fee
    to be paid by a person making an application to vary a registration under these provisions:
    s 40(1)(b) (not yet in force). As to such regulations and fees see further s 40(2)–(4); and PARA 216
    note 3.
14 See the Regulation and Inspection of Social Care (Wales) Act 2016 s 12(3) (not yet in force: see
    note 1), which provides that a variation under s 12 takes effect only if the requirements of ss 18–20
    (see PARA 217) are met (so far as applicable).
15 Regulation and Inspection of Social Care (Wales) Act 2016 s 47(b) (not yet in force: see note 1).
    As to offences see PARA 203 note 3.
16 Regulation and Inspection of Social Care (Wales) Act 2016 s 20(1)(b) (not yet in force: see note 1).
17 Regulation and Inspection of Social Care (Wales) Act 2016 s 20(2) (not yet in force: see note 1).
    A decision stated in a notice given under s 20(2) takes effect on the date on which the notice is
    given: s 20(3) (not yet in force).

E.   INFORMATION AND INSPECTIONS

224. Power to require information. As from a day to be appointed[1] the Welsh
Ministers[2] may require:

    (1)   a service provider[3];

    (2)   a responsible individual[4];

    (3)   a person employed by or otherwise working for a service provider[5]; and

    (4)   any person who has held any of those positions[6],

to provide them with any information relating to a regulated service[7] which the
Ministers think necessary or expedient to obtain for the purposes of exercising
their supervisory[8] functions[9]. However the Ministers may not require a person to
provide information if disclosure of that information is prohibited by any
enactment or other rule of law[10].

It is an offence for a person:

    (a)   to fail to comply with a requirement imposed on him by the Welsh
        Ministers under these provisions[11]; and

    (b)   to make a statement which he knows is false or materially misleading in
        responding to a requirement imposed by the Welsh Ministers under
        these provisions[12].

1   At the date at which this volume states the law the Regulation and Inspection of Social Care
    (Wales) Act 2016 Pt 1 (ss 1–64) had yet to be brought into force.
2   As to the Welsh Ministers see PARA 395.
3   Regulation and Inspection of Social Care (Wales) Act 2016 s 32(3)(a) (not in force: see note 1).
    As to the meaning of 'service provider' see PARA 203 note 4.
4   Regulation and Inspection of Social Care (Wales) Act 2016 s 32(3)(b) (not in force: see note 1).
    As to the responsible individual see PARA 212.
5   Regulation and Inspection of Social Care (Wales) Act 2016 s 32(3)(c) (not in force: see note 1).
6   Regulation and Inspection of Social Care (Wales) Act 2016 s 32(3)(d) (not in force: see note 1).
7   As to the meaning of 'regulated service' see PARA 203. The power to require information under
    these provisions includes power to require copies of any documents or records (including medical

and other personal records), and power to require the provision of information in legible form: Regulation and Inspection of Social Care (Wales) Act 2016 s 32(4) (not yet in force: see note 1).

8 Ie functions under the Regulation and Inspection of Social Care (Wales) Act 2016 Pt 1 Ch 2 (ss 5–31) and Pt 1 Ch 3 (ss 32–37) or under s 38–40 (see PARA 203 et seq).

9 Regulation and Inspection of Social Care (Wales) Act 2016 s 32(1) (not yet in force: see note 1).

10 Regulation and Inspection of Social Care (Wales) Act 2016 s 32(2) (not yet in force: see note 1).

11 Regulation and Inspection of Social Care (Wales) Act 2016 s 49(1) (not yet in force: see note 1). It is a defence for a person charged with an offence under s 49(1) to show that he had a reasonable excuse for failing to comply with the requirement: s 49(2) (not yet in force). As to offences see PARA 203 note 3. An offence under s 49 may be prescribed as an offence in relation to which a penalty notice may be issued: see s 52; and PARA 213 note 21.

12 Regulation and Inspection of Social Care (Wales) Act 2016 s 47(d) (not yet in force: see note 1). An offence under s 47 may be prescribed as an offence in relation to which a penalty notice may be issued: see s 52; and PARA 213 note 21.

225. Inspections. An 'inspection'[1] is an inspection:

(1)   of the standard of any care and support[2] provided by a service provider[3] in the course of providing a regulated service[4], measured in relation to any regulatory requirements[5] as to the standard of care and support to be provided[6]; and

(2)   of the organisation and co-ordination of regulated services provided by a service provider[7].

As from a day to be appointed only an individual authorised by the Welsh Ministers (an 'inspector') may carry out an inspection[8]. For the purposes of carrying out an inspection, an inspector may enter and inspect any premises[9] which he has reasonable grounds to believe is (or has been) used as a place at or from which a regulated service is (or has been) provided[10] or in connection with the provision of a regulated service[11]. The inspector may:

(a)   examine the state and management of the premises and assess the well-being[12] of any persons accommodated or receiving care and support there[13];

(b)   require the manager or any other person who appears to him to be responsible for the day to day management of the service at or from the premises or, where the service is no longer being provided, a person who appears to him to have responsibility for the day to day management of the premises, to produce any documents or records (including medical and other personal records) that he thinks may be relevant to the provision of the regulated service[14];

(c)   inspect and take copies of any documents or records (including medical and other personal records) that he thinks may be relevant to the provision of the regulated service[15];

(d)   seize and remove any document or other thing found at the premises which he has reasonable grounds to believe may be evidence of a failure to comply with any condition or other statutory[16] requirement[17];

(e)   require the manager or any other person who appears to him to be responsible for the day to day management of the service at or from the premises or, where the service is no longer being provided, a person who appears to him to have responsibility for the day to day management of the premises, to afford him such facilities and assistance as are necessary to enable him to carry out the inspection[18]; and

(f)   take such measurements and photographs and make such recordings as he inspector thinks necessary for the purpose of carrying out the inspection[19].

It is an offence for a person to:

(i)   intentionally obstruct an inspector exercising any information and inspection[20] function[21]; or

(ii)   fail to comply with any requirement imposed on him by an inspector exercising such a function[22].

1   Ie for the purposes of the Regulation and Inspection of Social Care (Wales) Act 2016 Pt 1 (ss 1–64).
2   As to the meanings of 'care' and 'support' see PARA 204.
3   As to the meaning of 'service provider' see PARA 203 note 4.
4   As to the meaning of 'regulated service' see PARA 203.
5   Ie requirements imposed by regulations under the Regulation and Inspection of Social Care (Wales) Act 2016 s 27(1): see PARA 214.
6   Regulation and Inspection of Social Care (Wales) Act 2016 s 33(1)(a) (at the date at which this volume states the law Pt 1 (ss 1–64) had yet to be brought into force).
7   Regulation and Inspection of Social Care (Wales) Act 2016 s 33(1)(b) (not yet in force: see note 6).
8   Regulation and Inspection of Social Care (Wales) Act 2016 s 33(2) (not yet in force: see note 6). The Welsh Ministers may by regulations make provision about the qualifications and other conditions to be met by an individual who may be an inspector (s 33(3) (not yet in force)): at the date at which this volume states the law no such regulations had been made. The Ministers must prepare and publish a code of practice about the manner in which inspections are to be carried out (including the frequency of inspections) (s 33(4) (not yet in force)), may revise the code and must publish a revised code (s 33(5) (not yet in force)). An inspector must have regard to the code when carrying out an inspection: s 33(6) (not yet in force). Where an inspector enters premises for the purposes of carrying out an inspection he must, if requested to do so by any person at the premises, produce a document showing his authorisation under s 33: s 34(3) (not yet in force).
9   'Premises' includes a vehicle: Regulation and Inspection of Social Care (Wales) Act 2016 s 34(6) (not yet in force: see note 6). An inspector may not pursuant to these provisions enter and inspect premises used wholly or mainly as a private dwelling unless the occupier consents: s 34(2) (not yet in force).
10 Regulation and Inspection of Social Care (Wales) Act 2016 s 34(1)(a) (not yet in force: see note 6).
11 Regulation and Inspection of Social Care (Wales) Act 2016 s 34(1)(b) (not yet in force: see note 6).
12 As to the meaning of 'well-being' see PARA 375.
13 Regulation and Inspection of Social Care (Wales) Act 2016 s 34(4)(a) (not yet in force: see note 6).
14 Regulation and Inspection of Social Care (Wales) Act 2016 s 34(4)(b) (not yet in force: see note 6). The powers in s 34(4)(b)–(d) include the power to gain access to and check the operation of any computer and associated apparatus which the inspector has reasonable grounds to believe is (or has been) used in connection with the documents or records, and require documents or records to be produced in a form which is legible and portable: s 34(5) (not yet in force).
15 Regulation and Inspection of Social Care (Wales) Act 2016 s 34(4)(c) (not yet in force: see note 6). See note 14.
16 Ie any requirement imposed by virtue of the Regulation and Inspection of Social Care (Wales) Act 2016 Pt 1.
17 Regulation and Inspection of Social Care (Wales) Act 2016 s 34(4)(d) (not yet in force: see note 6). See note 14.
18 Regulation and Inspection of Social Care (Wales) Act 2016 s 34(4)(e) (not yet in force: see note 6).
19 Regulation and Inspection of Social Care (Wales) Act 2016 s 34(4)(f) (not yet in force: see note 6).
20 Ie conferred on an inspector by the Regulation and Inspection of Social Care (Wales) Act 2016 Pt 1 Ch 3 (ss 32–37).
21 Regulation and Inspection of Social Care (Wales) Act 2016 s 50(1)(a) (not yet in force: see note 6). As to offences see PARA 203 note 3.
22 Regulation and Inspection of Social Care (Wales) Act 2016 s 50(1)(b) (not yet in force: see note 6). It is a defence for a person charged with an offence under s 50(1)(b) to show that he had a reasonable excuse for failing to comply with the requirement: s 50(2) (not yet in force).

226. Interviews and examinations. As from a day to be appointed[1] if an inspector[2] thinks it necessary or expedient for the purposes of carrying out an inspection[3], he may require any person to be interviewed by him in private[4], although he may not so interview:

(1)   a person to whom the service provider[5] provides (or has provided) care and support[6];

(2)   an individual with parental responsibility[7] for the person[8];

(3)   a relative[9] of the person[10];

(4)   the person's carer[11];

(5)   a donee of a lasting power of attorney[12] over the person[13],

without that person's consent[14].

An inspector may examine in private a person to whom the service provider provides (or has provided) care and support if:

(a)   the inspector is a registered medical practitioner or registered nurse[15];

(b)   the inspector thinks the examination is necessary or expedient for the purposes of assessing the effect of any such care and support on the well-being[16] of the person[17]; and

(c)   the person consents to the examination[18].

1   At the date at which this volume states the law the Regulation and Inspection of Social Care (Wales) Act 2016 Pt 1 (ss 1–64) had yet to be brought into force.

2   As to the meaning of 'inspector' see PARA 225. Where an inspector conducts an interview or examination under these provisions he must, if requested to do so by the person being interviewed or examined or an individual accompanying that person, produce a document showing his authorisation under the Regulation and Inspection of Social Care (Wales) Act 2016 s 33 (see PARA 225) and, in the case of an examination, a document showing that he is a registered medical practitioner or registered nurse: s 35(6) (not yet in force: see note 1). As to the meaning of 'registered medical practitioner' see MEDICAL PROFESSIONS vol 74 (2011) PARA 176. As to registered nurses see MEDICAL PROFESSIONS vol 74 (2011) PARA 713.

3   As to inspections see PARA 225.

4   Regulation and Inspection of Social Care (Wales) Act 2016 s 35(1) (not yet in force: see note 1). For the purposes of s 35(1), (4), an interview or examination is to be treated as conducted in private despite the presence of a third party if the person being interviewed or examined wants the third party to be present and the inspector does not object (s 35(5)(a) (not yet in force)) or the inspector wants the third party to be present and the person being interviewed or examined consents (s 35(5)(b) (not yet in force)).

5   As to the meaning of 'service provider' see PARA 203 note 4.

6   Regulation and Inspection of Social Care (Wales) Act 2016 s 35(3)(a) (not yet in force: see note 1). As to the meanings of 'care' and 'support' see PARA 204.

7   As to the meaning of 'parental responsibility' see the Children Act 1989 s 3; and CHILDREN AND YOUNG PERSONS vol 9 (2017) PARA 150 (definition applied by the Regulation and Inspection of Social Care (Wales) Act 2016 s 35(7) (not yet in force: see note 1)).

8   Regulation and Inspection of Social Care (Wales) Act 2016 s 35(3)(b) (not yet in force: see note 1).

9   'Relative', in relation to a person, means that person's parent, grandparent, child, grandchild, brother, half-brother, sister, half-sister, uncle, aunt, nephew or niece (including any person who is or has been in that relationship by virtue of a marriage or civil partnership or an enduring family relationship): Regulation and Inspection of Social Care (Wales) Act 2016 s 35(7) (not yet in force: see note 1). 'Child' means a person who is aged under 18: s 35(7) (not yet in force).

10 Regulation and Inspection of Social Care (Wales) Act 2016 s 35(3)(c) (not yet in force: see note 1).

11 Regulation and Inspection of Social Care (Wales) Act 2016 s 35(3)(d) (not yet in force: see note 1). As to the meaning of 'carer' see the Social Services and Well-being (Wales) Act 2014 s 3(4); and PARA 54 note 2 (definition applied by the Regulation and Inspection of Social Care (Wales) Act 2016 s 35(7) (not yet in force)).

12 As to the meaning of 'donee of a lasting power of attorney' see the Mental Capacity Act 2005 Pt 1 (ss 1–44); and AGENCY vol 1 (2008) PARA 217 et seq (definition applied by the Regulation and Inspection of Social Care (Wales) Act 2016 s 35(7) (not yet in force)).

13 Regulation and Inspection of Social Care (Wales) Act 2016 s 35(3)(e) (not yet in force: see note 1).

14 Regulation and Inspection of Social Care (Wales) Act 2016 s 35(2) (not yet in force: see note 1).

15 Regulation and Inspection of Social Care (Wales) Act 2016 s 35(4)(a) (not yet in force: see note 1).

16 As to the meaning of 'well-being' see PARA 375.

17 Regulation and Inspection of Social Care (Wales) Act 2016 s 35(4)(b) (not yet in force: see note 1).

18 Regulation and Inspection of Social Care (Wales) Act 2016 s 35(4)(c) (not yet in force: see note 1).

227. Inspection reports and ratings. As from a day to be appointed[1], as soon as is reasonably practicable after an inspection has been carried out[2], the Welsh Ministers[3] must prepare a report of the inspection and send a copy of it to the service provider[4]. Such report must include:

(1)   an assessment[5] of the standard of any care and support provided (or which had been provided) by the service provider[6];

(2) an assessment of the effect of any such care and support on the well-being[7] of persons to whom the care and support is (or had been) provided[8];

(3) an assessment of the organisation and co-ordination of regulated services[9] provided (or which had been provided) by the service provider[10]; and

(4) if regulations about inspection ratings are made are made[11], a rating of the service provider[12].

1 At the date at which this volume states the law the Regulation and Inspection of Social Care (Wales) Act 2016 Pt 1 (ss 1–64) had yet to be brought into force.

2 As to inspections see PARAS 225–226.

3 As to the Welsh Ministers see PARA 395.

4 Regulation and Inspection of Social Care (Wales) Act 2016 s 36(1) (not yet in force: see note 1). As to the meaning of 'service provider' see PARA 203 note 4. The Welsh Ministers must publish each report prepared under s 36(1) (s 36(3)(a)), ensure that copies are made available for inspection at such places and by such means as they think appropriate (s 36(3)(b) (not yet in force)), and send a copy of a report so prepared to any person who requests one (s 36(3)(c) (not yet in force)). The Ministers may by regulations make provision requiring a fee to be paid by a person for such a copy: s 40(1)(c) (not yet in force). As to such regulations and fees see further s 40(2)–(4); and PARA 216 note 3.

5 Ie, an assessment measured in relation to any requirements imposed by regulations under the Regulation and Inspection of Social Care (Wales) Act 2016 s 27(1) (see PARA 214) as to the standard of care and support to be provided: s 36(2)(a) (not yet in force: see note 1). As to the meanings of 'care' and 'support' see PARA 204.

6 Regulation and Inspection of Social Care (Wales) Act 2016 s 36(2)(a) (not yet in force: see note 1).

7 As to the meaning of 'well-being' see PARA 375.

8 Regulation and Inspection of Social Care (Wales) Act 2016 s 36(2)(b) (not yet in force: see note 1).

9 As to the meaning of 'regulated service' see PARA 203.

10 Regulation and Inspection of Social Care (Wales) Act 2016 s 36(2)(c) (not yet in force: see note 1).

11 Ie under the Regulation and Inspection of Social Care (Wales) Act 2016 s 37, which provides that the Welsh Ministers may by regulations make provision about ratings that may be given in relation to the quality of care and support provided by a service provider who has been inspected (s 37(1) (not yet in force: see note 1)). Such regulations:

    (1) may make provision requiring a service provider to display a rating included in a report prepared under d 36(1) in such manner, and at such place, as the regulations may specify (s 37(2)(a) (not yet in force));

    (2) may specify criteria to be applied when arriving at a rating (s 37(2)(b) (not yet in force)); and

    (3) must include provision for a service provider to appeal against a rating included in a report prepared under s 36(1) (s 37(2)(c) (not yet in force)).

Before making such regulations the Welsh Ministers must consult any persons they think appropriate: s 37(3) (not yet in force). However the requirement to consult does not apply to regulations which amend other regulations made under s 37(1) and do not, in the opinion of the Welsh Ministers, effect any substantial change in the provision made by the regulations to be amended: s 37(4) (not yet in force).

The Welsh Ministers may also by regulations provide that it is an offence for a service provider to fail to comply with a specified provision of regulations made under s 37(2)(a): s 45 (not yet in force). As to offences see PARA 203 note 3.

At the date at which this volume states the law no such regulations had been made.

12 Regulation and Inspection of Social Care (Wales) Act 2016 s 36(2)(d) (not yet in force: see note 1).

F.   FINANCIAL SUSTAINABILITY OF CARE PROVIDERS

228. Strategies for mitigating or eliminating financial risk. As from a day to be appointed[1], where the Welsh Ministers[2], in light of a financial sustainability assessment[3], considers that there is a significant risk to the financial sustainability of a service provider's business, they may require the provider to develop a plan for how to mitigate or eliminate the risk[4] and arrange for, or require the provider to arrange for, a person with appropriate professional expertise to carry out an independent review of the business[5].

The Welsh Ministers may by regulations make provision for enabling them to obtain from such persons as they think appropriate information which they believe will assist them to assess the financial sustainability of a service provider[6]. At the date at which this volume states the law no such regulations had been made.

1   At the date at which this volume states the law the Regulation and Inspection of Social Care (Wales) Act 2016 Pt 1 (ss 1–64) had yet to be brought into force.
2   As to the Welsh Ministers see PARA 395.
3   Ie an assessment under the Regulation and Inspection of Social Care (Wales) Act 2016 s 61(1). Where s 61 applies to a service provider, the Ministers must assess the financial sustainability of the service provider's business of carrying on regulated services: s 61(1) (not yet in force: see note 1). An assessment of the financial sustainability of the service provider's business under s 61(1) must include consideration of its corporate governance: s 61(2) (not yet in force). As to the meaning of 'service provider' see PARA 203 note 4. As to the meaning of 'regulated service' see PARA 203. The Welsh Ministers must by regulations specify criteria for determining whether (subject to regulations under s 59(4) (see below)) s 61 applies to a service provider in respect of regulated services: s 59(1) (not yet in force). In specifying the criteria, the Ministers must have regard in particular to:
   (1)   the amount of care and support provided by a service provider (s 59(2)(a) (not yet in force));
   (2)   the geographical concentration of a service provider's business (s 59(2)(b) (not yet in force)); and
   (3)   the extent to which a service provider specialises in the provision of particular types of regulated service (s 59(2)(c) (not yet in force)).
   As to the meanings of 'care' and 'support' see PARA 204. The Welsh Ministers must:
   (a)   at such times as they think appropriate, review the criteria for the time being specified in the regulations (s 59(3)(a) (not yet in force)); and
   (b)   publish information about how the matters mentioned in s 59(2), and any other matters to which they have regard in specifying the criteria, are to be measured (s 59(3)(b) (not yet in force)).
   The Ministers may by regulations provide that s 61 does not apply, or applies only to the extent specified, to a specified service provider or to a service provider of a specified description, regardless of whether that service provider or a service provider of that description would satisfy the criteria: s 59(4) (not yet in force). The circumstances in which regulations may be made under s 59(4) include those in which the Ministers are satisfied that certain service providers are already subject to a regulatory regime comparable to that provided for by ss 61, 62; and regulations made in such circumstances may, for example, make provision requiring specified persons to co-operate or to share information of a specified description: s 59(5) (not yet in force).
   Before making regulations under s 59 the Ministers must consult any persons they think appropriate: s 59(6) (not yet in force). However the requirement to consult does not apply to regulations which amend other regulations made under s 59 and do not, in the opinion of the Ministers, effect any substantial change in the provision made by the regulations to be amended: s 59(7) (not yet in force).
   The Ministers may also by regulations make provision about the making of the assessments required by s 61(1): s 61(9) (not yet in force).
   At the date at which this volume states the law no regulations had been made under s 59 or s 61.
4   Regulation and Inspection of Social Care (Wales) Act 2016 s 61(3)(a) (not yet in force: see note 1). Where the Ministers impose a requirement on a service provider under s 61(3)(a), they may also require the provider to co-operate with them in developing the plan (s 61(4)(a) (not yet in force)) and to obtain their approval of the finalised plan (s 61(4)(b) (not yet in force)).
5   Regulation and Inspection of Social Care (Wales) Act 2016 s 61(3)(b) (not yet in force: see note 1). Where the Ministers arrange for a review under s 61(3)(b), they may recover from the service provider such costs as they incur in connection with the arrangements (including such of their administrative costs in making the arrangements as they think it appropriate to recover): s 61(5) (not yet in force).
6   Ie a service provider to which the Regulation and Inspection of Social Care (Wales) Act 2016 s 61 (see note 3) applies: s 61(6) (not yet in force: see note 1). Before making regulations under s 61(6) the Welsh Ministers must consult any persons they think appropriate: s 61(7) (not yet in force). However the requirement to consult does not apply to regulations which amend other regulations made under s 61(6) and do not, in the opinion of the Welsh Ministers, effect any substantial change in the provision made by the regulations to be amended: s 61(8) (not yet in force).

229. Assessment of financial sustainability of service providers. As from a day to be appointed[1] the Welsh Ministers[2] must determine, in the case of each service provider[3], whether the service provider satisfies one or more of the financial sustainability[4] criteria[5]. If the Ministers determine that the service provider satisfies one or more of the criteria, the assessment provisions[6] apply to that service provider unless, or except in so far as, regulations[7] provide that it does not apply[8]. Where the assessment provisions apply to a service provider, the Welsh Ministers must inform the provider accordingly[9].

1   At the date at which this volume states the law the Regulation and Inspection of Social Care (Wales) Act 2016 Pt 1 (ss 1–64) had yet to be brought into force.
2   As to the Welsh Ministers see PARA 395.
3   As to the meaning of 'service provider' see PARA 203 note 4.
4   Ie the criteria specified in regulations under the Regulation and Inspection of Social Care (Wales) Act 2016 s 59 (see PARA 228).
5   Regulation and Inspection of Social Care (Wales) Act 2016 s 60(1) (not yet in force: see note 1).
6   Ie the Regulation and Inspection of Social Care (Wales) Act 2016 s 61 (see PARA 228).
7   Ie regulations under the Regulation and Inspection of Social Care (Wales) Act 2016 s 59(4) (see PARA 228).
8   Regulation and Inspection of Social Care (Wales) Act 2016 s 60(2) (not yet in force: see note 1).
9   Regulation and Inspection of Social Care (Wales) Act 2016 s 60(3) (not yet in force: see note 1).

230. Duty of local authority to meet needs in event of business failure. Where a person who is registered in respect of the provision of care and support through a business[1] becomes unable to continue to provide such care and support[2] because of business failure[3], a local authority in Wales[4] must for so long as it considers necessary (and in so far as it is not already required to do so) meet those of an adult's[5] needs for care and support[6] and those of a relevant carer's[7] needs for support which were[8] being met[9] by the person[10]. An authority is accordingly required to meet such needs regardless of:

    (1)   whether the relevant person[11] is ordinarily resident in its area[12];
    (2)   whether the authority has carried out a needs assessment or a financial assessment[13]; or
    (3)   whether the authority would otherwise have a duty[14] to meet those needs[15].

1   Ie, until a day to be appointed, a person who is registered under the Care Standards Act 2000 Pt 2 (ss 11–42: see CHILDREN AND YOUNG PERSONS vol 10 (2017) PARA 1017 et seq) in respect of an establishment or agency (within the meaning of the Care Standards Act 2000: see s 121(5); and CHILDREN AND YOUNG PERSONS vol 10 (2017) PARA 1017) or, as from that day, a person who is registered under the Regulation and Inspection of Social Care (Wales) Act 2016 s 7 (see PARA 216) to provide a regulated service (a 'service provider': see s 3(1)(c); and PARA 203 note 4): Social Services and Well-being (Wales) Act 2014 s 189(1), (9) (s 189(1) prospectively substituted, ss 189(2), (5)(a), (9), 190(1), 191(6), (7), prospectively amended, by the Regulation and Inspection of Social Care (Wales) Act 2016 Sch 3 paras 33–35)). At the date at which this volume states the law no day had been appointed for this purpose.
2   Ie, until the appointed day, becomes unable to carry on or manage the establishment or agency or, as from that day, becomes unable to provide a regulated service: Social Services and Well-being (Wales) Act 2014 s 189(1) (prospectively substituted: see note 1). As to the meaning of 'regulated service' see the Regulation and Inspection of Social Care (Wales) Act 2016 s 2(1); and PARA 203 (definition applied by the Social Services and Well-being (Wales) Act 2014 s 189(9) (as so prospectively amended)).
3   In the context of a person who is registered under the Care Standards Act 2000 Pt 2 (ie in the context of the operation of these provisions prior to the coming into force of the amendments referred to in note 1), 'business failure' is defined by the Care and Support (Business Failure) (Wales) Regulations 2015, SI 2015/1920 (made under the Social Services and Well-being (Wales) Act 2014 s 191(7) (prospectively amended: see note 1)). At the date at which this volume states the law 'business failure' had not been defined for the purposes of these provisions as so amended (ie in the context of a person who is registered under the Regulation and Inspection of Social Care (Wales) Act 2016 s 7).

4   As to the meanings of 'local authority' and 'Wales' see PARA 2. An authority becomes subject to the duty under these provisions as soon as it becomes aware of the business failure: Social Services and Well-being (Wales) Act 2014 s 191(1).

5   As to the meaning of 'adult' see PARA 2.

6   As to the meanings of 'care' and 'support' see PARA 2 note 1.

7   As to the meaning of 'carer' see PARA 54 note 2. 'Relevant carer' means a carer who is an adult and provides or intends to provide care for another adult: Social Services and Well-being (Wales) Act 2014 s 189(9).

8   Ie, until the appointed day, immediately before the person registered under the Care Standards Act 2000 Pt 2 of in respect of that establishment or agency (the 'registered person') became unable to carry on or manage the establishment or agency; or, as from that day, immediately before the service provider became unable to provide the regulated service: Social Services and Well-being (Wales) Act 2014 s 189(2), (9) (prospectively amended: see note 1).

9   Ie, until the appointed day, being met in the authority's area by the establishment or agency; or, as from that day, being met in the authority's area by the service provider: Social Services and Well-being (Wales) Act 2014 s 189(2) (prospectively amended: see note 1).

10 Social Services and Well-being (Wales) Act 2014 s 189(2) (prospectively amended: see note 1). Section 34 (how to meet needs: see PARAS 2, 3) and ss 46–49 (meeting needs: exceptions and restrictions: see PARAS 3–6) apply to meeting needs under s 189 as they apply to meeting needs under ss 35–45 (see PARAS 19–20, 30–32, 58–63): s 191(2). Regulations may make provision about the persons whom the local authority must involve in connection with meeting needs under s 189(2): s 191(3). At the date at which this volume states the law no such regulations had been made. Where a local authority considers it necessary to do so for the purpose of carrying out its duty under s 189(2), it may request the registered person, or such other person involved in the establishment or agency (until the appointed day), or the service provider, or such other person involved in the provider's business (as from that day) as it considers appropriate, to provide it with specified information: s 191(6) (as so prospectively amended). A local authority may impose a charge for meeting needs under s 189(2) (except in so far as those needs are met by the provision of information or advice) (s 189(4)); a charge under s 189(4):

    (1)   may be imposed only in respect of needs which were not, immediately before the registered person became unable to carry on or manage the establishment or agency (until the appointed day) or immediately before the service provider became unable to provide the regulated service (as from that day), being met either under arrangements made by a local authority discharging its duty under s 35 (see PARA 19) or s 40 (see PARAS 58–62), or exercising its power under s 36 (see PARA 20) or s 45 (see PARA 63), or by the provision of accommodation or services all or part of the cost of which was paid for by direct payments made by virtue of s 50 (see PARA 125) or s 52 (see PARA 127) (s 189(5)(a) (as so prospectively amended)); and

    (2)   may cover only the cost that the local authority incurs in meeting those needs (s 189(5)(b)).

    Sections 60–67, 70, 71, 73 apply to charging under s 189(4) as they apply to charging under s 59, and accordingly a local authority's power to impose a charge under s 189(4) is subject to the provision made in regulations under s 61 or s 62 (if any) and the authority's duties under ss 63, 66, 67 (if applicable): Social Services and Well-being (Wales) Act 2014 s 189(6). As to charging, reimbursement and contribution under the provisions referred to see PARAS 131–140.

11 'The relevant person' means (by virtue of the Social Services and Well-being (Wales) Act 2014 s 189(9)):

    (1)   in a case involving an adult's needs for care and support, that adult; or

    (2)   in a case involving a relevant carer's needs for support, the adult needing care.

12 Social Services and Well-being (Wales) Act 2014 s 189(3)(a). In connection with a person's residence see PARAS 84–87. If the relevant person is not ordinarily resident in the area of the local authority which is required to meet needs under s 189(2), that authority:

    (1)   must, in meeting needs under that provision which were being met under arrangements made by another local authority discharging its duty under s 35 or s 40 or exercising its power under s 36 or s 45, co-operate with that authority (s 189(7)(a));

    (2)   must, in meeting needs under that provision which were being met under arrangements all or part of the cost of which was paid for by another local authority by means of direct payments made by virtue of s 50 or s 52, co-operate with that authority (s 189(7)(b)); and

    (3)   may recover from the other local authority mentioned in head (1) or (2) above (as the case may be) the cost it incurs in meeting those of the adult's needs or the relevant carer's needs referred to in the provision in question (s 189(7)(c)).

    Any dispute between local authorities about the application of s 189 is to be determined under s 195 (see PARAS 96–99) as if it were a dispute of the type mentioned in s 189(1): s 189(8). Provision is also made in connection with cross-border cases: see s 190 (prospectively amended (see note 1); further amended by SI 2015/914).

13 Social Services and Well-being (Wales) Act 2014 s 189(3)(b). As to needs assessments see PARAS 66–77; as to financial assessments see PARA 141.
14 Ie under the Social Services and Well-being (Wales) Act 2014.
15 Social Services and Well-being (Wales) Act 2014 s 189(3)(c).

231. Duty to inform local authorities of provider failure. As from a day to be appointed[1], where the Welsh Ministers[2] are satisfied that a service provider[3] is likely to become unable to provide a regulated service[4] in respect of which it is registered because of provider failure[5], the Ministers must inform the local authorities[6] which they think will be required to carry out the duty[7] to meet the needs which that provider is likely to become unable to meet if the service provider becomes unable to provide the regulated service in question[8]. The Ministers may require the service provider, or such other person involved in the service provider's business as they think appropriate, to provide them with any information they think necessary or expedient to obtain for the purpose of assisting a local authority to carry out the intervention[9] duty[10]. However the Ministers may not require a person to provide information if disclosure of that information is prohibited by any enactment or other rule of law[11].

1 At the date at which this volume states the law the Regulation and Inspection of Social Care (Wales) Act 2016 Pt 1 (ss 1–64) had yet to be brought into force.
2 As to the Welsh Ministers see PARA 395.
3 Ie a service provider to whom the Regulation and Inspection of Social Care (Wales) Act 2016 s 61 (financial sustainability assessments: see PARAS 228–229) applies: s 62(1) (not yet in force: see note 1). As to the meaning of 'service provider' see PARA 203 note 4.
4 As to the meaning of 'regulated service' see PARA 203.
5 Ie as mentioned in the Social Services and Well-being (Wales) Act 2014 s 189: see PARA 230.
6 As to the meaning of 'local authority' see PARA 2.
7 Ie the duty under the Social Services and Well-being (Wales) Act 2014 s 189(2) (see PARA 230).
8 Regulation and Inspection of Social Care (Wales) Act 2016 s 62(1), (2) (not yet in force: see note 1).
9 See note 7.
10 Regulation and Inspection of Social Care (Wales) Act 2016 s 62(3) (not yet in force: see note 1). The power to require information under s 62(3) includes power to require copies of any documents or records (including medical and other personal records) and power to require the provision of information in legible form: s 62(5) (not yet in force).
11 Regulation and Inspection of Social Care (Wales) Act 2016 s 62(4) (not yet in force: see note 1).

232. National market stability report by Welsh Ministers. As from a day to be appointed[1] the Welsh Ministers[2] must prepare and publish a national market stability report at such times as may be prescribed[3]. A national market stability report must include an assessment of:

(1) the sufficiency of care and support[4] provided in Wales[5] during such period as may be prescribed[6];
(2) the extent to which regulated services[7] were provided in Wales during that prescribed period by applicable[8] service providers[9];
(3) the effect on the exercise of local authority social services functions[10] of the commissioning by local authorities[11] of services in connection with those functions during such period as may be prescribed[12]; and
(4) any other matter relating to the provision of care and support in Wales as may be prescribed[13].

A national market stability report must also include a report of any market oversight action[14] taken by the Ministers[15].

1 At the date at which this volume states the law the Regulation and Inspection of Social Care (Wales) Act 2016 Pt 1 (ss 1–64) had yet to be brought into force.
2 As to the Welsh Ministers see PARA 395.
3 Regulation and Inspection of Social Care (Wales) Act 2016 s 63(1) (not yet in force: see note 1). The Ministers must consult Social Care Wales when preparing a national market stability report

and may direct Social Care Wales to jointly prepare any part of the report with them as the Ministers think appropriate: s 63(2) (not yet in force). In preparing a market stability report the Ministers must have regard to the most recent local market stability report published by each local authority under the Social Services and Well-being (Wales) Act 2014 s 144B (see PARA 233): Regulation and Inspection of Social Care (Wales) Act 2016 s 63(4) (not yet in force). At the date at which this volume states the law no times had been prescribed for this purpose. As to Social Care Wales see PARAS 412–414.

4   Ie within the meaning of the Social Services and Well-being (Wales) Act 2014: see s 4; and PARA 2 note 1.
5   As to the meaning of 'Wales' see PARA 2.
6   Regulation and Inspection of Social Care (Wales) Act 2016 s 63(3)(a)(i) (not yet in force: see note 1). At the date at which this volume states the law no period had been prescribed for this purpose.
7   As to the meaning of 'regulated service' see PARA 203.
8   Ie service providers to whom the Regulation and Inspection of Social Care (Wales) Act 2016 s 61 (financial sustainability assessments: see PARAS 228–229) applies: s 63(3)(a)(ii) (not yet in force: see note 1). As to the meaning of 'service provider' see PARA 203 note 4.
9   Regulation and Inspection of Social Care (Wales) Act 2016 s 63(3)(a)(ii) (not yet in force: see note 1).
10 Ie within the meaning of the Social Services and Well-being (Wales) Act 2014: see Sch 2; and PARA 373.
11 As to the meaning of 'local authority' see PARA 2.
12 Regulation and Inspection of Social Care (Wales) Act 2016 s 63(3)(a)(iii) (not yet in force: see note 1). At the date at which this volume states the law no period had been prescribed for this purpose.
13 Regulation and Inspection of Social Care (Wales) Act 2016 s 63(3)(a)(iv) (not yet in force: see note 1). Before making regulations under s 63(3)(a)(iv) the Welsh Ministers must consult any persons they think appropriate: s 63(5) (not yet in force). However the requirement to consult does not apply to regulations which amend other regulations made under s 63(3)(a)(iv) and do not, in the opinion of the Ministers, effect any substantial change in the provision made by the regulations to be amended: s 63(6) (not yet in force). At the date at which this volume states the law no further matters had been prescribed for this purpose.
14 Ie action taken by the Ministers under the Regulation and Inspection of Social Care (Wales) Act 2016 ss 59–62 (see PARAS 228–229) during the period prescribed under s 63(3)(a)(i).
15 Regulation and Inspection of Social Care (Wales) Act 2016 s 63(3)(b) (not yet in force: see note 1).

233. Local market stability report by local authorities. As from a day to be appointed[1], a local authority in Wales[2] must prepare and publish a local market stability report at such times as may be prescribed[3]. A local market stability report must include an assessment of:

(1)   the sufficiency of care and support[4] provided in the local authority area during such period as may be prescribed[5];

(2)   the extent to which regulated services[6] were provided in the local authority area during that prescribed period by applicable[7] service providers[8];

(3)   the effect on the exercise of the local authority's social services functions[9] of the commissioning by the authority of any services in connection with those functions during such period as may be prescribed[10]; and

(4)   any other matter relating to the provision of regulated services in the local authority area as may be prescribed[11].

A local market stability report must also include a report of any market oversight action[12] taken by the authority[13].

1   The Social Services and Well-being (Wales) Act 2014 s 144B is added, as from a day to be appointed, by the Regulation and Inspection of Social Care (Wales) Act 2014 s 56(1). At the date at which this volume states the law no day had been appointed for this purpose.
2   As to the meanings of 'local authority' and 'Wales' see PARA 2.
3   Social Services and Well-being (Wales) Act 2014 s 144B(1) (prospectively added: see note 1). A local market stability report must be in such form as may be prescribed by regulations: s 144B(3) (as so prospectively added). At the date at which this volume states the law no such regulations had been made. In preparing a local market stability report a local authority must take account of the

assessment it has most recently published under s 14 (needs assessments: see PARA 389) and the plan it has most recently published under s 14A following the assessment (see PARA 389), and consult with each Local Health Board with which it carried out the assessment: s 144B(4) (as so prospectively added). At the date at which this volume states the law no times had been prescribed for this purpose. As to Local Health Boards see HEALTH SERVICES vol 54 (2017) PARA 97. A local authority must send a copy of a published local market stability report to the Welsh Ministers: s 144B(5) (as so prospectively added). As to the Welsh Ministers see PARA 395.

4 As to the meanings of 'care' and 'support' see PARA 2 note 1.

5 Social Services and Well-being (Wales) Act 2014 s 144B(2)(a)(i) (prospectively added: see note 1). At the date at which this volume states the law no period had been prescribed for this purpose.

6 As to the meaning of 'regulated service' see the Regulation and Inspection of Social Care (Wales) Act 2016 s 2(1); and PARA 203 (definition applied by the Social Services and Well-being (Wales) Act 2014 s 144B(8)(b) (prospectively added: see note 1)).

7 Ie service providers to whom the Regulation and Inspection of Social Care (Wales) Act 2016 s 61 (financial sustainability assessments: see PARAS 228–229) applies: Social Services and Well-being (Wales) Act 2014 s 144B(2)(a)(i) (prospectively added: see note 1). As to the meaning of 'service provider' see the Regulation and Inspection of Social Care (Wales) Act 2016 s 3(1)(c); and PARA 203 note 4 (definition applied by the Social Services and Well-being (Wales) Act 2014 s 144B(8)(a) (as so prospectively added)).

8 Social Services and Well-being (Wales) Act 2014 s 144B(2)(a)(ii) (prospectively added: see note 1).

9 As to local authority social services functions in Wales see PARA 373.

10 Social Services and Well-being (Wales) Act 2014 s 144B(2)(a)(iv) (prospectively added: see note 1). At the date at which this volume states the law no period had been prescribed for this purpose.

11 Social Services and Well-being (Wales) Act 2014 s 144B(2)(a)(iii) (prospectively added: see note 1). Before making regulations under s 144B(2)(a)(iii) the Welsh Ministers must consult any persons they think appropriate: s 144B(6) (as so prospectively added). However the requirement to consult does not apply to regulations which amend other regulations made under s 144B(2)(a)(iii) and do not, in the opinion of the Ministers, effect any substantial change in the provision made by the regulations to be amended: s 144B(7) (as so prospectively added). At the date at which this volume states the law no further matters had been prescribed for this purpose.

12 Ie action taken by the local authority in pursuance of its duty under the Social Services and Well-being (Wales) Act 2014 s 189(2) (see PARA 230) during the period prescribed under s 144B(2)(a)(i).

13 Social Services and Well-being (Wales) Act 2014 s 144B(2)(b) (prospectively added: see note 1).

4. PROTECTION OF CHILDREN AND VULNERABLE ADULTS

(1) SAFEGUARDING

(i) England

A.   SAFEGUARDING ADULTS

234.   Establishment of Safeguarding Adults Boards. Each local authority in England[1] must establish a Safeguarding Adults Board (an 'SAB')[2] for its area, the objective of which is to help and protect adults[3] in its area (other than those who are detained in prison or residing in approved premises[4]) who[5] are in need of protection from abuse and neglect[6]. The way in which an SAB must seek to achieve its objective is by co-ordinating and ensuring the effectiveness of what each of its members does[7]. An SAB may do anything which appears to it to be necessary or desirable for the purpose of achieving its objective[8]. If an SAB requests a person to supply information to it, or to some other person specified in the request, the person to whom the request is made must comply with the request if specified conditions are met[9]. Information may be used by the SAB, or other person to whom it is supplied[10], only for the purpose of enabling or assisting the SAB to exercise its functions[11].

1   As to the meaning of 'local authority' see PARA 1. Where two or more local authorities exercise their respective duties under these provisions by establishing an SAB for their combined area a reference in the Care Act 2014 s 43, s 44 or Sch 2 to the authority establishing the SAB is a reference to the authorities establishing it and a reference in s 43, s 44 or Sch 2 to the SAB's area is a reference to the combined area: s 43(6).
2   Provision about the membership, funding and other resources, and the strategy and annual report of an SAB is made by the Care Act 2014 ss 43(5), 76(10), (11)(b), (c), Sch 2.
3   As to the meaning of 'adult' see PARA 1 note 1.
4   See note 6.
5   Ie in cases of the kind described in the Care Act 2014 s 42(1) (see PARA 321).
6   Care Act 2014 s 43(1), (2). An SAB's objective under s 43(2) does not include helping and protecting adults who are detained in prison or residing in approved premises; but an SAB may nonetheless provide advice or assistance to any person for the purpose of helping and protecting such adults in its area in cases of the kind described in s 42(1): s 76(8). As to the meanings of 'prison' and 'approved premises' see PARA 87 notes 2, 4.
7   Care Act 2014 s 43(3).
8   Care Act 2014 s 43(4).
9   Ie if the request is made for the purpose of enabling or assisting the SAB to exercise its functions (Care Act 2014 s 45(1)(a), (2)) and to a person whose functions or activities the SAB considers to be such that the person is likely to have information relevant to the exercise of a function by the SAB (s 45(3)), and either:
    (1)   the information relates to the person to whom the request is made, a function or activity of that person, or a person in respect of whom that person exercises a function or engages in an activity (s 45(1)(b), (4)); or
    (2)   the information is information requested by the SAB from a person to whom information was supplied in compliance with another request under s 45 and is the same as, or is derived from, information so supplied (s 45(5)).
10   Ie under the Care Act 2014 s 45(1).
11   Care Act 2014 s 45(6).

235.   Safeguarding adults reviews. A Safeguarding Adults Board (an 'SAB')[1] must arrange for there to be a review of a case involving an adult[2] in its area with needs for care and support (whether or not the local authority[3] has been meeting any of those needs) if there is reasonable cause for concern about how the SAB, members of it or other persons with relevant functions worked together to safeguard the adult[4] and either:

(1)	the adult has died[5] and the SAB knows or suspects that the death resulted from abuse[6] or neglect (whether or not it knew about or suspected the abuse or neglect before the adult died)[7]; or

(2)	the adult is still alive[8] and the SAB knows or suspects that the adult has experienced serious abuse or neglect[9].

An SAB may arrange for there to be a review of any other case involving an adult in its area with needs for care and support (whether or not the local authority has been meeting any of those needs)[10]. Each member of the SAB must co-operate in and contribute to the carrying out of a review under this section with a view to identifying the lessons to be learnt from the adult's case[11] and applying those lessons to future cases[12].

1 As to the establishment and operation of SAB's see PARA 234.
2 As to the meaning of 'adult' see PARA 1 note 1. Where a local authority is to carry out such a review it must, where necessary, arrange for the provision of independent advocacy: see PARA 236.
3 As to the meaning of 'local authority' see PARA 234 note 1.
4 Care Act 2014 s 44(1)(a). The Care Act 2014 s 44 (see the text and notes 5–12) does not apply to any case involving an adult in so far as the case relates to any period during which the adult was detained in prison or residing in approved premises: s 76(9). As to the meanings of 'prison' and 'approved premises' see PARA 87 notes 2, 4.
5 Care Act 2014 s 44(1)(b), (2)(a).
6 As to the meaning of 'abuse' see PARA 8 note 12.
7 Care Act 2014 s 44(2)(b).
8 Care Act 2014 s 44(3)(a).
9 Care Act 2014 s 44(3)(b).
10 Care Act 2014 s 44(4).
11 Care Act 2014 s 44(5)(a).
12 Care Act 2014 s 44(5)(b).

236. Independent advocacy. Where a local authority in England[1] is to carry out an enquiry about a vulnerable adult[2], or a Safeguarding Adults Board (an 'SAB')[3] is to carry out a review of a case involving a living vulnerable adult[4], and the authority[5] considers that the adult would be disadvantaged by the absence of independent advocacy[6], it must arrange for a person who is independent of the authority (an 'independent advocate') to be available to represent and support the adult to whose case the enquiry or review relates for the purpose of facilitating his or her involvement in the enquiry or review[7]. This duty does not, however, apply in the case of an adult who is detained in prison[8] or residing in approved premises[9], or if the authority is satisfied that there is a person:

(1)	who would be an appropriate person[10] to represent and support the adult for the purpose of facilitating the adult's involvement[11]; and

(2)	who is not engaged in providing care or treatment for the adult in a professional capacity or for remuneration[12].

1 As to the meaning of 'local authority' see PARA 234 note 1.
2 Ie where there is to be an inquiry under the Care Act 2014 s 42(2) (see PARA 321): s 68(1)(a). As to the meaning of 'adult' see PARA 1 note 1.
3 As to the establishment and operation of SAB's see PARA 234.
4 Ie where there is to be a review under the Care Act 2014 s 44(1) of a case in which the condition in s 44(3) is met or a review under s 44(4): s 68(1)(b). As to reviews under s 44 see PARA 235.
5 Ie in a case within the Care Act 2014 s 68(1)(a), the authority making the enquiry or causing it to be made; and in a case within s 68(1)(b), the authority which established the SAB arranging the review: s 68(7).
6 Ie if the authority considers that, were an independent advocate not to be available, the individual would experience substantial difficulty in doing one or more of the following:

(1)   understanding relevant information (Care Act 2014 s 68(3)(a));

(2)   retaining that information (s 68(3)(b));

(3)   using or weighing that information as part of the process of being involved (s 68(3)(c));

(4)   communicating the individual's views, wishes or feelings (whether by talking, using sign language or any other means) (s 68(3)(d)).

7   Care Act 2014 s 68(2). If the enquiry or review needs to begin as a matter of urgency, it may do so even if the authority has not yet been able to comply with the duty under s 68(2) (and the authority continues to be subject to the duty): s 68(6).

8   Care Act 2014 s 76(7)(a). As to the meaning of 'prison' see PARA 87 note 2.

9   Care Act 2014 s 76(7)(b). As to the meaning of 'approved premises' see PARA 87 note 4.

10 For this purpose a person is not regarded as an appropriate person unless:

(1)   where the adult has capacity to consent to being represented and supported by that person, the adult does so consent (Care Act 2014 s 68(5)(a)); or

(2)   where the adult lacks capacity so to consent, the local authority is satisfied that being represented and supported by that person would be in the adult's best interests (s 68(5)(b)).

11 Care Act 2014 s 68(4)(a).

12 Care Act 2014 s 68(4)(b).

B.   SAFEGUARDING CHILDREN

237.   Establishment of local safeguarding children boards. Each local authority in England[1] must establish a local safeguarding children board (an 'LSCB')[2] for its area[3], the objective of which is to co-ordinate what is done by each person or body represented on the board[4] for the purposes of safeguarding and promoting the welfare of children[5] in the area of the authority by which it is established[6] and to ensure the effectiveness of what is done by each such person or body for those purposes[7]. An LSCB's functions, in relation to its objectives, are prescribed by statute[8]. If an LSCB requests a person or body to supply information specified in the request to it, or to another person or body specified in the request, the request must be complied with if specified conditions are met[9]. Information may be used by the LSCB, or other person or body to whom it is supplied[10], only for the purpose of enabling or assisting the LSCB to exercise its functions[11].

1   Ie a county council in England, a metropolitan district council, a non-metropolitan district council for an area for which there is no county council, a London borough council, the Common Council of the City of London (in its capacity as a local authority), and the Council of the Isles of Scilly: see the Children Act 2004 s 65(1); and CHILDREN AND YOUNG PERSONS vol 9 (2017) PARA 3. A local authority in England and each of its board partners (see note 2) must, in exercising its functions relating to a local safeguarding children board, have regard to any guidance given to it for the purpose by the Secretary of State: s 16(2) (ss 13(1), (3), (4), (5A), (8), 14A(3), 15(3), 16(2) amended by SI 2010/1158). As to the Secretary of State see PARA 333.

2   Provision about the membership, funding and other resources, and the strategy and annual report of an LSCB is made by the Children Act 2004 ss 13(2)–(5), (5A), (5B), (6), 14A, 15 (as amended (see note 1); s 13(3) amended by the Offender Management Act 2007 Sch 3 para 4; the Health and Social Care Act 2008 Sch 5 para 131; and by the Education and Skills Act 2008 Sch 1 para 85; Children Act 2004 ss 13(3), 15(3) amended by the Criminal Justice and Courts Act 2015 Sch 9 paras 15, 16; Children Act 2004 ss 13(5A), (5B), 14A added, s 14(1)(a) amended, by the Apprenticeships, Skills, Children and Learning Act 2009 ss 196, 197); and by the Local Safeguarding Children Boards Regulations 2006, SI 2006/90, regs 3, 3A, 4 (reg 3A added by SI 2010/622; amended by SI 2010/1172). Provision is also made for the periodic review of a board's performance by Her Majesty's Chief Inspector of Education, Children's Services and Skills: see the Local Safeguarding Children Boards (Review) Regulations 2013, SI 2013/2299 (made under the Children Act 2004 s 15A (ss 14B, 15A added by the Children, Schools and Families Act 2010 ss 8, 10)). As to Her Majesty's Chief Inspector of Education, Children's Services and Skills see EDUCATION vol 36 (2015) PARA 1133 et seq.

3   Children Act 2004 s 13(1) (as amended: see note 1). Two or more local authorities in England may discharge their respective duties by establishing a local safeguarding children board for their combined area: s 13(8) (as so amended).

4   Ie by virtue of the Children Act 2004 s 13(2), (4) or (5): see note 2. In the establishment and operation of a board, the authority establishing it must co-operate with each of its board partners and each board partner must co-operate with the authority: s 14(7).
5   Ie persons under the age of 18: see the Children Act 2004 s 65(1); and CHILDREN AND YOUNG PERSONS vol 9 (2017) PARA 3.
6   Children Act 2004 s 14(1)(a) (as amended: see note 2).
7   Children Act 2004 s 14(1)(b).
8   See PARA 238.
9   Ie if the request is made for the purpose of enabling or assisting the LSCB to perform its functions (Children Act 2004 s 14B(1), (2) (as added: see note 2)) and to a person or body whose functions or activities the LSCB considers to be such that the person or body is likely to have information relevant to the exercise of a function by the SAB (s 14B(3) (as so added)), and either:
    (1)   the information relates to the person or body to whom the request is made, a function or activity of that person or body, or a person in respect of whom a function is exercisable, or an activity is engaged in, by that person or body (s 14B(4) (as so added)); or
    (2)   the information is information requested by the LSCB from a person or body to whom information was supplied in compliance with another request under s 14B and is the same as, or is derived from, information so supplied (s 14B(5) (as so added)).
10 Ie under the Children Act 2004 s 14B(1).
11 Children Act 2004 s 14B(6) (as added: see note 9). An LSCB must have regard to any guidance given to it by the Secretary of State in connection with the exercise of its functions under s 14B: s 14B(7) (as so added).

238. Functions of local safeguarding children boards. The functions of a local safeguarding children board (an 'LSCB')[1] in relation to its objective[2] are:
    (1)   to develop policies and procedures for safeguarding and promoting the welfare of children[3] in the area of the local authority[4];
    (2)   communicating to persons and bodies in the area of the authority the need to safeguard and promote the welfare of children, raising their awareness of how this can best be done, and encouraging them to do so[5];
    (3)   monitoring and evaluating the effectiveness of what is done by the authority and its board partners individually and collectively to safeguard and promote the welfare of children, and advising them on ways to improve[6];
    (4)   participating in the planning of services for children in the area of the authority[7];
    (5)   undertaking reviews of serious cases[8] and advising the authority and its board partners on lessons to be learned[9].
The board may also engage in any other activity that facilitates, or is conducive to, the achievement of its objectives[10].

1   As to the establishment and operation of LSCB's see PARA 237.
2   Ie as defined in the Children Act 2004 s 14(1) (see PARA 237).
3   As to the meaning of 'children' see PARA 237 note 5.
4   Local Safeguarding Children Boards Regulations 2006, SI 2006/90 reg 5(1)(a) (made under the Children Act 2004 ss 14(2), (3), 16(1) (amended by SI 2010/1158)). This includes the development of policies and procedures in relation to:
    (1)   the action to be taken where there are concerns about a child's safety or welfare, including thresholds of intervention (Local Safeguarding Children Boards Regulations 2006, SI 2006/90 reg 5(1)(a)(i));
    (2)   training of persons who work with children or in services affecting the safety and welfare of children (reg 5(1)(a)(ii));
    (3)   recruitment and supervision of persons who work with children (reg 5(1)(a)(iii));
    (4)   investigation of allegations concerning persons who work with children (reg 5(1)(a)(iv));
    (5)   safety and welfare of children who are privately fostered (reg 5(1)(a)(v)); and
    (6)   co-operation with neighbouring local authorities and their board partners (reg 5(1)(a)(vi)) (amended by SI 2010/1172)).
    As to the meaning of 'local authority' in this context see PARA 237 note 1.

5   Local Safeguarding Children Boards Regulations 2006, SI 2006/90 reg 5(1)(b).
6   Local Safeguarding Children Boards Regulations 2006, SI 2006/90 reg 5(1)(c).
7   Local Safeguarding Children Boards Regulations 2006, SI 2006/90 reg 5(1)(d).
8   Ie cases where abuse or neglect of a child is known or suspected and either the child has died or
    the child has been seriously harmed and there is cause for concern as to the way in which the
    authority, its board partners or other relevant persons have worked together to safeguard the child:
    Local Safeguarding Children Boards Regulations 2006, SI 2006/90 reg 5(2). The purpose of a
    serious case review is so that lessons could be learned which might prevent repeat incidents: see *R
    (on the application of Webster) v Swindon Local Safeguarding Children Board* [2009] EWHC
    2755 (Admin), (2009) Times, 6 November (decision of board to hold limited review following
    potentially racially motivated attack in school grounds successfully challenged in judicial review
    proceedings).
9   Local Safeguarding Children Boards Regulations 2006, SI 2006/90 reg 5(1)(e).
10 Local Safeguarding Children Boards Regulations 2006, SI 2006/90 reg 5(3).

(ii) Wales

239. Establishment of the Safeguarding Boards and the National Independent Safeguarding Board. There are to be established in Wales Safeguarding Children Boards and Safeguarding Adult Boards, whose objectives are to protect children[1] and adults[2] within their areas from abuse and neglect[3]. The areas of Wales for which there are to be Safeguarding Boards are to be prescribed[4]. Provision may be made[5] for the Safeguarding Children Board and the Safeguarding Adults Board in each Safeguarding Board area to combine so as to form a single Safeguarding Board for the area ('a Safeguarding Children and Adult Board')[6]; the Safeguarding Children Board and the Safeguarding Adults Board for an area may also form a joint board for the area[7]. A Safeguarding Board must seek to achieve its objectives by co-ordinating and ensuring the effectiveness of what is done by each person or body represented on the Board[8]. A Safeguarding Board's functions, in relation to its objectives, are prescribed by statute[9]. There is also a National Independent Safeguarding Board[10], whose duties are:

(1)   to provide support and advice to Safeguarding Boards with a view to ensuring that they are effective[11];

(2)   to report on the adequacy and effectiveness of arrangements to safeguard children and adults in Wales[12]; and

(3)   to make recommendations to the Welsh Ministers as to how those arrangements could be improved[13].

1   As to the meaning of 'child' see PARA 2.
2   As to the meaning of 'adult' see PARA 2.
3   Ie, the objectives of a Safeguarding Children Board are to protect children within its area who are
    experiencing, or are at risk of, abuse, neglect or other kinds of harm (Social Services and
    Well-being (Wales) Act 2014 s 135(1)(a)), and to prevent children within its area from becoming
    at risk of abuse, neglect or other kinds of harm (s 135(1)(b)); and the objectives of a Safeguarding
    Adults Board are to protect adults within its area who have needs for care and support (whether
    or not a local authority is meeting any of those needs) (s 135(2)(a)(i)) and are experiencing, or are
    at risk of, abuse or neglect (s 135(2)(a)(ii)), and to prevent those adults within its area mentioned
    in s 135(2)(a)(i) from becoming at risk of abuse or neglect (s 135(2)(b)). As to the meanings of
    'abuse' and 'neglect' see PARA 15 note 11. As to the meanings of 'care' and 'support' see PARA 2
    note 1. As to the meaning of 'local authority' (in Wales) see PARA 2.
        Provision as to the membership of Safeguarding Boards and Safeguarding Board partners is
    made by s 134(2)–(11), s 139(2) (s 134(2) amended by SI 2016/413; Social Services and Well-being
    (Wales) Act 2014 s 134(8) amended by the Criminal Justice and Courts Act 2015 Sch 9 para 32)
    (regulations may make provision as to the functions of Safeguarding Board partners relating to the
    Boards on which they are represented: at the date at which this volume states the law none had
    been made) and the Social Services and Well-being (Wales) Act 2014 s 139(4) (each Safeguarding
    Board partner must take all reasonable steps to ensure that the Board on which it is represented
    operates effectively); provision for funding is made by s 138; provision for the procedures of

Boards is made by the Safeguarding Boards (Functions and Procedures) (Wales) Regulations 2015, SI 2015/1466, regs 5, 6 (made under the Social Services and Well-being (Wales) Act 2014 s 135(4)); provision for annual plans and reports is made by s 136. A Safeguarding Board partner must, in exercising its functions relating to a Board, have regard to any guidance given by the Welsh Ministers: s 139(3).

4   See the Social Services and Well-being (Wales) Act 2014 s 134(1) (regulations must set out those areas in Wales for which there are to be Safeguarding Boards ('Safeguarding Board areas'): at the date at which this volume states the law no such regulations had been made.

5   Ie by order of the Welsh Ministers, which may amend any provision of the Social Services and Well-being (Wales) Act 2014 Pt 7 (ss 126–142) as a consequence of there being a single Safeguarding Children and Adult Board for each Safeguarding Board area, and make other consequential provision including amendments of any other enactment (whenever passed or made): see s 140(2); and for the procedure for making regulations see s 141. As to the Welsh Ministers see PARA 395.

6   Social Services and Well-being (Wales) Act 2014 s 140(1).

7   Social Services and Well-being (Wales) Act 2014 s 135(7).The joint board is to have the objectives in both s 135(1) and (2) and references in Pt 7 to a Safeguarding Board are read as references to the joint board: s 135(7).

8   Social Services and Well-being (Wales) Act 2014 s 135(3). A Safeguarding Board may cooperate with another one or more Safeguarding Boards: s 135(5). A Safeguarding Board may act jointly with another one or more Safeguarding Boards in relation to their combined areas and if they do so, references in Pt 7 to a Safeguarding Board are read as references to the Boards acting jointly and references to a Safeguarding Board area are read as references to the combined area: s 135(6).

9   See PARA 240.

10 Provision for the constitution and proceedings of the National Board is made by the National Independent Safeguarding Board (Wales) (No 2) Regulations 2015, SI 2015/1803, regs 3–7 (made under the Social Services and Well-being (Wales) Act 2014 s 133). The National Board must make an annual report to the Welsh Ministers, must make such other reports to the Welsh Ministers as they require, and may make such other reports as it thinks fit: see the Social Services and Well-being (Wales) Act 2014 s 132(3); and in connection with the annual report see the National Independent Safeguarding Board (Wales) (No 2) Regulations 2015, SI 2015/1803, reg 8.

11 Social Services and Well-being (Wales) Act 2014 s 132(1), (2)(a). A Safeguarding Board must cooperate with the National Board, and must supply the National Board with any information it requests: s 139(1).

12 Social Services and Well-being (Wales) Act 2014 s 132(2)(b).

13 Social Services and Well-being (Wales) Act 2014 s 132(2)(c).

240.   Functions of Safeguarding Boards. The functions of a Safeguarding Board[1] in relation to its objectives[2] are:

(1)   to cooperate with other Safeguarding Boards and the National Board[3] with a view to contributing to the development and review of national policies and procedures for Safeguarding Boards and implementing national policies and procedures recommended by, and guidance and advice given by, the National Board[4];

(2)   to raise awareness throughout the Safeguarding Board area[5] of the Board's objectives and how these might be achieved[6];

(3)   to undertake relevant reviews, audits and investigations[7];

(4)   to review the efficacy of measures taken by the Board to achieve the Board's objectives[8];

(5)   to make recommendations in light of those reviews, to monitor the extent to which those recommendations are carried out and to take appropriate action where it is shown that the Board's objectives are not being fulfilled[9];

(6)   to disseminate information about those recommendations to other appropriate Safeguarding Boards and the National Board[10];

(7)   to facilitate research into protection of, and prevention of abuse and neglect of, children or adults at risk of harm[11];

(8)   to review the training needs of and promote the provision of suitable training for persons working to achieve the Board's objectives[12];

(9)   to arrange and facilitate an annual programme of multi-agency professional forums[13];

(10)   to cooperate or act jointly with any similar body situated in any jurisdiction where the Board considers that this will assist it to fulfil its objectives[14];

(11)   to obtain specialist advice or information relevant to the attainment of the Board's objectives[15];

(12)   to undertake[16] practice reviews[17].

A Safeguarding Board may, for the purpose of enabling or assisting the Board to perform its functions, ask a qualifying person or body[18] to supply specified information[19] to the Board or a person or body specified[20] by the Board[21], and the qualifying person or body to whom or to which such a request is made must comply with the request unless the person or body considers that doing so would be incompatible with the duties of the person or body or otherwise have an adverse effect on the exercise of the functions of the person or body[22]. Information so supplied may only be used by the Board or other person or body to whom or to which it is supplied for the specified[23] purpose[24].

1   As to the establishment and operation of Safeguarding Boards see PARA 238.
2   Ie as defined in the Social Services and Well-being (Wales) Act 2014 s 135(1) (Children Safeguarding Boards) or s 135(2) (Adult Safeguarding Boards) (see PARA 239).
3   As to the National Board see PARA 239.
4   Safeguarding Boards (Functions and Procedures) (Wales) Regulations 2015, SI 2015/1466, reg 3(1), (2)(a).
5   As to Safeguarding Board areas see PARA 238.
6   Safeguarding Boards (Functions and Procedures) (Wales) Regulations 2015, SI 2015/1466, reg 3(2)(b).
7   Safeguarding Boards (Functions and Procedures) (Wales) Regulations 2015, SI 2015/1466, reg 3(2)(c).
8   Safeguarding Boards (Functions and Procedures) (Wales) Regulations 2015, SI 2015/1466, reg 3(2)(d).
9   Safeguarding Boards (Functions and Procedures) (Wales) Regulations 2015, SI 2015/1466, reg 3(2)(e).
10 Safeguarding Boards (Functions and Procedures) (Wales) Regulations 2015, SI 2015/1466, reg 3(2)(f).
11 Safeguarding Boards (Functions and Procedures) (Wales) Regulations 2015, SI 2015/1466, reg 3(2)(g). 'Adults' and 'children' mean adults and children who are, or may be, affected by the exercise of a Board's functions (reg 2); as to the meanings of 'child' and 'adult' generally see PARA 2. As to the meanings of 'abuse' and 'neglect' see PARA 15 note 11.
12 Safeguarding Boards (Functions and Procedures) (Wales) Regulations 2015, SI 2015/1466, reg 3(2)(h).
13 Safeguarding Boards (Functions and Procedures) (Wales) Regulations 2015, SI 2015/1466, reg 3(2)(i). 'Multi-agency professional forums' means the forums, arranged and facilitated by a Board for practitioners and managers from representative bodies, and other bodies or persons deemed relevant by the Chair of the Board, with the purpose of learning from cases, audits, inspections and reviews in order to improve future child or adult protection policy and practice: reg 2.
14 Safeguarding Boards (Functions and Procedures) (Wales) Regulations 2015, SI 2015/1466, reg 3(2)(j).
15 Safeguarding Boards (Functions and Procedures) (Wales) Regulations 2015, SI 2015/1466, reg 3(2)(k).
16 Ie in accordance with the Safeguarding Boards (Functions and Procedures) (Wales) Regulations 2015, SI 2015/1466, reg 4.
17 Safeguarding Boards (Functions and Procedures) (Wales) Regulations 2015, SI 2015/1466, reg 3(2)(l).

18 'Qualifying person or body' means a person or body whose functions or activities are considered by the Board to be such that the person or body is likely to have information relevant to the exercise of a function of the Board: Social Services and Well-being (Wales) Act 2014 s 137(7).

19 Ie:

(1)   information relating to the qualifying person or body to whom or to which the request is made (Social Services and Well-being (Wales) Act 2014 s 137(2)(a));

(2)   information relating to a function or activity of that qualifying person or body (s 137(2)(b));

(3)   information relating to a person in respect of whom a function is exercisable, or an activity is engaged in, by that qualifying person or body (s 137(2)(c));

(4)   information which has been supplied to the qualifying person or body in compliance with another request under s 137 (s 137(2)(d)); or

(5)   information which is derived from information so supplied (s 137(2)(e)).

20 Ie specified in a request made under the Social Services and Well-being (Wales) Act 2014 s 137(1).

21 Social Services and Well-being (Wales) Act 2014 s 137(1).

22 Social Services and Well-being (Wales) Act 2014 s 137(4). A qualifying person or body who decides not to comply with a request under s 137(1) must give the Safeguarding Board which made the request written reasons for the decision: s 137(5).

23 Ie the purpose mentioned in the Social Services and Well-being (Wales) Act 2014 s 137(1).

24 Social Services and Well-being (Wales) Act 2014 s 137(6).

(2) DISCLOSURE AND BARRING

(i) The Regulated Activities

A.   REGULATED ACTIVITIES RELATING TO CHILDREN

241. Teaching, training and instruction. An activity is a regulated activity relating to children if it is any form of teaching, training or instruction of children, or it consists in or involves the day to day management or supervision of a person carrying out such an activity, unless the teaching, training or instruction is:

(1)   merely incidental to the teaching, training or instruction of persons who are not children[1]; or

(2)   provided to a child in the course of his employment[2] (unless the child has not attained the age of 16 and the activity is carried out by a person in respect of whom arrangements exist principally for that purpose)[3].

This does not include any form of teaching, training or instruction of children which is, on a regular basis, subject to the day to day supervision of another person who is engaging in regulated activity relating to children[4].

To qualify as a regulated activity relating to children the activity must be carried out frequently by the same person, or the period condition must be satisfied[5].

1 Safeguarding Vulnerable Groups Act 2006 s 5(1), Sch 4 paras 1(1)(a), (14), 2(1)(a). A person who is part of a group in relation to which another (P) engages in regulated activity relating to children does not engage in regulated activity only because he assists P or does anything on behalf of or under the direction of P which, but for this provision, would amount to engaging in regulated activity relating to children: Sch 4 para 5. 'Child' means a person who has not attained the age of 18: s 60(1).

2 In the Safeguarding Vulnerable Groups Act 2006 Sch 4 para 2(2) 'employment' includes any form of work which is carried out under the supervision or control of another, whether or not the person carrying it out is paid for doing so: Sch 4 para 2(6).

3 Safeguarding Vulnerable Groups Act 2006 Sch 4 para 2(2)(a), (3) (s 56(2), (3), Sch 4 paras 1(1)(b), 2(2), 10(2) amended, Sch 4 paras 1(15), 2(3A), (3C), 5A added, by the Protection of Freedoms Act 2012 ss 64(1), (2), (6), (7), (9), (10), 77(6), Sch 9 para 68, Sch 10 Pt 5).

4 Safeguarding Vulnerable Groups Act 2006 Sch 4 para 2(3A) (as added: see note 3). The references in Sch 4 para 2(3A), (3B)(b) (see PARA 242) to day to day supervision are references to such day

to day supervision as is reasonable in all the circumstances for the purpose of protecting any children concerned: Sch 4 para 2(3C) (as so added). Any activity which consists in or involves on a regular basis the day to day management or supervision of a person who would be carrying out an activity mentioned in Sch 4 para 1(1) (see the text and notes 1–3) but for the exclusion for supervised activity in Sch 4 para 2(3A) or (3B)(b) is a regulated activity relating to children: Sch 4 para 1(15) (as so added).

The Secretary of State must give guidance for the purpose of assisting regulated activity providers and personnel suppliers in deciding whether supervision is of such a kind that, as a result of Sch 4 para 1(2B)(b), Sch 4 para 2(3A) or Sch 4 para 2(3B)(b), the person being supervised would not be engaging in regulated activity relating to children: Sch 4 para 5A(1) (as so added). 'Personnel supplier' means a person carrying on an employment agency or an employment business, or an educational institution which supplies to another person a student who is following a course at the institution, for the purpose of enabling the student to obtain experience of engaging in regulated activity; and 'employment agency' and 'employment business' must be construed in accordance with the Employment Agencies Act 1973 (see s 13; and TRADE AND INDUSTRY vol 97 (2015) PARA 974): Safeguarding Vulnerable Groups Act 2006 s 60(1). Before giving guidance under these provisions, the Secretary of State must consult the Welsh Ministers: Sch 4 para 5A(2) (as so added). The Secretary of State must publish guidance given under these provisions: Sch 4 para 5A(3) (as so added). A regulated activity provider or a personnel supplier must, in exercising any functions under the Safeguarding Vulnerable Groups Act 2006, have regard to guidance for the time being given under these provisions: Sch 4 para 5A(4) (as so added).

Although the powers of the Secretary of State under many of the statutory provisions relating to social services have been transferred, so far as exercisable in relation to Wales, to the Welsh Ministers (see PARA 395), the powers of the Secretary of State under the Safeguarding Vulnerable Groups Act 2006 have not been. However, if the exercise of a power to make subordinate legislation (ie a power to make regulations or an order) under s 45(9) (see PARA 286), s 46(2) (see PARA 291), s 48(7) (see PARA 303) or s 49(7) (see PARA 303) will have effect in relation to any function of the Welsh Ministers to which the provision applies, or would apply in consequence of the exercise of the power, the Secretary of State must not exercise the power without the consent of the Welsh Ministers (s 56(2), (4) (s 56(2) as so amended)), and if the exercise of a power to make subordinate legislation under s 5(3) (see note 5), s 34ZA(7) (see PARA 294), s 35(1) (see PARA 280), s 36(1), (2) or (3) (see PARAS 281–283), s 37(2) (see PARA 290), s 40(2) (see PARA 291), s 41(8) (see PARA 285), s 42(2) (see PARA 291), s 64(2), Sch 3 para 1(1), 2(1), 7(1) or 8(1) (see PARAS 265–266, 270) or Sch 4 para 2(1)(f) or 7(1)(f) or (g) (see PARAS 245, 253, 257) will have effect in relation to Wales, the Secretary of State must not exercise the power unless he first consults the Welsh Ministers (s 56(3) (as so amended)).

5   Safeguarding Vulnerable Groups Act 2006 Sch 4 para 1(1)(b). The period condition is satisfied if the person carrying out the activity does so at any time on more than 3 days in any period of 30 days: Sch 4 para 10(1) (amended by SI 2010/1154). In relation to an activity that falls within the Safeguarding Vulnerable Groups Act 2006 Sch 4 para 2(1)(a), (b) or (c), the period condition is also satisfied if the person carrying out the activity does so at any time between 2 am and 6 am and the activity gives the person the opportunity to have face-to-face contact with children: Sch 4 para 10(2) (as amended: see note 3).

The Safeguarding Vulnerable Groups Act 2006 (Regulated Activity, Devolution and Miscellaneous Provisions) Order 2010, SI 2010/1154, is made under, inter alia, the Safeguarding Vulnerable Groups Act 2006 s 5(3)(a) (which provides that the Secretary of State may by order amend Sch 4 so as to vary the meaning of regulated activity relating to children) and s 54 (amended by the Protection of Freedoms Act 2012 Sch 9 para 67, Sch 10 Pt 5) (which provides that the Secretary of State may by order make provision for aligning the Safeguarding Vulnerable Groups Act 2006 with legislation passed by the devolved administrations in Scotland and Northern Ireland).

242.   Care and supervision. An activity is a regulated activity relating to children if it is any form of care for or supervision of children[1], or it consists in or involves the day to day management or supervision of a person carrying out such an activity, unless the care or supervision is:

(1)   merely incidental to care for or supervision of persons who are not children[2]; or

(2)   in the course of the child's employment (unless the child has not attained the age of 16 and the activity is carried out by a person in respect of whom arrangements exist principally for that purpose)[3].

This does not include any health care[4] provided otherwise than by (or under the direction or supervision of) a health care professional[5] and does not, except in the case of relevant personal care[6] or of health care provided by (or under the direction or supervision of) a health care professional, include any form of care for or supervision of children which is, on a regular basis, subject to the day to day supervision of another person who is engaging in regulated activity relating to children[7].

Unless the activity is relevant personal care or health care provided by or under the direction or supervision of a health care professional, in order to qualify as a regulated activity under this head the activity must be carried out frequently by the same person, or the period condition must be satisfied[8].

1 Safeguarding Vulnerable Groups Act 2006 Sch 4 paras 1(14), 2(1)(b). For an exclusion from these provisions for members of provider groups see Sch 4 para 5; and PARA 241 note 1. As to the meaning of 'child' see PARA 241 note 1.

2 Safeguarding Vulnerable Groups Act 2006 Sch 4 para 2(1)(b).

3 Safeguarding Vulnerable Groups Act 2006 Sch 4 para 2(2)(b), (3) (Sch 4 paras 1(1)(b), 2(2) amended, Sch 4 paras 1(1A)–(1D), 2(3B) added, by the Protection of Freedoms Act 2012 s 64(1)–(3), (7)). As to 'employment' see PARA 241 note 2.

4 'Health care' includes all forms of health care provided for children, whether relating to physical or mental health and also includes palliative care for children and procedures that are similar to forms of medical or surgical care but are not provided for children in connection with a medical condition: Safeguarding Vulnerable Groups Act 2006 Sch 4 para 1(1C) (as added: see note 3).

5 Safeguarding Vulnerable Groups Act 2006 Sch 4 para 2(3B)(a) (as added: see note 3). 'Health care professional' means a person who is a member of a profession regulated by a body mentioned in the National Health Service Reform and Health Care Professions Act 2002 s 25(3) (see MEDICAL PROFESSIONS vol 74 (2011) PARA 48): Safeguarding Vulnerable Groups Act 2006 Sch 4 para 1(1C) (as so added). References to health care provided by, or under the direction or supervision of, a health care professional includes a reference to first aid provided to a child by any person acting on behalf of an organisation established for the purpose of providing first aid: Sch 4 para 1(1D) (as so added).

6 'Relevant personal care' means:
   (1) physical assistance which is given to a child who is in need of it by reason of illness or disability and is given in connection with eating or drinking (including the administration of parenteral nutrition) (Safeguarding Vulnerable Groups Act 2006 Sch 4 para 1(1B)(a) (Sch 4 para 1(1B) as added: see note 3));
   (2) physical assistance which is given to a child who is in need of it by reason of age, illness or disability and is given in connection with toileting (including in relation to the process of menstruation) (Sch 4 para 1(1B)(b)(i) (as so added)), washing or bathing (Sch 4 para 1(1B)(b)(ii) (as so added)) or dressing (Sch 4 para 1(1B)(b)(iii) (as so added));
   (3) the prompting (together with supervision) of a child, who is in need of it by reason of illness or disability, in relation to the performance of the activity of eating or drinking where the child is unable to make a decision in relation to performing such an activity without such prompting and supervision (Sch 4 para 1(1B)(c) (as so added));
   (4) the prompting (together with supervision) of a child, who is in need of it by reason of age, illness or disability, in relation to the performance of any of the activities listed in Sch 4 para 1(1B)(b)(i)–(iii) (see head (2) above) where the child is unable to make a decision in relation to performing such an activity without such prompting and supervision (Sch 4 para 1(1B)(d) (as so added));
   (5) any form of training, instruction, advice or guidance which relates to the performance of the activity of eating or drinking (Sch 4 para 1(1B)(e)(i) (as so added)), is given to a child who is in need of it by reason of illness or disability (Sch 4 para 1(1B)(e)(ii) (as so added)) and does not fall within Sch 4 para 1(1B)(c) (see head (3) above) (Sch 4 para 1(1B)(e)(iii) (as so added)); or
   (6) any form of training, instruction, advice or guidance which relates to the performance of any of the activities listed in Sch 4 para 1(1B)(b)(i)–(iii) (Sch 4 para 1(1B)(f)(i) (as so added)), is given to a child who is in need of it by reason of age, illness or disability (Sch 4 para 1(1B)(f)(ii) (as so added)) and does not fall within Sch 4 para 1(1B)(d) (see head (4) above) (Sch 4 para 1(1B)(f)(iii) (as so added)).

7 Safeguarding Vulnerable Groups Act 2006 Sch 4 para 2(3B)(b) (as added: see note 3). As to references to day to day supervision, and as to the giving of guidance in this regard see PARA 241 note 4.

8 Safeguarding Vulnerable Groups Act 2006 Sch 4 para 1(1)(b), (1A), (3B)(a) (as added and amended: see note 3). As to when the period condition is satisfied see PARA 241 note 5.

243. Advice and guidance. An activity is a regulated activity relating to children if it is any form of advice or guidance provided wholly or mainly for children, or it consists in or involves the day to day management or supervision of a person carrying out such an activity, if the advice or guidance relates to their physical, emotional or educational well-being[1]. This does not include advice or guidance provided for a child in the course of his employment (unless the child has not attained the age of 16 and the activity is carried out by a person in respect of whom arrangements exist principally for that purpose)[2], or any legal advice[3]. To qualify as a regulated activity relating to children the activity must be carried out frequently by the same person, or the period condition must be satisfied[4].

1   Safeguarding Vulnerable Groups Act 2006 Sch 4 paras 1(14), 2(1)(c). As to the meaning of 'child' see PARA 241 note 1. For an exclusion from these provisions for members of provider groups see Sch 4 para 5; and PARA 241 note 1.
2   Safeguarding Vulnerable Groups Act 2006 Sch 4 para 2(2)(c), (3) (Sch 4 paras 1(1)(b), 2(2) amended, Sch 4 para 2(3D) added, by the Protection of Freedoms Act 2012 s 64(1), (2), (7)(b)). As to 'employment' see PARA 241 note 2.
3   Safeguarding Vulnerable Groups Act 2006 Sch 4 para 2(3D) (as added: see note 2).
4   Safeguarding Vulnerable Groups Act 2006 Sch 4 para 1(1)(b) (as amended: see note 2). As to when the period condition is satisfied see PARA 241 note 5.

244. Moderating a public electronic interactive communication service. An activity is a regulated activity relating to children if it is moderating a public electronic interactive communication service which is likely to be used wholly or mainly by children or it consists in or involves the day to day management or supervision of a person carrying out such an activity[1]. For these purposes a person moderates a public electronic interactive communication service if, for the purpose of protecting children, he has any function relating to:

(1)   monitoring the content of matter which forms any part of the service[2];
(2)   removing matter from, or preventing the addition of matter to, the service[3]; or
(3)   controlling access to, or use of, the service[4].

To qualify as a regulated activity relating to children the activity must be carried out frequently by the same person, or the period condition must be satisfied[5].

1   Safeguarding Vulnerable Groups Act 2006 Sch 4 paras 1(14), 2(1)(e). As to the meaning of 'child' see PARA 241 note 1. For an exclusion from these provisions for members of provider groups see Sch 4 para 5; and PARA 241 note 1.
2   Safeguarding Vulnerable Groups Act 2006 Sch 4 para 2(4)(a).
3   Safeguarding Vulnerable Groups Act 2006 Sch 4 para 2(4)(b). A person does not moderate a public electronic interactive communications service as mentioned in Sch 4 para 2(4)(b) or (c) unless he has access to the content of the matter and contact with users of the service: Sch 4 para 2(5).
4   Safeguarding Vulnerable Groups Act 2006 Sch 4 para 2(4)(c). See note 3.
5   Safeguarding Vulnerable Groups Act 2006 Sch 4 para 1(1)(b) (amended by the Protection of Freedoms Act 2012 s 64(1), (2)). As to when the period condition is satisfied see PARA 241 note 5.

245. Driving a vehicle. An activity is a regulated activity relating to children[1] if it is driving a vehicle which is being used only for the purpose of conveying children and any person supervising or caring for the children where:

(1)   a person (P) makes an arrangement (under a contract or otherwise) for children to be conveyed in a vehicle[2];
(2)   the arrangement is made between P and a person (B) or between P and a person with whom B is engaging in any form of work (whether or not for gain)[3]; and
(3)   B drives the vehicle and conveys the children pursuant to that arrangement[4].

An activity is also a regulated activity relating to children if it consists in or involves the day to day management or supervision of a person carrying out such an activity[5]. To qualify as a regulated activity relating to children the activity must be carried out frequently by the same person, or the period condition must be satisfied[6].

1 As to the meaning of 'child' see PARA 241 note 1.
2 Safeguarding Vulnerable Groups Act 2006 Sch 4 para 2(1)(f); Safeguarding Vulnerable Groups Act 2006 (Miscellaneous Provisions) Regulations 2009, SI 2009/1548, reg 3(a). For an exclusion from these provisions for members of provider groups see Sch 4 para 5; and PARA 241 note 1.
3 Safeguarding Vulnerable Groups Act 2006 (Miscellaneous Provisions) Regulations 2009, SI 2009/1548, reg 3(b).
4 Safeguarding Vulnerable Groups Act 2006 (Miscellaneous Provisions) Regulations 2009, SI 2009/1548, reg 3(b).
5 Safeguarding Vulnerable Groups Act 2006 Sch 4 para 1(14).
6 Safeguarding Vulnerable Groups Act 2006 Sch 4 para 1(1)(b) (amended by the Protection of Freedoms Act 2012 s 64(1), (2)). As to when the period condition is satisfied see PARA 241 note 5.

246. Peripheral functions in schools and other establishments for the care or accommodation of children. An activity is a regulated activity relating to children if:

(1)   it is carried out frequently by the same person or the period condition is satisfied[1];

(2)   it is carried out in an applicable educational establishment[2], a detention centre[3], a children's home or centre[4] or relevant childcare premises[5];

(3)   it is carried out by a person while engaging in any full-time work which is not teaching, training or instruction, care and supervision, advice and guidance, moderating a public electronic interactive communication service or driving a vehicle[6];

(4)   it is carried out for or in connection with the purposes of the establishment[7]; and

(5)   it gives that person the opportunity, in consequence of anything he is permitted or required to do in connection with the activity, to have contact with children[8].

Any activity which consists in or involves on a regular basis the day to day management or supervision of a person carrying out such an activity is also a regulated activity relating to children[9].

1 Safeguarding Vulnerable Groups Act 2006 Sch 4 para 1(2)(a). As to the meaning of 'child' see PARA 241 note 1. As to when the period condition is satisfied see PARA 241 note 5. For an exclusion from these provisions for members of provider groups see Sch 4 para 5; and PARA 241 note 1.
2 The applicable educational establishments for these purposes and for the purposes of the Safeguarding Vulnerable Groups Act 2006 Sch 4 para 1(9C) (see PARA 249) are:
    (1)   an educational institution which is exclusively or mainly for the provision of full-time education to children (Sch 4 para 3(1)(a) (Sch 4 para 3(1) amended, Sch 4 para 3(1)(aa) added, by SI 2010/1154));
    (2)   a school falling within the Education Act 1996 19(2) or (2B) (pupil referral units etc: see EDUCATION vol 35 (2015) PARA 427) which does not fall within the Safeguarding Vulnerable Groups Act 2006 Sch 4 para 3(1)(a) (Sch 4 para 3(1)(aa) (as so added));
    (3)   an alternative provision Academy which does not fall within Sch 4 para 3(1)(a) (Sch 4 para 3(1)(ab) (added by SI 2012/976)); and
    (4)   an establishment which is exclusively or mainly for the provision of nursery education (within the meaning of the School Standards and Framework Act 1998 s 117: see EDUCATION vol 35 (2015) PARA 95) (Safeguarding Vulnerable Groups Act 2006 Sch 4 para 3(1)(b)).
    'Educational institution' includes any training provider (within the meaning of the Education Act 2005 Pt 3 (ss 84A–100) (see s 100(1); and EDUCATION vol 36 (2015) PARA 1059), whether or not the training provider would otherwise be regarded as an institution: Safeguarding Vulnerable Groups Act 2006 s 60(1).

3   Ie an institution which is exclusively or mainly for the detention of children: Safeguarding
    Vulnerable Groups Act 2006 Sch 4 para 3(1)(d).
4   Ie a children's home within the meaning of the Care Standards Act 2000 s 1 (see CHILDREN AND
    YOUNG PERSONS vol 10 (2017) PARA 1003), a home provided in pursuance of arrangements
    under the Children Act 1989 s 82(5) (see CHILDREN AND YOUNG PERSONS vol 9 (2017)
    PARA 173), or a children's centre within the meaning of the Childcare Act 2006 s 5A(4) (see
    CHILDREN AND YOUNG PERSONS vol 10 (2017) PARA 1179): Safeguarding Vulnerable Groups
    Act 2006 Sch 4 para 3(1)(e), (f), (fa) (Sch 4 para 3(1)(fa) added by the Apprenticeships, Skills and
    Learning Act 2009 s 200).
5   Safeguarding Vulnerable Groups Act 2006 Sch 4 paras 1(2)(b), 3(1)(g). 'Relevant childcare
    premises' are any part of premises on which a person carries on any form of childcare (within the
    meaning of the Childcare Act 2006 s 18: see CHILDREN AND YOUNG PERSONS vol 10 (2017)
    PARA 1181) in respect of which he must be registered under that Act, any form of such childcare
    in respect of which he may be registered under the Childcare Act 2006, whether or not he is so
    registered, or any form of childminding or day care (within the meaning of the Children Act 1989
    s 79A or, as the case may be, the Children and Families (Wales) Measure 2010 s 19 (see
    CHILDREN AND YOUNG PERSONS vol 10 (2017) PARA 1242)) in respect of which he must be
    registered under the Childcare Act 2006: Safeguarding Vulnerable Groups Act 2006 Sch 4
    para 3(2) (Sch 4 para 3(2) amended, Sch 4 para 3(3)–(5) added, by SI 2009/2610; and further
    amended in relation to Wales by the Children and Families (Wales) Measure 2010 Sch 1 paras 27,
    28(c)). Premises on which a person carries on childcare or childminding are not relevant childcare
    premises for these purposes if the premises are the home of a parent (ie any person who has
    parental responsibility (as defined by the Children Act 1989: see s 3(1); and CHILDREN AND
    YOUNG PERSONS vol 9 (2017) PARA 150)) for a child or who has care of a child) of at least one
    child to whom the childcare or childminding is provided: Safeguarding Vulnerable Groups Act
    2006 Sch 4 para 3(3)–(5) (as so added).
6   Ie:
    (1)   any form of work for gain, other than any such work which is undertaken in pursuance
          of a contract for the provision of occasional or temporary services and is not an activity
          mentioned in the Safeguarding Vulnerable Groups Act 2006 Sch 4 para 2(1) (see
          PARAS 241–245) (disregarding for these purposes Sch 4 para 2(3A), (3B)(b)) (Sch 4
          para 1(2)(c), (2A) (Sch 4 para 1(2)(c), (14) amended, Sch 4 para 1(2A)–(2C), (15) added,
          by the Protection of Freedoms Act 2012 s 64(1), (4), (5), (6))); or
    (2)   any form of work which is not for gain, other than any such work which is carried out
          on a temporary or occasional basis, and is not an activity mentioned in the Safeguarding
          Vulnerable Groups Act 2006 Sch 4 para 2(1) (disregarding for these purposes Sch 4
          para 2(3A) and (3B)(b)), or any such work which is, on a regular basis, subject to the day
          to day supervision of another person who is engaging in regulated activity relating to
          children (that is to say, such day to day supervision as is reasonable in all the
          circumstances for the purpose of protecting any children concerned) (Sch 4 para 1(2B),
          (2C) (as so added)).
    Any activity which consists in or involves on a regular basis the day to day management or
    supervision of a person who would be carrying out an activity mentioned in Sch 4 para 1(2) (see
    the text and notes 1–5, 7, 8) but for the exclusion for supervised activity in Sch 4 para 1(2B) is a
    regulated activity relating to children: Sch 4 para 1(15) (as so added). As to the giving of guidance
    in this regard see Sch 4 para 5A; and PARA 241 note 4.
7   Safeguarding Vulnerable Groups Act 2006 Sch 4 para 1(2)(d).
8   Safeguarding Vulnerable Groups Act 2006 Sch 4 para 1(2)(e).
9   Safeguarding Vulnerable Groups Act 2006 Sch 4 para 1(14) (as amended: see note 6).

247. Childminding. Each of the following, if carried out in England, is a
regulated activity relating to children:

(1)   providing early years childminding[1] in respect of which a requirement to
      register[2] arises[3];

(2)   providing later years childminding[4] in respect of which a requirement to
      register[5] arises[6];

(3)   providing early years childminding or later years childminding, if it is
      provided by a person who is[7] registered[8]; and

(4)   providing later years childminding for a child[9] who has attained the age
      of eight, if a requirement to register would arise[10] in respect of that
      provision if the child had not attained that age[11].

Each of the following, if carried out in Wales, is a regulated activity relating to
children:

(a) acting as a childminder[12] so as to give rise to a requirement[13] to register[14]; and

(b) an activity which would give rise to such a requirement if the child in relation to whom the activity is carried out were under the age of eight[15].

1 As to the meaning of 'child' see PARA 241 note 1. As to the meaning of 'early years childminding' see the Childcare Act 2006 s 96(4), (5); and CHILDREN AND YOUNG PERSONS vol 10 (2017) PARA 1189 (definition applied by the Safeguarding Vulnerable Groups Act 2006 Sch 4 para 1(4)).

2 Ie by virtue of the Childcare Act 2006 s 33(1) (see CHILDREN AND YOUNG PERSONS vol 10 (2017) PARA 1190).

3 Safeguarding Vulnerable Groups Act 2006 Sch 4 para 1(3)(a). For an exclusion from these provisions for members of provider groups see Sch 4 para 5; and PARA 241 note 1.

4 As to the meaning of 'later years childminding' see the Childcare Act 2006 s 96(8), (9); and CHILDREN AND YOUNG PERSONS vol 10 (2017) PARA 1189 (definition applied by the Safeguarding Vulnerable Groups Act 2006 Sch 4 para 1(4)).

5 Ie by virtue of the Childcare Act 2006 s 52(1) (see CHILDREN AND YOUNG PERSONS vol 10 (2017) PARA 1202).

6 Safeguarding Vulnerable Groups Act 2006 Sch 4 para 1(3)(b).

7 Ie by virtue of the Childcare Act 2006 s 62(1) (see CHILDREN AND YOUNG PERSONS vol 10 (2017) PARA 1212).

8 Safeguarding Vulnerable Groups Act 2006 Sch 4 para 1(3)(c).

9 As to the meaning of 'child' see the Childcare Act 2006 s 60(1); and CHILDREN AND YOUNG PERSONS vol 10 (2017) PARA 1209 (definition applied by the Safeguarding Vulnerable Groups Act 2006 Sch 4 para 1(4)).

10 See note 5.

11 Safeguarding Vulnerable Groups Act 2006 Sch 4 para 1(3)(d). As to the meaning of 'England' see PARA 1 note 1.

12 For these purposes 'acting as a childminder' must be construed in accordance with the Children and Families (Wales) Measure 2010 s 19 (see CHILDREN AND YOUNG PERSONS vol 10 (2017) PARA 1242): Safeguarding Vulnerable Groups Act 2006 Sch 4 para 1(7) (amended by the Protection of Freedoms Act 2012 s 64(1), (6)).

13 Ie under the Children Act 1989 s 79D or, as the case may be, the Children and Families (Wales) Measure 2010 s 21 (see CHILDREN AND YOUNG PERSONS vol 10 (2017) PARA 1245).

14 Safeguarding Vulnerable Groups Act 2006 Sch 4 para 1(6)(a) (Sch 4 para 1(6)(a), (b) amended in relation to Wales by the Children and Families (Wales) Measure 2010 Sch 1 paras 27, 28).

15 Safeguarding Vulnerable Groups Act 2006 Sch 4 para 1(6)(b) (as amended: see note 14). Another age may be substituted for the age of 8 by order under s 19(4)(a): Sch 4 para 1(6)(b) (as so amended). As to the meaning of 'Wales' see PARA 2 note 4.

248. Fostering. It is a regulated activity relating to children to foster a child[1]. The fostering of a child (C) is not to be treated as a regulated activity where:

(1) a person (F) is barred from engaging in regulated activity relating to children[2];

(2) C is being looked after by a local authority[3];

(3) the local authority that looks after C is satisfied that C's welfare requires that C is fostered by F[4]; and

(4) either F or a member of F's household is a relative of C or C was being fostered by F immediately before F was barred from engaging in regulated activity relating to children[5].

1 Safeguarding Vulnerable Groups Act 2006 Sch 4 para 1(5). As to the meaning of 'child' see PARA 241 note 1. Despite s 58 (exemption for private, family and personal arrangements: see PARA 264), the Safeguarding Vulnerable Groups Act 2006 applies to activity that is regulated activity by virtue of Sch 4 para 1(5) (s 53(1)), although this does not affect the operation of the Safeguarding Vulnerable Groups Act 2006 in relation to any other activity that is carried out in connection with a foster child (s 53(2)). A person 'fosters' a child if he is a foster parent of the child (s 53(5), (6)); a person is a 'foster parent' if he is a local authority foster parent within the meaning of the Children Act 1989 s 23(3) (in relation to England) (see CHILDREN AND YOUNG PERSONS vol 10 (2017) PARA 921) or, in relation to Wales, within the meaning of s 105(1) as amended in relation to Wales by SI 2016/413), he is a person with whom a child has been placed by a voluntary organisation under the Children Act 1989 s 59(1)(a) (see CHILDREN AND YOUNG PERSONS vol 10 (2017) PARA 930), or he is a private foster parent (Safeguarding Vulnerable Groups Act

2006 s 53(7) (amended in relation to Wales by SI 2016/413)); and a person is a 'private foster parent' if he looks after a child for reward or in pursuance of an arrangement made by someone other than a member of the child's family (Safeguarding Vulnerable Groups Act 2006 s 53(8)) and he either:

    (1)   fosters the child privately within the meaning of the Children Act 1989 s 66(1) (see CHILDREN AND YOUNG PERSONS vol 10 (2017) PARA 984) (Safeguarding Vulnerable Groups Act 2006 s 53(9)(a));

    (2)   would be so fostering the child but for the Children Act 1989 s 66(2) (minimum period of 28 days: see CHILDREN AND YOUNG PERSONS vol 10 (2017) PARA 984) (Safeguarding Vulnerable Groups Act 2006 s 53(9)(b)); or

    (3)   (in the case of a child who has attained the age of 16) he would fall within head (1) or (2) above if he were under the age of 16 (s 53(9)(c)).

A person's family includes the person's foster child and the foster child of any member of the person's family; and references to a family relationship and family member are to be construed accordingly: s 53(10). For an exclusion from these provisions for members of provider groups see Sch 4 para 5; and PARA 241 note 1.

2   Safeguarding Vulnerable Groups Act 2006 (Miscellaneous Provisions) Order 2009, SI 2009/1797, art 3(2)(a) (amended by SI 2012/2157). A reference (however expressed) to a person being barred is construed in accordance with the Safeguarding Vulnerable Groups Act 2006 s 3 (see PARA 299 note 9): s 60(2). The Safeguarding Vulnerable Groups Act 2006 (Miscellaneous Provisions) Order 2009, SI 2009/1797, is made under the Safeguarding Vulnerable Groups Act 2006 Sch 4 para 6. As to the Secretary of State see PARA 333. See also PARA 241 note 4.

3   Safeguarding Vulnerable Groups Act 2006 (Miscellaneous Provisions) Order 2009, SI 2009/1797, art 3(2)(b). The reference to a local authority is a reference to a local authority within the meaning of the Children Act 1989 s 22 (see CHILDREN AND YOUNG PERSONS vol 10 (2017) PARAS 829–830) or, as the case may be, the Social Services and Well-being (Wales) Act 2014 s 74 (see CHILDREN AND YOUNG PERSONS vol 10 (2017) PARA 826): Safeguarding Vulnerable Groups Act 2006 (Miscellaneous Provisions) Order 2009, SI 2009/1797, art 3(2)(b) (amended in relation to Wales by SI 2016/211).

4   Safeguarding Vulnerable Groups Act 2006 (Miscellaneous Provisions) Order 2009, SI 2009/1797, art 3(2)(c).

5   Safeguarding Vulnerable Groups Act 2006 (Miscellaneous Provisions) Order 2009, SI 2009/1797, art 3(2)(d) (amended by SI 2012/2157).

249. Inspections and investigations of educational, family and health establishments and services in Wales. In Wales, the exercise of any of the following functions is a regulated activity relating to children so far as it gives the person exercising the function the opportunity, in consequence of anything the person is permitted or required to do in the exercise of that function, to have contact with children:

    (1)   the inspection of childminding or day care premises[1];

    (2)   the inspection of boarding schools and colleges[2];

    (3)   the inspection of teacher training[3];

    (4)   the inspection of local education authorities[4];

    (5)   until a day to be appointed, the inspection of residential family centres, fostering agencies, voluntary adoption agencies or adoption support agencies, and as from that day, the inspection of a residential family centre service, a fostering service or an adoption service[5];

    (6)   the inspection of education and training[6];

    (7)   until a day to be appointed, the review or investigation of the discharge of social services functions by local authorities, and as from that day, a review of local authority social services functions in Wales[7];

    (8)   the review or investigation of the functions of children's services authorities[8];

    (9)   the inspection of a school[9];

    (10)   the inspection of religious education[10];

    (11)   the inspection of a maintained school for a specific purpose[11];

    (12)   the inspection of careers services[12];

(13)   the exercise of a function of HM Chief Inspector of Education and Training in Wales[13], a body approved[14] to inspect a registered independent school in Wales[15], or the Welsh Ministers[16], so far as the function relates to the inspection of an applicable educational establishment[17], a detention centre[18], a children's home or centre[19] or relevant childcare premises[20]; and

(14)   the exercise of a function of the Welsh Ministers so far as the function relates to the inspection of an establishment, agency or body[21] which provides any form of treatment or therapy for children[22].

Any activity which consists in or involves on a regular basis the day to day management or supervision of a person carrying out such an activity is also a regulated activity relating to children[23].

1   Ie the exercise of a function so far as the function relates to the exercise of a power under the Children and Families (Wales) Measure 2010 s 41 or 42 (powers of inspection etc on entry onto childminding or day care premises in Wales or premises on which childminding or day care is suspected to be taking place: see CHILDREN AND YOUNG PERSONS vol 10 (2017) PARA 1257): Safeguarding Vulnerable Groups Act 2006 Sch 4 para 1(9A), (9B)(b) (Sch 4 para 1(9A)–(9C) added, Sch 4 para 1(10) amended, Sch 4 para 1(11) substituted, by SI 2010/1154; Safeguarding Vulnerable Groups Act 2006 Sch 4 paras 1(9B)(b)–(e), (h), (n), (14) amended by the Protection of Freedoms Act 2012 s 64(1), (6))). As to the meaning of 'child' see PARA 241 note 1. As to the meaning of 'Wales' see PARA 2 note 4.
    For an exclusion from these provisions for members of provider groups see Sch 4 para 5; and PARA 241 note 1.
2   Ie the exercise of a function so far as the function relates to any step taken in relation to Wales for the purposes of the Children Act 1989 s 87(3) (welfare of children in boarding schools and colleges: see CHILDREN AND YOUNG PERSONS vol 10 (2017) PARA 1276) (Safeguarding Vulnerable Groups Act 2006 Sch 4 para 1(9B)(c) (as added and amended: see note 1)), to an inspection in Wales under the Children Act 1989 s 87(6) (inspection of boarding school or college: see CHILDREN AND YOUNG PERSONS vol 10 (2017) PARA 1276) (Safeguarding Vulnerable Groups Act 2006 Sch 4 para 1(9B)(d) (as so added and amended)), or to any step taken in relation to Wales by a person appointed under the Children Act 1989 s 87A(1) (appointment as an inspector of boarding schools and colleges: see CHILDREN AND YOUNG PERSONS vol 10 (2017) PARA 1277) for the purposes of an agreement made in accordance with s 87A(2) or in order to comply with any requirement imposed on the person under s 87B (see CHILDREN AND YOUNG PERSONS vol 10 (2017) PARA 1278) (Safeguarding Vulnerable Groups Act 2006 Sch 4 para 1(9B)(e) (as so added and amended)).
3   Ie the exercise of a function so far as the function relates to an inspection under the Education Act 1994 s 18C (inspection of teacher training: see EDUCATION vol 36 (2015) PARA 1286): Safeguarding Vulnerable Groups Act 2006 Sch 4 para 1(9B)(f) (as added: see note 1).
4   Ie the exercise of a function so far as the function relates to an inspection under the Education Act 1997 s 38 (see EDUCATION vol 36 (2015) PARA 1293): Safeguarding Vulnerable Groups Act 2006 Sch 4 para 1(9B)(g) (as added: see note 1).
5   Ie the exercise of a function so far as the function relates to an inspection in Wales:
    (1)   until the appointed day, under the Care Standards Act 2000 s 31 (inspections of establishments and agencies or the inspection of premises suspected as being used as an establishment or agency: see CHILDREN AND YOUNG PERSONS vol 10 (2017) PARAS 1017, 1061) of a residential family centre, a fostering agency, a voluntary adoption agency or an adoption support agency (each of which has the meaning given in s 4: see CHILDREN AND YOUNG PERSONS vol 10 (2017) PARAS 1003, 1017) (Safeguarding Vulnerable Groups Act 2006 Sch 4 para 1(9B)(h) (as added and amended: see note 1)); and
    (2)   as from that day, under the Regulation and Inspection of Social Care (Wales) Act 2016 s 33 (inspections of regulated care and support services: see PARA 225) of a residential family centre service, a fostering service or an adoption service (each of which has the meaning given in Sch 1: see PARAS 206, 207) (Safeguarding Vulnerable Groups Act 2006 Sch 4 para 1(9B)(h) (Sch 4 para 1(9B)(h), (j), prospectively substituted, Sch 4 para 1(9B)(k) prospectively amended, in relation to Wales, by the Regulation and Inspection of Social Care (Wales) Act 2016 Sch 3 para 28)).
6   Ie the exercise of a function so far as the function relates to an inspection under the Learning and Skills Act 2000 Pt 4 (ss 73–88) (inspection of education and training within the remit of Her

Majesty's Chief Inspector of Education and Training in Wales: see EDUCATION vol 36 (2015) PARA 1268 et seq): Safeguarding Vulnerable Groups Act 2006 Sch 4 para 1(9B)(i) (as added: see note 1).

7　Ie the exercise of a function so far as the function relates:

(1)　until the appointed day, to a review or investigation under the Health and Social Care (Community Health and Standards) Act 2003 s 94 (review or investigation of the discharge of social services functions by local authorities in Wales: see PARA 400) (Safeguarding Vulnerable Groups Act 2006 Sch 4 para 1(9B)(j) (as added: see note 1)); and

(2)　as from that day, a review under the Social Services and Well-being (Wales) Act 2014 s 149B (reviews of local authority social services functions in Wales: see PARA 400) (Safeguarding Vulnerable Groups Act 2006 Sch 4 para 1(9B)(j) (prospectively substituted: see note 5)).

8　Ie the exercise of a function so far as the function relates to a review or investigation under the Health and Social Care (Community Health and Standards) Act 2003 s 94 or, as from a day to be appointed, a review under the Social Services and Well-being (Wales) Act 2014 s 149B, as applied by the Children Act 2004 s 30 (review or investigation of the functions of children's services authorities in Wales: see CHILDREN AND YOUNG PERSONS vol 9 (2017) PARA 224): Safeguarding Vulnerable Groups Act 2006 Sch 4 para 1(9B)(k) (as added and prospectively amended: see notes 1, 5).

9　Ie the exercise of a function so far as the function relates to an inspection under the Education Act 2005 s 28 (duty of Her Majesty's Chief Inspector of Education and Training in Wales to arrange regular inspections of certain schools: see EDUCATION vol 36 (2015) PARA 1182): Safeguarding Vulnerable Groups Act 2006 Sch 4 para 1(9B)(l) (as added: see note 1).

10　Ie the exercise of a function so far as the function relates to an inspection under the Education Act 2005 s 50 (inspection of religious education: see EDUCATION vol 36 (2015) PARA 1201): Safeguarding Vulnerable Groups Act 2006 Sch 4 para 1(9B)(m) (as added: see note 1).

11　Ie the exercise of a function so far as the function relates to an inspection in Wales under the Education Act 2005 s 51 (power of local education authorities to inspect maintained school for specific purpose: see EDUCATION vol 36 (2015) PARAS 1180, 1205): Safeguarding Vulnerable Groups Act 2006 Sch 4 para 1(9B)(n) (as added and amended: see note 1).

12　Ie the exercise of a function so far as the function relates to an inspection under the Education Act 2005 s 55 (see EDUCATION vol 36 (2015) PARA 1273): Safeguarding Vulnerable Groups Act 2006 Sch 4 para 1(9B)(o) (as added: see note 1).

13　Safeguarding Vulnerable Groups Act 2006 Sch 4 para 1(9C)(a), (b), (10)(b) (as added and amended: see note 1). As to HM Chief Inspector of Education and Training in Wales see EDUCATION vol 36 (2015) PARA 1148 et seq.

14　Ie in pursuance of the Education Act 2002 s 163(1)(b) (see EDUCATION vol 35 (2015) PARA 418).

15　Safeguarding Vulnerable Groups Act 2006 Sch 4 para 1(10)(c) (as added (see note 1); amended by the Education and Skills Act 2008 Sch 1 para 41(1), (2), (4)).

16　Safeguarding Vulnerable Groups Act 2006 Sch 4 para 1(10)(g) (as added (see note 1); amended by SI 2009/2610). As to the Welsh Ministers see PARA 395.

17　As to the applicable educational establishments for these purposes see the Safeguarding Vulnerable Groups Act 2006 Sch 4 para 3(1)(a), (aa), (ab), (b); and PARA 246 note 2.

18　Ie an institution which is exclusively or mainly for the detention of children: see the Safeguarding Vulnerable Groups Act 2006 Sch 4 para 3(1)(d); and PARA 246 note 3.

19　As to the children's homes and centres to which these provisions apply see the Safeguarding Vulnerable Groups Act 2006 Sch 4 para 3(1)(e), (f), (fa); and PARA 246 note 4.

20　As to the relevant childcare premises for these purposes see the Safeguarding Vulnerable Groups Act 2006 Sch 4 para 3(1)(g), (2)–(5); and PARA 246 note 5.

21　Ie an establishment or agency in relation to which a requirement to register arises under the Care Standards Act 2000 s 11 (see CHILDREN AND YOUNG PERSONS vol 10 (2017) PARA 1017) or an NHS body within the meaning of the Health and Social Care (Community Health and Standards) Act 2003 s 148 (see HEALTH SERVICES vol 54A (2017) PARA 659) which provides any form of treatment or therapy for children: Safeguarding Vulnerable Groups Act 2006 Sch 4 para 1(12). The reference to an NHS body includes a reference to any person who provides, or is to provide, health care for the body (wherever the health care is or is to be provided): Sch 4 para 1(13).

22　Safeguarding Vulnerable Groups Act 2006 Sch 4 para 1(11) (as substituted: see note 1).

23　Safeguarding Vulnerable Groups Act 2006 Sch 4 para 1(14) (as amended: see note 1).

250. Functions of the Children's Commissioner for Wales. The exercise of a function of the Children's Commissioner for Wales or the deputy Children's Commissioner for Wales is a regulated activity relating to children[1].

1 Safeguarding Vulnerable Groups Act 2006 Sch 4 para 1(9) (amended by the Protection of Freedoms Act 2012 s 64(1), (6)). As to the Children's Commissioner for Wales and the deputy Children's Commissioner for Wales see CHILDREN AND YOUNG PERSONS vol 9 (2017) PARA 205. As to the meaning of 'child' see PARA 241 note 1. As to the meaning of 'Wales' see PARA 2 note 4.

B.   REGULATED ACTIVITIES RELATING TO VULNERABLE ADULTS

251. Provision of health care. An activity is a regulated activity relating to vulnerable adults[1] if it is the provision to an adult of health care by, or under the direction or supervision of, a health care professional[2], or if it is any activity which consists in or involves on a regular basis the day to day management or supervision of a person carrying out such an activity[3]. 'Health care' includes all forms of health care provided for individuals, whether relating to physical or mental health and also includes palliative care and procedures that are similar to forms of medical or surgical care but are not provided in connection with a medical condition[4].

The provision to an adult of health care by a person who is not, but who acts under the direction or supervision of, a health care professional is not to be treated as a regulated activity relating to vulnerable adults where that health care is ophthalmic services provided[5] in practice premises[6] or as mobile services[7] or provided in a registered pharmacy[8].

1 'Vulnerable adult' means any adult to whom an activity which is a regulated activity relating to vulnerable adults by virtue of any provision of the Safeguarding Vulnerable Groups Act 2006 Sch 4 para 7(1) (see the text and notes 2–8; and PARAS 252–257) is provided; and 'adult' means a person who has attained the age of 18: s 60(1) (s 60(1) amended, Sch 4 para 7(1)–(3) substituted, Sch 4 para 7(3A) added, by the Protection of Freedoms Act 2012 ss 65(2), 66(2)).
2 Safeguarding Vulnerable Groups Act 2006 s 5(2), Sch 4 para 7(1)(a) (as substituted: see note 1). A 'health care professional' is a person who is a member of a profession regulated by a body mentioned in the National Health Service Reform and Health Care Professions Act 2002 s 25(3) (see MEDICAL PROFESSIONS vol 74 (2011) PARA 48) (Safeguarding Vulnerable Groups Act 2006 Sch 4 para 7(3) (as so substituted)); and any reference to health care provided by, or under the direction or supervision of, a health care professional includes a reference to first aid provided to an adult by any person acting on behalf of an organisation established for the purpose of providing first aid (Sch 4 para 7(3A) (as so added)).
     A person who is part of a group in relation to which another (P) engages in regulated activity relating to vulnerable adults does not engage in regulated activity only because he assists P or does anything on behalf of or under the direction of P which, but for this provision, would amount to engaging in regulated activity relating to vulnerable adults: Sch 4 para 7(10).
3 Safeguarding Vulnerable Groups Act 2006 Sch 4 para 7(5).
4 Safeguarding Vulnerable Groups Act 2006 Sch 4 para 7(2) (as substituted: see note 1).
5 Ie provided under regulations under the National Health Service Act 2006 Pt 6 (ss 115–125A) or the National Health Service (Wales) Act 2006 Pt 6 (ss 71–79) (see HEALTH SERVICES vol 54 (2017) PARA 350 et seq).
6 'Practice premises' means practice premises within the meaning of the General Ophthalmic Services Contracts Regulations 2008, SI 2008/1185 (see HEALTH SERVICES vol 54 (2017) PARA 337) or, in relation to services provided in Wales, means the address which is included in relation to the contractor in the ophthalmic list in accordance with the National Health Service (General Ophthalmic Services) Regulations 1986, SI 1986/975, Sch 1 para 3 (see HEALTH SERVICES vol 54 (2017) PARA 350) as the address at which services are provided: Safeguarding Vulnerable Groups Act 2006 (Miscellaneous Provisions) Order 2012, SI 2012/2113, art 5(a).
7 'Mobile services' means mobile services within the meaning of the General Ophthalmic Services Contracts Regulations 2008, SI 2008/1185 or the National Health Service (General Ophthalmic Services) Regulations 1986, SI 1986/975: Safeguarding Vulnerable Groups Act 2006 (Miscellaneous Provisions) Order 2012, SI 2012/2113, art 5(b).

8   Safeguarding Vulnerable Groups Act 2006 (Miscellaneous Provisions) Order 2012, SI 2012/2113, art 4 (made under the Safeguarding Vulnerable Groups Act 2006 Sch 4 para 9). 'Registered pharmacy' means a registered pharmacy within the meaning of the Medicines Act 1968 Pt 4 (ss 69–84A): see MEDICAL PROFESSIONS vol 74 (2011) PARA 784.

252. Provision of personal care. An activity is a regulated activity relating to vulnerable adults[1] if it is the provision to an adult of relevant personal care[2], that is to say:

(1)   physical assistance given to a person who is in need of it by reason of age, illness or disability[3];

(2)   the prompting, together with supervision, of a person who is in need of it by reason of age, illness or disability in relation to the performance of any of the physical assistance activities[4] where the person is unable to make a decision in relation to performing such an activity without such prompting and supervision[5]; or

(3)   any form of training, instruction, advice or guidance which relates to the performance of any of the physical assistance activities[6] is given to a person who is in need of it by reason of age, illness or disability, and does not fall within head (2) above[7].

An activity is also a regulated activity relating to vulnerable adults if it is an activity which consists in or involves on a regular basis the day to day management or supervision of a person carrying out such an activity[8].

1   As to the meanings of 'adult' and 'vulnerable adult' see PARA 251 note 1.
2   Safeguarding Vulnerable Groups Act 2006 Sch 4 para 7(1)(b) (Sch 4 para 7(1) substituted, Sch 4 para 7(3B) added, by the Protection of Freedoms Act 2012 s 66(2)). For an exclusion from these provisions for members of provider groups see the Safeguarding Vulnerable Groups Act 2006 Sch 4 para 7(10); and PARA 251 note 2.
3   Safeguarding Vulnerable Groups Act 2006 Sch 4 para 7(3B) (as added: see note 2). This includes the giving of physical assistance in connection with eating or drinking (including the administration of parenteral nutrition), toileting (including in relation to the process of menstruation), washing or bathing, dressing, oral care, or the care of skin, hair or nails: Sch 4 para 7(3B)(a) (as so added). The provision to an adult of physical assistance in connection with the care of hair (within the meaning Sch 4 para 7(3B)(a)) is not to be treated as a regulated activity relating to vulnerable adults where that assistance relates solely to the cutting of the adult's hair: Safeguarding Vulnerable Groups Act 2006 (Miscellaneous Provisions) Order 2012, SI 2012/2113, art 6.
4   Ie the activities listed in the Safeguarding Vulnerable Groups Act 2006 Sch 4 para 7(3B)(a) (see note 3).
5   Safeguarding Vulnerable Groups Act 2006 Sch 4 para 7(3B)(b) (as added: see note 2).
6   See note 4.
7   Safeguarding Vulnerable Groups Act 2006 Sch 4 para 7(3B)(c) (as added: see note 2).
8   Safeguarding Vulnerable Groups Act 2006 Sch 4 para 7(5).

253. Provision of psychotherapy and counselling related to health care. An activity is a regulated activity relating to vulnerable adults[1] if it is the provision of psychotherapy or counselling, but not life coaching, to an adult which is related to health care the adult is receiving from, or under the direction or supervision of, a health care professional[2], or if it is any activity which consists in or involves on a regular basis the day to day management or supervision of a person carrying out such an activity[3].

1   As to the meanings of 'adult' and 'vulnerable adult' see PARA 251 note 1.
2   Safeguarding Vulnerable Groups Act 2006 (Miscellaneous Provisions) Regulations 2012, SI 2012/2112, reg 27 (made under the Safeguarding Vulnerable Groups Act 2006 Sch 4 para 7(1)(g) (Sch 4 para 7(1) substituted by the Protection of Freedoms Act 2012 s 66(2))). As to the meaning of 'health care professional' see the Safeguarding Vulnerable Groups Act 2006 Sch 4 para 7(3); and PARA 251 note 2 (definition applied by the Safeguarding Vulnerable Groups Act 2006 (Miscellaneous Provisions) Regulations 2012, SI 2012/2112, reg 27). As to the meaning of 'health

care' see PARA 251. As to the meaning of 'relevant personal care' see PARA 252. For an exclusion
from these provisions for members of provider groups see the Safeguarding Vulnerable Groups Act
2006 Sch 4 para 7(10); and PARA 251 note 2.
3   Safeguarding Vulnerable Groups Act 2006 Sch 4 para 7(5).

254.   Provision of social work. An activity is a regulated activity relating to
vulnerable adults[1] if it is the provision by a social care worker[2] of relevant social
work[3] to an adult who is a client or potential client[4], or if it is any activity which
consists in or involves on a regular basis the day to day management or
supervision of a person carrying out such an activity[5].

1   As to the meanings of 'adult' and 'vulnerable adult' see PARA 251 note 1.
2   In relation to a vulnerable adult in England 'social care worker' means a person who is a social care
     worker by virtue of the Care Standards Act 2000 s 55(2)(a) (see PARA 335); in relation to a
     vulnerable adult in Wales 'social care worker' means a person who is a social care worker by virtue
     of the Regulation and Inspection of Social Care (Wales) Act 2016 s 79(1)(a) (see PARA 198):
     Safeguarding Vulnerable Groups Act 2006 Sch 4 para 7(3C), (3CA) (Sch 4 para 7(1) substituted,
     Sch 4 para 7(3C) added, by the Protection of Freedoms Act 2012 s 66(2)); Safeguarding Vulnerable
     Groups Act 2006 Sch 4 para 7(3C) amended, Sch 4 para 7(3CA) added, in relation to Wales only,
     by the Regulation and Inspection of Social Care (Wales) Act 2016 Sch 3 para 56).
3   As to the meaning of 'relevant social work' in relation to a vulnerable adult in England see the
     Care Standards Act 2000 s 55(4); and PARA 335; as to the meaning of 'relevant social work' in
     relation to a vulnerable adult in Wales see the Regulation and Inspection of Social Care (Wales)
     Act 2016 s 79(4); and PARA 198 (definitions applied by the Safeguarding Vulnerable Groups Act
     2006 Sch 4 para 7(3C), (3CA) (as added and (in relation to Wales) substituted and added: see note
     2)).
4   Safeguarding Vulnerable Groups Act 2006 Sch 4 para 7(1)(c) (as substituted: see note 2). For an
     exclusion from these provisions for members of provider groups see Sch 4 para 7(10); and
     PARA 251 note 2.
5   Safeguarding Vulnerable Groups Act 2006 Sch 4 para 7(5).

255.   Provision of assistance in relation to general household matters. An activity
is a regulated activity relating to vulnerable adults[1] if it is the provision of
assistance in relation to general household matters to an adult who is in need of
it by reason of age, illness or disability[2], or if it is any activity which consists in or
involves on a regular basis the day to day management or supervision of a person
carrying out such an activity[3]. Assistance in relation to general household matters
is day to day assistance in relation to the running of the household of the person
concerned where the assistance is the carrying out of one or more of the following
activities on behalf of that person: managing the person's cash; paying the
person's bills; and shopping[4].

1   As to the meanings of 'adult' and 'vulnerable adult' see PARA 251 note 1.
2   Safeguarding Vulnerable Groups Act 2006 Sch 4 para 7(1)(d) (Sch 4 para 7(1) substituted, Sch 4
     para 7(3D) added, by the Protection of Freedoms Act 2012 s 66(2)). For an exclusion from these
     provisions for members of provider groups see the Safeguarding Vulnerable Groups Act 2006
     Sch 4 para 7(10); and PARA 251 note 2.
3   Safeguarding Vulnerable Groups Act 2006 Sch 4 para 7(5).
4   Safeguarding Vulnerable Groups Act 2006 Sch 4 para 7(3D) (as added: see note 2).

256.   Provision of assistance in the conduct of an adult's own affairs. An activity
is a regulated activity relating to vulnerable adults[1] if it is any relevant assistance
in the conduct of an adult's own affairs[2], or if it is any activity which consists in
or involves on a regular basis the day to day management or supervision of a
person carrying out such an activity[3]. Relevant assistance in the conduct of a
person's own affairs is anything done on behalf of the person by virtue of:
  (1)   a lasting power of attorney[4];
  (2)   an enduring power of attorney[5] in respect of the person which is either
         registered[6] or the subject of an application to be so registered[7];
  (3)   an order made[8] in relation to the making of decisions on the
         person's behalf[9];

(4)   the appointment[10] of an independent mental health advocate or (as the case may be) an independent mental capacity advocate in respect of the person[11];

(5)   the provision of independent advocacy services[12] in respect of the person[13]; or

(6)   the appointment of a representative[14] to receive social security payments on behalf of the person[15].

In relation to England, relevant assistance in the conduct of a person's own affairs is also representing or supporting the person in pursuance of arrangements[16] for independent advocacy support in needs assessments or safeguarding inquiries[17].

1   As to the meanings of 'adult' and 'vulnerable adult' see PARA 251 note 1.
2   Safeguarding Vulnerable Groups Act 2006 Sch 4 para 7(1)(e) (Sch 4 para 7(1) substituted, Sch 4 para 7(3E) added, by the Protection of Freedoms Act 2012 s 66(2)). For an exclusion from these provisions for members of provider groups see the Safeguarding Vulnerable Groups Act 2006 Sch 4 para 7(10); and PARA 251 note 2.
3   Safeguarding Vulnerable Groups Act 2006 Sch 4 para 7(5).
4   Safeguarding Vulnerable Groups Act 2006 Sch 4 para 7(3E)(a) (as added: see note 2). The reference in the text to a lasting power of attorney is a reference to a lasting power of attorney created in respect of the person in accordance with the Mental Capacity Act 2005 s 9 (see AGENCY vol 1 (2008) PARAS 271–222): Safeguarding Vulnerable Groups Act 2006 Sch 4 para 7(3E)(a) (as so added).
5   Ie an enduring power of attorney within the meaning of the Mental Capacity Act 2005 Sch 4 (see AGENCY vol 1 (2008) PARAS 195–216).
6   Ie in accordance with the Mental Capacity Act 2005 Sch 4: see note 5.
7   Safeguarding Vulnerable Groups Act 2006 Sch 4 para 7(3E)(b) (as added: see note 2).
8   Ie under the Mental Capacity Act 2005 s 16 (see MENTAL HEALTH AND CAPACITY vol 75 (2013) PARAS 724, 734).
9   Safeguarding Vulnerable Groups Act 2006 Sch 4 para 7(3E)(c) (as added: see note 2).
10 Ie in pursuance of arrangements under the Mental Health Act 1983 s 130A (see MENTAL HEALTH AND CAPACITY vol 75 (2013) PARA 807) or the Mental Capacity Act 2005 s 35 (see MENTAL HEALTH AND CAPACITY vol 75 (2013) PARA 635).
11 Safeguarding Vulnerable Groups Act 2006 Sch 4 para 7(3E)(d) (as added: see note 2).
12 Ie within the meaning of the National Health Service Act 2006 s 248 or the National Health Service (Wales) Act 2006 s 187 (see HEALTH SERVICES vol 54A (2017) PARA 660).
13 Safeguarding Vulnerable Groups Act 2006 Sch 4 para 7(3E)(e) (as added: see note 2).
14 Ie in pursuance of regulations made under the Social Security Administration Act 1992 (see WELFARE BENEFITS AND PENSIONS).
15 Safeguarding Vulnerable Groups Act 2006 Sch 4 para 7(3E)(f) (as added: see note 2).
16 Ie arrangements made under the Care Act 2014 s 67 (see PARA 100–103) or s 68 (see PARA 236).
17 Safeguarding Vulnerable Groups Act 2006 Sch 4 para 7(3EA) (added by SI 2015/914).

257.   Driving a vehicle. An activity is a regulated activity relating to vulnerable adults[1] if it is the conveying of adults who need to be conveyed by reason of age, illness or disability by:

(1)   any person who is employed as a hospital porter[2];

(2)   any person who is employed as an emergency care assistant[3];

(3)   any person who is employed as an ambulance technician[4];

(4)   any driver who is employed in the Patient Transport Service or a person who is employed to assist that driver in carrying out the conveying[5],

where:

(a)   the conveying is on behalf of an organisation, whether or not the person who does, or assists in, such conveying is employed by that organisation[6];

(b)   the conveying is to or from a place in which the adult will receive, or has received, health care, relevant personal care or relevant social work[7]; and

(c)   the person does, or assists in, such conveying for the purpose of enabling the adult to receive that health care, relevant personal care or relevant social work (as the case may be)[8].

An activity is also a regulated activity relating to vulnerable adults if it is any activity which consists in or involves on a regular basis the day to day management or supervision of a person carrying out such an activity[9]. There is an exclusion in relation to licensed taxi drivers[10].

1 As to the meanings of 'adult' and 'vulnerable adult' see PARA 251 note 1.
2 Safeguarding Vulnerable Groups Act 2006 Sch 4 para 7(1)(f) (Sch 4 para 7(1) substituted by the Protection of Freedoms Act 2012 s 66(2)); Safeguarding Vulnerable Groups Act 2006 (Miscellaneous Provisions) Regulations 2012, SI 2012/2112, reg 24(a). For an exclusion from these provisions for members of provider groups see the Safeguarding Vulnerable Groups Act 2006 Sch 4 para 7(10); and PARA 251 note 2.
3 Safeguarding Vulnerable Groups Act 2006 (Miscellaneous Provisions) Regulations 2012, SI 2012/2112, reg 24(b).
4 Safeguarding Vulnerable Groups Act 2006 (Miscellaneous Provisions) Regulations 2012, SI 2012/2112, reg 24(c).
5 Safeguarding Vulnerable Groups Act 2006 (Miscellaneous Provisions) Regulations 2012, SI 2012/2112, reg 24(d).
6 Safeguarding Vulnerable Groups Act 2006 (Miscellaneous Provisions) Regulations 2012, SI 2012/2112, reg 25(a).
7 Safeguarding Vulnerable Groups Act 2006 (Miscellaneous Provisions) Regulations 2012, SI 2012/2112, reg 25(b). As to the meaning of 'relevant social work' see PARA 85 note 9.
8 Safeguarding Vulnerable Groups Act 2006 (Miscellaneous Provisions) Regulations 2012, SI 2012/2112, reg 25(c).
9 Safeguarding Vulnerable Groups Act 2006 Sch 4 para 7(5).
10 The Safeguarding Vulnerable Groups Act 2006 (Miscellaneous Provisions) Regulations 2012, SI 2012/2112, regs 24, 25 (see the text and notes 1–8) do not apply to any person who does, or assists in, such conveying in a vehicle which is licensed under the Town Police Clauses Act 1847 s 37 (see ROAD TRAFFIC vol 89 (2011) PARA 597), the Metropolitan Public Carriage Act 1869 s 6, the Local Government (Miscellaneous Provisions) Act 1976 s 48 (see ROAD TRAFFIC vol 90 (2011) PARA 1194), the Private Hire Vehicles (London) Act 1998 s 7 (see LONDON GOVERNMENT vol 71 (2013) PARA 234), or an equivalent provision of a local enactment: Safeguarding Vulnerable Groups Act 2006 (Miscellaneous Provisions) Regulations 2012, SI 2012/2112, reg 26.

258. Inspections and investigations of social services establishments in Wales. The exercise of any of the following 'inspection functions' of the Welsh Ministers[1], in so far as the inspection relates to social services, care, treatment or therapy provided for vulnerable adults[2] by the establishment, agency, person or body[3], is a regulated activity relating to vulnerable adults so far as the function gives the person exercising the function the opportunity, in consequence of anything the person is permitted or required to do in the exercise of that function, to have contact with vulnerable adults[4]:

(1)   a function relating to the inspection of the exercise by a local authority in the exercise of its social services functions[5];

(2)   a function relating to the inspection of an establishment or agency in relation to which a requirement to register[6] arises[7];

(3)   a function relating to the inspection of a person to whom the application of the registration requirements[8] have been[9] extended[10];

(4)   an NHS body[11]; or

(5)   any person, other than a local authority, providing Welsh local authority social services[12].

1 As to the Welsh Ministers see PARA 395.
2 As to the meanings of 'adult' and 'vulnerable adult' see PARA 251 note 1.
3 Safeguarding Vulnerable Groups Act 2006 Sch 4 para 7(7) (Sch 4 para 7(6) substituted, Sch 4 para 7(7), Sch 4 para 7(7)(d) amended, by SI 2010/1154 (made under, inter alia, the Safeguarding Vulnerable Groups Act 2006 s 5(3)).

4 Safeguarding Vulnerable Groups Act 2006 Sch 4 para 7(6) (as substituted: see note 3).
5 Safeguarding Vulnerable Groups Act 2006 Sch 4 para 7(7)(a) (Sch 7 para 7(7) as amended: see note 3). As to the social services functions of a local authority in Wales see PARA 373.
6 Ie a requirement to register under the Care Standards Act 2000 s 11 (see CHILDREN AND YOUNG PERSONS vol 10 (2017) PARA 1017).
7 Safeguarding Vulnerable Groups Act 2006 Sch 4 para 7(7)(b), (c) (Sch 7 para 7(7) as amended: see note 3).
8 Ie the Care Standards Act 2000 Pt 2 (ss 11–42): see CHILDREN AND YOUNG PERSONS vol 10 (2017) PARA 1017 et seq.
9 Ie in pursuance of regulations under the Care Standards Act 2000 s 42 (see CHILDREN AND YOUNG PERSONS vol 10 (2017) PARA 1002).
10 Safeguarding Vulnerable Groups Act 2006 Sch 4 para 7(7)(d) (as amended: see note 3).
11 Safeguarding Vulnerable Groups Act 2006 Sch 4 para 7(7)(e) (Sch 7 para 7(7) as amended: see note 3). The reference to an NHS body is to an NHS body within the meaning of the Health and Social Care (Community Health and Standards) Act 2003 s 148 (see HEALTH SERVICES vol 54A (2017) PARA 659), and includes a reference to any person who provides, or is to provide, health care for the body (wherever the health care is or is to be provided) (Safeguarding Vulnerable Groups Act 2006 Sch 4 para 7(8)).
12 Safeguarding Vulnerable Groups Act 2006 Sch 4 para 7(7)(f) (as amended: see note 3). The reference to Welsh local authority social services is a reference to Welsh local authority social services within the meaning of the Health and Social Care (Community Health and Standards) Act 2003 s 148 (see PARA 400).

259. Functions of the Commissioner for Older People in Wales. The exercise of a function of the Commissioner for Older People in Wales or the deputy Commissioner for Older People in Wales is a regulated activity relating to vulnerable adults[1].

1 Safeguarding Vulnerable Groups Act 2006 Sch 4 para 7(9) (amended by the Protection of Freedoms Act 2012 s 66(1), (7)). As to the Commissioner for Older People in Wales and his functions see the Commissioner for Older People (Wales) Act 2006; and DISCRIMINATION vol 33 (2013) PARA 292 et seq. As to the meanings of 'adult' and 'vulnerable adult' see PARA 251 note 1. As to the meaning of 'Wales' see PARA 2 note 4.

(ii) The Regulated Activity Providers

260. Persons responsible for the management or control of regulated activity. A person is a regulated activity provider if:

(1)   he is responsible for the management or control of regulated activity[1];
(2)   if the regulated activity is carried out for the purposes of an organisation, his exercise of that responsibility is not subject to supervision or direction by any other person for those purposes[2]; and
(3)   he makes, or authorises the making of, arrangements (whether in connection with a contract of service or for services or otherwise) for another person to engage in that activity[3].

1 Safeguarding Vulnerable Groups Act 2006 s 6(1), (2)(a). As to the meaning of 'regulated activity' see PARAS 241–250 (children), PARAS 251–259 (vulnerable adults). As to the duties of regulated activity providers to check if a person is barred see PARAS 294–296. If a regulated activity provider is an unincorporated association any requirement of or liability (including criminal liability) under the Safeguarding Vulnerable Groups Act 2006 must be taken to be a requirement on or liability of the person responsible for the management and control of the association or, if there is more than one such person, all of them jointly and severally: s 6(10). Section 6(2) does not apply in relation to any activity carried out by the Crown (s 51(4)), although the Safeguarding Vulnerable Groups Act 2006 and regulations and orders made thereunder do generally bind the Crown (s 51(1)–(3), (5)(a), (6), (7)).
    The Secretary of State may by order provide that in specified circumstances a person who makes, or authorises the making of, arrangements (of any description) for another to engage in regulated activity either is or is not a regulated activity provider: s 6(12). At the date at which this volume states the law no such order had been made. As to the Secretary of State see PARA 333. See also PARA 241 note 4.
2 Safeguarding Vulnerable Groups Act 2006 s 6(2)(b).

3   Safeguarding Vulnerable Groups Act 2006 s 6(2)(c). As to what amounts to the making of
    arrangements see PARA 157. For an exemption for private, family and personal arrangements see
    PARA 158.

261. Persons involved in making fostering arrangements. A person who makes
arrangements for another person to foster a child[1] as a private foster parent[2] and
has power to terminate the arrangements[3] is, if he would not otherwise be, a
regulated activity provider in relation to fostering carried out by the foster parent
in pursuance of the arrangements[4].

1   As to the meaning of 'child' see PARA 241 note 1. As to what amounts to the making of
    arrangements see PARA 263. For an exemption for private, family and personal arrangements see
    PARA 264. As to providers that are unincorporated associations see PARA 260 note 1.
2   Safeguarding Vulnerable Groups Act 2006 s 53(3)(a).
3   Safeguarding Vulnerable Groups Act 2006 s 53(3)(b).
4   Safeguarding Vulnerable Groups Act 2006 ss 6(3), 53(4). As to the duties of regulated activity
    providers to check if a person is barred see PARAS 294–296.

**262. Persons involved in the provision of care and support in registered
establishments.** A person is a regulated activity provider if he carries on a scheme
under which an individual agrees with him to provide care or support (which may
include accommodation) to an adult who is in need of it[1], and in respect of which
a requirement to register[2] arises[3].

1   Safeguarding Vulnerable Groups Act 2006 s 6(4)(a).
2   Ie under the Health and Social Care Act 2008 s 10 (see PARA 159) (in relation to England) or under
    the Care Standards Act 2000 s 11 (see CHILDREN AND YOUNG PERSONS vol 10 (2017)
    PARA 1017) (in relation to Wales).
3   Safeguarding Vulnerable Groups Act 2006 s 6(4)(b) (amended by SI 2010/813). As to the duties
    of regulated activity providers to check if a person is barred see PARAS 294–296. As to providers
    that are unincorporated associations see PARA 260 note 1.

263. What amounts to the making of arrangements. A person does not make
arrangements for another to engage in a regulated activity[1] merely because he
(alone or together with others) appoints that person:

   (1)   as the Children's Commissioner for Wales or the deputy
           Children's Commissioner for Wales[2];

   (2)   as the Commissioner for Older People in Wales or the
           Deputy Commissioner for Older People in Wales[3];

   (3)   as a deputy[4] in relation to a person lacking capacity[5];

   (4)   to any relevant position[6] in connection with the exercise of a lasting or
           enduring power of attorney or to exercise any function exercisable by
           virtue of that position[7].

The Secretary of State[8], the National Health Service Commissioning Board or
a clinical commissioning group do not make arrangements for another to engage
in a regulated activity by virtue of anything he does or they do[9] in connection with
the making of direct payments for the provision of healthcare[10]. Persons who
make decisions about direct payments for care on behalf of another also do not
make arrangements for these purposes[11].

1   As to the meaning of 'regulated activity' see PARAS 241–250 (children), PARAS 251–259
    (vulnerable adults).
2   Ie a position mentioned in the Safeguarding Vulnerable Groups Act 2006 Sch 4 para 1(9) (see
    PARA 250): s 6(8)(a) (s 6(8)(a), (d) amended by the Protection of Freedoms Act 2012 Sch 9
    paras 43, 46). As to the Children's Commissioner for Wales and the deputy
    Children's Commissioner for Wales see CHILDREN AND YOUNG PERSONS vol 9 (2017)
    PARA 188 et seq. As to the meaning of 'Wales' see PARA 2 note 4.
3   Ie a position mentioned in the Safeguarding Vulnerable Groups Act 2006 Sch 4 para 7(9) (see
    PARA 259): s 6(8)(a) (as amended: see note 2). As to the Commissioner for Older People in Wales
    and his functions see the Commissioner for Older People (Wales) Act 2006; and
    DISCRIMINATION vol 33 (2013) PARA 194 et seq.

4   Ie under the Mental Capacity Act 2005 s 16(2)(b) (see MENTAL HEALTH AND CAPACITY vol 75 (2013) PARA 724).
5   Safeguarding Vulnerable Groups Act 2006 s 6(8)(b).
6   Ie any position mentioned in the Safeguarding Vulnerable Groups Act 2006 Sch 4 para 7(3E)(a) or (b) (see PARA 256).
7   Safeguarding Vulnerable Groups Act 2006 s 6(8)(d) (as amended: see note 2).
8   As to the Secretary of State see PARA 333. See also PARA 241 note 4.
9   Ie under the National Health Service Act 2006 s 12A or s 12D, or regulations under s 12A or s 12B (see HEALTH SERVICES vol 54 (2017) PARAS 42, 43).
10 Safeguarding Vulnerable Groups Act 2006 s 6(8C), (8E) (s 6(8C) added by the Health Act 2009 Sch 1 paras 12, 13; Safeguarding Vulnerable Groups Act 2006 s 6(8D) added by the Health and Social Care Act 2012 Sch 5 paras 143, 144). As to the National Health Service Commissioning Board see HEALTH SERVICES vol 54 (2017) PARA 32; as to clinical commissioning groups see HEALTH SERVICES vol 54 (2017) PARA 35 et seq.
11 A person who is authorised as mentioned in the Care Act 2014 s 32(4)(a) (see PARA 106) does not make arrangements for another to engage in a regulated activity by virtue of anything that he does under s 32(4)(b): Safeguarding Vulnerable Groups Act 2006 s 6(8C) (added by SI 2015/914). As from a day to be appointed, an authority that is a local authority for the purposes of the Children Act 1989 s 17A (see CHILDREN AND YOUNG PERSONS vol 10 (2017) PARA 804), the Health and Social Care Act 2001 s 57 (see MENTAL HEALTH AND CAPACITY) (direct payments), the Care Act 2014 ss 31–33 (see PARAS 106–110) or, as from a day to be appointed, the Social Services and Well-being (Wales) Act 2014 ss 50–53 (see PARAS 125–130), or a person who is a person's surrogate within the meaning of the Health and Social Care Act 2001 s 57, or a person who is authorised as mentioned in the Social Services and Well-being (Wales) Act 2014 s 50(5)(a) (see PARA 125) does not make arrangements for another to engage in a regulated activity by virtue of anything the authority, surrogate or person does under (as the case may be) the Children Act 1989 s 17A, the Health and Social Care Act 2001 s 57(1B)(b), (1C)(b), the Care Act 2014 ss 31–33 or the Social Services and Well-being (Wales) Act 2014 s 50(5)(b), (6)(b): Safeguarding Vulnerable Groups Act 2006 s 6(8A), (8B), (8CA) (s 6(8A), (8B) prospectively added by the Health and Social Care Act 2008 Sch 14 para 8; Safeguarding Vulnerable Groups Act 2006 s 6(8A) amended by SI 2015/914; Safeguarding Vulnerable Groups Act 2006 s 6(8A) prospectively amended, s 6(8CA) prospectively added, in relation to Wales by SI 2016/413). At the date at which this volume states the law no day had been appointed for the coming into force of the amendments noted as prospective.

264. Exemption for private, family and personal arrangements. A person (P) is not a regulated activity provider if he is an individual and the arrangements he makes are private arrangements[1]. Arrangements are private arrangements if the regulated activity[2] is for, or for the benefit of, P himself[3] or a child[4] or vulnerable adult[5] who is a member of P's family[6] or a friend of P[7]. For these purposes it is immaterial whether P is also acting in any capacity other than as a family member or friend[8].

The Safeguarding Vulnerable Groups Act 2006 does not apply to any activity which is carried out in the course of a family relationship[9] or to any activity which is carried out in the course of a personal relationship[10] and for no commercial consideration[11].

1   Safeguarding Vulnerable Groups Act 2006 s 6(5).
2   As to the meaning of 'regulated activity' see PARAS 241–250 (children), PARAS 251–259 (vulnerable adults).
3   Safeguarding Vulnerable Groups Act 2006 s 6(6).
4   As to the meaning of 'child' see PARA 241 note 1.
5   As to the meanings of 'adult' and 'vulnerable adult' see PARA 251 note 1.
6   Safeguarding Vulnerable Groups Act 2006 s 6(7)(a). A family relationship includes a relationship between two persons who live in the same household and treat each other as though they were members of the same family: ss 6(11), 58(3). The Secretary of State may by order provide that an activity carried out in specified circumstances either is or is not carried out in the course of a family relationship or carried out in the course of a personal relationship: s 58(6). At the date at which this volume states the law no such order had been made. As to the Secretary of State see PARA 333. See also PARA 241 note 4.
7   Safeguarding Vulnerable Groups Act 2006 s 6(7)(b). A friend of a person (A) includes a person who is a friend of a member of A's family: ss 6(11), 58(5).
8   Safeguarding Vulnerable Groups Act 2006 s 6(9).

9 Safeguarding Vulnerable Groups Act 2006 s 58(1).
10 A personal relationship is a relationship between or among friends: Safeguarding Vulnerable Groups Act 2006 s 58(4).
11 Safeguarding Vulnerable Groups Act 2006 s 58(2).

(iii) The Barring System and the Barred Lists

A. CRITERIA FOR INCLUSION IN BARRED LISTS

265. Automatic inclusion in children's barred list. The Disclosure and Barring Service (DBS)[1] must include a person in the children's barred list[2] if it is satisfied that he has been convicted of, or cautioned in relation to, a specified sexual or violent offence[3]. DBS must also include a person in the children's barred list if before 20 January 2009[4] he had been made the subject of a disqualification order[5], or if he had been barred from working with children under the former barring provisions[6]. Provision is also made for DBS to include a person in the children's barred list if he is included in a specified list for the purposes of a country or territory outside the United Kingdom[7] or if an order or direction of a specified description requiring the person to do or not to do anything has been made against him for the purposes of a country or territory outside the United Kingdom[8], but at the date at which this volume states the law no such list, order or direction had been specified.

For the purposes of determining whether any of the criteria is satisfied in relation to a person any offence committed before he attained the age of 18, and any order or direction made before that time, must be ignored[9].

1 The Disclosure and Barring Service ('DBS') is a body corporate (Protection of Freedoms Act 2012 s 87(1), (2)), and is the regulatory body for the child and vulnerable adult protection systems under the Safeguarding Vulnerable Groups Act 2006 (see PARA 241 et seq). DBS also has functions under the Safeguarding Vulnerable Groups Act 2006 and under the Police Act 1997 Pt 5 (ss 112–127: see SENTENCING vol 92 (2015) PARA 636 et seq). Provision is made in relation to such matters as membership, terms of appointment of members, remuneration of members, staff, remuneration and pensions, delegation of functions, business plan, reports, funding, accounts, guidance, directions, status, use of information, payments in connection with maladministration, incidental powers, documents and transitional matters: see the Protection of Freedoms Act 2012 Sch 8; and the Disclosure and Barring Service (Core Functions) Order 2012, SI 2012/2522 (amended by SI 2014/238). DBS took over the role of the former Independent Safeguarding Authority which was dissolved, and its functions transferred to DBS, by the Protection of Freedoms Act 2012 (Disclosure and Barring Service Transfer of Functions) Order 2012, SI 2012/3006 (pursuant to the Protection of Freedoms Act 2012 s 88).
2 Ie the list that the Disclosure and Barring Service is required to maintain by virtue of the Safeguarding Vulnerable Groups Act 2006 s 2(1)(a) (amended by SI 2012/3006).
3 Safeguarding Vulnerable Groups Act 2006 s 2(2), Sch 3 paras 1, 24(1)(a), (2), (10) (Sch 3 para 1, Sch 8 para 2 amended by SI 2012/3006; Safeguarding Vulnerable Groups Act 2006 Sch 3 para 24(2) amended, Sch 3 para 24(10) added, by SI 2008/3050); Safeguarding Vulnerable Groups Act 2006 (Prescribed Criteria and Miscellaneous Provisions) Regulations 2009, SI 2009/37, reg 3(1), (3)(a), (4). In relation to a conviction or caution occurring on or after 20 January 2009 (ie the 'relevant date' for the purposes of the Safeguarding Vulnerable Groups Act 2006 (Prescribed Criteria and Miscellaneous Provisions) Regulations 2009, SI 2009/37 (reg 1(1), (2))), the offences are specified in Schedule para 1 (amended by SI 2012/2160). In relation to a conviction or caution occurring before that date, the offences are specified in the Education (Prohibition from Teaching or Working with Children) Regulations 2003, SI 2003/1184, Sch 2 Pt 2 (reg 8, Sch 2 substituted by SI 2007/195), and the person in question is required to be included in the list only if the Education (Prohibition from Teaching or Working with Children) Regulations 2003, SI 2003/1184, Sch 2 Pt 1 Condition C (as so substituted) is satisfied in relation to him, reg 8 (automatic prohibition: right to make representations) applied to him, and the Secretary of State had not made a direction under the Education Act 2002 s 142(1)(a) (prohibition from teaching: see EDUCATION vol 35 (2015) PARA 420) in relation to him: Safeguarding Vulnerable Groups Act 2006 (Prescribed Criteria and Miscellaneous Provisions) Regulations 2009, SI 2009/37, reg 3(3)(b)–(d). As to the procedure leading to inclusion in barred lists, including the making of

representations and appeals, see PARAS 270–275; as to challenging inclusions see PARAS 276–279. As to the provision of information about persons included in barred lists see PARAS 267, 293. As to the Secretary of State see PARA 333. See also PARA 241 note 4.

The offences referred to in reg 3, Schedule para 1 do not include any offence which a person has committed against a child before 12 October 2009 (ie the date on which the Safeguarding Vulnerable Groups Act 2006 s 2 was brought into force for all purposes by virtue of the Safeguarding Vulnerable Groups Act 2006 (Commencement No 6, Transitional Provisions and Savings) Order 2009, SI 2009/2611) if the court, having considered whether to make a disqualification order in connection with the commission of the offence, decided not to: see the Safeguarding Vulnerable Groups Act 2006 Sch 3 para 24(5), (6); and the Safeguarding Vulnerable Groups Act 2006 (Prescribed Criteria and Miscellaneous Provisions) Regulations 2009, SI 2009/37, reg 2(1), (2). The reference to an offence committed against a child must be construed in accordance with the Criminal Justice and Court Services Act 2000 Pt 2 (ss 26–42) (see s 26): Safeguarding Vulnerable Groups Act 2006 (Prescribed Criteria and Miscellaneous Provisions) Regulations 2009, SI 2009/37, reg 2(3).

Persons must be informed when a conviction or order will lead to inclusion in barred list: see PARA 267.

4   As to this date see note 3.
5   Safeguarding Vulnerable Groups Act 2006 Sch 3 para 24(1)(b); Safeguarding Vulnerable Groups Act 2006 (Prescribed Criteria and Miscellaneous Provisions) Regulations 2009, SI 2009/37, reg 3(2)(a). A disqualification order is an order of the court under the Criminal Justice and Court Services Act 2000 s 28, s 29 or s 29A (repealed): Safeguarding Vulnerable Groups Act 2006 (Prescribed Criteria and Miscellaneous Provisions) Regulations 2009, SI 2009/37, reg 1(2). A person who has been made the subject of a disqualification order is required to be included in the list under these provisions only if the Education (Prohibition from Teaching or Working with Children) Regulations 2003, SI 2003/1184, Sch 2 Pt 1 Condition C (substituted by SI 2007/195) is satisfied in relation to him, the Education (Prohibition from Teaching or Working with Children) Regulations 2003, SI 2003/1184, reg 8 (automatic prohibition: right to make representations) applied to him, and the Secretary of State had not made a direction under the Education Act 2002 s 142(1)(a) in relation to him: Safeguarding Vulnerable Groups Act 2006 (Prescribed Criteria and Miscellaneous Provisions) Regulations 2009, SI 2009/37, reg 3(2)(b)–(d).
6   See the Safeguarding Vulnerable Groups Act 2006 Sch 8 paras 2, 4 (as amended (see note 3); and also amended by the Policing and Crime Act 2009 s 81(2), (3); and by the Education Act 2011 Sch 2 para 27); the Safeguarding Vulnerable Groups Act 2006 (Transitional Provisions) Order 2008, SI 2008/473, arts 2, 3 (amended by SI 2008/2683; SI 2009/37; SI 2012/3006); the Safeguarding Vulnerable Groups Act 2006 (Barring Procedure) Regulations 2008, SI 2008/474, regs 3–7, 10 (amended by SI 2008/2683; SI 2012/3006); and the Safeguarding Vulnerable Groups Act 2006 (Prescribed Criteria) (Transitional Provisions) Regulations 2008, SI 2008/1062, reg 2, Schedule para 1 (reg 2 amended by SI 2012/3006), which make provision for the inclusion in the children's barred list of persons included (otherwise than provisionally) in the list kept under the Protection of Children Act 1999 s 1 (individuals considered unsuitable to work with children) (repealed), persons subject to disqualification orders and persons subject to a direction under the Education Act 2002 s 142(1).
7   Safeguarding Vulnerable Groups Act 2006 Sch 3 para 24(1)(c). The Secretary of State may specify a list for the purposes of Sch 3 para 24(1)(c) only if he thinks that inclusion in the list has a corresponding or similar effect to inclusion in a barred list: Sch 3 para 24(3).
8   Safeguarding Vulnerable Groups Act 2006 Sch 3 para 24(1)(d).
9   Safeguarding Vulnerable Groups Act 2006 Sch 3 para 24(4). For these purposes an offence committed over a period of time must be treated as committed on the last day of the period: Sch 3 para 24(7).

266. Automatic inclusion in adults' barred list. The Disclosure and Barring Service (DBS)[1] must include a person in the adults' barred list[2] if it is satisfied that on or after 20 January 2009[3], he has been convicted of, or cautioned in relation to, a specified sexual or violent offence[4] or if he had been barred from working with vulnerable adults under the former barring provisions[5]. Provision is also made for DBS to include a person in the adults' barred list if he is included in a specified list for the purposes of a country or territory outside the United Kingdom[6] or if an order or direction of a specified description requiring the person to do or not to do anything has been made against him either in the United

Kingdom or for the purposes of a country or territory outside the United Kingdom[7], but at the date at which this volume states the law no such list, order or direction had been specified.

For the purposes of determining whether any of the criteria is satisfied in relation to a person any offence committed before he attained the age of 18, and any order or direction made before that time, must be ignored[8].

1   As to the Disclosure and Barring Service see PARA 265.
2   Ie the list that the Disclosure and Barring Service is required to maintain by virtue of the Safeguarding Vulnerable Groups Act 2006 s 2(1)(b) (amended by SI 2012/3006).
3   Ie the 'relevant date': see PARA 265 note 3.
4   Safeguarding Vulnerable Groups Act 2006 s 2(3), Sch 3 paras 7(1), (2), 24(1)(a), (2), (10) (Sch 3 para 7(2) substituted, Sch 8 para 3 amended, by SI 2012/3006; Safeguarding Vulnerable Groups Act 2006 Sch 3 para 24(2) amended, Sch 3 para 24(10) added, by SI 2008/3050); Safeguarding Vulnerable Groups Act 2006 (Prescribed Criteria and Miscellaneous Provisions) Regulations 2009, SI 2009/37, reg 5. The offences are specified in Schedule para 3 (amended by SI 2012/2160). As to the procedure leading to inclusion in barred lists, including the making of representations and appeals, see PARAS 270–275; as to challenging inclusions see PARAS 276–279. As to the provision of information about persons included in barred lists see PARAS 267, 293.
    The offences referred to in the Safeguarding Vulnerable Groups Act 2006 (Prescribed Criteria and Miscellaneous Provisions) Regulations 2009, SI 2009/37, reg 5, Schedule para 3 do not include any offence which a person has committed against a child before 12 October 2009 if the court, having considered whether to make a disqualification order in connection with the commission of the offence, decided not to: see the Safeguarding Vulnerable Groups Act 2006 (Prescribed Criteria and Miscellaneous Provisions) Regulations 2009, SI 2009/37, reg 2(1), (2); and PARA 265 note 3.
    Persons must be informed when a conviction or order will lead to inclusion in barred list: see PARA 267.
5   See the Safeguarding Vulnerable Groups Act 2006 Sch 8 paras 3, 4 (as amended (see note 4); amended by the Policing and Crime Act 2009 s 81(2), (3)); the Safeguarding Vulnerable Groups Act 2006 (Transitional Provisions) Order 2008, SI 2008/473, art 4 (amended by SI 2008/2683; SI 2012/3006), the Safeguarding Vulnerable Groups Act 2006 (Barring Procedure) Regulations 2008, SI 2008/474, regs 8, 10 (amended by SI 2008/2683; SI 2012/3006), and the Safeguarding Vulnerable Groups Act 2006 (Prescribed Criteria) (Transitional Provisions) Regulations 2008, SI 2008/1062, reg 3, Schedule para 2 (reg 3 amended by SI 2012/3006) which make provision for the inclusion in the adults' barred list of persons included (otherwise than provisionally) in the list kept under the Care Standards Act 2000 s 81 (individuals considered unsuitable to work with vulnerable adults) (repealed).
6   Safeguarding Vulnerable Groups Act 2006 Sch 3 para 24(1)(c). The Secretary of State may specify a list for the purposes of Sch 3 para 24(1)(c) only if he thinks that inclusion in the list has a corresponding or similar effect to inclusion in a barred list: Sch 3 para 24(3). As to the Secretary of State see PARA 333. See also 241 note 4.
7   Safeguarding Vulnerable Groups Act 2006 Sch 3 para 24(1)(b), (d).
8   Safeguarding Vulnerable Groups Act 2006 Sch 3 para 24(4). For these purposes an offence committed over a period of time must be treated as committed on the last day of the period: Sch 3 para 24(7).

267. Persons must be informed that conviction or order will lead to inclusion in barred list. A court by or before which a person is convicted of an applicable offence[1] or which makes an applicable order[2] must inform the person at the time he is convicted or the order is made that the Disclosure and Barring Service (DBS)[3] will, or (as the case may be) may, include him in the barred list concerned[4].

1   Ie an offence of a description specified for the purposes of the Safeguarding Vulnerable Groups Act 2006 Sch 3 para 24(1)(a) (see PARAS 265, 266, 270).
2   Ie an order of a description specified for the purposes of the Safeguarding Vulnerable Groups Act 2006 Sch 3 para 24(1)(b) (see PARAS 265, 266, 270).
3   As to the Disclosure and Barring Service see PARA 265.
4   Safeguarding Vulnerable Groups Act 2006 Sch 3 para 25(1) (amended by the Protection of Freedoms Act 2012 Sch 9 para 72; SI 2008/3050; SI 2012/3006). As to the criteria for inclusion in the children's barred list see PARA 265. As to criteria for inclusion in the adults' barred list see PARA 266. These provisions do not apply to convictions by or before a court in a country or

territory outside England and Wales: Safeguarding Vulnerable Groups Act 2006 Sch 3 para 25(2) (added by SI 2008/3050). As to the meanings of 'England' and 'Wales' see PARAS 1, 2 note 4.

268. No damages for inclusion in barred list. No claim for damages lies[1] in respect of any loss or damage suffered by any person in consequence of the fact that an individual is included in a barred list[2], the fact that an individual is not included in a barred list[3], or the provision[4] of vetting and registration information[5].

1   Nothing in the Safeguarding Vulnerable Groups Act 2006 affects the Human Rights Act 1998 s 8 (judicial remedies: see RIGHTS AND FREEDOMS vol 88A (2013) PARA 29) as it relates to the power of a court to award damages in respect of an unlawful act of a public authority (within the meaning of the Human Rights Act 1998: see RIGHTS AND FREEDOMS vol 88A (2013) PARAS 26, 29): Safeguarding Vulnerable Groups Act 2006 s 57(3).
2   Safeguarding Vulnerable Groups Act 2006 s 57(1)(a). As to the criteria for inclusion in the children's barred list see PARA 159. As to criteria for inclusion in the adults' barred list see PARA 266.
3   Safeguarding Vulnerable Groups Act 2006 s 57(1)(b).
4   Ie in pursuance of any of the Safeguarding Vulnerable Groups Act 2006 ss 35, 36, 37, 39, 40, 41, 42, 45, 46 (see PARA 281 et seq).
5   Safeguarding Vulnerable Groups Act 2006 s 57(1)(c). Section 57(1)(c) does not apply to the provision of information which is untrue by a person who knows the information is untrue and either he is the originator of the information and he knew at the time he originated the information that it was not true, or he causes another person to be the originator of the information knowing, at the time the information is originated, that it is untrue: s 57(2).

269. Cross-border co-operation in compilation of lists. The Disclosure and Barring Service (DBS)[1] must inform the Scottish Ministers if a person is included in the children's barred list or the adults' barred list[2], and may provide further information to the Scottish Ministers and the Welsh Ministers[3].

Until a day to be appointed DBS must not include a person in the children's barred list or the adults' barred list only on a particular ground if a relevant Scottish authority[4] has already considered whether the person should be included in a corresponding list[5] on the same ground (whether or not it decided to include him in the list)[6] or if, in accordance with such criteria as the Secretary of State specifies by order, it is more appropriate for the person's case to be considered by the relevant Scottish authority[7]. As from that day DBS must not include a person in the children's barred list or the adults' barred list only on a particular ground if it knows that a relevant Scottish authority has already considered whether the person should be included in a corresponding list on the same ground and has decided not to include the person in the list[8], or if, in accordance with such criteria as the Secretary of State specifies by order, it is more appropriate for the person's case to be considered by the relevant Scottish authority[9].

As from the appointed day DBS must not include a person in the children's barred list or the adults' barred list if it knows that the person is included in a corresponding list[10], and must remove a person from the applicable list if it knows that the person is so included[11].

At the date at which this volume states the law no day had been appointed for these purposes.

1   As to the Disclosure and Barring Service see PARA 265.
2   Safeguarding Vulnerable Groups Act 2006 Sch 3 para 22 (Sch 3 paras 5A(1), (2), 6(1), (2), 11A(1), (2), 12(1), (2), 22, 22A, 23 amended by SI 2012/3006). As to the children's barred list see PARA 265 note 2. As to the adults' barred list see PARA 266 note 2. As to the provision of information about persons included in barred lists see PARAS 267, 293.
3   DBS may provide the Scottish Ministers with such information as it thinks may be relevant to the exercise by the Scottish Ministers of their functions under the Protection of Vulnerable Groups (Scotland) Act 2007 Pts 1, 2 (Safeguarding Vulnerable Groups Act 2006 Sch 3 para 22A (added

by SI 2011/565; as amended (see note 2))), and may, at the request of the Welsh Ministers, provide them with such information relating to the exercise of its functions as it thinks may be relevant to the exercise by the Welsh Ministers of any of their functions (Safeguarding Vulnerable Groups Act 2006 Sch 3 para 23 (as so amended)). As to the Welsh Ministers see PARA 395.

4   A relevant Scottish authority is such authority as the Secretary of State specifies by order as exercising for the purposes of the law of Scotland functions which correspond to those of DBS: Safeguarding Vulnerable Groups Act 2006 Sch 3 paras 6(2), 12(2) (as amended: see note 2). At the date at which this volume states the law no authorities had been specified for these purposes. As to the Secretary of State see PARA 333. See also PARA 241 note 4.

5   A corresponding list is a list maintained for the purposes of the law of Scotland which the Secretary of State specifies by order as corresponding to the children's barred list or, as the case may be, the adults' barred list: Safeguarding Vulnerable Groups Act 2006 Sch 3 paras 6(3), 12(3). At the date at which this volume states the law no lists had been specified for these purposes.

6   Safeguarding Vulnerable Groups Act 2006 Sch 3 paras 6(1)(a), 12(1)(a) (as amended: see note 2).

7   Safeguarding Vulnerable Groups Act 2006 Sch 3 paras 6(1)(b), 12(1)(b).

8   Safeguarding Vulnerable Groups Act 2006 Sch 3 paras 6(1)(a), 12(1)(a) (as amended (see note 2); Sch 3 paras 6, 12 prospectively further amended, Sch 3 paras 5A, 11A prospectively added, by the Protection of Freedoms Act 2012 s 74).

9   Safeguarding Vulnerable Groups Act 2006 Sch 3 paras 6(1)(b), 12(1)(b).

10 Safeguarding Vulnerable Groups Act 2006 Sch 3 paras 5A(1), 11A(1) (prospectively added and amended: see notes 2, 8). A corresponding list is a list maintained under the law of Scotland or Northern Ireland which the Secretary of State specifies by order as corresponding to the children's barred list: Sch 3 paras 5A(3), 11A(3) (as so prospectively added). At the date at which this volume states the law no lists had been specified for these purposes.

11 Safeguarding Vulnerable Groups Act 2006 Sch 3 paras 5A(2), 11A(2) (prospectively added and amended: see notes 2, 8).

B.   PROCEDURE LEADING TO INCLUSION IN BARRED LISTS

270.   Making and consideration of representations. If the Disclosure and Barring Service (DBS)[1] is satisfied that a person has been convicted of, or cautioned in relation to, a specified sexual or violent offence[2], has been made the subject of a risk of sexual harm order[3], or (in the case of inclusion in the children's barred list) has been made the subject of a disqualification order[4], and it appears to DBS that these provisions apply and the person is or has been, or might in future be, engaged in regulated activity relating to children or vulnerable adults[5], DBS must give the person the opportunity to make representations as to why the person should not be included in a barred list[6]. Provision is also made for DBS to give a person included in a specified list for the purposes of a country or territory outside the United Kingdom[7], or a person against whom an order or direction of a specified description requiring him to do or not to do anything has been made for the purposes of a country or territory outside the United Kingdom[8], the opportunity to make representations as to why he should not be included in a barred list, but at the date at which this volume states the law no such list, order or direction had been specified.

For the purposes of determining whether any of the criteria is satisfied in relation to a person any offence committed before he attained the age of 18, and any order or direction made before that time, must be ignored[9].

The making of representations will not necessarily preclude the person's inclusion in a barred list[10], and a person who fails to make representations must be included in the list[11].

1   As to the Disclosure and Barring Service see PARA 265.

2   Safeguarding Vulnerable Groups Act 2006 Sch 3 paras 2(1), 8(1), 24(1)(a), (2), (10) (Sch 3 para 24(2) amended, Sch 3 para 24(10) added, by SI 2008/3050); Safeguarding Vulnerable Groups Act 2006 (Prescribed Criteria and Miscellaneous Provisions) Regulations 2009, SI 2009/37, regs 4(1), (3)(a), (5), 6(b). For the purposes of representations about inclusion in the children's barred list:

(1)   in relation to a conviction or caution occurring on or after 20 January 2009 (ie the 'relevant date': see PARA 265 note 3), the offences are specified in Schedule para 2 (amended by SI 2009/2610; SI 2010/1146; SI 2012/2160; SI 2015/1472; SI 2016/554); and

(2)   in relation to a conviction or caution occurring before that date, the offences are specified in the Education (Prohibition from Teaching or Working with Children) Regulations 2003, SI 2003/1184, Sch 2 Pts 2–5 (Sch 2 substituted by SI 2007/195), and the person in question is required to be included in the list only if any of the Education (Prohibition from Teaching or Working with Children) Regulations 2003, SI 2003/1184, Sch 2 Pt 1 Conditions D–F (as so substituted) is satisfied in relation to him, reg 8 (automatic prohibition: right to make representations) applied to him, and the Secretary of State had not made a direction under the Education Act 2002 s 142(1)(a) (prohibition from teaching: see EDUCATION vol 35 (2015) PARA 420) in relation to him (Safeguarding Vulnerable Groups Act 2006 (Prescribed Criteria and Miscellaneous Provisions) Regulations 2009, SI 2009/37, reg 4(3)(b)–(d)).

As to the children's barred list see PARA 265 note 2. Representations about inclusion in the adults' barred list may be made only in respect of convictions or cautions on or after 20 January 2009, and the relevant offences are those set out in the Safeguarding Vulnerable Groups Act 2006 (Prescribed Criteria and Miscellaneous Provisions) Regulations 2009, SI 2009/37, Schedule para 4 (amended by SI 2009/2610; SI 2010/1146; SI 2012/2160; SI 2015/1472; SI 2016/554): Safeguarding Vulnerable Groups Act 2006 (Prescribed Criteria and Miscellaneous Provisions) Regulations 2009, SI 2009/37, reg 6(b). As to the adults' barred list see PARA 266 note 2. As to the Secretary of State see PARA 333. See also PARA 241 note 4.

The offences referred to in regs 4, 6 do not include any offence which a person has committed against a child before 12 October 2009 (see PARA 265 note 3) if the court, having considered whether to make a disqualification order in connection with the commission of the offence, decided not to: see the Safeguarding Vulnerable Groups Act 2006 Sch 3 para 24(5), (6); and the Safeguarding Vulnerable Groups Act 2006 (Prescribed Criteria and Miscellaneous Provisions) Regulations 2009, SI 2009/37, reg 2(1), (2).

Persons must be informed when a conviction or order will lead to inclusion in barred list: see PARA 267.

3   Safeguarding Vulnerable Groups Act 2006 Sch 3 para 24(1)(b); Safeguarding Vulnerable Groups Act 2006 (Prescribed Criteria and Miscellaneous Provisions) Regulations 2009, SI 2009/37, regs 4(4), 6(a). A risk of sexual harm order is an order made under the Sexual Offences Act 2003 s 123 (repealed) or the corresponding Scottish provision, and the person must have been made the subject of the order on or after 20 January 2009: Safeguarding Vulnerable Groups Act 2006 (Prescribed Criteria and Miscellaneous Provisions) Regulations 2009, SI 2009/37, regs 4(4), 6(a).

4   Safeguarding Vulnerable Groups Act 2006 (Prescribed Criteria and Miscellaneous Provisions) Regulations 2009, SI 2009/37, reg 4(2)(a), (6). As to the meaning of 'disqualification order' see PARA 265 note 5. A person who has been made the subject of a disqualification order on or after 20 January 2009 is required to be included under these provisions only if he does not meet any other criteria prescribed in reg 3 (see PARA 265) or reg 4 (see the text and notes 1–3): reg 4(6). A person who has been made the subject of a disqualification order before that date is required to be included under these provisions only if the Education (Prohibition from Teaching or Working with Children) Regulations 2003, SI 2003/1184, Sch 2 Pt 1 Condition C (substituted by SI 2007/195) is satisfied in relation to him, the Education (Prohibition from Teaching or Working with Children) Regulations 2003, SI 2003/1184, reg 8 (automatic prohibition: right to make representations) applied to him, and the Secretary of State had not made a direction under the Education Act 2002 s 142(1)(a) in relation to him: Safeguarding Vulnerable Groups Act 2006 (Prescribed Criteria and Miscellaneous Provisions) Regulations 2009, SI 2009/37, reg 4(2)(b)–(d).

5   Safeguarding Vulnerable Groups Act 2006 Sch 3 paras 2(2), 8(2) (Sch 3 paras 2(2), (4)–(8), 8(2), (4)–(8) substituted by the Protection of Freedoms Act 2012 s 67(2), (6); Safeguarding Vulnerable Groups Act 2006 Sch 3 paras 2(2), 8(2) further substituted, Sch 3 paras 2(4), (6), (8), 8(4), (6), (8) amended, by SI 2012/3006). As to the meaning of 'regulated activity' see PARAS 241–250 (children), PARAS 251–259 (vulnerable adults).

6   Safeguarding Vulnerable Groups Act 2006 Sch 3 paras 2(4), 8(4) (as substituted and amended: see note 5). As to the criteria for inclusion in the children's barred list see PARA 265. As to criteria for inclusion in the adults' barred list see PARA 266. As to the scope of the power to make representations, the making of representations where the whereabouts of a person is unknown, and procedure for the making of representations, see PARAS 273–274. As to the provision of information about persons included in barred lists see PARAS 267, 293.

7   Safeguarding Vulnerable Groups Act 2006 Sch 3 para 24(1)(c). The Secretary of State may specify a list for the purposes of Sch 3 para 24(1)(c) only if he thinks that inclusion in the list has a corresponding or similar effect to inclusion in a barred list: Sch 3 para 24(3).

8   Safeguarding Vulnerable Groups Act 2006 Sch 3 para 24(1)(d).

9   Safeguarding Vulnerable Groups Act 2006 Sch 3 para 24(4). For these purposes an offence committed over a period of time must be treated as committed on the last day of the period: Sch 3 para 24(7).
10 If the person makes representations before the end of any time prescribed for the purpose but DBS is satisfied that the Safeguarding Vulnerable Groups Act 2006 Sch 3 para 2 or Sch 3 para 8 (as the case may be) applies to the person, has reason to believe that the person is or has been, or might in future be, engaged in regulated activity relating to children or vulnerable adults, and is satisfied that it is appropriate to include the person in the appropriate list, it must include the person in the list: Sch 3 paras 2(7), (8), 8(7), (8) (as substituted and amended: see note 5).
11 If the person does not make representations before the end of any time prescribed for the purpose or the duty in Sch 3 paras 2(4), 8(4) (see the text and notes 1–6) does not apply by virtue of Sch 3 para 16(2) (see PARA 278), and DBS is satisfied that Sch 3 applies to the person and has reason to believe that the person is or has been, or might in future be, engaged in regulated activity relating to children or vulnerable adults, it must include the person in the list: Sch 3 paras 2(5), (6), 8(5), (6) (as substituted and amended: see note 5).

271. Representations concerning behaviour harmful to a child or vulnerable adult. If it appears to the Disclosure and Barring Service (DBS)[1] that a person is or has been, or might in future be, engaged in regulated activity relating to children or vulnerable adults[2], and has at any time engaged in:

(1)   conduct[3] which endangers a child (in the case of a person being considered for inclusion in the children's barred list) or vulnerable adult (in the case of a person being considered for inclusion in the adults' barred list) or is likely to endanger a child or vulnerable adult[4];

(2)   conduct which, if repeated against or in relation to a child or vulnerable adult, would endanger that child or vulnerable adult or would be likely to endanger him[5];

(3)   conduct involving sexual material relating to children (including possession of such material)[6];

(4)   conduct involving sexually explicit images depicting violence against human beings (including possession of such images), if it appears to DBS that the conduct is inappropriate[7]; or

(5)   conduct of a sexual nature involving a child, if it appears to DBS that the conduct is inappropriate[8],

then DBS must, if it proposes to include that person in the children's or adults' barred list[9], give him the opportunity to make representations as to why he should not be so included[10]. DBS must then include the person in the appropriate list if it is satisfied that the person has engaged in any of the conduct referred to above[11], it has reason to believe that the person is or has been, or might in future be, engaged in regulated activity relating to children or vulnerable adults[12], and it is satisfied that it is appropriate to include the person in the list[13].

1   As to the Disclosure and Barring Service see PARA 265.
2   Safeguarding Vulnerable Groups Act 2006 Sch 3 paras 3(1)(a)(ii), 9(1)(a)(ii) (Sch 3 paras 3(1)(a), (b), (2), (3), 4(1)(d), (e), (6), 9(1)(a), (b), (2), (3), 10(1)(d), (e) amended by SI 2012/3006; Safeguarding Vulnerable Groups Act 2006 Sch 3 paras 3(1)(a)(i), (ii), 9(1)(a)(i), (ii) substituted, Sch 3 paras 3(3)(aa), 9(3)(aa) added, Sch 3 paras 3(3)(b), 9(3)(b) amended, by the Protection of Freedoms Act 2012 s 67(3), (7)). As to the meaning of 'child' see PARA 241 note 1. As to the meanings of 'adult' and 'vulnerable adult' see PARA 251 note 1. As to the meaning of 'regulated activity' see PARAS 241–250 (children), PARAS 251–259 (vulnerable adults).
3   A person does not engage in the applicable conduct merely by committing an offence prescribed for these purposes: Safeguarding Vulnerable Groups Act 2006 Sch 3 paras 4(5), 10(5). 'Prescribed' means prescribed by regulations made by the Secretary of State: s 60(1). At the date at which this volume states the law no offences had been prescribed for this purpose. In connection with inclusion in the children's barred list, these provisions do not apply to a person if the relevant conduct consists only of an offence committed against a child before 12 October 2009 (ie the date on which s 2 was brought into force for all purposes by virtue of the Safeguarding Vulnerable Groups Act 2006 (Commencement No 6, Transitional Provisions and Savings) Order 2009, SI 2009/2611) and the court, having considered whether to make a disqualification order, decided

not to: Safeguarding Vulnerable Groups Act 2006 Sch 3 para 3(4); and see also (in relation to conduct engaged in before 12 October 2009) the Safeguarding Vulnerable Groups Act 2006 (Regulated Activity, Miscellaneous and Transitional Provisions and Commencement No 5) Order 2009, SI 2009/2610, art 23. The reference to an offence committed against a child must be construed in accordance with the Criminal Justice and Court Services Act 2000 Pt 2 (ss 26–42) (see s 26): Safeguarding Vulnerable Groups Act 2006 Sch 3 para 3(5)(a). A disqualification order is an order of the court under the Criminal Justice and Court Services Act 2000 s 28, s 29 or s 29A (repealed): Safeguarding Vulnerable Groups Act 2006 Sch 3 para 3(5)(b).

4   Safeguarding Vulnerable Groups Act 2006 Sch 3 paras 3(1)(a)(i), 4(1)(a), 9(1)(a)(i), 10(1)(a) (as amended and substituted: see note 2). As to the criteria for inclusion in the children's barred list see PARA 265. As to criteria for inclusion in the adults' barred list see PARA 266.

5   Safeguarding Vulnerable Groups Act 2006 Sch 3 paras 4(1)(b), 10(1)(b). A person's conduct endangers a child or vulnerable adult if he harms a child or vulnerable adult (Sch 3 paras 4(2)(a), 10(2)(a)), causes a child or vulnerable adult to be harmed (Sch 3 paras 4(2)(b), 10(2)(b)), puts a child or vulnerable adult at risk of harm (Sch 3 paras 4(2)(c), 10(2)(c)), attempts to harm a child or vulnerable adult (Sch 3 paras 4(2)(d), 10(2)(d)), or incites another to harm a child or vulnerable adult (Sch 3 paras 4(2)(e), 10(2)(e)).

6   Safeguarding Vulnerable Groups Act 2006 Sch 3 paras 4(1)(c), 10(1)(c). 'Sexual material relating to children' means indecent images of children or material (in whatever form) which portrays children involved in sexual activity and which is produced for the purposes of giving sexual gratification: Sch 3 paras 4(3), 10(3). 'Image' means an image produced by any means, whether of a real or imaginary subject: Sch 3 paras 4(4), 10(4).

7   Safeguarding Vulnerable Groups Act 2006 Sch 3 paras 4(1)(d), 10(1)(d) (as amended: see note 2). For the purposes of Sch 3 paras 4(1)(d), (e), 10(1)(d), (e), DBS must have regard to guidance issued by the Secretary of State as to conduct which is inappropriate: Sch 3 paras 4(6), 10(6) (as so amended). As to the Secretary of State see PARA 333. See also PARA 241 note 4.

8   Safeguarding Vulnerable Groups Act 2006 Sch 3 paras 4(1)(e), 10(1)(e) (as amended: see note 2). See note 7.

9   As to automatic inclusion in the barred lists see PARAS 265–266.

10 Safeguarding Vulnerable Groups Act 2006 Sch 3 paras 3(1)(b), (2), 9(1)(b), (2) (as amended: see note 2). As to the scope of the power to make representations, the making of representations where the whereabouts of a person is unknown, and procedure for the making of representations, see PARAS 273–274. As to the provision of information about persons included in barred lists see PARAS 267, 293.

11 Safeguarding Vulnerable Groups Act 2006 Sch 3 paras 3(3)(a), 9(3)(a) (as amended: see note 2).

12 Safeguarding Vulnerable Groups Act 2006 Sch 3 paras 3(3)(aa), 9(3)(aa) (as added: see note 2).

13 Safeguarding Vulnerable Groups Act 2006 Sch 3 paras 3(3)(b), 9(3)(b) (as amended: see note 2).

272. Representations concerning harm or potential harm to a child or vulnerable adult. If it appears to the Disclosure and Barring Service (DBS)[1] that a person is or has been, or might in future be, engaged in regulated activity relating to children or vulnerable adults[2], and it appears to DBS that that person may:

(1)   harm a child (in the case of a person being considered for inclusion in the children's barred list) or vulnerable adult (in the case of a person being considered for inclusion in the adults' barred list)[3];

(2)   cause a child or vulnerable adult to be harmed[4];

(3)   put a child or vulnerable adult at risk of harm[5];

(4)   attempt to harm a child or vulnerable adult[6]; or

(5)   incite another to harm a child or vulnerable adult[7].

then DBS must, if it proposes to include that person in the children's or adults' barred list[8], give him the opportunity to make representations as to why he should not be so included[9]. DBS must then include the person in the appropriate list if it is satisfied that the person has engaged in any of the conduct referred to above[10], it has reason to believe that the person is or has been, or might in future be, engaged in regulated activity relating to children or vulnerable adults[11], and it is satisfied that it is appropriate to include the person in the list[12].

1   As to the Disclosure and Barring Service see PARA 265.

2   Safeguarding Vulnerable Groups Act 2006 Sch 3 paras 5(1)(a)(ii), 11(1)(a)(ii) (Sch 3 paras 5(1)(a), (b), (2), (3) 11(1)(a), (b), (2), (3) amended by SI 2012/3006; Safeguarding Vulnerable Groups Act

2006 Sch 3 paras 5(1)(a)(i), (ii), 11(1)(a)(i), (ii) substituted, Sch 3 paras 5(3)(aa), 11(3)(aa) added, Sch 3 paras 5(3)(b), 11(3)(b) amended, by the Protection of Freedoms Act 2012 s 67(4)). As to the meaning of 'child' see PARA 241 note 1. As to the meanings of 'adult' and 'vulnerable adult' see PARA 251 note 1. As to the meaning of 'regulated activity' see PARAS 241–250 (children), PARAS 251–259 (vulnerable adults).

3 Safeguarding Vulnerable Groups Act 2006 Sch 3 paras 5(1)(a)(i), (4)(a), 11(1)(a)(i), (4)(a) (Sch 3 paras 5(1)(a)(i), 11(1)(a)(i) as amended: see note 2). As to the criteria for inclusion in the children's barred list see PARA 265. As to criteria for inclusion in the adults' barred list see PARA 266.

4 Safeguarding Vulnerable Groups Act 2006 Sch 3 paras 5(4)(b), 11(4)(b).

5 Safeguarding Vulnerable Groups Act 2006 Sch 3 paras 5(4)(c), 11(4)(c).

6 Safeguarding Vulnerable Groups Act 2006 Sch 3 paras 5(4)(d), 11(4)(d).

7 Safeguarding Vulnerable Groups Act 2006 Sch 3 paras 5(4)(e), 11(4)(e).

8 As to automatic inclusion in the barred lists see PARAS 265–266.

9 Safeguarding Vulnerable Groups Act 2006 Sch 3 paras 5(1)(b), (2), 11(1)(b), (2) (as amended: see note 2). As to the scope of the power to make representations, the making of representations where the whereabouts of a person is unknown, and procedure for the making of representations, see PARAS 273–274. As to the provision of information about persons included in barred lists see PARAS 267, 293.

10 Safeguarding Vulnerable Groups Act 2006 Sch 3 paras 5(3)(a), 11(3)(a) (as amended: see note 2).

11 Safeguarding Vulnerable Groups Act 2006 Sch 3 paras 5(3)(aa), 11(3)(aa) (as added: see note 2).

12 Safeguarding Vulnerable Groups Act 2006 Sch 3 paras 5(3)(b), 11(3)(b) (as amended: see note 2).

273. Scope of power to make representations. A person who is given an opportunity to make representations[1] must have the opportunity to make representations in relation to all of the information on which the Disclosure and Barring Service (DBS)[2] intends to rely in taking a decision relating to the inclusion of a person on a barred list[3]. The opportunity to make representations does not include the opportunity to make representations that findings of fact made by a competent body were wrongly made[4].

1 Ie in accordance with any provision of the Safeguarding Vulnerable Groups Act 2006 Sch 3 (see PARAS 270–272).

2 As to the Disclosure and Barring Service see PARA 265.

3 Safeguarding Vulnerable Groups Act 2006 s 2(4), Sch 3 para 16(1) (amended by SI 2012/3006).

4 Safeguarding Vulnerable Groups Act 2006 Sch 3 para 16(3). Findings of fact made by a competent body are findings of fact made in proceedings before the Secretary of State in the exercise of the Secretary of State's functions under the Education Act 2002 s 141B (see EDUCATION vol 36 (2015) PARA 1068), or in proceedings before one of the following bodies or any of its committees (or, in respect of Social Care Wales, any panel established under the Regulation and Inspection of Social Care (Wales) Act 2016 Pt 8 (ss 174–175) (see PARA 201)): the General Teaching Council for Wales (see EDUCATION vol 36 (2015) PARA 977 et seq); the Council of the Pharmaceutical Society of Great Britain (see MEDICAL PROFESSIONS vol 74 (2011) PARA 785 et seq); the General Medical Council (see MEDICAL PROFESSIONS vol 74 (2011) PARA 179 et seq); the General Dental Council (see MEDICAL PROFESSIONS vol 74 (2011) PARA 407 et seq); the General Optical Council (see MEDICAL PROFESSIONS vol 74 (2011) PARA 319 et seq); the General Osteopathic Council (see MEDICAL PROFESSIONS vol 74 (2011) PARA 526 et seq); the General Chiropractic Council (see MEDICAL PROFESSIONS vol 74 (2011) PARA 604 et seq); the Nursing and Midwifery Council (see MEDICAL PROFESSIONS vol 74 (2011) PARA 692 et seq); the Health and Care Professions Council (see MEDICAL PROFESSIONS vol 74 (2011) PARA 916 et seq); the General Social Care Council; or Social Care Wales (see PARAS 412–414): Safeguarding Vulnerable Groups Act 2006 Sch 3 para 16(4), (4A), (5) (Sch 3 para 16(4) amended by the Education Act 2011 Sch 2 para 27; and by the Health and Social Care Act 2012 Sch 15 para 56; Safeguarding Vulnerable Groups Act 2006 Sch 3 para 16(4) further amended, Sch 3 para 16(4A) added, in relation to Wales, by the Regulation and Inspection of Social Care (Wales) Act 2016 Sch 3 para 55). As to the Secretary of State see PARA 333. See also PARA 241 note 4.

274. Procedure for the making of representations. Where the Disclosure and Barring Service (DBS)[1] is required[2] to give a person the opportunity to make representations as to his inclusion in a barred list[3] it must give that person notice in writing that he may make such representations[4]. A person to whom such notice is given may make representations as to his inclusion in a barred list within the period of eight weeks starting on the day on which he is treated as having received the notice[5], although DBS may extend this period at its discretion[6].

1   As to the Disclosure and Barring Service see PARA 265.
2   Ie in accordance with any provision of the Safeguarding Vulnerable Groups Act 2006 Sch 3 (see PARAS 270–272).
3   As to the criteria for inclusion in the children's barred list see PARA 265. As to criteria for inclusion in the adults' barred list see PARA 266.
4   Safeguarding Vulnerable Groups Act 2006 (Barring Procedure) Regulations 2008, SI 2008/474, reg 2(1), (2) (reg 2(1)–(3), (6) amended by SI 2012/3006) (made under the Safeguarding Vulnerable Groups Act 2006 Sch 3 para 15 (amended by SI 2012/3006)). DBS must give such notice to the person in question by sending it to him by post (Safeguarding Vulnerable Groups Act 2006 (Barring Procedure) Regulations 2008, SI 2008/474, reg 2(3) (as so amended)), and any notice so sent must be treated as having been received by the person in question 48 hours after the date on which it was sent unless the contrary is proved (reg 2(4)). As to the provision of information about persons included in barred lists see PARAS 267, 293.
5   Safeguarding Vulnerable Groups Act 2006 (Barring Procedure) Regulations 2008, SI 2008/474, reg 2(5).
6   See the Safeguarding Vulnerable Groups Act 2006 (Barring Procedure) Regulations 2008, SI 2008/474, reg 2(6) (as amended: see note 4), which provides that a person has not completed making his representations within the period provided for under reg 2(5) and DBS is satisfied that the person has good reason for not doing so, DBS may allow that person such further period to make his representations as DBS considers reasonable.

C.   CHALLENGING INCLUSIONS IN BARRED LISTS

275. Appeals against inclusion in a list. An individual who is included in a barred list[1] may appeal to the Upper Tribunal[2] against a decision[3] to include him in the list[4]. Such an appeal may be made only on the grounds that the Disclosure and Barring Service (DBS)[5] has made a mistake on any point of law or in any finding of fact which it has made and on which the relevant decision was based[6], and only with the permission of the Upper Tribunal[7]. On such an appeal, the Tribunal must confirm the decision of DBS unless it finds that DBS has made a mistake of law or fact[8], and if the Tribunal finds that DBS has made such a mistake it must direct DBS to remove the person from the list or remit the matter to DBS for a new decision[9].

1   As to the criteria for inclusion in the children's barred list see PARA 265. As to criteria for inclusion in the adults' barred list see PARA 266. As to the making of representations about inclusion in barred lists see PARAS 270–274; as to challenging inclusions see further PARAS 276–279. As to the provision of information about persons included in barred lists see PARAS 267, 293.
2   As to the Upper Tribunal see COURTS AND TRIBUNALS vol 24 (2010) PARA 874 et seq.
3   Ie a decision under the Safeguarding Vulnerable Groups Act 2006 Sch 3 para 2, 3, 5, 8, 9 or 11 (see PARAS 270–272).
4   Safeguarding Vulnerable Groups Act 2006 s 4(1)(b) (s 4(1), (4)–(7) amended by SI 2008/2833; Safeguarding Vulnerable Groups Act 2006 s 4(1)(b) amended by the Protection of Freedoms Act 2012 Sch 9 para 44). Appeals may also be brought against a decision not to remove a person from a barred list: see PARA 279.
5   As to the Disclosure and Barring Service see PARA 265.
6   Safeguarding Vulnerable Groups Act 2006 s 4(2) (amended by SI 2012/3006). For these purposes the decision whether or not it is appropriate for an individual to be included in a barred list is not a question of law or fact: Safeguarding Vulnerable Groups Act 2006 s 4(3).
7   Safeguarding Vulnerable Groups Act 2006 s 4(4) (as amended: see note 4).
8   Safeguarding Vulnerable Groups Act 2006 s 4(5) (as amended (see note 4); s 4(5)–(7) amended by SI 2012/3006).
9   Safeguarding Vulnerable Groups Act 2006 s 4(6) (as amended: see notes 4, 8). If the Tribunal remits a matter to DBS under these provisions it may set out any findings of fact which it has made (on which DBS must base its new decision); and the person must be removed from the list until DBS makes its new decision, unless the Tribunal directs otherwise: s 4(7) (as so amended).

276. Reviews on application. A person who is included in a barred list[1] may apply to the Disclosure and Barring Service (DBS)[2] for a review of his inclusion[3].

An application for a review may be made only with the permission of DBS[4], and a person may apply for permission only if the application is made after the end of the minimum barred period[5] and in the prescribed period[6] ending with the time when he applies for permission, he has made no other such application[7]. DBS must not grant permission unless it thinks that the person's circumstances have changed since he was included in the list or since he last applied for permission (as the case may be)[8] and that the change is such that permission should be granted[9]. On a review of a person's inclusion, if DBS is satisfied that it is no longer appropriate for him to be included in the list it must remove him from it; otherwise it must dismiss the application[10].

1   As to the criteria for inclusion in the children's barred list see PARA 265. As to criteria for inclusion in the adults' barred list see PARA 266.
2   As to the Disclosure and Barring Service see PARA 265.
3   Safeguarding Vulnerable Groups Act 2006 Sch 3 para 18(1) (Sch 3 para 18(1), (2), (4), (5) amended by SI 2012/3006). As to the provision of information about persons included in barred lists see PARAS 267, 293.
4   Safeguarding Vulnerable Groups Act 2006 Sch 3 para 18(2) (as amended: see note 3).
5   Safeguarding Vulnerable Groups Act 2006 Sch 3 para 18(3)(a). The minimum barred period is the prescribed period (see note 6) beginning with such of the following as may be prescribed: the date on which the person was first included in the list; the date on which any criterion prescribed for the purposes of Sch 3 para 1, 2, 7 or 8 (see PARAS 265, 266, 270) is first satisfied; where the person is included in the list on the grounds that he has been convicted of an offence in respect of which a custodial sentence (within the meaning of the Powers of Criminal Courts (Sentencing) Act 2000 s 76: see SENTENCING vol 92 (2015) PARA 9) was imposed, the date of his release; and the date on which the person made any representations as to why he should not be included in the list: see the Safeguarding Vulnerable Groups Act 2006 Sch 3 para 18(6); and the Safeguarding Vulnerable Groups Act 2006 (Barring Procedure) Regulations 2008, SI 2008/474, regs 9, 10 (amended by SI 2012/3006).
6   The period prescribed for these purposes is:
    (1)   in relation to a person who has not reached the age of 18, one year (Safeguarding Vulnerable Groups Act 2006 (Barring Procedure) Regulations 2008, SI 2008/474, reg 11(1), (2));
    (2)   in relation to a person who has reached the age of 18, had been eligible before he reached that age to apply for permission pursuant to head (1) above, did not do so before he reached that age, and has not done so since he reached that age, one year (reg 11(3));
    (3)   in relation to a person who has not reached the age of 25 but to whom neither head (1) nor head (2) above applies, 5 years (reg 11(4));
    (4)   in relation to a person who has reached the age of 25, is not eligible to apply for permission pursuant to head (2) above, had been eligible before he reached the age of 25 to apply for permission pursuant to head (3) above, did not do so before he reached that age, and has not done so since he reached that age, 5 years (reg 11(5)); and
    (5)   in any other case, 10 years (reg 11(6)).
    For these purposes a reference to permission means the permission of DBS to make an application for review of a person's inclusion in a barred list: reg 11(7) (amended by SI 2012/3006).
7   Safeguarding Vulnerable Groups Act 2006 Sch 3 para 18(3)(b).
8   Safeguarding Vulnerable Groups Act 2006 Sch 3 para 18(4)(a) (as amended: see note 3).
9   Safeguarding Vulnerable Groups Act 2006 Sch 3 para 18(4)(b) (as amended: see note 3).
10 Safeguarding Vulnerable Groups Act 2006 Sch 3 para 18(5) (as amended: see note 3).

277. Reviews at discretion of Disclosure and Barring Service. If a person's inclusion in a barred list[1] is not subject to an application for review[2] the Disclosure and Barring Service (DBS)[3] may, at any time, review the person's inclusion in the list[4]. On any such review DBS may remove the person from the list if, and only if, it is satisfied that, in the light of information which it did not have at the time of the person's inclusion in the list, any change of circumstances relating to the person concerned, or any error by DBS, it is not appropriate for the person to be included in the list[5].

1 As to the criteria for inclusion in the children's barred list see PARA 265. As to criteria for inclusion in the adults' barred list see PARA 266.
2 Ie a review under the Safeguarding Vulnerable Groups Act 2006 Sch 3 para 18 (see PARA 276), or an application thereunder, which has not yet been determined: Sch 3 para 18A(1) (Sch 3 para 18A added by the Protection of Freedoms Act 2012 s 71).
3 As to the Disclosure and Barring Service see PARA 265.
4 Safeguarding Vulnerable Groups Act 2006 Sch 3 para 18A(2) (as added (see note 2); Sch 3 para 18A(2), (3) amended by SI 2012/3006). As to the provision of information about persons included in barred lists see PARAS 267, 293.
5 Safeguarding Vulnerable Groups Act 2006 Sch 3 para 18A(3) (as added and amended: see notes 2, 4).

278. Making of representations where the whereabouts of a person is unknown. Any requirement[1] to give a person an opportunity to make representations does not apply if the Disclosure and Barring Service (DBS)[2] does not know and cannot reasonably ascertain the whereabouts of the person[3].

Where a person is included in a barred list[4] and:

(1)   before he was included in the list, DBS was unable to ascertain his whereabouts[5]; or

(2)   he did not, before the end of any time prescribed for the purpose, make representations as to why he should not be included in the list[6] and DBS grants him permission to make such representations out of time[7],

then if he makes such representations after the prescribed time DBS must consider the representations[8] and if it thinks that it is not appropriate for the person to be included in the list concerned, must remove him from the list[9].

1 Ie any requirement of the Safeguarding Vulnerable Groups Act 2006 Sch 3 (see PARAS 270–272).
2 As to the Disclosure and Barring Service see PARA 265.
3 Safeguarding Vulnerable Groups Act 2006 Sch 3 para 16(2) (Sch 3 paras 16(2), 17(1), (2)(b), (3)(a) amended by SI 2012/3006).
4 Ie except a person included in pursuance of Safeguarding Vulnerable Groups Act 2006 Sch 3 para 1 or Sch 3 para 7 (automatic inclusion in barred lists: see PARAS 265, 266).
5 Safeguarding Vulnerable Groups Act 2006 Sch 3 para 17(1) (as amended: see note 3).
6 Safeguarding Vulnerable Groups Act 2006 Sch 3 para 17(2)(a).
7 Safeguarding Vulnerable Groups Act 2006 Sch 3 para 17(2)(b) (as amended: see note 3).
8 Safeguarding Vulnerable Groups Act 2006 Sch 3 para 17(3)(a) (as amended: see note 3). For these purposes it is immaterial that any representations mentioned in Sch 3 para 17(3) relate to a time after the person was included in the list concerned: Sch 3 para 17(4).
9 Safeguarding Vulnerable Groups Act 2006 Sch 3 para 17(3)(b).

279. Appeals against failure to remove. An individual who is included in a barred list[1] may appeal to the Upper Tribunal[2] against a decision[3] not to remove him from the list[4]. Such an appeal may be made only on the grounds that the Disclosure and Barring Service (DBS)[5] has made a mistake on any point of law or in any finding of fact which it has made and on which the relevant decision was based[6], and only with the permission of the Upper Tribunal[7]. On such an appeal, the Tribunal must confirm the decision of DBS unless it finds that DBS has made a mistake of law or fact[8], and if the Tribunal finds that DBS has made such a mistake it must direct DBS to remove the person from the list or remit the matter to DBS for a new decision[9].

1 As to the criteria for inclusion in the children's barred list see PARA 265. As to criteria for inclusion in the adults' barred list see PARA 266. As to the making of representations about inclusion in barred lists see PARAS 270–274; as to challenging inclusions see PARAS 275–278. As to the provision of information about persons included in barred lists see PARAS 267, 293.
2 As to the Upper Tribunal see COURTS AND TRIBUNALS vol 24 (2010) PARA 874 et seq.

3 Ie a decision under the Safeguarding Vulnerable Groups Act 2006 Sch 3 para 17, 18 or 18A (see PARAS 276–278).
4 Safeguarding Vulnerable Groups Act 2006 s 4(1)(c) (s 4(1), (4)–(7) amended by SI 2008/2833; Safeguarding Vulnerable Groups Act 2006 s 4(1)(c) amended by the Protection of Freedoms Act 2012 Sch 9 para 44).
5 As to the Disclosure and Barring Service see PARA 265.
6 Safeguarding Vulnerable Groups Act 2006 s 4(2) (amended by SI 2012/3006). For these purposes the decision whether or not it is appropriate for an individual to be included in a barred list is not a question of law or fact: Safeguarding Vulnerable Groups Act 2006 s 4(3).
7 Safeguarding Vulnerable Groups Act 2006 s 4(4) (as amended: see note 4).
8 Safeguarding Vulnerable Groups Act 2006 s 4(5) (as amended (see note 4); s 4(5)–(7) amended by SI 2012/3006).
9 Safeguarding Vulnerable Groups Act 2006 s 4(6) (as amended: see notes 4, 8). If the Tribunal remits a matter to DBS under these provisions it may set out any findings of fact which it has made (on which DBS must base its new decision); and the person must be removed from the list until DBS makes its new decision, unless the Tribunal directs otherwise: s 4(7) (as so amended).

(iv) Referrals of Persons for Inclusion on Barred Lists

A.   COMPULSORY REFERRALS

280. Compulsory referrals by regulated activity providers. A regulated activity provider[1] must refer a person to the Disclosure and Barring Service (DBS)[2] if the provider withdraws permission for that person to engage in regulated activity[3] provided by him[4] because it thinks that, on or after 12 October 2009[5], the criteria for inclusion in a barred list[6] applies to that person[7], he has engaged in conduct[8] endangering a child or vulnerable adult[9], or he may cause harm[10] to a child or vulnerable adult (ie the 'harm test' is satisfied)[11]. A regulated activity provider must also refer such a person to DBS if he does not withdraw permission for any of those reasons but would or might have done so if the person had not otherwise ceased to engage in the activity[12]. For this purpose 'referral' involves the regulated activity provider providing DBS with specified information it holds in relation to the person[13]. Failure to comply with this duty is an offence[14].

1 As to the meaning of 'regulated activity provider' see PARAS 260–264.
2 As to the Disclosure and Barring Service see PARA 265.
3 As to the meaning of 'regulated activity' see PARAS 241–250 (children), PARAS 251–259 (vulnerable adults).
4 Safeguarding Vulnerable Groups Act 2006 s 35(2)(a) (s 35(2) amended by SI 2012/3006).
5 Ie the date on which the Safeguarding Vulnerable Groups Act 2006 s 35 was brought into force for all purposes by virtue of the Safeguarding Vulnerable Groups Act 2006 (Commencement No 6, Transitional Provisions and Savings) Order 2009, SI 2009/2611): Safeguarding Vulnerable Groups Act 2006 s 35(7).
6 Ie the Safeguarding Vulnerable Groups Act 2006 Sch 3 para 1, 2, 7 or 8: see PARAS 265, 266, 270.
7 Safeguarding Vulnerable Groups Act 2006 s 35(3)(a).
8 Ie 'relevant conduct' within the meaning of the Safeguarding Vulnerable Groups Act 2006 Sch 3 para 4 or 10: see PARA 271.
9 Safeguarding Vulnerable Groups Act 2006 s 35(3)(b). As to the meaning of 'child' see PARA 241 note 1. As to the meanings of 'adult' and 'vulnerable adult' see PARA 251 note 1. For these purposes conduct is inappropriate if it appears to the regulated activity provider to be inappropriate having regard to the guidance issued by the Secretary of State under the Safeguarding Vulnerable Groups Act 2006 Sch 3 para 4(6) or 10(6) (see PARA 271): s 35(5). For the purposes of s 35(3)(b), (c) it is immaterial whether there is a finding of fact in any proceedings: s 52. As to the Secretary of State see PARA 333. See also PARA 241 note 4.
10 Ie may harm a child or vulnerable adult, cause a child or vulnerable adult to be harmed, put a child or vulnerable adult at risk of harm, attempt to harm a child or vulnerable adult, or incite another to harm a child or vulnerable adult: Safeguarding Vulnerable Groups Act 2006 s 35(4).
11 Safeguarding Vulnerable Groups Act 2006 s 35(3)(c). See note 9.
12 Safeguarding Vulnerable Groups Act 2006 s 35(2)(b).

13 Safeguarding Vulnerable Groups Act 2006 s 35(1)(a), (2) (as amended: see note 4). The information which must be provided is the information specified in the Safeguarding Vulnerable Groups Act 2006 (Prescribed Information) Regulations 2008, SI 2008/3265, Sch 1 (see PARA 289): reg 3.

14 A person commits an offence if he is required under the Safeguarding Vulnerable Groups Act 2006 s 35 to provide information to DBS and he fails without reasonable excuse, to provide the information: s 38(1). A person guilty of the offence is liable on summary conviction to a fine not exceeding level 5 on the standard scale: s 38(2). As to the powers of magistrates' courts to issue fines on summary conviction see SENTENCING vol 92 (2015) PARA 176.

If an offence under s 38 (or under s 9 (use of person for regulated activity: see PARAS 312–314)) is committed by a body corporate and is proved to have been committed with the consent or connivance of, or to be attributable to neglect on the part of a director (which, in relation to a body corporate whose affairs are managed by its members, means a member of the body), manager, secretary or other similar officer of the body, or a person purporting to act in such a capacity, he (as well as the body) commits the offence: s 18(1), (3). If an offence under s 38 or s 9 is committed by a partnership (whether or not a limited partnership) and is proved to have been committed with the consent or connivance of, or to be attributable to neglect on the part of a partner, or a person purporting to act as a partner, he (as well as the partnership) commits the offence: s 18(2).

281. Compulsory referrals by personnel suppliers. A personnel supplier[1] must refer to the Disclosure and Barring Service (DBS)[2] a person who has been supplied by that supplier to another person if the supplier knows that the supplied person has ceased to be engaged in regulated activity[3] because it was thought that, on or after 12 October 2009[4], the criteria for inclusion in a barred list[5] applied to that person[6], he has engaged in conduct[7] endangering a child or vulnerable adult[8], or the 'harm test' is satisfied[9]. A personnel supplier must also refer such a person to DBS if the supplied person has not ceased to be engaged in regulated activity for any of those reasons but would or might have done so if he had not otherwise ceased to engage in the activity[10]. For this purpose 'referral' involves the personnel supplier providing DBS with specified information it holds in relation to the person[11]. Failure to comply with this duty is an offence[12].

1 As to the meaning of 'personnel supplier' see PARA 241 note 4. As to the similar duties of personnel suppliers which are employment agencies or employment businesses see PARA 282; as to the similar duties of personnel suppliers which are educational institutions see PARA 283.
2 As to the Disclosure and Barring Service see PARA 265.
3 Safeguarding Vulnerable Groups Act 2006 ss 35(2)(a), 36(1) (ss 35(2), 36(1) amended by SI 2012/3006). As to the meaning of 'regulated activity' see PARAS 241–250 (children), PARAS 251–259 (vulnerable adults).
4 Ie the date on which the Safeguarding Vulnerable Groups Act 2006 ss 35, 36 was brought into force for all purposes by virtue of the Safeguarding Vulnerable Groups Act 2006 (Commencement No 6, Transitional Provisions and Savings) Order 2009, SI 2009/2611): Safeguarding Vulnerable Groups Act 2006 ss 35(7), 36(10).
5 Ie the Safeguarding Vulnerable Groups Act 2006 Sch 3 para 1, 2, 7 or 8: see PARAS 265, 266, 270.
6 Safeguarding Vulnerable Groups Act 2006 s 35(3)(a).
7 Ie 'relevant conduct' within the meaning of the Safeguarding Vulnerable Groups Act 2006 Sch 3 para 4 or 10: see PARA 271.
8 Safeguarding Vulnerable Groups Act 2006 s 35(3)(b). As to the meaning of 'child' see PARA 241 note 1. As to the meanings of 'adult' and 'vulnerable adult' see PARA 251 note 1. As to when conduct is 'inappropriate' for these purposes see s 35(5); and PARA 280 note 9. For the purposes of s 35(3)(b), (c) it is immaterial whether there is a finding of fact in any proceedings: s 52.
9 Safeguarding Vulnerable Groups Act 2006 s 35(3)(c). As to the 'harm test' see s 35(4); and PARA 280 note 10.
10 Safeguarding Vulnerable Groups Act 2006 s 35(2)(b).
11 Safeguarding Vulnerable Groups Act 2006 s 36(1) (as amended: see note 3). The information that must be provided under s 36(1) is the information specified in the Safeguarding Vulnerable Groups Act 2006 (Prescribed Information) Regulations 2008, SI 2008/3265, Sch 1 (see PARA 289): reg 4(1)(a). For the additional information to be provided where the personnel supplier is an employment business or employment agency, see reg 4(1)(b); and PARA 282 note 13.
12 A person commits an offence if he is required under the Safeguarding Vulnerable Groups Act 2006 s 36 to provide information to DBS and he fails without reasonable excuse, to provide the

information: s 38(1). A person guilty of the offence is liable on summary conviction to a fine not exceeding level 5 on the standard scale: s 38(2). As to the powers of magistrates' courts to issue fines on summary conviction see SENTENCING vol 92 (2015) PARA 176.

282. Compulsory referrals by employment agencies or employment businesses. A personnel supplier[1] which is an employment agency or an employment business[2] must refer a person to the Disclosure and Barring Service (DBS)[3] if it determines to cease to act for that person[4] because it thinks that, on or after 12 October 2009[5], the criteria for inclusion in a barred list[6] applies to that person[7], he has engaged in conduct[8] endangering a child or vulnerable adult[9], or he may cause harm[10] to a child or vulnerable adult (ie the 'harm test' is satisfied)[11]. An employment agency or employment business must also refer such a person to DBS if it does not determine to cease to act for the person for any of those reasons but would or might have done so if the arrangement with, or employment of, him had not otherwise come to an end[12]. For this purpose 'referral' involves the employment agency or employment business providing DBS with specified information it holds in relation to the person[13]. Failure to comply with this duty is an offence[14].

1 As to the meaning of 'personnel supplier' see PARA 241 note 4.
2 As to the meanings of 'employment agency' and 'employment business' see PARA 241 note 4. An employment agency acts for a person if it makes arrangements with him with a view to finding him relevant employment with an employer or supplying him to employers for relevant employment by them (Safeguarding Vulnerable Groups Act 2006 s 36(7)), and an employment business acts for a person if it employs him to act for and under the control of other persons (s 36(8)). As to the meaning of 'employment' see the Employment Agencies Act 1973 s 13; and TRADE AND INDUSTRY vol 97 (2015) PARA 974 (definition applied by the Safeguarding Vulnerable Groups Act 2006 s 36(9)).
3 As to the Disclosure and Barring Service see PARA 265.
4 Safeguarding Vulnerable Groups Act 2006 s 36(2)(a) (s 36(2) amended by SI 2012/3006).
5 Ie the date on which the Safeguarding Vulnerable Groups Act 2006 s 36 was brought into force for all purposes by virtue of the Safeguarding Vulnerable Groups Act 2006 (Commencement No 6, Transitional Provisions and Savings) Order 2009, SI 2009/2611): Safeguarding Vulnerable Groups Act 2006 s 36(10).
6 Ie the Safeguarding Vulnerable Groups Act 2006 Sch 3 para 1, 2, 7 or 8: see PARAS 265, 266, 270.
7 Safeguarding Vulnerable Groups Act 2006 s 36(4)(a).
8 Ie 'relevant conduct' within the meaning of the Safeguarding Vulnerable Groups Act 2006 Sch 3 para 4 or 10: see PARA 271.
9 Safeguarding Vulnerable Groups Act 2006 s 36(4)(b). As to the meaning of 'child' see PARA 241 note 1. As to the meanings of 'adult' and 'vulnerable adult' see PARA 251 note 1. For these purposes conduct is inappropriate if it appears to the personnel supplier to be inappropriate having regard to the guidance issued by the Secretary of State under the Safeguarding Vulnerable Groups Act 2006 Sch 3 para 4(6) or 10(6) (see PARA 271): s 36(6). For the purposes of s 36(4)(b), (c) it is immaterial whether there is a finding of fact in any proceedings: s 52. As to the Secretary of State see PARA 333. See also PARA 241 note 4.
10 Ie may harm a child or vulnerable adult, cause a child or vulnerable adult to be harmed, put a child or vulnerable adult at risk of harm, attempt to harm a child or vulnerable adult, or incite another to harm a child or vulnerable adult: Safeguarding Vulnerable Groups Act 2006 s 36(5).
11 Safeguarding Vulnerable Groups Act 2006 s 36(4)(c). See note 9.
12 Safeguarding Vulnerable Groups Act 2006 s 36(2)(b).
13 Safeguarding Vulnerable Groups Act 2006 s 36(2)(a) (as amended: see note 4). The information that must be provided under s 36(2) is the information specified in the Safeguarding Vulnerable Groups Act 2006 (Prescribed Information) Regulations 2008, SI 2008/3265, Sch 1 (see PARA 289) (reg 4(1)(a)), and, where the personnel supplier is an employment business or employment agency, any other information held by the supplier under the Conduct of Employment Agencies and Employment Business Regulations 2003, SI 2003/3319, Sch 4 (particulars relating to work-seekers) (except the information specified in Sch 4 para 10) (Safeguarding Vulnerable Groups Act 2006 (Prescribed Information) Regulations 2008, SI 2008/3265, reg 4(1)(b)).
14 A person commits an offence if he is required under the Safeguarding Vulnerable Groups Act 2006 s 36 to provide information to DBS and he fails without reasonable excuse, to provide the information: s 38(1). A person guilty of the offence is liable on summary conviction to a fine not

exceeding level 5 on the standard scale: s 38(2). As to the powers of magistrates' courts to issue fines on summary conviction see SENTENCING vol 92 (2015) PARA 176.

283. Compulsory referrals by educational institutions. A personnel supplier[1] which is an educational institution[2] must refer a student following a course at the institution to the Disclosure and Barring Service (DBS)[3] if it determines to cease to supply that student to another person for him to engage in regulated activity[4], or if it determines that he should cease to follow a course at the institution[5], because it thinks that, on or after 12 October 2009[6], the criteria for inclusion in a barred list[7] applies to that student[8], he has engaged in conduct[9] endangering a child or vulnerable adult[10], or he may cause harm[11] to a child or vulnerable adult (ie the 'harm test' is satisfied)[12]. An educational institution must also refer such a student to DBS if it does not determine to cease to supply him or that he should cease to follow a course at the institution for any of those reasons but would or might have done so if he had not otherwise ceased to engage in the activity or ceased to follow the course[13]. For this purpose 'referral' involves the institution providing DBS with specified information it holds in relation to the student[14]. Failure to comply with this duty is an offence[15].

1   As to the meaning of 'personnel supplier' see PARA 241 note 4.
2   As to the meaning of 'educational institution' see PARA 246 note 2.
3   As to the Disclosure and Barring Service see PARA 265.
4   Safeguarding Vulnerable Groups Act 2006 s 36(3)(a) (s 36(3) amended by SI 2012/3006). As to the meaning of 'regulated activity' see PARAS 241–250 (children), PARAS 251–259 (vulnerable adults).
5   Safeguarding Vulnerable Groups Act 2006 s 36(3)(b).
6   Ie the date on which the Safeguarding Vulnerable Groups Act 2006 s 36 was brought into force for all purposes by virtue of the Safeguarding Vulnerable Groups Act 2006 (Commencement No 6, Transitional Provisions and Savings) Order 2009, SI 2009/2611): Safeguarding Vulnerable Groups Act 2006 s 36(10).
7   Ie the Safeguarding Vulnerable Groups Act 2006 Sch 3 para 1, 2, 7 or 8: see PARAS 265, 266, 270.
8   Safeguarding Vulnerable Groups Act 2006 s 36(4)(a).
9   Ie 'relevant conduct' within the meaning of the Safeguarding Vulnerable Groups Act 2006 Sch 3 para 4 or 10: see PARA 271.
10 Safeguarding Vulnerable Groups Act 2006 s 36(4)(b). As to the meaning of 'child' see PARA 241 note 1. As to the meanings of 'adult' and 'vulnerable adult' see PARA 251 note 1. For these purposes conduct is inappropriate if it appears to the personnel supplier to be inappropriate having regard to the guidance issued by the Secretary of State under the Safeguarding Vulnerable Groups Act 2006 Sch 3 para 4(6) or 10(6) (see PARA 271): s 36(6). For the purposes of s 36(4)(b), (c) it is immaterial whether there is a finding of fact in any proceedings: s 52. As to the Secretary of State see PARA 333. See also PARA 241 note 4.
11 Ie may harm a child or vulnerable adult, cause a child or vulnerable adult to be harmed, put a child or vulnerable adult at risk of harm, attempt to harm a child or vulnerable adult, or incite another to harm a child or vulnerable adult: Safeguarding Vulnerable Groups Act 2006 s 36(5).
12 Safeguarding Vulnerable Groups Act 2006 s 36(4)(c). See note 10.
13 Safeguarding Vulnerable Groups Act 2006 s 36(3)(c).
14 Safeguarding Vulnerable Groups Act 2006 s 36(3) (as amended: see note 4). The information that must be provided under s 36(3) is:
    (1)   the information specified in the Safeguarding Vulnerable Groups Act 2006 (Prescribed Information) Regulations 2008, SI 2008/3265, Sch 1 paras 1–3, 5, 6, 9, 10 (see PARA 289) (reg 4(2)(a));
    (2)   details of the course that the person is following at the educational institution including the name and duration of the course and the qualification or other accreditation to which the course leads (reg 4(2)(b));
    (3)   a copy of the person's application for a place on the course (reg 4(2)(c));
    (4)   the date on which the person began the course (reg 4(2)(d));
    (5)   details of any regulated activity in which the person has engaged as a result of having been supplied to another person by the educational institution for the purposes of engaging in such activity including the date on which any placement began and the duration of the placement, the name and address of the person to whom P was supplied, the setting and location of the placement, whether the activity was one relating to children or to vulnerable adults, and a description of the position held and the duties undertaken (reg 4(2)(e));

(6) the date on which and the reasons why the educational institution determined to cease to supply the person to another person for him to engage in regulated activity or that the person should cease to follow a course at the institution (reg 4(2)(f));

(7) where an educational institution does not make a determination as mentioned in head (6) above but would or might have done so if the person had not otherwise ceased to engage in the activity or ceased to follow the course, the reasons why the institution would or might have made any such determination (reg 4(2)(g));

(8) details of any comments or reports made by persons to whom the person was supplied for the purposes of engaging in the regulated activity (reg 4(2)(h)); and

(9) an assessment of the person's progress on the course (including his placements with persons for the purposes of engaging in regulated activity) (reg 4(2)(i)).

15 A person commits an offence if he is required under the Safeguarding Vulnerable Groups Act 2006 s 36 to provide information to DBS and he fails without reasonable excuse, to provide the information: s 38(1). A person guilty of the offence is liable on summary conviction to a fine not exceeding level 5 on the standard scale: s 38(2). As to the powers of magistrates' courts to issue fines on summary conviction see SENTENCING vol 92 (2015) PARA 176.

B. VOLUNTARY REFERRALS

284. Voluntary referrals by local authorities. If a local authority[1] thinks that a person has engaged in conduct[2] endangering a child or vulnerable adult[3] the authority may, if it thinks that the person is or has been, or might in future be, engaged in regulated activity[4] and that the Disclosure and Barring Service (DBS)[5] may[6] consider it appropriate for the person to be included in a barred list[7], provide DBS with any information it holds relating to that person[8]. If the conduct thought to have been engaged in occurred on or after 12 October 2009[9] the authority may provide such information only if it additionally thinks that the criteria for inclusion in a barred list[10] applies to the person[11] and that person may cause harm[12] to a child or vulnerable adult (ie the 'harm test' is satisfied)[13].

1 As to the meaning of 'local authority' see the Local Authorities (Goods and Services) Act 1970 s 1; and LOCAL GOVERNMENT vol 69 (2009) PARA 495 (definition applied by the Safeguarding Vulnerable Groups Act 2006 s 39(7)).

2 Ie 'relevant conduct' within the meaning of the Safeguarding Vulnerable Groups Act 2006 Sch 3 para 4 or 10: see PARA 271.

3 Safeguarding Vulnerable Groups Act 2006 s 39(2)(b), (5)(a) (s 39(1), (4)(b), (5) amended by SI 2012/3006). As to the meaning of 'child' see PARA 241 note 1. As to the meanings of 'adult' and 'vulnerable adult' see PARA 251 note 1. For these purposes conduct is inappropriate if it appears to the authority to be inappropriate having regard to the guidance issued by the Secretary of State under the Safeguarding Vulnerable Groups Act 2006 Sch 3 para 4(6) or 10(6) (see PARA 271): s 39(6). For the purposes of s 39(2)(b), (5)(a) it is immaterial whether there is a finding of fact in any proceedings: s 52. As to the Secretary of State see PARA 333. See also PARA 241 note 4.

4 Safeguarding Vulnerable Groups Act 2006 s 39(4)(a), (5)(b) (s 39(1), (4)(a), (b) amended by the Protection of Freedoms Act 2012 s 77(2)). As to the meaning of 'regulated activity' see PARAS 241–250 (children), PARAS 251–259 (vulnerable adults). See also note 7.

5 As to the Disclosure and Barring Service see PARA 265.

6 Ie except in a case where the Safeguarding Vulnerable Groups Act 2006 Sch 3 para 1 or 7 (automatic inclusion: see PARAS 265, 266) applies.

7 Safeguarding Vulnerable Groups Act 2006 s 39(4)(b) (as amended: see notes 3, 4). If the authority thinks that the person is or has been, or might in future be, engaged in regulated activity and that DBS may consider it appropriate for the person to be included in a barred list, the 'second condition' is said to be satisfied: s 39(4). As to the criteria for inclusion in the children's barred list see PARA 265. As to criteria for inclusion in the adults' barred list see PARA 266.

8 Safeguarding Vulnerable Groups Act 2006 s 39(1), (5) (as amended: see notes 3, 4).

9 Ie the date on which the Safeguarding Vulnerable Groups Act 2006 s 39 was brought into force for all purposes by virtue of the Safeguarding Vulnerable Groups Act 2006 (Commencement No 6, Transitional Provisions and Savings) Order 2009, SI 2009/2611).

10 Ie the Safeguarding Vulnerable Groups Act 2006 Sch 3 para 1, 2, 7 or 8: see PARAS 265, 266, 270.

11 Safeguarding Vulnerable Groups Act 2006 s 39(2)(a).

12 Ie may harm a child or vulnerable adult, cause a child or vulnerable adult to be harmed, put a child or vulnerable adult at risk of harm, attempt to harm a child or vulnerable adult, or incite another to harm a child or vulnerable adult: Safeguarding Vulnerable Groups Act 2006 s 39(3).

13 Safeguarding Vulnerable Groups Act 2006 s 39(2)(c). For the purposes of s 39(2)(c) it is immaterial whether there is a finding of fact in any proceedings: s 52.

285. Voluntary referrals by keepers of registers. A person may be referred to the Disclosure and Barring Service (DBS)[1] by the keepers of the registers of pharmacists[2], medical practitioners[3], dentists[4], optometrists and dispensing opticians[5], osteopaths[6], chiropractors[7], nurses and midwives[8], and (in Wales) social workers and ancillary care professionals[9]. If a keeper of a relevant register[10] thinks that a person has engaged in conduct[11] endangering a child or vulnerable adult[12] the keeper may, if it thinks that the person is or has been, or might in future be, engaged in regulated activity[13] and that DBS may[14] consider it appropriate for the person to be included in a barred list[15], provide DBS with any information they hold relating to that person[16]. If the conduct thought to have been engaged in occurred on or after 12 October 2009[17] the keeper may provide such information only if it additionally thinks that the criteria for inclusion in a barred list[18] applies to the person[19] and that person may cause harm[20] to a child or vulnerable adult (ie the 'harm test' is satisfied)[21].

1   As to the Disclosure and Barring Service see PARA 265.
2   Ie the register maintained under the Pharmacy Order 2010, SI 2010/231, art 19 (see MEDICAL PROFESSIONS vol 74 (2011) PARA 821 et seq), the keeper of which for these purposes is the registrar appointed under art 18 (see MEDICAL PROFESSIONS vol 74 (2011) PARA 789): Safeguarding Vulnerable Groups Act 2006 s 41(7) (amended by SI 2010/231).
3   Ie any of the lists of medical practitioners kept under the Medical Act 1983 s 2 (see MEDICAL PROFESSIONS vol 74 (2011) PARA 211), the keeper of which for these purposes is the registrar of the General Medical Council (see MEDICAL PROFESSIONS vol 74 (2011) PARA 179 et seq): Safeguarding Vulnerable Groups Act 2006 s 41(7) (amended by the Protection of Freedoms Act 2012 Sch 9 para 64).
4   Ie the dentists register kept under the Dentists Act 1984 s 14 (see MEDICAL PROFESSIONS vol 74 (2011) PARA 410) or the dental care professionals register kept under s 36B (see MEDICAL PROFESSIONS vol 74 (2011) PARA 474), the keeper of which for these purposes is the registrar appointed under s 14: Safeguarding Vulnerable Groups Act 2006 s 41(7).
5   Ie the register of optometrists or the register of dispensing opticians maintained under the Opticians Act 1989 s 7 (see MEDICAL PROFESSIONS vol 74 (2011) PARA 344), or the register of persons undertaking training as optometrists or the register of persons undertaking training as dispensing opticians maintained under s 8A (see MEDICAL PROFESSIONS vol 74 (2011) PARA 345), the keeper of which for these purposes is the Registrar of the General Optical Council (see MEDICAL PROFESSIONS vol 74 (2011) PARA 319 et seq): Safeguarding Vulnerable Groups Act 2006 s 41(7).
6   Ie the register of osteopaths maintained under the Osteopaths Act 1993 s 2 (see MEDICAL PROFESSIONS vol 74 (2011) PARA 533), the keeper of which for these purposes is the Registrar of Osteopaths (see MEDICAL PROFESSIONS vol 74 (2011) PARA 533): Safeguarding Vulnerable Groups Act 2006 s 41(7).
7   Ie the register of chiropractors maintained under the Chiropractors Act 1994 s 2 (see MEDICAL PROFESSIONS vol 74 (2011) PARA 611), the keeper of which for these purposes is the Registrar of Chiropractors (see MEDICAL PROFESSIONS vol 74 (2011) PARA 611): Safeguarding Vulnerable Groups Act 2006 s 41(7).
8   Ie the register of qualified nurses and midwives maintained under the Nursing and Midwifery Order 2001, SI 2002/253, art 5 (see MEDICAL PROFESSIONS vol 74 (2011) PARA 713), the keeper of which for these purposes is the registrar appointed under art 4 (see MEDICAL PROFESSIONS vol 74 (2011) PARA 712): Safeguarding Vulnerable Groups Act 2006 s 41(7).
9   Ie:
    (1)   the register of social workers and social care workers in Wales maintained under the Regulation and Inspection of Social Care (Wales) Act 2016 s 80 (see PARA 201) (the keeper of which for these purposes is the Registrar appointed under s 81 (see PARA 412)) (Safeguarding Vulnerable Groups Act 2006 s 41(7) (amended by the Health and Social Care Act 2012 s 213(7)(m), Sch 15 para 52; and by the Regulation and Inspection of Social Care (Wales) Act 2016 Sch 3 para 54); and
    (2)   the register of members of relevant professions maintained under the Health and Social Work Professions Order 2001, SI 2001/254, art 5 (see MEDICAL PROFESSIONS vol 74 (2011) PARA 928) (the keeper of which for these purposes is the registrar appointed

under art 4 (see MEDICAL PROFESSIONS vol 74 (2011) PARA 922)) (Safeguarding Vulnerable Groups Act 2006 s 41(7) (amended by the Health and Social Care Act 2012 s 213(7)(m), Sch 15 para 52)).

10 See the text and notes 1–9.

11 Ie 'relevant conduct' within the meaning of the Safeguarding Vulnerable Groups Act 2006 Sch 3 para 4 or 10: see PARA 271.

12 Safeguarding Vulnerable Groups Act 2006 s 41(2)(b), (5)(a) (s 41(1), (4)(b), (5) amended by SI 2012/3006). As to the meaning of 'child' see PARA 241 note 1. As to the meanings of 'adult' and 'vulnerable adult' see PARA 251 note 1. For these purposes conduct is inappropriate if it appears to the keeper to be inappropriate having regard to the guidance issued by the Secretary of State under the Safeguarding Vulnerable Groups Act 2006 Sch 3 para 4(6) or 10(6) (see PARA 271): s 41(6). For the purposes of s 41(2)(b), (5)(a) it is immaterial whether there is a finding of fact in any proceedings: s 52. As to the Secretary of State see PARA 333. See also PARA 241 note 4.

13 Safeguarding Vulnerable Groups Act 2006 s 41(4)(a), (5)(b) (s 41(1), (4)(a), (b) amended by the Protection of Freedoms Act 2012 s 75(1)). As to the meaning of 'regulated activity' see PARAS 241–250 (children), PARAS 251–259 (vulnerable adults). See also note 16.

14 Ie except in a case where the Safeguarding Vulnerable Groups Act 2006 Sch 3 para 1 or 7 (automatic inclusion: see PARAS 265, 266) applies.

15 Safeguarding Vulnerable Groups Act 2006 s 41(4)(b) (as amended: see notes 12, 13). If the keeper thinks that the person is or has been, or might in future be, engaged in regulated activity and that DBS may consider it appropriate for the person to be included in a barred list, the 'second condition' is said to be satisfied: s 41(4). As to when the second condition is satisfied in particular circumstances see note 21. As to the criteria for inclusion in the children's barred list see PARA 265. As to criteria for inclusion in the adults' barred list see PARA 266.

16 Safeguarding Vulnerable Groups Act 2006 s 41(1), (5) (as amended: see notes 12, 13).

17 Ie the date on which the Safeguarding Vulnerable Groups Act 2006 s 39 was brought into force for all purposes by virtue of the Safeguarding Vulnerable Groups Act 2006 (Commencement No 6, Transitional Provisions and Savings) Order 2009, SI 2009/2611).

18 Ie the Safeguarding Vulnerable Groups Act 2006 Sch 3 para 1, 2, 7 or 8: see PARAS 265, 266, 270.

19 Safeguarding Vulnerable Groups Act 2006 s 41(2)(a).

20 Ie may harm a child or vulnerable adult, cause a child or vulnerable adult to be harmed, put a child or vulnerable adult at risk of harm, attempt to harm a child or vulnerable adult, or incite another to harm a child or vulnerable adult: Safeguarding Vulnerable Groups Act 2006 s 41(3).

21 Safeguarding Vulnerable Groups Act 2006 s 41(2)(c). For the purposes of s 41(2)(c) it is immaterial whether there is a finding of fact in any proceedings: s 52.

286. Voluntary referrals by supervisory authorities. A person may be referred to the Disclosure and Barring Service (DBS)[1] by the Secretary of State[2], the Welsh Ministers[3], the Care Quality Commission[4], the Public Guardian[5], Her Majesty's Chief Inspector of Education, Children's Services and Skills[6], Her Majesty's Chief Inspector of Education and Training in Wales[7], the Charity Commissioners for England and Wales[8], and a registration authority under the Care Standards Act 2000[9]. If any such authority (a 'supervisory authority') thinks that a person has engaged in conduct[10] endangering a child or vulnerable adult[11] the authority may, if it thinks that the person is or has been, or might in future be, engaged in regulated activity[12] and that DBS may[13] consider it appropriate for the person to be included in a barred list[14], provide DBS with any information they hold relating to that person[15]. If the conduct thought to have been engaged in occurred on or after 12 October 2009[16] the authority may provide such information only if it additionally thinks that the criteria for inclusion in a barred list[17] applies to the person[18] and that person may cause harm[19] to a child or vulnerable adult (ie the 'harm test' is satisfied)[20].

1 As to the Disclosure and Barring Service see PARA 265.

2 Ie in respect of his functions under the Education Act 2002 Pt 10 Ch 1 (ss 156A–171) (regulation of independent schools: see EDUCATION vol 35 (2015) PARA 416 et seq) (Safeguarding Vulnerable Groups Act 2006 s 45(7)(aa) (added by SI 2010/1073)) and, as from a day to be appointed under the Education Act 2011 s 82(3), in respect of his functions under the Education Act 2002 ss 141B–141E (teacher misconduct: see EDUCATION vol 36 (2015) PARAS 1068–1071) and the Education and Skills Act 2008 Pt 4 Ch 1 (ss 92–141) (independent educational institutions: see EDUCATION vol 35 (2015) PARA 382 et seq): Safeguarding Vulnerable Groups Act 2006

s 45(7)(aza), (azb) (prospectively added by the Education Act 2011 Sch 2 para 27). At the date at which this volume states the law no day had been appointed for the coming into force of these provisions. As to the Secretary of State see PARA 333. See also PARA 241 note 4.

3 Ie in respect of their functions under the Education Act 2002 Pt 10 Ch 1, the Health and Social Care (Community Health and Standards) Act 2003 Pt 2 Ch 4 (ss 70–75) (NHS Health Care: see HEALTH SERVICES vol 54A (2017) PARAS 656–657) and Pt 2 Ch 6 (ss 92–101) (social services), and the Children Act 1989 Pt 11 (ss 80–84) (supervisory functions: see CHILDREN AND YOUNG PERSONS vol 9 (2017) PARAS 171–175) and Pt 12 (ss 85–108) (miscellaneous and general: see CHILDREN AND YOUNG PERSONS): Safeguarding Vulnerable Groups Act 2006 s 45(7)(b), (e), (ea), (9) (s 45(7)(b), (e) amended by SI 2009/2610; Safeguarding Vulnerable Groups Act 2006 s 45(7)(c) substituted, s 45(7)(e) also amended, by the Health and Social Care Act 2008 Sch 5 para 91; Safeguarding Vulnerable Groups Act 2006 s 45(7)(ea) added by SI 2009/1797).

4 Ie in respect of its functions under the Health and Social Care Act 2008 Pt 1 (ss 1–97): Safeguarding Vulnerable Groups Act 2006 s 45(7)(c) (as substituted: see note 3).

5 Ie in the exercise of his functions (see MENTAL HEALTH AND CAPACITY vol 75 (2013) PARA 752): Safeguarding Vulnerable Groups Act 2006 s 45(7)(f).

6 Ie in the exercise of his functions (see EDUCATION vol 36 (2015) PARA 1151 et seq): Safeguarding Vulnerable Groups Act 2006 s 45(7)(g) (which refers to Her Majesty's Chief Inspector of Schools in England, an office that has been abolished and replaced by Her Majesty's Chief Inspector of Education, Children's Services and Skills: see EDUCATION).

7 Ie in the exercise of his functions (see EDUCATION vol 36 (2015) PARA 1148 et seq): Safeguarding Vulnerable Groups Act 2006 s 45(7)(h).

8 Ie in the exercise of their functions (see CHARITIES vol 8 (2015) PARA 543 et seq): Safeguarding Vulnerable Groups Act 2006 s 45(7)(i).

9 Ie a registration authority within the meaning of the Care Standards Act 2000 s 5 (see CHILDREN AND YOUNG PERSONS vol 10 (2017) PARA 1017) in respect of its functions under Pt 2 (ss 11–42) (establishments and agencies: see CHILDREN AND YOUNG PERSONS vol 10 (2017) PARA 1017 et seq): Safeguarding Vulnerable Groups Act 2006 s 45(7)(a).

10 Ie 'relevant conduct' within the meaning of the Safeguarding Vulnerable Groups Act 2006 Sch 3 para 4 or 10: see PARA 271.

11 Safeguarding Vulnerable Groups Act 2006 s 45(2)(b), (5)(a) (s 45(1), (4)(b), (5) amended by SI 2012/3006). As to the meaning of 'child' see PARA 241 note 1. As to the meanings of 'adult' and 'vulnerable adult' see PARA 251 note 1. For these purposes conduct is inappropriate if it appears to the authority to be inappropriate having regard to the guidance issued by the Secretary of State under the Safeguarding Vulnerable Groups Act 2006 Sch 3 para 4(6) or 10(6) (see PARA 271): s 45(10). For the purposes of s 45(2)(b), (5)(a) it is immaterial whether there is a finding of fact in any proceedings: s 52.

12 Safeguarding Vulnerable Groups Act 2006 s 45(4)(a), (5)(b) (s 45(1), (4)(a), (b) amended by the Protection of Freedoms Act 2012 s 76(1)). As to the meaning of 'regulated activity' see PARAS 241–250 (children), PARAS 251–259 (vulnerable adults). See also note 14.

13 Ie except in a case where the Safeguarding Vulnerable Groups Act 2006 Sch 3 para 1 or 7 (automatic inclusion: see PARAS 265, 266) applies.

14 Safeguarding Vulnerable Groups Act 2006 s 45(4)(b) (as amended: see notes 11, 12). If the authority thinks that the person is or has been, or might in future be, engaged in regulated activity and that DBS may consider it appropriate for the person to be included in a barred list, the 'second condition' is said to be satisfied: s 45(4). As to the criteria for inclusion in the children's barred list see PARA 265. As to criteria for inclusion in the adults' barred list see PARA 265.

15 Safeguarding Vulnerable Groups Act 2006 s 45(1), (5) (as amended: see notes 11, 12).

16 Ie the date on which the Safeguarding Vulnerable Groups Act 2006 s 45 was brought into force for all purposes by virtue of the Safeguarding Vulnerable Groups Act 2006 (Commencement No 6, Transitional Provisions and Savings) Order 2009, SI 2009/2611).

17 Ie the Safeguarding Vulnerable Groups Act 2006 Sch 3 para 1, 2, 7 or 8: see PARAS 265, 266, 270.

18 Safeguarding Vulnerable Groups Act 2006 s 45(2)(a).

19 Ie may harm a child or vulnerable adult, cause a child or vulnerable adult to be harmed, put a child or vulnerable adult at risk of harm, attempt to harm a child or vulnerable adult, or incite another to harm a child or vulnerable adult: Safeguarding Vulnerable Groups Act 2006 s 45(3).

20 Safeguarding Vulnerable Groups Act 2006 s 45(2)(c). For the purposes of s 45(2)(c) it is immaterial whether there is a finding of fact in any proceedings: s 52.

(v) Collection of Barring Information by the Disclosure and Barring Service

287. Information on persons included on barred lists. Where an individual is included in a barred list[1] the Disclosure and Barring Service (DBS)[2] must keep the following information in respect of that person:

(1)   any alternative names and aliases of the individual[3];

(2)   the individual's date and place of birth[4];

(3)   the address of the individual[5];

(4)   the Police National Computer identification number[6] relating to the individual[7];

(5)   the criminal record certificate number[8] relating to the individual[9];

(6)   the national insurance number of the individual[10]; and

(7)   all additional information relating to the identity of the individual[11].

1   As to the criteria for inclusion in the children's barred list see PARA 265. As to criteria for inclusion in the adults' barred list see PARA 266.
2   As to the Disclosure and Barring Service see PARA 265.
3   Safeguarding Vulnerable Groups Act 2006 s 2(5) (amended by SI 2012/3006); Safeguarding Vulnerable Groups Act 2006 (Barred List Prescribed Information) Regulations 2008, SI 2008/16, reg 2, 3(a) (reg 3 amended by SI 2012/3006; SI 2012/3006).
4   Safeguarding Vulnerable Groups Act 2006 (Barred List Prescribed Information) Regulations 2008, SI 2008/16, reg 3(b) (as amended: see note 3).
5   Safeguarding Vulnerable Groups Act 2006 (Barred List Prescribed Information) Regulations 2008, SI 2008/16, reg 3(c) (as amended: see note 3).
6   The 'Police National Computer identification number' means the reference number used on the Police National Computer to identify a particular individual: Safeguarding Vulnerable Groups Act 2006 (Barred List Prescribed Information) Regulations 2008, SI 2008/16, reg 1.
7   Safeguarding Vulnerable Groups Act 2006 (Barred List Prescribed Information) Regulations 2008, SI 2008/16, reg 3(f) (as amended: see note 3).
8   The 'criminal record certificate number' means the number relating to any criminal record certificate within the meaning of the Police Act 1997 s 113A (see SENTENCING vol 92 (2015) PARAS 641, 642) or any enhanced criminal record certificate within the meaning of 113B (see SENTENCING vol 92 (2015) PARAS 640–642): Safeguarding Vulnerable Groups Act 2006 (Barred List Prescribed Information) Regulations 2008, SI 2008/16, reg 1 (amended by SI 2012/2112).
9   Safeguarding Vulnerable Groups Act 2006 (Barred List Prescribed Information) Regulations 2008, SI 2008/16, reg 3(g) (substituted by SI 2012/2112).
10 Safeguarding Vulnerable Groups Act 2006 (Barred List Prescribed Information) Regulations 2008, SI 2008/16, reg 3(h) (as amended: see note 3).
11 Safeguarding Vulnerable Groups Act 2006 (Barred List Prescribed Information) Regulations 2008, SI 2008/16, reg 3(i) (as amended: see note 3).

288. Information relating to functions of Disclosure and Barring Service. Where an individual is included in a barred list[1] the Disclosure and Barring Service (DBS)[2] must keep the following information related to its functions in respect of that person's inclusion:

(1)   the date of the individual's inclusion on the barred list[3];

(2)   all information provided to DBS which it considers relevant to the decision of whether or not the individual should be barred[4];

(3)   any information provided to DBS[5] by keepers of relevant registers or supervisory authorities[6];

(4)   relevant police information provided to DBS but which DBS must not take account of for the purpose of deciding[7] whether or not the individual should be barred[8];

(5)   the reasons for DBS's decision to bar the individual, including any findings of fact made by DBS giving rise to that decision[9];

(6)   any information provided to DBS, including representations made to it by the individual, which DBS considers might be relevant to any subsequent appeal or review[10]; and

(7)   the outcome of any such appeal or review and any information provided to or held by DBS following such proceedings, including any findings of fact[11].

1   As to the criteria for inclusion in the children's barred list see PARA 265. As to criteria for inclusion in the adults' barred list see PARA 266.
2   As to the Disclosure and Barring Service see PARA 265.
3   Safeguarding Vulnerable Groups Act 2006 (Barred List Prescribed Information) Regulations 2008, SI 2008/16, reg 4(a) (reg 4 amended by SI 2012/3006).
4   Safeguarding Vulnerable Groups Act 2006 (Barred List Prescribed Information) Regulations 2008, SI 2008/16, reg 4(b) (as amended: see note 3).
5   Ie in accordance with the Safeguarding Vulnerable Groups Act 2006 s 41 (registers: power to refer: see PARA 285) and s 45 (supervisory authorities: power to refer: see PARA 286).
6   Safeguarding Vulnerable Groups Act 2006 (Barred List Prescribed Information) Regulations 2008, SI 2008/16, reg 4(c) (as amended: see note 3).
7   Ie in accordance with the Safeguarding Vulnerable Groups Act 2006 Sch 3 para 19(5), (6) (information which the chief officer of a relevant police force thinks that it would not be in the interests of the prevention or detection of crime to disclose to the individual: see PARA 292).
8   Safeguarding Vulnerable Groups Act 2006 (Barred List Prescribed Information) Regulations 2008, SI 2008/16, reg 4(d) (as amended: see note 3).
9   Safeguarding Vulnerable Groups Act 2006 (Barred List Prescribed Information) Regulations 2008, SI 2008/16, reg 4(e) (as amended: see note 3).
10 Safeguarding Vulnerable Groups Act 2006 (Barred List Prescribed Information) Regulations 2008, SI 2008/16, reg 4(f) (as amended: see note 3).
11 Safeguarding Vulnerable Groups Act 2006 (Barred List Prescribed Information) Regulations 2008, SI 2008/16, reg 4(g) (as amended: see note 3).

B.   INFORMATION ABOUT PROPOSED INCLUSIONS AND REMOVALS

289. Information to be provided in connection with the inclusion of persons in barred lists. Where regulated activity providers[1] are required, pursuant to the inclusion of a person in or the removal of a person from a barred list[2], to provide information about that person to the Disclosure and Barring Service (DBS)[3], the information which may be required may include all or some of the following:

(1)   specified information identifying the person in question[4];

(2)   a description of the regulated activity that the person is, or was, engaged in[5];

(3)   information as to whether or not the person is included in any relevant register[6] or any register established and maintained by a supervisory authority[7] and, if so, details of the relevant entries in any such register[8];

(4)   specified information (including copies of relevant documents) relating to the person's employment[9];

(5)   information (including copies of relevant documents) relating to the person's conduct[10];

(6)   information relating to the reason why the person providing information to DBS[11] considers that the harm test is satisfied in relation to that person[12];

(7)   details of any investigation undertaken by any person in relation to the person's conduct[13];

(8)   details of any disciplinary proceedings or measures taken, or to be taken, in relation to the person's conduct[14];

(9)   details of any other proceedings before any court, tribunal or any other person taken or to be taken in relation to the person's conduct[15]; and

(10) details of any action taken, or to be taken, by the person referring or providing information to DBS in relation to the person's conduct[16].

1 As to the meaning of 'regulated activity provider' see PARAS 260–264.
2 Ie pursuant to the Safeguarding Vulnerable Groups Act 2006 s 35 (duty of regulated activity providers who withdraw permission for a person to engage in a regulated activity to inform Disclosure and Barring Service (DBS): see PARA 280), s 36 (duty of personnel suppliers to inform Disclosure and Barring Service where a person has ceased to be engaged in regulated activity: see PARAS 282, 283), s 37 (information to be provided by regulated activity providers in relation to persons proposed to be included on or removed from barred lists: see PARA 290), s 40 (information to be provided by local authorities in relation to persons proposed to be included on barred lists: see PARA 291), s 42 (information to be provided by keepers of registers in relation to persons proposed to be included on barred lists: see PARA 291), or s 46 (information to be provided by supervisory authorities in relation to persons proposed to be included on barred lists: see PARA 291).
3 As to the Disclosure and Barring Service see PARA 265.
4 Ie the person's full name and title, any other name or names by which the person may be known, the person's date of birth, the person's national insurance number, the person's gender, and the person's last known address (including postcode): Safeguarding Vulnerable Groups Act 2006 (Prescribed Information) Regulations 2008, SI 2008/3265, Sch 1 para 1 (amended by SI 2012/2112).
5 Safeguarding Vulnerable Groups Act 2006 (Prescribed Information) Regulations 2008, SI 2008/3265, Sch 1 para 2.
6 Ie as defined in the Safeguarding Vulnerable Groups Act 2006 s 41(7): see PARA 285.
7 As to the supervisory authorities for the purposes of the Safeguarding Vulnerable Groups Act 2006: see s 45(7); and PARA 286.
8 Safeguarding Vulnerable Groups Act 2006 (Prescribed Information) Regulations 2008, SI 2008/3265, Sch 1 para 3.
9 Ie: the application for employment made by the person and the letter of appointment; the person's job description including the position held and the duties undertaken by him; the date on which the person started the employment; the person's qualifications, employment history and disciplinary record; details of any relevant training undertaken by the person; whether or not the person is still employed and if so, his current job description and a description of his duties; if the person is no longer employed, the date from which and the circumstances in which he ceased to be so employed; the reasons why permission was withdrawn for the person to engage in the regulated activity in question or, where such permission was not withdrawn (but would or might have been withdrawn had the person not otherwise ceased to engage in the activity), the reasons why such permission would have or might have been withdrawn: Safeguarding Vulnerable Groups Act 2006 (Prescribed Information) Regulations 2008, SI 2008/3265, Sch 1 para 4.
10 Ie: a summary of the conduct including details of the setting and location in which such conduct occurred; details of any harm suffered by any child or vulnerable adult resulting from or arising from the conduct or any risk of harm that a child or vulnerable adult was, or may have been, exposed to as a result of such conduct (and, in connection with any such child or vulnerable adult, his name and date of birth, details of the relationship between the person and the child or vulnerable adult, information relating to the vulnerability of the child or vulnerable adult that may be relevant to DBS's consideration of whether to include or remove the person in or from a barred list including any emotional, behavioural, medical or physical condition), whether the person has accepted responsibility for or admitted the conduct or any part of it, any explanation offered by the person for the conduct or any remorse or insight demonstrated by the person in relation to the conduct, and any information other than that relating to the person's conduct which is likely to, or may, be relevant in considering whether the person should be included in or removed from a barred list including information relating to any previous offences, allegations, incidents, behaviour or other acts or omissions): Safeguarding Vulnerable Groups Act 2006 (Prescribed Information) Regulations 2008, SI 2008/3265, Sch 1 para 5 (amended by SI 2012/3006). A reference to the person's conduct is a reference to any offence which he has committed or is alleged to have committed, any incident involving him or any behaviour or other act or omission of his that gave rise to the provision of information to DBS under the Safeguarding Vulnerable Groups Act 2006 s 35 (see PARAS 280, 281), s 36 (see PARAS 281, 282), s 39 (see PARA 284), s 41 (see PARA 285) or s 45 (see PARA 286) or in relation to which DBS is considering whether to include or remove the person in or from a barred list: Safeguarding Vulnerable Groups Act 2006 (Prescribed Information) Regulations 2008, SI 2008/3265, reg 2(2). As to the meaning of 'child' see PARA 241 note 1. As to the meanings of 'adult' and 'vulnerable adult' see PARA 251 note 1.
11 Ie under the Safeguarding Vulnerable Groups Act 2006 s 35 or s 36.

12 Safeguarding Vulnerable Groups Act 2006 (Prescribed Information) Regulations 2008, SI 2008/3265, Sch 1 para 6 (amended by SI 2012/3006).
13 Ie including the evidence and information obtained and considered in any such investigation, the outcome of the investigation (if known), and contact details (including a name, address, telephone number and e-mail address) of any person responsible for the investigation: Safeguarding Vulnerable Groups Act 2006 (Prescribed Information) Regulations 2008, SI 2008/3265, Sch 1 para 7.
14 Ie including the evidence and information obtained and considered in such proceedings or with respect to such measures and the outcome of any disciplinary proceedings or measures taken including a copy of any decision or other document evidencing the outcome of such action: Safeguarding Vulnerable Groups Act 2006 (Prescribed Information) Regulations 2008, SI 2008/3265, Sch 1 para 8.
15 Ie including the outcome of any such proceedings, and including proceedings commenced under the Children Act 1989: Safeguarding Vulnerable Groups Act 2006 (Prescribed Information) Regulations 2008, SI 2008/3265, Sch 1 para 9 (amended by SI 2012/2112).
16 Ie including whether or not the matter has been referred to the police or to any other person: Safeguarding Vulnerable Groups Act 2006 (Prescribed Information) Regulations 2008, SI 2008/3265, Sch 1 para 10 (amended by SI 2012/3006).

290. Collection of Information from regulated service providers. If the Disclosure and Barring Service (DBS)[1] is considering whether to include any person in a barred list[2] or whether to remove any person from a barred list[3] it may require the following persons to provide it with specified information relating to that person[4]:

(1)   any regulated activity provider[5] who has made arrangements for that person to engage in regulated activity (whether or not the arrangements are still in place)[6];

(2)   any personnel supplier[7] which is an employment agency or employment business and which acts for or has acted for that person[8]; and

(3)   any personnel supplier which is an educational institution[9] and which has supplied that person to another person for him to engage in regulated activity[10].

Failure to provide any such information is an offence[11].

1   As to the Disclosure and Barring Service see PARA 265.
2   Safeguarding Vulnerable Groups Act 2006 s 37(1)(a) (s 37(1), (2) amended by SI 2012/3006). As to the criteria for inclusion in the children's barred list see PARA 265. As to criteria for inclusion in the adults' barred list see PARA 266.
3   Safeguarding Vulnerable Groups Act 2006 s 37(1)(b) (as amended: see note 2).
4   The information that must be provided under the Safeguarding Vulnerable Groups Act 2006 s 37(2) is:
     (1)   the information specified in the Safeguarding Vulnerable Groups Act 2006 (Prescribed Information) Regulations 2008, SI 2008/3265, Sch 1 paras 1–3, 5, 6, 9, 10 (see PARA 289) (regs 4(2)(a), 5(3));
     (2)   details of the course that the person is following at the educational institution including the name and duration of the course and the qualification or other accreditation to which the course leads (reg 4(2)(b));
     (3)   a copy of the person's application for a place on the course (reg 4(2)(c));
     (4)   the date on which the person began the course (reg 4(2)(d));
     (5)   details of any regulated activity in which the person has engaged as a result of his having been supplied to another person by the educational institution for the purposes of engaging in such activity including the date on which any placement began and the duration of the placement, the name and address of the person to whom the person was supplied, the setting and location of the placement, whether the activity was one relating to children or to vulnerable adults, and a description of the position held and the duties undertaken by the person (reg 4(2)(e));
     (6)   the date on which and the reasons why the educational institution determined to cease to supply the person to another person for the person to engage in regulated activity or that the person should cease to follow a course at the institution (reg 4(2)(f));
     (7)   where an educational institution does not make a determination as mentioned in head (6) above but would or might have done so if the person had not otherwise ceased to engage in the activity or ceased to follow the course, the reasons why the institution would or might have made any such determination (reg 4(2)(g));

(8) details of any comments or reports made by persons to whom the person was supplied for the purposes of engaging in the regulated activity (reg 4(2)(h)); and

(9) an assessment of the person's progress on the course (including his placements with persons for the purposes of engaging in regulated activity) (reg 4(2)(i)).

As to the meaning of 'regulated activity' see PARAS 241–250 (children), PARAS 251–259 (vulnerable adults). As to the meaning of 'child' see PARA 241 note 1. As to the meanings of 'adult' and 'vulnerable adult' see PARA 251 note 1.

5 As to the meaning of 'regulated activity provider' see PARAS 260–264.

6 Safeguarding Vulnerable Groups Act 2006 s 37(2)(a) (as amended: see note 2). The information that must be provided under s 37(2)(a) is the information specified in the Safeguarding Vulnerable Groups Act 2006 (Prescribed Information) Regulations 2008, SI 2008/3265, Sch 1 (see PARA 289): reg 5(1).

7 As to the meaning of 'personnel supplier' see PARA 241 note 4.

8 Safeguarding Vulnerable Groups Act 2006 s 37(2)(c) (as amended: see note 2). The information that must be provided under s 37(2)(c) is the information specified in the Safeguarding Vulnerable Groups Act 2006 (Prescribed Information) Regulations 2008, SI 2008/3265, Sch 1 (regs 4(1)(a), 5(2)), and, where the personnel supplier is an employment business or employment agency, any other information held by that personnel supplier under the Conduct of Employment Agencies and Employment Business Regulations 2003, SI 2003/3319, Sch 4 (particulars relating to work-seekers: see TRADE AND INDUSTRY) (except the information specified in Sch 4 para 10) (Safeguarding Vulnerable Groups Act 2006 (Prescribed Information) Regulations 2008, SI 2008/3265, reg 4(1)(b)).

As to the meanings of 'employment agency' and 'employment business' see PARA 241 note 4. An employment agency acts for a person if it makes arrangements with him with a view to finding him relevant employment with an employer or supplying him to employers for relevant employment by them (Safeguarding Vulnerable Groups Act 2006 s 37(3)), and an employment business acts for a person if it employs him to engage in regulated activity for and under the control of other persons (s 37(5)). As to the meaning of 'employment' see the Employment Agencies Act 1973 s 13; and TRADE AND INDUSTRY vol 97 (2015) PARA 974 (definition applied by the Safeguarding Vulnerable Groups Act 2006 s 37(6)). Relevant employment is employment which consists in or involves engaging in regulated activity: s 37(4).

9 As to the meaning of 'educational institution' see PARA 246 note 2.

10 Safeguarding Vulnerable Groups Act 2006 s 37(2)(d) (as amended: see note 2).

11 A person commits an offence if he is required in pursuance of the Safeguarding Vulnerable Groups Act 2006 s 37 to provide information to DBS and he fails without reasonable excuse, to provide the information: s 38(1). A person guilty of the offence is liable on summary conviction to a fine not exceeding level 5 on the standard scale: s 38(2). As to the powers of magistrates' courts to issue fines on summary conviction see SENTENCING vol 92 (2015) PARA 176.

291. Collection of information from local authorities, register keepers and supervisory authorities. If the Disclosure and Barring Service (DBS)[1] is considering whether to include any person in a barred list[2] or remove any person from a barred list[3] and thinks that a local authority[4] hold any prescribed information relating to the person, it may require the authority to provide it with the information[5]. If DBS is considering whether to include in, or remove from, a barred list a person who appears on a relevant register[6] or a person in relation to whom DBS thinks that a supervisory authority[7] may have prescribed information[8], it may require the keeper of the register or, as the case may be, supervisory authority to provide it with any prescribed information he or it holds relating to the person[9]. The local authority, register keeper or supervisory authority must comply with any such requirement[10].

1 As to the Disclosure and Barring Service see PARA 265.

2 Safeguarding Vulnerable Groups Act 2006 s 40(1)(a) (ss 40(1), (2), 42(1), (2), 46(1), (2) amended by SI 2012/3006). As to the criteria for inclusion in the children's barred list see PARA 265. As to criteria for inclusion in the adults' barred list see PARA 266.

3 Safeguarding Vulnerable Groups Act 2006 s 40(1)(b) (as amended: see note 2).

4 Ie a local authority within the meaning of the Local Authority Social Services Act 1970 s 1 (see PARA 315): Safeguarding Vulnerable Groups Act 2006 s 40(4).

5 Safeguarding Vulnerable Groups Act 2006 s 40(2) (as amended: see note 2). The information prescribed for the purposes of s 40(2) is the information specified in the Safeguarding Vulnerable Groups Act 2006 (Prescribed Information) Regulations 2008, SI 2008/3265, Sch 1 paras 1–3, 5, 6, 9, 10 (see PARA 289) (reg 7(a)) and any information other than that relating to the

person's conduct which is likely to, or may, be relevant in considering whether the person should be included in or removed from a barred list including information contained in reports of and minutes of meetings arising from investigations relating to the protection of children or vulnerable adults (reg 7(b)). As to the meaning of 'child' see PARA 241 note 1. As to the meanings of 'adult' and 'vulnerable adult' see PARA 251 note 1.

6 Safeguarding Vulnerable Groups Act 2006 s 42(1)(a), (b) (as amended: see note 2). As to the registers in question and the keepers of those registers see the Safeguarding Vulnerable Groups Act 2006 s 41(7); and PARA 285 (s 42(4)).

7 As to the 'supervisory authorities' for these purposes see the Safeguarding Vulnerable Groups Act 2006 s 45(7); and PARA 286.

8 Safeguarding Vulnerable Groups Act 2006 s 46(1)(a), (b) (as amended: see note 2).

9 Safeguarding Vulnerable Groups Act 2006 ss 42(2), 46(2) (as amended: see note 2). The information prescribed for the purposes of s 42(2) is the information specified in the Safeguarding Vulnerable Groups Act 2006 (Prescribed Information) Regulations 2008, SI 2008/3265, Sch 1 paras 1–3, 5, 6, 9, 10 (reg 9(a)) and any information other than that relating to the person's conduct which is likely to, or may, be relevant in considering whether the person should be included in or removed from a barred list including information relating to any decisions made, actions taken or complaints received by the keeper in relation to that person (reg 9(b)). The information prescribed for the purposes of the Safeguarding Vulnerable Groups Act 2006 s 46(2) is the information specified in the Safeguarding Vulnerable Groups Act 2006 (Prescribed Information) Regulations 2008, SI 2008/3265, Sch 1 paras 1–3, 5, 6, 9, 10 (reg 11(a)) and any information other than that relating to the person's conduct which is likely to, or may, be relevant in considering whether the person should be included in or removed from a barred list including information relating to any decisions made, actions taken, complaints received or inspections undertaken by the authority in relation to the person (reg 11(b)).

10 Safeguarding Vulnerable Groups Act 2006 ss 40(3), 42(3), 46(3).

292. Powers of Disclosure and Barring Service to request information on convictions and cautions.

The Disclosure and Barring Service (DBS)[1] may require:

(1)   any person who holds records of convictions or cautions[2] for the use of police forces generally to provide to it any relevant information relating to a person[3] being considered for inclusion in a barred list or making representations in connection with such inclusion[4];

(2)   any person who holds such records to provide to it a description of the offence committed by the person in question, the date on which the offence was committed, and the date of conviction and sentence or (where applicable) the date and place of caution[5]; and

(3)   the relevant chief officer[6] to provide to it any such relevant information[7].

1 As to the Disclosure and Barring Service see PARA 265.

2 As to the meaning of 'caution' see the Police Act 1997 s 126; and CRIMINAL LAW vol 26 (2016) PARA 621 (definition applied by the Safeguarding Vulnerable Groups Act 2006 Sch 3 para 19(7)).

3 Ie a person to whom any of the Safeguarding Vulnerable Groups Act 2006 Sch 3 paras 1–5 or 7–11 (see PARA 265 et seq) applies or appears to apply: Sch 3 para 19(1)(a) (Sch 3 para 19(1), (4)–(7) amended by SI 2012/3006; Safeguarding Vulnerable Groups Act 2006 Sch 3 para 19(1)(a)–(c), (2), (3), (5), (7) amended, Sch 3 para 19(7A) added, by the Protection of Freedoms Act 2012 s 70(1), Sch 9 para 129(5)). For these purposes relevant information relating to a person is information which the person holding the records reasonably believes to be relevant in relation to the regulated activity concerned: Safeguarding Vulnerable Groups Act 2006 Sch 3 para 19(2) (as so amended). As to the meaning of 'regulated activity' see PARAS 241–250 (children), PARAS 251–259 (vulnerable adults).

4 Safeguarding Vulnerable Groups Act 2006 Sch 3 para 19(1)(a) (as amended: see note 3). As to the criteria for inclusion in the children's barred list see PARA 265. As to criteria for inclusion in the adults' barred list see PARA 266.

5 Safeguarding Vulnerable Groups Act 2006 Sch 3 para 19(1)(b) (as amended: see note 3); Safeguarding Vulnerable Groups Act 2006 (Prescribed Information) Regulations 2008, SI 2008/3265, reg 12.

6 'The relevant chief officer' means any chief officer of a police force who is identified by DBS for these purposes: Safeguarding Vulnerable Groups Act 2006 Sch 3 para 19(7) (as amended: see note 3). The Police Act 1997 s 113B(10), (11) (see SENTENCING vol 92 (2015) PARA 640) apply for the purposes of the definition of 'the relevant chief officer' as they apply for the purposes of s 113B: Safeguarding Vulnerable Groups Act 2006 Sch 3 para 19(7A) (as so added).

7 Safeguarding Vulnerable Groups Act 2006 Sch 3 para 19(1)(c) (as amended: see note 3). For these purposes relevant information relating to a person is information which the relevant chief officer reasonably believes to be relevant in relation to the regulated activity concerned: Sch 3 para 19(3) (as so amended). DBS must pay to the appropriate local policing body such fee as the Secretary of State thinks appropriate for information provided to DBS in accordance with these provisions: Sch 3 para 19(4) (as so amended). As to the Secretary of State see PARA 333. See also PARA 241 note 4.

For the purpose of deciding under Sch 3 whether or not a person is included in a barred list DBS must not take account of relevant police information (ie information obtained by DBS in pursuance of Sch 3 para 19(1)(c)) if the relevant chief officer thinks that it would not be in the interests of the prevention or detection of crime to disclose the information to the person: Sch 3 para 19(5), (6) (as so amended).

293. Duty to consider relevance of information. The Disclosure and Barring Service (DBS)[1] must ensure that in respect of any information it receives in relation to an individual from whatever source or of whatever nature it considers whether the information is relevant to its consideration as to whether the individual should be included in each barred list[2]. This duty does not, without more, require DBS to give an individual the opportunity to make representations as to why he should not be included in a barred list[3].

1 As to the Disclosure and Barring Service see PARA 265.
2 Safeguarding Vulnerable Groups Act 2006 Sch 3 para 13(1) (Sch 3 para 13(1), (2) amended by SI 2012/3006). As to the criteria for inclusion in the children's barred list see PARA 265. As to criteria for inclusion in the adults' barred list see PARA 266.
3 Safeguarding Vulnerable Groups Act 2006 Sch 3 para 13(2) (as amended: see note 2). As to the making of representations concerning inclusion in a barred list see PARAS 270–272.

(vi) Disclosure of Information about Barred Persons and Persons of Concern

A. DUTIES OF REGULATED ACTIVITY PROVIDERS AND PERSONNEL SUPPLIERS TO CHECK IF A PERSON IS BARRED

294. Regulated activity providers. As from a day to be appointed[1] a regulated activity provider[2] who is considering whether to permit an individual (B) to engage in regulated activity relating to children or vulnerable adults[3] must ascertain that B is not barred from the activity[4] concerned before permitting B to engage in it[5]. Particular provision is made in connection with where a person is to be treated as having complied with this duty[6].

1 The Safeguarding Vulnerable Groups Act 2006 s 34ZA (see the text and notes 2–5; and PARAS 295–296) is added, as from a day to be appointed under the Protection of Freedoms Act 2012 s 120(1), by s 73. At the date at which this volume states the law no such day had been appointed.
2 As to the meaning of 'regulated activity provider' see PARAS 260–264.
3 As to the meaning of 'child' see PARA 241 note 1. As to the meanings of 'adult' and 'vulnerable adult' see PARA 251 note 1. As to the meaning of 'regulated activity' see PARAS 241–250 (children), PARAS 251–259 (vulnerable adults).
4 As to when a person is barred from regulated activity see PARA 299 note 9.
5 Safeguarding Vulnerable Groups Act 2006 s 34ZA(1) (prospectively added: see note 1). The Secretary of State may by regulations provide for the duty under s 34ZA(1) not to apply in relation to persons of a prescribed description: s 34ZA(7)(a) (as so prospectively added). At the date at which this volume states the law no such regulations had been made. As to the Secretary of State see PARA 333. See also PARA 241 note 4.
6 See PARA 296.

295. Personnel suppliers. As from a day to be appointed[1] a personnel supplier[2] who is considering whether to supply an individual (B) to another (P) and knows, or has reason to believe, that P will make arrangements for B (if supplied) to engage in regulated activity relating to children or vulnerable adults[3], must ascertain that B is not barred from the activity[4] concerned before supplying B to P[5]. Particular provision is made in connection with where a person is to be treated as having complied with this duty[6].

1   The Safeguarding Vulnerable Groups Act 2006 s 34ZA (see the text and notes 2–5; and PARAS 294, 296) is added, as from a day to be appointed under the Protection of Freedoms Act 2012 s 120(1), by s 73. At the date at which this volume states the law no such day had been appointed.
2   As to the meaning of 'personnel supplier' see PARA 241 note 4.
3   As to the meaning of 'child' see PARA 241 note 1. As to the meanings of 'adult' and 'vulnerable adult' see PARA 251 note 1. As to the meaning of 'regulated activity' see PARAS 241–250 (children), PARAS 251–259 (vulnerable adults).
4   As to when a person is barred from regulated activity see PARA 299 note 9.
5   Safeguarding Vulnerable Groups Act 2006 s 34ZA(2) (prospectively added: see note 1). The Secretary of State may by regulations provide for the duty under s 34ZA(2) not to apply in relation to persons of a prescribed description: s 34ZA(7)(b) (as so prospectively added). At the date at which this volume states the law no such regulations had been made. As to the Secretary of State see PARA 333. See also PARA 241 note 4.
6   See PARA 296.

296. Compliance with the duty to check whether a person is barred. As from a day to be appointed[1] a regulated activity provider[2] or personnel supplier[3] who is under a duty to check whether a person is barred[4] will, in particular, be treated as having met this duty if:

(1)   he has[5] been informed[6] that B is not barred from the activity concerned[7];
(2)   he has[8] checked a relevant enhanced criminal record certificate[9] of B[10] and the certificate does not show that B is barred from the activity concerned[11]; or
(3)   he has[12] checked a relevant enhanced criminal record certificate of B and up-date information given[13] in relation to the certificate[14], the certificate does not show that B is barred from the activity concerned[15], and the up-date information is not advice to request B to apply for a new enhanced criminal record certificate[16].

1   The Safeguarding Vulnerable Groups Act 2006 s 34ZA (see the text and notes 2–16; and PARAS 294–295) is added, as from a day to be appointed under the Protection of Freedoms Act 2012 s 120(1), by s 73. At the date at which this volume states the law no such day had been appointed.
2   As to the meaning of 'regulated activity provider' see PARAS 260–264.
3   As to the meaning of 'personnel supplier' see PARA 241 note 4.
4   As to this duty see PARA 294 (regulated activity providers) and PARA 295 (personnel suppliers). As to when a person is barred from regulated activity see PARA 299 note 9.
5   Ie within the period prescribed by regulations: at the date at which this volume states the law no such regulations had been made.
6   Ie under the Safeguarding Vulnerable Groups Act 2006 s 30A (see PARAS 296, 299, 300).
7   Safeguarding Vulnerable Groups Act 2006 s 34ZA(3), (4) (prospectively added: see note 1).
8   See note 5.
9   'Enhanced criminal record certificate' means an enhanced criminal record certificate issued under the Police Act 1997 s 113B (see SENTENCING vol 92 (2015) PARAS 640–642); and 'relevant enhanced criminal record certificate' means an enhanced criminal record certificate which includes, by virtue of s 113BA (see SENTENCING vol 92 (2015) PARA 638), suitability information relating to children (in the case of regulated activity relating to children) and an enhanced criminal record certificate which includes, by virtue of s 113BB (see SENTENCING vol 92 (2015) PARA 638), suitability information relating to vulnerable adults (in the case of regulated activity relating to vulnerable adults): Safeguarding Vulnerable Groups Act 2006 s 34ZA(8) (prospectively added: see note 1).
10 Safeguarding Vulnerable Groups Act 2006 s 34ZA(5)(a) (prospectively added: see note 1). The certificate must have been obtained with the prescribed period: see s 34ZA(5)(a) (as so prospectively added); and note 5.
11 Safeguarding Vulnerable Groups Act 2006 s 34ZA(5)(b) (prospectively added: see note 1).
12 See note 5.

13 Ie given under the Police Act 1997 s 116A (see SENTENCING vol 92 (2015) PARA 645). The information must have been given with the prescribed period: see the Safeguarding Vulnerable Groups Act 2006 s 34ZA(6)(a) (prospectively added: see note 1); and note 5.
14 Safeguarding Vulnerable Groups Act 2006 s 34ZA(6)(a) (prospectively added: see note 1).
15 Safeguarding Vulnerable Groups Act 2006 s 34ZA(6)(b) (prospectively added: see note 1).
16 Safeguarding Vulnerable Groups Act 2006 s 34ZA(6)(c) (prospectively added: see note 1).

B. DISCLOSURE OF BARRING INFORMATION TO INTERESTED PARTIES

297. Persons who may apply for information about barring. A person may apply for information about barring[1] if he is:

(1) a person who permits, or is considering whether to permit, the person in respect of whom the information is requested (B) to engage in regulated activity relating to children[2];

(2) a person who permits, or is considering whether to permit, B to engage in regulated activity relating to vulnerable adults[3];

(3) a personnel supplier[4] in connection with the supply, or possible supply, of B to another person for B to engage in regulated activity relating to children[5];

(4) a personnel supplier in connection with the supply, or possible supply, of B to another person for B to engage in regulated activity relating to vulnerable adults[6];

(5) a person who has parental responsibility for a child[7] and is considering whether B is suitable to engage in regulated activity in relation to the child[8];

(6) a person who is considering whether B should be a private foster parent[9] in relation to his child[10];

(7) a person (except the parent of a child to be fostered) making, or who has made, arrangements for another to foster a child who is considering whether B is suitable to live in premises in which the child is fostered[11];

(8) a local authority[12] in the exercise of functions[13] considering whether B is suitable to foster a child privately[14] or to live in premises in which a child is so fostered[15];

(9) a person who is considering whether B is suitable to engage in regulated activity in relation to a vulnerable adult who is a friend or family member of the person[16];

(10) a person who carries on an adult placement scheme[17] and is considering whether B is suitable to live in premises in which an adult is provided with accommodation as part of the scheme[18];

(11) a person who is permitting, or considering whether to permit, B to have access to health or educational records relating to a child[19];

(12) a person who is permitting, or considering whether to permit, B to have access to health records relating to vulnerable adults[20];

(13) a person who is permitting, or is considering whether to permit, B to engage in an activity in respect of which financial resources are provided[21] if engaging in the activity gives B the opportunity to have contact with children[22]; and

(14) the Disclosure and Barring Service (DBS) in relation to members and employees and prospective members and employees of DBS[23].

1 Ie pursuant to the Safeguarding Vulnerable Groups Act 2006 ss 30–32 (see PARAS 298–301). As to the information on barred persons required to be kept by the Disclosure and Barring Service (DBS) see PARAS 287–288. As to the Disclosure and Barring Service see PARA 265.
2 Safeguarding Vulnerable Groups Act 2006 Sch 7 column 1 entry 1. As to the meaning of 'child' see PARA 241 note 1. As to the meaning of 'regulated activity' in relation to children see

PARAS 241–250. In entries 1, 5 the reference to 'regulated activity' must be construed by disregarding Sch 4 para 2(2) (see PARA 241) if the activity relates to a child who has not attained the age of 16 or is carried on for the purposes of the armed forces of the Crown (Sch 7 para 3(1)), and in entries 1, 5, 9 the reference to 'regulated activity' includes a reference to an activity which would be a regulated activity if it were carried out frequently (Sch 7 para 3(2)(a) (Sch 7 para 3(2) amended by SI 2012/2113)).

3 Safeguarding Vulnerable Groups Act 2006 Sch 7 column 1 entry 2. As to the meanings of 'adult' and 'vulnerable adult' see PARA 251 note 1. As to the meaning of 'regulated activity' in relation to vulnerable adults see PARAS 251–259.

4 As to the meaning of 'personnel supplier' see PARA 241 note 4.

5 Safeguarding Vulnerable Groups Act 2006 Sch 7 column 1 entry 5. As to the meaning of 'regulated activity' for these purposes see note 2.

6 Safeguarding Vulnerable Groups Act 2006 Sch 7 column 1 entry 6.

7 As to the meaning of 'parental responsibility' see the Children Act 1989 s 3(1); and CHILDREN AND YOUNG PERSONS vol 9 (2017) PARA 150 (definition applied by the Safeguarding Vulnerable Groups Act 2006 Sch 7 para 4).

8 Safeguarding Vulnerable Groups Act 2006 Sch 7 column 1 entry 9. As to the meaning of 'regulated activity' for these purposes see note 2. Such a person is not entitled to apply for information under these provisions if B is permitted to engage in regulated activity in relation to the child by an independent regulated activity provider: Sch 7 column 1 entry 9. As to the meaning of 'regulated activity provider' see PARAS 260–264: a regulated activity provider is an independent regulated activity provider unless it is a company wholly owned by B (Sch 7 para 5).

9 Ie within the meaning of the Safeguarding Vulnerable Groups Act 2006 s 53 (see PARA 142).

10 Safeguarding Vulnerable Groups Act 2006 Sch 7 column 1 entry 10.

11 Safeguarding Vulnerable Groups Act 2006 Sch 7 column 1 entry 11.

12 As to the meaning of 'local authority' see the Children Act 1989 s 105; and CHILDREN AND YOUNG PERSONS vol 9 (2017) PARA 154 (definition applied by the Safeguarding Vulnerable Groups Act 2006 Sch 7 column 1 entry 12).

13 Ie functions under the Children Act 1989 s 67 (see CHILDREN AND YOUNG PERSONS vol 10 (2017) PARAS 990–994).

14 Ie within the meaning of the Children Act 1989: see s 66; and CHILDREN AND YOUNG PERSONS vol 10 (2017) PARA 984.

15 Safeguarding Vulnerable Groups Act 2006 Sch 7 column 1 entry 12.

16 Safeguarding Vulnerable Groups Act 2006 Sch 7 column 1 entry 13. Such a person is not entitled to apply for information under these provisions if B is permitted to engage in the regulated activity by an independent regulated activity provider: Sch 7 column 1 entry 13.

17 An adult placement scheme is a scheme under which an individual agrees with the person carrying on the scheme to provide accommodation, in the home in which the individual ordinarily resides, to an adult who is in need of it, and in respect of which a requirement to register arises under the Health and Social Care Act 2008 s 10 (in relation to England: see PARA 159) or under the Care Standards Act 2000 s 11 (in relation to Wales: see CHILDREN AND YOUNG PERSONS vol 10 (2017) PARA 1017): Safeguarding Vulnerable Groups Act 2006 Sch 7 para 6.

18 Safeguarding Vulnerable Groups Act 2006 Sch 7 column 1 entry 14.

19 Safeguarding Vulnerable Groups Act 2006 Sch 7 column 1 entry 15.

20 Safeguarding Vulnerable Groups Act 2006 Sch 7 column 1 entry 16.

21 Ie pursuant to the Apprenticeships, Skills, Children and Learning Act 2009 s 61 (repealed) or s 100 (see EDUCATION vol 36 (2015) PARA 783), the Education Act 2002 s 14 (see EDUCATION vol 35 (2015) PARA 78), or the Learning and Skills Act 2000 s 34(1) (see EDUCATION vol 36 (2015) PARA 792).

22 Safeguarding Vulnerable Groups Act 2006 Sch 7 column 1 entry 18 (amended by the Education Act 2011 Sch 16 para 38; and by SI 2010/1080).

23 Safeguarding Vulnerable Groups Act 2006 Sch 7 column 1 entry 19 (added by SI 2012/2113; amended by SI 2012/3006).

298. Declaration to be made by person applying for information about barring. A person who wishes to apply for information about barring[1] (A) is required to make a declaration ('the appropriate declaration') in connection with the application[2]. The appropriate declaration is a declaration that the person making it is a person who may apply for information about barring[3] and that the person in respect of whom the information is requested (B) has consented to the provision of the information to A or, as the case may be, the application[4]. As from a day to be appointed the declaration must also include a declaration by A that the status by virtue of which he is entitled to apply for barring information[5] relates to children or, as the case may be, vulnerable adults[6], and a declaration made in connection with an application to the Secretary of State for information[7] may also be required to include a declaration by A as to whether the information is sought by him with a view to permitting or supplying B to carry out paid activity[8] or with a view to making a check[9] in relation to the appointment of B to a position in which B will carry out paid activity[10].

An individual commits an offence if, in an application made for any of the purposes for which an appropriate declaration is required[11], he makes a false declaration and he either knows that it is false or is reckless as to whether it is false[12].

1 Ie pursuant to the Safeguarding Vulnerable Groups Act 2006 ss 30–32 (see PARAS 298–301). As to the information on barred persons required to be kept by the Disclosure and Barring Service (DBS) see PARAS 287–288. As to the Disclosure and Barring Service see PARA 265.
2 See the Safeguarding Vulnerable Groups Act 2006 ss 30, 30A, 30B, 32; and PARAS 298–301.
3 Ie that he falls within the Safeguarding Vulnerable Groups Act 2006 Sch 7 column 1 (see PARA 297): ss 30(2)(a), (3), 30A(2)(a), 30B(3)(a), 32(3)(a), (4) (ss 30A, 30B prospectively substituted for ss 30–32, and s 34(1) prospectively amended, by the Protection of Freedoms Act 2012 s 72(1), (3); Safeguarding Vulnerable Groups Act 2006 ss 30(2)(a), 32(3)(a) prospectively amended, ss 30(2)(aa), (ab), (2A), (6A), (6B), 32(3)(aa) prospectively added, ss 30(3), 32(4) prospectively repealed, by the Policing and Crime Act 2009 ss 85, 86, Sch 8 Pt 8). At the date at which this volume states the law no day or days had been appointed for the commencement of these amendments, which are technical and will not materially affect the meaning of the text.
4 Safeguarding Vulnerable Groups Act 2006 ss 30(2)(b), 30A(2)(c), 30B(3)(c), 32(3)(c) (prospectively substituted: see note 3). If B consents to the provision of information to A in relation to an application under these provisions, the consent also has effect in relation to any subsequent such application by A: ss 30(6), 30A(4), 30B(7), 32(9) (as so prospectively substituted).
5 Ie the entry in the Safeguarding Vulnerable Groups Act 2006 Sch 7 column 1 (see PARA 297) which applies to A.
6 See the Safeguarding Vulnerable Groups Act 2006 ss 30(2)(aa), 30A(2)(b), 30B(3)(b), 32(3)(aa) (prospectively substituted and added: see note 3). As to the meaning of 'child' see PARA 241 note 1. As to the meanings of 'adult' and 'vulnerable adult' see PARA 251 note 1.
7 Ie an application under the Safeguarding Vulnerable Groups Act 2006 s 30 as that provision has effect before the coming into force of the substitution recorded in note 3. As to the Secretary of State see PARA 333. See also PARA 241 note 4.
8 'Paid activity' means an activity carried out for financial gain, and the Secretary of State may by regulations provide for an activity to be treated as, or not to be treated as, an activity carried out for financial gain: Safeguarding Vulnerable Groups Act 2006 ss 30(6A), (6B) (prospectively added: see note 3).
9 Ie in accordance with the Safeguarding Vulnerable Groups Act 2006 s 15(2)(a) (now repealed).
10 Safeguarding Vulnerable Groups Act 2006 ss 30(2)(ab) (prospectively added: see note 3).
11 Ie the Safeguarding Vulnerable Groups Act 2006 s 30 or s 30A (see PARA 300), or s 30B or s 32 (see PARA 301), as the case may be.
12 Safeguarding Vulnerable Groups Act 2006 s 34(1) (prospectively amended: see note 3). A person guilty of an offence under s 34(1) is liable on summary conviction to a fine not exceeding level 5 on the standard scale: s 34(2). As to the powers of magistrates' courts to issue fines on summary conviction see SENTENCING vol 92 (2015) PARA 176.

299. Barring information to be provided on application. Until a day to be appointed[1] the information about barring which must be provided[2] is whether the person in respect of whom the information is requested (B) is subject to monitoring in relation to regulated activity relating to children or (as the case may be) vulnerable adults[3] and if so, whether he is undergoing assessment[4]. Where the application refers to children, the information to be provided must be that relating to children[5]; and where the application refers to vulnerable adults, the information to be provided must be that relating to vulnerable adults[6].

As from the appointed day[7] the information about barring which must be provided[8] is whether B is barred from regulated activity[9] relating to children[10] or, as the case may be, vulnerable adults[11].

1 As from a day to be appointed, the Safeguarding Vulnerable Groups Act 2006 ss 30A, 30B (see the text and notes 7–11; and PARAS 300, 301) are substituted for s 31 by the Protection of Freedoms Act 2012 s 72(1). At the date at which this volume states the law no such day or days had been appointed.

2 Ie pursuant to an application under the Safeguarding Vulnerable Groups Act 2006 s 30 (see PARAS 298, 300). As to the information on barred persons required to be kept by the Disclosure and Barring Service (DBS) see PARAS 287–288. As to the Disclosure and Barring Service see PARA 265.

3 Safeguarding Vulnerable Groups Act 2006 s 31(1), (2)(a), (3)(a), (5) (prospectively substituted: see note 1). As to the meaning of 'child' see PARA 241 note 1. As to the meanings of 'adult' and 'vulnerable adult' see PARA 251 note 1. As to the meaning of 'regulated activity' see PARAS 241–250 (children), PARAS 251–259 (vulnerable adults).

4 Safeguarding Vulnerable Groups Act 2006 s 31(2)(b), (3)(b) (prospectively substituted: see note 1). B is undergoing assessment if:
    (1)   the Secretary of State is required to notify B as mentioned in s 24(4) (now repealed) in connection with B's monitoring application but has not yet done so (s 31(4)(a) (as so prospectively substituted));
    (2)   B has made a simultaneous application under the Police Act 1997 s 113B (see SENTENCING vol 92 (2015) PARAS 640–642) but the Secretary of State has not yet issued an enhanced criminal record certificate under that provision (Safeguarding Vulnerable Groups Act 2006 s 31(4)(b) (as so prospectively substituted)); and
    (3)   in relation to s 31(2)(b), (3)(b), B is being considered for inclusion in the children's barred list in pursuance of Sch 3 para 3 or 5 or, as the case may be, the adults' barred list in pursuance of Sch 3 para 9 or 11 (see PARAS 271–272) (s 31(4)(c) (as so prospectively substituted)).
    In s 31(4)(b) 'simultaneous application' means an application made simultaneously with B's monitoring application under s 24: s 31(5) (as so prospectively substituted). As to the Secretary of State see PARA 333. See also PARA 241 note 4.

5 See the Safeguarding Vulnerable Groups Act 2006 s 30(4)(a) (s 30(4)(a), (b) prospectively substituted (see note 1); and prospectively amended by the Policing and Crime Act 2009 s 85); and the Safeguarding Vulnerable Groups Act 2006 Sch 7 column 2. At the date at which this volume states the law no day had been appointed for the commencement of the amendment made by the Policing and Crime Act 2009 s 85.

6 See the Safeguarding Vulnerable Groups Act 2006 s 30(4)(b) (prospectively substituted and amended: see notes 1, 5); and Sch 7 column 2.

7 See note 1.

8 Ie pursuant to an application under the Safeguarding Vulnerable Groups Act 2006 s 30A (see PARAS 299–300) or s 30B (see PARA 301).

9 A person is barred from regulated activity relating to children if he is included in the children's barred list or the list maintained under the Safeguarding Vulnerable Groups (Northern Ireland) Order 2007, SI 2007/1351, art 6(1)(a), and a person is barred from regulated activity relating to vulnerable adults if he is included in the adults' barred list or the list maintained under the Safeguarding Vulnerable Groups (Northern Ireland) Order 2007, SI 2007/1351, art 6(1)(b): Safeguarding Vulnerable Groups Act 2006 s 3; Safeguarding Vulnerable Groups Act 2006 (Miscellaneous Provisions) Order 2009, SI 2009/1797, art 5.

10 See the Safeguarding Vulnerable Groups Act 2006 s 30A(3)(a) (prospectively substituted: see note 1); and Sch 7 column 2.

11 See the Safeguarding Vulnerable Groups Act 2006 s 30A(3)(b) (prospectively substituted: see note 1); and Sch 7 column 2.

300. Circumstances in which barring information must be provided. A person (A) must be provided with the relevant barring information[1] in relation to another (B) if:
    (1)   he makes an application for the information[2];
    (2)   the application contains the appropriate declaration[3]; and
    (3)   the person required to provide the information pursuant to such an application has no reason to believe that the declaration is false[4].

Until a day to be appointed the person required to provide the information pursuant to such an application is the Secretary of State[5]; as from that day it is the Disclosure and Barring Service (DBS)[6]. Provision is made for the prescription and levying of fees for these purposes[7].

1   As to the information to be provided under these provisions see PARA 299. As to the information on barred persons required to be kept by the Disclosure and Barring Service (DBS) see PARAS 287–288. As to the Disclosure and Barring Service see PARA 265.

2   Safeguarding Vulnerable Groups Act 2006 ss 30(1)(a), 30A(1)(a) (ss 30A, 30B prospectively substituted for s 30 by the Protection of Freedoms Act 2012 s 72(1)). At the date at which this volume states the law no day or days had been appointed for the commencement of these amendments.

3   Safeguarding Vulnerable Groups Act 2006 ss 30(1)(b), 30A(1)(b) (prospectively substituted: see note 2). As to the appropriate declaration see PARA 298.

4   Safeguarding Vulnerable Groups Act 2006 ss 30(1)(c), 30A(1)(c) (prospectively substituted (see note 2); s 30A(1), (6), (7) amended by SI 2012/3006).

5   Safeguarding Vulnerable Groups Act 2006 s 30(1) (prospectively substituted: see note 2). The Secretary of State may prescribe the form, manner and contents of an application for the purposes of s 30 (including the form and manner of a declaration contained in such an application) (s 30(7) (as so prospectively substituted)), and may by regulations make provision requiring a local authority which makes or proposes to make direct payments to or on behalf of a person in accordance with regulations under the Children Act 1989 s 17A (see CHILDREN AND YOUNG PERSONS vol 10 (2017) PARA 804) or the Health and Social Care Act 2001 s 57 (see MENTAL HEALTH AND CAPACITY), in accordance with the Care Act 2014 s 31 or s 32 (see PARA 106), or in accordance with regulations under the Social Services and Well-being (Wales) Act 2014 ss 50–53 (see PARAS 125–130), to inform the person of his right to obtain relevant information under the Safeguarding Vulnerable Groups Act 2006 s 30 (s 30(8) (as so prospectively substituted; amended by SI 2015/914 and, in relation to Wales, by SI 2016/413)). At the date at which this volume states the law no such regulations had been made for any of these purposes. As to the Secretary of State see PARA 333. See also PARA 241 note 4.

6   Safeguarding Vulnerable Groups Act 2006 s 30A(1) (prospectively substituted (see note 2); and amended (see note 4)). DBS may determine the form, manner and contents of an application for these purposes (including the form and manner of a declaration contained in such an application): s 30A(7) (as so prospectively substituted).

7   Until a day to be appointed, where the Secretary of State is the person required to provide the information pursuant to an application under these provisions he may refuse to provide A with the information if B has failed to pay a fee required by the Safeguarding Vulnerable Groups Act 2006 s 24A (now repealed): s 30(2A) (prospectively added by the Policing and Crime Act 2009 s 84(3); and prospectively substituted (see note 2)). At the date at which this volume states the law no day had been appointed for these purposes.

    As from a day to be appointed, where DBS is the person required to provide the information pursuant to an application under these provisions the Secretary of State may prescribe any fee payable in respect of an application under the Safeguarding Vulnerable Groups Act 2006 s 30A (s 30A(5) (as so prospectively substituted)), and DBS may refuse to provide the information if any such fee is not paid (s 30A(1)(a) (as so prospectively substituted)). Fees received by DBS by virtue of these provisions must be paid into the Consolidated Fund: s 30A(6) (as so prospectively substituted, and as amended (see note 4)). As to the Consolidated Fund see CONSTITUTIONAL AND ADMINISTRATIVE LAW vol 20 (2014) PARA 480.

301. Registration of applicants for barring information. There is required to be established and maintained a register in which a person (A) must be registered in relation to another (B) if:

(1)   A makes an application to be registered in relation to B[1];

(2)   the application contains the appropriate declaration[2];

(3)   the person required to establish and maintain the register has no reason to believe that the declaration is false[3]; and

(4)   until a day to be appointed[4], B is subject to monitoring in relation to the regulated activity[5] to which the application relates[6].

Until a day to be appointed[7] the person required to establish and maintain this register is the Secretary of State[8], who must notify A if B ceases to be subject to monitoring in relation to the regulated activity to which A's registration relates[9];

as from that day the register is required to be established and maintained by the Disclosure and Barring Service (DBS)[10], which must notify A if B is barred from regulated activity to which A's registration relates[11].

Once a person has been so notified his registration ceases[12]. DBS may also cancel a person's registration in prescribed circumstances[13], which as from a day to be appointed may in particular include circumstances where DBS has asked the registered person (A) to make a renewed declaration[14] within the prescribed period in relation to the person (B) in relation to whom A is registered[15] and either A has failed to make the declaration within that period[16] or A has made the declaration within that period but DBS has reason to believe that it is false[17], and must cancel a person's registration if the person applies for it to be cancelled[18] and, in prescribed circumstances, if the person in relation to whom he is registered applies for it to be cancelled[19].

Provision is made for the prescription and levying of fees for certain of these purposes[20].

1   Safeguarding Vulnerable Groups Act 2006 ss 30B(1), (2)(a), 32(1), (2)(a) (ss 30A, 30B prospectively substituted for ss 30–32, and ss 33(1), (2), 34(1) prospectively amended, and s 33(3A)–(3D) prospectively added by the Protection of Freedoms Act 2012 s 72(1)–(3); Safeguarding Vulnerable Groups Act 2006 ss 30B(1), (2), (5), (9), (10), 33(3), (3A), (3D), (4), (5) amended by SI 2012/3006). At the date at which this volume states the law no day or days had been appointed for the commencement of the amendments made by the Protection of Freedoms Act 2012.

2   Safeguarding Vulnerable Groups Act 2006 ss 30B(2)(b), 32(2)(b) (prospectively substituted: see note 1). As to the appropriate declaration see PARA 298.

3   Safeguarding Vulnerable Groups Act 2006 ss 30B(2)(c), 32(2)(c) (prospectively substituted: see note 1).

4   Ie until the appointed day referred to in note 1.

5   As to the meaning of 'regulated activity' see PARAS 241–250 (children), PARAS 251–259 (vulnerable adults).

6   Safeguarding Vulnerable Groups Act 2006 s 32(2)(d) (prospectively substituted: see note 1).

7   See note 1.

8   Safeguarding Vulnerable Groups Act 2006 s 32(1) (prospectively substituted: see note 1). Until the appointed day the Secretary of State may prescribe the form, manner and contents of an application for these purposes (including the form and manner of a declaration contained in such an application): s 32(10) (as so prospectively substituted). At the date at which this volume states the law nothing had been prescribed for these purposes. As to the Secretary of State see PARA 333. See also PARA 241 note 4.

9   Safeguarding Vulnerable Groups Act 2006 s 32(6) (prospectively substituted: see note 1). If the status by virtue of which A is entitled to apply for barring information relates to children (ie the applicant's declaration (see PARA 298) states that Sch 7 column 2 refers to children), A's application and registration relate to children; if the status by virtue of which A is entitled to apply for barring information relates to vulnerable adults (ie the applicant's declaration states that Sch 7 column 2 refers to vulnerable adults), A's application and registration relate to vulnerable adults: s 32(5) (as so prospectively substituted; amended by the Policing and Crime Act 2009 s 86(1), (4)). As to the meaning of 'child' see PARA 241 note 1. As to the meanings of 'adult' and 'vulnerable adult' see PARA 251 note 1. The requirement under the Safeguarding Vulnerable Groups Act 2006 s 32(6) is satisfied if notification is sent to any address recorded against A's name in the register: s 32(7) (as so prospectively substituted).

10   As to the Disclosure and Barring Service see PARA 265. As from a day to be appointed DBS may determine the form, manner and contents of an application for the purposes of the Safeguarding Vulnerable Groups Act 2006 s 30B (including the form and manner of a declaration contained in such an application): s 30B(10) (prospectively substituted and amended: see note 1).

11   Safeguarding Vulnerable Groups Act 2006 s 30B(5) (prospectively substituted and amended: see note 1). As to when a person is barred from regulated activity see PARA 299 note 9. If the status by virtue of which A is entitled to apply for barring information relates to children (ie the applicant's declaration states that Sch 7 column 2 refers to children), A's application and registration relate to children; if the status by virtue of which A is entitled to apply for barring information relates to vulnerable adults (ie the applicant's declaration states that Sch 7 column 2 refers to vulnerable adults), A's application and registration relate to vulnerable adults: s 30B(4) (as so prospectively substituted). The requirement under s 30B(5) is satisfied if notification is sent to any address recorded against A's name in the register: s 30B(6) (as so prospectively substituted).

12 Safeguarding Vulnerable Groups Act 2006 s 33(1), (2) (prospectively amended: see note 1).

13 Safeguarding Vulnerable Groups Act 2006 s 33(3) (as amended: see note 1). At the date at which this volume states the law no circumstances had been prescribed for these purposes. When a person's registration is cancelled under s 33(3) or (4)(b), DBS must notify him of that fact: s 33(5) (as so amended). The requirement under s 33(5) is satisfied if notification is sent to any address recorded against A's name in the register: s 33(6).

14 A renewed declaration is a declaration by A that he is a person who may apply for information about barring (ie that he falls within the Safeguarding Vulnerable Groups Act 2006 Sch 7 column 1 (see PARA 297) in relation to B, that the status by virtue of which he is entitled to apply for barring information relates to children or, as the case may be, vulnerable adults (ie that the entry in Sch 7 column 2 which applies to A refers to children or, as the case may be, vulnerable adults), and that B consents to the registration of A in relation to B: s 33(3B) (as so prospectively added). If B consents to the provision of information to A under s 30A (see PARA 299), the consent also has effect as consent to the registration of A in relation to B: s 33(3C) (as so prospectively added).

An individual commits an offence if, in relation to the making of a renewed declaration pursuant to these provisions, he makes a false declaration and he either knows that it is false or is reckless as to whether it is false: ss 33(3D), 34(1) (as so prospectively added and amended). A person guilty of an offence under s 34(1) is liable on summary conviction to a fine not exceeding level 5 on the standard scale: s 34(2). As to the powers of magistrates' courts to issue fines on summary conviction see SENTENCING vol 92 (2015) PARA 176.

15 Safeguarding Vulnerable Groups Act 2006 s 33(3A)(a) (prospectively added and amended: see note 1).

16 Safeguarding Vulnerable Groups Act 2006 s 33(3A)(b)(i) (prospectively added: see note 1).

17 Safeguarding Vulnerable Groups Act 2006 s 33(3A)(b)(ii) (prospectively added and amended: see note 1).

18 Safeguarding Vulnerable Groups Act 2006 s 33(4)(a) (as amended: see note 1).

19 Safeguarding Vulnerable Groups Act 2006 s 33(4)(b) (as amended: see note 1). See note 13. At the date at which this volume states the law no circumstances had been prescribed for these purposes.

20 As from a day to be appointed the Secretary of State may prescribe any fee payable in respect of an application under the Safeguarding Vulnerable Groups Act 2006 s 30B (s 30B(8) (prospectively substituted: see note 1) and DBS may refuse to register an applicant if any such fee is not paid (s 30B(2)(a) (as so prospectively substituted)). Fees received by DBS by virtue of these provisions must be paid into the Consolidated Fund: s 30B(9) (as so prospectively substituted and amended). As to the Consolidated Fund see CONSTITUTIONAL AND ADMINISTRATIVE LAW vol 20 (2014) PARA 480.

C. DISCLOSURE OF BARRING INFORMATION TO SUPERVISORY AUTHORITIES

302. Power of supervisory authorities to apply for barring information. The Secretary of State, the Welsh Ministers, the Care Quality Commission, the Public Guardian, Her Majesty's Chief Inspector of Education, Children's Services and Skills, Her Majesty's Chief Inspector of Education and Training in Wales, the Charity Commissioners for England and Wales, and a registration authority under the Care Standards Act 2000[1], may apply to the Disclosure and Barring Service (DBS)[2] for information as to whether a person is barred from regulated activity relating to children or, as the case may be, vulnerable adults[3], and if a supervisory authority makes such an application DBS must provide the authority with that information[4].

1 Ie the 'supervisory authorities' for the purposes of the Safeguarding Vulnerable Groups Act 2006: see s 45(7); and PARA 286. A supervisory authority may apply for information under these provisions only if the information is required in connection with the exercise of a function of the supervisory authority mentioned in s 45(7): s 47(4).

2 As to the Disclosure and Barring Service see PARA 265. As to the information on barred persons required to be kept by DBS see PARAS 287–288.

3 Safeguarding Vulnerable Groups Act 2006 s 47(2)(a), (3)(a), (6). As to the meaning of 'child' see PARA 241 note 1. As to the meanings of 'adult' and 'vulnerable adult' see PARA 251 note 1. As to the meaning of 'regulated activity' see PARAS 241–250 (children), PARAS 251–259 (vulnerable adults). As to when a person is barred from regulated activity see PARA 299 note 9. DBS may

determine the form, manner and contents of an application for these purposes: s 47(7) (amended by the Protection of Freedoms Act 2012; Safeguarding Vulnerable Groups Act 2006 s 47(1), (7) amended by SI 2012/3006).

4   Safeguarding Vulnerable Groups Act 2006 s 47(1) (as amended: see note 3).

303. Notification to supervisory authorities of changes in barring information.

The supervisory authorities[1] may apply to the Disclosure and Barring Service (DBS)[2] to be notified of changes in barring information[3] and, provided such an application is not withdrawn, will be 'interested supervisory authorities' for these purposes[4]. Until a day to be appointed[5] DBS must notify every interested supervisory authority if a person is newly included in the children's barred list or, as the case may be, the adults' barred list[6], DBS becomes aware that a person is subject to a relevant children's disqualification or, as the case may be, a relevant adults' disqualification[7], or having been subject to monitoring in relation to regulated activity relating to children or, as the case may be, vulnerable adults, a person ceases[8] to be so subject[9]; as from that day[10] DBS must, unless it is satisfied that the authority already has the information concerned[11], notify every interested supervisory authority if a person is included in the children's barred list or, as the case may be, the adults' barred list[12] or if DBS is aware that a person is subject to a relevant children's disqualification or, as the case may be, a relevant adults' disqualification[13].

1   As to the 'supervisory authorities' for these purposes see the Safeguarding Vulnerable Groups Act 2006 s 45(7); and PARA 286.

2   As to the Disclosure and Barring Service see PARA 265. As to the information on barred persons required to be kept by DBS see PARAS 287–288.

3   Ie may apply to DBS to be notified if any of the circumstances mentioned in the Safeguarding Vulnerable Groups Act 2006 s 48(1) or s 49(1) (see the text and notes 6–9) apply in relation to a person: ss 48(3)(a), 49(3)(a) (ss 48(1)(a), (b), (2), (3)(a), (5)(a), (8), 49(1)(a), (b), (2), (3)(a), (5)(a), (8) prospectively amended, ss 48(1)(c), 49(1)(c) prospectively repealed, ss 48(2A), (5)(b), 49(2A), (5)(b) prospectively added, by the Protection of Freedoms Act 2012 s 76(3), (4), as from a day to be appointed; Safeguarding Vulnerable Groups Act 2006 ss 48(1)(b), (2), (2A), (3), (4), (5)(a), (b), (8), 49(1)(b), (2), (2A), (3), (4), (5)(a), (b), (8) amended by SI 2012/3006). At the date at which this volume states the law no day or days had been appointed for the commencement of the prospective amendments.

     A supervisory authority may apply to DBS under the Safeguarding Vulnerable Groups Act 2006 s 48(3)(a) or s 49(3)(a) only if the notification is required in connection with the exercise of a function of the supervisory authority mentioned in s 45(7) (see PARA 180): ss 48(4), 49(4) (as so amended). DBS may determine the form, manner and contents of an application for these purposes: ss 48(8), 49(8) (as so amended).

4   Safeguarding Vulnerable Groups Act 2006 ss 48(3)(b), 49(3)(b). For the purposes of ss 48(3)(b), 49(3)(b) an application is withdrawn if the supervisory authority notifies DBS that it no longer wishes to be notified as referred to in note 3 above: ss 48(5)(a), 49(5)(a) (prospectively amended and amended: see note 3). As from a day to be appointed an application is also 'withdrawn' for these purposes if DBS cancels the application on the grounds that the supervisory authority has not answered, within such reasonable period as was required by DBS, a request from DBS as to whether the supervisory authority still wishes to be notified of any circumstance mentioned in s 48(1) or s 49(1) in relation to the person, or that the notification is not required in connection with the exercise of a function of the supervisory authority mentioned in s 45(7): ss 48(5)(b), 49(5)(b) (as so prospectively added and amended).

     The Secretary of State may provide that in prescribed circumstances a supervisory authority is not an interested supervisory authority for these purposes (ss 48(7), 49(7)); at the date at which this volume states the law no such circumstances had been prescribed. As to the Secretary of State see PARA 333. See also PARA 241 note 4.

5   See note 3.

6   Safeguarding Vulnerable Groups Act 2006 ss 48(1)(a), (2), 49(1)(a), (2) (prospectively amended: see note 3). As to the criteria for inclusion in the children's barred list see PARA 265. As to criteria for inclusion in the adults' barred list see PARA 266.

7   Safeguarding Vulnerable Groups Act 2006 ss 48(1)(b), 49(1)(b) (as amended and prospectively amended: see note 3). A person is subject to a relevant children's disqualification if he is included in a list maintained under the Protection of Vulnerable Groups (Scotland) Act 2007 s 1(1)(a) or the

Safeguarding Vulnerable Groups (Northern Ireland) Order 2007, SI 2007/1351, art 6(1)(a), and a person is subject to a relevant adults' disqualification if he is included in a list maintained under the Protection of Vulnerable Groups (Scotland) Act 2007 s 1(1)(b) or the Safeguarding Vulnerable Groups (Northern Ireland) Order 2007, SI 2007/1351, art 6(1)(b): Safeguarding Vulnerable Groups Act 2006 ss 48(6), 49(6); Safeguarding Vulnerable Groups Act 2006 (Miscellaneous Provisions) Order 2012, SI 2012/2113, arts 2, 3.

8 Ie by virtue of the Safeguarding Vulnerable Groups Act 2006 s 26 (now repealed).

9 Safeguarding Vulnerable Groups Act 2006 ss 48(1)(c), 49(1)(c) (prospectively repealed: see note 3). As to the meaning of 'child' see PARA 241 note 1. As to the meanings of 'adult' and 'vulnerable adult' see PARA 251 note 1.

10 See note 3.

11 Safeguarding Vulnerable Groups Act 2006 ss 48(2A), 49(2A) (prospectively added and amended: see note 3).

12 Safeguarding Vulnerable Groups Act 2006 ss 48(1)(a), 49(1)(b) (prospectively amended: see note 3).

13 Safeguarding Vulnerable Groups Act 2006 ss 48(1)(b), 49(1)(b) (amended and prospectively amended: see note 3). As to when a person is subject to a relevant children's disqualification or a relevant adults' disqualification see note 7.

304. Duty of Disclosure and Barring Service to inform supervisory authorities about persons of concern. The Disclosure and Barring Service (DBS)[1] may provide a supervisory authority[2] with any information it has[3] that it thinks:

(1) relates to the protection of children[4] or vulnerable adults[5] in general, or of any child or vulnerable adult in particular[6]; and

(2) is relevant to the exercise of any function[7] of the authority[8].

Disclosure may be made under these provisions either on an application by the authority or otherwise[9].

1 As to the Disclosure and Barring Service see PARA 265.

2 As to the supervisory authorities for the purposes of the Safeguarding Vulnerable Groups Act 2006 see s 45(7); and PARA 286.

3 Ie other than information falling within the Safeguarding Vulnerable Groups Act 2006 Sch 3 para 19(5) (provision of relevant police information for barring purposes: see PARA 292) or of any circumstance mentioned in s 48(1) or s 49(1) (notification of changes in barring information: see PARA 303) in relation to a person: s 50(3) (s 50(2), (3) amended, s 50(4), (5) added, by the Protection of Freedoms Act 2012 s 76(5)).

4 As to the meaning of 'child' see PARA 241 note 1.

5 As to the meanings of 'adult' and 'vulnerable adult' see PARA 251 note 1.

6 Safeguarding Vulnerable Groups Act 2006 s 50(1), (2), (3)(a) (s 50(1), (2), (4), (5) amended by SI 2012/3006).

7 Ie any function which is mentioned in the Safeguarding Vulnerable Groups Act 2006 s 45(7) (see PARA 286): s 50(3)(b) (as amended: see note 3).

8 Safeguarding Vulnerable Groups Act 2006 s 50(3)(b) (as amended: see note 3).

9 Safeguarding Vulnerable Groups Act 2006 s 50(2) (as amended: see note 3). A supervisory authority may apply to DBS under s 50 only if the information is required in connection with the exercise of a function of the supervisory authority which is mentioned in s 45(7): s 50(4) (as added and amended: see notes 3, 6). DBS may determine the form, manner and contents of an application for these purposes: s 50(5) (as so added and amended).

D. DISCLOSURE OF BARRING INFORMATION TO KEEPERS OF REGISTERS

305. Notification of keepers of registers. Provision is made for the keepers of professional registers[1] to be notified by the Disclosure and Barring Service (DBS)[2] when a person who appears on such a register is subject to the barring provisions[3]. Such notifications may be made either where DBS becomes aware that a person is or has become subject to the barring provisions[4] or on the application of the keeper of the relevant register[5]. Notifications need not be made[6] if DBS is satisfied that the keeper of the register already has the information concerned[7]. Provision is also made for the provision of other relevant information by DBS, whether on application or otherwise[8].

1   As to the registers in question and the keepers of those registers see the Safeguarding Vulnerable Groups Act 2006 ss 41(7), 43(6); and PARA 285.
2   As to the Disclosure and Barring Service see PARA 265. As to the information on barred persons required to be kept by DBS see PARAS 287–288.
3   See the Safeguarding Vulnerable Groups Act 2006 s 43; and PARAS 306, 307.
4   See PARA 306.
5   See PARA 307. DBS may determine the form, manner and contents of an application for the purposes of the Safeguarding Vulnerable Groups Act 2006 s 43: s 43(5F) (s 43(5E), (5F) added by the Protection of Freedoms Act 2012 s 75(3); amended by SI 2012/3006).
6   Ie the duties in the Safeguarding Vulnerable Groups Act 2006 s 43(2), (4), (5B): see PARAS 306, 307.
7   Safeguarding Vulnerable Groups Act 2006 s 43(5E) (as added and amended: see note 5).
8   See PARA 308.

306. Notification where persons are or have become subject to barring provisions. Until a day to be appointed[1] the Disclosure and Barring Service (DBS)[2] is required to notify the keepers of professional registers[3] where DBS knows or thinks that a person (A) appears on a relevant register[4] and either A is newly included in a barred list[5] or DBS becomes aware that A is subject to a relevant disqualification[6], or having been subject to monitoring, A ceases[7] to be so subject[8]; as from that day[9] the notification duty arises where DBS knows or thinks that A appears on a relevant register[10] and either A is included in a barred list[11] or DBS is aware that A is subject to a relevant disqualification[12]. Notification involves DBS notifying the keeper of the relevant register of the circumstances which triggered the notification duty[13].

1   The Safeguarding Vulnerable Groups Act 2006 s 43(1), (2) are substituted by the Protection of Freedoms Act 2012 s 75(3), as from a day to be appointed. At the date at which this volume states the law no such day had been appointed.
2   As to the Disclosure and Barring Service see PARA 265. As to the information on barred persons required to be kept by DBS see PARAS 287–288.
3   As to the registers in question and the keepers of those registers see the Safeguarding Vulnerable Groups Act 2006 ss 41(7), 43(6); and PARA 285. As to the application and notification duty generally see PARA 305.
4   A keeper of a relevant register may apply for information under the Safeguarding Vulnerable Groups Act 2006 s 43 (see PARA 307), or to be notified under s 43, in relation to a person (A) only if A appears in the register or A is being considered for inclusion in the register: s 43(5D) (added by the Protection of Freedoms Act 2012 s 75(3)).
5   As to the criteria for inclusion in the children's barred list see PARA 265. As to criteria for inclusion in the adults' barred list see PARA 266.
6   Safeguarding Vulnerable Groups Act 2006 s 43(1)(a) (prospectively substituted (see note 1); s 43(1), (2) amended by SI 2012/3006). A person is subject to a relevant disqualification for the purposes of the Safeguarding Vulnerable Groups Act 2006 s 43 if he is included in a list maintained under the Protection of Vulnerable Groups (Scotland) Act 2007 s 1(1)(a) or (b) or the Safeguarding Vulnerable Groups (Northern Ireland) Order 2007, SI 2007/1351, art 6(1)(a) or (b): Safeguarding Vulnerable Groups Act 2006 s 43(7); Safeguarding Vulnerable Groups Act 2006 (Miscellaneous Provisions) Order 2012, SI 2012/2113, arts 2, 3.
7   Ie by virtue of the Safeguarding Vulnerable Groups Act 2006 s 26 (now repealed).
8   Safeguarding Vulnerable Groups Act 2006 s 43(1)(b) (prospectively substituted: see note 1).
9   See note 1.
10 Safeguarding Vulnerable Groups Act 2006 s 43(1)(a) (prospectively substituted and amended: see notes 1, 6).
11 Safeguarding Vulnerable Groups Act 2006 s 43(1)(b)(i) (prospectively substituted and amended: see notes 1, 6).
12 Safeguarding Vulnerable Groups Act 2006 s 43(1)(b)(ii) (prospectively substituted and amended: see notes 1, 6).
13 Until a day to be appointed, DBS must notify the keeper of the register of the circumstances mentioned in the Safeguarding Vulnerable Groups Act 2006 s 43(1)(a) or (b) (as the case may be) (s 43(2)(a) (prospectively substituted: see notes 1, 6)) and in a case where A is newly included in

a barred list, must provide the keeper with all the information on which DBS relied in deciding to include A in the list (s 43(2)(b) (as so prospectively substituted and amended)). As from that day, DBS must notify the keeper of the register of the circumstances mentioned in s 43(1)(b)(i) or (as the case may be) s 43(1)(b)(ii) (s 43(2)(a) (as so prospectively substituted and amended)), and, in the case where A is included in a barred list, provide the keeper of the register with such of the information on which DBS relied in including A in the list as DBS considers to be relevant to the exercise of any function of the keeper and otherwise appropriate to provide (s 43(2)(b) (as so prospectively substituted and amended)).

307. Notification on application of register keeper. The Disclosure and Barring Service (DBS)[1] is required to notify the keeper of a relevant register[2] if a person (A) is included in a barred list[3], or if DBS is aware that A is subject to a relevant disqualification[4], if the keeper of the register makes an application to DBS for the purpose of ascertaining such information[5]. Applications may be made only in respect of persons appearing or being considered for inclusion in the register in question[6].

As from a day to be appointed, DBS must notify the keeper of a register if A is included in a barred list[7] or if DBS is aware that A is subject to a relevant disqualification[8], if the keeper has applied to DBS to be notified in relation to A of such circumstances[9] and the application has not been withdrawn[10].

1   As to the Disclosure and Barring Service see PARA 265. As to the information on barred persons required to be kept by DBS see PARAS 287–288.
2   As to the registers in question and the keepers of those registers see the Safeguarding Vulnerable Groups Act 2006 ss 41(7), 43(6); and PARA 285. As to applications and the notification duty generally see PARA 305.
3   Safeguarding Vulnerable Groups Act 2006 s 43(3)(a), (4) (s 43(3), (4) substituted by the Protection of Freedoms Act 2012 s 75(3); Safeguarding Vulnerable Groups Act 2006 s 43(3), (4), (5A)–(5C) amended by SI 2012/3006). As to the criteria for inclusion in the children's barred list see PARA 265. As to criteria for inclusion in the adults' barred list see PARA 266.
4   Safeguarding Vulnerable Groups Act 2006 s 43(3)(b) (as substituted: see note 3). As to when is subject to a relevant disqualification see PARA 306 note 6.
5   Safeguarding Vulnerable Groups Act 2006 s 43(3), (4) (as substituted and amended: see note 3).
6   See the Safeguarding Vulnerable Groups Act 2006 s 43(5D); and PARA 306 note 4.
7   Safeguarding Vulnerable Groups Act 2006 s 43(5A)(a)(i) (s 43(5A)–(5C) prospectively added by the Protection of Freedoms Act 2012 s 75(3), as from a day to be appointed). At the date at which this volume states the law no day had been appointed for the commencement of these provisions.
8   Safeguarding Vulnerable Groups Act 2006 s 43(5A)(a)(ii) (prospectively added (see note 7); as amended (see note 3)).
9   Safeguarding Vulnerable Groups Act 2006 s 43(5A), (5B) (prospectively added (see note 7); as amended (see note 3)).
10 Safeguarding Vulnerable Groups Act 2006 s 43(5A)(b) (prospectively added: see note 7). For these purposes an application is withdrawn if the keeper of the register notifies DBS that the keeper no longer wishes to be notified if the circumstances are, or become, as mentioned in s 43(5A)(a)(i) or (as the case may be) (ii) (see the text and notes 7–9) in relation to A, or DBS cancels the application on either of the following grounds: that the keeper has not answered, within such reasonable period as was required by DBS, a request from DBS as to whether the keeper still wishes to be notified if the circumstances are, or become, as mentioned in s 43(5A)(a)(i) or (as the case may be) (ii); or that A neither appears in the register nor is being considered for inclusion in the register: s 43(5C) (as so prospectively added; as amended (see note 3)).

308. Provision of relevant information. The Disclosure and Barring Service (DBS)[1] may provide to the keeper of a relevant register[2] such information[3] relating to the protection of children[4] or vulnerable adults[5] in general, or of any child or vulnerable adult in particular[6], and which is relevant to the exercise of any function of the keeper of the register[7], as DBS considers appropriate[8].

1   As to the Disclosure and Barring Service see PARA 265.
2   Ie whether on an application by the keeper of a relevant register or otherwise: Safeguarding Vulnerable Groups Act 2006 s 43(5) (s 43(5) substituted, s 43(5G) added, by the Protection of Freedoms Act 2012 s 75(3); Safeguarding Vulnerable Groups Act 2006 s 43(5) amended by SI

2012/3006). As to the registers in question and the keepers of those registers see the Safeguarding Vulnerable Groups Act 2006 ss 41(7), 43(6); and PARA 285. Applications and notifications may be made only in respect of persons appearing or being considered for inclusion in the register in question: see s 43(5D); and PARA 306 note 4. As to applications and the notification duty generally see PARA 305.

3 Ie excluding information which is information that the circumstances are as mentioned in the Safeguarding Vulnerable Groups Act 2006 s 43(1)(b)(i) or (ii) in relation to a person (inclusion in barred list or subject to disqualification: see PARA 306), any information provided under s 43(2)(b) (provision of barring information: see PARA 306), or information falling within Sch 3 para 19(5) (provision of relevant police information for barring purposes: see PARA 292): s 43(5G)(b) (as added: see note 2). The Secretary of State may by order amend s 43(5G): s 43(5H) (as so added). At the date at which this volume states the law no such order had been made. As to the Secretary of State see PARA 333. See also PARA 241 note 4.
4 As to the meaning of 'child' see PARA 241 note 1.
5 As to the meanings of 'adult' and 'vulnerable adult' see PARA 251 note 1.
6 Safeguarding Vulnerable Groups Act 2006 s 43(5G)(a)(i) (as added: see note 2).
7 Safeguarding Vulnerable Groups Act 2006 s 43(5G)(a)(ii) (as added: see note 2).
8 Safeguarding Vulnerable Groups Act 2006 s 43(5) (as substituted and amended: see note 2).

E.   DISCLOSURE OF BARRING INFORMATION TO POLICE AND SECRETARY OF STATE

309. Duty of Disclosure and Barring Service to inform police about matters of concern. The Disclosure and Barring Service (DBS)[1] may provide any information it has to a chief officer of police[2] for use for any of the following purposes:

(1)   the prevention, detection and investigation of crime[3];
(2)   the apprehension and prosecution of offenders[4];
(3)   the appointment of persons who are under the direction and control of the chief officer[5]; and
(4)   the disclosure of information[6] relating to criminal record certificates[7].

DBS must also, for use for any of those purposes, provide to any chief officer of police who has requested it a barred list[8] or information as to whether a particular person is barred[9].

For use for the purposes of the protection of children[10] or vulnerable adults[11] DBS may provide to a relevant authority[12] any information which DBS reasonably believes to be relevant to that authority[13] and must provide to any relevant authority who has requested it information as to whether a particular person is barred[14].

1 As to the Disclosure and Barring Service see PARA 265.
2 'A chief officer of police' includes the Chief Constables of the Police Services of Northern Ireland and Scotland: Safeguarding Vulnerable Groups Act 2006 s 50A(3) (Safeguarding Vulnerable Groups Act 2006 s 50A added by the Policing and Crime Act 2009 s 88; Safeguarding Vulnerable Groups Act 2006 s 50A(3) added by SI 2010/1154, and amended by SI 2013/602; Safeguarding Vulnerable Groups Act 2006 s 50A(1), (1A)–(1C), (2), (3) amended by SI 2012/3006).
3 Safeguarding Vulnerable Groups Act 2006 s 50A(1)(a) (as added: see note 2). The powers conferred by s 50A do not limit any other power of DBS to provide information for any purpose or to any person: s 50A(2) (as so added; s 50A(1)(c), (d), (1A)–(1C), (4) added, s 50A(2) amended, by the Protection of Freedoms Act 2012 s 77(3), (4), Sch 9 para 65).
4 Safeguarding Vulnerable Groups Act 2006 s 50A(1)(b) (as added: see notes 2, 3).
5 Safeguarding Vulnerable Groups Act 2006 s 50A(1)(c) (as added (see notes 2, 3).
6 Ie by the relevant chief officer under the Police Act 1997 s 113B(4) (see SENTENCING vol 92 (2015) PARA 640).
7 Safeguarding Vulnerable Groups Act 2006 s 50A(1)(d) (as added: see notes 2, 3); Safeguarding Vulnerable Groups Act 2006 (Miscellaneous Provisions) Regulations 2012, SI 2012/2112, reg 28.
8 As to the barred lists see PARAS 265–293.
9 Safeguarding Vulnerable Groups Act 2006 s 50A(1A) (as added and amended: see notes 2, 3).
10 As to the meaning of 'child' see PARA 241 note 1.
11 As to the meanings of 'adult' and 'vulnerable adult' see PARA 251 note 1.
12 Ie the Secretary of State exercising functions in relation to prisons or a provider of probation services (within the meaning given by the Offender Management Act 2007 s 3(6): see

SENTENCING vol 92 (2015) PARA 669): Safeguarding Vulnerable Groups Act 2006 s 50A(4) (as added: see notes 2, 3). As to the Secretary of State see PARA 333. See also PARA 241 note 4.
13 Safeguarding Vulnerable Groups Act 2006 s 50A(1B) (as added: see notes 2, 3).
14 Safeguarding Vulnerable Groups Act 2006 s 50A(1C) (as added: see notes 2, 3).

310. Information to be exchanged between Secretary of State and Disclosure and Barring Service. Where the Disclosure and Barring Service (DBS)[1] includes a person in a barred list[2], is considering whether to include a person in a barred list, or thinks that any of the prescribed criteria for inclusion[3] is satisfied in relation to him and that the Secretary of State does not already have the information, it must provide the Secretary of State with the following information:

(1)   full name and title[4];
(2)   any other name or names by which the person may be known[5];
(3)   date of birth[6];
(4)   national insurance number[7];
(5)   gender[8]; and
(6)   last known address (including postcode)[9].

Where DBS includes a person in a barred list it must additionally provide the Secretary of State with the date of and the reasons for inclusion in the list[10]. Where DBS is considering whether to include a person in a barred list it must additionally provide the Secretary of State with information as to whether that person is being considered by DBS for inclusion in the children's barred list or the adults' barred list (or both)[11]. Where DBS thinks that any of the prescribed criteria for inclusion is satisfied in relation to a person and that the Secretary of State does not already have the information, it must additionally provide the Secretary of State with any prescribed criterion that is satisfied in relation to the person and the date on which any such criterion was satisfied[12].

The Secretary of State may provide to DBS any information relating to a person which is held by him in connection with his functions under the former barring provisions[13], and DBS is also required to provide the Secretary of State with such advice as he requests in connection with decisions relating to those provisions[14].

1   As to the Disclosure and Barring Service see PARA 265.
2   As to the criteria for inclusion in the children's barred list see PARA 265. As to criteria for inclusion in the adults' barred list see PARA 266.
3   Ie the criteria prescribed for the purposes of the Safeguarding Vulnerable Groups Act 2006 Sch 3 para 1, 2, 7 or 8: see PARAS 265, 266, 270.
4   Safeguarding Vulnerable Groups Act 2006 Sch 3 para 21 (amended by SI 2012/3006); Safeguarding Vulnerable Groups Act 2006 (Prescribed Information) Regulations 2008, SI 2008/3265, reg 13(1), (2)(a), (3)(a), (4)(a), Sch 1 para 1(a). As to the Secretary of State see PARA 333. See also PARA 241 note 4.
5   Safeguarding Vulnerable Groups Act 2006 (Prescribed Information) Regulations 2008, SI 2008/3265, Sch 1 para 1(b).
6   Safeguarding Vulnerable Groups Act 2006 (Prescribed Information) Regulations 2008, SI 2008/3265, Sch 1 para 1(c).
7   Safeguarding Vulnerable Groups Act 2006 (Prescribed Information) Regulations 2008, SI 2008/3265, Sch 1 para 1(d).
8   Safeguarding Vulnerable Groups Act 2006 (Prescribed Information) Regulations 2008, SI 2008/3265, Sch 1 para 1(e).
9   Safeguarding Vulnerable Groups Act 2006 (Prescribed Information) Regulations 2008, SI 2008/3265, Sch 1 para 1(f).
10 Safeguarding Vulnerable Groups Act 2006 (Prescribed Information) Regulations 2008, SI 2008/3265, reg 13(2)(b). This must include information as to which of the Safeguarding Vulnerable Groups Act 2006 Sch 3 paras 1–5 or 7–11 (see PARA 265 et seq) DBS relied upon in including the person in the list: Safeguarding Vulnerable Groups Act 2006 (Prescribed Information) Regulations 2008, SI 2008/3265, reg 13(2)(b) (amended by SI 2012/3006).
11 Safeguarding Vulnerable Groups Act 2006 (Prescribed Information) Regulations 2008, SI 2008/3265, reg 13(3)(b) (amended by SI 2012/3006). DBS must inform the Secretary of State

which of the Safeguarding Vulnerable Groups Act 2006 Sch 3 paras 3, 5, 9 or 11 applies: Safeguarding Vulnerable Groups Act 2006 (Prescribed Information) Regulations 2008, SI 2008/3265, reg 13(3)(b) (amended by SI 2012/3006).

12 Safeguarding Vulnerable Groups Act 2006 (Prescribed Information) Regulations 2008, SI 2008/3265, reg 13(4)(b).

13 See the Safeguarding Vulnerable Groups Act 2006 Sch 3 para 20 (amended by SI 2012/3006), which provides that the Secretary of State may provide to DBS any information relating to a person which is held by him in connection with his functions under the repealed provisions of the Protection of Children Act 1999, the Care Standards Act 2000 Pt 7 (repealed), or the Education Act 2002 ss 142–144.

14 See the Safeguarding Vulnerable Groups Act 2006 Sch 8 para 1 (amended by SI 2012/3006), which provides that DBS must provide the Secretary of State with such advice as he requests in connection with any decision in relation to the inclusion of a person in the list kept under the Protection of Children Act 1999 s 1 (individuals considered unsuitable to work with children) (repealed) or the Care Standards Act 2000 s 81 (individuals considered unsuitable to work with vulnerable adults) (repealed), or any decision in relation to a direction under the Education Act 2002 s 142 (prohibition from teaching: see EDUCATION vol 35 (2015) PARA 420) in relation to a person.

(vii) Restriction on Activities of Barred Persons

311. Barred person not to engage in regulated activity. An individual commits an offence[1] if he:

(1)   seeks to engage in regulated activity[2] from which he is barred[3];

(2)   offers to engage in regulated activity from which he is barred[4]; or

(3)   engages in regulated activity from which he is barred[5].

There are a number of statutory defences available to a person charged with an offence under these provisions[6].

1 A person guilty of an offence under the Safeguarding Vulnerable Groups Act 2006 s 7(1) is liable, on conviction on indictment, to imprisonment for a term not exceeding five years, or to a fine, or to both; and on summary conviction, to imprisonment for a term not exceeding six months, or to a fine not exceeding the statutory maximum, or to both: s 7(2), (6). In relation to an offence committed on or after the day to be appointed for the coming into force of the Criminal Justice Act 2003 s 282(3), the maximum term of imprisonment on summary conviction is increased to 12 months: Safeguarding Vulnerable Groups Act 2006 s 7(6). At the date at which this volume states the law no such day had been appointed. As to the powers of magistrates' courts to issue fines on summary conviction see SENTENCING vol 92 (2015) PARA 176.

2 As to the meaning of 'regulated activity' see PARAS 241–250 (children), PARAS 251–259 (vulnerable adults). To qualify as a regulated activity for these purposes it is not necessary that the activity is carried out frequently by the same person, or that the period condition is satisfied (ie the Safeguarding Vulnerable Groups Act 2006 Sch 4 para 1(1)(b) (see PARA 241) and Sch 1 para 1(2)(a) (see PARA 246) are disregarded for these purposes): s 7(5)(a). As to when the period condition is satisfied see PARA 241 note 5.

3 Safeguarding Vulnerable Groups Act 2006 s 7(1)(a). As to when a person is barred from regulated activity see PARA 299 note 9.

4 Safeguarding Vulnerable Groups Act 2006 s 7(1)(b).

5 Safeguarding Vulnerable Groups Act 2006 s 7(1)(c).

6 See PARA 314.

312. Use of barred person for regulated activity. A person commits an offence[1] if:

(1)   he permits an individual (B) to engage in regulated activity[2] from which B is barred[3];

(2)   he knows or has reason to believe that B is barred from that activity[4]; and

(3)   B engages in the activity[5].

There are a number of statutory defences available to a person charged with an offence under these provisions[6].

1 A person guilty of an offence under the Safeguarding Vulnerable Groups Act 2006 s 9(1) is liable, on conviction on indictment, to imprisonment for a term not exceeding five years, or to a fine, or

to both; and on summary conviction, to imprisonment for a term not exceeding six months, or to a fine not exceeding the statutory maximum, or to both: s 9(3), (6). In relation to an offence committed on or after the day to be appointed for the coming into force of the Criminal Justice Act 2003 s 282(3), the maximum term of imprisonment on summary conviction is increased to 12 months: Safeguarding Vulnerable Groups Act 2006 s 9(6). At the date at which this volume states the law no such day had been appointed. As to offences committed by partnerships and bodies corporate see s 18; and PARA 280. As to the powers of magistrates' courts to issue fines on summary conviction see SENTENCING vol 92 (2015) PARA 176.

2 As to the meaning of 'regulated activity' see PARAS 241–250 (children), PARAS 251–259 (vulnerable adults). To qualify as a regulated activity for these purposes it is not necessary that the activity is carried out frequently by the same person, or that the period condition is satisfied (ie the Safeguarding Vulnerable Groups Act 2006 Sch 4 para 1(1)(b) (see PARA 241) and Sch 1 para 1(2)(a) (see PARA 246) are disregarded for these purposes): s 9(5)(a). As to when the period condition is satisfied see PARA 241 note 5.

3 Safeguarding Vulnerable Groups Act 2006 s 9(1)(a). As to when a person is barred from regulated activity see PARA 299 note 9.

4 Safeguarding Vulnerable Groups Act 2006 s 9(1)(b).

5 Safeguarding Vulnerable Groups Act 2006 s 9(1)(c).

6 See PARA 314.

313. Supply of barred persons for regulated activity. A personnel supplier[1], and a person in the course of acting or appearing to act on behalf of a personnel supplier[2], commits an offence[3] if:

(1)   he supplies an individual (B) to another (P)[4];

(2)   he knows or has reason to believe that P will make arrangements for B to engage in regulated activity[5] from which B is barred[6]; and

(3)   he knows or has reason to believe that B is barred from that activity[7].

There are a number of statutory defences available to a person charged with an offence under these provisions[8].

1 As to the meaning of 'personnel supplier' see PARA 241 note 4.

2 A person charged with an offence in the course of acting or appearing to act on behalf of a personnel supplier (ie an offence under the Safeguarding Vulnerable Groups Act 2006 s 19) does not commit the offence if B has not attained the age of 16: s 20(1).

3 A person guilty of an offence under the Safeguarding Vulnerable Groups Act 2006 s 9(2) or s 19(2) is liable, on conviction on indictment, to imprisonment for a term not exceeding five years, or to a fine, or to both; and on summary conviction, to imprisonment for a term not exceeding six months, or to a fine not exceeding the statutory maximum, or to both: ss 9(3), (6), 19(5), (10). In relation to an offence committed on or after the day to be appointed for the coming into force of the Criminal Justice Act 2003 s 282(3), the maximum term of imprisonment on summary conviction is increased to 12 months: Safeguarding Vulnerable Groups Act 2006 ss 9(6), 19(10). At the date at which this volume states the law no such day had been appointed. As to offences committed by partnerships and bodies corporate see s 18; and PARA 280. As to the powers of magistrates' courts to issue fines on summary conviction see SENTENCING vol 92 (2015) PARA 176.

4 Safeguarding Vulnerable Groups Act 2006 ss 9(2)(a), 19(2)(a).

5 As to the meaning of 'regulated activity' see PARAS 241–250 (children), PARAS 251–259 (vulnerable adults). To qualify as a regulated activity for these purposes it is not necessary that the activity is carried out frequently by the same person, or that the period condition is satisfied (ie the Safeguarding Vulnerable Groups Act 2006 Sch 4 para 1(1)(b) (see PARA 241) and Sch 1 para 1(2)(a) (see PARA 246) are disregarded for these purposes): ss 9(5)(a), 19(8)(a). As to when the period condition is satisfied see PARA 241 note 5.

6 Safeguarding Vulnerable Groups Act 2006 ss 9(2)(b), 19(2)(b). As to when a person is barred from regulated activity see PARA 299 note 9.

7 Safeguarding Vulnerable Groups Act 2006 ss 9(2)(c), 19(2)(c).

8 See PARA 314.

314. Defences. It is a defence for a person charged with the offences of engaging in regulated activity while being a barred person[1], of using a barred person for regulated activity[2] or of supplying a barred person for regulated activity[3] to prove:

(1)   that he reasonably thought that it was necessary for him, or the barred person being supplied or used, to engage in the activity for the purpose of preventing harm to a child[4] or vulnerable adult[5] (as the case may be)[6];

(2)   that he reasonably thought that there was no other person who could engage in the activity for that purpose[7]; and

(3)   that the barred person engaged in the activity for no longer than was necessary for that purpose[8].

In relation to the offence of engaging in regulated activity while being a barred person[9], it is also a defence for the person to prove that he did not know, and could not reasonably be expected to know, that he was barred from that activity[10].

1   Ie the offence under the Safeguarding Vulnerable Groups Act 2006 s 7(1): see PARA 311.
2   Ie the offence under the Safeguarding Vulnerable Groups Act 2006 s 9(1): see PARA 312.
3   Ie the offence under the Safeguarding Vulnerable Groups Act 2006 s 9(2): see PARA 313. These defences are not available to a person charged with an offence under s 19 (see PARA 313).
4   As to the meaning of 'child' see PARA 241 note 1.
5   As to the meanings of 'adult' and 'vulnerable adult' see PARA 251 note 1.
6   Safeguarding Vulnerable Groups Act 2006 ss 7(4)(a), 9(4)(a).
7   Safeguarding Vulnerable Groups Act 2006 ss 7(4)(b), 9(4)(b).
8   Safeguarding Vulnerable Groups Act 2006 ss 7(4)(c), 9(4)(c).
9   See note 1.
10 Safeguarding Vulnerable Groups Act 2006 s 7(3).

5. SUPERVISION, INTERVENTION AND ADMINISTRATION

(1) ENGLAND

(i) Local Authorities

A. PRINCIPLES GOVERNING THE PROVISION OF CARE

315. Local authority social services functions. The 'social services functions' of a local authority in England are[1] principally its functions relating to the provision of care and support under the Care Act 2014[2] and the protection of children under the Children Act 1989[3]. In addition, local authorities in England have a number of functions relating to the protection of young offenders and children in care[4], the establishment of local safeguarding children's boards[5], the employment and representation of disabled persons[6], the provision of welfare services to sick and disabled persons[7], the welfare and accommodation of mentally disordered persons[8], as well as certain residual and administrative functions[9], which are also 'social services functions' for these purposes. Further statutory functions may be designated 'social services functions' by the Secretary of State[10].

1   Ie for the purposes of the Local Authority Social Services Act 1970: s 1A(a) (s 1A added by the Local Government Act 2000 s 102(3)). The duties imposed by the Local Authority Social Services Act 1970 apply only in relation to local authorities in England: see s 1 (amended by the Local Government Act 1972 s 195(1); disapplied in relation to local authorities in Wales by the Social Services and Well-being (Wales) Act 2014 (Consequential Amendments) Regulations 2016, SI 2016/413, reg 20), which provides that the local authorities for the purposes of that Act are the councils of non-metropolitan counties and metropolitan districts in England, the councils of London boroughs and the Common Council of the City of London. As to the meaning of 'England' see PARA 1 note 1. As to local government areas and authorities in England see LOCAL GOVERNMENT vol 69 (2009) PARA 22 et seq. As to the London boroughs and their councils see LONDON GOVERNMENT vol 71 (2013) PARAS 15, 20, 34–38. As to the Common Council of the City of London see LONDON GOVERNMENT vol 71 (2013) PARA 16. The Local Authority Social Services Act 1970 has effect as if the Council of the Isles of Scilly were a local authority (see s 12; and the Isles of Scilly (Local Authority Social Services) Order 1980, SI 1980/328); and does not extend to Northern Ireland (see the Local Authority Social Services Act 1970 s 15).

2   Local Authority Social Services Act 1970 Sch 1 (amended by SI 2015/914). The functions are those under the Care Act 2014 Pt 1 (ss 1–80) (see PARA 1 et seq), and under the Community Care (Delayed Discharges) Act 2003 Pt 1 (ss 1–14), which correspond to the functions under the Care Act 2014 Sch 3 (discharge of hospital patients with care and support needs) where a patient is be discharged into local authority areas in England by an NHS body in Wales (see PARA 69) which are defined as 'social services functions' for these purposes: Local Authority Social Services Act 1970 Sch 1 (amended by the Community Care (Delayed Discharges etc) Act 2003 s 13). There are also functions relating to the provision of accommodation and other assistance for persons in need under the National Assistance Act 1948 ss 21–27, 45, 48, 49, 56(3) which have been superseded by the overall effect of the Care Act 2014 (see PARA 3 note 4), and associated functions under the Public Health (Control of Disease) Act 1984 s 46(2), (5) (burial and cremation of persons dying in accommodation provided under the National Assistance Act 1948 Pt III (ss 21–35)) and the Health and Social Care Act 2001 Pt 4 (ss 49–59) (functions in relation to the provision of residential accommodation; making of direct payments to person in respect of his securing provision of services or services to carers) which are defined as 'social services functions' for these purposes: Local Authority Social Services Act 1970 Sch 1 (amended by the Public Health (Control of Disease) Act 1984 Sch 2 para 6; the Health and Social Care Act 2001 Sch 5 para 15(3); the Mental Capacity Act 2005 Sch 7 para 16; and the Health and Social Care Act 2008 s 147(5)).

3   Ie functions under the Children Act 1989 (see CHILDREN AND YOUNG PERSONS) (except s 36, Sch 3 paras 12–18, 19(1)): Local Authority Social Services Act 1970 Sch 1 (entry added by the Children Act 1989 Sch 13 para 26(2); and amended by the National Health Service and Community Care Act 1990 Sch 9 para 11(a); the Adoption and Children Act 2002 Sch 3 para 14(b); the Care Standards Act 2000 Sch 4 para 4; the Health and Social Care Act 2012 Sch 5 para 15; the Children and Families Act 2014 Sch 2 para 44; SI 2002/2469; SI 2007/961; SI 2010/1158).

4 Ie functions under the Children and Young Persons Act 1933 Pt III (ss 31–59) (see CHILDREN
   AND YOUNG PERSONS) and Pt IV (ss 77–81); the Children and Young Persons Act 1963 Pt I
   (ss 16–32) (see CHILDREN AND YOUNG PERSONS); the Children and Young Persons Act 1969
   (see CHILDREN AND YOUNG PERSONS); the Social Work (Scotland) Act 1968 ss 75(2), 76(4)
   (welfare of child in care whose parent moves to Scotland); the Children and Young Persons Act
   2008 Pt 1 (ss 1–6) (making arrangements for the discharge of relevant care functions in relation
   to certain children and young persons: see CHILDREN AND YOUNG PERSONS vol 10 (2017)
   PARA 821), in so far as it confers on a local authority in England within the meaning of Pt 1; and
   the Legal Aid, Sentencing and Punishment of Offenders Act 2012 s 92 (functions in relation to a
   child remanded to local authority accommodation) (see CHILDREN AND YOUNG PERSONS vol 10
   (2017) PARA 1301): Local Authority Social Services Act 1970 Sch 1 (amended by the Child Care
   Act 1980 Sch 6; the Children Act 1989 Sch 15; the Children and Young Persons Act 2008 s 5; the
   Legal Aid, Sentencing and Punishment of Offenders Act 2012 Sch 12 para 13; and SI 2010/1158).
5 Ie functions under the Children Act 2004 ss 13–16 (see PARAS 237–238) and s 9A (functions
   relating to targets for safeguarding: see PARA 316): Local Authority Social Services Act 1970 Sch 1
   (amended by the Children Act 2004 s 56; and by the Apprenticeships, Skills, Children and
   Learning Act 2009 s 195(3)).
6 Ie functions under the Disabled Persons (Employment) Act 1958 s 3 (see EMPLOYMENT vol 40
   (2014) PARA 611) and the Disabled Persons (Services, Consultation and Representation) Act 1986
   ss 1–4, 5(5), 7, 8 (see PARAS 329, 331; and EDUCATION) (representation and assessment of
   disabled persons): Local Authority Social Services Act 1970 Sch 1 (amended by the Local
   Government Act 2000 Sch 5 para 7; and by SI 2010/1158).
7 Ie functions under the National Assistance Act 1948 ss 29, 30 (see PARA 329) and under the
   Chronically Sick and Disabled Persons Act 1970 ss 1, 2 (see PARA 330), s 2A (see PARA 25) and
   (to the extent that it remains applicable) s 18: Local Authority Social Services Act 1970 Sch 1
   (amended by SI 2015/914).
8 Ie functions under the Mental Health Act 1959 s 8 (see MENTAL HEALTH AND CAPACITY vol 75
   (2013) PARA 557); the Mental Health Act 1983 Pt II (ss 2–34); Pt III (ss 35–55), Pt VI (ss 80–92)
   (welfare of mentally disordered; guardianship; exercise of functions of nearest relative), ss 66, 67,
   s 69(1) (exercise of functions of nearest relative in relation to mental health review tribunals), s 114
   (appointment of approved social workers), s 115 (entry and inspection), s 116 (welfare of certain
   patients), ss 117, 117A (after-care), s 130 (prosecutions), s 130A (making arrangements to enable
   independent mental health advocates to be available to help qualifying patients); the Mental
   Health (Scotland) Act 1984 s 10 (in relation to persons in Scottish hospitals under the care of
   English local authorities); the National Health Service and Community Care Act 1990 s 47 (see
   MENTAL HEALTH AND CAPACITY); and the Mental Capacity Act 2005 ss 39, 39A, 39C, 39D
   (instructing independent mental capacity advocate), s 49 (reports in proceedings) and Sch A1 (any
   functions) (see MENTAL HEALTH AND CAPACITY): Local Authority Social Services Act 1970
   Sch 1 (amended by the Education (Handicapped Children Act 1970 Schedule; the National Health
   Service Reorganisation Act 1973 Sch 5; the Mental Health Act 1983 Sch 4 para 27; the Children
   Act 1989 Sch 13 para 26(1)(a); the Care Standards Act 2000 Sch 6; the Mental Capacity Act 2005
   Sch 7 para 16(1), (3); the Mental Capacity Act 2007 Sch 9 Pt 2 para 13; the Health and Social Care
   Act 2012 s 43(4); SI 2008/2828; SI 2008/2833; SI 2015/914).
9 Ie functions under the Local Authority Social Services Act 1970 s 6 (appointment of director: see
   PARA 324) and s 7B (complaints procedure: see PARA 325); the Health Services and Public Health
   Act 1968 s 45 (welfare of old people) and s 65 (assistance to voluntary organisations: see HEALTH
   SERVICES vol 54 (2017) PARA 287); the Adoption Act 1976 (see CHILDREN AND YOUNG
   PERSONS) (functions continuing to be exercisable by virtue of any transitional or saving provision
   made by or under the Adoption and Children Act 2002); the Housing (Scotland) Act 1987 s 38(b)
   and the Housing Act 1996 s 213(1)(b) (see HOUSING vol 56 (2011) PARA 306) (co-operation in
   relation to homeless persons and persons threatened with homelessness); the Carers (Recognition
   and Services) Act 1995 s 1 (see MENTAL HEALTH AND CAPACITY) (assessment of ability of carers
   to provide care); the Education Act 1996 s 322 (see EDUCATION vol 36 (2015) PARA 1025) (help
   for another local authority); the Adoption (Intercountry Aspects) Act 1999 ss 1, 2(4) (see
   CHILDREN AND YOUNG PERSONS vol 9 (2017) PARAS 582, 585) (functions under regulations
   made under s 1 giving effect to the Convention on Protection of Children and Co-operation in
   Respect of Intercountry Adoptions (The Hague, 29 May 1993; TS 40 (1994); Cm 2691)
   art 9(a)–(c)); the Adoption and Children Act 2002 (maintenance of Adoption Service; functions of
   local authority as adoption agency) (see CHILDREN AND YOUNG PERSONS); the Contracting Out
   (Local Authorities Social Services Functions) (England) Order 2014, SI 2014/829, art 3 (see LOCAL
   GOVERNMENT vol 69 (2009) PARA 407) (contracting out); and (as from a day to be appointed)
   the Health and Social Care (Community Health and Standards) Act 2003 s 114 (consideration of
   complaints: see PARA 325): Local Authority Social Services Act 1970 Sch 1 (amended by the
   National Health Service Reorganisation Act 1973 Sch 4 para 131(2); the National Health Service
   Act 1977 Sch 16; the Housing (Scotland) Act 1987 Sch 23 para 16; the Children Act 1989 Sch 15;
   the National Health Service and Community Care Act 1990 Sch 9 para 11(b); the Carers

(Recognition and Services) Act 1995 s 1(7); the Housing Act 1996 Sch 17 para 1; the Education Act 1996 Sch 37 para 18; the Adoption (Intercountry Aspects) Act 1999 Sch 2 para 1; the Care Standards Act 2000 s 112; the Adoption and Children Act 2002 Sch 3 para 14; the Children Act 2004 Sch 2 para 2(1), (3); the Childcare Act 2006 Sch 2 para 1; SI 2010/1158; SI 2014/829; and prospectively amended by the Health and Social Care (Community Health and Standards) Act 2003 Sch 9 para 4)).

10 Local Authority Social Services Act 1970 s 1A(b) (as added: see note 1). Such designation is by order under s 1A: s 1A (as so added). At the date at which this volume states the law no such order had been made. As to the Secretary of State see PARA 333.

316. Exercise of functions under ministerial guidance and direction. A local authority in England[1] must act under the general guidance of the Secretary of State[2] in the exercise of its social services functions[3]. Without prejudice to this, the Secretary of State may also give directions to local authorities which must exercise their social services functions in accordance with those directions[4].

The Secretary of State may, in accordance with regulations, set safeguarding targets (ie targets for safeguarding and promoting the welfare of children in a local authority's area) for a local authority in England[5]. In exercising their functions, a local authority in England must act in the manner best calculated to secure that any safeguarding targets so set (so far as relating to the area of the authority) are met[6].

1 As to the meanings of 'local authority' and 'England' see PARA 1. The duties imposed by the Local Authority Social Services Act 1970 apply only in relation to local authorities in England: see PARA 315 note 1.

2 As to the Secretary of State see PARA 333.

3 Care Act 2014 s 78(1); Local Authority Social Services Act 1970 s 7(1), (1A) (s 7(1A) added by SI 2015/914). As to the meaning of 'social services functions' (which for this purpose include the functions given to the authority by the Care Act 2014 Pt 1 (ss 1–80) or by regulations thereunder) see PARA 315. In relation to all social services functions other than those under Pt 1, this includes the exercise of any discretion conferred by any relevant enactment: Local Authority Social Services Act 1970 s 7(1). Before issuing any guidance for the purposes of the Care Act 2014 s 78(1), the Secretary of State must consult such persons as he considers appropriate: s 78(2). As to the effect of the guidance which has been issued by the Secretary of State under the Local Authority Social Services Act 1970 s 7 see *R v Islington London Borough Council, ex p Rixon* [1997] ELR 66, 32 BMLR 136. See also *R (on the application of AB and SB) v Nottingham County Council* [2001] EWHC 235 (Admin), [2001] 3 FCR 350; *B v Lewisham London Borough Council* [2008] EWHC 738 (Admin), [2008] 2 FLR 523, [2008] All ER (D) 248 (Apr); and CHILDREN AND YOUNG PERSONS vol 10 (2017) PARA 796.

4 Local Authority Social Services Act 1970 s 7A(1) (s 7A added by the National Health Service and Community Care Act 1990 s 50). Directions must be given in writing (Local Authority Social Services Act 1970 s 7A(2)(a) (as so added)) and may be given to a particular authority or to authorities of a particular class or to authorities generally (s 7A(2)(b)).

5 Children Act 2004 s 9A(1), (4) (s 9A added by the Apprenticeships, Skills, Children and Learning Act 2009 s 195(1); Children Act 2004 s 9A amended by SI 2010/1158). As to the meaning of 'local authority in England' in this context see the Children Act 2004 s 65(1); and CHILDREN AND YOUNG PERSONS vol 9 (2017) PARA 212. The regulations may, in particular:
   (1) make provision about matters by reference to which safeguarding targets may, or must, be set (s 9A(2)(a) (as so added));
   (2) make provision about periods to which safeguarding targets may, or must, relate (s 9A(2)(b) (as so added));
   (3) make provision about the procedure for setting safeguarding targets (s 9A(2)(c) (as so added));
   (4) specify requirements with which a local authority in England must comply in connection with the setting of safeguarding targets (s 9A(2)(d) (as so added and amended)).
   At the date at which this volume states the law no such regulations had been made.

6 Children Act 2004 s 9A(3) (as added and amended: see note 5).

317. Duty to promote an individual's well-being. The general duty of a local authority in England[1], in exercising a care and support function[2] in the case of an individual, is to promote that individual's well-being[3]. 'Well-being' means[4] well-being so far as relating to any of the following:
   (1) personal dignity (including treatment of the individual with respect)[5].

(2)   physical and mental health and emotional well-being[6];

(3)   protection from abuse and neglect[7];

(4)   control over day-to-day life[8];

(5)   participation in work, education, training and recreation[9];

(6)   social and economic well-being[10];

(7)   domestic, family and personal relationships[11];

(8)   suitability of living accommodation[12]; and

(9)   contribution to society[13].

1 As to the meanings of 'local authority' and 'England' see PARA 1.
2 Ie a function under the Care Act 2014 Pt 1 (ss 1–80).
3 Care Act 2014 s 1(1). The Secretary of State must have regard to the general duty of local authorities under s 1(1) in issuing guidance for the purposes of s 78(1) (see PARA 316) and in making regulations under Pt 1: s 78(3).
4 Ie in relation to an individual.
5 Care Act 2014 s 1(2)(a).
6 Care Act 2014 s 1(2)(b).
7 Care Act 2014 s 1(2)(c); As to the meaning of 'abuse' see PARA 8 note 12.
8 Care Act 2014 s 1(2)(d). This is specified as being control by the individual himself, and as including control over care and support, or support, provided to the individual and the way in which it is provided: s 1(2)(d).
9 Care Act 2014 s 1(2)(e).
10 Care Act 2014 s 1(2)(f).
11 Care Act 2014 s 1(2)(g).
12 Care Act 2014 s 1(2)(h).
13 Care Act 2014 s 1(2)(i). This is specified as being contribution by the individual himself: s 1(2)(i).

318. Prevention of need for care and support. A local authority in England[1] must provide or arrange for the provision of services, facilities or resources, or take other steps, which it considers will:

(1)   contribute towards preventing or delaying the development by adults[2] in its area of needs for care and support[3];

(2)   contribute towards preventing or delaying the development by carers[4] in its area of needs for support[5];

(3)   reduce the needs for care and support of adults in its area[6]; and

(4)   reduce the needs for support of carers in its area[7].

The authority may make a charge for such provision or arrangements[8]. In performing this duty the authority must have regard to:

(a)   the importance of identifying services, facilities and resources already available in the authority's area and the extent to which the authority could involve or make use of them in performing that duty[9];

(b)   the importance of identifying adults in the authority's area with needs for care and support which are not being met (by the authority or otherwise)[10];

(c)   the importance of identifying carers in the authority's area with needs for support which are not being met (by the authority or otherwise)[11].

These duties do not extend to the provision of services etc for, or the taking of steps, in relation to the support of, certain persons subject to immigration control, or in relation to the provision of health services and housing[12].

1 As to the meanings of 'local authority' and 'England' see PARA 1. In cases where a local authority performs the duty under the Care Act 2014 s 2(1) (see the text and notes 2–7) jointly with one or more other local authorities in relation to the authorities' combined area, references in s 2 to a local authority are to be read as references to the authorities acting jointly (s 2(6)(a)) and references to a local authority's area are to be read as references to the combined area (s 2(6)(b)).
2 As to the meaning of 'adult' see PARA 1 note 1.
3 Care Act 2014 s 2(1)(a).
4 As to the meaning of 'carer' see PARA 33 note 2.

5   Care Act 2014 s 2(1)(b).
6   Care Act 2014 s 2(1)(c).
7   Care Act 2014 s 2(1)(d).
8   As to charges which may be made, and exceptions to charging, see the Care and Support (Preventing Needs for Care and Support) Regulations 2014, SI 2014/2673 (made under the Care Act 2014 s 2(3), (4)). A charge under the regulations may cover only the cost that the local authority incurs in providing or arranging for the provision of the service, facility or resource or for taking the other step: s 2(5).
9   Care Act 2014 s 2(2)(a).
10 Care Act 2014 s 2(2)(b).
11 Care Act 2014 s 2(2)(c).
12 See the Care Act 2014 ss 2(7), 21–23; and PARA 5.

319. Individual's views and wishes to be taken into account in providing care. In exercising a care and support function[1] in the case of an individual, a local authority in England[2] must have regard to the following matters in particular:

(1)   the importance of beginning with the assumption that the individual is best-placed to judge the individual's well-being[3];

(2)   the individual's views, wishes, feelings and beliefs[4];

(3)   the importance of preventing or delaying the development of needs for care and support or needs for support and the importance of reducing needs of either kind that already exist[5];

(4)   the need to ensure that decisions about the individual are made having regard to all the individual's circumstances (and are not based only on the individual's age or appearance or any condition of the individual's or aspect of the individual's behaviour which might lead others to make unjustified assumptions about the individual's well-being)[6];

(5)   the importance of the individual participating as fully as possible in decisions relating to the exercise of the function concerned and being provided with the information and support necessary to enable the individual to participate[7];

(6)   the importance of achieving a balance between the individual's well-being and that of any friends or relatives who are involved in caring for the individual[8];

(7)   the need to protect people from abuse and neglect[9]; and

(8)   the need to ensure that any restriction on the individual's rights or freedom of action that is involved in the exercise of the function is kept to the minimum necessary for achieving the purpose for which the function is being exercised[10].

1   Ie a function under the Care Act 2014 Pt 1 (ss 1–80).
2   As to the meanings of 'local authority' and 'England' see PARA 1.
3   Care Act 2014 s 1(3)(a).
4   Care Act 2014 s 1(3)(b).
5   Care Act 2014 s 1(3)(c).
6   Care Act 2014 s 1(3)(d).
7   Care Act 2014 s 1(3)(e).
8   Care Act 2014 s 1(3)(f).
9   Care Act 2014 s 1(3)(g). As to the meaning of 'abuse' see PARA 8 note 12.
10 Care Act 2014 s 1(3)(h).

320. Duty to co-operate with partners. A local authority in England[1] must co-operate with each of its relevant partners[2], and each relevant partner must co-operate with the authority, in the exercise of:

(1)   their respective functions relating to adults with needs for care and support[3];

(2)   their respective functions relating to carers[4]; and

(3)   functions of theirs the exercise of which is relevant to functions referred to in head (1) above (2)[5].

A local authority must also co-operate[6] with such other persons as it considers appropriate who exercise functions, or are engaged in activities, in the authority's area relating to adults with needs for care and support or relating to carers[7].

A local authority must make arrangements for ensuring co-operation between:

(a)   the officers of the authority who exercise the authority's functions relating to adults with needs for care and support or its functions relating to carers[8];

(b)   the officers of the authority who exercise the authority's functions relating to housing (in so far as the exercise of those functions is relevant to functions referred to in head (a))[9];

(c)   the Director of Children's Services at the authority (in so far as the exercise of functions by that officer is relevant to the functions referred to in head (a))[10]; and

(d)   the authority's director of public health[11].

Where a request for co-operation is made[12], the partner or authority must comply with the request unless it considers that doing so would be incompatible with its own duties[13] or would otherwise have an adverse effect on the exercise of its functions[14].

Authorities must also make arrangements for public involvement in the scrutiny of care services[15].

1   As to the meanings of 'local authority' and 'England' see PARA 1. The references in the Care Act 2014 s 6(1), (4)(a) (see the text and notes 2–8) to a local authority's functions include a reference to the authority's functions under ss 58–65 (transition for children with needs etc: see PARAS 22–25): s 6(5).
2   Each of the following is a 'relevant partner' of a local authority in England:
    (1)   where the authority is a county council for an area for which there are district councils, each district council (Care Act 2014 ss 6(7)(a), 7(4));
    (2)   any local authority, or district council for an area in England for which there is a county council, with which the authority agrees it would be appropriate to co-operate under this section (s 6(7)(b));
    (3)   each NHS body in the authority's area (s 6(7)(c));
    (4)   the Minister of the Crown exercising functions in relation to social security, employment and training, so far as those functions are exercisable in relation to England (s 6(7)(d));
    (5)   the chief officer of police for a police area the whole or part of which is in the authority's area (s 6(7)(e));
    (6)   the Minister of the Crown exercising functions in relation to prisons, so far as those functions are exercisable in relation to England (s 6(7)(f));
    (7)   a relevant provider of probation services in the authority's area (s 6(7)(g)); and
    (8)   such person, or a person of such description, as regulations may specify (s 6(7)(h)).
    As to local government areas and authorities in England see LOCAL GOVERNMENT vol 69 (2009) PARA 22 et seq. The reference to an NHS body in a local authority's area is a reference to the National Health Service Commissioning Board (see HEALTH SERVICES vol 54 (2017) PARA 32), so far as its functions are exercisable in relation to the authority's area, a clinical commissioning group (see HEALTH SERVICES vol 54 (2017) PARA 35 et seq) the whole or part of whose area is in the authority's area, or an NHS trust or NHS foundation trust (see HEALTH SERVICES vol 54 (2017) PARAS 235, 244) which provides services in the authority's area: Care Act 2014 s 6(8). Where an adult whose case comes within s 48 (temporary duty on local authority to provide care in event of provider failure: see PARAS 180–185) is being provided with NHS continuing healthcare (as construed in accordance with standing rules under the National Health Service Act 2006 s 6E (see HEALTH SERVICES vol 54 (2017) PARA 22)) under arrangements made by a clinical commissioning group no part of whose area is in the local authority's area, the group is to be treated as a relevant partner of the authority for the purposes of the Care Act 2014 ss 6, 7: s 52(9), (10). As to the meaning of 'adult' see PARA 1 note 1. As to police forces, police areas and chief officers of police see POLICE AND INVESTIGATORY POWERS vol 84 (2013) PARAS 52 et seq, 123 et seq. As to the meaning of 'prison' see the Prison Act 1952 s 53(1); and PRISONS AND

PRISONERS vol 85 (2012) PARA 403 (definition applied by the Care Act 2014 s 6(9)). As to the meaning of 'relevant provider of probation services' seethe Criminal Justice Act 2003 s 325; and SENTENCING vol 92 (2015) PARAS 23–24 (definition applied by the Care Act 2014 s 6(10)). At the date at which this volume states the law no regulations had been made for the purposes of s 6(7)(h).

3　Care Act 2014 s 6(1)(a). The Care Act 2014 does not apply to the care of children (see PARA 21), and corresponding provision for co-operation in delivering care to children is made by the Children Act 2004 s 10: see CHILDREN AND YOUNG PERSONS vol 9 (2017) PARA 212.

4　Care Act 2014 s 6(1)(b). As to the meaning of 'carer' see PARA 33 note 2.

5　Care Act 2014 s 6(1)(c). The duties under s 6(1)–(4) are to be performed for the following purposes in particular:

   (1)　promoting the well-being of adults with needs for care and support and of carers in the authority's area (s 6(6)(a));

   (2)　improving the quality of care and support for adults and support for carers provided in the authority's area (including the outcomes that are achieved from such provision) (s 6(6)(b));

   (3)　smoothing the transition to the system provided for by Pt 1 (ss 1–80) for persons in relation to whom functions under ss 58–65 are exercisable (s 6(6)(c));

   (4)　protecting adults with needs for care and support who are experiencing, or are at risk of, abuse or neglect (s 6(6)(d)); and

   (5)　identifying lessons to be learned from cases where adults with needs for care and support have experienced serious abuse or neglect and applying those lessons to future cases (s 6(6)(e)).

As to the meaning of 'well-being' see PARA 317. As to the meaning of 'abuse' see PARA 8 note 12.

6　Ie in the exercise of its functions under the Care Act 2014 Pt 1.

7　Care Act 2014 s 6(2). The following are examples of persons with whom a local authority may consider it appropriate to co-operate for the purposes of s 6(2):

   (1)　a person who provides services to meet adults' needs for care and support, services to meet carers' needs for support or services, facilities or resources of the kind referred to in s 2(1) (see PARA 318) (s 6(3)(a));

   (2)　a person who provides primary medical services, primary dental services, primary ophthalmic services, pharmaceutical services or local pharmaceutical services under the National Health Service Act 2006 (see HEALTH SERVICES vol 54 (2017) PARAS 295, 316, 333; HEALTH SERVICES vol 54A (2017) PARA 367 et seq) (Care Act 2014 s 6(3)(b));

   (3)　a person in whom a hospital in England is vested which is not a health service hospital (as defined by the National Health Service Act 2006: see HEALTH SERVICES vol 54 (2017) PARA 26) (Care Act 2014 s 6(3)(c)); and

   (4)　·　a private registered provider of social housing (s 6(3)(d)).

8　Care Act 2014 s 6(4)(a).

9　Care Act 2014 s 6(4)(b).

10　Care Act 2014 s 6(4)(c).

11　Care Act 2014 s 6(4)(d). As to the authority's director of public health see the National Health Service Act 2006 s 73A; and HEALTH SERVICES vol 54 (2017) PARA 277.

12　Ie:

   (1)　where a local authority requests the co-operation of a relevant partner, or of a local authority which is not one of its relevant partners, in the exercise of a function under the Care Act 2014 Pt 1 in the case of an individual with needs for care and support or in the case of a carer, a carer of a child or a young carer (s 7(1)); or

   (2)　where a relevant partner of a local authority, or a local authority which is not one of its relevant partners, requests the co-operation of the local authority in its exercise of a function in the case of an individual with needs for care and support or in the case of a carer, a carer of a child or a young carer (s 7(2).

'Carer of a child' means a person who is a carer for the purposes of s 60 (see PARA 42): s 7(5).

13　Care Act 2014 s 7(1)(a), (2)(a). A person who decides not to comply with a request under s 7(1) or (2) must give the person who made the request written reasons for the decision: s 7(3).

14　Care Act 2014 s 7(1)(b), (2)(b). See note 13.

15　See the Local Government and Public Involvement in Health Act 2007 s 221; and HEALTH SERVICES vol 54A (2017) PARA 558.

321. Duty to make inquiries about vulnerable adults. Where a local authority in England[1] has reasonable cause to suspect that an adult[2] in its area (whether or not ordinarily resident[3] there):

(1)   has needs for care and support (whether or not the authority is meeting any of those needs)[4];

(2)   is experiencing, or is at risk of, abuse[5] or neglect[6]; and

(3)   as a result of those needs is unable to protect himself against the abuse or neglect or the risk of it[7],

the authority must make (or cause to be made) whatever enquiries it thinks necessary to enable it to decide whether any action should be taken in the adult's case[8] and, if so, what and by whom[9].

1   As to the meaning of 'local authority' see PARA 1.
2   As to the meaning of 'adult' see PARA 1 note 1.
3   In connection with a person's residence see PARAS 84–87.
4   Care Act 2014 s 42(1)(a).
5   As to the meaning of 'abuse' see PARA 8 note 12.
6   Care Act 2014 s 42(1)(b).
7   Care Act 2014 s 42(1)(c).
8   Ie whether under the Care Act 2014 Pt 1 (ss 1–80) or otherwise.
9   Care Act 2014 s 42(2). Where a local authority is to carry out such an inquiry it must, where necessary, arrange for the provision of independent advocacy: see PARA 236.

322. Integration with health services. A local authority in England[1] must exercise its care and support functions[2] with a view to ensuring the integration of care and support provision[3] with health provision[4] and health-related provision[5] where it considers that this would:

(1)   promote the well-being[6] of adults in the authority's area with needs for care and support, and carers in the authority's area[7];

(2)   contribute to the prevention or delay of the development by adults in its area of needs for care and support or the development by carers in its area of needs for support[8]; or

(3)   improve the quality of care and support for adults, and of support for carers, provided in its area (including the outcomes that are achieved from such provision)[9].

1   As to the meanings of 'local authority' and 'England' see PARA 1.
2   Ie functions under the Care Act 2014 Pt 1 (ss 1–80).
3   'Care and support provision' means:
      (1)   provision to meet the needs of adults for care and support (Care Act 2014 s 3(2)(a));
      (2)   provision to meet carers' needs for support (s 3(2)(b)); and
      (3)   provision of services, facilities or resources, or the taking of other steps, under s 2 (preventing needs for care and support: see PARA 318) (s 3(2)(c)).
    As to the meaning of 'adult' see PARA 1 note 1. As to the meaning of 'carer' see PARA 33 note 2.
4   'Health provision' means provision of health services as part of the health service: Care Act 2014 s 3(3).
5   'Health-related provision' means provision of services which may have an effect on the health of individuals but which are not health services provided as part of the health service (Care Act 2014 s 3(4)(a)) or services provided in the exercise of social services functions (as defined by the Local Authority Social Services Act 1970 s 1A: see PARA 315) (Care Act 2014 s 3(4)(b)). For these purposes the provision of housing is health-related provision: s 3(5).
6   As to the meaning of 'well-being' see PARA 317.
7   Care Act 2014 s 3(1)(a).
8   Care Act 2014 s 3(1)(b).
9   Care Act 2014 s 3(1)(c).

323. Duty to promote and provide choice in the provision of services. A local authority in England[1] must promote the efficient and effective operation of a market in services for meeting care and support needs[2] with a view to ensuring that any person in its area wishing to access services in the market:

(1)   has a variety of providers to choose from who (taken together) provide a variety of services[3];

(2)   has a variety of high quality services to choose from[4]; and

(3)   has sufficient information to make an informed decision about how to meet the needs in question[5].

In performing that duty, an authority must have regard to the following matters in particular:

(a)   the need to ensure that the authority has, and makes available, information about the providers of services for meeting care and support needs and the types of services they provide[6];

(b)   the need to ensure that it is aware of current and likely future demand for such services and to consider how providers might meet that demand[7];

(c)   the importance of enabling adults with needs for care and support, and carers with needs for support, who wish to do so to participate in work, education or training[8];

(d)   the importance of ensuring the sustainability of the market (in circumstances where it is operating effectively as well as in circumstances where it is not)[9];

(e)   the importance of fostering continuous improvement in the quality of such services and the efficiency and effectiveness with which such services are provided and of encouraging innovation in their provision[10]; and

(f)   the importance of fostering a workforce whose members are able to ensure the delivery of high quality services (because, for example, they have relevant skills and appropriate working conditions)[11].

In arranging for the provision by persons other than it of services for meeting care and support needs, a local authority in England must have regard to the importance of promoting the well-being of adults in its area with needs for care and support and the well-being of carers in its area[12]. In meeting an adult's needs for care and support or a carer's needs for support, a local authority in England must have regard to its duty under these provisions[13].

1   As to the meaning of 'local authority' in England see PARA 1. In cases where a local authority performs the duty under the Care Act 2014 s 5(1) (see the text and notes 2–5) jointly with one or more other local authorities in relation to persons who are in the authorities' combined area, references in s 5 to a local authority are to be read as references to the authorities acting jointly (s 5(6)(a)) and references in s 5 to a local authority's area are to be read as references to the combined area (s 5(6)(b)).

2   'Services for meeting care and support needs' means services for meeting adults' needs for care and support (Care Act 2014 s 5(7)(a)) and services for meeting carers' needs for support (s 5(7)(b)). As to the meaning of 'adult' see PARA 1 note 1. As to the meaning of 'carer' see PARA 33 note 2. The references in s 5(7) to services for meeting needs include a reference to services, facilities or resources the purpose of which is to contribute towards preventing or delaying the development of those needs: s 5(8).

3   Care Act 2014 s 5(1)(a).

4   Care Act 2014 s 5(1)(b).

5   Care Act 2014 s 5(1)(c).

6   Care Act 2014 s 5(2)(a).

7   Care Act 2014 s 5(2)(b). In having regard to the matters mentioned in s 5(2)(b), a local authority must also have regard to the need to ensure that sufficient services are available for meeting the needs for care and support of adults in its area and the needs for support of carers in its area: s 5(3).

8   Care Act 2014 s 5(2)(c).

9   Care Act 2014 s 5(2)(d).

10 Care Act 2014 s 5(2)(e).

11 Care Act 2014 s 5(2)(f).

12 Care Act 2014 s 5(4).

13 Care Act 2014 s 5(5).

B.   ADMINISTRATIVE MATTERS

324.   Appointment of director of social services. A local authority in England[1] must appoint an officer, to be known as the director of adult social services, for the purposes of its social services functions[2], other than those for which the authority's director of children's services is responsible[3]. Two or more local authorities may, if they consider that the same person can efficiently discharge, for both or all of them, the functions of director of adult social services or (as the case may be) director of social services, concur in the appointment of a person as director of adult social services or (as the case may be) director of social services for both or all of those authorities[4].

A local authority which has appointed or concurred in the appointment of a person under these provisions must secure the provision of adequate staff to assist him in the exercise of his functions[5].

1   As to the meaning of 'local authority' see PARA 315 note 1; as to the meaning of 'England' see PARA 1 note 1. The duties imposed by the Local Authority Social Services Act 1970 apply only in relation to local authorities in England: see PARA 315 note 1.
2   As to the meaning of 'social services functions' see PARA 315.
3   Local Authority Social Services Act 1970 s 6(A1) (s 6(A1) added, s 6(2), (6) amended, by the Children Act 2004 Sch 2 para 2(1), (2)). The reference is to those social services functions for which the local authority's director of children's services is responsible under the Children Act 2004 s 18: see CHILDREN AND YOUNG PERSONS vol 9 (2017) PARA 216. Corresponding provision in relation to local authorities in Wales is made by the Social Services and Well-being (Wales) Act 2014 s 144: see PARA 384.
4   Local Authority Social Services Act 1970 s 6(2) (as amended: see note 3).
5   Local Authority Social Services Act 1970 s 6(6) (as amended: see note 3).

325.   Consideration of complaints and holding of inquiries. Local authorities in England[1] are required[2] to consider complaints about the discharge of any of their social services functions, the provision of services by another person pursuant to arrangements made by such an authority in the discharge of those functions[3], and the provision of services by such an authority or any other person in pursuance of arrangements made by the authority[4] in relation to the functions of an NHS body[5]. Provision is made for the handling of such complaints[6], the carrying out of investigations deriving from complaints[7], and the publication and monitoring of outcomes[8].

The Secretary of State[9] may cause an inquiry to be held in any case where, whether on representations to it or otherwise, it considers it advisable to do so in connection with the exercise by any local authority in England[10] of any of its social services functions (except in so far as those functions relate to persons under the age of 18)[11].

1   As to the meaning of 'local authority' see PARA 315 note 1; as to the meaning of 'England' see PARA 1 note 1. The duties imposed by the Health and Social Care (Community Health and Standards) Act 2003 ss 114, 115 (see the text and note 2) apply only in relation to local authorities in England: see the Social Services and Well-being (Wales) Act 2014 (Consequential Amendments) Regulations 2016, SI 2016/413, regs 204–206.
2   Ie by the Local Authority Social Services and National Health Service Complaints (England) Regulations 2009, SI 2009/309 (made under the Health and Social Care (Community Health and Standards) Act 2003 ss 114(1), (2), (5)(a), (c), (6), 115). As to the meaning of 'social services functions' see PARA 315.
3   Health and Social Care (Community Health and Standards) Act 2003 s 114(1)(b).
4   Ie arrangements made under the National Health Service Act 2006 s 75 (see HEALTH SERVICES vol 54 (2017) PARA 282).
5   Health and Social Care (Community Health and Standards) Act 2003 s 114(1)(c) (amended by the National Health Service (Consequential Provisions) Act 2006 Sch 1 para 243).
6   See the Local Authority Social Services and National Health Service Complaints (England) Regulations 2009, SI 2009/309, regs 3–9, 11, 12 (amended by SI 2009/1768; SI 2013/235).

7   See the Local Authority Social Services and National Health Service Complaints (England) Regulations 2009, SI 2009/309, regs 13–14 (amended by SI 2013/235).
8   See the Local Authority Social Services and National Health Service Complaints (England) Regulations 2009, SI 2009/309, regs 15–18 (amended by SI 2013/235).
9   As to the Secretary of State see PARA 333.
10 The duties imposed by the Local Authority Social Services Act 1970 apply only in relation to local authorities in England: see PARA 315 note 1.
11 Local Authority Social Services Act 1970 s 7C(1) (s 7C added by the National Health Service and Community Care Act 1990 s 50). The Local Government Act 1972 s 250(2)–(5) (see LOCAL GOVERNMENT vol 69 (2009) PARA 105) applies in relation to inquiries under the Local Authority Social Services Act 1970 s 7C(1) as it applies in relation to inquiries under that provision: s 7C(2) (as so added).

326. Provision of information and advice. A local authority in England[1] must establish and maintain a service for providing people in its area with information and advice relating to care and support for adults[2] and support for carers[3]. The service must provide information and advice on the following matters in particular:

(1)   the statutory system governing the provision of care[4] and how the system operates in the authority's area[5];

(2)   the choice of types of care and support, and the choice of providers, available to those who are in the authority's area[6];

(3)   how to access the care and support that is available[7];

(4)   how to access independent financial advice on matters relevant to the meeting of needs for care and support[8]; and

(5)   how to raise concerns about the safety or well-being of an adult who has needs for care and support[9].

In providing information and advice under this section, a local authority must in particular:

(a)   have regard to the importance of identifying adults in the authority's area who would be likely to benefit from financial advice on matters relevant to the meeting of needs for care and support[10]; and

(b)   seek to ensure that what it provides is sufficient to enable adults to identify matters that are or might be relevant to their personal financial position that could be affected by the statutory system[11], to make plans for meeting needs for care and support that might arise[12], and to understand the different ways in which they may access independent financial advice on matters relevant to the meeting of needs for care and support[13].

Information and advice provided under these provisions must be accessible to, and proportionate to the needs of, those for whom it is being provided[14].

1   As to the meanings of 'local authority' and 'England' see PARA 1. In cases where a local authority performs the duty under the Care Act 2014 s 4(1) jointly with one or more other local authorities by establishing and maintaining a service for their combined area, references to a local authority are read as references to the authorities acting jointly and references to a local authority's area are read as references to the combined area: s 4(6).
2   As to the meaning of 'adult' see PARA 1 note 1. The Care Act 2014 does not apply to the care of children (see PARA 21).
3   Care Act 2014 s 4(1). As to the meaning of 'carer' see PARA 33 note 2.
4   Ie the system provided for by the Care Act 2014 Pt 1 (ss 1–80).
5   Care Act 2014 s 4(2)(a).
6   Care Act 2014 s 4(2)(b).
7   Care Act 2014 s 4(2)(c).
8   Care Act 2014 s 4(2)(d). 'Independent financial advice' means financial advice provided by a person who is independent of the local authority in question: s 4(5).
9   Care Act 2014 s 4(2)(e).
10 Care Act 2014 s 4(3)(a).

11 Care Act 2014 s 4(3)(b)(i).
12 Care Act 2014 s 4(3)(b)(ii).
13 Care Act 2014 s 4(3)(b)(iii).
14 Care Act 2014 s 4(4).

327. Protecting property of adults being cared for away from home. Where an adult[1] is having needs for care and support met[2] in a way that involves the provision of accommodation, or is admitted to hospital (or both)[3], and it appears to a local authority[4] that there is a danger of loss or damage to movable property of the adult's in the authority's area because the adult is unable (whether permanently or temporarily) to protect or deal with the property[5] and no suitable arrangements have been or are being made[6], the authority must take reasonable steps to prevent or mitigate the loss or damage[7]. For the purpose of performing that duty, the authority may at all reasonable times and on reasonable notice enter any premises which the adult was living in immediately before being provided with accommodation or admitted to hospital[8] and may deal with any of the adult's movable property in any way which is reasonably necessary for preventing or mitigating loss or damage[9]. This duty does not, however, apply in the case of an adult who is detained in prison[10] or residing in approved premises[11].

Obstruction of an authority's power of entry is an offence[12].

1 As to the meaning of 'adult' see PARA 1 note 1. A local authority may recover from an adult whatever reasonable expenses the authority incurs under these provisions in the adult's case: Care Act 2014 s 47(7).
2 Ie under the Care Act 2014 s 18 or s 19 (see PARAS 12, 13).
3 Care Act 2014 s 47(1)(a).
4 As to the meaning of 'local authority' see PARA 1.
5 Care Act 2014 s 47(1)(b)(i).
6 Care Act 2014 s 47(1)(b)(ii).
7 Care Act 2014 s 47(2).
8 Care Act 2014 s 47(3)(a). A local authority may not exercise the power under s 47(3)(a) unless it has obtained the consent of the adult concerned or, where the adult lacks capacity to give consent, the consent of a person authorised under the Mental Capacity Act 2005 to give it on the adult's behalf, or where the adult lacks capacity to give consent and there is no person so authorised, the local authority is satisfied that exercising the power would be in the adult's best interests: Care Act 2014 s 47(4). As to 'having' and 'lacking' capacity see PARA 8 note 10. As to a person being 'authorised' under the Mental Capacity Act 2005 see PARA 12 note 16. Where a local authority is proposing to exercise the power under the Care Act 2014 s 47(3)(a), the officer it authorises to do so must, if required, produce valid documentation setting out the authorisation to do so: s 47(5).
9 Care Act 2014 s 47(3)(b).
10 Care Act 2014 s 76(7)(a). As to the meaning of 'prison' see PARA 87 note 2.
11 Care Act 2014 s 76(7)(b). As to the meaning of 'approved premises' see PARA 87 note 4.
12 A person who, without reasonable excuse, obstructs the exercise of the power under the Care Act 2014 s 47(3)(a) commits an offence and is liable on summary conviction to a fine not exceeding level 4 on the standard scale: s 47(6). As to the powers of magistrates' courts to issue fines on summary conviction see SENTENCING vol 92 (2015) PARA 176.

328. Maintenance of register of sight-impaired and disabled adults. A local authority in England[1] must establish and maintain a register of sight-impaired and severely sight-impaired adults[2] who are ordinarily resident in its area[3]. A local authority may also establish and maintain, for the purposes in particular of planning the provision by the authority of services to meet needs for care and support[4] and monitoring changes over time in the number of adults in the authority's area with needs for care and support and the types of needs they have[5], one or more registers of adults[6] who:

(1)   have a disability[7];

(2)   have a physical or mental impairment which is not a disability but which gives rise, or which the authority considers may in the future give rise, to needs for care and support[8]; or

(3)   comes within any other category of persons the authority considers appropriate to include in a register of persons who have, or the authority considers may in the future have, needs for care and support[9].

1   As to the meanings of 'local authority' and 'England' see PARA 1.
2   A person is to be treated as being sight-impaired or severely sight-impaired if he is certified as such by a consultant ophthalmologist: Care and Support (Sight-impaired and Severely Sight-impaired Adults) Regulations 2014, SI 2014/2854, reg 2(1) (made under the Care Act 2014 s 77(2)). In this context 'consultant ophthalmologist' means a consultant or honorary consultant appointed in the medical speciality of ophthalmology, who is employed for the purposes of providing any service as part of the health service: Care and Support (Sight-impaired and Severely Sight-impaired Adults) Regulations 2014, SI 2014/2854, reg 1(2). As to the meaning of 'adult' see PARA 1 note 1. The Care Act 2014 does not apply to the care of children (see PARA 21).
3   Care Act 2014 s 77(1).
4   Care Act 2014 s 77(3)(a).
5   Care Act 2014 s 77(3)(b).
6   Ie adults who are ordinarily resident in the local authority's area: Care Act 2014 s 77(3).
7   Care Act 2014 s 77(4)(a). As to the meaning of 'disability' see the Equality Act 2010 s 6; and DISCRIMINATION vol 33 (2013) PARA 50 (definition applied by the Care Act 2014 s 77(5)).
8   Care Act 2014 s 77(4)(b).
9   Care Act 2014 s 77(4)(c).

329. Duty to promote welfare of sick and disabled persons. A local authority in England[1] may, with the approval of the Secretary of State[2], and to such extent as the Secretary of State may direct in relation to persons ordinarily resident in the area of the local authority[3] must, make arrangements for promoting the welfare of certain persons, namely persons aged 18 or over who are blind[4], deaf[5] or dumb, or who suffer from mental disorder of any description, and other persons aged 18 or over who are substantially and permanently handicapped by illness, injury or congenital deformity or such other disabilities[6] as may be prescribed by the Secretary of State[7]. Without prejudice to the generality of this power, a local authority in England may make arrangements:

(1)   for informing persons to whom such arrangements relate of the services available for them[8];

(2)   for instructing such persons in their own homes or elsewhere in methods of overcoming the effects of their disabilities[9];

(3)   for providing workshops where such persons may be engaged in suitable work, whether under a contract of service or otherwise, and hostels where persons engaged in the workshops, and other persons to whom such arrangements relate and for whom work or training is being provided[10], may live[11];

(4)   for providing such persons with suitable work, whether under a contract of service or otherwise, in their own homes or elsewhere[12];

(5)   for helping such persons in disposing of the produce of their work[13];

(6)   for providing such persons with recreational facilities in their own homes or elsewhere[14];

(7)   for compiling and maintaining classified registers of the persons to whom such arrangements relate[15].

Nothing in these provisions authorises or requires:

(a) the payment of money to any person to whom these provisions apply, other than persons for whom work is provided[16] or who are engaged in work which they are enabled to perform in consequence of anything done in pursuance of arrangements made under these provisions[17]; or (b)	the provision of any accommodation or services required to be provided under the National Health Service Act 2006[18].

A local authority may, in accordance with welfare arrangements[19], employ as its agent[20] any voluntary organisation[21] or any person carrying on, professionally or by way of trade or business, activities which consist of or include the provision of services[22], being an organisation or person which appears to the authority to be capable of providing the service to which the arrangements apply[23].

1	For the purposes of the National Assistance Act 1948 Pt III (ss 21–35) 'local authority' means a council which is a local authority for the purposes of the Local Authority Social Services Act 1970 in England (see PARA 315 note 1): see the National Assistance Act 1948 s 33 (amended by the Local Authority Social Services Act 1970 s 2(7), Sch 3; the Local Government Act 1972 Sch 23 para 2(6); and the Residential Homes Act 1980 Sch 2; and disapplied in relation to local authorities in Wales by the Social Services and Well-being (Wales) Act 2014 (Consequential Amendments) Regulations 2016, SI 2016/413, regs 6, 8). The provisions of the National Assistance Act 1948 extend to the Isles of Scilly (see s 66; and the Isles of Scilly (National Assistance) Order 1980, SI 1980/326); but do not, save as expressly provided, extend to Northern Ireland (National Assistance Act 1948 s 67).
2	As to the Secretary of State see PARA 333.
3	As to the duty of a local authority to inform itself of the number of persons within its area to whom these provisions apply and of the need for the making of arrangements for them see PARAS 330, 331.
4	'Blind person' means a person so blind as to be unable to perform any work for which eyesight is essential: National Assistance Act 1948 s 64(1).
5	These powers do not extent to the provision of a school for deaf children: *Royal Cross School for the Deaf Trustees v Morton (Valuation Officer)* [1975] 2 All ER 519, [1975] 1 WLR 1002, CA.
6	'Disability' includes mental as well as physical disability: National Assistance Act 1948 s 64(1).
7	National Assistance Act 1948 s 29(1) (amended by the Mental Health (Scotland) Act 1960 ss 113(1), 114; the Local Government Act 1972 Sch 23 para 2(4); and the Children Act 1989 Sch 13 para 11(2)). At the date at which this volume states the law, no such regulations prescribing other disabilities had been made. The National Assistance Act 1948 s 29(1) confers a power on a local authority to provide services for someone who is not ordinarily resident in its area, but not an ongoing duty: *R (on the application of Manchester City Council) v St Helens Metropolitan Borough Council* [2009] EWCA Civ 1348, [2010] PTSR 1157, [2010] All ER (D) 254 (Feb).
	The Disabled Persons (Services, Consultation and Representation) Act 1986 ss 1, 2 (amended by the Children Act 1989 Sch 12 para 44, Sch 13 para 59; the National Health Service and Community Care Act 1990 Sch 9 para 30, Sch 10; the Care Standards Act 2000 Sch 4 para 11; the Health and Social Care (Community Health and Standards) Act 2003 Sch 4 para 65; the National Health Service (Consequential Provisions) Act 2006 Sch 1 para 88; the Health and Social Care Act 2012 Sch 5 para 39, Sch 14 para 51; SI 2002/2469; SI 2007/961; and further amended so far as relating to local authorities in Wales by SI 2016/413) make provision for the appointment and rights of authorised representatives of disabled persons: however those provisions, while not having been repealed, have never been brought into force.
8	National Assistance Act 1948 s 29(4)(a).
9	National Assistance Act 1948 s 29(4)(b).
10	Ie under the Disabled Persons (Employment) Act 1944 or the Employment and Training Act 1973: see EMPLOYMENT.
11	National Assistance Act 1948 s 29(4)(c) (amended by the Employment and Training Act 1973 Sch 3 para 3).
12	National Assistance Act 1948 s 29(4)(d).
13	National Assistance Act 1948 s 29(4)(e).
14	National Assistance Act 1948 s 29(4)(f).
15	National Assistance Act 1948 s 29(4)(g).
16	Ie under arrangements made by virtue of the National Assistance Act 1948 s 29(4)(c) or s 29(4)(d).
17	National Assistance Act 1948 s 29(6)(a).
18	National Assistance Act 1948 s 29(6)(b) (amended by the National Health Service (Consequential Provisions) Act 2006 Sch 1 paras 5, 8). See generally HEALTH SERVICES.
19	Ie arrangements under the National Assistance Act 1948 s 29(1).
20	Ie for the purposes of the National Assistance Act 1948 s 29.
21	'Voluntary organisation' means a body whose activities are carried on otherwise than for profit, but does not include any public or local authority: National Assistance Act 1948 s 64(1).
22	Ie for any of the persons to whom the National Assistance Act 1948 s 29 applies.

23 National Assistance Act 1948 s 30(1) (amended by the Local Government Act 1972 Sch 23
    para 2(5); and the National Health Service and Community Care Act 1990 s 42(6)).

**330. Duty to monitor numbers of sick and disabled persons and to publicise
services.** It is the duty of every local authority in England[1] which is required to
make welfare arrangements for disabled persons[2] to inform itself of the number of
persons to whom that provision applies within its area and of the need for the
making by the authority of such arrangements for such persons[3]. Every such local
authority must cause to be published, at such times and in such manner as it
considers appropriate, general information as to the services provided under
welfare arrangements which are for the time being available in its area[4]. It must
also ensure that any person[5] who uses any of those services is informed of any
other service provided by the authority (whether under any such arrangements or
not) which in the authority's opinion is relevant to his needs and any service
provided by any other authority or organisation which in the opinion of the
authority is relevant to his needs and of which particulars are in the
authority's possession[6].

1   As to the meaning of 'local authority' see PARA 315 note 1; as to the meaning of 'England' see
    PARA 1 note 1. The duties imposed by the Chronically Sick and Disabled Persons Act 1970 s 1 (see
    the text and notes 2–6) apply only in relation to local authorities in England: see s 1(4) (s 1(4), (5)
    added by SI 2015/914); and the Social Services and Well-being (Wales) Act 2014 (Consequential
    Amendments) Regulations 2016, SI 2016/413, regs 25, 26.
2   Ie an authority having functions under the National Assistance Act 1948 s 29: see PARA 329.
3   Chronically Sick and Disabled Persons Act 1970 s 1(1).
4   Chronically Sick and Disabled Persons Act 1970 s 1(2)(a).
5   Ie any person to whom the National Assistance Act 1948 s 29 applies or any disabled child who
    uses services provided under arrangements made by the authority under the Children Act 1989 Pt 3
    (ss 16B–30) (see CHILDREN AND YOUNG PERSONS).
6   Chronically Sick and Disabled Persons Act 1970 s 1(2)(b), (5) (s 1(2)(b) amended by the Disabled
    Persons (Services, Consultation and Representation) Act 1986 s 9; Chronically Sick and Disabled
    Persons Act 1970 s 1(5) as added (see note 1)).

**331. Duty to make arrangements for the provision of practical assistance to sick
and disabled persons.** Where a local authority in England[1] which is required to
make welfare arrangements for disabled persons[2] is satisfied in the case of any
person[3] ordinarily resident[4] in its area that it is necessary in order to meet that
person's needs[5] for it to make arrangements for all or any of the following matters:

(1)   the provision of practical assistance for that person in his home[6];
(2)   the provision for him of, or assistance to him in obtaining, wireless,
       television, library or similar recreational facilities[7];
(3)   the provision for him of lectures, games, outings or other recreational
       facilities outside his home, or assistance to him in taking advantage of
       educational facilities available to him[8];
(4)   the provision for him of facilities for, or assistance in, travelling to and
       from his home for the purpose of participating in any services provided
       under the arrangements or, with the authority's approval, in any other
       similar services[9];
(5)   the provision of assistance for him in arranging for the carrying out of
       any works of adaptation in his home or the provision of any additional
       facilities designed to secure his greater safety, comfort or convenience[10];
(6)   facilitating the taking of holidays by him, whether at holiday homes or
       otherwise and whether provided under arrangements made by the
       authority or otherwise[11];
(7)   the provision of meals for him, whether in his home or elsewhere[12];

(8)   the provision for him of, or assistance to him in obtaining, a telephone
        and any equipment necessary to enable him to use a telephone[13],

it is its duty to make those arrangements in the exercise of its functions[14].

1   As to the meaning of 'local authority' see PARA 315 note 1; as to the meaning of 'England' see
    PARA 1 note 1. The duties imposed by the Chronically Sick and Disabled Persons Act 1970 s 2(1),
    (4)–(6) (see the text and notes 2–14) apply only in relation to local authorities in England: see s 2(3)
    (s 2(3)–(9) added by SI 2015/914); and the Social Services and Well-being (Wales) Act 2014
    (Consequential Amendments) Regulations 2016, SI 2016/413, reg 27.
2   Ie an authority having functions under the National Assistance Act 1948 s 29 (see PARA 329) or
    under the Children Act 1989 Pt 3 (ss 16B–30) (see CHILDREN AND YOUNG PERSONS).
3   Ie any person to whom the National Assistance Act 1948 or the Children Act 1989 Pt 3 applies.
4   Any question arising under these provisions as to a person's ordinary residence in an area in
    England or Wales is to be determined by the Secretary of State or by the Welsh Ministers:
    Chronically Sick and Disabled Persons Act 1970 s 2(7) (as added: see note 1). As to the Secretary
    of State see PARA 333; as to the Welsh Ministers see PARA 395. The Secretary of State and the
    Welsh Ministers must make and publish arrangements for determining which cases are to be dealt
    with by the Secretary of State and which are to be dealt with by the Welsh Ministers: s 2(8) (as so
    added). Those arrangements may include provision for the Secretary of State and the Welsh
    Ministers to agree, in relation to any question that has arisen, which of them is to deal with the
    case: s 2(9) (as so added).
        Where a person is in her present abode voluntarily and with a settled intention of remaining
    there for the time being and her disabilities do not appear to prevent her from having the requisite
    understanding for both those mental elements, that is sufficient to justify a finding that she is
    ordinarily resident in a particular area: *R v Kent County Council, ex p Salisbury* [1999] 3 FCR
    193, [2000] 1 FLR 155.
5   A local authority must decide whether the needs of a disabled person aged under 18 call for the
    provision by the authority of any services in accordance with the Chronically Sick and Disabled
    Persons Act 1970 s 2(1) when requested to do so by a disabled person or his carer: see the Disabled
    Persons (Services, Consultation and Representation) Act 1986 s 4(1)(a), (c), (2) (amended by SI
    2015/914). As from a day to be appointed under the Disabled Persons (Services, Consultation and
    Representation) Act 1986 s 18(2) the authorised representative (see ss 1, 2; and PARA 329 note 7)
    of a disabled person aged under 18 may also make such a request: see s 4(b). At the date at which
    this volume states the law, no such day had been appointed.
        In assessing the person's needs and whether it is necessary to make arrangements in order to
    meet his needs, a local authority is entitled to take account of the resources available to it: *R v
    Gloucestershire County Council, ex p Barry* [1997] AC 584, [1997] 2 All ER 1, HL. See also *R (on
    the application of Spink) v Wandsworth London Borough Council* [2005] EWCA Civ 302, [2005]
    2 All ER 954, [2005] 1 WLR 2884 (parental resources may be taken into account where claimant
    is a child).
6   Chronically Sick and Disabled Persons Act 1970 s 2(1)(a), (6)(a) (s 2(6) as added: see note 1).
7   Chronically Sick and Disabled Persons Act 1970 s 2(1)(b), (6)(b) (s 2(6) as added: see note 1).
8   Chronically Sick and Disabled Persons Act 1970 s 2(1)(c), (6)(c) (s 2(6) as added: see note 1).
9   See the Chronically Sick and Disabled Persons Act 1970 s 2(1)(d), (6)(d) (s 2(6) as added: see note
    1).
10 Chronically Sick and Disabled Persons Act 1970 s 2(1)(e), (6)(e) (s 2(6) as added: see note 1). See
    R (on the application of BG) v Medway Council [2005] EWHC 1932 (Admin), [2005] 3 FCR 199
    (provision of financial assistance to adapt claimant's home subject to the condition that it would
    have to be repaid if claimant ceased to live there within 20 years was reasonable).
11 Chronically Sick and Disabled Persons Act 1970 s 2(1)(f), (6)(f) (s 2(6) as added: see note 1). A
    local authority which has a duty to facilitate the taking of holidays by a person under s 2(1)(f) has
    the power to meet that duty by covering the basic costs of a holiday, and a policy which excludes
    the provision of the basic costs of holidays unlawfully fetters the authority's discretion: *R v North
    Yorkshire County Council, ex p Hargreaves* (1997) 96 LGR 39.
12 Chronically Sick and Disabled Persons Act 1970 s 2(1)(g), (6)(g) (s 2(6) as added: see note 1).
13 Chronically Sick and Disabled Persons Act 1970 s 2(1)(h), (6)(h) (s 2(6) as added: see note 1).
14 Ie its functions under the National Assistance Act 1948 s 29: Chronically Sick and Disabled
    Persons Act 1970 s 2(1), (4) (s 2(1) amended by the Local Authority Social Services Act 1970 Sch 2
    para 12; the Local Government Act 1972 Sch 30; and the National Health Service and Community
    Care Act 1990 Sch 9 para 12, Sch 10; Chronically Sick and Disabled Persons Act 1970 s 2(4) as
    added (see note 1)). This duty is subject to the provisions of the Local Authority Social Services Act
    1970 ss 7(1), 7A (see PARA 316): Chronically Sick and Disabled Persons Act 1970 s 2(1), (5) (as
    so amended and added).

The Chronically Sick and Disabled Persons Act 1970 s 2 and the National Assistance Act 1948 s 29 (see PARA 329) must be read together: *Wyatt v Hillingdon London Borough Council* (1978) 76 LGR 727, CA. There is no private law remedy sounding in damages for the failure to comply with this duty: see *Wyatt v Hillingdon London Borough Council* at 733–734 per Lane LJ.

As to clarification in relation to the test to be applied by local authorities when conducting an inquiry into the discharge of its duties under the Chronically Sick and Disabled Persons Act 1970 s 2, see *R (on the application of KM) (by his mother and litigation friend) v Cambridgeshire County Council* [2012] UKSC 23, [2012] 3 All ER 1218.

332. Appeals against local authority decisions. Regulations may make provision for appeals against decisions taken by a local authority in England[1] in the exercise of social services functions[2] in respect of an individual[3]. The regulations may in particular make provision about:

(1)   who may (and may not) bring an appeal[4];

(2)   grounds on which an appeal may be brought[5];

(3)   pre-conditions for bringing an appeal[6];

(4)   how an appeal is to be brought and dealt with (including time limits)[7];

(5)   who is to consider an appeal[8];

(6)   matters to be taken into account (and disregarded) by the person or body considering an appeal[9];

(7)   powers of the person or body deciding an appeal[10];

(8)   what action is to be taken by a local authority as a result of an appeal decision[11];

(9)   providing information about the right to bring an appeal, appeal procedures and other sources of information and advice[12];

(10)   representation and support for an individual bringing or otherwise involved in an appeal[13]; and

(11)   investigations into things done or not done by a person or body with power to consider an appeal[14].

The regulations may make provision for:

(a)   an appeal brought or complaint made under another procedure to be treated as, or as part of, an appeal brought under the regulations[15];

(b)   an appeal brought or complaint made under another procedure to be considered with an appeal brought under the regulations[16];

(c)   matters raised in an appeal brought under the regulations to be taken into account by the person or body considering an appeal brought or complaint made under another procedure[17].

The regulations may include provision conferring functions on a person or body established by or under an Act[18].

At the date at which this volume states the law no such regulations had been made.

1   As to the meaning of 'local authority' see PARA 315 note 1; as to the meaning of 'England' see PARA 1 note 1.
2   Ie functions under the Care Act 2014 Pt 1 (ss 1–80). This includes decisions taken before the coming into force of the first regulations made under these provisions: s 72(1). The regulations may make provision, in relation to a case where an appeal is brought under regulations under s 72(1) for any provision of Pt 1 to apply, for a specified period (not beginning earlier than the date on which the decision appealed against was made, or ending later than the date on which the decision on the appeal takes effect), as if a decision ('the interim decision') differing from the decision appealed against had been made; as to what the terms of the interim decision are, or as to how and by whom they are to be determined; and for financial adjustments to be made following a decision on the appeal: s 72(9), (10).
3   Care Act 2014 s 72(1).
4   Care Act 2014 s 72(2)(a).
5   Care Act 2014 s 72(2)(b).

6   Care Act 2014 s 72(2)(c). Provision about pre-conditions for bringing an appeal may require specified steps to have been taken before an appeal is brought s 72(3).

7   Care Act 2014 s 72(2)(d). Provision about how an appeal is to be dealt with may include provision for the appeal to be treated as, or as part of, an appeal brought or complaint made under another procedure, and the appeal to be considered with any such appeal or complaint: s 72(4).

8   Care Act 2014 s 72(2)(e). Provision about who is to consider an appeal may include provision establishing, or requiring or permitting the establishment of, a panel or other body to consider an appeal, and requiring an appeal to be considered by, or by persons who include, persons with a specified description of expertise or experience: s 72(5).

9   Care Act 2014 s 72(2)(f).

10 Care Act 2014 s 72(2)(g).

11 Care Act 2014 s 72(2)(h).

12 Care Act 2014 s 72(2)(i).

13 Care Act 2014 s 72(2)(j). Provision about representation and support for an individual may include provision applying any provision of or made under s 67 (role of independent advocate: see PARA 100), with or without modifications: s 72(6).

14 Care Act 2014 s 72(2)(k).

15 Care Act 2014 s 72(7)(a).

16 Care Act 2014 s 72(7)(b).

17 Care Act 2014 s 72(7)(c).

18 Care Act 2014 s 72(8). This includes an Act passed after 14 May 2014 (ie the date on which the Care Act 2014 received royal assent); and for that purpose, the regulations may amend, repeal, or revoke an enactment, or provide for an enactment to apply with specified modifications: s 72(8).

(ii) The Secretary of State

333. Ministerial functions and oversight. Ministerial functions relating to social services in England are exercisable by the Secretary of State[1], as are functions relating to the oversight of the Disclosure and Barring Service[2]. If satisfied that any local authority[3] has failed, without reasonable excuse, to comply with any of its duties which are social services functions[4], the Secretary of State may make an order declaring that authority to be in default with respect to the duty in question[5]. The order may contain such directions as appear to the Secretary of State to be necessary for the purposes of ensuring that the duty is complied with within such period as may be specified in the order[6].

1   In any enactment, 'Secretary of State' means one of Her Majesty's principal secretaries of state: see the Interpretation Act 1978 s 5, Sch 1. As to the meaning of 'England' see PARA 1 note 1. As to the office of Secretary of State see CONSTITUTIONAL AND ADMINISTRATIVE LAW vol 20 (2014) PARA 153. Functions relating to social services in Wales are exercised by the Welsh Ministers: see PARA 395.

2   See PARAS 241–314 (noting that functions relating to the oversight of DBS so far as relating to Wales have not been devolved to the Welsh Ministers).

3   Ie an authority which is a 'local authority' for the purposes of the Local Authority Social Services Act 1970: see s 1; and PARA 315 note 1.

4   Ie other than a duty imposed by or under the Children Act 1989 (see CHILDREN AND YOUNG PERSONS , the Adoption (Intercountry Aspects) Act 1999 s 1 (see CHILDREN AND YOUNG PERSONS vol 9 (2017) PARA 582) or s 2(4) (see CHILDREN AND YOUNG PERSONS vol 9 (2017) PARA 585) or the Adoption and Children Act 2002 (see CHILDREN AND YOUNG PERSONS): see the Local Authority Social Services Act 1970 s 7D(1) (s 7D added by the National Health Service and Community Care Act 1990 s 50; amended by the Adoption and Children Act 2002 Sch 3 para 13). As to the meaning of 'social services functions' see PARA 315.

5   Local Authority Social Services Act 1970 s 7D(1) (as added: see note 4). As to the exercise of functions under guidance of the Secretary of State see ss 7, 7A; and PARA 316. As to the related provisions on consideration of complaints and the holding of inquiries see ss 7B, 7C; and PARA 325.

6   Local Authority Social Services Act 1970 s 7D(2) (as added: see note 4). On the application of the Secretary of State, any such direction is enforceable by mandatory order: s 7D(3) (as so added). As to mandatory orders and judicial review see JUDICIAL REVIEW vol 61 (2010) PARA 703 et seq.

334. Inspection of premises used for care and support services. Any person authorised by the Secretary of State[1] may at any reasonable time enter and inspect any premises (other than regulated premises[2]) in which care and support services[3] are or are proposed to be provided by a local authority in England[4], whether directly or under arrangements made with another person[5]. Any person inspecting any premises under these provisions may:

(1)   make such examination into the state and management of the premises, and the facilities and services provided there, as he thinks fit[6];

(2)   inspect any records[7] relating to the premises, or to any person for whom services have been or are to be provided there[8]; and

(3)   require the owner of, or any person employed in, the premises to furnish him with such information as he may request[9].

Any person inspecting any premises under these provisions may:

(a)   interview any person residing there in private for the purpose of investigating any complaint as to those premises or the services provided there, or if he has reason to believe that the services being provided there for that person are not satisfactory[10]; and

(b)   examine any such person in private[11].

Any person who intentionally obstructs another in the exercise of this power is guilty of an offence[12].

1 As to the Secretary of State see PARA 333.
2 For these purposes 'regulated premises' means premises used for the carrying on of a regulated activity within the meaning the Health and Social Care Act 2008 Pt 1 (ss 1–97) by a person who is registered under Pt 1 Ch 2 (ss 8–44) (see PARAS 152–165) in respect of the activity: National Health Service and Community Care Act 1990 s 48(1A)(a) (s 48(1) amended, s 48(1A) added, by SI 2010/813).
3 Ie services under the Care Act 2014 Pt 1 (ss 1–80). These provisions also apply to premises in which services under the Mental Health Act 1983 s 117 (after-care for persons formerly detained: see MENTAL HEALTH AND CAPACITY vol 75 (2013) PARA 945): National Health Service and Community Care Act 1990 s 48(1) (as amended (see note 2); s 48(1), (2)(b) amended by SI 2015/914).
4 Ie a county council in England, a district council for an area in England for which there is no county council, a London borough council or the Common Council of the City of London: National Health Service and Community Care Act 1990 ss 47(8), 48(8). As to the meaning of 'England' see PARA 1 note 1. As to local government areas and authorities in England see LOCAL GOVERNMENT vol 69 (2009) PARA 22 et seq. As to the London boroughs and their councils see LONDON GOVERNMENT vol 71 (2013) PARAS 15, 20, 34–38. As to the Common Council of the City of London see LONDON GOVERNMENT vol 71 (2013) PARA 16.
5 National Health Service and Community Care Act 1990 s 48(1) (as amended: see notes 2, 3). Any person exercising the power of entry must, if so required, produce some duly authenticated document showing his authority to do so: s 48(6).
6 National Health Service and Community Care Act 1990 s 48(2)(a).
7 Ie any records in whatever form they are held: see the National Health Service and Community Care Act 1990 s 48(2). Any person exercising the power to inspect records:
    (1)   is entitled at any reasonable time to have access to, and inspect and check the operation of, any computer and any associated apparatus or material which is or has been in use in connection with the records in question (s 48(3)(a)); and
    (2)   may require reasonable assistance from the person by whom or on whose behalf the computer is or has been so used, or any person having charge of or otherwise concerned with the operation of the computer, apparatus or material (s 48(3)(b)).
8 National Health Service and Community Care Act 1990 s 48(2)(b) (as amended: see note 3). No person may exercise the power under s 48(2)(b) so as to inspect medical records, or exercise the power under s 48(4)(b), unless he is a registered medical practitioner and the records relate to medical treatment given at the premises in question; nor may any person exercise the power to examine a person unless he is a registered medical practitioner: s 48(5). As to the meaning of 'registered medical practitioner' see MEDICAL PROFESSIONS vol 74 (2011) PARA 176.
9 National Health Service and Community Care Act 1990 s 48(2)(c).
10 National Health Service and Community Care Act 1990 s 48(4)(a).

11 National Health Service and Community Care Act 1990 s 48(4)(b).
12 National Health Service and Community Care Act 1990 s 48(7). A person guilty of such an offence
   is liable on summary conviction to a fine not exceeding level 3 on the standard scale: s 48(7). As
   to the powers of magistrates' courts to issue fines on summary conviction see SENTENCING vol 92
   (2015) PARA 176.

335. Training of social workers. The Secretary of State[1] has the function of:
  (1)   ascertaining what training is required by persons who are or wish to
         become social care workers[2];
  (2)   ascertaining what financial and other assistance is required for
         promoting such training[3];
  (3)   encouraging the provision of such assistance[4];
  (4)   drawing up occupational standards for social care workers[5].
The Secretary of State must also encourage persons to take part in:
  (a)   courses approved by the Health and Social Care Professions Council[6]
         for persons who are or wish to become social workers[7]; and
  (b)   other courses relevant to the training of persons who are or wish to
         become social care workers[8].
If it appears to the Secretary of State that adequate provision is not being made
for training persons who are or wish to become social care workers he may
provide, or secure the provision of, courses for that purpose[9]. The Secretary
of State (or, if directed, a special health authority[10]) may also, upon such terms and
subject to such conditions as he considers appropriate make grants, and pay
travelling and other allowances, to persons resident in England, in order to secure
their training in the work of social care workers[11]; and the Secretary of State may
make grants to organisations providing training in the work of social care
workers[12].
For these purposes 'social care worker' means a person[13] who:
  (i)   engages in social work which is required in connection with any health,
         education or social services provided in England[14];
  (ii)   is employed at, or manages, a children's home in England[15], a care home
         in England[16] or a residential family centre in England[17];
  (iii) is employed for the purposes of, or manages, a domiciliary care agency,
         a fostering agency, a voluntary adoption agency or an adoption support
         agency, in so far as the agency provides services to persons in England[18];
         or
  (iv)   is supplied by a domiciliary care agency to provide personal care in their
         own homes for persons in England who by reason of illness, infirmity or
         disability are unable to provide it for themselves without assistance[19].
Additional categories of person may be prescribed[20].

1 As to the Secretary of State see PARA 333. Any functions of the Secretary of State under these
   provisions may be exercised by any person, or by employees of any person, authorised to do so by
   the Secretary of State: Care Standards Act 2000 s 67(5)(b). For the purpose of determining the
   terms and effect of such an authorisation and the effect of so much of any contract made between
   Secretary of State and the authorised person as relates to the exercise of the function, the
   Deregulation and Contracting Out Act 1994 Pt 2 (ss 69–79C: see CONSTITUTIONAL AND
   ADMINISTRATIVE LAW vol 20 (2014) PARA 163; LOCAL GOVERNMENT vol 69 (2009)
   PARA 407 et seq) has effect as if the authorisation were given by virtue of an order under s 69:
   Care Standards Act 2000 s 67(7) (s 67(1), (3), (4), (7) amended, ss 55(2)–(4), 67(2) substituted, in
   relation to Wales only but with the effect that s 67 now applies only to England, by the Regulation
   and Inspection of Social Care (Wales) Act 2016 Sch 3 paras 42, 43). As to the meaning of
   'employee' in this context see the Deregulation and Contracting Out Act 1994 s 79(1); and LOCAL
   GOVERNMENT vol 69 (2009) PARA 407 (definition applied by the Care Standards Act 2000
   s 67(7) (as so amended)).
2 Care Standards Act 2000 s 67(1)(a) (s 67(1) as amended: see note 1). The Secretary of State may
   not exercise the function under s 67(1)(a) or (d) in relation to a social worker who is registered as

such in a register maintained under the Health and Social Work Professions Order 2001, SI 2002/254, art 5 (see MEDICAL PROFESSIONS vol 74 (2011) PARA 928): Care Standards Act 2000 s 67(1A) (added by the Health and Social Care Act 2012 s 221(1).

3   Care Standards Act 2000 s 67(1)(b) (s 67(1) as amended: see note 1).

4   Care Standards Act 2000 s 67(1)(c) (s 67(1) as amended: see note 1).

5   Care Standards Act 2000 s 67(1)(d) (s 67(1) as amended: see note 1). See note 2.

6   Ie under the Health and Social Work Professions Order 2001, SI 2002/254, art 15 or by virtue of art 19(4) (see MEDICAL PROFESSIONS vol 74 (2011) PARAS 938, 942). As to the Health and Social Care Professions Council see MEDICAL PROFESSIONS vol 74 (2011) PARA 916 et seq.

7   Care Standards Act 2000 s 67(2)(a) (as substituted: see note 1).

8   Care Standards Act 2000 s 67(2)(b) (as substituted: see note 1).

9   Care Standards Act 2000 s 67(3) (as amended: see note 1).

10 As to special health authorities see HEALTH SERVICES vol 54 (2017) PARA 180 et seq. The Secretary of State may direct a special health authority to exercise such of his functions under the Care Standards Act 2000 s 67(4)(a) as may be specified in the directions: s 67A(1) (s 67A added by the Health Act 2006 s 72). If the Secretary of State gives such a direction the National Health Service Act 2006 has have effect as if the direction were a direction of the Secretary of State under s 7 (see HEALTH SERVICES vol 54 (2017) PARA 24) and the functions were exercisable by the special health authority under s 7: Care Standards Act 2000 s 67A(2) (as so added; amended by the National Health Service (Consequential Amendments) Act 2006 Sch 1 para 287). Directions under the Care Standards Act 2000 s 67A(1) must be given by an instrument in writing and may be varied or revoked by subsequent directions: s 67A(3) (as so added).

11 Care Standards Act 2000 s 67(4)(a) (as amended: see note 1).

12 Care Standards Act 2000 s 67(4)(b).

13 Ie other than a person excepted by regulations: Care Standards Act 2000 s 55(1), (2) (as substituted: see note 1). At the date at which this volume states the law no such regulations had been made.

14 Care Standards Act 2000 s 55(2)(a) (as substituted: see note 1). Such a person is referred to in this context as a 'social worker'.

15 As to the meaning of 'children's home' in this context see the Care Standards Act 2000 s 1; and CHILDREN AND YOUNG PERSONS vol 10 (2017) PARA 1003.

16 As to the meaning of 'care home' in this context see the Care Standards Act 2000 s 3; and PARA 3 note 3.

17 Care Standards Act 2000 s 55(2)(b), (c) (as substituted: see note 1). A person who manages such a agency is referred to as a 'Social care manager': s 55(4A) (added by SI 2016/1030).

18 Care Standards Act 2000 s 55(2)(d), (e) (as substituted: see note 1).

19 Care Standards Act 2000 s 55(2)(f) (as substituted: see note 1).

20 Regulations may provide that persons of any of the following descriptions are to be treated as social care workers:

(1)   a person engaged in work for the purposes of a local authority in England's social services functions (Care Standards Act 2000 s 55(3)(a) (as substituted: see note 1));

(2)   a person engaged in work in England comprising the provision of services similar to services which may or must be provided by a local authority in England in the exercise of its social services functions (s 55(3)(b) (as so substituted));

(3)   a person engaged in the provision of personal care for any person in England (s 55(3)(c) (as so substituted));

(4)   a person who is employed in, or promotes, an undertaking (other than an establishment or agency) which consists of or includes supplying, or providing services for the purpose of supplying, persons to provide personal care to persons in England (s 55(3)(d), (e) (as so substituted));

(5)   a person who is employed in connection with the discharge of the functions of the Secretary of State under the Children Act 1989 s 80 (inspection of children's homes etc: see CHILDREN AND YOUNG PERSONS vol 9 (2017) PARA 171) (Care Standards Act 2000 s 55(3)(f) (as so substituted));

(6)   a person who is employed as a member of staff of the Office for Standards in Education, Children's Services and Skills (see CHILDREN AND YOUNG PERSONS vol 9 (2017) PARA 240) who inspects premises under the Children Act 1989 s 87 (welfare of children accommodated in independent schools and colleges: see CHILDREN AND YOUNG PERSONS vol 10 (2017) PARA 1276), the Care Standards Act 2000 s 31 (inspection of establishments and agencies by persons authorised by registration authority: see CHILDREN AND YOUNG PERSONS vol 9 (2017) PARAS 1017, 1031), or the Education and Inspections Act 2006 s 139 (inspection by Chief Inspector: see EDUCATION vol 36 (2015) PARA 1291), or who manages such an employee (Care Standards Act 2000 s 55(3)(g), (i) (as so substituted));

(7)	a person who is employed as a member of staff of the Care Quality Commission who, under the Health and Social Care Act 2008 Pt 1 (ss 1–97) inspects premises used for or in connection with the provision of social care (within the meaning of s 9(3): see PARA 152 note 2), or who manages such an employee (Care Standards Act 2000 s 55(3)(h), (i) (as so substituted));

(8)	a person employed in a day centre in England (s 55(3)(j) (as so substituted)); or

(9)	a person participating in a course approved by the Health and Care Professions Council under Health and Social Work Professions Order 2001, SI 2002/254, art 15 for persons wishing to become social workers (Care Standards Act 2000 s 55(3)(k) (as so substituted)).

As to a local authority in England's social services functions see PARA 315. As to the Care Quality Commission see PARA 336 et seq. 'Day centre' means a place where nursing or personal care (but not accommodation) is provided wholly or mainly for persons mentioned in s 3(2) (see PARA 3 note 3): s 55(5). At the date at which this volume states the law no such additional persons had been prescribed.

(iii) The Care Quality Commission

### A.	ESTABLISHMENT AND FUNCTIONS

336. Establishment, objectives and functions. The Care Quality Commission ('the Commission') is a body corporate[1] whose functions are to regulate health and social care services in England[2]. The main objective of the Commission in performing its functions is to protect and promote the health, safety and welfare of people who use health and social care services[3]. The Commission performs its functions for the general purpose of encouraging the improvement of health and social care services[4], the provision of health and social care services in a way that focuses on the needs and experiences of people who use those services[5], and the efficient and effective use of resources in the provision of health and social care services[6].

1	Health and Social Care Act 2008 s 1(1). The Commission was established in 2008, replacing the Commission for Healthcare Audit and Inspection, the Commission for Social Care Inspection and the Mental Health Act Commission, which were dissolved: s 1(2), Sch 2 (making provision for the transfer of property, rights and liabilities in regard to the Commission). Section 1(3), Sch 1 (amended by the Health and Social Care Act 2012 ss 181, 292; and the Care Act 2014 s 88), the Care Quality Commission (Healthwatch England Committee) Regulations 2012, SI 2012/1640, and the Care Quality Commission (Membership) Regulations 2015, SI 2015/1479, make provision about the Commission's status, general powers and duties, membership, remuneration and allowances, employees, procedure, exercise of functions, assistance, payments and loans, accounts and the seal and evidence.

2	The Commission has the functions conferred on it by or under any enactment: Health and Social Care Act 2008 s 2(1). 'Enactment' includes an enactment comprised in subordinate legislation (within the meaning of the Interpretation Act 1978: see STATUTES AND LEGISLATIVE PROCESS vol 96 (2012) PARA 608): Health and Social Care Act 2008 s 97(1). Those functions include registration functions under Pt 1 Ch 2 (ss 8–44), (see PARAS 152–165), review and investigation functions under Pt 1 Ch 3 (ss 45A–51), and functions under the Mental Health Act 1983 (see generally MENTAL HEALTH AND CAPACITY) (Health and Social Care Act 2008 s 2(2)). For the purposes of Pt 1 (ss 1–97), the 'regulatory functions' of the Commission are its functions under Pt 1 Ch 2, Pt 1 Ch 3 and Pt 1 Ch 5 (ss 53–59) (except its functions under s 53 (information and advice: see PARA 352), s 57 (reviews of data, studies and research: see PARA 355) and regulations under s 59 (additional functions: see PARA 165) to the extent that the regulations provide that they are not to be treated as regulatory functions for the purposes of Pt 1), its functions under the Care Act 2014 ss 54(1), 55(1) (financial sustainability of care providers: see PARA 180), and the doing by the Commission of anything for the purpose of assisting a local authority to carry out the duty under s 48(2) (duty of local authority to meet needs in event of business failure: see PARA 184): Health and Social Care Act 2008 ss 60(2), 97(1); Care Act 2014 s 57(1), (2). The Commission also has functions relating to the provision of the high security psychiatric services at specified hospitals (see the Care Quality Commission (Additional Functions) Regulations 2011, SI 2011/1551 (amended by SI 2012/921; SI 2013/1413) (made under the Health and Social Care Act 2008 s 59 (amended by the by the Health and Social Care Act 2012 Sch 13 paras 14, 17))). The Commission also has functions relating to the making of arrangements for public involvement in the scrutiny of care services under the Local Government and Public Involvement in Health Act 2007 s 221(1)

(see HEALTH SERVICES vol 54A (2017) PARA 558), but must arrange for the Healthwatch England committee to exercise the functions on its behalf: see the Health and Social Care Act 2008 ss 45A–45D (added by the Health and Social Care Act 2012 ss 181(1), (4), 182(11)). As to Healthwatch England and its committee see HEALTH SERVICES vol 54A (2017) PARA 557 et seq.
3   Health and Social Care Act 2008 s 3(1). In Pt 1 Ch 1 (ss 1–7) 'health and social care services' means the services to which the Commission's functions relate: ss 3(3), 7.
4   Health and Social Care Act 2008 s 3(2)(a).
5   Health and Social Care Act 2008 s 3(2)(b).
6   Health and Social Care Act 2008 s 3(2)(c).

337. Matters to which the Commission must have regard. In performing its functions the Care Quality Commission[1] must have regard to:
- (1)   views expressed by or on behalf of members of the public about health and social care services[2];
- (2)   experiences of people who use health and social care services and their families and friends[3];
- (3)   views expressed by Local Healthwatch organisations[4] or Local Healthwatch contractors[5] about the provision of health and social care services[6];
- (4)   the need to protect and promote the rights of persons[7] who use health and social care services[8];
- (5)   the need to ensure that action by the Commission in relation to health and social care services is proportionate to the risks against which it would afford safeguards and is targeted only where it is needed[9];
- (6)   any developments in approaches to regulatory action[10]; and
- (7)   best practice among persons performing functions comparable to those of the Commission (including the principles under which regulatory action should be transparent, accountable and consistent)[11].

In performing its functions the Commission must also have regard to such aspects of government policy as the Secretary of State[12] may direct[13].

1   As to the Care Quality Commission's establishment, objectives and functions see PARA 336.
2   Health and Social Care Act 2008 s 4(1)(a). As to the meaning of 'health and social care services' see PARA 336 note 3.
3   Health and Social Care Act 2008 s 4(1)(b).
4   As to Local Healthwatch organisations see HEALTH SERVICES vol 54A (2017) PARA 558.
5   For these purposes, 'Local Healthwatch contractor' has the meaning given by the Local Government and Public Involvement in Health Act 2007 s 223 (see HEALTH SERVICES vol 54A (2017) PARA 558): Health and Social Care Act 2008 s 4(3) (s 4(1)(c) amended, s 4(3) substituted, by the Health and Social Care Act 2012 s 189(6)).
6   Health and Social Care Act 2008 s 4(1)(c) (as amended: see note 5).
7   Ie including, in particular, the rights of children, of persons detained under the Mental Health Act 1983, of persons who are deprived of their liberty in accordance with the Mental Capacity Act 2005, and of other vulnerable adults: Health and Social Care Act 2008 s 4(1)(d) (as amended: see note 5).
8   Health and Social Care Act 2008 s 4(1)(d).
9   Health and Social Care Act 2008 s 4(1)(e).
10 Health and Social Care Act 2008 s 4(1)(f).
11 Health and Social Care Act 2008 s 4(1)(g).
12 As to the Secretary of State see PARA 333.
13 Health and Social Care Act 2008 s 4(2). Any power of the Secretary of State or the Privy Council to give directions under the Health and Social Care Act 2008 includes power to vary or revoke the directions by subsequent directions: s 165(1). Subject to s 165(3), a direction under the Health and Social Care Act 2008 by the Secretary of State or the Privy Council must be given by an instrument in writing: s 165(2) (amended by the Health and Social Care Act 2012 s 294(5)).

338. Interaction with other authorities in exercise of functions. The Care Quality Commission[1] may act jointly with another public authority[2] where it is appropriate   to   do   so   for   the   efficient   and   effective   exercise   of the Commission's functions[3]. This[4] is without prejudice to any other power the Commission may have to act jointly with another public authority[5].

The Commission may, if it thinks it appropriate to do so, provide advice or assistance to another public authority[6] for the purpose of the exercise by that authority of that authority's functions[7], and may do anything it thinks appropriate to facilitate the carrying out of an inspection[8] of a best value authority[9].

1 As to the Care Quality Commission's establishment, objectives and functions see PARA 336.
2 In the Health and Social Care Act 2008 Sch 4, 'public authority' includes any person certain of whose functions are functions of a public nature but does not include either House of Parliament or a person exercising functions in connection with proceedings in Parliament: s 66, Sch 4 para 3(1). Subject to Sch 4 para 9(3) (see note 6), references in Sch 4 to a public authority do not include a public authority outside the United Kingdom: Sch 4 para 3(2). In relation to a particular act, a person is not a public authority by virtue of Sch 4 para 3(1) if the nature of the act is private: Sch 4 para 3(3). As to the meaning of 'United Kingdom' see PARA 4 note 12.
3 Health and Social Care Act 2008 Sch 4 para 8(1). As to interaction with other authorities regarding inspections see PARA 225.
4 Ie the Health and Social Care Act 2008 Sch 4 para 8(1).
5 Health and Social Care Act 2008 Sch 4 para 8(2).
6 For these purposes, the reference to another public authority includes a public authority in the Channel Islands or the Isle of Man: Health and Social Care Act 2008 Sch 4 para 9(3).
7 Health and Social Care Act 2008 Sch 4 para 9(1).
8 Ie an inspection under the Local Government Act 1999 s 10 (see LOCAL GOVERNMENT vol 69 (2009) PARA 699).
9 Health and Social Care Act 2008 Sch 4 para 9(1A) (s 9(1A) added, s 9(2) substituted, by the Local Audit and Accountability Act 2014 Sch 12 para 88). Anything done under the Health and Social Care Act 2008 Sch 4 para 9 may be done on such terms, including terms as to payment, as the Commission thinks fit: Sch 4 para 9(2) (as so substituted).

339. Co-operation and mutuality. The Care Quality Commission[1] and the Welsh Ministers[2] must co-operate with each other for the efficient and effective discharge of their corresponding functions[3]. The Commission and the Welsh Ministers may share information with each other for these purposes[4]. The Commission must also co-operate with Monitor[5] in the exercise of their respective functions[6].

The Auditor General for Wales[7] must, on request, provide the Commission with any information it may reasonably require for the purpose of making comparisons, in the exercise of certain of its functions[8] so far as relating to health care or English NHS bodies[9], between English NHS bodies and Welsh NHS bodies[10]. The Commission must, on request, provide the Comptroller and Auditor General[11] with any material relevant to a review or investigation[12] in respect of an English NHS body, a study[13] promoted, or undertaken, by the Commission and, until a day to be appointed, a review[14] in respect of an English NHS body[15].

The Commission and a Minister of the Crown[16] may make arrangements for the Commission to perform any of its functions in relation to a prescribed[17] health scheme[18], or a prescribed social care scheme[19], for which the Minister has responsibility, and to provide services or facilities in so far as they are required by the Minister in connection with such a scheme[20].

1 As to the Care Quality Commission's establishment, objectives and functions see PARA 336.
2 As to the Welsh Ministers see PARA 395.
3 Health and Social Care Act 2008 s 69(1). Their corresponding functions are the Commission's functions (see PARA 218) and any functions of the Welsh Ministers exercisable in or in relation to Wales which correspond or are similar to any of the Commission's functions: s 69(2). As to the meaning of 'Wales' see PARA 2 note 4.
4 Health and Social Care Act 2008 s 69(3).
5 The Health and Social Care Act 2008 refers to the Independent Regulator but this is now known as Monitor: see HEALTH SERVICES vol 54 (2017) PARA 195.
6 Health and Social Care Act 2008 s 70(1). In particular, the Commission must give Monitor any information the Commission has about the provision of health care which the Commission or

Monitor considers would assist Monitor in the exercise of its functions (s 70(2)(a) (s 70(2) substituted, s 70(3) amended, s 70(4) added, by the Health and Social Care Act 2012 s 289)), make arrangements with Monitor to ensure that a person applying both to be registered under Pt 1 Ch 2 (ss 8–44: see PARAS 152–165) and for a licence under the Health and Social Care Act 2012 may do so by way of a single application form, and such a person is granted a registration under the Health and Social Care Act 2008 Pt 1 Ch 2 and a licence under the Health and Social Care Act 2008 by way of a single document (Health and Social Care Act 2008 s 70(2)(b) (as so substituted)), and seek to secure that the conditions on a registration under Pt 1 Ch 2 in a case within s 70(2)(b) are consistent with the conditions included in the person's licence under that Act (s 70(2)(c) (as so substituted)). Without prejudice to s 70(2)(a) the Commission must, on request, provide Monitor with any material relevant to a review under s 46 (see PARA 179), a review or investigation under s 48 (see PARA 340), or a study promoted, or undertaken, by the Commission under s 54 (see PARA 354), so far as the material relates to the provision of health care by a person who holds a licence under the Health and Social Care Act 2012 Pt 3 Ch 3 (ss 81–114 see HEALTH SERVICES): Health and Social Care Act 2008 s 70(3), (4) (as so amended and added; s 70(3) amended by the Care Act 2014 s 91(9)(c)). As to the meaning of 'health care' see PARA 152 note 2. Except in the Health and Social Care Act 2008 Pt 1 Ch 2, any reference Pt 1 to the provision of health care includes a reference to the provision of services connected with the provision of health care and the promotion and protection of public health: s 97(2).

7   As to the Auditor General for Wales see LOCAL GOVERNMENT vol 69 (2009) PARA 796.
8   Ie its functions under the Health and Social Care Act 2008 s 54: see PARA 354.
9   As to the meaning of 'English NHS body' see PARA 158 note 6.
10 Health and Social Care Act 2008 s 71(1). For these purposes, 'Welsh NHS body' has the same meaning as in the Public Audit (Wales) Act 2004 Pt 3 (ss 60–64) (see LOCAL GOVERNMENT vol 69 (2009) PARA 799): Health and Social Care Act 2008 s 71(2).
11 As to the Comptroller and Auditor General see CONSTITUTIONAL AND ADMINISTRATIVE LAW vol 20 (2014) PARA 494.
12 Ie under the Health and Social Care Act 2008 s 48.
13 Ie under the Health and Social Care Act 2008 s 54.
14 Ie under the Health and Social Care Act 2008 s 46.
15 Health and Social Care Act 2008 s 72 (amended by the Care Act 2014 s 91(9)(d)); prospectively amended by the Health and Social Care Act 2012 s 164). At the date at which this volume states the law no day had been appointed for this purpose.
16 'Minister of the Crown' has the same meaning as in the Ministers of the Crown Act 1975 (see CONSTITUTIONAL AND ADMINISTRATIVE LAW vol 20 (2014) PARA 151): Health and Social Care Act 2008 s 97(1).
17 'Prescribed' means prescribed by regulations: Health and Social Care Act 2008 s 97(1). At the date at which this volume states the law nothing had been prescribed for this purpose.
18 For these purposes 'health scheme' means a scheme which appears to the Secretary of State to be a health or medical scheme paid for out of public funds: Health and Social Care Act 2008 s 73(4). As to the Secretary of State see PARA 333.
19 For these purposes, 'social care scheme' means a scheme which appears to the Secretary of State to be a social care scheme paid for out of public funds: Health and Social Care Act 2008 s 73(4). At the date at which this volume states the law nothing had been prescribed for this purpose.
20 Health and Social Care Act 2008 s 73(1). Such arrangements may be made on such terms and conditions as may be agreed between the parties to the arrangements (s 73(2)), and those terms and conditions may include provision with respect to the making of payments to the Commission in respect of the cost to it of giving effect to the arrangements (s 73(3)). Corresponding provision is made in relation to Northern Ireland Ministers: see s 74.

B.   REVIEWS, INSPECTIONS AND ASSESSMENTS

340. Special reviews and investigations. A 'special review or investigation' is a review[1] of or an investigation into:

(1)   the provision of NHS care[2];
(2)   the provision of adult social services[3];
(3)   the exercise of the functions of the National Health Service Commissioning Board or a clinical commissioning group in arranging for the provision[4] of NHS care[5];
(4)   the exercise of the functions of English local authorities[6] in arranging for the provision of adult social services[7]; or
(5)   the exercise of functions by English Health Authorities[8].

The Care Quality Commission[9] may conduct any special review or investigation, and must do so if the Secretary of State so requests[10]. Such a review or investigation may relate to the overall provision of NHS care or adult social services or to the provision of NHS care or adult social services of a particular description[11], to the overall exercise of functions or to the exercise of functions of a particular description[12], or to the provision of care or services or the exercise of functions by bodies or persons generally or by particular bodies or persons[13]. Where the Commission conducts such a review or investigation it must publish a report[14].

Where the Commission conducts a review or investigation under these provisions in respect of an English local authority and considers that the authority is failing to discharge any of its adult social services functions to an acceptable standard, the Commission must inform the Secretary of State of that fact and recommend any special measures which it considers the Secretary of State should take[15].

1   Ie other than a periodic review and performance assessment under the Health and Social Care Act 2008 s 46 (see PARA 179).
2   Health and Social Care Act 2008 s 48(2)(a) (s 48(1), (2) amended, s 48(2)(bb), (3A) added, by the Care Act 2014 s 91(4), (6)–(8)).
3   Health and Social Care Act 2008 s 48(2)(b). As to the meaning of 'adult social services' see PARA 179 note 13. A review or investigation under s 48(2)(b), in so far as it involves a review or investigation into the arrangements made for the provision of the adult social services in question, is to be treated as a review under s 48(2)(bb) (see the text and note 7) (and the requirement for approval under s 48(1) is accordingly to apply): s 48(3A) (as added: see note 2).
4   Ie under the National Health Service Act 2006 (see HEALTH SERVICES) or the Mental Health Act 1983 s 117 (after-care) (see MENTAL HEALTH AND CAPACITY vol 75 (2013) PARA 945).
5   Health and Social Care Act 2008 s 48(2)(ba) (s 48(2)(ba) added and amended, s 81(2) amended, by the Health and Social Care Act 2012 s 40, Sch 5 paras 159, 165). As to the National Health Service Commissioning Board see HEALTH SERVICES vol 54 (2017) PARA 32. As to clinical commissioning groups see HEALTH SERVICES vol 54 (2017) PARA 35 et seq. The Commission may not conduct a review or investigation under the Health and Social Care Act 2008 s 48(2)(ba) or (bb) without the approval of the Secretary of State: s 48(1) (as amended: see note 2).
6   As to the meaning of 'English local authority' see PARA 158 note 6.
7   Health and Social Care Act 2008 s 48(2)(bb) (as added: see note 2). See note 5.
8   Health and Social Care Act 2008 s 48(2)(c). For these purposes 'English Health Authority' means a Special Health Authority performing functions only or mainly in respect of England: s 48(8)(b). As to the meaning of 'England' see PARA 1 note 1. As to special health authorities see HEALTH SERVICES vol 54 (2017) PARA 180 et seq.
9   As to the Care Quality Commission's establishment, objectives and functions see PARA 336.
10 Health and Social Care Act 2008 s 48(1) (as amended (see note 2); amended by the Health and Social Care Act 2012 s 293(2)). The Commission must from time to time prepare and publish a document setting out the special reviews and investigations that it proposes to conduct under the Health and Social Care Act 2008 s 48: s 81(1)(a). Before preparing a document under s 81(1) the Commission must consult the Secretary of State, the National Health Service Commissioning Board and any other person or body specified by an order made by the Secretary of State, and it must send each of those persons or bodies a copy of the document once it is prepared: s 81(2) (as amended: see note 5). The Commission may determine that any document or combination of documents prepared for the purposes of any other enactment or enactments is to be treated as a document prepared for the purposes of s 81(1) (so long as the requirements of s 81(2) are complied with in relation to the document or documents concerned): s 81(3). Nothing in a document published under s 81(1) is to be regarded as affecting any power of the Secretary of State to require a review or investigation to be conducted or a study to be undertaken or as preventing the Commission from conducting an investigation under s 48 where the Commission considers there to be a risk to the health, safety or welfare of persons receiving health or social care: s 81(4). As to the Secretary of State see PARA 333.
11 Health and Social Care Act 2008 s 48(3)(a).
12 Health and Social Care Act 2008 s 48(3)(b).
13 Health and Social Care Act 2008 s 48(3)(c).

14 Health and Social Care Act 2008 s 48(4). As to reports see PARA 179 note 10. The Commission must consider whether the report raises anything on which it ought to give advice to the Secretary of State under s 53(2) (see PARA 352): s 48(5). If the review or investigation gives rise to a duty to act under s 50(2) or (3) (see also PARA 179) in respect of an English local authority, s 53(5) does not apply in relation to so much of the report as relates to that local authority: s 48(6).
15 Health and Social Care Act 2008 s 50(1), (2) (s 50(1) amended by the Care Act 2014 s 91(9)(a)). See further the Health and Social Care Act 2008 s 50(3)–(5); and PARA 179 note 14.

341. Inspections. The Care Quality Commission[1] may for the purposes of its regulatory functions[2] carry out inspections of the carrying on of a regulated activity[3], the provision of NHS care[4], the provision of adult social services[5] or the exercise of functions by an English NHS body[6]. The Commission may delegate any of its inspection functions[7] (to such extent as it may determine) to another public authority[8]. If the carrying out of an inspection is so delegated it is nevertheless to be regarded for the purposes of any enactment as carried out by the Commission[9].

1 As to the Care Quality Commission's establishment, objectives and functions see PARA 336.
2 As to the 'regulatory functions' of the Commission see PARA 336 note 2.
3 Health and Social Care Act 2008 s 60(1)(a). As to the meaning of 'regulated activity' for these purposes see PARA 152 note 2; as to the carrying on of regulated activities see Pt 1 Ch 2 (ss 8–44); and PARAS 152–165. Where an inspection is carried out for the purposes of the Commission's functions under Pt 1 Ch 2, the Commission must prepare a report on the matters inspected and without delay send a copy of the report to the person who carries on the regulated activity in question and, if a person is registered under Pt 1 Ch 2 as a manager in respect of the activity, that person: Health and Social Care Act 2008 s 61(2). The Commission must publish the report s 61(3). As to reports and information generally see s 84; and PARA 179 note 10.
4 Health and Social Care Act 2008 s 60(1)(b). 'NHS care' means health care commissioned by the National Health Service Commissioning Board (see HEALTH SERVICES vol 54 (2017) PARA 32) or by a clinical commissioning group (whether from an English NHS provider or not) (see HEALTH SERVICES vol 54 (2017) PARA 35 et seq): s 97(1) (amended by the Health and Social Care Act 2012 Sch 5 paras 154, 166(1), (3), (4)). 'English NHS provider' means an NHS foundation trust (see HEALTH SERVICES vol 54 (2017) PARA 244) or (until a day to be appointed) a National Health Service trust all or most of whose hospitals, establishments and facilities are situated in England: Health and Social Care Act 2008 s 97(1) (as so amended; prospectively amended by the Health and Social Care Act 2012 Sch 14 Pt 2 paras 108, 109(b)). At the date at which this volume states the law no such day had been appointed. As to the meaning of 'health care' see PARA 152 note 2.
5 As to the meaning of 'adult social services' see PARA 179 note 13.
6 Health and Social Care Act 2008 s 60(1). As to the meaning of 'English NHS body' see PARA 158 note 6.
7 Ie functions relating to, or connected with, inspections carried out by the Commission under the Health and Social Care Act 2008 s 60: Sch 4 para 2.
8 Health and Social Care Act 2008 Sch 4 para 4(1). As to the meaning of 'public authority' see PARA 338 note 2.
9 Health and Social Care Act 2008 Sch 4 para 4(2).

342. Powers to enter regulated premises. Premises[1] are 'regulated premises' if they fall within one or more of the following descriptions:

(1)   they are used for the carrying on of a regulated activity[2];
(2)   they are owned or controlled by an English NHS body[3] or English local authority[4]; or
(3)   they are used or proposed to be used for or in connection with the provision of NHS care, the exercise of any functions of an English NHS body or the provision of adult social services[5].

If the Care Quality Commission[6] considers it necessary or expedient for the purposes of any of its regulatory functions[7], a person authorised by the Commission may enter and inspect any premises which are, or which the person reasonably believes to be, regulated premises[8]. A person so authorised to enter and inspect such premises may, if he considers it necessary or expedient for relevant purposes[9]:

(a)	make any examination into the state and management of the premises or the treatment of persons receiving care[10] there[11];

(b)	inspect and take copies of any documents or records[12];

(c)	have access to, and check the operation of, any computer, and any associated apparatus or material, which is or has been in use in connection with any documents or records[13];

(d)	inspect any other item[14];

(e)	seize and remove from the premises any documents, records or other items[15];

(f)	interview in private any person who carries on or manages a regulated activity, or who manages the provision of NHS care or adult social services, at the premises[16], any person working at the premises[17], and any person receiving care at the premises who consents to be interviewed[18]; and

(g)	if certain conditions[19] are met, examine in private any person receiving care at the premises[20].

The authorised person may also require any person to afford him such facilities and assistance with respect to matters within the person's control as are necessary to enable him to exercise the relevant[21] powers[22] and take such measurements and photographs, and make such recordings, as he considers necessary to enable him to exercise those powers[23].

A person who without reasonable excuse obstructs the exercise of an inspection power[24] or fails to comply with a requirement[25] is guilty of an offence[26].

1	'Premises' includes a vehicle: Health and Social Care Act 2008 s 62(6).

2	Health and Social Care Act 2008 s 62(3)(a). As to the meaning of 'regulated activity' for these purposes see PARA 152 note 2; as to the carrying on of regulated activities see Pt 1 Ch 2 (ss 8–44); and PARAS 152–165.

3	As to the meaning of 'English NHS body' see PARA 158 note 6.

4	Health and Social Care Act 2008 s 62(3)(b). As to the meaning of 'English local authority' see PARA 158 note 6.

5	Health and Social Care Act 2008 s 62(3)(c). As to the meaning of 'NHS care' see PARA 341 note 4. As to the meaning of 'adult social services' see PARA 179 note 13. If NHS care or an adult social service is provided to a person in premises used wholly or mainly as a private dwelling, the premises are not to be regarded as used for or in connection with the provision of that care or service: s 62(4).

6	As to the Care Quality Commission's establishment, objectives and functions see PARA 336.

7	Health and Social Care Act 2008 s 62(1). As to the 'regulatory functions' of the Commission see PARA 336 note 2.

8	Health and Social Care Act 2008 s 62(2). A person who proposes to exercise this power must if so required produce some duly authenticated document showing the person's authority to exercise the power: s 62(5). For the Commission's power to require an explanation of material provided pursuant to these provisions see PARA 344.

9	For these purposes, 'relevant purposes' means the purposes of any of the Commission's regulatory functions: Health and Social Care Act 2008 s 63(8).

10	For these purposes, any reference to a person receiving care at premises includes a reference to a person who is accommodated there: Health and Social Care Act 2008 s 63(8).

11	Health and Social Care Act 2008 s 63(1), (2)(a).

12	Health and Social Care Act 2008 s 63(2)(b). For these purposes, any reference to documents or records includes a reference to personal and medical records: Health and Social Care Act 2008 s 63(8). The power under s 63(2)(b) (see head (b) in the text) includes power to require any person holding or accountable for documents or records (whether or not kept at the premises) to produce them for inspection at the premises and to require any records which are kept by means of a computer to be produced in a form in which they are legible and can be taken away: s 63(4).

13	Health and Social Care Act 2008 s 63(2)(c).

14	Health and Social Care Act 2008 s 63(2)(d).

15	Health and Social Care Act 2008 s 63(2)(e).

16 Health and Social Care Act 2008 s 63(2)(f)(i). The power under s 63(2)(f)(i) to interview a person
    in private includes power, in the case of a body corporate, to interview in private any director,
    manager, secretary or other similar officer of the body corporate and, where the body is an English
    NHS body or English local authority, any officer or member of the NHS body or local authority:
    s 63(5).
17 Health and Social Care Act 2008 s 63(2)(f)(ii).
18 Health and Social Care Act 2008 s 63(2)(f)(iii).
19 The conditions are:
    (1)   a person is a registered medical practitioner or registered nurse (Health and Social Care
             Act 2008 s 63(3)(a));
    (2)   that person has reason to believe that the person to be examined is not receiving proper
             care at the premises (s 63(3)(b)); and
    (3)   the person to be examined is capable of giving consent to the examination and does so
             or is incapable of giving consent to the examination (s 63(3)(c)).
    As to registered medical practitioners see MEDICAL PROFESSIONS vol 74 (2011) PARA 176.
    As to registered nurses see MEDICAL PROFESSIONS vol 74 (2011) PARA 713.
20 Health and Social Care Act 2008 s 63(2)(g).
21 Ie the powers under the Health and Social Care Act 2008 ss 62, 63.
22 Health and Social Care Act 2008 s 63(6)(a).
23 Health and Social Care Act 2008 s 63(6)(b).
24 Ie conferred by the Health and Social Care Act 2008 s 62 or s 63.
25 Ie imposed under the Health and Social Care Act 2008 s 63.
26 Health and Social Care Act 2008 s 63(7). Such a person is liable on summary conviction to a fine
    not exceeding level 4 on the standard scale: s 63(7). As to the powers of magistrates' courts to issue
    fines on summary conviction see SENTENCING vol 92 (2015) PARA 176. The offence under s 63
    is a fixed penalty offence: see the Health and Social Care Act 2008 (Regulated Activities)
    Regulations 2014, SI 2014/2936, reg 24, Sch 5; and PARA 159 note 4.

343. Powers to require information. The Care Quality Commission[1] may
require:

(1)   an English NHS body[2];
(2)   a person providing health care[3] commissioned by the National Health
         Service Commissioning Board or a clinical commissioning group[4];
(3)   an English local authority[5];
(4)   a person providing adult social services[6] commissioned by an English
         local authority[7];
(5)   a person who carries on or manages a regulated activity[8]; or
(6)   the Health and Social Care Information Centre[9],

to provide it with any information, documents, records (including personal and
medical records) or other items which the Commission considers it necessary or
expedient to have for the purposes of any of its regulatory functions[10]. A person
who without reasonable excuse fails to comply with such a requirement is guilty
of an offence[11].

1 As to the Care Quality Commission's establishment, objectives and functions see PARA 336.
2 Health and Social Care Act 2008 s 64(2)(a). As to the meaning of 'English NHS body' see
   PARA 158 note 6.
3 As to the meaning of 'health care' see PARA 152 note 2.
4 Health and Social Care Act 2008 s 64(2)(b) (s 64(2)(b), (d) amended, s 64(2)(f) added, by the
   Health and Social Care Act 2012 Sch 5 paras 154, 162, Sch 19 para 11). As to the National Health
   Service Commissioning Board see HEALTH SERVICES vol 54 (2017) PARA 32); as to clinical
   commissioning groups see HEALTH SERVICES vol 54 (2017) PARA 35 et seq.
5 Health and Social Care Act 2008 s 64(2)(c). As to the meaning of 'English local authority' see
   PARA 158 note 6.
6 As to the meaning of 'adult social services' see PARA 179 note 13.
7 Health and Social Care Act 2008 s 64(2)(d) (as amended: see note 4).
8 Health and Social Care Act 2008 s 64(2)(e). As to the meaning of 'regulated activity' for these
   purposes see PARA 152 note 2; as to the carrying on of regulated activities see Pt 1 Ch 2 (ss 8–44);
   and PARAS 152–165.
9 Health and Social Care Act 2008 s 64(2)(f) (as added: see note 4). As to the Health and Social Care
   Information Centre see PARA 372a; and HEALTH SERVICES vol 54 (2017) PARA 204.

10 Health and Social Care Act 2008 s 64(1). As to the 'regulatory functions' of the Commission see PARA 336 note 2. This power includes, in relation to information, documents or records kept by means of a computer, power to require the provision of the information, documents or records in legible form: s 64(3). For the Commission's power to require an explanation of material provided pursuant to these provisions see PARA 344.
11 Health and Social Care Act 2008 s 64(4). Such a person is liable on summary conviction to a fine not exceeding level 4 on the standard scale: s 64(4). As to the powers of magistrates' courts to issue fines on summary conviction see SENTENCING vol 92 (2015) PARA 176. The offence under s 64 is a fixed penalty offences: see the Health and Social Care Act 2008 (Regulated Activities) Regulations 2014, SI 2014/2936, reg 24, Sch 5; and PARA 159 note 4. As to proceedings for offences see PARA 158 note 6.

344. Power to require explanations. Where the Care Quality Commission[1] considers an explanation of:

(1)   any documents, records or other items inspected, copied or provided pursuant to its powers[2] of entry and inspection and its powers[3] to request information[4];

(2)   any information so provided[5];

(3)   any documents, records, other items or information otherwise provided to the Commission by any person for the purposes of the Commission's regulatory functions[6]; or

(4)   any matters which are the subject of the exercise of any such functions[7],

necessary or expedient for the purposes of any of its regulatory functions, the persons listed below must, if so requested, provide an explanation of that matter to the Commission or to persons authorised by it[8]:

(a)   a person carrying on a regulated activity[9];

(b)   a chair, director or employee of a person carrying on a regulated activity[10];

(c)   an English NHS body[11];

(d)   a member of an English NHS body other than an NHS foundation trust[12];

(e)   a member of a committee or sub-committee of an English NHS body other than an NHS foundation trust[13];

(f)   a member of a committee or sub-committee of the board of directors of an NHS foundation trust[14];

(g)   an employee of an English NHS body other than one falling within head(b) above[15];

(h)   a local authority[16];

(i)   a member or officer of a local authority[17];

(j)   a member of a committee or sub-committee of a local authority or a member of a joint committee of two or more local authorities[18];

(k)   an elected mayor[19] of a local authority[20];

(l)   a person (other than a person prescribed in heads (b) to (k) above) who is assisting in the carrying on of a regulated activity[21];

(m)   a person providing equipment or premises to a registered person[22];

(n)   a chair, director or employee of a person providing equipment or premises to a registered person[23]; and

(o)   a person (other than a person prescribed in head (n) above) who is assisting a person providing equipment or premises to a registered person[24].

A person who without reasonable excuse fails to comply with such a requirement is guilty of an offence[25].

1   As to the Care Quality Commission's establishment, objectives and functions see PARA 336.
2   Ie the Commission's powers under the Health and Social Care Act 2008 ss 62, 63 (see PARA 342).

3 Ie the Commission's powers under the Health and Social Care Act 2008 s 64 (see PARA 343).
4 Health and Social Care Act 2008 s 65(2)(a).
5 Health and Social Care Act 2008 s 65(2)(b).
6 Health and Social Care Act 2008 s 65(2)(c). As to the 'regulatory functions' of the Commission see PARA 336 note 2.
7 Health and Social Care Act 2008 s 65(2)(d).
8 Care Quality Commission (Registration) Regulations 2009, SI 2009/3112, reg 10(1) (made under the Health and Social Care Act 2008 s 65(1), (3)). Explanations required under these provisions must be provided at such times and such places as may be specified by the Commission: Care Quality Commission (Registration) Regulations 2009, SI 2009/3112, reg 10(2).
9 Care Quality Commission (Registration) Regulations 2009, SI 2009/3112, reg 10(1)(a). As to the meaning of 'regulated activity' for these purposes see PARA 152 note 2; as to the carrying on of regulated activities see the Health and Social Care Act 2008 Pt 1 Ch 2 (ss 8–44); and PARAS 152–165.
10 Care Quality Commission (Registration) Regulations 2009, SI 2009/3112, reg 10(1)(b).
11 Care Quality Commission (Registration) Regulations 2009, SI 2009/3112, reg 10(1)(c). As to the meaning of 'English NHS body' see PARA 158 note 6.
12 Care Quality Commission (Registration) Regulations 2009, SI 2009/3112, reg 10(1)(d). As to NHS foundation trusts see HEALTH SERVICES vol 54 (2017) PARA 244.
13 Care Quality Commission (Registration) Regulations 2009, SI 2009/3112, reg 10(1)(e).
14 Care Quality Commission (Registration) Regulations 2009, SI 2009/3112, reg 10(1)(f).
15 Care Quality Commission (Registration) Regulations 2009, SI 2009/3112, reg 10(1)(g).
16 Care Quality Commission (Registration) Regulations 2009, SI 2009/3112, reg 10(1)(h). As to the meaning of 'local authority' see PARA 187 note 2.
17 Care Quality Commission (Registration) Regulations 2009, SI 2009/3112, reg 10(1)(i).
18 Care Quality Commission (Registration) Regulations 2009, SI 2009/3112, reg 10(1)(j).
19 Ie within the meaning given in the Local Government Act 2000 s 39 (see LOCAL GOVERNMENT vol 69 (2009) PARA 320).
20 Care Quality Commission (Registration) Regulations 2009, SI 2009/3112, reg 10(1)(k).
21 Care Quality Commission (Registration) Regulations 2009, SI 2009/3112, reg 10(1)(l).
22 Care Quality Commission (Registration) Regulations 2009, SI 2009/3112, reg 10(1)(m).
23 Care Quality Commission (Registration) Regulations 2009, SI 2009/3112, reg 10(1)(n).
24 Care Quality Commission (Registration) Regulations 2009, SI 2009/3112, reg 10(1)(o).
25 Health and Social Care Act 2008 s 65(4). Such a person is liable on summary conviction to a fine not exceeding level 4 on the standard scale: s 65(4). As to the powers of magistrates' courts to issue fines on summary conviction see SENTENCING vol 92 (2015) PARA 176. The offence under s 65 is a fixed penalty offence: see the Health and Social Care Act 2008 (Regulated Activities) Regulations 2014, SI 2014/2936, reg 24, Sch 5; and PARA 159 note 4. As to proceedings for offences see PARA 158 note 6.

345. Inspections to be carried out in accordance with guidance given by Secretary of State. The Secretary of State[1] may publish guidance about steps which the Care Quality Commission[2] may take in exercising powers of inspection[3] with a view to avoiding the imposition of unreasonable burdens on those in respect of whom the powers are exercisable[4]. Such steps might include, for example, co-operating with other regulatory authorities and co-ordinating the exercise of relevant powers[5], sharing information or the results of inspections[6], and seeking to obtain information from other sources before exercising a relevant power to require the provision of that information[7]. In exercising powers of inspection[8], regulatory authorities must have regard to any guidance published[9]. Nothing in these provisions[10] is intended to limit the scope of a power or affect a person's obligation to comply with a requirement imposed in the exercise of such a power[11].

1 As to the Secretary of State see PARA 333.
2 As to the Care Quality Commission's establishment, objectives and functions see PARA 336. The Health and Social Care Act 2008 s 68 (see the text and notes 3–11) applies in respect of 'regulatory authorities', ie the Commission and such other bodies as may be prescribed: s 68(2). A body may not be so prescribed unless it has functions relating to the provision of health or social care: s 68(3). As to the meaning of 'health or social care' see PARA 152 note 2. At the date at which this volume states the law no bodies additional to the Commission had been prescribed for this purpose.

3 Ie powers conferred by or under an enactment to carry out inspections or require the provision of information (Health and Social Care Act 2008 s 68(4)) but, in relation to a body prescribed under s 68(2) (see note 2), such powers are 'relevant powers' only so far as they are exercisable in respect of a person in respect of whom the Commission has relevant powers (s 68(4)). In s 68, 'inspections' includes inspections of persons, premises or the carrying on of activities, a reference to a power to carry out inspections includes a reference to any power which is ancillary to that power (such as a power to enter premises or to require assistance), and a reference to a power to require the provision of information includes a reference to a power to require the production of documents, records or other items, a power to require the making of reports and a power to require explanations: s 68(8).
4 Health and Social Care Act 2008 s 68(1).
5 Health and Social Care Act 2008 s 68(5)(a).
6 Health and Social Care Act 2008 s 68(5)(b).
7 Health and Social Care Act 2008 s 68(5)(c).
8 See note 3.
9 Health and Social Care Act 2008 s 68(6). The reference in the text to the guidance is a reference to guidance published under s 68(1).
10 Ie in the Health and Social Care Act 2008 s 68.
11 Health and Social Care Act 2008 s 68(7).

346. Cancellation or variation of onerous inspections. If an inspection authority[1] is proposing to carry out an inspection[2] that would involve inspecting an English NHS provider[3] or a person[4] who is registered as a service provider[5] but only in relation to a regulated activity[6] (other than a provider or person who provides services in prisons or other places of detention[7]), and the Commission considers that the proposed inspection would impose an unreasonable burden on the provider or person or would do so if carried out in a particular way, the Commission must give a notice to the inspection authority requiring it not to carry out the proposed inspection, or not to carry it out in that way[8]. Where such a notice is given, the proposed inspection is not to be carried out, or (as the case may be) is not to be carried out in the manner mentioned in the notice[9]. The Secretary of State, if satisfied that the proposed inspection would not impose an unreasonable burden on the specified organisation in question, or would not do so if carried out in a particular manner, may give consent to the inspection being carried out, or being carried out in that manner[10].

1 Health and Social Care Act 2008 Sch 4 para 6(2)(a). For the purposes of Sch 4 paras 5–7 the 'inspection authorities' are:
   (1) Her Majesty's Chief Inspector of Prisons (see PRISONS AND PRISONERS vol 85 (2012) PARA 409) (Health and Social Care Act 2008 Sch 4 para 1(1), (2)(a), (3)(a));
   (2) Her Majesty's Chief Inspector of Constabulary (see POLICE AND INVESTIGATORY POWERS vol 84 (2013) PARA 152) (Sch 4 para 1(2)(b), (3)(b));
   (3) Her Majesty's Chief Inspector of the Crown Prosecution Service (see CRIMINAL PROCEDURE vol 27 (2015) PARA 26) (Sch 4 para 1(2)(c), (3)(c));
   (4) Her Majesty's Chief Inspector of the National Probation Service for England and Wales (see SENTENCING vol 92 (2015) PARA 682) (Sch 4 para 1(2)(d), (3)(d)); and
   (5) Her Majesty's Chief Inspector of Education, Children's Services and Skills (see EDUCATION vol 36 (2015) PARA 1133 et seq) (Sch 4 para 1(2)(f), (3)(f)).
   These provisions also apply to any other person or body specified by order made by the Secretary of State: Sch 4 para 6(2)(b). At the date at which this volume states the law no further persons or bodies had been specified for this purpose. As to the Secretary of State see PARA 333.
2 A notice may not be given under these provisions in the case of an inspection carried out by Her Majesty's Chief Inspector of Education, Children's Services and Skills under the Childcare Act 2006 s 49 or s 60 (inspections: see CHILDREN AND YOUNG PERSONS vol 10 (2017) PARAS 1199, 1209) and a review carried out under the Children Act 2004 s 20 (joint area reviews: see CHILDREN AND YOUNG PERSONS vol 9 (2017) PARA 217): Care Quality Commission (Specified Organisations etc) Order 2010, SI 2010/496, art 4 (made under the Health and Social Care Act 2008 Sch 4 para 6(6)).
3 Care Quality Commission (Specified Organisations etc) Order 2010, SI 2010/496, art 2(1)(a) (made under the Health and Social Care Act 2008 Sch 4 para 6(3)–(5)). As to the meaning of 'English NHS provider' see PARA 341 note 4.

4   Ie a person other than an English NHS provider or an English local authority: Care Quality Commission (Specified Organisations etc) Order 2010, SI 2010/496, art 2(1)(b). As to the meaning of 'English local authority' see PARA 158 note 6.
5   Ie registered under the Health and Social Care Act 2008: see Pt 1 Ch 2 (ss 8–44); and PARAS 152–165.
6   Ie within the meaning of the Health and Social Care Act 2008 Pt 1 (ss 1–97) (see PARA 152 et seq).
7   The persons and bodies referred to in the Care Quality Commission (Specified Organisations etc) Order 2010, SI 2010/496, art 2(1) (see the text and notes 1–6) are not, by virtue of art 2(2), specified for the purposes of the Health and Social Care Act 2008 Sch 4 para 6(3) (see note 2) in relation to the provision of services in:
    (1)   a prison within the meaning of the Prison Act 1952 (see s 53(1); and PRISONS AND PRISONERS vol 85 (2012) PARA 403);
    (2)   a contracted out prison as defined in the Criminal Justice Act 1991 s 84(4) (see PRISONS AND PRISONERS vol 85 (2012) PARA 521);
    (3)   a young offender institution as defined in the Prison Act 1952 s 43(1)(aa) (see PRISONS AND PRISONERS vol 85 (2012) PARA 487);
    (4)   a remand centre as defined in the Prison Act 1952 s 43(1)(a) (see PRISONS AND PRISONERS vol 85 (2012) PARA 485); and
    (5)   a removal centre or a short-term holding facility as defined in the Immigration and Asylum Act 1999 s 147 (see IMMIGRATION AND ASYLUM vol 57 (2012) PARA 192).
8   Health and Social Care Act 2008 Sch 4 para 6(1).
9   Health and Social Care Act 2008 Sch 4 para 6(7). This is subject to Sch 4 para 6(8) (see the text and note 10.
10 Health and Social Care Act 2008 Sch 4 para 6(8). The Secretary of State may also by order make supplementary provision: Sch 4 para 6(9). Supplementary provision includes, in particular, provision about the form of notices, provision prescribing the period within which notices are to be given, provision prescribing circumstances in which notices are, or are not, to be made public. provision for revising or withdrawing notices, and provision for setting aside notices not validly given: Sch 4 para 6(9).

347. Inspection programmes and inspection frameworks. The Care Quality Commission[1] must from time to time prepare:
(1)   a document setting out what inspections it proposes to carry out (an 'inspection programme')[2]; and
(2)   a document setting out the manner in which it proposes to exercise its functions of inspecting and reporting (an 'inspection framework')[3].

Before preparing an inspection programme or an inspection framework the Commission must consult:
(a)   the Secretary of State[4];
(b)   the inspection authorities[5]; and
(c)   any other person or body specified by an order made by the Secretary of State[6],

and it must send to each of those persons or bodies a copy of each programme or framework once it is prepared[7].

1   As to the Care Quality Commission's establishment, objectives and functions see PARA 336.
2   Health and Social Care Act 2008 Sch 4 para 5(1)(a).
3   Health and Social Care Act 2008 Sch 4 para 5(1)(b). The Commission may determine that any document or combination of documents prepared for the purposes of any other enactment or enactments is to be treated as a document prepared for the purposes of Sch 4 para 5(1)(b) (so long as any requirements applying under or by virtue of Sch 4 para 5 are complied with in relation to the document or documents concerned): Sch 4 para 5(4). Nothing in any inspection programme or inspection framework is to be read as preventing the Commission from making visits without notice: Sch 4 para 5(5).
4   Health and Social Care Act 2008 Sch 4 para 5(2)(a). As to the Secretary of State see PARA 333.
5   Health and Social Care Act 2008 Sch 4 para 5(2)(b). As to the inspection authorities see PARA 346 note 1.
6   Health and Social Care Act 2008 Sch 4 para 5(2)(c). At the date at which this volume states the law no order had been made for these purposes.
7   Health and Social Care Act 2008 Sch 4 para 5(2).

348. Co-operation with inspection authorities and co-ordination of reviews or assessments. The Care Quality Commission[1] must co-operate with the inspection authorities[2] where it is appropriate to do so for the efficient and effective exercise of the Commission's functions[3]. The Commission may also make arrangements with an inspection authority[4] to carry out, on behalf of the authority inspections in England[5] of any institution or matter which the Commission is not required or authorised to carry out by virtue of any other enactment[6]. Inspections[7] may be carried out on such terms, including terms as to payment, as the Commission thinks fit[8].

The Commission must promote the effective co-ordination of reviews or assessments carried out by public bodies or other persons in relation to the carrying on of regulated activities[9].

1　As to the Care Quality Commission's establishment, objectives and functions see PARA 336.
2　Health and Social Care Act 2008 Sch 4 para 7(a). As to the inspection authorities see PARA 346 note 1. These provisions also apply to any other public authority specified by order made by the Secretary of State: Sch 4 paras 7(b), 10(1)(b). At the date at which this volume states the law no further authorities had been specified for this purpose. As to the Secretary of State see PARA 333.
3　Health and Social Care Act 2008 Sch 4 para 7.
4　Health and Social Care Act 2008 Sch 4 para 10(1)(a). See note 2.
5　As to the meaning of 'England' see PARA 1 note 1.
6　Health and Social Care Act 2008 Sch 4 para 10(1).
7　Ie under the Health and Social Care Act 2008 Sch 4 para 10.
8　Health and Social Care Act 2008 Sch 4 para 10(2).
9　Health and Social Care Act 2008 s 67. As to the meaning of 'regulated activity' for these purposes see PARA 152 note 2; as to the carrying on of regulated activities see the Health and Social Care Act 2008 Pt 1 Ch 2 (ss 8–44); and PARAS 152–165.

C.　CONFIDENTIALITY AND DATA PROTECTION

349. Protection of individuals from disclosure and identification. A person is guilty of an offence[1] if, during the lifetime of an individual, he knowingly or recklessly discloses information which has been obtained by the Care Quality Commission[2] on terms or in circumstances requiring it to be held in confidence[3] and relates to and identifies that individual[4]. It is a defence for a person charged with such offence to prove:

(1)　that at the time of the alleged offence that the individual was not identified by the disclosure or consented to it[5], or that the disclosure was otherwise lawful or necessary[6], or that he reasonably believed such circumstances applied[7]; or

(2)　that the disclosure was made for the purpose of facilitating the exercise of any of the Commission's functions[8], in connection with the investigation of a criminal offence (whether or not in the United Kingdom)[9] or for the purpose of criminal proceedings (whether or not in the United Kingdom)[10].

If a person charged with an offence relies on a defence as above, and evidence is adduced which is sufficient to raise an issue with respect to that defence, the court must assume that the defence is satisfied unless the prosecution proves beyond reasonable doubt that it is not[11].

1　A person guilty of an offence under these provisions is liable on summary conviction to imprisonment for a term not exceeding 12 months, or to a fine not exceeding the statutory maximum, or to both, and on conviction on indictment, to imprisonment for a term not exceeding two years, or to a fine, or to both: Health and Social Care Act 2008 s 76(3). In relation to an offence committed before the commencement of the Criminal Justice Act 2003 s 154(1), the reference to 12 months is to be read as a reference to six months: Health and Social Care Act 2008 s 76(4). As to the powers of magistrates' courts to issue fines on summary conviction see SENTENCING vol 92 (2015) PARA 176. As to proceedings for offences see PARA 158 note 6.

2 As to the Care Quality Commission's establishment, objectives and functions see PARA 336. Reference in the Health and Social Care Act 2008 ss 76–80 (see the text and notes 3–11; and PARAS 350–351) to information obtained or disclosed by the Commission includes information obtained or disclosed by a person authorised by the Commission: s 76(6).

3 Health and Social Care Act 2008 s 76(1)(a), (2).

4 Health and Social Care Act 2008 s 76(1)(b). For the purposes of s 76(1)(b) information obtained by the Commission is to be treated as identifying an individual if the individual can be identified from a combination of that information and other information obtained by the Commission: s 76(5).

5 Ie that the disclosure was made in a form in which the individual to whom the information relates is not identified (Health and Social Care Act 2008 s 77(1)(a), (2)(a)) or was made with the consent of that individual (s 77(2)(b)). For the purposes of s 77(2)(a), information disclosed by a person is to be treated as being in a form in which an individual is identified if the individual can be identified from a combination of the information and other information disclosed by the person or by the Commission: s 77(5).

6 Ie that the information disclosed had previously been lawfully disclosed to the public (Health and Social Care Act 2008 s 77(2)(c)), that the disclosure was made under or pursuant to the Local Authority Social Services and National Health Service Complaints (England) Regulations 2009, SI 2009/309 (complaints: see PARA 325; and HEALTH SERVICES vol 54A (2017) PARA 663 et seq) (Health and Social Care Act 2008 s 77(2)(d)), that the disclosure was made in accordance with any enactment or court order (s 77(2)(e)), that the disclosure was necessary or expedient for the purposes of protecting the welfare of any individual (s 77(2)(f)), or that the disclosure was made to any person or body in circumstances where it was necessary or expedient for the person or body to have the information for the purpose of exercising functions of that person or body under any enactment (s 77(2)(g)).

7 Health and Social Care Act 2008 s 77(1)(b).

8 Health and Social Care Act 2008 s 77(3)(a).

9 Health and Social Care Act 2008 s 77(3)(b). As to the meaning of 'United Kingdom' see PARA 4 note 12.

10 Health and Social Care Act 2008 s 77(3)(c).

11 Health and Social Care Act 2008 s 77(4).

350. Use of information and permitted disclosures. Information obtained by, or documents or records produced to, the Care Quality Commission[1] in connection with any of its functions may be used by the Commission in connection with any of its other functions[2]. The Commission may disclose information[3] relating to an individual obtained by it in the course of exercising any of its functions if the disclosure is made either in a form in which the individual is not identified[4] or with the consent of the individual[5], and may disclose information so obtained in all cases (whether or not relating to an individual) if:

(1) the information has previously been lawfully disclosed to the public[6];

(2) the disclosure is made under or pursuant to[7] complaints proceedings[8];

(3) the disclosure is made in accordance with any enactment or court order[9];

(4) the disclosure is necessary or expedient for the purposes of protecting the welfare of any individual[10];

(5) the disclosure is made to any person or body in circumstances where it is necessary or expedient for the person or body to have the information for the purpose of exercising functions of that person or body under any enactment[11];

(6) the disclosure is made for the purpose of facilitating the exercise of any of the Commission's functions[12];

(7) the disclosure is made in connection with the investigation of a criminal offence (whether or not in the United Kingdom)[13]; or

(8) the disclosure is made for the purpose of criminal proceedings (whether or not in the United Kingdom)[14].

1 As to the Care Quality Commission's establishment, objectives and functions see PARA 336.
2 Health and Social Care Act 2008 s 78. As to information obtained or disclosed by the Commission see PARA 349 note 2.
3 The Health and Social Care Act 2008 s 79(2), (3) (see the text and notes 4–14) have effect notwithstanding any rule of common law which would otherwise prohibit or restrict the disclosure: s 79(4).
4 Health and Social Care Act 2008 s 79(1), (2)(a). For the purposes of s 79(2)(a), information disclosed by the Commission is to be treated as being in a form in which an individual is identified if the individual can be identified from a combination of the information and other information disclosed by the Commission: s 79(5).
5 Health and Social Care Act 2008 s 79(2)(b).
6 Health and Social Care Act 2008 s 79(3)(a).
7 Ie under or pursuant to the Local Authority Social Services and National Health Service Complaints (England) Regulations 2009, SI 2009/309 (complaints: see PARA 325; and HEALTH SERVICES vol 54A (2017) PARA 663 et seq).
8 Health and Social Care Act 2008 s 79(3)(b).
9 Health and Social Care Act 2008 s 79(3)(c).
10 Health and Social Care Act 2008 s 79(3)(d).
11 Health and Social Care Act 2008 s 79(3)(e).
12 Health and Social Care Act 2008 s 79(3)(f).
13 Health and Social Care Act 2008 s 79(3)(g).
14 Health and Social Care Act 2008 s 79(3)(h). As to the meaning of 'United Kingdom' see PARA 4 note 12.

351. Code of practice. The Care Quality Commission[1] must prepare and publish a code in respect of the practice it proposes to follow in relation to confidential personal information[2]. The code must in particular make provision about the obtaining by the Commission of information which, once obtained, will be confidential personal information; and about the handling, use and disclosure by the Commission of confidential personal information[3]. Before publishing the code, the Commission must consult the National Health Service Commissioning Board and such other persons as it considers appropriate[4]. The Commission must keep the code under review and, if it considers it appropriate, from time to time publish a revised code[5].

1 As to the Care Quality Commission's establishment, objectives and functions see PARA 336.
2 Health and Social Care Act 2008 s 80(1).
3 Health and Social Care Act 2008 s 80(2). As to information obtained or disclosed by the Commission see PARA 349 note 2. For these purposes, 'confidential personal information' means information which:
   (1) is obtained by the Commission on terms or in circumstances requiring it to be held in confidence (s 80(5)(a)); and
   (2) relates to and identifies an individual (s 80(5)(b)).
   For the purposes of s 80(5)(a), information obtained by the Commission is to be treated as identifying an individual if the individual can be identified from a combination of the information and other information obtained by the Commission: s 80(6).
4 Health and Social Care Act 2008 s 80(3) (amended by the Health and Social Care Act 2012 s 280(4). As to the National Health Service Commissioning Board see HEALTH SERVICES vol 54 (2017) PARA 32.
5 Health and Social Care Act 2008 s 80(4). References in s 80 to the code include any revised code: see s 80(4).

D. PUBLICATIONS AND REPORTS

352. Duty to keep Secretary of State informed about provision of care. The Care Quality Commission[1] must keep the Secretary of State[2] informed about the provision of NHS care[3], the provision of adult social services[4] and the carrying on of regulated activities[5], and may at any time give the Secretary of State advice on anything connected with those matters[6]. When requested to do so by the Secretary of State, the Commission must give the Secretary of State such advice or information in connection with those matters as may be specified in the request[7].

The Commission may give advice:

(1)   to the Secretary of State or an English NHS body[8] about the establishment or conduct of any inquiry held, or to be held, by the Secretary of State or NHS body in relation to the provision of health care[9] by or pursuant to arrangements made by that body[10]; and

(2)   to the Secretary of State or an English local authority[11] about the establishment or conduct of any inquiry held, or to be held, by the Secretary of State or local authority in relation to the provision of adult social services by or pursuant to arrangements made by that authority[12].

The Secretary of State may give a direction to the Commission if the Secretary of State considers that the Commission is failing or has failed to discharge any of its functions or is failing or has failed properly to discharge any of its functions[13], and that the failure is significant[14]. If the Commission fails to comply with such a direction the Secretary of State may discharge the functions to which the direction relates or make arrangements for any other person to discharge them on the Secretary of State's behalf[15].

1   As to the Care Quality Commission's establishment, objectives and functions see PARA 336.
2   As to the Secretary of State see PARA 333.
3   Health and Social Care Act 2008 s 53(1)(a). As to the meaning of 'NHS care' see PARA 341 note 4.
4   Health and Social Care Act 2008 s 53(1)(b). As to the meaning of 'adult social services' see PARA 179 note 13.
5   Health and Social Care Act 2008 s 53(1)(c). As to the meaning of 'regulated activity' for these purposes see PARA 152 note 2; as to the carrying on of regulated activities see the Health and Social Care Act 2008 Pt 1 Ch 2 (ss 8–44); and PARAS 152–165.
6   Health and Social Care Act 2008 s 53(2). Advice under s 53(2) may in particular include advice on any changes that the Commission thinks should be made to regulations under s 20 (regulation of regulated activities) (see PARA 107) or a code of practice under s 21 (code of practice relating to health care associated infections) (see PARA 196): s 53(3) (amended by the Health and Social Care Act 2012 Sch 17 para 12(1), (3)).
7   Health and Social Care Act 2008 s 53(4).
8   As to the meaning of 'English NHS body' see PARA 158 note 6.
9   As to the meaning of 'health care' see PARA 152 note 2; as to the provision of health care see PARA 339 note 6.
10 Health and Social Care Act 2008 s 53(5)(a).
11 As to the meaning of 'English local authority' see PARA 158 note 6.
12 Health and Social Care Act 2008 s 53(5)(b).
13 For these purposes a failure to discharge a function properly includes a failure to discharge it consistently with what the Secretary of State considers to be the interests of the health service in England or (as the case may be) with what otherwise appears to the Secretary of State to be the purpose for which it is conferred; and 'the health service' has the same meaning as in the National Health Service Act 2006 (see s 275(1); and HEALTH SERVICES vol 54 (2017) PARA 9): Health and Social Care Act 2008 s 82(5) (s 82(1) amended, ss 82(2A), (4), (5), 165(3) added, by the Health and Social Care Act 2012 s 294)).
14 Health and Social Care Act 2008 s 82(1) (as amended: see note 13). Such a direction may direct the Commission to discharge such of those functions, and in such manner and within such period or periods, as may be specified in the direction: s 82(2). The Secretary of State may not give such a direction in relation to the performance of functions in a particular case: s 82(2A) (as so added). Where the Secretary of State exercises a power under s 82(1) or (3), he must publish the reasons for doing so: s 82(4) (as so added). A direction under s 82 must be given by regulations or by an instrument in writing: s 165(3) (as so added).
15 Health and Social Care Act 2008 s 82(3).

353. Duty to publish statement on user involvement. The Care Quality Commission[1] must publish a statement describing how it proposes to:

(1)   promote awareness among service users[2] and carers[3] of its functions[4];

(2)   promote and engage in discussion with service users and carers about the provision of health and social care services and about the way in which the Commission exercises its functions[5];

(3)   ensure that proper regard is had to the views expressed by service users and carers[6]; and

(4)   arrange for any of its functions to be exercised by, or with the assistance of, service users and carers[7].

The Commission may from time to time revise the statement and must publish any revised statement[8]. Before publishing the statement (or revised statement) the Commission must consult such persons as it considers appropriate[9].

1   As to the Care Quality Commission's establishment, objectives and functions see PARA 336.
2   For these purposes, 'service users' means people who use health or social care services: Health and Social Care Act 2008 s 5(4)(a). As to the meanings of 'health or social care', 'health care' and 'social care' see PARA 152 note 2.
3   For these purposes 'carers' means people who care for service users as relatives or friends: Health and Social Care Act 2008 s 5(4)(b).
4   Health and Social Care Act 2008 s 5(1)(a).
5   Health and Social Care Act 2008 s 5(1)(b).
6   Health and Social Care Act 2008 s 5(1)(c).
7   Health and Social Care Act 2008 s 5(1)(d).
8   Health and Social Care Act 2008 s 5(2).
9   Health and Social Care Act 2008 s 5(3).

354. Studies aimed at improving economy and efficiency of care provision. The Care Quality Commission[1] may undertake or promote comparative or other studies designed to enable it to make recommendations[2]:

(1)   for improving economy, efficiency and effectiveness in the provision of health care[3] by an English NHS provider[4], the provision of adult social services[5] by an English local authority[6], and the making of arrangements by an English local authority for the provision of adult social services[7];

(2)   for improving the management, other than the financial management, of an English NHS body[8]; or

(3)   for improving the management of an English local authority in its provision of adult social services[9].

The Commission may also undertake or promote studies designed to enable it to prepare reports as to the impact of the operation of any particular statutory provisions[10] or any directions or guidance given by a Minister of the Crown (whether pursuant to any such provisions or otherwise), on economy, efficiency and effectiveness in an activity mentioned in head (2) or (3) above[11].

The Commission must undertake or promote such a study[12] if the Secretary of State so requests[13].

1   As to the Care Quality Commission's establishment, objectives and functions see PARA 336.
2   The Commission must from time to time prepare and publish a document setting out the studies that it proposes to undertake under the Health and Social Care Act 2008 s 54: s 81(1)(b). As to such a document see further s 81(2)–(4); and PARA 340 note 10. The Commission must publish any recommendations made by it and the result of any studies undertaken or promoted: s 55(1).
3   As to the meaning of 'health care' see PARA 152 note 2; as to the provision of health care see PARA 339 note 6.
4   Health and Social Care Act 2008 s 54(1)(a), (2)(a). As to the meaning of 'English NHS provider' see PARA 341 note 4.
5   As to the meaning of 'adult social services' see PARA 179 note 13.
6   Health and Social Care Act 2008 s 54(2)(c). As to the meaning of 'English local authority' see PARA 158 note 6.
7   Health and Social Care Act 2008 s 54(2)(d). The Commission may not exercise the power under s 54(1)(a), so far as it relates to the activity mentioned in s 54(2)(d), without the approval of the Secretary of State: s 54(2A) (added by the Care Act 2014 s 90(4)).

8   Health and Social Care Act 2008 s 54(1)(b). As to the meaning of 'English NHS body' see
    PARA 158 note 6. The reference in s 54(1) to an English NHS body does not include a reference
    to the National Health Service Commissioning Board, a clinical commissioning group or a Special
    Health Authority: s 54(5) (amended by the Health and Social Care Act 2012 Sch 5 para 160). As
    to the National Health Service Commissioning Board see HEALTH SERVICES vol 54 (2017)
    PARA 32; as to clinical commissioning groups and Special Health Authorities see HEALTH
    SERVICES vol 54 (2017) PARA 35 et seq.
9   Health and Social Care Act 2008 s 54(1)(c).
10 Health and Social Care Act 2008 s 54(3)(a). As to reports and information generally see s 84; and
    PARA 179 note 10.
11 Health and Social Care Act 2008 s 54(3)(b). As to the meaning of 'Minister of the Crown' see
    PARA 339 note 16. As to directions generally see s 165; and PARA 179 note 7.
12 Ie a study falling within the Health and Social Care Act 2008 s 54(1) or (3) (see the text and notes
    1–11).
13 Health and Social Care Act 2008 s 54(4).

355. Reviews of the provision and quality of care services. The Care
Quality Commission may review[1]:

(1)   studies and research undertaken by others, or the quality of data
       obtained by others, in relation to the provision of NHS care[2] or adult
       social services[3] or the carrying on of regulated activities[4];

(2)   the methods used in undertaking such studies and research or in
       collecting and analysing such data[5]; and

(3)   the validity of conclusions drawn from such studies and research or
       from such data[6].

The Commission must conduct such a review if the Secretary of State[7] so
requests[8].

1   As to the Care Quality Commission's establishment, objectives and functions see PARA 336.
    The Commission must from time to time prepare and publish a document setting out the reviews
    that it proposes to conduct under the Health and Social Care Act 2008 s 57: s 81(1)(c). As to such
    a document see further s 81(2)–(4); and PARA 340 note 10. If the Commission conducts a review
    under s 57 it must publish a report: s 57(3). As to reports and information generally see s 84; and
    PARA 179 note 10.
2   As to the meaning of 'NHS care' see PARA 341 note 4.
3   As to the meaning of 'adult social services' see PARA 179 note 13.
4   Health and Social Care Act 2008 s 57(1)(a). As to the meaning of 'regulated activity' for these
    purposes see PARA 152 note 2; as to the carrying on of regulated activities see the Health and
    Social Care Act 2008 Pt 1 Ch 2 (ss 8–44); and PARAS 152–165.
5   Health and Social Care Act 2008 s 57(1)(b).
6   Health and Social Care Act 2008 s 57(1)(c).
7   As to the Secretary of State see PARA 333.
8   Health and Social Care Act 2008 s 57(2).

356. Provision of information to the public. The Care Quality Commission[1]
may make available to the public[2] information relating to the provision of NHS
care[3], the provision of adult social services[4] and the carrying on of regulated
activities[5].

1   As to the Care Quality Commission's establishment, objectives and functions see PARA 336.
2   These provisions are subject to the Health and Social Care Act 2008 s 76 and s 79(2) (see
    PARA 349): s 58(2).
3   Health and Social Care Act 2008 s 58(1)(a). As to the meaning of 'NHS care' see PARA 341 note
    4.
4   Health and Social Care Act 2008 s 58(1)(b). As to the meaning of 'adult social services' see
    PARA 179 note 13.
5   Health and Social Care Act 2008 s 58(1)(c). As to the meaning of 'regulated activity' for these
    purposes see PARA 152 note 2; as to the carrying on of regulated activities see the Health and
    Social Care Act 2008 Pt 1 Ch 2 (ss 8–44); and PARAS 152–165.

357. Reports for financial year. As soon as possible after the end of each financial year[1], the Care Quality Commission must make a report[2] on each of the following matters:

(1)   the way in which it has exercised its functions during the year[3];

(2)   the provision of NHS care[4] during the year[5];

(3)   the provision of adult social services[6] during the year[7];

(4)   the carrying on of regulated activities[8] during the year[9]; and

(5)   the steps taken by it during the year to implement the proposals in its statement on user involvement[10].

The Commission may comply with these requirements by preparing a single document or separate documents on each of the matters mentioned[11].

1   For these purposes, 'financial year' means the period beginning with the date on which the Care Quality Commission is established and ending with the next 31 March following that date, and each successive period of 12 months ending with 31 March: Health and Social Care Act 2008 s 83(7).

2   As to the Care Quality Commission's establishment, objectives and functions see PARA 336. The Commission must lay before Parliament a copy of each report made under these provisions and send a copy of each such report to the Secretary of State: Health and Social Care Act 2008 s 83(4). As to the Secretary of State see PARA 333. The Commission must also provide the Secretary of State with such reports and information relating to the exercise of its functions as the Secretary of State may from time to time request: s 83(5).

3   Health and Social Care Act 2008 s 83(1)(a). Section 83(1)(a) does not apply to the Commission's functions under the Mental Health Act 1983 (see MENTAL HEALTH AND CAPACITY): Health and Social Care Act 2008 s 83(6). The reference in head (1) in the text to the Commission's functions does not include a reference to its functions under s 45A (see PARA 336): s 83(1A) (added by the Health and Social Care Act 2012 s 181(1), (11)).

4   As to the meaning of 'NHS care' see PARA 341 note 4.

5   Health and Social Care Act 2008 s 83(1)(b). The reports under the Health and Social Care Act 2008 s 83(1)(b), (c) must, in particular, set out (and identify as such) the contents of the report made by the Healthwatch England committee under s 45C(1)(a) (see PARA 336) in respect of the year concerned: s 83(2A) (added by the Health and Social Care Act 2012 s 181(1), (2)).

6   As to the meaning of 'adult social services' see PARA 179 note 13.

7   Health and Social Care Act 2008 s 83(1)(c). See note 5.

8   As to the meaning of 'regulated activity' for these purposes see PARA 152 note 2; as to the carrying on of regulated activities see the Health and Social Care Act 2008 Pt 1 Ch 2 (ss 8–44); and PARAS 152–165.

9   Health and Social Care Act 2008 s 83(1)(d).

10 Health and Social Care Act 2008 s 83(1)(e). The 'statement on user involvement' is the Commission's statement under s 5: see PARA 353. As to reports and information generally see s 84; and PARA 179 note 10.

11 Health and Social Care Act 2008 s 83(2).

(iv) Ombudsman

358. Matters which may be investigated. A Local Commissioner[1] may investigate a matter[2] which relates to action[3] taken by an adult social care provider[4] in connection with the provision of adult social care[5]. A matter may be investigated where:

(1)   a complaint about it[6] has been made to a Commissioner by or on behalf of[7] a member of the public who claims to have sustained injustice in consequence of the matter[8]; or

(2)   the matter has come to a Commissioner's attention during the course of an investigation[9] and it appears to the Commissioner that a member of the public has, or may have, suffered injustice in consequence of the matter[10].

A Commissioner may not conduct an investigation under these provisions[11] in respect of:

(a)   a matter which could be the subject of an investigation by a Commissioner under the local government maladministration provisions[12];

(b)   a matter which could be the subject of an investigation[13] by the Health Service Commissioner[14];

(c)   the commencement or conduct of civil or criminal proceedings before any court of law[15]; or

(d)   action taken in respect of appointments or removals, pay, discipline, superannuation or other personnel matters[16].

1   'Local commissioner' means a person, other than a Parliamentary Commissioner for Administration or an advisory member, who is a member of the Commission for Local Administration in England: see the Local Government Act 1974 s 23(3); and LOCAL GOVERNMENT vol 69 (2009) PARA 839 (definition applied by s 34T(2)(d), (e) (ss 34A–34T, Sch 5A (ie Pt 3A)) added by the Health Act 2009 Sch 5 paras 2, 3)).

2   Ie under the Local Government Act 1974 Pt 3A. In each financial year in which the Commission for Local Administration in England conducts a review under s 23(12) (see LOCAL GOVERNMENT vol 69 (2009) PARA 839), it must also review the operation (since the last review was made under this provision) of the provisions of Pt 3A about the investigation of matters: ss 34R(1), 34T(2)(b) (as added: see note 1). The Commission may convey to government departments and the Care Quality Commission any recommendations or conclusions reached in the course of a review under s 34R(1). The Commission may provide to adult social care providers (see note 3) or any adult social care provider such advice and guidance about good practice as appears to the Commission to be appropriate, and arrange for the advice and guidance to be published for the information of the public: s 34R(2) (as so added). Before providing such advice or guidance the Commission must consult such persons as appear to it to be appropriate: s 34R(3) (as so added). As to the Commission for Local Administration in England see LOCAL GOVERNMENT vol 69 (2009) PARA 839 et seq. As to the Care Quality Commission see PARA 336. Every Local Commissioner must for each financial year prepare a general report on the discharge of the Commissioner's functions under Pt 3A and submit it to the Commission not later than 2 months after the end of the year to which it relates: s 34S(1) (as so added). The Commission must for each financial year prepare a general report on the discharge of its functions under Pt 3A, which must be prepared as soon as may be after the Commission has received the reports for the year from Local Commissioners under s 34S(1) (s 34S(2), (3) (as so added)). The Commission must arrange for the publication of such annual report and the reports which are submitted under s 34S(1): s 34S(4) (as so added). The Commission must lay a copy of the annual report before Parliament: s 34S(5) (as so added).

3   'Action' includes a failure to act, and other expressions connoting action must be construed accordingly: Local Government Act 1974 s 34(1) (definition applied by s 34T(2)(a) (as added: see note 1)). 'Action' is to be treated as action taken by:
    (1)   an adult social care provider if it is taken by a person employed by that provider (s 34A(1), (4)(a) (as so added));
    (2)   a person acting on behalf of that provider (s 34A(4)(b) (as so added)), or;
    (3)   a person to whom that provider has delegated any functions (s 34A(4)(c) (as so added)).
    'Action' is also to be treated as action by an adult social care provider if that provider provides adult social care by means of an arrangement with another person (s 34A(5)(a) (as so added)), and the action is taken by or on behalf of the other person in carrying out the arrangement (s 34A(5)(b) (as so added)).

4   For these purposes 'adult social care provider' means a person who carries on an activity which involves, or is connected with, the provision of adult social care, and is a regulated activity within the meaning of the Health and Social Care Act 2008 Pt 1 (ss 1–97): Local Government Act 1974 s 34A(3) (as added: see note 1). As to the meaning of 'regulated activity' for these purposes see PARA 152 note 2; as to the carrying on of regulated activities see the Health and Social Care Act 2008 Pt 1 Ch 2 (ss 8–44); and PARAS 152–165. 'Adult social care' means social care within the meaning of the Health and Social Care Act 2008 Pt 1 (see PARA 152 note 2) which is provided to persons aged 18 or over: Local Government Act 1974 s 34A(2) (as added: see note 1).

5   Local Government Act 1974 s 34B(1)(a) (as added: see note 1).

6   Ie a complaint which satisfies the Local Government Act 1974 s 34C (see note 7) and s 34D (see PARA 359).

7   A complaint about a matter under the Local Government Act 1974 Pt 3A may only be made by a member of the public who claims to have sustained injustice in consequence of the matter (s 34C(1)(a) (as added: see note 1)), by a person authorised in writing by that person to act on his behalf (s 34C(1)(b) (as so added)) or, where a member of the public by whom a complaint about

a matter might have been made under Pt 3A has died or is otherwise unable to authorise a person to act on his behalf, made by that person's personal representatives (if any) or by a person who appears to a Local Commissioner to be suitable to represent the person (s 34C(1)(c), (2) (as so added)).

8 Local Government Act 1974 s 34B(1)(b), (3) (as added: see note 1). Any question whether this condition is met in relation to a matter is to be determined by a Local Commissioner: s 34B(4) (as so added). The Commissioner may, if he thinks fit, pay to the person by whom the complaint (if any) was made sums in respect of the expenses properly incurred by them and allowances by way of compensation for the loss of their time: s 34F(5) (as so added).

9 Local Government Act 1974 ss 34B(5), 34E(1)(a) (as added: see note 1). The investigations referred to are investigations under the Local Government Act 1974 Pt 3 (ss 23–34: see LOCAL GOVERNMENT vol 69 (2009) PARA 839 et seq) or Pt 3A: s 34E(1)(a) (as added: see note 1).

10 Local Government Act 1974 s 34E(1)(c) (as added: see note 1). In order to be investigated under this provision the matter must have come to the Commissioner's attention before the person affected or that person's personal representatives had notice of the matter or in any other case, before the end of the permitted period: s 34E(1)(b) (as so added). In this context 'the permitted period' means the period of 12 months beginning with the day on which the person affected first had notice of the matter, or, if the person affected has died without having notice of the matter, the day on which the personal representatives of the person affected first had notice of the matter: s 34E(2) (as so added). 'Person affected' means (by virtue of s 34T(1) (as so added)):

   (1) in relation to a matter which is the subject of a complaint made or to be made under Pt 3A, a member of the public who claims or is alleged to have sustained injustice in consequence of the matter; and

   (2) in relation to a matter coming to the attention of a Local Commissioner to which s 34E applies, the member of the public who the Local Commissioner considers has, or may have, sustained injustice in consequence of the matter.

   A Local Commissioner may disapply the requirement in s 34E(1)(b) in relation to a particular matter: s 34E(3) (as so added).

11 Ie under the Local Government Act 1094 Pt 3A.

12 Local Government Act 1974 s 34B(2), Sch 5A para 1 (as added: see note 1). 'The local government maladministration provisions' are Pt 3: see LOCAL GOVERNMENT vol 69 (2009) PARA 839 et seq. Her Majesty may by Order in Council amend Sch 5A by adding, omitting or changing a description of an action or matter: s 34B(10), (11) (as so added). At the date at which this volume states the law no such order had been made.

13 Ie under the Health Service Commissioners Act 1993 (see HEALTH SERVICES vol 54A (2017) PARA 681 et seq).

14 Local Government Act 1974 Sch 5A para 2 (as added: see note 1).

15 Local Government Act 1974 Sch 5A para 3 (as added: see note 1).

16 Local Government Act 1974 Sch 5A para 4 (as added: see note 1).

359. Procedure for making complaints. A complaint about a matter[1] must be made in writing[2] and before the end of the period of 12 months beginning with the day on which the person affected first had notice of the matter[3] or, if the person affected has died without having notice of the matter, the day on which the personal representatives of the person affected first had notice of the matter[4] or, if earlier, the day on which the complainant first had notice of the matter[5] ('the permitted period')[6].

1 Ie under the Local Government Act 1974 Pt 3A (ss 34A–34T, Sch 5A). A Local Commissioner may disapply either or both of the requirements in the Local Government Act 1974 s 34D(1)(a), (b) (see the text and notes 2–6) in relation to a particular complaint: s 34D(2) (Pt 3A added by the Health Act 2009 Sch 5 paras 2, 3). As to the meaning of 'Local Commissioner' see PARA 358 note 1.

2 Local Government Act 1974 s 34D(1)(a) (as added: see note 1).

3 Local Government Act 1974 s 34D(2)(a) (as added: see note 1). As to the meaning of 'person affected' see PARA 358 note 10.

4 Local Government Act 1974 s 34D(2)(b)(i) (as added: see note 1).

5 Local Government Act 1974 s 34D(2)(b)(ii) (as added: see note 1).

6 Local Government Act 1974 s 34D(1)(b) (as added: see note 1).

360. Commissioners' discretion in initiating and proceeding with investigation. Before investigating a matter[1] a Local Commissioner[2] must be satisfied that:

(1)   the matter has been brought, by or on behalf of the person affected[3], to the notice of the adult social care provider[4] to which it relates and that that provider has been afforded a reasonable opportunity to investigate the matter and to respond[5]; or

(2)   in the particular circumstances, it is not reasonable to expect the matter to be brought to the notice of that provider or for that provider to be afforded a reasonable opportunity to investigate the matter and to respond[6].

In deciding whether to initiate, continue or discontinue an investigation, a Commissioner must[7] act in accordance with the his own discretion[8], and without prejudice to the discretion so conferred, a Commissioner who is satisfied with action[9] which the adult social care provider concerned has taken or proposes to take may in particular decide not to investigate a matter[10] or to discontinue an investigation of a matter[11].

1   Ie under the Local Government Act 1974 Pt 3A (ss 34A–34T, Sch 5A): see PARA 358.
2   As to the meaning of 'Local Commissioner' see PARA 358 note 1.
3   The reference to a person affected includes a reference to that person's personal representatives: Local Government Act 1974 s 34B(7) (Pt 3A added by the Health Act 2009 Sch 5 paras 2, 3). As to the meaning of 'person affected' see PARA 358 note 10.
4   As to the meaning of 'adult social care provider' see PARA 358 note 4.
5   Local Government Act 1974 s 34B(6)(a) (as added: see note 2).
6   Local Government Act 1974 s 34B(6)(b) (as added: see note 2).
7   Ie subject to the provisions of Local Government Act 1974 ss 34B–34E (see PARAS 358–359).
8   Local Government Act 1974 s 34B(8) (as added: see note 2). The Commissioner must prepare a written statement if he decides not to investigate a matter or decides to discontinue an investigation: s   34H(1)(a),   (b) (as so added).   The   statement   must   set   out   the Local Commissioner's reasons for the decision: s 34H(2) (as so added). The Commissioner must send a copy of a statement prepared under s 34H to the complainant (if any) (s 34H(5), (6)(a) (as so added)), the adult social care provider concerned (s 34H(6)(b) (as so added)), any person who is alleged in the complaint (if any) to have taken or authorised the action which was the subject of the investigation (s 34H(6)(c) (as so added)), and any person who otherwise appears to the Local Commissioner to have taken or authorised such action (s 34H(6)(d) (as so added)). As to the meaning of 'action' see PARA 358 note 3. In connection with the application of s 34H(5) in the case of a joint investigation see s 34N(4); and PARA 364 note 3. The Commissioner may send a copy of a statement prepared under s 34H to the Care Quality Commission (s 34H(7)(a) (as so added)) and any local authority which appears to the Commissioner to have an interest in the subject matter of the statement (s 34H(7)(b) (as so added)). As to the Care Quality Commission see PARA 336; as to the meaning of 'local authority' see s 34; and LOCAL GOVERNMENT vol 69 (2009) PARA 23 (definition applied by s 34T(2)(c) (as so added)). The statement must identify the adult social care provider concerned unless the provider is an individual, or a particular individual would, in the opinion of the Local Commissioner, be likely to be identified as a result of identifying the provider (s 34H(8)(a) (as so added)), and the Commissioner considers that it is not appropriate for the individual to be identified (s 34H(8)(b) (as so added)). The statement must not mention the name of any person other than the provider (s 34H(9)(a) (as so added)) or contain any particulars which, in the opinion of the Commissioner, are likely to identify any other person and can be omitted without impairing the effectiveness of the statement(s 34H(9)(b) (as so added)), unless, after taking into account the public interest as well as the interests of that person, the complainant (if any) and of other persons, the Commissioner considers it necessary to mention the name of that person or to include in the statement any such particulars.
9   As to the meaning of 'action' see PARA 358 note 3.
10 Local Government Act 1974 s 34B(9)(a) (as added: see note 2).
11 Local Government Act 1974 s 34B(9)(b) (as added: see note 2).

361. Procedure for investigations. Subject to the requirement that every investigation[1] is to be conducted in private[2], the procedure for conducting an investigation is to be such as the Local Commissioner[3] considers appropriate in the circumstances of the case[4]. A Commissioner has the same powers as the High Court in respect of the attendance and examination of witnesses[5] and the production of documents[6]. To assist in any investigation, a Commissioner may obtain advice from any person who in his opinion is qualified to give it[7].

A Commissioner may also appoint and pay a mediator or other appropriate person to assist in the conduct of an investigation[8]. Commissioners also have duties to give specified persons opportunities to comment, and powers to require the provision of information[9].

1   Ie every investigation under the Local Government Act 1974 Pt 3A (ss 34A–34T, Sch 5A): see PARA 358.
2   Local Government Act 1974 s 34F(2) (Pt 3A added by the Health Act 2009 Sch 5 paras 2, 3).
3   As to the meaning of 'Local Commissioner' see PARA 358 note 1.
4   Local Government Act 1974 s 34F(3) (as added: see note 2). The Commission for Local Administration in England must divide the matters which may be investigated under Pt 3A into such categories as it considers appropriate and allocate, or make arrangements for allocating, responsibility for each category of matter to one or more of the Local Commissioners: s 34Q(1) (as so added). The Commission must make arrangements for Local Commissioners to deal with matters for which they do not have responsibility pursuant to s 34Q(1) and must publish information about the procedures for making complaints under Pt 3A: s 34Q(2) (as so added).
5   Local Government Act 1974 s 34G(3)(a) (as added: see note 2). No person may be compelled for the purposes of an investigation to give any evidence or produce any document which the person could not be compelled to give or produce in civil proceedings before the High Court: s 34G(8) (as so added).
6   Local Government Act 1974 s 34G(3)(b) (as added: see note 2). See note 5.
7   Local Government Act 1974 s 34G(4) (as added: see note 2). A Commissioner may pay to any such person giving advice such fees or allowances as he may determine: s 34G(5) (as so added).
8   Local Government Act 1974 s 34G(6) (as added: see note 2). Any person so appointed is to be deemed to be an officer of the Commission in carrying out functions under that appointment: s 34G(7) (as so added).
9   See PARA 362.

362. Persons who may be invited or compelled to contribute to the investigation. A Local Commissioner[1] who proposes to investigate a matter[2] must give the following persons an opportunity to comment on the matter:

(1)   the adult social care provider[3] concerned[4];
(2)   any person who is alleged in the complaint (if any) to have taken or authorised the action[5] which would be the subject of the investigation[6]; and
(3)   any person who otherwise appears to the Commissioner to have taken or authorised that action[7].

Pursuant to his powers to conduct an investigation in such manner as he considers appropriate[8], a Commissioner may, in particular:

(a)   obtain information from such persons and in such manner as he thinks fit[9];
(b)   make such inquiries as he thinks fit[10]; and
(c)   determine whether any person may be represented (by counsel, solicitor or otherwise) in the investigation[11],

and may require[12] the adult social care provider concerned[13], and any other person who in the Commissioner's opinion is able to furnish any such information or produce any such documents[14], to furnish information or produce documents relevant to the investigation[15].

1   As to the meaning of 'Local Commissioner' see PARA 358 note 1.
2   Ie under the Local Government Act 1974 Pt 3A (ss 34A–34T, Sch 5A): see PARAS 358–361.
3   As to the meaning of 'adult social care provider' see PARA 358 note 4.
4   Local Government Act 1974 s 34F(1)(a) (Pt 3A added by the Health Act 2009 Sch 5 paras 2, 3).
5   As to the meaning of 'action' see PARA 358 note 3.
6   Local Government Act 1974 s 34F(1)(b) (as added: see note 4).
7   Local Government Act 1974 s 34F(1)(c) (as added: see note 4).
8   See PARA 361.
9   Local Government Act 1974 s 34F(4)(a) (as added: see note 4).
10 Local Government Act 1974 s 34F(4)(b) (as added: see note 4).

11 Local Government Act 1974 s 34F(4)(c) (as added: see note 4).
12 Nothing in the Local Government Act 1974 s 34G(1) (see the text and notes 13–15) affects the restriction imposed by the Public Services Ombudsman (Wales) Act 2005 s 34X (disclosure of information: see LOCAL GOVERNMENT): Local Government Act 1974 s 34G(2) (as added: see note 4).
13 Local Government Act 1974 s 34G(1)(a) (as added: see note 4).
14 Local Government Act 1974 s 34G(1)(b) (as added: see note 4).
15 Local Government Act 1974 s 34G(1) (as added: see note 4). The Commissioner may, if he thinks fit, pay to any other person who attends or furnishes information for the purposes of an investigation under Pt 3A, sums in respect of the expenses properly incurred by them and allowances by way of compensation for the loss of their time: s 34F(5) (as so added).

363. Consultation and co-operation with other Commissioners. If at any stage in the course of a social care investigation[1] a Local Commissioner[2] forms the opinion that the matters which are the subject of the investigation include a matter which could be the subject of an investigation by another Commissioner or Ombudsman[3] the Commissioner must consult with the appropriate Commissioner or Ombudsman about the matter[4] and where a complaint was made about the matter must, if he considers it necessary, inform the person initiating the complaint of the steps necessary to initiate a complaint[5] to one of the Commissioners or Ombudsmen[6]. If, at any stage in the course of conducting an administrative investigation[7] the Parliamentary Commissioner forms the opinion that the complaint relates partly to a matter which could be the subject of a social care investigation[8] the Parliamentary Commissioner must consult with the appropriate Local Commissioner about the complaint[9] and if the Parliamentary Commissioner considers it necessary, must inform the person initiating the complaint of the steps necessary[10] to initiate a social care complaint[11].

If, at any stage in the course of a social care investigation a Local Commissioner forms the opinion that the matters which are the subject of the investigation include a matter within the jurisdiction of the Parliamentary Commissioner, the Health Service Commissioner or both, the Local Commissioner may conduct such investigation jointly with that Commissioner or those Commissioners[12]. If a Local Commissioner forms the opinion that a complaint being investigated by the Parliamentary Commissioner, the Health Service Commissioner or both, relates partly to a matter within the Local Commissioner's jurisdiction[13], the Local Commissioner may conduct a social care investigation jointly with that Commissioner or those Commissioners[14].

1 Ie an investigation under the Local Government Act 1974 Pt 3A (ss 34A–34T, Sch 5A): see PARAS 358–362.
2 As to the meaning of 'Local Commissioner' see PARA 358 note 1.
3 Ie the Parliamentary Commissioner, in accordance with the Parliamentary Commissioner Act 1967; the Health Service Commissioner, in accordance with the Health Service Commissioners Act 1993; the Scottish Public Services Ombudsman in accordance with the Scottish Public Services Ombudsman Act 2002; or the Public Services Ombudsman for Wales, in accordance with the Public Services Ombudsman (Wales) Act 2005: Local Government Act 1974 s 34M(1)(a)–(d) (Pt 3A added by the Health Act 2009 Sch 5 paras 2, 3). As to the Parliamentary Commissioner see CONSTITUTIONAL AND ADMINISTRATIVE LAW vol 20 (2014) PARA 633 et seq; as to the Health Service Commissioner for England see HEALTH SERVICES vol 54A (2017) PARA 681 et seq; as to the Public Services Ombudsman for Wales see LOCAL GOVERNMENT vol 69 (2009) PARA 843.
4 Local Government Act 1974 s 34M(2)(a) (as added: see note 3). Consultation under s 34M(2)(a) or s 34M(5)(a) in relation to a matter under investigation under Pt 3A or, as the case may be, under the Parliamentary Commissioner Act 1967 may be about anything relating to the matter, including the conduct of any investigation into the matter and the form, content and publication of any report or statement of the results of or conclusions on such an investigation: Local Government Act 1974 s 34M(3), (6) (as so added). Nothing in the Parliamentary Commissioner Act 1967

s 11(2) (see CONSTITUTIONAL AND ADMINISTRATIVE LAW vol 20 (2014) PARA 637), the Health Service Commissioners Act 1993 s 15 (see HEALTH SERVICES), the Scottish Public Services Ombudsman Act 2002 s 19, the Public Services Ombudsman (Wales) Act 2005 s 34X (disclosure of information: see LOCAL GOVERNMENT) or the Local Government Act 1974 s 34K(1) (see PARA 367) (confidentiality), applies in relation to the disclosure of information in the course of consultations held in accordance with s 34M: s 34M(7) (as so added).

5 Ie under the Parliamentary Commissioner 1967, the Health Service Commissioners Act 1993, the Scottish Public Services Ombudsman Act 2002 or the Public Services Ombudsman (Wales) Act 2005, as the case may be.
6 Local Government Act 1974 s 34M(2)(b) (as added: see note 3).
7 Ie an investigation under the Parliamentary Commissioner 1967: see CONSTITUTIONAL AND ADMINISTRATIVE LAW vol 20 (2014) PARA 633 et seq.
8 See note 1.
9 Local Government Act 1974 s 34M(4), (5)(a) (as added: see note 3). See note 4.
10 Ie a complaint under the Local Government Act 1974 Pt 3A.
11 Local Government Act 1974 s 34M(5)(b) (as added: see note 3).
12 Local Government Act 1974 s 34N(1) (as added: see note 3). A Local Commissioner must obtain the consent of the person affected or the complainant (if any) before agreeing to a joint investigation referred to in s 34N(1): s 34N(2) (as so added). As to the meaning of 'person affected' see PARA 358 note 10.
13 Ie by virtue of the Local Government Act 1974 Pt 3A.
14 Local Government Act 1974 s 34N(3) (as added: see note 3).

364. Statement of conclusions and recommendations. A Local Commissioner[1] must prepare a written statement if he completes an investigation[2] relating to a matter[3]. The statement must set out the Commissioner's conclusions on the investigation[4] and include any recommendations the Commissioner considers it appropriate to make[5]. The recommendations the Commissioner may make are recommendations with respect to action[6] which, in the Commissioner's opinion, the adult social care provider[7] concerned should take to remedy any injustice sustained by the person affected in consequence of the action of the provider which was the subject of the investigation[8] and to prevent injustice being caused in the future in consequence of similar action of the provider[9]. Where an adult social care provider receives a statement which contains recommendations it must consider the statement[10] and notify the Commissioner within the required period of the action which it has taken or proposes to take[11]. Failure to make such notification may result in the issuing of an adverse findings notice[12].

1 As to the meaning of 'Local Commissioner' see PARA 358 note 1.
2 Ie an investigation under the Local Government Act 1974 Pt 3A (ss 34A–34T, Sch 5A): see PARAS 358–363.
3 Local Government Act 1974 s 34H(1)(c) (Pt 3A added by the Health Act 2009 Sch 5 paras 2, 3). As to statements under the Local Government Act 1974 s 34H see further s 34H(5)–(9); and PARA 360 note 7. A Commissioner must not prepare a statement under s 34H which includes government information unless he has obtained the written consent of an officer of the government department concerned or given the department not less than one month's notice in writing of the intention to include the information in a statement: s 34K(3) (as so added). 'Government information' means information disclosed under s 34G(1) (see PARA 362) which is derived from a communication with a government department and has not been made public: s 34K(4) (as so added). If a Commissioner conducts an investigation jointly with another person (see s 34N; and PARA 363), the requirements of s 34H(1)(c), (5) (so far as relating to a case where the Local Commissioner conducts an investigation under Pt 3A) may be satisfied by a statement or report made jointly with that person: s 34N(4) (as so added).
    A Commissioner may publish all or part of a statement under s 34H, or publish a summary of a matter which is the subject of such a statement, if, after taking into account the public interest as well as the interests of the complainant (if any) and of other persons, he considers it appropriate to do so (s 34J(1)(a), (c) (as so added)), and may supply a copy of all or part of such a statement or summary to any person who requests it and charge a reasonable fee for doing so (s 34J(2) (as so added)). Section 34H(8), (9) (see PARA 360 note 7) applies to any part of a summary of a matter that is published, or a copy of which is supplied, under s 34J as they apply to a statement prepared under s 34H: s 34J(3) (as so added).
4 Local Government Act 1974 s 34H(3)(a) (as added: see note 3).

5   Local Government Act 1974 s 34H(3)(b) (as added: see note 3).
6   As to the meaning of 'action' see PARA 358 note 3.
7   As to the meaning of 'adult social care provider' see PARA 358 note 4.
8   Local Government Act 1974 s 34H(4)(a) (as added: see note 3). As to the meaning of 'person affected' see PARA 358 note 10.
9   Local Government Act 1974 s 34H(4)(b) (as added: see note 3).
10   Local Government Act 1974 s 34I(1), (2)(a) (as added: see note 3).
11   Local Government Act 1974 s 34I(2)(b) (as added: see note 3).
12   See PARA 365.

365. Adverse findings notices. If:

(1)   an adult social care provider[1] fails to notify the Local Commissioner[2] of the action[3] it has taken or proposes to take[4] in response to recommendations[5];

(2)   the Commissioner is satisfied[6] that the provider concerned has decided to take no action[7];

(3)   the Commissioner is not satisfied with the action which the provider concerned has taken or proposes to take[8]; or

(4)   the Commissioner does not[9] receive confirmation that the provider has taken action, as proposed, to the satisfaction of the Commissioner[10],

the Commissioner may by notice require the provider to arrange for an 'adverse findings notice' to be published[11]. An adverse findings notice is a notice[12] consisting of:

(a)   details of any action recommended in the statement which the provider has not taken[13]; and

(b)   if the provider so requires, an explanation of the provider's reasons for having taken no action on, or not the action recommended in, the statement[14].

If the provider fails to arrange[15] for the publication of the adverse findings notice[16] or is unable[17] to agree with the Commissioner the form of the notice to be published[18], the Commissioner must arrange for an adverse findings notice to be published in such manner as he considers appropriate[19].

1   As to the meaning of 'adult social care provider' see PARA 358 note 4.
2   Ie within the period of one month beginning with the date on which the provider concerned received the statement or such longer period as the Local Commissioner may agree in writing (the 'required period'): Local Government Act 1974 s 34I(8) (Pt 3A added by the Health Act 2009 Sch 5 paras 2, 3). As to the meaning of 'Local Commissioner' see PARA 358 note 1.
3   As to the meaning of 'action' see PARA 358 note 3.
4   Ie the notification mentioned in the Local Government Act 1974 s 34I(2)(b) (see PARA 364).
5   Local Government Act 1974 s 34I(3)(a) (as added: see note 2).
6   Ie before the end of the required period (see note 2).
7   Local Government Act 1974 s 34I(3)(a) (as added: see note 2).
8   Local Government Act 1974 s 34I(3)(b) (as added: see note 2).
9   Ie within a period of one month beginning with the end of the required period, or such longer period as the Local Commissioner may agree in writing: Local Government Act 1974 s 34I(3)(c) (as added: see note 2).
10   Local Government Act 1974 s 34I(3)(c) (as added: see note 2).
11   Local Government Act 1974 s 34I(3) (as added: see note 2). The adverse findings notice must be published by the provider in such manner as the Commissioner may direct: s 34I(5) (as so added). A Commissioner may arrange for further publication of all or part of an adverse findings notice published under s 34I(3) or (6), or publish a summary of a matter which is the subject of an adverse findings notice under s 34I, if, after taking into account the public interest as well as the interests of the complainant (if any) and of other persons, he considers it appropriate to do so (s 34J(1)(b), (c) (as so added)), and may supply a copy of all or part of such a notice or summary to any person who requests it and charge a reasonable fee for doing so (s 34J(2) (as so added)). Section 34H(8), (9) (see PARA 360 note 7) applies to any part of a summary of a matter that is published, or a copy of which is supplied, under s 34J as they apply to a statement prepared under s 34H: s 34J(3) (as so added).

12 Notices are in such form as the provider concerned and the Commissioner may agree: Local Government Act 1974 s 34I(4) (as added: see note 2).

13 Local Government Act 1974 s 34I(4)(a) (as added: see note 2). In this circumstance the notice must also contain such supporting material as the Commissioner may require: s 34I(4)(b) (as so added).

14 Local Government Act 1974 s 34I(4)(c) (as added: see note 2).

15 Ie in accordance with the Local Government Act 1974 s 34I(4), (5).

16 Local Government Act 1974 s 34I(6)(a) (as added: see note 2).

17 Ie within the period of one month beginning with the date on which the provider received the notice under the Local Government Act 1974 s 34I(3), or such longer period as the Local Commissioner may agree in writing: s 34I(6)(b) (as so added).

18 Local Government Act 1974 s 34I(6)(b) (as added: see note 2).

19 Local Government Act 1974 s 34I(6) (as added: see note 2). See note 11. The provider concerned must reimburse the Commission on demand any reasonable expenses incurred by the Local Commissioner in performing the duty under s 34I(6): s 34I(7) (as so added).

366. Obstruction of investigations. If any person without lawful excuse:

(1) obstructs a Local Commissioner[1] in the performance of his investigatory[2] functions[3];

(2) obstructs any person discharging or assisting in the discharge of those functions[4]; or

(3) is guilty of an act or omission in relation to an investigation which, if that investigation were a proceeding in the High Court, would constitute contempt of court[5],

the Commissioner may certify the offence to the High Court, and where an offence is so certified, the High Court may inquire into the matter and, after hearing any witnesses who may be produced against or on behalf of the person charged, and after hearing any statement that may be offered in defence, deal with that person in any manner in which the High Court could deal with him if he had committed the like offence in relation to the High Court[6].

1 As to the meaning of 'Local Commissioner' see PARA 358 note 1.

2 Ie functions under the Local Government Act 1974 Pt 3A (ss 34A–34T, Sch 5A): see PARAS 358–362.

3 Local Government Act 1974 s 34G(9)(a) (Pt 3A added by the Health Act 2009 Sch 5 paras 2, 3).

4 Local Government Act 1974 s 34G(9)(b) (as added: see note 3).

5 Local Government Act 1974 s 34G(9)(c) (as added: see note 3).

6 Local Government Act 1974 s 34G(10) (as added: see note 3).

367. Confidentiality. Information obtained by a Local Commissioner[1], or any person discharging or assisting in the discharge of a function of a Local Commissioner, in the course of or for the purposes of an investigation[2] must not be disclosed except:

(1) for the purposes of the investigation and of any statement, adverse findings notice or summary[3];

(2) for the purposes of an investigation under the local government maladministration provisions[4] and of any report, statement or summary[5] in relation to such an investigation[6];

(3) for the purposes of a complaint which is being investigated by the Parliamentary Commissioner or the Health Service Commissioner for England (or both)[7];

(4) for the purposes of any proceedings for an offence under the Official Secrets Acts 1911 to 1989[8] alleged to have been committed in respect of information obtained[9] by a Local Commissioner or by a person discharging or assisting in the discharge of a function of a Local Commissioner[10];

(5) for the purposes of any proceedings for an offence of perjury alleged to have been committed in the course of an investigation[11];

(6)   for the purposes of an inquiry with a view to the taking of proceedings of a kind mentioned in head (4) or (5) above[12]; or

(7)   for the purposes of obstruction proceedings[13].

A Local Commissioner or a person discharging or assisting in the discharge of a function of a Local Commissioner may not be called upon to give evidence in any proceedings[14] of matters coming to his or her knowledge in the course of an investigation[15].

1   As to the meaning of 'Local Commissioner' see PARA 358 note 1.
2   Ie information obtained for the purposes of an investigation under the Local Government Act 1974 Pt 3A (ss 34A–34T, Sch 5A): see PARA 358. Information obtained from the Information Commissioner by virtue of the Freedom of Information Act 2000 s 76 (see CONSTITUTIONAL AND ADMINISTRATIVE LAW vol 20 (2014) PARA 461) is to be treated for the purposes of the Local Government Act 1974 s 34K(1) as obtained for the purposes of an investigation under Pt 3A and, in relation to such information, the reference in s 34K(1)(a) to the investigation has effect as a reference to any investigation: Local Government Act 1974 s 34K(5) (Pt 3A added by the Health Act 2009 Sch 5 paras 2, 3).
3   Local Government Act 1974 s 34K(1)(a) (as added: see note 2). The reference in the text is to statement, adverse findings notice or summary under s 34H, 34I or 34J (see PARAS 364–365).
4   'The local government maladministration provisions' are the Local Government Act 1974 Pt 3: see LOCAL GOVERNMENT vol 69 (2009) PARA 839 et seq.
5   Ie under the Local Government Act 1974 s 30, s 31 or s 31B: see LOCAL GOVERNMENT vol 69 (2009) PARA 860.
6   Local Government Act 1974 s 34K(1)(b) (as added: see note 2).
7   Local Government Act 1974 s 34K(1)(c) (as added: see note 2). As to the Parliamentary Commissioner see CONSTITUTIONAL AND ADMINISTRATIVE LAW vol 20 (2014) PARA 633 et seq; as to the Health Service Commissioner for England see HEALTH SERVICES vol 54A (2017) PARA 681 et seq.
8   See CRIMINAL LAW vol 26 (2016) PARA 498 et seq.
9   Ie by virtue of the Local Government Act 1974 Pt 3A.
10 Local Government Act 1974 s 34K(1)(d) (as added: see note 2).
11 Local Government Act 1974 s 34K(1)(e) (as added: see note 2).
12 Local Government Act 1974 s 34K(1)(f) (as added: see note 2).
13 Local Government Act 1974 s 34K(1)(g) (as added: see note 2). The reference in the text is to proceedings under s 34G(10): see PARA 366.
14 Ie other than proceedings within the Local Government Act 1974 s 34K(1)(d), (e) or (g) (see the text and notes 8–11, 13).
15 Local Government Act 1974 s 34K(2) (as added: see note 2).

368. Disclosure of information. A Local Commissioner[1] may disclose to the Information Commissioner[2] any information obtained by, or furnished to, the Local Commissioner[3] if the information appears to the Local Commissioner to relate to:

(1)   a matter in respect of which the Information Commissioner could exercise any enforcement[4] power[5]; or

(2)   the commission of an offence under the data protection[6] provisions[7].

A Local Commissioner may disclose to the Care Quality Commission[8] any information obtained by, or furnished to, the Local Commissioner[9] if the information appears to the Local Commissioner to relate to a matter in respect of which the Commission has functions under any enactment[10].

1   As to the meaning of 'Local Commissioner' see PARA 358 note 1.
2   As to the Information Commissioner see CONFIDENCE AND INFORMATIONAL PRIVACY vol 19 (2011) PARA 109 et seq. Nothing in the Local Government Act 1974 s 34K(1) (see PARA 367) applies in relation to the disclosure of information in accordance with these provisions: ss 34O(2), 34P(2) (Pt 3A (ss 34A–34T, Sch 5A) added by the Health Act 2009 Sch 5 paras 2, 3).
3   Ie information obtained or furnished under or for the purposes of the Local Government Act 1974 Pt 3A: see PARA 358.
4   Ie power conferred by the Data Protection Act 1998 Pt 5 (ss 40–50) (enforcement: see CONFIDENCE AND INFORMATIONAL PRIVACY vol 19 (2011) PARA 151 et seq), the Freedom of Information Act 2000 s 48 (practice recommendations: see CONSTITUTIONAL AND

ADMINISTRATIVE LAW vol 20 (2014) PARA 633) or Pt 4 (ss 50–56) (enforcement: see
CONFIDENCE AND INFORMATIONAL PRIVACY vol 19 (2011) PARA 127; CONSTITUTIONAL
AND ADMINISTRATIVE LAW vol 20 (2014) PARAS 462–467).
5 Local Government Act 1974 s 34O(1)(a) (as added: see note 2).
6 Ie an offence under any provision of the Data Protection Act 1998 other than Sch 9 para 12
   (obstruction of execution of warrant) (see CONFIDENCE AND INFORMATIONAL PRIVACY) or
   under the Freedom of Information Act 2000 s 77 (offence of altering etc records with intent to
   prevent disclosure: see CONSTITUTIONAL AND ADMINISTRATIVE LAW vol 20 (2014)
   PARA 435).
7 Local Government Act 1974 s 34O(1)(b) (as added: see note 2).
8 As to the Care Quality Commission's establishment, objectives and functions see PARA 336.
9 See note 3.
10 Local Government Act 1974 s 34P(1) (as added: see note 2). See note 2.

369. Defamation and privilege. For the purposes of the law of defamation the
following are absolutely privileged:
   (1)   the publication of any matter in communications[1] between an adult
         social care provider[2] and a Local Commissioner[3], or any person
         discharging or assisting in the discharge of a function of a
         Local Commissioner[4];
   (2)   the publication of any matter by a Local Commissioner or by any
         person discharging or assisting in the discharge of a function of a
         Local Commissioner, in communicating[5] with a complainant or the
         person affected in relation to a matter[6], the
         Parliamentary Commissioner, the Health Service Commissioner or any
         officer of either such Commissioner[7], the Care Quality Commission or
         any officer of that Commission[8], or a local authority[9];
   (3)   the publication of any matter in[10] preparing, making and sending a
         statement[11];
   (4)   the publication of any matter by inclusion in an adverse findings
         notice[12];
   (5)   the publication of any matter by inclusion in a statement, adverse
         findings notice or summary[13]; and
   (6)   the publication of any matter contained in a report by a
         Local Commissioner which has been made available to the public[14].

1 Ie for the purposes of the Local Government Act 1974 Pt 3A (ss 34A–34T, Sch 5A): see PARA 358.
2 As to the meaning of 'adult social care provider' see PARA 358 note 4.
3 As to the meaning of 'Local Commissioner' see PARA 358 note 1.
4 Local Government Act 1974 s 34L(1)(a) (Pt 3A added by the Health Act 2009 Sch 5 paras 2, 3).
5 See note 1.
6 Local Government Act 1974 s 34L(1)(b), (2)(a) (as added: see note 4). As to the meaning of 'person
   affected' see PARA 358 note 10.
7 Local Government Act 1974 s 34L(2)(b) (as added: see note 4). As to the
   Parliamentary Commissioner see CONSTITUTIONAL AND ADMINISTRATIVE LAW vol 20 (2014)
   PARA 633 et seq; as to the Health Service Commissioner for England see HEALTH SERVICES
   vol 54A (2017) PARA 681 et seq.
8 Local Government Act 1974 s 34L(2)(c) (as added: see note 4). As to the Care Quality Commission
   see PARA 336.
9 Local Government Act 1974 s 34L(2)(d) (as added: see note 4). As to the meaning of 'local
   authority' see s 34; and LOCAL GOVERNMENT vol 69 (2009) PARA 23 (definition applied by
   s 34T(2)(c) (as so added)).
10 Ie in accordance with the Local Government Act 1974 s 34H (see PARA 364).
11 Local Government Act 1974 s 34L(1)(c) (as added: see note 4).
12 Local Government Act 1974 s 34L(1)(d) (as added: see note 4). The reference in the text to an
   'adverse findings notice' is a reference to a notice published in accordance with s 34I(3), (4), (5) or
   (6) (see PARA 365).

13 Local Government Act 1974 s 34L(1)(e) (as added: see note 4). The reference in the text to inclusion in a statement, adverse findings notice or summary is a reference to inclusion in a statement, adverse findings notice or summary under s 34J (see PARA 364).
14 Local Government Act 1974 s 34L(1)(f) (as added: see note 4). The reference in the text to publication is a reference to a notice publication by inclusion in a report made or published under s 34S (see PARA 415).

(v) Other Regulatory Bodies

370. The Professional Standards Authority for Health and Social Care. The general functions of the Professional Standards Authority for Health and Social Care[1] include the promotion of the interests of users of health care, users of social care in England[2], users of social work services in England and other members of the public in relation to the performance of their functions by regulatory bodies, the promotion of best practice in the performance of those functions, the formulation of good professional self-regulation, the promotion of co-operation between regulatory bodies, all in the interests of the health, safety and well-being of users of health care, users of social care in England, users of social work services in England and other members of the public; and recent developments include the power to establish voluntary registers of persons who are or have been unregulated health professionals and unregulated health care workers in the United Kingdom, and unregulated social care workers in England[3].

1 As to the establishment of this body see the National Health Service Reform and Health Care Professions Act 2002 s 25(1); and MEDICAL PROFESSIONS vol 74 (2011) PARAS 47, 48.
2 See generally the Health and Social Care Act 2012 ss 222–229; and MEDICAL PROFESSIONS.
3 See generally the National Health Service Reform and Health Care Professions Act 2002 Pt 2 (ss 25–35); and MEDICAL PROFESSIONS vol 74 (2011) PARA 47 et seq.

371. The National Institute for Health and Care Excellence. The National Institute for Health and Care Excellence was established under the Health and Social Care Act 2012[1]. In exercising its functions the Institute must have regard to:
  (1)   the broad balance between the benefits and costs of the provision of health services or of social care in England[2];
  (2)   the degree of need of persons for health services or social care in England[3]; and
  (3)   the desirability of promoting innovation in the provision of health services or of social care in England[4].
The Institute's functions principally relate to quality standards[5] and to advice and guidance[6].

1 See, generally, the Health and Social Care Act 2012 Pt 8 (ss 232–249); and HEALTH SERVICES vol 54 (2017) PARA 218 et seq.
2 See the Health and Social Care Act 2012 s 233(1)(a); and HEALTH SERVICES vol 54 (2017) PARA 219.
3 See the Health and Social Care Act 2012 s 233(1)(b); and HEALTH SERVICES vol 54 (2017) PARA 219.
4 See the Health and Social Care Act 2012 s 233(1)(c); and HEALTH SERVICES vol 54 (2017) PARA 219.
5 See the Health and Social Care Act 2012 ss 234–236; and HEALTH SERVICES vol 54 (2017) PARAS 220–222.
6 See the Health and Social Care Act 2012 ss 237–241; and HEALTH SERVICES vol 54 (2017) PARAS 223–227.

372. The Health and Social Care Information Centre. The Health and Social Care Information Centre is established under the Health and Social Care Act 2012[1]. In exercising its functions the Centre must have regard to:

(1) the information standards published by the Secretary of State or the National Health Service Commissioning Board[2];

(2) such guidance issued by the Secretary of State as the Secretary of State may require[3];

(3) such guidance issued by the Board as the Board may require[4];

(4) the need to respect and promote the privacy of recipients of health services and of adult social care in England[5]; and

(5) the need to promote the effective, efficient and economic use of resources in the provision of health services and of adult social care in England[6].

The Centre must seek to minimise the burdens it imposes on others[7] and exercise its functions effectively, efficiently and economically[8].

The Centre's functions principally include functions relating to information systems[9] and to the quality of health and social care information[10].

1 See the Health and Social Care Act 2012 s 252, Sch 18; and HEALTH SERVICES vol 54 (2017) PARA 204.
2 See the Health and Social Care Act 2012 s 253(1)(a); and HEALTH SERVICES vol 54 (2017) PARA 205.
3 See the Health and Social Care Act 2012 s 253(1)(b); and HEALTH SERVICES vol 54 (2017) PARA 205.
4 See the Health and Social Care Act 2012 s 253(1)(c); and HEALTH SERVICES vol 54 (2017) PARA 205.
5 See the Health and Social Care Act 2012 s 253(1)(ca); and HEALTH SERVICES vol 54 (2017) PARA 205.
6 See the Health and Social Care Act 2012 s 253(1)(d); and HEALTH SERVICES vol 54 (2017) PARA 205.
7 See the Health and Social Care Act 2012 s 253(2)(a); and HEALTH SERVICES vol 54 (2017) PARA 205.
8 See the Health and Social Care Act 2012 s 253(2)(b); and HEALTH SERVICES vol 54 (2017) PARA 205.
9 See the Health and Social Care Act 2012 ss 254–265; and HEALTH SERVICES vol 54 (2017) PARAS 206–212.
10 See the Health and Social Care Act 2012 ss 266, 267; and HEALTH SERVICES vol 54 (2017) PARA 213.

(2) WALES

(i) Local Authorities

A. PRINCIPLES GOVERNING THE PROVISION OF CARE

373. Local authority social services functions. The 'social services functions' of a local authority in Wales are[1] principally its functions relating to the provision of care and support under the Social Services and Well-being (Wales) Act 2014[2] and the protection of children under the Children Act 1989[3]. In addition, local authorities in Wales have a number of functions relating to the protection of young offenders and children in care[4], the welfare and accommodation of mentally disordered persons[5] and the representation of disabled persons[6], as well as certain residual and administrative functions[7], which are also 'social services functions' for these purposes. Further statutory functions may be designated 'social services functions' by the Welsh Ministers[8].

1 Ie for the purposes of the Social Services and Well-being (Wales) Act 2014: s 143(1). The duties imposed by the Social Services and Well-being (Wales) Act 2014 apply only in relation to local authorities in Wales: see s 197(1) (which provides that the local authorities for the purposes of that

Act are the councils of counties or county boroughs in Wales); and PARA 2. As to the meaning of 'Wales' see PARA 2 note 4. As to local government areas and authorities in Wales see LOCAL GOVERNMENT vol 69 (2009) PARA 22 et seq.

2 Social Services and Well-being (Wales) Act 2014 Sch 2. The functions are those under the Social Services and Well-being (Wales) Act 2014 (see PARA 1 et seq); under the Community Care (Delayed Discharges) Act 2003 Pt 1 (ss 1–14), which have never been brought into force in relation to Wales and correspond to the functions of English local authorities under the Care Act 2014 Sch 3 (discharge of hospital patients with care and support needs) where a patient is be discharged into local authority areas in England by an NHS body in Wales (see PARA 69), which are also defined as 'social services functions' for the purposes of English local authorities under the Local Authority Social Services Act 1970 Sch 1 (see PARA 315 note 2); and under the Care Act 2014 ss 50, 52 (duty of local authority to meet needs in event of business failure: cross border cases: see PARA 184): Social Services and Well-being (Wales) Act 2014 Sch 2. Not defined as 'social services functions' of a local authority in Wales are functions under the Social Services and Well-being (Wales) Act 2014 s 15(4) (see PARA 376) (in so far as it relates to other functions that are not social services functions), s 120(2) (see CHILDREN AND YOUNG PERSONS), s 128(1), (2) (see PARA 380), s 130(1), (2) (see PARA 380), s 162 (see PARA 378) and s 164 (see PARA 378): Sch 2.

3 Ie functions under the Children Act 1989 (see CHILDREN AND YOUNG PERSONS) (except s 36, Sch 3 paras 12–19(1)): Social Services and Well-being (Wales) Act 2014 Sch 2. Note the exclusion and modification of provisions of the Children Act 1989 in relation to local authorities in Wales by the Social Services and Well-being (Wales) Act 2014 (Consequential Amendments) Regulations 2016, SI 2016/413, regs 55–122.

4 Ie functions under the Children and Young Persons Act 1933 ss 34, 34A (see CHILDREN AND YOUNG PERSONS vol 10 (2017) PARAS 1287, 1295); the Children and Young Persons Act 1969 (see CHILDREN AND YOUNG PERSONS); and the Legal Aid, Sentencing and Punishment of Offenders Act 2012 s 92 (functions in relation to a child remanded to local authority accommodation) (see CHILDREN AND YOUNG PERSONS vol 10 (2017) PARA 1301): Social Services and Well-being (Wales) Act 2014 Sch 2. Note the modification of the Children and Young Persons Act 1933 ss 34, 34A in relation to local authorities in Wales by the Social Services and Well-being (Wales) Act 2014 (Consequential Amendments) Regulations 2016, SI 2016/413, regs 3–5.

5 Ie functions the Mental Health Act 1983 Pt II (ss 2–34); Pt III (ss 35–55), Pt VI (ss 80–92) (welfare of mentally disordered; guardianship; exercise of functions of nearest relative), ss 66, 67, s 69(1) (exercise of functions of nearest relative in relation to mental health review tribunals), s 114 (appointment of approved social workers), s 115 (entry and inspection), s 116 (welfare of certain patients), s 117 (after-care) and s 130 (prosecutions); the Mental Health (Scotland) Act 1984 s 10 (in relation to persons in Scottish hospitals under the care of Welsh local authorities); the Mental Capacity Act 2005 ss 39, 39A, 39C, 39D (instructing independent mental capacity advocate), s 49 (reports in proceedings) and Sch A1 (any functions); and the Mental Health (Wales) Measure 2010 Pt 1–3 (ss 1–30) (primary and secondary mental health services) (see MENTAL HEALTH AND CAPACITY): Social Services and Well-being (Wales) Act 2014 Sch 2. Note the modification of the Mental Health Act 1983, the Mental Capacity Act 2005 and the Mental Health (Wales) Measure 2010 in relation to local authorities in Wales by the Social Services and Well-being (Wales) Act 2014 (Consequential Amendments) Regulations 2016, SI 2016/413, regs 35–37, 226–229, 280–285.

6 Ie functions under the Disabled Persons (Services, Consultation and Representation) Act 1986 s 5(5) (see EDUCATION): Social Services and Well-being (Wales) Act 2014 Sch 2.

7 Ie functions under the Health Services and Public Health Act 1968 s 65 (assistance to voluntary organisations: see HEALTH SERVICES vol 54 (2017) PARA 287); the Adoption Act 1976 (see CHILDREN AND YOUNG PERSONS) (functions continuing to be exercisable by virtue of any transitional or saving provision made by or under the Adoption and Children Act 2002); the Public Health (Control of Disease) Act 1984 s 46(2), (5) (burial and cremation of persons dying in accommodation provided under the National Assistance Act 1948 Pt III (ss 21–35)); the Disabled Persons (Services, Consultation and Representation) Act 1986 ss 1, 2 (appointment and rights of authorised representatives of disabled persons) (which provisions, while not having been repealed, have never been brought into force), and s 3 (assessment of needs of disabled persons (disapplied in relation to local authorities in Wales by the Social Services and Well-being (Wales) Act 2014 (Consequential Amendments) Regulations 2016, SI 2016/413, reg 48); and the Housing (Scotland) Act 1987 s 38(b); the Education Act 1996 s 322 (see EDUCATION vol 36 (2015) PARA 1025) (help for another local authority); the s 1 (see CHILDREN AND YOUNG PERSONS vol 9 (2017) PARA 582) and s 2(4) (see CHILDREN AND YOUNG PERSONS vol 9 (2017) PARA 585) (functions under regulations made under s 1 giving effect to the Convention on Protection of Children and Co-operation in Respect of Intercountry Adoptions (The Hague, 29 May 1993; TS 40 (1994); Cm 2691) art 9(a)–(c)); the Adoption and Children Act 2002 (maintenance of Adoption Service; functions of local authority as adoption agency) (see CHILDREN AND YOUNG PERSONS); the Children and Families (Wales) Measure 2010 s 66 (family social work standards officers) (see

CHILDREN AND YOUNG PERSONS vol 9 (2017) PARA 219); and the Housing (Wales) Act 2014 s 95(2)–(4) (but only where those functions apply by virtue of s 95(5)(b) (co-operation and information sharing in relation to homeless persons: see HOUSING)): Social Services and Well-being (Wales) Act 2014 Sch 2 (amended by the Housing (Wales) Act 2014 Sch 3 para 22).
8   Social Services and Well-being (Wales) Act 2014 143(2). Such designation is by order under s 143: s 143(2). At the date at which this volume states the law no such order had been made. As to the Welsh Ministers see PARA 395.

374. Exercise of functions under ministerial guidance and direction. A local authority in Wales[1], or an officer of an authority, subject to a direction or instruction relating to its social services functions[2] must comply with it[3]. An authority must give the Welsh Ministers[4] and other specified persons[5] as much assistance in connection with the exercise of social services functions[6] as they are reasonably able to give[7]. A local authority must, when exercising its social services functions, act in accordance with any relevant requirements contained in a code[8] (unless such requirements are specifically excluded, in which case the authority must issue a policy statement in respect of the function[9], or it would be unreasonable for the authority to follow them[10]) and have regard to any relevant guidelines contained in it[11].

In exercising its broad social services functions an authority must act in accordance with any relevant requirements imposed upon it by a code[12] relating the statements of well-being outcomes[13] and have regard to any relevant guidance contained in that code[14].

1   As to the meanings of 'local authority' and 'Wales' see PARA 2.
2   Ie a direction or instruction under the Social Services and Well-being (Wales) Act 2014 Pt 8 (ss 143–161C). This includes a direction or an instruction to exercise a function that is contingent upon the opinion of the authority or an officer of the authority: s 159(2). As to a local authority's social services functions see PARA 373.
3   Social Services and Well-being (Wales) Act 2014 s 159(1). A direction under Pt 8 must be in writing may be varied or revoked by a later direction and is enforceable by mandatory order on application by, or on behalf of, the Welsh Ministers: s 159(3).
4   As to the Welsh Ministers see PARA 395.
5   Ie any person authorised for these purposes by the Welsh Ministers, any person acting under a direction under the Social Services and Well-being (Wales) Act 2014 Pt 8, and any person assisting the Welsh Ministers or any such person: s 160(2).
6   Ie the exercise of functions under or by virtue of the Social Services and Well-being (Wales) Act 2014 Pt 8.
7   Social Services and Well-being (Wales) Act 2014 s 160(1).
8   Social Services and Well-being (Wales) Act 2014 s 145(3)(a). As to such codes see s 145(1); and PARA 410.
9   Where the Social Services and Well-being (Wales) Act 2014 s 145 applies to a requirement in a code a local authority may exercise social services functions in a way that does not comply with the requirement so far as:
    (1)   the authority considers there is good reason for it not to comply with the requirement in particular categories of cases or at all (s 147(1)(a));
    (2)   it decides on an alternative policy for the exercise of its functions in respect of the subject matter of the requirement (s 147(1)(b)); and
    (3)   a policy statement issued by the authority in accordance with s 148 (see below) is in effect (s 147(1)(c)).
    Where heads (1) to (3) above apply, the authority:
    (a)   must follow the course set out in the policy statement (s 147(2)(a)); and
    (b)   is subject to the duty to comply with the requirement in the code only so far as the subject matter of the requirement is not displaced by the policy statement (s 147(2)(b)).
    A policy statement issued under s 147(1) must set out how the local authority proposes that social services functions should be exercised differently from the requirement in the relevant code and the authority's reasons for proposing that different course: s 148(1). An authority that has issued a policy statement may issue a revised policy statement (s 148(2)(a)) and give notice revoking a policy statement (s 148(2)(b)). A policy statement (or revised statement) must state that it is issued under s 147(1) and the date on which it is to take effect: s 148(3). An authority that

issues a policy statement (or revised statement), or gives a notice under s 148(2)(b) must arrange for the statement or notice to be published and send a copy of the statement or notice to the Welsh Ministers: s 148(4).

    If in relation to a policy statement issued by a local authority, the Welsh Ministers consider that the authority's alternative policy for the exercise of functions (in whole or in part) is not likely to lead to the exercise of social services functions to an adequate standard they may direct the authority to take any action which they consider appropriate for the purpose of securing the exercise of functions by the authority in accordance with the relevant requirement in the relevant code: s 149.

    A code may, however, specify that s 147 does not apply to a requirement contained in the code: see s 145(4); and PARA 410.

10 The duty to comply with a requirement in a code of practice or to follow the course set out in a policy statement (see note 9) does not apply to a local authority so far as it would be unreasonable for the authority to follow the code or policy statement in a particular case or category of case: Social Services and Well-being (Wales) Act 2014 s 147(3).

11 Social Services and Well-being (Wales) Act 2014 s 145(3).

12 Ie a code issued under the Social Services and Well-being (Wales) Act 2014 s 9 (see PARA 396).

13 Social Services and Well-being (Wales) Act 2014 s 10(1)(a). Where performance measures or performance targets are specified in a code issued under s 9, they are to be treated (so far as they apply to the performance of local authorities in exercising their functions) as having been specified as performance indicators or performance standards respectively under the Local Government (Wales) Measure 2009 s 8(1) (see LOCAL GOVERNMENT vol 69 (2009) PARA 714): Social Services and Well-being (Wales) Act 2014 s 10(2).

14 Social Services and Well-being (Wales) Act 2014 s 10(1)(b).

375. Duty to promote a person's well-being. A person exercising care and support functions[1] in Wales[2] must seek to promote the well-being of people who need care and support[3] and carers[4] who need support[5]. 'Well-being' means[6], in relation to a person, well-being so far as relating to any of the following:

    (1)   physical and mental health and emotional well-being[7];

    (2)   protection from abuse and neglect[8];

    (3)   control over day-to-day life[9];

    (4)   participation in work, education, training and recreation[10];

    (5)   social and economic well-being[11];

    (6)   domestic, family and personal relationships[12];

    (7)   suitability of living accommodation[13];

    (8)   contribution to society[14]; and

    (9)   securing rights and entitlements[15].

In relation to a child in Wales 'well-being' also includes physical, intellectual, emotional, social and behavioural development[16] and the child's welfare[17].

1 Ie functions under the Social Services and Well-being (Wales) Act 2014.

2 Care and support functions under the Social Services and Well-being (Wales) Act 2014 are generally exercisable by local authorities, although many of them are delegable: see PARA 2. As to the meanings of 'local authority' and 'Wales' see PARA 2.

3 Social Services and Well-being (Wales) Act 2014 s 5(a). As to the meanings of 'care' and 'support' see PARA 2 note 1.

4 As to the meaning of 'carer' see PARA 54 note 2.

5 Social Services and Well-being (Wales) Act 2014 s 5(b).

6 Ie for the purposes of the Social Services and Well-being (Wales) Act 2014 and the Regulation and Inspection of Social Care (Wales) Act 2016 (see s 189).

7 Social Services and Well-being (Wales) Act 2014 s 2(1), (2)(a).

8 Social Services and Well-being (Wales) Act 2014 s 2(2)(b). As to the meanings of 'abuse' and 'neglect' see PARA 15 note 11.

9 Social Services and Well-being (Wales) Act 2014 s 2(4)(a). Control over day-to-day life is identified as included as part of 'well-being' only in relation to an adult: s 2(4)(a). As to the meaning of 'adult' see PARA 2.

10 Social Services and Well-being (Wales) Act 2014 s 2(2)(c). Participation in work is identified as included as part of 'well-being' only in relation to an adult: s 2(4)(b).

11 Social Services and Well-being (Wales) Act 2014 s 2(2)(g).

12 Social Services and Well-being (Wales) Act 2014 s 2(2)(d).

13 Social Services and Well-being (Wales) Act 2014 s 2(2)(h).
14 Social Services and Well-being (Wales) Act 2014 s 2(2)(e).
15 Social Services and Well-being (Wales) Act 2014 s 2(2)(f).
16 Social Services and Well-being (Wales) Act 2014 s 2(3)(a).
17 Social Services and Well-being (Wales) Act 2014 s 2(3)(b). The reference is to 'welfare' as that word is interpreted for the purposes of the Children Act 1989: see s 1; and CHILDREN AND YOUNG PERSONS vol 9 (2017) PARA 315 et seq.

376. Prevention of need for care and support. A local authority in Wales[1] must provide or arrange for the provision of a range and level of services which it considers will achieve the following purposes in its area[2]:

(1)   contributing towards preventing or delaying the development of people's needs for care and support[3];

(2)   reducing the needs for care and support of people who have such needs[4];

(3)   promoting the upbringing of children[5] by their families, where that is consistent with the well-being of children[6];

(4)   minimising the effect on disabled people of their disabilities[7];

(5)   contributing towards preventing people from suffering abuse or neglect[8];

(6)   reducing the need for proceedings for care or supervision orders[9], criminal proceedings against children[10], any family or other proceedings in relation to children which might lead to them being placed in local authority care[11] or proceedings under the inherent jurisdiction of the High Court in relation to children[12];

(7)   encouraging children not to commit criminal offences[13];

(8)   avoiding the need for children to be placed in secure accommodation[14]; and

(9)   enabling people to live their lives as independently as possible[15],

and in discharging this duty the authority:

(a)   must identify the services already available in the authority's area which may help in achieving the listed purposes and consider involving or making use of those services in discharging the duty[16];

(b)   may take account of services which the authority considers might reasonably be provided or arranged by other persons in deciding what it should provide or arrange[17];

(c)   must make the best use of the authority's resources and in particular avoid provision which might give rise to disproportionate expenditure[18].

A local authority in Wales may not provide payments in the discharge of its duty to provide such services[19] unless it considers that the payments would achieve one or more of the purposes mentioned in heads (1)–(9) above[20] and that it would not be reasonably practicable to achieve that purpose or those purposes in any other way[21], the payments are provided under or by virtue of a contract which relates to the provision of services for the authority's area[22], or the payments are provided in circumstances specified in regulations[23]. It may, however, impose charges[24].

These duties do not extend to the provision of services etc for, or the taking of steps, in relation to the support of, certain persons subject to immigration control, or in relation to the provision of health services and housing[25].

1   As to the meanings of 'local authority' and 'Wales' see PARA 2. Two or more local authorities may jointly discharge the duty under Social Services and Well-being (Wales) Act 2014 s 15(1) (see the text and notes 2–3) in relation to their combined area, and where they do so references in s 15 to a local authority are to be read as references to the authorities acting jointly (s 15(8)(a)) and references to a local authority's area are to be read as references to the combined area (s 15(8)(b)).

2   The things that may be provided or arranged in discharging this duty include, but are not limited to, care and support (or in the case of carers, support) of the kind that must or may be provided under the Social Services and Well-being (Wales) Act 2014 ss 35–45 (see PARAS 19–20 (adults), PARAS 30–32 (children) and PARAS 58–63 (carers)): s 15(3). A local authority, in the exercise of its other functions, and a Local Health Board, in the exercise of its functions, must have regard to the importance of achieving the purposes in s 15(2) (see the text and notes 3–15) in its area: s 15(4), (5). Where advocacy services are being provided for a person under s 15 and regulations under s 181 (provision of advocacy services: see PARA 104) would (apart from this provision) impose a requirement upon a local authority to make advocacy services available to that person in respect of the same matters, that requirement does not apply: s 182(2). As to Local Health Boards see HEALTH SERVICES vol 54 (2017) PARA 97.

3   Social Services and Well-being (Wales) Act 2014 s 15(1), (2)(a). As to the meanings of 'care' and 'support' see PARA 2 note 1.

4   Social Services and Well-being (Wales) Act 2014 s 15(2)(b).

5   As to the meaning of 'child' see PARA 2.

6   Social Services and Well-being (Wales) Act 2014 s 15(2)(c).

7   Social Services and Well-being (Wales) Act 2014 s 15(2)(d).

8   Social Services and Well-being (Wales) Act 2014 s 15(2)(e). As to the meanings of 'abuse' and 'neglect' see PARA 15 note 11.

9   Social Services and Well-being (Wales) Act 2014 s 15(2)(f)(i). As to care and supervision orders see the Children Act 1989 Pt 4 (ss 31–42); and CHILDREN AND YOUNG PERSONS vol 9 (2017) PARA 351 et seq.

10 Social Services and Well-being (Wales) Act 2014 s 15(2)(f)(ii).

11 Social Services and Well-being (Wales) Act 2014 s 15(2)(f)(iii).

12 Social Services and Well-being (Wales) Act 2014 s 15(2)(f)(iv).

13 Social Services and Well-being (Wales) Act 2014 s 15(2)(g).

14 Social Services and Well-being (Wales) Act 2014 s 15(2)(h) (amended by SI 2016/413). The reference in the text is to secure accommodation within the meaning given in the Social Services and Well-being (Wales) Act 2014 s 119 (see CHILDREN AND YOUNG PERSONS vol 10 (2017) PARA 1075) and in the Children Act 1989 s 25 (see CHILDREN AND YOUNG PERSONS vol 10 (2017) PARA 1062).

15 Social Services and Well-being (Wales) Act 2014 s 15(2)(i).

16 Social Services and Well-being (Wales) Act 2014 s 15(6)(a).

17 Social Services and Well-being (Wales) Act 2014 s 15(6)(b).

18 Social Services and Well-being (Wales) Act 2014 s 15(6)(c). Provision is not to be considered as giving rise to disproportionate expenditure only because that provision is more expensive than comparable provision: s 15(7).

19 Ie the authority's duty under the Social Services and Well-being (Wales) Act 2014 s 15(1).

20 Social Services and Well-being (Wales) Act 2014 s 49(2)(a)(i).

21 Social Services and Well-being (Wales) Act 2014 s 49(2)(a)(ii).

22 Social Services and Well-being (Wales) Act 2014 s 49(2)(b).

23 Social Services and Well-being (Wales) Act 2014 s 49(2)(c). At the date at which this volume states the law no such regulations had been made.

24 A local authority in Wales may impose charges for services provided under the Social Services and Well-being (Wales) Act 2014 s 15 or for assistance provided under s 17 (information, advice and assistance: see PARA 392): Care and Support (Charging) (Wales) Regulations 2015, SI 2015/1843, reg 16(1) (made under the Social Services and Well-being (Wales) Act 2014 s 69). If an authority exercises this discretion in relation to a particular service or assistance, it may only do so to impose a flat-rate charge in relation to that service or assistance: Care and Support (Charging) (Wales) Regulations 2015, SI 2015/1843, reg 16(2). 'Flat-rate charge' means a fixed rate charge which is imposed by a local authority regardless of the means of the person who is liable to be charged for care and support arranged or provided by a local authority under the Social Services and Well-being (Wales) Act 2014 Pt 4 (ss 32–58) (meeting needs), for services provided under s 15 or for assistance provided under s 17: Care and Support (Financial Assessment) (Wales) Regulations 2015, SI 2015/1843, reg 1(4). A flat-rate charge imposed under reg 16 may not exceed the cost incurred in providing the services or the assistance to which the charge relates: reg 16(3). A local authority may not exercise its discretion under reg 16(1) to impose a charge on a child or in relation to any provision of a service or assistance in relation to which a charge is being imposed under the Social Services and Well-being (Wales) Act 2014 Pt 5 (ss 59–73) (charging and financial assessment: see PARAS 131–142): reg 16(4).

25 See the Social Services and Well-being (Wales) Act 2014 ss 15(9), 46–48; and PARA 5. The Social Services and Well-being (Wales) Act 2014 s 49 (restriction on provision of payments: see PARA 376) is also excluded.

377. Individual's views and wishes to be taken into account in providing care. A person exercising care and support functions in Wales[1] in relation to an individual who has, or may have, needs for care and support[2] or a carer[3] who has, or may have, needs for support[4] must[5]:

(1)   in so far as is reasonably practicable, ascertain and have regard to the individual's views, wishes and feelings[6];

(2)   have regard to the importance of promoting and respecting the dignity of the individual[7];

(3)   have regard to the characteristics, culture and beliefs of the individual (including, for example, language)[8]; and

(4)   have regard to the importance of providing appropriate support to enable the individual to participate in decisions that affect him or her to the extent that is appropriate in the circumstances, particularly where the individual's ability to communicate is limited for any reason[9].

A person exercising care and support functions in Wales in relation to an adult[10] must, in addition, have regard to the importance of beginning with the presumption that the adult is best placed to judge the adult's well-being[11] and the importance of promoting the adult's independence where possible[12], and a person exercising such functions in relation to a child[13] must also have regard to the importance of promoting the upbringing of the child by the child's family, in so far as doing so is consistent with promoting the well-being of the child[14], and where the child is under the age of 16, must ascertain and have regard to the views, wishes and feelings of the persons with parental responsibility for the child, in so far as doing so is consistent with promoting the well-being of the child and reasonably practicable[15].

1   Ie functions under the Social Services and Well-being (Wales) Act 2014. Care and support functions under the Act are generally exercisable by local authorities, although many of them are delegable: see PARA 2. As to the meanings of 'local authority' and 'Wales' see PARA 2.
2   Social Services and Well-being (Wales) Act 2014 s 6(1)(a). As to the meanings of 'care' and 'support' see PARA 2 note 1.
3   As to the meaning of 'carer' see PARA 2 note 2.
4   Social Services and Well-being (Wales) Act 2014 s 6(1)(b).
5   These duties are also owed to an individual in respect of whom functions are exercisable under the Social Services and Well-being (Wales) Act 2014 Pt 6 (ss 74–125D) (looked after children etc: see CHILDREN AND YOUNG PERSONS vol 10 (2017) PARA 826 et seq): Social Services and Well-being (Wales) Act 2014 s 6(1)(c).
6   Social Services and Well-being (Wales) Act 2014 s 6(2)(a).
7   Social Services and Well-being (Wales) Act 2014 s 6(2)(b).
8   Social Services and Well-being (Wales) Act 2014 s 6(2)(c).
9   Social Services and Well-being (Wales) Act 2014 s 6(2)(d).
10   Ie an adult falling within the Social Services and Well-being (Wales) Act 2014 s 6(1)(a), (b) or (c) (see the text and notes 1–5): s 6(3). As to the meaning of 'adult' see PARA 2.
11   Social Services and Well-being (Wales) Act 2014 s 6(3)(a). As to the meaning of 'well-being' see PARA 375.
12   Social Services and Well-being (Wales) Act 2014 s 6(3)(b).
13   Ie a child falling within the Social Services and Well-being (Wales) Act 2014 s 6(1)(a), (b) or (c) (see the text and notes 1–5): s 6(4). As to the meaning of 'child' in Wales see PARA 2.
14   Social Services and Well-being (Wales) Act 2014 s 6(4)(a).
15   Social Services and Well-being (Wales) Act 2014 s 6(4)(b).

378. Duty to co-operate with partners including other local authorities. A local authority in Wales[1] must make arrangements to promote co-operation between it[2], each of its relevant partners[3] in the exercise of their adult[4] care and support functions[5], and such other persons or bodies[6] as the authority considers appropriate[7]. An authority must also make arrangements to promote co-operation between the officers of the authority who exercise its functions[8]. Such arrangements are to be made with a view to:

(1)   improving the well-being[9] of adults within the authority's area with needs for care and support[10] and adults within the authority's area who are carers[11];

(2)   improving the quality of care and support for adults, and of support for adults who are carers, provided in the authority's area (including the outcomes that are achieved from such provision)[12]; and

(3)   protecting adults with needs for care and support who are experiencing, or are at risk of, abuse or neglect[13].

If, for the purpose of the exercise of any of its social services functions[14], a local authority in Wales requests the co-operation of, or requests the provision of information from:

(a)   a relevant partner of the local authority making the request[15];

(b)   a local authority, a Local Health Board or an NHS Trust which is not a relevant partner of the local authority making the request[16]; or

(c)   a youth offending team[17] for an area any part of which falls within the area of the local authority making the request[18],

the person must comply with the request unless he considers that doing so would be incompatible with his own duties[19] or otherwise have an adverse effect on the exercise of his functions[20].

1   As to the meanings of 'local authority' and 'Wales' see PARA 2.
2   Social Services and Well-being (Wales) Act 2014 s 162(1)(a).
3   For the purposes of the Social Services and Well-being (Wales) Act 2014 ss 162, 164 each of the following is a 'relevant partner' of a local authority in Wales:
    (1)   the local policing body and the chief officer of police for a police area any part of which falls within the area of the local authority (ss 128(4), 130(5)(a), 162(4)(a), 164(7));
    (2)   any other local authority with which the authority agrees that it would be appropriate to co-operate under s 162 (s 162(4)(b));
    (3)   the Secretary of State to the extent that he is discharging functions under the Offender Management Act 2007 ss 2, 3 (see SENTENCING vol 92 (2015) PARA 669) in relation to Wales (Social Services and Well-being (Wales) Act 2014 s 162(4)(c));
    (4)   any provider of probation services that is required by arrangements under the Offender Management Act 2007 s 3(2) to act as a relevant partner of the authority (Social Services and Well-being (Wales) Act 2014 s 162(4)(d));
    (5)   a Local Health Board for an area any part of which falls within the area of the authority (s 162(4)(e));
    (6)   an NHS Trust providing services in the area of the authority (s 162(4)(f) (amended in relation to local authorities in Wales by SI 2016/413));
    (7)   the Welsh Ministers to the extent that they are discharging functions under the Learning and Skills Act 2000 Pt 2 (ss 31–41) (see EDUCATION vol 36 (2015) PARA 789 et seq) (Social Services and Well-being (Wales) Act 2014 s 162(4)(g)); and
    (8)   such a person, or a person of such description, as regulations may specify (s 162(4)(h)).
    As to local government areas and authorities in Wales see LOCAL GOVERNMENT vol 69 (2009) PARA 22 et seq. As to police forces, police areas and chief officers of police see POLICE AND INVESTIGATORY POWERS vol 84 (2013) PARAS 52 et seq, 123 et seq. As to the Secretary of State see PARA 333. As to Local Health Boards see HEALTH SERVICES vol 54 (2017) PARA 97. As to NHS Trusts see HEALTH SERVICES vol 54 (2017) PARA 235. As to the Welsh Ministers see PARA 395. Regulations under s 162(4)(h) may not specify a Minister of the Crown or the governor of a prison (or, in the case of a contracted out prison, its director) unless the Secretary of State consents: s 162(5). In this context a reference to a prison includes a young offender institution and a reference to a contracted out prison has the meaning given by the Criminal Justice Act 1991 s 84(4) (see PRISONS AND PRISONERS vol 85 (2012) PARA 521): Social Services and Well-being (Wales) Act 2014 s 162(11).
    Where a person whose needs are being met by a local authority under s 189(2) (duty of local authority to meet needs in event of business failure: see PARA 230) is also being provided with continuing NHS care under arrangements made by a Local Health Board no part of whose area is in the local authority's area, the Local Health Board is to be treated as a 'relevant partner' of the authority for the purposes of ss 162, 164: s 191(4). In s 191(4) 'continuing NHS care' means

services or facilities provided by virtue of the National Health Service (Wales) Act 2006 ss 3(1)(e), 12 (see HEALTH SERVICES vol 54 (2017) PARA 97): Social Services and Well-being (Wales) Act 2014 s 191(5).

The relevant partners of a local authority must co-operate with the authority in the making of arrangements under s 162: s 162(6). An authority and any of its relevant partners may for the purposes of such arrangements:

    (a)   provide staff, goods, services, accommodation or other resources (s 162(7)(a));
    (b)   establish and maintain a pooled fund (s 162(7)(b)); and
    (c)   share information with each other (s 162(7)(c)).

For these purposes a 'pooled fund' is a fund which is made up of contributions by the authority and the relevant partner or partners concerned (s 162(8)(a)) and out of which payments may be made towards expenditure incurred in the discharge of functions of the authority and functions of the relevant partner or partners (s 162(8)(b)). An authority and each of its relevant partners must, in exercising their functions under s 162, have regard to any guidance given to them for the purpose by the Welsh Ministers: s 162(9). The Welsh Ministers must consult the Secretary of State before giving such guidance: s 162(10).

4   As to the meaning of 'adult' see PARA 2. Note that these provisions apply only to adults: corresponding provision relating to children is made by the Children Act 2004 s 25: see CHILDREN AND YOUNG PERSONS vol 9 (2017) PARA 218.
5   Social Services and Well-being (Wales) Act 2014 s 162(1)(b). The 'adult care and support functions' referred to are the relevant partner's functions relating to adults with needs for care and support or to adults who are carers (s 162(1)(b)(i)) and their other functions the exercise of which is relevant to such functions (s 162(1)(b)(ii)). As to the meanings of 'care' and 'support' see PARA 2 note 1. As to the meaning of 'carer' see PARA 54 note 2.
6   Ie, being persons or bodies of any nature who or which exercise functions or are engaged in activities in relation to adults within the authority's area with needs for care and support (Social Services and Well-being (Wales) Act 2014 s 162(1)(c)(i)) or adults within the authority's area who are carers (s 162(1)(c)(ii)).
7   Social Services and Well-being (Wales) Act 2014 s 162(1)(c).
8   Social Services and Well-being (Wales) Act 2014 s 162(2).
9   As to the meaning of 'well-being' see PARA 375.
10 Social Services and Well-being (Wales) Act 2014 s 162(3)(a)(i).
11 Social Services and Well-being (Wales) Act 2014 s 162(3)(a)(ii).
12 Social Services and Well-being (Wales) Act 2014 s 162(3)(b).
13 Social Services and Well-being (Wales) Act 2014 s 162(3)(c). As to the meanings of 'abuse' and 'neglect' see PARA 15 note 11.
14 As to a local authority's social services functions see PARA 373.
15 Social Services and Well-being (Wales) Act 2014 s 164(1), (2), (4)(a).
16 Social Services and Well-being (Wales) Act 2014 s 164(4)(b) (amended in relation to local authorities in Wales by SI 2016/413)).
17 As to youth offending teams see CHILDREN AND YOUNG PERSONS vol 10 (2017) PARA 1284.
18 Social Services and Well-being (Wales) Act 2014 s 164(4)(c).
19 Social Services and Well-being (Wales) Act 2014 s 164(1)(a), (2)(a).
20 Social Services and Well-being (Wales) Act 2014 s 164(1)(b), (2)(b). A person who decides not to comply with such a request must give the authority which made the request written reasons for the decision: s 164(3). A local authority and each of the persons mentioned in s 164(4) must in exercising their functions under s 164 have regard to any guidance given to them for the purpose by the Welsh Ministers: s 164(5). The Welsh Ministers must consult the Secretary of State before giving such guidance: s 164(6).

379. Duty to make inquiries about vulnerable adults.

If a local authority in Wales[1] has reasonable cause to suspect that a person within its area (whether or not ordinarily resident[2] there) is an 'adult at risk', that is, is an adult[3] who:

    (1)   is experiencing or is at risk of abuse or neglect[4];
    (2)   has needs for care and support[5] (whether or not the authority is meeting any of those needs)[6]; and
    (3)   as a result of those needs is unable to protect himself or herself against the abuse or neglect or the risk of it[7],

the authority must make (or cause to be made) whatever enquiries it thinks necessary to enable it to decide whether any action should be taken[8] and, if so, what and by whom[9], and decide whether any such action should be taken[10].

An 'adult protection and support order' is an order whose purposes are:

(a)   to enable an authorised officer of a local authority in Wales[11], and any other person accompanying the officer to speak in private with a person suspected of being an adult at risk[12];

(b)   to enable the authorised officer to ascertain whether that person is making decisions freely[13]; and

(c)   to enable the authorised officer properly to assess whether the person is an adult at risk and to make a decision[14] on what, if any, action should be taken[15].

An authorised officer of a local authority may apply to a justice of the peace for an adult protection and support order in relation to a person living in any premises within a local authority's area[16], and the justice may make order if satisfied that:

(i)   the authorised officer has reasonable cause to suspect that a person is an adult at risk[17];

(ii)   it is necessary for the authorised officer to gain access to the person in order properly to assess whether the person is an adult at risk and to make a decision[18] on what, if any, action should be taken[19];

(iii)   making an order is necessary in order to fulfil the order's[20] purposes[21]; and

(iv)   exercising the power of entry conferred by the order will not result in the person being at greater risk of abuse or neglect[22].

When an adult protection and support order is in force the authorised officer, a constable and any other specified person accompanying the officer in accordance with the order, may enter the premises specified in the order for the order' purposes[23].

1   As to the meanings of 'local authority' and 'Wales' see PARA 2. In exercising its functions under the Social Services and Well-being (Wales) Act 2014 ss 126, 127, a local authority, a person who is an authorised officer for the purposes of s 127 (see the text and notes 11–23), and a constable or other specified person accompanying an authorised officer in accordance with an adult protection and support order made under s 127, must have regard to any guidance given to it by the Welsh Ministers: s 131(1)(a)–(c). The Welsh Ministers must consult the Secretary of State before giving guidance under s 131(1): s 131(2). As to the Welsh Ministers see PARA 395; as to the Secretary of State see PARA 333.

2   In connection with a person's residence see PARAS 84–87.

3   As to the meaning of 'adult' see PARA 2. See PARA 380 (duty to report adults at risk).

4   Social Services and Well-being (Wales) Act 2014 s 126(1)(a). As to the meanings of 'abuse' and 'neglect' see PARA 15 note 11.

5   As to the meanings of 'care' and 'support' see PARA 2 note 1.

6   Social Services and Well-being (Wales) Act 2014 s 126(1)(b).

7   Social Services and Well-being (Wales) Act 2014 s 126(1)(c).

8   Ie whether under the Social Services and Well-being (Wales) Act 2014 or otherwise.

9   Social Services and Well-being (Wales) Act 2014 s 126(2)(a). In connection with the inclusion of the conclusions of such inquires in care and support plans see s 126(3); and PARA 81.

10 Social Services and Well-being (Wales) Act 2014 s 126(2)(b).

11 Ie a person authorised by a local authority in Wales for these purposes, who has received appropriate training: see the Social Services and Well-being (Wales) Act 2014 s 127(9); and the Adult Protection and Support Orders (Authorised Officer) (Wales) Regulations 2015, SI 2015/1465.

12 Social Services and Well-being (Wales) Act 2014 s 127(2)(a).

13 Social Services and Well-being (Wales) Act 2014 s 127(2)(b).

14 Ie as required by the Social Services and Well-being (Wales) Act 2014 s 126(2) (see the text and notes 1–10).

15 Social Services and Well-being (Wales) Act 2014 s 127(2)(c).

16 Social Services and Well-being (Wales) Act 2014 s 127(1). An adult protection and support order must specify the premises to which it relates (s 127(5)(a)), provide that the authorised officer

may be accompanied by a constable (s 127(5)(b)), and specify the period for which the order is to be in force (s 127(5)(c)). Other conditions may be attached to an adult protection and support order, for example:

(1)   specifying restrictions on the time at which the power of entry conferred by the order may be exercised (s 127(6)(a));

(2)   providing for the authorised officer to be accompanied by another specified person (s 127(6)(b));

(3)   requiring notice of the order to be given to the occupier of the premises and to the person suspected of being an adult at risk (s 127(6)(c)).

17   Social Services and Well-being (Wales) Act 2014 s 127(4)(a).
18   See note 14.
19   Social Services and Well-being (Wales) Act 2014 s 127(4)(b).
20   Ie the purposes set out in the Social Services and Well-being (Wales) Act 2014 s 127(2) (see the text and notes 11–15).
21   Social Services and Well-being (Wales) Act 2014 s 127(4)(c).
22   Social Services and Well-being (Wales) Act 2014 s 127(4)(d).
23   Social Services and Well-being (Wales) Act 2014 s 127(3). A constable accompanying the authorised officer may use reasonable force if necessary in order to fulfil the purposes of an adult protection and support order set out in s 127(2): s 127(7). On entering the premises in accordance with an adult protection and support order the authorised officer must:

(1)   state the object of the visit (s 127(8)(a));

(2)   produce evidence of the authorisation to enter the premises (s 127(8)(b)); and

(3)   provide an explanation to the occupier of the premises of how to complain about how the power of entry has been exercised (s 127(8)(c)).

380. Duty to report adults and children at risk. If a relevant partner[1] of a local authority in Wales[2] has reasonable cause to suspect that a person is an adult[3] at risk, or that a child[4] is a child at risk[5], and appears to be within the authority's area, it must inform the authority of that fact[6]. If the person that the relevant partner has reasonable cause to suspect is an adult at risk, or the child that the relevant partner has reasonable cause to suspect is a child at risk, appears to be within the area of a local authority other than one of which it is a relevant partner, it must inform that other authority[7]. If a local authority has reasonable cause to suspect that a person within its area at any time is an adult at risk, or that a child within its area at any time is a child at risk, and is living or proposing to live within the area of another local authority (or a local authority in England[8]), it must inform that other authority[9].

1   As to the meaning of 'relevant partner' see PARA 378 note 3; for the purposes of the Social Services and Well-being (Wales) Act 2014 s 130 (children at risk), a 'relevant partner' also includes a youth offending team for an area any part of which falls within the area of the authority (s 130(5)(b)). As to youth offending teams see CHILDREN AND YOUNG PERSONS vol 10 (2017) PARA 1284.

2   As to the meanings of 'local authority' and 'Wales' see PARA 2. In exercising its functions under the Social Services and Well-being (Wales) Act 2014 ss 128, 130, a local authority and a person who is a relevant partner for the purposes of s 128 or s 130 must have regard to any guidance given to it by the Welsh Ministers: s 131(1)(a), (d). The Welsh Ministers must consult the Secretary of State before giving guidance under s 131(1): s 131(2). As to the Welsh Ministers see PARA 395; as to the Secretary of State see PARA 333.

3   As to the meaning of 'adult' see PARA 2.

4   As to the meaning of 'child' see PARA 2.

5   For these purposes 'a child at risk' is a child who is experiencing or is at risk of abuse, neglect or other kinds of harm, and has needs for care and support (whether or not the authority is meeting any of those needs): Social Services and Well-being (Wales) Act 2014 s 130(4). As to the meanings of 'abuse' and 'neglect' see PARA 15 note 11. As to the meanings of 'care' and 'support' see PARA 2 note 1. For provision about a local authority's duty to investigate children at risk, see the Children Act 1989 s 47; and CHILDREN AND YOUNG PERSONS vol 9 (2017) PARAS 272–274.

6   Social Services and Well-being (Wales) Act 2014 ss 128(1), 130(1).

7   Social Services and Well-being (Wales) Act 2014 ss 128(2), 130(2).

8   As to the meaning of 'England' see PARA 1.

9   Social Services and Well-being (Wales) Act 2014 ss 128(3), 130(3).

381. Integration with health services. A local authority in Wales[1] must exercise its social services functions[2] with a view to ensuring the integration of care and support provision[3] with health provision[4] and health-related provision[5] where it considers that this would:

(1)   promote the well-being[6] of children within the authority's area[7], adults within the authority's area with needs for care and support[8], or carers within the authority's area with needs for support[9];

(2)   contribute to the prevention or delay of the development by adults or children in its area of needs for care and support or the development by carers in its area of needs for support[10]; or

(3)   improve the quality of care and support for adults and children, and of support for carers, provided in its area (including the outcomes that are achieved from such provision)[11].

1   As to the meanings of 'local authority' and 'Wales' see PARA 2.
2   As to the social services functions of local authorities in Wales generally see PARA 2.
3   'Care and support provision' means:
    (1)   provision to meet the needs of adults and children for care and support (Social Services and Well-being (Wales) Act 2014 s 165(2)(a)); and
    (2)   provision to meet carers' needs for support (s 165(2)(b)).
    As to the meanings of 'adult' and 'child' see PARA 2. As to the meaning of 'carer' see PARA 2 note 2. As to the meanings of 'care' and 'support' see PARA 2 note 1.
4   'Health provision' means provision of health services as part of the health service: Social Services and Well-being (Wales) Act 2014 s 165(3). The 'health service' means the health service continued under the National Health Service (Wales) Act 2006 s 1(1) (see HEALTH SERVICES vol 54 (2017) PARA 97): Social Services and Well-being (Wales) Act 2014 s 165(5).
5   'Health-related provision' means provision of services which may have an effect on the health of individuals but which are not health services provided as part of the health service (Social Services and Well-being (Wales) Act 2014 s 165(4)(a)) or services provided in the exercise of social services functions (s 165(4)(b)).
6   As to the meaning of 'well-being' see PARA 375.
7   Social Services and Well-being (Wales) Act 2014 s 165(1)(a)(i).
8   Social Services and Well-being (Wales) Act 2014 s 165(1)(a)(ii).
9   Social Services and Well-being (Wales) Act 2014 s 165(1)(a)(iii).
10   Care Act 2014 s 3(1)(b); Social Services and Well-being (Wales) Act 2014 s 165(1)(b).
11   Care Act 2014 s 3(1)(c); Social Services and Well-being (Wales) Act 2014 s 165(1)(c).

382. Promotion of social enterprises and the third sector in Wales. A local authority in Wales[1] must promote:

(1)   the development in its area of social enterprises[2] to provide care and support[3] and preventative services[4];

(2)   the development in its area of co-operative organisations[5] or arrangements to provide care and support and preventative services[6];

(3)   the involvement of persons for whom care and support or preventative services are to be provided in the design and operation of that provision[7]; and

(4)   the availability in its area of care and support and preventative services from third sector organisations[8] (whether or not the organisations are social enterprises[9] or co-operative organisations)[10].

1   As to the meanings of 'local authority' and 'Wales' see PARA 2.
2   For these purposes the following types of organisation are examples of organisations which are to be treated as 'social enterprises':
    (1)   a community interest company as referred to in the Companies (Audit, Investigations and Community Enterprise) Act 2004 s 26 (see COMPANIES vol 14 (2016) PARA 75) (Social Services and Well-being (Wales) Act 2014 (Social Enterprise, Co-operative and Third Sector) (Wales) Regulations 2015, SI 2015/1500, reg 7(1)(a)) (made under the Social Services and Well-being (Wales) Act 2014 s 16(3));

(2)   a community benefit society which meets the requirements for registration in
        the Co-operative and Community Benefit Societies Act 2014 s 2 (see FINANCIAL
        INSTITUTIONS vol 48 (2015) PARA 890) (Social Services and Well-being (Wales) Act
        2014 (Social Enterprise, Co-operative and Third Sector) (Wales) Regulations 2015, SI
        2015/1500, reg 7(1)(b));

(3)   a community enterprise (reg 7(1)(c));

(4)   a credit union which is registered and regulated under the Credit Unions Act 1979 (see
        FINANCIAL INSTITUTIONS vol 48 (2015) PARA 890 et seq) (Social Services and
        Well-being (Wales) Act 2014 (Social Enterprise, Co-operative and Third Sector) (Wales)
        Regulations 2015, SI 2015/1500, reg 7(1)(d));

(5)   a housing association (as defined in the Housing Associations Act 1985 s 1) (see
        HOUSING vol 56 (2011) PARA 11) (Social Services and Well-being (Wales) Act 2014
        (Social Enterprise, Co-operative and Third Sector) (Wales) Regulations 2015, SI
        2015/1500, reg 7(1)(e)).

In reg 7(1)(c) a 'community enterprise means a body which:

(a)   has the primary purpose of contributing to the economic and social development of a
        particular area of Wales (reg 7(2)(a)); and

(b)   by its written constitution, admits to membership only persons resident in, or employed
        in, that area (or both so resident and so employed) (reg 7(2)(b)(i)) or persons nominated
        by such persons as are mentioned in reg 7(2)(b)(i) (reg 7(2)(b)(ii)).

3   In this context 'care and support' includes support for carers: Social Services and Well-being
    (Wales) Act 2014 s 16(2). As to the meanings of 'care' and 'support' see PARA 2 note 1. As to the
    meaning of 'carer' in Wales see PARA 54 note 2.

4   Social Services and Well-being (Wales) Act 2014 s 16(1)(a). 'Preventative services' means services
    the local authority considers would achieve any of the purposes in s 15(2) (see PARA 376): s 16(2).

5   For the purposes of the Social Services and Well-being (Wales) Act 2014 s 16(1):

(1)   an organisation may be treated as a co-operative organisation whether or not it meets all
        the requirements for registration under the Co-operative and Community Benefit
        Societies Act 2014 (see Pt 1 (ss 1–9); and FINANCIAL INSTITUTIONS vol 48 (2015)
        PARAS 898–904, 1072–1079) (Social Services and Well-being (Wales) Act 2014 (Social
        Enterprise, Co-operative and Third Sector) (Wales) Regulations 2015, SI 2015/1500,
        reg 8(1)(a));

(2)   arrangements may be treated as co-operative arrangements whether or not the
        organisation making the arrangements meets all the requirements for registration under
        the Co-operative and Community Benefit Societies Act 2014 (Social Services and
        Well-being (Wales) Act 2014 (Social Enterprise, Co-operative and Third Sector) (Wales)
        Regulations 2015, SI 2015/1500, reg 8(1)(b)),

if the organisation, or the organisation making the arrangements, conforms sufficiently with the
principles for co-operatives, which require that the organisation:

(a)   is autonomous (reg 8(2)(a));

(b)   has voluntary membership (reg 8(2)(b));

(c)   has the purpose of meeting common economic, social and cultural needs and aspirations
        (reg 8(2)(c));

(d)   is jointly owned (reg 8(2)(d)); and

(e)   is democratically controlled (reg 8(2)(e)).

6   Social Services and Well-being (Wales) Act 2014 s 16(1)(b).

7   Social Services and Well-being (Wales) Act 2014 s 16(1)(c).

8   'Third sector organisation' means an organisation which a person might reasonably consider to
    exist wholly or mainly to provide benefits for society: Social Services and Well-being (Wales) Act
    2014 s 16(2). 'Society' includes a section of society (s 16(2)); and for the purposes of s 16 a
    'section' of society may be made up of:

(1)   those persons who need or may need care and support (Social Services and Well-being
        (Wales) Act 2014 (Social Enterprise, Co-operative and Third Sector) (Wales)
        Regulations 2015, SI 2015/1500, reg 9(a));

(2)   carers who need or may need support (reg 9(b)); or

(3)   children, care leavers and young persons in relation to whom a local authority have
        functions exercisable under the Social Services and Well-being (Wales) Act 2014 Pt 6
        (ss 74–125: see CHILDREN AND YOUNG PERSONS vol 10 (2017) PARA 826 et seq)
        (Social Services and Well-being (Wales) Act 2014 (Social Enterprise, Co-operative and
        Third Sector) (Wales) Regulations 2015, SI 2015/1500, reg 9(c)).

9   'Social enterprise' means (by virtue of the Social Services and Well-being (Wales) Act 2014 s 16(2))
    an organisation whose activities are wholly or mainly activities which a person might reasonably
    consider to be activities carried on for the benefit of society ('its social objects'), and which:

(1)   generates most of its income through business or trade;

(2)   reinvests most of its profits in its social objects;

(3)   is independent of any public authority; and

(4)   is owned, controlled and managed in a way that is consistent with its social objects.

For this purpose an activity is only to be treated as an activity which a person might reasonably consider to be an activity carried on for the benefit of society if:

(a)   it is inclusive (Social Services and Well-being (Wales) Act 2014 (Social Enterprise, Co-operative and Third Sector) (Wales) Regulations 2015, SI 2015/1500, reg 3(a));

(b)   it involves people (reg 3(b)); and

(c)   it promotes well-being (reg 3(c)),

and in this context:

(i)   an activity is 'inclusive' if the organisation that carries out the activity has, in relation to that activity, had regard to the factors to which a public authority must have regard in complying with the public sector equality duty set out in the Equality Act 2010 s 149 (see DISCRIMINATION vol 33 (2013) PARAS 266–272) (Social Services and Well-being (Wales) Act 2014 (Social Enterprise, Co-operative and Third Sector) (Wales) Regulations 2015, SI 2015/1500, reg 4);

(ii)   an activity 'involves people' if the organisation providing the activity promotes the involvement of persons for whom care and support or preventative services are to be provided in the design and operation of that provision (reg 5)); and

(iii)   an activity 'promotes well-being' if the organisation providing the activity has, in the design and operation of the activity, had regard to the aim of seeking to promote the well-being of people who need care and support, and carers who need support (reg 6).

10 Social Services and Well-being (Wales) Act 2014 s 16(1)(d).

383. United Nations instruments on the welfare of adults and children. A person exercising care and support functions in Wales[1] in relation to an individual who has, or may have, needs for care and support[2] or a carer[3] who has, or may have, needs for support[4] must have due regard to the United Nations Principles for Older Persons[5] or the United Nations Convention on the Rights of the Child[6], as the case may be[7].

1   Ie functions under the Social Services and Well-being (Wales) Act 2014. Care and support functions under the Act are generally exercisable by local authorities, although many of them are delegable: see PARA 2. As to the meaning of 'local authority' in Wales see PARA 2.

2   Social Services and Well-being (Wales) Act 2014 s 6(1)(a). As to the meanings of 'care' and 'support' see PARA 2 note 1.

3   As to the meaning of 'carer' in Wales see PARA 2 note 4.

4   Social Services and Well-being (Wales) Act 2014 s 6(1)(b).

5   Ie the United Nations Principles for Older Persons adopted by the General Assembly of the United Nations on 16 December 1991.

6   Ie the Convention on the Rights of the Child (20 November 1989) (UN General Assembly Resolution 44/25; Cmd 1976) Pt 1. For these purposes, Pt 1 is to be treated as having effect as set out for the time being in the Rights of Children and Young Persons (Wales) Measure 2011 Sch 1 Pt 1 (see CHILDREN AND YOUNG PERSONS vol 9 (2017) PARA 170) but subject to any declaration or reservation as set out for the time being in Pt 3: Social Services and Well-being (Wales) Act 2014 s 7(3). The Welsh Ministers are not required to have regard to the Convention, but rather to the Rights of Children and Young Persons (Wales) Measure 2011: Social Services and Well-being (Wales) Act 2014 s 7(4).

7   Social Services and Well-being (Wales) Act 2014 s 7(1), (2).

B.   ADMINISTRATIVE MATTERS

384. Duty to appoint Director of Social Services. A local authority in Wales[1] must appoint an officer, to be known as the director of social services, for the purposes of its social services functions[2]. A local authority may not appoint a person to be its director of social services unless it is satisfied that the person has demonstrated competencies specified by the Welsh Ministers[3]. Two or more local authorities may, if they consider that the same person can efficiently discharge, for both or all of them, the functions of a director of social services, appoint one person as director of social services for both or all of those authorities[4]. A local authority which has appointed, or jointly appointed, a person under these provisions must secure the provision of adequate staff for the purposes of its social services functions in order to assist the director[5].

1   As to the meanings of 'local authority' and 'Wales' see PARA 2.
2   Social Services and Well-being (Wales) Act 2014 144(1). As to a local authority's social services functions see PARA 373.
3   Social Services and Well-being (Wales) Act 2014 144(2). As to the Welsh Ministers see PARA 395. The Welsh Ministers must specify the competencies for the purpose of s 144(2) in a code issued under s 145 (see PARA 410) or in regulations: s 144(3). At the date at which this volume states the law no such regulations had been made.
4   Social Services and Well-being (Wales) Act 2014 144(4).
5   Social Services and Well-being (Wales) Act 2014 144(5).

385. Protecting property of persons being cared for away from home. Where a person is having needs for care and support[1] met[2] in a way that involves the provision of accommodation or is admitted to a hospital (or both)[3], and it appears to a local authority in Wales[4] that there is a danger of loss or damage to movable property of the person in the authority's area because the person is unable (whether permanently or temporarily) to protect or deal with the property[5] and no suitable arrangements have been or are being made[6], the authority must take reasonable steps to prevent or mitigate the loss or damage[7]. For the purpose of discharging that duty, the authority may at all reasonable times and on reasonable notice enter any premises which the person was living in immediately before being provided with accommodation or admitted to hospital[8] and may take any other steps which it considers reasonably necessary for preventing or mitigating loss or damage[9]. This duty does not, however, apply in the case of a person who is detained in prison or youth detention accommodation or residing in approved premises[10].

Obstruction of an authority's power of entry is an offence[11].

1   As to the meanings of 'care' and 'support' see PARA 2 note 1. A local authority may recover from whatever reasonable expenses it incurs under these provisions relation to an adult's movable property, from that adult: Social Services and Well-being (Wales) Act 2014 s 58(9). As to the meaning of 'adult' see PARA 2. An amount so recoverable is recoverable summarily as a civil debt (but this does not affect any other method of recovery): s 58(10).
2   Ie under the Social Services and Well-being (Wales) Act 2014 s 35, 36, 37 or 38 (see PARAS 19, 20 (adults) and PARAS 30, 31 (children).
3   Social Services and Well-being (Wales) Act 2014 s 58(1)(a) (amended by SI 2016/413).
4   As to the meanings of 'local authority' and 'Wales' see PARA 2.
5   Social Services and Well-being (Wales) Act 2014 s 58(1)(b)(i).
6   Social Services and Well-being (Wales) Act 2014 s 58(1)(b)(ii).
7   Social Services and Well-being (Wales) Act 2014 s 58(3).
8   Social Services and Well-being (Wales) Act 2014 s 58(3)(a). A local authority must (by virtue of s 58(4)) ensure that the following requirements are satisfied before taking any steps under s 58(3)(a) or (b) (and where the authority is unable to ensure that these requirements are satisfied, it's duty under s 58(2) ceases to apply (s 58(6))):
    (1)   where the authority is satisfied that the person is an adult or a child aged 16 or 17 who has capacity to consent to the taking of the steps, or a child aged under 16 who has sufficient understanding to make an informed decision about whether to consent to the taking of the steps, it must obtain the person's consent to the taking of the steps (CASE 1);
    (2)   where the authority is satisfied that the person is an adult who lacks capacity to consent to the taking of the steps, it must obtain consent to the taking of the steps from a person authorised under the Mental Capacity Act 2005 (whether in general or specific terms) to give consent on the adult's behalf, if any person is so authorised, or if there is no person so authorised, the authority must be satisfied that the taking of the steps would be in the adult's best interests (CASE 2);
    (3)   where the authority is satisfied that the person is a child aged 16 or 17 who lacks capacity to consent to the taking of the steps, it must obtain consent to the taking of the steps from a person authorised under the Mental Capacity Act 2005 (whether in general or specific terms) to give consent on the child's behalf, if any person is so authorised, or

if there is no person so authorised, the local authority must obtain consent to the taking of the steps from a person with parental responsibility for the child (CASE 3); and

(4)   where the authority is satisfied that the person is a child aged under 16 who does not have sufficient understanding to make an informed decision about whether to consent to the taking of the steps, it must obtain consent to the taking of the steps from a person with parental responsibility for the child (CASE 4).

As to the meaning of 'child' see PARA 2. The authority must take reasonable steps to obtain any consent which may be needed under the Social Services and Well-being (Wales) Act 2014 s 58(4): s 58(5). As to 'having' and 'lacking' capacity see PARA 8 note 10. As to a person being 'authorised' under the Mental Capacity Act 2005 see PARA 12 note 16.

Where a local authority is proposing to exercise the power under s 58(3)(a), the officer it authorises to do so must, if required, produce valid documentation setting out the authorisation to do so: s 58(7).

9   Social Services and Well-being (Wales) Act 2014 s 58(3)(b). See note 8.

10   Social Services and Well-being (Wales) Act 2014 s 187(4). As to the meanings of 'prison', 'youth detention accommodation' and 'approved premises': see PARA 87 notes 2–4.

11   A person who, without reasonable excuse, obstructs the exercise of the power under the Social Services and Well-being (Wales) Act 2014 s 58(3)(a) commits an offence and is liable on summary conviction to a fine not exceeding level 4 on the standard scale: s 58(8). As to the powers of magistrates' courts to issue fines on summary conviction see SENTENCING vol 92 (2015) PARA 176.

Where a body corporate is guilty of an offence under the Social Services and Well-being (Wales) Act 2014, and that offence is proved to have been committed with the consent or connivance of, or to have been attributable to any neglect on the part of any director, manager, secretary or other similar officer of the body corporate, or any person purporting to act in any such capacity, that person is guilty of the offence as well as the body corporate, and is liable to be proceeded against and punished accordingly: s 195A(1) (s 195A added in relation to Wales by SI 2016/413). For these purposes 'director', in relation to a body corporate whose affairs are managed by its members, means a member of the body corporate: Social Services and Well-being (Wales) Act 2014 s 195A(2) (as so added). Proceedings for an offence alleged to have been committed under the Social Services and Well-being (Wales) Act 2014 by an unincorporated body are to be brought in the name of that body (and not in that of any of its members) and, for the purposes of any such proceedings, any rules of court relating to the service of documents have effect as if that body were a corporation: s 195A(3) (as so added). Any fine imposed on an unincorporated body on its conviction of an offence under the Social Services and Well-being (Wales) Act 2014 is to be paid out of the funds of that body: s 195A(4) (as so added). If an unincorporated body is charged with an offence under the Social Services and Well-being (Wales) Act 2014, the Criminal Justice Act 1925 s 33 (see CRIMINAL PROCEDURE vol 27 (2015) PARAS 373–374) and the Magistrates' Courts Act 1980 Sch 3 (see CRIMINAL PROCEDURE vol 27 (2015) PARA 198) have effect as if a corporation had been charged: Social Services and Well-being (Wales) Act 2014 s 195A(5) (as so added). Where an offence under the Social Services and Well-being (Wales) Act 2014 committed by an unincorporated body (other than a partnership) is proved to have been committed with the consent or connivance of, or attributable to any neglect on the part of, any officer of the body or any member of its governing body, that person as well as the body is guilty of the offence and liable to be proceeded against and punished accordingly: s 195A(6) (as so added). Where an offence under the Social Services and Well-being (Wales) Act 2014 committed by a partnership or a Scottish partnership is proved to have been committed with the consent or connivance of, or to be attributable to any neglect on the part of, a partner, that partner as well as the partnership is guilty of the offence and liable to be proceeded against and punished accordingly: s 195A(7) (as so added).

386. Duty of Welsh Ministers and Social Care Wales to co-operate with each other and other authorities.

The Welsh Ministers[1] and Social Care Wales[2] must co-operate with each other in the exercise of their relevant functions[3] if they think that such co-operation will have a positive effect on the manner in which those functions are exercised[4] or will assist them in achieving their general objectives[5]; and must, in the exercise of those functions, seek to co-operate with a relevant authority[6] if they think such co-operation will have a positive effect on the manner in which the body exercises its functions[7] or will assist the body in achieving its general objectives[8]. Where a regulatory body requests the co-operation of a relevant authority[9], or a relevant authority requests the co-operation of the Welsh Ministers or Social Care Wales, the body or authority receiving the request must comply with it unless it is prevented from co-operating in the manner requested by any enactment or other rule of law[10], thinks that such co-operation would otherwise be incompatible with its own functions[11], or thinks that such co-operation would have an adverse effect on its functions or (in the case of the Welsh Ministers and Social Care Wales) on achieving its general objectives[12].

1 As to the Welsh Ministers see PARA 395: the Ministers are a 'regulatory body' for these purposes (Regulation and Inspection of Social Care (Wales) Act 2016 s 176(a)(i).
2 As to the establishment and objectives of Social Care Wales see PARA 412: Social Care Wales is a 'regulatory body' for these purposes (Regulation and Inspection of Social Care (Wales) Act 2016 s 176(a)(ii).
3 Ie the Welsh Ministers' regulatory functions (see PARA 399 note 2) and Social Care Wales' functions under Regulation and Inspection of Social Care (Wales) Act 2016: s 176(b). As to information sharing pursuant to such co-operation see PARA 388.
4 Regulation and Inspection of Social Care (Wales) Act 2016 s 178(1)(a).
5 Regulation and Inspection of Social Care (Wales) Act 2016 s 178(1)(b). The Welsh Ministers' general objectives are the objectives mentioned in s 4 (see PARA 395); Social Care Wales' general objective is the objective mentioned in s 68(1) (see PARA 412): s 176(c).
6 For these purposes the 'relevant authorities' are:
    (1)   Her Majesty's Chief Inspector for Education and Training in Wales (see EDUCATION vol 36 (2015) PARA 1147 et seq) (Regulation and Inspection of Social Care (Wales) Act 2016 s 177(1)(a));
    (2)   the Education Workforce Council (see EDUCATION vol 36 (2015) PARA 1075) (s 177(1)(b));
    (3)   each local authority (s 177(1)(c));
    (4)   each Local Health Board (s 177(1)(d));
    (5)   an NHS Trust (s 177(1)(e));
    (6)   a Welsh fire and rescue authority (s 177(1)(f));
    (7)   a Community Health Council (s 177(1)(g)); and
    (8)   such other person as may be prescribed (s 177(1)(h)).
    As to the meaning of 'local authority' see PARA 2. 'NHS Trust' means a National Health Service Trust constituted under the National Health Service (Wales) Act 2006; and 'community Health Council' means a Community Health Council continued or established under s 182: Regulation and Inspection of Social Care (Wales) Act 2016 s 177(2)(a), (c). As to Local Health Boards and community health councils see HEALTH SERVICES vol 54 (2017) PARA 97. As to NHS Trusts see HEALTH SERVICES vol 54 (2017) PARA 235. 'Welsh fire and rescue authority' means an authority in Wales constituted by a scheme under the Fire and Rescue Services Act 2004 s 2 or a scheme to which s 4 applies (see FIRE AND RESCUE SERVICE vol 51 (2013) PARAS 18–20): Regulation and Inspection of Social Care (Wales) Act 2016 s 177(2)(b).
7 Regulation and Inspection of Social Care (Wales) Act 2016 s 178(2)(a).
8 Regulation and Inspection of Social Care (Wales) Act 2016 s 178(2)(b).
9 Ie under the Regulation and Inspection of Social Care (Wales) Act 2016 s 178(2).
10 Regulation and Inspection of Social Care (Wales) Act 2016 s 178(3)(a), (4)(a).
11 Regulation and Inspection of Social Care (Wales) Act 2016 s 178(3)(b), (4)(b).
12 Regulation and Inspection of Social Care (Wales) Act 2016 s 178(3)(c), (4)(c).

387. Joint and delegated exercise of functions of Welsh Ministers and Social Care Wales. The Welsh Ministers and Social Care Wales[1] may arrange with each other for them to act together in exercising jointly one or more relevant functions[2] of one with one or more relevant functions of the other[3]. Either body may enter into such an arrangement only if it thinks that the arrangement will have a positive effect on the manner in which it exercises the function[4] or will assist the body in achieving its general objectives[5]. Such arrangements may include the establishment of a joint committee to exercise the relevant joint functions on behalf of the Welsh Ministers and Social Care Wales[6] and be on such other terms and conditions (including terms as to payment) as may be agreed between them[7].

The Welsh Ministers and Social Care Wales may each delegate any of their relevant functions to the other, if they agree that such delegation will have a positive effect on the manner in which the function is to be exercised[8] or will assist the delegating body in achieving its general objectives[9]; however, a function must not be delegated if the other body thinks that such a delegation may be detrimental to the manner in which the other body exercises its functions[10] or the achievement of the other body's general objectives[11]. Notwithstanding the general power to delegate[12], Social Care Wales may not delegate its rule-making functions or its functions relating to fitness to practise proceedings[13].

1 Ie the 'regulatory bodies': see PARA 386.
2 As to the Welsh Ministers' and Social Care Wales' 'relevant functions' see PARA 386 note 3.
3 Regulation and Inspection of Social Care (Wales) Act 2016 s 179(1). As to information sharing pursuant to such delegation see PARA 388.
4 Regulation and Inspection of Social Care (Wales) Act 2016 s 179(2)(a).
5 Regulation and Inspection of Social Care (Wales) Act 2016 s 179(2)(b).
6 Regulation and Inspection of Social Care (Wales) Act 2016 s 179(3)(a).
7 Regulation and Inspection of Social Care (Wales) Act 2016 s 179(3)(b).
8 Regulation and Inspection of Social Care (Wales) Act 2016 s 180(1)(a). A delegation under s 180(1) may be on such terms and conditions (including terms as to payment) as may be agreed between the Welsh Ministers and Social Care Wales: s 180(4). A function may be delegated under s 180(1) wholly or to any lesser extent as may be agreed by the Welsh Ministers and Social Care Wales: s 180(5). A delegation under s 180(1) does not affect any liability or responsibility of the body delegating the function for its exercise nor the ability of that body to exercise that function or make other arrangements in relation to it: s 180(6).
9 Regulation and Inspection of Social Care (Wales) Act 2016 s 180(1)(b).
10 Regulation and Inspection of Social Care (Wales) Act 2016 s 180(2)(a).
11 Regulation and Inspection of Social Care (Wales) Act 2016 s 180(2)(b).
12 Ie the Regulation and Inspection of Social Care (Wales) Act 2016 s 180(1).
13 Regulation and Inspection of Social Care (Wales) Act 2016 s 180(3). As to fitness to practice and fitness to practise proceedings see PARA 200.

388. Information sharing between Welsh Ministers and Social Care Wales. The Welsh Ministers and Social Care Wales[1] may provide information to one another, or to a relevant authority[2], in pursuance of an arrangement[3] to co-operate, jointly exercise functions or delegate functions[4]. Information must not so be provided if the person holding the information is prohibited from providing it by any enactment or other rule of law[5]; in the case of information relating to an individual, the information may be provided under these provisions only if it is provided in a form which does not identify the individual[6] or the person holding the information obtains the individual's consent to provide it[7]. Information provided in pursuance of such an arrangement must be used by the person to whom it is provided only for the purposes of co-operating, jointly exercising functions or exercising delegated functions in pursuance of the arrangement[8].

The Welsh Ministers and Social Care Wales must also disclose information obtained in the exercise of their relevant functions to any other person if it thinks that such disclosure is necessary or expedient to protect the well-being[9] of an individual in Wales[10]. Information must not be so disclosed if disclosure of the information is prohibited by any enactment or other rule of law[11]. In the case of information identifying an individual, it may be disclosed in a manner which identifies the individual only if the regulatory body thinks such identification is necessary to protect the well-being of any individual[12].

1 Ie the 'regulatory bodies': see PARA 386.
2 As to the meaning of 'relevant authority' see PARA 386 note 6.
3 Ie an arrangement made under the Regulation and Inspection of Social Care (Wales) Act 2016 Pt 9: as to such arrangements see PARA 386–387.
4 Regulation and Inspection of Social Care (Wales) Act 2016 s 181(1).
5 Regulation and Inspection of Social Care (Wales) Act 2016 s 181(2).
6 Regulation and Inspection of Social Care (Wales) Act 2016 s 181(3)(a). For the purposes of ss 181(3)(a), 182(3) information is to be treated as being in a form which identifies an individual if the individual can be identified from a combination of the information and other information provided to a regulatory body, relevant authority or other person (as it may be) by the same regulatory body: ss 181(4), 182(4).

7 Regulation and Inspection of Social Care (Wales) Act 2016 s 181(3)(b).
8 Regulation and Inspection of Social Care (Wales) Act 2016 s 181(5).
9 As to the meaning of 'well-being' see PARA 375.
10 Regulation and Inspection of Social Care (Wales) Act 2016 s 182(1). As to the meaning of 'Wales' see PARA 2 note 4. Section 181 (see the text and notes 1–9) does not affect the duty of the Welsh Ministers and Social Care Wales to disclose information for the purposes of protecting the well-being of an individual: s 181(6).
11 Regulation and Inspection of Social Care (Wales) Act 2016 s 182(2).
12 Regulation and Inspection of Social Care (Wales) Act 2016 s 182(3). See note 6.

389. Duty to assess needs for care and support and preventative services, and to enter into partnership arrangements. A local authority in Wales[1], and each Local Health Board[2] any part of whose area lies within the area of the authority, must assess[3]:

(1)   the extent to which there are people in the authority's area who need care and support[4];

(2)   the extent to which there are carers[5] in the authority's area who need support[6];

(3)   the extent to which there are people in the authority's area whose needs for care and support (or, in the case of carers, support) are not being met (by the authority, the Board or otherwise)[7];

(4)   the range and level of services required to meet the care and support needs of people in the authority's area (including the support needs of carers)[8];

(5)   the range and level of services required to provide preventative services[9] in the authority's area[10]; and

(6)   the actions required to provide the range and level of services identified in accordance with heads (4) and (5) through the medium of Welsh[11].

Authorities and Health Boards are required to enter into 'partnership arrangements' with one another in respect of the carrying out of these functions[12]. Each local authority and Health Board ('relevant body') which has carried out a joint assessment under these provisions must prepare and publish a plan[13] setting out:

(a)   the range and level of services the body proposes to provide, or arrange to be provided, in response to the assessment of needs under heads (1) to (3) above[14];

(b)   in the case of a local authority, the range and level of services the authority proposes to provide, or arrange to be provided, in seeking to provide[15] preventative services[16];

(c)   in the case of a Local Health Board, anything the Board proposes to do in connection with its duty[17] to have regard to the importance of preventative action when exercising its functions[18];

(d)   how the services set out in the plan are to be provided, including the actions the body proposes to take to provide, or arrange to provide, the services through the medium of Welsh[19];

(e)   any other action the body proposes to take in response to the assessment[20];

(f)   the details of anything the body proposes to do in response to the assessment jointly with another relevant body[21];

(g)   the resources to be deployed in doing the things set out in the plan[22].

1 As to the meanings of 'local authority' and 'Wales' see PARA 2.
2 As to Local Health Boards see HEALTH SERVICES vol 54 (2017) PARA 97.

3 Ie in accordance with regulations, which may, for example, provide for the timing and review of assessments: Social Services and Well-being (Wales) Act 2014 s 14(1), (2). At the date at which this volume states the law no such regulations had been made.

4 Social Services and Well-being (Wales) Act 2014 s 14(1)(a). As to the meanings of 'care' and 'support' see PARA 2 note 1. As to local government areas and authorities in Wales see LOCAL GOVERNMENT vol 69 (2009) PARA 22 et seq.

5 As to the meaning of 'carer' see PARA 2 note 2.

6 Social Services and Well-being (Wales) Act 2014 s 14(1)(b).

7 Social Services and Well-being (Wales) Act 2014 s 14(1)(c).

8 Social Services and Well-being (Wales) Act 2014 s 14(1)(d).

9 Ie required to achieve the purposes in the Social Services and Well-being (Wales) Act 2014 s 15(2) (see PARA 376).

10 Social Services and Well-being (Wales) Act 2014 s 14(1)(e).

11 Social Services and Well-being (Wales) Act 2014 s 14(1)(f).

12 See the Care and Support (Partnership Arrangements for Population Assessments) (Wales) Regulations 2015, SI 2015/1495 and the Partnership Arrangements (Wales) Regulations 2015, SI 2015/1989 (made under the Social Services and Well-being (Wales) Act 2014 s 166(1)–(5), 167(3), 168 (s 166(2) amended by SI 2016/413)), which set out the authorities between whom arrangements must be made and the form such arrangements are to take. See also the Social Services and Well-being (Wales) Act 2014 s 167(1), (2), (4) (resources for partnership arrangements). Partnership arrangements made pursuant to these provisions do not affect the liability of a Local Health Board for the exercise of any of its functions, the liability of a local authority for the exercise of any of its functions, or any power or duty to recover charges in respect of services provided in the exercise of any local authority functions: s 166(6). The Welsh Ministers must issue, and from time to time revise, guidance about partnership arrangements made under these provisions: s 169(1). In exercising functions conferred on them under or by virtue of these provisions a local authority, a Local Health Board, a team or person carrying out partnership arrangements in accordance with the Care and Support (Partnership Arrangements for Population Assessments) (Wales) Regulations 2015, SI 2015/1495, and a partnership board established under the Partnership Arrangements (Wales) Regulations 2015, SI 2015/1989, must have regard to that guidance and to any outcomes specified in a statement issued under the Social Services and Well-being (Wales) Act 2014 s 8 (see PARA 396): s 169(2).

13 A relevant body's plan may be published by including it within a local well-being plan published under the Well-being of Future Generations (Wales) Act 2015 s 39 or s 44(5) by a public services board of which the body is a member: Social Services and Well-being (Wales) Act 2014 s 14A(3) (s 14A added by the Well-being of Future Generations (Wales) Act 2015 Sch 4 para 34). A local authority and a Local Health Board who have carried out a joint assessment together under the Social Services and Well-being (Wales) Act 2014 s 14(1) may jointly prepare and publish a plan under these provisions: s 14A(4) (as so added). Two or more local authorities may jointly prepare and publish a plan under these provisions, but such a joint plan may be published by including it within a local well-being plan only if each local authority is a member of the public services board (see the Well-being of Future Generations (Wales) Act 2015 ss 47, 49 (merging of public services boards)): Social Services and Well-being (Wales) Act 2014 s 14A(5) (as so added). A relevant body must submit to the Welsh Ministers any part of a plan it has prepared under s 14A(2) which relates to the health and well-being of carers and any other part of such a plan as may be specified by regulations: s 14A(6) (as so added). Regulations may make provision about plans prepared and published under s 14A(2), including provision specifying when a plan is to be published, about reviewing a plan, about consulting persons when preparing or reviewing a plan, and about the monitoring and evaluation of services and other action set out in a plan: s 14A(7) (as so added). For the regulations so made see the Care and Support (Area Planning) (Wales) Regulations 2017, SI 2017/56.

14 Social Services and Well-being (Wales) Act 2014 s 14A(1), (2)(a) (as added: see note 13).

15 Ie in seeking achieve the purposes in the Social Services and Well-being (Wales) Act 2014 s 15(2).

16 Social Services and Well-being (Wales) Act 2014 s 14A(2)(b) (as added: see note 13).

17 Ie under the Social Services and Well-being (Wales) Act 2014 s 15(5) (see PARA 376).

18 Social Services and Well-being (Wales) Act 2014 s 14A(2)(c) (as added: see note 13).

19 Social Services and Well-being (Wales) Act 2014 s 14A(2)(d) (as added: see note 13).

20 Social Services and Well-being (Wales) Act 2014 s 14A(2)(e) (as added: see note 13).

21 Social Services and Well-being (Wales) Act 2014 s 14A(2)(f) (as added: see note 13).

22 Social Services and Well-being (Wales) Act 2014 s 14A(2)(g) (as added: see note 13).

390. Maintenance of register of sight-impaired, hearing impaired and disabled persons. A local authority in Wales[1] must establish and maintain a register[2] of the persons ordinarily resident in the authority's area who:

(1)   are sight-impaired or severely sight-impaired[3];

(2)   are hearing-impaired or severely hearing-impaired[4]; or

(3)   have sight and hearing impairments which, in combination, have a significant effect on their day to day lives[5].

Provision is also made for local authorities in Wales to establish and maintain a register of persons[6] who:

(a)   are disabled[7];

(b)   are not disabled but have a physical or mental impairment which gives rise, or which the authority considers may in the future give rise, to needs for care and support[8]; or

(c)   comes within any other category of persons the authority considers appropriate to include in a register of persons who have, or who the authority considers may in the future have, needs for care and support[9].

The registers so established and maintained may be used in the exercise of the authority's functions[10].

1   As to the meanings of 'local authority' and 'Wales' see PARA 2.
2   The register must identify, in respect of each person included in it:
    (1)   into which of heads (1) to (3) in the text that person falls (Social Services and Well-being (Wales) Act 2014 s 18(2)(a)); and
    (2)   the person's linguistic circumstances (s 18(2)(b)).
    Nothing in s 18 requires a local authority to include any person in a register unless the person has applied to be included in the register or an application to be so included has been made on the person's behalf: s 18(9). Where a local authority includes a person in a register maintained under this section, the authority must inform the person that he or she has been so included, and if a request is made by the person or on the person's behalf, must remove from the register any personal data (within the meaning of the Data Protection Act 1998: see s 1(1); and CONFIDENCE AND INFORMATIONAL PRIVACY vol 19 (2011) PARA 97) relating to that person: Social Services and Well-being (Wales) Act 2014 s 18(10).
3   Social Services and Well-being (Wales) Act 2014 s 18(1)(a). Regulations may specify, for the purposes of s 18(1), categories of persons who are, or are not, to be treated as falling within s 18(1)(a), (b) or (c): s 18(3). At the date at which this volume states the law no such regulations had been made.
4   Social Services and Well-being (Wales) Act 2014 s 18(1)(b). See note 2.
5   Social Services and Well-being (Wales) Act 2014 s 18(1)(c). See note 2.
6   The maintenance of such a register is compulsory in respect of children who are within the local authority's area (Social Services and Well-being (Wales) Act 2014 s 18(4)) and is discretionary in respect of adults who are ordinarily resident in the local authority's area (s 18(5)). A local authority may categorise people included in a register under s 18(4) or (5) as it thinks fit and must identify the linguistic circumstances of those people in the relevant register: s 18(7). As to the meanings of 'adult' and 'child' see PARA 2.
7   Social Services and Well-being (Wales) Act 2014 s 18(6)(a).
8   Social Services and Well-being (Wales) Act 2014 s 18(6)(b). As to the meanings of 'care' and 'support' see PARA 2 note 1.
9   Social Services and Well-being (Wales) Act 2014 s 18(6)(c).
10 Social Services and Well-being (Wales) Act 2014 s 18(8). For example, the registers may be used for the purpose of planning the provision by the authority of services to meet needs for care and support or support for carers (s 18(8)(a)) and monitoring changes over time in the number of people in the authority's area with needs for care and support and the types of needs they or their carers have (s 18(8)(b)). As to the meaning of 'carer' see PARA 2 note 2.

391. Complaints. Regulations may make provision about the consideration of complaints relating to:

(1)   the discharge by a local authority in Wales[1] of its social services functions[2];

(2)   the provision of services by another person pursuant to arrangements made by a local authority in the discharge of those functions[3];

(3)   the provision of services by a local authority or another person[4] in relation to the functions of an NHS body[5] so far as exercisable in relation to Wales[6].

The regulations may make provision about:

(a)   the persons who may make a complaint[7];

(b)   the complaints which may, or may not, be made[8];

(c)   the persons to whom complaints may be made[9];

(d)   complaints which need not be considered[10];

(e)   the period within which complaints must be made[11];

(f)   the procedure to be followed in making and considering a complaint[12];

(g)   matters which are excluded from consideration[13];

(h)   the making of a report or recommendations about a complaint[14]; and

(i)   the action to be taken as a result of a complaint[15].

The regulations may also provide for who may consider the complaint[16], the giving of assistance to complainants[17] and the referral of complaints[18], and may make administrative provision[19]. However the regulations may not make provision about complaints capable of being[20] considered as representations[21].

At the date at which this volume states the law no such regulations had been made.

1   As to the meanings of 'local authority' and 'Wales' see PARA 2.
2   Social Services and Well-being (Wales) Act 2014 s 171(1)(a). As to a local authority's social services functions see PARA 373.
3   Social Services and Well-being (Wales) Act 2014 s 171(1)(b).
4   Ie in pursuance of arrangements made by the authority under the National Health Service Act 2006 s 35 or the National Health Service (Wales) Act 2006 s 33 (see HEALTH SERVICES vol 54 (2017) PARAS 260, 282).
5   Ie within the meaning of the National Health Service (Wales) Act 2006 s 33 or the National Health Service Act 2006 s 35.
6   Social Services and Well-being (Wales) Act 2014 s 171(1)(c).
7   Social Services and Well-being (Wales) Act 2014 s 172(1), (2)(a).
8   Social Services and Well-being (Wales) Act 2014 s 172(2)(b).
9   Social Services and Well-being (Wales) Act 2014 s 172(2)(c).
10 Social Services and Well-being (Wales) Act 2014 s 172(2)(d).
11 Social Services and Well-being (Wales) Act 2014 s 172(2)(e).
12 Social Services and Well-being (Wales) Act 2014 s 172(2)(f).
13 Social Services and Well-being (Wales) Act 2014 s 172(2)(g).
14 Social Services and Well-being (Wales) Act 2014 s 172(2)(h).
15 Social Services and Well-being (Wales) Act 2014 s 172(2)(i).
16 The regulations may provide for a complaint to be considered by one or more of:
        (1)   the local authority in respect of whose functions the complaint is made (Social Services and Well-being (Wales) Act 2014 s 171(2)(a));
        (2)   an independent panel established under the regulations (s 171(2)(b)); and
        (3)   any other person or body other than a Minister of the Crown (s 171(2)(c)).
17 Regulations may require local authorities to:
        (1)   make arrangements to provide assistance (by way of representation or otherwise) to persons who make, or intend to make, a complaint under regulations made under the Social Services and Well-being (Wales) Act 2014 s 171 (s 173(1)(a)); and
        (2)   give publicity to the arrangements for the provision of that assistance (s 173(1)(b)).
    The regulations may, for example, make provision about:
        (a)   the persons to whom assistance must be provided (s 173(2)(a));
        (b)   the kind of assistance that must be provided to those persons (s 173(2)(b));
        (c)   the persons by whom that assistance may be provided (s 173(2)(c));
        (d)   the stage or stages in the consideration of a complaint in relation to which that assistance must be provided (s 173(2)(d)); and
        (e)   the kind of publicity that must be given to the arrangements for the provision of that assistance (s 173(2)(e)).

18 The regulations may provide for a complaint or any matter raised by the complaint:

   (1)   to be referred to the Public Services Ombudsman for Wales ('the Ombudsman') for the Ombudsman to consider whether to investigate the complaint or matter under the Public Services Ombudsman (Wales) Act 2005 (and to be treated by the Ombudsman as a complaint duly referred under s 2(3): LOCAL GOVERNMENT vol 69 (2009) PARA 849) (Social Services and Well-being (Wales) Act 2014 s 171(3)(a)); or

   (2)   to be referred to any other person or body for that person or body to consider whether to take any action otherwise than under the regulations (s 171(3)(b)).

19 The regulations may:

   (1)   require a person about whom, or a body about which, a complaint is made to make a payment in relation to the consideration of the complaint under the regulations (Social Services and Well-being (Wales) Act 2014 s 172(3)(a));

   (2)   require a payment of that kind to be made to a person or body specified in the regulations and to be of an amount specified in, or calculated or determined under, the regulations (s 172(3)(b)); and

   (3)   require an independent panel to review the amount chargeable under head (1) above in a particular case and, if the panel thinks fit, to substitute a lesser amount (s 172(3)(c)).

The regulations may require a person who, or a body which, considers complaints under the regulations to give publicity to the procedures to be followed under the regulations: s 172(4). The regulations may also:

   (a)   provide for different parts or aspects of a complaint to be treated differently (s 172(5)(a));

   (b)   require the production of information or documents to enable a complaint to be properly considered (s 172(5)(b)); and

   (c)   authorise the disclosure of information or documents relevant to a complaint to a person who, or a body which, is considering a complaint under the regulations or to whom a complaint has been referred (despite any rule of common law that would otherwise prohibit or restrict the disclosure) (s 172(5)(c)).

The regulations may make provision about complaints which raise both matters falling to be considered under the regulations and matters falling to be considered under other statutory complaints procedures (ie procedures established by or under an enactment within the legislative competence of the National Assembly for Wales) including (among other things) provision to:

   (i)   enable a complaint of that kind to be made under the regulations (s 172(6)(a), (7)); and

   (ii)   secure that matters falling to be considered under other statutory complaints procedures are treated as if they had been raised in a complaint made under the appropriate procedures (s 172(6)(b)).

20 Ie under the Social Services and Well-being (Wales) Act 2014 s 174 or s 176 (see CHILDREN AND YOUNG PERSONS vol 10 (2017) PARAS 1123, 1124.

21 Social Services and Well-being (Wales) Act 2014 s 171(4).

392. Provision of information and advice. A local authority in Wales[1] must secure the provision of a service for providing people with information[2] and advice relating to care and support[3] and assistance in accessing care and support[4]. The authority must seek to ensure that the service is sufficient to enable a person to make plans for meeting needs for care and support that might arise[5] and provides information, advice and assistance to a person in a manner which is accessible to that person[6]. The service must include, as a minimum, the publication of information and advice on:

   (1)   the statutory care and support system[7] and how the system operates in the authority's area[8];

   (2)   the types of care and support available in the authority's area[9];

   (3)   how to access the care and support that is available[10]; and

   (4)   how to raise concerns about the well-being of a person who appears to have needs for care and support[11].

1   As to the meanings of 'local authority' and 'Wales' see PARA 2. Two or more local authorities may jointly secure the provision of a service under these provisions for their combined area; and where they do so references to a local authority are read as references to the authorities acting jointly and references to a local authority's area are read as references to the combined area: Social Services and Well-being (Wales) Act 2014 s 17(6).

2   In this context 'information' includes, but is not limited to, financial information (including information about direct payments): Social Services and Well-being (Wales) Act 2014 s 17(2).
3   Social Services and Well-being (Wales) Act 2014 s 17(1)(a). As to direct payments see PARAS 125–130. As to the meanings of 'care' and 'support' see PARA 2 note 1; in this context 'care and support' includes support for carers: s 17(7). As to the meaning of 'carer' see PARA 2 note 2. Where advocacy services are being provided for a person under s 17 and regulations under s 181 (provision of advocacy services: see PARA 104) would (apart from this provision) impose a requirement upon a local authority to make advocacy services available to that person in respect of the same matters, that requirement does not apply: s 182(2).
4   Social Services and Well-being (Wales) Act 2014 s 17(1)(b). A local authority in Wales may impose charges for assistance provided under s 17: see the Care and Support (Charging) (Wales) Regulations 2015, SI 2015/1843, reg 16; and PARA 376 note 24.
5   Social Services and Well-being (Wales) Act 2014 s 17(3)(a).
6   Social Services and Well-being (Wales) Act 2014 s 17(3)(b).
7   Ie the system provided for by the Social Services and Well-being (Wales) Act 2014.
8   Social Services and Well-being (Wales) Act 2014 s 17(4)(a). As to local government areas and authorities in Wales see LOCAL GOVERNMENT vol 69 (2009) PARA 22 et seq.
9   Social Services and Well-being (Wales) Act 2014 s 17(4)(b). For this purpose a Local Health Board or an NHS Trust providing services in the area of a local authority must provide that authority with information about the care and support it provides in the authority's area: s 17(5).
10 Social Services and Well-being (Wales) Act 2014 s 17(4)(c).
11 Social Services and Well-being (Wales) Act 2014 s 17(4)(d).

393.   Power to promote and undertake studies and research. A local authority in Wales[1] may conduct, commission, or assist in the conduct of, research into any matter connected with any of its social services functions[2], any of its functions[3] as a local mental health partner[4], or the functions of Safeguarding Boards[5].

1   As to the meanings of 'local authority' and 'Wales' see PARA 2.
2   Social Services and Well-being (Wales) Act 2014 s 184(2)(a), (12)(a). As to the meanings of 'local authority' and 'Wales' see PARA 2; as to a local authority's social services functions see PARA 373. See note 2.
3   Ie under the Mental Health (Wales) Measure 2010 (see MENTAL HEALTH AND CAPACITY).
4   Social Services and Well-being (Wales) Act 2014 s 184(12)(b).
5   Social Services and Well-being (Wales) Act 2014 s 184(2)(b). 'Safeguarding Board' means a Safeguarding Children Board or a Safeguarding Adults Board established under s 134 (see PARAS 238): s 184(11).

394.   Annual reports. As from a day to be appointed[1], as soon as is reasonably practicable after the end of a financial year[2], a local authority in Wales[3] must prepare and publish an annual report about the exercise of its social services functions[4] in respect of that year[5]. The report must include details[6] of how the authority has exercised its social services functions during the financial year[7] such other information as may be prescribed by regulations[8]. A local authority must send a copy of a published annual report to the Welsh Ministers[9].

1   The Social Services and Well-being (Wales) Act 2014 s 144A is added, as from a day to be appointed, by the Regulation and Inspection of Social Care (Wales) Act 2014 s 56(1). At the date at which this volume states the law no day had been appointed for this purpose.
2   For these purposes 'financial year' means the period of one year beginning on 1 April and ending on 31 March: Social Services and Well-being (Wales) Act 2014 s 144A(6) (prospectively added: see note 1).
3   As to the meanings of 'local authority' and 'Wales' see PARA 2.
4   As to a local authority's social services functions see PARA 373.
5   Social Services and Well-being (Wales) Act 2014 s 144A(1) (prospectively added: see note 1). An annual report must be in the form prescribed by the Local Authority Social Services Annual Reports (Prescribed Form) (Wales) Regulations 2017, SI 2017/274 (made under the Social Services and Well-being (Wales) Act 2014 s 144A(4) (as so prospectively added)).
6   Ie, including details of the extent to which the authority has:
    (1)   acted in accordance with requirements imposed on local authorities by a code issued under the Social Services and Well-being (Wales) Act 2014 s 9 (codes to help achieve outcomes in relation to well-being: see PARA 396) (s 144A(2)(a)(i) (prospectively added: see note 1));

(2)   acted in accordance with any relevant requirements contained in a code issued under s 145 (codes about the exercise of social services functions: see PARA 410) (s 144A(2)(a)(ii) (as so prospectively added)); and

(3)   had regard to any relevant guidelines in a code issued under s 145 (s 144A(2)(a)(ii) (as so prospectively added)).

The details provided under s 144A(2)(a)(ii) must state how the authority has satisfied any requirements contained in a code relating to assessing the needs of an individual in accordance with Pt 3 (ss 19–31) and meeting needs under Pt 4 (ss 32–58): s 144A(3) (as so prospectively added).

7   Social Services and Well-being (Wales) Act 2014 s 144A(2)(a) (prospectively added: see note 1).

8   Social Services and Well-being (Wales) Act 2014 s 144A(2)(b) (prospectively added: see note 1). At the date at which this volume states the law no regulations had been made for this purpose.

9   Social Services and Well-being (Wales) Act 2014 s 144A(5) (prospectively added: see note 1). As to the Welsh Ministers see PARA 395.

(ii) The Welsh Ministers

A. GENERAL POWERS AND DUTIES

395. Ministerial functions and oversight. The principal enactments relating to the provision of social care in Wales, ie the Social Services and Well-being (Wales) Act 2014[1] and the Regulation and Inspection of Social Care (Wales) Act 2016[2], confer all ministerial functions on the Welsh Ministers[3], although the Secretary of State[4] has a consultative role. Ministerial functions relating to disclosure and barring under the Safeguarding Vulnerable Groups Act 2006 have not, however, been devolved to the Welsh Ministers and remain with the Secretary of State, although the Welsh Ministers have a consultative function where applicable[5]. Ministerial functions under other legislation relating to social services[6] have also been devolved to the Welsh Ministers by the operation of the devolution legislation[7].

1   As from a day to be appointed, in exercising functions under the Social Services and Well-being (Wales) Act 2014 Pt 8 (ss 143–161C) (social services functions) the Welsh Ministers must seek to promote and maintain high standards in the provision of local authority social services functions (s 144C (prospectively added by the Regulation and Inspection of Social Care (Wales) Act 2016 s 188(1)); until that day, the Ministers have the general function of encouraging improvement in the provision of Welsh local authority social services (Health and Social Care (Community Health and Standards) Act 2003 s 92 (ss 92, 96, 97 prospectively repealed by the Regulation and Inspection of Social Care (Wales) Act 2016 Sch 3 para 18)). Until the appointed day the matters to which the Ministers must have regard in exercising its functions under the Health and Social Care (Community Health and Standards) Act 2003 s 92 are the same as those to which they must have regard in conducting a review of local authority social services functions under s 94 (see PARA 400): see s 97(1)(a), (2); and PARA 400.

At the date at which this volume states the law no day had been appointed for these purposes.

2   The general objectives of the Welsh Ministers in exercising their functions under the Regulation and Inspection of Social Care (Wales) Act 2016 Pt 1 (ss 1–64) are to protect, promote and maintain the safety and well-being of people who use regulated services and to promote and maintain high standards in the provision of regulated services: s 4. As to the meaning of 'regulated services' see PARA 203.

3   As to the Welsh Ministers and the Welsh Assembly Government see the Government of Wales Act 2006 Pt 2 (ss 45–92); and CONSTITUTIONAL AND ADMINISTRATIVE LAW vol 20 (2014) PARA 373 et seq. As to the meaning of 'Wales' see PARA 2 note 4.

4   As to the Secretary of State see PARA 333.

5   See PARAS 241–314.

6   Ie under the Jobseekers Act 1995 s 30 (see PARA 151) and the Local Government Act 2000 s 93; and PARA 150.

7   Ie by the operation of the Government of Wales Act 2006 Sch 11 paras 26, 30 (see STATUTES AND LEGISLATIVE PROCESS vol 96 (2012) PARAS 1034–1035), which provide that instruments transferring functions to the National Assembly for Wales under the Government of Wales Act 1998 s 22 (repealed) continue to have effect following the transfer of the Assembly's executive functions to the Welsh Ministers as conferring those functions on those Ministers, and that

functions originally conferred on the Assembly by enactments made after the establishment of that body are also transferred to the Welsh Ministers. For provisions as to the exercise of transferred functions see the Government of Wales Act 2006 Sch 3, Sch 11 paras 33–35; and STATUTES AND LEGISLATIVE PROCESS vol 96 (2012) PARA 1035. Until the appointed day (see note 1) the Ministers also have power to confer on themselves, by regulations, functions corresponding to the functions of the Care Quality Commission under the Health and Social Care Act 2008 Pt 1 (ss 1–97) (see PARAS 336–357) and functions relating to the provision of services assigned to Her Majesty's Chief Inspector of Education, Children's Services and Skills under the Education and Inspections Act 2006 s 118(4) (see EDUCATION vol 36 (2015) PARA 1136), although that power has never been exercised: see the Health and Social Care (Community Health and Standards) Act 2003 s 96 (substituted by the Education and Inspections Act 2006 Sch 14 para 88; amended by the Health and Social Care Act 2008 Sch 5 para 42; prospectively repealed (see note 1)).

396. Duty to issue statement of well-being outcomes. The Welsh Ministers[1] must issue a statement[2] relating to the well-being[3] of persons in Wales who need care and support[4] and carers[5] in Wales who need support[6]. The statement must specify the outcomes that are to be achieved, in terms of the well-being of such persons, by means of care and support (or, in the case of carers, support) provided[7] by local authorities[8] and care and support (or, in the case of carers, support) provided by others which is of a kind that could be so provided by local authorities[9]. The statement must also specify measures by reference to which the achievement of those outcomes is to be assessed[10].

The Ministers must issue, and from time to time revise, a code to help achieve the outcomes specified in such a statement[11]. The code may give guidance to any person providing care and support (or, in the case of carers, support)[12] and impose requirements on local authorities in relation to provision of that kind[13]. The following are examples of the matters which may be set out in the code:

(1)   standards ('quality standards') to be achieved in the provision of care and support (or, in the case of carers, support)[14];

(2)   measures ('performance measures') by reference to which performance in achieving those quality standards can be assessed[15];

(3)   targets ('performance targets') to be met in relation to those performance measures[16]; and

(4)   steps to be taken in relation to those standards, measures and targets[17].

Local authorities must comply with the code[18], and the Ministers may do anything which they consider likely to help local authorities' compliance[19].

1   As to the Welsh Ministers see PARA 395.
2   The statement must be issued within 3 years beginning with 1 May 2014 (ie the date on which the Social Services and Well-being (Wales) Act 2014 received royal assent): s 8(2). The Ministers must keep the statement under review and may revise the statement whenever they consider it appropriate to do so: s 8(6). Before issuing or revising the statement, the Ministers must consult such persons as they think fit: s 8(7). The Ministers must, on issuing or revising the statement, lay a copy of the statement before the National Assembly for Wales and publish the statement on their website: s 8(8).
3   As to the meaning of 'well-being' see PARA 375.
4   Social Services and Well-being (Wales) Act 2014 s 8(1)(a). As to the meanings of 'care' and 'support' see PARA 2 note 1.
5   As to the meaning of 'carer' see PARA 54 note 2.
6   Social Services and Well-being (Wales) Act 2014 s 8(1)(b). The Welsh Ministers may publish reports on the progress made by local authorities and others towards the achievement of the outcomes specified in a statement under s 8: s 13(b)(i). As to the meanings of 'local authority' and 'Wales' see PARA 2.
7   Ie under the Social Services and Well-being (Wales) Act 2014.
8   Social Services and Well-being (Wales) Act 2014 s 8(3)(a). The Welsh Ministers may publish information about the provision of care and support (or, in the case of carers, support) of the kind described in s 8(3): s 13(a).
9   Social Services and Well-being (Wales) Act 2014 s 8(3)(b). See note 8.

10 Social Services and Well-being (Wales) Act 2014 s 8(4). The statement may specify different outcomes or measures for different categories of people who need care and support (or, in the case of carers, support): s 8(5).

11 Social Services and Well-being (Wales) Act 2014 s 9(1). The Ministers must publish on their website the code which is for the time being in force and make available to the public (whether on their website or otherwise) codes which are no longer in force: s 9(5). Before issuing or revising a code under s 9 the Welsh Ministers must consult such persons as they think fit on a draft of the code (or revised code): s 11(1). If the Ministers wish to proceed with the draft (with or without modifications) they must lay a copy of the draft before the National Assembly for Wales (s 11(2) and if before the end of the 40 day period beginning on the day on which the draft is laid before the Assembly (and not including any time during which the Assembly is dissolved or is in recess for more than four days) the Assembly resolves not to approve the draft, the Ministers must not issue the code (or revised code) in the form of that draft (this does not prevent a new draft of a code (or revised code) from being laid before the Assembly): s 11(3), (5), (6). If no such resolution is made before the end of that period the Ministers must issue the code (or revised code) in the form of the draft and the code (or revised code) comes into force on the date appointed by order of the Ministers: s 11(4). The Ministers may revoke a code (or revised code) issued under s 11 in a further code or by direction (s 11(7)); any such direction must be laid before the Assembly (s 11(8)).

12 Ie care and support, or support, of the kind described in the Social Services and Well-being (Wales) Act 2014 s 8(3) (see the text and notes 7–9).

13 Social Services and Well-being (Wales) Act 2014 s 9(2).

14 Social Services and Well-being (Wales) Act 2014 s 9(3)(a). The code may specify different quality standards for different categories of care and support (or, in the case of carers, support) and different categories of people who need care and support (or, in the case of carers, support) (s 9(4)(a)) and different quality standards to apply at different times (s 9(4)(c)). The Welsh Ministers may publish reports on the progress made by local authorities and others towards the achievement of the quality standards (if any) specified in a code under s 9: s 13(b)(ii).

15 Social Services and Well-being (Wales) Act 2014 s 9(3)(b). The code may specify different performance measures or performance targets for different categories of care and support (or, in the case of carers, support) and different categories of persons who provide care and support (or, in the case of carers, support) (s 9(4)(b)) and different performance measures or performance targets to apply at different times (s 9(4)(c)).

16 Social Services and Well-being (Wales) Act 2014 s 9(3)(c). See note 15. The Welsh Ministers may publish reports on the progress made by local authorities and others towards the achievement of the performance targets (if any) specified in a code under s 9: s 13(b)(ii).

17 Social Services and Well-being (Wales) Act 2014 s 9(3)(d).

18 See the Social Services and Well-being (Wales) Act 2014 s 10; and PARA 374.

19 Social Services and Well-being (Wales) Act 2014 s 12(1). This includes power:

    (1)   to enter into arrangements or agreements with any person (s 12(2)(a));

    (2)   to co-operate with, or facilitate or co-ordinate the activities of, any person (s 12(2)(b));

    (3)   to exercise on behalf of any person any functions of that person (s 12(2)(c));

    (4)   to provide staff, goods, services or accommodation to any person (s 12(2)(d)).

    If a local authority asks them to do so, the Welsh Ministers must consider whether to exercise their power under s 12(1): s 12(4). Unless the Ministers are exercising the power under s 12(1) in response to a request so made they must, before exercising that power, consult the local authority which they propose to assist by the exercise of the power and those persons who appear to the Welsh Ministers to be key stakeholders affected by the exercise of the power (s 12(3)).

397. Engagement with the public. As from a day to be appointed[1] the Welsh Ministers[2] must make information about the exercise of their regulatory functions available for the public[3] and prepare and publish a statement of their policy with respect to involving the public in the exercise of those functions (whether by consultation or other means)[4]. The Ministers may revise a statement of policy and must publish the revised statement[5] or may publish a new statement of policy[6]. A statement of policy (or revised statement) must, in particular, address:

(1)   the involvement of the public in inspections[7] of service providers[8]; and

(2)   the involvement of carers[9] in the exercise of the Ministers' regulatory functions[10].

The Ministers must have regard to the most recent policy statement published under these provisions when exercising their regulatory functions[11].

1   At the date at which this volume states the law the Regulation and Inspection of Social Care (Wales) Act 2016 s 41 (see the text and notes 2–11) had not been brought into force.
2   As to the Welsh Ministers see PARA 395.
3   Regulation and Inspection of Social Care (Wales) Act 2016 s 41(1)(a) (not yet in force). The Ministers must lay a copy of a published statement of policy (or revised statement) before the National Assembly for Wales: s 41(4).
4   Regulation and Inspection of Social Care (Wales) Act 2016 s 41(1)(b) (not yet in force).
5   Regulation and Inspection of Social Care (Wales) Act 2016 s 41(2)(a) (not yet in force).
6   Regulation and Inspection of Social Care (Wales) Act 2016 s 41(2)(b) (not yet in force).
7   Ie inspections carried out under the Regulation and Inspection of Social Care (Wales) Act 2016 Pt 1 Ch 3 (ss 32–37) (see PARAS 224–227).
8   Regulation and Inspection of Social Care (Wales) Act 2016 s 41(3)(a) (not yet in force).
9   Ie within the meaning of the Social Services and Well-being (Wales) Act 2014 s 3 (see PARA 54 note 2).
10 Regulation and Inspection of Social Care (Wales) Act 2016 s 41(3)(b) (not yet in force).
11 Regulation and Inspection of Social Care (Wales) Act 2016 s 41(5) (not yet in force).

398. Duty to keep register of service providers. As from a day to be appointed[1] the Welsh Ministers[2] must maintain a register of service providers[3]. An entry in the register in respect of a service provider must show the following information[4]:

    (1)   the regulated services[5] that the service provider is registered to provide[6];

    (2)   the places at, from or in relation to which the provider is registered to provide those services[7];

    (3)   the name of the responsible individual[8] registered in respect of each such place[9];

    (4)   the date on which the provider's registration took effect in respect of each such regulated service and place[10];

    (5)   details of any other conditions imposed on the service provider's registration[11];

    (6)   a summary of any inspection report relating to the service provider which has[12] been published[13];

    (7)   such other information as may be prescribed[14].

1   At the date at which this volume states the law the Regulation and Inspection of Social Care (Wales) Act 2016 Pt 1 (ss 1–64) had yet to be brought into force.
2   As to the Welsh Ministers see PARA 395.
3   Regulation and Inspection of Social Care (Wales) Act 2016 s 38(1) (not yet in force: see note 1). As to the meaning of 'service provider' see PARA 203 note 4. The Ministers must publish the register and make it available for public inspection free of charge, in such manner, and at such times, as they think appropriate (s 38(3)), and must comply with any reasonable request made by a person for a copy of, or an extract from, the register (s 38(4) (not yet in force)) (although they may refuse to comply with such a request in prescribed circumstances (s 38(5)(b) (not yet in force))). At the date at which this volume states the law no such circumstances had been prescribed. The Ministers may by regulations make provision requiring a fee to be paid by a person for a copy of the register published under s 38(3), or an extract of it: s 40(1)(e) (not yet in force). As to such regulations and fees see further s 40(2)–(4); and PARA 216 note 3.
4   The Welsh Ministers may omit prescribed information from the published register in prescribed circumstances: Regulation and Inspection of Social Care (Wales) Act 2016 s 38(5)(a) (not yet in force: see note 1). At the date at which this volume states the law no such circumstances had been prescribed.
5   As to the meaning of 'regulated service' see PARA 203.
6   Regulation and Inspection of Social Care (Wales) Act 2016 s 38(2)(a) (not yet in force: see note 1). As to the registration of service providers see PARAS 203–223.
7   Regulation and Inspection of Social Care (Wales) Act 2016 s 38(2)(b) (not yet in force: see note 1).
8   As to the responsible individual see PARA 212.
9   Regulation and Inspection of Social Care (Wales) Act 2016 s 38(2)(c) (not yet in force: see note 1).
10 Regulation and Inspection of Social Care (Wales) Act 2016 s 38(2)(d) (not yet in force: see note 1).
11 Regulation and Inspection of Social Care (Wales) Act 2016 s 38(2)(e) (not yet in force: see note 1).

12 Ie under the Regulation and Inspection of Social Care (Wales) Act 2016 s 36(3)(a) (see PARA 227).
13 Regulation and Inspection of Social Care (Wales) Act 2016 s 38(2)(f) (not yet in force: see note 1).
14 Regulation and Inspection of Social Care (Wales) Act 2016 s 38(2)(g) (not yet in force: see note 1).
   At the date at which this volume states the law no additional information had been prescribed for this purpose.

399. Annual report on regulatory functions. As from a day to be appointed[1], as soon as is reasonably practicable after the end of a financial year, the Welsh Ministers[2] must prepare and publish an annual report about the exercise of their regulatory functions[3] in respect of that financial year[4]. The annual report must include details of how the Ministers have exercised those functions during the year[5], the extent to which they have, in the exercise of those functions achieved the general[6] objectives[7] and had regard to the most recent statement[8] of policy[9], and how statutory equality and child protection duties[10] affected the exercise of those functions during the year[11]. The annual report may include any other information the Welsh Ministers think appropriate[12].

1 At the date at which this volume states the law the Regulation and Inspection of Social Care (Wales) Act 2016 Pt 1 (ss 1–64) had yet to be brought into force.
2 As to the Welsh Ministers see PARA 395.
3 'Regulatory functions' means the Welsh Ministers' functions under the Regulation and Inspection of Social Care (Wales) Act 2016 Pt 1 (ss 1–64), the Social Services and Well-being (Wales) Act 2014 s 94A (see CHILDREN AND YOUNG PERSONS vol 10 (2017) PARA 894) and ss 149A–161B (see PARAS 374, 404–405, 400–402, 408, 411), and the Adoption and Children Act 2002 s 15 (inspection of premises relating to adoption services: see CHILDREN AND YOUNG PERSONS vol 9 (2017) PARAS 551–552), although any function of making, confirming or approving subordinate legislation (as defined by the Government of Wales Act 2006 s 158(1)) is not a regulatory function: Regulation and Inspection of Social Care (Wales) Act 2016 s 3(1)(b) (not yet in force: see note 1).
4 Regulation and Inspection of Social Care (Wales) Act 2016 s 42(1) (not yet in force: see note 1). The Ministers must lay a copy of a published annual report before the National Assembly for Wales: s 42(5) (not yet in force: see note 1).
5 Regulation and Inspection of Social Care (Wales) Act 2016 s 42(2)(a) (not yet in force: see note 1).
6 Ie the objectives referred to in the Regulation and Inspection of Social Care (Wales) Act 2016 s 4 (see PARA 395).
7 Regulation and Inspection of Social Care (Wales) Act 2016 s 42(2)(b)(i) (not yet in force: see note 1).
8 Ie the most recent statement published under the Regulation and Inspection of Social Care (Wales) Act 2016 s 41 (see PARA 397).
9 Regulation and Inspection of Social Care (Wales) Act 2016 s 42(2)(b)(ii) (not yet in force: see note 1).
10 Ie (by virtue of the Regulation and Inspection of Social Care (Wales) Act 2016 s 42(4)(a)–(d) (not yet in force: see note 1)) the Welsh Ministers' duties under:
   (1)   the Equality Act 2010 s 149 (public sector equality duty) (see DISCRIMINATION vol 33 (2013) PARAS 264–269);
   (2)   the Rights of Children and Young Persons (Wales) Measure 2011 s 1(1) (duty to have due regard to the United Nations Convention on the Rights of the Child) (see CHILDREN AND YOUNG PERSONS vol 9 (2017) PARA 290; RIGHTS AND FREEDOMS vol 88A (2013) PARA 112);
   (3)   the Social Services and Well-being (Wales) Act 2014 s 7(1) (duty to have due regard to the United Nations Principles for Older Persons when exercising functions relating to adult social services) (see PARA 316); and
   (4)   the Welsh Language (Wales) Measure 2011 Pt 4 (ss 25–70) (standards) (see CONSTITUTIONAL AND ADMINISTRATIVE LAW vol 20 (2014) PARA 408 et seq).
11 Regulation and Inspection of Social Care (Wales) Act 2016 s 42(2)(c) (not yet in force: see note 1).
12 Regulation and Inspection of Social Care (Wales) Act 2016 s 42(3) (not yet in force: see note 1).

B.   POWERS OF REVIEW AND STUDY, INTERVENTION AND INSPECTION

(A)   Reviews, Studies and Research

400. Power to review local authority social services functions. The Welsh Ministers[1] have the function of conducting reviews of, and investigations into, the way in which local authorities in Wales[2] discharge their social services functions[3]. The Ministers may in particular conduct:

(1)   a review of the overall provision of Welsh local authority social services[4];

(2)   a review of the provision of any Welsh local authority social service of a particular description[5];

(3)   a review of, or investigation into, the provision of any Welsh local authority social service by a particular person or persons[6]; and

(4)   as from a day to be appointed, a review of the way in which the social services functions of a particular local authority are exercised[7].

Until the appointed day the Ministers may, in a review, assess performance against criteria[8] and award performance ratings[9]; as from that day, regulations may make provision about ratings that may be given in relation to the exercise of a specified local authority social services function[10] and ratings must be given in accordance with them[11]. When conducting such a review[12] the Welsh Ministers must, in relation to the local authority social services functions under review, have regard to:

(a)   the availability and accessibility of the services[13];

(b)   the quality and effectiveness of the services[14];

(c)   the management of the services[15];

(d)   the economy and efficiency of their provision and their value for money[16];

(e)   the availability and quality of information provided to people in the local authority area about the services[17];

(f)   until the appointed day, the need to safeguard and promote the rights and welfare of children[18] and the effectiveness of measures taken by the local authority for such purpose[19];

(g)   as from the appointed day, the duties imposed on local authorities to promote well-being[20], the other overarching duties[21] and the duties relating to UN Principles and Convention[22] in so far as they are relevant to the services and the effectiveness of measures taken by a local authority to fulfil those duties[23];

(h)   as from the appointed day, the effectiveness of measures taken by a local authority to achieve the outcomes specified in the statement of outcomes relating to well-being[24] in so far as they are relevant to the services[25];

(i)   as from the appointed day, any performance measures and performance targets[26] that they think are relevant[27];

(j)   as from the appointed day, any requirements or guidelines[28] that they think are relevant[29]; and

(k)   as from the appointed day, the extent to which a local authority has involved people in the local authority area in decisions about the way in which its social services functions are exercised and in reviewing the exercise of those functions[30].

1   As to the Welsh Ministers see PARA 395.
2   As to the meanings of 'local authority' and 'Wales' see PARA 2.
3   Health and Social Care (Community Health and Standards) Act 2003 s 94(1) (ss 94, 97 prospectively repealed by the Regulation and Inspection of Social Care (Wales) Act 2016 Sch 3 para 18). Until a day to be appointed these powers are exercisable pursuant to the Health and Social Care (Community Health and Standards) Act 2003 s 94 (as so prospectively repealed); as from that day they are exercisable pursuant to the Social Services and Well-being (Wales) Act 2014 ss 149B–149D (prospectively added by the Regulation and Inspection of Social Care (Wales) Act 2016 s 57(1)). At the date at which this volume states the law no day had been appointed for this purpose. As from the appointed day the power is expressed as the Ministers having power to

review the way in which the social services functions of local authorities are exercised: Social Services and Well-being (Wales) Act 2014 s 149B(1) (as so prospectively added). As to a local authority's social services functions see PARA 373.

Until the appointed day, where the Ministers conduct a review or investigation under these provisions they must publish a report; as from that day the Ministers must prepare and publish a report of a review conducted under the Social Services and Well-being (Wales) Act 2014 s 149B(1) and lay a copy of the report before the National Assembly for Wales: Health and Social Care (Community Health and Standards) Act 2003 s 94(5); Social Services and Well-being (Wales) Act 2014 s 149B(4) (as so prospectively repealed and added).

There are powers of inspection relating to reviews under these provisions (see PARA 407) and as from the appointed day there are powers to require information relating to such reviews (see PARA 408).

4   Health and Social Care (Community Health and Standards) Act 2003 s 94(2)(a); Social Services and Well-being (Wales) Act 2014 s 149B(2)(a) (prospectively repealed and added: see note 3). Until the appointed day 'Welsh local authority social service' means (by virtue of the Health and Social Care (Community Health and Standards) Act 2003 s 148):

     (1)   a service provided, in any place, by a local authority in Wales in the exercise of any of its social services functions;

     (2)   a service provided, in any place, by another person pursuant to arrangements made by a local authority in Wales in the exercise of its social services functions;

     (3)   a service which is provided, in any place, by a local authority in Wales, or by another person pursuant to arrangements made by a local authority in Wales, under the Local Government Act 2000 s 2(1)(b) (see LOCAL GOVERNMENT vol 69 (2009) PARA 463) and is similar in nature to a service which could be provided by the authority in the exercise of any of its social services functions.

No corresponding definition is in force as from the appointed day.

As from the appointed day this provision is cast as a review of the overall exercise of local authority social services functions in Wales: Social Services and Well-being (Wales) Act 2014 s 149B(2)(a) (as so prospectively added). A reference in s 149B(2) to the exercise by a local authority of local authority social services functions includes a reference to the commissioning of any services in connection with those functions: s 149B(3) (as so prospectively added).

Until the appointed day there is no fee for these purposes (see the Care Standards Act 2000 and Children Act 1989 (Abolition of Fees) (Wales) Regulations 2006, SI 2006/878, reg 5 (made under the Health and Social Care (Community Health and Standards) Act 2003 s 94(6)–(8))); however, as from the appointed day regulations may make provision for a local authority to pay a fee in respect of a review under the Social Services and Well-being (Wales) Act 2014 s 149B(1): s 149C(1) (as so prospectively added). Such regulations may include provision specifying the amount of any fee or permitting the Welsh Ministers to determine the amount of any fee (subject to any limits or other factors as may be specified in the regulations) and specifying the time by which a fee is to be payable or specifying factors by which that time is to be determined by the Welsh Ministers: s 149C(2) (as so prospectively added). At the date at which this volume states the law no regulations had been made under s 149C.

5   Health and Social Care (Community Health and Standards) Act 2003 s 94(2)(b); Social Services and Well-being (Wales) Act 2014 s 149B(2)(c) (prospectively repealed and added: see note 3). As from the appointed day this provision is cast as a review of the exercise of a local authority social services function of a particular description (whether exercised by a single local authority or by two or more authorities working together): s 149B(2)(c) (as so prospectively added). See also note 4.

6   Health and Social Care (Community Health and Standards) Act 2003 s 94(2)(c); Social Services and Well-being (Wales) Act 2014 s 149B(2)(d) (prospectively repealed and added: see note 3). As from the appointed day this provision is cast as a review of the exercise of a local authority social services function by a particular person or persons: s 149B(2)(d) (as so prospectively added). See also note 4.

7   Social Services and Well-being (Wales) Act 2014 s 149B(2)(b) (prospectively added: see note 3). See also note 4.

8   Health and Social Care (Community Health and Standards) Act 2003 s 94(3)(a) (prospectively repealed: see note 3).

9   Health and Social Care (Community Health and Standards) Act 2003 s 94(3)(b) (prospectively repealed: see note 3).

10   Social Services and Well-being (Wales) Act 2014 s 149B(5) (prospectively added: see note 3). Before making such regulations the Welsh Ministers must consult any persons they think appropriate: s 149B(7) (as so prospectively added). The requirement to consult does not apply to regulations which amend other regulations made under s 149B(5) and do not, in the opinion of the

Welsh Ministers, effect any substantial change in the provision made by the regulations to be amended: s 149B(8) (as so prospectively added). At the date at which this volume states the law no regulations had been made under s 149B.

11 If regulations are made under the Social Services and Well-being (Wales) Act 2014 s 149B (see the text and note 10) in relation to the exercise of a local authority social services function, the Welsh Ministers must:

    (1)   in conducting a review of the exercise of that function give a rating in accordance with the regulations (s 149B(6)(a) (prospectively added: see note 3)); and

    (2)   include the rating in their report of the review (s 149B(6)(b) (as so prospectively added)).

12 The Health and Social Care (Community Health and Standards) Act 2003 s 97(2) (see the text and notes 13–19) apply also for the purposes of the exercise of the Welsh Ministers' functions under s 92 (see PARA 395), s 93 (see PARA 402) and s 95 (see PARA 403), and the Social Services and Well-being (Wales) Act 2014 s 149D (see the text and notes 13–16, 20–30) apply also to reviews under s 149A (see PARA 402).

13 Health and Social Care (Community Health and Standards) Act 2003 s 97(1)(a), (2)(a) (prospectively repealed: see note 3); Social Services and Well-being (Wales) Act 2014 s 149D(a) (as so prospectively added).

14 Health and Social Care (Community Health and Standards) Act 2003 s 97(2)(b) (prospectively repealed: see note 3); Social Services and Well-being (Wales) Act 2014 s 149D(b) (as so prospectively added).

15 Health and Social Care (Community Health and Standards) Act 2003 s 97(2)(c) (prospectively repealed: see note 3); Social Services and Well-being (Wales) Act 2014 s 149D(c) (as so prospectively added).

16 Health and Social Care (Community Health and Standards) Act 2003 s 97(2)(d) (prospectively repealed: see note 3); Social Services and Well-being (Wales) Act 2014 s 149D(d) (as so prospectively added).

17 Health and Social Care (Community Health and Standards) Act 2003 s 97(2)(e) (prospectively repealed: see note 3); Social Services and Well-being (Wales) Act 2014 s 149D(e) (as so prospectively added).

18 Health and Social Care (Community Health and Standards) Act 2003 s 97(2)(f) (prospectively repealed: see note 3).

19 Health and Social Care (Community Health and Standards) Act 2003 s 97(2)(g) (prospectively repealed: see note 3).

20 Ie the duty imposed by the Social Services and Well-being (Wales) Act 2014 s 5: see PARA 375.

21 Ie the duty imposed by the Social Services and Well-being (Wales) Act 2014 s 6: see PARA 377.

22 Ie the duty imposed by the Social Services and Well-being (Wales) Act 2014 s 7: see PARA 383.

23 Social Services and Well-being (Wales) Act 2014 s 149D(f) (prospectively added: see note 3).

24 Ie a statement issued by the Welsh Ministers under the Social Services and Well-being (Wales) Act 2014 s 8: see PARA 396.

25 Social Services and Well-being (Wales) Act 2014 s 149D(g) (prospectively added: see note 3).

26 Ie set out in a code issued under the Social Services and Well-being (Wales) Act 2014 s 9: see PARA 396.

27 Social Services and Well-being (Wales) Act 2014 s 149D(h) (prospectively added: see note 3).

28 Ie contained in a code issued under the Social Services and Well-being (Wales) Act 2014 s 145: see PARA 410.

29 Social Services and Well-being (Wales) Act 2014 s 149D(i) (prospectively added: see note 3).

30 Social Services and Well-being (Wales) Act 2014 s 149D(j) (prospectively added: see note 3).

401. Inquiries into the provision of care and support. The Welsh Ministers[1] may cause an inquiry to be held into any matter connected with the provision of care and support[2]. Before an inquiry begins, the Ministers may direct that it is to be held in private[3]; if no such direction is given, the person holding the inquiry may decide to hold it, or any part of it, in private[4]. The report of the person holding the inquiry must be published unless the Welsh Ministers think there are exceptional circumstances for not publishing it (or any part of it)[5].

1   As to the Welsh Ministers see PARA 395.

2   Regulation and Inspection of Social Care (Wales) Act 2014 s 183(1). The Local Government Act 1972 s 250(2)–(5) (powers in relation to local inquiries: see LOCAL GOVERNMENT vol 69 (2009) PARA 105) apply in relation to an inquiry under the Regulation and Inspection of Social Care (Wales) Act 2014 s 183 as they apply in relation to a local inquiry under the Local Government Act 1972 s 250: Regulation and Inspection of Social Care (Wales) Act 2014 s 183(4).

3   Regulation and Inspection of Social Care (Wales) Act 2014 s 183(2).

4 Regulation and Inspection of Social Care (Wales) Act 2014 s 183(3).
5 Regulation and Inspection of Social Care (Wales) Act 2014 s 183(5).

402. Power to review studies and research. The Welsh Ministers[1] may review[2]:
(1)   studies and research undertaken by others in relation to the exercise of the social services functions of local authorities in Wales[3];
(2)   the methods used in such studies and research[4]; and
(3)   the validity of conclusions drawn from such studies and research[5].
The matters to which the Ministers must have regard when conducting such a review are the same as those to which they must have regard in conducting a review[6] of local authority social services functions[7].

1 As to the Welsh Ministers see PARA 395.
2 Until a day to be appointed these powers are exercisable pursuant to the Health and Social Care (Community Health and Standards) Act 2003 s 93 (ss 93, 97 prospectively repealed by the Regulation and Inspection of Social Care (Wales) Act 2016 Sch 3 para 18); as from that day they are exercisable pursuant to the Social Services and Well-being (Wales) Act 2014 s 149A (ss 149A, 149D prospectively added by the Regulation and Inspection of Social Care (Wales) Act 2016 s 57(1)). At the date at which this volume states the law no day had been appointed for this purpose. Until the appointed day, where the Ministers conduct a review under the Health and Social Care (Community Health and Standards) Act 2003 s 93 they must publish such report as they consider appropriate; as from that day, the Ministers must prepare and publish a report of a review conducted under these provisions and lay a copy of the report before the National Assembly for Wales: Health and Social Care (Community Health and Standards) Act 2003 s 93(2); Social Services and Well-being (Wales) Act 2014 s 149A(2) (as so prospectively repealed and added). As from the appointed day there are powers of inspection for the purposes of reviews under these provisions (see PARA 407) and powers to require information relating to such reviews (see PARA 408).
3 Health and Social Care (Community Health and Standards) Act 2003 s 93(1)(a); Social Services and Well-being (Wales) Act 2014 s 149A(1)(a) (prospectively repealed and added: see note 2). As to the meanings of 'local authority' and 'Wales' see PARA 2; as to a local authority's social services functions see PARA 373.
4 Health and Social Care (Community Health and Standards) Act 2003 s 93(1)(b); Social Services and Well-being (Wales) Act 2014 s 149A(1)(b) (prospectively repealed and added: see note 2).
5 Health and Social Care (Community Health and Standards) Act 2003 s 93(1)(c); Social Services and Well-being (Wales) Act 2014 s 149A(1)(c) (prospectively repealed and added: see note 2).
6 Ie under the Health and Social Care (Community Health and Standards) Act 2003 s 94 or, as from the appointed day (see note 2), the Social Services and Well-being (Wales) Act 2014 s 149B: see PARA 400.
7 See the Health and Social Care (Community Health and Standards) Act 2003 s 97(1)(a), (2) (prospectively repealed: see note 2); the Social Services and Well-being (Wales) Act 2014 s 149D (as so prospectively added); and PARA 400.

403. Power to promote and undertake studies and research. The Welsh Ministers[1] may conduct, commission, or assist in the conduct of, research into any matter connected with:
(1)   their social services functions[2];
(2)   any social services function of a local authority in Wales[3];
(3)   any function[4] of a local authority in Wales as a local mental health partner[5];
(4)   the functions[6] of Local Health Boards[7]; or
(5)   the functions of Safeguarding Boards[8].
Until a day to be appointed[9] the Welsh Ministers also have the function of promoting or undertaking comparative or other studies designed to enable them to make recommendations:
(a)   for improving economy, efficiency and effectiveness in the discharge by local authorities in Wales of their social services functions[10]; and
(b)   for improving the management of such authorities in the discharge of those functions[11].

Until that day[12] the Ministers may also promote or undertake studies designed to enable them to prepare reports as to the impact of the operation of any particular statutory provisions on economy, efficiency and effectiveness in the discharge by local authorities in Wales of their social services functions[13]. The matters to which the Ministers must have regard in exercising these functions are the same as those to which they must have regard in conducting a review[14] of local authority social services functions[15]. The Ministers must publish or otherwise make available any such recommendations made by them and a report on the result of any such studies[16].

1   As to the Welsh Ministers see PARA 395.
2   Social Services and Well-being (Wales) Act 2014 s 184(1)(a). The Welsh Ministers' and local authorities' social services functions are their functions under the Social Services and Well-being (Wales) Act 2014.
3   Social Services and Well-being (Wales) Act 2014 s 184(1)(b), (12)(a). As to the meanings of 'local authority' and 'Wales' see PARA 2; as to a local authority's social services functions see PARA 373. See note 2.
4   Ie under the Mental Health (Wales) Measure 2010 (see MENTAL HEALTH AND CAPACITY).
5   Social Services and Well-being (Wales) Act 2014 s 184(12)(b).
6   Ie under the Social Services and Well-being (Wales) Act 2014.
7   Social Services and Well-being (Wales) Act 2014 s 184(1)(c). As to Local Health Boards see HEALTH SERVICES vol 54 (2017) PARA 97. A Local Health Board may conduct, commission, or assist in the conduct of, research into any matter connected with its functions under the Social Services and Well-being (Wales) Act 2014: s 184(3).
8   Social Services and Well-being (Wales) Act 2014 s 184(1)(d). As to the meaning of 'safeguarding Board' see PARA 393 note 5.
9   The Health and Social Care (Community Health and Standards) Act 2003 ss 95, 97 (see the text and notes 10–16) are repealed, as from a day to be appointed, by the Regulation and Inspection of Social Care (Wales) Act 2016 Sch 3 para 18. At the date at which this volume states the law no day had been appointed for this purpose.
10   Health and Social Care (Community Health and Standards) Act 2003 s 95(1)(a) (prospectively repealed: see note 9).
11   Health and Social Care (Community Health and Standards) Act 2003 s 95(1)(b) (prospectively repealed: see note 9).
12   See note 9.
13   Health and Social Care (Community Health and Standards) Act 2003 s 95(2) (prospectively repealed: see note 9).
14   Ie under the Health and Social Care (Community Health and Standards) Act 2003 s 94: see PARA 400.
15   See the Health and Social Care (Community Health and Standards) Act 2003 s 97(1)(a), (2) (prospectively repealed: see note 9); and PARA 400.
16   Health and Social Care (Community Health and Standards) Act 2003 s 95(3) (prospectively repealed: see note 9).

(B)   Interventions

404. Power to intervene in exercise of local authority social services functions. The Welsh Ministers[1] have grounds for intervention in the exercise by a local authority in Wales[2] of its social services functions[3] if[4]:

(1)   the authority has failed, or is likely to fail, to comply with a duty that is a social services function[5];

(2)   the authority has acted, or is proposing to act, unreasonably in the exercise of a social services function[6]; or

(3)   the authority is failing, or is likely to fail, to perform a social services function to an adequate standard[7].

If the Ministers are satisfied that one or more of these grounds exist in relation to the local authority they may give it a warning notice[8], and having done so[9], will have the power to intervene in the exercise of the authority's social services functions if the authority has failed to comply, or secure compliance, with the notice to the Ministers' satisfaction within the compliance period[10]. The power to intervene also arises if the Ministers are satisfied that one or more of Grounds 1 to 3 exist in relation to the authority and have reason to believe that there is a related risk to the health or safety of any person that calls for urgent intervention[11] or the authority is unlikely to be able to comply, or secure compliance, with a warning notice[12]. Where the Ministers exercise the power to intervene they have a number of powers pursuant to such exercise[13].

1 As to the Welsh Ministers see PARA 395.
2 As to the meanings of 'local authority' and 'Wales' see PARA 2.
3 As to a local authority's social services functions see PARA 373.
4 For the purposes of the Social Services and Well-being (Wales) Act 2014 Pt 8 (ss 143–161C), the grounds for intervention in the exercise by a local authority of its social services functions are as listed in heads (1)–(3) in the text: s 150.
5 This is referred to as Ground 1: Social Services and Well-being (Wales) Act 2014 s 150.
6 This is referred to as Ground 2: Social Services and Well-being (Wales) Act 2014 s 150.
7 This is referred to as Ground 3: Social Services and Well-being (Wales) Act 2014 s 150.
8 Social Services and Well-being (Wales) Act 2014 s 151(1). The Ministers must specify each of the following in the warning notice:
    (1)   the grounds for intervention (s 151(2)(a));
    (2)   the reasons why they are satisfied that the grounds exist (s 151(2)(b));
    (3)   the action they require the authority to take in order to deal with the grounds for intervention (s 151(2)(c));
    (4)   the period within which the action is to be taken by the authority ('the compliance period') (s 151(2)(d)); and
    (5)   the action they are minded to take if the authority fails to take the required action (s 151(2)(e)).
    Where the Ministers give a warning notice under s 151(1) they must within 21 days of the giving of the notice, lay a copy of the notice before the National Assembly for Wales and within 90 days of the giving of the notice, report to the National Assembly for Wales on the action taken by the local authority in response to the warning notice: s 151(3).
9 Social Services and Well-being (Wales) Act 2014 s 152(1), (2)(a). The Ministers must, within 90 days of the date on which they begin to intervene in the exercise of a local authority's social services functions, report to the National Assembly for Wales on the steps taken pursuant to the intervention: s 152(4). Where the Ministers have the power to intervene, they must keep the circumstances giving rise to the power under review: s 152(5). If the Ministers conclude that the grounds for intervention have been dealt with to their satisfaction or that the exercise of their powers under Pt 8 would not be appropriate for any other reason, they must notify the local authority of their conclusion in writing: s 152(6). The Ministers' power to intervene continues in effect until they give such a notice: s 152(7). Until such time as notice is given under s 152(6), the Ministers must, every 6 months from the date on which they begin to intervene in the exercise of a local authority's social services functions, report to the Assembly on the steps being taken pursuant to the intervention: s 152(8). Where the Ministers have the power to intervene, they are not limited to taking the action they said they were minded to take in a warning notice: s 152(9).
10 Social Services and Well-being (Wales) Act 2014 s 152(2)(b).
11 Social Services and Well-being (Wales) Act 2014 s 152(3)(a). The reference is to intervention under Pt 8.
12 Social Services and Well-being (Wales) Act 2014 s 152(3)(b).
13 See the Social Services and Well-being (Wales) Act 2014 ss 153–160; and PARA 405.

405. Powers of Ministers pursuant to intervention. If the Welsh Ministers[1] have the power to intervene[2] in the exercise of social services functions[3] by a local authority in Wales[4] they may:
    (1)   direct the authority to enter into a contract or other arrangement with a specified person[5], or a person falling within a specified class, for the provision to the authority of specified services of an advisory nature[6];
    (2)   give such a direction to the authority or any of its officers as they think is appropriate for securing that the functions to which the grounds for intervention relate are performed on behalf of the authority by a person specified in the direction[7];

(3)   direct that the functions to which the grounds for intervention relate are
        to be exercised by them or a person nominated by them[8]; and

(4)   if they think it is appropriate in order to deal with the grounds for
        intervention, direct the authority or any of its officers or take any other
        steps[9].

1   As to the Welsh Ministers see PARA 395.
2   Ie pursuant to the Social Services and Well-being (Wales) Act 2014 s 152: see PARA 404. As to
    powers of entry and inspection pursuant to these powers see PARA 407.
3   As to a local authority's social services functions see PARA 373.
4   As to the meanings of 'local authority' and 'Wales' see PARA 2.
5   In the Social Services and Well-being (Wales) Act 2014 ss 153, 154 'specified' means specified in
    a direction: s 153(4).
6   Social Services and Well-being (Wales) Act 2014 s 153(1), (2). The direction may require the
    contract or other arrangement to contain specified terms and conditions: s 153(3).
        As to directions under Pt 8 (ss 143–161C) and the local authority's duty to comply with them,
    and the authority's duty to assist persons in the exercise of social services functions, see ss 159,
    160; and PARA 374. Where the Welsh Ministers exercise their power of direction under s 153,
    s 154, s 155 or s 157, they must within 21 days of the giving of the direction, lay a copy of the
    direction before the National Assembly for Wales, and within 90 days of the giving of the
    direction, report to the Assembly on the steps taken by the authority to comply with the direction:
    s 158.
7   Social Services and Well-being (Wales) Act 2014 s 154(1), (2). As to 'specified' see note 5; as to
    directions generally see note 6. A direction under s 154(2) may require that any contract or other
    arrangement made by the authority with the specified person contains terms and conditions
    specified in the direction: s 154(3). If a direction under s 154(2) is in force, the functions of the
    authority to which it relates are to be treated for all purposes as being exercisable by the specified
    person: s 154(4).
        If the Ministers think it is expedient, a direction under s 154 or 155 may relate to the
    performance of social services functions in addition to the functions to which the grounds for
    intervention relate: s 156(1). The Welsh Ministers may have regard (among other things) to
    financial considerations in deciding whether it is expedient that a direction should relate to social
    services functions other than the functions relating to the grounds for intervention: s 156(2).
8   Social Services and Well-being (Wales) Act 2014 s 155(1), (2). As to directions generally see note
    6. If a direction is made under s 155(2), the authority must comply with the instructions of the
    Ministers or their nominee in relation to the exercise of the functions: s 155(3). If such a direction
    is in force, the functions of the authority to which it relates are to be treated for all purposes as
    being exercisable by the Ministers or their nominee: s 155(4).
9   Social Services and Well-being (Wales) Act 2014 s 157(1), (2). As to directions generally see note
    6.

406. Power to intervene in exercise of Social Care Wales' functions. If the Welsh
Ministers[1] are satisfied that Social Care Wales[2] has without reasonable excuse
failed to discharge any of its functions[3] or, in discharging any of its functions, has
without reasonable excuse failed to comply with any directions given[4] by the
Welsh Ministers in relation to those functions[5], they may publish a statement
declaring Social Care Wales to be in default[6] and direct it to discharge such of its
functions, and in such manner and within such period or periods, as may be
specified in the direction[7]. If Social Care Wales fails to comply with such a
direction, the Ministers may discharge the functions to which the direction relates
themselves[8] or make arrangements for any other person to discharge those
functions on their behalf[9].

1   As to the Welsh Ministers see PARA 395.
2   As to the establishment and objectives of Social Care Wales see PARA 412.
3   Regulation and Inspection of Social Care (Wales) Act 2016 s 78(1)(a).
4   Ie under the Regulation and Inspection of Social Care (Wales) Act 2016 s 77: see PARA 413.
5   Regulation and Inspection of Social Care (Wales) Act 2016 s 78(1)(b).
6   Regulation and Inspection of Social Care (Wales) Act 2016 s 78(2)(a).
7   Regulation and Inspection of Social Care (Wales) Act 2016 s 78(2)(b). A direction under s 78(2)(b)
    must be in writing and may be varied or revoked by a subsequent direction: s 78(4).

8 Regulation and Inspection of Social Care (Wales) Act 2016 s 78(3)(a).
9 Regulation and Inspection of Social Care (Wales) Act 2016 s 78(3)(b).

(C) Inspections

407. Powers of Welsh Ministers to enter and inspect local authority premises.
Until a day to be appointed[1] a person authorised to do so by the Welsh Ministers[2]
may, if the Welsh Ministers consider it necessary or expedient for the purposes of
their powers to oversee the provision of Welsh local authority social services[3], at
any reasonable time enter and inspect any premises owned or controlled by a local
authority in Wales[4] and any associated premises[5], other than premises used wholly
or mainly as a private dwelling[6]. A person so authorised to enter and inspect
premises may, if he considers it necessary or expedient:

(1)   inspect, take copies of and remove from the premises any documents or
       records (including personal records) relating to the discharge by the
       local authority of its social services functions[7];
(2)   inspect any other item and remove it from the premises[8];
(3)   interview in private any person working at the premises; or any person
       accommodated or cared for there who consents to be interviewed[9]; and
(4)   make any other examination into the state and management of the
       premises and treatment of persons accommodated or cared for there[10].

A person so authorised to enter and inspect premises may require any person
to afford him such facilities and assistance with respect to matters within the
person's control as are necessary to enable him to exercise his powers[11] of entry[12]
and take such measurements and photographs and make such recordings as he
considers necessary to enable him to exercise those powers[13].

Until the appointed day[14], if the Welsh Ministers have the power to intervene[15]
in the exercise of social services functions[16] by a local authority in Wales, a person
exercising intervention functions[17] has at all reasonable times a right of entry to
the premises of the local authority in question[18] and a right to inspect, and take
copies of, any records or other documents[19] kept by the authority, and any other
documents containing information relating to the authority, which the person
considers relevant to the exercise of his or her social services functions[20]. As from
that day these powers are extended to also apply where the Welsh Ministers
consider their application to be necessary or expedient for the purposes of a
review of local authority social services functions[21], and are modified so that a
person exercising intervention functions[22] no longer has a right of entry but
instead may authorise an inspector[23] to enter and inspect relevant premises[24]. The
inspector may:

(a)   examine the state and management of the premises and, if any persons
       are accommodated or receive care and support[25] at the premises,
       examine the treatment of those persons[26];
(b)   require the manager of the premises or any other person who appears to
       the inspector to hold or be accountable for documents or records kept
       at the premises to produce any documents or records (including medical
       and other personal records) that the inspector considers may be relevant
       to the exercise of social services functions[27] by the person who
       authorised the inspector[28];
(c)   inspect and take copies of any documents or records (including medical
       and other personal records) that the inspector considers may be relevant
       to the exercise of social services functions by the person who authorised
       the inspector[29];

(d)   require any person to afford the inspector such facilities and assistance with respect to matters within the person's control as are necessary to enable the inspector to carry out the inspection[30];

(e)   take such measurements and photographs and make such recordings as the inspector considers necessary for the purpose of carrying out the inspection[31]; and

(f)   interview in private the manager of the premises or any other person who appears to the inspector to be responsible for the premises, any person working there, and any person accommodated or receiving care and support there who consents to be interviewed[32].

It is an offence to obstruct the exercise of these powers or to fail to comply with these requirements[33].

1   The Health and Social Care (Community Health and Standards) Act 2003 ss 98, 99 (see the text and notes 2–13) are repealed, and the Social Services and Well-being (Wales) Act 2014 s 161 is substituted, and new ss 161A, 161C (see the text and notes 14–33) are added, as from a day to be appointed, by the Regulation and Inspection of Social Care (Wales) Act 2016 s 57(2), Sch 3 para 18. At the date at which this volume states the law no day had been appointed for this purpose.

2   As to the Welsh Ministers see PARA 395. A person who proposes to exercise any power of entry or inspection conferred by these provisions must if so required produce some duly authenticated document showing his authority to exercise the power: Health and Social Care (Community Health and Standards) Act 2003 s 98(3) (prospectively repealed: see note 1).

3   Ie for the purposes of the Health and Social Care (Community Health and Standards) Act 2003 Pt 2 Ch 6 (ss 92–101). As to the meanings of 'local authority' and 'Wales' see PARA 2. As to the meaning of 'Welsh local authority social service' see PARA 400 note 4.

4   Health and Social Care (Community Health and Standards) Act 2003 s 98(1)(a) (prospectively repealed: see note 1).

5   Ie premises which are used, or proposed to be used, by any person in connection with the provision of a Welsh local authority social service or which the Welsh Ministers reasonably believe to be so used, or proposed to be so used: Health and Social Care (Community Health and Standards) Act 2003 s 98(2) (prospectively repealed: see note 1).

6   Health and Social Care (Community Health and Standards) Act 2003 s 98(1)(b) (prospectively repealed: see note 1).

7   Health and Social Care (Community Health and Standards) Act 2003 s 99(1)(a) (prospectively repealed: see note 1). This includes power to require any person holding or accountable for documents or records kept on the premises to produce them and in relation to records which are kept by means of a computer, power to require the records to be produced in a form in which they are legible and can be taken away: s 99(2) (as so prospectively repealed). A person authorised by virtue of s 99(1)(a) to inspect any records is entitled to have access to, and to check the operation of, any computer and any associated apparatus or material which is or has been in use in connection with the records in question: s 99(3) (as so prospectively repealed).

8   Health and Social Care (Community Health and Standards) Act 2003 s 99(1)(b) (prospectively repealed: see note 1).

9   Health and Social Care (Community Health and Standards) Act 2003 s 99(1)(c) (prospectively repealed: see note 1).

10   Health and Social Care (Community Health and Standards) Act 2003 s 99(1)(d) (prospectively repealed: see note 1).

11   Ie his powers under the Health and Social Care (Community Health and Standards) Act 2003 s 98.

12   Health and Social Care (Community Health and Standards) Act 2003 s 99(4)(a) (prospectively repealed: see note 1).

13   Health and Social Care (Community Health and Standards) Act 2003 s 99(4)(b) (prospectively repealed: see note 1).

14   See note 1.

15   Ie pursuant to the Social Services and Well-being (Wales) Act 2014 s 152: see PARA 404.

16   As to a local authority's social services functions see PARA 373.

17   Ie a person specified in a direction under the Social Services and Well-being (Wales) Act 2014 s 153 or, where the direction specifies a class of persons, the person with whom the local authority enters into the contract or other arrangement required by the direction, a person specified in a direction under s 154, the Welsh Ministers in pursuance of a direction under s 155 and a person nominated

by a direction under s 155: s 161(2). Any reference in this section to a person falling within s 161(2) includes a reference to any person assisting that person: s 161(4). As to the exercise of functions under ss 153–155 see PARA 405.

18 Social Services and Well-being (Wales) Act 2014 s 161(1)(a).

19 For this purpose 'document' and 'records' each include information recorded in any form: Social Services and Well-being (Wales) Act 2014 s 161(5).

20 Social Services and Well-being (Wales) Act 2014 s 161(1)(b). The reference to 'social services functions' is a reference to functions under Pt 8 (ss 143–161C). In exercising the right under s 161(1)(b) to inspect records or other documents, a person is entitled to have access to, and inspect and check the operation of, any computer and any associated apparatus or material which is or has been in use in connection with the records or other documents in question (s 161(3)(a)) and may require the person by whom or on whose behalf the computer is or has been so used, and any person having charge of, or otherwise concerned with the operation of, the computer, apparatus or material, to provide any assistance he may reasonably require (including, among other things, the making of information available for inspection or copying in a legible form) (s 161(3)(b)).

21 Ie a review conducted under the Social Services and Well-being (Wales) Act 2014 s 149B(1) (see PARA 400). Until the appointed day, for the purposes of their powers of review under the Health and Social Care (Community Health and Standards) Act 2003 s 94 (see PARA 400) the Ministers may carry out an inspection of any local authority in Wales and any other person providing a Welsh local authority social service: Health and Social Care (Community Health and Standards) Act 2003 s 94(4) (prospectively repealed by the Regulation and Inspection of Social Care (Wales) Act 2016 Sch 3 para 18).

22 Ie a person falling within the Social Services and Well-being (Wales) Act 2014 s 161(2) (see note 17), and the Welsh Ministers in the circumstances described in the text and note 21.

23 The Welsh Ministers may by regulations make provision about the qualifications and other conditions to be met by an individual who may be an inspector: Social Services and Well-being (Wales) Act 2014 s 161(5) (prospectively substituted: see note 1). At the date at which this volume states the law no such regulations had been made. When entering premises, an inspector must, if requested to do so by any person at the premises, produce a document showing the inspector's authorisation given under s 161(1): s 161(6) (as so prospectively substituted). An inspector must have regard to the most recently published code of practice under s 161A (see PARA 411) when carrying out an inspection under s 161: s 161A(3) (as so prospectively added). In ss 161, 161A–161C 'inspector' means an individual authorised under s 161(1): s 161(15) (as so prospectively substituted).

24 Social Services and Well-being (Wales) Act 2014 s 161(1), (2) (prospectively substituted: see note 1). 'Premises' includes a vehicle (s 161(4) (as so prospectively substituted)), and the following premises are 'relevant' for these purposes:
  (1)   premises owned or controlled by a local authority (s 161(3)(a) (as so prospectively substituted)); and
  (2)   premises which are used, or proposed to be used, by any person in connection with the exercise of a local authority social services function, or which the Welsh Ministers reasonably believe is being used, or may be used, for that purpose (s 161(3)(b) (as so prospectively substituted)),
but premises used wholly or mainly as a private dwelling do not fall within these provisions unless the occupier of the premises consents to the inspector entering and inspecting them (s 161(3) (as so prospectively substituted)). As soon as is reasonably practicable after an inspector has concluded an inspection under s 161 he must send a report of the inspection to the person who gave the authorisation under s 161(1): s 161(13) (as so prospectively substituted). That person must send a copy of the inspector's report to the local authority being reviewed or subject to the direction and, if the person is not the Welsh Ministers, to the Welsh Ministers: s 161(14) (as so prospectively substituted).

25 As to the meanings of 'care' and 'support' see PARA 2 note 1.

26 Social Services and Well-being (Wales) Act 2014 s 161(7)(a) (prospectively substituted: see note 1). Where persons are accommodated or receiving care and support at the inspected premises, the inspector is a registered medical practitioner or registered nurse, and the inspector has reasonable grounds to believe that a person accommodated or receiving care and support at the premises is not receiving (or has not received) proper care and support, the inspector may examine the person in private but only if the person gives consent to the examination: s 161(9), (10) (as so prospectively substituted). For the purposes of s 161(7)(f), (10), an interview or examination is to be treated as conducted in private despite the presence of a third party if the person being interviewed or examined wants the third party to be present and the inspector does not object or the inspector wants the third party to be present and the person being interviewed or examined consents: s 161(11) (as so prospectively substituted). Where an inspector conducts an interview or

examination under s 161 he must, if requested to do so by the person being interviewed or examined or an individual accompanying that person, produce a document showing his authorisation given under s 161(1) and, in the case of an examination, a document showing that the inspector is a registered medical practitioner or registered nurse: s 161(12) (as so prospectively substituted). As to the meaning of 'registered medical practitioner' see MEDICAL PROFESSIONS vol 74 (2011) PARA 176; as to registered nurses see MEDICAL PROFESSIONS vol 74 (2011) PARA 713.

27 Ie functions under the Social Services and Well-being (Wales) Act 2014 Pt 8 (ss 143–161C).

28 Social Services and Well-being (Wales) Act 2014 s 161(7)(b) (prospectively substituted: see note 1). The powers in s 161(7)(b)–(d) include the power to gain access to and check the operation of any computer and associated apparatus which the inspector has reasonable grounds to believe is (or has been) used in connection with the documents or records and require documents or records to be produced in a form which is legible and portable: s 161(8) (as so prospectively substituted).

29 Social Services and Well-being (Wales) Act 2014 s 161(7)(c) (prospectively substituted: see note 1). See note 28.

30 Social Services and Well-being (Wales) Act 2014 s 161(7)(d) (prospectively substituted: see note 1). See note 28.

31 Social Services and Well-being (Wales) Act 2014 s 161(7)(e) (prospectively substituted: see note 1).

32 Social Services and Well-being (Wales) Act 2014 s 161(7)(f) (prospectively substituted: see note 1). See s 161(11), (12); and note 26.

33 See the Health and Social Care (Community Health and Standards) Act 2003 s 99(5) (prospectively repealed: see note 1), which provides that any person who without reasonable excuse obstructs the exercise of any power conferred by the Health and Social Care (Community Health and Standards) Act 2003 s 98 or s 99, or fails to comply with any requirement of those provisions, is guilty of an offence and liable on summary conviction to a fine not exceeding level 4 on the standard scale; and the Social Services and Well-being (Wales) Act 2014 s 161C (as so prospectively added), which provides, as from the appointed day, that it is an offence to intentionally obstruct the carrying out of an inspection of premises under s 161 by an inspector (s 161C(1)(a) (as so prospectively added) or to fail to comply with any requirement imposed on the person by an inspector carrying out such an inspection (s 161C(1)(b) (as so prospectively added). It is a defence for a person charged with an offence under s 161C(1)(b) to show that he had a reasonable excuse for not complying with the requirement: s 161C(3) (as so prospectively added). A person guilty of an offence under s 161C is liable on summary conviction, to a fine, or to imprisonment for a term not exceeding 6 months, or to both, and on conviction on indictment, to a fine, or to imprisonment for a term not exceeding 2 years, or to both: s 161C(4) (as so prospectively added). As to the powers of magistrates' courts to issue fines on summary conviction see SENTENCING vol 92 (2015) PARA 176. The Regulation and Inspection of Social Care (Wales) Act 2016 ss 53–55 (offences by bodies corporate and unincorporated bodies; and proceedings for offences: see PARA 203 note 2) apply to an offence under the Social Services and Well-being (Wales) Act 2014 s 161C as they apply to offences under the Regulation and Inspection of Social Care (Wales) Act 2016 Pt 1: Social Services and Well-being (Wales) Act 2014 s 161C(5) (as so prospectively added).

408. Power to require information. The Welsh Ministers[1] may require:

(1) a local authority in Wales[2] to provide them with information in connection with the performance by the authority any of its social services functions[3] and any of its functions[4] as a local mental health partner[5], and the persons in relation to whom it has exercised those functions[6];

(2) a Local Health Board[7] to provide them with information in connection with the performance of its social services functions[8] and the persons in relation to whom it has exercised those functions[9];

(3) the lead partner of a Safeguarding Board[10] to provide them with information in connection with the performance by that Board of its functions[11]; and

(4) a voluntary organisation to provide them with information in connection with adults[12] accommodated by the organisation or on its behalf[13].

Until a day to be appointed[14] the Welsh Ministers:

(a)   may at any time require a local authority in Wales[15], a person providing
a Welsh local authority social service[16] for the authority[17], or any Welsh
NHS body or cross-border SHA[18], to provide them with any
information, documents, records (including personal records)[19] or other
items which relates or relate to the discharge by a local authority in
Wales of its social services functions[20] and which the Ministers consider
it necessary or expedient to have for the purpose of any of their
functions[21]; and

(b)   may require specified persons[22] to provide to them, or to a person
authorised by them, an explanation of any documents, records or items
inspected, copied or produced[23], any information so provided, and any
matters which are the subject of the exercise of any Ministerial
functions[24], in cases where the Ministers consider the explanation
necessary or expedient for the purposes of those functions[25].

It is an offence to obstruct the exercise of these powers or to fail to comply with
these requirements[26].

As from the appointed day[27] the Welsh Ministers may require a local authority
in Wales, a person providing a service in connection with the exercise of a local
authority social services function in Wales, a Local Health Board or an NHS trust
to provide them with:

(i)   any documents, records (including medical or other personal records)[28]
or other information which relate to the exercise of a social services
function of a local authority and which the Welsh Ministers consider it
necessary or expedient to have for the purposes of a review of studies
and research[29] or local authority social services functions[30];

(ii)   an explanation of the content of any documents, records or other
information so provided or any documents or records provided to an
inspector conducting an inspection of premises[31] in connection with a
review of studies and research[32].

It is an offence to obstruct the exercise of these powers or to fail to comply with
these requirements[33].

1   As to the Welsh Ministers see PARA 395.
2   As to the meanings of 'local authority' and 'Wales' see PARA 2.
3   Social Services and Well-being (Wales) Act 2014 s 184(4)(a), (12)(a). As to a local
authority's social services functions see PARA 373. A requirement under s 184(4), (5), (6) or (7)
must be complied with by providing the information in such form and at such time as the Welsh
Ministers may require: s 184(8). Information required to be provided under s 184(4) may include
information relating to and identifying individual children, but only if that information is needed
to inform the review and development of policy and practice relating to the well-being of children
or the conduct of research relating to the well-being of children: s 184(9). The Ministers must in
each year lay before the National Assembly for Wales a summary of the information provided to
them under s 184(4), (5), (6) and (7), but the summary must not include information that identifies
an individual child or allows an individual child to be identified: s 184(10).
4   Ie under the Mental Health (Wales) Measure 2010 (see MENTAL HEALTH AND CAPACITY).
5   Social Services and Well-being (Wales) Act 2014 s 184(12)(b).
6   Social Services and Well-being (Wales) Act 2014 s 184(4)(b). See note 3.
7   As to Local Health Boards see HEALTH SERVICES vol 54 (2017) PARA 97.
8   Social Services and Well-being (Wales) Act 2014 s 184(5)(a). A Local Health Board's social
services functions are its functions under the Social Services and Well-being (Wales) Act 2014. See
note 3.
9   Social Services and Well-being (Wales) Act 2014 s 184(5)(b). See note 3.
10 'The lead partner of a Safeguarding Board' is the Safeguarding Board partner specified as the lead
partner in the Safeguarding Boards (Functions and Procedures) (Wales) Regulations 2015, SI
2015/1466 (see PARA 238): Social Services and Well-being (Wales) Act 2014 s 184(11). As to the
meaning of 'safeguarding Board' see PARA 393 note 5.
11 Social Services and Well-being (Wales) Act 2014 s 184(6). See note 3.

12　As to the meaning of 'adult' see PARA 2.

13　Social Services and Well-being (Wales) Act 2014 s 184(7). See note 3.

14　The Health and Social Care (Community Health and Standards) Act 2003 ss 100, 101 (see the text and notes 15–26) are repealed, and the Social Services and Well-being (Wales) Act 2014 ss 161B, 161C (see the text and notes 27–33) are added, as from a day to be appointed, by the Regulation and Inspection of Social Care (Wales) Act 2016 s 57(2), Sch 3 para 18. At the date at which this volume states the law no day had been appointed for this purpose.

15　Health and Social Care (Community Health and Standards) Act 2003 s 100(2)(a) (prospectively repealed: see note 14).

16　As to the meaning of 'Welsh local authority social service' see PARA 400 note 4.

17　Health and Social Care (Community Health and Standards) Act 2003 s 100(2)(b) (prospectively repealed: see note 14).

18　Health and Social Care (Community Health and Standards) Act 2003 s 100(2)(c) (prospectively repealed: see note 14). 'Welsh NHS body' means a Local Health Board, an NHS trust (until a day to be appointed, an NHS trust all or most of whose hospitals, establishments and facilities are situated in Wales), and a Special Health Authority performing functions only or mainly in respect of Wales (see generally HEALTH SERVICES vol 54 (2017) PARA 180): s 148 (prospectively amended by the Health and Social Care Act 2012 Sch 14 para 90(b)). At the date at which this volume states the law no such day had been appointed. 'Cross-border SHA' means a Special Health Authority not performing functions only or mainly in respect of England or only or mainly in respect of Wales: Health and Social Care (Community Health and Standards) Act 2003 s 148.

19　The power to require the provision of information includes, in relation to records kept by means of a computer, power to require the provision of the records in legible form: Health and Social Care (Community Health and Standards) Act 2003 s 100(3) (prospectively repealed: see note 14).

20　Health and Social Care (Community Health and Standards) Act 2003 s 100(1)(a) (prospectively repealed: see note 14). The reference in the text is a reference to functions under Pt 2 Ch 6 (ss 92–101).

21　Health and Social Care (Community Health and Standards) Act 2003 s 100(1)(b) (prospectively repealed: see note 14).

22　Ie (by virtue of the National Assembly for Wales (Social Services Explanations) Regulations 2005, SI 2005/1510, reg 2(3) (made under the Health and Social Care (Community Health and Standards) Act 2003 s 101(1), (2) (prospectively repealed: see note 14))):
　　(1)　a local authority;
　　(2)　a member or former member of a local authority;
　　(3)　an elected mayor or former elected mayor of a local authority, within the meaning of the Local Government Act 2000 s 39(1) (see LOCAL GOVERNMENT vol 69 (2009) PARA 320);
　　(4)　an officer or former officer of a local authority;
　　(5)　a service provider (ie a person other than a local authority who provides, has provided or has agreed to provide a Welsh local authority social service);
　　(6)　an employee or former employee of a service provider or any other person who is assisting or has assisted that provider in the provision of a Welsh local authority social service; and
　　(7)　a person (other than one listed in any of heads (2)–(6) above) who is assisting or has assisted a local authority in the provision of a Welsh local authority social service.

23　Ie under the Health and Social Care (Community Health and Standards) Act 2003 ss 98–100 (see PARA 407; and the text and notes 14–22).

24　Ie under the Health and Social Care (Community Health and Standards) Act 2003 Pt 2 Ch 6 (ss 92–101) (see PARA 395 et seq).

25　National Assembly for Wales (Social Services Explanations) Regulations 2005, SI 2005/1510, reg 2(1). A requirement under reg 2(1) must be given in a written notice which must also set out the why the explanation is required, specify whether the explanation is to be provided in person or in writing (save that where the person required to provide the explanation is a body of persons corporate or unincorporate, the explanation must be required in writing), and, where the explanation is to be provided in person, specify, and give reasonable notice of, the time and place at which it is to be provided: reg 2(2).

26　See the Health and Social Care (Community Health and Standards) Act 2003 ss 100(4), 101(3) (prospectively repealed: see note 14), which provide that any person who without reasonable excuse fails to comply with any requirement imposed by virtue of s 100 or s 101 is guilty of an offence and liable on summary conviction to a fine not exceeding level 4 on the standard scale. As to the powers of magistrates' courts to issue fines on summary conviction see SENTENCING vol 92 (2015) PARA 176.

27　See note 14.

28 The power in the Social Services and Well-being (Wales) Act 2014 s 161B(1) includes power to require documents or records to be produced in a form which is legible and portable: s 161B(4) (prospectively added: see note 14). A person is not required to provide documents, records or other information under these provisions if he is prohibited from providing them by any enactment or other rule of law: s 161B(3) (as so prospectively added).

29 Ie a review under the Social Services and Well-being (Wales) Act 2014 s 149A (see PARA 402).

30 Social Services and Well-being (Wales) Act 2014 s 161B(1)(a) (prospectively added: see note 14). The reference to a review local authority social services functions is a reference to a review under s 149B (see PARA 400): s 161B(1)(a) (as so prospectively added).

31 Ie under the Social Services and Well-being (Wales) Act 2014 s 161.

32 Social Services and Well-being (Wales) Act 2014 s 161B(1)(b) (prospectively added: see note 14). A Local Health Board or NHS trust cannot be required to provide an explanation of the content of any documents or records provided to an inspector conducting an inspection of premises under s 161 (see PARA 407): s 161B(2) (as so prospectively added).

33 See the Social Services and Well-being (Wales) Act 2014 s 161C(2) (prospectively added: see note 14), which provides, as from the appointed day, that it is an offence to fail to comply with a requirement imposed on a person by s 161B(1). It is a defence for a person charged with an offence under s 161C(2) to show that he had a reasonable excuse for not complying with the requirement: s 161C(3) (as so prospectively added). As to the punishment etc offences under s 161C see PARA 407 note 22.

409. Inspection of premises used for care and support services. Any person authorised by the Welsh Ministers[1] may at any reasonable time enter and inspect any premises (other than regulated premises[2]) in which care and support services[3] are or are proposed to be provided by a local authority in Wales[4], whether directly or under arrangements made with another person[5]. Any person inspecting any premises under these provisions may:

(1)   make such examination into the state and management of the premises, and the facilities and services provided there, as he thinks fit[6];

(2)   inspect any records[7] relating to the premises, or to any person for whom services have been or are to be provided there[8]; and

(3)   require the owner of, or any person employed in, the premises to furnish him with such information as he may request[9].

Any person inspecting any premises under these provisions may:

(a)   interview any person residing there in private for the purpose of investigating any complaint as to those premises or the services provided there, or if he has reason to believe that the services being provided there for that person are not satisfactory[10]; and

(b)   examine any such person in private[11].

Any person who intentionally obstructs another in the exercise of this power is guilty of an offence[12].

1 As to the Welsh Ministers see PARA 395.

2 For these purposes 'regulated premises' means premises in respect of which a person is registered under the Care Standards Act 2000 Pt II (ss 11–42) (see CHILDREN AND YOUNG PERSONS vol 10 (2017) PARA 1017 et seq): National Health Service and Community Care Act 1990 s 48(1A)(b) (s 48(1) amended, s 48(1A) added, by SI 2010/813).

3 Ie services under the Social Services and Well-being (Wales) Act 2014 Pt 4 (ss 32–58). These provisions also apply to premises in which services under the Mental Health Act 1983 s 117 (after-care for persons formerly detained: see MENTAL HEALTH AND CAPACITY vol 75 (2013) PARA 945): National Health Service and Community Care Act 1990 s 48(1) (as amended (see note 2); s 48(1), (2)(b) amended by SI 2015/914).

4 Ie the council of a county or county borough in Wales: National Health Service and Community Care Act 1990 ss 47(8), 48(8) (s 47(8) amended by SI 2016/413). As to the meaning of 'Wales' see PARA 2 note 4. As to local government areas and authorities in Wales see LOCAL GOVERNMENT vol 69 (2009) PARA 22 et seq.

5 National Health Service and Community Care Act 1990 s 48(1) (as amended: see notes 2, 3). Any person exercising the power of entry must, if so required, produce some duly authenticated document showing his authority to do so: s 48(6).

6 National Health Service and Community Care Act 1990 s 48(2)(a).

7   Ie any records in whatever form they are held: see the National Health Service and Community
    Care Act 1990 s 48(2). Any person exercising the power to inspect records:
    (1)   is entitled at any reasonable time to have access to, and inspect and check the operation
           of, any computer and any associated apparatus or material which is or has been in use
           in connection with the records in question (s 48(3)(a)); and
    (2)   may require reasonable assistance from the person by whom or on whose behalf the
           computer is or has been so used, or any person having charge of or otherwise concerned
           with the operation of the computer, apparatus or material (s 48(3)(b)).
8   National Health Service and Community Care Act 1990 s 48(2)(b) (as amended: see note 3). No
    person may exercise the power under s 48(2)(b) so as to inspect medical records, or exercise the
    power under s 48(4)(b), unless he is a registered medical practitioner and the records relate to
    medical treatment given at the premises in question; nor may any person exercise the power to
    examine a person unless he is a registered medical practitioner: s 48(5). As to the meaning of
    'registered medical practitioner' see MEDICAL PROFESSIONS vol 74 (2011) PARA 176.
9   National Health Service and Community Care Act 1990 s 48(2)(c).
10 National Health Service and Community Care Act 1990 s 48(4)(a).
11 National Health Service and Community Care Act 1990 s 48(4)(b).
12 National Health Service and Community Care Act 1990 s 48(7). A person guilty of such an offence
    is liable on summary conviction to a fine not exceeding level 3 on the standard scale: s 48(7). As
    to the powers of magistrates' courts to issue fines on summary conviction see SENTENCING vol 92
    (2015) PARA 176.

C.   CODES OF PRACTICE

410. Power to issue codes. The Welsh Ministers[1] may issue, and from time to
time revise, one or more codes on the exercise of social services functions[2] ('a
code')[3]. A code may impose requirements, and may include guidelines setting out
aims, objectives and other matters[4]. The Welsh Ministers must publish each code
for the time being in force on their website and make available to the public codes
that have been replaced or revoked (whether on their website or otherwise)[5].

Before issuing or revising a code the Welsh Ministers must consult such persons
as they think fit on a draft of the code (or revised code)[6], and if they wish to
proceed with the draft (with or without modifications) must lay a copy of the draft
before the National Assembly for Wales[7]. If[8] the Assembly resolves not to approve
the draft, the Ministers must not issue the code (or revised code) in the form of
that draft[9]: if no such resolution is made[10] the Ministers must issue the code (or
revised code) in the form of the draft[11]. The Ministers may revoke a code (or
revised code) in a further code or by direction[12].

1   As to the Welsh Ministers see PARA 395.
2   As to social services functions see PARA 373.
3   Social Services and Well-being (Wales) Act 2014 s 145(1). For local authority's duty to act in
    accordance with the code see s 145(3); and PARA 374.
4   Social Services and Well-being (Wales) Act 2014 s 145(2). A code may specify that s 147
    (exclusions) does not apply to a requirement contained in the code: s 145(4).
5   Social Services and Well-being (Wales) Act 2014 s 145(5).
6   Social Services and Well-being (Wales) Act 2014 s 146(1).
7   Social Services and Well-being (Wales) Act 2014 s 146(2).
8   Ie before the end of the 40 day period, that is, the period which begins on the day on which the
    draft is laid before the Assembly and does not include any time during which the Assembly is
    dissolved or is in recess for more than four days: Social Services and Well-being (Wales) Act 2014
    s 146(5).
9   Social Services and Well-being (Wales) Act 2014 s 146(3). Section 146(3) does not prevent a new
    draft of a code (or revised code) from being laid before the Assembly: s 146(6).
10 Ie before the end of the 40 day period: see note 8.
11 Social Services and Well-being (Wales) Act 2014 s 146(4)(a). The code (or revised code) came into
    force on 10 April 2017: see the Revised Code of Practice on the exercise of social services functions
    in relation to Part 4 (direct payments and choice of accommodation) and Part 5 (charging and
    financial assessment) of the Social Services and Well-being (Wales) Act 2014 (Appointed Day)
    (Wales) Order 2017, SI 2017/557 (made under the Social Services and Well-being (Wales) Act
    2014 s 146(4)(b)).

12 Social Services and Well-being (Wales) Act 2014 s 146(7). A direction under s 146(7) must be laid before the Assembly: s 146(8).

411. Code of practice about inspections. As from a day to be appointed[1] the Welsh Ministers[2] must prepare and publish a code of practice about the manner in which inspections of premises[3] are to be carried out (including about the frequency of such inspections)[4]. The Ministers may revise the code and must publish a revised code[5].

1 The Social Services and Well-being (Wales) Act 2014 s 161A is added, as from a day to be appointed, by the Regulation and Inspection of Social Care (Wales) Act 2016 s 57(2). At the date at which this volume states the law no day had been appointed for this purpose.
2 As to the Welsh Ministers see PARA 395.
3 Ie under the Social Services and Well-being (Wales) Act 2014 s 161: see PARA 407.
4 Social Services and Well-being (Wales) Act 2014 s 161A(1) (prospectively added: see note 1).
5 Social Services and Well-being (Wales) Act 2014 s 161A(2) (prospectively added: see note 1).

(iii) Social Care Wales

412. Establishment and objectives. Social Care Wales is a body corporate whose principal objective in carrying out its functions is to protect, promote and maintain the safety and well-being of the public in Wales[1]. In pursuing that objective Social Care Wales must exercise its functions with a view to promoting and maintaining:

(1)   high standards in the provision of care and support services[2];
(2)   high standards of conduct and practice among social care workers[3];
(3)   high standards in the training of social care workers[4]; and
(4)   public confidence in social care workers[5].

In exercising its functions Social Care Wales must have regard to any guidance, and comply with nay directions, given to it by the Welsh Ministers[6].

1 Regulation and Inspection of Social Care (Wales) Act 2016 ss 67(2), (3), 68(1). Social Care Wales is the former Care Council for Wales, which was constituted under the Care Standards Act 2000 s 54 (repealed): Regulation and Inspection of Social Care (Wales) Act 2016 s 67(1), (2). Social Care Wales must appoint a registrar: s 81(1). Provision for the constitution, staff etc of Social Care Wales is made by ss 67(4), 81(2), (3), Sch 2; and provision as to the exercise of Social Care Wales' rule-making powers is made by ss 73–75 (s 74 amended by SI 2016/1030). See also PARA 386 (duty of Welsh Ministers and Social Care Wales to co-operate with each other and other authorities), PARA 387 (joint and delegated exercise of functions of Welsh Ministers and Social Care Wales), and PARA 388 (information sharing between Welsh Ministers and Social Care Wales).
2 Regulation and Inspection of Social Care (Wales) Act 2016 s 68(2)(a).'Care and support service' means a regulated service or any other service in Wales which involves the provision of care and support by social care workers: s 69(3). As to the meanings of 'care' and 'support' see PARA 204; as to the meaning of 'regulated service' see PARA 203; as to the meaning of 'social care worker' see (by virtue of ss 68(3), 69(4)) PARA 198 (noting in particular note 9).
3 Regulation and Inspection of Social Care (Wales) Act 2016 s 68(2)(b).
4 Regulation and Inspection of Social Care (Wales) Act 2016 s 68(2)(c).
5 Regulation and Inspection of Social Care (Wales) Act 2016 s 68(2)(d).
6 Regulation and Inspection of Social Care (Wales) Act 2016 ss 76(1), 77(1). The Welsh Ministers must publish any guidance they give to Social Care Wales: s 76(2). A direction must be in writing and may be varied or revoked by a subsequent direction: s 77(2). As to the Welsh Ministers see PARA 395. The Ministers also have default powers of intervention: see s 78; and PARA 406.

413. Advice, assistance and public engagement. Social Care Wales[1] may give any person providing a care and support service[2] advice or other assistance (including grants) for the purpose of encouraging improvement in the provision of that service[3]. It may also promote or undertake comparative or other studies designed to enable it to make recommendations[4] for improving economy, efficiency and effectiveness in the provision of a care and support service[5]. It must:

(1)   make information about it and the exercise of its functions available to the public, and social care workers[6];

(2)   prepare and publish a statement of its policy with respect to involving the public and social care workers in the exercise of those functions (whether by consultation or other means)[7]; and

(3)   prepare and publish a statement of its policy with respect to the bringing of criminal proceedings by it[8].

1   As to the establishment and objectives of Social Care Wales see PARA 412.
2   As to the meaning of 'care and support service' see PARA 412 note 1.
3   Regulation and Inspection of Social Care (Wales) Act 2016 s 69(1). Social Care Wales may attach such conditions to a grant given under s 69(1) as it thinks appropriate: s 69(2).
4   Ie under the Regulation and Inspection of Social Care (Wales) Act 2016 s 69 (see the text and notes 1–3).
5   Regulation and Inspection of Social Care (Wales) Act 2016 s 70.
6   Regulation and Inspection of Social Care (Wales) Act 2016 s 71(1)(a).
7   Regulation and Inspection of Social Care (Wales) Act 2016 s 71(1)(b). Social Care Wales may revise its statements of policy under ss 71, 72 and must publish the revised statement, or may publish a new statement of policy (ss 71(2), 72(2)), and must have regard to the most recent policy statement published under s 71 or, as the case may be, s 72 when exercising its functions (ss 71(3), 72(3)).
8   Regulation and Inspection of Social Care (Wales) Act 2016 s 72(1). See note 7.

414. Duty to keep register of social workers and social care workers. Social Care Wales[1] must keep a register of social workers[2], social care workers of any other description specified by the Welsh Ministers by regulations[3], visiting social workers from relevant European States[4] and visiting social care managers from relevant European states[5]. There must be a separate part of the register for social workers[6], for each description of social care worker specified in such regulations[7], for visiting social workers from relevant European States[8] and for visiting social care managers from relevant European states[9]. An entry in the register in respect of a person must show[10]:

(1)   the date on which the person was entered onto the register[11];

(2)   the person's qualifications to practise work of the kind to which his registration relates[12];

(3)   such other qualifications, knowledge or experience relevant to the person's registration as may be prescribed[13]; and

(4)   such information relating to the person's fitness to practise as may be prescribed[14].

Social Care Wales must by rules require a person registered in a part of the register to give notice to the registrar of changes to the information recorded in the register in respect of that person[15]. It must also keep a list of persons whose entries in the register have been removed by order[16].

1   As to the establishment and objectives of Social Care Wales see PARA 412. Social Care Wales must publish the register in such manner, and at such times, as it thinks appropriate (Regulation and Inspection of Social Care (Wales) Act 2016 s 108(1)) and must comply with any reasonable request made by a person for a copy of, or an extract from, the register (s 108(2)).
2   Regulation and Inspection of Social Care (Wales) Act 2016 s 80(1)(a). As to the meanings of 'social worker' and 'social care worker' see PARA 198. As to the registration of social workers and social care workers see PARA 201.
3   Regulation and Inspection of Social Care (Wales) Act 2016 s 80(1)(b). See the Social Care Wales (Specification of Social Care Workers) (Registration) Regulations 2016, SI 2016/1235. As to the Welsh Ministers see PARA 395.
4   Regulation and Inspection of Social Care (Wales) Act 2016 s 80(1)(c). As to visiting social workers from relevant European States see s 90; and PARA 201.
5   Regulation and Inspection of Social Care (Wales) Act 2016 s 80(1)(d) (added by SI 2016/1030).
6   Regulation and Inspection of Social Care (Wales) Act 2016 s 80(2)(a). This is referred to as the 'social worker part' of the register: s 80(3)(a).

7 Regulation and Inspection of Social Care (Wales) Act 2016 s 80(2)(b). This is referred to as the 'added part' of the register: s 80(3)(b).
8 Regulation and Inspection of Social Care (Wales) Act 2016 s 80(2)(c). This is referred to as the 'visiting European social worker part' of the register: s 80(3)(c) (amended by SI 2016/1030).
9 Regulation and Inspection of Social Care (Wales) Act 2016 s 80(2)(d) (added by SI 2016/1030). This is referred to as the 'visiting European social care manager part' of the register: Regulation and Inspection of Social Care (Wales) Act 2016 s 80(3)(d) (added by SI 2016/1030).
10 Social Care Wales may by rules require or authorise the registrar to include in an entry in the register information not required by virtue of these provisions or to remove from an entry in the register information of a kind specified in the rules: Regulation and Inspection of Social Care (Wales) Act 2016 s 91(2). Rules under s 91(2) may not require or authorise the registrar to record information relating to a person's physical or mental health: s 91(3).
11 Regulation and Inspection of Social Care (Wales) Act 2016 s 91(1)(a).
12 Regulation and Inspection of Social Care (Wales) Act 2016 s 91(1)(b).
13 Regulation and Inspection of Social Care (Wales) Act 2016 s 91(1)(c). See the Social Care Wales (Content of Register) Regulations 2016, SI 2016/1097.
14 Regulation and Inspection of Social Care (Wales) Act 2016 s 91(1)(d). See the Social Care Wales (Content of Register) Regulations 2016, SI 2016/1097. As to fitness to practice see PARA 200.
15 Regulation and Inspection of Social Care (Wales) Act 2016 s 106(1). Rules under s 106(1) may, in particular, include provision about the changes to be notified, the manner in which and the time within which a notice must be given and the consequences of failing to comply with any requirements contained in the rules (which may include referral of the matter to a fitness to practise panel): s 106(2).
16 Ie:
   (1) where a person is subject to a removal order made by a fitness to practise panel under the Regulation and Inspection of Social Care (Wales) Act 2016 s 138(9) (disposal following a finding of impairment of fitness to practise), or s 152(8)(e), s 153(9)(d) or s 154(8)(d) (disposal in a review case following a finding of impairment of fitness to practise) (although an entry may not be made in the list relating to a person subject to such a removal order until the decision has taken effect under s 141(5) or s 157(6) (as the case may be)) (s 110(1)–(3); and see the Social Care Wales (List of Persons Removed from the Register) Regulations 2016, SI 2016/1111);
   (2) where a person is subject to an order for removal by agreement made by a fitness to practise panel under the Regulation and Inspection of Social Care (Wales) Act 2016 s 135 (removal from register on consensual basis) or s 152(2), s 153(2), s 154(2) or s 155(5) (disposal in a review case) (and where a person is subject to such an order for removal by agreement the list must give details of the statement of facts agreed under s 135(2) or s 150(2) (as the case may be) (s 110(4), (5)).
   As to the disposal of allegations of impaired fitness to practice see PARA 200. The Welsh Ministers may by regulations make provision about the form and content of the list, the publication of the list or specified information from the list, and circumstances in which an entry relating to a person must be removed from the list: s 110(6).

(iv) Ombudsman

415. Matters which may be investigated. The Ombudsman[1] may investigate[2]:
   (1) action[3] taken by a care home provider[4] in connection with the provision of accommodation, nursing or personal care in a care home in Wales[5];
   (2) action taken by a domiciliary care provider[6] in connection with the provision of domiciliary care in Wales[7]; and
   (3) action taken by an independent palliative care provider[8] in connection with the provision of a palliative care service in Wales[9].

A matter may be investigated where a complaint about it has been duly made or referred[10] to the Ombudsman by or on behalf of[11] a member of the public who claims or claimed to have sustained injustice or hardship as a result of the matter[12]. In the case of a complaint which relates to an independent palliative care provider, it is also necessary[13] that the provider has received public funding[14], within the three years before the date of the action to which the complaint relates, in respect of a palliative care service that it provides in Wales[15]. However, the Ombudsman may not investigate, under these provisions[16]:

(a)   matters which may be investigated pursuant to existing powers[17] for the investigation of complaints[18];

(b)   the commencement or conduct of proceedings before a court of competent jurisdiction[19]; or

(c)   action taken in respect of appointments or removals, pay, discipline, superannuation or other personnel matters[20].

1   As to the Ombudsman see LOCAL GOVERNMENT vol 69 (2009) PARA 843.

2   Ie pursuant to the Public Services Ombudsman (Wales) Act 2005 Pt 2A (ss 34A–34T, Sch 3A).

3   As to the meaning of 'action' see the Public Services Ombudsman (Wales) Act 2005 s 41(1); and LOCAL GOVERNMENT vol 69 (2009) PARA 847.

4   As to the meaning of 'care home' see, until a day to be appointed, the Care Standards Act 2000 s 3; and PARA 3 note 3 (definition applied by the Public Services Ombudsman (Wales) Act 2005 ss 34A(6), 34R(1), (2) (Pt 2A (ss 34A–34T, Sch 3A) added by the Social Services and Well-being (Wales) Act 2014 Sch 3 paras 2, 4; Public Services Ombudsman (Wales) Act 2005 s 34R(2), (3), (5)(a) prospectively amended, s 34R(6) prospectively added, by the Regulation and Inspection of Social Care (Wales) Act 2016 Sch 3 para 26)); as from the appointed day 'care home' means premises at which a care home service within the meaning of the Regulation and Inspection of Social Care (Wales) Act 2016 Pt 1 (ss 1–64) (see Sch 1 para 1; and PARA 205) is provided wholly or mainly to persons aged 18 or over: Public Services Ombudsman (Wales) Act 2005 s 34R(2) (as so added and prospectively amended). Until the appointed day 'care home provider' means a person who carries on a care home; as from that day a 'care home provider' is a service provider of a care home service within the meaning of the meaning of the Regulation and Inspection of Social Care (Wales) Act 2016 Pt 1 where the service is provided wholly or mainly to persons aged 18 or over: Public Services Ombudsman (Wales) Act 2005 s 34R(3) (as so added and prospectively amended).

Action is to be treated as action taken by a care home provider if it is taken by a person employed by that provider, a person acting on behalf of that provider, or a person to whom that provider has delegated any functions: s 34R(4) (as so added). Until the appointed day action is also to be treated as action taken by a care home provider if he provides, by means of an arrangement with another person, accommodation, nursing or personal care in a care home in Wales for a person falling within the Care Standards Act 2000 s 3(2) and, the action is taken by or on behalf of the other person in carrying out the arrangement; as from that day, action is also to be treated as action taken by a care home provider if he provides, by means of an arrangement with another person, accommodation, nursing or care in a care home in Wales for an individual because of the individual's vulnerability or need, and, the action is taken by or on behalf of the other person in carrying out the arrangement: Public Services Ombudsman (Wales) Act 2005 s 34R(5) (as so added and prospectively amended). As from the appointed day 'care' has the same meaning as in the Regulation and Inspection of Social Care (Wales) Act 2016 Pt 1 (see s 3(1); and PARA 204): Public Services Ombudsman (Wales) Act 2005 s 34R(6) (as so added and prospectively added)

At the date at which this volume states the law no day had been appointed for this purpose.

5   Public Services Ombudsman (Wales) Act 2005 s 34A(1)(a) (as added: see note 4).

6   'Domiciliary care' means personal care provided in their own homes for persons who by reason of illness, infirmity or disability are unable to provide it for themselves without assistance: Public Services Ombudsman (Wales) Act 2005 s 34S(1), (2) (as added: see note 4). 'Domiciliary care provider' means a person who carries on an activity which involves the provision of domiciliary care, but it does not include an individual who:

(1)   carries on the activity otherwise than in partnership with others (s 34S(3)(a) (as so added));

(2)   is not employed by a body corporate or unincorporated association to carry it on (s 34S(3)(b) (as so added));

(3)   does not employ any other person to carry out the activity (s 34S(3)(c) (as so added)); and

(4)   provides or arranges the provision of domiciliary care to fewer than four persons (s 34S(3)(d) (as so added)).

Action is to be treated as action taken by a domiciliary care provider if it is taken by:

(a)   a person employed by that provider (s 34S(4)(a) (as so added));

(b)   a person acting on behalf of that provider (s 34S(4)(b) (as so added)); or

(c)   a person to whom that provider has delegated any functions (s 34S(4)(c) (as so added)).

Action is also to be treated as action taken by a domiciliary care provider if he provides domiciliary care by means of an arrangement with another person and the action is taken by or on behalf of the other person in carrying out the arrangement: s 34S(5) (as so added).

7 Public Services Ombudsman (Wales) Act 2005 s 34A(1)(b) (as added: see note 4).

8 'Independent palliative care provider' means a person who provides a palliative care service and is not a Welsh health service body: Public Services Ombudsman (Wales) Act 2005 s 34T(1), (3) (as added: see note 4). 'Palliative care service' means a service the main purpose of which is to provide palliative care: s 34T(2) (as so added). Action is to be treated as action taken by an independent palliative care provider if it is taken by:
   (1)   a person employed by that provider (s 34T(4)(a) (as so added));
   (2)   a person acting on behalf of that provider (s 34T(4)(b) (as so added)); or
   (3)   a person to whom that provider has delegated any functions (s 34T(4)(c) (as so added)).
   Action is also to be treated as action taken by an independent palliative care provider if he provides palliative care by means of an arrangement with another person and the action is taken by or on behalf of the other person in carrying out the arrangement: s 34T(5) (as so added).

9 Public Services Ombudsman (Wales) Act 2005 s 34A(1)(c) (as added: see note 4).

10 As to when complaints are duly made or referred see PARA 416. The Ombudsman retains a discretion to consider a complaint which has not been duly made or referred: see PARA 417.

11 A complaint about a matter under the Public Services Ombudsman (Wales) Act 2005 Pt 2A may only be made by a member of the public ('the person aggrieved') who claims or claimed to have sustained injustice or hardship as a result of a matter to which Pt 2A applies (s 34D(1)(a) (as added: see note 4)), a person authorised in writing by the person aggrieved to act on that person's behalf (s 34D(1)(b) (as so added)) or, if the person aggrieved is not capable of authorising a person to act on his or her behalf (for example because the person has died), a person who appears to the Ombudsman to be appropriate to act on behalf of the person aggrieved (s 34D(1)(c) (as so added)). 'Member of the public' does not include a person acting in his or her capacity as a care home provider, a domiciliary care provider, an independent palliative care provider or a listed authority: s 34D(2) (as so added). It is for the Ombudsman to determine any question of whether a person is entitled under these provisions to make a complaint: see s 34D(3); and PARA 417. As to the listed authorities see LOCAL GOVERNMENT vol 69 (2009) PARA 854.

12 Public Services Ombudsman (Wales) Act 2005 s 34B(1)(a) (as added: see note 4). The Ombudsman may pay to the person who made the complaint and to any other person who attends or supplies information for the purposes of the investigation sums in respect of the expenses properly incurred by them and allowances to compensate for the loss of their time: s 34H(6) (as so added). The Ombudsman may attach conditions to those payments: s 34H(7) (as so added).

13 Ie the complaint cannot otherwise be investigated.

14 For this purpose 'public funding' means funding from the Welsh Ministers, a Local Health Board established under the National Health Service (Wales) Act 2006 s 11, an NHS Trust or a county council or county borough council in Wales: Public Services Ombudsman (Wales) Act 2005 s 34B(3) (as so added). As to the Welsh Ministers see PARA 395. As to Local Health Boards see HEALTH SERVICES vol 54 (2017) PARA 97. As to NHS Trusts see HEALTH SERVICES vol 54 (2017) PARA 235. As to local government areas and authorities in Wales see LOCAL GOVERNMENT vol 69 (2009) PARA 22 et seq.

15 Public Services Ombudsman (Wales) Act 2005 s 34B(1)(b), (2) (as added: see note 4).

16 Ie the Public Services Ombudsman (Wales) Act 2005 Pt 2A does not apply.

17 Ie matters which may be investigated under the Public Services Ombudsman (Wales) Act 2005 Pt 2 (ss 2–34) (see LOCAL GOVERNMENT vol 69 (2009) PARA 847 et seq).

18 Public Services Ombudsman (Wales) Act 2005 s 34A(2)(a) (as added: see note 4).

19 Public Services Ombudsman (Wales) Act 2005 s 34A(2)(b), Sch 3A para 1 (as added: see note 4). The Welsh Ministers may by order amend Sch 3A by adding an entry, removing an entry, or changing an entry: s 34A(3). Before making an order under s 34A(3), the Welsh Ministers must consult the Ombudsman: s 34A(4) (as so added). No order is to be made under s 34A(3) unless a draft of the statutory instrument containing it has been laid before, and approved by a resolution of, the Assembly: s 34A(5) (as so added). At the date at which this volume states the law no such order had been made.

20 Public Services Ombudsman (Wales) Act 2005 Sch 3A para 2 (as added: see note 4).

416. Procedure to be followed before making a complaint. Before making a complaint to the Ombudsman[1] the person affected[2] must have brought the matter to which it relates to the notice of the provider to whom it relates[3], and the provider must have been given a reasonable opportunity to investigate the matter and to respond[4]. Before a complaint can be referred to the Ombudsman it must have been made to the provider by or on behalf of the person affected[5] before the end of the period of twelve months beginning with the day on which the person aggrieved first had notice of the matter[6]. A complaint will be 'duly made' or, as the case may be, 'duly referred' if these requirements, and specified procedural requirements[7], are complied with[8].

1   As to the Ombudsman see LOCAL GOVERNMENT vol 69 (2009) PARA 843. As to the making of complaints see PARA 415.
2   A complaint will be 'duly made' or 'duly referred' under these provisions only if it is made (in the case of a referral, previously made) by a person who is entitled under the Public Services Ombudsman (Wales) Act 2005 s 34D (see PARA 415) to make a complaint to the Ombudsman: ss 34B(4)(a), (5)(b), 34F(1)(a)(i) (Pt 2A (ss 34A–34T, Sch 3A) added by the Social Services and Well-being (Wales) Act 2014 Sch 3 para 2).
3   Public Services Ombudsman (Wales) Act 2005 s 34B(4)(b)(i) (as added: see note 2).
4   Public Services Ombudsman (Wales) Act 2005 s 34B(4)(b)(ii) (as added: see note 2).
5   Public Services Ombudsman (Wales) Act 2005 s 34B(5)(a) (as added: see note 2). See note 2.
6   Public Services Ombudsman (Wales) Act 2005 s 34F(1)(a)(ii) (as added: see note 2).
7   The complaint must be made or referred in writing and before the end of the period of 12 months beginning with the day on which the person aggrieved first has notice of the matter or, in the case of a referral, the complaint was made to the provider: Public Services Ombudsman (Wales) Act 2005 ss 34B(4)(c), 34E(1), (2)(b), 34F(1)(b) (as added: see note 2). It is for the Ombudsman to determine whether these requirements are met in respect of a complaint: s 34E(3) (as so added).
8   Public Services Ombudsman (Wales) Act 2005 s 34B(4), (5) (as added: see note 2). The Ombudsman retains a discretion to consider a complaint which has not been duly made or referred: see PARA 417.

417. Ombudsman's discretion in initiating and proceeding with investigation. It is for the Ombudsman[1] to determine any question of whether a person is entitled[2] to make a complaint[3]. It is also for the Ombudsman to determine whether a complaint has been duly made or referred[4], and if he determines that a complaint has not been duly made because the provider has been given insufficient notice of it[5], or that a complaint has not been duly made or referred for procedural reasons[6], he may nonetheless investigate the complaint if it is a matter which may be investigated[7] and he thinks it reasonable to do so[8]. It is also for the Ombudsman to decide whether to begin, continue or discontinue an investigation[9]: if his decision is not to begin or continue, or to discontinue, the investigation he is required to notify that decision to the affected parties[10].

The Ombudsman may take any action he considers appropriate with a view to resolving a complaint which he has the power[11] to investigate[12]. He may take such action in addition to or instead of conducting an investigation into the complaint[13].

1   As to the Ombudsman see LOCAL GOVERNMENT vol 69 (2009) PARA 843. As to the making of complaints see PARA 415.
2   Ie under the Public Services Ombudsman (Wales) Act 2005 s 34D (see PARA 415).
3   Public Services Ombudsman (Wales) Act 2005 s 34D(3) (Pt 2A (ss 34A–34T, Sch 3A) added by the Social Services and Well-being (Wales) Act 2014 Sch 3 para 2).
4   Ie whether the requirements of the Public Services Ombudsman (Wales) Act 2005 s 34B(1) (see PARA 416) have been met in respect of a complaint: s 34B(6) (as added: see note 3).
5   Ie where the Ombudsman determines that the requirements of the Public Services Ombudsman (Wales) Act 2005 s 34B(1) have not been met in respect of the complaint because the requirements of s 34(4)(b) (see PARA 416) have not been met in respect of that complaint.
6   Ie where the Ombudsman determines that the requirements of the Public Services Ombudsman (Wales) Act 2005 s 34B(1) have not been met in respect of a complaint because the requirements of s 34E or s 34F(1)(a)(ii) or (b)(ii) (see PARA 416) have not been met in respect of that complaint.
7   Ie it is a complaint which relates to a matter to which the Public Services Ombudsman (Wales) Act 2005 Pt 2 applies (see PARA 416).
8   Public Services Ombudsman (Wales) Act 2005 s 34B(7) (as added: see note 3).

9   Public Services Ombudsman (Wales) Act 2005 s 34B(8) (as added: see note 3). The Ombudsman
    may take any action which he thinks may assist in making a decision under s 34B(8) (s 34B(9) (as
    so added)), and may begin or continue an investigation into a complaint even if the complaint has
    been withdrawn (s 34B(10) (as so added)).

10 If the Ombudsman decides under the Public Services Ombudsman (Wales) Act 2005 s 34B(8) not
    to begin an investigation into a complaint or to discontinue an investigation, he must prepare a
    statement of the reasons for that decision (s 34G(1) (as so added)) and must send a copy of the
    statement to the person who made the complaint (s 34G(2)(a) (as so added)) and the provider to
    whom the complaint relates (s 34G(2)(b) (as so added)). He may also send a copy of the statement
    to any other persons he thinks appropriate: s 34G(3) (as so added). The Ombudsman may publish
    a statement under s 34G if, after taking account of the interests of the person aggrieved and any
    other persons he thinks appropriate, he considers that it would be in the public interest to do so:
    s 34G(4) (as so added). The Ombudsman may supply a copy of the published statement, or part
    of that statement, to any person who requests it (s 34G(5) (as so added)), and may charge a
    reasonable fee for supplying such a copy (s 34G(6) (as so added)). The following information must
    not be included in a version of a statement sent to a person under s 34G(2)(b) or (3) or published
    under s 34G(4): the name of a person other than the provider to whom the complaint relates
    (s 34G(7)(a) (as so added)) and information which, in the opinion of the Ombudsman, is likely to
    identify such a person and which, in the Ombudsman's opinion, can be omitted without impairing
    the effectiveness of the statement (s 34G(7)(b) (as so added)). Section 34G(7) does not apply if,
    after taking account of the interests of the person aggrieved and any other persons the
    Ombudsman thinks appropriate, the Ombudsman considers that it would be in the public interest
    to include that information in that version of the statement: s 34G(8) (as so added).

11 Ie under the Public Services Ombudsman (Wales) Act 2005 s 34B (see PARAS 415–416)

12 Public Services Ombudsman (Wales) Act 2005 s 34C(1) (as added: see note 3). Any such action
    must be taken in private: s 34C(3) (as so added). Where a complaint is resolved and the
    Ombudsman concludes that the person aggrieved has sustained injustice or hardship as a result of
    the matter complained of, or that insufficient remedial action has been taken, the Ombudsman
    may prepare a 'special report': see PARA 421.

13 Public Services Ombudsman (Wales) Act 2005 s 34C(2) (as added: see note 3).

418. Procedure for investigations. Subject to the requirement that every
investigation[1] must be conducted in private[2] and that affected persons be given an
opportunity to comment on the matter[3], the procedure for conducting an
investigation is that which the Ombudsman[4] thinks appropriate in the
circumstances of the case[5]. The Ombudsman has the same powers as the
High Court in relation to the attendance and examination of witnesses (including
the administration of oaths and affirmations and the examination of witnesses
abroad)[6] and the production of documents[7]. The Ombudsman may, among other
things:

(1)   make any inquiries which he thinks appropriate[8]; and
(2)   determine whether any person may be represented in the investigation
       by an authorised person[9] or another person[10].

1   Ie every investigation pursuant to the Public Services Ombudsman (Wales) Act 2005 Pt 2A
    (ss 34A–34T, Sch 3A): see PARA 415 et seq.

2   Public Services Ombudsman (Wales) Act 2005 s 34H(2) (Pt 2A added by the Social Services and
    Well-being (Wales) Act 2014 Sch 3 para 2).

3   See the Public Services Ombudsman (Wales) Act 2005 s 34H(1); and PARA 419.

4   As to the Ombudsman see LOCAL GOVERNMENT vol 69 (2009) PARA 843.

5   Public Services Ombudsman (Wales) Act 2005 s 34H(3) (as added: see note 2).

6   Public Services Ombudsman (Wales) Act 2005 s 34I(1), (3)(a) (as added: see note 2). No person
    may be compelled to give any evidence or produce any document which the person could not be
    compelled to give or produce in civil proceedings before the High Court (s 34I(5) (as so added)),
    and the Crown is not entitled to any privilege in relation to the production of documents or the
    giving of evidence that would otherwise be allowed by law in legal proceedings (s 34I(6) (as so
    added)). Where an obligation to maintain secrecy or other restriction on the disclosure of
    information obtained by or supplied to persons in Her Majesty's service has been imposed by an
    enactment or rule of law, the obligation or restriction does not to apply to the disclosure of
    information for the purposes of the investigation: s 34I(7) (as so added).

7   Public Services Ombudsman (Wales) Act 2005 s 34I(3)(b) (as added: see note 2).

8   Public Services Ombudsman (Wales) Act 2005 s 34H(4)(a) (as added: see note 2).
9   For this purpose 'authorised person' means a person who, for the purposes of the Legal Services
    Act 2007, is an authorised person in relation to an activity which constitutes the exercise of a right
    of audience or the conduct of litigation (within the meaning of the Legal Services Act 2007): Public
    Services Ombudsman (Wales) Act 2005 s 34H(5) (as added: see note 2). As to the meaning of
    'authorised person' the Legal Services Act 2007 see s 1(4); and LEGAL PROFESSIONS vol 65
    (2015) PARA 202; as to rights of audience and the conduct of litigation see s 12(1); and LEGAL
    PROFESSIONS vol 65 (2015) PARA 352.
10 Public Services Ombudsman (Wales) Act 2005 s 34H(4)(b) (as added: see note 2).

419. Persons who may be invited or compelled to contribute to the investigation. If the Ombudsman decides[1] to conduct an investigation into a complaint[2] he must:

(1)   give the provider to whom the complaint relates an opportunity to comment on the allegations contained in the complaint[3]; and

(2)   give any other person who is alleged in the complaint to have taken or authorised the action complained of an opportunity to comment on the allegations relating to that person[4].

The Ombudsman may require a person he thinks is able to supply information or produce a document relevant to the investigation to do so[5], and may require a person he thinks is able to supply information or produce a document relevant to the investigation to provide any facility he may reasonably require[6].

1   As to the Ombudsman see LOCAL GOVERNMENT vol 69 (2009) PARA 843. As to the making of
    complaints see PARA 415.
2   Ie under the Public Services Ombudsman (Wales) Act 2005 s 34B(8) (see PARA 417).
3   Public Services Ombudsman (Wales) Act 2005 s 34H(1) (Pt 2A (ss 34A–34T, Sch 3A) added by
    the Social Services and Well-being (Wales) Act 2014 Sch 3 para 2).
4   Public Services Ombudsman (Wales) Act 2005 s 34H(2) (as added: see note 3).
5   Public Services Ombudsman (Wales) Act 2005 s 34I(2) (as added: see note 3).
6   Public Services Ombudsman (Wales) Act 2005 s 34I(4) (as added: see note 3).

420. Reporting on investigations and acting on investigation reports. After conducting an investigation[1] the Ombudsman[2] must prepare a report on the findings of the investigation (an 'investigation report')[3]. Where the Ombudsman has concluded in such a report that the person aggrieved has sustained injustice or hardship as a result of the matter investigated, the provider to whom the matter relates must consider the report and notify the Ombudsman[4] of the action he has taken or proposes to take in response to the report[5]. If such notification is not given, or satisfactory remedial action is not taken, the Ombudsman may recommend further action in a 'special report'[6].

Alternatively, instead of preparing an investigation report, the Ombudsman may prepare a report on his findings[7]. He may do this if he is satisfied that the public interest does not require[8] an investigation report[9] because he has concluded either:

(1)   that the person aggrieved[10] has not sustained injustice or hardship as a result of the matter complained of[11]; or

(2)   that the person aggrieved has sustained such injustice or hardship[12] and the provider to whom the complaint relates agrees to implement[13] any recommendations that the Ombudsman makes[14].

If having prepared such a report the Ombudsman is not satisfied that the provider has implemented his recommendations, he may recommend further action in a 'special report'[15].

Provision is made for the publicising of reports[16].

1   Ie an investigation into a complaint about a matter to which the Public Services Ombudsman
    (Wales) Act 2005 Pt 2A (ss 34A–34T) applies.

2 As to the Ombudsman see LOCAL GOVERNMENT vol 69 (2009) PARA 843.
3 Public Services Ombudsman (Wales) Act 2005 s 34K(2)(a) (Pt 2A (ss 34A–34T, Sch 3A) added by the Social Services and Well-being (Wales) Act 2014 Sch 3 para 2).
4 Ie before the end of the period of one month beginning on the date on which the authority receives the report or a longer period specified by the Ombudsman in writing (if any): Public Services Ombudsman (Wales) Act 2005 s 34M(3) (as added: see note 3).
5 Public Services Ombudsman (Wales) Act 2005 s 34M(1), (2)(a) (as added: see note 3). The provider must also notify the period before the end of which he proposes to take that action (if that action has not already been taken): s 34M(2)(b) (as so added).
6 See the Public Services Ombudsman (Wales) Act 2005 ss 34O, 34P; and PARA 422.
7 Public Services Ombudsman (Wales) Act 2005 s 34N(4) (as added: see note 3). If the Ombudsman decides to prepare such a report ss 34K–34M (investigation reports) do not apply: ss 34K(1), 34N(4) (as so added).
8 Ie the public interest does not require the Public Services Ombudsman (Wales) Act 2005 ss 34K–34M to apply.
9 Public Services Ombudsman (Wales) Act 2005 s 34N(1)(b), (2)(c) (as added: see note 3).
10 As to the person aggrieved see PARA 415.
11 Public Services Ombudsman (Wales) Act 2005 s 34N(1)(a) (as added: see note 3).
12 Public Services Ombudsman (Wales) Act 2005 s 34N(2)(a) (as added: see note 3).
13 Ie before the end of 'the permitted period', that is:
  (1) a period agreed between the Ombudsman, the provider and the person who made the complaint (Public Services Ombudsman (Wales) Act 2005 s 34N(3)(a) (as added: see note 3)); or
  (2) if the Ombudsman thinks that no such agreement can be reached, a period specified by him in writing (s 34N(3)(b) (as so added)).
14 Public Services Ombudsman (Wales) Act 2005 s 34N(2)(b) (as added: see note 3).
15 See note 6.
16 See PARA 422.

421. Special reports and recommendations. A 'special report' is a report which makes such recommendations as the Ombudsman[1] thinks fit as to the action which, in his opinion, should be taken to remedy the injustice or hardship to the person aggrieved[2] and to prevent similar injustice or hardship being caused in the future[3]. The Ombudsman may prepare a special report if:

(1) he has concluded in an investigation report[4] that the person aggrieved has sustained injustice or hardship as a result of the matter investigated[5] and either the provider has not notified the Ombudsman of the remedial action it has taken or the Ombudsman is not satisfied with the provider's response[6];

(2) he has prepared a report on his findings[7] and is not satisfied that the provider has[8] implemented his recommendations[9].

The Ombudsman may also prepare a special report if:

(a) a complaint in respect of a provider has been[10] resolved[11];

(b) in resolving the complaint, the Ombudsman has concluded that the person aggrieved has sustained injustice or hardship as a result of the matter complained of[12],

(c) the provider has agreed to take particular action before the end of a particular period[13]; and

(d) the Ombudsman is not satisfied that the provider has[14] taken that action[15].

Provision is made for the publicising of special reports[16].

1 As to the Ombudsman see LOCAL GOVERNMENT vol 69 (2009) PARA 843.
2 Public Services Ombudsman (Wales) Act 2005 s 34P(1)(b)(i) (Pt 2A (ss 34A–34T, Sch 3A) added by the Social Services and Well-being (Wales) Act 2014 Sch 3 para 2). As to the person aggrieved see PARA 415. A special report must also set out the facts which entitle the Ombudsman to prepare it (ie the facts on the basis of which Case 1, 2 or 3 of s 34O (see the text and notes 4–15) applies): Public Services Ombudsman (Wales) Act 2005 s 34P(1)(a) (as so added).
3 Public Services Ombudsman (Wales) Act 2005 s 34P(1)(b)(ii) (as added: see note 2).

4   As to the making of investigation reports see PARA 420.
5   Public Services Ombudsman (Wales) Act 2005 s 34O(1), (2)(a) (as added: see note 2).
6   Ie the Ombudsman:
    (1)   has not received the notification required under the Public Services Ombudsman (Wales)
          Act 2005 s 34M (see PARA 420) before the end of the period permitted under s 34
          (s 34O(2)(b), (3)(a) (as so added));
    (2)   has received that notification but is not satisfied with the action which the provider has
          taken or proposes to take or the period before the end of which the provider proposes
          to have taken that action (s 34O(3)(b) (as so added)); or
    (3)   has received that notification but is not satisfied that the provider has, before the end of
          the period referred to in s 34M(2)(b) (see PARA 420) or such longer period specified by
          the Ombudsman in writing (if any), taken the action that the provider proposed to take
          (s 34O(3)(c), (4)(as so added)).
    The circumstances referred to in s 34O(2)–(4) are referred to as 'Case 1': s 34O(2) (as so
    added).
7   Public Services Ombudsman (Wales) Act 2005 s 34O(5)(a) (as added: see note 2). This is a report
    on the Ombudsman's findings under s 34N by virtue of s 34N(2) (see PARA 420).
8   Ie before the end of the period referred to in the Public Services Ombudsman (Wales) Act 2005
    s 34N(2)(b) (see PARA 420 note 9) or a longer period specified by the Ombudsman in writing (if
    any): s 34O(6) (as added: see note 2).
9   Public Services Ombudsman (Wales) Act 2005 s 34O(5)(b) (as added: see note 2). The
    circumstances referred to in s 34O(5), (6) are referred to as 'Case 2': s 34O(5) (as so added).
10 Ie under the Public Services Ombudsman (Wales) Act 2005 s 34C (see PARA 417).
11 Public Services Ombudsman (Wales) Act 2005 s 34O(7)(a) (as added: see note 2).
12 Public Services Ombudsman (Wales) Act 2005 s 34O(7)(b) (as added: see note 2).
13 Public Services Ombudsman (Wales) Act 2005 s 34O(7)(c) (as added: see note 2).
14 Ie before the end of the period referred to in the Public Services Ombudsman (Wales) Act 2005
    s 34O(7)(c) (see the text and note 13) or a longer period specified by the Ombudsman in writing
    (if any): s 34O(8) (as added: see note 2).
15 Public Services Ombudsman (Wales) Act 2005 s 34O(7)(d) (as added: see note 2). The
    circumstances referred to in s 34O(7), (8) are referred to as 'Case 3': s 34O(7) (as so added).
16 See PARA 422.

422. Publicising of reports. The Ombudsman[1] must send a copy of an investigation report[2] or a special report[3] arising out of a failure to address the findings of an investigation report[4] to the person who made the complaint and other appropriate persons[5]. The Ombudsman must send a copy of a report of his findings[6], and a copy of any other special report[7], to the person who made the complaint and the provider to whom the complaint relates[8]. The Ombudsman may also send a copy of any type of report to any other persons he thinks appropriate[9], and may publish any report[10]. Certain information may not be included in copies of reports[11].

The Ombudsman may arrange for a notice about an investigation report or a special report[12] to be published in one or more newspapers or by means of broadcast or other electronic media[13]. In deciding whether it is appropriate to make such arrangements the Ombudsman must take into account:

(1)   the public interest[14];
(2)   the interests of the person aggrieved[15]; and
(3)   the interests of any other persons the Ombudsman thinks appropriate[16].

1   As to the Ombudsman see LOCAL GOVERNMENT vol 69 (2009) PARA 843.
2   Ie a report under the Public Services Ombudsman (Wales) Act 2005 s 34K (see PARA 420).
3   Ie a report under the Public Services Ombudsman (Wales) Act 2005 s 34P (see PARA 421).
4   Ie a special report prepared because the Public Services Ombudsman (Wales) Act 2005
    s 34O(2)–(4) ('Case 1') (see PARA 421) applies.
5   Public Services Ombudsman (Wales) Act 2005 ss 34K(2)(b), 34P(2) (Pt 2A (ss 34A–34T, Sch 3A)
    added by the Social Services and Well-being (Wales) Act 2014 Sch 3 para 2). The appropriate
    persons are:
    (1)   the person who made the complaint (Public Services Ombudsman (Wales) Act 2005
          s 34K(3)(a) (as so added));
    (2)   the provider to whom it relates (s 34K(3)(b) (as so added));

(3)   any other person who is alleged in the complaint to have taken or authorised the action complained of (s 34K(3)(c) (as so added)); and

(4)   the Welsh Ministers (see PARA 395) (s 34K(3)(d) (as so added)).

6 Ie a report under the Public Services Ombudsman (Wales) Act 2005 s 34N (see PARA 420).

7 Ie a special report prepared because the Public Services Ombudsman (Wales) Act 2005 s 34O(5), (6) ('Case 2') or s 34O(7), (8) ('Case 3') (see PARA 421) applies.

8 Public Services Ombudsman (Wales) Act 2005 ss 34K(5)(a), 34P(3) (as added: see note 5).

9 Public Services Ombudsman (Wales) Act 2005 ss 34K(4), 34N(5)(b), 34P(4) (as added: see note 5).

10 The Ombudsman may publish a special report under any circumstances (Public Services Ombudsman (Wales) Act 2005 s 34P(5)), and may publish a report under s 34K or s 34N if, after taking account of the interests of the persons aggrieved and any other persons the Ombudsman thinks appropriate, he considers it to be in the public interest to do so (ss 34K(5), 34N(6) (as added: see note 5)). He may supply a copy of a report so published, or a part of that report, to any person who requests it (ss 34K(6), 34N(7), 34P(6) (as so added)), and may charge a reasonable fee for such supply (ss 34K(7), 34N(8), 34P(7) (as so added)).

11 The following information must not be included in a version of a report or special report sent to a person under the Public Services Ombudsman (Wales) Act 2005 s 34K(3)(b), (c) or (4), s 34N(5) or s 34P(2), (3) or (4), or published under s 34K(5), s 34N(6) or s 34P(5):

(1)   the name of a person other than the provider to whom the complaint relates (ss 34K(8)(a), 34N(9)(a), 34P(8)(a) (as added: see note 5));

(2)   information which, in the opinion of the Ombudsman, is likely to identify such a person and which, in the Ombudsman's opinion, can be omitted without impairing the effectiveness of the report (ss 34K(8)(b), 34N(9)(b), 34P(8)(b) (as so added)).

Sections 34K(8), 34N(9), 34P(8) do not apply if, after taking account of the interests of the person aggrieved and any other persons the Ombudsman thinks appropriate, the Ombudsman considers that it would be in the public interest to include that information in that version of the report or special report: ss 34K(9), 34N(10), 34P(9) (as so added).

12 The notice may, for example:

(1)   provide a summary of the Ombudsman's findings (Public Services Ombudsman (Wales) Act 2005 ss 34L(2)(a), 34Q(2)(a) (as added: see note 5));

(2)   specify an address or addresses at which a copy of the published report can be inspected during ordinary office hours and from which a copy of that report (or part of that report) may be obtained (ss 34L(2)(b), 34Q(2)(b) (as so added)); and

(3)   specify a website address at which a copy of the published report can be viewed (ss 34L(2)(c), 34Q(2)(c) (as so added)).

13 Public Services Ombudsman (Wales) Act 2005 ss 34L(1), 34Q(1) (as added: see note 5). The provider to whom the report relates must, if required to do so by the Ombudsman, reimburse the Ombudsman for the reasonable costs of arranging the publication of the notice: ss 34L(3), 34Q(3) (as so added).

14 Public Services Ombudsman (Wales) Act 2005 ss 34L(4)(a), 34Q(4)(a) (as added: see note 5).

15 Public Services Ombudsman (Wales) Act 2005 ss 34L(4)(b), 34Q(4)(b) (as added: see note 5).

16 Public Services Ombudsman (Wales) Act 2005 ss 34L(4)(c), 34Q(4)(c) (as added: see note 5).

423. Co-operation, data protection, and privilege of information.

Supplementary provision is made[1] in connection with investigations of complaints relating to the provision of social and palliative care carried out by the ombudsman[2]. Where the matter under consideration is one which could fall within the remit of another ombudsman or Commissioner, provision is made for an ombudsman conducting any such investigation to consult and co-operate with that other ombudsmen or Commissioner[3]. Provision is also made restricting the disclosure of information obtained in the course of such investigations[4], and for a specified communications and publications made pursuant to such investigations to be absolutely privileged and therefore not susceptible to defamation claims[5].

1 Ie by the Public Services Ombudsman (Wales) Act 2005 Pt 2B (ss 34U–34Z).

2 Ie pursuant to his powers under the Public Services Ombudsman (Wales) Act 2005 Pt 2A (ss 34A–34T). The new provisions also apply to investigations of alleged maladministration by listed authorities carried out by the Ombudsman pursuant to his powers under the Public Services Ombudsman (Wales) Act 2005 Pt 2 (ss 2–34) (see LOCAL GOVERNMENT vol 69 (2009) PARAS 847–866).

3 See the Public Services Ombudsman (Wales) Act 2005 ss 34U–34W; and LOCAL GOVERNMENT vol 69 (2009) PARAS 847–866.

4 See the Public Services Ombudsman (Wales) Act 2005 ss 34X, 34Y; and LOCAL GOVERNMENT vol 69 (2009) PARAS 847–866.
5 See the Public Services Ombudsman (Wales) Act 2005 s 34Z; and LOCAL GOVERNMENT vol 69 (2009) PARAS 847–866.

424–500. Obstruction of investigations. If the Ombudsman[1] is satisfied that a person:

(1)   without lawful excuse, has obstructed the discharge of any of the Ombudsman's functions[2] relating to the investigation of complaints about the provision of social and palliative care[3]; or

(2)   has done an act in relation to an investigation which, if the investigation were proceedings in the High Court, would constitute contempt of court[4],

he may issue a certificate to that effect to the High Court[5] and if he issues such a certificate, the High Court may inquire into the matter[6]. If the High Court is satisfied that either of heads (1) or (2) above is met in relation to the person, it may deal with that person in the same manner as it may deal with a person who has committed contempt in relation to the High Court[7].

1   As to the Ombudsman see LOCAL GOVERNMENT vol 69 (2009) PARA 843.
2   Ie functions under the Public Services Ombudsman (Wales) Act 2005 Pt 2A (ss 34A–34T) (see PARA 415 et seq).
3   Public Services Ombudsman (Wales) Act 2005 s 34J(2)(a) (Pt 2A (ss 34A–34T, Sch 3A) added by the Social Services and Well-being (Wales) Act 2014 Sch 3 para 2).
4   Public Services Ombudsman (Wales) Act 2005 s 34J(2)(b) (as added: see note 3).
5   Public Services Ombudsman (Wales) Act 2005 s 34J(1) (as added: see note 3).
6   Public Services Ombudsman (Wales) Act 2005 s 34J(3) (as added: see note 3).
7   Public Services Ombudsman (Wales) Act 2005 s 34J(4) (as added: see note 3).

SPECIFIC PERFORMANCE

1. THE REMEDY AND ITS SCOPE

(1) THE NATURE OF SPECIFIC PERFORMANCE

501. The remedy by specific performance. Specific performance is equitable relief, given by the court to enforce against a defendant the duty of doing what he agreed by contract to do. Therefore, it would appear that technically a claimant may obtain judgment for specific performance[1] even though there has not, in the strict sense, been any default by the defendant before the issue of the writ[2]. In practice the modern cases invariably proceed on the basis of an actual or threatened breach of contract of a type sufficient to justify the intervention of equity[3].

In early times a court of equity assumed jurisdiction to compel a party to a contract to perform his part of the contract when damages recoverable at law were not an adequate remedy[4]. The remedy of specific performance is thus in contrast with the remedy by way of damages for breach of contract, which gives pecuniary compensation for failure to carry out the terms of the contract[5]. The remedy is exceptional in character[6], and the court has a discretion either to grant it or to leave the parties to their rights at law[7]. The discretion, however, is not an arbitrary or capricious one; it is to be exercised on fixed principles in accordance with authority[8], though a court is not in modern times perhaps so constrained as once it was by previous decisions or black letter rules[9]. The judge must exercise his discretion in a judicial manner[10]. If the contract is within the category of contracts of which specific performance is ordinarily granted[11], is valid in form, has been made between competent parties and is unobjectionable in its nature and circumstances, specific performance is in effect granted as a matter of course[12] even though the judge may think it is very favourable to one party and unfavourable to the other[13], unless the defendant can rely on one of the recognised equitable defences[14]. Where such a defence is available, the existence of a valid contract is not in itself enough to bring about the interference of the court. The conduct of the claimant, such as delay, acquiescence, breach on his part, or some other circumstance outside the contract, may render it inequitable to enforce it[15], or the contract itself may, for example on the ground of misdescription, be such that the court will refuse to enforce it[16].

The jurisdiction to grant specific performance, formerly exercisable only by a court of equity, is now vested in all branches of the High Court[17], but actions for the specific performance of contracts relating to the sale, exchange or partition of land, or the raising of charges on land, are assigned to the Chancery Division[18]. The relief still retains its character as an equitable remedy, and the old principles of equitable relief apply[19]. Specific performance is now also made available in the County Court for the specific performance of any agreement for the sale, purchase or lease of any property where, in the case of a sale or purchase, the purchase money, or, in the case of a lease, the value of the property, does not exceed the County Court limit[20] or where the parties agree that the County Court is to have jurisdiction[21]. District judges have jurisdiction to grant specific performance in resolving small claims referred[22] for arbitration[23]. Arbitrators can order specific performance, save in the case of a contract relating to land[24].

The availability of the remedy of specific performance does not of itself import the existence of some equitable interest; all it imports is the inadequacy of the common law remedy of damages in the particular circumstances[25].

1 Such a judgment is enforceable by proceedings for contempt of court or by other means, eg by appointing another person to do the act: see PARA 636; and CONTEMPT OF COURT vol 22 (2012) PARAS 65, 111. An order for specific performance often falls into two parts. The first can be of a declaratory nature, the second containing consequential directions: see *Hasham v Zenab* [1960] AC 316 at 329, [1960] 2 WLR 374 at 377, PC, per Lord Tucker. It is intended to put both parties in the same position as if their respective contractual obligations had been timeously performed by both of them: *Harvela Investments Ltd v Royal Trust Co of Canada (CI) Ltd* [1986] AC 207 at 227, [1985] 2 All ER 966 at 971, HL, per Lord Diplock.

2 *Hasham v Zenab* [1960] AC 316, [1960] 2 WLR 374, PC; *Oakacre Ltd v Claire Cleaners (Holdings) Ltd* [1982] Ch 197, [1981] 3 All ER 667, where damages 'in addition to' specific performance were awarded for delay after the issue of the writ, even though no decree of specific performance was made because the contract had been completed by the date of the hearing. Damages could not be awarded at law because the writ was premature, having been issued five days before the completion date, at which time there had been no breach of contract. See generally Ibbetson *A Historical Introduction to the Law of Obligations* (1999) p 88.

3 See *Zucker v Tyndall Holdings plc* [1993] 1 All ER 124.

4 For a short historical introduction to the jurisdiction see EQUITABLE JURISDICTION vol 47 (2014) PARAS 1–5; and *Zucker v Tyndall Holdings plc* [1993] 1 All ER 124, [1992] 1 WLR 1127, CA.

5 As to damages for breach of contract see DAMAGES vol 29 (2014) PARA 499 et seq. See also PARA 632 et seq.

6 *Co-operative Insurance Society v Argyll Stores* [1998] AC 1 at 11.

7 *Re Scott and Alvarez's Contract, Scott v Alvarez* [1895] 2 Ch 603 at 612, 615, CA. See also the unusual case of *Jobson v Johnson* [1989] 1 All ER 621, [1989] 1 WLR 1026, CA.

8 See *Re Hallett's Estate, Knatchbull v Hallett* (1880) 13 ChD 696 at 710, CA, per Jessel MR; *Bennett v Smith* (1852) 16 Jur 421 (sale of land); *Lamare v Dixon* (1873) LR 6 HL 414 at 423 per Lord Chelmsford.

9 See *Internet Trading Clubs Ltd v Freeserve (Investments) Ltd* [2001] 1 EBLR 142 at [30]. See also *Posner v Scott-Lewis* [1987] Ch 25, [1986] 3 All ER 513, [1986] 3 WLR 531 (services in apartment block); *Rainbow Estates Ltd v Tokenhold Ltd* [1999] Ch 64, [1998] 2 All ER 860, [1999] 3 WLR 980 (tenant's repair covenant); *Thames Valley Power Ltd v Total Gas & Power Ltd* [2005] EWHC 2208 (Comm), [2006] 1 Lloyd's Rep 441, [2005] ArbLR 60 (commercial supply of gas), where previous practice was not regarded as an absolute barrier.

10 See *Goring v Nash* (1744) 3 Atk 186; *White v Damon* (1802) 7 Ves 30 at 35; *Buckle v Mitchell* (1812) 18 Ves 100 at 111; *Revell v Hussey* (1813) 2 Ball & B 280 at 288; *Conlon v Murray* [1958] NI 17.

11 As to the classes of contracts which are not specifically enforceable see PARA 506 et seq.

12 *Hall v Warren* (1804) 9 Ves 605 at 608; *Sudbrook Trading Estates Ltd v Eggleton* [1983] 1 AC 444 at 478, [1982] 3 All ER 1 at 6 per Lord Diplock; *Patel v Ali* [1984] Ch 283, [1984] 1 All ER 978 at 981 per Goulding J; *Mungalsingh v Juman* [2015] UKPC 38; [2016] 1 P & CR 128, [2016] 1 P & CR D7 at [32] per Lord Neuberger.

13 *Haywood v Cope* (1858) 25 Beav 140; *Matila Ltd v Lisheen Properties Ltd* [2010] EWHC 1832 (Ch), [2010] All ER (D) 221 (Jul). As to refusing specific performance on the ground of hardship see PARA 556 et seq.

14 As to equitable defences generally see PARA 540 et seq.

15 *Clowes v Higginson* (1813) 1 Ves & B 524 at 527; *Leech v Schweder* (1874) 9 Ch App 465n at 467n; *Re Terry and White's Contract* (1886) 32 ChD 14 at 27, CA; *Langen & Wind Ltd v Bell* [1972] Ch 685, [1972] 1 All ER 296 (regard had to unpaid vendor's equitable lien). See also PARA 550 et seq. As to delay and acquiescence see PARA 579. See also EQUITABLE JURISDICTION vol 47 (2014) PARAS 112, 252 et seq.

16 See eg *Re Davis and Cavey* (1888) 40 ChD 601 at 606; *Re Scott and Alvarez's Contract, Scott v Alvarez* [1895] 2 Ch 603, CA; *Charles Hunt Ltd v Palmer* [1931] 2 Ch 287. See also PARA 623 et seq.

17 See COURTS AND TRIBUNALS vol 24 (2010) PARA 699 et seq. See also the Senior Courts Act 1981 s 49(1); and EQUITABLE JURISDICTION vol 47 (2014) PARA 99.

18 See the Senior Courts Act 1981 s 61(1), Sch 1 para 1(a); and PARA 583. 'Land' includes buildings and other structures, land covered with water, and any estate, interest, easement, servitude or right in or over land: Interpretation Act 1978 s 5, Sch 1.

19 See EQUITABLE JURISDICTION vol 47 (2014) PARA 99.

20 See the County Courts Act 1984 s 23(d); and PARA 584.
21 See the County Courts Act 1984 s 24; and COURTS AND TRIBUNALS vol 24 (2010) PARA 776.
22 See COURTS AND TRIBUNALS vol 24 (2010) PARA 787.
23 See *Joyce v Liverpool City Council, Wynne v Liverpool City Council* [1995] 3 All ER 110, [1995] 3 WLR 439, CA.
24 See the Arbitration Act 1996 s.48(5)(b); and PARA 532. For what amounts to a contract relating to land in this context see *Telia Sonera AB v Hilcourt (Docklands) Ltd* [2003] EWHC 3540 (Ch), [2003] ArbLR 42, [2003] All ER (D) 91 (Jul).
25 *Re Stapylton Fletcher Ltd (in administrative receivership), Re Ellis, Son & Vidler Ltd (in administrative receivership)* [1995] 1 All ER 192 at 213, [1994] 1 WLR 1181 at 1203 per Paul Baker J.

502. Principles governing the granting of equitable relief. Before the fusion of the administration of law and equity, certain rules resulted from the nature and origin of equitable jurisdiction, and from its relation to the system of law enforced by the courts of common law, which limited and determined the method on which equity acted.[1] The most fundamental principles were that equity followed the law[2] and that it applied its remedies as supplementary to legal remedies and on the ground of their inadequacy[3].

Despite some early statements to the contrary[4], it became established that a court of equity could order specific performance of a contract which was not enforceable at law[5]. The court would not, however, interfere except on the ground that, while relief should in conscience be given, no adequate relief was obtainable at law[6]; hence it would not interfere where adequate damages were recoverable at law, or no damage had in law been suffered, as in the case of an agreement entirely unperformed to grant a loan[7]. A further principle which affected the granting of equitable relief was that equity acted in personam[8]. Since the fusion of the administration of law and equity, the above rules still limit the exercise of the jurisdiction to grant specific performance[9].

1 See generally EQUITABLE JURISDICTION vol 47 (2014) PARAS 1–5, 103 et seq. See also *Re Scott and Alvarez's Contract, Scott v Alvarez* [1895] 2 Ch 603 at 612, 615, CA.
2 Eg equity followed the law as regards limitation of actions but, in practice, actions for specific performance are generally subject to an even shorter period of limitation than at law: see EQUITABLE JURISDICTION vol 47 (2014) PARA 253 et seq.
3 See EQUITABLE JURISDICTION vol 47 (2014) PARAS 8, 10. For illustrations see PARA 514 et seq.
4 *Normanby (Marquis) v Duke of Devonshire* (1697) Freem Ch 216; *Bettesworth v Dean and Chapter of St Paul's* (1726) Sel Cas Ch 66. Cf *Cannel v Buckle* (1724) 2 P Wms 243.
5 Thus a claimant would fail at law for a non-essential misdescription, but equity could enforce with compensation (see *Mortlock v Buller* (1804) 10 Ves 292 at 305–306), and similarly where the claimant has substantially, but not exactly performed a condition (see *Davis v Hone* (1805) 2 Sch & Lef 341 at 347). See further PARA 503.
6 Cf *Wright v Bell* (1818) 5 Price 325 (purchase of a debt). See also PARA 514.
7 *Rogers v Challis* (1859) 27 Beav 175; *South African Territories v Wallington* [1898] AC 309, HL. Cf *Beech v Ford* (1848) 7 Hare 208 (annuity); *Ashton v Corrigan* (1871) LR 13 Eq 76 (mortgage). See also PARA 534.
8 See PARA 521; and EQUITABLE JURISDICTION vol 47 (2014) PARAS 103–104.
9 See further EQUITABLE JURISDICTION vol 47 (2014) PARAS 95–100.

503. Obligations enforceable by specific performance. The remedy is not confined to cases where there is a cause of action at law; all that is necessary is to show circumstances which will justify intervention by a court of equity[1].

In addition to contracts enforceable at law[2], the following obligations are potentially enforceable by specific performance:

(1)   contracts which are not yet enforceable at law[3];
(2)   contracts which are unenforceable at law but are enforceable in equity because equity does not regard time as being of the essence[4];
(3)   contracts which are unenforceable at law because of a failure to pay money on time but where equity gives relief against forfeiture[5];

(4) proprietary estoppel[6];
(5) compulsory purchase[7].

In addition there are statutory rights to specific performance pursuant to the Landlord and Tenant Act 1985[8], the Consumer Rights Act 2015[9] and certain other legislation[10].

1 *Marks v Lilley* [1959] 2 All ER 647, [1959] 1 WLR 749; *Hasham v Zenab* [1960] AC 316 at 329, [1960] 2 WLR 374 at 376–377, PC; *R v Bradford Metropolitan District Council, ex p Pickering* (2000) 33 HLR 409 at 415–417 per Munby J.
2 See 526 et seq.
3 The innocent party may apply for an order even before the contractual date for completion provided he can satisfy the court that a serious breach of contract is likely to occur if the court does not intervene: see *Hasham v Zenab* [1960] AC 316, [1960] 2 WLR 374, PC. See also PARA 501 note 2.
4 See *Parkin v Thorold* (1852) 16 Beav 59, 22 LJ Ch 170, 16 Jur 959; *Starside Properties Ltd v Mustapha* [1974] 2 All ER 567, [1974] 1 WLR 816, 28 P & CR 95; *Graham v Pitkin* [1992] 2 All ER 235, [1992] 1 WLR 403, 64 P & CR 522. See further CONTRACT vol 22 (2012) PARA 502; EQUITABLE JURISDICTION vol 47 (2014) PARA 227. As to when time is of the essence see PARA 576 et seq.
5 See *Re Dagenham Dock Co* (1873) LR 8 Ch App 1022, 38 JP 180; *Kilmer v British Columbia Orchard Lands Ltd* [1913] AC 319, 82 LJPC 77, 57 Sol Jo 338; *Transag Haulage Ltd (IAR) v Leyland DAF Finance plc* [1994] 2 BCLC 88, [1994] BCC 356, [1994] CCLR 111; *The Jotunheim* [2004] EWHC 671 (Comm), [2005] 1 Lloyd's Rep 181; *Celestial Aviation Trading 71 Ltd v Paramount Airways Private Ltd* [2010] EWHC 185 (Comm), [2011] 1 All ER (Comm) 259, [2011] 1 Lloyd's Rep 9. As to relief against forfeiture see EQUITABLE JURISDICTION vol 47 (2014) PARAS 223–227.
6 See PARA 506; and ESTOPPEL vol 47 (2014) PARA 392 et seq.
7 See PARA 538.
8 Ie the Landlord and Tenant Act 1985 s 17. See PARA 507 note 7; and LANDLORD AND TENANT vol 62 (2016) PARA 358.
9 Ie the Consumer Rights Act 2015 s 58. See PARA 515 note 9; and CONSUMER PROTECTION vol 21 (2016) PARA 369.
10 Ie the Companies Act 2006 s 740 (contract to underwrite debenture issue) (see PARA 515); the Trade Union and Labour Relations (Consolidation) Act 1992 Sch A1 para 31(6) (duty to bargain collectively in certain cases) (see EMPLOYMENT vol 41A (2014) PARA 1123).

504. Specific performance and injunctions. It is sometimes appropriate to compel the performance of a contract by the equitable remedy of an injunction rather than by specific performance. In general, an injunction is the proper method of restraining a defendant from committing a breach of a negative obligation[1] or from interfering with the claimant's exercise of his rights under the contract[2], whereas specific performance is the proper method of compelling a defendant to perform a positive obligation of his own under the contract. An injunction may sometimes be used as a method of putting pressure on a defendant to perform his part of a contract which the court would not be prepared to enforce directly by an order for specific performance[3]; for example, the court might grant an injunction to enforce a valid covenant against accepting employment with a competitor[4] contained in a contract of personal service which is not directly enforceable by an action for specific performance[5]. In connection with contracts of personal service, it has been said that the court will exercise this power only where there is an express negative covenant in the agreement, and will not imply such a covenant from a positive obligation to work full-time for the employer[6], but in connection with other types of contract the absence or presence of an express negative covenant does not appear to have been regarded as significant[7]. The court may also enforce a negative stipulation not to sell goods to other buyers contained in an agreement for the sale of goods, even if that agreement is incapable of being directly enforced by specific performance[8].

The court may grant an interim injunction in aid of specific performance[9]. For example, it may forbid the removal of the subject matter of the contract from the jurisdiction pending the trial[10] or a disposal of the subject matter by the defendant[11], although if there is doubt as to the existence or enforceability of the contract the defendant will not be restrained from disposing of the subject matter to a third person if the balance of convenience favours allowing him to do so[12].

The court has power to grant a mandatory injunction to protect contractual rights, either at the trial or on an interlocutory application[13]. A party who has committed (or, in the case of an interlocutory application, is alleged to have committed) a breach of a negative obligation may be ordered to take action to restore the status quo[14]. A vendor may be ordered to take positive action to prevent serious damage to the property[15]. In certain circumstances, the court may even grant a mandatory injunction directly requiring a party to the contract to perform his contractual obligations, either on an interlocutory application[16] or at the trial of the action[17]. An interlocutory injunction will be refused where the court concludes there was not a sufficient likelihood that the applicant would be able to establish its entitlement at trial[18] or that the risk of injustice if the injunction is not given does not significantly outweigh the risk of injustice if it was granted[19].

1   As to the protection of contractual rights by injunction see CIVIL PROCEDURE vol 12 (2015) PARA 1173 et seq.
2   *Jones (James) & Sons Ltd v Earl of Tankerville* [1909] 2 Ch 440.
3   *Lauritzencool AB v Lady Navigation Inc* [2005] EWCA Civ 579, [2006] 1 All ER 866, [2005] 1 WLR 3686 (time charter not specifically enforceable but injunction against conflicting use of ship). See also *Evans Marshall & Co Ltd v Bertola SA* [1973] 1 All ER 992 at 1005, [1973] 1 WLR 349 at 379, CA, per Sachs LJ (revsd on another ground [1976] 2 Lloyd's Rep 17, HL); *Decro-Wall International SA v Practitioners in Marketing Ltd* [1971] 2 All ER 216, [1971] 1 WLR 361, CA.
4   As to the validity of such covenants and other covenants in restraint of trade see COMPETITION vol 18 (2009) PARA 377 et seq.
5   See *Lumley v Wagner* (1852) 1 De GM & G 604, and the other cases cited in PARA 509 note 1. See also CIVIL PROCEDURE vol 12 (2015) PARA 1185. See also *Whitwood Chemical Co v Hardman* [1891] 2 Ch. 416: see further the text to note 6.
6   *Whitwood Chemical Co v Hardman* [1891] 2 Ch 416, CA. Cf *Wolverhampton and Walsall Rly Co v London and North Western Rly Co* (1873) LR 16 Eq 433 at 440 per Lord Selborne LC. See also *Mutual Reserve Fund Life Association v New York Life Insurance Co and Harvey* (1896) 75 LT 528; *Davis v Foreman* [1894] 3 Ch 654. See also PARA 509.
7   See eg *Evans Marshall & Co Ltd v Bertola SA* [1973] 1 All ER 992, [1973] 1 WLR 349, CA (sole agency contract).
8   *Donnell v Bennett* (1883) 22 ChD 835. See also *Sky Petroleum Ltd v VIP Petroleum Ltd* [1974] 1 All ER 954, [1974] 1 WLR 576.
9   See CIVIL PROCEDURE vol 12 (2015) PARA 1194. As to applications for interim relief in specific performance actions generally see PARA 605.
10 *Hart v Herwig* (1873) 8 Ch App 860. Cf the freezing (formerly 'Mareva') injunction: *Mareva Cia Naviera SA v International Bulkcarriers SA, The Mareva* [1980] 1 All ER 213, [1975] 2 Lloyd's Rep 509, CA; and see CIVIL PROCEDURE vol 12 (2015) PARA 595 et seq.
11 *Preston v Luck* (1884) 27 ChD 497, CA.
12 *Hadley v London Bank of Scotland Ltd* (1865) 3 De GJ & Sm 63, where an injunction was refused because the contract, if established at the trial, would be binding on the third person by reason of the registration by the plaintiff of his claim as a lis pendens.
13 As to the circumstances in which mandatory injunctions will be granted see CIVIL PROCEDURE vol 12 (2015) PARA 1102 et seq. In *Channel Tunnel Group Ltd v Balfour Beatty Construction Ltd* [1993] AC 334, [1993] 1 All ER 664, HL, Lord Mustill said at 366 and at 689 that the claim for a final mandatory injunction was the same as one for specific performance of the obligation to work continuously on the contract; and in *Parker v Camden London Borough Council, Newman v Camden London Borough Council* [1986] Ch 162 at 173, [1985] 2 All ER 141 at 146, CA, Sir John Donaldson MR referred to 'a mandatory injunction in the form of an order for specific performance'. See also *Dance v Welwyn Hatfield District Council* [1990] 3 All ER 572, [1990] 1 WLR 1097, CA; *Scandinavian Trading Tanker Co AB v Flota Petrolera Ecuatoriana, The Scaptrade* [1983] 2 AC 694, [1983] 2 All ER 763, HL (injunction restraining shipowner from

exercising his right of withdrawal of vessel from service of charterer said to be indistinguishable from a decree for specific performance of a contract to render services: see PARAS 508–509); *Worldwide Dryers Ltd v Warner Howard Ltd* (1982) Times, 9 December.

14 See *Shepherd Homes Ltd v Sandham* [1971] Ch 340 at 348, [1970] 3 All ER 402 at 409 per Megarry J.

15 *Strelley v Pearson* (1880) 15 ChD 113.

16 *Smith v Peters* (1875) LR 20 Eq 511, where a vendor was ordered to give a valuer access to premises; *Sky Petroleum Ltd v VIP Petroleum Ltd* [1974] 1 All ER 954, [1974] 1 WLR 576, where the defendants were ordered not to withhold supplies of motor fuel from the plaintiffs' filling stations, no alternative sources of supply being available; *Astro Exito Navegacion SA v Southland Enterprise Co Ltd (No 2) (Chase Manhattan Bank NA intervening), The Messiniaki Tolmi* [1982] QB 1248, [1982] 3 All ER 335, CA (cited in CIVIL PROCEDURE vol 12 (2015) PARA 1194), where the buyers of a ship were ordered to sign a notice of readiness in order to enable money secured by a confirmed letter of credit to be paid out before the expiration of the letter; *Acrow (Automation) Ltd v Rex Chainbelt Inc* [1971] 3 All ER 1175, [1971] 1 WLR 1676, CA, where the Court of Appeal granted a mandatory order to use all reasonable endeavours to supply goods; *Land Rover Group Ltd v UPF (UK) Ltd (in administrative receivership) and others* [2002] EWHC 303 (QB), [2003] 2 BCLC 222, where a chassis manufacturer was required to continue supplies to a car manufacturer that was in receivership; *Aston Martin Lagonda Ltd v Automotive Industrial Partnership Ltd* [2010] All ER (D) 131 (Feb), where an obligation to supply car windscreens and associated parts was enforced.

17 *Puddephatt v Leith* [1916] 1 Ch 200, where a shareholder was ordered to exercise voting rights in accordance with a contractual undertaking (cf *Greenwell v Porter* [1902] 1 Ch 530, where an injunction was granted restraining shareholders from voting contrary to their undertakings); *Bourne v McDonald* [1950] 2 KB 422, [1950] 2 All ER 183, CA, where the defendant was ordered to carry out his contractual undertaking to build a fence in an action commenced in a county court but not within the court's statutory jurisdiction relating to specific performance.

18 *OT Africa Line Ltd v Vickers* [1996] 1 Lloyd's Rep 700, CC, *Seecomm Networks Services Corpn v Colt Telecommunications* [2002] EWHC 2638 (QB), [2002] All ER (D) 14 (Nov).

19 *Zockoll Group Ltd v Mercury Communications Ltd* [1998] FSR 354, [1999] EMLR 385, CA; *Co-operative Insurance Society Ltd v Argyll Stores (Holdings) Ltd* [1998] AC 1, [1997] 3 All ER 297, [1997] 2 WLR 898; *Seecomm Networks Services Corpn v Colt Telecommunications* [2002] EWHC 2638 (QB), [2002] All ER (D) 14 (Nov); *Youatwork Ltd v Motivano Ltd* [2003] EWHC 1047 (Ch), [2003] All ER (D) 37 (May).

505. Enforcement of trusts and charges distinguished from specific performance.

Actions for the enforcement of trusts differ from actions for specific performance in that trusts are not matters of contract but involve obligations of a purely equitable nature to which formerly only the Court of Chancery could have given effect[1]. However, a claim for specific performance may arise in the case of a contract to make a settlement. In such a case, specific performance may be ordered at the suit of another party to the contract, but not at the suit of a trustee or beneficiary who provided no consideration for the contract[2], although a contract to make a marriage settlement may be enforced by a beneficiary who is issue of the marriage[3].

Where for good consideration a mortgage or charge has been created in a form not enforceable at law, the court can enforce the charge as an equitable right, but this is not a case of specific performance; in a proper case the court may also enforce the execution of a legal mortgage or charge, and this is a case of specific performance[4].

1 See EQUITABLE JURISDICTION vol 47 (2014) PARAS 6, 228 et seq.

2 *Green v Paterson* (1886) 32 ChD 95, CA; *Re Pryce, Nevill v Pryce* [1917] 1 Ch 234; *Re Kay's Settlement, Broadbent v Macnab* [1939] Ch 329, [1939] 1 All ER 245; *Re Cook's Settlement Trusts, Royal Exchange Assurance v Cook* [1965] Ch 902, [1964] 3 All ER 898. If, however, a covenant creates a debt enforceable at law or an immediate trust, the beneficiary does not need to claim specific performance and can enforce the covenant directly: *Williamson v Codrington* (1750) 1 Ves Sen 511; *Fletcher v Fletcher* (1844) 4 Hare 67; *Re Cavendish Browne's Settlement Trusts, Horner v Rawle* [1916] WN 341. See *Briggs v Parsloe* [1937] 3 All ER 831. See also PARA 506; and PERSONAL PROPERTY vol 80 (2013) PARA 874.

3 *Harvey v Ashley* (1748) 3 Atk 607 at 610; *Hill v Gomme* (1839) 5 My & Cr 250 at 254; *A-G v Jacobs-Smith* [1895] 2 QB 341 at 353, CA; *Re Cook's Settlement Trusts, Royal Exchange*

Assurance v Cook [1965] Ch 902 at 915, [1964] 3 All ER 898 at 904. Issue of the marriage are said to be within the marriage consideration. See also SETTLEMENTS vol 91 (2012) PARA 540.
4   See MORTGAGE vol 77 (2016) PARA 251. See also *Bank of Scotland Plc v Waugh (No 2)* [2014] EWHC 2835 (Ch).

(2) GENERAL LIMITS OF JURISDICTION

(i) Contracts which may be outside the Scope of the Remedy

506.   Voluntary promises. In many older cases it was said that the court does not enforce specific performance of voluntary promises, whether under seal or not, and a party claiming specific performance must show some consideration[1]. Past consideration does not suffice[2]. This rule will apply equally whether the volunteer seeks to enforce a contract or a settlement, except where the legal title has been completed[3]; but the court is not concerned with the adequacy of the consideration and will, if it is otherwise appropriate, enforce a contract entered into for slight or even token consideration[4]. It could now be argued that if specific performance is available to enforce an obligation supported by nominal consideration it should also be available in the case of a purely voluntary undertaking which is otherwise enforceable on account of being contained in a deed[5].

Even if consideration has been given, a benefit to be provided under a contract for a person who did not give consideration cannot at common law[6], as a rule be directly enforced by him in his personal capacity, but the contract may be enforced for his benefit by the party who provided the consideration[7]. A beneficiary under the contract can enforce it if it appears that one of the parties was contracting as trustee on his behalf[8]. A trust cannot be inferred in the absence of any indication that the beneficiary was intended to have a directly enforceable right against the party promising to confer a benefit on him[9]. Contracts can be enforced by a person to whom the rights of the original contracting party pass by assignment, devolution or operation of law[10].

The court may enforce the performance of a gratuitous promise by an owner of property to confer on the promisee some estate or interest in that property through the principle of proprietary (sometimes called equitable) estoppel[11]. Such an equitable estoppel will be created if, to the knowledge of the owner, the promisee spends money on the property or otherwise acts to his detriment in reliance on the promise[12]. The principle applies not only where the owner makes an express promise but also where he encourages or creates a belief or expectation that the promisee has or will acquire some estate or interest in the property[13]. A proprietary estoppel will not arise when both parties to commercial negotiations were aware that their agreement to date was partial and incomplete[14]. In such a case the court has a wide discretion to grant whatever relief is necessary to give effect to the promisee's equity. This may be the grant of a decree of specific performance[15], but alternatively, where appropriate, the court may order the owner to transfer the property or some interest in it to the promisee[16], or may make a declaration as to the promisee's rights over the property[17]. An order of one of the latter kinds is not strictly speaking an order for specific performance, since there is no contract to enforce, but it is very similar in its operation, and, as in specific performance in the strict sense, the court may award equitable damages in addition to or in lieu of performance[18]. It has, however, been said that the court can only invoke this principle in order to compel the owner to create or transfer an interest in land or, perhaps, in other forms of property[19].

A claimant seeking to enforce a contract may, of course, make use of the principle of estoppel, whether equitable by convention or by representation, in the normal way by relying on it to bar the defendant from raising some particular defence to the action[20].

1 *Penn v Lord Baltimore* (1750) 1 Ves Sen 444 at 450. See also *Brownsmith v Gilborne* (1727) 2 Stra 738 (voluntary settlement); *Morris v Burroughs* (1737) 1 Atk 399 at 401; *Colman v Sarrel* (1789) 1 Ves 50; *Groves v Groves* (1828) 3 Y & J 163; *Jefferys v Jefferys* (1841) Cr & Ph 138; *Ord v Johnston* (1855) 1 Jur NS 1063; *Walrond v Walrond* (1858) John 18; *Kennedy v May* (1863) 11 WR 358; *Cheale v Kenward* (1858) 3 De G & J 27, where, in an agreement to transfer shares, the assumption of liability by the transferee was sufficient consideration; *Stephens v Green, Green v Knight* [1895] 2 Ch 148, CA, where in a postnuptial contract mutual covenants of husband and wife were sufficient consideration. Cf *Burrows v Greenwood* (1840) 4 Y & C Ex 251 (voluntary contract). See also GIFTS vol 52 (2014) PARA 267.
2 *Robertson v St John* (1786) 2 Bro CC 140, where a promise to renew a lease in consequence of money already laid out was held nudum pactum and specific performance was refused.
3 *Jefferys v Jefferys* (1841) Cr & Ph 138 at 141 per Lord Cottenham LC.
4 *Wycherley v Wycherley* (1763) 2 Eden 175; *Houghton v Lees* (1854) 1 Jur NS 862; *Mountford v Scott* [1975] Ch 258, [1975] 1 All ER 198, CA (£1 consideration for grant of option).
5 In *Mountford v Scott* [1975] Ch 258 at 264 Russell LJ described the older rule supporting the unavailability of specific performance in cases involving nominal consideration as 'startling'.
6 Note that a third party entitled to sue under the Contracts (Rights of Third Parties) Act 1999 may obtain an order of specific performance: see s 1(5) and CONTRACT vol 22 (2012) PARA 341 et seq.
7 *Keenan v Handley* (1864) 2 De GJ & Sm 283; *Hohler v Aston* [1920] 2 Ch 420; *Beswick v Beswick* [1968] AC 58, [1967] 2 All ER 1197, HL.
8 *Gregory v Williams* (1817) 3 Mer 582; *Gandy v Gandy* (1885) 30 ChD 57, CA; *Vandepitte v Preferred Accident Insurance Corpn of New York* [1933] AC 70, PC; *Harmer v Armstrong* [1934] Ch 65, CA; *Re Webb, Barclays Bank Ltd v Webb* [1941] Ch 225, [1941] 1 All ER 321; *Re Foster's Policy, Menneer v Foster* [1966] 1 All ER 432, [1966] 1 WLR 222. See also PERSONAL PROPERTY vol 80 (2013) PARA 874. As to the enforcement of contracts to settle property see *Re Cook's Settlement Trusts, Royal Exchange Assurance v Cook* [1965] Ch 902, [1964] 3 All ER 898; and PARA 505.
9 *Vandepitte v Preferred Accident Insurance Corpn of New York* [1933] AC 70, PC; *Re Schebsman, ex p Official Receiver, Trustee v Cargo Superintendents (London) Ltd and Schebsman* [1944] Ch 83, [1943] 2 All ER 768, CA; *Re Miller's Agreement, Uniacke v A-G* [1947] Ch 615, [1947] 2 All ER 78; *Beswick v Beswick* [1968] AC 58, [1967] 2 All ER 1197, HL. See generally discussion in *Barbados Trust Co Ltd v Bank of Zambia* [2007] EWCA Civ 148 at [99], [2007] 2 All ER (Comm) 445 at [99], [2007] 1 Lloyd's Rep 495 at [99].
10 *Beswick v Beswick* [1968] AC 58, [1967] 2 All ER 1197, HL. As to specific performance at the suit of personal representatives or assignees see PARAS 590–591.
11 As to equitable estoppel see ESTOPPEL vol 47 (2014) PARA 392 et seq; and EQUITABLE JURISDICTION vol 47 (2014) PARA 252.
12 *Thorner v Major* [2009] UKHL 18, [2009] 3 All ER 945, [2009] 1 WLR 776.
13 *Ramsden v Dyson* (1866) LR 1 HL 129 at 170 per Lord Kingsdown; *Chalmers v Pardoe* [1963] 3 All ER 552, [1963] 1 WLR 677, PC; *Price v Strange* [1978] Ch 337, [1977] 3 All ER 371, CA; *JT Developments Ltd v Quinn* (1990) 62 P & CR 33, CA. See *Taylor Fashions Ltd v Liverpool Victoria Trustees Co Ltd, Old & Campbell Ltd v Liverpool Victoria Friendly Society* [1982] QB 133n, [1981] 1 All ER 897; *Habib Bank Ltd v Habib Bank AG Zurich* [1981] 2 All ER 650, [1981] 1 WLR 1265, CA; *Matharu v Matharu* [1994] 3 FCR 216, [1994] 2 FLR 597, CA; *Thorner v Major* [2009] UKHL 18, [2009] 3 All ER 945. Cf *A-G of Hong Kong v Humphreys Estate (Queen's Gardens) Ltd* [1987] AC 114, [1987] 2 All ER 387, where specific performance was not awarded because commercial parties retained their right to cease negotiations; *Clarke v Swaby* [2007] UKPC 1, [2007] 2 P & CR 12, [2007] All ER (D) 78 (Jan), where the Privy Council questioned whether there was a sufficient causal link between expenditure and any possible encouragement, though this was not subject to appeal.
14 *Yeoman's Row Management Ltd v Cobbe* [2008] UKHL 55, [2008] 4 All ER 713, [2008] 1 WLR 1752. As to proprietary estoppel see ESTOPPEL vol 47 (2014) PARA 309.
15 *Taylor Fashions Ltd v Liverpool Victoria Trustees Co Ltd, Old & Campbell Ltd v Liverpool Victoria Trustees Co Ltd* [1982] QB 133, [1981] 1 All ER 897 (decree of specific performance of the renewal option in the lease).

16 *Duke of Beaufort v Patrick* (1853) 17 Beav 60; *Dillwyn v Llewellyn* (1862) 4 De GF & J 517; *Pascoe v Turner* [1979] 2 All ER 945, [1979] 1 WLR 431, CA; *Voyce v Voyce* (1991) 62 P & CR 290, CA. See also *Thomas v Thomas* [1956] NZLR 785.

17 *Crabb v Arun District Council* [1976] Ch 179, [1975] 3 All ER 865, CA. See also *Plimmer v City of Wellington Corpn* (1884) 9 App Cas 699, PC; *Inwards v Baker* [1965] 2 QB 29, [1965] 1 All ER 446, CA; *Ives (ER) Investment Ltd v High* [1967] 2 QB 379, [1967] 1 All ER 504, CA; *Salvation Army Trustee Co Ltd v West Yorkshire Metropolitan County Council* (1980) 41 P & CR 179, DC.

18 *Crabb v Arun District Council (No 2)* (1976) 121 Sol Jo 86, CA, where damages were refused because of the staleness of the claim. As to equitable damages see PARA 632.

19 *Western Fish Products Ltd v Penwith District Council* [1981] 2 All ER 204 at 218, CA; *Baird Textile Holdings Ltd v Marks and Spencer plc* [2001] EWCA Civ 274, [2002] 1 All ER (Comm) 737. Cf, however, *Salvation Army Trustee Co Ltd v West Yorkshire Metropolitan County Council* (1980) 41 P & CR 179, DC, where, on unusual facts, the defendants were ordered to purchase property from the plaintiffs; *Amalgamated Investment and Property Co Ltd (in liquidation) v Texas Commerce International Bank Ltd* [1982] QB 84 at 131, [1981] 3 All ER 577 at 591, CA, per Brandon J. *Strover v Strover* [2005] EWHC 860 (Ch), (2005) Times, 30 May, where proprietary estoppel was applied to a policy of life assurance; *Fisher v Brooker* [2009] UKHL 41, [2009] 4 All ER 789, [2009] 1 WLR 1764 where it was applied with respect to copyright.

20 See eg *Spiro v Lintern* [1973] 3 All ER 319, [1973] 1 WLR 1002, CA, where the owner was estopped by conduct from denying his wife's authority to contract for the sale of a house; *Taylors Fashions Ltd v Liverpool Victoria Trustees Co Ltd, Old & Campbell Ltd v Liverpool Victoria Trustees Co Ltd* [1982] QB 133, [1981] 1 All ER 897.

507. Acts the performance of which would require continued supervision. It was long thought that the court would not enforce the performance of contracts which involved continuous acts and which required the watching and supervision of the court[1]. The scope and application of this limitation has been the subject of some debate in more recent cases, however; and it may now best be regarded as a situation where the court often will refuse an order as a matter of discretion. The 'constant supervision' limitation was associated with, and the partial justification for, another older restriction that the court did not normally order the specific performance of a contract to build or repair[2]. However, this rule is subject to important exceptions[3], and a decree for specific performance of a contract to build will be made if the following conditions are fulfilled:

(1)   that the building work is defined by the contract between the parties;
(2)   that the claimant has a substantial interest in the performance of the contract of such a nature that he cannot be adequately compensated in damages;
(3)   that the defendant is in possession of the land on which the work is contracted to be done[4].

It is no objection to granting specific performance of an agreement for a lease that the lease is to contain a covenant by the defendant to repair[5]. Further it is now settled that the court, in appropriate cases, can order specific performance of a tenant's covenant to repair[6] and the court now has a statutory power to order specific performance of a landlord's covenant to repair a dwelling house[7].

In a line of cases from 1970 to 1998, the courts became more ready to enforce contracts requiring supervision. The question was whether the contract sufficiently defined the work to be done, expressly or by implication, to permit the court to make an order which enabled the defendant to know what he has to do to comply with it[8].

However, this does not mean that the 'constant supervision' objection has ceased to have any force, especially when coupled with difficulties in stating with precision what is required of the defendant, or the potential difficulties inherent in ordering a defendant to carry on a business[9]. Even here, however, the objection may on occasion be avoided by the restrained and careful drafting of the order sought[10] or exceptionally by the award of a different remedy[11].

The court has power to direct that if an order for the specific performance of a contract is not complied with, the act required to be done may so far as practicable be done by the party by whom the order or judgment was obtained or some other person appointed by the court, at the cost of the disobedient party[12].

1   *Pollard v Clayton* (1855) 1 K & J 462 at 481 (contract to supply coal from a particular mine); *Peto v Brighton, Uckfield and Tunbridge Wells Rly Co* (1863) 1 Hem & M 468 (contracts to construct railways); *Blackett v Bates* (1865) 1 Ch App 117 (contract to supply engine power and keep railway line in repair); *Powell Duffryn Steam Coal Co v Taff Vale Rly Co* (1874) 9 Ch App 331 (contract to grant running powers); *Ryan v Mutual Tontine Westminster Chambers Association* [1893] 1 Ch 116, CA (contract that porter will perform his duties); *Dominion Coal Co Ltd v Dominion Iron and Steel Co Ltd and National Trust Co Ltd* [1909] AC 293, PC (contract for delivery of coal by instalments); *Barnes v City of London Real Property Co* [1918] 2 Ch 18 (agreement by landlord to provide housekeeper); *Joseph v National Magazine Co Ltd* [1959] Ch 14, [1958] 3 All ER 52 (contract to publish article of which exact terms not agreed); and see *Rayner v Stone* (1762) 2 Eden 128; *Phipps v Jackson* (1887) 56 LJ Ch 550; *Keith, Prowse & Co v National Telephone Co* [1894] 2 Ch 147; *Dowty Boulton Paul Ltd v Wolverhampton Corpn* [1971] 2 All ER 277, [1971] 1 WLR 204. Cf *Cooke v Chilcott* (1876) 3 ChD 694 (covenant running with land).

2   This rule is not only based on the court's inability to supervise performance, but also on the want of definiteness usually involved in such contracts, and further on the principle that damages are generally an adequate remedy: see *Errington v Aynsly* (1788) 2 Bro CC 341; *Lucas v Commerford (or Comerford)* (1790) 3 Bro CC 166; *Hill v Barclay* (1810) 16 Ves 402 (tenant's covenant to repair); *Kay v Johnson* (1864) 2 Hem & M 118; *Wheatley v Westminster Brymbo Coal Co* (1869) LR 9 Eq 538 (covenant to work a coal mine); *Merchants' Trading Co v Banner* (1871) LR 12 Eq 18 (agreement to alter a ship); *Greenhill v Isle of Wight (Newport Junction) Rly Co* (1871) 23 LT 885. See also *Flint v Brandon* (1803) 8 Ves 159 (covenant to make good a gravel pit); *Booth v Pollard* (1840) 4 Y & C Ex 61; *South Wales Rly Co v Wythes* (1854) 1 K & J 186 (affd 5 De GM & G 880, CA); *Brace v Wehnert* (1858) 25 Beav 348; *Norris v Jackson* (1860) 1 John & H 319. Cf *Soames v Edge* (1860) John 669 (specific performance of contract to accept lease; damages for failure to build); *Middleton v Greenwood* (1864) 2 De GJ & Sm 142. See also *Female Orphans' Asylum v Waterlow* (1868) 16 WR 1102 (agreement to grant lease); *Wood v Silcock* (1884) 50 LT 251 (preliminary building agreement).

3   *Wolverhampton Corpn v Emmons* [1901] 1 KB 515, CA. This was not adopted in *New Zealand Downer Construction (NZ) Ltd v Silverfield Developments Ltd* [2006] 1 NZLR 785.

4   *Wolverhampton Corpn v Emmons* [1901] 1 KB 515, CA (see note 3). See also *Molyneux v Richard* [1906] 1 Ch 34; *Carpenters Estates Ltd v Davies* [1940] Ch 160, [1940] 1 All ER 13; *City of London v Nash* (1747) 3 Atk 512. See also *Storer v Great Western Rly* (1842) 2 Y & C Ch Cas 48; *Sanderson v Cockermouth and Workington Rly Co* (1849) 11 Beav 497; *Lytton v Great Northern Rly Co* (1856) 2 K & J 394; *Wilson v Furness Rly Co* (1869) LR 9 Eq 28; *Hood v North Eastern Rly Co* (1870) 5 Ch App 525; *Wilson v Northampton and Banbury Junction Rly Co* (1874) 9 Ch App 279 (all cases of accommodation works). Cf *Greene v West Cheshire Rly Co* (1871) LR 13 Eq 44; *Todd & Co v Midland Great Western Rly of Ireland Co* (1881) 9 LR Ir 85; *Fortescue v Lostwithiel and Fowey Rly Co* [1894] 3 Ch 621; *Price v Penzance Corpn* (1845) 4 Hare 506; *Pembroke v Thorpe* (1740) 3 Swan 437n; *Oxford v Provand* (1868) LR 2 PC 135; *Audenshaw UDC v Manchester Corpn* (1907) 71 JP 342, which cases illustrate the same rule. In *South Wales Rly Co v Wythes* (1854) 1 K & J 186 (affd 5 De GM & G 880, CA), specific performance was refused on the ground that damages would be an adequate remedy, the plaintiffs being in a position to have the railway constructed, as the land was in their possession and the same proposition was stated obiter in *North East Lincolnshire Borough Council v Millennium Park (Grimsby) Limited* [2002] EWCA Civ 1719, [2002] All ER (D) 346 (Oct). See also *Cubitt v Smith* (1864) 11 LT 298; *Hepburn v Leather* (1884) 50 LT 660; *Hounslow London Borough Council v Twickenham Garden Developments Ltd* [1971] Ch 233 at 251, [1970] 3 All ER 326 at 340 per Megarry J; *Airport Industrial GP Ltd, Airport Industrial Nominees Ltd v Heathrow Airport Ltd, AP16 Ltd* [2015] EWHC 3753 (Ch).

5   *Paxton v Newton* (1854) 2 Sm & G 437.

6   *Rainbow Estates Ltd v Tokenhold Ltd* [1999] Ch 64, [1998] 2 All ER 860. See also LANDLORD AND TENANT vol 62 (2016) PARAS 347, 357.

7   See the Landlord and Tenant Act 1985 s 17; and LANDLORD AND TENANT vol 62 (2016) PARA 358. Query whether s 17 applies to an obligation not contained in a deed; see *Gordon v Selico Co Ltd* [1985] 2 EGLR 79; affd [1986] 1 EGLR 71, CA (held that, given a deed, the word 'covenant' extended to implied promises).

8 *Hounslow London Borough Council v Twickenham Garden Developments Ltd* [1971] Ch 233 at
   251, [1970] 3 All ER 326 at 340 per Megarry J; *Giles (CH) & Co Ltd v Morris* [1972] 1 All ER
   960 at 969, [1972] 1 WLR 307 at 318 per Megarry J; *Shiloh Spinners Ltd v Harding* [1973] AC
   691 at 724, [1973] 1 All ER 90 at 102, HL, per Lord Wilberforce; *Jeune v Queens Cross
   Properties Ltd* [1974] Ch 97, [1973] 3 All ER 97; *Barrow v Chappell & Co Ltd* [1976] RPC 355
   (contract to publish music); *Tito v Waddell (No 2)* [1977] Ch 106 at 321–323, [1977] 3 All ER
   129 at 307–309 per Megarry V-C; *Price v Strange* [1978] Ch 337 at 359, [1977] 3 All ER 371 at
   385, CA, per Goff LJ; *Gyllenhammar & Partners International Ltd v Sour Brodogrodevna
   Industrija* [1989] 2 Lloyd's Rep 403; *Posner v Scott-Lewis* [1987] Ch 25, [1986] 3 All ER 513. See
   also *Ford Sellar Morris Developments Ltd v Grant Seward Ltd* [1989] 2 EGLR 40 at 41–42 per
   Hoffmann J, where it was said that there is no doubt as to the jurisdiction of the court to
   order specific performance of a building contract, though an order will not usually be made as it
   may be difficult to make clear what the defendant has to do, and damages will normally be an
   adequate remedy; *Tustian v Johnston* [1993] 2 All ER 673; revsd [1993] 3 All ER 534n, CA. See
   also LANDLORD AND TENANT vol 62 (2016) PARA 165.
9 In *Cooperative Insurance Society Ltd v Argyll Stores (Holdings) Ltd* [1998] AC 1, [1997] 3 All ER
   297, [1997] 2 WLR 898, HL, the House of Lords reviewed recent developments in the law (see text
   and note 8) when, reversing the decision of the Court of Appeal [1996] 3 All ER 934, [1996] Ch
   286, [1996] 3 WLR 27, CA and refused specific performance of a covenant in a 35 year lease to
   a supermarket obliging the business to remain open during local business hours. Lord Hoffman
   stated that arguments based upon difficulty of supervision remained powerful. He noted that the
   risk of a court having to give an indefinite set of rulings to ensure execution of the order was more
   compelling where the obligation in question like the supermarket 'keep open' clause was one to
   carry on, an activity, rather than to procure a result. For obligations to carry on a business see also
   Woolworth (FW) plc v Charlwood Alliance Properties [1987] 1 EGLR 53 applying *Braddon
   Towers Ltd v International Stores Ltd* (1979) reported in [1987] 1 EGLR 209, and distinguishing
   Posner v Scott-Lewis [1987] Ch 25, [1986] 3 All ER 513; *Flogas v Warrington* [2007] EWHC
   1303 (QB).
10 *Jet2.com Ltd v Blackpool Airport Ltd* [2010] EWHC 3166 (Comm), [2010] All ER (D) 58 (Dec)
   upholding the continuance of an injunction preventing the defendant from reducing the
   airport's hours.
11 *XY v Facebook Ireland Limited* [2012] NIQB 96, where *Cooperative Insurance v Argyll Stores Ltd*
   [1997] 3 All ER 297, [1998] AC 1, [1997] 2 WLR 898, HL was applied in a human rights context
   (the potential difficulty of monitoring a 'Facebook web page' which constituted prima facie
   unlawful harassment of the defendant was avoided by instead requiring the removal of the page).
12 CPR r 70.2A, which is expressed to be without prejudice to the court's power under the
   Senior Courts 1981 s 39 to nominate a person to execute any necessary contract etc and its power
   to punish the disobedient party for contempt. The commonest example is a lease or conveyance of
   land, but it is not the only one: see eg *Astro Exito Navegacion SA v Southland Enterprise Co (No
   2)* [1983] 2 AC 787, [1983] 2 All ER 725, [1983] 3 WLR 130 (execution in defendant's name of
   paperwork necessary to allow claimant to draw on letter of credit).

508. Contracts for personal work or services. A judgment for specific
performance of a contract for personal work or services is not pronounced, either
at the suit of the employer or the employee[1]. If services are supplied which are not
personal in nature no prohibition applies[2]. The court does not seek to compel
persons against their will to maintain continuous personal and confidential
relations[3]; but this rule is not absolute and without exception[4]. It has been held
that an employer may be restrained from dismissing an employee in breach of
contract if there is no loss of confidence between employer and employee[5] or if (at
least in a contract of employment to carry out a public duty) the employee has
been dismissed in a manner which does not comply with statutory or contractual
regulations governing dismissal[6]. In one case this practice has given way to a
statutory prohibition: no court may, whether by way of an order for specific
performance of a contract of employment or an injunction restraining a breach or
threatened breach of such a contract, compel an employee to do any work or
attend at any place for the doing of any work[7].

This principle applies not merely to contracts of employment, but to all
contracts which involve the rendering of continuous services by one person to

another, such as a contract to work a railway line[8]. Contracts of agency, such as that of a shipbroker[9] or an auctioneer[10], an arbitration agreement[11], come under the same rule, and a contract of apprenticeship is not enforced against a minor[12]. A time charter, unless it is a charter by demise, is a contract for services to be rendered to the charterer by the shipowner through the use of the vessel by the shipowner's own servants and accordingly falls within the principle[13]. One contractual provision which by itself would not be specifically enforceable (because, for example, it requires the performance of personal services) does not, however, prevent the contract as a whole from being specifically enforced, and the court may refuse to let the difficulties of specifically enforcing the obligation to perform personal services outweigh the desirability of the contract as a whole being enforced[14]. The court may order the execution of a service agreement even if it would not specifically enforce the obligations under that agreement[15]. Furthermore, the general rule does not apply so as to prevent a person or group of persons given the right to appoint or nominate a director of a company from exercising such a right, although a company will not be forced to accept as a director a person to whose appointment it has reasonable objections[16].

1   *Pickering v Bishop of Ely* (1843) 2 Y & C Ch Cas 249; *Fitzpatrick v Nolan* (1851) 1 I Ch R 671 (personal service); *Stocker v Brockelbank* (1851) 3 Mac & G 250; *Stocker v Wedderburn* (1857) 3 K & J 393; *Gillis v M'Ghee* (1861) 13 I Ch R 48 (personal service); *Ogden v Fossick* (1862) 4 De GF & J 426; *Firth v Ridley* (1864) 33 Beav 516; *White v Boby* (1877) 37 LT 652, CA; *Frith v Frith* [1906] AC 254, PC; *Clarke v Price* (1819) 2 Wils Ch 157 (law reporting); *Baldwin v Society for the Diffusion of Useful Knowledge* (1838) 9 Sim 393; *Chaplin v North Western Rly Co* (1862) 5 LT 601, sub nom *Horne v London and North Western Rly Co* [1862] 10 WR 170 (personal service); *McGhee v Midlands British Road Services Ltd* [1985] ICR 503 at 508, EAT; *Ashworth v Royal National Theatre* [2014] EWHC 1176 (QB), [2014] 4 All ER 238, [2014] IRLR 526. Such decrees were made in earlier cases (see *Ball v Coggs* (1710) 1 Bro Parl Cas 140; *East India Co v Vincent* (1740) 2 Atk 83), but later judges have refused to follow these precedents (see the cases cited in this note above).

2   *Ferrara Quay Ltd v Carillion Construction* [2009] BLR 367. On this basis specific performance of a contract to publish music was enforced in *Barrow v Chappel & Co Ltd* (1951) reported at [1976] RPC 355.

3   *Johnson v Shrewsbury and Birmingham Rly Co* (1853) 3 De GM & G 914; *Bainbridge v Smith* (1889) 41 ChD 462 at 464, CA; *De Francesco v Barnum* (1890) 45 ChD 430; *Whitwood Chemical Co v Hardman* [1891] 2 Ch 416, CA; *City and Hackney Health Authority v National Union of Public Employees* [1985] IRLR 252, CA. In *Rigby v Connol* (1880) 14 ChD 482 at 487, Jessel MR seems to confine the principle to cases where no rights of property are involved, but see *Lee v Showmen's Guild of Great Britain* [1952] 2 QB 329 at 341, [1952] 1 All ER 1175 at 1180, CA, per Denning LJ; *Vertex Data Science Ltd v Powergen Retail Ltd* [2006] EWHC 1340 (Comm), [2006] 2 Lloyd's Rep 591; *Akai Holdings Ltd v RMS Robson Rhodes LLP* [2007] EWHC 1641 (Ch); *Mission Capital plc v Sinclair and another* [2008] EWHC 1339 (Ch), [2010] 1 BCLC 304.

4   *Giles (CH) & Co Ltd v Morris* [1972] 1 All ER 960 at 969, [1972] 1 WLR 307 at 318 per Megarry J. See also *Regent International Hotels (UK) Ltd v Pageguide Ltd* (1985) Times, 13 May, CA.

5   *Hill v CA Parsons & Co Ltd* [1972] Ch 305, [1971] 3 All ER 1345, CA (where an employer was ordered not to dismiss an employee for failure to join a specified trade union); *Irani v Southampton and South West Hampshire Health Authority* [1985] ICR 590, [1985] IRLR 203; and see *Jaber v Science and Information Technology Ltd* [1992] BCLC 764. Cf *Chappell v Times Newspapers Ltd* [1975] 2 All ER 233, [1975] 1 WLR 482, CA; *Powell v Brent London Borough Council* [1988] ICR 176, [1987] IRLR 466, CA; *Hughes v Southwark London Borough Council* [1988] IRLR 55; *MacPherson v London Borough of Lambeth* [1988] IRLR 470; *Wishart v National Assocn of Citizens' Advice Bureaux Ltd* [1990] ICR 794, [1990] IRLR 393, CA; *Wadcock v London Borough of Brent* [1990] IRLR 223; *Robb v Hammersmith and Fulham London Borough Council* [1991] ICR 514; *Alexander v Standard Telephones and Cables plc* [1990] ICR 291, [1990] IRLR 55; *Gryf-Lowczowski v Hinchingbrooke Healthcare NHS Trust* [2005] EWHC 2407 (QB), [2006] IRLR 100, [2006] ICR 425; *Edwards v Chesterfield Royal Hospital NHS Foundation Trust*; *Botham v Ministry of Defence* [2011] UKSC 58, [2012] 2 AC 22, [2012] 2 All ER 278; and see

discussion in *Geys v Socieìteì Geineìrale, London Branch* [2012] UKSC 63 at [73], [74], [2013] AC 523 at [73], [74], [2013] 1 All ER 1061 at [73], [74].

6   *Malloch v Aberdeen Corpn* [1971] 2 All ER 1278, [1971] 1 WLR 1578, HL; *Jones v Lee and Guilding* [1980] IRLR 67, [1980] ICR 310, CA. Cf *Gunton v Richmond-upon-Thames London Borough Council* [1981] Ch 448, [1980] 3 All ER 577, CA; *Powell v Brent London Borough Council* [1988] ICR 176, [1987] IRLR 466, CA, (1987); *Gryf-Lowczowski v Hinchingbrooke Healthcare NHS Trust* [2005] EWHC 2407 (QB), [2006] IRLR 100, [2006] ICR 425.

7   Trade Union and Labour Relations (Consolidation) Act 1992 s 236. See also EMPLOYMENT vol 41A (2014) PARA 1348; and EMPLOYMENT vol 41 (2014) PARA 826. In contrast an Employment Tribunal may, where an employee has been unfairly dismissed in contravention of statutory requirements, order the employee's reinstatement or re-engagement. However, the only sanction for failure to abide by such an order is a monetary award.

8   *Johnson v Shrewsbury and Birmingham Rly Co* (1853) 3 De GM & G 914. See also *Horne v London and North Western Rly Co* (1861) 10 WR 170, and cf *Pickering v Bishop of Ely* (1843) 2 Y & C Ch Cas 249, where specific performance was refused of a contract to grant an office the holder of which would have had the right and duty of performing work of a confidential character. See also *Warren v Mendy* [1989] 3 All ER 103, [1989] ICR 525, CA.

9   *Brett v East India and London Shipping Co Ltd* (1864) 2 Hem & M 404. See AGENCY vol 1 (2008) PARA 71.

10 *Chinnock v Sainsbury* (1860) 6 Jur NS 1318. See also *Bertram v Ball* (1882) 27 Sol Jo 39. Note, however, *Folioshield Ltd v Pleamere Ltd* [1990] 2 EGLR 1, where it was said that specific performance could be granted requiring the defendant to permit the plaintiff to carry out its duties as the defendant's sole letting agent. See AUCTION vol 4 (2011) PARA 29.

11 *Vertex Data Science Ltd v Powergen Retail Ltd* [2006] EWHC 1340 (Comm), [2006] 2 Lloyd's Rep 591. See also ARBITRATION vol 2 (2008) PARA 1213.

12 *De Francesco v Barnum* (1889) 43 ChD 165. Conversely, an order is not made against the master: *Webb v England* (1860) 29 Beav 44. See generally CHILDREN AND YOUNG PERSONS vol 9 (2017) PARA 22.

13 *Scandinavian Trading Tanker Co AB v Flota Petrolera Ecuatoriana, The Scaptrade* [1983] 2 AC 694, [1983] 2 All ER 763, HL; *Sport International Bussum BV v Inter-Footwear Ltd* [1984] 1 All ER 376, [1984] 1 WLR 776, CA (affd [1984] 2 All ER 321, [1984] 1 WLR 776, HL); cf *LauritzenCool AB v Lady Navigation Inc* [2005] EWCA Civ 579, [2005] 2 All ER (Comm) 183, [2005] 1 WLR 3686.

14 *Fortescue v Lostwithiel and Fowey Rly Co* [1894] 3 Ch 621; *Giles (CH) & Co Ltd v Morris* [1972] 1 All ER 960 at 969, [1972] 1 WLR 307 at 317 per Megarry J.

15 *Giles (CH) & Co Ltd v Morris* [1972] 1 All ER 960, [1972] 1 WLR 307. See also *Granville v Betts* (1848) 18 LJ Ch 32; *Wilson v West Hartlepool Rly Co* (1865) 2 De GJ & Sm 475; *Chelsfield Advisers LLP v Qatari Diar Real Estate Investment Co* [2015] EWHC 1322 (Ch), [2015] All ER (D) 180 (May) (court refusing to make an order requiring the defendant to continue instructing an expert).

16 *British Murac Syndicate Ltd v Alperton Rubber Co Ltd* [1915] 2 Ch 186. See also *Plantations Trust Ltd v Bila (Sumatra) Rubber Lands Ltd* (1916) 85 LJ Ch 801; and COMPANIES vol 14 (2016) PARA 519.

509. Indirect enforcement of contracts for personal services. In certain circumstances, although refusing to order specific performance of a contract for personal services, the court may put pressure on an employee to comply with the contract by granting an injunction restraining him from committing a breach of a negative covenant in the contract which restricts his freedom to take other employment[1]. The court will not generally grant an injunction in the absence of such a covenant, and will not imply a negative covenant from an obligation of the employee to devote the whole of his time to his employer's business[2], although the question whether the covenant is negative or positive is one of substance rather than form[3]. The court will refuse to grant an injunction in terms which would prevent the employee from accepting other employment of any kind[4], but may enforce a covenant not to engage in any other occupation during the subsistence of the contract by granting the injunction in a more restricted form[5]. The court will not grant an injunction where the parties owe each other reciprocal obligations of trust and confidence and the defendant has lost confidence in the claimant⁶, but the fact that some degree of mutual co-operation is needed does not preclude the court from granting a negative injunction designed to encourage the party in breach to perform his part⁷.

1   *Lumley v Wagner* (1852) 1 De GM & G 604; *Grimston v Cuningham* [1894] 1 QB 125; *Robinson (William) & Co Ltd v Heuer* [1898] 2 Ch 451, CA; *Warner Bros Pictures Inc v Nelson* [1937] 1 KB 209, [1936] 3 All ER 160; *Marco Productions Ltd v Pagola* [1945] KB 111, [1945] 1 All ER 155. See also *Morris v Colman* (1812) 18 Ves 437, as explained in *Clarke v Price* (1819) 2 Wils Ch 157. See generally CIVIL PROCEDURE vol 12 (2015) PARA 1185 et seq. An injunction of this kind operates as a form of indirect order for specific performance only if the employer continues to offer employment, but if the employer has accepted the employee's repudiation he may still be entitled to enforce a negative covenant: *Marshall (Thomas) (Exports) Ltd v Guinle* [1979] Ch 227, [1978] 3 All ER 193. In *Evening Standard Co Ltd v Henderson* [1987] ICR 588, [1987] IRLR 64, CA, an interlocutory injunction was granted of a negative term not to work for anyone else during the currency of the contract on the basis of an undertaking by the employer to pay the employee his salary and other contractual benefits throughout the remainder of the contractual period whether he chose to continue working for the employer or not. It was, however, refused in *Provident Financial Group plc v Hayward* [1989] 3 All ER 298, [1989] ICR 160, CA, where the employer was prepared to continue to pay the employee during the remaining period but was not prepared to allow him to continue to work. See also *Warren v Mendy* [1989] 3 All ER 103, [1989] ICR 525, CA; and see *Lotus Cars Ltd v Jaguar Cars Ltd* [1982] LS Gaz R 1214, where an injunction against the defendants was refused where the effect of granting it would have been, in effect, to grant a decree of specific performance of P's contract with the plaintiff, P not being a party to the action. As to the validity of covenants in restraint of trade generally see COMPETITION vol 18 (2009) PARA 377 et seq.
2   *Whitwood Chemical Co v Hardman* [1891] 2 Ch 416, CA; *Mortimer v Beckett* [1920] 1 Ch 571. Cf *William Robinson & Co Ltd v Heuer* [1898] 2 Ch 451 at 456, CA, per Lindley LJ.
3   *Wolverhampton and Walsall Rly Co v London and North Western Rly Co* (1873) LR 16 Eq 433 at 440 per Lord Selborne LC; *Davis v Foreman* [1894] 3 Ch 654; *Mutual Reserve Fund Life Association v New York Life Insurance Co and Harvey* (1896) 75 LT 528 at 529, CA, per Lindley LJ. Cf *Manchester Ship Canal Co v Manchester Racecourse Co* [1901] 2 Ch 37, CA; *Metropolitan Electric Supply Co Ltd v Ginder* [1901] 2 Ch 799; *Jones (James) & Sons Ltd v Earl of Tankerville* [1909] 2 Ch 440; *Esso Petroleum Co Ltd v Harper's Garage (Stourport) Ltd* [1968] AC 269, [1967] 1 All ER 699, HL.
4   *Ehrman v Bartholomew* [1898] 1 Ch 671; *Palace Theatre Ltd v Clensy and Hackney and Shepherd's Bush Empire Palaces Ltd* (1909) 26 TLR 28, CA; *Chapman v Westerby* [1913] WN 277; *Rely-a-Bell Burglar and Fire Alarm Co Ltd v Eisler* [1926] Ch 609.
5   *William Robinson & Co Ltd v Heuer* [1898] 2 Ch 451, CA; *Warner Bros Pictures Inc v Nelson* [1937] 1 KB 209, [1936] 3 All ER 160 (film star restrained from rendering services in any film or stage production for anyone other than the plaintiffs); *Araci v Fallon* [2011] EWCA Civ 668, [2011] All ER (D) 37 (Jun) (jockey prevented from riding rival horse in the Derby). Some doubt was cast on *Warner Bros Pictures Inc v Nelson* in *Warren v Mendy* [1989] 3 All ER 103, [1989] ICR 525, CA, where Nourse LJ, giving the judgment of the court, cited the observation of Oliver J in *Nichols Advance Vehicle Systems Inc v De Angelis* (21 December 1979, unreported), that it represents the high water mark of the application of *Lumley v Wagner* (1852) 1 De GM & G 604 (cited in note 1).
6   *Page One Records Ltd v Britton (t/a The Troggs)* [1967] 3 All ER 822, [1968] 1 WLR 157.
7   *Evans Marshall & Co Ltd v Bertola SA* [1973] 1 All ER 992 at 1005, [1973] 1 WLR 349 at 379, CA, per Sachs LJ; revsd on another ground [1976] 2 Lloyd's Rep 17, HL.

510. Absence of mutuality. The court may refuse to order specific performance on the ground of absence of mutuality; thus it will not as a rule compel a defendant to perform his obligations specifically if it cannot at the same time ensure that any unperformed obligation of the claimant will be specifically performed¹. Lack of mutuality does not deprive the court of jurisdiction to order specific performance, but is a matter to be taken into account by the court in deciding whether to exercise its discretion to order specific performance². The court will not order specific performance at the suit of a claimant who is a minor³, since the contract cannot be enforced against him⁴. A claimant cannot normally obtain a specific performance order to enforce a contract which could not be enforced against himself on the ground that it involves the future performance by him of personal services or of work which is not defined with sufficient precision⁵.

A claimant may, however, be granted an injunction restraining the defendant from preventing the execution of the contract by the claimant, even if the execution involves the performance of work which the claimant could not be ordered to perform[6].

The defence of want of mutuality must be judged on the facts and circumstances as they exist at the date of the hearing[7]. If the work or services required of the claimant under the contract have been performed before the hearing, the defendant cannot rely on the defence of want of mutuality, even if the work has in fact been done by the defendant[8]. The fact that at the date of the contract a claimant vendor had no title to the property which he contracted to sell does not entitle the defendant to refuse to perform the contract if the claimant has acquired title before the date of the hearing and the defendant did not, immediately upon discovering the absence of title, elect to treat the contract as discharged[9]. However, where a contract is illegal, the fact that the illegal part of it has been performed does not entitle the claimant to enforce performance of the rest of it[10].

1   *Price v Strange* [1978] Ch 337 at 367, [1977] 3 All ER 371 at 392, CA, per Buckley LJ.
2   *Price v Strange* [1978] Ch 337 at 359, 370, [1977] 3 All ER 371 at 385, 395, CA.
3   *Flight v Bolland* (1828) 4 Russ 298.
4   *Flight v Bolland* (1828) 4 Russ 298; *Lumley v Ravenscroft* [1895] 1 QB 683, CA.
5   *Hill v Gomme* (1839) 1 Beav 540; *Pickering v Bishop of Ely* (1843) 2 Y & C Ch Cas 249; *Johnson v Shrewsbury and Birmingham Rly Co* (1853) 3 De GM & G 914; *Stocker v Wedderburn* (1857) 3 K & 393; *Ord v Johnston* (1855) 1 Jur NS 1063; *Ogden v Fossick* (1862) 4 De GF & J 426; *Peto v Brighton, Uckfield and Tunbridge Wells Rly Co* (1863) 1 H & M 468.
6   *Jones (James) & Sons Ltd v Earl of Tankerville* [1909] 2 Ch 440, where an injunction was granted restraining the defendant from interfering with the plaintiff's right to enter on the defendant's land to cut timber.
7   *O'Regan v White* [1919] 2 IR 339; *Kirkland v Bird* (1968) 112 Sol Jo 440 at 441; *Wakeham v Mackenzie* [1968] 2 All ER 783 at 785, [1968] 1 WLR 1175 at 1177; *Price v Strange* [1978] Ch 337, [1977] 3 All ER 371, CA. See also *Macaulay v Great Paramount Theatre Ltd* (1921) 22 SRNSW 66 at 74; *Williamson (JC) Ltd v Lukey* (1931) 45 CLR 282 at 298.
8   *Price v Strange* [1978] Ch 337, [1977] 3 All ER 371, CA, where an order for specific performance was made with an allowance for the cost of work done by the defendant as a set-off against costs. See also *Sutton v Sutton* [1984] Ch 184, [1984] 1 All ER 168 (where the plaintiff could not have been ordered to carry out her part of agreement, but carried it out, the defendant could not rely on defence of want of mutuality).
9   *Hoggart v Scott* (1830) 1 Russ & M 293; *Eyston v Simonds* (1842) 1 Y & C Ch Cas 608; *Salisbury v Hatcher* (1842) 2 Y & C Ch Cas 54; *Murrell v Goodyear* (1860) 1 De GF & J 432; *Forrer v Nash* (1865) 35 Beav 167; *Brewer v Broadwood* (1882) 22 ChD 105; *Bellamy v Debenham* [1891] 1 Ch 412, CA; *Halkett v Earl of Dudley* [1907] 1 Ch 590; *Stickney v Keeble* [1915] AC 386 at 417, HL, per Lord Parker; *Elliott and H Elliott (Builders) Ltd v Pierson* [1948] Ch 452; *Price v Strange* [1978] Ch 337 at 354, 364, [1977] 3 All ER 371 at 381, 389, CA; *Pips (Leisure Productions) Ltd v Walton* (1980) 43 P & CR 415.
10 *Hope v Hope* (1857) 8 De GM & G 731.

511. Contracts enforceable despite absence of mutuality. A defendant cannot rely on a want of mutuality caused by his own default; for example, he cannot rely on the fact that his own laches has deprived him of the right to claim specific performance against the claimant[1]. A contract by a trustee to purchase trust property can be enforced against him, although it cannot be enforced by him[2].

Where at the time of the contract a vendor did not have the full interest he agreed to sell, the purchaser can, as a rule, claim a conveyance of such interest as the vendor possessed, with compensation, although the vendor would not have a corresponding right against the purchaser[3].

The right to rely on want of mutuality as a defence may be waived, for example by standing by and allowing the claimant to spend time and money in carrying out his part of the contract[4].

There is no need for mutuality where the tenant of a dwelling sues his landlord for breach of a repairing covenant[5].

1 *South Eastern Rly Co v Knott* (1852) 10 Hare 122. See also *Eastern Counties Rly Co v Hawkes* (1855) 5 HL Cas 331, where the defendant's statutory power of compulsory acquisition had expired.
2 *Ex p Lacey* (1802) 6 Ves 625.
3 See PARA 624; and CONVEYANCING vol 23 (2016) PARA 453 et seq.
4 *Halkett v Earl of Dudley* [1907] 1 Ch 590; *Price v Strange* [1978] Ch 337 at 356, [1977] 3 All ER 371 at 384, CA, per Goff LJ; *Sutton v Sutton* [1984] Ch 184, [1984] 1 All ER 168.
5 See the Landlord and Tenant Act 1985 s 17; and LANDLORD AND TENANT vol 62 (2016) PARA 358.

512. Inability to order performance of the whole contract. It was previously thought that a court could not order specific performance of part only of a contract[1]. However, it is now generally accepted that that is incorrect[2]. By a principle which overlaps with that of mutuality, the court will not as a general rule order specific performance of part of a contract unless it can order the performance of the whole contract[3]. This principle does not, however, apply to the grant of an injunction to restrain a breach of the contract[4], even if that may in practice compel the performance of the contract[5]; and where the contract is to execute a document, specific performance may be ordered even though the court might not be able to order specific performance of some of the obligations created by that document[6]. If the contract, although in form a single contract, is divisible into two or more parts which can be treated as being in substance separate contracts, specific performance can be ordered of one part even if it cannot be ordered of another[7]. Conversely, if two contracts are in form separate but are in substance interdependent, specific performance will not be ordered of one if it cannot be ordered of both[8]. If the contract itself provides for completion in stages, the court may order specific performance of one stage even though it cannot at that time direct performance of a subsequent stage[9]. If the obligations which cannot be enforced are an insubstantial part of the whole contract, the court can grant specific performance of the major part of the contract with damages as compensation for the obligations which cannot be performed[10]; and in cases relating to agreements for the construction of a building and the lease of the completed building the court has ordered specific performance of a lease of the site with damages for failure to erect the building[11].

1 See *Merchants Trading Co v Banner* (1871) LR 12 Eq 18; and *Kerr on Injunctions* (6th edn, 1927), p 409.
2 See *Lytton v Great Northern Rly Co* (1856) 2 K & J 394; *Rainbow Estates Ltd v Tokenhold Ltd* [1999] Ch 64, [1998] 2 All ER 860; and Jones and Goodhart, *Specific Performance* (2nd edn, 1996) pp 57-60. See also *Internet Trading Clubs Ltd v Freeserve (Investments) Ltd* [2001] EBLR 142, [2001] All ER (D) 185 (Jun), where it was said that the fact that the claimants were seeking specific performance of part only of a contract was not in itself an insuperable obstacle.
3 *Gervais v Edwards* (1848) 2 Dr & War 80; *Stocker v Wedderburn* (1857) 3 K & J 393 at 407; *Kernot v Potter* (1862) 3 De GF & J 447; *Ogden v Fossick* (1862) 4 De GF & J 426; *Merchants Trading Co v Banner* (1871) LR 12 Eq 18; *Ryan v Mutual Tontine Westminster Chambers Association* [1893] 1 Ch 116, CA; *Barnes v City of London Real Property Co etc* [1918] 2 Ch 18.
4 *Rigby v Great Western Rly Co* (1846) 15 LJ Ch 266; affd 2 Ph 44.
5 *Dietrichsen v Cabburn* (1846) 2 Ph 52; *Lumley v Wagner* (1852) 1 De GM & G 604. See also the other cases cited in PARA 509 note 1; and *De Mattos v Gibson* (1859) 4 De G & J 276 at 299 per Lord Hatherley LC; *Sevin v Deslandes* (1860) 30 LJ Ch 457; *Decro-Wall International SA v Practitioners in Marketing Ltd* [1971] 2 All ER 216, [1971] 1 WLR 361, CA; *Evans Marshall & Co Ltd v Bertola SA* [1973] 1 All ER 992, [1973] 1 WLR 349, CA (revsd on the question of damages [1976] 2 Lloyd's Rep 17, HL). Cf *Fothergill v Rowland* (1873) LR 17 Eq 132.
6 *England v Curling* (1844) 8 Beav 129 (partnership agreement); *Paxton v Newton* (1854) 2 Sm & G 437 (lease containing repairing covenants); *Stocker v Wedderburn* (1857) 3 K & J 393 at 403;

Wilson v West Hartlepool Rly Co (1865) 2 De GJ & Sm 475; *Giles (CH) & Co Ltd v Morris* [1972] 1 All ER 960, [1972] 1 WLR 307 (service agreement).

7   *Wilkinson v Clements* (1872) 8 Ch App 96; *Lowther v Heaver* (1889) 41 ChD 248, CA.
8   *Casamajor v Strode* (1834) 2 My & K 706 at 722; *Holliday v Lockwood* [1917] 2 Ch 47.
9   *Odessa Tramways Co v Mendel* (1878) 8 ChD 235, CA; *Langen and Wind Ltd v Bell* [1972] Ch 685, [1972] 1 All ER 296.
10 *Middleton v Greenwood* (1864) 2 De GJ & Sm 142.
11 *Soames v Edge* (1860) John 669; *Kay v Johnson* (1864) 2 Hem & M 118.

513.   Agreements ancillary to unenforceable principal contract. The court does not enforce an agreement if it is merely ancillary to a principal contract which is itself unenforceable; the adjunct must go along with the principal agreement. Thus specific performance of an agreement to execute a bond may be refused where the bond is to secure performance of a contract to execute works, which could not be enforced, the bond being merely ancillary to the works which form the substance of the contract[1]. Similarly, where a person agrees to employ another as broker and also agrees to insert his name as broker in all his advertisements, the court, being unable to order performance of the former, which is the substantial agreement, refuses to enforce the latter[2].

1   *South Wales Rly Co v Wythes* (1854) 5 De GM & G 880, CA, affg 1 K & J 186. Cf the cases cited in PARA 509, where a negative covenant which was enforced was distinct from the positive contract which was unenforceable.
2   *Brett v East India and London Shipping Co Ltd* (1864) 2 Hem & M 404.

(ii) Where Money Payment Adequate or Decree Valueless

514.   Principle as to damages being adequate remedy. The ground on which a court of equity would interfere to enforce specific performance of a contract was the inadequacy of the remedy at common law, which was by payment of a sum of money as damages[1]; so it follows that the court does not so interfere in cases where a money payment affords an adequate remedy[2]. The principle appears to be the same whether the contract leaves the amount of damages in the event of breach unliquidated, or whether it specifies a sum by way of penalty or liquidated damages[3]. It has been said that the test is now whether it is just, in all the circumstances, that a claimant should be confined to his remedy in damages[4].

1   See PARA 502.
2   *Harnett v Yielding* (1805) 2 Sch & Lef 549 at 553; *Adderley v Dixon* (1824) 1 Sim & St 607 at 610 per Leach V-C; *Wilson v Northampton and Banbury Junction Rly Co* (1874) 9 Ch App 279 at 284 per Lord Selborne LC; *Tito v Waddell (No 2)* [1977] Ch 106 at 327, [1977] 3 All ER 129 at 312 per Megarry V-C; *Anders Utkilens Rederi A/S v O/Y Lovisa Stevedoring Co A/B, The Golfstraum* [1985] 2 All ER 669 at 673 per Goulding J; *Flogas v Warrington* [2007] EWHC 1303 (QB).
3   See PARAS 515–519.
4   *Evans Marshall & Co Ltd v Bertola SA* [1973] 1 All ER 992 at 1005, [1973] 1 WLR 349 at 379, CA, per Sachs LJ; revsd on the question of assessment of damages [1976] 2 Lloyd's Rep 17, HL. See also *Coulls v Bagot's Executor and Trustee Co Ltd* (1967) 119 CLR 460 at 503 (Aust HC), per Windeyer J; *Beswick v Beswick* [1968] AC 58, [1967] 2 All ER 1197, HL; *Sudbrook Trading Estate Ltd v Eggleton* [1982] 3 All ER 1 at 6, [1982] 3 WLR 315 at 321, HL, per Lord Diplock; *CN Marine Inc v Stena Line A/B and Regie Voor Maritiem Transport, The Stena Nautica (No 2)* [1982] 2 Lloyd's Rep 336, CA; *Chiswell Shipping Ltd v State Bank of India, The World Symphony* [1987] 1 Lloyd's Rep 165. As to damages generally see DAMAGES.

515.   Adequacy of damages. The following illustrations may be given of contracts in which the court refuses specific performance on the ground that damages in money would afford a sufficient remedy.

The court as a rule refuses specific performance of a sale of government stock[1]. On the other hand, the court may enforce a contract for the sale or purchase of shares in a company[2], especially where the shares are unquoted[3] or will give the purchaser a controlling interest[4]. Where there is a free market in the shares, in which event the vendor or purchaser may easily make a substituted contract and be compensated for any difference in price by means of damages[5], specific performance will not be awarded[6]. In an action by a company to enforce specific performance of an underwriting contract, that is, a contract to take up shares in the company which are not fully paid, a decree will normally be granted[7]. The court may also enforce a contract to take up debentures[8].

The court generally refuses specific performance of a contract to sell or purchase chattels[9] which are not specific or ascertained[10] unless there is no alternative source of supply[11]. It may specifically enforce a contract to deliver specific or ascertained chattels[12], but this power is discretionary and will not be exercised if damages are an adequate remedy[13]. The court will enforce such a contract to deliver chattels if the goods are of so unique or special a character that money compensation is not adequate[14] and where the goods are of such a nature that it would damage the land to remove them, or where there is a contract for the sale of a house and chattels in it, with the furnishings in situ, if damages would not be an adequate remedy[15]. A contract for the sale of a ship may be specifically enforced, at least where, as usually is the case, the ship is of exceptional value to the claimant[16] and it has been said that a court would order specific performance of a contract to lease an aircraft, since each aircraft has unique features peculiar to itself[17].

Damages may be an adequate remedy even if the chattel which is the subject matter of the contract is not an ordinary article of commerce and substantial delay and loss of profit will be involved in obtaining a substitute[18]. Damages have in the past also been held to be an adequate remedy for breach of a tenant's covenant to repair the demised premises[19], a covenant to provide a resident porter for a block of flats[20] and a contract to lend money[21]. Where there is doubt, it is for the claimant to prove that damages are not an adequate remedy[22]. The modern authorities suggest that the discretion is to be exercised more flexibly than in the past[23].

Since land may have 'a peculiar and special value' to a purchaser[24], a claim for specific performance of an agreement to sell or grant an interest in land will not be refused on the ground that damages would be an adequate remedy, even if the interest to be granted is a lease for a short term[25] or a mere contractual licence to enter on land for a temporary purpose[26].

The principle of mutuality is applicable, so that a vendor of an interest in land, or of other property of such a nature that damages would be an inadequate remedy to the purchaser, may be entitled to an order for specific performance even though damages would be an adequate remedy for the vendor himself[27]. Other contracts for breach of which damages have been held to be an inadequate remedy include a contract for the sale of a patent[28], a contract under which the defendant agreed to erect buildings on his own land[29], a contract to pay an annuity to the other contracting party[30], a contract to grant an annuity to, or confer another benefit on a third person for which any damages recoverable by the claimant would be nominal[31], and a contract for the assignment of a debt[32].

Damages rather than specific performance are often the appropriate remedy if some of the persons entitled to the benefit of an order for specific performance are not before the court, since they might prefer to claim damages rather than enforce the contract[33].

1   *Cud v Rutter* (1720) 1 P Wms 570; *Cappur v Harris* (1723) Bunb 135; and *Nutbrown v Thornton* (1804) 10 Ves 159 at 161. As to government stock see FINANCIAL INSTRUMENTS AND TRANSACTIONS vol 49 (2015) PARA 122 et seq. The decisions of Leach V-C in *Doloret v Rothschild* (1824) 1 Sim & St 590 (contract for sale of Neapolitan stock; specific performance granted, and decree for delivery of certificates) and in *Withy v Cottle* (1822) 1 Sim & St 174 (specific performance on vendor's bill or contract for sale of life annuity payable out of dividends of stock) are contrary to the general current of authority; cf *Gardener v Pullen and Philips*(1700) 2 Vern 394, where the sale of East India stock was decreed in specie.
2   *Duncuft v Albrecht* (1841) 12 Sim 189; *Cheale v Kenward* (1858) 3 De G & J 27; and *Jobson v Johnson* [1989] 1 All ER 621, [1989] 1 WLR 1026. Cf *Colt v Nettervill* (1725) 2 P Wms 304; *Buxton v Lister* (1746) 3 Alk 383. See further COMPANIES vol 14 (2016) PARA 400; COMPANIES vol 15A (2016) PARA 1907. See also *Langen and Wind Ltd v Bell* [1972] Ch 685, [1972] 1 All ER 296. As to specific performance of a contract to purchase shares see further PARAS 527–529.
3   *Peña v Dale* [2003] EWHC 1065 (Ch), [2004] 2 BCLC 508.
4   *Harvela Investments Ltd v Royal Trust Co of Canada (CI) Ltd* [1986] AC 207, [1985] 2 All ER 966.
5   In such cases damages afford an adequate remedy, so that the basis of the court's jurisdiction is gone: see *Re Schwabacher*, and *Stern v Schwabacher, Koritschoner's Claim* (1907) 98 LT 127 at 128.
6   See PARA 527.
7   *New Brunswick and Canada Rly and Land Co v Muggeridge* (1859) 4 Drew 686 (not following *Sheffield Gas Consumers' Co v Harrison* (1853) 17 Beav 294); *Oriental Inland Steam Co Ltd v Briggs* (1861) 2 John & H 625 (on appeal 4 De GF & J 191), where specific performance was refused on the facts.
8   See the Companies Act 2006 s 740; and COMPANIES vol 15A (2016) PARA 1495.
9   In contrast to a contract to supply chattels, a remedy of repair or replacement is now available under the Consumer Rights Act 2015 in relation to both consumer contracts goods and for digital content: see CONSUMER PROTECTION vol 21 (2016) PARA 374.
10 *Holroyd v Marshall* (1862) 10 HL Cas 191 at 209, explained in *Re Wait* [1927] 1 Ch 606, CA. See also *Buxton v Lister* (1746) 3 Atk 383 at 384; *Hoare v Dresser* (1859) 7 HL Cas 290 at 317; *Fothergill v Rowland* (1873) LR 17 Eq 132; *Donnell v Bennett* (1883) 22 ChD 835; *Dominion Coal Co Ltd v Dominion Iron and Steel Co Ltd and National Trust Co Ltd* [1909] AC 293, PC, where specific performance was refused of a contract by a colliery company to deliver coal from its colliery to a steel company for the requirements of the steel company over a term of years; but see *Taylor v Neville* (prior to 1746) cited in 3 Atk at 384, which appears to be wrongly decided. See also *Pollard v Clayton* (1855) 1 K & J 462. Where delivery of the chattels is only part of an otherwise enforceable contract, delivery may be enforced: *Marsh v Milligan* (1857) 3 Jur NS 979.
11 *Sky Petroleum Ltd v VIP Petroleum Ltd* [1974] 1 All ER 954, [1974] 1 WLR 576; *Land Rover Group Ltd v UPF (UK) Ltd (in administrative receivership)* [2002] EWHC 303 (QB), [2003] 2 BCLC 222; *Thames Valley Power Ltd v Total Gas & Power Ltd* [2005] EWHC 2208 (Comm), [2006] 1 Lloyd's Rep 441, [2005] ArbLR 60; *Aston Martin Lagonda Ltd v Automotive Industrial Partnership Ltd* [2010] All ER (D) 131 (Feb).
12 See the Sale of Goods Act 1979 s 52; *Jones (James) & Sons Ltd v Earl of Tankerville* [1909] 2 Ch 440 at 445; and SALE OF GOODS AND SUPPLY OF SERVICES vol 91 (2012) PARA 303.
13 *Cohen v Roche* [1927] 1 KB 169 (Hepplewhite chairs); *Société des Industries Metallurgiques SA v Bronx Engineering Co Ltd* [1975] 1 Lloyd's Rep 465, CA; *Eximenco Handels AG v Partrederiet Oro Chief and Levantes Maritime Corpn, The Oro Chief* [1983] 2 Lloyd's Rep 509 (ship).
14 *Falcke v Gray* (1859) 4 Drew 651 (contract for sale of china jars); *Thorn v Public Works Comrs* (1863) 32 Beav 490; see *Phillips v Lamdin* [1949] 2 KB 33, [1949] 1 All ER 770 (ornate Adam door). In *Hexter v Pearce* [1900] 1 Ch 341, specific performance was granted of a contract relating to an undivided moiety of mineral property. Cf *Burrow v Scammell* (1881) 19 ChD 175. As to the analogous remedy of an order for specific delivery of chattels in cases not involving performance of a contract see EQUITABLE JURISDICTION vol 47 (2014) PARA 11.
15 *Record v Bell* [1991] 4 All ER 471, [1991] 1 WLR 853.
16 See *Lynn v Chaters* (1837) 2 Keen 521; *Claringbould v Curtis* (1852) 21 LJ Ch 541; *Hart v Herwig* (1873) 8 Ch App 860 at 866; *Batthyany v Bouch* (1881) 4 Asp MLC 380; *Behnke v Bede Shipping Co Ltd* [1927] 1 KB 649 at 661; *Astro Exito Navegacion SA v Southland Enterprise Co Ltd (No 2) (Chase Manhattan Bank NA intervening), The Messiniaki Tolmi* [1982] QB 1248, [1982] 3 All ER 335, CA; *Allseas International Management Ltd v Panroy Bulk*

      Transport SA, The Star Gazer and Star Delta [1985] 1 Lloyd's Rep 370. Cf *Société des Industries Metallurgiques SA v Bronx Engineering Co Ltd* [1975] 1 Lloyd's Rep 465 at 468, CA, per Lord Edmund-Davies; *CN Marine Inc v Stena Line AB* [1982] 2 Lloyd's Rep 336, CA. So too with a contract to charter a ship by demise: see *Scandinavian Trading Tanker Co AB v Flota Petrolera Ecuatoriana, The Scaptrade* [1983] 2 AC 694 at 702-703 per Lord Diplock, [1983] 2 All ER 763, and cf *The Jotunheim* [2004] EWHC 671 (Comm), [2005] 1 Lloyd's Rep 181.

17 *Bristol Airport plc v Powdrill* [1990] Ch 744 at 759, [1990] 2 All ER 493 at 502, CA, per Browne-Wilkinson V-C. Cf *Blue Sky One Ltd v Blue Airways LLC* [2009] EWHC 3314 (Comm) at [313] per Beatson J, [2010] All ER (D) 09 (Jan).

18 *Société des Industries Metallurgiques SA v Bronx Engineering Co Ltd* [1975] 1 Lloyd's Rep 465, CA (large industrial machine built to order).

19 *City of London v Nash* (1747) 3 Atk 512. See also *Rainbow Estates Ltd v Tokenhold Ltd* [1999] Ch 64, [1998] 2 All ER 860 and PARA 507.

20 *Ryan v Mutual Tontine Westminster Chambers Association* [1893] 1 Ch 116, CA; but cf *Posner v Scott-Lewis* [1987] Ch 25, [1986] 3 All ER 513.

21 *Rogers v Challis* (1859) 27 Beav 175, approved in *Larios v Bonany y Gurety* (1873) LR 5 PC 346. See also PARA 534. Cf *Hermann v Hodges* (1873) LR 16 Eq 18, where specific performance was ordered of an agreement to execute a legal mortgage as security.

22 *CN Marine Inc v Stena Line AB and Regie Voor Maritiem Transport, The Stena Nautica (No 2)* [1982] 2 Lloyd's Rep 336, CA.

23 *Re BA Peters plc (in administration)* [2008] EWHC 2205 (Ch), [2010] 1 BCLC 110. See also *RVB Investments Ltd v Bibby* [2013] EWHC 65 (Ch), [2013] All ER (D) 206 (Jan), where the court granted an order for specific performance requiring a surety to execute and complete a lease in circumstances where the surety was insolvent, despite the fact that the term of the lease would already have expired.

24 *Adderley v Dixon* (1824) 1 Sim & St 607 at 610. See also *Sudbrook Trading Estate Ltd v Eggleton* [1983] 1 AC 444 at 478, [1982] 3 All ER 1 at 6, HL, per Lord Diplock.

25 *Lever v Koffler* [1901] 1 Ch 543. See also LANDLORD AND TENANT vol 62 (2016) PARA 89.

26 *Verrall v Great Yarmouth Borough Council* [1981] QB 202, [1980] 1 All ER 839, CA.

27 *Kenney v Wexham* (1822) 6 Madd 355 (sale of an annuity); *Adderley v Dixon* (1824) 1 Sim & St 607 at 612; *Clifford v Turrell* (1841) 1 Y & C Ch Cas 138 at 150 (on appeal (1845) 14 LJ Ch 390); *Cogent v Gibson* (1864) 33 Beav 557 (sale of a patent); *Beswick v Beswick* [1968] AC 58, [1967] 2 All ER 1197, HL (sale of a business). See also *Eastern Counties Rly Co v Hawkes* (1855) 5 HL Cas 331 at 376 per Lord St Leonards, where it was said that damages would not be an adequate remedy for a vendor because he would not have divested himself of the estate. The explanation based on the principle of mutuality has been said to be 'perhaps not wholly satisfying': *Anders Utkilens Rederi A/S v O/Y Lovisa Stevedoring Co A/B, The Golfstraum* [1985] 2 All ER 669 at 673 per Goulding J.

28 *Cogent v Gibson* (1864) 33 Beav 557.

29 *Wolverhampton Corpn v Emmons* [1901] 1 QB 515, CA. Cf *South Wales Rly Co v Wythes* (1854) 1 K & J 186 (affd 5 De GM & G 880, CA), where it was held that damages were an adequate remedy as the plaintiffs had powers of compulsory purchase which would enable them to carry out the works themselves.

30 *Swift v Swift* (1841) 3 I Eq R 267.

31 *Beswick v Beswick* [1968] AC 58, [1967] 2 All ER 1197, HL.

32 *Wright v Bell* (1818) 5 Price 325; *Adderley v Dixon* (1824) 1 Sim & St 607.

33 *Tito v Waddell (No 2)* [1977] Ch 106 at 324, 326, [1977] 3 All ER 129 at 309, 311.

516. Contract stipulating for payment of money on non-performance. Where a contract contains a stipulation that in the event of non-performance a certain sum of money is to be paid, that fact is not in itself decisive in considering whether or not specific performance should be granted[1]. The answer is to be found by considering the intention of the parties, that is, whether the party bound to performance has a choice given to him by the contract to perform or to pay the agreed sum, or whether he is bound to do a certain thing, with a penal sum or sum by way of liquidated damages attached as security. In the second instance, notwithstanding the penal clause, the court enforces performance if the contract is such that without the penal clause it would have been proper for specific performance[2].

1 *Howard v Hopkyns* (1742) 2 Atk 371; *Roper v Bartholomew, Butler v Bartholomew* (1823) 12 Price 797; *French v Macale* (1842) 2 Dr & War 269.

2 *Roper v Bartholomew, Butler v Bartholomew* (1823) 12 Price 797 at 821; *French v Macale* (1842) 2 Dr & War 269; *Coles v Sims* (1854) 5 De GM & G 1. Cf the injunction cases of *Bath & North East Somerset District Council v Mowlem plc* [2004] EWCA Civ 115 at [14] per Mance LJ, [2015] 1 WLR 785 (Note); and *AB v CD* [2014] EWCA Civ 229, [2015] 1 WLR 771. See also DEEDS AND OTHER INSTRUMENTS vol 32 (2012) PARAS 326–329, 472–473.

517. Choice of remedy in case of penalty clause. Where a contract contains a clause providing for the forfeiture of money by the payer upon his non-performance of some obligation, the party entitled to performance has his right in law upon the contract for the money payable under the clause, and also his right in equity to specific relief; he can, at his election, obtain either form of relief, but he cannot obtain both[1]. Thus the ordinary provision on a sale of land that in case of default by the purchaser he is to forfeit his deposit and the seller is to be entitled to resell and claim any deficiency as liquidated damages does not exclude a claim for specific performance by the seller[2].

The court may treat the penal sum as security, and not as an alternative mode of performance, notwithstanding that the obligation is expressed in an alternative form[3].

Specific performance may also be ordered where the benefit of performance will go to one person and that of the penalty to another[4].

1 *Fox v Scard* (1863) 33 Beav 327 at 328. See *Gedge v Duke of Montrose* (1857) 5 WR 537 (assignment of lease); *General Accident Assurance Corpn v Noel* [1902] 1 KB 377 (injunction). On the avoidance of 'double recovery' see *Elsley v JG Collins Insurance Agencies Ltd* (1978) 83 DLR (3d) 1 (Supreme Court of Canada).
2 For instances see *Crutchley v Jerningham* (1817) 2 Mer 502 at 506; *Long v Bowring* (1864) 33 Beav 585; and CONVEYANCING vol 23 (2016) PARA 57. For other instances of specific performance notwithstanding a penalty clause see *Howard v Hopkyns* (1742) 2 Atk 371; *Jeudwine v Agate* (1829) 3 Sim 129 at 141; *Logan v Wienholt* (1833) 1 Cl & Fin 611, HL; *Butler v Powis* (1845) 2 Coll 156; *National Provincial Bank of England v Marshall* (1888) 40 ChD 112, CA. It is no bar to specific performance that the penalty is by bond: cf *Hobson v Trevor* (1723) 2 P Wms 191; *Clarkson v Edge* (1863) 33 Beav 227; *Roper v Bartholomew, Butler v Bartholomew* (1823) 12 Price 797.
3 *Chilliner v Chilliner* (1754) 2 Ves Sen 528 (contract to renew a lease or answer in damages).
4 *French v Macale* (1842) 2 Dr & War 269.

518. Payment as an alternative to performance. There are cases where the court holds, on the construction of a contract, that the intention of the parties is that the act may be done by the contracting party or that payment may be made by him of the stipulated amount, so that the contracting party has in effect the option either of doing the act which he has contracted to do or paying the specified sum, the contract being either to do or abstain from doing on payment of the sum in money[1]. The court may treat covenants to perform or to pay as alternative where specific performance would work unreasonable results[2].

1 *Ranger v Great Western Rly Co* (1854) 5 HL Cas 72 at 94. Cf *Astley v Weldon* (1801) 2 Bos & P 346.
2 *Magrane v Archbold* (1813) 1 Dow 107, HL.

519. Where performance would be valueless. Specific performance is not decreed if the defendant would be entitled to revoke or dissolve a contract when executed, as in the case of a contract containing an express power of revocation, since it would be idle to do that which might instantly be undone by one of the parties. Instances of the application of this principle are afforded by the refusal to order specific performance of an agreement for a partnership at will[1] or of a contract for a lease which is to contain a proviso for re-entry on breach of a covenant which has already been broken in such a way by the claimant as to entitle the defendant to re-enter[2]. Conversely, specific performance has been refused on the ground that performance has become valueless to the defendant[3].

A contract for the grant of a lease for a term which has expired before the date of the hearing[4] and a promise to issue share warrants when the opportunity to exercise the option they contained had long passed is not specifically enforced[5]. The principle is that equity does nothing in vain[6], and the court will refuse to order specific performance of a contract whenever the performance of the order would be a waste of time and money[7].

It should be noted, however, that there is no bar to the apparently pointless grant of specific performance if some purpose would be served thereby[8]. A straightforward example is enforcement of a surety's obligation to take over a lease disclaimed by a bankrupt tenant[9], or a bankrupt tenant's own obligation to execute a lease that when executed will trigger a surety's obligation to pay rent[10].

1 *Hercy v Birch* (1804) 9 Ves 357; *Sheffield Gas Consumers' Co v Harrison* (1853) 17 Beav 294: see PARA 536. Cf *Wheeler v Trotter* (1737) 3 Swan 174n, where specific performance was refused of an agreement by the registrar of a consistory court to delegate his office, such delegation being obviously revocable.
2 *Jones v Jones* (1803) 12 Ves 186; *Gregory v Wilson* (1852) 9 Hare 683; *Swain v Ayres* (1888) 21 QBD 289, CA. It must be clear that the right to forfeit exists.
3 — *v White* (circa 1709) 3 Swan 108n. See *Parker v Taswell* (1858) 2 De G & J 559.
4 *Western v Perrin* (1814) 3 Ves & B 197; *Nesbitt v Meyer* (1818) 1 Swan 223; *Walters v Northern Coal Mining Co* (1855) 5 De GM & G 629; *De Brassac v Martyn* (1863) 9 LT 287.
5 *De Jongh Weill v Mean Fiddler Holdings* [2005] All ER (D) 331 (Jul). See also *North East Lincolnshire Borough Council v Millennium Park (Grimsby) Ltd* [2002] EWCA Civ 1719, [2002] All ER (D) 346 (Oct), where specific performance of a promise to build a 'roundabout to nowhere' was refused. The court may, however, be prepared to grant specific performance of a contract to grant a licence to occupy land for a few days, as in the case of an agreement to provide a hall for a public meeting: see *Verrall v Great Yarmouth Borough Council* [1981] QB 202, [1980] 1 All ER 839, CA.
6 *New Brunswick and Canada Rly and Land Co v Muggeridge* (1859) 4 Drew 686 at 699 per Kindersley V-C; and see *Udall v Capri Lighting Ltd (in liquidation)* [1988] QB 907, [1987] 3 All ER 262, CA (a case relating to enforcement of a solicitor's undertaking).
7 *Tito v Waddell (No 2)* [1977] Ch 106 at 326, [1977] 3 All ER 129 at 311.
8 'It may be fitting for a court of equity to decree the execution of a lease, after the expiration of the term; a case of important rights and losses arising in the interval, and where a strong necessity is presented to the Court': *Nesbitt v Meyer* (1818) 1 Swan 223 at 226. See also *Walters v Northern Coal Mining Co* (1855) 5 De GM & G 629 at 638.
9 *RVB Investments Ltd v Bibby* [2013] EWHC 65 (Ch); [2013] All ER (D) 206 (Jan).
10 *AMEC Properties Ltd v Planning Research and Systems plc* [1992] BCLC 1149, [1992] 1 EGLR 70, [1992] 13 EG 109.

(iii) Where Performance would be Substantially Impossible

520. Performance substantially impossible. A decree of specific performance will not be granted if it would be substantially impossible to carry it out[1], for example where there is a contract to grant a lease at a rent greater than that which can lawfully be recovered at the time when the contract is due to be performed[2].

1 *Watts v Spence* [1976] Ch 165, [1975] 2 All ER 528; *North East Lincolnshire Borough Council v Millennium Park (Grimsby) Ltd* [2002] EWCA Civ 1719, [2002] All ER (D) 346 (Oct); *Coles and others (Trustees of the Ward Green Working Men's Club) v Samuel Smith Old Brewery (Tadcaster)* [2007] EWCA Civ 1461, [2008] 2 EGLR 159. See also *Clark v Lucas Solicitors LLP* [2009] EWHC 1952 (Ch), [2010] 2 All ER 955 for reasoning by analogy to the rules applicable to specific performance (solicitor's undertaking to redeem an existing charge was enforced and not regarded as incapable of later performance despite the sum then required being double the sale price of the property).
2 See *Newman v Dorrington Developments Ltd* [1975] 3 All ER 928, [1975] 1 WLR 1642, where, however, the principle did not apply on the facts of the case and specific performance was granted.

(iv) Defendant or Subject Matter out of the Jurisdiction

521. Service of writ outside the jurisdiction. Equity acts in personam[1], and cannot therefore pronounce a judgment for specific performance against a defendant who is not personally subject to the jurisdiction of the English courts.

A judgment for specific performance is not generally given against a person who is not capable of being served within the jurisdiction[2]. Service of a writ of summons may, however, be allowed out of the jurisdiction by leave of the court[3] in certain cases. Where leave is given to serve a writ out of the jurisdiction, judgment for specific performance may be given if a case for it is established[4].

1   As to this principle see EQUITABLE JURISDICTION vol 47 (2014) PARAS 103–104. See also CONFLICT OF LAWS vol 19 (2011) PARA 363.
2   See, however, the anomalous case of *Hart v Herwig* (1873) 8 Ch App 860, where a contract was made abroad for the sale of a foreign ship, and substituted service on the master was allowed when the ship was within the jurisdiction.
3   As to applications for leave see CIVIL PROCEDURE vol 11 (2015) PARA 267 et seq.
4   As to the jurisdiction of the English courts to entertain actions relating to contracts wherever made where the parties are effectively before the court (eg where leave has been given to serve the writ out of the jurisdiction) see CONFLICT OF LAWS PARA 396 et seq.

522. Subject matter of contract outside the jurisdiction. By virtue of the principle that equity acts in personam[1], the court may enforce a contract for the sale of or other dealing with land or other property outside the jurisdiction against a defendant who is within the jurisdiction[2] or has submitted to it, or who has been properly served out of the jurisdiction[3]. The order can be enforced by committal for contempt or an order for sequestration of the defendant's assets within the jurisdiction[4]. The court will not, however, enforce a contract for the purchase of land out of the jurisdiction against a third person who has bought it from the contractual vendor, even with notice of the prior contract, unless the prior contract is binding on the subsequent purchaser under the lex situs[5]. The court ought not to decree specific performance if the dispute between the parties is the subject matter of prior proceedings before a tribunal in the jurisdiction in which the property is situated, or if the order can have no operation without the intervention of a foreign court and would probably be ignored by that court[6]. The court will not order specific performance of a contract relating to foreign land if, under the lex situs, the defendant lacks the capacity to make such a contract[7] or if the recognition of the interest created by the contract would be contrary to the law of the lex situs[8].

1   Cf PARA 521 note 1.
2   *Archer v Preston*, cited in *Earl of Arglasse v Muschamp* (1682) 1 Vern 76; *Penn v Lord Baltimore* (1750) 1 Ves Sen 444; *Lord Cranstown v Johnson* (1796) 3 Ves 170; *Re Courtney, ex p Pollard* (1840) Mont & Ch 239 at 251 per Lord Cottenham LC; *Ewing v Orr Ewing* (1883) 9 App Cas 34 at 40, HL, per Lord Selborne LC; *Richard West & Partners (Inverness) Ltd v Dick* [1969] 2 Ch 424, [1969] 1 All ER 943, CA; *Chellaram v Chellaram* [1985] Ch 409, [1985] 1 All ER 1043. See also *Webb v Webb* [1992] 1 All ER 17, [1991] 1 WLR 1410 (further proceedings Case C–294/92 [1994] QB 696, [1994] 3 All ER 911, ECJ); *Mackinnon v Donaldson Lufkin & Jenrette Securities Corpn* [1986] Ch 482, [1986] 1 All ER 653. See also EQUITABLE JURISDICTION vol 47 (2014) PARAS 103–104; CONFLICT OF LAWS vol 19 (2011) PARA 363.
3   See *Duder v Amsterdamsch Trustees Kantoor* [1902] 2 Ch 132. European Parliament and Council Regulation (EU) 1215/2012 (OJ L351, 20.12.2012, p 1) on jurisdiction and the recognition and enforcement of judgments in civil and commercial matters ('Brussels I (Recast)'), makes it clear that English courts retain jurisdiction in such cases even if the defendant is EU-domiciled. The Convention on Jurisdiction and the Recognition and Enforcement of Judgments in Civil and Commercial Matters (Lugano, 30 October 2007; OJ L147, 10.6.2009, p 5) ('the Lugano Convention') 2007, does the same for EEA-domiciled defendants.
4   See *British South Africa Co v Companhia de Moçambique* [1892] 2 QB 358, CA at 364.

5   *Norris v Chambres, Chambres v Norris* (1861) 3 De GF & J 583; *Norton v Florence Land and Public Works Co* (1877) 7 ChD 332. See, however, *Mercantile Investment and General Trust Co v River Plate Trust, Loan and Agency Co* [1892] 2 Ch 303, where an English company acquired land in Mexico subject to a previous equitable charge which was void under Mexican law, and the charge was held to be enforceable against the company in England after the sale of the land.
6   *Norris v Chambres* (1861) 3 De GF & J 583; *Norton v Florence Land and Public Works Co* (1877) 7 ChD 332.
7   *Bank of Africa Ltd v Cohen* [1909] 2 Ch 129, CA.
8   *Waterhouse v Stansfield* (1852) 10 Hare 254; *Hicks v Powell* (1869) 4 Ch App 741.

(v) The Crown, States and Diplomats

523.   The Crown. Although civil proceedings may be brought against the Crown[1], where any such relief is sought as might in proceedings between subjects be granted by way of specific performance, the court must not make an order for specific performance but may in lieu make an order declaratory of the rights of the parties[2].

1   See CROWN AND CROWN PROCEEDINGS vol 29 (2014) PARA 84 et seq.
2   See the Crown Proceedings Act 1947 s 21(1) proviso (a): and CROWN AND CROWN PROCEEDINGS vol 29 (2014) PARA 110. As to the parallel provisions in s 21(1) proviso (a) relating to injunctions see *Factortame Ltd v Secretary of State for Transport* [1990] 2 AC 85, [1989] 2 All ER 692, HL (further proceedings Case C–213/89 [1991] 1 AC 603, [1991] 1 All ER 70, ECJ); cf *M v Home Office* [1994] 1 AC 377, [1993] 3 All ER 537, HL.

524.   States. Relief may not be given against a state by way of an order for specific performance[1] without the written consent of the state concerned[2], which may be contained in a prior agreement[3], but a provision merely submitting to the jurisdiction of the courts is not to be regarded as a consent for this purpose[4].

This immunity applies to any foreign or commonwealth state other than the United Kingdom[5].

1   See the State Immunity Act 1978 s 13(2)(a); and INTERNATIONAL RELATIONS LAW vol 61 (2010) PARA 257. See also *JH Rayner (Mincing Lane) Ltd v Department of Trade and Industry, Maclaine Watson & Co Ltd v Department of Trade and Industry, Maclaine Watson & Co Ltd v International Tin Council* [1990] 2 AC 418, sub nom *Maclaine Watson & Co Ltd v Department of Trade and Industry, Maclaine Watson & Co Ltd v International Tin Council* [1989] 3 All ER 523, HL; *Intpro Properties (UK) Ltd v Sauvel* [1983] QB 1019, [1983] 2 All ER 495, CA.
2   See the State Immunity Act 1978 s 13(3); and INTERNATIONAL RELATIONS LAW vol 61 (2010) PARA 257.
3   See the State Immunity Act 1978 ss 13(3); and INTERNATIONAL RELATIONS LAW vol 61 (2010) PARA 257.
4   See the State Immunity Act 1978 s 13(3); and INTERNATIONAL RELATIONS LAW vol 61 (2010) PARA 257.
5   See the State Immunity Act 1978 s 14(1); and INTERNATIONAL RELATIONS LAW vol 61 (2010) PARA 245.

525.   Diplomats. A diplomatic agent[1] is immune from civil jurisdiction[2], with exceptions which include a real action relating to private immovable property situated in the United Kingdom (unless he holds it on behalf of the sending state for the purposes of the mission)[3] and an action relating to any professional or commercial activity exercised by the diplomatic agent in the United Kingdom outside his official functions[4]. Members of the administrative, technical and service staff of a diplomatic mission and consular staff enjoy more limited immunities which, in general, protect them from a specific performance action only if they entered into the contract in the course of their duties[5].

1   As to the meaning of 'diplomatic agent' see the Diplomatic Privileges Act 1964 s 2(1), Sch 1 art 1(e); and INTERNATIONAL RELATIONS LAW vol 61 (2010) PARA 273. The immunity also extends to members of the agent's family forming part of his household if they are not nationals

of the United Kingdom and Colonies: see s 2(2), Sch 1 art 37 para 1. As to categories of citizenship see BRITISH NATIONALITY vol 4 (2011) PARA 406 et seq.

2   See the Diplomatic Privileges Act 1964 Sch 1 art 31 para 1; and INTERNATIONAL RELATIONS LAW vol 61 (2010) PARA 274. As to waiver of the immunity see Sch 1 art 32.

3   See the Diplomatic Privileges Act 1964 Sch 1 art 31 para 1(a); and INTERNATIONAL RELATIONS LAW vol 61 (2010) PARA 274.

4   See the Diplomatic Privileges Act 1964 Sch 1 art 31 para 1(c); and INTERNATIONAL RELATIONS LAW vol 61 (2010) PARA 274. 'United Kingdom' means Great Britain and Northern Ireland: Interpretation Act 1978 s 5, Sch 1. 'Great Britain' means England, Scotland and Wales: Union with Scotland Act 1706, preamble art I; Interpretation Act 1978 s 22(1), Sch 2 para 5(a). Neither the Channel Islands nor the Isle of Man are within the United Kingdom, nor are they colonies. As to the constitutional status of the Channel Islands see COMMONWEALTH vol 13 (2009) PARAS 790–798; and as to the constitutional status of the Isle of Man see COMMONWEALTH vol 13 (2009) PARAS 799–800. See further CONSTITUTIONAL AND ADMINISTRATIVE LAW vol 20 (2014) PARA 3.

5   See the Diplomatic Privileges Act 1964 Sch 1 art 37 paras 2, 3; the Consular Relations Act 1968 s 1(1), Sch 1 art 43; and INTERNATIONAL RELATIONS LAW vol 61 (2010) PARAS 280–281, 296.

(3) APPLICATION OF SPECIFIC PERFORMANCE TO PARTICULAR CONTRACTS

(i) Contracts for the Grant of an Interest in Land

526.   Contracts relating to land. In general specific performance of a contract relating to land, including a contractual licence[1], is granted as a matter of course[2] in England and Wales unless one of the defences discussed below can be established[3].

1   See *Verrall v Great Yarmouth Borough Council* [1981] QB 202, [1980] 1 All ER 839, CA.

2   *Sudbrook Trading Estates Ltd v Eggleton* [1983] 1 AC 444 at 478, [1982] 3 All ER 1 at 6 per Lord Diplock; *Patel v Ali* [1984] Ch 283, [1984] 1 All ER 978 at 981 per Goulding J; *Mungalsingh v Juman* [2015] UKPC 38 at [32] per Lord Neuberger, [2016] 1 P & CR 7. See also *AMEC Properties Ltd v Planning Research and Systems plc* [1992] BCLC 1149, [1992] 1 EGLR 70, CA, where it was held that the fact that the defendant was an insolvent company was not a basis for refusing specific performance on the ground that this would undermine the statutory scheme for the distribution of the assets of an insolvent company.

3   See PARA 540 et seq.

(ii) Sale of Shares

527.   Contracts relating to shares. It is the practice of the court to grant specific performance of contracts for the sale of shares in companies[1], unless they are freely available in the market[2]. This means that specific performance will usually be ordered of a contract for the sale of unquoted shares. Where, however, all or part of the purchase money is to remain outstanding after the transfer, the court ought not to order specific performance unless the order is in a form which will effectively safeguard the unpaid vendor's equitable lien[3].

In an order for specific performance of a contract for the sale of shares, any party whose execution of the transfer is required will be ordered to execute it[4], and directions will be given to ensure that the purchaser is registered as the shareholder[5].

Summary judgment[6] for specific performance of a contract for the sale of shares can be given[7]. An order for specific performance may be made even if the directors have a power to refuse to register the transferee as a shareholder, unless there is evidence that the directors may exercise that power[8]. The fact that the claimant is not the registered owner of shares, but merely the equitable owner, is not a bar to his suing a purchaser for specific performance[9].

The effect of a specifically enforceable contract for the sale of shares is to transfer the beneficial ownership of the shares immediately to the purchaser[10].

The above principles apply equally to other kinds of securities, for example bonds, debentures and certificates of deposit.

1   Where a company has issued shares on terms that they are or are liable to be redeemed, or has agreed to purchase any of its own shares, the court cannot grant an order for specific performance of the terms of redemption or purchase if the company shows that it is unable to meet the costs of redeeming or purchasing the shares in question out of distributable profits: see the Companies Act 2006 s 735(1), (3); and COMPANIES vol 15A (2016) PARA 1429. If, however, the company is wound up and at the commencement of the winding up any of the shares have not been redeemed or purchased, the terms of redemption or purchase may be enforced against the company unless either the terms provided for the redemption or purchase to take place at a date later than that of the commencement of the winding up, or during the period beginning with the date on which the redemption or purchase was to have taken place and ending with the commencement of the winding up the company could not at any time have lawfully made a distribution equal in value to the price at which the shares were to have been redeemed or purchased: see the Companies Act 2006 s 735(4), (5); and COMPANIES vol 15A (2016) PARA 1429.

2   *Duncuft v Albrecht* (1841) 12 Sim 189 at 199 per Shadwell V-C; *Re Schwabacher, Stern v Schwabacher, Koritschoner's Claim* (1907) 98 LT 127. See also *Sainsbury (J) plc v O' Connor (Inspector of Taxes)* [1991] STC 318 at 324–325, [1991] 1 WLR 963 at 971–972, CA, per Lloyd LJ; *Peña v Dale* [2003] EWHC 1065 (Ch), [2004] 2 BCLC 508. See also PARA 515; and COMPANIES vol 14 (2016) PARA 333. Cf *Bishop v Bonham* [1988] 1 WLR 742, 4 BCC 347, CA.

3   *Langen and Wind Ltd v Bell* [1972] Ch 685, [1972] 1 All ER 296, where an order for specific performance was made on condition that the purchasers' solicitors should hold the share certificates as stakeholders until payment in full of the purchase price.

4   As to the form and execution of the instrument of transfer see the Stock Transfer Acts 1963 and 1982; and COMPANIES vol 14 (2016) PARAS 411, 441.

5   As to the form of the order see *Evans v Wood* (1867) LR 5 Eq 9; *Paine v Hutchinson* (1868) 3 Ch App 388; 3 Seton's Judgments and Orders (7th Edn) 2209.

6   Ie generally under CPR Pt 24: see PARA 602 et seq.

7   *Woodlands v Hind* [1955] 2 All ER 604, [1955] 1 WLR 688; *Man UK Properties Ltd v Falcon Investments Ltd* [2015] EWHC 1324 (Ch), [2015] All ER (D) 67 (Jun).

8   *Evans v Wood* (1867) LR 5 Eq 9. See also *Poole v Middleton* (1861) 4 LT 631; cf *Hughes-Hallett v Indian Mammoth Gold Mines Co* (1882) 22 ChD 561 (registration already refused by directors; no order for specific performance).

9   *Paine v Hutchinson* (1868) 3 Ch App 388; *Loring v Davis* (1886) 32 ChD 625.

10 *Paine v Hutchinson* (1868) 3 Ch App 388 at 390; *Oughtred v IRC* [1960] AC 206, [1959] 3 All ER 623, [1959] 3 WLR 898; *Wood Preservation Ltd v Prior* [1969] 1 All ER 364, [1969] 1 WLR 1007, CA. See also *Hawks v McArthur* [1951] 1 All ER 22.

528. Effect of winding up. Any transfer of shares in a company made after the commencement of the winding up of the company by the court is void unless the court otherwise orders[1]. After the commencement of the winding up, the court will not order specific performance of a contract entered into before that event except in remarkable circumstances[2]. It will not order specific performance of a contract entered into after the commencement of the winding up and in ignorance of it[3]. The vendor may, however, obtain an order for an indemnity against calls on the shares after the date of the contract even if specific performance is not available[4].

1   See the Insolvency Act 1986 s 127(1); and COMPANY AND PARTNERSHIP INSOLVENCY vol 17 (2011) PARA 658. The winding up is deemed to commence at the time of the presentation of the petition (see s 129(2)), unless the company has previously passed a resolution for a voluntary winding up (see s 129(1)), or the court has made a winding-up order on hearing an administration application (see s 129(1A)); see COMPANY AND PARTNERSHIP INSOLVENCY vol 17 (2011) PARA 439.

2   *Sullivan v Henderson* [1973] 1 All ER 48, [1973] 1 WLR 333. But see *Paine v Hutchinson* (1868) 3 Ch App 388.

3 *Re London, Hamburg and Continental Exchange Bank, Emmerson's Case* (1866) 1 Ch App 433.
4 See the cases cited in PARA 529 note 2.

529. Calls on shares. It appears that a call made on the shares before the date of a contract for their sale, being a call of which the purchaser is ignorant, is not a ground for resisting specific performance of the contract[1]. The vendor is entitled to an indemnity against any calls made after the date of the contract and repayment of money already paid on such a call[2].

1 See *Hawkins v Maltby* (1867) LR 4 Eq 572 (on appeal 3 Ch App 188); *Hawkins v Maltby* (1868) LR 6 Eq 505 (on appeal (1869) 4 Ch App 200).
2 *Evans v Wood* (1867) LR 5 Eq 9; *Paine v Hutchinson* (1868) 3 Ch App 388; *Coles v Bristowe* (1868) 4 Ch App 3; *Hawkins v Maltby* (1869) 4 Ch App 200; *Cruse v Paine* (1869) 4 Ch App 441; *Nickalls v Merry* (1875) LR 7 HL 530; *Bowring v Shepherd* (1871) LR 6 QB 309, Ex Ch.

(iii) Other Particular Contracts

530. Contracts relating to choses or things in action and expectant interests. It is generally not necessary to seek an order for specific performance of a contract to assign for consideration a chose or thing in action, since such a contract will as a rule operate as an equitable assignment of the chose in action and no further action by the assignor will be required to perfect it[1]. The rights of the assignee will therefore be protected by the grant of an injunction or the appointment of a receiver rather than by making an order for specific performance[2].

A disposition of an equitable interest or trust subsisting at the time of the disposition must be in writing[3], and the assignee under an oral contract for the disposition of such an interest will be entitled to an order for the execution of a disposition in writing[4]. The court will order specific performance of an agreement for the assignment of a chose or thing in action if a formal instrument of assignment or other act is required to make the contract fully effective; thus the court will order specific performance of a contract for the sale of shares[5] or for the assignment of a patent[6] or copyright[7]. In such a case, specific performance may be granted to the vendor even though he only requires the purchase money[8]. A contract to assign an expectancy for consideration will likewise be enforced by an order for specific performance if it is necessary to execute some further instrument to give full effect to the contract[9]. The court will not, however, enforce a voluntary covenant for the assignment of future property[10].

Certain choses or things in action are incapable of assignment[11], and in such cases the question of specific performance does not arise.

1 *Metcalfe v Archbishop of York* (1836) 1 My & Cr 547; *Tailby v Official Receiver* (1888) 13 App Cas 523, HL (see in particular at 543–547 per Lord Macnaghten); *Re Lind, Industrials Finance Syndicate Ltd v Lind* [1915] 2 Ch 345, CA; *Re Warren, ex p Wheeler v Trustee in Bankruptcy* [1938] Ch 725, [1938] 2 All ER 331, DC. In the case of the assignment of the benefit of a contract, the assignee may of course have to take proceedings for specific performance against the other party to the original contract: see PARA 591.
2 *Tailby v Official Receiver* (1888) 13 App Cas 523 at 547, HL, per Lord Macnaghten. As to future debts, expectancies and other forms of future property see *Tailby v Official Receiver* (1888) 13 App Cas 523, HL; and CHOSES IN ACTION vol 13 (2009) PARA 30.
3 See the Law of Property Act 1925 s 53(1)(c); and DEEDS AND OTHER INSTRUMENTS vol 32 (2012) PARA 224.
4 See *Oughtred v IRC* [1960] AC 206, [1959] 3 All ER 623, HL.
5 See PARA 527.
6 *Bewley v Hancock* (1856) 6 De GM & G 391; *Printing and Numerical Registering Co v Sampson* (1875) LR 19 Eq 462; *Worthington Pumping Engine Co and Engine Co v Moore* (1902) 20 RPC 41.

7 *Thombleson v Black* (1837) 1 Jur 198; *Western Front Ltd v Vestron Inc* [1987] FSR 66. See also *Macdonald (Erskine) Ltd v Eyles* [1921] 1 Ch 631. As to assignment of patents see PATENTS AND REGISTERED DESIGNS vol 79 (2014) PARA 373. As to assignment of copyright see COPYRIGHT vol 23 (2016) PARA 641 et seq.

8 *Withy v Cottle* (1822) 1 Sim & St 174; *Cogent v Gibson* (1864) 33 Beav 557.

9 *Hobson v Trevor* (1723) 2 P Wms 191; *Wethered v Wethered* (1828) 2 Sim 183; *Hyde v White* (1832) 5 Sim 524; *Lyde v Mynn* (1833) 1 My & K 683; *Persse v Persse* (1840) 7 Cl & Fin 279.

10 *Re Ellenborough, Towry Law v Burne* [1903] 1 Ch 697. See also *Meek v Kettlewell* (1842) 1 Hare 464.

11 Eg a bare cause of action: *Trendtex Trading Corpn v Crédit Suisse* [1982] AC 679, [1981] 3 All ER 520, HL. See CHOSES IN ACTION vol 13 (2009) PARA 98 et seq.

531. Matrimonial and civil partnership proceedings. Agreements between spouses to compromise financial relief proceedings are generally not enforceable by means of specific performance and normal contractual principles do not apply[1].

Specific performance of an executory agreement for separation[2] between spouses[3] may be granted by the court, provided that there is a binding contract for valuable consideration[4], and provided that the contract neither contains provisions which are void as being against public policy[5] nor is objectionable on the ground of duress or other like grounds[6].

1 See *Xydhias v Xydhias* [1999] 2 All ER 386, [1999] 1 FCR 289, CA, where it was held that an agreement for the compromise of an ancillary relief application does not give rise to a contract enforceable at law; the only way of rendering the bargain enforceable was to covert the concluded agreement into an order of the court. However, it has been suggested that an agreement between spouses to compromise proceedings for financial relief may still be an enforceable contract if all the normal requirements for formation of a valid contract have been complied with: see *Warwick (formerly Yarwood) v Trustee in Bankruptcy of Yarwood* [2010] EWHC 2272 (Ch), [2010] 3 FCR 311, 154 Sol Jo (no 36) 33. See also *DN v HN* [2014] EWHC 3435 (Fam), [2015] Fam Law 1044, [2015] All ER (D) 250 (Jun), where an agreement which was found to be distinct from the financial remedy claim was held to be enforceable. See further MATRIMONIAL AND CIVIL PARTNERSHIP LAW vol 72 (2015) PARAS 254, 628, 868.

2 As to contracts for separation between spouses and civil partners see generally MATRIMONIAL AND CIVIL PARTNERSHIP LAW vol 72 (2015) PARA 343 et seq.

3 The court's jurisdiction in this respect was established in *Wilson v Wilson* (1848) 1 HL Cas 538. See also *Gibbs v Harding* (1870) 5 Ch App 336 (separation deed); *Besant v Wood* (1879) 12 ChD 605; *Hart v Hart* (1881) 18 ChD 670; *Evershed v Evershed* (1882) 46 LT 690 (agreement to compromise).

4 As to what constitutes consideration see MATRIMONIAL AND CIVIL PARTNERSHIP LAW vol 72 (2015) PARA 349.

5 In *Vansittart v Vansittart* (1858) 4 K & J 62 (affd 2 De G & J 249), it was held that, where the agreement was executory, the presence of any unlawful stipulation would be a bar to a decree, whereas in *Hamilton v Hector* (1872) LR 13 Eq 511, where the suit was on a deed, relief by injunction was granted in respect of covenants which were valid, irrespective of void covenants also contained in the deed. As to void provisions see the Matrimonial Causes Act 1973 s 34; and MATRIMONIAL AND CIVIL PARTNERSHIP LAW vol 72 (2015) PARAS 333–334.

6 See MATRIMONIAL AND CIVIL PARTNERSHIP LAW vol 72 (2015) PARA 348. Provisions in a separation agreement as to the residence of, and contact with, children will not be enforced unless the court is of opinion that it is for the benefit of the child to do so, since where the upbringing of a child is in question the court must regard his welfare as the paramount consideration; see the Children Act 1989 s 1(1); and CHILDREN AND YOUNG PERSONS vol 9 (2017) PARA 315 et seq. See also *Jump v Jump* (1883) 8 PD 159; and MATRIMONIAL AND CIVIL PARTNERSHIP LAW vol 73 (2015) PARA 359. The same principle would, it is submitted, apply in the case of a parental responsibility agreement under the Children Act 1989 s 4(1)(b). As to parental responsibility agreements see CHILDREN AND YOUNG PERSONS vol 9 (2017) PARA 155 et seq.

532. Arbitration and awards. The court does not enforce the specific performance of agreements to refer to arbitration[1], although an indirect method of enforcing performance of such an agreement is provided by the Arbitration Act 1996, which gives the court discretion to stay an action in respect of any dispute which the parties have by writing agreed to refer to arbitration[2].

The performance of an award may, however, be specifically enforced by the judgment of the court if what is ordered by the award is a matter which, if the subject of an agreement, would have been proper for specific performance[3], and, where a reference has been ordered by the court, the award may be enforced before it has been made a ruling of the court[4]. Where an action is brought for the specific performance of an award, the defendant may raise such grounds of defence as would be available on general principles in resisting such an action; thus, he may object that the award is invalid in law[5], is uncertain[6] or is in excess of the arbitrator's authority, or does not fully deal with the matters submitted, or that the agreement to refer the matter to arbitration is not one that the court would enforce because of unfairness, unreasonableness or other like grounds[7]. It seems that a party may not claim specific performance of an award after taking proceedings to have it set aside[8].

Parties to an arbitration are free to agree on the powers exercisable by the arbitral tribunal as regards remedies, and the tribunal has the same powers as the court to order specific performance of a contract other than one relating to land[9].

1   *Street v Rigby* (1802) 6 Ves 815; *Gourlay v Duke of Somerset* (1815) 19 Ves 429; *Agar v Macklew* (1825) 2 Sim & St 418; *Gervais v Edwards* (1848) 2 Dr & War 80; *South Wales Rly Co v Wythes* (1854) 5 De GM & G 880, CA; *Vertex Data Science Ltd v Powergen Retail Ltd* [2006] EWHC 1340 (Comm), [2006] 2 Lloyd's Rep 591. The court may, however, appoint an arbitrator if both parties request it to do so: *Medov Lines SpA v Traelandsfos A/S* [1969] 2 Lloyd's Rep 225. In certain circumstances the High Court has power to appoint an arbitrator or umpire: as to the court's powers to appoint an arbitrator see the Arbitration Act 1996 ss 16–19, 27; and ARBITRATION vol 2 (2008) PARAS 1226–1228.
2   See the Arbitration Act 1996 s 9(1); and ARBITRATION vol 2 (2008) PARA 1222. As to the staying of legal proceedings generally see ss 9–11. See also *Cheslyn v Dalby* (1836) 2 Y & C Ex 170, which illustrates how refusal to perform an agreement to refer may raise an equity to which the court will give effect.
3   *Reignolds v Latham* (1579) Cary 106; *Norton v Mascall* (1687) 2 Vern 24; *Hall v Hardy* (1733) 3 P Wms 187; *Wood v Griffith* (1818) 1 Swan 43; *Clay v Rufford* (1849) 8 Hare 281; *Peel v Peel* (1869) 17 WR 586. Cf *Thompson v Noel* (1738) 1 Atk 60 at 62. In *Blackett v Bates* (1865) 1 Ch App 117 specific performance was refused on the ground that the order would have involved the enforcement of continuous performance: see PARA 507. As to the effect of part performance of an award see *Norton v Mascall* above. As to the methods of enforcing an award see *Selby v Whitbread & Co* [1917] 1 KB 736 at 753–754 per McCardie J; and ARBITRATION vol 2 (2008) PARA 1274–1275.
4   *Wood v Taunton* (1849) 11 Beav 449.
5   *Blundell v Brettargh* (1810) 17 Ves 232. Cf *Norton v Mascall* (1687) 2 Vern 24. As to various grounds of invalidity see ARBITRATION vol 2 (2008) PARA 1276 et seq.
6   *Wakefield v Llanelly Rly and Dock Co* (1865) 3 De GJ & Sm 11.
7   *Nickels v Hancock* (1855) 7 De GM & G 300. Distinguish the unreasonableness of the award itself, if not involving invalidity: see *Wood v Griffith* (1818) 1 Swan 43, where it was held that the parties, having chosen their tribunal, must abide by its decision.
8   *Blackett v Bates* (1865) 1 Ch App 117.
9   Arbitration Act 1996 s 48(1), (5)(b). For what amounts to a contract relating to land in this context, see *Telia Sonera AB v Hilcourt (Docklands) Ltd* [2003] EWHC 3540 (Ch), [2003] ArbLR 42, [2003] All ER (D) 91 (Jul). As to the various remedies available in arbitral proceedings see generally the Arbitration Act 1996 s 48; and ARBITRATION vol 2 (2008) PARA 1259.

533.   Appointment of a valuer. If a contract for sale provides for the purchase price to be fixed by a valuer or valuers to be nominated by the parties and one party prevents the machinery from operating by refusing to nominate a valuer, the court will treat the contract as a contract for sale at a fair and reasonable price[1]. The court will itself determine, on expert evidence, what that price is, and will order specific performance of the contract[2]. In such a case the provision in the contract for ascertainment of the price is regarded as subsidiary and non-essential. If, however, the contract provides for the price to be fixed by a named valuer or someone who has special knowledge relevant to the question of value, the prescribed mode of valuation may be regarded as an essential term and specific performance may be refused if the nominated valuer is unable or unwilling to act[3].

Where a valuer has been appointed, the court has power to make a mandatory order directing a party to allow the valuer to have access to the property which he is required to value[4].

1 See CONVEYANCING vol 23 (2016) PARA 40.
2 *Sudbrook Trading Estate Ltd v Eggleton* [1983] 1 AC 444, [1982] 3 All ER 1, HL, overruling *Milnes v Gery* (1807) 14 Ves 400, *Agar v Macklew* (1825) 2 Sim & St 418, and *Vickers v Vickers* (1867) LR 4 Eq 529. It is possible that the court might alternatively compel the party in default to appoint a valuer: *Sudbrook Trading Estate Ltd v Eggleton* above at 479 and at 7 per Lord Diplock.
3 *Sudbrook Trading Estate Ltd v Eggleton* [1983] 1 AC 444 at 479, [1982] 3 All ER 1 at 6, HL, per Lord Diplock and at 483–484 and 10 per Lord Fraser of Tullybelton.
4 *Morse v Merest* (1821) 6 Madd 26; *Smith v Peters* (1875) LR 20 Eq 511.

534. Contracts for the loan or payment of money. It is the general rule that the court will not order specific performance of a contract to pay money[1]. In particular, the court will not normally compel an intended borrower to take or an intended lender to make a loan, whether the loan is secured or unsecured, but will leave the claimant to his remedy in damages[2]. There are, however, significant exceptions to this rule[3]. Contracts to lend or pay money have been specifically enforced in the following circumstances:

(1) if a loan has already been made in consideration of the defendant's promise to execute a mortgage or other security, the court will decree specific performance of the agreement[4];

(2) if the agreement to lend is collateral to the main contract and that contract is specifically enforceable, the agreement to lend may also be specifically enforceable[5];

(3) if the agreement is for the grant of an annuity[6];

(4) if an employer has promised to pay its national insurance contributions to a pension fund for the employee[7];

(5) if a person has entered into an indemnity agreement to relieve a debtor by undertaking to discharge the debt on his behalf (and not merely to reimburse the debtor after he has paid the debt), the court will specifically enforce the obligation by ordering the indemnifying party to pay the debt, provided that the debt has become a present and enforceable liability[8]; and similarly a surety is entitled to an order directing the principal debtor to discharge the debt as soon as it has become a present liability[9];

(6) if the contract is of such a kind that a purchaser can sue for specific performance (for example a contract for the sale of land), the vendor can also sue for specific performance even though his only claim is for a liquidated sum of money[10].

By statute, a contract with a company to take up and pay for any debentures of the company may be enforced by an order for specific performance[11]. Specific performance has also been granted of an agreement to surrender tax losses[12].

1 *Crampton v Varna Rly Co* (1872) 7 Ch App 562.
2 *Rogers v Challis* (1859) 27 Beav 175 (action by potential lender); *Sichel v Mosenthal* (1862) 30 Beav 371 (action by potential borrower); *Larios v Bonany y Gurety* (1873) LR 5 PC 346; *Western Wagon and Property Co v West* [1892] 1 Ch 271 at 275 per Chitty J; *South African Territories v Wallington* [1898] AC 309, HL; *Loan Investment Corpn of Australasia v Bonner* [1970] NZLR 724, PC.
3 See *Loan Investment Corpn of Australasia v Bonner* [1970] NZLR 724 at 742, PC, per Sir Garfield Barwick.
4 *Ashton v Corrigan* (1871) LR 13 Eq 76; *Hermann v Hodges* (1873) LR 16 Eq 18.

5   *Starkey v Barton* [1909] 1 Ch 284. Cf *Loan Investment Corpn of Australasia v Bonner* [1970] NZLR 724, PC, where a contract which was essentially one of loan was not enforceable.

6   *Clifford v Turrell* (1841) 1 Y & C Ch 138 (on appeal (1845) 14 LJ Ch 390); *Swift v Swift* (1841) 3 I Eq R 267; *Keenan v Handley* (1864) 2 De GJ & S 283; *Beswick v Beswick* [1968] AC 58 at 97, [1967] 2 All ER 1197 at 1218, HL, per Lord Upjohn. See also *Nives v Nives* (1880) 15 ChD 649 (purchase money payable by instalments).

7   *The Halcyon Skies* [1977] QB 14, [1976] 1 All ER 856, [1976] 2 WLR 514.

8   *Re Richardson, ex p St Thomas's Hospital (Governors)* [1911] 2 KB 705 at 709–710, CA; *McIntosh v Dalwood (No 4)* (1930) 30 SRNSW 415. Cf *Hughes-Hallett v Indian Mammoth Gold Mines Co* (1882) 22 ChD 561 (liability contingent).

9   *Ascherson v Tredegar Dry Dock and Wharf Co Ltd* [1909] 2 Ch 401. Cf *Bradford v Gammon* [1925] Ch 132.

10 *Kenney v Wexham* (1822) 6 Madd 355; *Adderley v Dixon* (1824) 1 Sim & St 607 at 612; *Clifford v Turrell* (1841) 1 Y & C Ch 138 at 150; *Cogent v Gibson* (1864) 33 Beav 557; *Beswick v Beswick* [1968] AC 58, [1967] 2 All ER 1197, HL. See also *Eastern Counties Rly Co v Hawkes* (1855) 5 HL Cas 331 at 376; *Nives v Nives* (1880) 15 ChD 649; *Gorringe v London Improvement Society* [1899] 1 IR 142 at 152; *Starkey v Barton* [1909] 1 Ch 284 at 290; *Turner v Bladin* (1951) 82 CLR 463 at 473. See also PARA 515.

11 See the Companies Act 2006 s 740; and COMPANIES vol 15A (2016) PARA 1495.

12 *Charterhouse Investment Trust Ltd v Tempest Diesels Ltd* [1986] BCLC 1.

535. Contract of indemnity. An ordinary contract of indemnity can be directed to be specifically performed by ordering that the indemnifier should pay the amount concerned directly to the third party to whom the liability was owed or, in some cases, to the party to be indemnified[1].

1   *Johnston v Salvage Association and McKiver* (1887) 19 QBD 458 at 460, CA, per Lindley LJ; *British Union and National Insurance Co v Rawson* [1916] 2 Ch 476 at 481–482, CA, per Pickford LJ; *Firma C-Trade SA v Newcastle Protection and Indemnity Association, The Fanti, Socony Mobil Oil Inc v West of England Ship Owners Mutual Insurance Assocn (London) Ltd, The Padre Island (No 2)* [1991] 2 AC 1, [1990] 2 All ER 705, HL (where, however, the express provisions of the rules of the protection and indemnity associations concerned precluded the application of the remedy).

536. Agreements relating to partnerships. The court does not as a general rule enforce an agreement to form and carry on a partnership[1], but it does enforce such an agreement by ordering the parties to execute a formal deed where they have actually entered on performance by carrying on the partnership business[2], and it also enforces a contract for the purchase of a share in a partnership[3], or for an option to enter into partnership[4]. It seems doubtful whether the court would specifically enforce a contract to execute a deed of partnership as distinguished from a contract to enter into a partnership[5].

1   *New Brunswick and Canada Rly and Land Co v Muggeridge* (1859) 4 Drew 686 at 697 et seq per Kindersley V-C; *Sichel v Mosenthal* (1862) 30 Beav 371; *Scott v Rayment* (1868) LR 7 Eq 112. Where the proposed partnership is at will, interference by the court would in any event be nugatory, as either party could instantly dissolve the partnership: cf *Hercy v Birch* (1804) 9 Ves 357; *Sheffield Gas Consumers' Co v Harrison* (1853) 17 Beav 294 (partnership to make secret medicines). See also *Vivers v Tuck* (1863) 1 Moo PCCNS 516, where specific performance of a partnership agreement was refused on the ground of hardship. As to partnerships generally see PARTNERSHIP.

2   *Hibbert v Hibbert* (1807) cited in *Scott v Rayment* (1868) LR 7 Eq 112; *England v Curling* (1844) 8 Beav 129; *Crowley v O' Sullivan* [1900] 2 IR 478. See also EQUITABLE JURISDICTION vol 47 (2014) PARA 64.

3   *Dodson v Downey* [1901] 2 Ch 620. The court inserts the term that the purchaser indemnify the vendor against the liabilities of the business: *Dodson v Downey*. See also *Charlesworth v Jennings* (1864) 11 LT 439 (misrepresentation); *Homfray v Fothergill* (1866) LR 1 Eq 567.

4   *Lisle v Reeve* [1902] 1 Ch 53 CA; affd sub nom *Reeve v Lisle* [1902] AC 461, HL.

5   See G Jones & W Goodhart, *Specific Performance* (2nd ed, 1996), p 184. Cf *Stocker v Wedderburn* (1857) 3 K & J 393.

537. Contracts to leave property by will, to settle property or to exercise powers. A contract for good consideration to leave by will ascertainable property[1] to a particular person may be enforced by an order for specific performance as against all persons claiming as volunteers under the person who so agreed[2]. Specific performance is not, however, ordered where the person who entered into the contract was merely acting in exercise of a testamentary power of appointment[3]. An agreement to make ample provision for a person by will is too vague to be enforced[4]; a definite agreement must be proved in order that relief may be granted[5]. If the property in question is an interest in land and the contract is made on or after 27 September 1989, the contract is a complete nullity if the statutory requirements as to form are not complied with[6].

Specific performance may also be granted of certain contracts to settle property on marriage[7] or to exercise a power to jointure[8].

1   As to contracts to leave property by will see WILLS AND INTESTACY vol 102 (2016) PARAS 20–21.
2   *Synge v Synge* [1894] 1 QB 466 at 470–471, CA; *Schaefer v Schuhmann* [1972] AC 572, [1972] 1 All ER 621, PC. See also *Goilmere v Battison* (1682) 1 Vern 48, sub nom *Goylmer v Paddiston* (1682) 2 Vent 353; *Ridley v Ridley* (1865) 34 Beav 478; *Coverdale v Eastwood* (1872) LR 15 Eq 121; *Alderson v Maddison* (1880) 5 Ex D 293 (revsd on the facts (1881) 7 QBD 174, CA, and sub nom *Maddison v Alderson* (1883) 8 App Cas 467, HL); *Re Broadwood, Edwards v Broadwood (No 2)* (1912) 56 Sol Jo 703, CA; *Wakeham v Mackenzie* [1968] 2 All ER 783, [1968] 1 WLR 1175. Cf *Re Gonin* [1979] Ch 16, [1977] 2 All ER 720. As to voluntary contracts see PARA 506.
3   *Re Parkin, Hill v Schwarz* [1892] 3 Ch 510 at 517. As to a covenant not to revoke such a will see *Re Lawley, Zaiser v Lawley* [1902] 2 Ch 799 at 804, 805, CA; *Robinson v Ommanney* (1882) 21 ChD 780; and WILLS AND INTESTACY vol 102 (2016) PARA 21.
4   *Macphail v Torrance* (1909) 25 TLR 810.
5   *Walpole (Lord) v Lord Orford* (1797) 3 Ves 402, discussed and explained in *Re Oldham, Hadwen v Myles* [1925] Ch 75 at 85, and *Gray v Perpetual Trustee Co* [1928] AC 391 at 400, PC.
6   See the Law of Property (Miscellaneous Provisions) Act 1989 ss 2, 5(3), (4) (which replaced the Law of Property Act 1925 s 40 in relation to contracts made on or after 27 September 1989). See also LANDLORD AND TENANT vol 62 (2016) PARA 73.
7   See SETTLEMENTS vol 91 (2012) PARA 540.
8   See TRUSTS AND POWERS vol 98 (2013) PARA 505.

538. Compulsory purchase. There are numerous and extensive statutory provisions which enable government departments, local authorities and other public bodies to acquire land compulsorily, and in certain circumstances an owner may require an authority to purchase land from him[1]. Once the price or compensation has been ascertained, there is a complete agreement which can be enforced by an order for specific performance[8] or, in the case of the acquiring authority, by the payment of compensation into court and the execution of a deed poll vesting the land in itself[9].

Whether specific performance will be granted after the price or compensation has been agreed or determined will depend on the application of the ordinary rules[10]. The acquiring authority may insist that the owner shows a good title and specific performance will then be granted only on condition that the owner does so[11]. In the case of unregistered land, the owner must execute a conveyance, and it is a defence to an action for the price that no conveyance has been executed[12]. Where a lease is acquired, the acquiring authority must give the usual covenants by an assignee against breach of the covenants in the lease[13]. Interest is payable from the time when a good title is shown or, if title has been accepted before the date when the price is agreed or ascertained, from the latter date[14]. If possession is taken by the acquiring authority at an earlier time interest is payable (in the absence of statutory provision to the contrary) from the date of possession[15].

1   See generally COMPULSORY ACQUISITION OF LAND.

8 *Regent's Canal Co v Ware* (1857) 23 Beav 575; *Mason v Stokes Bay Rly and Pier Co* (1862) 32 LJ
   Ch 110; *Harding v Metropolitan Rly Co* (1872) 7 Ch App 154; *Re Cary-Elwes' Contract* [1906]
   2 Ch 143. See further COMPULSORY ACQUISITION OF LAND vol 18 (2009) PARA 651.
9 See the Compulsory Purchase Act 1965 s 9; and COMPULSORY ACQUISITION OF LAND vol 18
   (2009) PARAS 661, 663, 664. See also *IRC v Metrolands (Property Finance) Ltd* [1982] 2 All ER
   557 at 561, [1982] 1 WLR 341 at 346, HL (deemed notice to treat).
10 *Re Pigott and Great Western Rly Co* (1881) 18 ChD 146 at 150 per Jessel MR.
11 *Gunston v East Gloucestershire Rly Co* (1868) 18 LT 8.
12 *East London Union v Metropolitan Rly Co* (1869) LR 4 Exch 309. Transfers of registered land are
   executed by the transferee. See generally CONVEYANCING.
13 *Harding v Metropolitan Rly Co* (1872) 7 Ch App 154.
14 *Re Pigott and Great Western Rly Co* (1881) 18 ChD 146.
15 *Inglewood Pulp and Paper Co v New Brunswick Electric Power Commission* [1928] AC 492, PC.
   Accrued interest is payable on an advance payment on account of compensation: see the
   Land Compensation Act 1973 s 52A; and COMPULSORY ACQUISITION OF LAND vol 18 (2009)
   PARA 657. As to the power of the Upper Tribunal to direct that interest be paid from the date of
   the award or previous entry see COMPULSORY ACQUISITION OF LAND vol 18 (2009) PARA 745.

539. Provision of information. Specific performance may be granted in respect
of the provision of information[1].

A doctor is under a duty to answer his patient's questions as to the treatment
proposed[2], and he may be under a like duty in respect of treatment that has
already been given[3]. It has been suggested that if a patient is refused information
to which he is entitled, he may be able to bring an action claiming specific
performance of the duty to inform[4].

1 See *Transport for Greater Manchester (formerly Greater Manchester Passenger Transport
   Executive) v Thales Transport & Security Ltd* [2012] EWHC 3717 (TCC); 146 ConLR 194 (where
   an order was made for specific performance requiring the defendant to disclose various
   documentation relating to the costs of an infrastructure project); *Personal Management
   Solutions Ltd v Brakes Bros Ltd* [2014] EWHC 3495 (QB) (where specific performance was
   ordered of an undertaking by one of the defendants to identify confidential information which he
   had in his possession); *Alfa Finance Holdings AD v Quarzwerke GmbH* [2015] EWHC 243 (Ch)
   (where specific performance was ordered of an obligation to grant the claimant reasonable access
   to certain 'books, records and documents').
2 See *Sidaway v Board of Governors of the Bethlem Royal Hospital and the Maudsley Hospital*
   [1985] AC 871, [1985] 1 All ER 643, HL.
3 See *Lee v South West Thames Regional Health Authority* [1985] 2 All ER 385 at 389–390, [1985]
   1 WLR 845 at 850–851, CA.
4 See *Lee v South West Thames Regional Health Authority* [1985] 2 All ER 385 at 390, [1985] 1
   WLR 845 at 851, CA, per Sir John Donaldson MR.

2. FACTORS RELEVANT TO THE GRANT OF SPECIFIC PERFORMANCE

(1) REQUIREMENTS FOR SPECIFIC PERFORMANCE

540. Definite concluded contract. Where it is sought to enforce specific performance of a contract[1], the court must be satisfied:

(1)   that there is a concluded contract[2] which is binding at law[3], and in particular that the parties have agreed, expressly or impliedly[4], on all the essential terms of the contract; and

(2)   that the terms are sufficiently certain and precise that the court can order and supervise the exact performance of the contract[5].

1   It has been questioned what is included in the term 'contract'. A judge's order made by consent is from many aspects a contract, with further elements added by reason of the order of the court (see *Wentworth v Bullen* (1829) 9 B & C 840; *Lievesley v Gilmore* (1866) LR 1 CP 570; *Conolan v Leyland* (1884) 27 ChD 632), but specific performance of such an order was refused in *Thames Iron Works Co v Patent Derrick Co* (1860) 1 John & H 93 by Page Wood V-C, it being the order of another court and providing its own method of enforcement. In *Caton v Caton* (1867) LR 2 HL 127, the House of Lords differed in opinion as to whether instructions for a settlement were a contract for a settlement or instructions for a contract. A recital in a deed may be evidence of a contract: *Wilson v Keating* (1859) 4 De G & J 588 (affg 27 Beav 121), where the transferee of shares was held bound to pay on a contract evidenced by a transfer, even though he was a mere nominee.

2   As to contracts not concluded see PARAS 543–544.
3   See CONTRACT vol 22 (2012) PARA 231 et seq.
4   Lack of agreement may result eg by reason of misrepresentation (see generally MISREPRESENTATION vol 76 (2013) PARA 740 et seq), mistake (see CONTRACT vol 22 (2012) PARA 317; MISTAKE vol 77 (2016) PARAS 41–46) or defects in the subject matter of the contract (see PARAS 562–563).
5   See PARA 545 et seq.

541. Grounds for refusing specific performance. The grounds on which specific performance will be refused do not fall into rigid categories. There is a general jurisdiction to deny specific performance if the court, on the particular facts, considers it just to do so[1]. Thus specific performance will not be granted if the contract is illegal[2] or oppressive[3], if the claimant has failed to perform conditions of the contract[4] or done acts amounting to a repudiation of the contract[5] or been guilty of undue delay in performing his part of the contract[6], if it has become impossible for the defendant to perform the contract[7], if the contract has been rescinded or varied[8], it is contrary to public policy to order performance[9], or if the parties have contracted out of the right to specific performance[10].

1   *Conlon v Murray* [1958] NI 17.
2   As to the general nature and effect of illegality in contracts see CONTRACT vol 22 (2012) PARA 424 et seq.
3   As to oppressiveness see PARA 550 et seq.
4   As to non-performance see PARA 565 et seq.
5   As to repudiation see PARAS 572–573.
6   As to lapse of time see PARA 576 et seq.
7   As to impossibility see PARAS 574–575.
8   As to rescission see PARA 598.
9   As to public policy see PARA 582.
10   As to contracting out see PARA 542.

542. Contracting out. Parties can contract out of the right to specific performance[1], although it is generally not possible to contract in[2].

1   This is presumably on the basis that equity follows the law. See *Mills v Sportsdirect.com Retail Ltd* [2010] EWHC 1072 (Ch), [2010] 2 P & CR D45, [2010] 2 BCLC 143 (an agreement which set

out a complete code of remedies available to the parties had not included specific performance; the parties were found to have agreed (or to be taken to have agreed) that specific performance would not be available; accordingly the contract had not been specifically enforceable).

2   See *Quadrant Visual Communications Ltd v Hutchinson Telephone (UK) Ltd* [1993] BCLC 442, [1992] 3 LS Gaz R 31, 136 Sol Jo LB 32 (the discretion of the court could not be fettered by the agreement of the parties so as to exclude the absence of 'clean hands' from the consideration of the judge in circumstances where an equitable remedy was sought by one party); *Co-Operative Insurance Society Ltd v Argyll Stores (Holdings) Ltd* [1998] AC, [1997] 3 All ER 297, [1997] 2 WLR 898 (an order for specific performance of a contract containing a covenant to carry on a business was overturned by the House of Lords). See also PARA 565.

(2) CONTRACT NOT CONCLUDED

543. Factors determining a concluded contract. The court will specifically enforce a contract only if that contract is binding at law[1]. At one time the Court of Chancery would refuse specific performance if there was any doubt as to whether there was a binding contract, leaving the parties to their rights at common law[2]. Since the fusion of the administration of law and equity, the court will decide at the same hearing whether the contract is binding and whether it should be specifically enforced[3].

1   See CONTRACT vol 22 (2012) PARA 231 et seq; CONVEYANCING vol 23 (2016) PARA 25 et seq; SALE OF GOODS AND SUPPLY OF SERVICES vol 91 (2012) PARA 28 et seq.
2   *Huddleston v Briscoe* (1805) 11 Ves 583; *Stratford v Bosworth* (1813) 2 Ves & B 341; *Skelton v Cole* (1857) 1 De G & J 587.
3   See the Senior Courts Act 1981 s 49(2); and cf *Bigg v Boyd Gibbins Ltd* [1971] 2 All ER 183, [1971] 1 WLR 913, CA.

544. Representations inducing conduct. One party may make a representation to another with the object of inducing him to act in a certain way. The other does so. In certain cases the court will compel the representor to perform the letter of his representation even though there is no binding oral contract because of the absence of valuable consideration.

The circumstances in which the court will intervene are still not clear. It has been suggested that the equitable doctrine of proprietary estoppel[1] is directed to ascertaining, in particular individual circumstances, whether one party could be permitted to deny the validity of an agreement which, knowingly or unknowingly, he has allowed another to assume to be a valid agreement[2]. For that reason the true owner of land may not be allowed to assert title against another who, to his knowledge, acts to his detriment in the belief that he has entered into a valid contract to buy the land from the owner[3]. Indeed, the courts appear to be ready specifically to enforce such an agreement where, having regard to the previous dealings between the parties, it would be inequitable not to do so. To establish such inequity it is necessary to show detriment[4].

1   For the formative cases on equitable proprietary estoppel see *Huning v Ferrers* (1710) Gilb Ch 85; *Savage v Foster* (1723) 9 Mod Rep 35; *Stiles v Cowper* (1748) 3 Atk 692; *Dillwyn v Llewelyn* (1862) 4 De GF & J 517; *Ramsden v Dyson and Thornton* (1866) LR 1 HL 129; *Willmott v Barber* (1880) 15 ChD 96; *Plimmer v City of Wellington Corpn* (1884) 9 App Cas 699, PC; *Chalmers v Pardoe* [1963] 3 All ER 552, [1963] 1 WLR 677, PC. See also PARAS 502, 506; and ESTOPPEL vol 47 (2014) PARA 392 et seq.
2   See generally *Inwards v Baker* [1965] 2 QB 29, [1965] 1 All ER 446, CA; *Ives (ER) Investment Ltd v High* [1967] 2 QB 379, [1967] 1 All ER 504, CA; *Spiro v Lintern* [1973] 3 All ER 319, [1973] 1 WLR 1002, CA; *Crabb v Arun District Council* [1976] Ch 179, [1975] 3 All ER 865, CA; *Salvation Army Trustee Co Ltd v West Yorkshire Metropolitan County Council* (1980) 41 P & CR 179, DC; *Taylors Fashions Ltd v Liverpool Victoria Trustees Co Ltd, Old & Campbell Ltd v Liverpool Victoria Trustees Co Ltd* [1982] QB 133, [1981] 1 All ER 897; *Coombes v Smith* [1986] 1 WLR 808; *Hammersmith and Fulham London Borough Council v Top Shop Centres Ltd,*

Hammersmith and Fulham London Borough Council v Glassgrove Ltd [1990] Ch 237, [1989] 2 All ER 655; *Lim Teng Huan v Ang Swee Chuan* [1992] 1 WLR 113, PC; *A-G of Hong Kong v Humphreys Estate (Queen's Gardens) Ltd* [1987] AC 114, [1987] 2 All ER 387; *Clarke v Swaby* [2007] UKPC 1, [2007] 2 P & CR 12, [2007] All ER (D) 78 (Jan); *Yeoman's Row Management Ltd v Cobbe* [2008] UKHL 55, [2008] 4 All ER 713; *Thorner v Major* [2009] UKHL 18, [2009] 3 All ER 945, [2009] 1 WLR 776.

3 *Spiro v Lintern* [1973] 3 All ER 319, [1973] 1 WLR 1002, CA.
4 *Taylors Fashions Ltd v Liverpool Victoria Trustees Co Ltd* [1982] QB 133n, [1981] 1 All ER 897; *Gillett v Holt* [2001] Ch 210, [2000] 2 All ER 289, CA; *Jennings v Rice* [2002] EWCA Civ 159, [2003] 1 FCR 501; *Henry v Henry* [2010] UKPC 3, [2010] 1 All ER 988, 75 WIR 254. This was said not to be necessary in *Greasley v Cooke* [1980] 3 All ER 710 at 713, [1980] 1 WLR 1306 at 1311, CA, per Lord Denning MR but this view is based upon a confusion between the distinct doctrines and requirements of proprietary and promissory estoppel. See generally R Halson 'The offensive limits of promissory estoppel' [1999] LMCLQ 256. As to proprietary estoppel see ESTOPPEL vol 47 (2014) PARA 392 et seq. As to promissory estoppel see ESTOPPEL vol 47 (2014) PARA 385 et seq.

(3) UNCERTAINTY AS A DEFENCE TO SPECIFIC PERFORMANCE

545. Requirements in respect of contract. Before the court will order specific performance of a contract it must be satisfied not only that there is a contract binding at law but also that the terms of the contract are sufficiently precise so that the court can order and supervise the exact performance of the contract[1].

1 See *Waring & Gillow Ltd v Thompson* (1912) 29 TLR 154, CA; *Fountain Forestry Ltd v Edwards* [1975] Ch 1, [1974] 2 All ER 280 (administrator purported to enter into a contract for the sale of land on behalf of himself and his co-administrator, who never ratified the contract; purchaser refused specific performance against administrator); *Sudbrook Trading Estate Ltd v Eggleton* [1983] 1 AC 444, [1981] 3 All ER 105, CA (option to purchase at price to be fixed by valuers nominated by parties; one party refused to appoint valuer; no concluded contract); revsd [1983] 1 AC 444, [1982] 3 All ER 1, HL, on the ground that there was on its true construction a complete contract for a sale at a fair and reasonable price, and the court would substitute its own machinery for ascertaining the value of the property for the agreed machinery which had broken down. Cf *Bigg v Boyd Gibbins Ltd* [1971] 2 All ER 183, [1971] 1 WLR 913, CA; *Tito v Waddell (No 2)* [1977] Ch 106, [1977] 3 All ER 129. See also *118 Data Resource Ltd v IDS Data Services Ltd* [2014] EWHC 3629 (Ch), [2014] All ER (D) 57 (Nov).

546. Time at which certainty is determined. Whether a contract is sufficiently certain must be determined at the commencement of the action[1] since it is at that time that non-performance must be justified[2]. However specific performance is ordered even if the contract is incomplete at that date if the defect is such that it can be remedied or compensated[3], or where a term which is not then ascertained is capable of being ascertained by the court[4].

1 *Adams v Broke* (1842) 1 Y & C Ch Cas 627; *Shardlow v Cotterell* (1881) 20 ChD 90, CA (revsg 18 ChD 280).
2 *Right d Fisher, Nash and Hyrons v Cuthell* (1804) 5 East 491.
3 *Lord Kensington v Phillips* (1817) 5 Dow 61, HL; *Pritchard v Ovey* (1820) 1 Jac & W 396; *Soames v Edge* (1860) John 669; *Norris v Jackson* (1860) 1 John & H 319; *Middleton v Greenwood* (1864) 2 De GJ & Sm 142. As to specific performance with compensation see PARA 621 et seq.
4 *Owen v Thomas* (1834) 3 My & K 353; *Walker v Eastern Counties Rly Co* (1848) 6 Hare 594; *Monro v Taylor* (1848) 8 Hare 51; *Pickles v Sutcliffe* [1902] WN 200; and see PARA 549 et seq.

547. Effect of partial performance on uncertainty. Although a contract may be challenged on the ground that its terms are too uncertain to be enforced in equity[1], the court will nonetheless be anxious to enforce the contract if there has been partial performance of its terms from which the party seeking to resist the enforcement has derived a benefit, and the circumstances are such that the claimant can be fully compensated only by an order of specific performance[2].

1   See PARA 549 et seq.
2   See *Parker v Taswell* (1858) 2 De G & J 559 at 571; *Oxford v Provand* (1868) LR 2 PC 135 at 149–150; *Hart v Hart* (1881) 18 ChD 670 at 685; *Sanderson v Cockermouth and Workington Rly Co* (1849) 11 Beav 497 (affd (1850) 2 H & Tw 327), followed in *South Eastern Rly Co v Associated Portland Cement Manufacturers (1900) Ltd* [1910] 1 Ch 12, CA, where a railway company, having obtained possession under a grant, was held bound to permit the making of the necessary accommodation works. See also *Waring and Gillow Ltd v Thompson* (1912) 29 TLR 154 at 156, CA (proposals to found new company).

548.   Effect of fraud. The court will be reluctant to deny specific performance on the ground of uncertainty if the contract was induced by the defendant's fraud[1].

1   *Chattock v Muller* (1878) 8 ChD 177, where there was an agreement by which A promised to grant a portion of an estate on purchase to B in consideration of B not competing at the sale. An inquiry was directed to ascertain the boundaries; apparently, if unascertainable, A would be ordered to convey the whole. Cf *Pallant v Morgan* [1953] Ch 43, [1952] 2 All ER 951, where there was an agreement by the agents of A and B at an auction that B's agent should bid and A's agent should refrain and that B, if his agent were successful, would divide the land according to a certain formula, which, however, left certain details to be agreed later. The agreement was held to be too vague to be specifically enforced, but a declaration was made that B should hold as trustee for A and B jointly. The suggestion of Malins V-C in *Chattock v Muller* above that the defendant could become bound to hand over the whole property to the plaintiff at the price which he paid for it was not followed. As to the formal requirements which must now be satisfied in order to enforce a contract for the sale of land see the Law of Property (Miscellaneous Provisions) Act 1989 s 2; and CONVEYANCING vol 23 (2016) PARA 27.

549.   Uncertainty in terms. The court does not as a rule enforce specific performance of an agreement unless its terms are certain and unambiguous so that the obligations of the parties can be clearly ascertained and hence the defendant can know with some degree of precision what he is being ordered to do[1]. Specific Performance will nevertheless be granted provided that there is such a degree of certainty as is reasonably required in the circumstances[2]; or the original uncertainty has been removed by a subsequent election[3] or by a course of dealing between the parties[4]; or if the term is ancillary or collateral[5]; or by terms reasonably implied in law[6].

1   *Douglas v Baynes* [1908] AC 477 at 485, PC; *Bushwall Properties Ltd v Vortex Properties Ltd* [1976] 2 All ER 283, [1976] 1 WLR 591, CA, where there was a contract for the sale of land with completion in phases; no term could be implied that the purchaser had power to select which part of the land was to be included in each phase. See also *Legh v Haverfield* (1800) 5 Ves 452, where an agreement was established but the evidence as to its terms was contradictory, and specific performance was refused; *Hodges v Horsfall* (1829) 1 Russ & M 116 (sale of land according to plan insufficiently identified); *Kemble v Kean* (1829) 6 Sim 333 (engagement as actor, but terms vague); *Reynolds v Waring* (1831) 1 You 346 (uncertain evidence of oral agreement); *Callaghan v Callaghan* (1841) 8 Cl & Fin 374, HL (inconsistent terms); *Webb v Direct London and Portsmouth Rly Co* (1852) 1 De GM & G 521; *Lord James Stuart v London and North Western Rly Co* (1852) 1 De GM & G 721 (revsg 15 Beav 513) (agreement for sale of land required for a railway); *South Wales Rly Co v Wythes* (1854) 5 De GM & G 880, CA (agreement to build railway to plans of specified surveyor); *Paris Chocolate Co v Crystal Palace Co* (1855) 3 Sm & G 119 (agreement to provide accommodation for sale of chocolate); *Williamson v Wootton* (1855) 3 Drew 210 (reservation of mines); *Lancaster v De Trafford* (1862) 8 Jur NS 873 (description of land vague); *Pearce v Watts* (1875) LR 20 Eq 492 at 493 per Jessel MR (agreement for sale of land subject to reservation of land 'necessary for a railway' held too vague, but if the conveyance is executed the exception, being uncertain, is bad); *Smith v Wheatcroft* (1878) 9 ChD 223 (sale of land); *Oxford Corpn v Crow* [1893] 3 Ch 535; *Savill Bros Ltd v Bethell* [1902] 2 Ch 523, CA; *Macphail v Torrance* (1909) 25 TLR 810 (agreement to make ample provision by will). In *Pilling v Armitage* (1805) 12 Ves 78, the plaintiff, having failed to prove the agreement which he had set up, was refused specific performance of a different agreement admitted by the defendant. Cf *Legal v Miller* (1750) 2 Ves Sen 299 (lease of house).

2   *Great Northern Rly Co v Manchester, Sheffield and Lincolnshire Rly Co* (1851) 5 De G & Sm 138.
    Cf *Roberts v Smith* (1859) 4 H & N 315; *Baumann v James* (1868) 3 Ch App 508 (an agreement
    to do specified 'and other' works, where the other works were clearly of small amount); *Scammell
    (G) & Nephew Ltd v Ouston* [1941] AC 251, [1941] 1 All ER 14, HL; *Fawcett Properties Ltd v
    Buckingham County Council* [1961] AC 636, [1960] 3 All ER 503, HL (condition in planning
    permission); *Greater London Council v Connolly* [1970] 2 QB 100, [1970] 1 All ER 870, CA (rent
    liable to be changed on notice); *Brown v Gould* [1972] Ch 53, [1971] 2 All ER 1505.
3   *Jenkins v Green* (1858) 27 Beav 437 (agreement to lease land 'less 37 acres'; defect capable of cure
    by selection by lessor before execution). Cf *South Eastern Rly Co v Associated Portland Cement
    Manufacturers (1900) Ltd* [1910] 1 Ch 12, CA, and contrast *Bushwall Properties Ltd v Vortex
    Properties Ltd* [1976] 2 All ER 283, [1976] 1 WLR 591, CA.
4   Cf *Oxford v Provand* (1868) LR 2 PC 135; *Waring and Gillow Ltd v Thompson* (1912) 29 TLR
    154, CA; *Hillas & Co Ltd v Arcos Ltd* (1932) 147 LT 503, HL.
5   Cf *Richardson v Smith* (1870) 5 Ch App 648.
6   Cf *South Wales Rly Co v Wythes* (1854) 5 De GM & G 880, CA.

(4) UNFAIRNESS OR OPPRESSIVENESS AS A DEFENCE TO SPECIFIC PERFORMANCE

550. Contract unfair or oppressive. The court's discretion to grant specific
performance is, it is said, not exercised if the contract is not 'equal and fair'[1]. Even
though no fraud, duress or undue influence such as to justify rescission is shown,
the court may still not enforce the contract[2] if it would not be consistent with
equity and good conscience to do so[3].

1   *Walpole (Lord) v Lord Orford* (1797) 3 Ves 402 at 420. Cf *Buxton v Lister* (1746) 3 Atk 383 at
    386; *Rees v Marquis of Bute* [1916] 2 Ch 64.
2   *Willan v Willan* (1810) 16 Ves 72 at 83. See also *Savage v Taylor* (1736) Cas *temp* Talb 234;
    Twining v Morrice (1788) 2 Bro CC 326; *Davis v Symonds* (1787) 1 Cox Eq Cas 402; *Redshaw
    v Bedford Level (Governor & Co)* (1759) 1 Eden 346; *Clark v Malpas* (1862) 31 Beav 80; *Conlon
    v Murray* [1958] NI 17; *Buckley v Irwin* [1960] NI 98; and CONVEYANCING vol 23 (2016)
    PARAS 65, 456. Oral evidence is admissible to show unfairness depending not on the terms of the
    contract but on extrinsic circumstances: see *Davis v Symonds* above. As to rescission see
    PARA 598; and MISREPRESENTATION vol 76 (2013) PARA 811 et seq.
3   *Mortlock v Buller* (1804) 10 Ves 292 at 305; *Blomley v Ryan* (1956) 99 CLR 362 at 401, 402
    (Aust HC); *Pateman v Pay* (1974) 232 Estates Gazette 457 (sharp practice: vendor mistaken);
    Heath v Heath [2009] EWHC 1908 (Ch), [2010] 1 FLR 610, where specific performance was
    refused on the basis of both a serious misapprehension about the basis of the agreement and also
    because of subsequent delay in seeking specific performance. However contrast *Harrop v
    Thompson* [1975] 2 All ER 94, [1975] 1 WLR 545, where the plaintiff was granted specific
    performance even though he and another had agreed that that other should stay away from an
    auction, and consequently he had acquired the defendant's property cheaply. See also *Dudley
    Metropolitan Borough Council v Dudley Muslim Association* [2015] EWCA Civ 1123, [2016] 1
    P & C R 10, where it was held that there was no public law defence available to the defendant
    based on a legitimate expectation or a general appeal to abuse of power; the terms of the contract
    that the claimant sought to enforce had been perfectly clear.

551. Time at which unfairness must be determined. As a general rule, the
question of unfairness must be determined as at the date of the making of the
contract[1]. For instance, a family arrangement or other compromise is fair if
entered into by both parties who have equal knowledge and means of knowledge,
and who contract in view of some future and uncertain event or the future
ascertainment of facts past but unknown[2]. That the contingency turns out
adversely to one party does not render the contract unfair[3]. Where, however, the
actual facts are such as to render what is sold worthless, and are known to one
party but not to the other, the contract will not be enforced, even if it expressly
deals with an uncertainty[4]; and, if the contingency is outside the contemplation of

the parties, and different in kind and degree from such uncertainty as the parties contemplated, the court may refuse specific performance even though the contract is not discharged at law[5].

A contract may be fair when it is made but subsequently circumstances may change to such an extent that it is oppressive specifically to enforce it[6]. For example, there may be unfairness or impropriety in the valuation made by a third person where under the contract the price is to be fixed by such a valuation[7], but such circumstances will be rare.

1   *Revell v Hussey* (1813) 2 Ball & B 280 at 288.
2   *Williams v Williams* (1867) 2 Ch App 294 at 304 per Turner LJ. See also *Frank v Frank* (1667) 1 Cas in Ch 84; *Stapilton v Stapilton* (1739) 1 Atk 2; *Pickering v Pickering* (1839) 2 Beav 31 at 56; *Heap v Tonge* (1851) 9 Hare 90; *Bucknell v Bucknell* (1858) 7 I Ch R 130; and SETTLEMENTS vol 91 (2012) PARA 903 et seq.
3   *Emery v Wase* (1803) 8 Ves 505 at 517–518; *Lawton v Campion* (1854) 18 Beav 87. See also *Parker v Palmer* (1662) 1 Cas in Ch 42; *Anon* (1717–38) before Jekyll MR, cited in 6 Ves at 24 (future allotment sold for £20; subsequently allotted and worth £200); *Re Lightoller, ex p Peake* (1816) 1 Madd 346 (partner agreeing to give to retiring partner large sum for business although it was known to be insolvent).
4   *Smith v Harrison* (1857) 3 Jur NS 287.
5   *Baxendale v Seale* (1855) 19 Beav 601; *Davis v Shepherd* (1866) 1 Ch App 410 (uncertain amount of coal demised, but actual extent far in excess of parties' estimate).
6   *Patel v Ali* [1984] Ch 283, [1984] 1 All ER 978, where it was said that to make an order would inflict on the defendant 'a hardship amounting to injustice'.
7   *Emery v Wase* (1803) 8 Ves 505. Cf *Chichester v M' Intire* (1830) 4 Bli NS 78; *Eads v Williams* (1854) 4 De GM & G 674; *Collier v Mason* (1858) 25 Beav 200; *Price v Strange* [1978] Ch 337, [1977] 3 All ER 371, CA.

552. Suppression of fact. Specific performance may be denied because the claimant has suppressed some relevant facts, even though he is under no duty to disclose them and the suppression does not amount to an actionable fraudulent, negligent or innocent misrepresentation so as to impugn the contract at law[1]. For example a lessee may obtain the renewal of a lease while suppressing the fact that the person on whose life the old lease depended is in extremis[2].

1   *Beyfus v Lodge* [1925] Ch 350; *Citytowns Ltd v Bohemian Properties Ltd* [1986] 2 EGLR 258.
2   *Ellard v Lord Llandaff* (1810) 1 Ball & B 241; *Hesse v Briant* (1856) 6 De GM & G 623, where a solicitor acting for both parties failed to make full disclosure to both.

553. Relationship of the parties. There may be circumstances in the position or mental state of the party against whom specific performance is sought which render it inequitable that the court should force him to perform his contract. The burden of proof lies on the party against whom specific performance is sought to establish such circumstances[1]. He must show that he is the victim of equitable fraud on the part of the other party, 'fraud' in its equitable context meaning an unconscientious use of the power arising out of the circumstances and conditions of the contracting parties[2].

These circumstances include intoxication[3], intimidating and pressurising conduct which need not amount to duress or undue influence[4], mental weakness not amounting to incapacity to contract[5], distress[6], illiteracy, lack of education[7], want of advice[8] or similar circumstances appearing inconsistent with intelligent consent[9]. The court will certainly not grant specific performance if the claimant knew of the defendant's incapacity[10]. However it need not be shown that the claimant was guilty of intentional unfairness[11]; it is enough that he has contributed, albeit unintentionally, to the defendant's state of mind[12].

1   *Broughton v Snook* [1938] Ch 505 at 512–513, [1938] 1 All ER 411 at 418–419. Cf *Blomley v Ryan* (1956) 99 CLR 362 at 428–429 (Aust HC).

2 *Earl of Aylesford v Morris* (1873) 8 Ch App 484 at 490–491; *Hart v O' Connor* [1985] AC 1000, [1985] 2 All ER 880, PC. See EQUITABLE JURISDICTION vol 47 (2014) PARA 30.

3 *Cooke v Clayworth* (1811) 18 Ves 12; — *v Ogden* (1827) 5 LJOS 104; *Nagle v Baylor* (1842) 3 Dr & War 60; *Cox v Smith* (1868) 19 LT 517 (sale of land: mistake). Distinguish *Shaw v Thackray* (1853) 1 Sm & G 537, where the intoxicated party was not the real defendant. In *Lightfoot v Heron* (1839) 3 Y & C Ex 586 drinking had not affected the parties' intelligence, and the contract was enforced. As to the effect of intoxication on the validity of contracts see *Matthews v Baxter* (1873) LR 8 Exch 132; and CONTRACT vol 22 (2012) PARA 299. As to its effect on gifts see GIFTS vol 52 (2014) PARA 213. As to suspicious circumstances generally as constituting a ground for refusing specific performance see *Rochfort v Creswick* (1721) 1 Bro Parl Cas 171 (sale of land: part execution); *West v Habgood* (1837) 6 LJ Ch 369 (sale of land); *Valentine v Dickinson* (1861) 7 Jur NS 857 (sale of houses).

4 *Dewar v Elliott* (1824) 2 LJOS 178: see CONTRACT vol 22 (2012) PARA 291 et seq.

5 *Clarkson v Hanway* (1723) 2 P Wms 203; *Bridgeman v Green* (1757) Wilm 58 at 61; *Gartside v Isherwood* (1783) 1 Bro CC 558; *Broughton v Snook* as reported in [1938] 1 All ER 411; *Watkin v Watson-Smith* (1986) Times, 3 July. It must be pleaded and proved that the incapacity was known, or ought to have been known, to the other party: *Broughton v Snook* above at 417. Even where a contract was entered into by a person of unsound mind, if his affliction was not apparent and his consequent incapacity was not known to the other contracting party the validity of the contract is judged by the same standards as a contract made by a person of sound mind: *Hart v O' Connor* [1985] AC 1000, [1985] 2 All ER 880, PC. See PARA 596; and EQUITABLE JURISDICTION vol 47 (2014) PARAS 30, 33. See also CONTRACT vol 22 (2012) PARA 250; MENTAL HEALTH AND CAPACITY vol 75 (2013) PARA 614.

6 *Johnson v Nott* (1684) 1 Vern 271; *Kemeys v Hansard* (1815) Coop G 125.

7 *Clark v Malpas* (1862) 4 De GF & J 401; *Johnson v Buttress* (1936) 56 CLR 113 (Aust HC).

8 *Stanley v Robinson* (1830) 1 Russ & M 527; *Helsham v Langley* (1841) 1 Y & C Ch Cas 175; *Vivers v Tuck* (1863) 1 Moo PCCNS 516 at 527. See however *Lightfoot v Heron* (1839) 3 Y & C Ex 586, and *Haberdashers' Co v Issac* (1857) 3 Jur NS 611 (affd 29 LTOS 350), cases which show that mere want of legal advice is not enough.

9 *Bell v Howard* (1742) 9 Mod Rep 302; *Martin v Mitchell* (1820) 2 Jac & W 413; *Stanley v Robinson* (1830) 1 Russ & M 527; *Blomley v Ryan* (1956) 99 CLR 362 at 405 (Aust HC). If, however, the court is satisfied that the contract is fair and properly concluded, it grants specific performance: *Brinkley v Hann* (1843) Drury *temp* Sug 175. As to transactions impeachable from the position of the parties see MISREPRESENTATION vol 76 (2013) PARA 834 et seq. As to equitable relief in cases of fiduciary relationship see EQUITABLE JURISDICTION vol 47 (2014) PARA 228 et seq.

10 *Baskcomb v Beckwith* (1869) LR 8 Eq 100; *Denny v Hancock* (1870) 6 Ch App 1.

11 *Twining v Morrice* (1788) 2 Bro CC 326, where a purchase was not enforced against the vendor by reason of the solicitor's inadvertent conduct which 'damped' the sale; *Mortlock v Buller* (1804) 10 Ves 292; *Baskcomb v Beckwith* (1869) LR 8 Eq 100; *Denny v Hancock* (1870) 6 Ch App 1.

12 *Cooke v Clayworth* (1811) 18 Ves 12 at 15–16.

554. Unfairness to third persons. A species of unfairness which may stay the hand of the court is that the contract, if enforced, would be injurious to third persons[1], or would involve a breach of trust[2] or a breach of a prior contract with a third person[3], or would compel the defendant to do an act which he is not lawfully competent to do[4], or would involve a gross breach of duty as between principal and agent[5].

1 *Thomas v Dering* (1837) 1 Keen 729 (tendency to injure remaindermen); *McKewan v Sanderson* (1875) LR 20 Eq 65 (undue advantage over other creditors); *De Cordova v De Cordova* (1879) 4 App Cas 692, PC. Cf the decisions as to hardship to third persons cited in PARA 558.

2 *Byrne v Acton* (1721) 1 Bro Parl Cas 186; *Mortlock v Buller* (1804) 10 Ves 292 (extreme disadvantageousness of contract); *Harnett v Yielding* (1805) 2 Sch & Lef 549 (act in excess of power); *Ord v Noel* (1820) 5 Madd 438; *Thompson v Blackstone* (1843) 6 Beav 470 (contract entitling the purchaser to retain out of the purchase money a debt due from the trustee in his personal capacity); *Bellringer v Blagrave* (1847) 1 De G & Sm 63 (covenant ultra vires). See also *Hill v Buckley* (1811) 17 Ves 394; *Magrane v Archbold* (1813) 1 Dow 107, HL; *Bridger v Rice* (1819) 1 Jac & W 74; *Neale v Mackenzie* (1837) 1 Keen 474; *Wood v Richardson* (1840) 4 Beav 174; *White v Cuddon* (1842) 8 Cl & Fin 766, HL (revsg *Cudden v Cartwright* (1840) 4 Y & C Ex 25); *Goodwin v Fielding* (1853) 4 De GM & G 90 (unbusinesslike character of transaction); *Maw v Topham* (1854) 19 Beav 576; *Sneesby v Thorne* (1855) 1 Jur NS 536 (affd 7 De GM & G 399); *Rede v Oakes* (1864) 4 De GJ & Sm 505; *Trappes v Cobb* (1867) 16 WR 117; *Naylor v*

Goodall (1877) 47 LJ Ch 53; *Dunn v Flood* (1855) 28 ChD 586, CA (affg (1883) 25 ChD 629); *Briggs v Parsloe* [1937] 3 All ER 831. Where an innocent breach of trust has been committed as the result of a contract, the court may nevertheless enforce the contract by making the other party carry out his part of the bargain: *Briggs v Parsloe*.

3 *Willmott v Barber* (1880) 15 ChD 96 (contract to assign a lease containing a covenant not to assign); *Warmington v Miller* [1973] QB 877, [1973] 2 All ER 372 (contract to sublease in breach of prohibition in head lease). However, the rule is not absolute: see eg *PSM International plc v Whitehouse and Willenhall Automation Ltd* [1992] IRLR 279, [1992] FSR 489, CA. Cf *Weatherall v Geering* (1806) 12 Ves 504 at 511; *Mulholland v Belfast Corpn* (1859) 9 I Ch R 204; *Manchester Ship Canal Co v Manchester Racecourse Co* [1900] 2 Ch 352 at 367 (affd [1901] 2 Ch 37 at 50, CA).

4 *Byrne v Acton* (1721) 1 Bro Parl Cas 186; *Harnett v Yielding* (1805) 2 Sch & Lef 549 at 554; *Tolson v Sheard* (1877) 5 ChD 19, CA; *Oceanic Steam Navigation Co v Sutherberry* (1880) 16 ChD 236, CA; *New Windsor Corpn v Stovell* (1884) 27 ChD 665; *Delves v Gray* [1902] 2 Ch 606. See also *Mansfield v Childerhouse* (1876) 4 ChD 82.

5 *Shrewsbury and Birmingham Rly Co v London and North Western Rly Co etc* (1853) 4 De GM & G 115; affd (1857) 6 HL Cas 113 (railway directors). Cf *Mortlock v Buller* (1804) 10 Ves 292 at 313. Injury to the public is not a sufficient ground for refusing specific performance: *Raphael v Thames Valley Rly Co* (1867) 2 Ch App 147, revsg (1866) LR 2 Eq 37.

555. Inadequacy of consideration. Despite some earlier decisions to the contrary[1], mere inadequacy of consideration is not in itself a ground for resisting specific performance unless it is so gross as to lead the court to infer fraud[2], or there are other circumstances which, combined with the inadequacy, will induce the court not to enforce the contract[3]. Whenever the question of inadequacy of consideration is raised it must generally be determined as at the date of the contract[4]. Subsequent events are only relevant if they are of such a nature as to make it oppressive to enforce the contract[5].

1 *Savile v Savile* (1721) 1 P Wms 745; *Vaughan v Thomas* (1783) 1 Bro CC 556; *Day v Newman* (1788) 2 Cox Eq Cas 77; *Tilly v Peers* (1791) cited in 10 Ves at 301. See also *Nott v Hill* (1682) 2 Cas in Ch 120.

2 *Griffith v Spratley* (1787) 1 Cox Eq Cas 383; *Collier v Brown* (1788) 1 Cox Eq Cas 428; *White v Damon* (1802) 7 Ves 30; *Coles v Trecothick* (1804) 9 Ves 234 at 246; *Underhill v Horwood* (1804) 10 Ves 209; *Burrowes v Lock* (1805) 10 Ves 470; *Lowther v Lord Lowther* (1806) 13 Ves 95 at 103; *Stilwell v Wilkins* (1821) Jac 280 at 282; *Bower v Cooper* (1843) 2 Hare 408 at 411; *Borell v Dann* (1843) 2 Hare 440; *Stephens v Hotham* (1855) 1 K & J 571; *Harrison v Guest* (1855) 6 De GM & G 424 (affd (1860) 8 HL Cas 481); *Haywood v Cope* (1858) 25 Beav 140; *Holmes v Howes* (1872) 20 WR 310. See also *Axelsen v O'Brien* (1949) 80 CLR 219 at 226 (Aust HC); *Blomley v Ryan* (1956) 99 CLR 362 at 405 (Aust HC). In *Abbott v Sworder* (1852) 4 De G & Sm 448, the excessive price to be paid by the purchaser (£5,000 for an estate worth £3,500) was held to be no defence to an action by the vendor. *Falcke v Gray* (1859) 4 Drew 651 is contrary to the course of authority. As to unconscionable bargains generally see EQUITABLE JURISDICTION vol 47 (2014) PARAS 30, 32, 38.

3 For instances see *Young v Clerk* (1720) Prec Ch 538 (ignorance); *Deane v Rastron* (1792) 1 Anst 64 (deliberate suppression of true value). Cf *Lewis v Lord Lechmere* (1722) 10 Mod Rep 503; *Callaghan v Callaghan* (1841) 8 Cl & Fin 374, HL, where the transaction was held to be in the nature of a gift, not a sale; *Cockell v Taylor* (1851) 15 Beav 103, where there was great undervalue coupled with illiteracy and humble circumstances. In this connection the court is not debarred from considering the question of inadequacy simply because the consideration has been determined by a valuer to whom it has been referred by the parties: see *Emery v Wase* (1803) 8 Ves 505 and *Parken v Whitby* (1823) Turn & R 366. See also PARA 553.

4 *Mortimer v Capper* (1782) 1 Bro CC 156.

5 See PARA 551.

(5) HARDSHIP AS A DEFENCE TO SPECIFIC PERFORMANCE

556. Hardship resulting from performance. Specific performance may not be ordered where performance would involve, even without any impropriety on the part of the claimant[1], great hardship to the defendant[2], so much so that it would be unreasonable and harsh to grant equitable relief[3]. Such hardship may be apparent on the face of the contract, or latent and the result of collateral matters, in which event the court is more likely to refuse performance[4].

1　*Falcke v Gray* (1859) 4 Drew 651 at 660.
2　— *v White* (circa 1709) 3 Swan 108n (wayleave); *Gould v Kemp* (1834) 2 My & K 304 at 308; *Re Highett and Bird's Contract* [1903] 1 Ch 287 at 293–294, CA.
3　*Wedgwood v Adams* (1843) 6 Beav 600 at 605; *Watson v Marston* (1853) 4 De GM & G 230; *Eastes v Russ* [1914] 1 Ch 468 at 480, CA. See *Patel v Ali* [1984] Ch 283, [1984] 1 All ER 978 (defendant contracted to sell her house; after date of contract she became disabled; specific performance of completion of contract refused).
4　See eg *Faine v Brown* (1750) cited in 2 Ves Sen 307, where the defendant would forfeit half the purchase price if the sale was specifically enforced. More recently the court has not ordered specific performance of a contract if this would mean that there was a reasonable possibility that the claimant would be in a position to evict the defendant husband and possibly his daughter, thereby splitting up the family: *Wroth v Taylor* [1974] Ch 30, [1973] 1 All ER 897 (where the husband was the defendant: see PARA 559).

557. Time at which hardship must arise. As a general rule, hardship must exist at the time of the contract if it is to be a defence to a claim for specific performance. Thus the court may refuse to enforce an award on a submission to arbitration if the submission involves hardship[1], but not on the ground of mere hardship and unreasonableness in the award itself[2]. Similarly a covenant to renew a sublease without fine may be enforced even though the terms of the renewal of the head lease are changed and made more onerous[3]. Exceptionally, however, hardship subsequently arising may be treated as a ground for refusing specific performance[4]. This is more likely to be so if the change of conditions involving hardship to the defendant has resulted from some act of the claimant[5], especially if the claimant's conduct operated as something in the nature of a trap[6].

1　*Nickels v Hancock* (1855) 7 De GM & G 300. See generally ARBITRATION vol 2 (2017) PARA 501 et seq.
2　*Wood v Griffith* (1818) 1 Swan 43; *Weekes v Gallard* (1869) 18 WR 331.
3　*Evans v Walshe* (1805) 2 Sch & Lef 519; *Revell v Hussey* (1813) 2 Ball & B 280; *Lawder v Blatchford* (1815) Beat 522.
4　*City of London v Nash* (1747) 3 Atk 512 (covenant to rebuild houses in good condition and repair); *Webb v Direct London and Portsmouth Rly Co* (1852) 1 De GM & G 521 (contract by railway to buy land: railway project then abandoned). See also *Patel v Ali* [1984] Ch 283, [1984] 1 All ER 978 (defendant contracted to sell her house; after date of contract she became disabled; specific performance of completion of contract refused).
5　*Bedford (Duke) v British Museum Trustees* (1822) 2 My & K 552, where an alteration in the character of the neighbourhood due to the plaintiff 's acts was the ground for not enforcing restrictive covenants. See, however, REAL PROPERTY AND REGISTRATION vol 87 (2012) PARA 1092 et seq (discharge or modification of restrictive covenants). See also *Davis v Hone* (1805) 2 Sch & Lef 341; *Shrewsbury and Birmingham Rail Co v Stour Valley Rail Co* (1852) 2 De GM & G 866 at 882; *Sayers v Collyer* (1884) 28 ChD 103, CA; *Chatsworth Estates Co v Fewell* [1931] 1 Ch 224.
6　*Dowson v Solomon* (1859) 1 Drew & Sm 1.

558. Hardship flowing from defendant's conduct. Hardship which flows from the conduct of the defendant[1], or hardship which results to the defendant simply because the purpose he had in view when he made the contract has now failed[2], or because his speculation has proved unfortunate to him[3], cannot be set up by way of defence. Where the defendant is a company it is not relevant that performance may involve hardship to individual members as distinguished from the company[4].

1　*Storer v Great Western Rly* (1842) 2 Y & C Ch Cas 48 at 52; *Hawkes v Eastern Counties Rly Co* (1852) 1 De GM & G 737 (affd (1855) 5 HL Cas 331).

2 *Adams v Weare* (1784) 1 Bro CC 567; *Emery v Wase* (1803) 8 Ves 505 at 517–518; *Webb v Direct London and Portsmouth Rly Co* (1851) 9 Hare 129 at 140 per Turner V-C; *Lord James Stuart v London and North Western Rly Co* (1852) 15 Beav 513 at 523 per Romilly MR; *Morley v Clavering* (1860) 29 Beav 84.

3 *Haywood v Cope* (1858) 25 Beav 140; *Mountford v Scott* [1975] Ch 258 at 264, [1975] 1 All ER 198 at 200–201, CA; *Matila Ltd v Clarke* [2010] EWHC 1832 (Ch), [2010] All ER (D) 221 (Jun).

4 *Edwards v Grand Junction Rly Co* (1836) 1 My & Cr 650; *Hawkes v Eastern Counties Rly Co* (1852) 1 De GM & G 737 (affd sub nom *Eastern Counties Rly Co v Hawkes* (1855) 5 HL Cas 331).

559. Hardship to third persons. In certain circumstances a court may refuse to grant specific performance on the ground that it would cause hardship to a third person, for example, if it would compel the third person to join in a sale when he had no wish to do so[1] or would lead to the eviction of the defendant's children from the family home[2].

1 *Thomas v Dering* (1837) 1 Keen 729 at 747–748; *Watts v Spence* [1976] Ch 165, [1975] 2 All ER 528, where a husband who owned the home jointly with his wife contracted to sell without his wife's authority. Cf *Cedar Holdings Ltd v Green* [1981] Ch 129 at 147, [1979] 3 All ER 117, CA. This decision was overruled in *Williams and Glyn's Bank Ltd v Boland, Williams and Glyn's Bank Ltd v Brown* [1981] AC 487, [1980] 2 All ER 408, HL, but for different reasons, namely that it was unreal to describe a spouse's interest in a matrimonial home simply as an interest in the proceeds of sale.

2 *Wroth v Tyler* [1974] Ch 30, [1973] 1 All ER 897. See *Patel v Ali* [1984] Ch 283, [1984] 1 All ER 978 (specific performance of completion of sale of house would make it difficult for disabled defendant to care for her children). See also *Thames Guaranty Ltd v Campbell* [1985] QB 210, [1984] 2 All ER 585, CA (husband, now bankrupt, was co-owner of house with his wife and purported to charge the whole legal and beneficial interest; order for partial performance of husband's contract to create an equitable charge refused because an order, if made, would expose the wife to proceedings under the Law of Property Act 1925 s 30 (now repealed) likely to result in an order for the sale of the matrimonial home she occupied). See PARAS 624–625.

560. Relief granted on terms to prevent hardship. A claimant is sometimes granted specific performance only on certain terms imposed to avoid hardship which would otherwise result to the defendant. Thus a vendor liable to covenants in respect of the land can compel the purchaser to elect either to rescind the contract or to execute an indemnity against such covenants as a term of specific performance[1]. Moreover, in certain circumstances the purchaser may be granted specific performance with compensation if the vendor is not able to convey what he has contracted to sell[2].

1 *Moxhay v Inderwick* (1847) 1 De G & Sm 708; *Lukey v Higgs* (1855) 1 Jur NS 200; *Re Poole and Clarke's Contract* [1904] 2 Ch 173, CA; *Reckitt v Cody* [1920] 2 Ch 452. Cf *Hutchinson v Payne* [1975] VR 175 (Vict).

2 As to specific performance with compensation see PARA 621 et seq.

561. Other circumstances in which no relief is granted. The following are examples of circumstances in which the court is unwilling, on the ground of hardship, to enforce contracts:

(1) where there is no right of way to the land sold[1];

(2) where, without the knowledge of either vendor or purchaser, the property is being used by the tenant as a disorderly house[2];

(3) where the vendors have personally agreed to discharge the estate from incumbrances, and some of the vendors are trustees[3];

(4) where trustees have sold in circumstances which would constitute a breach of trust[4];

(5) where a mortgagee who has foreclosed and intended to sell as absolute owner has by inadvertence purported to sell as a mortgagee with a power of sale[5]; and

(6)   where the defendant, if required to perform, would be left with a remedy against an insolvent person[6] or would have to bear the risk of a criminal prosecution[7] or would be involved in costly and hazardous litigation which might lead to his eviction and the splitting up of his family[8].

The fact that performance would expose the defendant to forfeiture constitutes such hardship as induces the court to refuse performance, at least if forfeiture would clearly result[9]. A mere possibility is not enough[10], and forfeiture not resulting directly from performance of the contract, but proximately caused by other acts of the defendant, constitutes no defence[11].

1   *Denne v Light* (1857) 8 De GM & G 774. See *Tomlinson v Manchester and Birmingham Rly Co* (1840) 2 Ry & Can Cas 104.
2   *Hope v Walter* [1900] 1 Ch 257, CA (revsg [1899] 1 Ch 879), where a counterclaim for rescission and return of deposit failed in both courts.
3   *Wedgwood v Adams* (1843) 6 Beav 600.
4   *Mortlock v Buller* (1804) 10 Ves 292; *White v Cuddon* (1842) 8 Cl & Fin 766, HL: see TRUSTS AND POWERS vol 98 (2013) PARA 628.
5   *Watson v Marston* (1853) 4 De GM & G 230. Such a sale would open the foreclosure: see MORTGAGE vol 77 (2016) PARA 619. For other cases of hardship see *Ely (Dean and Chapter) v Stewart (or Steward)* (1740) 2 Atk 44 (covenant to leave buildings in repair); *Hamilton v Grant* (1815) 3 Dow 33, HL; *Kimberley v Jennings* (1836) 6 Sim 340; *Talbot v Ford* (1842) 13 Sim 173; *Shrewsbury and Birmingham Rly Co v London and North Western Rly Co etc* (1853) 4 De GM & G 115 (affd (1857) 6 HL Cas 113), where the parties were companies.
6   *Neale v Mackenzie* (1837) 1 Keen 474.
7   *Pottinger v George* (1967) 116 CLR 328 at 337 (Aust HC).
8   *Wroth v Tyler* [1974] Ch 30, [1973] 1 All ER 897.
9   *Faine v Brown* (1750) cited in 2 Ves Sen 307, where a sale would have involved forfeiture of half the purchase money to the vendor's brother; *Peacock v Penson* (1848) 11 Beav 355, where a covenant to make a road was not enforced on the ground of risk of forfeiting the land, but compensation was given; *Becker v Partridge* [1966] 2 QB 155, [1966] 2 All ER 266, CA, where rescission was granted on the ground that breaches of covenant were defects in the vendor's title. Cf *Warmington v Miller* [1973] QB 877, [1973] 2 All ER 372, CA, following *Willmott v Barber* (1880) 15 ChD 96, where (in each case) a contract was made in breach of a covenant in a lease not to assign.
10   *Rankin v Lay* (1860) 2 De GF & J 65.
11   *Helling v Lumley* (1858) 3 De G & J 493.

(6) DEFECTS IN SUBJECT MATTER OF CONTRACT AS A DEFENCE TO SPECIFIC PERFORMANCE

562. Defect apart from fraud. Apart from any question of fraud[1] or misrepresentation[2], the existence of a defect in the subject matter of the contract is in certain instances a ground for refusing specific performance[3].

Most of the cases concern contracts for the sale of land. The vendor is under a duty to prove his title and to convey what he has contracted to convey[4]. Consequently if there is any substantial variation[5] between the property offered and the property contracted to be sold, the purchaser can resist specific performance even though the variation is beneficial to him[6]. Whether the difference is substantial is a question of fact. If the purchaser has knowledge of an irremovable defect of title at the date of the contract, it cannot be implied that the vendor promised to convey an unincumbered freehold interest[7]; if the defect is removable[8], then, subject to any agreement to the contrary, the purchaser may assume that the vendor will remove it[9]. If the purchaser did not know of the defect and is to resist specific performance he must show that the defect is substantial and latent, in the sense that a purchaser could not have discovered its existence by exercising reasonable care[10] in his inspection of the title or the property. The latent defect may be that the property is subject to unusual or onerous covenants[11] or may relate to the physical nature of the property[12].

The question has frequently arisen as to the effect of an exclusion clause, such as 'no error, misstatement or omission in the particulars shall annul a sale'. Despite such a clause, specific performance will be denied if the vendor failed to make disclosure of a substantial defect of the existence of which he was aware (he cannot compel a purchaser to assume what he knows to be untrue[13]), or if he innocently misrepresents the state of the title when the true facts are within his knowledge[14]. Again it has long been established that if the defect is substantial not only will specific performance be denied but the purchaser may be entitled to rescind the contract[15]. If the defect is trivial or insubstantial, a vendor may be denied specific performance simply because the purchaser's claim for compensation is excluded, or limited by, the contract[16].

In this connection it should be noted that, quite apart from any discretion in the court to refuse relief on equitable grounds, an exclusion clause may be invalidated by statute. Thus a clause which attempts to exclude or limit the liability for misrepresentation is valid only if the representor can satisfy the court that it is fair and reasonable having regard to the circumstances which were, or ought reasonably to have been, known to or in the contemplation of the parties when the contract was made[17]. Occasionally consumer protection law may also intervene, as where provision is made by Part 2 of the Consumer Rights Act 2015[18] for the protection of consumers from unfair terms and notices contained in a contract between a trader and a consumer[19].

1   As to the effect of fraud see EQUITABLE JURISDICTION vol 47 (2014) PARA 12 et seq; MISREPRESENTATION vol 76 (2013) PARA 754 et seq generally.
2   As to misrepresentation generally see MISREPRESENTATION vol 76 (2013) PARA 740 et seq.
3   *Whitmel v Farrel* (1749) 1 Ves Sen 256 (marriage settlement); *Bentley v Craven* (1853) 17 Beav 204. Cf *Crosse v Lawrence* (1852) 9 Hare 462; *Crosse v Keene* (1852) 9 Hare 469; *Sun Permanent Benefit Building Society v Western Suburban and Harrow Road Permanent Building Society* [1921] 2 Ch 438, CA.
4   *Pips (Leisure Productions) Ltd v Walton* (1982) 43 P & CR 415; *Pinekerry Ltd v Kenneth Needs (Contractors) Ltd* (1992) 64 P & CR 245, CA.
5   As to what is a substantial variation see inter alia *Re Arnold, Arnold v Arnold* (1880) 14 ChD 270, CA; *Jacobs v Revell* [1900] 2 Ch 858; *Shepherd v Croft* [1911] 1 Ch 521; *Holliday v Lockwood* [1917] 2 Ch 47; *Watson v Burton* [1956] 3 All ER 929, [1957] 1 WLR 19; *Citytowns Ltd v Bohemian Properties Ltd* [1986] 2 EGLR 258.
6   *Ayles v Cox* (1852) 16 Beav 23.
7   *Timmins v Moreland Street Property Co Ltd* [1958] Ch 110 at 132, [1957] 3 All ER 265 at 277, CA. It is otherwise if the contract contains an express term that good title should be conveyed: see *Cato v Thompson* (1882) 9 QBD 616, CA.
8   Cf *Burnell v Brown* (1820) 1 Jac & W 168; *Castle v Wilkinson* (1870) 5 Ch App 534.
9   *English v Murray* (1883) 49 LT 35; *Lett v Randall* (1883) 49 LT 71; *Re Gloag and Miller's Contract* (1883) 23 ChD 320.
10 See *Denny v Hancock* (1870) 6 Ch App 1 at 12 per James LJ. Cf *Yandle & Sons v Sutton* [1922] 2 Ch 199; *Simpson v Gilley* (1922) 92 LJ Ch 194.
11 An example is the sale of leaseholds where the vendor is silent as to unusual and onerous covenants (*Hampshire v Wickens* (1878) 7 ChD 555; *Re Lander and Bagley's Contract* [1892] 3 Ch 41; *Molyneux v Hawtrey* [1903] 2 KB 487, CA), unless the purchaser ought himself to have ascertained their existence (*Reeve v Berridge* (1888) 20 QBD 523, CA; *Re White and Smith's Contract* [1896] 1 Ch 637), since it is the vendor's duty in a case relating to real property to disclose any material defect not ascertainable in the ordinary course by the purchaser (*Carlish v Salt* [1906] 1 Ch 335; *Re Haedicke and Lipski's Contract* [1901] 2 Ch 666; see CONVEYANCING vol 23 (2016) PARA 61). See also *Stevens v Adamson* (1818) 2 Stark 422 (fact of notice of re-entry not disclosed to purchaser of leaseholds); *Ballard v Way* (1836) 1 M & W 520; *Darlington v Hamilton* (1854) Kay 550 ('leaseholds' held by underlease, the head lease comprising other property); *Turner v Turner* [1881] WN 70; *Heywood v Mallalieu* (1883) 25 ChD 357 (claim to an easement stated by the vendor to be negligible); *Re Lloyds Bank Ltd and Lillington's Contract* [1912] 1 Ch 601; *Allen v Smith* [1924] 2 Ch 308 (long leaseholds; lease stated to be in 'ordinary'

form, but containing onerous and unusual covenant); *Beyfus v Lodge* [1925] Ch 350 (leaseholds; non-disclosure of landlord's notice to repair); *Flexman v Corbett* [1930] 1 Ch 672 (leaseholds; onerous and unusual covenant and proviso for re-entry).

12 *Dyer v Hargrave, Hargrave v Dyer* (1805) 10 Ves 505, where a farm described as lying within a ring fence was seen by the purchaser and specific performance was denied.

13 *Heywood v Mallalieu* (1883) 25 ChD 357; *Nottingham Patent Brick and Tile Co v Butler* (1885) 15 QBD 261 (affd (1886) 16 QBD 778, CA); *Beyfus v Lodge* [1925] Ch 350. But if the purchaser takes the risk that title may be bad, specific performance will be decreed unless it is manifest that the title is plainly indefensible: see *Re Scott and Alvarez's Contract, Scott v Alvarez* [1895] 2 Ch 603, CA.

14 *Walker v Boyle* [1982] 1 All ER 634, [1982] 1 WLR 495. See also *Charles Hunt Ltd v Palmer* [1931] 2 Ch 287; *Laurence v Lexcourt Holdings Ltd* [1978] 2 All ER 810, [1978] 1 WLR 1128; *Atlantic Estates plc v Ezekiel* [1991] 2 EGLR 202, CA.

15 *Flight v Booth* (1834) 1 Bing NC 370; *King Bros (Finance) Ltd v North Western British Road Services Ltd* [1986] 2 EGLR 253.

16 *Watson v Burton* [1956] 3 All ER 929 at 934, [1957] 1 WLR 19 at 25. For that reason a prudent vendor may waive the benefit of the clause and agree to pay compensation: see *Shepherd v Croft* [1911] 1 Ch 521 at 529–530. It is a distinct question whether an appropriately drafted exclusion clause can prevent a purchaser recovering damages at law. In *Nottingham Patent Brick and Tile Co v Butler* (1885) 15 QBD 261 the purchaser was allowed to rescind and recover the deposit: see the Law of Property Act 1925 s 49(2); and PARA 620. However, in *Photo Production Ltd v Securicor Transport Ltd* [1980] AC 827, [1980] 1 All ER 556, HL, the House of Lords held that an appropriately drafted clause could, as a matter of construction, exclude or limit the liability of a contracting party. It is unlikely that such a clause could protect a vendor who knew of the defect of title. But the position is uncertain if the seller innocently misrepresents the title or (an even more difficult case) if he is ignorant of the defect. Cf *Ward v Hobbs* (1878) 4 App Cas 13, HL (sale of pigs with all faults). If such a clause attempts to exclude or limit the liability of a representor, it may be held to be unreasonable: see the Misrepresentation Act 1967 s 3(1); and MISREPRESENTATION vol 76 (2013) PARA 802. The Misrepresentation Act 1967 s 3 does not apply to a term in a consumer contract within the meaning of the Consumer Rights Act 2015 Pt 2 (ss 61–76) (see CONSUMER PROTECTION vol 21 (2016) PARA 391 et seq): see the Misrepresentation Act 1967 s 3(2) (added by added by the Consumer Rights Act 2015 s 75, Sch 4 para 1).

17 See the Misrepresentation Act 1967 s 3(1) (see note 16); and MISREPRESENTATION vol 76 (2013) PARA 802.

18 Ie the Consumer Rights Act 2015 Pt 2 (ss 61–76): see CONSUMER PROTECTION vol 21 (2016) PARAS 391–402. It was held in *R (on the application of Khatun) v Newham London Borough Council* [2004] EWCA Civ 55, [2005] QB 37, [2004] 3 WLR 417 that the predecessor of Part 2 applied to land sales, and it seems the same will apply to the present legislation.

19 See CONSUMER PROTECTION vol 21 (2016) PARA 391 et seq.

563. Proof of title on a sale of land. A particular instance in which non-performance of a condition by the claimant is a bar to his action is where he is a vendor of land suing for specific performance of the contract, but is unable to prove a good title[1]. Although the rule[2], established in the early part of the eighteenth century[3], that specific performance will be refused if the court, although not actually pronouncing a title to be bad, considers it too doubtful to be forced on a purchaser[4] is still in force[5], the defence that a title is too doubtful to be forced on a purchaser has in modern times found little favour with the court, and the general rule now is that it is the court's duty, unless there are exceptional circumstances[6], to decide the rights between vendor and purchaser and to ascertain and determine as best it may what the law is[7]. The mere possibility that a claimant to an incumbrance, not bound by a decision of the court in proceedings to which he was not a party, may involve the purchaser in future litigation should not deter the court from finding the title good. This is so whether the doubt as to the title is one of law or of fact. It is difficult to define with precision what degree of doubt as to title will lead the court to refuse specific performance[8]. The general principle appears to be this: if the facts and circumstances of the case are so compelling that the court concludes beyond reasonable doubt that the purchaser will not be at risk of a successful assertion against him of the incumbrance[9], the court should declare in favour of a good title shown[10]. The case law suggests the following specific rules:

(1)   the existence of a decision of a court of co-ordinate jurisdiction, which the court thinks wrong, leads the court to refuse performance both where such decision is adverse to the title and where it is in favour of it[11]; where the decision is that of an inferior court which a higher court thinks wrong, the higher court does not treat the title as doubtful if the decision of the inferior court was adverse to the title[12], although, on the other hand, the title is treated as doubtful if the decision was in its favour[13];

(2)   where the title depends on the particular words of an inartistic and ambiguous document, the court treats the title as doubtful[14], but not if the difficulty can be solved by the application of general rules of construction[15], or if it depends on the general law of the land[16];

(3)   where the proof of the title depends on doubtful facts as to which no clear presumption in favour of the title can be drawn[17], or as to which the presumption, although not necessarily conclusive, is adverse[18], the title is treated as doubtful; but it is not so treated where there is a presumption in favour of the facts supporting the title[19], or where the objection amounts simply to a suspicion of bad faith, so that the presumption in favour of good faith may be invoked[20];

(4)   where there is substantial doubt whether all the relevant evidence is before the court, specific performance will be refused[21]; and

(5)   if the defect does not detract from the purchaser's enjoyment of the property, the court may order specific performance with compensation[22].

1   As to title generally see CONVEYANCING vol 23 (2016) PARA 112 et seq. As to the practice on reference of title see PARA 608 et seq. As to the covenants for title implied by statute on the actual disposition of a property see the Law of Property (Miscellaneous Provisions) Act 1994 Pt I (ss 1–13); and CONVEYANCING vol 23 (2016) PARAS 181–182.

2   For a statement of the general principle see *Parker v Tootal* (1865) 11 HL Cas 143 at 158 per Lord Westbury LC; *Re Nichols' and Von Joel's Contract* [1910] 1 Ch 43 at 46, CA. See also *Marlow v Smith* (1723) 2 P Wms 198; *Shapland v Smith* (1780) 1 Bro CC 75; *Cooper v Denne* (1792) 1 Ves 565; *Sheffield v Lord Mulgrave* (1795) 2 Ves 526; *Roake v Kidd* (1800) 5 Ves 647; *Vancouver v Bliss* (1805) 11 Ves 458 at 465; *Jervoise v Duke of Northumberland* (1820) 1 Jac & W 559 at 568; *Willcox v Bellaers* (1825) Turn & R 491; *Smith v Colbourne* [1914] 2 Ch 533 at 541, 544, CA; *Johnson v Clarke* [1928] Ch 847. The practical justification of the rule is that the court's decision in an action of specific performance would not bind third persons not present before the court: see *Glass v Richardson* (1852) 9 Hare 698 at 701 per Turner V-C (on appeal 2 De GM & G 658); *Osborne v Rowlett* (1880) 13 ChD 774 at 781 per Jessel MR. Cf *Re Reilly and Brady's Contract* [1910] 1 IR 258.

3   The original practice of the Court of Chancery was to decide for or against the title, and to grant or refuse specific performance accordingly: see Fry on Specific Performance (6th Edn) 410 et seq.

4   See *Marlow v Smith* (1723) 2 P Wms 198; *Sloper v Fish* (1813) 2 Ves & B 145 at 149.

5   *Re Nichols' and Von Joel's Contract* [1910] 1 Ch 43, CA. The rule was recognised by the House of Lords in *Parker v Tootal* (1865) 11 HL Cas 143.

6   These exist where there is a real difficulty in construing a document, for example where extrinsic evidence has to be obtained to resolve a latent ambiguity of description in the document, and the point of construction can be determined conclusively by a very easy procedure such as an originating summons between the proper parties: see *Wilson v Thomas* [1958] 1 All ER 871, [1958] 1 WLR 422, where vendors, beneficiaries under an ambiguous will, were not entitled to have the title cleared at the purchaser's expense (following *Re Nichols' and Von Joel's Contract* [1910] 1 Ch 43, CA). The reported cases do not indicate what other circumstances will be considered as exceptional.

7   *MEPC Ltd v Christian-Edwards* [1981] AC 205, [1979] 3 All ER 752, HL. See also *Alexander v Mills* (1870) 6 Ch App 124; *Re Nichols' and Von Joel's Contract* [1910] 1 Ch 43, CA; *Smith v Colbourne* [1914] 2 Ch 533, CA; *Johnson v Clarke* [1928] Ch 847, where the vendor was given no costs; *Mungalsingh v Juman* [2015] UKPC 38, [2016] 1 P & CR 128, where it was held that the question of whether certain documents had to be produced by a seller and, if so, whether their production was a matter of title, had to, at least to some extent, be governed by the general practice of conveyancers in the jurisdiction in question.

8   *MEPC Ltd v Christian-Edwards* [1981] AC 205, [1979] 3 All ER 752, HL, is now the leading case. The earlier authorities include *Sheffield v Lord Mulgrave* (1795) 2 Ves 526; *Rose v Calland* (1800) 5 Ves 186; *Lord Braybroke v Inskip* (1803) 8 Ves 417 at 428; *Jervoise v Duke of Northumberland* (1820) 1 Jac & W 559; *Price v Strange* (1820) 6 Madd 159; *Pyrke v Waddingham* (1852) 10 Hare 1 at 8; *Rogers v Waterhouse* (1858) 4 Drew 329; *Collier v McBean* (1865) 1 Ch App 81; *Hamilton v Buckmaster* (1866) LR 3 Eq 323; *Williams v Scott* [1900] AC 499, PC. See also *Wrigley v Sykes* (1856) 21 Beav 337; *Bull v Hutchens* (1863) 32 Beav 615; *Austin v Tawney* (1867) 2 Ch App 143; *Beioley v Carter* (1869) 4 Ch App 230; *Mullings v Trinder* (1870) LR 10 Eq 449; *Alexander v Mills* (1870) 6 Ch App 124; *Highgate Archway Co v Jeakes* (1871) LR 12 Eq 9; *Radford v Willis* (1871) 7 Ch App 7; *Bell v Holtby* (1873) LR 15 Eq 178; *Wise v Piper* (1880) 13 ChD 848; *Palmer v Locke* (1881) 18 ChD 381, CA.

    The doubt which influences the court may be one of general law (*Sloper v Fish* (1813) 2 Ves & B 145; *Blosse v Lord Clanmorris* (1821) 3 Bli 62, HL; *Re Thackwray and Young's Contract* (1888) 40 ChD 34), or of the construction of the particular documents (*Earl of Lincoln v Arcedeckne* (1844) 1 Coll 98; *Bristow v Wood* (1844) 1 Coll 480), or of facts on the title or extrinsic to it (*Pyrke v Waddingham* above), and the facts may be doubtful either as not being satisfactorily established (*Smith v Death* (1820) 5 Madd 371), or as being negative and not admitting of satisfactory proof (*Lowes v Lush* (1808) 14 Ves 547).

9   *MEPC Ltd v Christian-Edwards* [1981] AC 205, [1979] 3 All ER 725, HL.

10   In *MEPC Ltd v Christian-Edwards* [1981] AC 205 at 220, [1979] 3 All ER 752 at 757–758, HL, Lord Russell suggested that, where the doubt is one of fact, the old test as to whether it would be the duty of a judge to direct a jury to find in favour of the fact may be too stringent. For the earlier authorities see *Price v Strange* (1820) 6 Madd 159; *Sharp v Adcock* (1828) 4 Russ 374; *Cattell v Corrall* (1840) 4 Y & C Ex 228 at 237; *Heseltine v Simmons* (1858) 6 WR 268; *Potter v Perry* (1859) 7 WR 182; *Pegler v White* (1864) 33 Beav 403; *Burnell v Firth* (1867) 15 WR 546. Cf *Re New Land Development Association and Gray* [1892] 2 Ch 138, CA; *Re Calcott and Elvin's Contract* [1898] 2 Ch 460, CA; *Williams v Scott* [1900] AC 499, PC. As further illustrations see *Re Maskell and Goldfinch's Contract* [1895] 2 Ch 525; *Re Hollis' Hospital Trustees and Hague's Contract* [1899] 2 Ch 540; *Re Marshall and Salt's Contract* [1900] 2 Ch 202; *Re Douglas and Powell's Contract* [1902] 2 Ch 296; *Re Verrell's Contract* [1903] 1 Ch 65. Where the probability of litigation was not great, specific performance was denied: see *Lyddall v Weston* (1739) 2 Atk 19 (mathematical certainty impossible); *Seaman v Vawdrey* (1810) 16 Ves 390 at 393; *Martin v Cotter* (1846) 3 Jo & Lat 496; *Spencer v Topham* (1856) 22 Beav 573; *Falkner v Equitable Reversionary Society* (1858) 4 Drew 352; *Noyes v Paterson* [1894] 3 Ch 267; *Hepworth v Pickles* [1900] 1 Ch 108; *Re Summerson, Downie v Summerson* [1900] 1 Ch 112n. In *George v Thomas* (1904) 90 LT 505 the action was adjourned to give a third person, who was a claimant, an opportunity of establishing his claim.

11   *Mullings v Trinder* (1870) LR 10 Eq 449.

12   *Sheppard v Doolan* (1842) 3 Dr & War 1 at 8; *Beioley v Carter* (1869) 4 Ch App 230.

13   *Mullings v Trinder* (1870) LR 10 Eq 449.

14   *Alexander v Mills* (1870) 6 Ch App 124 at 132 per James LJ.

15   *Radford v Willis* (1871) 7 Ch App 7.

16   *Alexander v Mills* (1870) 6 Ch App 124; *Forster v Abraham* (1874) LR 17 Eq 351; *Osborne to Rowlett* (1880) 13 ChD 774; *Mogridge v Clapp* [1892] 3 Ch 382, CA; *Re Thompson and M'Williams' Contract* [1896] 1 IR 356; *Re Carter and Kenderdine's Contract* [1897] 1 Ch 776, CA (overruling *Re Briggs and Spicer* [1891] 2 Ch 127). Cf *Re Handman and Wilcox's Contract* [1902] 1 Ch 599 at 609, CA; *Johnson v Clarke* [1928] Ch 847.

17   See *Lowes v Lush* (1808) 14 Ves 547 (no creditor able to take advantage of act of bankruptcy); *Eyton v Dicken* (1817) 4 Price 303 (presumption from mere fact of possession); *Freer v Hesse* (1853) 4 De GM & G 495 (absence of notice of incumbrance); *Re Handman and Wilcox's Contract* [1902] 1 Ch 599, CA (absence of notice); *Re Douglas and Powell's Contract* [1902] 2 Ch 296 (complicated and ambiguous facts).

18   *Warde v Dixon* (1858) 28 LJ Ch 315.

19   *Barnwell v Harris* (1809) 1 Taunt 430; *Emery v Grocock* (1821) 6 Madd 54; *Prosser v Watts* (1821) 6 Madd 59; *Causton v Macklew* (1828) 2 Sim 242; *Magennis v Fallon* (1829) 2 Mol 561.

20 *M'Queen v Farquhar* (1805) 11 Ves 467; *Cattell v Corrall* (1840) 4 Y & C Ex 228 (criticising dicta in *Hartley v Smith* (1819) Buck 368); *Green v Pulsford* (1839) 2 Beav 70; *Grove v Bastard* (1848) 2 Ph 619 (subsequent proceedings (1851) 1 De GM & G 69); *Re Huish's Charity* (1870) LR 10 Eq 5; *Alexander v Mills* (1870) 6 Ch App 124. When title depended on a will, the absence of the heir and the fact that the will had been proved against him were not in themselves enough to prevent performance: see *Colton v Wilson* (1733) 3 P Wms 190; *Morrison v Arnold* (1817) 19 Ves 670; *Weddall v Nixon* (1853) 17 Beav 160.

21 *Mullings v Trinder* (1870) LR 10 Eq 449 at 455; *Wilson v Thomas* [1958] 1 All ER 871 at 877–878, [1958] 1 WLR 422 at 430–431. Cf *Bigg v Boyd Gibbins Ltd* [1971] 2 All ER 183, [1971] 1 WLR 913, CA (a 'plain case' under RSC Ord 86).

22 As to specific performance with compensation see PARA 621 et seq.

564. Title depending on adverse possession. In some cases the court has compelled a purchaser to take a title depending on adverse possession[1], but he has not been compelled to take a leap in the dark[2]. In those cases, objections apparent on the face of the title as shown were covered by the possession[3].

1 See *Scott v Nixon* (1843) 3 Dr & War 388.
2 *Re Nisbet and Potts' Contract* [1905] 1 Ch 391 at 402; affd [1906] 1 Ch 386, CA. See CONVEYANCING vol 23 (2016) PARA 121.
3 *Games v Bonnor* (1884) 54 LJ Ch 517, CA; *Re Atkinson and Horsell's Contract* [1912] 2 Ch 1, CA. See further LIMITATION PERIODS vol 68 (2016) PARA 1095.

(7) NON-PERFORMANCE BY CLAIMANT AS DEFENCE TO SPECIFIC PERFORMANCE

565. Failure to be ready, willing and able to perform the contract. A claimant seeking to enforce a contract must show that all conditions precedent have been fulfilled[1] and that he has performed, or been ready and willing to perform, all the terms which ought to have been performed by him, and also that he is ready and willing to perform all future obligations under the contract[2]. Subject to certain exceptions[3], any failure on his part or breach of his own obligation also bars his claim to specific performance[4]. This rule is applied strictly. Thus the Privy Council declined to award specific performance of a contract of sale where time was made of the essence and payment was made a mere ten minutes late[5].

A contractual term purporting to oust this principle cannot fetter the court's discretion to grant or refuse specific performance after taking account of the claimant's conduct[6].

1 As to conditions precedent generally see CONTRACT vol 22 (2012) PARA 531 et seq. See also LANDLORD AND TENANT vol 62 (2016) PARAS 89, 129, 133, 135.
2 Cf *General Billposting Co Ltd v Atkinson* [1909] AC 118, HL; *Measures Bros Ltd v Measures* [1910] 2 Ch 248, CA; *Australian Hardwoods Pty Ltd v Railways Comr* [1961] 1 All ER 737, [1961] 1 WLR 425, PC; *Sport International Bussum BV v Inter-Footwear Ltd* [1984] 1 All ER 376, [1984] 1 WLR 776, CA (affd [1984] 2 All ER 321, [1984] 1 WLR 776, HL). See also *Stratford v Earl of Aldborough* (1786) 1 Ridg Parl Rep 287; *Acraman v Price, Davies v Price* (1870) 18 WR 540. Cf *Sun Permanent Benefit Building Society v Western Suburban and Harrow Road Permanent Building Society* [1921] 2 Ch 438, CA, where a vendor unable to transfer the full benefit of the subject matters covered by the contract was held not to be 'ready and willing', and accordingly was refused specific performance. Repudiation by the defendant does not excuse the plaintiff from showing performance or readiness to perform on his part: *Ellis v Rogers* (1884) 29 ChD 661 (left open on appeal at 671, CA) (building lease); *Morrow v Carty* [1957] NI 174; and see PARA 599.
3 As to impossibility see PARA 570.
4 *Strong v Stringer* (1889) 61 LT 470; *Hooper v Bromet* (1904) 90 LT 234, CA; *Australian Hardwoods Pty Ltd v Railways Comr* [1961] 1 All ER 737, [1961] 1 WLR 425, PC; *Doyle v East* [1972] 2 All ER 1013, [1972] 1 WLR 1080 (where a builder failed to build a house in substantial accordance with the agreement); *Groveholt Ltd v Hughes* [2012] EWHC 3351 (Ch); [2013] 1 EGLR 15. See also *Cardiothoracic Institute v Shrewdcrest Ltd* [1986] 3 All ER 633,

[1986] 1 WLR 368. There is an apparent exception where the separate parts of an agreement are severable and in truth amount to separate contracts; in such instances, failure by the plaintiff to fulfil conditions as to one part does not bar his claim for performance of a separate part in respect of which he has fulfilled his obligations: see *Wilkinson v Clements* (1872) 8 Ch App 96 (building agreement). However, as a rule, a contract must be specifically performed as a whole, or the court will entirely refuse to enforce it: see *Wood v Rowe* (1820) 2 Bli 595, HL (agreement to settle litigation); *Ford v Stuart* (1852) 15 Beav 493 (mortgage and settlement).

5   *Union Eagle Ltd v Golden Achievement Ltd* [1997] AC 514, [1997] 2 All ER 215, PC.
6   *Quadrant Visual Communications Ltd v Hutchison Telephone (UK) Ltd* [1993] BCLC 442.

566. Effect of non-performance of terms of contract. In addition to conditions[1], the claimant seeking specific performance must prima facie show that he has performed all the terms of the contract which he has undertaken to perform, whether expressly or by implication[2], and which he ought to have performed at the date of the claim form[3]. This rule, however, is subject to a qualification: it does not apply to obligations placed on the claimant unless the latter are essential and considerable[4]. Hence the court does not bar a claim on the ground that the claimant has failed in literal performance, or is in default in some non-essential or unimportant term[5], although in such cases it may grant compensation to the defendant[6].

Where a condition or essential term ought to have been performed by the claimant at the date of the claim form, the court does not accept his undertaking to perform in lieu of performance, but dismisses the claim[7].

1   As to conditions see PARA 565 et seq.
2   *Tildesley v Clarkson* (1862) 30 Beav 419. Distinguish *Chappell v Gregory* (1864) 34 Beav 250, where no such term was held to be implied.
3   *Quadrangle Development and Construction Co Ltd v Jenner* [1974] 1 All ER 729, [1974] 1 WLR 68, CA; *Cole v Rose* [1978] 3 All ER 1121, DC; *Singh (Sudagar) v Nazeer* [1979] Ch 474, [1978] 3 All ER 817; *Groveholt Ltd v Hughes* [2012] EWHC 3351 (Ch); [2013] 1 EGLR 15. Cf *Rightside Properties Ltd v Gray* [1975] Ch 72, [1974] 2 All ER 1169.
4   *Modlen v Snowball* (1861) 4 De GF & J 143; *Reeves v Greenwich Tanning Co Ltd* (1864) 2 Hem & M 54.
5   *Dyster v Randall & Sons* [1926] Ch 932 at 942–943. Nevertheless the claimant might on that ground have failed in an action at law: *Davis v Hone* (1805) 2 Sch & Lef 341 at 347; see *Craven v Tickell* (1789) 1 Ves 60 (small deviation from agreed plan); *Lord v Stephens* (1835) 1 Y & C Ex 222. It seems that *Oxford v Provand* (1868) LR 2 PC 135 ought to be considered as emphasising the distinction between essential and non-essential terms.
6   As to specific performance with compensation see PARA 621 et seq.
7   *Williams v Brisco* (1882) 22 ChD 441, CA. Cf *Holmes v Trench* [1898] 1 IR 319.

567. Separate or collateral contract irrelevant. The claimant may enter into a contract which is separate from but collateral to the contract which he seeks specifically to enforce. Where the claimant does so, it is not open to the defendant to say that specific performance should be dependent on the performance of the collateral contract, even though it relates to the same subject matter[1]. For example, there may be independent[2] covenants in the same contract, non-performance of one of which does not prevent enforcement of performance of the other covenants[3].

1   *Phipps v Child* (1857) 3 Drew 709.
2   As to dependent and independent covenants generally see DEEDS AND OTHER INSTRUMENTS vol 32 (2012) PARA 467 et seq.
3   *Green v Low* (1856) 22 Beav 625, where a contract for a lease and also for an option to purchase were held to be independent. Cf *Raffety v Schofield* [1897] 1 Ch 937; *Starkey v Barton* [1909] 1 Ch 284. See also *Gibson v Goldsmid* (1854) 5 De GM & G 757, and distinguish *Measures Bros Ltd v Measures* [1910] 2 Ch 248, CA (interdependent covenants). Breach of an intended covenant in a lease may prevent a tenant under an agreement for a lease obtaining a lease: *Coatsworth v Johnson* (1886) 55 LJQB 220, CA; and see LANDLORD AND TENANT vol 62 (2016) PARA 71.

568. Waiver or wrongful act by the defendant. Non-performance by the claimant cannot be relied on by the defendant as a defence to specific performance where he has waived performance[1], or where the non-performance was caused by his own breach of contract or by his preventing the claimant from performing his obligations under the contract[2], or where his failure to perform specifically resulted in land being sold by the claimant's mortgagees[3].

1 *Lamare v Dixon* (1873) LR 6 HL 414. See also *Strong v Stringer* (1889) 61 LT 470, where rent was accepted after a breach of covenant.
2 *Hotham v East India Co* (1787) 1 Term Rep 638; *Murrell v Goodyear* (1860) 1 De GF & J 432, where a purchaser prevented the vendor from completing his title. See also CONTRACT vol 22 (2012) PARA 536.
3 *Johnson v Agnew* [1980] AC 367, [1979] 1 All ER 883, HL: see PARA 574.

569. Waiver by claimant of term for his benefit. If there is a stipulation in a contract intended to benefit the claimant, he may waive it and obtain specific performance, provided the stipulation is in terms for the exclusive benefit of the claimant[1].

1 *Heron Garage Properties Ltd v Moss* [1974] 1 All ER 421, [1974] 1 WLR 148; *Federated Homes Ltd v Turner* (1974) 233 Estates Gazette 845; *Balbosa v Ayoub Ali* [1990] 1 WLR 914, PC. Cf *Scott v Bradley* [1971] Ch 850, [1971] 1 All ER 583.

570. Performance by claimant impossible. A similar rule applies where performance by the claimant of his own obligations becomes impossible. Where the impossibility, although of a nature to affect the right to performance, relates to subsidiary, non-essential matters (such as where there is a deficiency in the acreage to be sold) or merely to literal fulfilment, the court seeks to grant performance with compensation[1]. Similarly, if after substantial performance by a claimant of his obligation it has, without any default on his part, become impossible for him to make complete performance and the status quo ante cannot be restored, the court may enforce performance by the other party[2]. The appointment of a receiver does not of itself afford a vendor company a defence to a claim by the purchaser for specific performance of the contract[3].

1 *Norris v Jackson* (1862) 3 Giff 396. As to specific performance with compensation see PARA 621 et seq.
2 See Gilbert's History and Practice of Chancery 240–242, citing *Earl of Feversham v Watson* (1680) Cas temp Finch 445; *Medith v Wynn* (1711) 1 Eq Cas Abr 70. See also 1 Fonblanque's Treatise of Equity 385–386; Story's Equity Jurisprudence (14th Edn) 1060–1062.
3 *Freevale Ltd v Metrostore (Holdings) Ltd* [1984] Ch 199, [1984] 1 All ER 495.

571. No specific performance where right of set-off. A claim to specific performance will fail if it is dependent on the non-payment of a money claim to which there is a complete defence by way of a legal or equitable right of set-off. Thus where the claimant had a right to require the defendant to assign certain property to him if specified payments were not made, the claimant failed in his claim for specific performance, notwithstanding non-payment, where the defendant would have had a complete defence by way of set-off against the claimant's money claim[1].

1 *BICC plc v Burndy Corpn* [1985] Ch 232, [1985] 1 All ER 417, CA.

(8) CLAIMANT'S BREACH OF CONTRACT AS A DEFENCE TO SPECIFIC PERFORMANCE

572. Effect of repudiation by the claimant. It is obvious that a claimant who has expressly repudiated his obligations under a contract is debarred from claiming specific performance of the contract by the other party, provided that the other party has accepted the repudiation[1]. The same principles apply where, although the claimant has not in express terms refused to perform his part of the contract, he has done acts which show an intention no longer to be bound by it, and which amount to a complete and total repudiation of everything which has to be done by him[2]. To hold otherwise might result in the award of specific performance which could then be rendered valueless by the defendant's termination[3]. Thus where an employer has wrongfully dismissed his employee, he is not allowed to enforce against the employee, by specific performance or injunction, a restrictive covenant contained in the contract of employment[4]. However, the innocent party may refuse to terminate the contract and sue for specific performance[5], though if he accepts a repudiatory breach the contract is at an end and specific performance ceases to be available[6].

1   Cf PARA 565 et seq.
2   See CONTRACT vol 22 (2012) PARA 560 et seq. See also *Freeth v Burr* (1874) LR 9 CP 208 at 213; *Mersey Steel and Iron Co v Naylor, Benzon & Co* (1884) 9 App Cas 434, HL; *Shaffer (James) Ltd v Findlay, Durham and Brodie* [1953] 1 WLR 106, CA; *Federal Commerce and Navigation Ltd v Molena Alpha Inc, The Nanfri, The Benfri, The Lorfri* [1979] AC 757, [1979] 1 All ER 307, HL; *Woodar Investment Development Ltd v Wimpey Construction UK Ltd* [1980] 1 All ER 571, [1980] 1 WLR 277, HL.
3   It follows a fortiori that specific performance is unavailable when termination has actually taken place: see *Supportways Community Services Ltd v Hampshire County Council* [2006] EWCA Civ 1035, [2006] LGR 836.
4   See EMPLOYMENT vol 39 (2014) PARA 19. For an authoritative discussion of the jurisprudential basis of repudiations in the context of contracts of employment see *Geys v Societe Generale, London Branch* [2012] UKSC 63, [2013] AC 523, [2013] 1 All ER 1061.
5   Cf *Johnson v Agnew* [1980] AC 367, [1979] 1 All ER 883, HL, where specific performance, however, became impossible: see PARA 574.
6   *Walker v Standard Chartered Bank plc, Jasaro SA v Standard Chartered Bank plc* [1992] BCLC 535, CA.

573.   Effect of acts done in contravention of contract. Where a claimant claiming specific performance of a contract has acted in contravention of its terms, the court may refuse in its discretion to enforce the contract in his favour. Thus, for example, where a vendor who has agreed to give immediate possession retakes possession, he is not entitled to specific performance[1]. Similarly, where there is an agreement for a lease and the lessee commits breaches of the terms of the agreement, such as waste[2], failure to insure or repair[3], or, if the agreement is for a sublease, knowingly commits acts which are inconsistent with the covenants of the head lease[4], the contract is not specifically enforced. So, also, a covenant to renew is not enforced where the lessee has been guilty of serious breaches of the expiring lease[5].

In the past it has been said that to constitute a bar to specific performance, such acts must be gross and wilful[6]; and in relation to leases they must, as a rule, be not only such as would work a forfeiture of the legal interest, but also such that the court would not relieve against the forfeiture[7]. Today it is more likely, even in a claim for equitable relief, that a court will consider not only the nature of the particular term which is breached[8], but also the consequences which flow from the breach in determining whether to grant specific performance[9]. Consequently specific performance may be granted where the wrongful acts are trifling[10] or, in relation to leases, are such that the court would relieve against a forfeiture of the legal estate[11]. However, this always gives way to the agreement between the parties. Thus, in the absence of waiver or estoppel, the Privy Council declined to award specific performance of a contract of sale where time was made of the essence[12].

1 *Knatchbull v Grueber* (1815) 1 Madd 153; affd (1817) 3 Mer 124. Cf *Royou v Paul* (1858) 28 LJ Ch 555 (vendor giving notice of intention to resell) (explained in *Laughton v Port Erin Comrs* [1910] AC 565, PC); *Bedford and Cambridge Rly Co v Stanley* (1862) 2 John & H 746, where a railway company agreed to purchase land, then resorted to compulsory powers, and it was held that such resort was inconsistent with the agreement and a bar to the company's enforcing it. See also *Blackett v Bates* (1865) 1 Ch App 117, where it was doubted whether proceedings to set aside an award would not be a bar to a subsequent claim to enforce it specifically.

2 See *Hill v Barclay* (1811) 18 Ves 56 at 63; *Gregory v Wilson* (1852) 9 Hare 683; *Lewis v Bond* (1853) 18 Beav 85. Apparently, a gross instance of waste would have this result even where the lease, if executed, would not have contained a proviso for re-entry: *Gourlay v Duke of Somerset* (1812) 1 Ves & B 68 at 73.

3 *Nunn v Truscott* (1849) 3 De G & Sm 304; *Gregory v Wilson* (1852) 9 Hare 683.

4 *Lewis v Bond* (1853) 18 Beav 85.

5 *Thompson v Guyon* (1831) 5 Sim 65; *Greville v Parker* [1910] AC 335, PC: see LANDLORD AND TENANT vol 62 (2016) PARAS 89, 433.

6 *Hare v Burges* (1857) 5 WR 585; *Parker v Taswell* (1858) 2 De G & J 559.

7 As to relief against forfeiture see EQUITABLE JURISDICTION vol 47 (2014) PARA 223 et seq; LANDLORD AND TENANT vol 62 (2016) PARA 510 et seq.

8 Cf *A/S Awilco v Fulvia SpA di Navigazione, The Chikuma* [1981] 1 All ER 652, [1981] 1 WLR 314, HL. Cf *Bunge Corpn v Tradax SA* [1981] 2 All ER 513, [1981] 1 WLR 711, HL.

9 Cf *Bunge Corpn v Tradax SA* [1981] 2 All ER 513, [1981] 1 WLR 711, HL, explaining *Hongkong Fir Shipping Co Ltd v Kawasaki Kisen Kaisha Ltd* [1962] 2 QB 26, [1962] 1 All ER 474, CA.

10 *Besant v Wood* (1879) 12 ChD 605 (separation deed). See also *Gorton v Smart* (1822) 1 Sim & St 66; *Trant v Dwyer* (1828) 2 Bli NS 11, HL; *Walker v Jeffreys* (1842) 1 Hare 341; *Holmes v Eastern Counties Rly Co* (1857) 3 Jur NS 737; *Hare v Burges* (1857) 5 WR 585; *Parker v Taswell* (1858) 2 De G & J 559.

11 *Parker v Taswell* (1858) 2 De G & J 559.

12 *Union Eagle Ltd v Golden Achievement Ltd* [1997] AC 514, [1997] 2 All ER 215, PC (specific performance was not awarded when the purchaser of high value property where time was made of the essence was ten minutes late tendering cheques and documents).

(9) PERFORMANCE BY THE DEFENDANT IMPOSSIBLE

574. Frustration and impossibility. At law it is no defence to a claim for damages that the contract has become impossible of performance through the defendant's own acts, or for that matter without any fault on his part[1]. However, equity does not act in vain: from which it follows that if performance is genuinely impossible for any reason, specific performance will be denied[2]. So there can be no specific performance of a contract to allot shares already allotted to someone else[3], or a contract to buy realty when the buyer has no chance whatever of being able to pay for it[4] and again, it is a defence to a claim for specific performance that the defendant (who is generally a vendor of land) is not able to put an end to the rights of a third person over the land or to compel him to concur in the conveyance[5]. However, in cases short of complete impossibility an order to the defendant to use his best endeavours is entirely appropriate. So a defendant who promises to provide a performance bond can be ordered to do all he can to obtain it[6]; and a vendor of land whose ability to give good title is conditional on the consent of third parties must do his best to obtain any necessary consents[7]. He must take proceedings to eject a tenant by sufferance, a tenant at will or a trespasser who has no right to be there[8], but he need not embark on any dangerous and uncertain litigation to secure any consents; thus a husband need not take legal proceedings against his wife in order to secure her eviction from the matrimonial home[9].

If, however, the impossibility does not relate to the substance of the contract, the court may order the defendant to perform the contract so far as he can[10] and pay compensation for the part unperformed[11].

1   As to the effect of impossibility of performance and frustration on contracts generally see CONTRACT vol 22 (2012) PARA 467 et seq. As to frustration in relation to leases see LANDLORD AND TENANT vol 63 (2016) PARA 492.
2   *Green v Smith* (1738) 1 Atk 572 at 573; *Denton v Stewart* (1786) 1 Cox Eq Cas 258; *Smith v Morris* (1788) 2 Bro CC 311; *Ferguson v Wilson* (1866) 2 Ch App 77. Cf *Ellis v Colman, Bates and Husler* (1858) 25 Beav 662; *Wycombe Rly Co v Donnington Hospital* (1866) 1 Ch App 268; *Castle v Wilkinson* (1870) 5 Ch App 534. Cf *Johnson v Agnew* [1980] AC 367, [1979] 1 All ER 883, HL. See also PARA 572.
3   *Ferguson v Wilson* (1866) 2 Ch App 77.
4   *Titanic Quarter Ltd v Rowe* [2010] NICh 14.
5   *Wroth v Tyler* [1974] Ch 30 at 48, [1973] 1 All ER 897 at 911; *Watts v Spence* [1976] Ch 165, [1975] 2 All ER 528. See also *Lehmann v McArthur* (1868) 3 Ch App 496.
6   *Liberty Mercian Ltd v Cuddy Civil Engineering Ltd* [2013] EWHC 4110 (TCC), [2014] All ER (D) 118 (Jan).
7   Cf *Costigan v Hastler* (1804) 2 Sch & Lef 160 at 166; *Malhotra v Choudhury* [1980] Ch 52, [1979] 1 All ER 186, CA.
8   For the form of order in such a case see *Wroth v Tyler* [1974] Ch 30 at 51, [1973] 1 All ER 897 at 913.
9   *Wroth v Tyler* [1974] Ch 30, [1973] 1 All ER 897.
10 *Errington v Aynsly* (1788) 2 Bro CC 340, where there was a contract to build a bridge, but it proved impossible to lay the foundations, and it was ordered that the bridge be built on the nearest possible site and that compensation be paid. Cf *A-G v Day* (1749) 1 Ves Sen 218 at 224 per Lord Eldon LC; *Paxton v Newton* (1854) 2 Sm & G 437; *Barnes v Wood* (1869) LR 8 Eq 424.
11 As to compensation see PARA 621 et seq.

575.   Time at which impossibility is judged. The time at which impossibility is judged is the proper time for performance of the contract, not the date of the contract[1].

1   For instance, if a person enters into a contract which at the time he is not able to perform, but afterwards becomes able to do so, he is bound to perform it. Thus a person may contract to convey an estate on a future day even though he is not the owner of the estate at the date of the contract, or similarly may contract to sell goods which are not then his property. Such contracts would be enforced if the vendor has become possessed of the land or goods: see *Browne v Warner* (1808) 14 Ves 409 at 412; *Carne v Mitchell* (1846) 10 Jur 909; *Holroyd v Marshall* (1862) 10 HL Cas 191; CONVEYANCING vol 23 (2016) PARA 39; SALE OF GOODS AND SUPPLY OF SERVICES vol 91 (2012) PARAS 55–56. As to the validity of such contracts at law see *Cuddee v Rutter* (1720) 5 Vin Abr 538, pl 21 (which appears inconsistent with the later authorities); *Hibblewhite v M' Morine* (1839) 5 M & W 462; *De Medina v Norman* (1842) 9 M & W 820; and cf *Clayton v Duke of Newcastle* (1682) 2 Cas in Ch 112. Similarly, where contracts dealing with property require parliamentary sanction for their performance, the court protects the property while the sanction is being obtained: *Frederick v Coxwell* (1829) 3 Y & J 514; *Great Western Rly Co v Birmingham and Oxford Junction Rly Co* (1848) 2 Ph 597; *Hawkes v Eastern Counties Rly Co* (1852) 1 De GM & G 737; *Devenish v Brown* (1856) 26 LJ Ch 23. In *Walker v Barnes* (1818) 3 Madd 247, where an indemnity was to be secured on real property, the court rejected the plea that the contractor had not sufficient realty and ordered him to purchase sufficient to enable him to give the security. Cf *Carey v Stafford* (1725) 3 Swan 427n.

(10)   LAPSE OF TIME AS A DEFENCE TO SPECIFIC PERFORMANCE

(i)   Time of the Essence of the Contract

576.   When time is made of the essence of a contract. In the past, stipulations in a contract as to time were construed differently at law and in equity[1]. It is now provided by statute that in the event of a conflict the rules of equity are to prevail[2].

It has been held that these statutory provisions, and their predecessors, make it clear that there is now only one set of rules for the courts to apply[3].

Time is always of the essence of a unilateral contract because the offeree's acceptance must scrupulously observe the terms of the offer; so an option to renew a lease or to terminate a lease (the so-called 'break-clause') must be punctually exercised because the offeror must know with certainty whether or not the option has been exercised so that he may, if he so wishes, dispose of the property to another[4].

In a bilateral or synallagmatic contract time is of the essence if:

(1)   the parties state expressly that stipulations as to the time by which any step provided for by the particular clause is to be taken are treated as being of the essence[5]; or it may be implied from the interrelationship of the particular clause or clauses with the other clauses of the contract or from the surrounding circumstances including trade custom that the parties have agreed that the time is to be of the essence[6];

(2)   time was made of the essence by subsequent notice[7];

(3)   the delay has been so great as to be evidence of an abandonment of the contract[8], although delay has no such effect if waived by the conduct of the parties[9].

This position is also affected by two important general principles. Firstly, the courts will not order specific performance when to do so would subvert the commercial purpose of a time stipulation[10]. Secondly, consistency and certainty is recognised as of huge importance in all commercial dealings[11].

Although actions founded on simple contract are subject to a six years' statutory limitation period[12], claims for specific performance strictly do not come within this provision[13]. However, courts of equity may by analogy apply this six-year limitation period to claims for specific performance[14].

1   Supreme Court of Judicature Act 1873 s 25(7) (repealed); Law of Property Act 1925 s 41; and see CONTRACT vol 22 (2012) PARA 502.
2   Senior Courts Act 1981 s 49(1).
3   *United Scientific Holdings Ltd v Burnley Borough Council, Cheapside Land Development Co Ltd v Messels Service Co* [1978] AC 904 at 924, 927, 937, 944–945, 949, 957, [1977] 2 All ER 62 at 68, 70, 77–78, 83–84, 88, 93–94, HL.
4   *United Scientific Holdings Ltd v Burnley Borough Council, Cheapside Land Development Co Ltd v Messels Service Co* [1978] AC 904 at 929, 945, 951–952, [1977] 2 All ER 62 at 71, 84, 88–90, HL. See also *Chiltern Court (Baker Street) Residents Ltd v Wallabrook Property Co Ltd* [1988] 2 EGLR 253. As to the exercise of an option to purchase land, see *Di Luca v Juraise (Springs) Ltd* [1998] 18 EG 131, CA.
5   *United Scientific Holdings Ltd v Burnley Borough Council, Cheapside Land Development Co Ltd v Messels Service Co* [1978] AC 904, [1977] 2 All ER 62, HL. See also *Baynham v Guy's Hospital* (1796) 3 Ves 295, where the right of renewal of the lease was forfeited; *Honeyman v Marryat* (1855) 21 Beav 14 (affd (1857) 6 HL Cas 112); *Hudson v Temple* (1860) 29 Beav 536, where the vendor was at liberty to rescind if the purchase was not completed by the date specified; *Barclay v Messenger* (1874) 43 LJ Ch 449, which shows that if time is originally of the essence but is extended, the substituted time is also essential; *Kilmer v British Columbia Orchard Lands Ltd* [1913] AC 319, PC, where time was originally of the essence but the stipulation was waived; *Stickney v Keeble* [1915] AC 386, HL; *Steedman v Drinkle* [1916] 1 AC 275, PC; *Brickles v Snell* [1916] 2 AC 599, PC; *Guerin v Heffernan* [1925] 1 IR 57; *Maredelanto Compania Naviera SA v Bergbau-Handel GmbH, The Mihalis Angelos* [1971] 1 QB 164, [1970] 3 All ER 125; *Bunge Corpn v Tradax SA* [1981] 2 All ER 513, [1981] 1 WLR 711; *Greenwich Marine Inc v Federal Commerce and Navigation Co Ltd, The Mavro Vetranic* [1985] 1 Lloyd's Rep 580; *PT Berlian Laju Tanker TBK v Nuse Shipping Ltd, The Aktor* [2008] EWHC 1330 (Comm), [2008] 2 All ER (Comm) 784, [2008] 2 Lloyd's Rep 246; *Lombard North Central plc v Butterworth* [1987] QB 527, [1987] 1 All ER 267, CA. Cf *Re Sandwell Park Colliery Co, Field v Sandwell Park Colliery Co* [1929] 1 Ch 277, [1928] WN 297 et seq. Equity does not apply its liberal views as to time to the performance of a condition: *Re Sandwell Park Colliery Co, Field v The Co* at 282

per Maugham J; *Factory Holdings Group Ltd v Leboff International Ltd* [1987] 1 EGLR 135 (rent review clause). See also *Lock v Bell* [1931] 1 Ch 35; *Harold Wood Brick Co Ltd v Ferris* [1935] 2 KB 198, CA. But merely specifying a date for performance is not enough: *Vernon v Stephens* (1722) 2 P Wms 66; *Hearne v Tenant* (1807) 13 Vest 287; *Roberts v Berry* (1852) 16 Beav 31 (affd (1853) 3 De GM & G 284); *Parkin v Thorold* (1852) 16 Beav 59. See also CONVEYANCING vol 23 (2016) PARA 246.

6   *United Scientific Holdings Ltd v Burnley Borough Council, Cheapside Land Development Co Ltd v Messels Service Co* [1978] AC 904, [1977] 2 All ER 62, HL. See PARA 577. See also *Parkin v Thorold* (1852) 16 Beav 59 at 65.
7   See PARA 578.
8   See PARA 579.
9   See PARA 581. See also the Limitation Act 1980 s 36(2); and LIMITATION PERIODS vol 68 (2016) PARA 906. As to synallagmatic contracts see further CONTRACT vol 22 (2012) PARA 204.
10 *Union Eagle Ltd v Golden Achievement Ltd* [1997] AC 514, [1997] 2 All ER 215 where the Privy Council refused to order specific performance of a property sale contract when documents were tendered 10 minutes late.
11 *Jindal Iron and Steel Co Ltd v Islamic Solidarity Shipping Co Jordan Inc, The Jordan II* [2004] UKHL 49, [2005] 1 All ER 175, [2005] 1 All ER (Comm) 1.
12 See the Limitation Act 1980 s 5: and LIMITATION PERIODS vol 68 (2016) PARA 956.
13 See the Limitation Act 1980 s 36(1): and LIMITATION PERIODS vol 68 (2016) PARA 954. *P&O Nedlloyd BV v Arab Metals Co (The UB Tiger)* [2006] EWCA Civ 1717, [2007] 2 All ER (Comm) 401, [2007] 1 WLR 2288.
14 See the Limitation Act 1980 s 36(1): and LIMITATION PERIODS vol 68 (2016) PARA 954. See *Firth v Slingsby* (1888) 58 LT 481 at 483. Cf *Talmash v Mugleston* (1826) 4 LJOS 200, where it was held that actions for specific performance were not subject to a six-year limitation period. In practice they are subject to a shorter limitation period: see PARA 579. See also EQUITABLE JURISDICTION vol 47 (2014) PARAS 262–263.

577. **When time is of the essence of a contract.** Time is of the essence of the contract if the parties have expressly stipulated that it should be so[1]. The intention of the parties may also be implied from the interrelationship of various clauses of the contract or otherwise from the surrounding circumstances[2].

If a party has stipulated that, as to certain provisions in his favour, time is to be of the essence of the contract, prima facie the court will hold time as essential in respect of other provisions which are against him[3].

The court may also infer an intention of the parties to treat time as essential by reason of the nature of the contract. Such an intention is inferred in contracts in respect of a reversionary interest[4], or contracts for the sale of land to be used directly for purposes of trade and commerce[5], and, in particular, public houses as going concerns[6], and of mines[7], or contracts relating to things which are subject to fluctuations in value[8]. That time is of the essence may also be inferred from the surrounding circumstances including trade customs[9] in contemplation of which the contract is made, for example the purchase of a reversionary interest which becomes progressively more valuable[10] or a house for immediate occupation as a residence[11]. In all these instances delay in completing the contract would involve hardship to the other party[12]. In contrast, a provision that the purchaser is to pay interest on the purchase money in the event of non-completion by the day appointed is a sufficient indication that the time fixed for completion was not intended to be of the essence of the contract[13]. Similarly, if a clause in a contract which makes a time stipulation as to the exercise of a right is entered into for the benefit of both parties (such as a rent review clause), then time is not presumptively of the essence of the contract unless the delay is so prolonged as to deprive the other party of substantially the whole benefit which it was intended that he should obtain under the contract[14]. However, a stipulation that a contract ceases to be enforceable after a certain period may well preclude both an action for performance and an action for damages founded upon that contract[15].

1   See PARA 576.

2   *United Scientific Holdings Ltd v Burnley Borough Council, Cheapside Land Development Co Ltd v Messels Service Co* [1978] AC 904, [1977] 2 All ER 62, HL; *Hammond v Allen* [1994] 1 All ER 307.

3   *Seaton v Mapp* (1846) 2 Coll 556 at 564 ('the plaintiffs' proposition is that the purchaser shall be held by a cable, and the vendors by a skein of silk'); *Upperton v Nickolson* (1871) 6 Ch App 436, where time was specified to be of the essence in the case of the purchaser's obligation, but not of the vendors; *C Richards & Son v Karenita Ltd* (1971) 221 Estates Gazette 25, where the tenant's right to break the lease was interlocked with the landlord's right to serve a notice for rent review, as interpreted in *United Scientific Holdings Ltd v Burnley Borough Council, Cheapside Land Development Co Ltd v Messels Service Co* [1978] AC 904 at 962, [1977] 2 All ER 62 at 98, HL. Cf *Re Todd and M' Fadden's Contract* [1908] 1 IR 213.

4   *Newman v Rogers* (1793) 4 Bro CC 391; *Spurrier v Hancock* (1799) 4 Ves 667. Cf *Levy v Stogdon* [1899] 1 Ch 5, CA, and distinguish *Patrick v Milner* (1877) 2 CPD 342 (special conditions).

5   *Wright v Howard* (1823) 1 Sim & St 190 (mills); *Coslake v Till* (1826) 1 Russ 376; *Walker v Jeffreys* (1842) 1 Hare 341; *Dyas v Rooney* (1890) 27 LR Ir 4 (Ir CA) (pasture land for stocking).

6   *Cowles v Gale* (1871) 7 Ch App 12, CA. Cf *Seaton v Mapp* (1846) 2 Coll 556; *Day v Luhke* (1868) LR 5 Eq 336; *Claydon v Green* (1868) LR 3 CP 511; *Tadcaster Tower Brewery Co v Wilson* [1897] 1 Ch 705 at 711 per Romer J; *Lock v Bell* [1931] 1 Ch 35 (sale to be completed 'on or about' a specified date).

7   *London (City) v Mitford* (1807) 14 Ves 41 at 58; *Parker v Frith* (1819) 1 Sim & St 199n; *Walker v Jeffreys* (1842) 1 Hare 341; *Eads v Williams* (1854) 4 De GM & G 674; *MacBryde v Weekes* (1856) 22 Beav 533; *Clegg v Edmondson* (1857) 8 De GM & G 787; *Alloway v Braine* (1859) 26 Beav 575; *Huxham v Llewellyn* (1873) 21 WR 570 at 766; *Glasbrook v Richardson* (1874) 23 WR 51; *Nicholson v Smith* (1822) 22 ChD 640.

8   *Withy v Cottle* (1823) Turn & R 78 (annuities); *Doloret v Rothschild* (1824) 1 Sim & St 590 (government stock); *Payne v Banner* (1846) 15 LJ Ch 227 (contract relating to patents); *Pollard v Clayton* (1855) 1 K & J 462 (coal). The position is similar in the case of contracts relating to shares: see *Sparks v Liverpool Waterworks Co* (1807) 13 Ves 428; *Campbell v London and Brighton Rly Co* (1846) 5 Hare 519; *Re Schwabacher, Stern v Schwabacher, Koritschoner's Claim* (1907) 98 LT 127 at 129; *Hare v Nicoll* [1966] 2 QB 130, [1966] 1 All ER 285, CA (highly speculative shares; commercial transaction). Where no time is fixed, the obligation is to deliver in a reasonable time: *De Waal v Adler* (1886) 12 App Cas 141, PC; and see COMPANIES vol 15A (2016) PARA 1907.

9   See *Maredelanto Compania Naviera SA v Bergbau-Handel GmbH, The Mihalis Angelos* [1971] 1 QB 164, [1970] 3 All ER 125 (considering on 'expected ready to load' clause in a charterparty) and *Bunge Corpn v Tradax SA* [1981] 2 All ER 513, [1981] 1 WLR 711 (generalising mercantile custom to a general presumption that time stipulations in commercial contracts were intended to be 'conditions').

10 *Newman v Rogers* (1793) 4 Bro CC 391.

11 *Seaton v Mapp* (1846) 2 Coll 556; *Nokes v Lord Kilmorey* (1847) 1 De G & Sm 444; *Tilley v Thomas* (1867) 3 Ch App 61. However, this inference may be excluded by the conditions of the contract: see *Webb v Hughes* (1870) LR 10 Eq 281. The purchaser's motives will not be taken into consideration in construing stipulations as to time unless they are expressed in the contract or were made known to the vendor: *Boehm v Wood* (1820) 1 Jac & W 419; *Nokes v Lord Kilmorey* above.

12 *Coslake v Till* (1826) 1 Russ 376; *Carter v Dean and Chapter of Ely* (1834) 7 Sim 211, where the contract was for the grant of a lease by an ecclesiastical corporation for a consideration divisible among the existing members; *Roberts v Berry* (1853) 3 De GM & G 284; *Green v Sevin* (1879) 13 Ch 589. See CONVEYANCING vol 23 (2016) PARA 246.

13 *Patrick v Milner* (1877) 2 CPD 342; *Hatten v Russell* (1888) 38 ChD 334.

14 *United Scientific Holdings Ltd v Burnley Borough Council, Cheapside Land Development Co Ltd v Messels Service Co* [1978] AC 904, [1977] 2 All ER 62, HL, overruling *Samuel Properties (Developments) Ltd v Hayek* [1972] 3 All ER 473, [1972] 1 WLR 1296, CA, and *Mount Charlotte Investments Ltd v Leek and Westbourne Building Society* [1976] 1 All ER 890, 30 P & CR 410.

15 See *Smith v Lindsay & Kirk* (No 1) [2000] SC 200, [2000] SLT 287, Ct of Sess, Inner House.

578.   Time made of the essence by notice. Even though time is not initially of the essence of the contract, it may be made so by notice given by one party to the contract to the other. If the contract for the sale of property fixed a date for completion or performance of some intermediate obligation, such as delivery of an abstract of title, the failure of one party to the contract either to complete or to perform the intermediate obligation by the stipulated date entitles the other party then and there to serve a notice making time of the essence, even though the time fixed by the contract was not of the essence of the contract[1]. He does not have to wait until there has been unreasonable delay by the party in breach before serving such a notice[2]. In the case of an open contract where no date for completion or for the performance of any intermediate obligation is fixed, the law implies a term that the contract will be completed or the obligation performed within a reasonable time from the date of the contract. In this case, a notice making time of the essence of the contract cannot be given until there has been an unreasonable delay, because it is only then that there is a breach of the contract[3]. There may, of course, be a special provision in the conditions of sale of a particular contract[4].

The notice is essential[5], and must be clear and unequivocal[6]. It may, it seems, be given orally[7]. It must limit a time within which the party in default must perform his obligation and, if the notice fixes a time which in all the circumstances is reasonable, the time so fixed will be considered by the court as having become of the essence of the contract[8].

Unless the contract otherwise provides, the time specified in the notice must be reasonable[9]. Whether the time given in the notice is reasonable is a question of fact[10] depending on the circumstances; for example, the person pressing for completion may have given a similar notice in the past, compliance with which he has waived, or there may be a special need for early completion or the parties may have been in negotiation as to the matter[11]. If, however, the contract provides for a specific period of notice which must be given for the purpose of making time of the essence, the question whether the specified period is reasonable in the circumstances does not arise[12].

Since strictly speaking an action for specific performance may be begun even where the defendant is not in breach[13], it follows that proceedings may be brought before any notice making time of the essence has expired or even been served.

1 *Behzadi v Shaftesbury Hotels Ltd* [1992] Ch 1, [1991] 2 All ER 477, CA, disapproving *Smith v Hamilton* [1951] Ch 174, [1950] 2 All ER 928, and following *Neeta (Epping) Pty Ltd v Phillips* (1974) 131 CLR 286 (Aust HC); *Winchcombe Carson Trustee Co Ltd v Ball-Rand Pty Ltd* [1974] 1 NSWLR 477 (NSW); *O' Sullivan v Moodie* [1977] 1 NZLR 643 (NZ SC); *Louinder v Leis* (1982) 149 CLR 509 (Aust HC); and see *Re Olympia & York Canary Wharf Ltd, American Express Europe Ltd v Adamson* [1993] BCC 154. As to payment of a deposit see *Willmott (John) Homes Ltd v Read* (1986) 51 P & CR 90, (1985) Times, 6 May but note *Willmott (John) Homes Ltd v Read* overruled in *Samarenko v Dawn Hill House Ltd* [2011] EWCA Civ 1445, [2013] Ch 36, [2012] 2 All ER 476. See also *Raineri v Miles* [1981] AC 1050, [1980] 2 All ER 145, HL; and see *Urban 1 (Blonk Street) Ltd v Ayres* [2013] EWCA Civ 816, [2014] 1 WLR 756, [2013] All ER (D) 77 (Jul) (failure to comply with notice to complete on ground of alleged repudiatory breach by party serving notice).
2 Prior to *Behzadi v Shaftesbury Hotels Ltd* [1992] Ch 1, [1991] 2 All ER 477, CA, it was thought that an innocent party could not serve a notice making time of the essence until there had been an unreasonable delay on the part of the other party: see *Taylor v Brown* (1839) 2 Beav 180; *King v Wilson* (1843) 6 Beav 124; *Benson v Lamb* (1846) 9 Beav 502; *Pegg v Wisden* (1852) 16 Beav 239; *Green v Sevin* (1879) 13 ChD 589; *Compton v Bagley* [1892] 1 Ch 313; *Stickney v Keeble* [1915] AC 386; *Irani (Jamshed Khodaram) v Burjorji Dhunjibhai* (1915) 32 TLR 156, PC; *Smith v Hamilton* [1951] Ch 174, [1950] 2 All ER 928; *British and Commonwealth Holdings plc v Quadrex Holdings Inc* [1989] QB 842, [1989] 3 All ER 492, CA; *Delta Vale Properties Ltd v Mills* [1990] 2 All ER 176, [1990] 1 WLR 445, CA. See CONTRACT vol 22 (2012) PARA 499 et seq; CONVEYANCING vol 23 (2016) PARA 246.
3 *Behzadi v Shaftesbury Hotels Ltd* [1992] Ch 1, [1991] 2 All ER 477, CA.
4 *Cumberland Court (Brighton) Ltd v Taylor* [1964] Ch 29, [1963] 2 All ER 536. See *Re Barr's Contract, Moorwell Holdings Ltd v Barr* [1956] Ch 551, [1956] 2 All ER 853.
5 *Urban 1 (Blonk Street) Ltd v Ayres* [2013] EWCA Civ 816, [2014] 1 WLR 756, [2014] 1 P & CR 1.

6 *Reynolds v Nelson* (1821) 6 Madd 18; *Delta Vale Properties Ltd v Mills* [1990] 2 All ER 176, [1990] 1 WLR 445, CA. The notice should require completion by the date named and state that in default the contract will be rescinded: *Hatten v Russell* (1888) 38 ChD 334 at 346.

7 *Nokes v Lord Kilmorey* (1847) 1 De G & Sm 444. Cf *Spiro v Glencrown Properties Ltd* [1991] Ch 537, [1991] 1 All ER 600.

8 *King v Wilson* (1843) 6 Beav 124. As to the question of reasonableness see *King v Wilson*; *Parkin v Thorold* (1852) 16 Beav 59; *Pegg v Wisden* (1852) 16 Beav 239; *Nott v Riccard* (1856) 22 Beav 307, where short notice was justified by the previous refusal of the party in default; *Wells v Maxwell* (1863) 32 Beav 408 (affd 33 LJ Ch 44); *Crawford v Toogood* (1879) 13 ChD 153; *Re Barr's Contract, Moorwell Holdings Ltd v Barr* [1956] Ch 551, [1956] 2 All ER 853, where the failure of an anticipated subsale for which the vendors were agents meant that notice to complete within 28 days, in accordance with the conditions of sale, was not reasonable and was therefore ineffective; *Behzadi v Shaftesbury Hotels Ltd* [1992] Ch 1, [1991] 2 All ER 477, CA. Where the nature of the contract involves expedition, a notice that would in other cases be unreasonably short may suffice: see *MacBryde v Weekes* (1856) 22 Beav 533, where, in a contract to grant a mining lease, one month's notice was good; *Compton v Bagley* [1892] 1 Ch 313, where 14 days' notice was enough on the purchase of a farm for the purchaser's personal occupation. A notice conditionally waived revives on failure of the condition: *Stewart v Smith* (1824) 6 Hare 222n.

9 *Re Barr's Contract, Moorwell Holdings Ltd v Barr* [1956] Ch 551, [1956] 2 All ER 853.

10 *United Scientific Holdings Ltd v Burnley Borough Council, Cheapside Land Development Co Ltd v Messels Service Co* [1978] AC 904 at 946, [1977] 2 All ER 62 at 85, HL.

11 *Stickney v Keeble* [1915] AC 386 at 419, HL; *Ajit (Chintamanie) v Joseph Mootoo Sammy* [1967] AC 255, [1966] 3 WLR 983, PC.

12 *Cumberland Court (Brighton) Ltd v Taylor* [1964] Ch 29, [1963] 2 All ER 536.

13 *Hasham v Zenab* [1960] AC 316, [1960] 2 WLR 374, 104 Sol Jo 125.

(ii) Acquiescence, Laches and Waiver

579. Delay constituting evidence of abandonment. Where time is not originally of the essence of the contract and has not been made so by notice, delay by a party in performing his part of the contract, or in commencing or prosecuting the enforcement of his rights, may constitute such laches or acquiescence as will debar him from obtaining specific performance[1].

Normally the delay will arise from the claimant's failure to issue his writ in the action, but his laches may bar his equitable relief if, having issued the writ, he delays in bringing the action to trial[2].

The extent of delay which has this effect varies with circumstances, but as a rule must be capable of being construed as amounting to an abandonment of the contract[3]. Any period of delay may be fatal if it is delay in declaring an option or exercising any other unilateral right such as a tenant's right to exercise an option to determine a lease[4]; and if the other party has already given notice that he does not intend to perform the contract, the party aggrieved must take proceedings promptly if he desires to obtain specific performance[5].

1 *Lloyd v Collett* (1793) 4 Bro CC 469; *Fordyce v Ford* (1794) 4 Bro CC 494; *Harrington v Wheeler* (1799) 4 Ves 686; *Moore v Blake* (1808) 1 Ball & B 62; *Eads v Williams* (1854) 4 De GM & G 674 at 691 per Lord Cranworth LC; *Rich v Gale* (1871) 24 LT 745; *Lamare v Dixon* (1873) LR 6 HL 414; *Dean v Upton* (1990) Times, 10 May, CA; *Heath v Heath* [2009] EWHC 1908 (Ch), [2010] 1 FLR 610 (specific performance was refused of an agreement based upon a serious misunderstanding and where there was a long delay in seeking specific performance. Either factor alone would have justified the refusal). Cf *Simpson v Connolly* [1953] 2 All ER 474, [1953] 1 WLR 911, where on an agreement to extinguish a debt which was conditional on certain land being transferred there was undue delay in transferring the land; *Amherst v James Walker Goldsmith & Silversmith Ltd* [1983] Ch 305, [1983] 2 All ER 1067, CA. As to laches generally see EQUITABLE JURISDICTION vol 47 (2014) PARA 253 et seq. See also LIMITATION PERIODS vol 68 (2016) PARA 906.

2 *Towli v Fourth River Property Co Ltd, Michaelides v Cormican Properties Ltd* (1976) Times, 24 November, where a delay of nine years between the issue of the writ and the hearing was fatal.

Cf *Du Sautoy v Symes* [1967] Ch 1146 at 1168, [1967] 1 All ER 25 at 37, where three years' delay was not fatal.
3   *Marquis of Hertford v Boore* (1801) 5 Ves 719 (14 months' delay not a bar); *Southcomb v Bishop of Exeter* (1847) 6 Hare 213 (18 months' delay a bar); *Eads v Williams* (1854) 4 De GM & G 674 (lease of coal mines; three and a half years' delay a bar); *Lazard Bros & Co Ltd v Fairfield Properties Co (Mayfair) Ltd* (1977) 121 Sol Jo 793 (delay of two years before issue of writ); see [1978] The Conveyancer and Property Lawyer 184. See *Lord James Stuart v London and North Western Rly Co* (1852) 1 De GM & G 721; *Moore v Marrable* (1866) 1 Ch App 217.
4   *United Scientific Holdings Ltd v Burnley Borough Council, Cheapside Land Development Co Ltd v Messels Service Co* [1978] AC 904, [1977] 2 All ER 62, HL. See also *Brooke v Garrod* (1857) 3 K & J 608; *Lord Ranelagh v Mellon* (1864) 2 Drew & Sm 278; *Weston v Collins* (1865) 34 LJ Ch 353. Cf *Austin v Tawney* (1867) 2 Ch App 143; *Lord Darnley v London, Chatham and Dover Rly Co* (1867) LR 2 HL 43; *Nicholson v Smith* (1882) 22 ChD 640. The rule does not apply if no time is fixed originally: *Moss v Barton* (1866) LR 1 Eq 474; *Buckland v Papillon* (1866) 2 Ch App 67; *Re Adams and Kensington Vestry* (1883) 24 ChD 199; affd (1884) 27 ChD 394, CA.
5   *Heaphy v Hill* (1824) 2 Sim & St 29; *Watson v Reid* (1830) 1 Russ & M 236; *Parkin v Thorold* (1852) 16 Beav 59 at 73; *Lehmann v McArthur* (1868) 3 Ch App 496; *Huxham v Llewellyn* (1873) 21 WR 570, 766.

580. Delay in enforcing judgment. Leave to enforce a decree of specific performance will be refused if it is inequitable to the party in breach so to decree, as where the claimant has been guilty of extraordinary delay and has no reasonable explanation or excuse for allowing the judgment to remain unenforced for so long[1]. If the claimant has acted reasonably in waiting, the mere fact that the defendant has suffered detriment through the lapse of time is not sufficient ground for refusing specific performance[2].

1   *Easton v Brown* [1981] 3 All ER 278, applying *McKenna v Richey* [1950] VLR 360 (Vict).
2   *Easton v Brown* [1981] 3 All ER 278, applying *McKenna v Richey* [1950] VLR 360 (Vict).

581. When delay is no bar to relief. Delay does not bar a claim to specific performance if the claimant has been in substantial possession of the benefits under the contract, and is merely claiming the completion of the legal estate[1], or if the delay is due to negotiations between the parties on the question in dispute[2]. Nor can the benefit of delay be claimed by the party causing it, for example where it has been caused by improper objections which he has taken[3].

Delay may, however, be fatal when the contract which is the basis of the claimant's title is in dispute[4]. Moreover, the defence of delay is waived if, after such a lapse of time as would entitle a party to resist specific performance on that ground, the party so entitled proceeds to deal with the other party regardless of the delay[5]. He is held to have waived the defence only if he acted with full knowledge of the facts[6].

1   *Crofton v Ormsby* (1806) 2 Sch & Lef 583 at 603; *Clarke v Moore* (1844) 1 Jo & Lat 723, where the tenant was in possession under an agreement, and delay was no bar to claiming specific performance of the agreement to accept the lease; *Burke v Smyth* (1846) 3 Jo & Lat 193; *Sharp v Milligan* (1856) 22 Beav 606; *Shepheard v Walker* (1875) LR 20 Eq 659; *Williams v Greatrex* [1956] 3 All ER 705, [1957] 1 WLR 31, CA, where a delay of ten years was not fatal. Such possession must purport to be under the contract and be recognised as such: *Mills v Haywood* (1877) 6 ChD 196, CA. Cf *Lamare v Dixon* (1873) LR 6 HL 414, where objections by the intending lessee were not waived by his continuing in possession and paying rent under protest. The mere leaving of a deposit does not constitute acquiescence on the part of a purchaser: *Watson v Reid* (1830) 1 Russ & M 236. See also *Voyce v Voyce* (1991) 62 P & CR 290, CA.
2   *Southcomb v Bishop of Exeter* (1847) 6 Hare 213; *Gee v Pearse* (1848) 2 De G & Sm 325; *McMurray v Spicer* (1868) LR 5 Eq 527.
3   *Morse v Merest* (1821) 6 Madd 26; *Shrewsbury and Birmingham Rly Co v London and North Western Rly Co etc* (1850) 2 Mac & G 324; *Monro v Taylor* (1852) 3 Mac & G 713.
4   *Joyce v Joyce* [1979] 1 All ER 175, [1978] 1 WLR 1170.
5   *Seton v Slade, Hunter v Seton* (1802) 7 Ves 265 (examining abstract after time expired); *King v Wilson* (1843) 6 Beav 124. Cf *Pincke v Curteis* (1793) 4 Bro CC 329; *Hudson v Bartram* (1818) 3 Madd 440 (waiver by accepting payment after forfeiture by non-payment); *Hipwell v Knight*

(1835) 1 Y & C Ex 401; *Re Eastern Counties Railway Act, ex p Gardner* (1841) 4 Y & C Ex 503; *Pegg v Wisden* (1852) 16 Beav 239; *Webb v Hughes* (1870) LR 10 Eq 281. Other instances of waiver by conduct are *Boehm v Wood* (1820) 1 Jac & W 419 at 420; *Cutts v Thodey* (1842) 13 Sim 206; *Eads v Williams* (1854) 4 De GM & G 674; but see *Barclay v Messenger* (1874) 43 LJ Ch 449, where there was held to be no waiver of the time of payment by giving permission before that time.

6   *Lord Darnley v London, Chatham and Dover Rly Co* (1863) 1 De GJ & Sim 204.

(11) PUBLIC POLICY

582.   Enforcement contrary to public policy. Specific performance may be denied if it would be contrary to public policy to enforce the contract specifically. The fact that the public would be misled as to the authorship of a literary work if the contract, which provided for the naming as author of a person who had not written the work, were to be performed has been held to be a good ground for refusing specific performance, for this would be fraud on the public[1]. In an appropriate case specific performance may also be refused where there is a risk of public disorder if a contract to grant a licence to use a public building were to be enforced[2]. Against such a consideration must be weighed the individual's right to exercise his freedom of speech and of assembly[3].

Specific performance may be refused if it would be contrary to the European Convention on Human Rights[4].

1   *Post v Marsh* (1880) 16 ChD 395. Fry on Specific Performance (6th Edn) 343 suggests that the fraud of a third person, without the plaintiff's connivance, which induced the defendant to enter into the contract might be a sufficient defence. But there has been no such case, and in *Union Bank of London v Munster* (1887) 37 ChD 51, Jessel MR was sceptical whether such a defence could ever succeed.

2   Cf *Verrall v Great Yarmouth Borough Council* [1981] QB 202, [1980] 1 All ER 839, CA, where this argument was rejected on the particular facts.

3   See *Miller v Jackson* [1977] QB 966, [1977] 3 All ER 338, CA, where an injunction was refused on the ground of public interest; cf *Kennaway v Thompson* [1981] QB 88, [1980] 3 All ER 329, CA, where an injunction was granted. See *Imutran Ltd v Uncaged Campaigns Ltd* [2001] 2 All ER 385, [2002] FSR 20, [2001] IP & T 573, where an interim injunction was continued and the court discussed whether the availability of injunctive relief was restricted by the right to free expression and the Human Rights Act 1998 s 12 (see RIGHTS AND FREEDOMS vol 88A (2013) PARA 430).

4   See *Ashworth v Royal National Theatre* [2014] EWHC 1176 (QB), [2014] 4 All ER 238.

3. PROCEEDINGS FOR SPECIFIC PERFORMANCE

(1) INSTITUTION OF PROCEEDINGS

(i) Tribunals having Jurisdiction

583. The High Court. Claims for the specific performance of contracts relating to the sale, exchange or partition of land[1] or the raising of charges on land[2] are expressly assigned to the Chancery Division[3]. Claims for the specific performance of an agreement relating to the carriage of goods in a ship[4] or to the use or hire of a ship[5] are assigned to the Queen's Bench Division and taken by the Admiralty Court[6]. Claims for the specific performance of contracts of any other kind may be instituted at the claimant's option in any Division of the High Court[7] subject to the power to transfer claims from one Division to another[8] or from the High Court to the County Court[9]. If a counterclaim for specific performance[10] of a contract relating to the sale, exchange or partition of land is raised in proceedings commenced in the Queen's Bench Division, the court will generally accede to an application for transfer of the proceedings to the Chancery Division[11].

1   As to the formation of contracts for the sale of land see CONVEYANCING vol 23 (2016) PARA 25 et seq; as to specific performance of contracts for the sale of land see CONVEYANCING vol 23 (2016) PARA 453 et seq; and as to the exchange of land see REAL PROPERTY AND REGISTRATION vol 87 (2012) PARA 253 et seq.
2   As to charges on land see MORTGAGE vol 77 (2016) PARA 261 et seq.
3   See the Senior Courts Act 1981 s 61(1), Sch 1 para 1(a); and CIVIL PROCEDURE vol 11 (2015) PARA 136. As to the meaning of 'land' see PARA 501 note 18.
4   As to the carriage of goods by sea see *Petrofina SA v AOT Ltd, The Maersk Nimrod* [1992] QB 571, [1991] 3 All ER 161; and CARRIAGE AND CARRIERS vol 7 (2015) PARA 206 et seq.
5   As to contracts for the hire of a ship see SHIPPING AND MARITIME LAW vol 93 (2008) PARA 111 et seq.
6   See the Senior Courts Act 1981 ss 20(1)(a), (2)(h), 62(2), Sch 1 para 2(c); and SHIPPING AND MARITIME LAW vol 93 (2008) PARAS 85, 111.
7   See the Senior Courts Act 1981 s 64; and CIVIL PROCEDURE vol 11 (2015) PARA 95. In practice, specific performance claims are not heard in the Family Division, since specific performance of an agreement relating to any matters involving the upbringing of a child will not be granted: see PARA 531.
8   See the Senior Courts Act 1981 s 65; and CIVIL PROCEDURE vol 11 (2015) PARA 106.
9   See the County Courts Act 1984 s 40; and CIVIL PROCEDURE vol 11 (2015) PARA 108.
10   As to counterclaims for specific performance see CIVIL PROCEDURE vol 11 (2015) PARA 367 et seq.
11   *Hillman v Mayhew* (1876) 1 Ex D 132; *Holloway v York* (1877) 2 Ex D 333, CA; *London Land Co v Harris* (1884) 13 QBD 540. *Cf Storey v Waddle* (1879) 4 QBD 289, CA.

584. The County Court. The County Court[1] has jurisdiction to hear and determine proceedings for the specific performance of any agreement for the sale, purchase or lease of property[2] where, in the case of a sale or purchase, the purchase money[3] or, in the case of a lease, the value of the property[4] does not exceed the County Court limit[5], or where the parties have agreed that the County Court is to have jurisdiction in the proceedings[6]. Claims commenced in the County Court may be transferred to the High Court by order of the High Court or the County Court[7].

The County Court may also grant a mandatory injunction, which operates in effect as a specific performance order, as ancillary relief in an action claiming damages for breach of contract within the statutory jurisdiction of the court[8].

1   As to the County Court generally see COURTS AND TRIBUNALS vol 24 (2010) PARA 758 et seq. As to transfers within the County Court see CPR 30.2, 30.4, 30.7; and as to classification of courts see COURTS AND TRIBUNALS vol 24 (2010) PARA 616 et seq.
2   As to specific performance of contracts for the sale of land see CONVEYANCING vol 23 (2016) PARA 453 et seq. It appears that an agreement for the exchange of property or for some other transaction in which the consideration for the transfer does not consist primarily of money is not an agreement for the sale or purchase of property: see *Robshaw Bros Ltd v Mayer* [1957] Ch 125, [1956] 3 All ER 833; *Doyle v East* [1972] 2 All ER 1013, [1972] 1 WLR 1080.
3   In the case of sale or purchase, it does not matter that the value of the property may exceed the statutory limit if the purchase price is within it: *R v Judge Whitehorne* [1904] 1 KB 827, DC. As to purchase money on a contract for the sale of land see CONVEYANCING vol 23 (2016) PARA 228.
4   In the case of a lease, it is the value of the freehold, and not the value of the leasehold interest, which governs jurisdiction: *Angel v Jay* [1911] 1 KB 666, DC.
5   County Courts Act 1984 s 23(d) (amended by the Crime and Courts Act 2013 Sch 9 paras 1, 10(1)). 'The County Court limit' means the limit for the time being specified by an order under the County Courts Act 1984 s 145: s 147(1). For this purpose the current limit is £350,000: County Court Jurisdiction Order 2014, SI 2014/503, art 3, Table. As to the general equity jurisdiction of the County Court see COURTS AND TRIBUNALS vol 24 (2010) PARA 776.
6   See the County Courts Act 1984 s 24; and COURTS AND TRIBUNALS vol 24 (2010) PARA 776.
7   See the County Courts Act 1984 s 41; and CIVIL PROCEDURE vol 11 (2015) PARA 108. See also CPR 30.3, 30.4, 30.8; and as to the original jurisdiction of the County Court see COURTS AND TRIBUNALS vol 24 (2010) PARA 767.
8   See the County Courts Act 1984 s 38(1); and CIVIL PROCEDURE vol 12 (2015) PARA 1082; COURTS AND TRIBUNALS vol 24 (2010) PARA 768. See also *Bourne v McDonald* [1950] 2 KB 422, [1950] 2 All ER 183, CA. As to mandatory injunctions generally see CIVIL PROCEDURE vol 12 (2015) PARA 1102 et seq.

585. **Arbitrators.** Where a written agreement contains a provision for submitting disputes as to the performance of a contract, other than a contract relating to land, to arbitration and does not express a contrary intention, the arbitrators or umpire have the same power as the High Court[1] to order specific performance of the contract[2].

1   As to the court's power to order specific performance see PARA 532.
2   See the Arbitration Act 1996 s 48 (s 48(5)(b) in particular); and ARBITRATION vol 2 (2017) PARA 559.

(ii) Nature of Proceedings

586. **Form of proceedings.** Proceedings in the High Court to obtain a judgment for specific performance are usually commenced in the Chancery Division, even if not expressly assigned to it[1], as the machinery of the Chancery Division is better adapted to the complicated procedure which is often necessary for the carrying into effect of an order for specific performance[2]. In relatively simple claims the claimant will generally wish to apply for summary judgment[3].

1   As to the assignment of claims for specific performance to the Chancery Division or the Queen's Bench Division see PARA 583. As to the jurisdiction of the County Court see PARA 584.
2   As to proceedings after judgment see PARA 636 et seq.
3   Ie in most cases summary judgment pursuant to CPR Pt 24: see PARA 602 et seq; and CIVIL PROCEDURE vol 12 (2015) PARA 549 et seq. As to how to start the proceedings and the claim form see CPR Pt 7; CPR PD 7A—How to Start Proceedings–The Claim Form; and CIVIL PROCEDURE vol 11 (2015) PARA 138 et seq.

587. **Vendor and purchaser summonses.** A vendor or purchaser of any interest in land or their representatives respectively may apply in a summary way to the court

in respect of any requisitions[1] or objections or any claim for compensation or any other question arising out of or connected with the contract, not being a question affecting the existence or validity of the contract[2]. Such an application is made by originating summons and is known as a 'vendor and purchaser summons'[3]. This procedure can be used as a relatively cheap and quick alternative to a full specific performance claim, particularly where a specific objection to title is raised and the parties accept that the contract must stand or fall by the validity of that objection[4]. The jurisdiction is not limited to issues of title but can be invoked to decide such matters as a question of construction of the contract, a dispute over the proper form of the conveyance or transfer, or a question as to the validity of a notice to rescind[5]. The jurisdiction can be exercised even if the validity or enforceability of the contract is not admitted[6]. However, especially if it decides that this is not appropriate for deciding disputed areas of fact, the court may order the claim to continue as if it had not used this procedure and give appropriate directions[7]. The court cannot make an order for specific performance or award damages on a vendor and purchaser summons, but if the court sustains an objection to title it may grant consequential relief, such as a declaration that the contract is rescinded and an order that the vendor return the deposit with interest and pay the purchaser's costs of investigating title[8]. The court cannot make an award of 'compensation' if the claim is in truth for damages over and above interest and the costs of investigating title[9].

The County Court has jurisdiction under the above provisions where the land which is to be dealt with in the court does not exceed £30,000 in capital value[10].

1 As to requisitions on title see CONVEYANCING vol 23 (2016) PARA 199 et seq.
2 See the Law of Property Act 1925 s 49(1): and CONVEYANCING vol 23 (2016) PARA 470. The jurisdiction extends to contracts for exchange (see s 49(3)), and has been exercised in relation to contracts for the grant of leases (*Re Anderton and Milner's Contract* (1890) 45 ChD 476 (lease at a premium); *Re Lander and Bagley's Contract* [1892] 3 Ch 41 (lease without a premium)). Cf, however, *Young v Markworth Properties Ltd* [1965] Ch 475, [1965] 1 All ER 834, Lands Tribunal, where the grant of a lease at a premium was held not to be a 'sale'.
3 As to vendor and purchaser summonses generally see CONVEYANCING vol 23 (2016) PARA 470.
4 See CONVEYANCING vol 23 (2016) PARA 470.
5 *Re Jackson and Woodburn's Contract* (1887) 37 ChD 44.
6 *Re Lander and Bagley's Contract* [1892] 3 Ch 41; *Re Hughes and Ashley's Contract* [1900] 2 Ch 595, CA.
7 See eg now CPR 8.1(3); CIVIL PROCEDURE vol 11 (2015) PARA 150 et seq; and see also *Re Hare and O' More's Contract* [1901] 1 Ch 93.
8 *Re Hargreaves and Thompson's Contract* (1886) 32 ChD 454, CA; *Re Higgins and Percival* (1888) 57 LJ Ch 807; *Re Walker and Oakshott's Contract* [1901] 2 Ch 383.
9 *Re Hargreaves and Thompson's Contract* (1886) 32 ChD 454, CA; *Re Wilson's and Stevens' Contract* [1894] 3 Ch 546.
10 See the Law of Property Act 1925 s 49(4); and CONVEYANCING vol 23 (2016) PARA 470.

(iii) Parties

588. Parties to the contract. Usually, the parties to a claim for specific performance will be the parties to the contract[1]. For this purpose, a contract entered into by an agent having actual, implied or ostensible authority to contract on behalf of his principal[2] or which is subsequently ratified by the principal[3] will be treated as having been made by the principal, and can generally be enforced directly by or against the principal[4]. Where there has been a novation of the contract[5] resulting from an agreement by all parties that a new person should be introduced as party to the contract in place of an original party who is discharged, the contract is enforceable against the new party to the contract and not against his predecessor[6]. A person purporting to act as agent for a third party but in fact

acting on his own behalf may enforce the contract in his own name against the
other party to the contract unless that other party has been prejudiced by the
former's representation that he was acting as an agent[7].

1   As to parties to contracts for the sale of land see CONVEYANCING vol 23 (2016) PARA 157 et seq;
    and as to parties to claims generally see CIVIL PROCEDURE vol 11 (2015) PARA 469 et seq.
2   As to the authority of an agent see AGENCY vol 1 (2008) PARA 29 et seq; and as to the liability
    of the principal see AGENCY vol 1 (2008) PARA 121 et seq.
3   As to ratification of an agent's acts see AGENCY vol 1 (2008) PARA 57 et seq.
4   As to the principal's liability for contracts entered into by the agent see AGENCY vol 1 (2008)
    PARA 125 et seq; and as to exceptions to a principal's liability see AGENCY vol 1 (2008)
    PARAS 127–131.
5   As to novation of contracts see CONTRACT vol 22 (2012) PARAS 598–604.
6   *Holden v Hayn and Bacon* (1815) 1 Mer 47; *Stanley v Chester and Birkenhead Rly Co* (1838) 9
    Sim 264; *Shaw v Fisher* (1855) 5 De GM & G 596; *Coles v Bristowe* (1868) 4 Ch App 3; *Hawkins
    v Maltby* (1869) 4 Ch App 200.
7   *Fellowes v Lord Gwydyr* (1829) 1 Russ & M 83; *Gewa Chartering BV v Remco Shipping
    Lines Ltd, The Remco* [1984] 2 Lloyd's Rep 205.

589. Strangers to the contract. As a general rule, the obligation to perform a
contract cannot be assigned by the promisor to a third person except by novation
with the consent of the promisee[1]. This means that the contract cannot be
enforced against a stranger[2]. There are certain exceptions to this rule; in
particular, contracts may in certain circumstances be enforced against a transferee
of the subject matter of the contract[3]. By contrast, the benefit of a contract can be
assigned and the assignee will normally be able to enforce the contract against a
party who contracted with the assignor[4]. In the case of the death or bankruptcy
of a contracting party, both the benefit and burden of a contract may pass by
operation of law to the personal representatives[5] or trustee in bankruptcy[6]. Apart
from cases of assignment or transfer of the benefit of a contract by operation of
law, a stranger to the contract cannot normally enforce it[7]. The Contracts (Rights
of Third Parties) Act 1999 provides that a third party may, when the provisions
of the Act have not been excluded and the third party is expressly identified[8],
enforce a contractual provision in his own right if either, the contract expressly
states that he may[9] or the term purports to confer a benefit on him[10]. It now seems
that the identification of the third party in the contract as the recipient of a benefit
creates a rebuttable presumption that it was intended thereby to confer on him an
enforceable right[11]. The Contracts (Rights of Third Parties) Act 1999 also
expressly preserves all previous common law exceptions to the doctrine of privity
of contract[12] including any right of action available to a contracting party which
will directly secure the benefit for the third party[13].

As an exception to this rule, if a party enters into a contract as trustee for a
third person, the third person may enforce the contract directly[14]. However, it is
necessary to prove that the person entering into the contract intended to enter into
it in a fiduciary capacity[15]. It is not enough to show that the terms of the contract
conferred a benefit on the third person, since this fact does not by itself give rise
to any implication that the promisee was acting in a fiduciary capacity[16]. In some
cases it may be necessary or desirable to make a stranger to the contract a
co-defendant together with a contracting party, for example if the stranger claims
an interest in the purchase money[17] or if the stranger has been let into possession
of the property by the vendor and the purchaser needs an order for possession
against him[18].

1   *Tolhurst v Associated Portland Cement Manufacturers (1900) Ltd* [1902] 2 KB 660 at 668, CA,
    per Collins MR; affd on other grounds [1903] AC 414, HL. As to the assignment of rights and

liabilities see CONTRACT vol 22 (2012) PARAS 335–336; and as to novation of contracts see CONTRACT vol 22 (2012) PARAS 598–604. See also PARA 506.

2 'There is no equitable principle by virtue of which land can be taken away from the true owner under colour of specific performance of a contract to which he was not a party and which he did not authorise to be made on his behalf ': *Howard v Miller* [1915] AC 318 at 323, PC, per Lord Parker. See also *Robertson v Great Western Rly Co* (1839) 1 Ry & Can Cas 459; *Hare v London and North Western Rly Co* (1860) 1 John & H 252.

3 See PARA 592.

4 *Crosbie v Tooke* (1833) 1 My & K 431; *Morgan v Rhodes* (1834) 1 My & K 435. See also PARA 591.

5 See PARA 590.

6 See PARA 594.

7 *Tweddle v Atkinson* (1861) 1 B & S 393; *Dunlop Pneumatic Tyre Co Ltd v Selfridge & Co Ltd* [1915] AC 847, HL; *Scruttons Ltd v Midland Silicones Ltd* [1962] AC 446, [1962] 1 All ER 1, HL. See also CONTRACT vol 22 (2012) PARAS 327, 328.

8 See the Contracts (Rights of Third Parties) Act 1999 s 1(3); and CONTRACT vol 22 (2012) PARA 343.

9 See the Contracts (Rights of Third Parties) Act 1999 s 1(1)(a); and CONTRACT vol 22 (2012) PARA 343.

10 See the Contracts (Rights of Third Parties) Act 1999 s 1(1)(b); and CONTRACT vol 22 (2012) PARA 343.

11 *Nisshin Shipping Co Ltd v Cleaves & Co Ltd* [2003] EWHC 2602 (Comm), [2004] 1 All ER (Comm) 481, [2004] 1 Lloyd's Rep 38.

12 See the Contracts (Rights of Third Parties) Act 1999 s 7(1); and CONTRACT vol 22 (2012) PARA 343.

13 See the Contracts (Rights of Third Parties) Act 1999 s 4; and CONTRACT vol 22 (2012) PARA 343.

14 *Touche v Metropolitan Railway Warehousing Co* (1871) 6 Ch App 671; *Kelly v Larkin and Carter* [1910] 2 IR 550. However, it is normally necessary for the beneficiary to sue the trustee as well as the other party to the contract, unless that other party waives this requirement: see *Les Affréteurs Réunis SA v Leopold Walford (London) Ltd* [1919] AC 801, HL. See also CONTRACT vol 22 (2012) PARAS 338–339. A covenant in a marriage settlement will be enforced at the suit of a person within the marriage consideration: *Re D'Angibau, Andrews v Andrews* (1880) 15 ChD 228 at 242, CA, per Cotton LJ.

15 As to intention to create a trust see CONTRACT vol 22 (2012) PARA 340.

16 *Re Schebsman, ex p Official Receiver, The Trustee v Cargo Superintendents (London) Ltd and Schebsman* [1944] Ch 83, [1943] 2 All ER 768, CA; *Green v Russell* [1959] 2 QB 226, [1959] 2 All ER 525, CA; *Beswick v Beswick* [1968] AC 58, [1967] 2 All ER 1197, HL; see generally the discussion in *Barbados Trust Co v Bank of Zambia* [2007] EWCA Civ 148 at [99], [2007] 2 All ER (Comm) 445 at [99]; [2007] 1 Lloyd's Rep 495 at [99].

17 *West Midland Rly Co v Nixon* (1863) 1 Hem & M 176.

18 *Bishop of Winchester v Mid-Hants Rly Co* (1867) LR 5 Eq 17.

590. Death of party to the contract. If a party to a contract dies before performance is completed, an order for specific performance can normally be obtained by or against the personal representatives of the deceased, but only if such an order could have been obtained by or against the deceased[1]. Consequently, specific performance will not be ordered of a contract requiring the exercise by the deceased of some personal skill or discretion[2]. If the deceased has entered into a contract to take a lease, his personal representatives are entitled to have the lease so framed that they incur no personal liability under the covenants[3].

1 See *Hinton v Hinton* (1755) 2 Ves Sen 631; *Phillips v Everard* (1831) 5 Sim 102. As to proceedings against estates generally see CIVIL PROCEDURE vol 12A (2015) PARA 1311. As to the effect of the death of a party on a contract for the sale of land see CONVEYANCING vol 23 (2016) PARA 204 et seq; and as to claims by and against personal representatives see WILLS AND INTESTACY vol 103 (2016) PARA 1271 et seq.

2 See *Siboni v Kirkman* (1836) 1 M & W 418 at 423 per Parke B (affd sub nom *Kirkman v Siboni* (1838) 4 M & W 339, Ex Ch); and WILLS AND INTESTACY vol 103 (2016) PARA 1213. Cf *Re Worthington, ex p Pathé Frères* [1914] 2 KB 299, CA. As to the enforceability of contracts for personal services see PARAS 508–509.

3 *Stephens v Hotham* (1855) 1 K & J 571. The liability of the personal representatives is limited to
   the assets of the estate, and they do not incur the unrestricted liability to which they would
   otherwise have been subject as the original grantees of the lease: *Stephens v Hotham*. See also
   LANDLORD AND TENANT vol 62 (2016) PARA 38.

591. Enforcement by assignee of the contract. Where the benefit of a contract
has been assigned, the assignee may as a general rule enforce specific performance
provided that the assignee can himself perform or procure the performance of the
assignor's obligations under the contract[1]. On the assignment of a contract to take
a lease, the lessor can require the assignor to join in the lease for the purpose of
guaranteeing performance of the lessee's covenants[2]. On a sale of leaseholds, if the
contract is not entered into on grounds personal to the purchaser, completion may
be enforced in favour of a solvent nominee of the purchaser, but upon the terms
that the purchaser joins in the assignment for the purpose of guaranteeing the
performance of the covenants in the lease[3]. Where, however, there is a personal
element in the contract[4], or where there is an express proviso against assignment[5],
or the assignment is illegal or contrary to public policy[6], the assignee cannot
enforce specific performance.

As a rule, it is not necessary for the assignee to join the assignor as a party to
a claim for specific performance brought against the other party to the contract[7].
There are, however, many circumstances in which it may be necessary or desirable
to join the assignor as a party to the claim. If there has been an equitable
assignment of a legal chose or thing in action, any claim to the chose or thing in
action must be brought in the name of the assignor[8]; and if the assignor refuses to
consent to the use of his name, the assignee sues in his own name and must make
the assignor a defendant to the claim[9]. The assignor should be joined if it is
necessary to ensure that he is bound by the decision or if he is required to perform
any obligations under the original contract or the assignment.

A person who has taken an assignment of the benefit of a contract by way of
charge or mortgage is entitled to claim specific performance of the contract[10].

The rights of a sub-purchaser to enforce a contract against the original vendor
are substantially the same as those of an assignee of the benefit of a contract[11].

If a contract between the vendor and the original purchaser can be treated as
severable into a series of independent contracts, an assignee or sub-purchaser of
a severable part of the original contract can require completion of that part
without having to procure completion of the original contract in its entirety[12].

1 *Crosbie v Tooke* (1833) 1 My & K 431; *Morgan v Rhodes* (1834) 1 My & K 435. See also
   CONTRACT vol 22 (2012) PARA 335.
2 *Dowell v Dew* (1842) 1 Y & C Ch Cas 345.
3 *Curtis Moffat Ltd v Wheeler* [1929] 2 Ch 224. How far the solvency or other personal quality of
   the intended lessee is relied on by the lessor in the ordinary cases of leases is a question of fact, but
   that such contracts are assignable appears clearly from *Dowell v Dew* (1843) 12 LJ Ch 158 at 164
   per Lord Lyndhurst LC; *Buckland v Papillon* (1866) 2 Ch App 67 at 71 per Lord Chelmsford LC.
4 *Gibson v Carruthers* (1841) 8 M & W 321 at 343; *Rayner v Grote* (1846) 15 M & W 359 at 365;
   Tolhurst v Associated Portland Cement Manufacturers (1900) Ltd [1901] 2 KB 811 at 816 (revsd
   on another point [1902] 2 KB 660, CA; [1903] AC 414, HL); *Barnes v Wilson* (1913) 29 TLR 639.
   See also CHOSES IN ACTION vol 13 (2009) PARA 100; CONTRACT vol 22 (2012) PARA 335.
5 *Weatherall v Geering* (1806) 12 Ves 504. Cf *Jalabert v Duke of Chandos* (1759) 1 Eden 372. See
   also *Dowell v Dew* (1842) 1 Y & C Ch Cas 345.
6 *Johnson v Shrewsbury and Birmingham Rly Co* (1853) 3 De GM & G 914.
7 *Tolhurst v Associated Portland Cement Manufacturers (1900) Ltd and Imperial Portland
   Cement Co Ltd* [1903] AC 414 at 424–425, HL, per Lord Lindley.
8 *Durham Bros v Robertson* [1898] 1 QB 765, CA. See also CHOSES IN ACTION vol 13 (2009)
   PARA 68.
9 *Hammond v Messenger* (1838) 9 Sim 327; *Crouch v Crédit Foncier of England* (1873) LR 8 QB
   374 at 380 per Blackburn J. See CHOSES IN ACTION vol 13 (2009) PARA 68.

10 *Browne v London Necropolis and National Mausoleum Co* (1857) 6 WR 188; *Shaw v Foster* (1872) LR 5 HL 321.
11 *Shaw v Foster* (1872) LR 5 HL 321 at 338–339 per Lord Cairns.
12 *Wilkinson v Clements* (1872) 8 Ch App 96.

592. Enforcement against transferee of property. Where there is a contract for the sale or demise of property and the property is thereafter transferred to a third person, the general principle is that specific performance may be granted against the transferee, if he is a volunteer, or takes with notice of the prior contract, or has acquired only an equitable title and has no better equity than the purchaser or intended lessee[1]. The relevant time for notice is the time of completion of the transfer, and it is no defence to the transferee that he had no notice of the claimant's contract at the time when he entered into his own contract[2]. If the subject matter of the contract is a legal estate in land, the above principle takes effect subject to important modifications[3].

If the vendor sells the subject matter of the contract to a company controlled by him, both he and the company may be ordered to perform the contract[4].

1 *Taylor v Stibbert* (1794) 2 Ves 437. The principle applies to contracts for the sale of shares: *Graham v O' Connor* (1895) 73 LT 712. See also EQUITABLE JURISDICTION vol 47 (2014) PARA 119 et seq. Cf *Meng Leong Development Pte Ltd v Jip Hong Trading Co Pte Ltd* [1985] AC 511, [1985] 1 All ER 120, PC.
2 *Mumford v Stohwasser* (1874) LR 18 Eq 556.
3 Ie modifications contained in the Land Charges Act 1972 (in relation to land with unregistered title), and the Land Registration Act 2002 (in relation to land with registered title): see PARA 593.
4 *Jones v Lipman* [1962] 1 All ER 442, [1962] 1 WLR 832.

593. Contracts relating to land. Estate contracts and other interests in registered land may be protected by notices and restrictions under the Land Registration Act 2002[1]. If they are not so protected, any disponee for valuable consideration automatically takes free of them[2]. There are also unregistered interests which override registered dispositions, notably interests (including estate contracts) held by persons in actual occupation[3].

An uncompleted contract for the purchase of a legal estate in unregistered land will be void and unenforceable against a subsequent purchaser for money or money's worth of a legal estate in the land, unless registered in the register of land charges kept under the Land Charges Act 1972 before completion of the subsequent purchase[4]. Conversely, registration of a contract in the register of land charges or any local land charges register is deemed to constitute actual notice to all persons and for all purposes connected with the land affected[5]. The Land Charges Act 1972 does not apply to estate contracts affecting land registered under the Land Registration Act 2002[6].

1 For more detail and discussion see the Land Registration Act 2002 Pt 4 (ss 32–47); and REAL PROPERTY AND REGISTRATION vol 87 (2012) PARA 512 et seq.
2 See the Land Registration Act 2002 s 29; and REAL PROPERTY AND REGISTRATION vol 85 (2012) PARA 455.
3 See the Land Registration Act 2002 ss 11, 12, Sch 1 para 2, ss 29, 30, Sch 3 para 2; and REAL PROPERTY AND REGISTRATION vol 87 (2012) PARAS 391, 482.
4 See the Law of Property Act 1925 s 199(1)(i); the Land Charges Act 1972 ss 2(4)(iv), 4(6); and REAL PROPERTY AND REGISTRATION vol 87 (2012) PARAS 708, 724, 735. The first contract will be void even if the sale to the subsequent purchaser was for nominal consideration and was effected for the purpose of defeating the earlier contract: *Midland Bank Trust Co Ltd v Green* [1981] AC 513, [1981] 1 All ER 153, HL. Where an option to purchase is registered as an estate contract under the Land Charges Act 1972 s 2(4)(iv), the contract for the sale of land resulting from the exercise of the option need not be so registered to preserve priority: *Armstrong & Holmes Ltd v Holmes* [1994] 1 All ER 826, [1993] 1 WLR 1482. An unregistered contract may become binding on a subsequent purchaser through the principle of equitable estoppel if the subsequent purchaser stands by while the original contracting party spends money or otherwise acts to his detriment in the belief that the contract is effective: *Ives (ER) Investment Ltd v High*

[1967] 2 QB 379, [1967] 1 All ER 504, CA; *Taylors Fashions Ltd v Liverpool Victoria Trustees Co Ltd, Old & Campbell Ltd v Liverpool Victoria Friendly Society* [1982] QB 133n, [1981] 1 All ER 897. See PARA 506.

5   See the Law of Property Act 1925 s 198(1); and REAL PROPERTY AND REGISTRATION vol 87 (2012) PARA 708. Such registration does not, however, exclude a vendor's liability in respect of certain covenants as to title implied by statute: see the Law of Property (Miscellaneous Provisions) Act 1994 s 6(3); and REAL PROPERTY AND REGISTRATION vol 87 (2012) PARA 490.

6   See the Land Charges Act 1972 s 14(1); and REAL PROPERTY AND REGISTRATION vol 87 (2012) PARA 697. See also the Land Registration Act 2002 s 87(1); and REAL PROPERTY AND REGISTRATION vol 87 (2012) PARAS 537–538.

594. Bankruptcy of contracting party. Bankruptcy does not, as a general rule, determine a contract[1]. Property held by the bankrupt on trust for any other person does not vest in his trustee in bankruptcy[2]. There is therefore no barrier to specific performance being ordered for or against a bankrupt in respect of property held by him on trust for others.

When an individual is adjudicated bankrupt his estate[3] vests automatically in his trustee in bankruptcy immediately on his appointment taking effect or, in the case of the official receiver, on his becoming trustee[4], and all rights of the bankrupt under contracts to which he was a party are deemed to have been assigned to the trustee[5].

A trustee in bankruptcy is entitled to specific performance of a contract for the sale or purchase of property entered into by the bankrupt before the commencement of the bankruptcy if the contract is of a kind which the bankrupt would have been able to enforce and the performance of it does not require the exercise of any skill or discretion which is personal to the bankrupt[6]. Specific performance of a contract by the bankrupt to purchase property will not, however, normally be granted against the trustee[7]. A trustee in bankruptcy who seeks specific performance of a contract for the grant of a lease to the bankrupt may be required personally to enter into the lessee's covenants in the lease as a condition of obtaining the order[8].

A trustee in bankruptcy is normally entitled to disclaim an unprofitable contract entered into by the bankrupt, and if he does so the contract can no longer be enforced against the trustee and the other party is left to submit a proof in the bankruptcy for any damage suffered[9]. The trustee in bankruptcy of a vendor cannot disclaim the contract if the equitable interest in the property has already passed to the purchaser, and in such a case the trustee can be ordered to complete the sale upon receipt of the purchase price[10].

A trustee will be deemed to have adopted an unprofitable contract if a written application has been made to him to decide whether he will disclaim or not and the period of 28 days beginning with the day on which that application was made has expired without a notice of disclaimer having been given in respect of that property[11].

The trustee in bankruptcy will, of course, often enter into contracts for the sale of property of the bankrupt in the course of realising his assets, in which case the trustee himself is the contracting party and any claim to enforce the contract by or against the trustee is governed by the general principles of the law of specific performance.

Property which is acquired by, or devolves upon, the bankrupt after the commencement of the bankruptcy does not automatically vest in the trustee. The trustee may, however, by notice in writing claim for the bankrupt's estate any property which has been so acquired by, or has so devolved upon, the bankrupt[12]. Except with the leave of the court, such a notice cannot be served after the end of the period of 42 days beginning with the day on which it first came to the knowledge of the trustee that the property in question had been acquired by, or had devolved upon, the bankrupt[13]. Upon service of the notice, the property to which it relates vests in the trustee as part of the bankrupt's estate and his title relates back to the time at which the property was acquired by, or devolved upon, the bankrupt[14]. However, no such remedy is available in respect of property acquired in good faith, for value and without notice of the bankruptcy[15], nor in respect of a transaction entered into by a banker before service on the banker of a notice[16].

1   *Brooke v Hewitt* (1796) 3 Ves 253 at 255; *Re Edwards, ex p Chalmers* (1873) 8 Ch App 289 at 293–294; *Re Sneezum, ex p Davis* (1876) 3 ChD 463 at 473, CA; *Jennings' Trustee v King* [1952] Ch 899 at 908, [1952] 2 All ER 608 at 612. See BANKRUPTCY AND INDIVIDUAL INSOLVENCY vol 5 (2013) PARA 431.
2   See the Insolvency Act 1986 s 283(3)(a); and BANKRUPTCY AND INDIVIDUAL INSOLVENCY vol 5 (2013) PARA 412 et seq.
3   As to the meaning of a bankrupt's 'estate' see the Insolvency Act 1986 s 283; and BANKRUPTCY AND INDIVIDUAL INSOLVENCY vol 5 (2013) PARA 211.
4   See the Insolvency Act 1986 s 306(1);and BANKRUPTCY AND INDIVIDUAL INSOLVENCY vol 5 (2013) PARA 398.
5   See the Insolvency Act 1986 s 311(4); and BANKRUPTCY AND INDIVIDUAL INSOLVENCY vol 5 (2013) PARA 410.
6   See *Brooke v Hewitt* (1796) 3 Ves 253; *Powell v Lloyd* (1828) 2 Y & J 372; *Crosbie v Tooke* (1833) 1 My & K 431; *Morgan v Rhodes* (1834) 1 My & K 435; *Buckland v Papillon* (1866) 2 Ch App 67. Where the contract requires personal skill the trustee in bankruptcy cannot obtain an order for specific performance by offering to perform the bankrupt's obligations himself: *Knight v Burgess* (1864) 33 LJ Ch 727 (building contract); *Gibson v Carruthers* (1841) 8 M & W 321 at 343 per Lord Abinger CB. See further BANKRUPTCY AND INDIVIDUAL INSOLVENCY vol 5 (2013) PARA 431.
7   *Holloway v York* (1877) 25 WR 627. See BANKRUPTCY AND INDIVIDUAL INSOLVENCY vol 5 (2013) PARA 432.
8   See *Powell v Lloyd* (1828) 2 Y & J 372; *Crosbie v Tooke* (1833) 1 My & K 431.
9   See the Insolvency Act 1986 s 315; and BANKRUPTCY AND INDIVIDUAL INSOLVENCY vol 5 (2013) PARAS 431, 490 et seq. The Insolvency Act 1986 s 315 does not, however, apply in relation to, among other things, a market contract or a contract effected by the exchange or clearing house for the purpose of realising property provided as margin in relation to market contracts: see the Companies Act 1989 s 164(1); and FINANCIAL SERVICES REGULATION vol 50A PARA 737. As to the meaning of 'market contract' see s 155; and FINANCIAL SERVICES REGULATION vol 50A (2016) PARA 729.
10 *Re Scheibler, ex p Holthausen* (1874) 9 Ch App 722; *Re Bastable, ex p Trustee* [1901] 2 KB 518, CA; *Pearce v Bastable's Trustee in Bankruptcy* [1901] 2 Ch 122; and see *Freevale Ltd v Metrostore (Holdings) Ltd* [1984] Ch 199 at 207–208, [1984] 1 All ER 495 at 501. If the purchaser has paid the purchase money to the bankrupt without notice of the act of bankruptcy, he cannot obtain an order directing the assignment of the property to him without paying the purchase money over again to the trustee: *Re Pooley, ex p Rabbidge* (1878) 8 ChD 367, CA. However, the trustee cannot be ordered to perform any work on the land which the bankrupt agreed to carry out as part of the contract: *Re Gough, Hanning v Lowe* (1927) 96 LJ Ch 239, DC.
11 See the Insolvency Act 1986 s 316; and BANKRUPTCY AND INDIVIDUAL INSOLVENCY vol 5 (2013) PARA 498.
12 See the Insolvency Act 1986 s 307(1); and BANKRUPTCY AND INDIVIDUAL INSOLVENCY vol 5(2013) PARAS 458–461.
13 See the Insolvency Act 1986 s 309(1)(a); and BANKRUPTCY AND INDIVIDUAL INSOLVENCY vol 5(2013) PARA 459. Knowledge of the bankrupt's acquisition is acquired by the trustee when it has become clear to him, on cogent evidence verified to his reasonable satisfaction, that the property in question has been acquired by the bankrupt, and has been acquired after the commencement of the bankruptcy: *Viscount St Davids v Lewis* [2015] EWHC 2826 (Ch), [2015] BPIR 1471, [2015] All ER (D) 73 (Oct).
14 See the Insolvency Act 1986 s 307(3); and BANKRUPTCY AND INDIVIDUAL INSOLVENCY vol 5 (2013) PARA 459.
15 See the Insolvency Act 1986 s 307(4); and BANKRUPTCY AND INDIVIDUAL INSOLVENCY vol 5 (2013) PARA 459.
16 See the Insolvency Act 1986 s 307(4A); and BANKRUPTCY AND INDIVIDUAL INSOLVENCY vol 5 (2013) PARA 459.

595. Company insolvency. Although the functions of a liquidator[1] in the winding up of a company resemble those of a trustee in bankruptcy[2], there are important differences. In particular, the property of the company does not vest in the liquidator, but remains vested in the company. A liquidator has power to disclaim any onerous property[3], and may do so notwithstanding that he has taken possession of it, endeavoured to sell it, or otherwise exercised rights of ownership in relation to it[4]. The company will be deemed to have adopted an unprofitable contract if a written application has been made to the liquidator by any person interested in the contract requiring him to decide whether he will or will not disclaim and the liquidator has not, within a 28-day period after receipt of the application or such further period as the court may allow, given the prescribed notice[5]. In a winding up by the court, any disposition of the property of the company made after the commencement of the winding up[6] is void unless the court orders otherwise[7]. The court will normally direct completion of a contract of sale by the company entered into in good faith in the ordinary course of business if an equitable title has passed to the purchaser between the presentation of the petition and the making of the winding-up order, but if title has not passed the purchaser will be left to prove for damages in the liquidation[8].

In a winding up by the court, the court has power to stay proceedings against the company before the winding-up order[9], and after the order has been made no claim may be begun or proceeded with against the company without the leave of the court[10]. In a claim for specific performance a stay will normally be refused, or leave to proceed given, if the claim relates to a contract for sale under which equitable title has passed from the company to the purchaser[11] or if there is an arguable defence to the claim and it is more convenient to resolve the issues in the claim than in proceedings in the liquidation[12].

The commencement of the liquidation or the making of a winding-up order does not affect the powers of a receiver appointed under a debenture to deal with the property charged by the debenture, so a contract relating to such property entered into by the receiver in the name of the company can be specifically enforced notwithstanding the making of a winding-up order[13].

Where a company enters into a contract to sell land, the fact that it is placed in receivership prior to completion is not of itself a defence to a claim by the purchaser for specific performance[14].

1 As to the appointment and duties of a liquidator see COMPANY AND PARTNERSHIP INSOLVENCY vol 17 (2011) PARAS 505 et seq, 909 et seq.
2 As to the position of a trustee in bankruptcy see PARA 594.
3 'Onerous property' comprises any unprofitable contract and any other property of the company which is unsaleable or not readily saleable or is such that it may give rise to a liability to pay money or perform any other onerous act: Insolvency Act 1986 s 178(3).
4 See the Insolvency Act 1986 s 178(2); and COMPANY AND PARTNERSHIP INSOLVENCY vol 17 (2011) PARA 824 et seq. Section 178 does not, however, apply in relation to, among other things, a market contract or a contract effected by the exchange or clearing house for the purpose of realising property provided as margin in relation to market contracts: see the Companies Act 1989 s 164(1); and FINANCIAL SERVICES REGULATION vol 50A PARA 737. As to the meaning of 'market contract' see s 155 (amended by SI 1991/880; SI 1998/1748; SI 2009/853; SI 2013/504); and FINANCIAL SERVICES REGULATION vol 50A (2016) PARA 729. It seems that, by analogy with the cases cited in PARA 594 note 10, a liquidator cannot disclaim a contract for a sale by the company under which an equitable interest in the property has passed to the purchaser before the commencement of the winding up.
5 See the Insolvency Act 1986 s 178(5); and see Insolvency Rules 1986, SI 1986/1925, rr 4.187–4.194; and COMPANY AND PARTNERSHIP INSOLVENCY vol 17 (2011) PARA 830. As to the disclaimer of leaseholds see the Insolvency Act 1986 s 179; and as to the right of the other party to the company's contract to apply to the court for an order rescinding the contract see s 186. See further COMPANY AND PARTNERSHIP INSOLVENCY vol 17 (2011) PARA 833.

6 As to the time of the commencement of the winding up see the Insolvency Act 1986 s 129; and COMPANY AND PARTNERSHIP INSOLVENCY vol 16 (2011) PARA 439.

7 See the Insolvency Act 1986 s 127; and COMPANY AND PARTNERSHIP INSOLVENCY vol 17 (2011) PARA 658. Section 127 does not affect the liquidator's powers to dispose of the property of the company, which in the case of a winding up by the court are conferred by s 167: see COMPANY AND PARTNERSHIP INSOLVENCY vol 16 (2011) PARA 527. Nor does s 127 apply to in relation to, among other things a market contract, or a contract effected by the exchange or clearing house for the purpose of realising property provided as margin in relation to market contracts: see the Companies Act 1989 s 164(1); and FINANCIAL SERVICES REGULATION vol 50A PARA 737. See note 4.

  See further the Companies Act 1989 s 164(4)–(6); and FINANCIAL SERVICES REGULATION vol 50A (2016) PARA 737.

8 *Re Wiltshire Iron Co, ex p Pearson* (1868) 3 Ch App 443; *Re Oriental Bank Corpn, ex p Guillemin* (1884) 28 ChD 634. A fortiori, completion will be ordered if equitable title passed to the purchaser before the commencement of the winding up: cf the bankruptcy cases cited in PARA 594 note 10. See *Re French's (Wine Bar) Ltd* [1987] BCLC 499, 3 BCC 173.

9 See the Insolvency Act 1986 s 126; and COMPANY AND PARTNERSHIP INSOLVENCY vol 17 (2011) PARA 845.

10 See the Insolvency Act 1986 s 130(2); and COMPANY AND PARTNERSHIP INSOLVENCY vol 16 (2011) PARA 440; COMPANY AND PARTNERSHIP INSOLVENCY vol 17 (2011) PARA 851 et seq.

11 See *Marshall v Glamorgan Iron and Coal Co* (1868) LR 7 Eq 129.

12 *Thames Plate Glass Co v Land and Sea Telegraph Construction Co* (1871) 6 Ch App 643. See also *Re Coregrange* [1984] BCLC 453 (claim to enforce specific performance against company in liquidation permitted).

13 *Gough's Garages Ltd v Pugsley* [1930] 1 KB 615.

14 *Freevale Ltd v Metrostore (Holdings) Ltd* [1984] Ch 199, [1984] 1 All ER 495. See also *Bristol Alliance Nominee No 1 Ltd and others v Bennett and others* [2013] EWCA Civ 1626, [2014] 1 EGLR 9, [2014] 1 P & CR D42 (successful claim by landlords to enforce specific performance of agreements for surrender and variation of leases against company in administration).

596. Incapacity. The general rule of law is that any person, natural or artificial, may sue or be sued in the English courts although this is subject to exceptions[1]. A person under disability, whether a child or a protected party, may sue or be sued, but proceedings by or against him are subject to special rules of procedure[2] and there may be special rules about granting particular relief or a particular remedy in such cases[3].

The law regarding people who lack capacity is covered elsewhere in this work[4]. The common law rule is that a contract made by a person who at the time lacked the capacity to make it is voidable but not void[5].

The Court of Protection[6] has power under the Mental Capacity Act 2005 to make a declaration in relation to a person's property and affairs including in particular the carrying out of any contract entered into by that person[7]. Thus specific performance is available subject to the above.

1 See generally CIVIL PROCEDURE vol 11 (2015) PARA 469 et seq.

2 See CPR Pt 21; and CIVIL PROCEDURE vol 11 (2015) PARA 469.

3 For instance, it seems that specific performance cannot be granted in favour of or against a minor: see *Flight v Bolland* (1828) 4 Russ 298; *Lumley v Ravenscroft* [1895] 1 QB 683, CA. However, this may be subject to exceptions: see G Jones and W Goodhart, *Specific Performance* (2nd edn, 1996) p 94.

4 See MENTAL HEALTH AND CAPACITY vol 75 (2013) PARA 601 et seq. As to the capacity of children in regard to contracts see CHILDREN AND YOUNG PERSONS vol 9 (2017) PARA 12 et seq.

5 See MENTAL HEALTH AND CAPACITY vol 75 (2013) PARA 614.

6 As to the Court of Protection see MENTAL HEALTH AND CAPACITY vol 75 (2013) PARA 720 et seq.

7 See the Mental Capacity Act 2005 s 18(1)(f); and MENTAL HEALTH AND CAPACITY vol 75 (2013) PARA 727.

(iv) Statement of Case

597. Additional and alternative relief. In addition to specific performance, the claim form should claim any additional or alternative relief which the claimant may wish to seek in the claim[1]. Such relief may include one or more of the following:

(1) damages in lieu of or in addition to specific performance[2];
(2) rescission of the contract[3];
(3) in a purchaser's claim, return of the deposit and a declaration that the purchaser is entitled to a lien for its repayment[4];
(4) in a vendor's claim, a declaration that the deposit has been forfeited or that the claimant is entitled to a lien for the balance of the purchase money[5];
(5) an injunction to restrain the defendant from dealing with the subject matter of the contract in a manner inconsistent with his obligations under it[6];
(6) rectification[7];
(7) a vesting order[8].

Where the claimant obtains judgment on motion for judgment in default of defence[9], no relief can be obtained unless it has been claimed in the statement of claim[10].

1 As to the contents of particulars of claim see CPR 16.4, CPR PD 16—*Statements of Case*.
2 As to damages see PARA 632 et seq.
3 As to rescission see PARA 598.
4 As to claims for the return of a deposit see CONVEYANCING vol 23 (2016) PARA 452.
5 As to claims for forfeiture of a deposit see CONVEYANCING vol 23 (2016) PARA 452.
6 As to injunctions in aid of specific performance see CIVIL PROCEDURE vol 12 (2015) PARA 1194.
7 As to rectification of contracts for the sale of land see CONVEYANCING vol 23 (2016) PARA 463.
8 As to vesting orders see TRUSTS AND POWERS vol 98 (2013) PARA 309 et seq.
9 As to default judgments see CIVIL PROCEDURE vol 12 (2015) PARA 535 et seq.
10 *Stone v Smith* (1887) 35 ChD 188; *Kingdon v Kirk* (1887) 37 ChD 141; *Tacon v National Standard Land Mortgage and Investment Co* (1887) 56 LJ Ch 529; *Palmer v Lark* [1945] Ch 182, [1954] 1 All ER 355.

598. Rescission and repudiation. The word 'rescission' is used in two different senses. In the strict sense, it means the exercise by a party to a contract of a right to have the contract avoided ab initio. Such a right may arise by virtue of a term in the contract itself or for some reason such as fraud, misrepresentation or mistake[1]. A person who has a right to rescind the contract in the strict sense will lose that right if, at a time when he knows that he has the right of rescission, he affirms the contract by taking some step which indicates an intention to proceed with it[2]. The commencement of a claim for specific performance of a contract clearly affirms the contract[3], so that rescission in the strict sense cannot in practice be claimed as alternative relief in a claim for specific performance.

'Rescission' is, however, frequently and confusingly used in a broader sense to describe a different act, namely, the acceptance by one party to a contract of a repudiatory breach of contract by the other party[4]. Acceptance of repudiation discharges both parties from further performance of their executory obligations under the contract, but the contract is not avoided ab initio and the innocent party may claim damages for breach of contract[5]. A claimant may claim both specific performance and rescission (in the sense of acceptance of repudiation) in the alternative, but as these claims are inconsistent with each other he must elect between them at the trial if he has not done so previously[6]. Rescission ab initio is very different from a failure of performance which entitles the innocent party to treat the contract as discharged[7].

A person pursuing a claim for specific performance is treating the contract as still in existence, and therefore cannot elect to rescind after the defendant has remedied his breach and is able and willing to perform his part of the contract[8]. If the repudiatory breach is not of a continuing nature, the innocent party will be treated as having affirmed the contract and lost the right to rescind if, after acquiring full knowledge of the breach, he takes steps which indicate an intention to proceed with the contract[9] or delays in exercising the right to terminate it[10].

It has been held that, where a claimant commenced a claim for specific performance claiming damages as alternative relief but not rescission, he could not terminate the contract by accepting the repudiation without first discontinuing the claim[11].

1 As to rescission generally see CONTRACT vol 22 (2012) PARA 553 et seq. As to claims for rescission see MISREPRESENTATION vol 76 (2013) PARA 811 et seq. As to the effect of fraud see EQUITABLE JURISDICTION vol 47 (2014) PARA 12 et seq; MISREPRESENTATION vol 76 (2013) PARA 754 et seq generally. As to misrepresentation generally see MISREPRESENTATION vol 76 (2013) PARA 740 et seq. As to the effect of mistake see CONTRACT vol 22 (2012) PARA 317; MISTAKE vol 77 (2016) PARAS 41–46.
2 As to affirmation see MISREPRESENTATION vol 76 (2013) PARA 827.
3 *Re Murray, Dickson v Murray* (1887) 57 LT 223.
4 Further discussion of the semantic confusion can be found in *Hurst v Bryk* [2002] 1 AC 185, [2000] 2 All ER 193, [2000] 2 WLR 740 per Lord Millett. As to 'rescission' in this sense see CONTRACT vol 22 (2012) PARA 344 et seq. As to repudiation of contracts generally see CONTRACT vol 22 (2012) PARA 560 et seq.
5 *Heyman v Darwins Ltd* [1942] AC 356 at 399, [1942] 1 All ER 337 at 360, HL, per Lord Porter; *Johnson v Agnew* [1980] AC 367 at 393, [1979] 1 All ER 883 at 889, HL, per Lord Wilberforce.
6 *Farrant v Olver* (1922) 91 LJ Ch 758; *Glover v Broome* [1926] WN 46; *Johnson v Agnew* [1980] AC 367 at 392, [1979] 1 All ER 883 at 889, HL, per Lord Wilberforce.
7 *Howard-Jones v Tate* [2011] EWCA Civ 1330, [2012] 2 All ER 369, [2012] 1 P & CR 247.
8 *Frost v Knight* (1872) LR 7 Exch 111 at 112, Ex Ch, per Cockburn CJ; *Halkett v Earl of Dudley* [1907] 1 Ch 590.
9 *Hain Steamship Co Ltd v Tate and Lyle Ltd* [1936] 2 All ER 597, HL; *Aquis Estates Ltd v Minton* [1975] 3 All ER 1043, [1975] 1 WLR 1452, CA.
10 *Halkett v Earl of Dudley* [1907] 1 Ch 590 at 597 per Parker J, approved in *Berners v Fleming* [1925] Ch 264, CA.
11 *Public Trustee v Pearlberg* [1940] 2 KB 1, [1940] 2 All ER 270, CA, not followed in *Ogle v Comboyuro Investments Pty Ltd* (1976) 136 CLR 444 (Aust HC). Cf *Johnson v Agnew* [1980] AC 367, [1979] 1 All ER 883, HL.

599. Statements of case. The normal rules of statements of case[1] apply to specific performance claims. It is customary but not essential for the claimant to plead that he is ready, willing and able to perform his part of the contract[2]. If the claimant wishes to claim interest under a provision in the contract he should plead it[3].

1 As to statements of case generally see CPR Pt 16; and CIVIL PROCEDURE vol 11 (2015) PARA 340 et seq.
2 *Public Trustee v Pearlberg* [1940] 2 KB 1 at 11, [1940] 2 All ER 270 at 275, CA, per Slesser LJ. Cf *Ellis v Rogers* (1884) 29 ChD 661.
3 *Palmer v Lark* [1945] Ch 182, [1945] 1 All ER 355; and see also *Ward v Chief Constable of Avon and Somerset* (1985) 129 Sol Jo 606, CA.

600. Statements of case concerning title to land. Unless the purchaser has accepted the vendor's title, an inquiry as to title will be directed as part of the order for specific performance of a contract for the sale of land[1]. In a vendor's claim for specific performance it is therefore unnecessary for the claimant to plead or prove at the trial that he has a good title to the land[2], and it is unnecessary for the defendant to plead any defect in the title or put the claimant to proof of title[3]. However, if the purchaser has accepted the vendor's title[4] the vendor should plead that fact in order to obviate the need for an inquiry as to title. If the vendor claims that the purchaser has waived an objection to title the vendor must plead the waiver[5] and prove it at the trial; the issue of waiver cannot be raised at the inquiry as to title[6]. A purchaser who has admitted the vendor's title in his statement of case is held to have waived any objection to title and is not entitled to an inquiry as to title[7]. A purchaser may plead a defect in the vendor's title with a view to having the vendor's claim dismissed at the trial without having to wait for the subsequent inquiry[8]. If a serious and irremediable defect in the vendor's title is disclosed at the trial, his claim for specific performance will be dismissed even though the defect was not pleaded by the purchaser[9]. Compensation may be granted for a defect appearing on an investigation of title, even though no claim to compensation was made in the statement of case and no order for compensation was made at the trial[10].

1 *Jenkins v Hiles* (1802) 6 Ves 646; *Lesturgeon v Martin* (1834) 3 My & K 255. As to inquiries as to title see PARA 608 et seq. As to specific performance of contracts for the sale of land see CONVEYANCING vol 23 (2016) PARA 453 et seq.
2 As to what constitutes a good title see CONVEYANCING vol 23 (2016) PARA 39. As to the covenants for title implied by statute on the disposition of a property see the Law of Property (Miscellaneous Provisions) Act 1994 Pt I (ss 1–13); and CONVEYANCING vol 23 (2016) PARA 181.
3 As to proof of title see CONVEYANCING vol 23 (2016) PARA 123 et seq.
4 As to acceptance of title see CONVEYANCING vol 23 (2016) PARA 201.
5 *Clive v Beaumont* (1848) 1 De G & Sm 397; *Gaston v Frankum* (1848) 2 De G & Sm 561.
6 *McGrory v Alderdale Estate Co Ltd* [1918] AC 503, HL.
7 *Phipps v Child* (1857) 3 Drew 709.
8 *Lucas v James* (1849) 7 Hare 410 at 425. Where the only defence to a claim for specific performance is an objection to title, a vendor and purchaser summons may be used as an alternative: see PARA 587.
9 *Baskcomb v Phillips* (1859) 29 LJ Ch 380.
10 *Wilson v Williams* (1857) 3 Jur NS 810.

601. Default judgments. If the claimant in a High Court claim has served a claim and the defendant has not served a defence within the requisite time, the claimant may apply for judgment for specific performance and any ancillary or alternative relief claimed[1]. The claimant will not be granted any relief not claimed[2] and cannot rely on any facts not pleaded in the claim. Thus a claimant will not usually be given judgment for interest at the contractual rate unless he has pleaded the relevant term of the contract[3]. An application for a default judgment is normally made[4] and usually the application must specify or be accompanied by a draft of the precise form of order sought by the claimant[5].

1 As to default judgments generally see CPR Pt 12; and CIVIL PROCEDURE vol 12 (2015) PARA 535 et seq. As to ancillary or alternative relief see PARA 597.
2 *Stone v Smith* (1887) 35 ChD 188; *Kingdon v Kirk* (1887) 37 ChD 141; *Tacon v National Standard Land Mortgage and Investment Co* (1887) 56 LJ Ch 529.
3 *Palmer v Lark* [1945] Ch 182, [1945] 1 All ER 355.
4 As to the procedure on application for a default judgment see CPR 12.10; and CIVIL PROCEDURE vol 12 (2015) PARA 543.
5 *De Jongh v Newman* (1887) 56 LT 180.

(2) PROCEEDINGS FOR SUMMARY JUDGMENT

602. Form of procedure. If a remedy sought by a claimant in his claim form[1] includes a claim:

(1)   for specific performance of an agreement (whether in writing or not) for the sale, purchase, exchange, mortgage or charge of any property, or for the grant or assignment of a lease of any property[2], with or without an alternative claim for damages[3]; or

(2)   for rescission of such an agreement[4]; or

(3)   for the forfeiture or return of the deposit made under such an agreement[5],

then, any time after the claim form has been served whether or not the defendant has acknowledged service of the claim form, whether or not the time for acknowledging service has expired and whether or not any particulars of claim have been served[6], the claimant may apply for judgment[7].

The orders the court may make on such an application include judgment on the claim, the striking-out or dismissal of the claim, the dismissal of the application, or a conditional order[8].

There may be provision as to costs[9]. If an order for summary judgment is made against a respondent who does not appear at the hearing of the application, the respondent may apply for the order to be set aside or varied[10], and on the hearing of such an application the court may make such order as it thinks just[11].

Summary judgment may be ordered for specific performance of a contract for the sale of property situated outside the jurisdiction[12].

1   As to claim forms, commencement of proceedings, etc see PARA 586; and CIVIL PROCEDURE vol 11 (2015) PARA 135 et seq.
2   This includes personal as well as real property, and an agreement either to purchase shares or to find a purchaser for them is an agreement for the sale or purchase of property: *Woodlands v Hind* [1955] 2 All ER 604, [1955] 1 WLR 688. The words 'sale' and 'purchase' are used in their strict primary meaning, namely a sale or purchase in consideration of a money payment: *Robshaw Bros Ltd v Mayer* [1957] Ch 125, [1956] 3 All ER 833; *Young v Markworth Properties Ltd* [1965] Ch 475, [1965] 1 All ER 834. A contract to transfer a house to a builder in consideration of the erection by him of another house on a plot belonging to the transferor is not a sale or exchange: *Doyle v East* [1972] 2 All ER 1013, [1972] 1 WLR 1080.
3   CPR PD 24—*The Summary Disposal of Claims* para 7.1(1)(a). This covers a case where the claimant elects to treat the contract as repudiated (see PARA 598), and only asks for damages: *Woodlands v Hind* [1955] 2 All ER 604, [1955] 1 WLR 688.
4   CPR PD 24—*The Summary Disposal of Claims* para 7.1(1)(b).
5   CPR PD 24—*The Summary Disposal of Claims* para 7.1(1)(c). As to pleading additional and alternative relief see PARA 597.
6   CPR PD 24—*The Summary Disposal of Claims* para 7.1(2).
7   CPR PD 24—*The Summary Disposal of Claims* para 7.1(1). Such application is under CPR Pt 24: for details see further CIVIL PROCEDURE vol 12 (2015) PARA 549 et seq.
8   CPR PD 24—*The Summary Disposal of Claims* para 5.1. A conditional order is an order which requires a party to pay a sum of money into court, or to take a specified step in relation to his claim or defence, as the case may be, and provides that that party's claim will be dismissed or his statement of case will be struck out if he does not comply: CPR PD 24—*The Summary Disposal of Claims* para 5.2.
9   As to costs see CPR PD 24—*The Summary Disposal of Claims* paras 9.1–9.3.
10   CPR PD 24—*The Summary Disposal of Claims* para 8.1.
11   CPR PD 24—*The Summary Disposal of Claims* para 8.2.
12   *Richard West & Partners (Inverness) Ltd v Dick* [1969] 2 Ch 424, [1969] 1 All ER 943, CA. As to jurisdiction over foreign property see CONFLICT OF LAWS vol 19 (2011) PARA 668 et seq.

603. Directions where dismissal etc. Where the court dismisses the application for summary judgment for specific performance[1] or makes an order that does not completely dispose of the claim, the court will give case management directions as to the future conduct of the case[2].

1   As to applications for summary judgment see PARA 602.
2   CPR PD 24—*The Summary Disposal of Claims* para 10.

604. Costs. The general rule is that the costs of any proceedings or any part of the proceedings are not to be assessed by the detailed procedure until the conclusion of the proceedings, but the court may order them to be assessed immediately[1].

1 See CPR 47.1. As to further guidance about when proceedings are concluded for this purpose see CPR PD47. As to discussion generally of CPR Pt 47–Procedure for Assessment of Costs and Default Provision see CIVIL PROCEDURE vol 12A (2015) PARA 1749 et seq.

(3) INTERIM PROCEEDINGS

605. Interim relief. The court has power to make an interim order to enforce the performance of a contractual obligation[1]. In a purchaser's claim, the defendant may be restrained by injunction from: disposing of the property, ceasing to supply the claimant with goods or services[2] or creating rights over it inconsistent with the terms of the contract[3]. The defendant may also be restrained by injunction from damaging the subject matter of the contract[4] or taking it out of the jurisdiction[5]. The court has power to make an order for the detention, custody or preservation of any property which is the subject matter of the claim or for the inspection of any such property in the possession of a party[6]. If it is necessary for the preservation of the property, the court may appoint some person to act as receiver pending the determination of the proceedings[7]. If the subject matter of the sale is property (such as farm land) which needs to be worked in order to prevent deterioration, the receiver may also be appointed to act as manager[8].

1 *Smith v Peters* (1875) LR 20 Eq 511 (order to permit valuer to enter premises); *Astro Exito Navegacion SA v Southland Enterprise Co Ltd and Nan Jong Iron and Steel Co Ltd, The Messiniaki Tolmi* [1981] 2 Lloyd's Rep 595, [1982] Com LR 106, CA; further proceedings [1982] QB 1248, [1982] 3 All ER 335, CA; affd [1983] 2 AC 787, [1983] 2 All ER 725, HL (order directing buyer to give instructions for payment under letter of credit). As to interim applications generally see CIVIL PROCEDURE vol 12 (2015) PARAS 581 et seq, 1076, 1176. As to interim remedies generally see CIVIL PROCEDURE vol 12 (2015) PARA 566 et seq.
2 *Sky Petroleum Ltd v VIP Petroleum Ltd* [1974] 1 All ER 954, [1974] 1 WLR 576; *Land Rover Group Ltd v UPF (UK) Ltd (in administrative receivership)* [2002] EWHC 303 (QB), [2003] 2 BCLC 222; *Aston Martin Lagonda Ltd v Automotive Industrial Partnership Ltd* [2010] All ER (D) 131 (Feb); *Jet2.com Ltd v Blackpool Airport Ltd* [2010] EWHC 3166 (Comm), [2010] All ER (D) 58 (Dec).
3 *Curtis v Marquis of Buckingham* (1814) 3 Ves & B 168. In the case of contracts for the sale of land, however, relief of this kind is usually unnecessary because an estate contract can be protected by registration under the Land Charges Act 1972 (in the case of unregistered land) or by entry of a notice or restriction on the register of title under the Land Registration Act 2002: see REAL PROPERTY AND REGISTRATION vol 87 (2012) PARA 724. As to injunctions in aid of specific performance see CIVIL PROCEDURE vol 12 (2015) PARA 1194.
4 *Crockford v Alexander* (1808) 15 Ves 138.
5 *Hart v Herwig* (1873) 8 Ch App 860. As to the grant of interim injunctions see CIVIL PROCEDURE vol 12 (2015) PARA 581 et seq.
6 See CPR 25.1(1)(c)(i), (d), 25.3, 25.5, CPR PD 25A—Interim Injunctions paras 2.1-4.5. As to CPR Pt 25 generally see CIVIL PROCEDURE vol 12 (2015) PARA 566 et seq.
7 See *Boehm v Wood* (1820) 2 Jac & W 236; *Stilwell v Wilkins* (1821) Jac 280. See generally RECEIVERS vol 88 (2012) PARA 30 et seq.
8 *Hyde v Warden* (1876) 1 Ex D 309, CA. See also RECEIVERS vol 88 (2012) PARA 184 et seq. A similar appointment can be made where the claim is for rescission of the contract: *Gibbs v David* (1875) LR 20 Eq 373; *Cook v Andrews* [1897] 1 Ch 266.

606. Payment into court. If the purchaser has been let into possession of the property the court may make an interim order directing him to pay the purchase price into court[1], although the order will usually give the purchaser the option of giving up possession of the property instead[2]. If the purchaser has done something to prejudice the value of the property he may be ordered to pay the purchase price into court without an option to give up possession[3], but in view of the possibility of obtaining summary judgment this power should be exercised only in an extreme case[4]. Payment into court will not be ordered if the contract expressly provides for the purchaser to take possession before completion[5], unless the purchaser has performed acts of ownership which alter the nature of the property[6]. If the purchaser of a lease at a premium is let into possession and pays rent, it is inappropriate to order him to pay the premium into court or give up possession[7]. An order for payment into court will also be refused if the delay in completion is due to the fault of the vendor[8] or if the purchaser is in possession by virtue of some independent right such as a tenancy[9]. Payment into court under a court order does not release the purchaser from the obligation to pay interest at the rate specified in the contract[10]. An order may be made for payment of royalties into court in a claim for specific performance of a lease of a mine where the defendant has been allowed into possession[11]. A stakeholder may be ordered to pay the deposit into court[12].

1   *Buck v Lodge* (1812) 18 Ves 450; *Lilley v Allen* (1866) 14 LT 52.
2   *Clarke v Wilson* (1808) 15 Ves 317; *Gibson v Clarke* (1813) 1 Ves & B 500; *Tindal v Cobham* (1835) 2 My & K 385; *Greenwood v Turner* [1891] 2 Ch 144; *Re Cassano and Mackay's Contract* [1920] WN 7.
3   *Pope v Great Eastern Rly Co* (1866) LR 3 Eq 171.
4   *Maskell v Ivory* [1970] Ch 502, [1970] 1 All ER 488.
5   *Pryse v Cambrian Rly Co* (1867) 2 Ch App 444.
6   *Dixon v Astley* (1816) 1 Mer 133; *Cutler v Simons* (1816) 2 Mer 103. Cf *Gell v Watson* (1818) 3 Madd 225.
7   *Joel v Montgomery and Taylor Ltd* [1967] Ch 272, [1966] 3 All ER 763.
8   *Fox v Birch* (1815) 1 Mer 105.
9   *Freebody v Perry* (1815) Coop G 91; *Robertshaw v Bray* (1866) 35 LJ Ch 844.
10   *Pearlberg v May* [1951] Ch 699, [1951] 1 All ER 1001, CA.
11   *Lewis v James* (1886) 32 ChD 326, CA. Cf *Faulkner v Llewellin* (1862) 31 LJ Ch 549.
12   *Yates v Farebrother* (1819) 4 Madd 239.

(4) RELIEF

(i) Judgment for Specific Performance

607. Form of judgment. The judgment for specific performance generally commences with a declaration that the agreement in question ought to be specifically performed and orders and adjudges the same accordingly. The judgment then usually includes directions consequent on the declaration, which vary according to the circumstances of the case. Thus the judgment may include an inquiry as to damages suffered by the claimant by reason of the defendant's delay[1], and a reference to chambers for an inquiry as to the vendor's title[2]. Where the vendor has a lien[3] for unpaid purchase money on the property sold, a declaration of the lien may be embodied in the judgment, with liberty to apply to enforce the lien if the vendor so desires[4]. Again, where the vendor's title has been accepted by or forced on the purchaser, the judgment may contain directions for the ascertainment of how much is payable by the purchaser in respect of the purchase money, whether with or without interest[5], and whether with or without compensation or abatement[6]. It may also contain special directions as to the rents or the deterioration of the property[7]. On payment of what is due from the purchaser the judgment may direct a conveyance by the vendor, a vesting order or the appointment of a person to convey[8]. Orders dealing with the deposit may also be necessary[9], and, in the case of agreements for leases, special forms of order are required[10].

If an inquiry as to the vendor's title is ordered, any provisions of the order which are dependent on the outcome of the inquiry may be omitted, and the case will be restored for further consideration after the inquiry has been held.

1   See *Bennett v Stone* [1902] 1 Ch 226 at 236–238; affd [1903] 1 Ch 509, CA (order for accounts not on footing of wilful default; vendors occupying and farming the land not charged with occupation rent, but with proceeds of crops less expenses of realisation, without allowance for losses in farming). As to damages for delay see PARA 635. As to a successful purchaser bringing into account, against the purchase money due to vendor, the costs payable by the vendor see *Green v Sevin* (1879) 13 ChD 589 at 602; distinguish *Phillips v Howell* [1901] 2 Ch 773 at 778 (rule limited to cases where debts are between the parties in the same capacity); and see CIVIL PROCEDURE vol 11 (2015) PARA 438.
2   See PARA 608 et seq.
3   As to the lien of an unpaid vendor of land see LIEN vol 68 (2016) PARA 859 et seq.
4   *Walker v Ware, Hadham and Buntingford Rly Co* (1865) LR 1 Eq 195; *Sedgwick v Watford and Rickmansworth Rly Co* (1867) 36 LJ Ch 379, where an immediate sale was ordered; *Vyner v Hoylake Rly Co* (1868) 17 WR 92; *Wing v Tottenham and Hampstead Junction Rly Co* (1868) 3 Ch App 740; *Munns v Isle of Wight Rly Co* (1870) 5 Ch App 414; *Keane v Athenry and Ennis Junction Rly Co* (1870) 19 WR 43; *Bee v Stafford and Uttoxeter Rly Co* (1875) 23 WR 868.
5   For a form of judgment where a purchaser who had been let into possession at a rent failed to complete see *Mutual Investment Society v Johns* [1934] WN 59. As to interest on purchase money see PARAS 615–617.
6   As to specific performance with compensation see PARA 621 et seq.
7   As to right to rents see PARA 614; and as to deterioration see PARA 618.
8   The order should provide for the simultaneous delivery of the conveyance and payment of the purchase money with interest and costs: see *Cooper v Morgan* [1909] 1 Ch 261; *Palmer v Lark* [1945] Ch 182, [1945] 1 All ER 355. See also CONVEYANCING vol 23 (2016) PARA 453 et seq.
9   As to the deposit see PARAS 619–620.
10 See *Strelley v Pearson* (1880) 15 ChD 113; *Eadie v Addison* (1882) 52 LJ Ch 80. As to specific performance of agreements for leases see LANDLORD AND TENANT vol 62 (2016) PARAS 89–90.

(ii) Reference of Title

608. Nature and purpose of reference of title. In claims for specific performance it is often necessary to determine whether or not the vendor can make a good title[1], since the court does not grant the remedy of specific enforcement of a sale unless it is satisfied that the vendor has such a title as the purchaser either is willing, or can be forced, to accept[2]. It follows that a reference of title is generally ordered in a vendor's claim on the purchaser's application[3], and will also be ordered in a purchaser's claim, unless the purchaser has accepted the title or waived any objection to it[4]. A vendor cannot be permitted to take exception to his own title[5].

1   As to the extent of the vendor's obligation to make a good title and the mode of investigation and proof of the vendor's title, so far as they relate to contracts for the sale of land, see CONVEYANCING vol 23 (2016) PARA 133 et seq. An inquiry into title may, of course, be directed in other matters than sale of land, such as contracts for sale of shares: *Shaw v Fisher* (1848) 2 De G & Sm 11; *Curling v Flight* (1848) 2 Ph 613.
2   As to adequacy of title see PARA 563.
3   *Jenkins v Hiles* (1802) 6 Ves 646, where the purchaser admitted that he had no specific objection, but an inquiry was ordered; *Lesturgeon v Martin* (1834) 3 My & K 255, where a general inquiry was ordered, even though the purchaser admitted that he had only one particular objection. Cf *Fleetwood v Green* (1809) 15 Ves 594. Where a defect of title appears on the statements of case or is proved at the hearing the court may decide against the title without ordering an inquiry: cf *Lucas v James* (1849) 7 Hare 410 at 425 per Wigram V-C; *Baskcomb v Phillips* (1859) 29 LJ Ch

380. See also PARA 600. A delay by a purchaser in raising a patent objection may result in his being ordered to pay the costs of the inquiry: see *Curling v Austin* (1862) 2 Drew & Sm 129; *Upperton v Nickolson* (1871) 6 Ch App 436.

4 However, the purchaser may have to bear the costs of the inquiry if it appears that the vendor had at the proper time disclosed a good title (*Lyle v Earl of Yarborough* (1859) John 70), or if he afterwards waives his objections (*Bennett v Fowler* (1840) 2 Beav 302).

5 *Bradley v Munton* (1852) 15 Beav 460.

609. Limitations on the inquiry. The reference of title, although in general terms, is confined to such title as under the conditions of the contract the vendor is bound to show. These conditions may restrict the purchaser's right to object to the title, or to make requisitions or inquiries from the vendor as to his title, or may preclude the purchaser from inquiring into or objecting to certain parts of the title[1].

A reference of title is not ordered where the vendor expressly sells merely such interest as he has[2], or such title as he himself bought with[3], or where the contract is not so much a contract of sale as a compromise of disputed rights[4], or where the contract was for the sale of the vendor's share and interest in property and not the property itself[5].

1 As to the effect and validity of conditions restricting the vendor's obligations to prove his title see CONVEYANCING vol 23 (2016) PARA 112 et seq. As to the covenants for title implied by statute on the disposition of a property see the Law of Property (Miscellaneous Provisions) Act 1994 Pt I (ss 1–13); and CONVEYANCING vol 23 (2016) PARA 181 et seq.

2 *Southby v Hutt* (1837) 2 My & Cr 207 at 212. See also CONVEYANCING vol 23 (2016) PARA 60 et seq.

3 *Re Haedicke and Lipski's Contract* [1901] 2 Ch 666 at 669. See also *Re Duthy and Jesson's Contract* [1898] 1 Ch 419 (best title vendors can give).

4 *Godson v Turner* (1851) 15 Beav 46. Cf *Ashton v Wood* (1857) 3 Jur NS 146.

5 *Phipps v Child* (1857) 3 Drew 709.

610. Waiver as a bar to reference. A reference of title is not ordered even though the party claiming it is prima facie entitled to have it, if he has waived the right to it either expressly[1] or by implication[2]. The waiver may go to the whole of the title, or merely to some particular objection or objections[3].

Even where the purchaser's acts have been held to constitute a waiver of his right to investigate the vendor's title, the court may not enforce the contract where it has appeared by other means that the vendor's title was defective[4]. Conversely, a purchaser may himself cure a defect, which he will thus be debarred from objecting to, and specific performance will be ordered[5].

A waiver must be expressly pleaded[6], and must be established at the hearing, so that a vendor cannot adduce evidence of waiver on an inquiry as to title[7].

1 Eg by admitting the claimant's title in the defence in a claim for specific performance: cf *Phipps v Child* (1857) 3 Drew 709. An express waiver may be either absolute or conditional: *Townley v Bond* (1843) 4 Dr & War 240 at 261.

2 The implied waiver must be clear and free from surprise or misrepresentation on the part of the vendor: see *Jenkins v Hiles* (1802) 6 Ves 646 at 655; *Haydon v Bell* (1838) 1 Beav 337; *Blacklow v Laws* (1842) 2 Hare 40. As to acceptance of title generally see CONVEYANCING vol 23 (2016) PARA 201.

3 *Corless v Sparling* (1874) 8 IR Eq 335.

4 *Warren v Richardson* (1830) You 1. See also CONVEYANCING vol 23 (2016) PARA 112 et seq.

5 *Murrell v Goodyear* (1860) 1 De G F & J 432, where the purchaser was allowed to claim the cost of curing the defect as a deduction from the purchase price.

6 *Clive v Beaumont* (1848) 1 De G & Sm 397. See also PARA 600.

7 *McGrory v Alderdale Estate Co Ltd* [1918] AC 503, HL.

611. Form and scope of reference. The reference of title may be expressly limited in accordance with the requirements of the case[1] or it may be open and general[2].

It is directed not merely to the question of whether or not a good title is made out, but also, where necessary, to the time when such title was shown[3].

Ordering a reference of title at an interim stage[4] is rarely done because where the only issue is whether the vendor can show a good title, the issue can usually be more quickly and cheaply resolved by a vendor and purchaser summons[5].

1   *Hume v Pocock* (1865) LR 1 Eq 423; affd (1866) 1 Ch App 379. See also *Remnant v Holt* (1847), cited in 3 Seton's Judgments and Orders (7th Edn) 2160; *Saul v Bolton* (1852), cited in 3 Seton's Judgments and Orders (7th Edn) 2159.
2   *Harnett v Baker* (1875) LR 20 Eq 50, where the conditions were held to be misleading; an open reference was offered, and, being refused by the vendor, the claim was dismissed.
3   *Foxlowe v Amcoats* (1840) 3 Beav 496. This inquiry is generally necessary for the purpose of determining the date from which interest is payable by the purchaser (see PARAS 615–617), and also in connection with the question of liability for costs (see PARA 613). A good title is shown, as opposed to being made, when the necessary facts and documents are set out in the abstract: *Parr v Lovegrove* (1858) 4 Drew 170 at 176; see also *Sherwin v Shakspear* (1853) 17 Beav 267 at 275; and CONVEYANCING vol 23 (2016) PARA 113 et seq.
4   See *Phillipson v Gibbon* (1871) 6 Ch App 428.
5   See the Law of Property Act 1925 s 49(1); and PARA 587.

612.   Consequences of failure to prove title. If the master's order is against title, the contract is not automatically discharged and the purchaser must apply to the court for an order that the contract be discharged[1]. The court may refuse to order the discharge of the contract if the defect in title has been cured after the date of the master's order[2]. If the contract is discharged, the purchaser will be entitled to damages[3]. The order discharging the contract will normally direct repayment of the deposit, together with interest, unless the right to interest on repayment of a deposit is excluded by the contract[4]. The court may also declare that the purchaser is entitled to a lien on the subject matter of the contract for repayment of the deposit, costs and any interest on damages to which he is entitled[5].

1   *Halkett v Earl of Dudley* [1907] 1 Ch 590; *Austins of East Ham Ltd v Macey* [1941] Ch 338 at 341, CA, per Sir Wilfred Greene MR; *Singh (Sudagar) v Nazeer* [1979] Ch 474, [1978] 3 All ER 817. These cases, and the cases cited in notes 2–3, were decided on the old master's certificate procedure.
2   *Coffin v Cooper* (1807) 14 Ves 205; *Hume v Pocock* (1866) 1 Ch App 379; *Halkett v Earl of Dudley* [1907] 1 Ch 590.
3   *Johnson v Agnew* [1980] AC 367, [1979] 1 All ER 883, HL. The rule in *Bain v Fothergill* (1874) LR 7 HL 158, which formerly limited the damages to the expenses incurred by the purchaser, has been abolished in relation to contracts made on or after 27 September 1989: see the Law of Property (Miscellaneous Provisions) Act 1989 ss 3, 5(3), (4)(a).
4   As to recovery of the deposit see CONVEYANCING vol 23 (2016) PARA 452.
5   As to purchaser's lien see LIEN vol 68 (2016) PARA 864 et seq.

613.   Costs. In a claim for specific performance, as in other claims, the costs are in the general discretion of the court subject to the provisions of rules of court[1]. Nevertheless a number of practices have grown up, and may still guide courts in their assessment. Generally, where the dispute is as to title, the vendor has to pay the costs up to the time when he first showed a good title[2]. However, a purchaser who has caused the litigation by his objections may have to pay the costs if the objections are overruled, even though in some other respect a good title has not been shown at the time of the objection[3]. A purchaser may be deprived of his costs if he raises a successful objection at too late a stage[4], and a purchaser who raises a successful objection but waives it may be ordered to pay the costs[5]. Costs may be awarded to the vendor if he is unable to show title to the whole subject matter of the contract but the court orders specific performance with compensation[6], but a vendor may be deprived of his costs if the title is subject to a defect of which he should have known, even though he is able to cure it[7].

Where a claimant issued proceedings claiming specific performance after the date on which completion was due to take place, but without having previously served a notice making time of the essence, he was nevertheless awarded the costs of the claim as, there clearly being no defence, his equitable right to specific performance had accrued at the date when the claim form was issued[8].

Considerations of costs also turn on whether the case was one proper for determination, without a claim, by a vendor and purchaser summons[9].

1   See the Senior Courts Act 1981 s 51; CPR 44–CPR 47; *Gomba Holdings (UK) Ltd v Minories Finance Ltd (No 2)* [1993] Ch 171, [1992] 4 All ER 588, CA; *Seavision Investment SA v Evennett and Clarkson Puckle Ltd, The Tiburon* [1992] 2 Lloyd's Rep 26, CA; *Steele Ford & Newton v Crown Prosecution Service (No 2)* [1994] 1 AC 22, [1993] 2 All ER 769, HL; and CIVIL PROCEDURE vol 12A (2015) PARA 1684. As to the costs of proceedings for summary judgment see PARA 604.
2   *Freer v Hesse* (1853) 4 De GM & G 495 at 505; *Phillipson v Gibbon* (1871) 6 Ch App 428 at 434; *Halkett v Earl of Dudley* [1907] 1 Ch 590 at 607.
3   *Bridges v Longman* (1857) 24 Beav 27.
4   *Upperton v Nickolson* (1871) 6 Ch App 436.
5   *Bennett v Fowler* (1840) 2 Beav 302.
6   *Carver v Richards* (1860) 3 LT 142.
7   *Phillipson v Gibbon* (1871) 6 Ch App 428.
8   *Marks v Lilley* [1959] 2 All ER 647, [1959] 1 WLR 749. See also *Horton v Kurzke* [1971] 2 All ER 577, [1971] 1 WLR 769.
9   See *Lawes v Gibson* (1865) LR 1 Eq 135. As to vendor and purchaser summonses, and the questions properly determinable on them, see PARA 587.

(iii) Interest, Rents and Deterioration

614. Rights as between vendor and purchaser to rents and profits. On a contract for the sale of real property, as regards registered land, the legal title does not pass until the buyer has become the registered proprietor of the land[1]. If the contract is one of which specific performance can be decreed[2], then between the date of the contract and the date of completion the legal estate remains in the vendor, but the equitable estate passes to the purchaser[3]. The vendor is entitled to the rents and profits and is liable to bear outgoings up to the time, if any, fixed for completion[4], or, if no time is fixed, up to the time at which completion ought to take place, that is, as a rule, when a good title is shown[5]. After that date the purchaser is, as a rule, entitled to the rents and profits, but is liable to bear the outgoings and to pay the vendor interest on the unpaid purchase money[6]. Where the purchase price is to be fixed subsequently to the contract, interest does not run until the price is ascertained[7].

It is a general principle of equity that one party cannot claim simultaneously the benefit of the money and of the land. Hence, unless the contract unequivocally provides otherwise, a purchaser who has been relieved of the obligation to pay interest cannot claim the rents and profits; conversely, a vendor who has elected under the terms of the contract to retain the rents and profits cannot claim interest on the purchase money as well[8].

Until actual completion, the rents and profits will normally continue to be collected by the vendor, but if the purchaser is entitled to them in equity the vendor will receive them as trustee for the purchaser and will have to account for them to the purchaser on completion[9].

1   See CONVEYANCING vol 23 (2016) PARA 264. As regards unregistered land, the title to the property passes to the buyer on completion.
2   As to contracts of which specific performance will not be decreed see PARA 506 et seq.
3   The interest conferred by the agreement is an interest commensurate with the relief which equity would give by way of specific performance: see *Howard v Miller* [1915] AC 318 at 326, PC, per

Lord Parker; *Central Trust and Safe Deposit Co v Snider* [1916] 1 AC 266 at 272, PC, per Lord
Parker. See also *Rose v Watson* (1864) 10 HL Cas 672 at 678 per Lord Westbury LC; *Raffety v
Schofield* [1897] 1 Ch 937 at 943 per Romer J; *Cornwall v Henson* [1899] 2 Ch 710 at 714
per Cozens-Hardy J. If the contract goes off, the equitable estate revests in the vendor: see *Wall v
Bright* (1820) 1 Jac & W 494 at 501 per Plumer MR. For a fuller discussion of the respective rights
of a vendor and purchaser between contract and conveyance see CONVEYANCING vol 23 (2016)
PARA 190 et seq; and as to equitable interests under contracts for sale see EQUITABLE
JURISDICTION vol 47 (2014) PARAS 214–215.
4   See *Binks v Lord Rokeby* (1818) 2 Swan 222 at 225; *Esdaile v Stephenson* (1822) 1 Sim & St 122;
    Carrodus v Sharp (1855) 20 Beav 56 at 58; *Wells v Maxwell (No 2)* (1863) 32 Beav 550; *Re Keeble
    and Stillwell's Fletton Brick Co* (1898) 78 LT 383; *Plews v Samuel* [1904] 1 Ch 464.
5   *Pincke v Curteis* (1793) 4 Bro CC 329; *Enraght v Fitzgerald* (1842) 2 Dr & War 43; *Carrodus v
    Sharp* (1855) 20 Beav 56; *Barsht v Tagg* [1900] 1 Ch 231 at 235; *Halkett v Earl of Dudley* [1907]
    1 Ch 590. See also CONVEYANCING vol 23 (2016) PARA 309 et seq.
6   See *Fletcher v Lancashire and Yorkshire Rly Co* [1902] 1 Ch 901 at 908. See also the cases cited
    in notes 4–5. As to the rate of interest see CONVEYANCING vol 23 (2016) PARA 278 note 3. See
    also CONVEYANCING vol 23 (2016) PARA 276 et seq.
7   *Catling v Great Northern Rly Co* (1869) 18 WR 121.
8   See *Re Hewitt's Contract* [1963] 3 All ER 419, [1963] 1 WLR 1298.
9   *Lysaght v Edwards* (1876) 2 ChD 499; *Clarke v Ramuz* [1891] 2 QB 456, CA; *Plews v Samuel*
    [1904] 1 Ch 464. See also CONVEYANCING vol 23 (2016) PARA 191.

615. Interest on purchase money where the vendor is in possession. Apart from
the special terms of the contract, the following rules as to interest[1] apply:
   (1)   if there is delay in completion which is due to the default of the vendor,
         and the interest is in excess of the rents, the purchaser is not liable to pay
         interest during the period of delay, but the vendor retains the rents[2],
         although where the delay is due to the fault of the purchaser, interest
         runs from the proper date for completion[3];
   (2)   if, where completion is delayed through the vendor's fault, the purchaser
         appropriates the purchase money and gives notice of the appropriation
         to the vendor, it appears that the vendor is only entitled to the interest,
         if any, accruing on the money so appropriated[4].

1   As to the rate of interest where none is specified by the contract see PARA 614 note 6.
2   *Esdaile v Stephenson* (1822) 1 Sim & St 122; *Paton v Rogers* (1822) 6 Madd 256; *Jones v Mudd*
    (1827) 4 Russ 118; *Re Hewitt's Contract* [1963] 3 All ER 419, [1963] 1 WLR 1298. As to the
    proper date for completion see CONVEYANCING vol 23 (2016) PARA 247 et seq.
3   *Binks v Lord Rokeby* (1818) 2 Swan 222; *Monro v Taylor* (1852) 3 Mac & G 713; *Wells v
    Maxwell (No 2)* (1863) 32 Beav 550; *Halkett v Earl of Dudley* [1907] 1 Ch 590 at 606.
4   *Regent's Canal Co v Ware* (1857) 23 Beav 575; *Re Monckton and Gilzean* (1884) 27 ChD 555.
    Cf *Re Riley to Streatfield* (1886) 34 ChD 386, where it was held that this principle does not apply
    to a case of delay by a willing vendor and only applies if there has been a purported repudiation
    by the vendor.

616. Express contractual provisions. The rules as to interest[1] may be varied by
the special terms of a contract. For instance:
   (1)   rents until completion may be expressly reserved to the vendor[2]; or
   (2)   the contract may provide that the purchaser is to pay interest from the
         date fixed for completion, notwithstanding delay from any cause
         whatever, in which case interest is payable even if delay is due to the
         fault of the vendor[3], so long as there is on his part no vexatious conduct,
         bad faith or gross negligence[4]; or
   (3)   the contract may exempt the purchaser from payment of interest only in
         the case of wilful default[5] on the part of the vendor, this involving actual
         default on the vendor's part and more than mere mistake or oversight,
         although not necessarily meaning intentional delay or wilful
         obstruction[6].

A vendor in possession himself[7] is charged a fair occupation rent[8], unless he simply remained in possession owing to the purchaser's default[9]. Liability for outgoings as a rule goes with the right to receive rents[10].

1 As to interest see PARAS 614–615.
2 In such a case the vendor cannot claim interest unless the contract unequivocally provides otherwise: *Brooke v Champernowne* (1837) 4 Cl & Fin 589 at 611, HL; *Re Hewitt's Contract* [1963] 3 All ER 419, [1963] 1 WLR 1298.
3 *Sherwin v Shakspear* (1854) 5 De GM & G 517; *Williams v Glenton* (1866) 1 Ch App 200. See also *Greenwood v Churchill* (1845) 8 Beav 413 (great delay on vendor's part; purchaser ordered to pay interest, but left to apply for compensation); *Rowley v Adams* (1850) 12 Beav 476 (vendor's failure to deliver abstract at due date); *Cowpe v Bakewell* (1851) 13 Beav 421; *Dyson v Hornby* (1851) 4 De G & Sm 481; *Bannerman v Clarke* (1856) 3 Drew 632 (delay through death of vendor); *Vickers v Hand* (1859) 26 Beav 630; *Lord Palmerston v Turner* (1864) 33 Beav 524 (delay through proceedings necessary to perfect vendor's power to sell). See also CONVEYANCING vol 23 (2016) PARA 276 et seq. Cf *De Visme v De Visme* (1849) Mac & G 336.
4 *Sherwin v Shakspeare* (1854) 5 De GM & G 517 at 529 per Knight Bruce LJ. See also *Re Kissock and Taylor's Contract* [1916] 1 IR 393; *Sheridan v Higgins* [1971] IR 291.
5 Delay may be due to wilful default if it is caused by the vendor's absence abroad (*Re Young and Harston's Contract* (1885) 31 ChD 168, CA; *Re Hetling and Merton's Contract* [1893] 3 Ch 269, CA) or his failure to apply in good time for any necessary consent (*Re Wilson and Stevens' Contract* [1894] 3 Ch 546). See also *Re Bayley-Worthington and Cohen's Contract* [1909] 1 Ch 648; *Re Hewitt's Contract* [1963] 3 All ER 419, [1963] 1 WLR 1298. For cases where it was held that delay had not been due to wilful default see *Re London Corpn and Tubbs' Contract* [1894] 2 Ch 524, CA (erroneous description of title); *Re Woods and Lewis' Contract* [1898] 1 Ch 433 (on appeal [1898] 2 Ch 211, CA) (unknown defect of title); *North v Percival* [1898] 2 Ch 128 (vendor's unsuccessful resistance to claim for specific performance). See also *Bennett v Stone* [1902] 1 Ch 226 (affd [1903] 1 Ch 509, CA); *Re Kissock and Taylor's Contract* [1916] 1 IR 393.
6 *Bennett v Stone* [1902] 1 Ch 226 at 232; affd [1903] 1 Ch 509, CA.
7 As to the liability of a vendor in receipt of rents to account see PARA 614.
8 *Dyer v Hargrave, Hargrave v Dyer* (1805) 10 Ves 505; *Metropolitan Rly Co v Defries* (1877) 2 QBD 189 (on appeal 2 QBD 387, CA). See also CONVEYANCING vol 23 (2016) PARA 196.
9 *Dakin v Cope* (1827) 2 Russ 170 at 181; *Leggott v Metropolitan Rly Co* (1870) 5 Ch App 716.
10 See *Lawes v Gibson* (1865) LR 1 Eq 135 (ground rent apportioned up to date of completion). Cf *Carrodus v Sharp* (1855) 20 Beav 56; *Williams v East London Rly Co* (1869) 1 LT 524. As to outgoings see CONVEYANCING vol 23 (2016) PARA 190.

617. Interest on purchase money where the purchaser is in possession. If, instead of the vendor remaining in possession[1], the purchaser has taken possession, he pays interest on the unpaid purchase money from the time of possession[2], even though the delay in completion has been due to the vendor's fault, and even though no profits have been made out of the land[3]. There must, of course, be a specifically enforceable obligation to purchase, and the purchaser must have taken or obtained, in advance of completion and payment of the price, a sufficient benefit over the property to be purchased or acquired; and the imposition of an obligation to pay interest must, in all the circumstances, be an equitable arrangement[4]. Where delay has arisen, the purchaser may, however, appropriate the purchase money for the purposes of the contract and give notice to the vendor, who is then only entitled to claim such interest as the money so appropriated produces[5].

1 See PARAS 614–616.
2 *Fludyer v Cocker* (1805) 12 Ves 25 at 27; *Binks v Lord Rokeby* (1818) 2 Swan 222 at 226; *Ballard v Shutt* (1880) 15 ChD 122; *Re Priestley's Contract* [1947] Ch 469, [1947] 1 All ER 716. Where a purchaser has been dispossessed after taking possession he is charged with interest during the period of possession: *Johnston v Johnston* (1869) 3 IR Eq 328. As to contracts exempting a purchaser from paying interest see *Birch v Joy* (1852) 3 HL Cas 565, where possession was held for 40 years before completion and the court refused to give effect to the exemption in the circumstances of the case.

3 *Fludyer v Cocker* (1805) 12 Ves 25; *Ballard v Shutt* (1880) 15 ChD 122; *Beresford v Clarke* [1908]
   2 IR 317. In *Cowpe v Bakewell* (1851) 13 Beav 421, the purchaser was put to his election to pay
   interest or give up the rents. See also *Herbert v Salisbury and Yeovil Rly Co* (1866) LR 2 Eq 221
   (interest at increasing rate); *A-G v Dean of Christ Church, Oxford* (1842) 13 Sim 214.
4 *Harrison v Thompson* [1993] BCLC 784, CA.
5 *Kershaw v Kershaw* (1869) LR 9 Eq 56. Cf *Winter v Blades* (1825) 2 Sim & St 393. See also
   CONVEYANCING vol 23 (2016) PARA 276.

618. Deterioration. A vendor, as constructive trustee, is liable for deterioration
to the property while he is in possession in the interval before completion,
provided the deterioration is due to his wilful default or want of reasonable care[1],
but he is not liable for deterioration occurring without his fault[2], and still less for
deterioration due to the purchaser's own fault[3]. The vendor's obligation to take
reasonable care of the property continues until actual completion unless delay in
completion is due to the fault of the purchaser[4]. As a rule the vendor is not entitled
to be indemnified for the cost of taking care of the property[5], but in special
circumstances he may have a right to an indemnity.

Thus where, in the case of the sale of a business as a going concern, a vendor
carries on the business up to the date fixed for completion and within a reasonable
time thereafter notifies the purchaser that the business is being carried on at a loss,
the vendor is, as against a purchaser who is in default as regards completion,
entitled to be indemnified against the loss incurred by carrying on the business[6].
So, also, where a purchaser contracts to buy leaseholds with knowledge of their
dilapidated condition subject to the landlord's consent to an assignment, and the
vendor has to spend money on repairs in order to obtain that consent, the vendor
is entitled to an indemnity from the purchaser against the cost of the repairs[7].

1 *Foster v Deacon* (1818) 3 Madd 394; *Earl of Egmont v Smith, Smith v Earl of Egmont* (1877) 6
   ChD 469 (failure to take steps to keep property in cultivation); *Royal Bristol Permanent Building
   Society v Bomash* (1887) 35 ChD 390; *Phillips v Lamdin* [1949] 2 KB 33, [1949] 1 All ER 770,
   where the vendor removed an ornate door and substituted a plain one, and was ordered to replace
   the ornate door; *Abdulla v Shah* [1959] AC 124, PC (letting of property without consent of
   purchaser). The purchaser's right to claim for deterioration may be enforced by action after
   conveyance in ignorance of the facts (*Clarke v Ramuz* [1891] 2 QB 456, CA; *Connolly v Keating
   (No 2)* [1903] 1 IR 356), and the claim may be set off against the balance of the purchase money
   (*Ferguson v Tadman* (1827) 1 Sim 530), or interest (*Phillips v Silvester* (1872) 8 Ch App 173). See
   further CONVEYANCING vol 23 (2016) PARA 193.
2 *Re Sweeny's Estate* (1890) 25 LR Ir 252.
3 *Harford v Purrier* (1816) 1 Madd 532.
4 *Binks v Lord Rokeby* (1818) 2 Swan 222; *Minchin v Nance* (1841) 4 Beav 332; *Sherwin v
   Shakspear* (1854) 5 De GM & G 517; *Regent's Canal Co v Ware* (1857) 23 Beav 575.
5 *Re Watford Corpn's and Ware's Contract* [1943] Ch 82, [1943] 1 All ER 54.
6 *Golden Bread Co Ltd v Hemmings* [1922] 1 Ch 162, following *Shaw v Foster* (1872) LR 5 HL
   321, and distinguishing *Dakin v Cope* (1827) 2 Russ 170.
7 *Lockharts v Bernard Rosen & Co* [1922] 1 Ch 433.

(iv) The Deposit

619. Questions as to deposit. In a claim for specific performance questions may
arise as to the deposit paid by the purchaser on the making of the contract[1], such
deposit being in the nature of part payment if the contract is duly completed, or,
if the contract fails owing to the default of the purchaser, serving as earnest or
security for the due performance of his contract and therefore liable to forfeiture[2].
It follows that if the contract is terminated as the result of a default by the vendor
or of the exercise by either party of a right of rescission the purchaser is entitled

to repayment of his deposit[3]. The deposit is also returnable if the contract is avoided by the non-occurrence of a condition precedent[4].

1 A deposit must be carefully distinguished from a payment made on account of the purchase price but not by way of deposit: see *Harrison v Holland and Hannen and Cubitts Ltd* [1922] 1 KB 211, CA; *Mayson v Clouet* [1924] AC 980, PC; *Dies v British and International Mining and Finance Corpn Ltd* [1939] 1 KB 724. See also *Hyundai Heavy Industries Co Ltd v Papadopoulos* [1980] 2 All ER 29, [1980] 1 WLR 1129, HL; *Stocznia Gdanska SA v Latvian Shipping Co and Latreefers Inc* [1998] 1 All ER 883, [1998] 1 WLR 574, [1998] 1 Lloyd's Rep 609 and *McDonald v Dennys Lascelles Ltd* (1933) 48 CLR 457 at 477 (Aust HC), per Dixon J. A deposit may only be forfeited if it is reasonable: *Workers Trust & Merchant Bank Ltd v Dojap Investments Ltd* [1993] AC 573, [1993] 2 All ER 370, PC, where a 25% deposit in a land sale contract was considered unreasonable.
2 See CONVEYANCING vol 23 (2016) PARA 57.
3 See CONVEYANCING vol 23 (2016) PARA 452.
4 *Shires v Brock* (1977) 247 Estates Gazette 127, CA, where the landlord's consent to the assignment of a lease was refused.

620. Purchaser's claim and counterclaim. A purchaser claiming specific performance may, in the alternative, claim a return of the deposit and enforcement of his lien on the property for that amount[1]. Similarly, in a vendor's claim for specific performance, the purchaser in resisting the claim may counterclaim for the return of the deposit with interest[2] (unless the right to interest is excluded by the contract) and for enforcement of his lien in respect of it[3].

It does not, however, necessarily follow that because a vendor is unsuccessful in his claim for specific performance the purchaser is entitled to a return of his deposit[4].

Similarly, if the purchaser is in default, the fact that the court has refused or might refuse to order specific performance of the contract gives the purchaser no automatic right to return of the deposit[5]. However, the court has a statutory power to order the repayment of the deposit if it thinks fit where it has refused to grant specific performance or in a claim for repayment of the deposit[6]. In exercise of this power the court has a wide and general discretion to do justice between the parties, having regard to all relevant considerations, including the terms of the contract[7], although it may not exercise its powers so as to deprive a purchaser of a legal right to the return of a deposit[8]. A term in a contract between a trader and a consumer[9] which has the object or effect of permitting the trader to retain sums paid by the consumer where the consumer decides not to conclude or perform the contract, without providing for the consumer to receive compensation of an equivalent amount from the trader where the trader is the party cancelling the contract, may be regarded as unfair[10].

It has recently been held that if the contractual deposit is due but has not in fact been paid, a vendor who has accepted the purchaser's repudiation of the contract can still obtain an order for payment of the deposit[11].

1 See CONVEYANCING vol 23 (2016) PARAS 452.
2 As to the appropriate rate of interest see PARA 614 note 6.
3 As to the purchaser's lien for repayment of his deposit see *Rose v Watson* (1864) 10 HL Cas 672; *Whitbread & Co Ltd v Watt* [1901] 11 Ch 911 (affd [1902] 1 Ch 835, CA) (purchaser's lien where contract rescinded under a condition of the contract); *Lee-Parker v Izzet* [1971] 3 All ER 1099 at 1106, [1971] 1 WLR 1688 at 1692. See also LIEN vol 68 (2016) PARA 864 et seq. There is no lien if the deposit has been paid to a stakeholder: *Combe v Lord Swaythling* [1947] Ch 625, [1947] 1 All ER 838.
4 *Re Scott and Alvarez's Contract, Scott v Alvarez* [1895] 2 Ch 603, CA. Cf *Re Hughes and Ashley's Contract* [1900] 2 Ch 595 at 602, CA; *Beyfus v Lodge* [1925] Ch 350.
5 *Re National Provincial Bank of England and Marsh* [1895] 1 Ch 190; *Re Scott and Alvarez's Contract, Scott v Alvarez* [1895] 2 Ch 603, CA; *Beyfus v Lodge* [1925] Ch 350.

6   See the Law of Property Act 1925 s 49(2); and CONVEYANCING vol 23 (2016) PARA 452. For an exercise of this discretionary power see *Charles Hunt Ltd v Palmer* [1931] 2 Ch 287.
7   *Universal Corpn v Five Ways Properties Ltd* [1979] 1 All ER 552 at 555, CA, per Buckley LJ. Cf *Omar v El-Wakil* [2001] EWCA Civ 1090 at [37], [2002] 2 P & CR 36 at [37] for the view that its exercise was exceptional. See *Schindler v Pigault* (1975) 30 P & CR 328; *Faruqi v English Real Estates Ltd* [1979] 1 WLR 963; *Maktoum v South Lodge Flats Ltd* (1980) Times, 22 April; *Dimsdale Developments (South East) Ltd v De Haan* (1984) 47 P & CR 1; *Midill (97PL) Ltd v Park Lane Estates Ltd* [2008] EWCA Civ 1227, [2009] 2 All ER 1067, [2009] 1 WLR 2460.
8   *Macara (James) Ltd v Barclay* [1945] KB 148, [1944] 2 All ER 589, CA.
9   See CONSUMER PROTECTION vol 21 (2016) PARA 391.
10 See the Consumer Rights Act 2015 s 63, Sch 2; and CONSUMER PROTECTION vol 21 (2016) PARA 396. An unfair term of a consumer contract or an unfair consumer notice is not binding on the consumer: see s 62(1)–(3).
11 See *Griffon Shipping* LLC *v Farodi Shipping Ltd, The Griffon* [2013] EWCA Civ 1567, [2014] 1 All ER (Comm) 593, [2014] 1 Lloyd's Rep 471; *Hardy* v *Griffiths* [2014] EWHC 3947 (Ch), [2015] Ch 417, [2014] All ER (D) 39 (Dec).

(5) SPECIFIC PERFORMANCE WITH COMPENSATION

(i) Compensation where there is no Condition for it

621. Where the vendor is entitled to specific performance on paying compensation. A vendor may obtain specific performance conditionally on paying compensation to a purchaser under a contract of sale[1], even where the vendor is unable to fulfil the exact terms of the bargain, provided that the purchaser will on completion obtain substantially what he bargained for[2] and that the difference in value between the thing contracted for and the thing sold can be fairly computed.

Thus, specific performance may be granted subject to compensation at the instance of the vendor where an estate is described as freehold and in fact a very small portion is held only from year to year[3]; where, in the case of a large estate, there is an objection to the title of a very small part not material to the enjoyment of the rest[4]; where a small portion of a property is wrongly described[5]; and where, on a purchase by a tenant in possession, the measurements are given inaccurately[6]. Specific performance has also been granted subject to compensation where, on the sale of a colliery, the profits were overstated[7]; where the estate sold was subject to quit rents[8]; and where the vendor was unable to give vacant possession of part of the property[9].

1   As to compensation under an open contract, and as to conditions providing for the case of errors in description of land and allowing or excluding compensation, see CONVEYANCING vol 23 (2016) PARA 83. Cf *SB Property Co Ltd v Chelsea Football and Athletic Co Ltd* (1992) 64 P & CR 440, CA.
2   *Rutherford v Acton-Adams* [1915] AC 866 at 869–870, PC, per Viscount Haldane.
3   *Calcraft v Roebuck* (1790) 1 Ves 221 (2 acres out of 186 acres).
4   *M'Queen v Farquhar* (1805) 11 Ves 467.
5   *Scott v Hanson* (1829) 1 Russ & M 128, where 2 acres out of 14 acres were wrongly described as 'meadow'.
6   *King v Wilson* (1843) 6 Beav 124, where property was described as 46 feet in depth, instead of 33 feet. Cf *Corless v Sparling* (1875) IR 9 Eq 595, where specific performance was ordered without compensation where there had been an overstatement as to the acreage of waste land of negligible value included in the contract.
7   *Powell v Elliot* (1875) 10 Ch App 424, where the vendor was allowed to enforce the contract on making compensation to the purchaser by submitting to an abatement from the purchase money bearing the same proportion to the excess as the total purchase money bore to the capitalised value of profits as stated by the vendor.
8   *Esdaile v Stephenson* (1822) 1 Sim & St 122 at 124.

9 *Topfell Ltd v Galley Properties Ltd* [1979] 2 All ER 388, [1979] 1 WLR 446. See also *Frasers Islington Ltd v Hanover Trustee Co Ltd* [2010] EWHC 1514 (Ch), [2010] 27 EG 85 (CS), [2010] 2 P & CR D49.

622. Where the vendor is entitled to specific performance without paying compensation. The court will order specific performance without compensation where the defect in the subject matter of the contract was visible to everybody at the time of the purchase[1]. Where a purchaser, after knowing of a defect, acts in a manner implying a waiver of his right to compensation for that defect, the vendor may insist on completion of the purchase without compensation[2].

Although it may award damages in such a case[3], the court will not grant compensation for a misrepresentation which is not contained in the contract[4]; nor will compensation be awarded for non-disclosure of something which is not an incumbrance on the title[5].

1 *Dyer v Hargrave, Hargrave v Dyer* (1805) 10 Ves 505 (misdescription of a farm described as lying within a ring fence which did not in fact so lie). Cf *Grant v Munt* (1815) Coop G 173 (compensation given for dry rot); *King v Wilson* (1843) 6 Beav 124.
2 *Burnell v Brown* (1820) 1 Jac & W 168; cf *Hughes v Jones* (1861) 3 De GF & J 307. As to waiver of objections to title generally see CONVEYANCING vol 23 (2016) PARA 201.
3 See the Misrepresentation Act 1967 s 2; and MISREPRESENTATION vol 76 (2013) PARA 800.
4 *Rutherford v Acton-Adams* [1915] AC 866, PC.
5 *Greenhalgh v Brindley* [1901] 2 Ch 324 (no compensation for non-disclosure of deed postponing acquisition of prescriptive right to light; but as it ought in fairness to have been disclosed, no order for costs).

623. Where the vendor is not entitled to specific performance on paying compensation. Where a material part of the subject matter of a contract is wanting, and the vendor cannot substantially give to the purchaser that which he agreed to buy, the court does not grant specific performance with compensation at the instance of the vendor[1]. Thus specific performance with compensation may be refused where third persons have prejudicial rights over the property sold[2]; where, on the sale of a house with land adjoining, the vendor has no title to a strip of land between the house and a road[3]; where the vendor cannot show a title to a substantial part of the property which is material to the enjoyment of the property[4]; where the measurements of the property are substantially less in a material particular than those by which it is described[5]; where the tenure of an estate contracted to be sold is different from that which the vendor represented himself to be selling[6]; where an estate is sold free from incumbrances and is in fact subject to an incumbrance amounting to a substantial part of the purchase money[7]; where there are restrictive covenants rendering the title to the land sold unmarketable[8]; and where there are very serious departures from specification in newly-built appartments[9].

Specific performance with compensation is also refused where the amount to be awarded as compensation cannot be fairly ascertained[10].

1 See also PARA 629. As to damages see PARA 632 et seq.
2 *Peers v Lambert* (1844) 7 Beav 546 (right to remove a jetty); *Shackleton v Sutcliffe* (1847) 1 De G & Sm 609 (right of way).
3 *Perkins v Ede* (1852) 16 Beav 193. A part of an estate may be material if in the hands of some person other than the purchaser it could be turned to some purpose prejudicial to the enjoyment of the estate: *Knatchbull v Grueber* (1815) 1 Madd 153 at 167 per Plumer V-C; affd (1817) 3 Mer 124.
4 *Re Arnold, Arnold v Arnold* (1880) 14 ChD 270, CA (material part of frontage).
5 *Re Deptford Creek Bridge Co and Bevan* (1884) 28 Sol Jo 327, CA (wharf 11 feet less than description, which affected use).
6 *Re Lloyds Bank Ltd and Lillington's Contract* [1912] 1 Ch 601 (property described as leasehold held on underlease of part of property demised by head lease). Cf *Cox v Coventon* (1862) 31 Beav 378.

7 *Wood v Bernal* (1812) 19 Ves 220 at 221 per Lord Eldon LC.
8 *Cato v Thompson* (1882) 9 QBD 616, CA. See also the cases cited in PARA 625 note 4.
9 *Donnelly v Weybridge Construction Ltd* [2006] EWHC 2678 (TCC), (2006) 111 ConLR 112, [2006] All ER (D) 62 (Nov).
10 *Nouaille v Flight* (1844) 7 Beav 521; *Lord Brooke v Rounthwaite* (1846) 5 Hare 298, where the amount of timber to be included in the sale was not defined by the contract; *Cato v Thompson* (1882) 9 QBD 616 at 618, CA, per Jessel MR; *Rudd v Lascelles* [1900] 1 Ch 815 (compensation for restrictive covenants held to be incapable of assessment). Cf *Halkett v Earl of Dudley* [1907] 1 Ch 590 at 593, and *Westmacott v Robins* (1862) 4 De GF & J 390.

624.   Where the purchaser is entitled to specific performance with compensation.
A purchaser may obtain specific performance with compensation against a vendor under a contract of sale where the vendor is unable to fulfil the exact terms of the bargain, but the difference in value between the actual subject matter and that stated in the contract can be measured by the court and form the subject of abatement in the amount of the purchase money[1]. However, the court will not hear the objection by the vendor that the purchaser cannot have the whole[2].

Thus, specific performance with compensation may be granted where the vendor, who has agreed to sell the fee, has only a partial interest[3]; where the vendor is only entitled to a moiety of the land he has agreed to sell[4]; where there is a deficiency in the acreage of the property sold[5]; where there is a misrepresentation as to the state of the roads on the property sold[6]; and where the property is subject to a mortgage which the purchaser has had to discharge[7]. Where, however, the representation is not made in the contract but is collateral, a purchaser cannot obtain specific performance with compensation[8] and his remedy is rescission of the contract, or a claim for damages[9]. If an injunction is granted to prevent future breaches, damages may be awarded as compensation for breaches in the past[10].

1 This principle was referred to as 'the doctrine of partial performance' by Slade LJ giving the judgment of the court in *Thames Guaranty Ltd v Campbell* [1985] QB 210 at 235, [1984] 2 All ER 585 at 595, CA. It is to be distinguished from the former doctrine of part performance under the Law of Property Act 1925 s 40 (repealed).
2 *Mortlock v Buller* (1804) 10 Ves 292 at 315 per Lord Eldon LC; *Rudd v Lascelles* [1900] 1 Ch 815 at 818. See also *A-G v Day* (1749) 1 Ves Sen 218 at 224; *Dale v Lister* (circa 1800) cited in 16 Ves at 7; *Milligan v Cooke* (1808) 16 Ves 1; *Western v Russell* (1814) 3 Ves & B 187; *Barnes v Wood* (1869) LR 8 Eq 424; *Rutherford v Acton-Adams* [1915] AC 866 at 870, PC, per Viscount Haldane. Cf *Thomas v Dering* (1837) 1 Keen 729; *Earl of Durham v Sir Francis Legard* (1865) 34 Beav 611. See also *Rignall Developments Ltd v Halil* [1988] Ch 190, [1987] 3 All ER 170 (specific performance on payment of purchase price less the costs of the plaintiff obtaining the removal of the relevant entries on the local land charges register). See also CONVEYANCING vol 23 (2016) PARA 453.
3 *Mortlock v Buller* (1804) 10 Ves 292 at 315; *Wilson v Williams* (1857) 3 Jur NS 810, where the vendor was entitled only to a reversion. See also the cases cited in CONVEYANCING vol 23 (2016) PARA 453.
4 *Hooper v Smart* (1874) LR 18 Eq 683; *Barker v Cox* (1876) 4 ChD 464; *Horrocks v Rigby* (1878) 9 ChD 180. In *Basma v Weekes* [1950] AC 441, [1950] 2 All ER 146, PC, three tenants in common agreed to sell their interests but one had no power to convey; and an order was made against the others. See also the cases cited in CONVEYANCING vol 23 (2016) PARA 453. Cf *Maw v Topham* (1854) 19 Beav 576; *Cedar Holdings Ltd v Green* [1981] Ch 129 at 147, [1979] 3 All ER 117 at 127, CA, per Goff LJ.
5 *Hill v Buckley* (1811) 17 Ves 394; *McKenzie v Hesketh* (1877) 7 ChD 675; *Connor v Potts* [1897] 1 IR 534 at 539. See also *Wheatley v Slade* (1830) 4 Sim 126.
6 *Re Chifferiel, Chifferiel v Watson* (1888) 40 Ch D 45 (method of estimating compensation in such a case).
7 *Grant v Dawkins* [1973] 3 All ER 897, [1973] 1 WLR 1406.
8 *Rutherford v Acton-Adams* [1915] AC 866, PC; *Gilchester Properties Ltd v Gomm* [1948] 1 All ER 493.
9 See the Misrepresentation Act 1967 s 2; and MISREPRESENTATION vol 76 (2013) PARA 800.

10 *Experience Hendrix LLC v PPX Enterprise Inc* [2003] EWCA Civ 323 at [34], [2003] 1 All ER
    (Comm) 830 at [34], [2003] FSR 853 at [34].

625. Where the purchaser is not entitled to specific performance with compensation. Compensation cannot be granted where the vendor has exercised a contractual right to determine the contract rather than complete with compensation[1]; or where the alienation of the partial interest of the vendor might prejudice the rights of third persons[2]; or where the purchaser has from the first been aware of the vendor's incapacity to convey the whole of the property sold[3]; or where the amount of compensation is incapable of computation[4]; or where the enforcement of the contract with compensation would be inequitable[5]; or where it would require the vendor to commit a breach of a pre-existing contract with a third person[6].

1 *Re Terry and White's Contract* (1886) 32 ChD 14, CA; *Lipman's Wallpaper Ltd v Mason and
   Hodghton Ltd* [1969] 1 Ch 20, [1968] 1 All ER 1123.
2 *Thomas v Dering* (1837) 1 Keen 729; *Thames Guaranty Ltd v Campbell* [1985] QB 210, [1984]
   2 All ER 585, CA.
3 *Castle v Wilkinson* (1870) 5 Ch App 534; see also *Carroll v Keayes* (1873) IR 8 Eq 97; *Re Edwards
   to Daniel Sykes & Co Ltd* (1890) 62 LT 445; *Hopcraft v Hopcraft* (1897) 76 LT 341.
4 *Westmacott v Robins* (1862) 3 De GF & J 390; *Cato v Thompson* (1882) 9 QBD 616 at 618, CA;
   Rudd v Lascelles [1900] 1 Ch 815. Cf *Halkett v Earl of Dudley* [1907] 1 Ch 590 at 593. See also
   Thomas v Dering (1837) 1 Keen 729; and cf *Powell v Elliot* (1875) 10 Ch App 424.
5 *Price v North* (1837) 2 Y & C Ex 620 at 626 per Lord Abinger CB; *Earl of Durham v Legard*
   (1865) 34 Beav 611. Cf *Hill v Buckley* (1811) 17 Ves 394; *McKenzie v Hesketh* (1877) 7 ChD 675;
   Rudd v Lascelles [1900] 1 Ch 815 at 819.
6 *Lipman's Wallpaper Ltd v Mason and Hodghton Ltd* [1969] 1 Ch 20, [1968] 1 All ER 1123.

626. Indemnity against defect or loss. Where the defect or loss is not certain but contingent, then, unless the parties have contracted for it, the vendor will not generally be compelled to give[1], nor the purchaser to take[2], an indemnity against such defect or loss.

1 *Balmanno v Lumley* (1813) 1 Ves & B 224; *Aylett v Ashton* (1835) 1 My & Cr 105; *Bainbridge
   v Kinnaird* (1863) 32 Beav 346. Where, however, there was a possible claim for estate duty (now
   replaced by inheritance tax) and the contract contained no mention of a deed of gift or the
   contingent claim to duty which might flow from it, it was said that specific performance would
   have been ordered if the vendor had provided an insurance policy within a reasonable time:
   Manning v Turner [1956] 3 All ER 641 at 645, [1957] 1 WLR 91 at 94 per Sir Leonard Stone V-C.
2 *Balmanno v Lumley* (1813) 1 Ves & B 224 at 225 per Lord Eldon LC. See also *Wood v Bernal*
   (1812) 19 Ves 220 at 221; *Fildes v Hooker* (1818) 3 Madd 193; *Nouaille v Flight* (1844) 7 Beav
   521 (ambiguous covenant); *Ridgeway v Gray* (1849) 1 Mac & G 109 (misdescription); *Re Weston
   and Thomas's Contract* [1907] 1 Ch 244 (small contingent incumbrance).

627. Compensation after completion. If the contract provides for compensation for any error or misstatement in the contract[1], the purchaser's right to compensation is not lost by completion if he was not then aware of the defect[2]. However, where there is no express condition for payment of compensation and the purchaser could have discovered the defect before completion by the exercise of due diligence, he cannot claim compensation after completion[3].

1 As to such conditions see CONVEYANCING vol 23 (2016) PARA 456 et seq.
2 *Cann v Cann* (1830) 3 Sim 447; *Bos v Helsham* (1866) LR 2 Exch 72; *Re Turner and Skelton*
   (1879) 13 ChD 130; *Palmer v Johnson* (1884) 13 QBD 351, CA.
3 *Besley v Besley* (1878) 9 ChD 103; *Clayton v Leech* (1889) 41 ChD 103, CA.

628. Alternative relief to the purchaser. When a purchaser fails to establish his right to specific performance with compensation, but would be entitled to rescind the contract, he may be given the option of completing without compensation or having the contract rescinded[1].

1   See *Earl of Durham v Legard* (1865) 34 Beav 611; *Re Hare and O'More's Contract* [1901] 1 Ch 93 at 96; *Rutherford v Acton-Adams* [1915] AC 866, PC. As to alternative relief see PARA 597.

(ii) Compensation where there is a Condition for it

629. Factors determining whether the vendor is entitled to specific performance. Conditions of sale are construed strictly against a vendor[1]. Where, therefore, a vendor seeks to enforce specific performance of a contract of sale against a purchaser, a condition in the contract providing for compensation in the event of any error or misstatement in the particulars applies only when on completion the purchaser will get substantially what he contracted for[2].

If, however, there are material misdescriptions[3], so that the purchaser will get something substantially different from that which he agreed to buy, specific performance is not ordered against him[4]. Thus, such an order has been refused where property described as copyhold was partly freehold[5], or where an underlease is described as a lease[6], or where there is serious misrepresentation as to the rent at which the property has been let[7]. A mere puffing description of the property sold, however, does not of necessity entitle a purchaser to resist specific performance on the ground of misrepresentation[8].

A condition which provides that errors and misstatements are not to annul a sale and that no compensation is to be allowed does not enable a vendor to enforce specific performance without compensation if the error or misstatement is a substantial one[9].

The court will not order specific performance with compensation unless the amount of such compensation can be reasonably estimated[10].

A vendor of several lots to the same purchaser is entitled to compensation for an understatement of the area of one lot on giving compensation for an overstatement in relation to others[11].

Compensation will not be awarded in respect of a misrepresentation which is not a term of the contract, but in such a case damages for the misrepresentation can be awarded to the purchaser[12]. A provision in the contract excluding any liability for such a misrepresentation will be of no effect unless it was a fair and reasonable one to be included, having regard to the circumstances which were or ought reasonably to have been known to or in the contemplation of the parties when the contract was made[13].

1   See DEEDS AND OTHER INSTRUMENTS vol 32 (2012) PARAS 378–379; CONVEYANCING vol 23 (2016) PARA 45. As to compensation after completion see CONVEYANCING vol 23 (2016) PARA 456.
2   *Re Fawcett and Holmes' Contract* (1889) 42 ChD 150, CA, where a house and yard were described as measuring 1,372 square yards, being really 1,033 square yards. The condition may apply even though the error is not a mere triviality: *Re Terry and White's Contract* (1886) 32 ChD 14 at 28, CA, per Lindley LJ; *Re Fawcett and Holmes' Contract* above at 156 per Lord Esher MR; *Ashburner v Sewell* [1891] 3 Ch 405 at 409 per Chitty J.
3   As to what are material misdescriptions see *Dykes v Blake* (1838) 4 Bing NC 463; *Ayles v Cox* (1852) 16 Beav 23; *Brewer v Brown* (1884) 28 ChD 309; *Jacobs v Revell* [1900] 2 Ch 858 (where the cases are reviewed); *Re Puckett and Smith's Contract* [1902] 2 Ch 258, CA. Cf *Re Brewer and Hankins' Contract* (1899) 80 LT 127, CA; *Shepherd v Croft* [1911] 1 Ch 521; *Citytowns Ltd v Bohemian Properties Ltd* [1986] 2 EGLR 258; and the cases cited in note 9.
4   *Flight v Booth* (1834) 1 Bing NC 370 (only two of many prohibited businesses mentioned); *Re Arnold, Arnold v Arnold* (1880) 14 ChD 270 at 279, CA. See also *Duke of Norfolk v Worthy*

(1808) 1 Camp 337 at 340; *Powell v Doubble* (1832), cited in Sugden's Vendors and Purchasers (14th Edn) 29; *Dobell v Hutchinson* (1835) 3 Ad & El 355; and CONVEYANCING vol 23 (2016) PARA 456.

5 *Ayles v Cox* (1852) 16 Beav 23. See also *Stewart v Alliston* (1815) 1 Mer 26, where a rack rent was described as a ground rent; cf *Price v Macaulay* (1852) 2 De GM & G 339, where specific performance with compensation was granted; *Evans v Robins* (1862) 8 Jur NS 846; *Hudson v Cook* (1872) LR 13 Eq 417 at 420.

6 *Madeley v Booth* (1848) 2 De G & Sm 718, followed in *Re Beyfus and Master's Contract* (1888) 39 ChD 110, CA, and *Broom v Phillips* (1896) 74 LT 459, although disapproved in *Camberwell and South London Building Society v Holloway* (1879) 13 ChD 754 at 760 per Jessel MR, where however, the conditions in effect gave notice that the lease sold was an underlease. Cf *Tompkins v Tratt* (1915) 139 LT Jo 541, where the conditions provided for the inspection of the 'lease' and that the purchaser should buy with full notice of its contents. See also *Turner v Turner* [1881] WN 70; *Re Lloyds Bank Ltd and Lillington's Contract* [1912] 1 Ch 601; *Re Russ and Brown's Contract* [1934] Ch 34, CA; and *Becker v Partridge* [1966] 2 QB 155, [1966] 2 All ER 266, CA, where a sub-underlease was described as an underlease.

7 *Dimmock v Hallett* (1866) 2 Ch App 21.

8 *Johnson v Smart* (1859) 2 Giff 151 (affd (1860) 2 LT 783); *Dimmock v Hallett* (1866) 2 Ch App 21 at 27.

9 *Whittemore v Whittemore* (1869) LR 8 Eq 603; *Jacobs v Revell* [1900] 2 Ch 858. See also *Portman v Mill* (1826) 2 Russ 570; *Lee v Rayson* [1917] 1 Ch 613; *Watson v Burton* [1956] 3 All ER 929, [1957] 1 WLR 19; and MISREPRESENTATION vol 76 (2013) PARAS 784–786; CONVEYANCING vol 23 (2016) PARA 456 et seq.

10 See the cases cited in PARA 625 note 4; *Magennis v Fallon* (1829) 2 Mol 561 at 589; *Lord Brooke v Rounthwaite* (1846) 5 Hare 298; *Cox v Coventon* (1862) 31 Beav 378.

11 *Leslie v Tompson* (1851) 9 Hare 268.

12 See the Misrepresentation Act 1967 s 2; and MISREPRESENTATION vol 76 (2013) PARA 800.

13 See the Misrepresentation Act 1967 s 3(1); and MISREPRESENTATION vol 76 (2013) PARA 802. See also *Walker v Boyle* [1982] 1 All ER 634, [1982] 1 WLR 495. The Misrepresentation Act 1967 s 3 does not apply to a term in a consumer contract within the meaning of Consumer Rights Act 2015 Pt 2 (ss 61–76) (see CONSUMER PROTECTION vol 21 (2016) PARA 391 et seq): see the Misrepresentation Act 1967 s 3(2) (added by Consumer Rights Act 2015 s 75, Sch 4 para 1(1), (3)).

630. Factors determining whether purchaser entitled to compensation. Similar principles to those determining whether a vendor is entitled to specific performance[1] apply where a purchaser seeks to enforce against a vendor specific performance with compensation of a contract of sale which contains a condition for compensation[2], except that in such case the rule as to strict construction does not apply, but the condition is interpreted according to the ordinary rules of construction[3]. Specific performance with compensation is accordingly granted where there is a misstatement in the particulars[4], and even, in some cases, where the purchaser knew of the inaccuracy of the statement[5].

Compensation may, however, be refused on the ground that the misstatement or omission does not affect the value of the property[6], or that the misdescription was orally corrected by the auctioneer even though the purchaser did not hear the correction[7].

A purchaser's right to compensation may be abrogated by the operation of another term of the contract, for example a condition giving the vendor the right to rescind[8], or by the impossibility of estimating the amount of the compensation to be paid[9].

1 As to the principles for determining whether a vendor is entitled to specific performance see PARA 629.

2 As to conditions for compensation see CONVEYANCING vol 23 (2016) PARA 456.

3 *Cordingley v Cheeseborough* (1862) 4 De GF & J 379 at 384 per Lord Westbury LC. See *White v Cuddon* (1842) 8 Cl & Fin 766, HL; *Debenham v Sawbridge* [1901] 2 Ch 98 (a defect of title is not 'an error or misstatement in the particulars of sale'); *Re Jackson and Haden's Contract* [1905] 1 Ch 603 (affd [1906] 1 Ch 412, CA).

4 *Painter v Newby* (1853) 11 Hare 26; *Aspinalls to Powell and Scholefield* (1889) 60 LT 595. Cf
   Cordingley v Cheeseborough (1862) 4 De GF & J 379; *Earl of Durham v Legard* (1865) 34 Beav
   611; *Re Hurlbalt and Chaytor's Contract* (1888) 57 LJ Ch 421.
5 *Lett v Randall* (1883) 49 LT 71. Cf *Cobbett v Locke-King* (1900) 16 TLR 379.
6 *Re Leyland and Taylor's Contract* [1900] 2 Ch 625, CA. Cf *Re Ward and Jordan's Contract*
   [1902] 1 IR 73; *Carlish v Salt* [1906] 1 Ch 335 at 340 per Joyce J.
7 *Re Hare and O' More's Contract* [1901] 1 Ch 93, where the purchaser was given the option of
   rescinding or completing without compensation.
8 *Mawson v Fletcher* (1870) LR 10 Eq 212 (affd 6 Ch App 91); *Re Terry and White's Contract*
   (1886) 32 ChD 14, CA; *Ashburner v Sewell* [1891] 3 Ch 405; *Watson v Burton* [1956] 3 All ER
   929, [1957] 1 WLR 19. Cf *Painter v Newby* (1853) 11 Hare 26; and see *Williams v Edwards*
   (1827) 2 Sim 78 (contract avoided if good title not shown).
9 *White v Cuddon* (1842) 8 Cl & Fin 766, HL. See also the cases cited in PARA 629 note 10.

631. Condition excluding compensation for misdescription. A clause which
provides that no misdescription or omission in the particulars of sale is to annul
the sale and that no compensation is to be allowed in respect of any
misdescription or omission prevents a purchaser from obtaining specific
performance with compensation[1].

However, such a clause does not deprive the purchaser of the right to rescind
the contract and recover his deposit if it may reasonably be supposed that, but for
the misdescription or omission, he might never have entered into the contract[2],
and the misdescription or omission relates to a matter which is within the
vendor's knowledge[3], even though the vendor does not regard it as a matter of
importance[4]. The same principle applies to clauses excluding liability for
pre-contract misrepresentation[5]. A vendor cannot by means of such a
clause exclude or restrict his liability for negligence or for a pre-contract
misrepresentation made by him unless the clause was a fair and reasonable one to
be included having regard to the circumstances which were or ought reasonably
to have been known to or in the contemplation of the parties when the contract
was made[6].

1 *Cordingley v Cheeseborough* (1862) 4 De G F & J 379; *Re Terry and White's Contract* (1886) 32
   ChD 14, CA. Cf *Whittemore v Whittemore* (1869) LR 8 Eq 603; *Molphy v Coyne* (1919) 53 ILT
   177. See also CONVEYANCING vol 23 (2016) PARA 456.
2 *Flight v Booth* (1834) 1 Bing NC 370 at 377 per Tindal CJ. See also CONVEYANCING vol 23
   (2016) PARA 83.
3 *Heywood v Mallalieu* (1883) 25 ChD 357; *Nottingham Patent Brick and Tile Co v Butler* (1885)
   15 QBD 261 (affd (1886) 16 QBD 778, CA); *Faruqi v English Real Estates Ltd* [1979] 1 WLR
   963. Cf *Beyfus v Lodge* [1925] Ch 350, where specific performance was refused on the ground of
   misdescription but the purchaser's claim for rescission was dismissed.
4 *Walker v Boyle* [1982] 1 All ER 634, [1982] 1 WLR 495.
5 *Charles Hunt Ltd v Palmer* [1931] 2 Ch 287; *Laurence v Lexcourt Holdings Ltd* [1978] 2 All ER
   810, [1978] 1 WLR 1128; *Walker v Boyle* [1982] 1 All ER 634, [1982] 1 WLR 495.
6 See the Misrepresentation Act 1967 s 3(1); the Unfair Contract Terms Act 1977 ss 2(2), 11;and
   MISREPRESENTATION vol 76 (2013) PARA 802; CONTRACT vol 22 (2012) PARAS 410, 419. See
   also *Walker v Boyle* [1982] 1 All ER 634, [1982] 1 WLR 495. The Misrepresentation Act 1967
   s 3 does not apply to a term in a consumer contract within the meaning of Consumer Rights Act
   2015 Pt 2 (ss 61–76) (see CONSUMER PROTECTION vol 21 (2016) PARA 391 et seq): see the
   Misrepresentation Act 1967 s 3(2) (added by the Consumer Rights Act 2015 s 75, Sch 4 para 1(1),
   (3)). The Unfair Contract Terms Act 1977 s 2 does not apply to a term in a consumer contract or
   a notice to the extent that it is a consumer notice (see CONSUMER PROTECTION vol 21 (2016)
   PARA 393): see the Unfair Contract Terms Act 1977 s 2(4) (added by Consumer Rights Act 2015
   s 75, Sch 4 paras 2, 4).
      As to the validity of exclusion clauses generally see *Photo Production Ltd v Securicor
   Transport Ltd* [1980] AC 827, [1980] 1 All ER 556, HL. See also MISREPRESENTATION vol 76
   (2013) PARA 826.

(6) DAMAGES WITH OR INSTEAD OF
SPECIFIC PERFORMANCE

632. Damages in equity. Where a court has jurisdiction[1] to entertain an application for an injunction or specific performance, it may award damages in equity in addition to or in substitution for an injunction or specific performance[2]. If specific performance is impossible or is refused the claimant will usually be entitled to damages at law for breach of contract[3] and will not need to claim equitable damages, but equitable damages can be claimed in some cases where damages at law cannot be recovered[4] or in circumstances where the court would not normally exercise its discretion to grant specific performance[5]. However, equitable damages cannot be awarded if the court has no jurisdiction to order specific performance[6] and, like any other equitable remedy, the award of damages is presumably subject to equitable considerations such as delay, mistake, acquiescence and unconscionable conduct[7].

It has been held that there is no jurisdiction to award equitable damages in respect of a contract of loan[8] or agency[9] or a partnership agreement[10]. Damages have also been refused where specific performance was impossible because the subject matter of the contract had been disposed of before the commencement of the claim[11], or where the right to specific performance had been extinguished by laches[12]. Equitable damages cannot be awarded where there is no concluded agreement[13] or where the claimant by his own act has rendered specific performance impossible[14]. Equitable damages can, however, be awarded where specific performance has become impossible because the subject matter of the contract has been disposed of between the commencement of the claim and the hearing[15] or where during that time the contract sued upon has been actually performed[16]. The power to grant equitable damages is a discretionary remedy; thus acquiescence may induce the court to refuse both damages and specific performance, while a lesser degree of acquiescence may induce the court to refuse specific performance but grant equitable damages[17]. An award of damages for breach of part of a contract may be coupled with an order for specific performance of the rest of the contract[18].

Where the statement of claim does not contain a claim for equitable damages the court may give leave for the statement of claim to be amended to include such a claim[19]. This is, perhaps, not strictly necessary for in some cases the court has awarded damages in lieu of specific performance even though there was no claim for equitable damages in the statements of case[20]. If there is no claim for specific performance in the statement of claim it has been observed that there are obvious difficulties in awarding damages as a substitute for what is not claimed[21], but it now appears that a claim for specific performance is not vital provided it is made clear that damages are being claimed[22] in substitution for the equitable remedy[23].

1 'Jurisdiction' includes powers: Senior Courts Act 1981 s 151(1). The question of jurisdiction must be determined as at the date of the writ: see *Jaggard v Sawyer* [1995] 2 All ER 189 at 205, [1995] 1 WLR 269 at 284–285, CA, per Millett LJ.

2 Senior Courts Act 1981 s 50 (Court of Appeal and High Court). The power is extended to county courts by the County Courts Act 1984 ss 23, 38; see COURTS AND TRIBUNALS vol 24 (2010) PARAS 768, 776. Damages under this power are referred to as equitable damages to distinguish them from damages at law awarded for breach of contract. See also *Jaggard v Sawyer* [1995] 2 All ER 189, [1995] 1 WLR 269, CA.

3 Apart from a claim in contract, it is sometimes possible to bring a claim for damages in tort. As to damages in tort see DAMAGES vol 29 (2014) PARA 408 et seq. Thus there may be a claim in deceit if there has been a fraudulent misrepresentation, or a claim under the Misrepresentation Act 1967 if there has been an innocent misrepresentation.

4   Damages in equity may be claimed, for example, where the action was begun before the contractual date for completion: see *Oakacre Ltd v Claire Cleaners (Holdings) Ltd* [1982] Ch 197, [1981] 3 All ER 667.

5   *Tamplin v James* (1880) 15 ChD 215, CA; *McKenna v Richey* [1950] VLR 360, [1950] ALR 778 (Vict). Cf *Lavery v Pursell* (1888) 39 ChD 508 at 519 per Chitty J.

6   It has been stated that for this purpose the court has no jurisdiction to entertain an action for specific performance if the contract is of a class of contracts of which the court, acting on accepted principles, would not in any circumstances decree specific performance: *Price v Strange* [1978] Ch 337 at 369, [1977] 3 All ER 371 at 393, CA, per Buckley LJ, giving as examples contracts for the sale and purchase of commodities readily available upon the market at an ascertainable price and contracts for personal services. However, cf *Price v Strange* at 359 and at 385 per Goff LJ.

7   As to delay see EQUITABLE JURISDICTION vol 47 (2014) PARA 253 et seq; as to mistake see EQUITABLE JURISDICTION vol 47 (2014) PARA 39 et seq; as to acquiescence see EQUITABLE JURISDICTION vol 47 (2014) PARA 252; and as to unconscionable conduct see EQUITABLE JURISDICTION vol 47 (2014) PARA 16 et seq.

8   *Rogers v Challis* (1859) 27 Beav 175. It is submitted that this is not an absolute rule, for it is based on the principle that the court will not award specific performance of a contract of loan, to which it is now established that there are numerous exceptions: see PARA 534.

9   *Chinnock v Sainsbury* (1860) 30 LJ Ch 409.

10   *Scott v Rayment* (1868) LR 7 Eq 112. See PARA 536.

11   *Ferguson v Wilson* (1866) 2 Ch App 77 (contract to allot shares; shares allotted to third persons before commencement of claim).

12   *Lavery v Pursell* (1888) 39 ChD 508. But see *McKenna v Richey* [1950] VLR 360, [1950] ALR 778 (Vict).

13   *Lewers v Earl of Shaftesbury* (1866) LR 2 Eq 270 (affd (1867) 16 LT 135); *Stimson v Gray* [1929] 1 Ch 629.

14   *Hipgrave v Case* (1885) 28 ChD 356, CA.

15   *Johnson v Agnew* [1980] AC 367, [1979] 1 All ER 883, HL. See also *Davenport v Rylands* (1865) LR 1 Eq 302 at 307 per Wood V-C; *Ferguson v Wilson* (1866) 2 Ch App 77 at 91 per Cairns LJ.

16   *Cory v Thames Ironworks & Shipbuilding Co Ltd* (1863) 8 LT 237.

17   *Sayers v Collyer* (1884) 28 ChD 103 at 110, CA, per Fry LJ.

18   *Soames v Edge* (1860) John 669; *London Corpn v Southgate* (1868) 38 LJ Ch 141.

19   *Surrey County Council v Bredero Homes Ltd* [1992] 3 All ER 302 at 315; affd [1993] 3 All ER 705, [1993] 1 WLR 1361, CA.

20   *Wedmore v Bristol Corpn* (1862) 7 LT 459; *Catton v Wyld* (1863) 32 Beav 266 at 268; *Betts v Neilson, Betts v De Vitre* (1868) 3 Ch App 429 at 441; *Lady Stanley of Alderley v Earl of Shrewsbury* (1875) LR 19 Eq 616 at 621.

21   See *Horsler v Zorro* [1975] Ch 302 at 307, [1975] 1 All ER 584 at 588 per Megarry J. In Australia and Canada, however, it seems that damages can be awarded even though there is no claim for specific performance but the circumstances are such that that remedy could have been claimed: *Masai Minerals Ltd v Heritage Resources Ltd* (1979) 95 DLR(3d) 488 at 494; affd (1981) 119 DLR(3d) 393; *Barbagallo v J & F Catelan Pty Ltd* [1986] 1 Qd R 245.

22   Ie under the Supreme Court Act 1981 s 50: see the text and notes 1–2.

23   *Jaggard v Sawyer* [1995] 2 All ER 189, [1995] 1 WLR 269, CA (a case on injunctions to which the same principles apply).

633. The measure of damages. Where the court has jurisdiction to award damages either at law or in equity, the measure of damages and the date at which they are to be assessed are the same in either case. The general principle is that the innocent party is entitled to be placed, so far as money can do so, in the same position as if the contract had been performed[1]. Prima facie the measure of damages will be the 'loss of bargain', that is, the extent to which the market value of the property in question exceeds the contract price (if the claimant is the purchaser) or falls short of it (if the claimant is the vendor)[2]. It is irrelevant that the purchaser wishes to acquire the property for personal occupation and not for resale[3]. If it is more beneficial to him, the innocent party can claim instead to be put in the same position as if the contract had never been made, by being reimbursed for expenditure (including pre-contract expenditure) which it was within the contemplation of the parties that he would incur and which has been wasted as a result of the breach[4]. A further possibility is that the claimant is awarded damages by reference to the defendant's gain rather than the claimant's loss[5]. If the defendant has incorrectly represented that he has power to sell the property, he may be liable for damages for misrepresentation even if damages for loss of bargain cannot be claimed for breach of contract[6].

Where damages are awarded in lieu of specific performance, the principle that damages should be assessed as at the date of the breach of contract (which is the usual rule in relation to commercial contracts) does not normally apply[7]. The selection of the appropriate date is a matter for the court's discretion, but the date usually chosen is the date at which the remedy of specific performance ceases to be available. Thus damages have been ordered to be assessed as at the date on which it ceased to be within the vendor's power to convey the property[8], as at the date on which the purchaser elected to abandon his claim to specific performance[9], and as at the date of judgment[10] and in a contract to sell shares, at the date at when the shares were sold to a third party[11]. If the purchaser has been guilty of delay in pursuing his claim, assessment may be directed as at an earlier date[12].

In calculating the damages due to a vendor, credit must be given for any deposit which has been forfeited[13].

Any claim to damages must be limited to the loss which is reasonably foreseeable as arising from the breach, either in the ordinary course of things or because of special circumstances known to the party committing the breach[14]. For this purpose, special circumstances are necessary to justify imputing to a vendor of land knowledge that the purchaser intends to use it in any particular manner[15].

1   *Johnson v Agnew* [1980] AC 367 at 400, [1979] 1 All ER 883 at 895, HL, per Lord Wilberforce; *Suleman v Shahsavari* [1989] 2 All ER 460, [1988] 1 WLR 1181; *William Sindall plc v Cambridgeshire County Council* [1994] 3 All ER 932, [1994] 1 WLR 1016, CA. As to the measure of damages for breach of contract see DAMAGES vol 29 (2014) PARA 499 et seq. See also the following cases on damages in lieu of an injunction: *Wrotham Park Estate Co v Parkside Homes Ltd* [1974] 2 All ER 321, [1974] 1 WLR 798; *Bracewell v Appleby* [1975] Ch 408, [1975] 1 All ER 993; *Tanner v Tanner* [1975] 3 All ER 776, [1975] 1 WLR 1346, CA; *Carr-Saunders v Dick McNeil Associates Ltd* [1986] 2 All ER 888, [1986] 1 WLR 922. The method of assessment in *Wrotham Park Estate Co v Parkside Homes Ltd* above was doubted in *Wrotham Park Settled Estates v Hertsmere Borough Council* [1993] 2 EGLR 15, CA; and see *Stoke-on-Trent City Council v W & J Wass Ltd* [1988] 3 All ER 394, [1988] 1 WLR 1406, CA; *Surrey County Council v Bredero Homes Ltd* [1993] 3 All ER 705, [1993] 1 WLR 1361, CA. *Wrotham Park Estate Co v Parkside Homes Ltd* above was, however, approved and applied in *Jaggard v Sawyer* [1995] 2 All ER 189, [1995] 1 WLR 269, CA.
2   See CONVEYANCING vol 23 (2016) PARA 456.
3   *Ridley v De Geerts* [1945] 2 All ER 654, CA.
4   *Lloyd v Stanbury* [1971] 2 All ER 267, [1971] 1 WLR 535; *Anglia Television Ltd v Reed* [1972] 1 QB 60, [1971] 3 All ER 690, CA. See also *McRae v Commonwealth Disposals Commission* (1951) 84 CLR 377, [1951] ALR 771 (Aust HC), where the costs of searching for a non-existent subject matter of the contract were held to have been reasonably incurred. Where the vendor fails to complete but the purchaser cannot prove any damages by way of loss of bargain, he may (in addition to recovering his deposit) recover interest on the deposit and the costs of approving and executing the contract, investigating title, searching and preparing the conveyance: *Wallington v Townsend* [1939] Ch 588, [1939] 2 All ER 225.
5   In *A-G v Blake (Jonathan Cape Ltd third party)* [2001] 1 AC 268, [2000] 4 All ER 385, HL, the majority of the House of Lords recognised that in exceptional cases ie where the claimant had a legitimate interest in restraining the defendants' profit making, gain based damages could be awarded. The British government was held entitled to an account of profits made by the defendant, a convicted and escaped Russian spy, from the publication of his memoirs in breach of a lifelong obligation of secrecy arising from his former employment by the British Intelligence Service. The House of Lords explained a number of different cases including *Wrotham Park Estate Co v Parkside Homes Ltd* [1974] 2 All ER 321, [1974] 1 WLR 798, 27 P & CR 296 noted above as illustrating gain rather than loss based damages. The facts of *A-G v Blake* are perhaps less unusual than they first seem see *Snepp v US* 444 US 507 (1980) (CIA employee); *A-G of England and Wales v R* [2002] 2 NZLR 91, NZ CA (elite SAS soldier). Subsequent attempts to follow *A-G v Blake*

do not appear consistent see *Esso Petroleum Co Ltd v Niad Ltd* [2001] EWHC 6 (Ch), [2001] All ER (D) 324 (Nov); *WWF-World Wide Fund for Nature (formerly World Wildlife Fund) v World Wrestling Federation Entertainment Inc* [2007] EWCA Civ 286, [2008] 1 All ER 74, [2008] 1 WLR 445.

6   See the Misrepresentation Act 1967 s 2(1); *Watts v Spence* [1976] Ch 165, [1975] 2 All ER 528; *Royscot Trust Ltd v Rogerson* [1991] 2 QB 297, [1991] 3 All ER 294, CA; *Gran Gelato Ltd v Richcliff (Group) Ltd* [1992] Ch 560, [1992] 1 All ER 865; MISREPRESENTATION vol 76 (2013) PARA 800; CONVEYANCING vol 23 (2016) PARA 459.

7   See CONVEYANCING vol 23 (2016) PARA 455.

8   *Johnson v Agnew* [1980] AC 367, [1979] 1 All ER 883, HL. See also *Techno Land Improvements Ltd v British Leyland (UK) Ltd* (1979) 252 Estates Gazette 805; *Ricci v Masons (a firm)* [1993] 2 EGLR 159.

9   *Domb v Isoz* [1980] Ch 548, [1980] 1 All ER 942, CA.

10 *Wroth v Tyler* [1974] Ch 30, [1973] 1 All ER 897; *Malhotra v Choudhury* [1980] Ch 52, [1979] 1 All ER 186, CA. See also *Grant v Dawkins* [1973] 3 All ER 897, [1973] 1 WLR 1406.

11 *Bear Stearns Bank plc v Forum Global Equity Ltd* [2007] EWHC 1576 (Comm), [2007] All ER (D) 103 (Jul).

12 *Malhotra v Choudhury* [1980] Ch 52, [1979] 1 All ER 186, CA.

13 *Shuttleworth v Clews* [1910] 1 Ch 176. As to the statutory power to order the return of the deposit see PARA 620.

14 See *Hadley v Baxendale* (1854) 9 Exch 341; and DAMAGES vol 29 (2014) PARA 532 et seq.

15 *Diamond v Campbell-Jones* [1961] Ch 22, [1960] 1 All ER 583, applying *Hadley v Baxendale* (1854) 9 Exch 341. Cf *Cottrill v Steyning and Littlehampton Building Society* [1966] 2 All ER 295, [1966] 1 WLR 753, where the vendor knew of the purchaser's intention to develop the property and damages were assessed on that footing.

634. Election between remedies. A claimant claiming specific performance or damages in the alternative[1] may, before the trial, elect to accept the repudiation[2] of the contract by the defendant and abandon the claim to specific performance, by communicating his election to the defendant or by other acts showing an unequivocal election to terminate the contract[3]. The right of election will cease, however, if the defendant remedies the breach before the claimant accepts the repudiation and the defendant is able and willing to perform his part of the contract[4]; or if the breach is not of a continuing nature and the claimant with full knowledge of the breach has taken steps which show an intention to proceed with the contract[5] or has delayed in exercising his right to terminate the contract[6]. The claimant must in any event elect at the trial between his claim to specific performance and his claim to damages[7].

If the claimant elects at the trial to claim specific performance but the defendant fails to comply with the court's directions for performance of the contract, the claimant must apply to the court for an order discharging the contract and cannot terminate the contract himself by treating the defendant's continued non-performance as a repudiation of the contract[8]. A claimant who has obtained an order for the discharge of the contract is entitled to the same relief by way of damages and otherwise as if he had accepted a repudiation of the contract by the defendant prior to the trial[9].

1   As to pleading alternative claims see PARA 597.

2   As to rescission and repudiation see PARA 598; and MISREPRESENTATION vol 76 (2013) PARA 811 et seq.

3   *Scarf v Jardine* (1882) 7 App Cas 345 at 361, HL, per Lord Blackburn; *Car and Universal Finance Co Ltd v Caldwell* [1965] 1 QB 525, [1964] 1 All ER 290, CA.

4   *Frost v Knight* (1872) LR 7 Exch 111 at 112, Ex Ch, per Cockburn CJ; *Halkett v Earl of Dudley* [1907] 1 Ch 590.

5   *Hain SS Co Ltd v Tate and Lyle Ltd* [1936] 2 All ER 597, HL; *Aquis Estates Ltd v Minton* [1975] 3 All ER 1043, [1975] 1 WLR 1452, CA.

6   *Halkett v Earl of Dudley* [1907] 1 Ch 590 at 597 per Parker J, approved in *Berners v Fleming* [1925] Ch 264, CA.

7   *Farrant v Olver* (1922) 91 LJ Ch 758; *Glover v Broome* [1926] WN 46; *Johnson v Agnew* [1980] AC 367 at 392, [1979] 1 All ER 883 at 889, HL, per Lord Wilberforce; *Tilcon Ltd v Land and Real Estate Investments Ltd* [1987] 1 All ER 615, [1987] 1 WLR 46, CA.

8   *Halkett v Earl of Dudley* [1907] 1 Ch 590; *Austins of East Ham Ltd v Macey* [1941] Ch 338, CA; *Sudagar Singh v Nazeer* [1979] Ch 474, [1978] 3 All ER 817; *Johnson v Agnew* [1980] AC 367, [1979] 1 All ER 883, HL; *GKN Distributors Ltd v Tyne Tees Fabrication Ltd* (1985) 50 P & CR 403. As to the discharge of specific performance orders see PARA 637.

9   *Johnson v Agnew* [1980] AC 367, [1979] 1 All ER 883, HL.

635. Damages in addition to specific performance. In certain circumstances a claimant may be entitled to damages for breach of contract as well as to an order for specific performance[1]. An agreement may be specifically enforced in part, leaving the claimant to his claim in damages for breach of the remainder[2]. Damages may be awarded for delay in completion[3]. Damages have also been awarded where a purchaser elected to complete a contract for the purchase of property which was charged to secure sums greater than the contract price[4].

1   As to damages as additional or alternative relief see CIVIL PROCEDURE vol 12 (2015) PARA 1117.

2   *Soames v Edge* (1860) John 669; *London Corpn v Southgate* (1868) 17 WR 197.

3   *Raineri v Miles* [1981] AC 1050, [1980] 2 All ER 145, HL; *Oakacre Ltd v Claire Cleaners (Holdings) Ltd* [1982] Ch 197, [1981] 3 All ER 667 (damages awarded where land had been conveyed to plaintiffs after issue of writ so that claim for specific performance did not fall to be considered). See also *Jaques v Millar* (1877) 6 ChD 153; *Royal Bristol Permanent Building Society v Bomash* (1887) 35 ChD 390; *Jones v Gardiner* [1902] 1 Ch 191; *Phillips v Lamdin* [1949] 2 KB 33, [1949] 1 All ER 770; *Ford-Hunt v Raghbir Singh* [1973] 2 All ER 700, [1973] 1 WLR 738; *Easton v Brown* [1981] 3 All ER 278 (damages for delay in complying with specific performance order); *Seven Seas Properties Ltd v Al-Essa* [1989] 1 All ER 164, [1988] 1 WLR 1272 (combination of specific performance and 'Mareva' injunctions (now freezing orders) by order for retention of purchase price pending inquiry into damages).

4   *Grant v Dawkins* [1973] 3 All ER 897, [1973] 1 WLR 1406, where the damages were limited to the excess of the value of the property, as assessed at the date of the discharge of the mortgages, over the purchase price.

(7) RELIEF AFTER JUDGMENT

636. Enforcement of the order. If the defendant fails to comply with the master's directions for completion, the claimant cannot immediately proceed to execution but must apply for a further order directing the defendant to complete[1]. The further order should specify the time within which the defendant must comply[2].

It is, however, usually possible to enforce an order for specific performance without resort to proceedings for contempt. In a vendor's claim, the order may be enforced by one or more of the various forms of execution available for enforcement of a money judgment[3]. In a purchaser's claim for specific performance of a contract concerning any interest in land or for the sale or exchange of any interest in land, the purchaser may apply to the court for a declaration that the vendor is a trustee of the interest and for a vesting order vesting that interest in the purchaser or, if it is more convenient, for the appointment of some person to convey the land or any interest in it to the purchaser[4].

Alternatively, where the High Court or family court has given or made a judgment or order directing a person to execute any conveyance, contract or other document and that person neglects or refuses to comply with the judgment or order or cannot after reasonable inquiry be found, that court may, on such terms and conditions, if any, as may be just, order that the conveyance, contract or other document be executed by such person as the court may nominate for the purpose[5]. An order vesting property or directing or authorising some person to assign or convey may be made by a master[6].

An order for the delivery of any goods which does not give the person against whom the order is made the alternative of paying the assessed value of the goods may be enforced by a writ of specific delivery[7].

If an order for specific performance of a contract is not complied with, the court may direct that the act required to be done may, so far as practicable, be done by the party by whom the order was obtained or some other person appointed by the court, at the cost of the disobedient party[8].

An unpaid vendor is entitled to a lien over the property for the balance of the purchase price, which he can enforce by obtaining a court order for sale of the property[9] and, where appropriate, an order for the appointment of a receiver pending sale[10]. The court may give the vendor leave to bid at the sale[11].

If there is long delay in seeking to enforce an order for specific performance, the court will refuse to direct the enforcement of the order if the claimant does not give a sufficient explanation of the delay and the defendant has suffered some detriment as a result of it[12]. Where the claimant has suffered damage as a result of the defendant's delay in complying with an order for specific performance, the court can direct a supplementary inquiry as to the amount of such damages and order payment of that amount to the claimant[13].

1   See *Morgan v Brisco* (1886) 32 ChD 192; *Palmer v Lark* [1945] Ch 182 at 184, [1945] 1 All ER 355 at 356.
2   See CPR 40.11. See *Liemann v Rightside Properties Ltd* (1973) 229 Estates Gazette 1347.
3   See CPR PD 70—*Enforcement of Judgments and Orders* para 1.1; and CIVIL PROCEDURE vol 12A (2015) PARA 1295.
4   See the Trustee Act 1925 ss 48, 50; and TRUSTS AND POWERS vol 98 (2013) PARAS 319, 323. See also *Wellesley v Wellesley, Mornington v Mornington, ex p Countess of Mornington* (1853) 4 De GM & G 537; *Hall v Hale* (1884) 51 LT 226. The procedure under the Trustee Act 1925 cannot be used to create an obligation binding on the defendant, such as a lessor's covenant for quiet enjoyment: *Cowper v Harmer* (1887) 57 LJ Ch 460.
5   See the Senior Courts Act 1981 s 39(1); and CIVIL PROCEDURE vol 12A (2015) PARA 1219. See also *Mir v Mir* [1992] Fam 79, [1992] 1 All ER 765; *Bank of Scotland Plc v Waugh (No 2)* [2014] EWHC 2835 (Ch). Unlike the power under the Trustee Act 1925 (see note 4), this power is not restricted to contracts concerning interests in land. Subject to any limitation on the court's jurisdiction to make the underlying order whose implementation is being frustrated, there is no limitation either on the class of document which may be so executed or on the purpose for which such a document may be used: *Astro Exito Navegacion SA v Chase Manhattan Bank NA* [1983] 2 AC 787, sub nom *Astro Exito Navegacion SA v Southland Enterprise Co Ltd, The Messiniaki Tolmi* [1983] 2 All ER 725, HL (where a court had jurisdiction over a letter of credit because it was a contract governed by English law and consequently the court also had jurisdiction to order that the notice of readiness required to operate the letter of credit be executed by a master of the Supreme Court).
    A conveyance, contract, document or instrument executed under the Senior Courts Act 1981 s 39(1) operates as if it had been executed by the person originally directed to execute it: see s 39(2); and CIVIL PROCEDURE vol 12A (2015) PARA 1219. Before making an order under this provision, the court ought to satisfy itself that there has been a neglect or refusal to execute the document, and ought not to make an anticipatory order unless the party in question has already shown by his conduct that he will refuse to execute: *Savage v Norton* [1908] 1 Ch 290 at 297 per Parker J, decided under earlier corresponding legislation.
6   As to the jurisdiction and powers of Chancery masters generally see CPR 2.4; and CIVIL PROCEDURE vol 11 (2015) PARA 97.
7   See CPR 83.14; and CIVIL PROCEDURE vol 12A (2015) PARA 1383.
8   See CPR 70.2A(2), (3)(a); and. CIVIL PROCEDURE vol 12A (2015) PARA 1298. The expenses incurred may be ascertained in such manner as the court may direct, and execution may issue against the disobedient party for the amount so ascertained and for costs: see CPR 70.2A(3)(b), (c).
9   *Munns v Isle of Wight Rly Co* (1870) 5 Ch App 414; *Lycett v Stafford and Uttoxeter Rly Co* (1872) LR 13 Eq 261; *Williams v Aylesbury and Buckingham Rly Co* (1873) 28 LT 547. See further LIEN vol 68 (2016) PARA 880.

10 *Munns v Isle of Wight Rly Co* (1870) 5 Ch App 414; *Ware v Aylesbury and Buckingham Rly Co* (1873) 28 LT 893. As to the appointment of a receiver see RECEIVERS vol 88 (2012) PARA 30 et seq.

11 *Lycett v Stafford and Uttoxeter Rly Co* (1872) LR 13 Eq 261; *Ware v Aylesbury and Buckingham Rly Co* (1873) 28 LT 893.

12 *Easton v Brown* [1981] 3 All ER 278, where there was a seven-year delay but a stay of proceedings was refused because the plaintiff had acted reasonably and the defendant had suffered no detriment. See also *McKenna v Richey* [1950] VLR 360, [1950] ALR 778 (Vict).

13 *Ford-Hunt v Raghbir Singh* [1973] 2 All ER 700, [1973] 1 WLR 738; *Easton v Brown* [1981] 3 All ER 278.

637. Discharge of the order. If the defendant fails to comply with an order for specific performance and the claimant no longer wishes to obtain specific performance or it has become impossible, the claimant is not entitled to treat the contract as having been terminated; he must apply to the court for an order discharging the contract[1]. The court's directions supersede the provisions of the contract, so that, for example, after an order for specific performance has been made neither party may serve on the other a completion notice purporting to make time of the essence of the contract[2]. The defendant may also apply for the discharge of the order if the claimant has failed to comply with the time-limit fixed by the court or is otherwise unable or unwilling to fulfil his obligations[3].

The court will not make an order for the discharge of the contract if it would be unjust to do so[4]. Where the innocent party gives notice that he proposes to ask the court to permit him to rescind the contract on the ground of the other party's repudiatory breach, the essential question which the court must ask itself is whether in the circumstances as they obtained at the date when the notice was given, it would be unconscionable for the innocent party to exercise his legal right to treat himself as discharged by the other's breach. If so, it would be unjust to deny him his contractual right and the decree of specific performance will be discharged[5]. If the ground of the application is that the vendor has failed to show a good title, the court may refuse to discharge the contract if the defect has been cured before the hearing[6]. A conditional order may be made directing that the contract be discharged if the party in default does not complete it within some specified time[7].

Until a specific performance order is made, a party who has committed a repudiatory breach of contract may escape liability if before the repudiation has been accepted by the innocent party an event occurs which makes it impossible for the innocent party to perform his own obligations under the contract[8]. This rule does not, however, apply after a specific performance order has been made, because in such a case the claimant is no longer free to accept the repudiation at his own discretion. Consequently, if after a specific performance order has been made an event occurs, without fault on the part of the claimant, which makes it impossible for him to complete the contract (for example a sale of the subject matter of the contract by the claimant's mortgagee at a time when the claimant cannot raise the money to discharge the mortgage), the defendant cannot rely on the claimant's inability to complete the contract as a defence to a claim for damages[9].

A party who has obtained an order for the discharge of the contract because of the other party's breach of contract or failure to comply with the court order is entitled to the same relief as if he had elected to accept a repudiation of the contract by the other party[10].

1 *Halkett v Earl of Dudley* [1907] 1 Ch 590; *Austins of East Ham Ltd v Macey* [1941] Ch 338, CA; *Sudagar Singh v Nazeer* [1979] Ch 474, [1978] 3 All ER 817; *Johnson v Agnew* [1980] AC 367,

[1979] 1 All ER 883, HL; *GKN Distributors Ltd v Tyne Tees Fabrication Ltd* (1985) 50 P & CR 403. See also *Ahmed v Wingrove* [2007] EWHC 1777 (Ch), [2007] 31 EG 81 (CS).

2   *Sudagar Singh v Nazeer* [1979] Ch 474, [1978] 3 All ER 817; *GKN Distributors Ltd v Tyne Tees Fabrication Ltd* (1985) 50 P & CR 403. See also *Ahmed v Wingrove* [2007] EWHC 1777 (Ch), [2007] 31 EG 81 (CS). As to notices to complete see CONVEYANCING vol 23 (2016) PARA 279.

3   *Sudagar Singh v Nazeer* [1979] Ch 474, [1978] 3 All ER 817. See also *Ahmed v Wingrove* [2007] EWHC 1777 (Ch), [2007] 31 EG 81 (CS).

4   *Johnson v Agnew* [1980] AC 367 at 399, [1979] 1 All ER 883 at 895, HL, per Lord Wilberforce.

5   *Hillel v Christoforides* (1991) 63 P & CR 301.

6   *Coffin v Cooper* (1807) 14 Ves 205; *Hume v Pocock* (1866) 1 Ch App 379; *Halkett v Earl of Dudley* [1907] 1 Ch 590.

7   *Foligno v Martin* (1853) 16 Beav 586; *Simpson v Terry* (1865) 34 Beav 423.

8   *Avery v Bowden* (1856) 6 E & B 953 at 962, Ex Ch.

9   *Johnson v Agnew* [1980] AC 367, [1979] 1 All ER 883, HL.

10 As to damages see PARA 632 et seq; and as to repayment or forfeiture of the deposit see PARAS 619–620.

INDEX

Social Services

References are to paragraph numbers; superior figures refer to notes

References are to paragraph numbers; superior figures refer to notes

References are to paragraph numbers; superior figures refer to notes

VULNERABLE ADULT—*continued*
  regulated activity—
    Commissioner for Older People in
      Wales 259
    conduct of adult's own affairs,
      provision of assistance in 256
    driving vehicles 257
    health care, provision of 251
    health care professional: meaning
      251n[2]
    household matters, provision of
      assistance as to 255
    inspections and investigations of
      social service establishments in
      Wales 258
    mental health, provision of
      counselling related to 253
    mobile services: meaning 251n[7]
    personal care, provision of 252
    practice premises: meaning 251n[6]
    providers. *See* regulated activity
      providers *below*
    psychotherapy, provision of 253
    registered pharmacy: meaning
      251n[8]
    social work, provision of 254
    vulnerable adult: meaning 251n[1]
  regulated activity providers—
    care and support in registered
      establishments, persons
      involved in provision of 262
    exemption for private, family and
      personal arrangements 264
    fostering arrangements, persons
      involved in 261
    making arrangements: meaning 263
    management or control of activity,
      persons responsible for 260
VULNERABLE ADULTS
  Safeguarding Adults Boards
    (England)—
    establishment of 234
    independent advocacy 236
    review of cases, role in 235
WALES
  Ombudsman—
    acting on investigation reports 420
    action: meaning 415n[4]
    authorised person: meaning 418n[9]
    care home: meaning 415n[4]
    care home provider: meaning 415n[4]
    cooperation by 423
    data protection 423

WALES—*continued*
  Ombudsman—*continued*
    discretion in initiating and
      proceeding with investigation
      417
    domiciliary care: meaning 415n[6]
    domiciliary care provider: meaning
      415n[6]
    independent palliative care provider:
      meaning 415n[8]
    investigation report: meaning 421
    matters subject to investigation by
      415
    member of the public: meaning
      415n[11]
    obstruction of investigations 424
    palliative care service: meaning
      415n[8]
    persons invited or compelled to
      contribute to investigations 419
    privilege of information 423
    procedure before making
      complaint 416
    procedure for investigations 418
    public funding: meaning 415n[14]
    publicising of reports 422
    recommendations by 421
    reports 420–422
    special reports 420, 421
  social care workers, regulation of—
    meaning 198
    appropriately qualified person:
      meaning 201n[4]
    barred list: meaning 200n[4]
    fitness to practise 200
    offence of falsely claiming to be
      199
    persons prohibited from social care
      work 202
    registration of 201
    social care worker: meaning 198
  social services in—
    adults, care needs of—
      circumstances allowing local
        authority to meet needs 20
      circumstances requiring local
        authority to meet needs 19
      determination of eligibility 17
      duty as to assessment of care
        needs 15
      duty to consider what can be
        done 18
      eligibility criteria 17

References are to paragraph numbers; superior figures refer to notes

Specific Performance

References are to paragraph numbers; superior figures refer to notes